Constant-Growth Dividend Discount Model

If the initial dividend is \$1 (paid in 1 year), and if the dividend grows thereafter at a [illegible] rate of g, the present value of the dividend stream is $P_0 = \dfrac{\text{DIV}_1}{r - g}$ (page 151)

Capital Budgeting

Break-Even Point

The sales revenue necessary for the firm to break even (in terms of accounting profits) is

$$\text{Break-even revenue} = \frac{\text{fixed costs including depreciation}}{\text{additional profit from each additional dollar of sales}} \quad \text{(page 253)}$$

Operating Leverage

The degree of operating leverage, DOL, is the sensitivity of profits to changes in sales:

$$\text{DOL} = \frac{\text{percentage change in profits}}{\text{percentage change in sales}} = 1 + \frac{\text{fixed costs}}{\text{profits}} \quad \text{(page 255)}$$

Risk and Return

Measures of Risk and Return

Mean or expected return = probability-weighted average of possible outcomes (page 281)

Variance = σ^2 = probability-weighted average of squared deviations around the mean (page 282)

Standard deviation = $\sigma = \sqrt{\text{Variance}}$ (page 282)

Variance of a sample of observations = sum of the square deviations around the average return, divided by the number of observations minus 1 (page 283)

Standard deviation of a sample = $\sqrt{\text{sample variance}}$ (page 283)

Beta = Expected increase in stock return for an extra 1 percent increase in the return on the market index (page 305)

Capital Asset Pricing Model

The expected rate of return on a risky security equals the rate of return on risk-free assets plus a risk premium that depends on the security beta:

$$r = r_f + \beta(r_m - r_f) \quad \text{(page 312)}$$

Capital Structure

Return on Assets

Return on assets equals the weighted average of the returns of the firm's outstanding securities:

$$r_{\text{assets}} = r_{\text{debt}} \frac{D}{V} + r_{\text{equity}} \frac{E}{V}$$

(assuming no taxes) (page 337)

Weighted-Average Cost of Capital

$$\text{WACC} = \frac{D}{V} \times r_{\text{debt}}(1 - T_c) + \frac{E}{V} \times r_{\text{equity}}$$

where T_c is the corporate tax rate, D is debt, E is equity, and $V = D + E$ (page 339)

Fundamentals of Corporate Finance

second
canadian
edition

Richard A. Brealey
Bank of England and London Business School

Stewart C. Myers
Sloan School of Management,
Massachusetts Institute of Technology

Alan J. Marcus
Wallace E. Carroll School of Management,
Boston College

Elizabeth M. Maynes
Schulich School of Business, York University

Devashis Mitra
University of New Brunswick

Toronto Montréal Boston Burr Ridge, IL Dubuque, IA Madison, WI New York San Francisco St. Louis
Bangkok Bogotá Caracas Kuala Lumpur Lisbon London Madrid Mexico City Milan New Delhi Santiago
Seoul Singapore Sydney Taipei

McGraw-Hill
Ryerson Limited

A Subsidiary of The McGraw·Hill Companies

Fundamentals of Corporate Finance
Second Canadian Edition

ISBN: 0-07-089866-9

2 3 4 5 6 7 8 9 10 TCP 0 9 8 7 6 5

Printed and bound in Canada.

Vice President and Editorial Director: Patrick Ferrier
Senior Sponsoring Editor: Lynn Fisher
Developmental Editor: Daphne Scriabin
Copy Editor: Double Space
Production Coordinator: Paula Brown
Marketing Manager: Kelly Smyth
Page Layout: Bill Renaud/Accutype
Art Director: Dianna Little
Cover Design: Sharon Lucas
Cover Image Credit: Copyright © Photodisc
Printer: Transcontinental Printing Group

National Library of Canada Cataloguing in Publication

Main entry under title:

Fundamentals of corporate finance / Richard Brealey ... [et al.]. — 2nd Canadian ed.

Includes index.
ISBN 0-07-089866-9

1. Corporations—Finance. I. Brealey, Richard A.

HG4026.F85 2002 658.15 C2002-903109-5

E.M.M. *To Bruce and David*
D.M. *To Koumari*

About the Authors

Richard A. Brealey

Special Adviser to the Governor of the Bank of England and Visiting Professor at the London Business School. For many years Professor Brealey was the Tokai Bank Professor of Finance at the London Business School. He is a fellow of the British Academy, a former President of the European Finance Association, and a former Director of the American Finance Association. He is co-author (with Stewart Myers) of Principles of Corporate Finance, the leading graduate-level corporate finance textbook.

Stewart C. Myers

Gordon Y. Billard Professor of Finance at MIT's Sloan School of Management. Dr. Myers is past President of the American Finance Association and a Research Associate of the National Bureau of Economic Research. His research has focused on financing decisions, valuation methods, the cost of capital, and financial aspects of government regulation of business. Dr. Myers is a Director of The Brattle Group, Inc. and is active as financial consultants.

Alan J. Marcus

Professor of Finance in the Wallace E. Carroll School of Management at Boston College and Visiting Professor at MIT's Sloan School of Management. His main research interests are in derivatives and securities markets. He is co-author (with Alex Kane and Zvi Bodie) of *Investments*, the leading graduate-level investments textbook. Professor Marcus spent two years at Freddie Mac where he helped to develop mortgage pricing and credit risk models. He currently serves on the Research Foundation Advisory Board of the Association for Investment Management and Research (AIMR) and the Advisory Council for the Currency Risk Management Alliance of State Street Bank and Windham Capital Management, Boston.

Elizabeth M. Maynes

Associate Professor of Finance at the Schulich School of Business, York University, Toronto. Her current research interests are in experimental economics and finance, where theories are tested with human subjects. Through this research, she has examined peoples' decisions whether to evade tax, whether to tender shares in a takeover bid and how much to contribute towards a public good. In addition, Professor Maynes conducts research on the role and value of voting rights of shareholders, initial public offerings and takeovers. Her research has been funded by the Social Sciences and Humanities Research Council of Canada and the Financial Research Foundation. Professor Maynes has extensive experience teaching introductory and corporate finance to undergraduate and MBA students and to managers.

Devashis Mitra

Professor of Finance at the Faculty of Administration, University of New Brunswick, Fredericton. He has extensive experience teaching introductory and advanced courses, in Corporate Finance and International Finance, to undergraduate and MBA students. Professor Mitra has conducted research in areas such as dividend policy, working capital, capital structure, international capital budgeting, financial markets and venture capital. His present research examines accounting and market measures of performance. Professor Mitra's research projects have been funded by Social Sciences and Humanities Research Council of Canada and the Shastri Indo-Canadian Institute. He has served as a past Finance Division Chair, Academic Reviewer and Program Chair at conferences of the Administrative Sciences Association of Canada.

Contents in Brief

PART ONE Introduction 1

CHAPTER 1 *The Firm and the Financial Manager* 2

CHAPTER 2 *Accounting and Finance* 34

PART TWO Value 61

CHAPTER 3 *The Time Value of Money* 62

CHAPTER 4 *Valuing Bonds* 112

CHAPTER 5 *Valuing Stocks* 138

CHAPTER 6 *Net Present Value and Other Investment Criteria* 169

CHAPTER 7 *Using Discounted Cash-Flow Analysis to Make Investment Decisions* 203

CHAPTER 8 *Project Analysis* 242

PART THREE Risk 270

CHAPTER 9 *Introduction to Risk, Return, and the Opportunity Cost of Capital* 271

CHAPTER 10 *Risk, Return, and Capital Budgeting* 304

CHAPTER 11 *The Cost of Capital* 332

PART FOUR Financing 358

CHAPTER 12 *Corporate Financing and the Lessons of Market Efficiency* 359

CHAPTER 13 *An Overview of Corporate Financing* 377

CHAPTER 14 *How Corporations Issue Securities* 409

PART FIVE Capital Structure and Dividend Policy 444

CHAPTER 15 *The Capital Structure Decision* 445

CHAPTER 16 *Dividend Policy* 479

PART SIX Financial Planning 504

CHAPTER 17 *Financial Statement Analysis* 505

CHAPTER 18 *Financial Planning* 543

CHAPTER 19 *Working Capital Management and Short-Term Planning* 571

PART SEVEN Short-Term Financial Decisions 603

CHAPTER 20 *Cash and Inventory Management* 604

CHAPTER 21 *Credit Management and Collection* 629

PART EIGHT Special Topics 655

CHAPTER 22 *Leasing* 656

CHAPTER 23 *Mergers, Acquisitions, and Corporate Control* 679

CHAPTER 24 *International Financial Management* 711

CHAPTER 25 *Options* 738

CHAPTER 26 *Risk Management* 767

Contents

PART ONE Introduction 1

CHAPTER 1

The Firm and the Financial Manager 2

1.1 Organizing a Business 3
Sole Proprietorships 3
Partnerships 3
Corporations 3
Hybrid Forms of Business Organization 5

1.2 The Role of the Financial Manager 6
The Capital Budgeting Decision 7
The Financing Decision 8

1.3 Financial Institutions and Markets 9
Financial Institutions 9
Financial Markets 11
Other Functions of Financial Markets and Institutions 13

1.4 Who Is the Financial Manager? 14
Careers in Finance 15

1.5 Goals of the Corporation 17
Shareholders Want Managers to Maximize Market Value 17
Ethics and Management Objectives 19
Do Managers Really Maximize Firm Value? 21

1.6 Topics Covered in This Book 26
Snippets of History 27

1.7 Summary 27
Related Web Links 30
Key Terms 30
Questions and Problems 30
Basic 30
Practice 31
Solutions to Check Points 32

CHAPTER 2

Accounting and Finance 34

2.1 The Balance Sheet 35
Book Values and Market Values 37

2.2 The Income Statement 40
Profits versus Cash Flow 41

2.3 The Statement of Cash Flows 42

2.4 Accounting for Differences 47

2.5 Taxes 48
Corporate Tax 48
Personal Tax 51

2.6 Summary 54
Related Web Links 55
Key Terms 55
Questions and Problems 55
Basic 55
Practice 56
Challenge 59
Internet Problems 59
Solutions to Check Points 59

PART TWO Value 61

CHAPTER 3

The Time Value of Money 62

3.1 Future Values and Compound Interest 63

3.2 Present Values 67
Finding the Interest Rate 72

3.3 Multiple Cash Flows 75
Future Value of Multiple Cash Flows 75
Present Value of Multiple Cash Flows 77

3.4 Level Cash Flows: Perpetuities and Annuities 78
How to Value Perpetuities 78
How to Value Annuities 79
Annuities Due 82
Future Value of an Annuity 86
Cash Flows Growing at a Constant Rate—Variations on Perpetuities and Annuities 88

3.5 Inflation and the Time Value of Money 90
Real versus Nominal Cash Flows 90
Inflation and Interest Rates 92
Valuing Real Cash Payments 94
Real or Nominal? 95

3.6 Effective Annual Interest Rates 95

3.7 Summary 98
Related Web Links 99
Key Terms 99
Questions and Problems 99
Basic 99
Practice 101
Challenge 104
Internet Problems 107
Solutions to Check Points 108
Minicase 111

CHAPTER 4

Valuing Bonds 112

4.1 Bond Characteristics 113
Reading the Financial Pages 113

4.2 Bond Prices and Yields 115
How Bond Prices Vary with Interest Rates 117
Yield to Maturity versus Current Yield 118
Rate of Return 121
Taxes and Rates of Return 123
Interest Rate Risk 125
The Yield Curve 126
Nominal and Real Rates of Interest 126
Default Risk 129
Variations in Corporate Bonds 131

4.3 Summary 131
Related Web Links 132
Key Terms 132
Questions and Problems 132
Basic 132
Practice 133
Challenge 135
Internet Problems 135
Solutions to Check Points 136

CHAPTER 5

Valuing Stocks 138

5.1 Stocks and the Stock Market 139
Reading the Stock Market Listings 140

5.2 Book Values, Liquidation Values, and Market Values 142

5.3 Valuing Common Stocks 145
Today's Price and Tomorrow's Price 145
The Dividend Discount Model 147

5.4 Simplifying the Dividend Discount Model 150
The Dividend Discount Model with No Growth 150
The Constant-Growth Dividend Discount Model 151
Estimating Expected Rates of Return 152
Nonconstant Growth 154

5.5 Growth Stocks and Income Stocks 155
The Price-Earnings Ratio 157
What Do Earnings Mean? 157
Valuing Entire Businesses 157

5.6 Summary 159
Related Web Links 159
Key Terms 160
Questions and Problems 160
Basic 160
Practice 160
Challenge 163
Internet Problems 165
Solutions to Check Points 165
Minicase 167

CHAPTER 6

Net Present Value and Other Investment Criteria 169

6.1 Net Present Value 170
A Comment on Risk and Present Value 171
Valuing Long-Lived Projects 172

6.2 Other Investment Criteria 175
Internal Rate of Return 176
A Closer Look at the Rate of Return Rule 176
Calculating the Rate of Return for Long-Lived Projects 177
A Word of Caution 179
Payback 180
Discounted Payback 181
Book Rate of Return 182

6.3 Investment Criteria When Projects Interact 183

Mutually Exclusive Projects 183
Investment Timing 184
Long- versus Short-Lived Equipment 186
Replacing an Old Machine 187
Mutually Exclusive Projects and the IRR Rule 188
Other Pitfalls of the IRR Rule 190

6.4 Capital Rationing 192
Soft Rationing 192
Hard Rationing 192
Pitfalls of the Profitability Index 193

6.5 Summary 194
Related Web Links 194
Key Terms 194
Questions and Problems 195
Basic 195
Practice 196
Challenge 200
Solutions to Check Points 200

CHAPTER 7

Using Discounted Cash-Flow Analysis to Make Investment Decisions 203

7.1 Discount Cash Flows, Not Profits 204

7.2 Discount Incremental Cash Flows 206
Include All Indirect Effects 206
Forget Sunk Costs 207
Include Opportunity Costs 207
Recognize the Investment in Working Capital 208
Beware of Allocated Overhead Costs 209

7.3 Discount Nominal Cash Flows by the Nominal Cost of Capital 209

7.4 Separate Investment and Financing Decisions 211

7.5 Calculating Cash Flow 211
Capital Investment 212
Investment in Working Capital 212
Cash Flow from Operations 213

7.6 Business Taxes in Canada and the Capital Budgeting Decision 215
Depreciation and Capital Cost Allowance 215
The Asset Class System 215
Sale of Assets 217
Termination of Asset Pool 217
Present Values of CCA Tax Shields 218

7.7 Example: Blooper Industries 221
Calculating Blooper's Project Cash Flows 223
Calculating the NPV of Blooper's Project 225
Further Notes and Wrinkles Arising from Blooper's Project 228

7.8 Summary 229
Related Web Links 229
Key Terms 229
Questions and Problems 230
Basic 230
Practice 231
Challenge 234
Solutions to Excel Spreadsheet Model Questions 234
Solutions to Check Points 236
Minicase 238

Appendix 7A: Deriving the CCA Tax Shield 239

CHAPTER 8

Project Analysis 242

8.1 How Firms Organize the Investment Process 243
Stage 1: The Capital Budget 243
Stage 2: Project Authorizations 243
Problems and Some Solutions 244

8.2 Some "What If" Questions 245
Sensitivity Analysis 245
Scenario Analysis 248

8.3 Break-Even Analysis 249
Accounting Break-Even Analysis 249
NPV Break-Even Analysis 251
Operating Leverage 254

8.4 Flexibility in Capital Budgeting 256
Decision Trees 256
The Option to Expand 258
Abandonment Options 259
Flexible Production Facilities 260
Investment Timing Options 260

8.5 Capital Budgeting Practices in Canadian Firms 261

8.6 Summary 262
Related Web Links 263
Key Terms 263
Questions and Problems 263
Basic 263
Practice 263
Challenge 266
Solutions to Check Points 267
Minicase 269

PART THREE Risk 270

CHAPTER 9

Introduction to Risk, Return, and the Opportunity Cost of Capital 271

9.1 Rates of Return: A Review 272

9.2 Seventy-Five Years of Capital Market History 273
Market Indexes 273
The Historical Record 275
Using Historical Evidence to Estimate Today's Cost of Capital 278

9.3 Measuring Risk 280
Variance and Standard Deviation 280
Measuring the Variation in Stock Returns 283

9.4 Risk and Diversification 285
Diversification 285
Asset versus Portfolio Risk 286
Correlation and Portfolio Diversification 289
Market Risk versus Unique Risk 293

9.5 Thinking about Risk 294
Message 1: Some Risks Look Big and Dangerous but Really Are Diversifiable 294
Message 2: Market Risks Are Macro Risks 296
Message 3: Risk Can Be Measured 297

9.6 Summary 297
Related Web Links 298
Key Terms 298
Questions and Problems 298
Basic 298
Practice 299
Internet Problems 301
Solutions to Check Points 302

CHAPTER 10

Risk, Return, and Capital Budgeting 304

10.1 Measuring Market Risk 305
Measuring Beta 305
Betas for Inco and Westcoast Energy 308
Portfolio Betas 309

10.2 Risk and Return 312
Why the CAPM Works 313
The Security Market Line 314
How Well Does the CAPM Work? 316
Using the CAPM to Estimate Expected Returns 317

10.3 Capital Budgeting and Project Risk 319
Company versus Project Risk 319
Determinants of Project Risk 320
Don't Add Fudge Factors to Discount Rates 322

10.4 Summary 323
Related Web Links 323
Key Terms 324
Questions and Problems 324
Basic 324
Practice 325
Challenge 329
Internet Problems 330
Solutions to Check Points 330

CHAPTER 11

The Cost of Capital 332

11.1 Geothermal's Cost of Capital 333

11.2 Calculating the Weighted-Average Cost of Capital 334
Calculating Company Cost of Capital as a Weighted Average 336
Market versus Book Weights 337
Taxes and the Weighted-Average Cost of Capital 338
What If There Are Three (or More) Sources of Financing? 339
Wrapping Up Geothermal 340
Checking Our Logic 340

11.3 Measuring Capital Structure 341

11.4 Calculating Required Rates of Return 343
The Expected Return on Bonds 343
The Expected Return on Common Stock 344
The Expected Return on Preferred Stock 345

11.5 Big Oil's Weighted-Average Cost of Capital 346
Real Oil Company WACCs 346

11.6 Interpreting the Weighted-Average Cost of Capital 347
When You Can and Can't Use WACC 347
Some Common Mistakes 347
How Changing Capital Structure Affects Expected Returns 348
What Happens If Capital Structure Changes and the Corporate Tax Rate Is Not Zero? 349
Revisiting the Project Cost of Capital 349

11.7 Flotation Costs and the Cost of Capital 350

11.8 Summary 351
Related Web Links 351
Key Terms 351
Questions and Problems 352
Basic 352
Practice 352
Challenge 354
Solutions to Check Points 354
Minicase 355

PART FOUR Financing 358

CHAPTER 12

Corporate Financing and the Lessons of Market Efficiency 359

12.1 Differences between Investment and Financing Decisions 360

12.2 What Is an Efficient Market? 361
A Startling Discovery: Price Changes Are Random 361
Three Forms of the Efficient-Market Theory 363
No Theory Is Perfect 365
The Crash of 1987 368

12.3 Lessons of Market Efficiency 370
Markets Have No Memory 370
There Are No Financial Illusions 370
There Are No Free Lunches on Wall Street or Bay Street 371

12.4 Summary 372
Related Web Links 373
Key Terms 373
Questions and Problems 373
Basic 373
Practice 374
Challenge 375
Internet Problems 375
Solutions to Check Points 376

CHAPTER 13

An Overview of Corporate Financing 377

13.1 Common Stock 378
Book Value versus Market Value 379
Dividends 380
Shareholders' Rights 380
Voting Procedures 381
Classes of Stock 381
Corporate Governance in Canada and Elsewhere 382

13.2 Preferred Stock 383

13.3 Corporate Debt 386
Debt Comes in Many Forms 387
Innovation in the Debt Market 391

13.4 Convertible Securities 394

13.5 Patterns of Corporate Financing 395
Do Firms Rely Too Heavily on Internal Funds? 395
External Sources of Capital 396

13.6 Summary 399
Related Web Links 400
Key Terms 400
Questions and Problems 400
Basic 400
Practice 401
Solutions to Check Points 402

13.7 Appendix 13A: The Bond Refunding Decision 404
Net Investment Costs Associated with Refunding 404
Net Savings Associated with Refunding 406
Net Present Value Associated with Refunding 406
Practice Problems 408

CHAPTER 14

How Corporations Issue Securities 409

14.1 Venture Capital 410

14.2 The Initial Public Offering 412
Arranging a Public Issue 413

14.3 The Underwriters 418
Who Are the Underwriters? 419

14.4 Listing on the Stock Market 420

14.5 Rights Issues and General Cash Offers by Public Companies 421
Rights Issues 422
General Cash Offers 423
Costs of the General Cash Offer 424
Market Reaction to Stock Issues 424

14.6 The Private Placement 426

14.7 Summary 427

Related Web Links 428
Key Terms 428
Questions and Problems 428
BASIC 428
PRACTICE 429
CHALLENGE 431
Solutions to Check Points 431
Minicase 432

14.8 Appendix 14A: The Financing of New and Small Enterprises 432
Venture Capital in Canada 432
TYPES OF VENTURE CAPITAL FUNDS 433
STAGES OF DEVELOPMENT FINANCED BY CANADIAN VENTURE CAPITAL FIRMS 434
RECENT VENTURE CAPITAL INVESTMENT ACTIVITY 436
Angel Investing 436
Other Sources of Small Business Financing 437
FINANCING UNDER THE CANADA SMALL BUSINESS FINANCING ACT 437
BUSINESS DEVELOPMENT BANK OF CANADA 437
REGIONAL AND PROVINCIAL LENDING PROGRAMS 438
INTERNET AND PRACTICE PROBLEMS 438

14.9 Appendix 14B: Hotch Pot's New Issue Prospectus 439

PART FIVE Capital Structure and Dividend Policy 444

CHAPTER 15

The Capital Structure Decision 445

15.1 How Borrowing Affects Value in a Tax-Free Economy 446
MM's Argument 447
How Borrowing Affects Earnings per Share 448
How Borrowing Affects Risk and Return 450
Debt and the Cost of Equity 452

15.2 Capital Structure and Corporate Taxes 455
Debt and Taxes at River Cruises 455
How Interest Tax Shields Contribute to the Value of Shareholders' Equity 457
Corporate Taxes and the Weighted-Average Cost of Capital 457
The Implications of Corporate Taxes for Capital Structure 459

15.3 Costs of Financial Distress 459
Bankruptcy Costs 461
Evidence on Bankruptcy Costs 461
Direct versus Indirect Costs of Bankruptcy 462
Financial Distress without Bankruptcy 462
Costs of Distress Vary with Type of Asset 465

15.4 Explaining Financial Choices 466
The Trade-Off Theory 466
A Pecking Order Theory 467
The Two Faces of Financial Slack 468

15.5 Summary 470
Related Web Links 471
Key Terms 471
Questions and Problems 472
BASIC 472
PRACTICE 472
CHALLENGE 475
Solutions to Check Points 476
Minicase 477

CHAPTER 16

Dividend Policy 479

16.1 How Dividends Are Paid 480
Cash Dividends 480
Some Legal Limitations on Dividends 480
Stock Dividends, Stock Splits, and Reverse Splits 482
Share Repurchase 483

16.2 How Do Companies Decide on Dividend Payments? 484

16.3 Why Dividend Policy Should Not Matter 485
Dividend Policy Is Irrelevant in Competitive Markets 486
The Assumptions behind Dividend Irrelevance 489

16.4 Why Dividends May Increase Firm Value 489
Market Imperfections 489
Dividends as Signals 490

16.5 Why Dividends? A Look at Tax Law Implications 492
Dividends versus Capital Gains 492
Dividend Clientele Effects 495
Share Repurchases Instead of Cash Dividends? 496

16.6 Summary 498
Related Web Links 498
Key Terms 499

Questions and Problems 499
Basic 499
Practice 499
Challenge 502
Solutions to Check Points 502

PART SIX Financial Planning 504

CHAPTER 17

Financial Statement Analysis 505

17.1 Financial Ratios 506
Leverage Ratios 511
Liquidity Ratio 513
Efficiency Ratios 515
Profitability Ratios 517

17.2 The DuPont System 520
Other Important Financial Ratios 521

17.3 Analysis of the Statement of Cash Flows 522

17.4 Using Financial Ratios 525
Choosing a Benchmark 526

17.5 Measuring Company Performance 529

17.6 The Role of Financial Ratios 531

17.7 Summary 533
Related Web Links 535
Key Terms 535
Questions and Problems 535
Basic 535
Practice 536
Challenge 538
Internet Problems 539
Solutions to Check Points 540
Minicase 540

CHAPTER 18

Financial Planning 543

18.1 What Is Financial Planning? 544
Financial Planning Focuses on the Big Picture 544
Financial Planning Is Not Just Forecasting 545
Three Requirements for Effective Planning 546

18.2 Financial Planning Models 547
Components of a Financial Planning Model 548
An Example of a Planning Model 548
An Improved Model 550

18.3 Planners Beware 555
Pitfalls in Model Design 555
The Assumption in Percentage of Sales Models 555
The Role of Financial Planning Models 556

18.4 External Financing and Growth 557

18.5 Summary 561
Related Web Links 562
Key Terms 562
Questions and Problems 562
Basic 562
Practice 563
Challenge 566
Internet Problems 567
Solutions to Check Points 567
Minicase 568

CHAPTER 19

Working Capital Management and Short-Term Planning 571

19.1 Working Capital 572
The Components of Working Capital 572
Working Capital and the Cash Conversion Cycle 573
The Working Capital Trade-Off 576

19.2 Links between Long-Term and Short-Term Financing 578

19.3 Tracing Changes in Cash and Working Capital 580

19.4 Cash Budgeting 582
Forecast Sources of Cash 582
Forecast Uses of Cash 584
The Cash Balance 584

19.5 A Short-Term Financing Plan 585
Options for Short-Term Financing 585
Evaluating the Plan 588

19.6 Sources of Short-Term Financing 589
Bank Loans 589
Commercial Paper 589
Banker's Acceptance 590
Secured Loans 590

19.7 The Cost of Bank Loans 592
Simple Interest 592

Discount Interest 593
Interest with Compensating Balances 593

19.8 Summary 594
Related Web Links 595
Key Terms 595
Questions and Problems 595
Basic 595
Practice 596
Challenge 598
Solutions to Check Points 599
Minicase 601

PART SEVEN Short-Term Financial Decisions 603

CHAPTER 20

Cash and Inventory Management 604

20.1 Cash Collection, Disbursement, and Float 605
Float 605
Valuing Float 606

20.2 Canada's Payments Systems 608

20.3 Managing Float 609
Speeding Up Collections 610
Controlling Disbursements 612
Electronic Funds Transfer 613

20.4 Inventories and Cash Balances 614
Managing Inventories 615
Managing Inventories of Cash 618
Uncertain Cash Flows 619
Cash Management in the Largest Corporations 621
Investing Idle Cash: The Money Market 621

20.5 Summary 623
Related Web Links 624
Key Terms 624
Questions and Problems 624
Basic 624
Practice 625
Challenge 627
Solutions to Check Points 627

CHAPTER 21

Credit Management and Collection 629

21.1 Terms of Sale 630

21.2 Credit Agreements 632

21.3 Credit Analysis 633
Financial Ratio Analysis 634
Numerical Credit Scoring 634
When to Stop Looking for Clues 635

21.4 The Credit Decision 636
Credit Decisions with Repeat Orders 638
Some General Principles 639

21.5 Collection Policy 640

21.6 Bankruptcy 641
Bankruptcy Procedures 641
The Choice between Liquidation and Reorganization 645

21.7 Summary 647
Related Web Links 648
Key Terms 648
Questions and Problems 648
Basic 648
Practice 649
Challenge 650
Solutions to Check Points 651
Minicase 653

PART EIGHT Special Topics 655

CHAPTER 22

Leasing 656

22.1 What is a Lease 657

22.2 Why Lease? 658
Sensible Reasons for Leasing 658
Some Dubious Reasons for Leasing 659

22.3 Valuing Leases 662
Operating Leases 662
Financial Leases 663

Cash Flows of a Financial Lease 663
Who Really Owns the Leased Asset? 664
Leasing and the Canada Customs and Revenue Agency (CCRA) 665
First Pass at Valuing a Financial Lease Contract 666
Financial Lease Evaluation 668

22.4 When Do Financial Leases Pay? 670

22.5 Summary 672
Related Web Links 672
Key Terms 672
Questions and Problems 673
Basic 673
Practice 674
Challenge 675
Internet Problems 676
Solutions to Check Points 676
Minicase 677

CHAPTER 23

Mergers, Acquisitions, and Corporate Control 679

23.1 The Market for Corporate Control 680
Method 1: Proxy Contests 681
Method 2: Mergers and Acquisitions 682
Method 3: Leveraged Buyouts 683
Method 4: Divestitures and Spin-Offs 684
Ownership Structure and the Market for Corporate Control 685

23.2 Sensible Motives for Mergers 685
Increased Revenues 687
Economies of Scale 687
Economies of Vertical Integration 688
Combining Complementary Resources 688
Merging to Reduce Taxes 689
Mergers as a Use for Surplus Funds 689

23.3 Dubious Reasons for Mergers 690
Diversification 690
The Bootstrap Game 690

23.4 Evaluating Mergers 692
Mergers Financed by Cash 692
Mergers Financed by Stock 694
A Warning 695
Another Warning 695
A Note on Tax Complications 696

23.5 Merger Tactics 697
Who Gets the Gains? 699

23.6 Leveraged Buyouts 700
Barbarians at the Gate? 702

23.7 Mergers and the Economy 703
Merger Waves 703
Do Mergers Generate Net Benefits? 704

23.8 Summary 705
Related Web Links 706
Key Terms 706
Questions and Problems 707
Basic 707
Practice 707
Challenge 708
Internet Problems 709
Solutions to Check Points 710
Minicase 710

CHAPTER 24

International Financial Management 711

24.1 Foreign Exchange Markets 712

24.2 Some Basic Relationships 715
Exchange Rates and Inflation 716
Inflation and Interest Rates 720
Interest Rates and Exchange Rates 721
The Forward Rate and the Expected Spot Rate 723
Some Implications 724

24.3 Hedging Exchange Rate Risk 725

24.4 International Capital Budgeting 727
Net Present Value Analysis 727
The Cost of Capital for Foreign Investment 729
Political Risk 729
Avoiding Fudge Factors 729

24.5 Summary 731
Related Web Links 732
Key Terms 732
Questions and Problems 732
Basic 732
Practice 733
Challenge 735
Internet Problems 735
Solutions to Check Points 735
Minicase 737

CHAPTER 25

Options 738

25.1 Calls and Puts 739
Selling Calls and Puts 741

Financial Alchemy with Options 743

25.2 What Determines Option Values? 745
Upper and Lower Limits on Option Values 745
The Determinants of Option Value 746
Option-Valuation Models 748

25.3 Spotting the Option 749
Options on Real Assets 749
Options on Financial Assets 752

25.4 Summary 755
Related Web Links 755
Key Terms 756
Questions and Problems 756
Basic 756
Practice 757
Challenge 759
Internet Problems 759
Solutions to Check Points 760

25.5 Appendix 25A: The Black-Scholes Option Valuation Model 762
Questions and Problems 765
Basic 765
Practice 765
Solutions to Check Points 766

CHAPTER 26

Risk Management 767

26.1 Why Hedge? 768

26.2 Reducing Risk with Options 768

26.3 Futures Contracts 771
The Mechanics of Futures Trading 774
Commodity and Financial Futures 775

26.4 Forward Contracts 776

26.5 Swaps 777

26.6 Is "Derivative" a Four-Letter Word? 780

26.7 Summary 781
Related Web Links 782
Key Terms 782
Questions and Problems 782
Basic 782
Practice 783
Challenge 784
Internet Problems 784
Solutions to Check Points 784

Appendix A: Present Value Tables 787

Appendix B: Solutions to Selected End-of-Chapter Problems 797

Glossary 813

Index 818

Preface

This book is about corporate finance. It focuses on how companies invest in real assets and how they raise the money to pay for these investments.

Financial management is important, interesting, and challenging. It is important because today's capital investment decisions may determine the businesses that the firm is in 10, 20, or more years ahead. Also, a firm's success or failure depends in large part on its ability to find the capital that it needs.

Finance is interesting for several reasons. Financial decisions often involve huge sums of money. Large investment projects or acquisitions may involve billions of dollars. Also, the financial community is international and fast moving with colourful heroes and a sprinkling of unpleasant villains.

Finance is challenging. Financial decisions are rarely cut and dried, and the financial markets in which companies operate are changing rapidly. Good managers can cope with routine problems but only the best managers can respond to change. To handle new problems, you need more than rules of thumb; you need to understand why companies and financial markets behave as they do and when common practice may not be best practice. Once you have a consistent framework for making financial decisions, complex problems become more manageable.

This book provides that framework. It is not an encyclopedia of finance. It focuses instead on setting out the basic principles of financial management and applying them to the main decisions faced by the financial manager. It explains why the firm's owners would like the manager to increase firm value, and it shows how managers value investments that may pay off at different points of time or have different degrees of risk. It also describes the main features of financial markets and discusses why companies may prefer a particular source of finance.

Some texts shy away from modern finance, sticking instead to more traditional, procedural, or institutional approaches. These are supposed to be easier or more practical. We disagree emphatically. The concepts of modern finance, properly explained, make the subject simpler not more difficult. They are also more practical. The tools of financial management are easier to grasp and can be used effectively when presented in a consistent conceptual framework. Modern finance provides that framework.

Modern financial management is not "rocket science." It is a set of ideas that can be made clear by words, graphs, and numerical examples. The ideas provide the "why" behind the tools that good financial managers use to make investment and financing decisions.

We wrote this book to make financial management clear, useful, interesting, and fun for beginners. We set out to show that modern finance and good financial practice go together—even for the financial novice.

Fundamentals and Principles of Corporate Finance

This book is derived in part from its sister text *Principles of Corporate Finance*. The spirit of the two books is similar: both apply modern finance, giving students a working ability to make financial decisions. However, there are also substantial differences between the two books.

First, we provide much more detailed discussion of the principles and mechanics of the time value of money. This material underlies almost all of this text, and we spend a lengthy chapter providing extensive practice with this key concept.

Second, we use numerical examples in this text to a greater degree than in *Principles*. Each chapter presents several detailed numerical examples to help the reader become familiar and comfortable with the material.

Third, we have streamlined the treatment of most topics. Whereas *Principles* has 35 chapters, *Fundamentals* has only 26. The relative brevity of *Fundamentals* necessitates a broader-brush coverage of some topics, but we feel that this is an advantage for beginners.

Fourth, we don't assume users will have a lot of background knowledge. While most will have had an introductory accounting course, we review the concepts of accounting that are important to the financial manager in Chapter 2.

Principles is known for its relaxed and informal writing style, and we continue this tradition in *Fundamentals*. In addition, we use as little mathematical notation as possible. Even when we present an equation, we usually write it in words rather than symbols. This approach has two advantages: It is less intimidating, and it focuses attention on the underlying concept rather than the formula.

Changes in The Second Canadian Edition

This second Canadian edition of *Fundamentals* includes many changes. After thoroughly researching the market, we have rewritten and rearranged material to improve readability, and we have expanded the treatment of some topics and introduced others for the first time. Here are some examples of the changes that we have made in various chapters:

Chapter 1 includes a whole new section on careers in finance. This overview introduces students to different possible career paths and also conveys a richer sense of the various roles of financial managers. The chapter has an expanded discussion of financial markets and institutions. Our discussion of whether managers maximize firm value includes updated coverage of compensation plans.

In Chapter 2 we have extended the discussion of the statement of cash flows to include the concepts of free cash flow and financial flows to bondholders and shareholders. We show how to use the statement of cash flows to calculate free cash flow. The taxation material has been updated to reflect the new provincial tax-on-income system.

In response to user requests, we have slightly reorganized Chapter 3. It now includes a section on inflation and the time value of money, formerly in Chapter 4, and the material on effective annual rates and compounding periods has been placed at the end of the chapter. We show how to use various financial calculators to solve time value of money problems. We have included present value formulas for growing annuities and growing perpetuities as well as the present and future values of ordinary annuities.

Chapter 4 is now devoted solely to bonds and includes the discussion of credit risk that was formerly part of a later chapter. A detailed example of valuing a bond with semiannual coupons has been added. Chapter 5 covers the stock market and stock valuation. Also, each chapter now includes a discussion of calculating before- and after-tax rates of return.

Chapter 6 on net present value and other investment criteria includes a new segment on the discounted payback period. This chapter also details the steps for finding NPV and IRR values using a financial calculator. Chapter 7 on discounted cash flow analysis has been extensively rewritten with careful attention to improving and clarifying the computation of project cash flows. This material has been expanded and enhanced with several worked examples. The chapter includes a detailed discussion of the capital cost allowance (CCA) system and an extensive conceptual treatment of the cash-flow implications of this system on capital budgeting decisions. We also provide a simple spreadsheet model that shows students how spreadsheets can enhance and simplify cash-flow analysis and capital budgeting decisions. The steps for arriving at a general formula for the CCA tax shield are provided in the chapter's appendix.

The material on risk and return in Part Three has been revised. The data in Chapter 9 has been updated. Chapter 10 on the capital asset pricing model contains new material on the firm's use of the CAPM in capital budgeting. The discussion of both theoretical and empirical calculations of beta has been extended. The treatment of taxes in measuring cost of capital (Chapter 11) has been simplified. A new section on flotation costs and the cost of capital has been added.

Part Four has also been revised. Chapter 13 (An Overview of Corporate Financing) has been updated with new material on asset-backed and index bonds as well as more recent data on trends in corporate financing. A new appendix to the chapter takes us through the process of deciding on whether or not to refund a bond issue. A spreadsheet example of the bond refunding decision is also included. Chapter 14 contains additional material on IPOs and an expanded discussion of rights issues. A new section examines issues germane to listing on Canada's stock markets. This chapter features a new appendix that discusses the environment for the financing of new and small enterprises in Canada. The appendix also describes the venture capital industry and angel investing in Canada. The section also includes a write-up on small business financing available under the Canada Small Business Financing Act, lending programs sponsored by the Business Development Bank of Canada as well as other regional and provincial lending programs. The material on capital structure in Chapter 15 has been considerably rewritten and simplified. Chapter 16 includes new discussion on reverse splits and the tax treatment of dividend decisions.

Part Six contains a significant amount of new material. Chapter 17 has three new Finance in Action articles relating accounting issues to finance, including a discussion of Enron's off-balance sheet accounting practices. Chapter 17 now discusses the analysis of the statement of cash flows and also the measurement and interpretation of economic value added (EVA). An Excel spreadsheet with a long-term financial plan has been integrated into Chapter 18. Chapter 19 similarly contains a cash management spreadsheet. Chapter 20 includes new material on Canada's payments system and electronic funds transfer. Chapter 21 has expanded coverage of bankruptcy.

Part Seven has been extended and updated. A new chapter on leasing, Chapter 22, has been added. It covers types of leases, reasons for leasing, and the valuation of financial leases. In Chapter 23, we illustrate the issues surrounding mergers with many new Canadian examples, including the story of the hostile takeover battle for Chapters, Inc. We have expanded our coverage of cash and stock offers. Chapter 24 reflects on the European Monetary Union and the creation of the euro. Chapter 25 contains actual applications of real options analysis and a new appendix on the Black-Scholes Option Valuation Model and how to use it has been added. Chapter 26 has additional examples and figures illustrating hedging with options and futures.

ORGANIZATIONAL DESIGN

Fundamentals is organized in eight parts.

Part One (Introduction) provides essential background material. In the first chapter we discuss how businesses are organized, the role of the financial manager, and the financial markets in which the manager operates. We explain how shareholders want managers to take actions that increase the value of their investment, and we describe some of the mechanisms that help to align the interests of managers and shareholders. Of course the task of increasing shareholder value does not justify corrupt and unscrupulous behaviour. We therefore discuss some of the ethical issues that confront managers.

A large corporation is a team effort, and so companies produce financial statements to help the players monitor their progress. Chapter 2 provides a brief overview of these financial statements and introduces two key distinctions—between market and book values and cash flows and profits. The chapter concludes with a summary of corporate and personal taxation.

Part Two (Value) is concerned with valuation. In Chapter 3 we introduce the concept of the time value of money, and since most readers will be more familiar with their own financial affairs rather than the big leagues of finance, we motivate our discussion by looking first at some personal financial decisions. We show how to value long-lived streams of cash flows and work through the valuation of perpetuities and annuities. Chapter 3 also contains a short concluding section on inflation and the distinction between real and nominal returns.

Chapters 4 and 5 introduce the basic features of bonds and stocks and give students a chance to apply the ideas of Chapter 3 to the valuation of these securities. We show how to find the value of a bond given its yield, and we show how prices of bonds fluctuate as interest rates change. We look at what determines stock prices and how stock valuation formulas can be used to infer the return that investors expect. Finally, we see how investment opportunities are reflected in the stock price and why analysts focus on the price-earnings multiple.

The remaining chapters of Part Two are concerned with the company's investment decisions. In Chapter 6 we introduce the concept of net present value (NPV) and show how to calculate the NPV of a simple investment project. We also look at other measures of an investment's attractiveness—the internal rate of return rule, payback, discounted payback, and the return on book. We then turn to more complex investment proposals, including choices between alternative projects, machine replacement decisions, and decisions of when to invest. Finally, we show how the profitability index can be used to choose between investment projects when capital is scarce.

The first step in any NPV calculation is to decide what to discount. Therefore, in Chapter 7 we work through a realistic example of a capital budgeting analysis, showing how the manager needs to recognize the investment in working capital and how taxes and capital cost allowance affect cash flows.

We start Chapter 8 by looking at how companies organize the investment process and ensure everyone works toward a common goal. We then go on to look at various techniques to help managers identify the key assumptions in their estimates, such as sensitivity analysis, scenario analysis, and break-even analysis. We describe how managers try to build future flexibility into projects so that they can capitalize on good luck and mitigate the consequences of bad luck. We conclude the chapter with a discussion of capital budgeting practices in corporate Canada.

Part Three (Risk) is concerned with the cost of capital. Chapter 9 starts with a historical survey of returns on bonds and stocks and goes on to distinguish between the unique risk and market risk of individual stocks. Chapter 10 shows how to measure market risk and discusses the relationship between risk and expected return. Chapter 11 introduces the weighted-average cost of capital and provides a practical illustration of how to estimate it.

Part Four (Financing) begins our discussion of the financing decision. In Chapter 12 we introduce the notion of market efficiency. Few other introductory texts include a chapter on this topic. We believe that without a solid understanding of market efficiency it is difficult to think through the issues that arise when firms issue securities or make capital structure and dividend decisions. Chapter 13 looks at the role of shareholders in large corporations and compares corporate governance in Canada and elsewhere. It also provides an overview of the securities that firms issue and their relative importance as sources of finance. An appendix to the chapter takes us through the process of deciding on whether or not to refund a bond issue. In Chapter 14 we look at how firms issue securities, and we follow a firm from its first need for venture capital through its initial public offering to its continuing need to raise debt or equity. Chapter 14 contains additional material on IPOs and an expanded discussion of rights issues. We have added a section on listing in Canada's stock markets. An appendix to the chapter describes the environment for the financing of new and small enterprises in Canada.

Part Five (Capital Structure and Dividend Policy) focuses on the two classic long-term financing decisions. How much the firm should borrow is addressed in Chapter 15 and how it should set its dividend policy is addressed in Chapter 16. In each case we start with Modigliani and Miller's (MM) observation that in well-functioning markets the decision should not matter, but we use this observation to help the reader understand why financial managers in practice do pay attention to these decisions. The material on capital structure in Chapter 15 has been considerably rewritten and simplified. In Chapter 16, we have added new discussion on reverse splits and have expanded the coverage of the tax implications of dividends payments.

Part Six (Financial Planning) starts with financial statement analysis in Chapter 17 and shows how analysts summarize the large volume of accounting information by calculating some key financial ratios. Long-term financial planning is discussed in Chapter 18, where we look at how the financial manager considers the combined effects of investment and financing decisions on the firm as a whole. We also show how measures of internal and sustainable growth help managers check that the firm's planned growth is consistent with its financing plans. Chapter 19 is an introduction to working capital management. It also shows how the manager ensures that the firm will have enough cash to pay its bills over the coming year, and it describes the principal sources of short-term borrowing.

Part Seven (Short-Term Financial Decisions) is concerned with two important short-term problems. Chapter 20 explains the mechanics of cash collection and disbursement and shows how firms invest idle cash. It also looks at the problem of managing inventories and shows how the decision to stock up on cash is similar to the decision to stock up on inventories of raw materials or finished goods. The parallel between the task of inventory management and cash management enables us to cover these topics with less repetition than in most other texts. In Chapter 21 we describe the basic steps of credit management, and we summarize bankruptcy procedures when customers cannot pay their bills.

Part Eight (Special Topics) covers several important but somewhat more advanced topics—leasing (Chapter 22), mergers (Chapter 23), international financial management (Chapter 24), options (Chapter 25), and risk management (Chapter 26). Some of these topics are touched on in earlier chapters. For example, the impact of leasing on financial statements comes up in Chapter 17, but we delve more deeply into the topic in Chapter 22. We introduce the idea of options in Chapter 8, when we show how companies build flexibility into capital projects. However, Chapter 25 generalizes this material, explains at an elementary level how options are valued, and provides some examples of why the financial manager needs to be concerned about options. In the appendix to Chapter 25, the Black-Scholes Option Valuation Model is presented. International finance is also not confined to Chapter 24. As one might expect from a book that is written by an international group of authors, examples from different countries and financial systems are scattered throughout the book. However, Chapter 24 tackles the specific problems that arise when a corporation is confronted by different currencies.

ROUTES THROUGH THE BOOK

There are about as many effective ways to organize a course in corporate finance as there are teachers. For this reason, we have ensured that the text is modular, so that topics can be introduced in different sequences.

We discuss the principles of valuation before plunging into detailed financial statement analysis or issues of financial planning. Nevertheless, we recognize that many instructors will prefer to move directly from Chapter 2 (Accounting and Finance) to Chapter 17 (Financial Statement Analysis) in order to provide a gentler transition from the typical prerequisite accounting course. We have made sure that Part Six (Financial Planning) can easily follow Part One.

Similarly, we discuss working capital after the student is familiarized with the basic principles of valuation and financing, but we recognize that many instructors prefer to reverse our order. There should be no difficulty in using Part Seven out of order.

When we discuss project valuation in Part Two, we stress that the opportunity cost of capital depends on project risk. But we do not discuss how to measure risk or how return and risk are linked until Part Three. This ordering can easily be modified. For example, the chapters on risk and return can be introduced before, after, or midway through the material on project valuation.

Walk-Through

New and Enhanced Pedagogy

A great deal of effort has gone into expanding and enhancing the features in *Fundamentals of Corporate Finance.*

CHAPTER OPENING

Each chapter begins with an overview relating the material to be covered in the chapter to the real world. Learning goals are contained in this section which are referred to again in the Summary that closes each chapter. See chapter 3, pages 62 and 98.

After studying this chapter you should be able to

- Calculate the future value to which money invested at a given interest rate will grow.
- Calculate the present value of a future payment.
- Calculate present and future values of streams of cash payments.
- Find the interest rate implied by the present or future value.
- Understand the difference between real and nominal cash flows and between real and nominal interest rates.
- Compare interest rates quoted over different time intervals—for example, monthly versus annual rates.

EXAMPLES

Separated numbered and titled examples are extensively integrated into the chapters providing detailed applications and illustrations of the text material. See chapter 4, page 116 and chapter 9, page 293.

EXAMPLE 4.3 *Calculating Yield to Maturity for the Canada Bond*

We found the value of the 6.5 percent coupon Canada bond by discounting at a 5.1 perce interest rate. We could have phrased the question the other way around: If the price of t bond is $1,038.05, what return do investors expect? We need to find the yield to maturit in other words, the discount rate r that solves the following equation:

FINANCE IN ACTION BOXES

Almost every chapter includes at least one "Finance in Action" box. These are excerpts, usually from the financial press, providing real-life illustrations of the chapter's topics, such as ethical choices in finance, new views about stock valuation, Internet IPOs, and corporate takeover battles abroad. See chapter 4, page 115, and chapter 8, page 259.

FINANCE IN ACTION

Syncrude Consortium's Staged I
Alberta's Oil Sands Operations

Buoyed by market and political momentum, Syncrude Canada Ltd., the consortium that runs northern Alberta's largest oil sands operation, will seek owner approval by July for the next and largest stage of its $8 billion expansion.

The Imperial Oil–led plant has also begun work on Stage 4, the final stage of its Syncrude 21 suite of projects, which may be larger than originally planned, Eric Newell, chairperson and chief executive, said in an interview.

"We continue at Syncrude to spend between $30 million and $40 million a year on research and development and we are continuing to find better ways. And who knows, you may see that investment even larger," he said. "The oil sands has a tremendous future and Syncrude is going to continue to be

while Suncor Energy, Inc.'s is alr wrapping up this year.

Shell has said the cost of its $ sands project could escalate by ab of a tight market for skilled labour, lar cost pressures could further incr which have already jumped to $2.8 timates of about $2 billion.

Newell said he is encouraged b said new development must wait un underway were completed.

"In 1995, we didn't have any p now we have $51 billion in terms

INTERNATIONAL ICON

An international icon now appears where the authors discuss global issues.

HOW TO VALUE PERPETUITIES

Some time ago the British government borrowed by issuing perpetuities. Instead ing these loans, the British government pays the investors holding these securitie annual payment in perpetuity.

The rate of interest on a perpetuity is equal to the promised annual payment C d the present value. For example, if a perpetuity pays $10 per year and you can buy it you will earn 10 percent interest each year on your investment. In general,

...must be ...
...osts to the firm's projects, a charge for overhead is usually made. But our principl...
...remental cash flows says that in investment appraisal we should include only the e...
...enses that would result from the project.

A project may generate extra overhead costs, but then again, it may not. W... should be cautious about assuming that the accountant's allocation of overhead costs represents the *incremental* cash flow that would be incurre... by accepting the project.

...firm is considering an investment in a new manufacturing plant. The... ...pany, but ex...ildings woul...

KEY POINTS

Located every few pages throughout the text, these points underscore and summarize the importance of the immediately preceding material, at the same time helping students focus on the most relevant topics critical to their understanding.

☑ CHECK POINT 3.5

Suppose you are planning a 1-month European vacation whe... now. The cost of the trip will be $3,500. Right now you have... bank account that pays 6 percent interest. How much more m... 1 year from now to have enough money for the trip 2 years f...

CHECK POINT QUESTION

Check Point questions are provided within each chapter, and enable students to check their understanding as they read. Answers are provided at the end of the chapter. See chapter 3, pages 75 and 108.

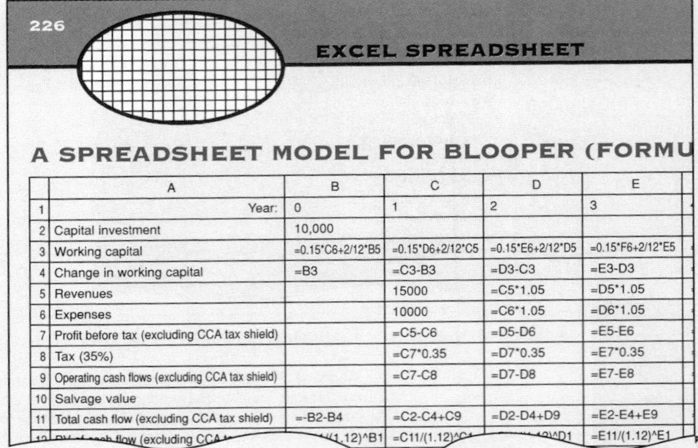

226

EXCEL SPREADSHEET

A SPREADSHEET MODEL FOR BLOOPER (FORMU...

	A	B	C	D	E
1	Year:	0	1	2	3
2	Capital investment	10,000			
3	Working capital	=0.15*C6+2/12*B5	=0.15*D6+2/12*C5	=0.15*E6+2/12*D5	=0.15*F6+2/12*E5
4	Change in working capital	=B3	=C3-B3	=D3-C3	=E3-D3
5	Revenues		15000	=C5*1.05	=D5*1.05
6	Expenses		10000	=C6*1.05	=D6*1.05
7	Profit before tax (excluding CCA tax shield)		=C5-C6	=D5-D6	=E5-E6
8	Tax (35%)		=C7*0.35	=D7*0.35	=E7*0.35
9	Operating cash flows (excluding CCA tax shield)		=C7-C8	=D7-D8	=E7-E8
10	Salvage value				
11	Total cash flow (excluding CCA tax shield)	=-B2-B4	=C2-C4+C9	=D2-D4+D9	=E2-E4+E9
12	PV of cash flow (excluding CCA ta...	...(1.12)^B1	=C11/(1.12)^C...	...12)^D1	=E11/(1.12)^E1

KEY FORMULAS

Called out in the text, key formulas are identified by a number. A summary of key formulas can be found on the Brealey web page.

EXCEL SPREADSHEET

New Excel spreadsheet boxes provide the student with detailed examples of how to use spreadsheets when applying financial concepts. See chapter 7, pages 226 and 227.

FINANCIAL CALCULATOR

An Introduction to Financial Cal...

Financial calculators are designed with present value and future value formulas already programmed. Therefore, you can readily solve many problems simply by entering the inputs for the problem and punching a key for the solution.

The basic financial calculator uses five keys that correspond to the inputs for common problems involving the time value of money.

...input:

Future Values

Recall Example 3.1, where we calc... of Peter Minuit's $24 investment. ... register. (You enter the value by typin... the *PV* key.) We assumed an interes... enter 8 into the *i* register. Because t... to compound, enter 377 into the *n* re... *PMT* register because there is no recu... in the calculation. Now ask the calc... On some calculators you simply pres... you need to first press...

CALCULATOR BOXES AND EXERCISES

In a continued effort to help students grasp the critical concept of Time Value of Money, many pedagogical tools have been added throughout the first section of the text. Financial Calculator boxes provide examples for solving a variety of problems with directions for the three most popular financial calculators. See chapter 3, pages 72–73, and chapter 6, page 179.

Walk-Through

End of Chapter

A variety of end-of-chapter features are offered to support the concepts presented throughout each chapter and include the following: Related Web Links, Key Terms, Questions and Problems, Spreadsheet Icons, Internet Problems, and Minicases.

Related Web Links

www.ganesha.org/invest/index.html Links to information useful for val
www.tsx.ca Information about stocks trading on the Toronto Stock Exchange
www.nasdaq.com Information about Nasdaq and Amex-traded stocks
www.nyse.com Information about stocks and trading on the New York S
www.fool.com/School/HowtoValueStocks.htm How investors value firr
www.zacks.com Information and analyses from Zacks Investment Resea
www.investools.com Investing tools, links to research reports on public con
www.brill.com Information on mutual funds, as well as articles and othe

Related Web Links

Web citations listed at the end of each chapter immediately direct students to the best sources of financial information on the Internet. While the authors have listed only relatively stable websites, some change in Web addresses is inevitable. Visit the text's Online Learning Centre at www.mcgrawhill.ca/college/brealey for updated information

Key Terms

Throughout each chapter, key terms appear in bold type with margin definitions and are listed in the end of chapter material for easy reference.

Key Terms

common stock	139	price-earnings (P/E) multiple	142	constant discou
primary market	139	book value	142	payout r
initial public offering (IPO)	139	liquidation value	143	plowbac
secondary market	139	market-value balance sheet	145	present v oppor
dividend	141	dividend discount model	147	sustainal

Basic

d. current yield

2. **Bond Yields.** If a bond with par value of $1,000 and a coupon rate of 8 percent is selling at a price of $970, is the bond's yield to maturity more or less than 8 percent? What about the current yield?

*3. **Bond Yields.** A bond with par value $1,000 has a current yield of 7.5 percent and a coupon rate of 8 percent. What is the bond's price?

Practice

*11. **Bond Prices and Returns.** One bond has a coupon rate of 8 percent, another a coupon rate of 12 percent. Both bonds have 10-year maturities and sell at a yield to maturity of 10 percent. If their yields to maturity next year are still 10 percent, what is the rate of return on each bond? Does the higher coupon bond give a higher rate of return?

*12. **Bond Returns.**

a. If the BCE bond in problem 6 has a yield to maturity of 8 percent 1 year from now, what will its

Challenge

32. **Interest Rate Risk.** Suppose interest rates increase from 8 percent to 9 percent. Which bond will suffer the greater percentage decline in price: a 30-year bond paying annual coupons of 8 percent, or a 30-year zero coupon bond? Can you explain intuitively why the zero exhibits greater interest rate risk even though it has the same maturity as the coupon bond?

*33. **After-Tax Rate of Return.** Using the information in problem 26, calculate your after-tax rate of return on your bond investment assuming that your marginal tax rate is 35 percent. You pay

Questions and Problems

New end-of-chapter problems are included for even more hands-on practice. Each question is labeled by topic and is separated by level of difficulty. Answers to selected questions (identified by an asterisk) are provided in Appendix B.

Walk-Through

SPREADSHEET ICON

To better understand important spreadsheet based problems, spreadsheet icons indicate problems specially linked to Excel based templates for further practice. These templates are available for download at the text's Online Learning Centre.

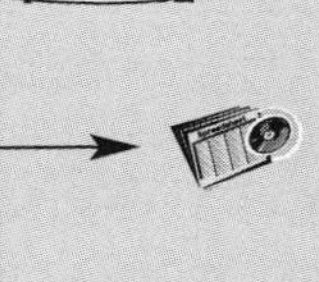

*8. **Stock** ... Potato Chips paid ... to grow steadily at a rate of 4 percent per year.

a. What is the expected dividend in each of the next 3 years?
b. If the discount rate for the stock is 12 percent, at what price will the stock s
c. What is the expected stock price 3 years from now?
d. If you buy the stock and plan to hold it for 3 years, what payments will you present value of those payments? Compare your answer to part (b).

9. **Constant-Growth Model.** A stock sells for $40. The next dividend will be $4 p return earned on reinvested funds is 15 percent and the company reinvests 40 the firm, what must be the discount rate?

INTERNET PROBLEMS

Students are presented with problems to solve using the wealth of material available on the Internet. See chapter 5, page 165 and chapter 10, page 330.

INTERNET PROBLEMS

1. Information about companies and their shares abounds on the web. and http://ca.finance.yahoo.com. Click on "Symbol Lookup" to find M tory. What other types of information are reported on these websites?
2. Visit the Toronto Stock Exchange website at www.tsx.ca, click on "List information and compare it to what is found on www.globeinvestor.com
3. Pick two Canadian companies listed on either the TSX or the Venture stock price data and dividend payments. Go to each company's website a better job of providing information to shareholders.
4. Create a list of preferred shares traded on the Toronto Stock Exchange on Globeinvestor.com. Select "Preferred" from the pull-down menu BCE.PR.P-T, which pays a fixed annual dividend of $1.60 per share. U ferred share to calculate the expected rate of return on the preferred sh 35 percent and your dividend tax rate is 20 percent, what is the expe these preferred shares?
5. It is difficult to get detailed information about companies' preferred sha however, provides one exception. Look at www.rbc.com/investorrel about the specific features of the various classes of preferred shares th on each class and compare them to each other. What conclusions ca assessment of these securities?

MINICASE

Jack Tar, CFO of Sheetbend & Halyard, Inc., opened the company confidential envelope. It contained a draft of a competitive bid for a contract to supply duffel canvas to the Canadian Armed Forces. The cover memo from Sheetbend's CEO asked Mr. Tar to review the bid before it was submitted.

The bid and its supporting documents had been prepared by Sheetbend's sales staff. It called for Sheetbend to supply 100,000 yards of duffel canvas per year for 5 years. The proposed selling price was fixed at $30 per yard.

Mr. Tar was not usually involved in sales, but this bid was unusual in at least two respects. First, if accepted by the navy, it would commit Sheetbend to a fixed price, long-term contract. Second, producing the duffel canvas would require an investment of $1.5 million to purchase machinery and to refurbish Sheetbend's plant in Saint John, New Brunswick.

Mr. Tar set to work and by the end of the week had collected the following facts and ... tions:

could be depreciated in an ass 30 percent.

- The refurbished plant and new years. However, the remaining small, and it was not clear that tained once the Forces contrac was custom built and could be second-hand value at the end
- Table 7.11 shows the sales staf navy contract. Mr. Tar reviewe its assumptions were reasonab book, not tax, depreciation.
- But the forecast income state working capital. Mr. Tar thou average about 10 percent of sa

Armed with this information, Mr ... the N...

MINICASES

Integrative minicases end most chapters and allow students to apply their knowledge to relatively complex, practical situations. See chapter 7, page 238, and chapter 15, page 477.

Supplements for The Instructor

INSTRUCTOR'S ONLINE LEARNING CENTRE (www.mcgrawhill.ca/college/brealey)

The Online Learning Centre includes a password-protected Web site for instructors. The OLC contains downloadable instructor supplements, solutions to Excel spreadsheets found on the student site, projects for use with Standard & Poor's Educational Version of Market Insight ©, and PageOut, the McGraw-Hill Ryerson course Web site development centre.

INSTRUCTOR'S CD-ROM INCLUDES:

INSTRUCTOR'S MANUAL

Updated and enhanced by the authors, this supplement includes a descriptive preface containing alternative course formats and case teaching methods, a chapter overview and outline, and key terms and concepts. The second section includes complete solutions to all end of chapter problems.

MICROSOFT® POWERPOINT® PRESENTATIONS

Prepared by Carol Edwards of the British Columbia Institute of Technology, these visually stimulating slides have been fully updated with graphs, charts, and lists. These slides can be edited or manipulated to fit the needs of a particular course.

COMPUTERIZED TEST BANK

Brian Buchanan of Langara College has adapted the test questions (approximately 2,600 in total), which consist of true or false, multiple choice, and discussion questions and problems. Questions are identified by level of difficulty and comprehension. Complete answers are provided for all questions and problems along with a reference to their location in the text. The Test Bank is available in the Diploma software program.

PageOut (www.mhhe.com/pageout) To create a Web page for your course using our resources, you can visit PageOut, the McGraw-Hill Ryerson Web site development centre. The Web-page-generation software is free to adopters and is designed to help faculty create an online course, complete with assignments, quizzes, links to relevant Web sites, lecture notes, and more, in a matter of minutes.

In addition, content cartridges are available for course management systems, such as WebCT and Blackboard.

THE STUDENT ONLINE LEARNING CENTRE (www.mcgrawhill.ca/college/brealey)

The OLC includes online study material including Quiz Questions, annotated Web links, Internet Questions, Excel templates, key terms and searchable glossary, a link to the Standard & Poor's Educational Version of Market Insight © site and Finance Around the World.

STUDY GUIDE (ISBN: 007-089868-5)

Keith Cheung, University of Windsor, prepared a valuable resource that provides students with an overview and additional review problems for each chapter. *The Study Guide* contains a thorough list of activities for students, including chapter introductions and outlines, sources of business information, key concepts and terms, completion questions, and problems with accompanying solutions. Ask for it at your bookstore!

FINANCIAL ANALYSIS SPREADSHEET TEMPLATES (FAST)

These Excel-based templates allow students to work with spreadsheets and are connected to over 100 problems in the text, which are identified by an icon. These files are available to students for downloading on the Online Learning Centre.

STANDARD
&POOR'S

STANDARD & POOR'S EDUCATIONAL VERSION OF MARKET INSIGHT©

McGraw-Hill Ryerson is proud to partner with Standard & Poor's to offer access to the Educational Version of Standard & Poor's Market Insight ©. This rich online resource provides six years of financial data for over 350 top companies, including 60 Canadian firms. The password-protected site is the perfect way to bring real data into today's classroom. Access is included with every new copy of this textbook. A link to the site is provided at the student OLC.

Acknowledgements

We want to thank everyone who helped us prepare this second edition. We want to express our appreciation to those instructors whose insightful comments and suggestions were invaluable to us during this revision.

Thank you!

Larry Bauer, *Memorial University of Newfoundland*
Harjeet Bhabra, *Concordia University, John Molson School of Business*
Nalinaksh Bhattacharyya, *University of Manitoba*
Brian Buchanan, *Langara College*
Bram Cadsby, *University of Guelph*
Richard Hudson, *Mount Allison University*
Anne Inglis, *Ryerson University*
Neil Longley, *University of Regina*
Keith MacInnes, *Ryerson University*
Bonnie Martel, *Niagara College*
Clifton Philpott, *Kwantlen University College*
Nancy Ursel, *University of Windsor*
Ganesh Vaidyanathan, *University of Saskatchewan*
Eric Wang, *Athabasca University*
Terry Zinger, *Laurentian University*

We owe much to our colleagues at the University of New Brunswick and the Schulich School of Business, York University. Special thanks to professors John Friedlan and Amin Mawani, York University, and Robert Maher, University of New Brunswick, for their willingness to share their accounting expertise, and professor Gopalan Srinivasan, University of New Brunswick, for many useful suggestions.

In addition, we'd like to thank our supplement authors Carol Edwards, Brian Buchanan, and Keith Cheung. Their efforts will help students and instructors alike.

We would like to thank Henry Chau, York University; and Calvin Milbury, University of New Brunswick, for research assistance; Marilyn Davis, University of New Brunswick, for secretarial assistance; and Josephine McMurray at the University of Guelph and Runu Kumari at the University of New Brunswick for checking calculations. As well, we would like to thank Bonnie Martel of Niagara College for her technical review of the solutions contained within the *Instructor's Manual*.

We are also grateful to the talented staff at McGraw-Hill Ryerson, especially Lynn Fisher, Senior Sponsoring Editor, Daphne Scriabin, Developmental Editor, Kelly Dickson, Manager, Editorial Services, and Christine Lomas, Editorial Coordinator. We want to thank the energetic copy editors Megan MacDonald and Kelly Lamorie of Double Space.

Finally, we cannot overstate the thanks due to our spouses, Bruce Rhodes and Koumari Mitra, and to David Rhodes, Elizabeth's son. They supported us and forgave us when we were very absorbed in the project.

Elizabeth M. Maynes
Devashis Mitra
Richard A. Brealey
Stewart C. Myers
Alan J. Marcus

McGraw-Hill Ryerson

Online Learning Centre

McGraw-Hill Ryerson offers you an online resource that combines the best content with the flexibility and power of the Internet. Organized by chapter, the BREALEY Online Learning Centre (OLC) offers the following features to enhance your learning and understanding of Corporate Finance:

- Online Quizzes
- Internet Questions
- Annotated Web Links
- Key Terms
- Microsoft® PowerPoint® Powernotes
- Searchable Glossary
- (FAST) Financial Analysis Spreadsheet Templates
- Link to Standard & Poor's Educational Version of Market Insight
- Finance Around the World

By connecting to the "real world" through the OLC, you will enjoy a dynamic and rich source of current information that will help you get more from your course and improve your chances for success, both in this course and in the future.

For the Instructor

Downloadable Supplements

All key supplements are available, password-protected for instant access!

PageOut

Create your own course Web page for free, quickly and easily. Your professionally designed Web site links directly to OLC material, allows you to post a class syllabus, offers an online gradebook, and much more! Visit www.pageout.net

Primis Online

Primis Online gives you access to our resources in the best medium for your students: printed textbooks or electronic ebooks. There are over 350,000 pages of content available from which you can create customized learning tools from our online database at www.mhhe.com/primis

eServices

McGraw-Hill Ryerson offers a unique services package designed for Canadian faculty. Our mission is to equip providers of higher education with superior tools and resources required for excellence in teaching. For additional information visit http://www.mcgrawhill.ca/highereducation/eservices/

Higher Learning. Forward Thinking.™

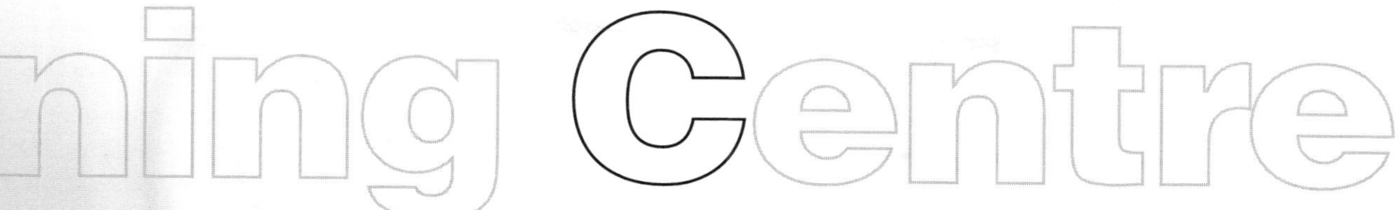

For the Student

Online Quizzes

Do you understand the material? You'll know after taking an Online Quiz!

Internet Exercises

Go online to learn how companies use the Internet in their day-to-day activities. Answer questions based on current organization Web sites and strategies.

Financial Analysis Spreadsheet Templates (FAST)

These Excel-based templates allow students to work with spreadsheets and are tied to over 100 problems in the text which are identified by an icon. These files are available to students for downloading on the Online Learning Centre.

Link to Standard & Poor's Educational Version of Market Insight

STANDARD &POOR'S

This Website provides access to **six years** of fundamental financial data from the renowned Standard & Poor's Compustat database for 355 companies including 60 leading Canadian firms. With the Excel Analytics functionality within Market Insight, 14 reports are generated from the COMPUSTAT database. These reports include annual and quarterly balance sheets, income statements, ratio reports, and cash flow statements, daily, weekly, and monthly adjusted price reports, and profitability, forecasted values, and monthly valuation data reports.

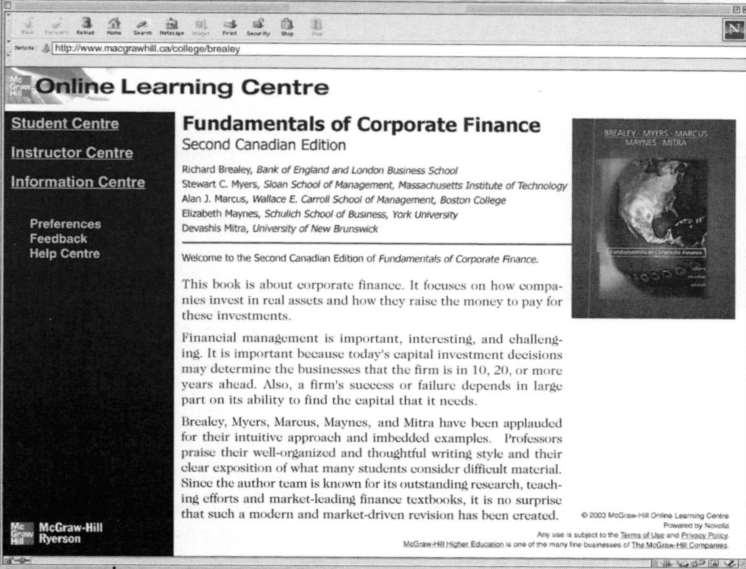

Your Internet companion to the most exciting educational tools on the Web!

The Online Learning Centre can be found at:
www.mcgrawhill.ca/college/brealey

PART ONE

Introduction

1 The Firm and the Financial Manager

2 Accounting and Finance

CHAPTER 1

The Firm and the Financial Manager

1.1 Organizing a Business
1.2 The Role of the Financial Manager
1.3 Financial Institutions and Markets
1.4 Who Is the Financial Manager?
1.5 Goals of the Corporation
1.6 Topics Covered in This Book
1.7 Summary

This book is an introduction to corporate finance. In the following chapters we will discuss the various responsibilities of the corporation's financial managers and show you how to tackle many of the problems that these managers are expected to solve. We begin in this chapter with a discussion of the corporation, the financial decisions it needs to make, and why they are important.

To survive and prosper, a company must satisfy its customers. It must also produce and sell products and services at a profit. In order to produce, it needs many assets—plant, equipment, offices, computers, technology, and so on. The company has to decide (1) which assets to buy and (2) how to pay for them. The financial manager plays a key role in both these decisions. The *investment decision,* that is, the decision to invest in assets like plant, equipment, and know-how, is in large part a responsibility of the financial manager. So is the *financing decision,* the choice of how to pay for such investments.

We start this chapter by explaining how businesses are organized. We then provide a brief introduction to the role of the financial manager and show you why corporate managers need a sophisticated understanding of financial markets. Next we turn to the goals of the firm and ask what makes for a good financial decision. Is the firm's aim to maximize profits? To avoid bankruptcy? To be a good citizen? We consider some conflicts of interest that arise in large organizations and review some mechanisms that align the interests of the firm's managers with the interests of its owners. Finally, we provide an overview of what is to come in the rest of the text.

After studying this chapter you should be able to

- Explain the advantages and disadvantages of the most common forms of business organization and determine which forms are most suitable to different types of businesses.
- Cite the major business functions and decisions that the firm's financial managers are responsible for and understand some of the possible career choices in finance.
- Explain the role of financial markets and institutions.
- Explain why it makes sense for corporations to maximize their market values.
- Show why conflicts of interest may arise in large organizations and discuss how corporations can provide incentives for everyone to work toward a common end.

Organizing a Business

SOLE PROPRIETORSHIPS

In 1934, Roy Thomson acquired his first newspaper, the *Timmins Press*, in Timmins, Ontario. Today, with 36,000 employees worldwide, the Thomson Corporation is a leading global e-information and solutions company, with sales revenues of over $9 billion in 2000. Thomson Corporation's income was recently ranked number 10 on the *Financial Post*'s list of Canada's largest corporations. If, like Roy Thomson, you start a business on your own, with no partners or shareholders, you are said to be a **sole proprietor**. You bear all of the costs and keep all of the profits after Canada Customs and Revenue Agency (CCRA) has taken its cut. The advantages of a proprietorship are the ease with which it can be established and the lack of regulations governing it. This makes it well-suited for a small company with an informal business structure.

sole proprietor Sole owner of a business which has no partners and no shareholders. The proprietor is personally liable for all the firm's obligations.

As a sole proprietor, you are responsible for all the business's debts and other liabilities. If the business borrows from the bank and subsequently cannot repay the loan, the bank has a claim against your personal belongings. It could force you into personal bankruptcy if the business debts are big enough. Thus as sole proprietor you have *unlimited liability.*

PARTNERSHIPS

Instead of starting on your own, you may wish to pool money and expertise with friends or business associates. If so, a sole proprietorship is obviously inappropriate. Instead, you can form a **partnership.** Your *partnership agreement* will set out how management decisions are to be made and the proportion of the profits to which each partner is entitled. The partners then pay personal income tax on their share of these profits.

partnership Business owned by two or more people who are personally responsible for all its liabilities.

Partners, like sole proprietors, have the disadvantage of unlimited liability. If the business runs into financial difficulties, each partner has unlimited liability for *all* the business's debts, not just his or her share. The moral is clear and simple: "Know thy partner."

Many professional businesses are organized as partnerships. They include the large accounting, legal, and management consulting firms. Several large Canadian investment dealers, such as BMO Nesbitt Burns, Scotia Capital, and CIBC World Markets, have their origins in partnerships, as do most large investment banks in the United States, such as Morgan Stanley, Salomon, Smith Barney, Merrill Lynch, and Goldman Sachs.[1] A number of large and growing Canadian companies, such as Saputo Inc. and the Jean Coutu Group, and international companies, such as Microsoft and Apple Computer, also started life as partnerships. But eventually these companies and their financing requirements grew too large for them to continue as partnerships.

CORPORATIONS

As your firm grows, you may decide to form a **corporation**. You may *incorporate* your firm federally, under the *Canadian Business Corporation Act*, or provincially, under the relevant provincial laws. A provincially incorporated firm may conduct its business in that

corporation Business owned by shareholders who are not personally liable for the business's liabilities.

[1] Investment dealers assist investors in buying and selling securities for a fee. They also assist firms in issuing new securities.

province but may need additional permissions to do business elsewhere. The incorporation documents are called *articles of incorporation* in most provinces.[2] When approved by the relevant government agency, these documents provide the charter to the firm to conduct its business as a corporation. Unlike a proprietorship or partnership, a corporation is legally distinct from its owners. As such, it is treated like a human being for many legal purposes and given rights and responsibilities. For example, it can borrow or lend money, and it can sue or be sued. It pays its own taxes—but it cannot vote!

limited liability The owners of the corporation are not personally responsible for its obligations.

The corporation is owned by its shareholders and they get to vote on important matters. Unlike proprietorships or partnerships, corporations have **limited liability,** which means that the shareholders cannot be held personally responsible for the obligations of the firm. If, say, Corel Corporation were to fail, no one could demand that its shareholders put up more money to pay off the debts. The most a shareholder can lose is the amount invested in the stock.

While the shareholders of a corporation own the firm, they do not usually manage it. Instead, they elect a *board of directors,* which in turn appoints the top managers. The board is the representative of shareholders and is supposed to ensure that management is acting in their best interests.

This *separation of ownership and management* is one distinctive feature of corporations. In other forms of business organization, such as proprietorships and partnerships, the owners are the managers.

The separation between management and ownership gives a corporation more flexibility and permanence than a partnership. Even if managers of a corporation quit or are dismissed and replaced by others, the corporation can survive. Similarly, today's shareholders may sell all their shares to new investors without affecting the business. In contrast, ownership of a proprietorship cannot be transferred without selling out to another owner-manager.

By organizing as a corporation, a business may be able to attract a wide variety of investors. The shareholders may include individuals who hold only a single share worth a few dollars, receive only a single vote, and are entitled to only a tiny proportion of the profits. Shareholders may also include giant pension funds and insurance companies the investment of which may run into the millions of shares and which are entitled to a correspondingly large number of votes and proportion of the profits.

Given these advantages, you might be wondering why all businesses are not organized as corporations. One reason is the time and cost required to manage a corporation's legal machinery. There can also be an important tax reason. Because the corporation is a separate legal entity, it is taxed separately. So corporations pay tax on their profits, and, in addition, shareholders pay tax on any dividends that they receive from the company.[3] By contrast, income received by partners and sole proprietors is taxed only once as personal income.

When you first establish a corporation, the shares may all be held by a small group, perhaps the company's managers and a small number of backers who believe the business will grow into a profitable investment. Your shares are not publicly traded and your company is *closely held.* Eventually, when the firm grows and new shares are issued to raise

[2] They are also called *letters patent* or *memorandum of association* in some provinces.

[3] To avoid taxing the same income twice, Canada's tax system, like that of several other countries, allows shareholders some credit for the taxes their company has already paid. Although this feature of Canadian tax law reduces the "double taxation" of dividend income, it does not usually eliminate it completely. We will discuss the dividend tax credit in more detail in Chapter 2.

additional capital, the shares will be widely traded. Such corporations are known as *public companies.* Most well-known corporations are public companies.[4]

To summarize, the corporation is a distinct, permanent legal entity. Its advantages are limited liability and the ease with which ownership and management can be separated. These advantages are especially important for large firms. The disadvantage of corporate organization is double taxation.

The financial managers of a corporation are responsible, by way of top management and the board of directors, to the corporation's shareholders. Financial managers are supposed to make financial decisions that serve shareholders' interests. Table 1.1 presents the distinctive features of the major forms of business organization.

HYBRID FORMS OF BUSINESS ORGANIZATION

Businesses do not always fit into these neat categories. Some are hybrids of the three basic types: proprietorships, partnerships, and corporations.

For example, businesses can be set up as *limited partnerships.* In this case, partners are classified as general or limited. General partners manage the business and have unlimited personal liability for the business's debts. Limited partners, however, are liable only for the money they contribute to the business. They can lose everything they put in, but not more.

Limited partners usually have a restricted role and cannot take part in the day-to-day management of the partnership, but they have the right to share in partnership profits and to have their contributions returned if the business is dissolved. Forming a limited partnership requires that a written agreement be registered provincially which details the capital contributions of the limited partners and identifies the general partners.

Now firms can also be set up as *limited liability partnerships (LLP)*, which are relatively new in Canada and are often designed to meet the liability concerns of

TABLE 1.1
Characteristics of business organizations

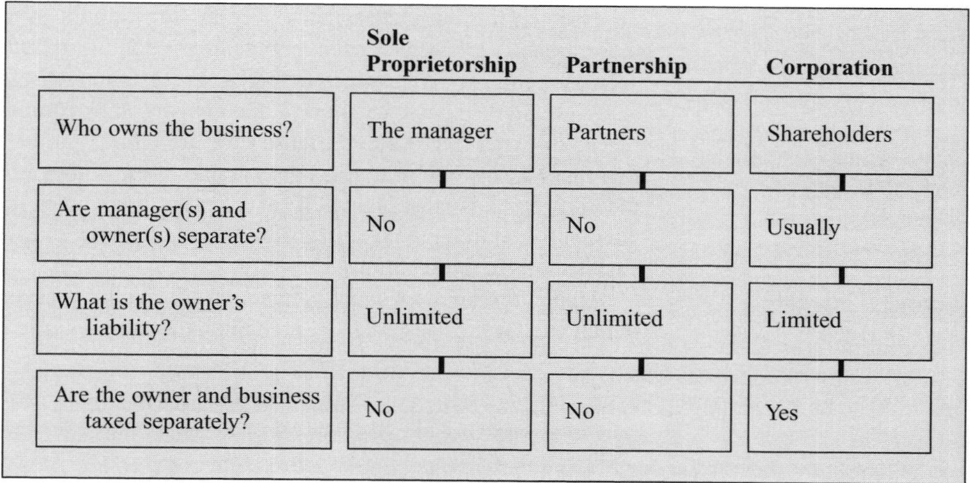

	Sole Proprietorship	Partnership	Corporation
Who owns the business?	The manager	Partners	Shareholders
Are manager(s) and owner(s) separate?	No	No	Usually
What is the owner's liability?	Unlimited	Unlimited	Limited
Are the owner and business taxed separately?	No	No	Yes

[4] For example, when Microsoft was initially established as a corporation, its shares were closely held by a small number of employees and backers. Microsoft shares were issued to the public in 1986. In contrast, McCain Foods is still closely held despite being one of Canada's largest multinational food manufacturers.

professionals such as accountants or lawyers.[5] Individual partners in an LLP continue to have unlimited liability for their own professional negligence or malpractice, as in an ordinary partnership, but they are not liable for the negligence or malpractice of their other partners. The firm retains overall liability and so its assets and any insurance policies it owns can be used to meet losses. Provincial laws determine whether members of individual professions are allowed to form LLPs. Limited liability partnerships combine the tax advantage of a partnership with the limited liability advantage of incorporation.

Professionals such as engineers or accountants may also incorporate using *limited liability corporations (LLC)* provided they are specifically permitted to do so by the laws governing the particular profession in that province.[6] Typically incorporation does not protect the professional from personal liability for negligence. Another variation on the theme is the *professional corporation (PC)*, which is commonly used by doctors, lawyers, and accountants. In this case, the business has limited liability but the professional can still be sued personally for malpractice, even if the malpractice occurs in the role of corporation employee. Despite their advantages, these forms of business organization still do not suit the largest firms for which widespread share ownership and separation of ownership and management are essential.

CHECK POINT 1.1

Which form of business organization might best suit the following?

a. A consulting firm with several senior consultants and support staff.
b. A house painting company owned and operated by a college student who hires some friends for occasional help.
c. A paper goods company with sales of $100 million and 2,000 employees.

1.2

The Role of the Financial Manager

real assets Assets used to produce goods and services.

financial assets Claims to the income generated by real assets. Also called securities.

financial markets Markets in which financial assets are traded.

To carry on business, companies need an almost endless variety of **real assets.** Many of these assets are tangible, such as machinery, factories, and offices; others are intangible, such as technical expertise, trademarks, and patents. All of them must be paid for.

To obtain the necessary money, the company sells **financial assets,** or *securities.*[7] These pieces of paper have value because they are claims on the firm's real assets and the cash that those assets will produce. For example, if the company borrows money from the bank, the bank has a financial asset. That financial asset gives it a claim to a stream of interest payments and to repayment of the loan. The company's real assets need to produce enough cash to satisfy these claims.

Financial managers stand between the firm's real assets and the **financial markets** in which the firm raises cash. The financial manager's role is shown in Figure 1.1, which

[5] *Limited Liability Partnerships*, Report 77 (Edmonton: The Alberta Law Reform Institute, 1999) p. 5. The report also recommends that LLPs in Canada should be available to enterprises generally as is the case in many states in the United States.

[6] For further discussion, see D. Duplessis, S. Enman, S. Gunz, and S. O'Byrne, *Canadian Business Law* (Scarborough, Ontario: Nelson Thomson Learning, 2001) pp. 530–532.

[7] For present purposes we are using *financial assets* and *securities* interchangeably, though "securities" usually refers to financial assets that are widely held, like the shares of Nortel Networks. An IOU ("I owe you") from your brother-in-law, which you might have trouble selling outside the family, is also a financial asset, but most people would not think of it as a security.

FIGURE 1.1
*Flow of cash between capital markets and the firm's operations. Key: (1) cash raised by selling financial assets to investors; (2) cash invested in the firm's operations; (3) cash generated by the firm's operations; (4*a*) cash reinvested; (4*b*) cash returned to investors.*

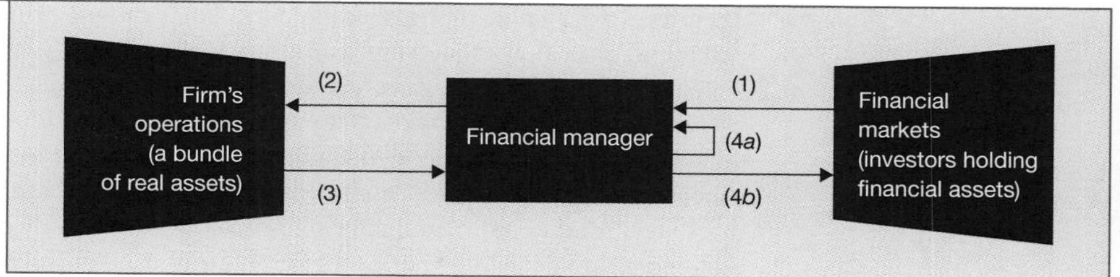

traces how money flows from investors to the firm and back to investors again. The flow starts when financial assets are sold to raise cash (arrow 1 in the figure). The cash is employed to purchase the real assets used in the firm's operations (arrow 2). Later, if the firm does well, the real assets generate enough cash inflow to more than repay the initial investment (arrow 3). Finally, the cash is either reinvested (arrow 4*a*) or returned to the investors who contributed the money in the first place (arrow 4*b*). Of course the choice between arrows 4*a* and 4*b* is not a completely free one. For example, if a bank lends the firm money at stage 1, the bank has to be repaid this money plus interest at stage 4*b*.

This flow chart suggests that the financial manager faces two basic problems. First, how much money should the firm invest, and what specific assets should the firm invest in? This is the firm's *investment decision,* or **capital budgeting decision.** Second, how should the cash required for an investment be raised? This is the **financing decision.**

capital budgeting decision Decision as to which real assets the firm should acquire.

financing decision Decision as to how to raise the money to pay for investments in real assets.

THE CAPITAL BUDGETING DECISION

Capital budgeting decisions are central to the company's success or failure. For example, in the late 1980s, the Walt Disney Company committed to construction of a Disneyland Paris theme park at a total cost of well over $2 billion. The park, which opened in 1992, turned out to be a financial bust, and Euro Disney had to reorganize in May 1994. Instead of providing profits on the investment, accumulated losses on the park by that date were more than $200 million.

Contrast that with Boeing's decision to "bet the company" by developing the 757 and 767 jets. Boeing's investment in these planes was $3 billion, more than double the total value of shareholders' investment as shown in the company's accounts at the time. By 1997, estimated cumulative profits from this investment were approaching $8 billion, and the planes were still selling well.

Consider also the case of Canada's Bombardier which decided to diversify into aerospace in 1986, and within a few years, invested over $5 billion to acquire, develop, and market product lines of small regional and business aircraft that the larger aircraft manufacturers such as Boeing do not produce. The company's bet on this niche market for 20- to 90-seat aircraft appears to have paid off as this sector now accounts for well over 50 percent of Bombardier's revenues. The company has a large and growing number of orders for its Dash 8 turboprops, CRJ regional jets and the Canadair and Learjet business jets.

Disney's decision to invest in Euro Disney or Boeing's and Bombardier's decisions to invest in a new generation of airliners are all examples of capital budgeting decisions. The success of such decisions is usually judged in terms of value. Good investment projects are worth more than they cost. Adopting such projects increases the value of the firm and therefore the wealth of its shareholders. For example, Boeing's investment produced a stream of cash flows that were worth much more than its $3 billion outlay.

Not all investments are in physical plant and equipment. For example, the plans of Nintendo's Canadian subsidiary to spend about $15 million in 2001/2002 to promote its new GameCube home game machine on television, and in print and online advertising in Canada represent an investment in intangible assets—brand recognition and acceptance. Moreover, traditional manufacturing firms are not the only ones that make important capital budgeting decisions. For example, in 1999, Nortel Networks had the highest expenditures on research and development (R&D) of any Canadian company, spending in excess of $2.9 billion.[8] This investment in future products and product improvement will be crucial to the company's ability to retain its existing customers and attract new ones.

Today's investments provide benefits in the future. Thus the financial manager is concerned not solely with the size of the benefits but also with how long the firm must wait for them. The sooner the profits come in, the better. In addition, these benefits are rarely certain; a new project may be a great success—but then again it could be a dismal failure. The financial manager needs a way to place a value on these uncertain future benefits.

We will spend considerable time in later chapters on project evaluation. While no one can guarantee that you will avoid disasters like Euro Disney or that you will be blessed with successes like the 757 or the CRJ regional jets, a disciplined, analytical approach to project proposals will weight the odds in your favour.

THE FINANCING DECISION

The financial manager's second responsibility is to raise the money to pay for the investment in real assets. This is the financing decision. When a company needs financing, it can invite investors to put up cash in return for a share of profits or it can promise investors a series of fixed payments. In the first case, the investor receives newly issued shares of stock and becomes a shareholder, a part-owner of the firm. In the second, the investor becomes a lender who must one day be repaid. The choice of the long-term financing mix is often called the **capital structure** decision, since *capital* refers to the firm's sources of long-term financing, and the markets for long-term financing are called **capital markets.**[9]

capital structure Firm's mix of long-term financing.

capital markets Markets for long-term financing.

Within the basic distinction—issuing new shares of stock versus borrowing money—there are endless variations. Suppose the company decides to borrow. Should it go to capital markets for long-term debt financing or should it borrow from a bank? Should it borrow in Paris, receiving and promising to repay euros, or should it borrow Canadian dollars in Toronto? Should it demand the right to pay off the debt early if future interest rates fall? We will look at these and other choices in later chapters.

The decision to invest in a new factory or to issue new shares of stock has long-term consequences. But the financial manager is also involved in some important short-term decisions. For example, she needs to make sure that the company has enough cash on hand to pay next week's bills and that any spare cash is put to work to earn interest. Such short-term financial decisions involve both investment (how to invest spare cash) and financing (how to raise cash to meet a short-term need).

Businesses are inherently risky, but the financial manager needs to ensure that risks are managed. For example, the manager will want to be certain that the firm cannot be wiped

[8] Accountants may treat investments in R&D differently than investments in plant and equipment but it is clear that both investments are creating real assets. Whether those assets are physical capital or know-how, both investments are essential capital budgeting activities.

[9] *Money markets* are used for short-term financing.

out by a sudden rise in oil prices or a fall in the value of the dollar. In later chapters, we will look at the techniques that managers use to explore the future and some of the ways that the firm can be protected against nasty surprises.

CHECK POINT 1.2

Are the following capital budgeting or financing decisions?

a. Ballard Power decides to spend $500 million to develop a new fuel cell.
b. Volkswagen decides to raise 350 million euros through a bank loan.
c. Nova Corporation constructs a pipeline to transport natural gas to Chile's remote southern Magallanes region.
d. Royal Caribbean Cruises sells $300 million (US) of new debt to upgrade its cruise liners.
e. Biochem Pharma buys a licence to produce and sell a new drug developed by a biotech firm.
f. Loblaw issues new shares to help finance the acquisition of Provigo, a retail grocery company.

1.3 Financial Institutions and Markets

If a corporation needs to borrow from the bank or issue new securities, then its financial manager had better understand how financial markets work. Perhaps less obviously, the capital budgeting decision also requires an understanding of financial markets. We have said that a successful investment is one that increases firm value. But how do investors value a firm? The answer to this question requires a theory of how the firm's stock is priced in financial markets.

Of course, theory is not the end of it. The financial manager is in day-by-day—sometimes minute-by-minute—contact with financial markets and must understand their institutions, regulations, and operating practices. We can give you a flavour for these issues by considering briefly some of the ways that firms interact with financial markets and institutions. We will treat most of these issues more completely in later chapters.

FINANCIAL INSTITUTIONS

financial intermediary Firm that raises money from many small investors and provides financing to businesses or other organizations by investing in their securities.

Most firms are too small to raise funds by selling stocks or bonds directly to investors. When these companies need to raise funds to help pay for a capital investment, the only choice is to borrow money from a **financial intermediary** like a bank or insurance company. The financial intermediary, in turn, raises funds from individual households, often in small amounts. For example, a bank raises funds when customers deposit money into their bank accounts. The bank can then lend this money to borrowers.

The bank saves borrowers and lenders from finding and negotiating with each other directly. For example, a firm that wishes to borrow $2.5 million could in principle try to arrange loans from many individuals:

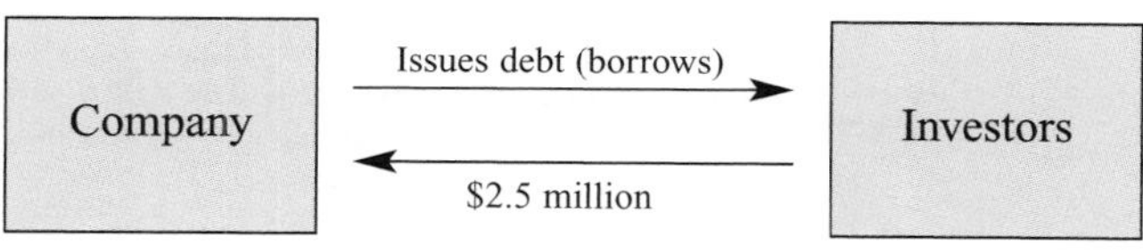

However, it is far more convenient and efficient for a bank, which has ongoing relations with thousands of depositors, to raise the funds from them, and then lend the money to the company:

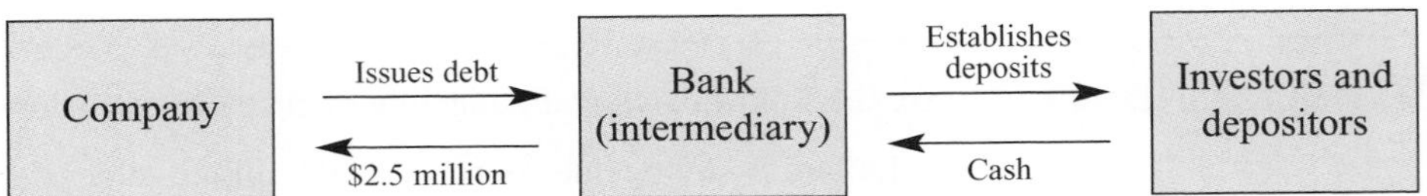

The bank provides a service. To cover the costs of this service, it charges borrowers a higher interest rate than it pays its depositors.

At present, Canadian residents are served by 54 banks that operate in different parts of the country and manage over $1.4 trillion in assets. Of these, 13 are domestic banks, while the remaining 41 are foreign bank subsidiaries and branches. The Big Six domestic chartered banks are perhaps the country's most familiar financial intermediaries. They account for about 90 percent of the country's bank industry assets and over 50 percent of the total domestic assets held by the financial sector.[10] But there are many others such as caisses populaires, credit unions, insurance companies, pension funds, and trust companies. Let us describe these financial intermediaries in a little more detail.

Like banks, trust companies, credit unions, and caisses populaires accept deposits and make loans. In addition, trust companies engage in fiduciary services such as managing assets, like registered retirement savings plans, for estates or pension plans. Some major trust companies experienced difficulties following the collapse of the real estate market in the early 1990s and, over the years, they have been consolidated with the chartered banks. A recent example is the assimilation of Canada Trust with Toronto Dominion Bank.

Credit unions and caisses populaires are typically run as cooperatives and are an important source of financing for residential mortgages as well as small and medium enterprises. Caisses populaires are mainly located in Québec although a number operate in Manitoba, Ontario, and the Maritime provinces; for example, there are over 45 caisses populaires acadiennes in New Brunswick. Credit unions can be found across Canada but are particularly active in British Columbia and Saskatchewan. Some of Canada's caisses populaires and credit unions are very large. Québec-based Mouvement Desjardins is a conglomerate involved in a wide array of activities and ranks among the top eight financial institutions in the country based on assets. Mouvement des caisses Desjardins includes a network of 739 caisses populaires in Québec and over 85 caisses populaires outside Québec.

Insurance companies includes health, life, property, and casualty insurance companies. Life insurance companies make loans from funds received from the sale of life insurance policies and products such as registered retirement savings plans (RRSP) and registered retirement income funds (RRIF).

Pension funds receive contributions from employers and employees, which they invest in a variety of financial securities. Some pension plans, such as Caisse de dépôt et

[10] In 2000, the largest chartered banks, in order of assets, were Royal Bank of Canada, Canadian Imperial Bank of Commerce, the Toronto Dominion Bank, Bank of Nova Scotia, Bank of Montreal, and National Bank of Canada. Shares in these banks are widely held by a large number of shareholders. For more information and statistics about Canada's banking industry, you can visit the website of the *Canadian Bankers Association* at www.cba.ca.

placement du Québec or the Ontario Teachers' Plan are among the largest and most influential investors in the country.

In Canada, large pension funds and insurance companies, particularly life and health insurance firms, invest more in the *long-term financing* of business than banks. They are massive investors in corporate stocks and bonds and occasionally make long-term loans directly to corporations.

Suppose a company needs a loan for 9 years, not 9 months. It could issue a bond directly to investors, or it could negotiate a 9-year loan with an insurance company:

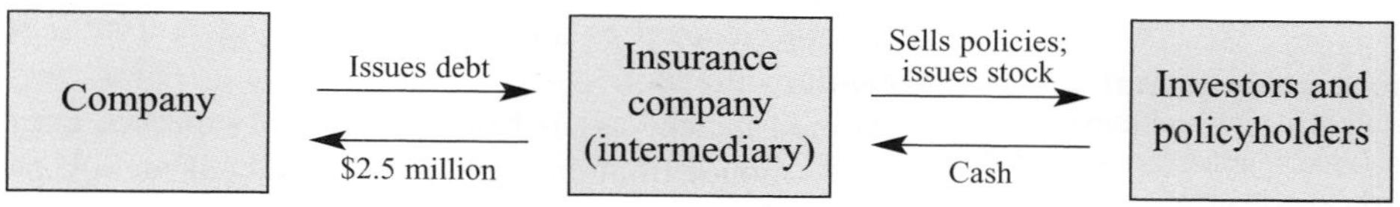

The money to make the loan comes mainly from the sale of insurance policies. Say you buy a fire insurance policy on your home. You pay cash to the insurance company and get a financial asset (the policy) in exchange. You receive no interest payments on this financial asset, but if a fire does strike, the company is obliged to cover the damages up to the policy limit. This is the return on your investment.

The company will issue not just one policy, but thousands. Normally the incidence of fires "averages out," leaving the company with a predictable obligation to its policyholders as a group. Of course the insurance company must charge enough for its policies to cover selling and administrative costs, pay policyholders' claims, and generate a profit for its shareholders.

Why is a financial intermediary different from a manufacturing corporation? First, it may raise money differently; for example, by taking deposits or selling insurance policies. Second, it invests that money in *financial* assets; for example, in stocks, bonds, or loans to businesses or individuals. The manufacturing company's main investments are in plant, equipment, and other *real* assets.

FINANCIAL MARKETS

As firms grow, their need for capital can expand dramatically. At some point, the firm may find that "cutting out the middle-man" and raising funds directly from investors is advantageous. At this point, it is ready to sell new financial assets, such as shares of stock, to the public. The first time the firm sells shares to the general public is called the *initial public offering,* or *IPO.* The corporation, which until now was privately owned, is said to "go public." The sale of the securities is usually managed by a group of investment dealers such as CIBC World Markets or RBC Dominion Securities. Investors who buy shares are contributing funds that will be used to pay for the firm's investments in real assets. In return, they become part-owners of the firm and share in the future success of the enterprise. Anyone who followed the market for Internet IPOs in 1999 and the subsequent price performance of these shares in 2000 and 2001 knows that these expectations for future success can be on the optimistic side (to put it mildly).

An IPO is not the only occasion on which newly issued stock is sold to the public. Established firms also issue new shares from time to time. For example, suppose Alcan needs to raise funds to renovate an aluminum smelting plant. It might hire an investment banking firm to sell $500 million of Alcan stock to investors. Some of this stock may be bought by individuals; the remainder will be bought by financial institutions such as pension funds and insurance companies. In fact, about a quarter of the shares of U.S. companies are owned by pension funds.

primary market Market for the sale of new securities by corporations.

A new issue of securities increases both the amount of cash held by the company and the amount of stocks or bonds held by the public. Such an issue is known as a *primary issue* and it is sold in the **primary market.** But in addition to helping companies raise new cash, financial markets also allow investors to trade stocks or bonds between themselves. For example, Smith might decide to raise some cash by selling her BCE stock at the same time that Jones invests his spare cash in BCE. The result is simply a transfer of ownership from Smith to Jones, which has no effect on the company itself. Such purchases and sales of existing securities are known as *secondary transactions* and they take place in the **secondary market.**

secondary market Market in which already issued securities are traded among investors.

Some financial assets have no secondary market. For example, when a small company borrows money from the bank, it gives the bank an IOU promising to repay the money with interest. The bank will keep the IOU and will not sell it to another bank. Other financial assets are regularly traded. Thus when a large public company raises cash by selling new shares to investors, it knows that many of these investors will subsequently decide to sell their shares to others.

Most trading in the shares of large Canadian corporations takes place on stock exchanges such as the Toronto Stock Exchange (TSE), now part of the TSX Group. As of April 2001, the TSE had 1399 companies listed with a daily average value of shares traded of about $3.2 billion. Trading in the shares of smaller and emerging companies was done through the Canadian Venture Exchange (CDNX), which in 2001, listed about 2650 companies. In 2001, CDNX became a wholly owned subsidiary of the TSE, although it continued to operate as a separate exchange.[11] Trading in shares can also be done in *over-the-counter (OTC)* markets, which do not have a centralized physical location like the TSX but consist of a network of security dealers who trade with each other over the phone, and increasingly nowadays, over electronic networks. In Canada, the volume of OTC equity trading has traditionally been quite small and until recently was conducted through a large network linking dealers across Canada called the Canadian Dealing Network (CDN). The most actively traded stocks on the CDN moved to the CDNX, now part of the TSX group. In November 2000, a new electronic entrant, Nasdaq Canada, launched operations in Montreal for the purpose of trading in shares listed on the Nasdaq stock market. Based in the United States, this stock market consists of a network of security dealers who use an electronic system known as NASDAQ[12] to quote prices at which they will buy and sell shares. In this respect, it is a large *over-the-counter (OTC)* market and lists a wide range of stocks, from small, upcoming companies to giants such as Microsoft and Intel. When Nasdaq Canada was started, 146 of the approximately 5000 Nasdaq-listed companies were Canadian.

While shares of stock may be traded either on exchanges or over-the-counter, most corporate debt is traded over-the-counter if it is traded at all. Government debt is also traded over-the-counter, a large component of it being Government of Canada bonds.

Many other things trade in financial markets; claims on commodities such as corn, crude oil, and silver; and options, which we dissect in Chapter 25. The market for foreign currencies is discussed in Chapter 24.

Now may be a good point to stress that the financial manager plays on a global stage

[11] Recently, CDNX has been replaced by the TSX Venture Exchange. The exchange is now part of the TSX Group which also includes the Toronto Stock Exchange. The symbols for the two exchanges, CDNX and TSE, have been replaced by TSX. The website for exchanges is at www.tsx.ca.

[12] National Association of Security Dealers Automated Quotation system.

and needs to be familiar with markets around the world. For example, larger Canadian companies having sizable global operations, such as Alcan or Canadian Imperial Bank of Commerce, tend to be *cross-listed* on the TSX as well as other large international exchanges such as the New York Stock Exchange (NYSE).

OTHER FUNCTIONS OF FINANCIAL MARKETS AND INSTITUTIONS

Financial markets and institutions provide financing for business. They also contribute in many other ways to our individual well-being and the smooth functioning of the economy. Here are some examples.[13]

The Payment Mechanism. Think how inconvenient life would be if you had to pay for every purchase in cash or if General Motors of Canada had to ship truckloads of $100 bills round the country to pay its suppliers. Chequing accounts, credit cards, and electronic transfers allow individuals and firms to send and receive payments quickly and safely over long distances. Banks are the obvious providers of payment services, but they are not alone. For example, if you buy shares in a money-market mutual fund, your money is pooled with that of other investors and used to buy safe, short-term securities. You can then write cheques on this mutual fund investment, just as if you had a bank deposit.

Borrowing and Lending. Financial institutions allow individuals to transfer expenditures across time. If you have more money now than you need and you wish to save for a rainy day, you can (for example) put the money on deposit in a bank. If you wish to anticipate some of your future income to buy a car, you can borrow money from the bank. Both the lender and the borrower are happier than if they were forced to spend cash as it arrived. Of course, individuals are not alone in needing to raise cash from time to time. Firms with good investment opportunities raise cash by borrowing or selling new shares. Many governments run at a deficit.

In principle, individuals or firms with cash surpluses could take out newspaper advertisements or surf the Net looking for counterparts with cash shortages. But it is usually cheaper and more convenient to use financial markets or institutions to link the borrower and the lender. For example, banks are equipped to check the borrower's creditworthiness and to monitor the use of the cash.

Almost all financial institutions are involved in channelling savings toward those who can best use them.

Pooling Risk. Financial markets and institutions allow individuals and firms to pool their risks. Insurance companies are an obvious example. Here is another. Suppose that you have only a small sum to invest. You could buy the stock of a single company, but then you could be wiped out if that company went belly-up. It's generally better to buy shares in a mutual fund that invests in a diversified portfolio of common stocks or other securities. In this case you are exposed only to the risk that security prices as a whole may fall.[14]

[13] Robert Merton gives an excellent overview of these functions in "A Functional Perspective of Financial Intermediation," *Financial Management* 24 (Summer 1995), pp. 23–41.

[14] Mutual funds provide other services. For example, they take care of much of the paperwork of holding shares. Investors also hope that the fund's professional managers will be able to outsmart the market and secure higher returns. Over the last decade, assets of these funds grew by leaps and bounds as many new investors tried to take advantage of ever-increasing stock prices.

CHECK POINT 1.3

Do you understand the following distinctions? Briefly explain in each case.

a. Real versus financial assets.
b. Investment versus financing decisions.
c. Capital budgeting versus capital structure decisions.
d. Primary versus secondary markets.
e. Financial intermediation versus direct financing from financial markets.

Who Is the Financial Manager?

In this book we will use the term *financial manager* to refer to anyone responsible for a significant corporate investment or financing decision. But except in the smallest firms, no *single* person is responsible for all the decisions discussed in this book. Responsibility is dispersed throughout the firm. Top management is, of course, constantly involved in financial decisions. But the engineer who designs a new production facility is also involved: the design determines the kind of asset the firm will invest in. Likewise the marketing manager who undertakes a major advertising campaign is making an investment decision: the campaign is an investment in an intangible asset that will pay off in future sales and earnings.

treasurer Manager responsible for financing, cash management, and relationships with financial markets and institutions.

controller Officer responsible for budgeting, accounting, and auditing.

chief financial officer (CFO) Officer who oversees the treasurer and controller and sets overall financial strategy.

Nevertheless, there are managers who specialize in finance, and their functions are summarized in Figure 1.2. The **treasurer** is usually the person most directly responsible for looking after the firm's cash, raising new capital, and maintaining relationships with banks and other investors who hold the firm's securities.

For small firms, the treasurer is likely to be the only financial executive. Larger corporations usually also have a **controller,** who prepares the financial statements, manages the firm's internal accounting, and looks after its tax affairs. You can see that the treasurer and controller have different roles: the treasurer's main function is to obtain and manage the firm's capital, whereas the controller ensures that the money is used efficiently.

The largest firms usually appoint a **chief financial officer (CFO)** to oversee both the treasurer's and the controller's work. The CFO is deeply involved in financial policymaking and corporate planning. Often he or she will have general responsibilities beyond strictly financial issues.

FIGURE 1.2
The financial managers in large corporations

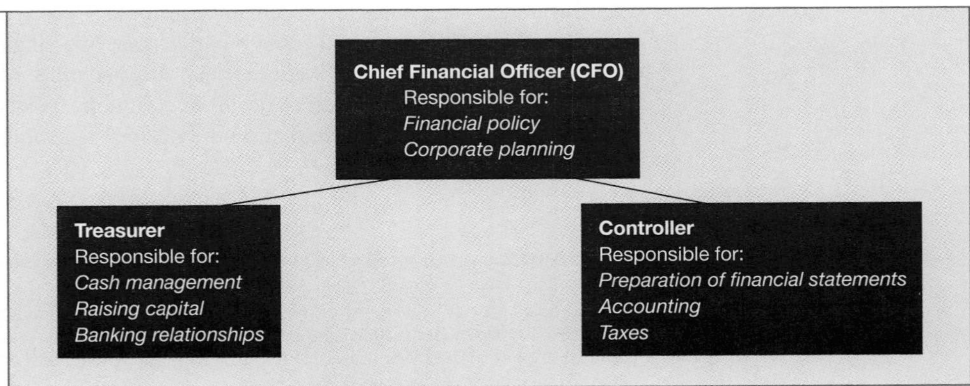

Usually the treasurer, controller, or CFO is responsible for organizing and supervising the capital budgeting process. However, major capital investment projects are so closely tied to plans for product development, production, and marketing that managers from these other areas are inevitably drawn into planning and analyzing the projects. If the firm has staff members specializing in corporate planning, they are naturally involved in capital budgeting too.

Because of the importance of many financial issues, ultimate decisions often rest by law or by custom with the board of directors.[15] For example, only the board has the legal power to declare a dividend or to sanction a public issue of securities. Boards usually delegate decision-making authority for small- or medium-sized investment outlays, but the authority to approve large investments is almost never delegated.

CHECK POINT 1.4

Sal and Sally went to business school together 10 years ago. They have just been hired by a midsized corporation that wants to bring in new financial managers. Sal studied finance, with an emphasis on financial markets and institutions. Sally majored in accounting and became a chartered accountant (CA) 5 years ago. Who is more suited to be treasurer? Controller? Briefly explain.

CAREERS IN FINANCE

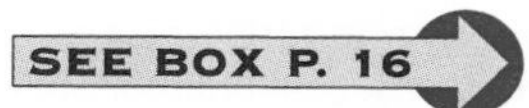
SEE BOX P. 16

In Canada, well over half a million people work in financial services, and many others work in the finance departments of corporations. We can't tell you what each person does all day, but we can give you some idea of the variety of careers in finance. The nearby Finance in Action box summarizes the experience of a small sample of recent (fictitious) graduates.

We explained earlier that corporations face two principal financial decisions: the investment decision and the financing decision. Therefore, as a newly recruited financial analyst, you may help to analyze a major new investment project. Or you may instead help to raise the money to pay for it, perhaps by a new issue of debt or by arranging to lease the plant and equipment. Other financial analysts work on short-term financial issues, such as collecting and investing the company's cash or checking whether customers are likely to pay their bills. Financial analysts are also involved in monitoring and controlling risk. For example, they may help to arrange insurance for the firm's plant and equipment, or they may assist with the purchase and sale of options, futures, and other exotic tools for managing risk.

Instead of working in the finance department of a corporation, you may join a financial institution. The largest employers are the commercial banks. We noted earlier that banks collect deposits and re-lend the cash to corporations and individuals. If you join a bank, at some point you may well work in a branch, where individuals and small businesses come to deposit cash or to seek a loan. Alternatively, you may be employed in the head office, helping to analyze a $100 million loan to a large corporation.

Banks do many things in addition to lending money, and they probably provide a greater variety of jobs than other financial institutions. For example, individuals and businesses use banks to make payments to each other. So if you work in the cash management department of a large bank, you may help companies electronically transfer huge sums of money as wages, taxes, and payments to suppliers. Banks also buy and sell foreign exchange, so you could find yourself working in front of one of those computer screens in a foreign exchange

[15] Often the firm's chief financial officer is also a member of its board of directors.

FINANCE IN ACTION

Working in Finance

Susan Webb, Research Analyst, Mutual Fund Group

After majoring in biochemistry, I joined the research department of a large mutual fund group. Because of my background, I was assigned to work with the senior pharmaceuticals analyst. I start the day by reading the business sections of the *Globe and Mail* and *Financial Post* and reviewing the analyses that come in each day from stockbroking firms. I also read about market activity and news worldwide from the Bloomberg website on my personal computer. Sometimes we need to revise our earnings forecasts and meet with the portfolio managers to discuss possible trades. The remainder of my day is spent mainly in analyzing companies and developing forecasts of revenues and earnings. I meet frequently with pharmaceutical analysts in stockbroking firms and we regularly visit company management. In the evenings I study for the Chartered Financial Analyst exam. Since I did not study finance at college, this is quite challenging. I hope eventually to move from a research role to become a portfolio manager.

Richard Gradley, Project Finance, Large Energy Company

After leaving college, I joined the finance department of a large engineering and construction company. I spent my first year helping to analyze capital investment proposals. I then moved to the project finance group, which is responsible for analyzing engineering infrastructure and construction projects around the world. Recently, I have been involved in a turnkey contract proposal to set up a large sulphuric acid plant in Europe. We built a spreadsheet model of the project to make sure that it was viable and we had to check that the contracts with the builders, operators, suppliers, and so on, were all in place before we could arrange bank finance for the project.

Albert Rodriguez, Emerging Markets Group, Major Toronto Bank

I joined the bank after majoring in finance. I spent the first 6 months in the bank's training program, rotating between departments. I was assigned to the Latin America team just before the 1998 Brazilian crisis when interest rates jumped to nearly 50 percent and the currency fell by 40 percent. There was a lot of activity, with everyone trying to figure out what was likely to happen next and how it would affect our business. My job is largely concerned with analyzing economies and assessing the prospects for bank business. There are plenty of opportunities to work abroad and I hope to spend some time in one of our Latin American offices, such as Argentina or Brazil.

Emma Kuletsky, Customer Service Representative, Regional Bank

My job is to help look after customers in a large branch. They seem to expect me to know about everything. I help them with financial planning and with their applications for loans. In a typical day, I may have to interview a new customer who wants to open an account with the bank and calm an old one who thinks she has been overcharged for a wire transfer. I like dealing with people, and one day I hope to be manager of a branch like this one.

dealing room. Another glamorous bank job is in the derivatives group, which helps companies to manage their risk by buying and selling options, futures, and so on. This is where the mathematicians and the computer buffs thrive.

Investment dealers such as Scotia Capital or CIBC World Markets help companies sell their securities to investors. They also have large corporate finance departments, which assist firms in major reorganizations such as takeovers. When firms issue securities or try to take over another firm, frequently a lot of money is at stake and the firms may need to move fast. Thus working for an investment bank can be a high-pressure activity with long hours. It can also be very well paid.

The distinction between commercial banks and investment dealers is narrowing. For example, commercial banks may also be involved in new issues of securities, while investment dealers are major traders in options and futures. The same company may own both investment dealers and commercial banks; for example, RBC Dominion Securities (an investment dealer and brokerage house) and the Royal Bank of Canada (a commercial bank) are both owned by Royal Bank Financial Group.

The insurance industry is another large employer. Much of the insurance industry is involved in designing and selling insurance policies on people's lives and property, but businesses are also major customers. So if you work for an insurance company or a large insurance broker, you could find yourself arranging insurance on a CRJ 200 regional jet in Canada or a pipeline in Chile.

A mutual fund collects money from individuals and invests in a portfolio of stocks or bonds. A financial analyst for a mutual fund analyzes the prospects for the securities and works with the investment manager to decide which ones should be bought and sold. Many other financial institutions also contain investment management departments. For example, you might work as a financial analyst in the investment department of an insurance company and help to invest the premiums. Or you could be a financial analyst in the trust department of a bank that manages money for retirement funds, universities, and charitable bodies.

Stockbroking firms and bond dealers help investment management companies and private individuals to invest in securities. They employ sales staff and dealers who make the trades. They also employ financial analysts to analyze the securities and help customers to decide which ones to buy or sell. Many stockbroking firms are owned by chartered banks, such as Bank of Montreal.

The big commercial banks, investment dealers, insurance companies, and stockbroking firms are mostly headquartered in and around Toronto. Of course, large financial institutions have their headquarters in other cities as well. For instance, National Bank of Canada, Caisse de dépôt et placement du Québec and Desjardins-Laurentian Financial Corporation are headquartered in Montreal while Great-West Life Assurance and Investors Group are headquartered in Winnipeg. Many financial institutions have significant business interests outside Canada. Finance is a global business, so you may spend some time working in an overseas branch or travel occasionally to one of the major international financial centres, such as New York, London, Frankfurt, Hong Kong, or Singapore.

Finance professionals tend to be well paid. Starting salaries for new graduates are in the region of $35,000, rather more in a major Toronto investment bank and somewhat less in a small regional bank. But let us look ahead a little: Table 1.2 gives you an idea of the compensation that you can look forward to when you become a senior financial manager. Table 1.3 directs you to some Internet sites that provide useful information about careers in finance.

1.5 Goals of the Corporation

SHAREHOLDERS WANT MANAGERS TO MAXIMIZE MARKET VALUE

For small firms, shareholders and management may be one and the same. But for large companies, separation of ownership and management is a practical necessity. For example, BCE has over 800 million outstanding shares, which are owned by some large institutional investors and thousands of small shareholders. There is no way that these shareholders can be actively involved in management; it would be like trying to run the City of Toronto by town meetings. Authority has to be delegated.

How can shareholders decide how to delegate decision making when they all have different tastes, wealth, time horizons, and personal opportunities? Delegation can work only if the shareholders have a common objective. Fortunately there is a natural financial

TABLE 1.2
Representative salaries for senior jobs in finance

Career	Annual Salary
Banking, large-size chartered bank[a]	
Chief executive officer	$1,080,874 + bonus
President	646,923 + bonus
Vice president, wealth management	375,000 + bonus
Corporate Finance, large-size company[b]	
Chief financial officer	$230,000
Vice president, finance	199,000
Corporate controller	172,000
Assistant controller	118,000
Investment banking	
Chief executive officer[a]	$302,000 + bonus
Managing director, finance[a]	260,000 + bonus
Financial analyst, manager[b]	85,000
Money management[a]	
Chief financial officer	$306,250 + bonus
Senior vice president, funds division	225,000 + bonus
Insurance[a]	
Chief investment officer	$330,000 + bonus
Chief financial officer	300,000 + bonus

Sources: a. Management proxy information circulars from www.sedar.com.
b. 2001 Robert Half/Accountemps Salary Guide, pp. 15–16. (The amounts represent maximums reported.)

TABLE 1.3
Internet sites for careers in finance

Site	URL	Comment
Canadian Careers	www.canadiancareers.com	This site provides a collection of resources by occupation, occupational profiles, and Canadian career planning and occupational links. Information on Canadian labour market trends is also provided.
Canada Work*info*NET	www.workinfonet.ca	This is a good source of career, education, and labour market information for Canadians. Links to provincial and regional information resources are also provided.
Human Resources Development Canada (HRDC)	www.hrdc-drhc.gc.ca	This federal government site provides occupation descriptions, salary and wage information, employment prospects, and access to related publications. You can access the HRDC site by province by entering the province's abbreviation in the Web address. For instance, you can access the HRDC site for the Ontario region by going to www.on.hrdc-drhc.gc.ca.
The Career Organization	www.careers.org	The site provides exhaustive links to employment and university resources available in the U.S. and Canada. This site also gives a detailed list of financial services and organizations in the U.S. and Canada, and offers links to financial company sites.
University of British Columbia Library	http://toby.library.ubc.ca/subjects/subjpage2.cfm?id=31	This site provides a collection of Web links to various compensation, salary, and wage information resources.
University of Waterloo	www.adm.uwaterloo.ca/infocecs/CRC/manual-home.html	A comprehensive career development manual is provided on this site.

objective on which almost all shareholders can agree: this is to maximize the current value of their investment.

A smart and effective financial manager makes decisions which increase the current value of the company's shares and the wealth of its shareholders. That increased wealth can then be put to whatever purposes the shareholders want. They can give their money to charity or spend it in glitzy nightclubs; they can save it or spend it now. Whatever their personal tastes or objectives, they can all do more when their shares are worth more.

Sometimes you hear managers speak as if the corporation has other goals. For example, they may say that their job is to "maximize profits." That sounds reasonable. After all, don't shareholders want their company to be profitable? But taken literally, profit maximization is not a well-defined corporate objective. Here are three reasons:

1. "Maximizing profits" leaves open the question of "which year's profits?" The company may be able to increase current profits by cutting back on maintenance or staff training, but shareholders may not welcome this if profits are damaged in future years.
2. A company may be able to increase future profits by cutting this year's dividend and investing the freed-up cash in the firm. That is not in the shareholders' best interests if the company earns only a very low rate of return on the extra investment.
3. Different accountants may calculate profits in different ways. So you may find that a decision that improves profits using one set of accounting rules may reduce them using another.

In a free economy a firm is unlikely to survive if it pursues goals that reduce the firm's value. Suppose, for example, that a firm's only goal is to increase its market share. It aggressively reduces prices to capture new customers, even when the price discounts cause continuing losses. What would happen to such a firm? As losses mount, it will find it more and more difficult to borrow money, and it may not even have sufficient profits to repay existing debts. Sooner or later, however, outside investors would see an opportunity for easy money. They could offer to buy the firm from its current shareholders and, once they have tossed out existing management, increase the firm's value by changing its policies. They would profit by the difference between the price paid for the firm and the higher value it would have under new management. Managers who pursue goals that destroy value often land in early retirement.

We conclude that managers as a general rule will act to maximize the value of the firm to its shareholders. Management teams that deviate too far from this rule are likely to be replaced.

ETHICS AND MANAGEMENT OBJECTIVES

We have suggested that managers should try to maximize market value. But some idealists say that managers should not be obliged to act in the selfish interests of their shareholders. Some realists argue that, regardless of what managers ought to do, they in fact look after themselves rather than their shareholders.

Let us respond to the idealists first. Does a focus on value mean that managers must act as greedy mercenaries riding roughshod over the weak and helpless? Most of this book is devoted to financial policies that increase firm value. None of these policies require galloping over the weak and helpless. In most instances there is little conflict between doing well (maximizing value) and "doing good."

The first step in doing well is doing good by your customers. Here is how Adam Smith put the case in 1776:

> It is not from the benevolence of the butcher, the brewer, or the baker, that we expect our dinner, but from their regard to their own interest. We address ourselves, not to their humanity but to their self-love, and never talk to them of our own necessities but of their advantages.[16]

By striving to enrich themselves and their shareholders, businesspeople have to provide their customers with the products and services they truly desire.

Of course ethical issues do arise in business as in other walks of life. So when we say that the objective of the firm is to maximize shareholder wealth, we do not mean that anything goes.

In part, the law deters managers from blatantly illegal action. But when the stakes are high, competition is intense, and a deadline is looming, it's easy for managers to blunder, and not inquire as deeply as they should about the legality or morality of their actions.

Written rules and laws can help only so much. In business, as in other day-to-day affairs, there are also unwritten rules of behaviour. These work because everyone knows that such rules are in the general interest. But they are reinforced because good managers know that their firm's reputation is one of its most important assets and therefore playing fair and keeping one's word are simply good business practices. Thus huge financial deals are regularly completed on a handshake and each side knows that the other will not renege later if things turn sour.[17]

Reputation is particularly important in financial management. If you buy a well-known brand in a store, you can be fairly sure what you are getting. But in financial transactions the other party often has more information than you and it is more difficult to be sure of the quality of what you are buying. This opens up plenty of opportunities for sharp practice and outright fraud, and because the activities of rogues are more entertaining than those of honest people, bookshelves are packed with accounts of financial fraudsters.

The reaction of honest financial firms is to build long-term relationships with their customers and establish a name for fair dealing and financial integrity. Major banks and securities firms know that their most valuable asset is their reputation and they emphasize their long history and their responsible behaviour when seeking new customers. When something happens to undermine that reputation the costs can be enormous.

Consider the case of the recent stock-trading scandal at RT Capital Management, the pension and institutional asset management subsidiary of the Royal Bank. Nine employees of the investment fund, including several top officials, were charged by the *Ontario Securities Commission (OSC)* with artificially inflating the closing prices of stocks traded on the TSE between October 1998 and March 1999. Six of the nine employees resigned, including RT Capital's then chief executive officer (CEO). RT Capital settled OSC's charges by agreeing to pay a $3 million fine. Concerned about unethical behaviour, 700 clients closed their accounts with the fund, resulting in Royal Bank losing in excess of $670 million of assets under management. A more dramatic and much more costly case is the Salomon Brothers 1991 bidding scandal in the United States.[18] A Salomon trader tried to evade rules limiting its participation in auctions of U.S. Treasury bonds by submitting bids in the names of the company's customers without the customers' knowledge. When this was discovered, Salomon settled the case by paying almost $200 million (US) in fines and establishing a $100 million (US) fund for payments of claims from civil lawsuits. Yet the

[16] Adam Smith, *An Inquiry into the Nature and Causes of the Wealth of Nations* (New York: Random House, 1937; first published 1776), p. 14.

[17] For example, the motto of the London Stock Exchange is "My word is my bond."

[18] This discussion is based on Clifford W. Smith, Jr., "Economics and Ethics: The Case of Salomon Brothers," *Journal of Applied Corporate Finance,* 5 (Summer 1992), pp. 23–28.

value of Salomon Brothers stock fell by far more than $300 million. In fact, the price dropped by about a third, representing a $1.5 billion (US) decline in market value.

Why did the value of Salomon drop so dramatically? Largely because investors were worried that the firm would lose business from customers that now distrusted the company. In both these examples, the damage to RT Capital's and Salomon's reputations was far greater than the explicit costs of the scandals, and hundreds or thousands of times as costly as the potential gains the firms could have reaped from the illegal trades.[19]

It is not always easy to know what is ethical behaviour and there can be many grey areas. For example, should the firm be prepared to do business with a corrupt or repressive government? Should it employ child labour in countries where that is the norm? The nearby Finance in Action box presents several simple situations that call for an ethically based decision, along with survey responses to the proper course of action in each circumstance. Compare your decisions with those of the general public.

CHECK POINT 1.5

Without knowing anything about the personal ethics of the owners, which company would you trust more to keep its word in a business deal?

a. Harry's Hardware has been in business for 50 years. Harry's grandchildren, now almost adults, plan to take over and operate the business. Hardware stores require considerable investment in customer relations to become established.
b. Victor's Videos just opened for business. It rents a storefront in a strip mall and has financed its inventory with a bank loan. Victor has little of his own money invested in the business. Video shops usually command little customer loyalty.

DO MANAGERS REALLY MAXIMIZE FIRM VALUE?

Owner-managers have no conflicts of interest in their management of the business. They work for themselves, reaping the rewards of good work and suffering the penalties of bad work. Their *personal* well-being is tied to the value of the firm.

In most large companies the managers are not the owners and they might be tempted to act in ways that are not in the best interests of the owners. For example, they might buy luxurious corporate jets for their travel, or overindulge in expense-account dinners. They might shy away from attractive but risky projects because they are worried more about the safety of their jobs than the potential for superior profits. They might engage in empire building, adding unnecessary capacity or employees. Such problems can arise because the managers of the firm, who are hired as agents of the owners, may have their own axes to grind. Therefore these conflicts are called **agency problems.**

agency problems Conflict of interest between the firm's owners and managers.

Think of the company's net revenue as a pie that is divided among a number of claimants. These include the management and the work force as well as the lenders and shareholders who put up the money to establish and maintain the business. The government is a claimant, too, since it gets to tax the profits of the enterprise. It is common to hear these claimants called **stakeholders** in the firm. Each has a stake in the firm and their interests may not coincide.

stakeholder Anyone with a financial interest in the firm.

[19] At the time of writing, RBC Dominion Securities, Royal Bank's underwriting and brokerage subsidiary, had announced that it was investigating a senior official on suspicion of illegal insider trading. By taking strict action against possible unethical behaviour by an employee, the firm seeks to maintain its reputation and credibility with investors.

FINANCE IN ACTION

Things Are Not Always Fair in Love or Economics

What constitutes *fair* behaviour by companies? One survey asked a number of individuals to state whether they regarded a particular action as acceptable or unfair. Before we tell you how they responded, think how *you* would rate each of the following actions:

1a. A small photocopying shop has one employee who has worked in the shop for 6 months and earns $9 per hour. Business continues to be satisfactory, but a factory in the area has closed and unemployment has increased. Other small shops in the area have now hired reliable workers at $7 an hour to perform jobs similar to those done by the photocopying shop employee. The owner of the photocopying shop reduces the employee's wage to $7.

1b. Now suppose that the shop does not reduce the employee's wage but he or she leaves. The owner decides to pay a replacement $7 an hour.

2. A house painter employs two assistants and pays them $9 per hour. The painter decides to quit house painting and go into the business of providing landscape services, where the going wage is lower. He reduces the workers' wages to $7 per hour for the landscaping work.

3a. A small company employs several workers and has been paying them average wages. There is severe unemployment in the area and the company could easily replace its current employees with good workers at a lower wage. The company has been making money. The owners reduce the current workers' wages by 5 percent.

3b. Now suppose instead that the company has been losing money and the owners reduce wages by 5 percent.

4. A grocery store has several months' supply of peanut butter in stock on shelves in the storeroom. The owner hears that the wholesale price of peanut butter has increased and immediately raises the price on the current stock of peanut butter.

5. A hardware store has been selling snow shovels for $15. The morning after a large snowstorm, the store raises the price to $20.

6. A store has been sold out of the popular Beanie Baby dolls for a month. A week before Christmas a single doll is discovered in a storeroom. The managers know that many customers would like to buy the doll. They announce over the store's public address system that the doll will be sold by auction to the customer who offers to pay the most.

Now compare your responses with the responses of a random sample of individuals:

	Percent Rating the Action As	
Action	**Acceptable**	**Unfair**
1a	17	83
1b	73	27
2	63	37
3a	23	77
3b	68	32
4	21	79
5	18	82
6	26	74

Source: Adapted from D. Kahneman, J. L. Knetsch, and R. Thaler, "Fairness as a Constraint on Profit Seeking: Entitlements in the Market," *American Economic Review* 76 (September 1986), pp. 728–741. Reprinted by permission of American Economic Association and the authors.

All these stakeholders are bound together in a complex web of contracts and understandings. For example, when banks lend money to the firm, they insist on a formal contract stating the rate of interest and repayment dates, perhaps placing restrictions on dividends or additional borrowing. Similarly, large companies have carefully worked out personnel policies that establish employees' rights and responsibilities. But you can't devise written rules to cover every possible future event. So the written contracts are supplemented by understandings. For example, managers understand that in return for a fat salary they are expected to work hard and not spend the firm's money on unwarranted personal luxuries.

What enforces these understandings? Is it realistic to expect managers always to act on behalf of the shareholders? The shareholders can't spend their lives watching through binoculars to check that managers are not shirking or dissipating company funds on the latest executive jet.

A closer look reveals several arrangements that help to ensure that the shareholders and managers are working toward common goals.

Compensation Plans. Managers are spurred on by incentive schemes that provide big returns if shareholders gain but are valueless if they do not. For example, when Michael Eisner was hired as CEO by the Walt Disney Company, his compensation package had three main components: a base annual salary of $750,000 (US); an annual bonus of 2 percent of Disney's net income above a threshold of "normal" profitability; and a 10-year option that allowed him to purchase 2 million shares of stock for $14 (US) per share, which was about the price of Disney stock at the time. Those options would be worthless if Disney's shares were selling for below $14 but highly valuable if the shares were worth more. This gave Eisner a huge personal stake in the success of the firm.

As it turned out, by the end of Eisner's 6-year contract the value of Disney shares had increased by $12 billion, more than sixfold. Eisner's compensation over the period was $190 million (US).[20] Was he overpaid? We don't know (and we suspect nobody else knows) how much Disney's success was due to Michael Eisner or how hard Eisner would have worked with a different compensation scheme.

Of course, a CEO can appear to be overpaid if the company is not performing as well as it used to and its share price is down. When it was announced that John Roth, then CEO of Nortel Networks, had received a total compensation of over $12 million (US) in 2000 and earned $135 million from exercising stock options, there was a volley of criticism in the news media. Although John Roth is widely admired for having transformed Nortel Networks into a leading international powerhouse in the field of Internet-based systems and the most valuable Canadian company ever, in just 3 years, his pay was perceived to be excessive at a time when the company's shareholders were seen to be suffering. Nortel's shares were trading at around $22, well below the July 2000 price of $124 per share, and shareholders had collectively lost over $300 billion in share value. Powerful shareholders such as the Ontario Teachers' Pension Plan called for the company's executive stock option plans to be revised. Soon afterwards, John Roth announced his resignation from the company.

SEE BOX P. 24

While stock option plans are sometimes criticized for being too favourable to managers (see the nearby Finance in Action box), they are still used widely by companies in order to provide managers with a strong financial incentive to increase firm value. Table 1.4 lists some of Canada's top-earning CEOs and their company's performance in 2000. Notice the importance of long-term incentives, including stock options, in the total compensation package. Does the CEO's pay always reflect the company's performance?

The Board of Directors. Boards of directors are sometimes portrayed as passive supporters of top management. But when company performance starts to slide, and managers don't offer a credible recovery plan, boards do act. In recent years, the chief executives of IBM, Eastman Kodak, General Motors, and Apple Computer were all forced out. The nearby Finance in Action box points out that in countries such as the United States and the United Kingdom boards recently have become more aggressive in their willingness to replace underperforming managers.

[20] This discussion is based on Stephen F. O'Byrne, "What Pay for Performance Looks Like: The Case of Michael Eisner," *Journal of Applied Corporate Finance* 5 (Summer 1992), pp. 135–136.

FINANCE IN ACTION

Pay CEOs with Stock Options or Stocks?

Pay for performance at many companies means doling out stock options on the principle that the interests of executives will then be aligned with shareholders.

Critics argue that rather than align the interests of CEOs with shareholders, stock options tend to have the opposite effect. Richard Rooney, president of Toronto-based Burgundy Asset Management Ltd., argues, "The worst thing about it is the behavioural aspects stock options encourage. Those differences in behaviour make you too interested in short-term stock price performance rather than corporate performance."

Executives face few of the risks their shareholders do. Suppose a CEO's options are worthless at the end of the grant period due to a steady decline in the share price over a number of years. The CEO has still earned an annual salary and bonus, but moreover, the CEO has suffered no loss in net worth. The same can't be said for the shareholders who have suffered a real decline in their portfolios.

Options don't cost anything to the bottom line so companies have little to lose in the short term by handing them out like candy.

In the long term, the more stock options are exercised, the further total shareholdings are diluted—lowering such measures as earnings per share and stock prices. Rooney suggests the only way for CEOs to truly have their interests tied to those of shareholders is for them to own shares, not options.

Source: Excerpted from *Financial Post*, "Shareholders No Longer Whisper about CEO's Pay," May 22, 2001, C5.

If shareholders believe that the corporation is underperforming and that the board of directors is not sufficiently aggressive in holding the managers to task, they can try to replace the board in the next election. The dissident shareholders will attempt to convince other shareholders to vote for their slate of candidates to the board. If they succeed, a new board will be elected and it can replace the current management team.

Takeovers. Poorly performing companies are also more likely to be taken over by another firm. After the takeover, the old management team may find itself out on the street. In

TABLE 1.4
CEO earnings[1] and company performance in 2000

Individual	Base salary	Bonus	Long-term incentive[2]	Total direct compensation	Company	Revenue in millions	Earnings per share
Jacques Bougie	$1,188	$1,388	$21,287	$23,863	Alcan Aluminium Ltd.	$13,717	$ 3.67
Anthony Comper	$ 900	$1,400	$ 4,022	$ 6,322	Bank of Montreal	$18,403	$ 3.31
Randall Oliphant	$ 814	$1,221	$ 5,168	$ 7,203	Barrick Gold Corporation	$ 1,994	($ 2.89)
John Hunkin	$ 900	$3,500	$ 7,753	$12,153	CIBC	$22,796	$ 4.97
George Heller	$1,200	$1,500	$ 1,337	$ 4,037	Hudson's Bay	$ 7,519	$ 1.60
Donald Walker	$ 149	$7,717	$ 145	$ 8,011	Magna International	$15,764	$10.56
Dominic D'Alessandro	$1,075	$3,000	$13,758	$17,833	Manulife Financial Ltd.	$14,152	$ 2.22
John Roth	$1,857	$8,371	$60,527	$70,754	Nortel Networks Corp.	$45,424	($ 1.50)
Jim Shaw	$ 850	$2,000	$ 7,829	$10,679	Shaw Communications	$ 974	$ .45
Charles Baillie	$1,081	$3,500	$ 5,432	$10,013	TD Bank	$20,075	$ 1.56
Richard Harrington	$1,708	$2,733	$12,851	$17,291	Thomson Corp.	$ 9,768	$ 1.38

[1]The amounts for base salary, bonus, long-term incentives, and total direct compensation are in thousands of dollars.

[2]The value of long-term incentives includes the estimated value of stock options as well as the present value of other long-term awards granted during the period.

Source: Financial Post, "Bullet Proof Pay Pockets; the Perks and Paycheques of Canada's Blue-Chip CEO's," May 22, 2001, C4.

FINANCE IN ACTION

Thank You and Goodbye

When it happens, says a wise old headhunter, it is usually a quick killing. It takes about a week. "Nobody is more powerful than a chief executive, right up until the end. Then suddenly, at the end, he has no power at all."

In the past few months, some big names have had the treatment: Eckhard Pfeiffer left Compaq, a computer company; Derek Wanless has left NatWest, a big British bank that became a takeover target. Others, such as Martin Grass, who left Rite Aid, an American drugstore chain, resigned unexpectedly without a job to go to.

It used to be rare for a board to sack the boss. In many parts of the world, it still is. But in big American and British companies these days, bosses who fail seem to be more likely to be sacked than ever before. Rakesh Khurana of the Sloan School of Management at Massachusetts Institute of Technology has recently examined 1,300 occasions when chief executives of Fortune 500 firms left their jobs. He found that, in a third of cases, the boss was sacked. For a similar level of performance, a chief executive appointed after 1985 is three times as likely to be fired as one appointed before that date.

What has changed? In the 1980s, the way to dispose of an unsatisfactory boss was by a hostile takeover. Nowadays, legal barriers make those much harder to mount. Indeed, by the beginning of the 1990s, chief executives were probably harder to dislodge than ever before. That started to change when, after a catastrophic fall in the company's share of the American car market, the board of General Motors screwed up the courage in 1992 to replace Robert Stempel.

The result seems to be that incompetent chief executives in large companies are rarer than they were in 1990 . . . . In Silicon Valley, sacking the boss has become so routine that some firms find that they spend longer looking for a chief executive than the new boss does in the job.

Source: © 1999 The Economist Newspaper Group, Inc. Reprinted with permission. www.economist.com.

recent years, the CEOs of Canadian Airlines and Chapters were replaced following such takeovers. We discuss takeovers in Chapter 23.

Specialist Monitoring. Finally, managers are subject to the scrutiny of specialists. Their actions are monitored by the security analysts who advise investors to buy, hold, or sell the company's shares. They are also reviewed by banks, which keep an eagle eye on the progress of firms receiving their loans.

We do not want to leave the impression that corporate life is a series of squabbles and endless micromanagement. It isn't, because practical corporate finance has evolved to reconcile personal and corporate interests—to keep everyone working together to increase the value of the whole pie, not merely the size of each person's slice.

The agency problem is mitigated in practice through several devices: compensation plans that tie the fortune of the manager to the fortunes of the firm; monitoring by lenders, stock market analysts, and investors; and ultimately, the threat that poor performance will result in the removal of the manager.

☑ CHECK POINT 1.6

Corporations are now required to publish the amount and form of compensation (e.g., stock options versus salary versus performance bonuses) received by their top executives. Of what use would that information be to a potential investor in the firm?

Topics Covered in This Book

This book covers investment decisions first, then financing decisions, and then a variety of planning issues that require understanding of both investments and financing.

In Parts Two and Three we look at different aspects of the investment decision. The first is the problem of how to value assets, and the second is the link between risk and value. Our discussion of these topics occupies Chapters 3 through 11.

Nine chapters devoted to the simple problem of finding real assets that are worth more than they cost may seem excessive, but that problem is not so simple in practice. We will require a theory of how long-lived, risky assets are valued, and that requirement will lead us to basic questions about capital markets. For example:

- How are corporate bonds and stocks valued in capital markets?
- What risks are borne by investors in corporate securities? How can these risks be measured?
- What compensation do investors demand for bearing risk?
- What rate of return can investors in common stocks reasonably expect to receive?

Intelligent capital budgeting and financing decisions require answers to these and other questions about how capital markets work.

Financing decisions occupy Parts Four and Five. We begin in Chapter 12 with another basic question about capital markets: Do security prices reflect the fair value of the underlying assets? This question is crucially important because the financial manager must know whether securities can be issued at a fair price. The remaining chapters in Part Four describe the kinds of securities corporations use to raise money and explain how and when they are issued. These chapters also describe the sources of financing of new and small business ventures.

Part Five continues the analysis of the financing decision, covering dividend policy and debt policy. We will also describe what happens when firms find themselves in financial distress because of poor operating performance, excessive borrowing, or both.

Part Six covers financial planning. Decisions about investment, dividend policy, debt policy, and other financial issues cannot be reached independently. They have to add up to a sensible overall financial plan for the firm, one which increases the value of the shareholders' investment yet still retains enough flexibility for the firm to avoid financial distress and pursue unexpected new opportunities.

Part Seven is devoted to decisions about the firm's short-term assets and liabilities. We discuss channels for short-term borrowing or investment, management of liquid assets (cash and marketable securities), and management of accounts receivable (money lent by the firm to its customers) and inventories.

Part Eight covers four important problems which require decisions about both investment and financing. First, we discuss the concept of leasing and the analysis of leasing decisions. Next, we look at mergers and acquisitions. Then we consider international financial management. All the financial problems of doing business at home are present overseas, but the international financial manager faces the additional complications created by multiple currencies, different tax systems, and special regulations imposed by foreign institutions and governments. Finally, we look at risk management and the specialized securities, including futures and options, that managers can use to hedge or lay off risks.

SNIPPETS OF HISTORY

Now let's lighten up a little. In this book we are going to describe how financial decisions are made today. But financial markets also have an interesting history. Look at the accompanying Finance in Action box, which lays out bits of this history, starting in prehistoric times, when the growth of bacteria anticipated the mathematics of compound interest, and continuing nearly to the present. We have keyed each of these episodes to the chapter of the book that discusses it.

1.7 Summary

1. What are the advantages and disadvantages of the most common forms of business organization? Which forms are most suitable to different types of businesses?

Businesses may be organized as **proprietorships, partnerships,** or **corporations.** A corporation is legally distinct from its owners. Therefore, the shareholders who own a corporation enjoy **limited liability** for its obligations. Ownership and management of corporations are usually separate, which means that the firm's operations need not be disrupted by changes in ownership. On the other hand, corporations are subject to double taxation. Larger companies, for which the separation of ownership and management is more important, tend to be organized as corporations.

2. What are the major business functions and decisions for which the firm's financial managers are responsible?

The overall task of financial management can be broken down into (1) the **investment**, or **capital budgeting, decision** and (2) the **financing decision.** In other words, the firm has to decide (1) how much to invest and what assets to invest in and (2) how to raise the necessary cash. The objective is to increase the value of the shareholders' stake in the firm.

The financial manager acts as the intermediary between the firm and **financial markets,** where companies raise funds by issuing securities directly to investors, and where investors can trade already-issued securities among themselves. The financial manager also may raise funds by borrowing from **financial intermediaries** like banks or insurance companies. The financial intermediaries in turn raise funds from individual households, often in small amounts.

In small companies there is often only one financial executive. However, larger corporations usually have both a treasurer and a controller. The **treasurer**'s job is to obtain and manage the company's financing. By contrast, the **controller**'s job is one of inspecting to see that the money is used correctly. Large firms may also appoint a **chief financial officer,** or **CFO**.

3. Why does it make sense for corporations to maximize their market values?

Value maximization is usually taken to be the goal of the firm. Such a strategy maximizes shareholders' wealth, thereby enabling shareholders to pursue their personal goals. However, value maximization does not imply a disregard for ethical decision making, in part because the firm's reputation as an employer and business partner depends on its past actions.

4. Why may conflicts of interest arise in large organizations? How can corporations provide incentives for everyone to work toward a common end?

Agency problems imply that managers may have interests that differ from those of the firm. These problems are kept in check by compensation plans that link the well-being of employees to that of the firm, by monitoring of management by the board of directors, security holders, and creditors, and by the threat of takeover.

FINANCE IN ACTION

Finance through the Ages

Date unknown ***Compound Growth.*** Bacteria start to propagate by subdividing. They thereby demonstrate the power of compound growth. (*Chapter 3*)

c. 1800 B.C. ***Interest Rates.*** In Babylonia, Hammurabi's Code established maximum interest rates on loans. Borrowers often mortgaged their property and sometimes their spouses, but in these cases the lender was obliged to return the spouse in good condition within 3 years. (*Chapter 4*)

c. 1000 B.C. ***Options.*** One of the earliest recorded options is described by Aristotle. The philosopher Thales knew by the stars that there would be a great olive harvest, so having a little money, he bought options for the use of olive presses. When the harvest came Thales was able to rent the presses at great profit. Today financial managers need to be able to evaluate options to buy or sell a wide variety of assets. (*Chapter 25*)

15th century ***International Banking.*** Modern international banking has its origins in the great Florentine banking houses. But the entire European network of the Medici empire employed only 57 people in eight offices. Today the Royal Bank of Canada has over 53,000 employees and an international network of 99 offices in over 30 countries. (*Chapter 13*)

1650 ***Futures.*** Futures markets allow companies to protect themselves against fluctuations in commodity prices. During the Tokugawa era in Japan, feudal lords collected rents in the form of rice but often they wished to trade their future rice deliveries. In Canada, the Winnipeg Commodity Exchange started operating in 1887 and established futures markets in wheat, oats, and flaxseed in 1904. (*Chapter 26*)

17th century ***Joint Stock Corporations.*** Although for a long time investors have combined together as joint owners of an enterprise, the modern corporation with a large number of shareholders originates with the formation in England of the great trading firms like the East India Company (est. 1599). Another early trading firm, Hudson's Bay (est. 1670), still survives and is one of Canada's largest companies. (*Chapter 14*)

17th century ***Money.*** Through the 17th century until well into the 19th, coins from many countries, such as England, France, Portugal, and Spain, circulated freely in the French and British colonies in North America. Different colonies rated coins differently, sometimes deliberately overrating (overvaluing) or underrating (undervaluing) them relative to others, based on their weight in gold or silver, in order to encourage or discourage their use. In such circumstances, overrated coins drove underrated coins from circulation—an application of Gresham's Law, "bad money drives out good." A chronic coin shortage encouraged the introduction of paper money. For instance, in 1685, card money was introduced in New France, which initially consisted of playing cards cut to different sizes according to denomination and signed by colonial officials. The first bank notes in Canada denominated in dollars were issued by the Montreal Bank in 1817. A distinctive Canadian currency came into being when the Province of Canada revised the Currency Act in 1857, requiring all provincial accounts to be kept in dollars. Silver and bronze coins bearing "Canada" were issued for the first time. Private bank notes were gradually phased out when the Bank of Canada started operations in 1935 and was given monopoly power to print money.[21] (*Chapter 20*)

1720 ***New Issue Speculation.*** From time to time investors have been tempted by speculative new issues. During the South Sea Bubble in England one company was launched to develop perpetual motion. Another enterprising individual announced a company "for carrying on an undertaking of great advantage but nobody to know what it is." Within 5 hours he had raised £2000; within 6 hours he was on his way out of the country. (*Chapter 14*)

1792 ***Formation of Stock Exchanges.*** In North America the New York Stock Exchange (NYSE) was founded in 1792 when a group of brokers met under a buttonwood tree and arranged to trade shares with one another at agreed rates of commission. Today the NYSE is the largest stock exchange in the world, trading on average about a billion shares a day. The Toronto Stock Exchange (TSE) was established in 1852. Today the TSE belongs to the TSX, Canada's largest stock exchange. The TSE traded an average of about 155 million shares valued at over $3.2 billion each day. (*Chapter 5*)

1929 ***Stock Market Crashes.*** Common stocks are risky investments. In September 1929, stock prices in the

[21] Information for this excerpt was compiled from J. Powell, "A History of the Canadian Dollar" at the Bank of Canada website, www.bankofcanada.ca/en/currency.htm.

United States reached an all-time high and the economist Irving Fisher forecast that they were at "a permanently high plateau." Some 3 years later stock prices were almost 90 percent lower and it was to be a quarter of a century before the prices of September 1929 were seen again. Contrary to popular impression, no Wall Street broker jumped out the window. (*Chapter 9*)

1960s ***Eurodollar Market.*** In the 1950s, the Soviet Union transferred its dollar holdings from the United States to a Russian-owned bank in Paris. This bank was best known by its telex address, EUROBANK, and consequently dollars held outside the United States came to be known as eurodollars. In the 1960s, U.S. taxes and regulation made it much cheaper to borrow and lend dollars in Europe rather than in the United States and a huge market in eurodollars arose. (*Chapter 13*)

1972 ***Financial Futures.*** Financial futures allow companies to protect themselves against fluctuations in interest rates, exchange rates, and so on. It is said that they originated from a remark by the economist Milton Friedman that he was unable to profit from his view that sterling was overpriced. The Chicago Mercantile Exchange founded the first financial futures market. Today futures exchanges in the United States trade 200 million contracts a year of financial futures. In Canada, a new market for futures contracts on treasury coupons and long-term government bonds was created in 1979. Canadian financial futures are traded on the Montreal Exchange. (*Chapter 26*)

1986 ***Capital Investment Decisions.*** The largest investment project undertaken by private companies was the construction of the tunnel under the English Channel. It started in 1986 and was completed in 1994 at a total cost of $15 billion (US). (*Chapter 6*)

1988 ***Mergers.*** The 1980s saw a wave of takeovers culminating in the $25 billion (US) takeover of RJR Nabisco. Over a period of 6 weeks, three groups battled for control of the company. As one of the contestants put it, "We were charging through the rice paddies, not stopping for anything and taking no prisoners." The takeover was the largest in history and generated almost $1 billion in fees for the banks and advisers. (*Chapter 23*)

1993 ***Inflation.*** Financial managers need to recognize the effect of inflation on interest rates and on the profitability of the firm's investments. In the United States inflation has been relatively modest, but some countries have suffered from hyperinflation. In Hungary after World War II the government issued banknotes worth 1000 trillion pengoes. In Yugoslavia in October 1993 prices rose by nearly 2000 percent and a dollar bought 105 million dinars. (*Chapter 3*)

1780 and 1997 ***Inflation-Indexed Debt.*** In 1780, Massachusetts paid Revolutionary War soldiers with interest-bearing notes rather than its rapidly eroding currency. Interest and principal payments on the notes were tied to the rate of subsequent inflation. After a 217-year hiatus, the United States Treasury issued 10-year inflation-indexed notes. Many other countries, including Britain and Israel, had done so previously. (*Chapter 4*)

1993 ***Controlling Risk.*** When a company fails to keep close tabs on the risks being taken by its employees, it can get into serious trouble. This was the fate of Barings, a 220-year-old British bank that numbered the queen among its clients. In 1993 it discovered that Nick Leeson, a trader in its Singapore office, had hidden losses of $1.3 billion (US) (£869 million) from unauthorized bets on the Japanese equity market. The losses wiped out Barings and landed Leeson in jail with a 6-year sentence. (*Chapter 26*)

1999 ***The Euro.*** Large corporations do business in many currencies. In 1999 a new currency came into existence when 11 European countries adopted the euro in place of their separate currencies. This was not the first time that different countries have agreed on a common currency. In 1865, France, Belgium, Switzerland, and Italy came together in the Latin Monetary Union, and they were joined by Greece and Romania the following year. Members of the European Monetary Union (EMU) hope that the euro will be a longer lasting success than earlier experiments. (*Chapter 24*)

2002 ***The Euro (An Update).*** In early 2001, Greece became the 12th country to adopt the euro and join the euro zone. By January 2002, euro notes and coins were in circulation in the 12 countries. More than 90 percent of cash payments in these countries are now carried out in euros. Consumers can still use the respective national currencies, although they are being phased out. (*Chapter 24*).[22]

[22] For more information about the euro, you can visit the website of the *Financial Times* at http://specials.ft.com/euro.

Related Web Links

www.financewise.com A search engine for finance-related sites
www.forbes.com News about financial management
www.wiso.gwdg.de/ifbg/finance.html Links to all kinds of finance sites
www.edgeonline.com Information for the small business financial manager
www.corpmon.com/index.htm The corporate monitoring project dedicated to inducing firms to make good decisions
www.bombardier.com
www.cba.ca Canadian Bankers Association
www.nortelnetworks.com
www.desjardins.com
www.ontarioteachers.com Ontario Teachers' Pension Plan information from Armquest investment counsellors and portfolio managers
www.alcan.com
www.tsx.ca Toronto Stock Exchange
www.bmo.com Bank of Montreal
www.bankofcanada.ca Bank of Canada

Key Terms

sole proprietor	3	capital budgeting decision	7	treasurer	14
partnership	3	financing decision	7	controller	14
corporation	3	capital structure	8	chief financial officer (CFO)	14
limited liability	4	capital markets	8	agency problems	21
real assets	6	financial intermediary	9	stakeholder	21
financial assets	6	primary market	12		
financial markets	6	secondary market	12		

Questions and Problems

*Answers in Appendix B

Basic

*1. **Financial Decisions.** Fit each of the following terms into the most appropriate space: *financing, real, stock, investment, executive airplanes, financial, capital budgeting, brand names.*
Companies usually buy ___ assets. These include both tangible assets such as ___ and intangible assets such as ___. In order to pay for these assets, they sell ___ assets such as ___. The decision regarding which assets to buy is usually termed the ___ or ___ decision. The decision regarding how to raise the money is usually termed the ___ decision.

2. **Value Maximization.** Give an example of an action that might increase profits but at the same time reduce stock price.

3. **Corporate Organization.** You may own shares of IBM, but you still can't enter corporate headquarters whenever you feel like it. In what sense then are you an owner of the firm?

4. **Corporate Organization.** What are the advantages and disadvantages of organizing a firm as a proprietorship, partnership, or corporation? In what sense are LLPs or professional corporations *hybrid* forms of business organization?

5. **Corporate Organization.** What do we mean when we say that corporate income is subject to *double taxation*?

6. **Financial Managers.** Which of the following statements more accurately describes the treasurer than the controller?
   a. Likely to be the only financial executive in small firms
   b. Monitors capital expenditures to make sure that they are not misappropriated
   c. Responsible for investing the firm's spare cash

d. Responsible for arranging any issue of common stock
e. Responsible for the company's tax affairs

PRACTICE

*7. **Real versus Financial Assets.** Which of the following are real assets and which ones are financial?

a. A share of stock
b. A personal IOU
c. A trademark
d. A truck
e. Undeveloped land
f. The balance in the firm's chequing account
g. An experienced and hardworking sales force
h. A bank loan agreement

8. **The Financial Manager.** Give two examples of capital budgeting decisions and financing decisions.

9. **Financial Markets.** What is meant by over-the-counter trading? Is this trading mechanism used for stocks, bonds, or both?

*10. **Financial Institutions.** We gave banks and insurance companies as two examples of financial institutions. What other types of financial institutions can you identify?

11. **Financial Markets.** In most years, new issues of stock are a tiny fraction of total stock market trading. In other words, secondary market volume is much greater than primary market volume. Does the fact that firms only occasionally sell new shares mean that the stock market is largely irrelevant to the financial manager? *Hint:* How is the price of the firm's stock determined, and why is it important to the financial manager?

12. **Goals of the Firm.** You may have heard big business criticized for focusing on short-term performance at the expense of long-term results. Explain why a firm that strives to maximize stock price should be less subject to an overemphasis on short-term results than one that maximizes profits.

13. **Goals of the Firm.** We claim that the goal of the firm is to maximize stock price. Are the following actions necessarily consistent with that goal?

a. The firm donates $3 million to the local art museum.
b. The firm reduces its dividend payment, choosing to reinvest more of earnings in the business.
c. The firm buys a corporate jet for its executives.

14. **Goals of the Firm.** Explain why each of the following may not be appropriate corporate goals:

a. Increase market share
b. Minimize costs
c. Underprice any competitors
d. Expand profits

*15. **Agency Issues.** Sometimes lawyers work on a contingency basis. They collect a percentage of their client's settlement instead of receiving a fixed fee. Why might clients prefer this arrangement? Would this sort of arrangement be more appropriate for clients that use lawyers regularly or infrequently?

16. **Reputation.** As you drive down a deserted highway you are overcome with a sudden desire for a hamburger. Fortunately, just ahead are two hamburger outlets; one is owned by a national brand, the other appears to be owned by "Joe." Which outlet has the greater incentive to serve you cat meat? Why?

*17. **Agency Problems.** If agency problems can be mitigated by tying the manager's compensation to the fortunes of the firm, why don't firms compensate managers *exclusively* with shares in the firm?

*18. **Agency Problems.** Many firms have devised defences that make it much more costly or difficult for other firms to take them over. How might such takeover defences affect the firm's agency problems? Are managers of firms with formidable takeover defences more or less likely to act in the firm's interests rather than their own?

19. **Agency Issues.** One of the "Finance through the Ages" episodes that we cite on page 29 is the 1993 collapse of Barings Bank when one of its traders lost $1.3 billion (US). Traders are compensated in large part according to their trading profits. How might this practice have contributed to an agency problem?

20. **Agency Issues.** Discuss which of the following forms of compensation is most likely to align the interests of managers and shareholders:
   a. A fixed salary
   b. A salary linked to company profits
   c. A salary that is paid partly in the form of the company's shares
   d. An option to buy the company's shares at an attractive price

21. **Agency Issues.** When a company's stock is widely held, it may not pay an individual shareholder to spend time monitoring the manager's performance and trying to replace poor management. Explain why. Do you think that a bank that has made a large loan to the company is in a different position?

*22. **Ethics.** In some countries, such as Japan and Germany, corporations develop close long-term relationships with one bank and rely on that bank for a large part of their financing needs. In the United States companies are more likely to shop around for the best deal. Do you think that this practice is more or less likely to encourage ethical behaviour on the part of the corporation?

23. **Ethics.** Is there a conflict between "doing well" and "doing good"? In other words, are policies that increase the value of the firm (doing well) necessarily at odds with socially responsible policies (doing good)? When there are conflicts, how might government regulations or laws tilt the firm toward doing good? For example, how do taxes or fees charged on pollutants affect the firm's decision to pollute? Can you cite other examples of "incentives" used by governments to align private interests with public ones?

24. **Ethics.** The following report appeared in the *Financial Times* (October 28, 1999, p. 1): "Coca-Cola is testing a vending machine that automatically raises the price of the world's favourite soft drink when the temperature increases . . . [T]he new machine, believed to have been tested in Japan, may well create controversy by using hot weather to charge extra. One rival said the idea of charging more when temperatures rose was 'incredible.'" Discuss.

Solutions to Check Points

1.1
   a. The consulting firm is most suited to a partnership. Each senior consultant might be a partner, with partial responsibility for managing the firm and its clients.
   b. The college student would set up the business as a sole proprietorship. He or she is the only manager, and has little need for partners to contribute capital.
   c. The large firm would be set up as a corporation. It requires great amounts of capital, and with the budgetary, payroll, and management issues that arise with such a large number of employees, it probably needs a professional management team.

1.2
   a. The development of a fuel cell is a capital budgeting decision. The investment of $500 million will purchase a real asset, the fuel cell.
   b. The bank loan is a financing decision. This is how Volkswagen will raise money for its investment.
   c. Capital budgeting.
   d. Financing.

e. Capital budgeting. Though intangible, the licence is a real asset that is expected to produce future sales and profits.

f. Financing.

1.3 a. Real assets support the operations of the business. They are necessary to produce future profits and cash inflows. Financial assets or securities are claims on the profits and cash inflows generated by the firm's real assets and operations.

b. A company *invests* in real assets to support its operations. It *finances* the investment by raising money from banks, shareholders, or other investors.

c. Capital budgeting deals with investment decisions. Capital structure is the composition of the company's sources of financing.

d. When a company raises money from investors, it sells financial assets or securities in the primary market. Later trades among investors occur in the secondary market.

e. A company can raise money by selling securities directly to investors in financial markets, or it can deal with a financial intermediary. The intermediary raises money from investors and reinvests it in the company's securities. The intermediary invests primarily in financial assets.

1.4 Sal would more likely be the treasurer and Sally the controller. The treasurer raises money from the credit and financial markets and requires background in financial institutions. The controller is more of an overseer who requires background in accounting.

1.5 Harry's has a far bigger stake in the reputation of the business than Victor's. The store has been in business for a long time. The owners have spent years establishing customer loyalty. In contrast, Victor's has just been established. The owner has little of his own money tied up in the firm, and so has little to lose if the business fails. In addition, the nature of the business results in little customer loyalty. Harry's is probably more reliable.

1.6 An investor would like top management to be compensated according to the fortunes of the firm. If management is willing to bet its own compensation on the success of the firm, that is good news; first, because it shows management has confidence in the firm, and second, because it gives managers greater incentives to work hard to make the firm succeed.

CHAPTER 2

Accounting and Finance

2.1 The Balance Sheet

2.2 The Income Statement

2.3 The Statement of Cash Flows

2.4 Accounting for Differences

2.5 Taxes

2.6 Summary

p. 41-46.

In Chapter 1 we pointed out that a large corporation is a team effort. All the players—the shareholders, lenders, directors, management, and employees—have a stake in the company's success and all therefore need to monitor its progress. For this reason the company prepares regular financial accounts and arranges for an independent firm of auditors to certify that these accounts present a "true and fair view."

Until the mid-19th century most businesses were owner-managed and seldom required outside capital beyond personal loans to the proprietor. When businesses were small and there were few outside stakeholders in the firm, accounting could be less formal. But with the industrial revolution and the creation of large railroad and canal companies, the shareholders and bankers demanded information that would help them gauge a firm's financial strength. That was when the accounting profession began to come of age.

We don't want to discuss the details of accounting practice. But because we will be referring to financial statements throughout this book, it may be useful to review their main features briefly. In this chapter we introduce the major financial statements, the balance sheet, the income statement, and the statement of cash flows. We discuss the important differences between income and cash flow and between book values and market values. We also discuss the Canadian tax system.

After studying this chapter you should be able to

- Interpret the information contained in the balance sheet, income statement, and statement of cash flows.
- Distinguish between market and book value.
- Explain why income differs from cash flow.
- Understand the essential features of the taxation of corporate and personal income.

The Balance Sheet

balance sheet Financial statement that shows the value of the firm's assets and liabilities at a particular time.

The company we have chosen to look at is Molson Inc., a major Canadian beer brewery. To see their 2001 annual report, go to www.molson.com/home/main.ghtml and select "Investor Relations," then "Financial Information." We will look first at the **balance sheet,** which presents a snapshot of the firm's assets and the source of the money that was used to buy those assets. The assets are listed on the left-hand side of the balance sheet. Some assets can be turned more easily into cash than others; these are known as *liquid* assets. The accountant puts the most liquid assets at the top of the list and works down to the least liquid.

Look, for example, at the left-hand column of Table 2.1, the balance sheet for Molson Inc. at its 2001 year-end.[1] You can see that Molson had $70.1 million of cash and marketable securities. In addition it had sold goods worth $102.3 million but had not yet received payment. These payments are due soon and therefore the balance sheet shows the unpaid bills, or *accounts receivable* (or simply *receivables*), as an asset. The next asset consists of inventories. These may be (1) raw materials and ingredients that the firm bought from suppliers, (2) work in process, and (3) finished products waiting to be shipped from the warehouse. Furthermore, in Molson's case, inventories included $45.2 million worth of returnable containers, including refillable kegs and bottles. Of course there are always some items that don't fit into neat categories. So the current assets category includes a fourth entry, *other current assets.*

Up to this point all the assets in Molson's balance sheet are likely to be used or turned into cash in the near future. They are therefore described as *current assets.* The second part of the balance sheet includes long-term assets not likely to be turned into cash soon. The first group of long-term assets is known as *fixed assets* such as buildings, equipment, and vehicles.

TABLE 2.1
Balance sheet for Molson Inc.

BALANCE SHEET FOR MOLSON INC.
(Figures in millions of dollars)

Assets	2001	2000	Liabilities and Shareholders' Equity	2001	2000
Current assets			Current liabilities		
Cash and marketable securities	70.1	61.7	Bank debt	—	39.4
Accounts receivable	102.3	153.6	Accounts payable	365.7	295.7
Inventories	138.9	131.6	Other current liabilities	252.7	263.6
Other current assets	121.1	105.5	Total current liabilities	618.4	598.7
Total current assets	432.4	452.4	Long-term debt	1,204.4	1,111.9
			Other long-term liabilities	662.6	375.5
Fixed assets			Total liabilities	2,485.4	2,086.1
Property, plant, and equipment, gross	1,308.2	1,118.9	Shareholders' equity		
Less accumulated depreciation	393.3	342.4	Capital stock	477.6	468.6
Net fixed assets	914.9	776.5	Retained earnings	317.8	557.1
Intangible assets	1,518.8	1,266.8	Total shareholders' equity	795.4	1,025.7
Other assets	414.7	616.1			
Total assets	3,280.8	3,111.8	Total liabilities and shareholders' equity	3,280.8	3,111.8

Source: Molson Inc., *Annual Report*, 2001.

[1]Molson has chosen March 31 as its year-end.

The balance sheet shows that the gross value of Molson's fixed assets is $1,308.2 million. This is what the assets originally cost. But they are unlikely to be worth that now. For example, suppose the company bought a delivery van 2 years ago; that van may be worth far less now than Molson paid for it. It might in principle be possible for the accountant to estimate separately the value today of the van, but this would be costly and somewhat subjective. Accountants rely instead on rules of thumb to estimate the depreciation in the value of assets and with rare exceptions they stick to these rules. For example, in the case of that delivery van the accountant may deduct a third of the original cost each year to reflect its declining value. So if Molson bought the van 2 years ago for $15,000, the balance sheet would show that accumulated depreciation is 2 × $5,000 = $10,000. Net of depreciation the value is only $5,000. Table 2.1 shows that Molson's total accumulated depreciation on fixed assets is $393.3 million. So while the assets cost $1,308.2 million, their net value in the accounts is only $1,308.2 – $393.3 = $914.9 million.

The fixed assets in Molson's balance sheet are all tangible assets. But Molson also has valuable intangible assets, such as its brand name, skilled management, and a well-trained labour force. Accountants are generally reluctant to record these intangible assets in the balance sheet unless they can be readily identified and valued.

There is, however, one important exception. When Molson has acquired other businesses and brand names in the past, it has paid more for these assets than the value shown in the other firms' accounts. This difference is shown in Molson's balance sheet as *intangible assets*. Note 14 to the financial statement states that $1,320.8 million of the intangible assets is the value attached to brand names acquired from other companies.[2] The final assets listed, *other assets*, are long-term assets that do not fit elsewhere. In Molson's case, these include assets associated with discontinued operations and its interest in Brewers Retail Inc., the beer distribution operation in Ontario.

Now look at the right-hand portion of Molson's balance sheet, which shows where the money to buy the assets came from. The accountant starts by looking at the company's liabilities—that is, the money owed by the company. First come those liabilities that are likely to be paid off most rapidly. *Bank debt* is often the first current liability listed; it indicates the amount of money the company must pay their bankers within the next year. Molson borrowed $39.4 million in 2000 but repaid it and made no new short-term bank loans in 2001. It also owes its suppliers $365.7 million for goods that have been delivered but not yet paid for. These unpaid bills are shown as *accounts payable* (or *payables*). Both the borrowings and the payables are debts that Molson must repay within the year. They are therefore classified as *current liabilities*.

Molson's current assets total $432.4 million; its current liabilities amount to $618.4 million. Therefore the difference between the value of Molson's current assets and its current liabilities is $432.4 – $618.4 = –$186 million. This figure is known as Molson's *net current assets* or *net working capital*. It roughly measures the company's potential reservoir of cash. Unlike Molson, most companies maintain positive net working capital.

Below the current liabilities Molson's accountants have listed the firm's long-term liabilities—that is, debts that come due after the end of a year. You can see that banks and other investors have made long-term loans to Molson of $1,204.4 million.

Molson's liabilities are financial obligations to various parties. For example, when Molson buys goods from its suppliers, it has a liability to pay for them; when it borrows from the bank, it has a liability to repay the loan. Thus the suppliers and the bank have first claim on the firm's assets. What is left over after the liabilities have been paid off belongs to the shareholders. This figure is known as the *shareholders' equity*. For Molson the total value

[2] Each year, Molson writes off, or amortizes, a small portion of its goodwill and brand names against its profits.

FIGURE 2.1

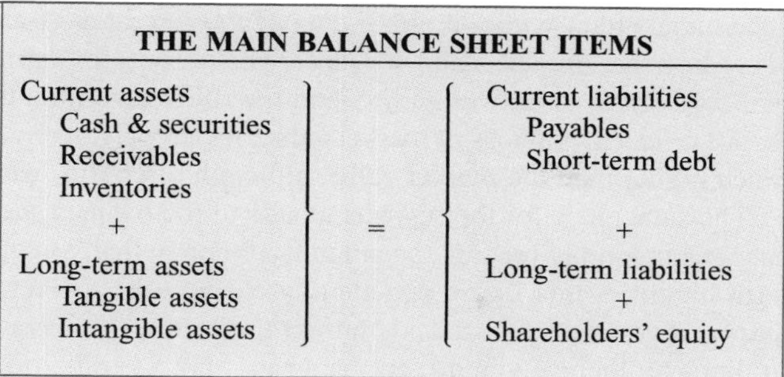

of shareholders' equity amounts to $795.4 million. Part of this sum ($477.6 million) has resulted from the sale of shares to investors. The remainder ($317.8 million) has come from earnings that Molson has retained and invested on shareholders' behalf.

Figure 2.1 shows how the separate items in the balance sheet link together. There are two classes of assets—current assets, which will soon be used or turned into cash, and long-term assets, which may be either tangible or intangible.[3] There are also two classes of liability—current liabilities, which are due for payment shortly, and long-term liabilities. The difference between the assets and the liabilities represents the amount of the shareholders' equity.

THE MAIN BALANCE SHEET ITEMS
Current assets
Cash & securities
Receivables
Inventories
+
Long-term assets
Tangible assets
Intangible assets
=
Current liabilities
Payables
Short-term debt
+
Long-term liabilities
+
Shareholders' equity

CHECK POINT 2.1

Suppose that Molson borrows $500 million by issuing new long-term bonds. It places $100 million of the proceeds in the bank and uses $400 million to buy new machinery. What items of the balance sheet would change? Would shareholders' equity change?

BOOK VALUES AND MARKET VALUES

Throughout this book we will frequently make a distinction between the book values of the assets shown in the balance sheet and their market values.

generally accepted accounting principles (GAAP) Procedures for preparing financial statements.

book value Net worth of the firm according to the balance sheet.

Items in the balance sheet are valued according to **generally accepted accounting principles,** commonly called **GAAP.** These state that assets must be shown in the balance sheet at their *historical cost* adjusted for depreciation. These **book values** are therefore "backward-looking" measures of value. They are based on the past cost of the asset, not its current market price or value to the firm. For example, suppose that a printing press cost McGraw-Hill Ryerson $1 million 2 years ago, but in today's market such presses sell for $1.3 million. The book value of the press would be less than its market value and the balance sheet would understate the value of McGraw-Hill Ryerson's assets.

Or consider a specialized plant that Intel develops for producing special-purpose computer chips at a cost of $100 million. The book value of the plant is $100 million less depreciation. But suppose that shortly after the plant is constructed, a new chip makes the existing one obsolete. The market value of Intel's new plant could fall by 50 percent. In this case market value would be less than book value.

The difference between book value and market value is greater for some assets than for others. It is zero in the case of cash but potentially very large for fixed assets where the

[3] Sometimes long-term assets are called "fixed assets." However, the term "fixed assets" is best used to describe tangible long-term assets, such as property, plant, and equipment.

accountant starts with the initial cost of the fixed assets and then depreciates that figure according to a pre-specified schedule. The purpose of depreciation is to allocate the original cost of the asset over its life, and the rules governing the depreciation of asset values do not reflect actual loss of market value. As a result, the book value of fixed assets is often much higher than the market value, although often it is less.

The same goes for the right-hand side of the balance sheet. In the case of liabilities the accountant simply records the amount of money that you have promised to pay. For short-term liabilities this figure is generally close to the market value of that promise. For example, if you owe the bank $1 million tomorrow, the accounts show a book liability of $1 million. As long as you are not bankrupt, that $1 million is also roughly the value to the bank of your promise. But now suppose that $1 million is not due to be repaid for several years. The accounts still show a liability of $1 million, but how much your debt is worth depends on what happens to interest rates. If interest rates rise after you have issued the debt, lenders may not be prepared to pay as much as $1 million for your debt; if interest rates fall, they may be prepared to pay more than $1 million.[4] Thus the market value of a long-term liability may be higher or lower than the book value.

To summarize, the market values of neither assets nor liabilities will generally equal their book values. Book values are based on historical or *original* values. Market values measure *current* values of assets and liabilities.

The difference between book value and market value is likely to be greatest for shareholders' equity. The book value of equity measures the cash that shareholders have contributed in the past plus the cash that the company has retained and reinvested in the business on their behalf. But this often bears little resemblance to the total market value that investors place on the shares.

This is the case for Molson. At year-end, March 31, 2001, the market value of Molson's outstanding common equity was $2,611.8 million, based on a closing stock price of $43.70, but the book value of equity was only $795.4 million.

If the market price of the firm's shares falls through the floor, don't try telling the shareholders that the book value is satisfactory—they won't want to hear it. Shareholders are concerned with the market value of their shares; market value, not book value, is the price at which they can sell their shares. Managers who wish to keep their shareholders happy will focus on market values.

We will often find it useful to think about the firm in terms of a *market-value balance sheet.* Like a conventional balance sheet, a market-value balance sheet lists the firm's assets, but it records each asset at its current market value rather than at historical cost less depreciation. Similarly, each liability is shown at its market value.

The difference between the market values of assets and liabilities is the market value of the shareholders' equity claim. The stock price is simply the market value of shareholders' equity divided by the number of outstanding shares.

[4] We will show you how changing interest rates affect the market value of debt in Chapter 4.

EXAMPLE 2.1 *Market- versus Book-Value Balance Sheets*

Jupiter has developed a revolutionary auto production process that enables it to produce cars 20 percent more efficiently than any rival. It has invested $10 billion in building its new plant. To finance the investment, Jupiter borrowed $4 billion and raised the remaining funds by selling new shares of stock in the firm. There are currently 100 million shares of stock outstanding. Investors are very excited about Jupiter's prospects. They believe that the flow of profits from the new plant justifies a stock price of $75.

If these are Jupiter's only assets, the book-value balance sheet immediately after it has made the investment is as follows:

BOOK-VALUE BALANCE SHEET FOR JUPITER MOTORS
(Figures in billions of dollars)

Assets		**Liabilities and Shareholders' Equity**	
Auto plant	$10	Debt	$4
		Shareholders' equity	6

Investors are placing a *market value* on Jupiter's equity of $7.5 billion ($75 per share times 100 million shares). We assume that the debt outstanding is worth $4 billion.[5] Therefore, if you owned all Jupiter's shares and all its debt, the value of your investment would be 7.5 + 4 = $11.5 billion. In this case you would own the company lock, stock, and barrel and would be entitled to all its cash flows. Because you can buy the entire company for $11.5 billion, the total value of Jupiter's assets must also be $11.5 billion. In other words, the market value of the assets must be equal to the market value of the liabilities plus the market value of the shareholders' equity.

We can now draw up the market-value balance sheet as follows:

MARKET-VALUE BALANCE SHEET FOR JUPITER MOTORS
(Figures in billions of dollars)

Assets		**Liabilities and Shareholders' Equity**	
Auto plant	$11.5	Debt	$4
		Shareholders' equity	7.5

Notice that the market value of Jupiter's plant is $1.5 billion more than the plant cost to build. The difference is due to the superior profits that investors expect the plant to earn. Thus in contrast to the balance sheet shown in the company's books, the market-value balance sheet is forward-looking. It depends on the benefits that investors expect the assets to provide.

Is it surprising that market value exceeds book value? It shouldn't be. Firms find it attractive to raise money to invest in various projects because they believe the projects will be worth more than they cost. Otherwise why bother? One of the basic tenets of finance is that the value of an asset is based on the future cash flows that it is expected to generate. You will usually find that shares of stock sell for more than the value shown in the company's books.

[5] Jupiter has borrowed $4 billion to finance its investment, but if the interest rate has changed in the meantime, the debt could be worth more or less than $4 billion.

CHECK POINT 2.2

a. What would be Jupiter's price per share if the auto plant had a market value of $14 billion?

b. How would you reassess the value of the auto plant if the value of outstanding stock were $8 billion?

2.2 The Income Statement

income statement Financial statement that shows the revenues, expenses, and net income of a firm over a period of time.

If Molson's balance sheet resembles a snapshot of the firm at a particular time, its **income statement** is like a video. It shows how profitable the firm has been during the past year.

Look at the summary income statement in Table 2.2. You can see that during 2001 Molson sold goods worth $2,483.4 million and paid brewing excise and sales taxes of $626.3 million, leaving them with net sales (or net revenues) of $1,857.1 million. The total expenses of producing and selling goods were $1,505.6 million. Included in these expenses are the costs of raw materials, labour, advertising and other marketing expenses, and head office costs. Molson's earnings before interest, taxes, depreciation, and amortization (EBITDA) were $351.5 million.

In addition to these out-of-pocket expenses, Molson also made a deduction for the value of the plant and equipment used up in producing the goods. In 2001 this charge for depreciation was $49.4 million. An additional $38.5 million charge for amortization of intangible assets was made. Thus Molson's total *earnings before interest and taxes* (*EBIT*) were

$$\begin{aligned} \text{EBIT} &= \text{net sales} - \text{costs} - \text{depreciation and amortization} \\ &= \$1{,}857.1 - \$1{,}505.6 - \$87.9 \\ &= \$263.6 \text{ million} \end{aligned}$$

TABLE 2.2 *Income statement for Molson Inc., 2001*

INCOME STATEMENT FOR MOLSON INC., 2001
(Figures in millions of dollars)

Sales and other revenues	2,483.4
Brewing excise and sale taxes	626.3
Net sales	1,857.1
Cost of sales, selling, and administrative costs	1,505.6
Earnings before interest, taxes, depreciation, and amortization (EBITDA)	351.5
Depreciation and amortization of property, plant, and equipment	49.4
Amortization of intangible assets	38.5
Earnings before interest and taxes (EBIT)	263.6
Net interest expense	68.7
Earnings before taxes	194.9
Taxes	57.7
Earnings (loss) from continuing operations	137.2
Earnings (loss) from discontinued operations	(3.3)
Net Earnings	133.9
Allocation of net income	
Cash dividends	40.6
Addition to retained earnings	93.3

Source: Molson, Inc., *Annual Report*, 2001.

The remainder of the income statement shows where these earnings went. As we saw earlier, Molson has partly financed its investment in plant and equipment by borrowing. In 2001 it paid $68.7 million of interest on this borrowing. A further slice of the profit went to the government in the form of taxes. This amounted to $57.7 million in 2001. The $137.2 million left over after paying interest and taxes were the earnings from Molson's *continuing* operations, the part of the business that Molson intended to keep going. Molson also sold part of its business during the year, including ownership of the Molson Centre and 80.1 percent of the Montreal Canadiens Hockey Club. Molson reported the earnings (losses) of these *discontinued* operations separately. The combined earnings from continuing and discontinued operations of $133.9 million belong to the shareholders. Of this sum, Molson paid out $40.6 million in dividends and reinvested the remaining $93.3 million in the business. Presumably, these invested funds made the company more valuable.

PROFITS VERSUS CASH FLOW

It is important to distinguish between Molson's profits and the cash that the company generates. Here are three reasons why profits and cash are not the same:

1. When Molson's accountants prepare the income statement, they do not simply count the cash coming in and the cash going out. Instead the accountant starts with the cash payments but then divides these payments into two groups—current expenditures (such as wages) and capital expenditures (such as the purchase of new machinery). Current expenditures are deducted from current revenues. However, rather than deducting the cost of machinery in the year it is purchased, the accountant makes an annual charge for depreciation. Thus the cost of machinery is spread over its forecast life.

   When calculating profits, the accountant *does not* deduct the expenditure on new equipment that year, even though cash is paid out. However, the accountant *does* deduct depreciation on assets previously purchased, even though no cash is currently paid out.

To calculate the cash produced by the business it is necessary to *add back* the depreciation charge (which is not a cash payment) and to *subtract* the expenditure on new capital equipment (which is a cash payment).

2. Consider the following stages in a manufacturing business. In period 1 the firm produces the goods; it sells them in period 2 for $100; and it gets paid for them in period 3. Although the cash does not arrive until period 3, the sale shows up in the income statement for period 2. The figure for accounts receivable in the balance sheet for period 2 shows that the company's customers owe an extra $100 in unpaid bills. Next period, after the customers have paid their bills, the receivables decline by $100.

The cash that the company *receives* is equal to the sales shown in the income statement less the increase in unpaid bills:

Period:	2	3
Sales	100	0
– Change in receivables	100	(100)
= Cash received	0	+100

3. The accountant also tries to match the costs of producing the goods with the revenues from the sale. For example, suppose that it costs $60 in period 1 to produce the goods

that are then sold in period 2 for $100. It would be misleading to say that the business made a loss in period 1 (when it produced the goods) and was very profitable in period 2 (when it sold them). Therefore, to provide a fairer measure of the firm's profitability, the income statement will not show the $60 as an expense of producing the goods until they are sold in period 2. This practice is known as *accrual accounting.* The accountant gathers together all expenses that are associated with a sale and deducts them from the revenues to calculate profit, even though the expenses may have occurred in an earlier period.

Of course the accountant cannot ignore the fact that the firm spent money on producing the goods in period 1. So the expenditure will be shown in period 1 as an *investment* in inventories. Subsequently in period 2, when the goods are sold, the inventories would decline again.

In our example, the cash is paid out when the goods are manufactured in period 1 but this expense is not recognized until period 2 when the goods are sold.

The cash *outflow* is equal to the cost of goods sold, which is shown in the income statement, plus the change in inventories:

Period:	1	2
Costs of goods sold	0	60
+ Change in inventories	60	(60)
= Cash paid out	+ 60	0

CHECK POINT 2.3

A firm pays $100 in period 1 to produce some goods. It sells those goods for $150 in period 2 but does not collect payment from its customers until period 3. Calculate the cash flows to the firm in each period by completing the following table. Do the resulting values for net cash flow in each period make sense?

Period:	1	2	3
Sales			
Change in accounts receivable			
Cost of goods sold			
Change in inventories			
Net cash flow			

2.3 The Statement of Cash Flows

The firm requires *cash* when it buys new plant and machinery or when it pays interest to the bank and dividends to the shareholders. Therefore, the financial manager needs to keep track of the cash that is coming in and going out.

We have seen that the firm's cash flow can be quite different from its net income. These differences can arise for at least two reasons:

1. The income statement does not recognize capital expenditures as expenses in the year that the capital goods are paid for. Instead, it spreads those expenses over time in the form of an annual deduction for depreciation.
2. The income statement uses the accrual method of accounting, which means that revenues and expenses are recognized as they are incurred rather than when the cash is received or paid out.

statement of cash flows
Financial statement that shows the firm's cash receipts and cash payments over a period of time.

The **statement of cash flows** shows the firm's cash inflows and outflows from operations as well as from its investments and financing activities. Table 2.3 is the cash-flow statement for Molson. It contains three sections. The first shows the cash flow from operating activities. This is the cash generated from Molson's normal business activities. Next comes the cash that Molson has invested in plant and equipment or in the acquisition of new businesses. The final section reports cash flows from financing activities such as the sale of new debt or stocks. We will look at these sections in turn.

The first section, cash flow from operating activities, starts with earnings from continuing operations but adjusts that figure for those parts of the income statement that do not involve cash coming in or going out. Therefore, it adds back the allowances for depreciation and amortization because these are not cash flows even though they are treated as expenses in the income statement.

Any additions to current assets need to be *subtracted* from net income, since these absorb cash but do not show up in the income statement. Conversely, any additions to current liabilities need to be *added* to net income because these release cash. In 2001, Molson reported that total cash provided from (used for) working capital decreased, resulting in a cash inflow of $44.5 million. They do not report changes in individual

TABLE 2.3
Statement of cash flows for Molson Inc.

STATEMENT OF CASH FLOWS FOR MOLSON INC., 2001
(Figures in millions of dollars)

Cash provided by operating activities	
Earnings (loss) from continuing operations	137.2
Depreciation and amortization of property, plant, and equipment	49.4
Amortization of intangible assets	38.5
Future income taxes	21.8
Other	(14.9)
Cash provided by operations	232.0
Cash provided from (used for) working capital	44.5
Rationalization costs	(48.3)
Cash provided by operating activities	228.2
Investing Activities	
Business acquisitions (net)	(277.0)
Additions to property, plant, and equipment (net)	(57.0)
Additions to investments and other assets	(8.3)
Proceeds from disposal of investments and other assets	39.0
Cash provided by (used for) investing activities	(303.3)
Financing Activities	
Increase in long-term debt	261.6
Reduction in long-term debt	(166.8)
Securitization of accounts receivable	57.0
Cash dividends	(40.6)
Other	6.8
Cash provided by (used for) financing activities	118.0
Increase(decrease) in cash from continuing operations	42.9
Increase(decrease) in cash from discontinued operations	8.8
Net increase in cash	51.7

Source: Molson Inc., *Annual Report*, 2001.

working capital accounts. However, from the balance sheet in Table 2.1, you can see the sources of this change, at least in part.[6] For example, accounts receivable decreased by $51.3 million, from $153.6 million in 2000 to $102.3 in 2001, representing cash the company received but was not included in the year's sales. Inventories increased by $7.3 million but the cost of producing these goods was not included in the cost of goods sold reported on the income statement. The increase in inventories must be subtracted from earnings to convert to cash flow. Accounts payable, on the other hand, increased $70 million. The accountant deducted this figure as part of the cost of goods sold by Molson in 2001, even though the company had not yet paid for these goods. Thus the $70 million increase in accounts payable must be added back to calculate the cash flow from operating activities.

We have pointed out that depreciation is not a cash payment; it is simply the accountant's allocation to the current year of the original cost of the capital equipment. However, cash does flow out the door when the firm actually buys and pays for new capital equipment. Therefore, these capital expenditures are set out in the second section of the cash-flow statement. You can see that Molson spent $57 million on new capital equipment and $277 million to purchase new businesses. It also raised $39 million on the sale of some investments. Total cash used for investments was $303.3 million.

cash flow from assets or free cash flow
Cash flow generated by the firm after investment in net working capital and fixed assets; also equal to *cash flow to bondholders and shareholders.*

free cash flow
See *cash flow from assets.*

The difference between the cash flows from operating activities and for investing activities is sometimes called **cash flow from assets** or **free cash flow**. It is called free cash flow because it is cash flow available to distribute to bondholders and shareholders. Molson's cash flow from assets is $228.2 – $303.3 = –$75.1 million. In other words, Molson spent more on new investments than it generated from its existing operations. The negative cash flow from assets must be paid for by new financing, or by using its pool of cash and marketable securities. Negative cash flows from assets are not necessarily a bad event—growing firms often have more investments than cash flow from operating activities. However, continued negative cash flows from assets are not sustainable: investors will tire of pouring money into the business without hope of ever receiving any return of cash flows.

The third section of the cash-flow statement shows the cash from financing activities and reveals how Molson dealt with the negative cash flow from assets. Molson raised $261.6 million in new long-term debt but also spent $166.8 million to retire long-term debt, resulting in a net increase in long-term debt of $94.8 million. In addition, they *securitized* $57 million of its accounts receivable by selling some of its receivables to lenders for immediate cash of $57 million. As Molson's customers pay for their purchases, the cash is then paid to the lenders, not to Molson. The company also paid $40.6 million in dividends to its shareholders.[7] In total, Molson raised $118 million in new financing during the year.

To summarize, the cash-flow statement tells us that Molson generated cash of $228.2 million from operating activities and spent $303.3 million on new investments, producing negative cash flows from assets amounting to –$75.1 million. However, it raised a net amount of $118 million in new finance, $42.9 million more than it needed to cover the negative cash flows from assets. This excess cash flow ended up in its bank account, increasing net cash by $42.9 million. It also generated $8.8 million in cash from its discontinued operations

[6] Sometimes the numbers don't add up because of rounding and procedures followed. For example, in Molson's case, having both continuing and discontinued operations affects the calculation of the change in working capital.

[7] You might think that interest payments should also be listed in this section. Accountants tend to view interest as a business expense because interest must be paid when it is due. However, to separate operating activities from all financing activities, move the interest expense to the financing section.

(although no details are provided), generating a total increase in cash of $51.7 million in 2001. To calculate this change in cash balance, we subtract the uses of cash from the sources:

			In millions
	Cash flow from operating activities		$228.2
−	Cash flow used for new investment	−	303.3
+	Cash raised by new financing	+	118.0
=	Change in cash balance from continuing operations	=	42.9
+	Change in cash balance from discontinued operations	+	8.8
=	Total change in cash balances	=	$ 51.7

CHECK POINT 2.4

Would the following activities increase or decrease the firm's cash balance?

a. Inventories are increased.
b. The firm reduces its accounts payable.
c. The firm issues additional common stock.
d. The firm buys new equipment.

Another way to think about Molson's financing activities is in terms of the cash flow that its bondholders and shareholders *receive* from Molson Inc. This is useful because the cash flows to bondholders and shareholders plus the increase in cash balances must equal the company's cash flow from assets. We saw that Molson raised net new financing of $118 million. This is a *negative* cash flow from the investors' perspective—they paid in more cash than Molson paid out to them. Cash balances from continuing operations increased $42.9 million. Thus the cash flow to bondholders and shareholders was –$118 million + $42.9 million, or –$75.1 million, exactly equal to Molson's cash flow from assets.

EXAMPLE 2.2 *Calculating Cash Flow from Assets and Cash Flow to Bondholders and Shareholders*

During 2002, Small Time Products generated net income of $63 and paid cash dividends of $22. However, as the new CFO, you want to assess how much cash flow the business generated. Here are the income statement and balance sheet prepared by the auditors.

SMALL TIME PRODUCTS INCOME STATEMENT, 2002

Revenues	$1,301
Cost of goods sold	1,031
Depreciation	140
Interest expense	38
Earnings before taxes	92
Taxes	29
Net income	63
Allocation of net income	
Dividends	22
Addition to retained earnings	41

SMALL TIME PRODUCTS BALANCE SHEET, 2001 AND 2002

Assets	**2002**	**2001**	**Liabilities and Shareholders' Equity**	**2002**	**2001**
Current assets			Current liabilities		
Cash	$ 42	$ 41	Bank loan	$ 40	$ 40
Accounts receivable	86	70	Accounts payable	120	108
Inventory	14	12	Total current liabilities	160	148
Total current assets	142	123	Long-term debt	464	420
			Total liabilities	624	568
Fixed assets			Shareholders' equity		
Net property and			Common shares	110	100
equipment	974	886	Retained earnings	382	341
Total assets	1,116	1,009	Total liabilities and shareholders' equity	1,116	1,009

Start with net income and add back depreciation, a noncash expense, to give cash flow from operations of $63 + $140 = $203. Next, calculate the changes in current assets and current liabilities, excluding changes in cash and bank loans. Accounts receivable increased $16 ($86 – $70) and inventory increased $2 ($14 – $12). Both of these changes reduced cash flow. Accounts payable increased $12 ($120 – $108) and this increased cash flow. Adding them gives the change in noncash net working capital: $16 + $2 – $12 = $6. It is positive, which results in a decrease in cash flow.

Finding capital expenditures requires a bit of detective work. At the beginning of the year 2002, the company had net fixed assets of $886. During the year, depreciation of $140 was taken, reducing net fixed assets to $886 – $140, or $746. However, the year-end net fixed assets on the balance sheet is $974. What accounts for the $228 difference ($974 – $746)? This is the capital expenditure made during the year.

Putting all of the pieces together gives the cash flow from assets:

Cash flow from operations	$203
Cash used in noncash net working capital	(6)
Cash used for capital expenditures	(228)
Cash flow from assets	($31)

The company spent $31 more cash than was generated by the business! Where did the money come from? Look at the changes in each of the sources of financing. No change occurred in the bank loan. Long-term debt increased $44 ($464 – $420) and common shares increased $10 ($110 – $100). Thus, the investors lent $44 and purchased $10 of new equity. In addition, shareholders received dividends of $22. Finally, the company used $1 of its cash ($42 – $41) to fund its activities. To summarize, the cash flow to bondholders and shareholders is

Increase in long-term debt	($44)
Increase in common shares	(10)
Dividends	22
Increase (decrease) in cash	1
Cash flow to bondholders and shareholders	($31)

Although Small Time Products' net income is positive, it spent more cash than the business generated, producing a negative cash flow from assets. The company had to find $31 of new financing to meet its needs for cash.

Accounting for Differences

While generally accepted accounting principles go a long way to standardize accounting practice in Canada, accountants still have some leeway in reporting earnings and book values. Financial analysts have even more leeway in how to use those reports; for example, some analysts will include profits or losses from extraordinary or nonrecurring events when they report net income, but others will not. For example, as an analyst of Molson's financial performance, would you only consider earnings from continuing operations or would you also include the loss from the discontinued operations? Your decision would reflect why you were analyzing the statements—to forecast future earnings or assess past performance. Similarly, accountants have discretion concerning the treatment of intangible assets such as patents, trademarks, or franchises. Some believe that including these intangibles on the balance sheet provides the best measure of the company's value as an ongoing concern. Others take a more conservative approach, and they exclude intangible assets. This approach is better suited for measuring the liquidation value of the firm.

Another source of imprecision arises from the fact that firms are not required to include all their liabilities on the balance sheet. For example, firms are not always required to include as liabilities on the balance sheet the value of their lease obligations.[8] They likewise are not required to include the value of several potential obligations such as warrants[9] sold to investors or issued to employees.

Even bigger differences can arise in international comparisons. Accounting practices can vary greatly from one country to another. For example, in Canada and the United States firms generally maintain one set of accounts that is sent to investors and a different set of accounts that is used to calculate their tax bill.[10] That would not be allowed in most countries. On the other hand, Canadian and United States standards are more stringent in most other regards. For example, German firms have far greater leeway to tuck money away in hidden reserve accounts.

When Daimler-Benz AG, producer of the Mercedes-Benz automobile, decided to list its shares on the New York Stock Exchange in 1993, it was required to revise its accounting practices to conform to United States standards. While it reported a modest profit in the first half of 1993 using German accounting rules, it reported a *loss* of $1 billion marks ($592 million US) under the much more revealing United States rules, primarily because of differences in the treatment of reserves.

Such differences in international accounting standards pose a problem for financial analysts who attempt to compare firms using data from their financial statements. This is why foreign firms must restate their financial results using the generally accepted accounting principles (GAAP) of Canada before their shares can be listed on a Canadian stock exchange. Likewise, the United States requires foreign companies wishing to list on a U.S. stock exchange to restate their financial results using U.S. GAAP. However, some larger Canadian companies wishing to list shares and sell debt to Americans enjoy special access to the U.S. market through the multi-jurisdictional disclosure system (MJDS), which allows them less

[8] Some airlines, at times, actually have not had any aircraft on their balance sheets because their aircraft were all leased. In contrast, General Electric owns the world's largest private airfleet because of its leasing business.

[9] A warrant is the right to purchase a share of stock from the corporation for a specified price, called the *exercise price.*

[10] For example, in their published financial statements most firms in Canada use straight-line depreciation. In other words, they make the same deduction for depreciation in each year of the asset's life. However, when they calculate taxable income, the same companies calculate their *capital cost allowance*, a form of accelerated depreciation—that is, they make larger deductions for depreciation in the early years of the asset's life and smaller deductions in the later years.

extensive disclosure requirements than other foreign issuers. Many foreign firms do make the accounting accommodations required to be able to access the large U.S. financial market. However, many firms have been reluctant to do this and list their shares elsewhere.

Other countries allow foreign firms to be listed on stock exchanges if their financial statements are prepared according to International Accounting Standards (IAS) rules, which impose considerable uniformity in accounting practices and are nearly as revealing as Canadian and U.S. standards. The nearby Finance in Action box reports on negotiations for international accounting standards.

SEE BOX P. 49

The lesson here is clear. While accounting values are often the starting point for the financial analyst, it is usually necessary to probe more deeply. The financial manager needs to know how the values on the statements were computed and whether there are important assets or liabilities missing altogether.

The trend today is toward greater recognition of the market values of various assets and liabilities. Firms are now required to acknowledge on the balance sheet the value of unfunded pension liabilities and other postemployment benefits, such as medical benefits.[11] In addition, a growing trend toward "market-value accounting" would have them record many assets at market value rather than at historical book value. Indeed, the Canadian Accounting Standards Board, in conjunction with nine other organizations that set accounting standards, including the U.S. Financial Accounting Standards Board and the International Accounting Standards Committee, has proposed major changes to the accounting of financial instruments, including the measurement of all financial assets at market value.[12] If adopted, these new standards will bring financial statements significantly closer to reporting market value; however, fixed assets will be valued at historical cost and most intangible assets will be omitted entirely.[13] Financial statements are a long way from market value.

2.5 Taxes

Taxes often have a major effect on financial decisions; therefore, we should explain how corporations and investors are taxed.

CORPORATE TAX

Companies pay tax on their income. For most companies in Canada, the corporate tax rate is the federal rate plus the appropriate provincial tax rate. The basic federal corporate tax rate is 27 percent.[14] However, to assist small businesses, the federal tax rate is only 12 percent on the first $200,000 of the taxable income of Canadian-controlled private corporations. In addition, companies engaged in manufacturing and processing are taxed at only 21 percent. The appropriate provincial corporate tax rate is added to the federal rate to give the overall tax rate. For example, a small business operating in New Brunswick pays 12 percent federal tax plus 4 percent provincial tax, giving a 16 percent total tax rate. Table 2.4 summarizes the main federal and provincial rates for 2001.[15] However, at the time

[11] When General Motors recognized the value of its postemployment obligations to GM employees, it resulted in the largest quarterly loss in United States history.

[12] Ian Hague, "Fair Debate for Fair Value," *CA Magazine*, May 2001, pp. 47–48.

[13] In the United Kingdom, Australia, and 40 other countries, current market value, not historical cost, is already reported on the balance sheet for property, plant, and equipment.

[14] Not all corporate income is subject to provincial taxation; for instance, income earned outside Canada. In this case, 10 percentage points are added to the federal rate, giving a basic federal rate of 37 percent. Tax rates were current at the time of writing.

[15] We have not included any federal or provincial surtaxes.

FINANCE IN ACTION

A Hill of Beans

The world cannot have a truly global financial system without the help of its accountants. They are letting investors down.

The biggest impediment to a global capital market is not volatile exchange rates, nor timid investors. It is that firms from one country are not allowed to sell their shares in many others, including, crucially, in the United States. And the reason for that is the inability of different countries to settle on an international standard for reporting.

In order to change this, the International Accounting Standards Committee has been trying for years to persuade as many companies as possible to adopt its standards, and to convince securities regulators such as America's Securities and Exchange Commission to let such firms list on their stock exchanges. But the IASC has so far failed to produce standards that the SEC is willing to endorse. It should produce them now.

The purpose of accounting standards is simple: to help investors keep track of what managers are doing with their money. Countries such as America and Britain, in which managers are accountable to lots of dispersed investors, have had to develop standards that are more transparent and rigorous than those of other countries. And since the purpose of international standards is to encourage such markets on a global scale, it makes sense to use these countries' standards as a guide.

British and American accounting standards have their respective flaws, debated ad nauseam by accountancy's aficionados. But they are both superior to the IASC's existing standards in two main ways. First, they promote transparency by making firms attach to their aggregate financial tables (such as the profit-and-loss statement) a set of detailed notes disclosing exactly how the main items (such as inventories and pension liabilities) are calculated. Second, they lay down rules on how to record certain transactions. In many cases, there is no intellectually "right" way to do this. The point is simply that there is a standard method, so that managers cannot mislead investors by choosing the method for themselves.

Let the Markets Do the Talking

If the merits of Anglo-American accounting are so obvious, why has the IASC not adopted its standards? Even in their present state, the international standards are more rigorous than many domestic ones, and therefore unpopular with local firms. But by introducing a rigorous set of international standards, acceptable to the SEC, the committee could unleash some interesting competition. Companies which adopted the new standards would enjoy the huge advantage of being able to sell their shares anywhere; those opting for less disclosure would be punished by investors. It is amazing how persuasive the financial markets can be.

of writing, future cuts to federal and provincial corporate tax rates had been announced. For current rates, visit PricewaterhouseCooper's tax website, www.ca.taxnews.com, or the Canadian Tax Foundation website, www.ctf.ca.

When firms calculate taxable income they are allowed to deduct expenses such as labour and material costs, marketing and selling costs, and administration expenditures. However, the costs of equipment and new factories cannot be deducted all at once, but instead, are deducted over time, depreciating the value of the assets. The allowable depreciation for tax purposes is determined by the Income Tax Act and is called the *capital cost allowance*.[16] Although the capital cost allowance is similar in concept to the GAAP depreciation charge reported in financial statements, the two systems are sufficiently different that taxes paid to the Canada Customs and Revenue Agency (CCRA) may be very different from the tax expense reported in the income statement.[17]

[16] We will tell you more about these allowances in Chapter 7.

[17] The capital cost allowance is a type of accelerated depreciation, allowing bigger deductions at the beginning of the life of an asset. This reduces taxable income and taxes relative to what they would be according to the GAAP straight-line depreciation used in the income statement. Deferred tax, a liability account on the balance sheet, is the difference between taxes shown on the income statement and the actual taxes paid.

TABLE 2.4
Federal and provincial corporate tax rates, 2001

	Small Business Rate, %	Manufacturing and Processing Rate, %	General Rate, %
Federal Government	12.0	21.0	27.0
British Columbia	4.5	16.5	16.5
Alberta	5.3	13.9	13.9
Saskatchewan	7.0	10.0	17.0
Manitoba	6.0	17.0	17.0
Ontario	6.5	12.0	14.0
Quebec	9.04	9.04	16.51
New Brunswick	4.0	16.0	16.0
Nova Scotia	5.0	16.0	16.0
Prince Edward Island	7.5	7.5	16.0
Newfoundland	5.0	5.0	14.0
Nothwest Territories	5.0	14.0	14.0
Nunavut	5.0	14.0	14.0
Yukon	6.0	2.5	15.0
Provincial/Territorial Average	5.8	11.8	15.4
Average Federal and Provincial Rates	17.8	32.8	42.4

Source: From Deborah L. Ort and David B. Perry, *Provincial Budget Roundup*, 2001, (2001 vol. 49, no. 3, *Canadian Tax Journal* 674–707).

Interest paid to debtholders is another important deduction allowed to companies when calculating their taxable income. Dividends paid to shareholders are not deductible but are paid out of after-tax income. Table 2.5 provides an example of how interest payments reduce corporate taxes. Although both companies have earnings before interest and taxes of \$100, Firm A pays only \$21 in tax, leaving it with \$100 – \$21, or \$79, to pay to bondholders and shareholders. Firm B has only \$100 – \$35, or \$65, to distribute.

The bad news about taxes is that each extra dollar of revenues increases taxable income by \$1 and results in 35 cents of extra taxes. The good news is that each extra dollar of expense *reduces* taxable income by \$1 and therefore reduces taxes by 35 cents. For example, if the firm borrows money, every dollar of interest it pays on the loan reduces taxes by 35 cents. Therefore, after-tax income is reduced by only 65 cents.

TABLE 2.5
Firms A and B both have earnings before interest and taxes (EBIT) of \$100 million, but A pays out part of its profits as debt interest. This reduces the corporate tax paid by A.

	Firm A	Firm B
EBIT	\$100	\$100
Interest	40	0
Pretax income	60	100
Tax (35% of pretax income)	21	35
Net income	39	65

Note: Figures in millions of dollars.

☑ CHECK POINT 2.5

Recalculate the figures in Table 2.5 assuming that Firm A now has to make interest payments of \$60 million. What happens to taxes paid? Does net income fall by the additional

$20 million interest payment compared with the case considered in Table 2.5, where interest expense was only $40 million?

When firms make profits, they pay 35 percent of the profits to the CCRA. But the process doesn't work in reverse; if the firm takes a loss, the CCRA does not send it a cheque for 35 percent of the loss. However, the firm can carry the losses back and deduct them from taxable income in earlier years, or it can carry them forward and deduct them from taxable income in the future.[18]

PERSONAL TAX

Table 2.6 shows federal and provincial tax rates for 2001. All provinces and territories in Canada now use "tax on income" systems, replacing the old system of charging provincial tax as a percentage of federal tax. The new system gives provinces and territories more flexibility in their tax policies, although they must still abide by the federal-provincial tax collection agreement. For the individual taxpayer, the changes mean that federal and provincial taxes are calculated separately. (Computerized tax preparation software never looked so attractive!) The Canada Customs and Revenue Agency (CCRA) collects income tax on behalf of the federal government and all provinces and territories (except Québec).

marginal tax rate Additional taxes owed per dollar of additional income.

The tax rates presented in Table 2.6 are **marginal tax rates** and they apply to various income tax brackets. The marginal tax rate is the tax the individual pays on each *extra* dollar of income. As a federal taxpayer, you would pay 16 cents for each extra dollar of income you earn when your income is below $30,754, but you would pay 22 cents of tax on each dollar of income in excess of $30,754 and up to $61,560. As outlined in Table 2.6, the federal personal tax system has four income brackets and marginal tax rates. This is a progressive tax system—the higher the income, the higher the tax rate. Almost all provincial and territorial systems are progressive. Alberta is the exception, where a flat tax rate of 10 percent is charged on all income.

For example, suppose you live in Saskatchewan and your taxable income is $50,000. Your federal tax is 16 percent of the first $30,754 and 22 percent on the remaining $19,246:

$$\text{Federal tax} = (.16 \times \$30{,}754) + (.22 \times \$19{,}246) = \$9{,}154.76$$

From Table 2.6 we see that the Saskatchewan provincial tax rate is 11.5 percent on the first $30,000 of taxable income and 13.5 percent on income in excess of $30,000. Your provincial tax is

$$\text{Provincial tax} = (.115 \times \$30{,}000) + (.135 \times \$20{,}000) = \$6{,}150$$

average tax rate Total taxes owed divided by total income.

What is your tax rate? The **average tax rate** is simply the total tax bill divided by total income. In this example, total tax is $9,154.76 + $6,150, or $15,304.76, giving an average tax rate of $15,304.76/$50,000 = .306, or 30.6 percent. At the margin, however, an extra dollar of income is taxed at 22 percent federally and 13.5 percent provincially, making a combined marginal tax rate of 22 percent plus 13.5 percent, or 35.5 percent. The marginal tax rate is usually the most important for making financial decisions because different types of income are taxed at different marginal rates, as we will discuss next.

The tax rates in Table 2.6 apply to salary and interest income. In Canada, dividend income received by individuals from Canadian corporations is taxed at a lower rate than

[18] Losses can be carried back for a maximum of 3 years and forward for up to 7 years.

TABLE 2.6
Federal and provincial personal income tax rates, 2001

	Tax Rate (%)	Income Bracket $
Federal	16.00	0–30,754
	22.00	30,755–61,560
	26.00	61,561–100,000
	29.00	100,001 and over
British Columbia	8.40	0–30,484
	11.90	30,485–60,969
	16.70	60,970–70,000
	18.70	70,001–85,000
	19.70	85,001 and over
Alberta	10.00	All income levels
Saskatchewan	11.50	0–30,000
	13.50	30,001–60,000
	16.00	60,001 and over
Manitoba	10.90	0–30,544
	16.20	30,545–61,089
	17.40	61,090 and over
Ontario	6.20	0–30,814
	9.24	30,815–61,629
	13.39	61,630 and over
Québec	17.00	0–26,000
	21.25	26,001–52,000
	24.50	52,001 and over
New Brunswick	9.68	0–29,590
	14.82	29,591–59,180
	16.52	59,181–100,000
	17.84	100,001 and over

	Tax Rate (%)	Income Bracket $
New Brunswick	9.68	0–29,590
	14.82	29,591–59,180
	16.52	59,181–100,000
	17.84	100,001 and over
Nova Scotia	9.77	0–29,590
	14.95	29,591–59,180
	16.67	59,181 and over
Prince Edward Island	9.80	0–30,754
	13.80	30,755–61,560
	18.37	61,561 and over
Newfoundland	10.57	0–29,590
	16.16	29,591–59,180
	18.02	59,181 and over
Northwest Territories	7.20	0–30,754
	9.90	30,755–61,560
	11.70	61,561–100,000
	13.05	100,001 and over
Nunavut	7.20	0–30,754
	9.90	30,755–61,560
	11.70	61,561–100,000
	13.05	100,001 and over
Yukon	7.36	0–30,754
	10.12	30,755–61,560
	11.96	61,561–100,000
	14.01	100,001 and over

Note: All surtaxes have been ignored.

Source: From Deborah L. Ort and David B. Perry, *Provincial Budget Roundup*, 2001, (2001 vol. 49, no. 3, *Canadian Tax Journal* 674–707).

salary or interest income. Since dividends are not tax-deductible at the corporate level, the tax system gives individuals a *dividend tax credit* designed to give credit for some of the corporate tax already paid. The system is different in the United States where the personal tax rates on dividends and interest income are identical and they equal the personal tax rate on salary income.

The calculation of tax on dividends is a bit messy but not tough. Suppose you receive \$50 of dividend income and your marginal federal tax rate is 26 percent. To calculate your federal tax, first "gross up" your dividend to 125 percent of the actual dividend received, to get *grossed-up* or *taxable* dividends:

$$\text{Grossed-up (taxable) dividends} = 1.25 \times \$50, \text{ or } \$62.50$$

The gross federal tax on this grossed-up dividend is

$$\text{Gross federal tax} = .26 \times \$62.50, \text{ or } \$16.25$$

However, you don't pay this amount! Subtract the *federal dividend tax credit* of 13.33 percent of the grossed-up dividend (or 16.66 percent of the actual dividend paid):

$$\text{Federal dividend tax credit} = .1333 \times \$62.50, \text{ or } \$8.33,$$

which results in net federal tax on dividends of \$16.25 – \$8.33, or \$7.92.

With the present system of tax on income, the federal government and each province or territory decides its own dividend tax credit rate. The federal dividend tax credit is 13.33 percent of the grossed-up dividend. It is 5.13 percent of the grossed-up dividend in Ontario, 7.7 percent in Nova Scotia, and 7.8 percent in New Brunswick. The provincial tax on dividend income is calculated in the same way as federal tax, using the appropriate provincial tax rate and dividend tax credit.

▸ EXAMPLE 2.3 *Calculating the Tax on Dividends*

You live in Ontario. Your federal marginal tax rate is 26 percent and your provincial marginal tax rate is 13.39 percent. The federal dividend tax is \$7.92, calculated above. The provincial tax on \$50 of dividend income is the tax on the grossed-up dividend less the 5.13 percent dividend tax credit:

$$\text{Provincial dividend tax} = .1339\ (1.25 \times \$50) - .0513 \times (1.25 \times \$50) = \$5.16$$

The total dividend tax is \$7.92 + \$5.16, or \$13.08.

In Example 2.3, the after-tax dividend income is the actual dividend of \$50 less the \$13.08 in taxes, or \$36.92. The effective tax rate on dividend income equals the dividend tax divided by dividends received, \$13.08/\$50, or 26.16 percent. This is substantially less than the combined federal-provincial marginal tax rate on salary and interest income of 26 percent + 13.39 percent, or 39.39 percent.

In addition to salary, interest, and dividend income, individuals can also earn capital gains income. A capital gain occurs when an asset is sold for more than its original purchase price. If you sell the asset for less than the original purchase price, you have a capital loss. Currently, 50 percent of capital gains are taxable; in other words, capital gains are taxed at one-half of the regular or full personal tax rate. Capital losses can be used to reduce your capital gains. If you don't have a capital gain in the current year to offset capital loss, you can carry the loss back up to 3 years or carry it forward indefinitely to reduce capital gains from another year. Capital gains and losses are *realized* only when you sell the asset. If you don't sell, you pay no tax.

▸ EXAMPLE 2.4 *Figuring Out Capital Gains Tax*

You bought shares in Bio-technics stock when it was selling for 10 cents a share. Its market price is now \$1 a share. As long as you hold on to the stock, there is no tax to pay on your gain. But if you sell for \$1, you realize a capital gain of 90 cents and must pay tax. If your combined marginal federal and provincial tax rate is 40 percent, the capital gains tax is .40 x .5 (\$0.90), or \$0.18, giving you an after-tax capital gain of \$0.90 – \$0.18, or \$0.72 per share sold.

✔ CHECK POINT 2.6

Suppose in 2001 you lived in Ontario and earned interest income of $1,000, dividend income of $1,000, and realized a capital gain of $1,000. Calculate the incremental tax, the after-tax income, and the tax rate for each of the different types of income assuming you are in the lowest tax bracket. Redo the calculations assuming you are in the highest tax bracket.

The tax rates in Table 2.6 apply to individuals. But financial institutions are major investors in shares and bonds. These institutions often have special rates of tax. For example, pension funds, which hold huge numbers of shares, are not taxed on either dividend income or capital gains.

2.6 Summary

1. What information is contained in the balance sheet, income statement, and statement of cash flows?

Investors and other stakeholders in the firm need regular financial information to help them monitor the firm's progress. Accountants summarize this information in a balance sheet, income statement, and statement of cash flows.

The **balance sheet** provides a snapshot of the firm's assets and liabilities. The assets consist of current assets that can be rapidly turned into cash and long-term assets, which may be fixed assets such as plant and machinery. The liabilities consist of current liabilities that are due for payment shortly and long-term debts. The difference between the assets and the liabilities represents the amount of the shareholders' equity.

The **income statement** measures the profitability of the company during the year. It shows the difference between revenues and expenses.

The **statement of cash flows** measures the sources and uses of cash during the year. The change in the company's cash balance is the difference between the sources and uses.

2. What is the difference between market and book value?

It is important to distinguish between the book values that are shown in the company accounts and the market values of the assets and liabilities. **Book values** are historical measures based on the original cost of an asset. For example, the assets in the balance sheet are shown at their historical cost less an allowance for depreciation. Similarly, the figure for shareholders' equity measures the cash that shareholders have contributed in the past or that the company has contributed on their behalf.

3. Why does accounting income differ from cash flow?

Income is not the same as cash flow. There are two reasons for this: (1) investment in fixed assets is not deducted immediately from income but is instead spread over the expected life of the equipment, and (2) the accountant records revenues when a sale is made rather than when the customer actually pays the bill, and at the same time, deducts the production costs even though those costs may have been incurred earlier.

4. What are the essential features of the taxation of corporate and personal income?

For large companies the **marginal rate of tax** on income is around 42 percent and around 18 percent for small businesses. In calculating taxable income the company deducts an allowance for depreciation and interest payments. It cannot deduct dividend payments to the shareholders.

Individuals are also taxed on their income, which includes dividends and interest on their investments. Dividends are taxed at lower rates than interest and salary income. Capital gains are taxed at one-half the personal tax rate, but only when the investment is sold and the gain realized.

RELATED WEB LINKS

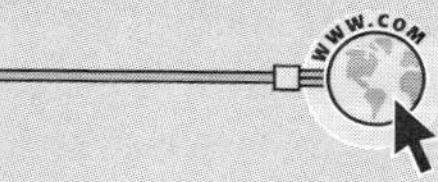

www.ibm.com/investor/financialguide Guide to understanding financial data in an annual report from IBM

www.fool.com/Features/1996/sp0708a.htm#4 A look at the balance sheet and how its components are related

www.ca.taxnews.com PricewaterhouseCoopers tax site

www.ctf.ca Canadian Tax Foundation

www.sedar.com Annual reports and other documents from public Canadian companies

KEY TERMS

balance sheet	35	book value	37	free cash flow	44
generally accepted accounting principles (GAAP)	37	income statement	40	marginal tax rate	51
		statement of cash flows	43	average tax rate	51
		cash flow from assets	44		

QUESTIONS AND PROBLEMS

*Answers in Appendix B

BASIC

*1. **Balance Sheet.** Construct a balance sheet for Sophie's Sofas given the following data. What is shareholders' equity?

Cash balances = $10,000
Inventory of sofas = $200,000
Store and property = $100,000
Accounts receivable = $22,000
Accounts payable = $17,000
Long-term debt = $170,000

2. **Financial Statements.** Earlier in the chapter, we characterized the balance sheet as providing a snapshot of the firm at one point in time and the income statement as providing a video. What did we mean by this? Is the statement of cash flows more like a snapshot or a video?

3. **Income versus Cash Flow.** Explain why accounting revenue generally differs from a firm's cash inflows.

4. **Working Capital.** QuickGrow is in an expanding market, and its sales are increasing by 25 percent per year. Would you expect its net working capital to be increasing or decreasing?

*5. **Tax Rates.** Using Table 2.6, calculate the combined federal and provincial marginal and average tax rates for both an Albertan and Newfoundlander with the following incomes:

a. $20,000
b. $60,000
c. $100,000
d. $3,000,000

6. **Tax Rates.** What would be the marginal and average tax rates for a Manitoban *corporation* with an income level of $100,000?

7. **Taxes.** John Smith lives in British Columbia. In 2001 he earned $1,500 in interest income, $3,000 in dividend income, and realized a $2,000 capital gain. Calculate his after-tax income for each type of income, assuming that his marginal federal tax rate was 26 percent, his marginal provincial tax rate was 18.7 percent, the dividend gross-up factor is 125 percent, the federal dividend tax credit is 13.33 percent of grossed-up dividends, and the provincial dividend tax credit is 6.6 percent of grossed-up dividends.

8. **Cash Flows.** What impact will the following actions have on the firm's cash balance?

a. The firm sells some goods from inventory.
b. The firm sells some machinery to a bank and leases it back for a period of 20 years.
c. The firm buys back 1 million shares of stock from existing shareholders.

PRACTICE

*9. **Balance Sheet/Income Statement.** The year-end 2002 balance sheet of Brandex Inc. lists common stock at $1,100,000 and retained earnings at $3,400,000. The next year, retained earnings were listed at $3,700,000. The firm's net income in 2003 was $900,000. There were no stock repurchases during the year. What were dividends paid by the firm in 2003?

*10. **Taxes.** You set up your tax preparation firm as an incorporated business in Nova Scotia. You took $70,000 from the firm as your salary. The firm's taxable income for the year (net of your salary) was $30,000. How much tax must be paid, including both your personal taxes and the firm's taxes? By how much will you reduce the total tax bill by reducing your salary to $50,000, thereby leaving the firm with taxable income of $50,000? Use the tax rates presented in tables 2.4 and 2.6.

*11. **Market versus Book Values.** The founder of Alchemy Products, Inc., discovered a way to turn lead into gold and patented this new technology. He then formed a corporation and invested $200,000 in setting up a production plant. He believes that he could sell his patent for $50 million.

a. What are the book value and market value of the firm?
b. If there are 2 million shares of stock in the new corporation, what would be the price per share and the book value per share?

*12. **Income Statement.** Sheryl's Shingles had sales of $10,000 in 2003. The cost of goods sold was $6,500, general and administrative expenses were $1,000, interest expenses were $500, and depreciation was $1,000. The firm's tax rate is 35 percent. Assume depreciation equals CCA.

a. What is earnings before interest and taxes?
b. What is net income?
c. What is cash flow from operations?

13. **Cash Flow.** Can cash flow from operations be positive if net income is negative? Can operating cash flow be negative if net income is positive? Give examples.

14. **Cash Flows.** Ponzi Products produced 100 chain letter kits this quarter, resulting in a total cash outlay of $10 per unit. It will sell 50 of the kits next quarter at a price of $11, and the other 50 kits in two quarters at a price of $12. It takes a full quarter for it to collect its bills from its customers. (Ignore possible sales in earlier or later quarters.)

a. Prepare an income statement for Ponzi for today and for each of the next three quarters. Ignore taxes.
b. What are the cash flows for the company today and in each of the next three quarters?
c. What is Ponzi's net working capital in each quarter?

*15. **Profits versus Cash Flow.** During the last year of operations, accounts receivable increased by $10,000, accounts payable increased by $5,000, and inventories decreased by $2,000. What is the total impact of these changes on the difference between profits and cash flow?

16. **Income Statement.** A firm's income statement includes the following data. The firm's average tax rate was 20 percent.

Cost of goods sold	$8,000
Income taxes paid	2,000
Administrative expenses	3,000
Interest expense	1,000
Depreciation	1,000

a. What was the firm's net income?
b. What must have been the firm's revenues?
c. What was EBIT?

*17. **Profits versus Cash Flow.** Butterfly Tractors had $14 million in sales last year. Cost of goods sold was $8 million, depreciation expense was $2 million, interest payment on outstanding debt was $1 million, capital expenditures were $1 million, and the firm's tax rate was 35 percent.

a. What were the firm's net income and cash flows from operations and assets?

b. What would happen to net income and cash flows if depreciation were increased by $1 million? How do you explain the differing impact of depreciation on income versus cash flow?

c. Would you expect the change in income and cash flows from the change in depreciation to have a positive or negative impact on the firm's stock price?

d. Now consider the impact on net income and cash flow if the firm's interest expense were $1 million higher. Why is this case different from part (b)?

18. **Cash Flow.** Candy Canes, Inc., spends $100,000 to buy sugar and peppermint in April. It produces its candy and sells it to distributors in May for $150,000, but it does not receive payment until June. For each month, find the firm's sales, net income, and operating cash flow.

19. **Financial Statements.** Here are the 2002 and 2003 (incomplete) balance sheets for Nobel Oil Corp.

NOBEL OIL CORP. BALANCE SHEET, AS OF END OF YEAR

Assets	2002	2003	Liabilities and Shareholders' Equity	2002	2003
Current assets	$ 310	$ 420	Current liabilities	$210	$240
Net fixed assets	1,200	1,420	Long-term debt	830	920

a. What was owners' equity at the end of 2002 and 2003?

b. If Nobel paid dividends of $100 in 2003, what must have been net income during the year?

c. If Nobel purchased $300 in fixed assets during the year, what must have been the depreciation charge on the income statement?

d. What was the change in net working capital between 2002 and 2003?

e. If Nobel issued $200 of new long-term debt, how much debt must have been paid off during the year?

f. What are the cash flow from operations, free cash flow, and cash flow to bondholders and shareholders?

g. Did Nobel Oil generate enough cash flow from operations to cover the dividends?

*20. **Financial Statements.** South Sea Baubles has the following (incomplete) balance sheet and income statement.

SOUTH SEA BAUBLES BALANCE SHEET, AS OF END OF YEAR
(Figures in millions of dollars)

Assets	2002	2003	Liabilities and Shareholders' Equity	2002	2003
Current assets	$ 90	$140	Current liabilities	$ 50	$ 60
Net fixed assets	800	900	Long-term debt	600	750

INCOME STATEMENT, 2003
(Figures in millions of dollars)

Revenue	$1,950
Cost of goods sold	1,030
Depreciation	350
Interest expense	240

a. What is shareholders' equity in 2002 and 2003?

b. What is net working capital in 2002 and 2003?

c. What is taxable income and taxes paid in 2003? Assume the firm pays taxes equal to 35 percent of taxable income.

d. What is cash flow provided by operations during 2003? Pay attention to changes in net working capital, using Table 2.3 as a guide.

e. Net fixed assets increased from $800 million to $900 million during 2003. What must have been South Sea's *gross* investment in fixed assets (capital expenditures) during 2003?

f. If South Sea reduced its outstanding accounts payable by $35 million during the year, what must have happened to its other current liabilities?

g. What are the cash flow from assets and cash flow to bondholders and shareholders?

Here are some data on Fincorp, Inc., that you should use for problems 21 to 28. The balance sheet items correspond to values at year-end of 2002 and 2003, while the income statement items correspond to revenues or expenses during the year ending in either 2002 or 2003. All values are in thousands of dollars.

	2002	2003
Revenue	$4,000	$4,100
Cost of goods sold	1,600	1,700
Depreciation	500	520
Inventories	300	350
Administrative expenses	500	550
Interest expense	150	150
Federal and provincial taxes[a]	400	420
Accounts payable	300	350
Accounts receivable	400	450
Net fixed assets[b]	5,000	5,800
Long-term debt	2,000	2,400
Notes payable	1,000	600
Dividends paid	410	410
Cash and marketable securities	800	300

[a] Taxes are paid in their entirety in the year that the tax obligation is incurred.

[b] Net fixed assets are fixed assets net of accumulated depreciation since the asset was installed.

21. **Balance Sheet.** Construct a balance sheet for Fincorp for 2002 and 2003. What is shareholders' equity?

*22. **Working Capital.** What happened to net working capital during the year? What about noncash net working capital?

23. **Income Statement.** Construct an income statement for Fincorp for 2002 and 2003. What was the addition to retained earnings for 2003? How does that compare with the increase in shareholders' equity between the two years?

*24. **Earnings per Share.** Suppose that Fincorp has 500,000 shares outstanding. What were earnings per share?

25. **Taxes.** What was the firm's average tax bracket for each year? Do you have enough information to determine the marginal tax bracket?

26. **Balance Sheet.** Examine the values for depreciation in 2003 and net fixed assets in 2002 and 2003. What was Fincorp's *gross* investment in plant and equipment during 2003?

27. **Cash Flows.** Construct a statement of cash flows for Fincorp for 2003 using Table 2.3 as a guide.

*28. **Book versus Market Value.** Now suppose that the *market value* (in thousands of dollars) of Fincorp's fixed assets in 2003 is $6,000, and that the value of its long-term debt is only $2,400. In addition, the consensus among investors is that Fincorp's past investments in developing the skills of its employees are worth $2,900. This investment of course does not show up on the balance sheet. What will be the price per share of Fincorp stock?

CHALLENGE

29. **Taxes.** Reconsider the data in problem 10. What are the total personal and corporate taxes if you pay yourself a salary of $50,000 and a dividend of $20,000?

30. **Free Cash Flows.**
    a. Using the data for Fincorp, determine the free cash flow and cash flow to bondholders and shareholders, using Example 2.2 as a guide.
    b. Up to now, interest has been included as an operating cash flow. Rework the free cash flow calculation for Fincorp, classifying interest expense as a financial flow and not as an operating cash flow.
    c. Why might an analyst want to separate all financial cash flows from the firm's operating cash flows?
    d. Rework the financial flows to bondholders and shareholders with interest classified as a financial cash flow, not an operating cash flow.

INTERNET PROBLEM

1. **Read an annual report.** Go to www.sedar.com, the website where public Canadian companies must post their annual reports and other corporate documents. Click on "Search Database," then "Public Company." Select document type "Annual Report" then "Search" and you will get a list of recent annual reports. Pick one and read it. What do you learn about the nature of the business and of the company's successes and failures? What type of assets and liabilities do they list on their balance sheet? Look at the cash flow statement and calculate the cash flows from assets. What were the financing flows to bondholders and shareholders?

SOLUTIONS TO CHECK POINTS

2.1 Cash and equivalents would increase by $100 million. Property, plant, and equipment would increase by $400 million. Long-term debt would increase by $500 million. Shareholders' equity would *not* increase: assets and liabilities have increased equally, leaving shareholders' equity unchanged.

2.2 a. If the auto plant were worth $14 billion, the equity in the firm would be worth $14 – $4 = $10 billion. With 100 million shares outstanding, each share would be worth $100.
b. If the outstanding stock were worth $8 billion, we would infer that the market values the auto plant at $8 + $4 = $12 billion.

2.3

	Period:	1	2	3
	Sales	0	150	0
–	Change in accounts receivable	0	150	(150)
–	Cost of goods sold	0	100	0
–	Change in inventories	100	(100)	0
	Net cash flow	–100	0	+150

The net cash flow pattern does make sense. The firm expends $100 in period 1 to produce the product but it is not paid its $150 sales price until period 3. In period 2 no cash is exchanged.

2.4 a. An increase in inventories uses cash, reducing the firm's net cash balance.
b. A reduction in accounts payable uses cash, reducing the firm's net cash balance.
c. An issue of common stock is a source of cash.
d. The purchase of new equipment is a use of cash, and it reduces the firm's net cash balance.

2.5

	Firm A	Firm B
EBIT	100	100
Interest	60	0
Pretax income	40	100
Tax (35% of pre-tax income)	14	35
Net income	26	65

Note: Figures in millions of dollars.

Taxes owed by Firm A fall from $21 million to $14 million. The reduction in taxes is 35 percent of the extra $20 million of interest income. Net income does not fall by the full $20 million of extra interest expense. It instead falls by interest expense less the reduction in taxes, or $20 million – $7 million = $13 million.

2.6

	Lowest Tax Bracket	Highest Tax Bracket
Federal tax rate	16%	29%
Ontario tax rate	6.2%	13.39%
Combined tax rate	22.2%	42.39%
1. **Interest income**	$1,000	$1,000
Tax on interest income	.222 × $1,000 = $222	.4239 × $1,000 = $423.90
After-tax interest income	$1,000 – $222 = $778	$1,000 – $423.9 = $576.1
Interest tax rate	$222/$1,000 = 22.2%	$423.9/$1,000 = 42.39%
2. **Dividend income**	$1,000	$1,000
Grossed-up dividend	1.25 × $1,000 = $1,250	1.25 × $1,000 = $1,250
Gross federal tax	.16 × $1,250 = $200	.29 × $1,250 = $362.5
Less: Federal dividend tax credit	.1333 × $1,250 = $166.63	.1333 × $1,250 = $166.63
Net federal dividend tax	$200 – $166.63 = $33.37	$362.5 – $166.63 = $195.88
Gross provincial tax	.062 × $1,250 = $77.50	.1339 × $1,250 = $167.38
Less: Provincial dividend tax credit	.0513 × $1,250 = $64.13	.0513 × $1,250 = $64.13
Net provincial dividend tax	$77.50 – 64.13 = $13.38	$167.38 – $64.13 = $103.25
Net tax on dividend income	$33.37 + $13.38 = $46.75	$195.88 + $103.25 = $299.13
After-tax dividend income	$1,000 – $46.75 = $953.25	$1,000 – $299.13 = $700.87
Dividend tax rate	$46.75/$1,000 = 4.68%	$299.13/$1,000 = 29.91%
3. **Capital gains income**	$1,000	$1,000
Tax on capital gains	.222 × .5 × $1,000 = $111	.4239 × .5 × $1,000 = $211.95
After-tax capital gains	$1,000 – $111 = $889	$1,000 – $211.95 = $788.05
Capital gains tax rate	$111/$1,000 = 11.1%	$211.95/$1,000 = 21.195%

PART TWO

Value

3 The Time Value of Money

4 Valuing Bonds

5 Valuing Stocks

6 Net Present Value and Other Investment Criteria

7 Using Discounted Cash-Flow Analyis to Make Investment Decisions

8 Project Analysis

CHAPTER 3

The Time Value of Money

3.1 Future Values and Compound Interest

3.2 Present Values

3.3 Multiple Cash Flows

3.4 Level Cash Flows: Perpetuities and Annuities

3.5 Inflation and the Time Value of Money

3.6 Effective Annual Interest Rates

3.7 Summary

Companies invest in lots of things. Some are *tangible assets*—that is, assets you can kick, like factories, machinery, and offices. Others are *intangible assets,* such as patents or trademarks. In each case the company lays out some money to start in the hopes of receiving even more money later. Individuals also make investments. For example, your university or college education may cost you $10,000 per year. That is an investment you hope will pay off in the form of a higher salary later in life. You are sowing now and expecting to reap later.

Companies pay for their investments by raising money and in the process assume liabilities. For example, they may borrow money from a bank and promise to repay it with interest later. You may also have financed your investment in a higher education by borrowing money that you plan to pay back out of that fat salary.

All these financial decisions require comparisons of cash payments at different dates. Will your future salary be sufficient to justify the current expenditure on university or college tuition? How much will you have to repay the bank if you borrow to finance your education?

In this chapter we take the first steps toward understanding the relationship between the value of the dollar today and in the future. We start by looking at how funds invested at a specific interest rate will grow over time. We next ask how much you would need to invest today to produce a specified sum of money in the future, and we describe some shortcuts for working out the value of a series of cash payments. Then we consider how inflation affects these financial calculations.

After studying this chapter you should be able to

- Calculate the future value to which money invested at a given interest rate will grow.
- Calculate the present value of a future payment.
- Calculate present and future values of streams of cash payments.
- Find the interest rate implied by the present or future value.
- Understand the difference between real and nominal cash flows and between real and nominal interest rates.
- Compare interest rates quoted over different time intervals—for example, monthly versus annual rates.

There is nothing complicated about these calculations, but if they are to become second nature, you should read the chapter thoroughly, work carefully through the examples (we have provided plenty), and make sure you tackle the Check Point questions. We are asking you to make an investment now in return for a payoff later.

3.1 Future Values and Compound Interest

You have \$100 invested in a bank account. Suppose banks are currently paying an interest rate of 6 percent per year on deposits. So after a year, your account will earn interest of \$6:

$$\text{Interest} = \text{interest rate} \times \text{initial investment}$$
$$= .06 \times \$100 = \$6$$

You start the year with \$100 and you earn interest of \$6, so the value of your investment will grow to \$106 by the end of the year:

$$\text{Value of investment after 1 year} = \$100 + \$6 = \$106$$

Notice that the \$100 invested grows by the factor $(1 + .06) = 1.06$. In general, for any interest rate, r, the value of the investment at the end of 1 year is $(1 + r)$ times the initial investment:

$$\text{Value after 1 year} = \text{initial investment} \times (1 + r)$$
$$= \$100 \times (1.06) = \$106$$

What if you leave this money in the bank for a second year? Your balance, now \$106, will continue to earn interest of 6 percent. So

$$\text{Interest in Year 2} = .06 \times \$106 = \$6.36$$

You start the second year with \$106 on which you earn interest of \$6.36. So by the end of the year the value of your account will grow to \$106 + \$6.36 = \$112.36.

In the first year your investment of \$100 increases by a factor of 1.06 to \$106; in the second year the \$106 again increases by a factor of 1.06 to \$112.36. Thus the initial \$100 investment grows twice by a factor 1.06:

$$\text{Value of account after 2 years} = \$100 \times 1.06 \times 1.06$$
$$= \$100 \times (1.06)^2 = \$112.36$$

If you keep your money invested for a third year, your investment multiplies by 1.06 each year for 3 years. By the end of the third year, it will total $\$100 \times (1.06)^3 = \$119.10$, scarcely enough to put you in the millionaire class, but even millionaires have to start somewhere.

future value Amount to which an investment will grow after earning interest.

Clearly for an investment horizon of t years, the original \$100 investment will grow to $\$100 \times (1.06)^t$. For an interest rate of r and a horizon of t years, the **future value** of your investment will be

$$\textbf{Future value of \$100} = \$100 \times (1 + r)^t$$

compound interest Interest earned on interest.

simple interest Interest earned only on the original investment; no interest is earned on interest.

Notice in our example that your interest income in the first year is \$6 (6 percent of \$100), and in the second year it is \$6.36 (6 percent of \$106). Your income in the second year is higher because you now earn interest on *both* the original \$100 investment *and* the \$6 of interest earned in the previous year. Earning interest on interest is called *compounding* or **compound interest.** In contrast, if the bank calculated the interest only on your original investment, you would be paid **simple interest.** With simple interest your bank balance is only \$112 after two years, \$100 + 2 × \$6.

Table 3.1 and Figure 3.1 illustrate the mechanics of compound interest. Table 3.1 shows that in each year, you start with a greater balance in your account—your savings have been increased by the previous year's interest. As a result, your interest income also is higher.

TABLE 3.1
Mechanics of compound interest—interest is earned on previous years' interest

Year	Balance at Start of Year	Interest Earned During Year	Balance at End of Year
1	\$100.00	.06 × \$100.00 = \$6.00	\$106.00
2	\$106.00	.06 × \$106.00 = \$6.36	\$112.36
3	\$112.36	.06 × \$112.36 = \$6.74	\$119.10
4	\$119.10	.06 × \$119.10 = \$7.15	\$126.25
5	\$126.25	.06 × \$126.25 = \$7.57	\$133.82

Obviously, the higher the rate of interest, the faster your savings will grow. Figure 3.2 shows that a few percentage points added to the (compound) interest rate can dramatically affect the future balance of your savings account. For example, after 10 years \$1,000 invested at 10 percent will grow to $\$1,000 \times (1.10)^{10} = \$2,594$. If invested at 5 percent, it will grow to only $\$1,000 \times (1.05)^{10} = \$1,629$.

Calculating future values is easy using almost any calculator. If you have the patience, you can multiply your initial investment by $1 + r$ (1.06 in our example) once for each year of your investment. A simpler procedure is to use the power key (the y^x key) on your calculator. For example, to compute $(1.06)^{10}$, enter 1.06, press the y^x key, enter 10, press = and discover that the answer is 1.791. (Try this!)

If you don't have a calculator, you can use a table of future values such as Table 3.2. Check that you can use it to work out the future value of a 10-year investment at 6 percent. First find the row corresponding to 10 years. Now work along that row until you reach the column for a 6 percent interest rate. The entry shows that \$1 invested for 10 years at 6 percent grows to \$1.791.

Now try one more example. If you invest \$1 for 20 years at 10 percent and do not withdraw any money, what will you have at the end? Your answer should be \$6.727.

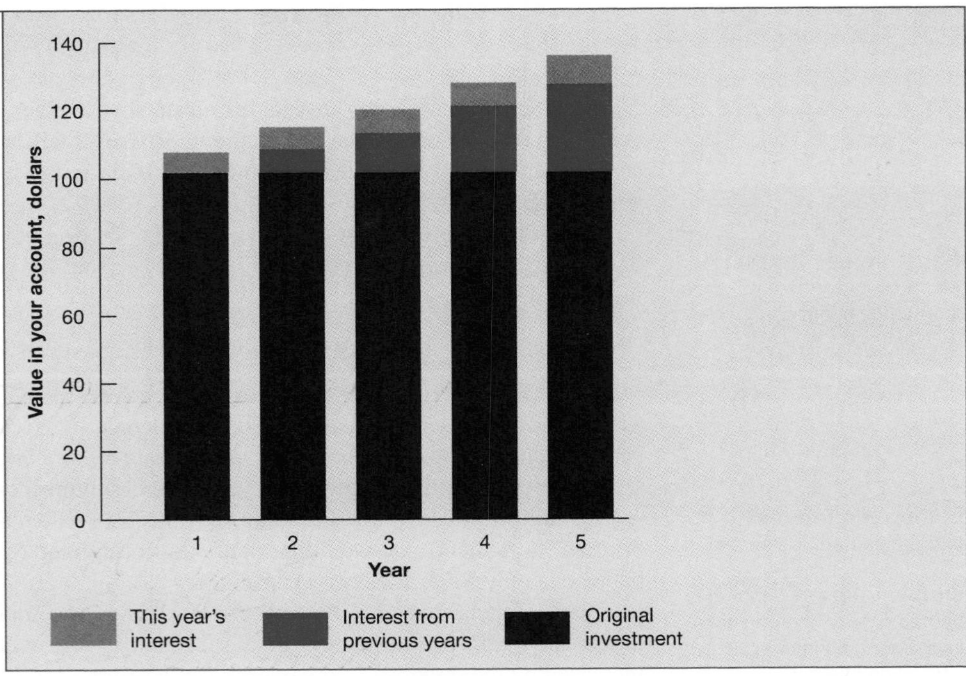

FIGURE 3.1
Compound interest. Future value of \$100 invested at 6 percent in each of the 5 years

FIGURE 3.2
Future values of $1 invested at various interest rates, with compound interest

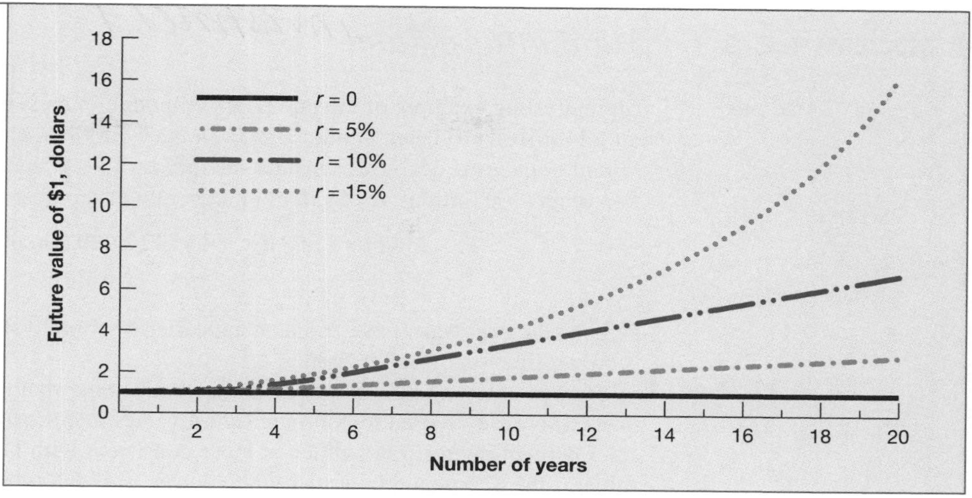

Table 3.2 gives future values for only a small selection of years and interest rates. Table A.1 at the end of the book is a bigger version of Table 3.2. It presents the future value of a $1 investment for a wide range of time periods and interest rates.

Future value tables are tedious, and as Table 3.2 demonstrates, they show future values only for a limited set of interest rates and time periods. For example, suppose that you want to calculate future values using an interest rate of 7.835 percent. The power key on your calculator will be faster and easier than future value tables. A third alternative is to use a financial calculator, which is discussed in the Financial Calculator box later in this chapter. No matter what method you pick, in each case the future value, FV, of investing I dollars for t periods at an interest rate r is calculated as

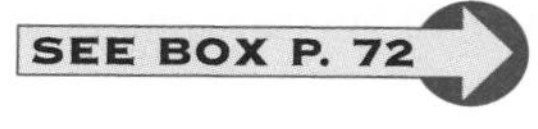
SEE BOX P. 72

$$FV = I \times (1 + r)^t$$

future value factor
Future value of a current cash flow of $1.

The expression $(1 + r)^t$ is called the **future value factor**. It measures the future value of a $1 investment at r percent per period for t periods.

TABLE 3.2
Future value factors—future values of $1, invested at various interest rates for different periods

Number of Years	Interest Rate per Year					
	5%	6%	7%	8%	9%	10%
1	1.050	1.060	1.070	1.080	1.090	1.100
2	1.103	1.124	1.145	1.166	1.188	1.210
3	1.158	1.191	1.225	1.260	1.295	1.331
4	1.216	1.262	1.311	1.360	1.412	1.464
5	1.276	1.338	1.403	1.469	1.539	1.611
10	1.629	1.791	1.967	2.159	2.367	2.594
20	2.653	3.207	3.870	4.661	5.604	6.727
30	4.322	5.743	7.612	10.063	13.268	17.449

▶ EXAMPLE 3.1 *Manhattan Island*

An interesting example of the power of compound interest is the sale of Manhattan Island for \$24 in 1626 to Peter Minuit. Based on New York real estate prices today, it seems that Minuit got a great deal. But consider the future value of that \$24 if it had been invested for 377 years (2003 minus 1626) at an interest rate of 8 percent per year:

$$\$24 \times (1.08)^{377} = \$95{,}712{,}000{,}000{,}000$$
$$= \$95.712 \text{ trillion}$$

Perhaps the deal wasn't as good as it appeared. The total value of land in Manhattan today is only a fraction of \$96 trillion.

Though entertaining, this analysis is actually somewhat misleading. First, the 8 percent interest rate we've used to compute future values is quite high by historical standards. At a 3.5 percent interest rate, which is more consistent with historical experience, the future value of the \$24 would be *dramatically* lower, only $\$24 \times (1.035)^{377} = \$10{,}297{,}294$! Second, we have understated the returns to Mr. Minuit and his successors: We have ignored the rental income that the island's land has generated over the last three or four centuries.

All things considered, if we had been around in 1626, we would have gladly paid \$24 for the island.

The power of compounding is not restricted to money. Foresters try to forecast the compound growth rate of trees, demographers the compound growth rate of population. An American social commentator once observed that the number of lawyers in the United States is increasing at a higher compound rate than the population as a whole (3.6 versus .9 percent in the 1980s), and in about two centuries there will be more lawyers than people! In all these cases, the principle is the same:

Compound growth means that value increases each period by the factor (1 + growth rate). The value after *t* periods will equal the initial value times (1 + growth rate)^t. When money is invested at compound interest, the growth rate is the interest rate.

☑ CHECK POINT 3.1

Suppose that Peter Minuit did not become the first real estate tycoon in New York, but instead had invested his \$24 at a 5 percent interest rate in New Amsterdam Savings Bank. What would have been the balance in his account after 5 years? 50 years?

☑ CHECK POINT 3.2

Start-up Enterprises had sales last year of only \$.5 million. However, a stock market analyst is bullish on the company and predicts that sales will double each year for 4 years. What are projected sales at the end of this period?

3.2 Present Values

Money can be invested to earn interest. If you are offered the choice between $100,000 now and $100,000 at the end of the year, you naturally take the money now to get a year's interest. Financial managers make the same point when they say that money in hand today has a *time value* or perhaps when they quote the most basic financial principle:

A dollar today is worth more than a dollar tomorrow.

present value (PV) Value today of a future cash flow.

We have seen that $100 invested for 1 year at 6 percent will grow to a future value of 100 × 1.06 = $106. Let's turn this around: How much do we need to invest now in order to produce $106 at the end of the year? Financial managers refer to this as the **present value (PV)** of the $106 payoff.

Future value is calculated by multiplying the present investment by one plus the interest rate, .06, or 1.06. To calculate present value, we simply reverse the process and divide the future value by 1.06:

$$\text{Present value} = \text{PV} = \frac{\text{future value}}{1.06} = \frac{\$106}{1.06} = \$100$$

What is the present value of, say, $112.36 to be received 2 years from now? Again we ask, how much would we need to invest now to produce $112.36 after 2 years? The answer is obviously $100; we've already calculated that at 6 percent $100 grows to $112.36:

$$\$100 \times (1.06)^2 = \$112.36$$

However, if we don't know, or forgot the answer, we just divide future value by $(1.06)^2$:

$$\text{Present value} = \text{PV} = \frac{\$112.36}{(1.06)^2} = \$100$$

In general, for a future value or payment t periods away, present value is

$$\textbf{Present value} = \frac{\textbf{future value after } t \textbf{ periods}}{(1 + r)^t} \qquad \textbf{(3.1)}$$

discount rate Interest rate used to compute present values of future cash flows.

In this context the interest rate r is known as the **discount rate**, and the present value is often called the *discounted value* of the future payment. To calculate present value, we discounted the future value at the interest r.

EXAMPLE 3.2 *Saving to Buy a New Computer*

Suppose you need $3,000 next year to buy a new computer. The interest rate is 8 percent per year. How much money should you set aside now in order to pay for the purchase? Just calculate the present value at an 8 percent interest rate of a $3,000 payment at the end of 1 year. This value is

$$\text{PV} = \frac{\$3{,}000}{1.08} = \$2{,}778$$

Notice that \$2,778 invested for 1 year at 8 percent will prove just enough to buy your computer:

$$\text{Future value} = \$2{,}778 \times 1.08 = \$3{,}000$$

The longer the period before you must make a payment, the less you need to invest today. For example, suppose that you can postpone buying that computer until the end of 2 years. In this case we calculate the present value of the future payment by dividing \$3,000 by $(1.08)^2$:

$$\text{PV} = \frac{\$3{,}000}{(1.08)^2} = \$2{,}572$$

Thus you need to invest \$2,778 today to provide \$3,000 in 1 year but only \$2,572 to provide the same \$3,000 in 2 years.

We repeat the basic procedure:

To work out how much you will have in the future if you invest for *t* years at an interest rate *r*, *multiply* the initial investment by $(1 + r)^t$. To find the present value of a future payment, run the process in reverse and *divide* by $(1 + r)^t$.

Present values are always calculated using compound interest. Whereas the ascending lines in Figure 3.2 show the future value of \$1 invested with compound interest, when we calculate present values we move back along the lines from future to present.

Thus present values decline, other things being equal, when future cash payments are delayed. The longer you have to wait for money, the less it's worth today, as we see in Figure 3.3. Notice how very small variations in the interest rate can have a powerful effect on the value of distant cash flows. At an interest rate of 10 percent, a payment of \$1 in Year 20 is worth \$.15 today. If the interest rate increases to 15 percent, the value of the future payment falls by about 60 percent to \$.06.

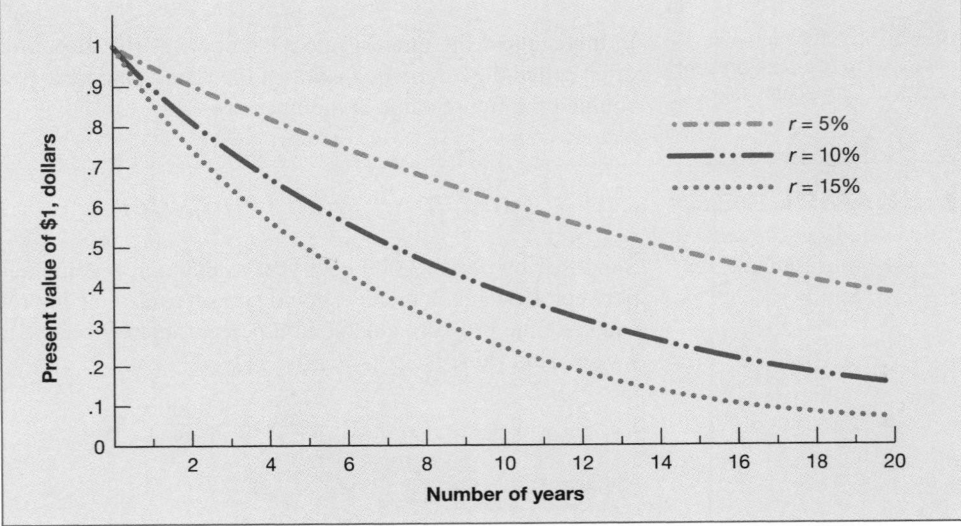

FIGURE 3.3
Present value of a future cash flow of \$1, using various interest rates

The present value formula is sometimes written differently. Instead of dividing the future payment by $(1 + r)^t$, we could just as easily multiply it by $1/(1 + r)^t$:

$$PV = \frac{\text{future payment}}{(1 + r)^t}$$

$$= \text{future payment} \times \frac{1}{(1 + r)^t}$$

discount factor Present value of a $1 future payment.

The expression $1/(1 + r)^t$ is called the **discount factor.** It measures the present value of $1 to be received in t years from today.

The simplest way to find the discount factor is to use a calculator, but financial managers sometimes find it convenient to use tables of discount factors. For example, Table 3.3 shows discount factors for a small range of years and interest rates. Table A.2 at the end of the book provides a set of discount factors for a wide range of years and interest rates.

Try using Table 3.3 to figure out how much to put aside for that $3,000 computer purchase. If the interest rate is 8 percent, the present value of $1 paid at the end of 1 year is $.926. So the present value of $3,000 is

$$PV = \$3{,}000 \times \frac{1}{1.08} = \$3{,}000 \times .926 = \$2{,}778$$

which matches the value we obtained in Example 3.2.

What if the computer purchase is postponed until the end of 2 years? Table 3.3 shows that the present value of $1 paid at the end of 2 years is .857. So the present value of $3,000 is

$$PV = \$3{,}000 \times \frac{1}{(1.08)^2} = \$3{,}000 \times .857 = \$2{,}571$$

which differs from the calculation in Example 3.2 only because of a rounding error.

Notice that as you move along the rows in Table 3.3, moving to higher interest rates, present values decline. As you move down the columns, moving to longer discounting periods, present values again decline. Why does this make sense?

EXAMPLE 3.3 *Coca-Cola Enterprises Borrows Some Cash*

In 1995 Coca-Cola Enterprises needed to borrow about a quarter of a billion dollars for 25 years. It did so by selling IOUs, each of which simply promised to pay the holder $1,000

TABLE 3.3
Discount factors—present value of $1 for various interest rates and different periods

Number of Years	Interest Rate per Year					
	5%	6%	7%	8%	9%	10%
1	.952	.943	.935	.926	.917	.909
2	.907	.890	.873	.857	.842	.826
3	.864	.840	.816	.794	.772	.751
4	.823	.792	.763	.735	.708	.683
5	.784	.747	.713	.681	.650	.621
10	.614	.558	.508	.463	.422	.386
20	.377	.312	.258	.215	.178	.149
30	.231	.174	.131	.099	.075	.057

at the end of 25 years.[1] The market interest rate at the time was 8.53 percent. How much would you have been prepared to pay for one of the company's IOUs?

To calculate present value we multiply the $1,000 future payment by the 25-year discount factor:

$$\text{PV} = \$1{,}000 \times \frac{1}{(1.0853)^{25}}$$
$$= \$1{,}000 \times .129 = \$129$$

Instead of using a calculator to find the discount factor, we could use Table A.2 at the end of the book. You can see that the 25-year discount factor is .146 if the interest rate is 8 percent and .116 if the rate is 9 percent. For an interest rate of 8.5 percent, the discount factor is roughly halfway between at .131, a shade higher than the exact figure.

CHECK POINT 3.3

Suppose that Coca-Cola had promised to pay $1,000 at the end of 10 years. If the market interest rate was 8.53 percent, how much would you have been prepared to pay for a 10-year IOU of $1,000?

EXAMPLE 3.4 *Finding the Value of Free Credit*

Kangaroo Autos is offering free credit on a $10,000 car. You pay $4,000 down and then the balance at the end of 2 years. Turtle Motors next door does not offer free credit but will give you $500 off the list price. If the interest rate is 10 percent, which company is offering the better deal?

Notice that you pay more in total by buying through Kangaroo, but since part of the payment is postponed, you can keep this money in the bank where it will continue to earn interest. To compare the two offers, you need to calculate the present value of the payments to Kangaroo. The *time line* in Figure 3.4 shows the cash payments to Kangaroo. The first payment, $4,000, takes place today. The second payment, $6,000, takes place at the end of 2 years. To find its present value, we need to multiply by the 2-year discount factor. The total present value of the payments to Kangaroo is therefore

$$\text{PV} = \$4{,}000 + \$6{,}000 \times \frac{1}{(1.10)^2}$$
$$= \$4{,}000 + \$4{,}958.68 = \$8{,}958.68$$

Suppose you start with $8,958.68. You make a down payment of $4,000 to Kangaroo Autos and invest the balance of $4,958.68. At an interest rate of 10 percent, this will grow over 2 years to $\$4{,}958.68 \times 1.10^2 = \$6{,}000$, just enough to make the final payment on your automobile. The total cost of $8,958.68 is a better deal than the $9,500 charged by Turtle Motors.

These calculations illustrate how important it is to use present values when comparing alternative patterns of cash payment.

[1] "IOU" means "I owe you." Coca-Cola's IOUs are called *bonds.* Usually bond investors receive a regular *interest* or *coupon* payment. The Coca-Cola Enterprises bond will make only a single payment at the end of Year 25. It was therefore known as a *zero-coupon bond.* More on this in the next chapter.

FINANCE IN ACTION

From Here to Eternity

Politicians, you may be aware, are fond of urging people to invest in the future. It would appear that some investors are taking them a bit too literally of late. The latest fad among emerging-market bond investors, eager to get a piece of the action, is to queue up for bonds with 100-year maturities, such as those issued by the Chinese government and Tenaga Nasional, a Malaysian electrical utility.

Not to be outdone by these century bonds, Eurotunnel, the beleaguered company that operates the railway beneath the English Channel, is trying to tempt investors with a millennium's worth of profits. Last week, in a bid to sweeten the pot for its shareholders and creditors, who must agree on an unpalatable financial restructuring, it asked the British and French governments to extend its operating franchise from a mere 65 years to 999 years. By offering investors some windfall profits, the firm hopes they will be more likely to ratify its plan. Has the distant future become the latest place to make a financial killing?

Alas, the future is not all that it is cracked up to be. Although at first glance, 999 years of profits would seem far better than 65 years, those last nine centuries are really nothing to get excited about. The reason is that a dollar spent today (human nature being what it is) is worth more to people than a dollar spent tomorrow. So when comparing profits in the future with those in the present, the future profits must be "discounted" by a suitable interest rate.

Under the relentless pressures of compound interest, the value of future profits is ground to nothing as the years go by. Suppose, for example, that you had a choice between making the following two gifts to a university: You could write a cheque for $10,000 today or give $1,000 a year for the next century. The latter donation might seem the more generous one, but at a 10% interest rate, they are worth the same amount. By the time compound discounting had finished with it, that final $1,000 payment would be worth only $.07 today (see diagram).

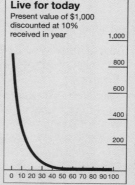

Live for today
Present value of $1,000 discounted at 10% received in year

What does this mean for Eurotunnel's investors? Extending its franchise by 934 years should increase its value to today's investors by only 10–15%, after discounting. If they are feeling generous, perhaps the British and French governments should toss in another year and make the franchise an even 1,000.

You should *never* compare cash flows occurring at different times without first discounting them to a common date. By calculating present values, we see how much cash must be set aside today to pay future bills.

The importance of discounting is highlighted in the Finance in Action box above, which examines the value of an extension of Eurotunnel's operating franchise from 65 to 999 years. While such an extension sounds as if it would be extremely valuable, the article (and its accompanying diagram) points out that profits 65 years or more from now have negligible present value.

FIGURE 3.4
Present value of the cash flows to Kangaroo Autos

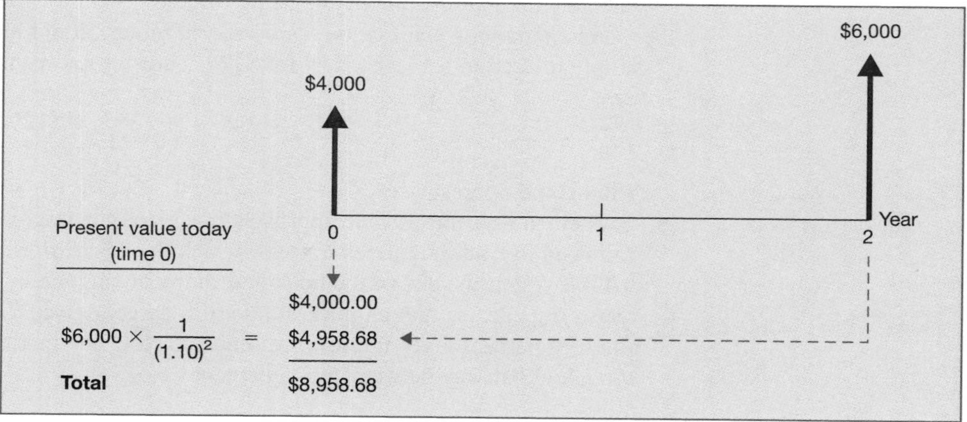

An Introduction to Financial Calculators

Financial calculators are designed with present value and future value formulas already programmed. Therefore, you can readily solve many problems simply by entering the inputs for the problem and punching a key for the solution.

The basic financial calculator uses five keys that correspond to the inputs for common problems involving the time value of money.

Each key represents the following input:

- *n* is the number of periods. (We have been using *t* to denote the length of time, or number of periods. Most calculators use *n* for the same concept.)
- *i* is the interest rate per period, expressed as a percentage (not a decimal). For example, if the interest rate is 8 percent, you would enter 8, not .08. On some calculators this key is written I/Y or I/YR. (We have been using *r* to denote the interest rate or discount rate.)
- *PV* is the present value.
- *FV* is the future value.
- *PMT* is the amount of any recurring payment (called an annuity). In single cash-flow problems such as those we have considered so far, *PMT* is zero.

Given any four of these inputs, the calculator will solve for the fifth. We will illustrate with several examples.

Future Values

Recall Example 3.1, where we calculated the future value of Peter Minuit's $24 investment. Enter 24 into the *PV* register. (You enter the value by typing 24 and then pushing the *PV* key.) We assumed an interest rate of 8 percent, so enter 8 into the *i* register. Because the $24 had 377 years to compound, enter 377 into the *n* register. Enter 0 into the *PMT* register because there is no recurring payment involved in the calculation. Now ask the calculator to compute *FV*. On some calculators you simply press the *FV* key. On others you need to first press the "compute" key (which may be labelled *COMP* or *CPT*), and then press *FV*. The exact sequence of keystrokes for three popular financial calculators are as follows:[1]

Hewlett-Packard HP-10B	Sharpe EL-733A	Texas Instruments BA II Plus
24 [PV]	24 [PV]	24 [PV]
377 [n]	377 [n]	377 [n]
8 [I/YR]	8 [i]	8 [I/Y]
0 [PMT]	0 [PMT]	0 [PMT]
[FV]	[COMP] [FV]	[CPT] [FV]

You should find after hitting the *FV* key that your calculator shows a value of –95.712 trillion, which, except for the minus sign, is the future value of the $24.

Why does the minus sign appear? Most calculators treat cash flows as either inflows (shown as positive numbers) or

FINDING THE INTEREST RATE

When we looked at Coca-Cola's IOUs in the previous section, we used the interest rate to compute a fair market price for each IOU. Sometimes you are given the price and have to calculate the interest rate that is being offered.

For example, when Coca-Cola borrowed money, it did not announce an interest rate. It simply offered to sell each IOU for $129. Thus we know that

$$\text{PV} = \$1{,}000 \times \frac{1}{(1+r)^{25}} = \$129$$

What is the interest rate?

There are several ways to approach this. First, you might use a table of discount factors. You need to find the interest rate for which the 25-year discount factor equals .129. Look at Table A.2 at the end of the book and run your finger along the row corresponding to 25 years. You can see that an interest rate of 8 percent gives too high a discount factor and a rate of 9 percent gives too low a discount factor. The interest rate on the Coca-Cola loan was about halfway between at 8.5 percent.

outflows (negative numbers). For example, if you borrow \$100 today at an interest rate of 12 percent, you receive money now (a *positive* cash flow), but you will have to pay back \$112 in a year, a *negative* cash flow at that time. Therefore, the calculator displays *FV* as a negative number. The following time line of cash flows shows the reasoning employed. The final negative cash flow of \$112 has the same present value as the \$100 borrowed today.

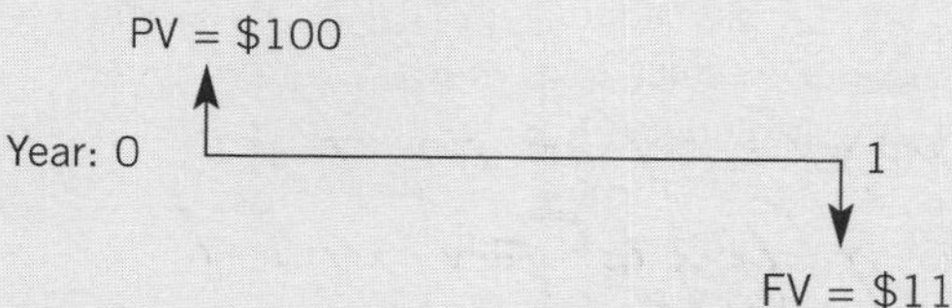

If, instead of borrowing, you were to *invest* \$100 today to reap a future benefit, you would enter *PV* as a negative number (first press 100, then press the +/– key to make the value negative, and finally press *PV* to enter the value into the *PV* register). In this case, *FV* would appear as a positive number, indicating that you will reap a cash inflow when your investment comes to fruition.

Present Values

Suppose your savings goal is to accumulate \$10,000 by the end of 30 years. If the interest rate is 8 percent, how much would you need to invest today to achieve your goal? Again, there is no recurring payment involved, so *PMT* is zero. We therefore enter the following: $n = 30$; $i = 8$; $FV = 10{,}000$; $PMT = 0$. Now compute *PV*, and you should get an answer of –993.77. The answer is displayed as a negative number because you need to make a cash outflow (an investment) of \$993.77 now in order to enjoy a cash inflow of \$10,000 in 30 years.

Finding the Interest Rate

The 25-year IOU from Coca-Cola Enterprises in Example 3.3 sold at \$129 and promised a final payment of \$1,000. We may obtain the market interest rate by entering $n = 25$, $FV = 1{,}000$, $PV = -129$, and $PMT = 0$. Compute *i* and you will find that the interest rate is 8.53 percent. This is the value we computed directly (but with more work) in the example.

How Long an Investment?

In Example 3.5, we consider how long it would take for an investment to double in value. This sort of problem is easily solved using a calculator. If the investment is to double, we enter $FV = 2$ and $PV = -1$. If the interest rate is 9 percent, enter $i = 9$ and $PMT = 0$. Compute *n* and you will find that $n = 8.04$ years. If the interest rate is 9.05 percent, the doubling period falls to 8 years, as we found in the example.

[1] The BA II Plus calculator requires a little extra work to initialize. When you buy the calculator, it is set to automatically interpret each period as a year and assumes that interest compounds monthly. In our experience, it is best to change the compounding frequency to once per period. To do so, press [2nd] {P/Y} 1 [ENTER], then press [↓] 1 [ENTER] and finally press [2nd] {QUIT} to return to standard calculator mode. You should only need to do this once, even if the calculator is shut off.

Second, you can rearrange the equation and use your calculator:

$$\$129 \times (1 + r)^{25} = \$1{,}000$$

$$(1 + r)^{25} = \frac{\$1{,}000}{\$129} = 7.75$$

$$(1 + r) = (7.75)^{1/25} = 1.0853$$

$$r = .0853, \text{ or } 8.53\%$$

In general this is more accurate. You can also use a financial calculator (see the Financial Calculator box above).

▶ EXAMPLE 3.5 *Double Your Money*

How many times have you heard of an investment adviser who promises to double your money? Is this really an amazing feat? That depends on how long it will take for your money to double. With enough patience, your funds eventually will double even if they

FINANCE IN ACTION

Confused by Investing? Maybe It's the New Math

If there's something about your investment portfolio that doesn't seem to add up, maybe you should check your math.

Lots of folks are perplexed by the mathematics of investing, so a refresher course might help. Here's a look at some key concepts:

10 Plus 10 Is 21

Imagine you invest $100, which earns 10% this year and 10% next year. How much have you made? If you answered 21%, go to the head of the class.

Here's how the math works: This year's 10% gain turns your $100 into $110. Next year, you also earn 10%, but you start the year with $110. Result? You earn $11, boosting your wealth to $121.

Thus, your portfolio has earned a *cumulative* 21% return over two years, but the *annualized* return is just 10%. The fact that 21% is more than double 10% can be attributed to the effect of investment compounding, the way that you earn money each year not only on your original investment but also on earnings from prior years that you've reinvested.

The Rule of 72

To get a feel for compounding, try the Rule of 72. What's that? If you divide a particular annual return into 72, you'll find out how many years it will take to double your money. Thus, at 10% a year, an investment will double in value in a tad over 7 years.

What Goes Down Comes Back Slowly

In the investment world, winning is nice, and losses can really sting. Let's say you invest $100, which loses 10% in the first year but bounces back 10% the next. Back to even? Not at all. In fact, you're down to $99.

Here's why: The initial 10% loss turns your $100 into $90. But the subsequent 10% gain earns you just $9, boosting your account's value to $99. The bottom line: To recoup any percentage loss, you need an even greater percentage gain. For instance, if you lose 25%, you need to make 33% to get back to even.

Not All Losses Are Equal

Which is less damaging, inflation of 50% or a 50% drop in your portfolio's value? If you said inflation, join that other bloke at the head of the class.

Confused? Consider the following example: If you have $100 to spend on cappuccino and your favourite cappuccino costs $1, you can buy 100 cups. What if your $100 then drops in value to $50? You can only buy 50 cups. And if the cappuccino's price instead rises 50% to $1.50? If you divide $100 by $1.50, you'll find you can still buy 66 cups and even leave a tip.

earn only a very modest interest rate. Suppose your investment adviser promises to double your money in 8 years. What interest rate is implicitly being promised?

The adviser is promising a future value of $2 for every $1 invested today. Therefore, we find the interest rate by solving for r as follows:

$$\begin{aligned} \text{Future value} &= \text{PV} \times (1 + r)^t \\ \$2 &= \$1 \times (1 + r)^8 \\ 1 + r &= 2^{1/8} = 1.0905 \\ r &= .0905, \text{ or } 9.05\% \end{aligned}$$

By the way, there is a convenient rule of thumb that one can use to approximate the answer to this problem. The *Rule of 72* states that the time it will take for an investment to double in value equals approximately $72/r$, where r is expressed as a percentage. Therefore, if the doubling period is 8 years, the Rule of 72 implies an (approximate) interest rate of 9 percent (since $72/9 = 8$ years). This is quite close to the exact solution of 9.05 percent.

SEE BOX P. 74

In the nearby Finance in Action box, the Rule of 72 is discussed as well as other issues of compound interest. By now you should easily be able to explain why, as the box suggests, "10 + 10 = 21." In addition, the impact of inflation on the purchasing power of your investments is discussed. We will consider these issues later in the chapter.

CHECK POINT 3.4

The Rule of 72 works best with relatively low interest rates. Suppose the time it will take for an investment to double in value is 12 years. Find the interest rate. What is the approximate rate implied by the Rule of 72? Now suppose that the doubling period is only 2 years. Is the approximation better or worse in this case?

3.3

Multiple Cash Flows

So far, we have considered problems involving only a single cash flow. This is obviously limiting. Most real-world investments, after all, will involve many cash flows over time. When there are many payments, you'll hear businesspeople refer to a *stream of cash flows.*

FUTURE VALUE OF MULTIPLE CASH FLOWS

Recall the computer you hope to purchase in 2 years (see Example 3.2). Now suppose that instead of putting aside a lump sum in the bank to finance the purchase, you plan to save a bit of money each year. You might be able to put \$1,200 in the bank now, and another \$1,400 in 1 year. If you earn an 8 percent rate of interest, how much will you be able to spend on a computer in 2 years?

The time line in Figure 3.5 shows how your savings grow. There are two cash inflows into the savings plan. The first cash flow will have 2 years to earn interest and, therefore, will grow to $\$1,200 \times (1.08)^2 = \$1,399.68$ while the second deposit, which comes a year later, will be invested for only 1 year and will grow to $\$1,400 \times (1.08) = \$1,512$. Therefore after 2 years, your total savings will be the sum of these two amounts, or \$2,911.68.

EXAMPLE 3.6 *Even More Savings*

Suppose that the computer purchase can be put off for an additional year and that you can make a third deposit of \$1,000 at the end of the second year. How much will be available to spend 3 years from now?

Again we organize our inputs using a time line as in Figure 3.6. The total cash available will be the sum of the future values of all three deposits. Notice that when we save for 3 years, the first two deposits each have an extra year for interest to compound:

$\$1,200 \times (1.08)^3$	=	\$1,511.65
$\$1,400 \times (1.08)^2$	=	1,632.96
$\$1,000 \times 1.08$	=	1,080.00
Total future value	=	\$4,224.61

FIGURE 3.5
Future value of two cash flows

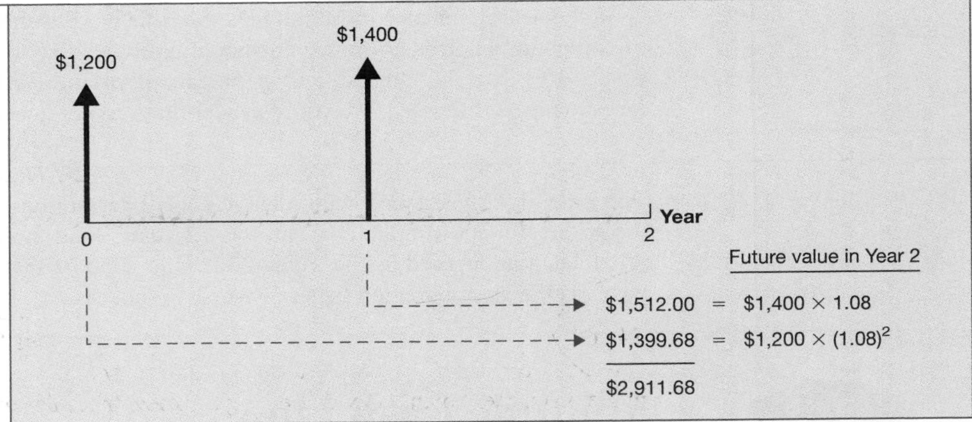

CHECK POINT 3.5

Suppose you are planning a 1-month European vacation when you graduate 2 years from now. The cost of the trip will be $3,500. Right now you have $1,500 and will put it into a bank account that pays 6 percent interest. How much more money will you need to deposit 1 year from now to have enough money for the trip 2 years from now?

We conclude that problems involving multiple cash flows are simple extensions of single cash-flow analysis.

To find the value at some future date of a stream of cash flows, calculate what each cash flow will be worth at that future date, and then add up these future values.

As we will now see, a similar adding-up principle works for present value calculations.

FIGURE 3.6
Future value of a stream of cash flows

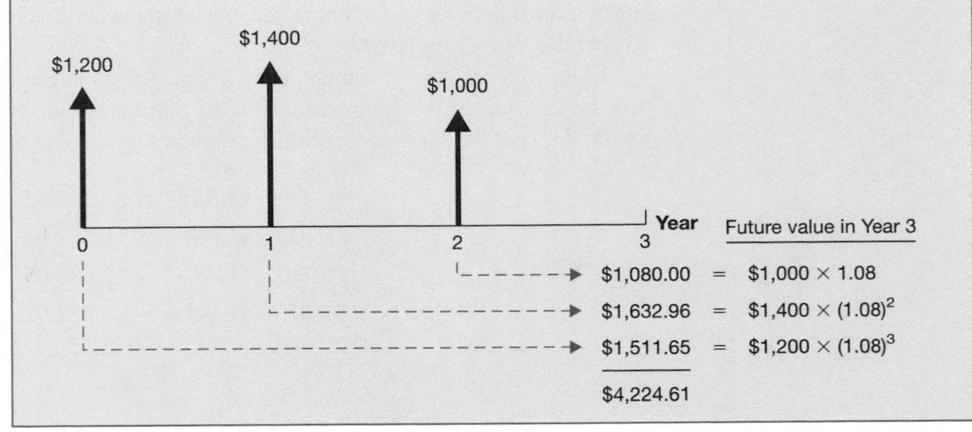

PRESENT VALUE OF MULTIPLE CASH FLOWS

When we calculate the present value of a future cash flow, we are asking how much that cash flow would be worth today. If there is more than one future cash flow, we simply need to work out what each flow would be worth today and then add these present values.

EXAMPLE 3.7 *Cash Up Front versus an Installment Plan*

Suppose that your auto dealer gives you a choice between paying $15,500 for a new car or entering into an installment plan where you pay $8,000 down today and make payments of $4,000 in each of the next 2 years. Which is the better deal? Before reading this chapter, you might have compared the total payments under the two plans: $15,500 versus $16,000 in the installment plan. Now, however, you know that this comparison is wrong, because it ignores the time value of money. For example, the last installment of $4,000 is less costly to you than paying out $4,000 now. The true cost of that last payment is the present value of $4,000.

Assume that the interest rate you can earn on safe investments is 8 percent. Suppose you choose the installment plan. As the time line in Figure 3.7 illustrates, the present value of the plan's three cash flows is:

	Present Value		
Immediate payment	$8,000	=	$8,000.00
Second payment	$4,000/1.08	=	3,703.70
Third payment	$4,000/(1.08)^2	=	3,429.36
Total present value		=	$15,133.06

Because the present value of the three payments is less than $15,500, the installment plan is in fact the cheaper alternative.

The installment plan's present value equals the amount that you would need to invest now to cover the three future payments. Let's check to see that this works. If you start with the present value of $15,133.06 in the bank, you could make the first $8,000 payment and be left with $7,133.06. After 1 year, your savings would grow with interest to

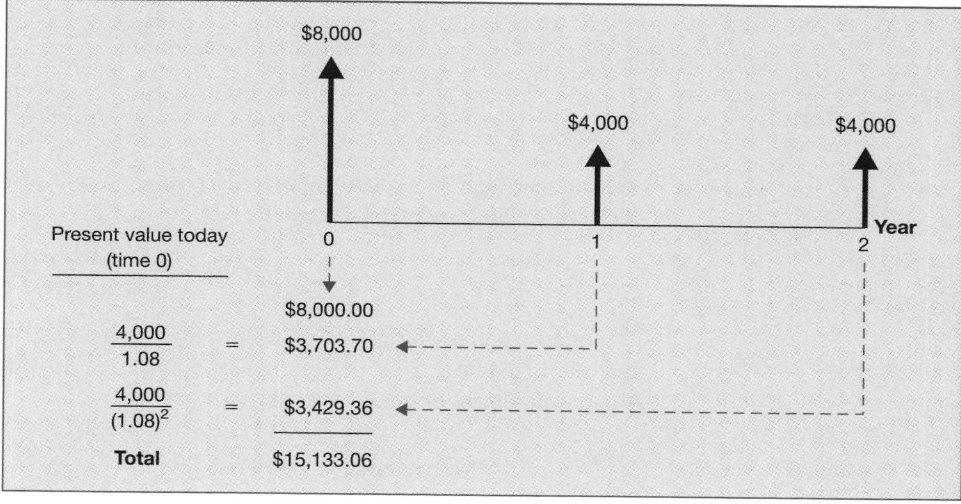

FIGURE 3.7
Present value of a stream of cash flows

$7,133.06 × 1.08 = $7,703.70. You then would make the second $4,000 payment and be left with $3,703.70. This sum left in the bank would grow in the last year to $3,703.70 × 1.08 = $4,000, just enough to make the last payment.

The present value of a stream of future cash flows is the amount you would have to invest today to generate that stream.

CHECK POINT 3.6

In order to avoid estate taxes, your rich aunt Frederica will pay you $10,000 per year for 4 years, starting 1 year from now. What is the present value of your benefactor's planned gifts? The interest rate is 7 percent. How much will you have 4 years from now if you invest each gift at 7 percent?

3.4 Level Cash Flows: Perpetuities and Annuities

annuity Equally spaced and level stream of cash flows.

perpetuity Stream of level cash payments that never end.

Frequently, you may need to value a stream of equal cash flows. For example, a home mortgage might require the homeowner to make equal monthly payments for the life of the loan. For a 30-year loan, this would result in 360 equal payments. A 4-year car loan might require 48 equal monthly payments. Any such sequence of equally spaced, level cash flows is called an **annuity.** If the payment stream lasts forever, it is called a **perpetuity.**

HOW TO VALUE PERPETUITIES

Some time ago the British government borrowed by issuing perpetuities. Instead of repaying these loans, the British government pays the investors holding these securities a fixed annual payment in perpetuity.

The rate of interest on a perpetuity is equal to the promised annual payment C divided by the present value. For example, if a perpetuity pays $10 per year and you can buy it for $100, you will earn 10 percent interest each year on your investment. In general,

$$\text{Interest rate on a perpetuity} = \frac{\text{cash payment}}{\text{present value}}$$

$$r = \frac{C}{\text{PV}}$$

We can rearrange this relationship to derive the present value of a perpetuity, given the interest rate r and the cash payment C:

$$\textbf{PV of perpetuity} = \frac{C}{r} = \frac{\textbf{cash payment}}{\textbf{interest rate}} \qquad \textbf{(3.2)}$$

Suppose some worthy person wishes to endow a chair in finance at your university. If the rate of interest is 10 percent, and the aim is to provide $100,000 a year forever, the amount that must be set aside today is

$$\text{Present value of perpetuity} = \frac{C}{r} = \frac{\$100{,}000}{.10} = \$1{,}000{,}000$$

Two warnings about the perpetuity formula. First, at a quick glance you can easily confuse the formula with the present value of a single cash payment. A payment of \$1 at the end of 1 year has a present value $1/(1 + r)$. The perpetuity has a value of $1/r$. These are quite different.

Second, the perpetuity formula tells us the value of a regular stream of payments starting one period from now. Thus our endowment of \$1 million would provide the university with its first payment of \$100,000 1 year hence. If the worthy donor wants to provide the university with an additional payment of \$100,000 up front, he or she would need to put aside \$1,100,000.

Sometimes you may need to calculate the value of a perpetuity that does not start to make payments for several years. For example, suppose that our philanthropist decides to provide \$100,000 a year with the first payment 4 years from now. As the time line in Figure 3.8 shows, we know that in Year 3, this endowment will be an ordinary perpetuity with payments starting at the end of 1 year. So our perpetuity formula tells us that in Year 3 the endowment will be worth $\$100{,}000/r$. But it is not worth that much now. To find today's value we need to multiply by the 3-year discount factor. Thus, the "delayed" perpetuity is worth

$$\$100{,}000 \times \frac{1}{r} \times \frac{1}{(1 + r)^3} = \$1{,}000{,}000 \times \frac{1}{(1.10)^3} = \$751{,}315$$

CHECK POINT 3.7

A British government perpetuity pays £4 a year forever and is selling for £48. What is the interest rate?

HOW TO VALUE ANNUITIES

There are two ways to value an annuity, that is, a limited number of cash flows. The slow way is to value each cash flow separately and add up the present values. The quick way is to take advantage of the following simplification. Figure 3.9 shows the cash payments and values of three investments.

Row 1. The investment shown in the first row provides a perpetual stream of \$1 payments starting in Year 1. We have already seen that this perpetuity has a present value of $1/r$.

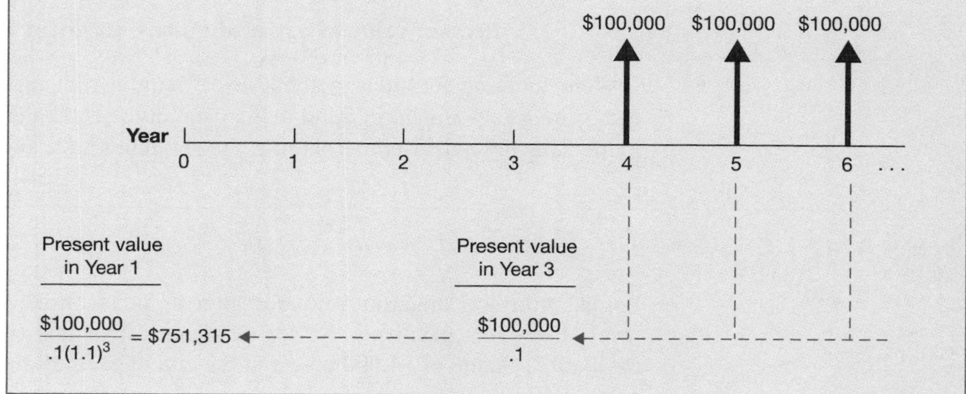

FIGURE 3.8
Time line for a delayed perpetuity—\$100,000 per year forever, to start in 4 years

FIGURE 3.9
Valuing an annuity as the difference between an immediate perpetuity (A) and a delayed perpetuity (B)

	Present value (Year 0)	Cash flow each year 1	2	3	4	5	6 ...
1. Perpetuity A	$\frac{1}{r}$	\$1	\$1	\$1	\$1	\$1	\$1...
2. Perpetuity B	$\frac{1}{r(1+r)^3}$	0	0	0	\$1	\$1	\$1...
3. Three-year annuity	$\frac{1}{r} - \frac{1}{r(1+r)^3}$	\$1	\$1	\$1			

Row 2. Now look at the investment shown in the second row of Figure 3.9. It also provides a perpetual stream of \$1 payments, but these payments don't start until Year 4. This stream of payments is identical to the delayed perpetuity that we just valued. In Year 3, the investment will be an ordinary perpetuity with payments starting in 1 year and will therefore be worth $1/r$ in Year 3. To find the value today, we simply multiply this figure by the 3-year discount factor. Thus

$$\text{PV} = \frac{1}{r} \times \frac{1}{(1+r)^3} = \frac{1}{r(1+r)^3}$$

Row 3. Finally, look at the investment shown in the third row of Figure 3.9. This provides a level payment of \$1 a year for each 3 years. In other words, it is a 3-year annuity. You can also see that, taken together, the investments in rows 2 and 3 provide exactly the same cash payments as the investment in row 1. Thus the value of our annuity (row 3) must be equal to the value of the row 1 perpetuity minus the value of the delayed row 2 perpetuity:

$$\text{Present value of a 3-year \$1 annuity} = \frac{1}{r} - \frac{1}{r(1+r)^3}$$

The general formula for the value of an annuity that pays C dollars a year for each of t years is

$$\textbf{Present value of } \boldsymbol{t}\textbf{-year annuity} = C\left[\frac{1}{r} - \frac{1}{r(1+r)^t}\right] \qquad \textbf{(3.3)}$$

annuity factor Present value of a \$1 annuity.

The expression in square brackets shows the present value of a t-year annuity of \$1 a year. It is generally known as the t-year **annuity factor.** Therefore, another way to write the value of an annuity is

Present value of *t*-year annuity = payment × annuity factor

Remembering formulas is about as difficult as remembering other people's birthdays. But as long as you bear in mind that an annuity is equivalent to the difference between an immediate and a delayed perpetuity, you shouldn't have any difficulty.

▸ EXAMPLE 3.8 *Back to Kangaroo Autos*

Let us return to Kangaroo Autos for, almost, the last time. Most installment plans call for level streams of payments. So let us suppose that this time Kangaroo offers an "easy payment" scheme of \$4,000 a year at the end of each of the next 3 years. First let's do the calculations the slow way; to show that if the interest rate is 10 percent, the present value

FIGURE 3.10
Time line for Kangaroo Autos' "Easy Payment" scheme of $4,000 a year for 3 years, Example 3.8

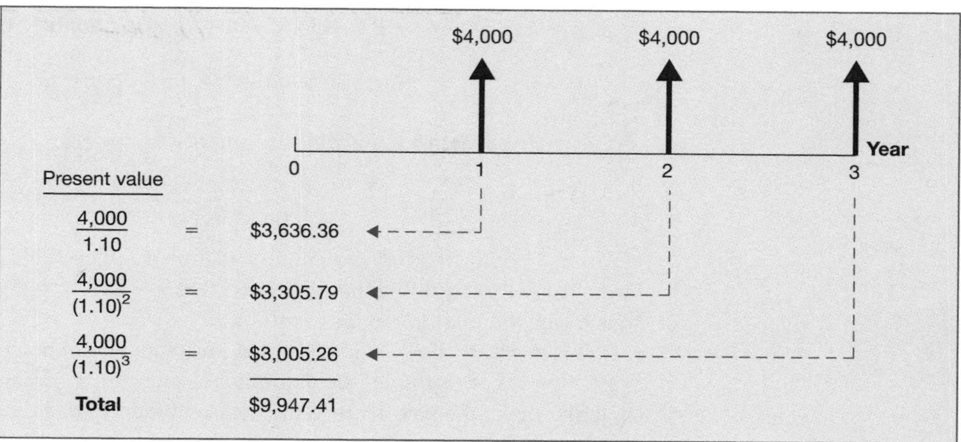

of the three payments is $9,947.41. The time line in Figure 3.10 shows these calculations. The present value of each cash flow is calculated and then the three present values are summed. The annuity formula, however, is much quicker:

$$\text{Present value} = \$4{,}000 \times \left[\frac{1}{.10} - \frac{1}{.10(1.10)^3}\right]$$
$$= \$4{,}000 \times 2.48685 = \$9{,}947.41$$

You can use a calculator to work out annuity factors or you can use a set of annuity tables. Table 3.4 is an abridged annuity table (an extended version is shown in Table A.3 at the end of the book). Check that you can find the 3-year annuity factor for an interest rate of 10 percent.

CHECK POINT 3.8

If the interest rate is 8 percent, what is the 4-year discount factor? What is the 4-year annuity factor? What is the relationship between these two numbers? Explain.

▶ EXAMPLE 3.9 *Winning Big at a Slot Machine*

In May 1992, a 60-year-old nurse plunked down $12 in a Reno casino and walked away with the biggest jackpot to that date—$9.3 million. We suspect she received unsolicited congratulations, good wishes, and requests for money from dozens of more or less worthy charities, relatives, and newly devoted friends. In response she could fairly point out that her prize wasn't really worth $9.3 million. That sum was to be paid in 20 annual installments of $465,000 each. What is the present value of the jackpot? The interest rate at the time was about 8 percent.

The present value of these payments is simply the sum of the present values of each payment. But rather than valuing each payment separately, it is much easier to treat the cash payments as a 20-year annuity. To value this annuity we simply multiply $465,000 by the 20-year annuity factor:

$$\text{PV} = \$465{,}000 \times \text{20-year annuity factor}$$
$$= \$465{,}000 \times \left[\frac{1}{r} - \frac{1}{r(1+r)^{20}}\right]$$

At an interest rate of 8 percent, the annuity factor is

$$\left[\frac{1}{.08} - \frac{1}{.08(1.08)^{20}}\right] = 9.818$$

(We also could look up the annuity factor in either Table 3.4 or Table A.3.) The present value of the \$465,000 annuity is \$465,000 × 9.818 = \$4,565,000. That \$9.3 million prize has a true value of about \$4.6 million.

This present value is the price that investors would be prepared to offer for the series of cash flows. For example, the gambling casino might arrange for an insurance company to actually make the payments to the lucky winner. In this case, the company would charge a bit less than \$4.6 million to take over the obligation. With this amount in hand today, it could generate enough interest income to make the 20 payments before running its "account" down to zero.

ANNUITIES DUE

The perpetuity and annuity formulas assume that the first payment occurs at the end of the period. They tell you the value of a stream of cash payments start one period hence.

However, streams of cash payments often start immediately. For example, Kangaroo Autos in Example 3.8 might have required three annual payments of \$4,000 starting immediately. A level stream of payments starting immediately is known as an **annuity due.**

annuity due Level stream of cash flows starting immediately.

If Kangaroo's loan was paid as an annuity due, you could think of the three payments as equivalent to an immediate payment of \$4,000, plus an ordinary annuity of \$4,000 for the remaining 2 years. This is made clear in Figure 3.11, which compares the cash-flow stream of the Kangaroo Autos loan, treating the three payments as an annuity (panel *a*) and as an annuity due (panel *b*).

In general, the present value of an annuity due of t payments of \$1 per year is the same as \$1 plus the present value of an ordinary annuity providing the remaining $t - 1$ payments. The present value of an annuity due of \$1 for t years is therefore

$$\text{PV annuity due} = 1 + \text{PV ordinary annuity of } t - 1 \text{ payments}$$
$$= 1 + \left[\frac{1}{r} - \frac{1}{r\,(1+r)^{t-1}}\right]$$

TABLE 3.4
Annuity table: present value of \$1 a year for each of t years at various interest rates

Number of Years	Interest Rate per Year: 5%	6%	7%	8%	9%	10%
1	.952	.943	.935	.926	.917	.909
2	1.859	1.833	1.808	1.783	1.759	1.736
3	2.723	2.673	2.624	2.577	2.531	2.487
4	3.546	3.465	3.387	3.312	3.240	3.170
5	4.329	4.212	4.100	3.993	3.890	3.791
10	7.722	7.360	7.024	6.710	6.418	6.145
20	12.462	11.470	10.594	9.818	9.129	8.514
30	15.372	13.765	12.409	11.258	10.274	9.427

By comparing the two panels in Figure 3.11, you can see that each of the three cash flows in the annuity due comes one period earlier than the corresponding cash flow of the ordinary annuity. Therefore, the present value of an annuity due is $(1 + r)$ times the present value of an annuity.[2] Figure 3.11 shows that the purpose of bringing the Kangaroo loan payments forward by 1 year was to increase their value from \$9,947.41 (as an annuity) to \$10,942.15 (as an annuity due). Notice that \$10,942.15 = \$9,947.41 × 1.10.

FIGURE 3.11

Annuity versus annuity due: (a) 3-year ordinary annuity (b) 3-year anuity due

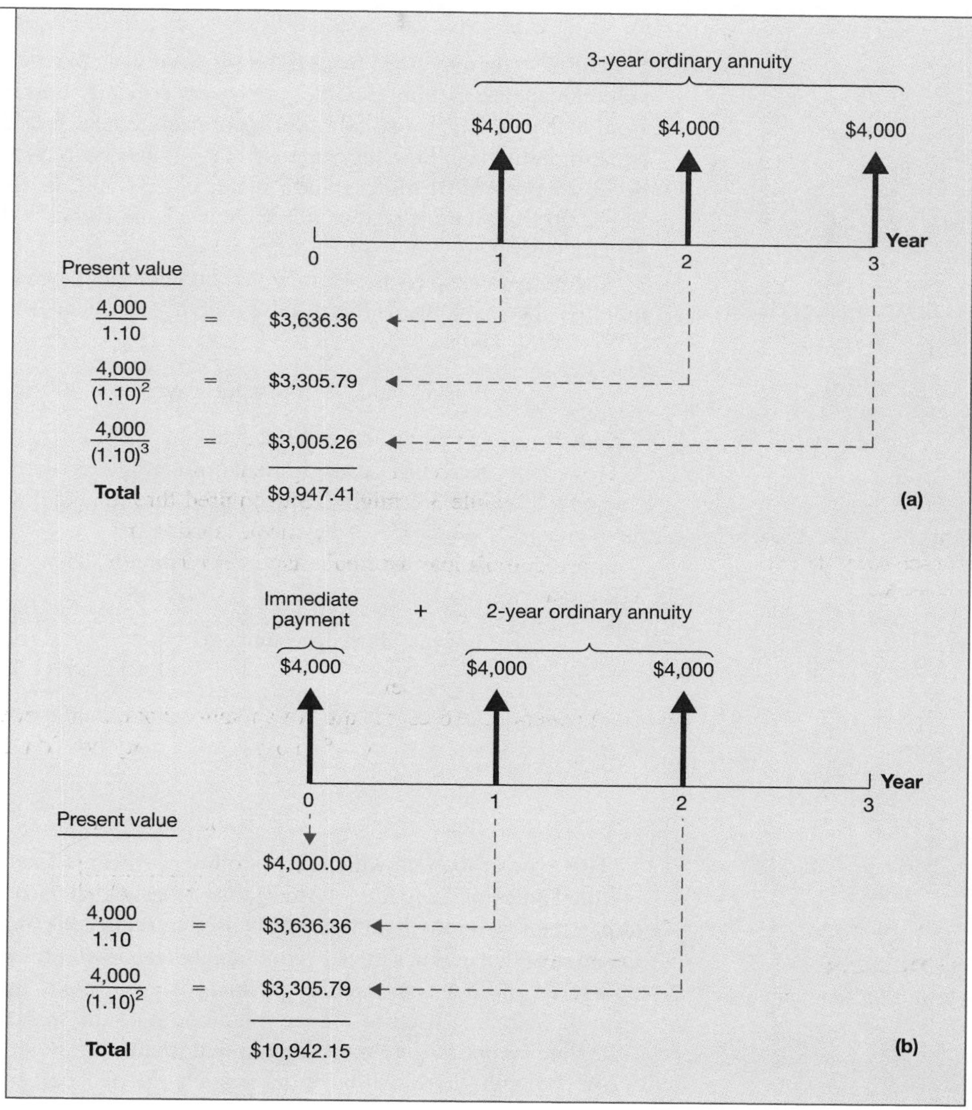

[2] Your financial calculator is equipped to handle annuities due. You simply need to put the calculator in "begin" mode, and the stream of cash flows will be interpreted as starting immediately. The begin key is labelled *BGN* or *BEG/END*. Each time you press the key, the calculator will toggle between ordinary annuity versus annuity due mode.

CHECK POINT 3.9

When calculating the value of the slot machine winnings in Example 3.9, we assumed that the first of the 20 payments occurs at the end of 1 year. However, the payment was probably made immediately, with the remaining payments spread over the following 19 years. What is the present value of the $9.3 million prize?

EXAMPLE 3.10 *Home Mortgages*

Sometimes you may need to find the series of cash payments that would provide a given value today. For example, home purchasers typically borrow the bulk of the house price from a lender. The most common loan arrangement is a 25-year loan that is repaid in equal monthly installments. Suppose that a house costs $150,000, and that the buyer puts down 25 percent of the purchase price, or $37,500, in cash, borrowing the remaining $112,500 from a mortgage lender such as a bank. What is the appropriate monthly mortgage payment?

The borrower repays the loan by making monthly payments over the next 25 years (300 months). The bank needs to set these monthly payments so that they have a present value of $112,500. Thus

$$\text{Present value} = \text{mortgage payment} \times \text{300-month annuity factor}$$
$$= \$112{,}500$$
$$\text{Mortgage payment} = \frac{\$112{,}500}{\text{300-month annuity factor}}$$

Suppose that the interest rate is 1 percent a month. Then

$$\text{Mortgage payment} = \frac{\$112{,}500}{\left[\frac{1}{.01} - \frac{1}{.01(1.01)^{300}}\right]}$$
$$= \frac{\$112{,}500}{94.9466}$$
$$= \$1{,}184.88$$

This type of loan, in which the monthly payment is fixed over the life of the mortgage, is called an *amortizing loan.* "Amortizing" means that part of the monthly payment is used to pay interest on the loan and part is used to reduce the amount of the loan. For example, the interest that accrues after 1 month on this loan will be 1 percent of $112,500, or $1,125. So $1,125 of your first monthly payment is used to pay interest on the loan and the balance of $59.88 is used to reduce the amount of the loan to $112,440.12. The $59.88 is called the *amortization* on the loan in that month.

Next month, there will be an interest charge of 1 percent of $112,440.12 = $1,124.40. So $1,124.40 of your second monthly payment is absorbed by the interest charge and the remaining $60.48 of your monthly payment ($1,184.88 – $1,124.40 = $60.48) is used to reduce the amount of your loan. Amortization in the second month is higher than in the first month because the amount of the loan has declined, and therefore less of the payment is taken up in interest. This procedure continues each month until the last month, when the amortization is just enough to reduce the outstanding amount on the loan to zero, and then, the loan is paid off.

Because the loan is progressively paid off, the fraction of the monthly payment devoted to interest steadily falls, while the fraction used to reduce the loan (the amortization) steadily increases. Thus the reduction in the size of the loan is much more rapid in the later years of the mortgage. Figure 3.12 illustrates how in the early years almost all of the mortgage payments are for interest. Even after 15 years, the bulk of the monthly payment is interest.

CHECK POINT 3.10

What will be the monthly payment if you take out a $100,000 15-year mortgage at an interest rate of 1 percent per month? How much of the first payment is interest and how much is amortization?

EXAMPLE 3.11 *How Much Luxury and Excitement Can $54 Billion Buy?*

Bill Gates is reputedly the world's richest person, with wealth estimated at $54 billion (US) at the beginning of 2002. We haven't yet met Mr. Gates, so we cannot fill you in on his plans for allocating the $54 billion between his charitable works and the cost of his life of luxury and excitement (L&E). So to keep things simple, we will just ask the following, entirely hypothetical, question: How much could Mr. Gates spend yearly on 40 more years of L&E if he were to devote the entire $54 billion to those purposes? Assume that his money is invested at 9 percent interest.

The 40-year 9 percent annuity factor is 10.757. Thus

$$\text{Present value} = \text{annual spending} \times \text{annuity factor}$$
$$\$54{,}000{,}000{,}000 = \text{annual spending} \times 10.757$$
$$\text{Annual spending} = \$5{,}019{,}987{,}000$$

Warning to Mr. Gates: We haven't considered inflation. The cost of buying L&E will increase, so $5 billion won't buy as much L&E in 40 years as it will today. More on that later.

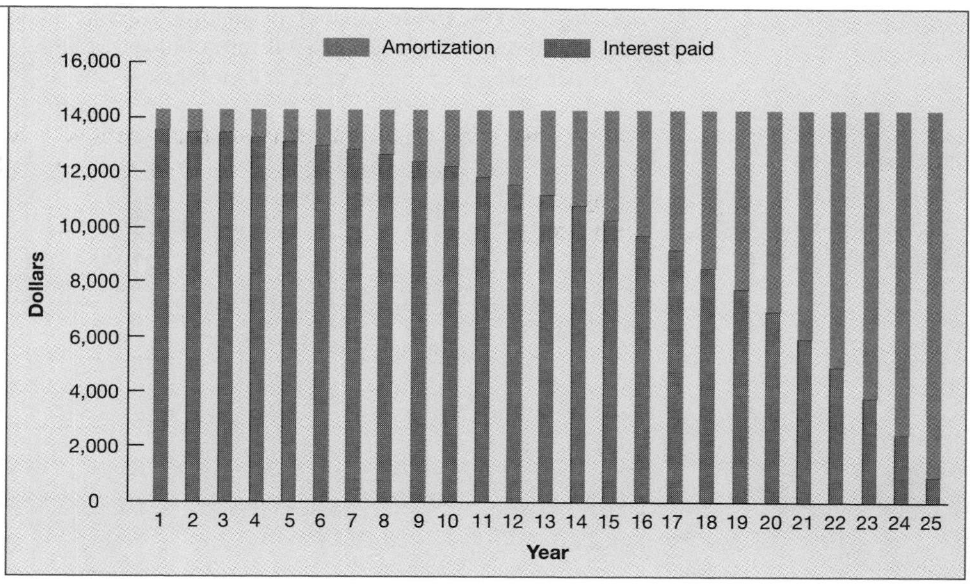

FIGURE 3.12
Mortgage amortization. This figure shows the breakdown of mortgage payments between interest and amortization. Monthly payments within each year are summed, so the figure shows the annual payment on the mortgage.

✓ CHECK POINT 3.11

Suppose you retire at age 70. You expect to live 20 more years and to spend \$55,000 per year during your retirement. How much money do you need to save by age 70 to support this consumption plan? Assume an interest rate of 7 percent.

FUTURE VALUE OF AN ANNUITY

You are back in savings mode again. This time you are setting aside \$3,000 at the end of every year in order to buy a car. If your savings earn interest of 8 percent per year, how much will they be worth at the end of 4 years? We can answer this question with the help of the time line in Figure 3.13. Your first year's savings will earn interest for 3 years, the second will earn interest for 2 years, the third will earn interest for 1 year, and the final savings in Year 4 will earn no interest. The sum of the future values of the four payments is

$$(\$3{,}000 \times 1.08^3) + (\$3{,}000 \times 1.08^2) + (\$3{,}000 \times 1.08) + \$3{,}000 = \$13{,}518$$

But wait a minute! We are looking here at a level stream of cash flows—an annuity. We have seen that there is a short-cut formula to calculate the *present* value of an annuity. So there ought to be a similar formula for calculating the *future* value of a level stream of cash flows.

Think first how much your stream of savings is worth today. You are setting aside \$3,000 in each of the next 4 years. The *present* value of this 4-year annuity is therefore equal to

$$\begin{aligned} PV &= \$3{,}000 \times \text{4-year annuity factor} \\ &= \$3{,}000 \times \left[\frac{1}{.08} - \frac{1}{.08(1.08)^4}\right] = \$9{,}936 \end{aligned}$$

Now think how much you would have after 4 years if you invested \$9,936 today. Simple! Just multiply by $(1.08)^4$:

$$\text{Value at end of Year } 4 = \$9{,}936 \times 1.08^4 = \$13{,}518$$

We calculated the future value of the annuity by first calculating the present value and then multiplying by $(1 + r)^t$. The general formula for the future value of a stream of cash flows of \$1 per year for each of t years is therefore

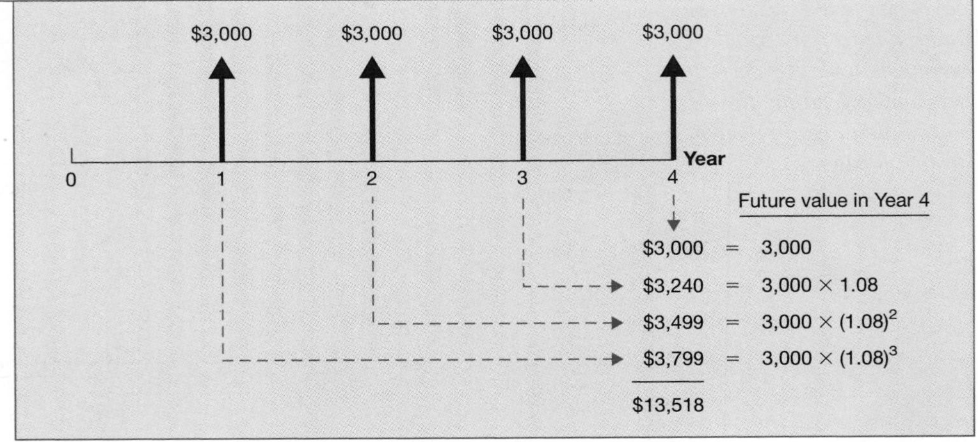

FIGURE 3.13
Future value of a 4-year, \$3,000 per year annuity invested at 8 percent

$$\textbf{Future value of annuity of \$1 per year} = \textbf{present value of annuity of \$1 per year} \times (1+r)^t$$

$$= \left[\frac{1}{r} - \frac{1}{r(1+r)^t}\right] \times (1+r)^t \qquad (3.4)$$

$$= \frac{(1+r)^t - 1}{r}$$

If you need to find the future value of just four cash flows, as in our example, it is a toss up whether it is quicker to calculate the future value of each cash flow separately (as we did in Figure 3.13) or to use the annuity formula. If you are faced with a stream of 10 or 20 cash flows, there is no contest.

You can find a table of the future value of an annuity in Table 3.5, or use the more extensive Table A.4 at the end of the book. You can see that in the row corresponding to $t = 4$ and the column corresponding to $r = 8\%$, the future value of an annuity of \$1 a year is \$4.506. Therefore, the future value of the \$3,000 annuity is \$3,000 × 4.506 = \$13,518.

Remember that all our annuity formulas assume that the first cash flow does not occur until the end of the first period. If the first cash flow comes immediately, the future value of the cash-flow stream is greater, since each flow has an extra year to earn interest. For example, at an interest rate of 8 percent, the future value of an annuity starting with an immediate payment would be exactly 8 percent greater than the figure given by our formula.

EXAMPLE 3.12 *Saving for Retirement*

In only 45 more years, you will retire. Have you started saving yet? Suppose you believe you will need to accumulate \$500,000 by your retirement date in order to support your desired standard of living. How much must you save *each year* between now and your retirement to meet that future goal? Let's say that the interest rate is 10 percent per year. You need to find how large the annuity in the following figure must be to provide a future value of \$500,000:

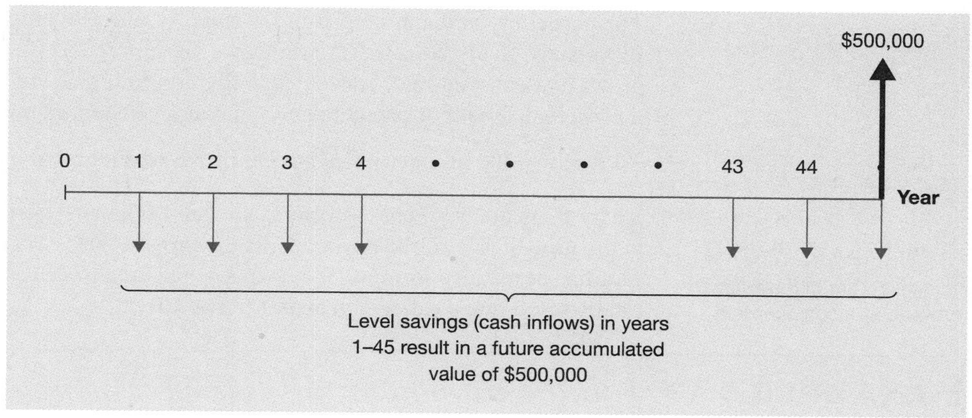

We know that if you were to save \$1 each year your funds would accumulate to

$$\text{Future value of annuity of \$1 a year} = \frac{(1+r)^t - 1}{r} = \frac{(1.10)^{45} - 1}{.10}$$

$$= \$718.90$$

TABLE 3.5
Future value factors—future value of a $1 annuity invested at various interest rates for different periods

Number of Years	Interest Rate per Year 5%	6%	7%	8%	9%	10%
1	1.000	1.000	1.000	1.000	1.000	1.000
2	2.050	2.060	2.070	2.080	2.090	2.100
3	3.153	3.184	3.215	3.246	3.278	3.310
4	4.310	4.375	4.440	4.506	4.573	4.641
5	5.526	5.637	5.751	5.867	5.985	6.105
10	12.578	13.181	13.816	14.487	15.193	15.937
20	33.066	36.786	40.995	45.762	51.160	57.275
30	66.439	79.058	94.461	113.283	136.308	164.494

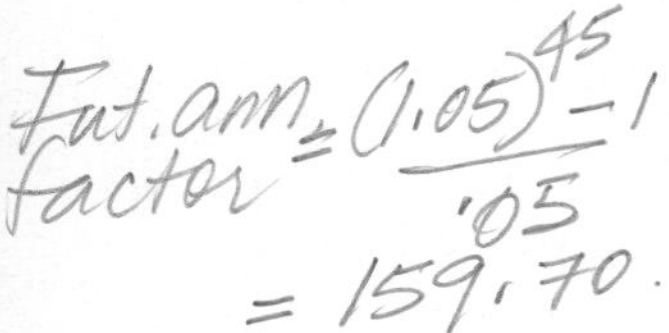

SEE BOX P. 89

(Rather than compute the future value formula directly, you could look up the future value annuity factor in Table 3.5 or Table A.4. Alternatively, you can use a financial calculator as we describe in the nearby Financial Calculator box.) Therefore, if we save an amount of $\$C$ each year, we will accumulate $\$C \times 718.90$.

We need to choose C to ensure that $\$C \times 718.90 = \$500{,}000$. Thus $C = \$500{,}000/718.90 = \$695.50$. This appears to be surprisingly good news. Saving $695.50 a year does not seem to be an extremely demanding savings program. Don't celebrate yet, however. The news will get worse when we consider the impact of inflation.

CHECK POINT 3.12

What is the required savings level if the interest rate is only 5 percent? Why has the amount increased?

CASH FLOWS GROWING AT A CONSTANT RATE—VARIATIONS ON PERPETUITIES AND ANNUITIES

The perpetuity and annuity formulas make valuing streams of *equal* cash flows easy. Unfortunately, many streams of cash flows are not equal. If, however, the cash-flow stream grows at a constant rate, convenient valuation formulas are available. The present value of a perpetual stream of payments growing at a constant rate is:

$$\text{Present value of a perpetual stream of payments growing at a constant rate} = \frac{C_1}{r-g}$$

where C_1 is the payment to occur at the end of the first period, r is the discount rate and g is the growth rate of the payments. If the growth rate, g, is zero, the formula becomes the familiar perpetuity formula, C/r. A perpetual stream of cash flows growing at a constant rate is some times called a **growing perpetuity**.

growing perpetuity An infinite stream of cash flows growing at a constant rate.

▶ EXAMPLE 3.13 *Valuing a Condo*

You are considering purchasing a condominium as an investment. Currently, the type of condo you want generates $12,000 in cash flow (rent minus expenses) annually. If the cash flow grows 3 percent per year, the building lasts forever, and the interest rate is 8 percent, what is the present value of the condo's cash flows?

$$\text{Present value} = \frac{\$12{,}000}{.08 - .03} = \$240{,}000$$

Solving Annuity Problems Using a Financial Calculator

The formulas for both the present value and future value of an annuity are also built into your financial calculator. Again, we can input all but one of the five financial keys, and let the calculator solve for the remaining variable. In these applications, the *PMT* key is used to either enter or solve for the value of an annuity.

Solving for an Annuity

In Example 3.12, we determined the savings stream that would provide a retirement goal of $500,000 after 45 years of saving at an interest rate of 10 percent. To find the required savings each year, enter n = 45, i = 10, *FV* = 500,000, and *PV* = 0 (because your "savings account" is currently empty). Compute *PMT* and find that it is –$695.50. Again, your calculator is likely to display the solution as –695.50, since the positive $500,000 cash value in 45 years will require 45 cash payments (outflows) of $695.50.

The sequence of key strokes necessary to solve this problem on three popular calculators are as follows:

Hewlett-Packard HP-10B	Sharpe EL-733A	Texas Instruments BA II Plus
0 [PV]	0 [PV]	0 [PV]
45 [n]	45 [n]	45 [n]
10 [I/YR]	10 [i]	10 [I/Y]
500,000 [FV]	500,000 [FV]	500,000 [FV]
[PMT]	[COMP] [PMT]	[CPT] [PMT]

Your calculator displays a negative number, as the 45 cash-outflows of $695.50 are necessary to provide for the $500,000 cash value at retirement.

Present Value of an Annuity

In Example 3.10 we considered a 25-year mortgage with monthly payments of $1,184.88 and an interest rate of 1 percent per month. Suppose we didn't know the amount of the mortgage loan. Enter n = 300 (months), i = 1, *PMT* = –1,184.88 (we enter the annuity level paid by the borrower to the lender as a negative number since it is a cash outflow), and *FV* = 0 (the mortgage is paid off after 25 years; there are no final future payments beyond the normal monthly payment). Compute *PV* to find that the value of the loan is $112,500.

What about the balance left on the mortgage after 7 years have passed? This is easy: The monthly payment is still *PMT* = –1,184.88, and we continue to use i = 1 and *FV* = 0. The only change is that the number of monthly payments remaining has fallen from 300 to 216 (18 years are left on the loan). So enter n = 216 and compute *PV* as 104,675.97. This is the balance remaining on the mortgage.

Future Value of an Annuity

In Figure 3.13, we showed that a 4-year annuity of $3,000 invested at 8 percent would accumulate to a future value of $13,518. To solve this on your calculator, enter n = 4, i = 8, *PMT* = –3,000 (we enter the annuity paid by the investor to her savings account as a negative number since it is a cash outflow), and *PV* = 0 (the account starts with no funds). Compute *FV* to find that the future value of the savings account after 3 years is $13,518.

Calculator Self-Test Review (answers below)

1. Turn back to Kangaroo Autos in Example 3.8. Can you now solve for the present value of the three installment payments using your financial calculator? What key strokes must you use?
2. Now use your calculator to solve for the present value of the three installment payments if the first payment comes immediately, that is, as an annuity due.
3. Find the annual spending available to Bill Gates using the data in Example 3.11 and your financial calculator.

Solutions to Calculator Self-Test Review Questions

1. Inputs are n = 3, i = 10, *FV* = 0, and *PMT* = 4,000. Compute *PV* to find the present value of the cash flows as $9,947.41.
2. If you put your calculator in "begin" mode and recalculate *PV* using the same inputs, you will find that *PV* has increased by 10 percent to $10,942.15. Alternatively, as depicted in Figure 3.11, you can calculate the value of the $4,000 immediate payment plus the value of a 2-year annuity of $4,000. Inputs for the 2-year annuity are n = 2, i = 10, *FV* = 0, and *PMT* = 4,000. Compute *PV* to find the present value of the cash flows as $6,942.15. This amount plus the immediate $4,000 payment results in the same total present value: $10,942.15.
3. Inputs are n = 40, i = 9, *FV* = 0, *PV* = –54,000 million. Compute *PMT* to find that the 40-year annuity with present value of $54 billion is $5,020 million.

Another useful present value formula can be used if the cash flows grow at a constant rate for a limited or finite period, say T years. The present value of a finite stream of cash flows growing at a constant rate is

$$\text{Present value of a finite stream of payments growing at a constant rate} = \frac{C_1}{r-g}\left(1-\left[\frac{1+g}{1+r}\right]^T\right)$$

growing annuity A finite stream of cash flows growing at a constant rate.

where C_1 is the payment to occur at the end of the first period, r is the discount rate, T is the number of payments, and g is the growth rate of the payments. If the growth rate, g, is zero, after a bit of jiggling, the formula becomes the familiar present value of an annuity formula. A finite stream of cash flows growing at a constant rate is some times referred to as a **growing annuity**.

▶ EXAMPLE 3.14 *Another Look at the Value of a Condo*

Upon reflection, the condo in Example 3.13 will not likely be around forever. If the building is torn down in 20 years, what is the present value of the cash flows if the first cash flow is $12,000, the growth rate 3 percent, and the interest rate 8 percent?

$$\text{Present value} = \frac{\$12{,}000}{.08-.03}\left(1-\left[\frac{1.03}{1.08}\right]^{20}\right) = \$147{,}000.50$$

3.5 Inflation and the Time Value of Money

When a bank offers to pay 6 percent on a savings account, it promises to pay interest of $60 for every $1,000 you deposit. The bank fixes the number of dollars that it pays, but it doesn't provide any assurance of how much those dollars will buy. If the value of your investment increases by 6 percent, while the prices of goods and services increase by 10 percent, you actually lose ground in terms of the goods you can buy.

REAL VERSUS NOMINAL CASH FLOWS

inflation Rate at which prices as a whole are increasing.

Prices of goods and services continually change. Textbooks may become more expensive (Sorry!) while computers become cheaper. An overall rise in prices is known as **inflation.** If the inflation rate is 5 percent per year, then goods that cost $1 a year ago, typically cost $1.05 this year. The increase in the general level of prices means that the purchasing power of money has eroded. If a dollar bill bought a loaf of bread last year, the same dollar this year buys only part of a loaf.

Economists track the general level of prices using several different price indexes. The best known of these is the *consumer price index,* or *CPI.* This measures the number of dollars that it takes to buy a specified basket of goods and services, which is supposed to represent the typical family's purchases.[3] Thus the percentage increase in the CPI from 1 year to the next measures the rate of inflation.

Figure 3.14 graphs the CPI since 1950. We have set the index for the end of 1950 to 100, so the graph shows the price level in each year as a percentage of 1950 prices. For example, the index in 1951 was 110. This means that on average $110 in 1951 would have bought the same quantity of goods and services as $100 in 1950. The inflation rate between

[3] Don't ask how you buy a "basket" of services.

FIGURE 3.14
Consumer Price Index, 1950–2001

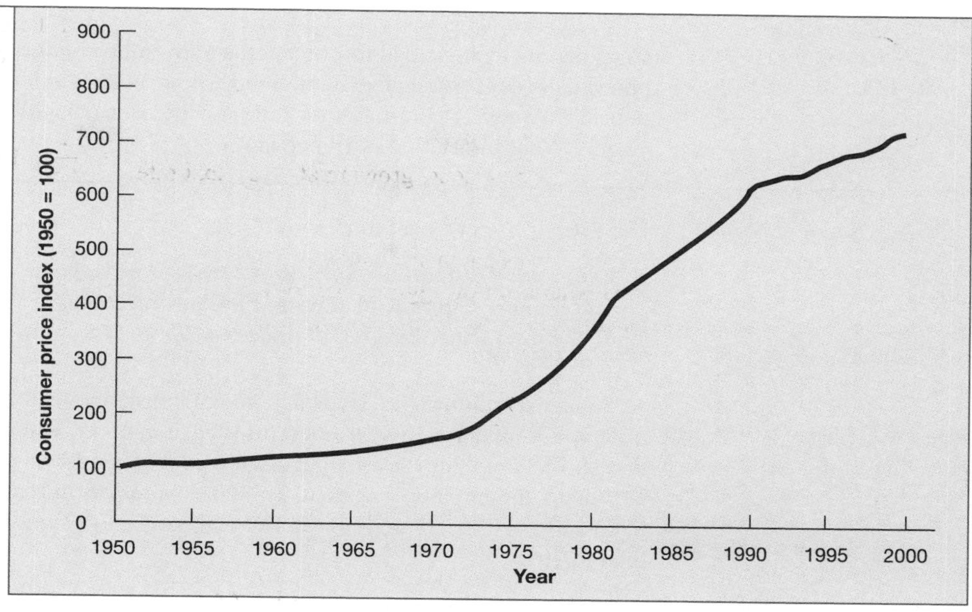

1950 and 1951 was therefore 10 percent. By mid-2001, the index was 770, meaning that 2001 prices were 7.70 times as high as 1950 prices.[4]

real value of $1 Purchasing power-adjusted value of a dollar.

The purchasing power of money fell by a factor of 7.7 between 1950 and 2001. A dollar in 2001 would buy only 13 percent of the goods it could buy in 1950 (1/7.7 = .13). In this case, we would say that the **real value of $1** declined by 100 – 14 = 86 percent from 1950 to 2001.

Although substantial inflation has occurred since 1950, inflation rates in the 1990s were less than 2 percent per year. However, as we write this in the summer of 2001, inflation is over 3 percent, causing concern among economists and policymakers. In Canada, the Bank of Canada is responsible for setting monetary policy to control inflation. Visit their website to learn more about their efforts to control inflation at www.bankofcanada.ca.

▶ EXAMPLE 3.15 *Talk Is Cheap*

Suppose that in 1975 a telephone call to your Aunt Hilda in London cost $10, while the price to airmail a letter was $.50. By 2001 the price of the phone call had fallen to $3, while that of the airmail letter had risen to $1. What was the change in the *real* cost of communicating with your aunt?

In 2001 the consumer price index was 3.33 times its level in 1975. If the price of telephone calls had risen in line with inflation, they would have cost 3.33 × $10 = $33 in 2001. That was the cost of a phone call measured in terms of 2001 dollars rather than 1975 dollars. Thus over the 26 years the *real* cost of an international phone call declined from $33 to $3, a fall of over 90 percent.

What about the cost of sending a letter? If the price of an airmail letter had kept pace with inflation, it would have been 3.33 × $.50 = $1.67 in 2001. The actual price was only $1. So the *real* cost of letter writing has also declined.

[4] The choice of 100 for the index in 1950 is arbitrary. For example, we could have set the index at 50 in 1950. In this case, the index in 1951 would have been 10 percent higher at 55 (that is, $50 in 1950 and $55 in 1951 would have bought the same basket of goods).

CHECK POINT 3.13

Consider a telephone call to London that currently would cost \$5. If the real price of telephone calls does not change in the future, how much will it cost you to make a call to London in 50 years, if the inflation rate is 5 percent (roughly its average over the past 25 years)? What if inflation is 10 percent?

Economists sometimes talk about *current* or *nominal dollars* versus *constant* or *real dollars.* Current or nominal dollars refer to the actual number of dollars of the day; constant or real dollars refer to the amount of purchasing power.

Some expenditures are fixed in nominal terms, and therefore *decline* in real terms. Suppose you took out a 10-year house mortgage in 1995. The monthly payment was \$800. It was still \$800 in 2001, even though the CPI increased by a factor of 1.10 over those years.

What's the monthly payment for 2001 expressed in real 1995 dollars? The answer is \$800/1.10, or \$727.27 per month. The real burden of paying the mortgage was less in 2001 than in 1995.

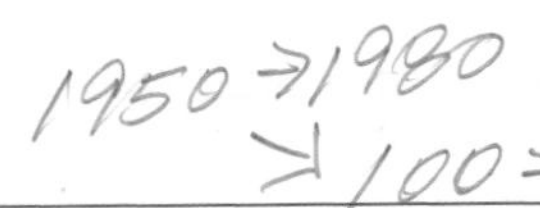

CHECK POINT 3.14

The price index in 1980 was 352. If a family spent \$250 a week on their typical purchases in 1950, how much would those purchases have cost in 1980? If your salary in 1980 was \$30,000 a year, what would be the real value of that salary in terms of 1950 dollars?

INFLATION AND INTEREST RATES

Whenever anyone quotes an interest rate, you can be fairly sure that it is a *nominal* rate, not a *real* rate. It sets the actual number of dollars you will be paid with no offset for future inflation.

nominal interest rate Rate at which money invested grows.

If you deposit \$1,000 in the bank at a **nominal interest rate** of 6 percent, you will have \$1,060 at the end of the year. But this does not mean you are 6 percent better off. Suppose that the inflation rate during the year is also 6 percent. Then the goods that cost \$1,000 last year will now cost \$1,000 × 1.06 = \$1,060, so you've gained nothing:

$$\text{Real future value of investment} = \frac{\$1{,}000 \times (1 + \text{nominal interest rate})}{(1 + \text{inflation rate})}$$

$$= \frac{\$1{,}000 \times 1.06}{1.06} = \$1{,}000$$

real interest rate Rate at which the purchasing power of an investment increases.

In this example, the nominal rate of interest is 6 percent, but the **real interest rate** is zero.

The real rate of interest is calculated by

$$\mathbf{1 + real\ interest\ rate} = \frac{\mathbf{1 + nominal\ interest\ rate}}{\mathbf{1 + inflation\ rate}} \qquad (3.5)$$

In our example, both the nominal interest rate and the inflation rate were 6 percent. So

$$1 + \text{real interest rate} = \frac{1.06}{1.06} = 1$$

$$\text{real interest rate} = 0$$

What if the nominal interest rate is 6 percent but the inflation rate is only 2 percent? In that case the real interest rate is 1.06/1.02 – 1 = .039, or 3.9 percent. Imagine that the price of a loaf of bread is $1, so that $1,000 would buy 1,000 loaves today. If you invest that $1,000 at a nominal interest rate of 6 percent, you will have $1,060 at the end of the year. However, if the price of bread has risen in the meantime to $1.02, then your money will buy you only 1,060/1.02 = 1,039 loaves. The real rate of interest is 3.9 percent.

CHECK POINT 3.15

a. Suppose that you invest your funds at an interest rate of 8 percent. What will be your real rate of interest if the inflation rate is zero? What if it is 5 percent?
b. Suppose that you demand a real rate of interest of 3 percent on your investments. What nominal interest rate do you need to earn, if the inflation rate is zero? If it is 5 percent?

Here is a useful approximation. The real rate approximately equals the difference between the nominal rate and the inflation rate:[5]

$$\textbf{Real interest rate} \approx \textbf{nominal interest rate} - \textbf{inflation rate}$$

Our example used a nominal interest rate of 6 percent, an inflation rate of 2 percent, and a real rate of 3.9 percent. If we round to 4 percent, the approximation gives the same answer:

$$\begin{aligned} \text{Real interest rate} &\approx \text{nominal interest rate} - \text{inflation rate} \\ &\approx 6 - 2 = 4\% \end{aligned}$$

The approximation works best when both the inflation rate and the real rate are small.[6] When they are not small, throw the approximation away and do it right.

EXAMPLE 3.16 *Real and Nominal Rates*

In Canada in 2001, the interest rate on 1-year government borrowing was about 4.5 percent. The inflation rate was 3 percent. Therefore, the real rate can be found by computing

$$\begin{aligned} 1 + \text{real interest rate} &= \frac{1 + \text{nominal interest rate}}{1 + \text{inflation rate}} \\ &= \frac{1.045}{1.03} = 1.0146 \\ \text{real interest rate} &= .01, \text{ or } 1.46\% \end{aligned}$$

The approximation rule gives a similar value of 4.5 – 3.0 = 1.5 percent. But the approximation would not have worked in the German hyperinflation of 1922/1923, when the inflation rate was well over 100 percent per *month* (at one point you needed one million marks to mail a letter), or in Peru in 1990, when prices increased by nearly 7,500 percent.

---

[5] The squiggle (≈) means "approximately equal to."

[6] When the interest and inflation rates are expressed as decimals (rather than percentages), the approximation error equals the product (real interest rate × inflation rate).

VALUING REAL CASH PAYMENTS

Think again about how to value future cash payments. Earlier in the chapter you learned how to value payments in current dollars by discounting at the nominal interest rate. For example, suppose that the nominal interest rate is 10 percent. How much do you need to invest now to produce \$100 in a year's time? Easy! Calculate the present value of \$100 by discounting by 10 percent:

$$\text{PV} = \frac{\$100}{1.10} = \$90.91$$

You get exactly the same result if you discount the *real* payment by the *real interest rate.* For example, assume that you expect inflation of 7 percent over the next year. The real value of that \$100 is therefore only \$100/1.07 = \$93.46. In one year's time your \$100 will buy only as much as \$93.46 today. Also with a 7 percent inflation rate, the real rate of interest is only about 3 percent. We can calculate it exactly from the formula:

$$\begin{aligned}(1 + \text{real interest rate}) &= \frac{1 + \text{nominal interest rate}}{1 + \text{inflation rate}} \\ &= \frac{1.10}{1.07} = 1.028 \\ \text{real interest rate} &= .028, \text{ or } 2.8\%\end{aligned}$$

If we now discount the \$93.46 real payment by the 2.8 percent real interest rate, we have a present value of \$90.91, just as before:

$$\text{PV} = \frac{\$93.46}{1.028} = \$90.91$$

The two methods should always give the same answer.[7] Remember:

Current dollar cash flows must be discounted by the nominal interest rate; real cash flows must be discounted by the real interest rate.

Mixing up nominal cash flows and real discount rates (or real rates and nominal flows) is an unforgivable sin. It is surprising how many sinners one finds.

CHECK POINT 3.16

You are owed \$5,000 by a relative who will pay you back in 1 year. The nominal interest rate is 8 percent and the inflation rate is 5 percent. What is the present value of your relative's IOU? Show that you get the same answer (a) discounting the nominal payment at the nominal rate, and (b) discounting the real payment at the real rate.

[7] If they don't equal there must be an error in your calculations. All we have done in the second calculation is to divide both the numerator (the cash payment) and the denominator (1 plus the nominal interest rate) by the same number (1 plus the inflation rate):

$$\begin{aligned}\text{PV} &= \frac{\text{payment in current dollars}}{1 + \text{nominal interest rate}} \\ &= \frac{(\text{payment in current dollars})/(1 + \text{inflation rate})}{(1 + \text{nominal interest rate})/(1 + \text{inflation rate})} \\ &= \frac{\text{payment in constant dollars}}{1 + \text{real interest rate}}\end{aligned}$$

EXAMPLE 3.17 *How Inflation Might Affect Bill Gates*

We showed earlier (Example 3.11) that at an interest rate of 9 percent, Bill Gates could, if he wished, turn his $54 billion (US) wealth into a 40-year annuity of $5 billion per year of luxury and excitement (L&E). Unfortunately L&E expenses inflate just like gasoline and groceries. Thus Mr. Gates would find the purchasing power of that $5 billion steadily declining. If he wants the same luxuries in 2042 as in 2002, he'll have to spend less in 2002, and then increase expenditures in line with inflation. How much should he spend in 2002? Assume the long-run inflation rate is 5 percent.

Mr. Gates needs to calculate a 40-year *real* annuity. The real interest rate is a little less than 4 percent:

$$1 + \text{real interest rate} = \frac{1 + \text{nominal interest rate}}{1 + \text{inflation rate}}$$

$$= \frac{1.09}{1.05} = 1.038$$

so the real rate is 3.8 percent. The 40-year annuity factor at 3.8 percent is 20.4. Therefore, annual spending (in 2002 dollars) should be chosen so that

$$\$54{,}000{,}000{,}000 = \text{annual spending} \times 20.4$$

$$\text{annual spending} = \$2{,}647{,}000{,}000$$

Mr. Gates could spend that amount on L&E in 2002 and 5 percent more (in line with inflation) in each subsequent year. This is only about half the value we calculated when we ignored inflation. Life has many disappointments, even for tycoons.

CHECK POINT 3.17

You have reached age 60 with a modest fortune of $3 million and are considering early retirement. How much can you spend each year for the next 30 years? Assume that your spending is stable in real terms. The nominal interest rate is 10 percent and the inflation rate is 5 percent.

REAL OR NOMINAL?

Any present value calculation done in nominal terms can also be done in real terms, and vice versa. Most financial analysts forecast in nominal terms and discount at nominal rates. However, in some cases real cash flows are easier to deal with. In our example of Bill Gates, the *real* expenditures were fixed. In this case, it was easiest to use real quantities. On the other hand, if the cash-flow stream is fixed in nominal terms (for example, the payments on a loan), it is easiest to use all nominal quantities.

3.6 Effective Annual Interest Rates

Thus far in this chapter we have used *annual* interest rates to value a series of *annual* cash flows. But interest rates may be quoted for days, months, years, or any convenient interval. How should we compare rates when they are quoted for different periods, such as monthly versus annually?

Consider your credit card. Suppose you have to pay interest on any unpaid balances at the rate of 1 percent *per month.* What is it going to cost you if you neglect to pay off your unpaid balance for a year?

Don't be put off because the interest rate is quoted per month rather than per year. The important thing is to maintain consistency between the interest rate and the number of periods. If the interest rate is quoted as a percent per month, then we must define the number of periods in our future value calculation as number of months. So if you borrow $100 from the credit card company at 1 percent per month for 12 months, you will need to repay $\$100 \times (1.01)^{12} = \$112.68$. Thus your debt grows after 1 year to $112.68. Therefore, we can say that the interest rate of 1 percent a month is equivalent to an **effective annual interest rate (EAR)**, or *annually compounded rate*, of 12.68 percent.

effective annual interest rate (EAR) Interest rate that is annualized using compound interest.

In general, the effective annual interest rate is defined as the annual growth rate allowing for the effect of compounding. Therefore,

$$(1 + \text{annual rate}) = (1 + \text{monthly rate})^{12}$$

When comparing interest rates, it is best to use effective annual rates. This compares interest paid or received over a common period (1 year) and allows for possible compounding during the period. Unfortunately, short-term rates are sometimes annualized by multiplying the rate per period by the number of periods in a year. In fact, truth in lending laws in Canada *require* that rates be annualized in this manner. Such rates are called **annual percentage rates (APRs).**[8] The interest rate on your credit card loan was 1 percent per month. Since there are 12 months in a year, the APR on the loan is $12 \times 1\% = 12\%$.

annual percentage rate (APR) Interest rate that is annualized using simple interest.

If the credit card company quotes an APR of 12 percent, how can you find the effective annual interest rate? The solution is simple:

Step 1. Take the quoted APR and divide by the number of compounding periods in a year to recover the rate per period actually charged. In our example, the interest was calculated monthly. So we divide the APR by 12 to obtain the interest rate per month:

$$\text{Monthly interest rate} = \frac{\text{APR}}{12} = \frac{12\%}{12} = 1\%, \text{ or } .01$$

Step 2. Now convert to an annually compounded interest rate:

$$(1 + \text{annual rate}) = (1 + \text{monthly rate})^{12} = (1 + .01)^{12} = 1.1268$$

The annual interest rate is .1268, or 12.68 percent.

In general, if an investment of $1 is worth $\$(1 + r)$ after one period, and there are m periods in a year, the investment will grow after 1 year to $\$(1 + r)^m$, and the effective annual interest rate is $(1 + r)^m - 1$. For example, a credit card loan that charges a monthly interest rate of 1 percent has an APR of 12 percent but an effective annual interest rate of $(1.01)^{12} - 1 = .1268$, or 12.68 percent. To summarize:

The effective annual rate is the rate at which invested funds will grow over the course of a year. It equals the rate of interest per period compounded for the number of periods in a year.

[8] Although the APR must be disclosed in the loan document, financial institutions typically (though not always) advertise effective rates when marketing their products. APRs are not commonly used or quoted for securities used in the big leagues of finance.

TABLE 3.6
Compounding frequency and effective annual interest rate (APR = 6%)

Compounding Period	Periods per Year (*m*)	Per-Period Interest Rate	Growth Factor of Invested Funds	Effective Annual Rate
1 year	1	6%	1.06	6.0000%
Semiannually	2	3	$1.03^{2} = 1.0609$	6.0900
Quarterly	4	1.5	$1.015^{4} = 1.061364$	6.1364
Monthly	12	.5	$1.005^{12} = 1.061678$	6.1678
Weekly	52	.11538	$1.0011538^{52} = 1.061800$	6.1800
Daily	365	.01644	$1.0001644^{365} = 1.061831$	6.1831

▶ EXAMPLE 3.18 *The Effective Interest Rates on Bank Accounts*

Back in the 1960s and 1970s, U.S. federal regulation limited the (APR) interest rates banks could pay on savings accounts. Banks were hungry for depositors, and they searched for ways to increase the *effective* rate of interest that could be paid within the rules. Their solution was to keep the same APR but to calculate the interest on deposits more frequently. As interest is calculated at shorter and shorter intervals, less time passes before interest can be earned on interest. Therefore, the effective annually compounded rate of interest increases. Table 3.6 shows the calculations assuming that the maximum APR that banks could pay is 6 percent. (Actually, it was a bit less than this, but 6 percent is a nice round number to use for illustration.)

You can see from Table 3.6 how U.S. banks were able to increase the effective interest rate simply by calculating interest at more frequent intervals.

The ultimate step was to assume that interest was paid in a continuous stream rather than at fixed intervals. With one year's *continuous compounding,* \$1 grows to e^{APR}, where $e = 2.718$ (a figure that may be familiar to you as the base for natural logarithms). Thus if you deposited \$1 with a bank that offered a continuously compounded rate of 6 percent, your investment would grow by the end of the year to $(2.718)^{.06} = \$1.061837$, just a hair's breadth more than if interest were compounded daily.

☑ CHECK POINT 3.18

A car loan requiring quarterly payments carries an APR of 8 percent. What is the effective annual rate of interest?

▶ EXAMPLE 3.19 *Figuring Out Canadian Mortgages*

In Example 3.10 we showed you how a mortgage works. In that example the interest rate was 1 percent per month. Now you know how to convert that to an effective annual rate of interest. However, before you apply for a job at your bank, you need to know how mortgage interest rates are calculated in Canada. For reasons unclear to us, although mortgage payments are typically made monthly, the posted mortgage interest rate is the APR for a *6-month* interest rate. We say that mortgage interest rates are quoted with semiannual compounding. To work out the monthly payments on a mortgage, the equivalent monthly rate of interest must be calculated. For example, if the posted mortgage interest rate is 7.75 percent, we know that this is the APR for 3.875 percent per 6 months (6-month interest rate = APR/2). The EAR of this interest rate is $(1.03875)^{2} - 1$, or 7.9 percent. The EAR must now be converted to its monthly equivalent rate:

$$\text{Monthly interest rate} = (1 + \text{EAR})^{1/12} - 1$$
$$= (1.079)^{1/12} - 1 = 0.00635646163, \text{ or about } 0.636\%$$

One final point about Canadian mortgages: Typically, the mortgage payment is calculated over a period (the amortization period), which is much longer than the term of the mortgage. For example, a bank commits to lend the money at the posted rate of 7.75 percent for a term of 5 years, but calculates the mortgage payment as if the mortgage will last 25 years. This mortgage has a term of 5 years and an amortization period of 25 years. Suppose you arrange a $200,000 mortgage. The 300-month, 0.636 percent annuity factor is 133.76 and your payments will be

$$\text{Mortgage payment} = \frac{\text{mortgage amount}}{\text{annuity factor}}$$

$$= \frac{\$200{,}000}{133.76} = \$1{,}495.22$$

You can check your calculations by visiting a website of a Canadian bank. We went to www.royalbank.com/mortgage. Keeping in mind that bankers use 10 decimal places, prove to yourself that *they* and *you* know how to convert the posted mortgage interest rate into the correct monthly interest rate.

3.7 Summary

1. **To what future value will money invested at a given interest rate grow after a given period of time?**

An investment of $1 earning an interest rate of r will increase in value each period by the factor $(1 + r)$. After t periods its value will grow to $\$(1 + r)^t$. This is the **future value** of the $1 investment with compound interest.

2. **What is the present value of a cash flow to be received in the future?**

The **present value** of a future cash payment is the amount that you would need to invest today to match that future payment. To calculate present value, we divide the cash payment by $(1 + r)^t$ or, equivalently, multiply by the **discount factor** $1/(1 + r)^t$. The discount factor measures the value today of $1 received in period t.

3. **How can we calculate present and future values of streams of cash payments?**

A level stream of cash payments that continues indefinitely is known as a **perpetuity**; one that continues for a limited number of years is called an **annuity**. The present value of a stream of cash flows is simply the sum of the present value of each cash flow. Similarly, the future value of an annuity is the sum of the future value of each individual cash flow. Shortcut formulas make the calculations for perpetuities and annuities easy. Variations of these formulas make it easy to calculate the present value of cash flows growing at a constant rate.

4. **What is the difference between real and nominal cash flows and real and nominal interest rates?**

A dollar is a dollar but the amount of goods that a dollar can buy is eroded by **inflation.** If prices double, the **real value of a dollar** halves. Financial managers and economists often find it helpful to re-express future cash flows in terms of real dollars—that is, dollars of constant purchasing power.

Be careful to distinguish the **nominal interest rate** and the **real interest rate**—that is, the rate at which the real value of the investment grows. Discount nominal cash flows (that is, cash flows measured in current dollars) at nominal interest rates. Discount real cash flows (cash flows measured in constant dollars) at real interest rates. *Never* mix and match nominal and real.

5. **How should we compare interest rates quoted over different time intervals—for example, monthly versus annual rates?**

Interest rates for short time periods are often quoted as annual rates by multiplying the per-period rate by the number of periods in a year. These **annual percentage rates** (APRs) do not recognize the effect of compound interest, that is, they annualize, assuming simple interest. The **effective annual rate** (EAR) annualizes using compound interest. It equals the rate of interest per period compounded for the number of periods in a year.

Related Web Links

http://invest-faq.com/articles/analy-fut-prs-val.html Understanding the concepts of present and future value
www.bankrate.com/brm/default.asp U.S. interest rates for a variety of purposes, and some calculators
www.financenter.com Calculators for evaluating financial decisions of all kinds
www.cannex.com Canadian interest rates for various financial products
www.financialplayerscenter.com An introduction to time value of money with several calculators
www.bankofcanada.ca Canadian interest rates and Canadian monetary policy
www.royalbank.com/mortgage Mortgage information and calculator
www.hsbc.ca/english/interactive_tools Mortgage calculator and other financial calculators
www.tdcanadatrust.com Mortgage calculator
www.scotiabank.com Mortgage calculator
www.financialservicesguide.net/tools.html Mortgage calculator
www.hrdc.gc.ca/hrib/learnlit/cesg/011/003_e.shtml RESP calculator
www.retireweb.com/respcalculator.html RESP calculator
www.lumpsum.com/lottery.html A business based on the time value of money

Key Terms

future value	63	annuity	78	real value of $1	91
compound interest	63	perpetuity	78	nominal interest rate	92
simple interest	63	annuity factor	80	real interest rate	92
future value factor	65	annuity due	82	effective annual interest rate (EAR)	96
present value (PV)	67	growing perpetuity	88	annual percentage rate (APR)	96
discount rate	67	growing annuity	90		
discount factor	69	inflation	90		

Questions and Problems

*Answers in Appendix B

Basic

*1. **Present Values.** Compute the present value of a $100 cash flow for the following combinations of discount rates and times:

a. $r = 10$ percent, $t = 10$ years
b. $r = 10$ percent, $t = 20$ years
c. $r = 5$ percent, $t = 10$ years
d. $r = 5$ percent, $t = 20$ years

2. **Future Values.** Compute the future value of a $100 cash flow for the same combinations of rates and times as in problem 1.

*3. **Future Values.** In 1880, five Aboriginal trackers were each promised the equivalent of $100 Australian for helping to capture the notorious outlaw Ned Kelley. In 1993 the granddaughters of two of the trackers claimed that this reward had not been paid. The Australian prime minister stated that if this was true, the government would be happy to pay the $100. However, the granddaughters also claimed that they were entitled to compound interest. How much was each entitled to if the interest rate was 5 percent? What if it was 10 percent?

4. **Future Values.** You deposit $1,000 into your bank account. If the bank pays 4 percent simple interest, how much will you accumulate in your account after 10 years? What if the bank pays compound interest? How much of your earnings will be interest on interest?

*5. **Present Values.** You will require $700 in 5 years. If you earn 6 percent interest on your funds, how much will you need to invest today in order to reach your savings goal?

*6. **Calculating Interest Rate.** Find the interest rate implied by the following combinations of present and future values:

Present Value	Years	Future Value
$400	11	$684
$183	4	$249
$300	7	$300

*7. **Present Values.** Would you rather receive $1,000 per year for 10 years or $800 per year for 15 years if

a. the interest rate is 5 percent?
b. the interest rate is 20 percent?

Why do your answers to parts (a) and (b) differ?

8. **Calculating Interest Rate.** Find the annual interest rate.

Present Value	Future Value	Time Period
100	115.76	3 years
200	262.16	4 years
100	110.41	5 years

*9. **Present Values.** What is the present value of the following cash-flow stream if the interest rate is 5 percent?

Year	Cash Flow
1	$200
2	$400
3	$300

*10. **Number of Periods.** How long will it take for $400 to grow to $1,000 at the interest rate specified?

a. 4 percent
b. 8 percent
c. 16 percent

*11. **Calculating Interest Rate.** Find the effective annual interest rate for each case:

APR	Compounding Period
12%	1 month
8%	3 months
10%	6 months

*12. **Calculating Interest Rate.** Find the APR (the stated interest rate) for each case:

Effective Annual Interest Rate	Compounding Period
10.00%	1 month
6.09%	6 months
8.24%	3 months

*13. **Growth of Funds.** If you earn 8 percent per year on your bank account, how long will it take an account with $100 to double to $200?

14. **Comparing Interest Rates.** Suppose you can borrow money at 8.5 percent per year (APR), compounded semiannually or 8.4 percent per year (APR) compounded monthly. Which is the better deal?

*15. **Calculating Interest Rate.** Lenny Loanshark charges "one point" per week (that is, 1 percent per week) on his loans. What APR must he report to consumers? Assume there are exactly 52 weeks in a year. What is the effective annual rate?

16. **Compound Interest.** Investments in the stock market have increased at an average compound rate of about 10 percent per year since 1926.

a. If you invested $1,000 in the stock market in 1926, how much would that investment be worth today?

b. If your investment in 1926 has grown to $1 million, how much did you invest in 1926?

17. **Compound Interest.** Old Time Savings Bank pays 5 percent interest on its savings accounts. If you deposit $1,000 in the bank and leave it there, how much interest will you earn in the first year? The second year? The 10th year?

18. **Compound Interest.** New Savings Bank pays 4 percent interest on its deposits. If you deposit $1,000 in the bank and leave it there, will it take more or less than 25 years for your money to double? You should be able to answer this without a calculator or interest rate tables.

19. **Calculating Interest Rate.** A zero-coupon bond which will pay $1,000 in 10 years is selling today for $422.41. What interest rate does the bond offer?

*20. **Present Values.** A famous quarterback just signed a $15 million contract providing $3 million a year for 5 years. A less famous receiver signed a $14 million 5-year contract providing $4 million now and $2 million per year for 5 years. Who is better paid? The interest rate is 12 percent.

PRACTICE

21. **Loan Payments.** If you take out an $8,000 car loan that calls for 48 monthly payments at an APR of 10 percent, what is your monthly payment? What is the effective annual interest rate on the loan?

22. **Annuity Values.**

 a. What is the present value of a 3-year annuity of $100 if the discount rate is 8 percent?
 b. What is the present value of the annuity in part (a) if you have to wait 2 years instead of 1 year for the payment stream to start?

*23. **Annuities and Interest Rates.** Professor's Annuity Corp. offers a lifetime annuity to retiring professors. For a payment of $80,000 at age 65, the firm will pay the retiring professor $600 a month until death.

 a. If the professor's remaining life expectancy is 20 years, what is the monthly rate on this annuity? What is the effective annual rate? What is the APR?
 b. If the monthly interest rate is .5 percent, what monthly annuity payment can the firm offer to the retiring professor?

24. **Annuity Values.** You want to buy a new car, but you can make an initial payment of only $2,000 and can afford monthly payments of, at most, $400.

 a. If the APR on auto loans is 12 percent and you finance the purchase over 48 months, what is the maximum price you can pay for the car?
 b. How much can you afford if you finance the purchase over 60 months?

*25. **Calculating Interest Rate.** In a *discount interest loan,* you pay the interest payment up front. For example, if a 1-year loan is stated as $10,000 and the interest rate is 10 percent, the borrower "pays" .10 × $10,000 = $1,000 immediately, thereby receiving net funds of $9,000 and repaying $10,000 in a year.

 a. What is the effective interest rate on this loan?
 b. If you call the discount d (for example, $d = 10\%$ using our numbers), express the effective annual rate on the loan as a function of d.
 c. Why is the effective annual rate always greater than the stated rate d?

26. **Annuity Due.** Recall that an annuity due is like an ordinary annuity except that the first payment is made immediately instead of at the end of the first period.

 a. Why is the present value of an annuity due equal to $(1 + r)$ times the present value of an ordinary annuity?
 b. Why is the future value of an annuity due equal to $(1 + r)$ times the future value of an ordinary annuity?

*27. **Rate on a Loan.** If you take out an $8,000 car loan that calls for 48 monthly payments of $225 each, what is the APR of the loan? What is the effective annual interest rate on the loan?

28. **Loan Payments.** Reconsider the car loan in the previous question. What if the payments are made in four annual year-end installments? What annual payment would have the same present value as the monthly payment you calculated? Use the same effective annual interest rate as in the previous question. Why is your answer not simply 12 times the monthly payment?

29. **Annuity Value.** Your landscaping company can lease a truck for $8,000 a year (paid at year-end) for 6 years. It can instead buy the truck for $40,000. The truck will be valueless after 6 years. If the interest rate your company can earn on its funds is 7 percent, is it cheaper to buy or lease?

*30. **Annuity Due Value.** Reconsider the previous problem. What if the lease payments are an annuity due, so that the first payment comes immediately? Is it cheaper to buy or lease?

*31. **Annuity Due.** A store offers two payment plans. Under the installment plan, you pay 25 percent down and 25 percent of the purchase price in each of the next 3 years. If you pay the entire bill immediately, you can take a 10 percent discount from the purchase price. If you can borrow or lend funds at a 6 percent interest rate which is the better deal?

32. **Annuity Value.** Reconsider the previous question. How will your answer change if the payments on the 4-year installment plan do not start for a full year?

*33. **Annuity and Annuity Due Payments.**

a. If you borrow $1,000 and agree to repay the loan in five equal annual payments at an interest rate of 12 percent, what will your payment be?

b. What if you make the first payment on the loan immediately instead of at the end of the first year?

*34. **Valuing Delayed Annuities.** Suppose that you will receive annual payments of $10,000 for a period of 10 years. The first payment will be made 4 years from now. If the interest rate is 6 percent, what is the present value of this stream of payments?

*35. **Mortgage.** You take out a $175,000 mortgage with a 25-year amortization period, a 5-year term, and a 6 percent posted mortgage interest rate. What is your monthly mortgage payment? When the mortgage expires in 5 years, what is the unpaid balance?

*36. **Mortgage.** You are arranging a $350,000 mortgage with a 25-year amortization period and a 7 percent posted interest rate. What is the monthly mortgage payment? Suppose the bank offers you the opportunity to pay your monthly payments in two equal installments (pay one-half of the monthly payment every 2 weeks). How much faster will you pay off your mortgage this way?

37. **Amortizing Loan.** Consider a 4-year amortizing loan. You borrow $1,000 initially, and repay it in four equal annual year-end payments.

a. If the interest rate is 10 percent, show that the annual payment is $315.47.

b. Fill in the following table, which shows how much of each payment is comprised of interest versus principal repayment (that is, amortization) and the outstanding balance on the loan at each date.

c. Show that the loan balance after 1 year is equal to the year-end payment of $315.47 times the 3-year annuity factor.

Time	Loan Balance	Year-End Interest Due on Balance	Year-End Payment	Amortization of Loan
0	$1,000	$100	$315.47	$215.47
1	______	______	315.47	______
2	______	______	315.47	______
3	______	______	315.47	______
4	0	0	—	—

38. **Annuity Value.** You've borrowed $4,248.68 and agreed to pay back the loan with monthly payments of $200. If the interest rate is 12 percent stated as an APR, how long will it take you to pay back the loan? What is the effective annual rate on the loan?

39. **Annuity Value.** The $40 million lottery payment that you just won actually pays $2 million per year for 20 years. If the discount rate is 10 percent, and the first payment comes in 1 year, what is the present value of the winnings? What if the first payment comes immediately?

*40. **Real Annuities.** A retiree wants level consumption in real terms over a 30-year retirement. If the inflation rate equals the interest rate she earns on her $450,000 of savings, how much can she spend in real terms each year over the rest of her life?

41. **EAR versus APR.** You invest $1,000 at a 6 percent annual interest rate, stated as an APR. Interest is compounded monthly. How much will you have in 1 year? In 1.5 years?

42. **Annuity Value.** You just borrowed $100,000 to buy a condo. You will repay the mortgage in equal monthly payments of $804.62 over the next 30 years. What monthly interest rate are you paying on the mortgage? What is the effective annual rate on that mortgage? What rate is the lender more likely to quote on the mortgage?

43. **EAR.** If a bank pays 10 percent interest with continuous compounding, what is the effective annual rate?

44. **Annuity Values.** You can buy a car that is advertised for $12,000 on the following terms: (a) pay $12,000 and receive a $1,000 rebate from the manufacturer, or (b) pay $250 a month for 4 years, for total payments of $12,000, implying zero percent financing. Which is the better deal if the interest rate is 1 percent per month?

*45. **Continuous Compounding.** How much will $100 grow to if invested at a continuously compounded interest rate of 10 percent for 6 years? What if it is invested for 10 years at 6 percent?

*46. **Future Values.** I now have $20,000 in the bank earning interest of .5 percent per month. I need $30,000 to make a down payment on a house. I can save an additional $100 per month. How long will it take me to accumulate the $30,000?

*47. **Perpetuities.** A bank advertises the following deal: "Pay us $100 a year for 10 years and then we will pay you (or your beneficiaries) $100 a year *forever*." Is this a good deal if the interest rate available on other deposits is 8 percent?

48. **Perpetuities.** A bank will pay you $100 a year for your lifetime if you deposit $2,500 in the bank today. If you plan to live forever, what interest rate is the bank paying?

*49. **Perpetuities.** A property will provide $10,000 a year forever. If its value is $125,000, what must be the discount rate?

50. **Applying Time Value.** You can buy property today for $3 million and sell it in 5 years for $4 million. (You earn no rental income on the property.)

    a. If the interest rate is 8 percent, what is the present value of the sales price?
    b. Is the property investment attractive to you? Why or why not?
    c. Would your answer to part (b) change if you also could earn $200,000 per year rent on the property?

51. **Applying Time Value.** A factory costs $400,000. You forecast that it will produce cash inflows of $120,000 in Year 1, $180,000 in Year 2, and $300,000 in Year 3. The discount rate is 12 percent. Is the factory a good investment? Explain.

*52. **Applying Time Value.** You invest $1,000 today and expect to sell your investment for $2,000 in 10 years.

    a. Is this a good deal if the discount rate is 5 percent?
    b. What if the discount rate is 10 percent?

53. **Calculating Interest Rate.** A store will give you a 3 percent discount on the cost of your purchase if you pay cash today. Otherwise, you will be billed the full price with payment due in 1 month. What is the implicit borrowing rate being paid by customers who choose to defer payment for the month?

*54. **Quoting Rates.** Banks sometimes quote interest rates in the form of "add-on interest." In this case, if a 1-year loan is quoted with a 20 percent interest rate and you borrow $1,000, then you pay back $1,200. But you make these payments in monthly installments of $100 each. What are the true APR and effective annual rate on this loan? Why should you have known that the true rates must be greater than 20 percent even before doing any calculations?

55. **Compound Interest.** Suppose you take out a $1,000, 3-year loan using add-on interest (see previous problem) with a quoted interest rate of 20 percent per year. What will your monthly payments be? (Total payments are $\$1{,}000 + \$1{,}000 \times .20 \times 3 = \$1{,}600$.) What are the true APR and effective annual rate on this loan? Are they the same as in the previous problem?

56. **Calculating Interest Rate.** What is the effective annual rate on a 1-year loan with an interest rate quoted on a discount basis (see problem 25) of 20 percent?

57. **Effective Rates.** First National Bank pays 6.2 percent interest compounded semiannually. Second National Bank pays 6 percent interest, compounded monthly. Which bank offers the higher effective annual rate?

58. **Calculating Interest Rate.** You borrow $1,000 from the bank and agree to repay the loan over the next year in 12 equal monthly payments of $90. However, the bank also charges you a loan-initiation fee of $20, which is taken out of the initial proceeds of the loan. Taking into account the impact of the initiation fee, what is the effective annual interest rate on the loan?

59. **Retirement Savings.** You believe you will need to save $500,000 by the time you retire in 40 years, in order to live comfortably. If the interest rate is 5 percent per year, how much must you save each year to meet your retirement goal?

60. **Retirement Savings.** How much would you need in the previous problem if you believe that you will inherit $100,000 in 10 years?

*61. **Retirement Savings.** You believe you will spend $40,000 per year for 20 years once you retire in 40 years. If the interest rate is 5 percent per year, how much must you save each year until retirement to meet your retirement goal?

*62. **Retirement Planning.** A couple thinking about retirement decide to put aside $3,000 each year in a savings plan that earns 8 percent interest. In 5 years they will receive a gift of $10,000, which can also be invested.

   a. How much money will they have accumulated 30 years from now?
   b. If their goal is to retire with $800,000 of savings, how much extra do they need to save every year?

63. **Retirement Planning.** A couple will retire in 50 years; they plan to spend about $30,000 per year in retirement, which should last about 25 years. They believe that they can earn 10 percent interest on retirement savings.

   a. If they make annual payments into a savings plan, how much will they need to save each year? Assume the first payment comes in 1 year.
   b. How would the answer to part (a) change if the couple also realize that in 20 years, they will need to spend $60,000 on their child's college education?

CHALLENGE

64. **Real versus Nominal Dollars.** An engineer in 1950 was earning $6,000 a year. Today she earns $60,000 a year. However, on average, goods today cost 7.7 times what they did in 1950. What is her real income today in terms of constant 1950 dollars?

*65. **Real versus Nominal Rates.** If investors are to earn a real interest rate at 4 percent, what nominal interest rate must they earn if the inflation rate is

a. zero
b. 4 percent
c. 6 percent

66. **Real Rates.** If investors receive an 8 percent interest rate on their bank deposits, what real interest rate will they earn if the inflation rate over the year is

a. zero
b. 3 percent
c. 6 percent

*67. **Real versus Nominal Rates.** You will receive $100 from a savings bond in 3 years. The nominal interest rate is 8 percent.

a. What is the present value of the proceeds from the bond?
b. If the inflation rate over the next few years is expected to be 3 percent, what will the real value of the $100 payoff be in terms of today's dollars?
c. What is the real interest rate?
d. Show that the real payoff from the bond in part (b), discounted at the real interest rate in part (c) gives the same present value for the bond as you found in part (a).

68. **Real versus Nominal Dollars.** Your consulting firm will produce cash flows of $100,000 this year, and you expect cash flow to keep pace with any increase in the general level of prices. The interest rate currently is 8 percent, and you anticipate inflation of about 2 percent.

a. What is the present value of your firm's cash flows for years 1 through 5?
b. How would your answer to part (a) change if you anticipated no growth in cash flow?

*69. **Real versus Nominal Annuities.** Good news: You will almost certainly be a millionaire by the time you retire in 45 years. Bad news: The inflation rate over your lifetime will average about 3 percent.

a. What will be the real value of $1 million by the time you retire, in terms of today's dollars?
b. What real annuity (in today's dollars) will $1 million support if the real interest rate at retirement is 2 percent and the annuity must last for 20 years?

*70. **Rule of 72.** Use the Rule of 72 to figure out how long it will take for your money to *quadruple* in value if the interest rate is 8 percent per year?

*71. **Inflation.** Inflation in Brazil in 1992 averaged about 23 percent per month. What was the annual inflation rate?

72. **Perpetuities.** British government perpetuities at 4 percent pay £4 interest each year forever. Another bond, 2.5 percent perpetuities, pays £2.50 per year forever. What is the value of 4 percent perpetuities if the long-term interest rate is 6 percent? What is the value of 2.5 percent perpetuities?

73. **Real versus Nominal Annuities.**

a. You plan to retire in 30 years and want to accumulate enough by then to have $30,000 per year for 15 years. If the interest rate is 10 percent, how much must you accumulate by the time you retire?
b. How much must you save each year until retirement in order to finance your retirement consumption?
c. You remember that the annual inflation rate is 4 percent. If a loaf of bread costs $1 today, what will it cost by the time you retire?
d. You really want to consume $30,000 a year in *real* dollars during retirement and wish to save an equal *real* amount each year until then. What is the real amount of savings that you need to accumulate by the time you retire?

e. Calculate the required preretirement real annual savings necessary to meet your consumption goals. Compare your answer to part (b). Why is there a difference?

f. What is the nominal value of the amount you need to save during the first year? (Assume the savings are put aside at the end of each year.) The 30th year?

74. **Retirement and Inflation.** Redo part (a) of problem 63, but now assume that the inflation rate over the next 50 years will average 4 percent.

a. What is the real annual savings the couple must set aside?

b. How much do they need to save in nominal terms in the first year?

c. How much do they need to save in nominal terms in the last year?

d. What will be their nominal expenditures in the first year of retirement? The last?

75. **Annuity Value.** What is the value of a perpetuity that pays $100 every 3 months forever? The discount rate quoted on an APR basis is 12 percent.

*76. **Changing Interest Rates.** If the interest rate this year is 8 percent and the interest rate next year will be 10 percent, what is the future value of $1 after 2 years? What is the present value of a payment of $1 to be received in 2 years?

*77. **Changing Interest Rates.** Your wealthy uncle established a $1,000 bank account for you when you were born. For the first 8 years of your life, the interest rate earned on the account was 8 percent. Since then, rates have been only 6 percent. Now you are 21 years old and ready to cash in. How much is in your account?

78. **Applying Time Value.** You would like to travel around the world in a sailboat for 2 years, leaving in 5 years from now. One year before you leave, you will purchase the sailboat at an expected cost of $150,000. During the pretrip year, you will learn how to sail the boat. Once the trip is underway, you forecast that your monthly expenses will be $2,200, payable at the start of the month. In addition, you would like to have an emergency fund of $45,000 available on the day you depart. How much do you need to save every month-end if you can earn an effective annual interest of 6 percent?

79. **Applying Time Value.** You are thinking of buying a used car for $4,000 for driving to school. Your parents are willing to lend you the $4,000 and charge only 2.4 percent APR. They want the loan repaid equally in 48 monthly payments, with the first payment due at the end of the month in which you buy the car. You estimate that the monthly cost of operating the car, including gas, insurance, maintenance and licence fees, will be $200 and payable at the start of each month. The cost of a monthly bus pass is $80. You expect that the car will be totally worn out in 4 years, with zero resale value, when you are finished school. Your discount rate is 6 percent.

a. If you have three roommates who also need transportation to and from school, how much do you need to charge them a month in order to cover all your costs? (You all plan to go to summer school, so you can assume 12 payments a year.)

b. Does it make financial sense to buy the car? Explain your answer.

80. **Applying Time Value.** You and your friend are avid snowboarders and bike racers. Nearly every other weekend you travel to a race in a rented van. Now that both of you have full-time jobs, your friend is pressuring you to seriously consider purchasing a van.

Here's how the conversation goes:

Friend: "Just think of how much we will save on rentals. The rented van costs us $100 a weekend, plus $.50 per kilometre. Most trips are 100 km, one-way. With our own van, we will only have to pay for fuel, about $.75 per km; and maintenance, about $.25 per km. A used van will only cost about $20,000. Think of the convenience!"

You: "What about insurance? What about depreciation?"

Friend: "Insurance will only be $1,200 per year. The salesperson says the van will depreciate slowly, only 10 percent per year. If we retire from the race circuit in 5 years, the van will still have value. Shouldn't we at least think about it?"

You: "I guess. I think a nominal discount rate of 9 percent is about right."

a. Do you think you should buy the van? Be sure to state your assumptions.

b. What if all costs are subject to a 3 percent annual inflation? Do you change your mind?

81. **Applying Time Value.** You are working as a financial planner. A couple has asked you to put together an investment plan for the education of their daughter. She is a bright 7 year old (her birthday is today), and everyone hopes she will go to college or university after high school in 10 years, on her 17th birthday. You estimate that today the cost of a year of college is $10,000, including the cost of tuition, books, accommodation, food, and clothing. You forecast that the annual inflation rate will be 4 percent. You may assume that these costs are incurred at the start of each college year. A typical college program lasts 4 years. The effective annual interest rate is 6 percent and is nominal.

    a. Suppose the couple invests money on her birthday, starting today and ending one year before she starts college. How much must they invest each year to have money to send their daughter to college?

    b. If the couple waits one year, until their daughter's 8th birthday, how much more do they need to invest annually?

82. **Growing Perpetuity.** A cottage is for sale for $580,000. Currently it generates annual cash flows, net of all expenses and taxes, of $35,000. If the cottage lasts forever, what rate of growth of the annual cash flows will be necessary for you to earn an 8 percent annual rate of return on your investment?

83. **Growing Annuity.** A real estate appraiser is assessing the value of a piece of land in Vancouver. Currently the land is unoccupied but is zoned for commercial use. Plans have been approved to build a five-story office building. Construction is expected to start in 1 year and will take 2 years to complete, at a total cost of $3 million. For simplicity, assume that the costs are paid in equal amounts at the start of each construction year.

    a. Suppose a constant annual cash flow of $400,000, net of all taxes and operating costs, is expected at the end of each year of operation, and the building lasts for 50 years. What is the maximum you would be willing to pay for the land if the discount rate is 8 percent? Explain your answer.

    b. If the cash flow from the tenants grows at 1.5 percent per year, after the first year of occupancy, recalculate the price you would be willing to pay for the land.

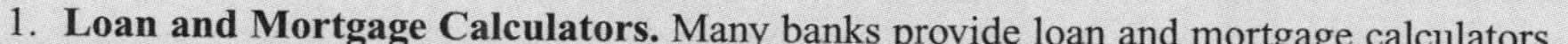

INTERNET PROBLEMS

1. **Loan and Mortgage Calculators.** Many banks provide loan and mortgage calculators.

    a. For example, go to the HSBC Bank of Canada website at www.hsbc.ca/english/interactive_tools, and under "Interactive Tools" on the left side of the page, select "Financial Planning Calculators." A list of different calculators will appear on the left. Select the "Personal Loan Calculator" and check that your answer to problem 21 is correct.

    b. At the same website, select the "Mortgage Calculator," then select "Mortgage Payment Calculator." For a $200,000 mortgage, with a 25 percent down payment at annual interest of 6 percent, compare the payments if you pay monthly, semi-monthly, biweekly, or weekly. Can you figure out how they got these numbers? Do your own calculations.

    c. Find another mortgage calculator for another Canadian bank. For example, see www.tdcanadatrust.com and www.scotiabank.com. Compare their biweekly payments. Are they the same? What does that tell you about the importance of assumptions in the time value of money calculations and the need to be careful using Internet calculators?

    d. Another mortgage calculator is found at www.financialservicesguide.net. How does it differ? Is it more useful? Repeat the mortgage calculation in part (b) and compare a Canadian mortgage to a U.S. mortgage.

2. **RESP Calculators.** The Canadian government is encouraging saving funds for post-secondary education through registered education savings plans (RESPs) and the Canada Education Savings Grant (www.hrdc.gc.ca/hrib/learnlit/cesg/011/003_e.shtml). Under current rules, a maximum of $4,000 may be saved each year, with a total lifetime maximum of $42,000. The Canada Education Savings Grant, paid annually by the federal government, is 20 percent of the contribution to a maximum of $400 per year. Although the contributions are not tax-deductible, they grow tax-free, and then are taxed at the student's, presumably lower, tax rate when he or she attends college or university. Compare the RESP calculator at HSBC Bank (see problem 1, select "RESP Calculator" from the list of "Financial Planning Calculators") with the one at www.retireweb.com/respcalculator.html. Both websites allow you to select the current cost of tuition plus living costs and the expected inflation rate. However, they calculate different items.
   a. Explain what each calculator is determining. How do the calculations differ?
   b. Set up a scenario and compare the two calculators.
   c. One of the calculators does not pay attention to the Canadian government's rules for RESPs. Which one?
3. **Cash for lottery winnings.** In the United States, lottery winnings are often paid in annual installments. Many companies are willing to pay the winner cash up front for the right to receive the future lottery payments. Search for "lottery winnings" with your favourite Internet search engine. Check out www.lumpsum.com/lottery.html. How do companies make money in this business? Why do you think that this is a popular business to get into? How would you protect winners from being exploited?

SOLUTIONS TO CHECK POINTS

3.1 Value after 5 years would have been $24 \times (1.05)^5 = \$30.63$; after 50 years, $24 \times (1.05)^{50} = \$275.22$.

3.2 When an amount doubles, it increases by 100 percent of itself, giving a growth rate of 100 percent. The future value factor for doubling in 1 year is (1 + 100%), or (1 + 1), which of course is 2. So at the end of the first year, sales will be \$.5 million × 2, or \$1 million. With 4 years of doubling each year, the future value factor is $(2)^4 = 16$, and projected sales after 4 years are $\$.5 \times 16 = \$8$ million.

3.3 Multiply the \$1,000 payment by the 10-year discount factor:

$$PV = \$1{,}000 \times \frac{1}{(1.0853)^{10}} = \$441.06$$

3.4 If the doubling time is 12 years, then $(1 + r)^{12} = 2$, which implies that $1 + r = 2^{1/12} = 1.0595$, or $r =$ 5.95 percent. The Rule of 72 would imply that a doubling time of 12 years is consistent with an interest rate of 6 percent: 72/6 = 12. Thus the Rule of 72 works quite well in this case. If the doubling period is only 2 years, then the interest rate is determined by $(1 + r)^2 = 2$, which implies that $1 + r = 2^{1/2} =$ 1.414, or $r = 41.4$ percent. The Rule of 72 would imply that a doubling time of 2 years is consistent with an interest rate of 36 percent: 72/36 = 2. Thus the Rule of 72 is quite inaccurate when the interest rate is high (or the time to double is short).

3.5 Let D be the unknown deposit to be made in 1 year. The future value of that deposit in 2 years is D × 1.06. It will have only 1 year to grow at 6 percent. We also know that the future value in 2 years of the \$1,500 you have right now will be $\$1{,}500 \times (1.06)^2$. The time line below summarizes all of the information:

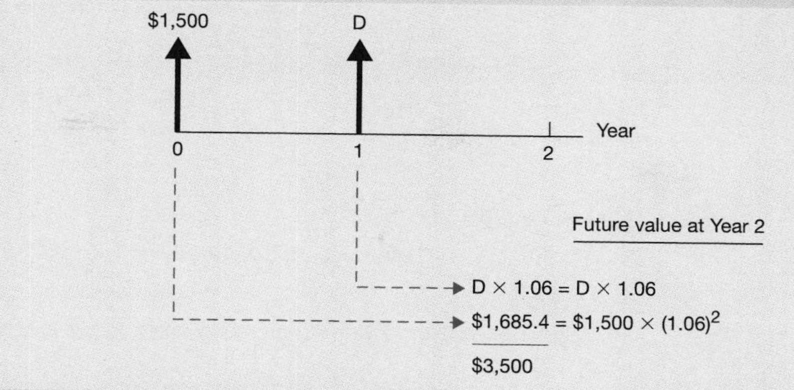

Since the future value of the two deposits must add up to the needed $3,500, you can rearrange to see that D × 1.06 = $3,500 – $1,685.4. Solving for D gives:

$$D = \$1{,}814.6/(1.06) = \$1{,}711.89$$

You will need to deposit about $1,712 in 1 year to have enough. Perhaps you better start lobbying your family for a large cash present in one year!

3.6

Gift at Year	Present Value
1	$10{,}000/(1.07)$ = $ 9,345.79
2	$10{,}000/(1.07)^2$ = 8,734.39
3	$10{,}000/(1.07)^3$ = 8,162.98
4	$10{,}000/(1.07)^4$ = 7,628.95
	$33,872.11

Gift at Year	Future Value at Year 4
1	$10{,}000/(1.07)^3$ = $12,250.43
2	$10{,}000/(1.07)^2$ = 11,449
3	$10{,}000/(1.07)$ = 10,700
4	10,000 = 10,000
	$44,399.43

3.7 The rate is 4/48 = .0833, about 8.3 percent.

3.8 The 4-year discount factor is $1/(1.08)^4 = .735$. The 4-year annuity factor is $[1/.08 - 1/(.08 \times 1.08^4)] = 3.312$. This is the difference between the present value of a $1 perpetuity starting next year and the present value of a $1 perpetuity starting in Year 5:

$$\text{PV (perpetuity starting next year)} = \frac{1}{.08} = 12.50$$

$$- \text{ PV (perpetuity starting in Year 5)} = \frac{1}{.08} \times \frac{1}{(1.08)^4} = 12.50 \times .735 = 9.188$$

$$= \text{ PV (4-year annuity)} = 12.50 - 9.188 = 3.312$$

3.9 Calculate the value of a 19-year annuity, then add the immediate $465,000 payment:

$$\text{19-year annuity factor} = \frac{1}{r} - \frac{1}{r(1+r)^{19}}$$

$$= \frac{1}{.08} - \frac{1}{.08(1.08)^{19}}$$

$$= 9.604$$

$$\text{PV} = \$465{,}000 \times 9.604 = \$4{,}466{,}000$$

$$\text{Total value} = \$4{,}466{,}000 + \$465{,}000$$

$$= \$4{,}931{,}000$$

Starting the 20-year cash-flow stream immediately, rather than waiting 1 year, increases value by nearly $400,000.

3.10 Fifteen years means 180 months. Then

$$\text{Mortgage payment} = \frac{100{,}000}{\text{180-month annuity factor}}$$

$$= \frac{100{,}000}{83.32}$$

$$= \$1{,}200.17 \text{ per month}$$

$1,000 of the payment is interest. The remainder, $200.17, is amortization.

3.11 You will need the present value at 7 percent of a 20-year annuity of $55,000:

Present value = annual spending × annuity factor
The annuity factor is $[1/.07 - 1/(.07 \times 1.07^{20})]$ = 10.594.
Thus you need 55,000 × 10.594 = $582,670.

3.12 If the interest rate is 5 percent, the future value of a 45-year, $1 annuity will be

$$\frac{(1.05)^{45} - 1}{.05} = 159.70$$

Therefore, we need to choose the cash flow, C, so that $C \times 159.70 = \$500{,}000$. This requires that $C = \$500{,}000/159.70 = \$3{,}130.87$. This required savings level is much higher than we found in Example 3.12. At a 5 percent interest rate, current savings do not grow as rapidly as when the interest rate was 10 percent; with less of a boost from compound interest, we need to set aside greater amounts in order to reach the target of $500,000.

3.13 The cost in dollars will increase by 5 percent each year to a value of $\$5 \times (1.05)^{50} = \$57.34$. If the inflation rate is 10 percent, the cost will be $\$5 \times (1.10)^{50} = \$586.95$.

3.14 The weekly cost in 1980 is $250 × (352/100) = $880. The real value of a 1980 salary of $30,000, expressed in real 1950 dollars, is $30,000 × (100/352) = $8,523.

3.15 a. If there's no inflation, real and nominal rates are equal at 8 percent. With 5 percent inflation, the real rate is (1.08/1.05) – 1 = .02857, a bit less than 3 percent.
b. If you want a 3 percent *real* interest rate, you need a 3 percent nominal rate if inflation is zero and an 8.15 percent rate if inflation is 5 percent. Note 1.03 × 1.05 = 1.0815.

3.16 The present value is

$$\text{PV} = \frac{\$5{,}000}{1.08} = \$4{,}629.63$$

The real interest rate is 2.857 percent (see Check Point 3.15*a*). The real cash payment is \$5,000/(1.05) = \$4,761.90. Thus

$$PV = \frac{\$4,761.90}{1.02857} = \$4,629.63$$

3.17 Calculate the real annuity. The real interest rate is 1.10/1.05 – 1 = .0476. We'll round to 4.8 percent. The real annuity is

$$\text{Annual payment} = \frac{\$3,000,000}{\text{30-year annuity factor}}$$

$$= \frac{\$3,000,000}{\frac{1}{.048} - \frac{1}{.048(1.048)^{30}}}$$

$$= \frac{\$3,000,000}{15.73} = \$190,728$$

You can spend this much each year in dollars of constant purchasing power. The purchasing power of each dollar will decline at 5 percent per year, so you'll need to spend more in nominal dollars: \$190,728 × 1.05 = \$200,264 in the second year, \$190,728 × 1.05^2 = \$210,278 in the third year, and so on.

3.18 The quarterly rate is 8/4 = 2 percent. The effective annual rate is $(1.02)^4 - 1 = .0824$, or 8.24 percent.

MINICASE

Alfred Road has reached his 70th birthday and is ready to retire. Mr. Road has no formal training in finance but has saved his money and invested carefully.

Mr. Road owns his home—the mortgage is paid off—and does not want to move. He is a widower, and he wants to bequeath the house and any remaining assets to his daughter.

He has accumulated savings of \$180,000, conservatively invested. The investments are yielding 9 percent interest. Mr. Road also has \$12,000 in a savings account at 5 percent interest. He wants to keep the savings account intact for unexpected expenses or emergencies.

Mr. Road's basic living expenses now average about \$1,500 per month, and he plans to spend \$500 per month on travel and hobbies. To maintain this planned standard of living, he will have to rely on his investment portfolio. The interest from the portfolio is \$16,200 per year (9 percent of \$180,000), or \$1,350 per month.

Mr. Road will also receive \$750 per month in Canada Pension and Old Age Security payments for the rest of his life. These payments are indexed for inflation. That is, they will be automatically increased in proportion to changes in the consumer price index.

Mr. Road's main concern is with inflation. The inflation rate has been below 3 percent recently, but a 3 percent rate is unusually low by historical standards. His pension payments will increase with inflation, but the interest on his investment portfolio will not.

What advice do you have for Mr. Road? Can he safely spend all the interest from his investment portfolio? How much could he withdraw at year-end from that portfolio if he wants to keep its real value intact?

Suppose Mr. Road will live for 20 more years and is willing to use up all of his investment portfolio over that period. He also wants his monthly spending to increase along with inflation over that period. In other words, he wants his monthly spending to stay the same in real terms. How much can he afford to spend per month?

Assume that the investment portfolio continues to yield a 9 percent rate of return and that the inflation rate is 4 percent.

CHAPTER 4

Valuing Bonds

4.1 Bond Characteristics

4.2 Bond Prices and Yields

4.3 Summary

Investment in a new plant and equipment requires money—often a lot of money. Sometimes firms may be able to save enough out of previous earnings to cover the cost of investments, but often they need to raise cash from investors. In broad terms, we can think of two ways to raise new money from investors: borrow the cash or sell additional shares of common stock.

If companies need the money for only a short while, they may borrow it from a bank; if they need it to make long-term investments, they generally issue bonds, which are simply long-term loans. When companies issue bonds, they promise to make a series of fixed interest payments and then to repay the debt. As long as the company generates sufficient cash, the payments on a bond are certain. In this case bond valuation involves straightforward time value of money computations. But there is some chance that even the most blue-chip company will fall on hard times and will not be able to repay its debts. Investors take this default risk into account when they price the bonds and demand a higher interest rate to compensate.

In the first part of this chapter we sidestep the issue of default risk and we focus on Government of Canada bonds. We show how bond prices are determined by market interest rates and how those prices respond to changes in rates. We also consider the yield to maturity and discuss why a bond's yield may vary with its time to maturity.

Later in the chapter we look at corporate bonds where there is also a possibility of default. We will see how bond ratings provide a guide to the default risk and how low-grade bonds offer higher promised yields.

In Chapter 13 we will look in more detail at the securities that companies issue, and we will see that there are many variations on bond design. But for now, we'll keep our focus on garden variety bonds and general principles of bond valuation.

After studying this chapter you should be able to

- Distinguish among the bond's coupon rate, current yield, and yield to maturity.
- Find the market price of a bond given its yield to maturity, find a bond's yield given its price, and demonstrate why prices and yields vary inversely.
- Show why bonds exhibit interest rate risk.
- Understand why investors pay attention to bond ratings and demand a higher interest rate for bonds with low ratings.

4.1

Bond Characteristics

bond Security that obligates the issuer to make specified payments to the bondholder.

coupon The interest payments paid to the bondholder.

face value Payment at the maturity of the bond. Also called *par value*, or *maturity value*, or *principal*.

coupon rate Annual interest payment as a percentage of face value.

Governments and corporations borrow money by selling **bonds** to investors. The money they collect when the bond is *issued,* or sold to the public, is the amount of the loan. In return, they agree to make specified payments to the bondholders, who are the lenders. When you own a bond, you generally receive a fixed interest payment each year until the bond matures. This payment is known as the **coupon** because most bonds used to have coupons that the investors clipped off and mailed to the bond issuer to claim the interest payment. At maturity, the debt is repaid: The borrower pays the bondholder the bond's **face value** (equivalently, its *par value*, *maturity value* or *principal*).

How do bonds work? Several years ago, the federal government raised money by selling 6.5 percent coupon, June 1, 2004 maturity, Government of Canada bonds. Each bond has a face value of $1,000. Because the **coupon rate** is 6.5 percent, the government makes coupon payments of 6.5 percent of $1,000, or $65 each year.[1] When the bond matures on June 1, 2004, the government must pay the face value of the bond, $1,000, in addition to the final coupon payment.

Suppose that in 2001 you decided to buy the 6.5s of 2004, that is, the 6.5 percent coupon bonds maturing in 2004. If you planned to hold the bond until maturity, you would then have looked forward to the cash flows depicted in Figure 4.1. The initial cash flow is negative and equal to the price you have to pay for the bond. Thereafter, the cash flows equal the annual coupon payment until the maturity date in 2004, when you receive the face value of the bond, $1,000, in addition to the final coupon payment.

READING THE FINANCIAL PAGES

Bond prices are reported in the financial press and are always for the previous day's trading activity. Figure 4.2 is an excerpt from the bond quotations for June 12, 2001, reported in the *Globe and Mail*, on June 13, 2001. The entry for the 6.5 percent Canada bonds maturing in June 2004 that we just looked at is highlighted. The prices reported in this newspaper were provided by RBC Dominion Securities, one of Canada's largest bond dealers (www.rbcds.com).

The prices quoted are the "final bid-side price as of 5 pm." The *bid* price is the price

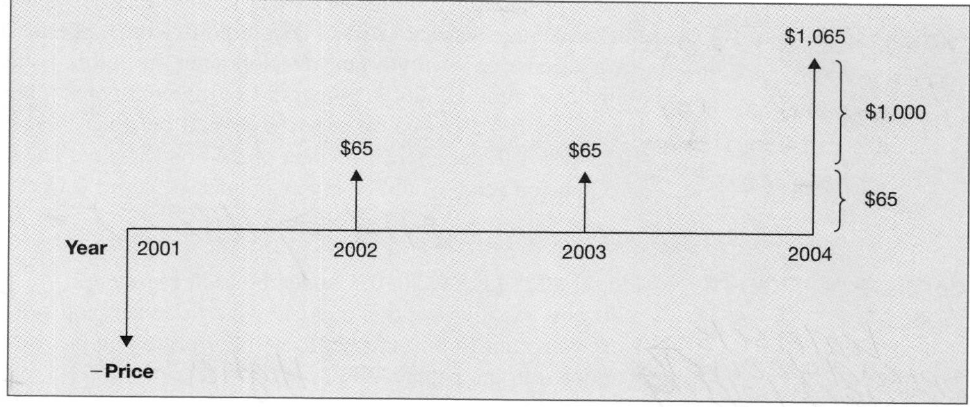

FIGURE 4.1
Cash flows to an investor in the 6.5 percent coupon bond, maturing in the year 2004

[1] In Canada, these coupon payments typically would come in two semiannual installments of $32.50 each. To keep things simple for now, we will assume one coupon payment per year.

FIGURE 4.2

Government of Canada bond quotes from the Globe and Mail, *June 13, 2001*

CANADIAN BONDS

Provided by RBC Dominion Securities

Selected quotations, with changes since the previous day, on actively traded bond issues yesterday. Yields are calculated to full maturity. Price is the final bid-side price as of 5 pm yesterday.

Issuer	Coupon	Maturity	Price	Yield	Price $ Chg
GOVERNMENT OF CANADA					
Canada	5.500	Sep 01/02	101.15	4.51	−0.01
Canada	6.000	Dec 01/02	101.96	4.60	−0.01
Canada	11.250	Dec 15/02	109.49	4.64	−0.02
Canada	11.750	Feb 01/03	110.90	4.73	−0.02
Canada	7.250	Jun 01/03	104.58	4.78	−0.01
Canada	5.750	Jun 01/03	101.80	4.78	−0.01
Canada	5.250	Sep 01/03	100.74	4.89	0.00
Canada	7.500	Dec 01/03	105.81	4.97	0.00
Canada	10.250	Feb 01/04	112.62	5.06	0.02
Canada	6.500	Jun 01/04	103.77	5.11	0.03
Canada	5.000	Sep 01/04	99.51	5.17	0.05
Canada	9.000	Dec 01/04	111.82	5.22	0.05
Canada	12.000	Mar 01/05	122.28	5.30	0.07
Canada	6.000	Sep 01/05	102.53	5.32	0.08
Canada	12.250	Sep 01.05	125.83	5.32	0.08
Canada	8.750	Dec 01/05	113.28	5.36	0.08
Canada	5.750	Sep 01/06	101.59	5.39	0.10
Canada	14.000	Oct 01/06	138.78	5.46	0.11
Canada	7.000	Dec 01/06	107.29	5.44	0.11
Canada	7.250	Jun 01/07	108.87	5.48	0.12
Canada	12.750	Mar 01/08	139.49	5.60	0.23
Canada	10.000	Jun 01/08	125.44	5.54	0.22
Canada	6.000	Jun 01/08	102.54	5.55	0.20
Canada	5.500	Jun 01/09	99.36	5.60	0.26
Canada	9.500	Jun 01/10	127.03	5.62	0.34
Canada	5.500	Jun 01/10	99.10	5.63	0.30
Canada	9.000	Mar 01/11	124.39	5.69	0.37
Canada	6.000	Jun 01/11	102.61	5.65	0.34
Canada	10.250	Mar 15/14	140.04	5.77	0.48
Canada	11.250	Jun 01/15	151.93	5.78	0.54
Canada	9.750	Jun 01/21	144.05	5.95	0.48
Canada	9.250	Jun 01/22	138.75	5.98	0.48
Canada	8.000	Jun 01/23	125.28	5.93	0.46
Canada	9.000	Jun 01/25	138.16	5.98	0.51
Canada	8.000	Jun 01/27	127.14	5.94	0.45
Canada	5.750	Jun 01/29	98.70	5.84	0.35
Real Return	4.250	Dec 01/21	109.66	3.58	0.00
Real Return	4.250	Dec 01/26	111.11	3.58	0.00
Real Return	4.000	Dec 01/31	107.65	3.59	0.00

Source: The *Globe and Mail*, June 13, 2001.

you receive if you *sell* the bond to a bond dealer. Prices are quoted as percentage of face value. Thus for the 6.5 percent bond, the price of 103.77 means 103.77 percent of the $1,000 face value, or $1,037.7. If you want to *buy* the bond, you pay the *asked* price. Just as used car dealers earn their living by reselling cars at higher prices than they paid for them, so the bond dealer needs to charge a *spread* between the bid and asked prices.

The next column, Yield, shows the *yield to maturity*, the rate of return investors will receive if they buy the bond at the quoted bond price and hold it to maturity in 2004. You can see that the Canada bonds at 6.5 percent offer investors a return of 5.11 percent. We will explain shortly how this figure was calculated. The final column, Price $ Chg, shows the change in price from the previous day. Thus the Canada 6.5s of 2004 price on June 11 was 103.74.

If you wanted to buy the Canada 6.5s of 2004, you would contact a bond dealer. Dealers hold inventories of bonds and are typically part of financial institutions such as banks and brokerage houses. This is an *over-the-counter market*, where securities are not traded in one central place. For example, TD Waterhouse offers bonds to retail investors through its on-line brokerage service (www.TDWaterhouse.com). See the nearby Finance in Action box for a discussion of important developments in online bond trading. At TD Waterhouse's website on June 12, 2001, you could sell the 6.5 percent bond for 103.289 (bid price) and buy it for 104.299 (ask price). The spread between the bid and ask prices is 104.299 – 103.289 = 1.01, or about 1 percent of the bond's value. The spread for a large investor, such as a pension fund, would be much smaller, closer to 0.1 percent of the bond's value.

CHECK POINT 4.1

Find the 5.5 June 1, 2010, Canada bond in Figure 4.2.

a. If you already own this bond, at what price can you sell it?

b. If you want to buy the bond, will the price you pay be higher or lower than the price quoted in the paper? Why?

c. How much did the price change from the previous day?

d. What annual interest payment does the bond make?

e. What is the bond's yield to maturity?

FINANCE IN ACTION

Hope for Retail Bond Traders

The development by the banks and independent dealers of online bond trading systems is good news for retail investors. It should help bond trading become more visible and comparable to what online investors in stocks now have—eventually.

Why Is Visibility a Problem for Individual Bond Investors?

Most bonds are fixed-income investments—that is, the owner receives a fixed amount of dollars of interest at intervals of usually six months, over the fixed life of the bond.

At the end, the owner receives the full face value amount of the bond as well. This means the rate of return on your investment depends directly on the price you pay. The more you pay, the lower the interest you get on each dollar you invest.

How Do You Know What's a Reasonable Price?

In the stock market you can easily find a reasonable starting point. Investors are accustomed to being able to check the last price at which a stock traded from information that's available to everyone. But when did you last see a ticker tape showing bond prices?

This lack of reliable price information is because there is no central reporting system for actual bond transaction prices. The usual industry excuse is that it's because bonds are traded over a telecommunications network by bond dealers, scattered around the country, and buying and selling them as owners not agents.

But so are the well-known stocks that trade on the Nasdaq stock market in the United States. Recent transaction prices in that market are as widely available as the [stock trading] prices on the New York and Toronto stock exchanges. There are other problems with the Nasdaq market but that is not one of them.

A would-be investor in bonds has to go to a bond dealer and ask for a quote on available issues. Oddly, for stock investors who first encounter this, there will be no mention of commission. What's on the broker's mind is how much he or she can mark up the bond price to a buyer, over the so-called transfer price. This is an internal price set by the firm at which the bond is transferred to the broker from the firm's inventory. This may or may not be what the bond cost the firm.

If the client wants to sell the bond instead, the broker has to decide how much to mark down the price the client gets. The broker gets the mark up or the markdown instead of a commission.

What decides the size of the mark ups or markdowns? They vary from firm to firm, from broker to broker, and from one minute to the next. If you are a good client who provides a lot of business and are not a pest, your "commission" may be small or even zero. You may do similarly well if your broker is hungry.

But these hidden charges provide less scrupulous brokers an opportunity to levy an unconscionably high "commission" without the client being aware of what's happening. That's because, unlike stocks, no commission charge is indicated to the client on an order confirmation, and there is no widely available, reliable source of the current market price for bonds against which you can check what your broker quotes.

The arrival of more online bond trading firms will be welcome because their published quotes improve the visibility of bond prices.

But until the Canadian investment industry stops dragging its feet on a long delayed project to provide an online source of actual bond transaction prices, there will be nothing for bond investors comparable to the ubiquitous stock market ticker.

Source: Adapted from Hugh Anderson, "Light Appears at the End of the Online Bond Tunnel: Consortium of Industry Players Ready to Launch Site," *Financial Post* (*National Post*), F 24'01, C5.

4.2 Bond Prices and Yields

In Figure 4.1, we examined the cash flows that an investor in 6.5 percent Canada bonds would receive. How much would you be willing to pay for this stream of cash flows? To find out, you need to look at the interest rate that investors could earn on similar securities. In 2001, Canada bonds with 3-year maturities offered a return of about 5.1 percent. Therefore, to value the 6.5s of 2004, we need to discount the prospective stream of cash flows at 5.1 percent:

$$\text{PV} = \frac{\$65}{(1+r)} + \frac{\$65}{(1+r)^2} + \frac{\$1{,}065}{(1+r)^3}$$
$$= \frac{\$65}{(1.051)} + \frac{\$65}{(1.051)^2} + \frac{\$1{,}065}{(1.051)^3} = \$1{,}038.05$$

Bond prices are usually expressed as a percentage of their face value. Thus we can say that our 6.5 percent Canada bond is worth 103.805 percent of face value, and its price would usually be quoted as 103.805.

Did you notice that the coupon payments on the bond are an annuity? In other words, the holder of our 6.5 percent Canada bond receives a level stream of coupon payments of \$65 per year for each of the 3 years. At maturity the bondholder gets an additional payment of \$1,000. Therefore, you can use the annuity formula to value the coupon payments and then add on the present value of the final payment of face value:

$$\begin{aligned} \textbf{PV} &= \textbf{PV (coupons)} + \textbf{PV (face value)} \\ &= \textbf{(coupon} \times \textbf{annuity factor)} + \textbf{(face value} \times \textbf{discount factor)} \qquad (4.1) \\ &= \$65 \times \left[\frac{1}{.051} - \frac{1}{.051(1.051)^3}\right] + 1{,}000 \times \frac{1}{1.051^3} \\ &= \$176.68 + \$861.37 = \$1{,}038.05 \end{aligned}$$

If you need to value a bond with many years to run before maturity, it is usually easiest to value the coupon payments as an annuity and then add on the present value of the final payment.

CHECK POINT 4.2

Calculate the present value of a 6-year bond with a 9 percent coupon. The interest rate is 12 percent.

EXAMPLE 4.1 *Bond Prices and Semiannual Coupon Payments*

Thus far we've assumed that interest payments occur annually. This is the case for bonds in many European countries, but in Canada most bonds make coupon payments *semiannually.* So when you hear that a bond in Canada has a coupon rate of 6.5 percent, you can generally assume that the bond makes a payment of \$65/2 = \$32.50 every 6 months. Similarly, when investors in Canada refer to the bond's interest rate, they usually mean the semiannually compounded interest rate. Thus an interest rate quoted at 5.1 percent really means that the 6-month rate is 5.1/2 = 2.55 percent.[2] The actual cash flows on the Canada bond are illustrated in Figure 4.3. To value the bond a bit more precisely, we should have discounted the series of semiannual payments by the semiannual rate of interest as follows:

[2] You may have noticed that the interest rate compounded semiannually on the bond is also the bond's APR, although this term is generally not used by bond investors. To find the effective rate, we can use a formula that we used in Section 3.6:

$$\text{Effective annual rate} = \left(1 + \frac{\text{APR}}{m}\right)^m - 1$$

where m is the number of payments each year. In the case of our Canada bond,

$$\text{Effective annual rate} = \left(1 + \frac{.051}{2}\right)^2 - 1 = 1.0255^2 - 1 = .0517, \text{ or } 5.17\%$$

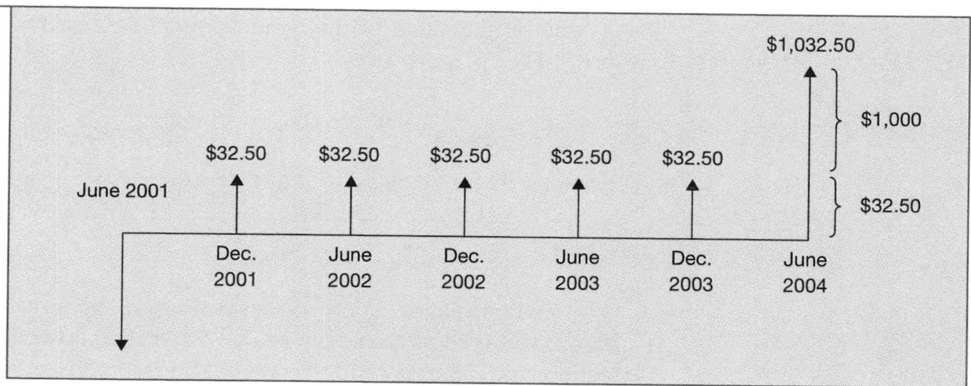

FIGURE 4.3
Cash flows to an investor in the 6.5 percent coupon bond, maturing in 2004. The bond pays semiannual coupons, so there are two payments of $32.50 each year.

$$
\begin{aligned}
\text{PV} &= \frac{\$32.5}{(1.0255)} + \frac{\$32.5}{(1.0255)^2} + \frac{\$32.5}{(1.0255)^3} + \frac{\$32.5}{(1.0255)^4} + \frac{\$32.5}{(1.0255)^5} + \frac{\$1{,}032.5}{(1.0255)^6} \\
&= \$1{,}038.49
\end{aligned}
$$

which is slightly more than the value of $1,038.05 that we obtained when we treated the coupon payments as annual rather than semiannual.[3] Since semiannual coupon payments just add to the arithmetic, we will stick to our approximation for the rest of the chapter and assume annual interest payments.

HOW BOND PRICES VARY WITH INTEREST RATES

As interest rates change, so do bond prices. For example, suppose that investors demanded an interest rate of 6.5 percent on 3-year government bonds. What would be the price of the Canada 6.5s of 2004? Just repeat the last calculation with a discount rate of $r = .065$:

$$
\text{PV at } 6.5\% = \frac{\$65}{(1.065)} + \frac{\$65}{(1.065)^2} + \frac{\$1{,}065}{(1.065)^3} = \$1{,}000.00
$$

Thus when the interest rate is the same as the coupon rate (6.5 percent in our example), the bond sells for its face value.

We first valued the Canada bond with an interest rate of 5.1 percent, which is lower than the coupon rate. In that case the price of the bond was *higher* than its face value. We then valued it using an interest rate that is equal to the coupon rate and found that bond price equalled face value. You have probably already guessed that when the cash flows are discounted at a rate that is *higher* than the bond's coupon rate, the bond is worth *less* than its face value. The following example confirms that this is the case.

EXAMPLE 4.2 *Bond Prices and Interest Rates*

Investors will pay $1,000 for a 6.5 percent, 3-year Canada bond, when the interest rate is 6.5 percent. Suppose that the interest rate is higher than the coupon rate at, say, 15 percent.

[3] Why is the present value a bit higher in this case? Because now we recognize that half the annual coupon payment is received only 6 months into the year, rather than at year-end. Because part of the coupon income is received earlier, its present value is higher.

Now what is the value of the bond? Simple! We just repeat our initial calculation but with $r = .15$:

$$\text{PV at 15\%} = \frac{\$65}{(1.15)} + \frac{\$65}{(1.15)^2} + \frac{\$1{,}065}{(1.15)^3} = \$805.93$$

The bond sells for 80.59 percent of face value.

We conclude that when the market interest rate exceeds the coupon rate, bonds sell for less than face value. When the market interest rate is below the coupon rate, bonds sell for more than face value.

YIELD TO MATURITY VERSUS CURRENT YIELD

Suppose you are considering the purchase of a 3-year bond with a coupon rate of 10 percent. Your investment adviser quotes a price for the bond. How do you calculate the rate of return the bond offers?

For bonds priced at face value the answer is easy. The rate of return is the coupon rate. We can check this by setting out the cash flows on your investment:

	Cash Paid to You in Year			
You Pay	**1**	**2**	**3**	**Rate of Return**
$1,000	$100	$100	$1,100	10%

Notice that in each year you earn 10 percent on your money ($100/$1,000). In the final year you also get back your original investment of $1,000. Therefore, your total return is 10 percent, the same as the coupon rate.

Now suppose that the market price of the 3-year bond is $1,136.16. Your cash flows are as follows:

	Cash Paid to You in Year			
You Pay	**1**	**2**	**3**	**Rate of Return**
$1,136.16	$100	$100	$1,100	?

current yield Annual coupon payments divided by bond price.

What's the rate of return now? Notice that you are paying out $1,136.16 and receiving an annual income of $100. So your income as a proportion of the initial outlay is $100/$1,136.16 = .088, or 8.8 percent. This is sometimes called the bond's **current yield.**

However, total return depends on both interest income and any capital gains or losses. A current yield of 8.8 percent may sound attractive, only until you realize that the bond's price must fall. The price today is $1,136.16, but when the bond matures 3 years from now, the bond will sell for its face value, or $1,000. A price decline (i.e., a *capital loss*) of $136.16 is guaranteed, so the overall return over the next 3 years must be less than the 8.8 percent current yield.

Let us generalize. A bond that is priced above its face value is said to sell at a *premium.* Investors who buy a bond at a premium face a capital loss over the life of the bond, so the return on these bonds is always *less* than the bond's current yield. A bond priced below face value sells at a *discount.* Investors in discount bonds face a capital *gain* over the life of the bond; the return on these bonds is *greater* than the current yield:

Because it focuses only on current income and ignores prospective price increases or decreases, the current yield mismeasures the bond's total rate of return. It overstates the return of premium bonds and understates that of discount bonds.

yield to maturity Interest rate for which the present value of the bond's payments equals the price.

We need a measure of return that takes account of both current yield and the change in a bond's value over its life. The standard measure is called **yield to maturity.** The yield to maturity is the answer to the following question: At what interest rate would the bond be correctly priced?

The yield to maturity is defined as the discount rate that makes the present value of the bond's payments equal to its price.

If you can buy the 3-year bond at face value, the yield to maturity is the coupon rate, 10 percent. We can confirm this by noting that when we discount the cash flows at 10 percent, the present value of the bond is equal to its \$1,000 face value:

$$\text{PV at 10\%} = \frac{\$100}{(1.10)} + \frac{\$100}{(1.10)^2} + \frac{\$1,100}{(1.10)^3} = \$1,000.00$$

But if you have to buy the 3-year bond for \$1,136.16, the yield to maturity is only 5 percent. At that discount rate, the bond's present value equals its actual market price, \$1,136.16:

$$\text{PV at 5\%} = \frac{\$100}{(1.05)} + \frac{\$100}{(1.05)^2} + \frac{\$1,100}{(1.05)^3} = \$1,136.16$$

EXAMPLE 4.3 *Calculating Yield to Maturity for the Canada Bond*

We found the value of the 6.5 percent coupon Canada bond by discounting at a 5.1 percent interest rate. We could have phrased the question the other way around: If the price of the bond is \$1,038.05, what return do investors expect? We need to find the yield to maturity, in other words, the discount rate r that solves the following equation:

$$\text{Price} = \frac{\$65}{(1+r)} + \frac{\$65}{(1+r)^2} + \frac{\$1,065}{(1+r)^3} = \$1,038.05$$

To find the yield to maturity, most people use a financial calculator. For our Government of Canada bond you would enter a PV of \$1,038.05.[4] The bond provides a regular payment of \$65, entered as PMT = 65. The bond has a future value of \$1,000, so FV = 1,000. The bond life is 3 years, so $n = 3$. Now compute the interest rate, and you will find that the yield to maturity is 5.1 percent. The nearby Financial Calculator box reviews the use of the financial calculator in bond valuation problems.

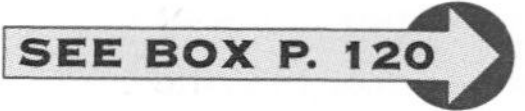

Example 4.3 illustrates that the yield to maturity depends on the coupon payments that you receive each year (\$65), the price of the bond (\$1,038.05), and the final repayment of face value (\$1,000). Thus it is a measure of the total return on this bond, accounting for

[4] Actually on most calculators you would enter 1,038.05 as a negative number, (–1,038.05), because the purchase of the bond represents a cash *outflow*.

FINANCIAL CALCULATOR

Bond Valuation on a Financial Calculator

In Chapter 3 we saw that financial calculators can compute the present values of level annuities as well as the present values of one-time future cash flows. Coupon bonds present both of these characteristics: The coupon payments are level annuities and the final payment of par value is an additional one-time payment. Thus for the coupon bond we looked at in Example 4.3, you would treat the periodic payment as PMT = \$65, the final or future one-time payment as FV = \$1,000, the number of periods as $n = 3$ years, and the interest rate as the yield to maturity of the bond, $i = 5.1$ percent. You would thus compute the value of the bond using the following sequence of key strokes. By the way, the order in which the various inputs for the bond valuation problem are entered does not matter.

Hewlett-Packard HP-10B	Sharp EL-733A	Texas Instruments BA II Plus
65 [PMT]	65 [PMT]	65 [PMT]
1000 [FV]	1000 [FV]	1000 [FV]
3 [N]	3 [n]	3 [N]
5.1 [I/YR]	5.1 [i]	5.1 [I/Y]
[PV]	[COMP] [PV]	[CPT] [PV]

Your calculator should now display a value of –1,038.05. The minus sign reminds us that the initial cash flow is negative: You have to pay to buy the bond.

You can also use the calculator to find the yield to maturity of a bond. For example, if you buy this bond for \$1,038.05, you should find that its yield to maturity is 5.1 percent. Let's check that this is so. You enter the PV as –1,038.05 because you buy the bond for this price. Thus to solve for the interest rate, use the following key strokes:

Hewlett-Packard HP-10B	Sharp EL-733A	Texas Instruments BA II Plus
65 [PMT]	65 [PMT]	65 [PMT]
1000 [FV]	1000 [FV]	1000 [FV]
3 [N]	3 [n]	3 [N]
–1038.05 [PV]	–1038.05 [PV]	–1038.05 [PV]
[I/YR]	[COMP] [i]	[CPT] [I/Y]

Your calculator should now display 5.1 percent, the yield to maturity of the bond.

both coupon income and price change for someone who buys the bond today and holds it until maturity. Bond investors often refer loosely to a bond's "yield." It's a safe bet that they are talking about its yield to maturity rather than its current yield.

The only *general* procedure for calculating yield to maturity is trial and error. You guess at an interest rate and calculate the present value of the bond's payments. If the present value is greater than the actual price, your discount rate must have been too low, so try a higher interest rate (since a higher rate results in a lower PV). Conversely, if PV is less than price, you must reduce the interest rate. In fact, when you use a financial calculator to compute yield to maturity, you will notice that it takes the calculator a few moments to compute the interest rate. This is because it must perform a series of trial-and-error calculations.[5]

☑ CHECK POINT 4.3

A 4-year maturity bond with a 14 percent coupon rate can be bought for \$1,200. What is the yield to maturity? You will need to use the trial-and-error method, or a financial calculator to answer this question.

[5] If you don't have a financial calculator, estimate the yield to maturity with an approximation formula. Check the estimate and fine tune it using the trial-and-error method to be confident of its accuracy. The approximation formula is

$$\text{YTM} = \frac{\text{annual coupon payment} + (\text{par value} - \text{current price})/\text{years to maturity}}{(\text{par value} + \text{current price})/2}$$

Figure 4.4 is a graphical view of yield to maturity. It shows the present value of the 6.5 percent Canada bond for different interest rates. The actual bond price, $1,038.05, is marked on the vertical axis. A line is drawn from this price over to the present value curve and then down to the interest rate, 5.1 percent. If we picked a higher or lower figure for the interest rate, then we would not obtain a bond price of $1,038.05. Thus we know that the yield to maturity on the bond must be 5.1 percent.

Figure 4.4 also illustrates a fundamental relationship between interest rates and bond prices:

> **When the interest rate rises, the present value of the payments to be received by the bondholder falls, and bond prices fall. Conversely, declines in the interest rate increase the present value of those payments and result in higher prices.**

A gentle warning! People sometimes confuse the *interest rate*—that is, the return that investors currently require—with the interest, or coupon, payment on the bond. Although interest rates change from day to day, the $65 coupon payments on our Canada bonds are fixed when the bond is issued. Changes in interest rates affect the *present value* of the coupon payments but not the payments themselves.

RATE OF RETURN

rate of return Total income per period per dollar invested.

When you invest in a bond, you receive a regular coupon payment. As bond prices change, you may also make a capital gain or loss. For example, suppose you buy the 6.5 percent Canada bond today for a price of $1,038.05 and sell it next year at a price of $1,045. The return on your investment is the $65 coupon payment plus the price change of ($1,045 – $1,038.05) = $6.95. The **rate of return** on your investment of $1,038.05 is

$$\textbf{Rate of return} = \frac{\textbf{coupon income + price change}}{\textbf{investment}} \tag{4.2}$$

$$= \frac{\$65 + \$6.95}{\$1,038.05} = .0693, \text{ or } 6.93\%$$

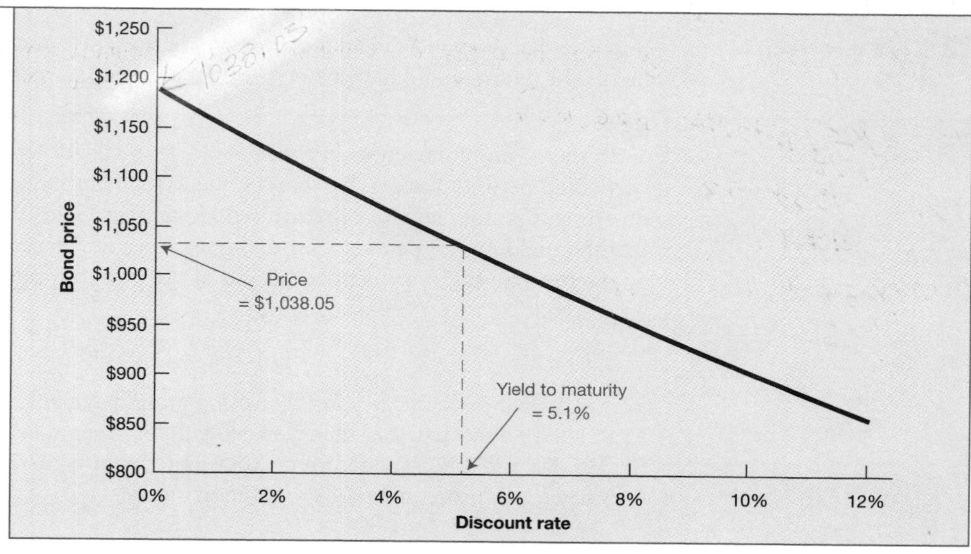

FIGURE 4.4
The value of the 6.5 percent bond is lower at higher discount rates. The yield to maturity is the discount rate at which price equals present value of cash flows.

Because bond prices fall when market interest rates rise and rise when market rates fall, the rate of return that you earn on a bond will also fluctuate with market interest rates. This is why we say bonds are subject to interest rate risk.

Do not confuse the bond's rate of return over a particular investment period with its yield to maturity. The yield to maturity is defined as the discount rate that equates the bond's price to the present value of all its promised cash flows. It is a measure of the average rate of return you will earn over the bond's life if you hold it to maturity. In contrast, the rate of return can be calculated for any particular holding period and is based on the actual income and the capital gain or loss on the bond over that period. The difference between yield to maturity and rate of return for a particular period is emphasized in the following example.

▶ EXAMPLE 4.4 *Rate of Return versus Yield to Maturity*

Our 6.5 percent coupon bond with maturity 2004 currently has 3 years left until maturity and sells today for \$1,038.05. Its yield to maturity is 5.1 percent. Suppose that by the end of the year, interest rates have fallen and the bond's yield to maturity is now only 4 percent. What will be the bond's rate of return?

At the end of the year, the bond will have only 2 years to maturity. If investors then demand an interest rate of 4 percent, the value of the bond will be

$$\text{PV at } 4\% = \frac{\$65}{(1.04)} + \frac{\$1{,}065}{(1.04)^2} = \$1{,}047.15$$

You invested \$1,038.05. At the end of the year you receive a coupon payment of \$65 and have a bond worth \$1,047.15. Your rate of return is therefore

$$\text{Rate of return} = \frac{\$65 + (\$1{,}047.15 - \$1{,}038.05)}{\$1{,}038.05} = .0714, \text{ or } 7.14\%$$

The yield to maturity at the start of the year was 5.1 percent. However, because interest rates fell during the year, the bond price rose, and this increased the rate of return.

☑ CHECK POINT 4.4

Suppose that the bond's yield to maturity had risen to 7 percent during the year. Show that its rate of return would have been *less* than the yield to maturity.

Is there *any* connection between yield to maturity and the rate of return during a particular period? Yes: If the bond's yield to maturity remains unchanged during an investment period, its rate of return will equal that yield. We can check this by assuming that the yield on 6.5 percent Canada bonds stays at 5.1 percent. If investors still demand an interest rate of 5.1 percent at the end of the year, the value of the bond will be

$$\text{PV} = \frac{\$65}{(1.051)} + \frac{\$1{,}065}{(1.051)^2} = \$1{,}025.99$$

At the end of the year you receive a coupon payment of \$65 and have a bond worth \$1,025.99, somewhat less than you paid for it. Your total profit is \$65 + (\$1,025.99 – \$1,038.05) = \$52.94. The return on your investment is therefore \$52.94/\$1,038.05 = .051, or 5.1 percent, just equal to the yield to maturity.

When interest rates do not change, the bond price changes with time so that the total return on the bond is equal to the yield to maturity. If the bond's yield to maturity increases, the rate of return during the period will be less than that yield. If the yield decreases, the rate of return will be greater than the yield.

CHECK POINT 4.5

Suppose you buy the bond next year for $1,025.99, and hold it for yet another year, so that at the end of that time it has only 1 year to maturity. Show that if the bond's yield to maturity is still 5.1 percent, your rate of return also will be 5.1 percent and the bond price will be $1,013.32.

The solid curve in Figure 4.5 plots the price of a 30-year maturity, 6.5 percent Canada bond over time assuming that its yield to maturity remains at 5.1 percent. The price declines gradually until the maturity date, when it finally reaches face value. In each period, the price decline offsets the coupon income by just enough to reduce total return to 5.1 percent. The dotted curve in Figure 4.5 shows the corresponding price path for a 30-year maturity, 3 percent coupon Canada bond, also assuming its yield to maturity remains at 5.1 percent. This low-coupon bond currently sells at a discount to face value. The coupon income provides less than a competitive rate of return, so the bond sells below par. Its price gradually approaches face value, however, and the price gain each year brings its total return up to the market interest rate of 5.1 percent.

TAXES AND RATES OF RETURN

Taxes reduce the rate of return on an investment. Let's go back to Example 4.4. You bought a bond for $1,038.05 and sold it 1 year later for $1,047.15 and received one coupon payment of $65. The *before-tax* rate of return on your 1-year investment was 7.14 percent. However, as we discussed in Chapter 2, interest income is fully taxable, and 50 percent of

FIGURE 4.5
Bond prices over time, assuming an unchanged yield to maturity. Prices of both premium and discount bonds approach face value as their maturity date approaches.

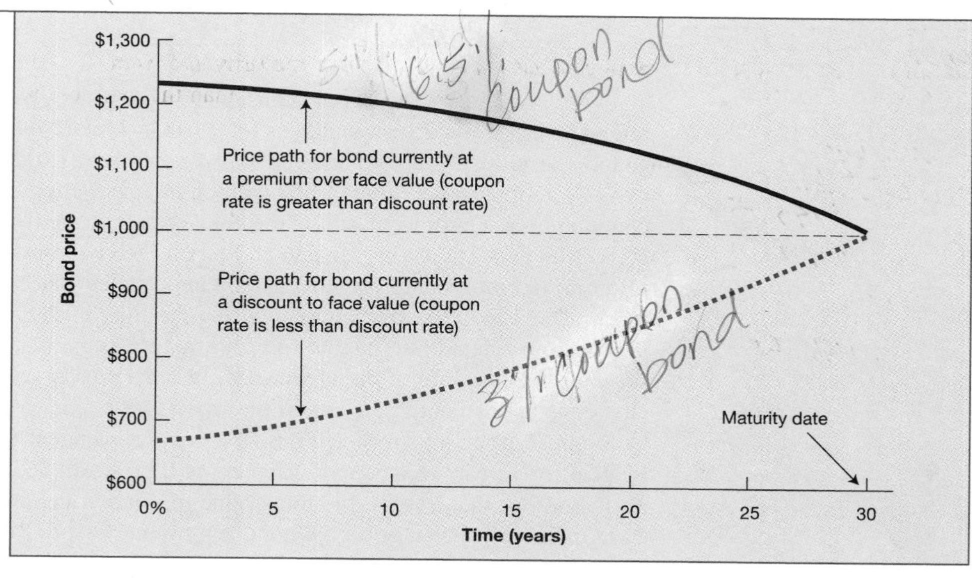

capital gains are taxable. To figure out the *after-tax* rate of return on the investment, convert the cash flows to their after-tax values by subtracting the relevant taxes. If your personal tax rate is 35 percent, the tax on the coupon payment of \$65 is

$$\text{Tax on coupon income} = \text{personal tax rate} \times \text{coupon income}$$
$$= .35 \times \$65 = \$22.75$$

After taxes, the coupon income is

$$\text{After-tax coupon income} = \text{coupon income} - \text{tax on coupon income}$$
$$= \$65 - \$22.75 = \$42.25$$

Likewise, the tax on the capital gain is

$$\text{Tax on capital gain} = \text{personal tax rate} \times .5 \times \text{capital gain}$$
$$= .35 \times .5 \times (\$1{,}047.15 - \$1{,}038.05) = \$1.5925$$

and the after-tax capital gain is

$$\text{After-tax capital gain} = \text{capital gain} - \text{tax on capital gain}$$
$$= (\$1{,}047.15 - \$1{,}038.05) - \$1.5925 = \$7.5075$$

Your after-tax rate of return is therefore

$$\text{After-tax rate of return} = \frac{\text{after-tax coupon income} + \text{after-tax capital gain}}{\text{investment}}$$
$$= \frac{\$42.25 + \$7.5075}{\$1{,}038.05} = .0479, \text{ or } 4.79\%$$

As you can see, taxes have a material effect on the rate of return on your investment! Here, the 7.14 percent before-tax rate of return is only 4.79 percent once you consider the taxes you must pay on your investment income.

CHECK POINT 4.6

Suppose you bought an 8 percent coupon bond for \$1,200 and sold it 1 year later for \$1,150. Calculate the before-tax and after-tax rate of return on your investment, if your personal tax rate is 40 percent and you can use the capital loss to reduce your taxes.

In our examples we have only considered 1-year investments. How do you calculate the rate of return if the investment lasts longer than 1 year? Suppose you buy the 6.5 percent coupon bond for \$1,038.05 and sell it in 2 years for \$1,015.25. You receive cash flows at two different points in time: a \$65 coupon payment after one year, and then another \$65 coupon plus the cash from selling the bond after 2 years. If you ignore the fact that you received the first \$65 early, you can add up all the coupon payments and calculate the rate of return like we did above. This method understates your rate of return—you ignored the value of investing the first coupon during the time of the bond investment. The standard approach to calculating the rate of return is to assume that the first coupon is reinvested for the remaining life of the investment. In other words, calculate the future value of that first coupon payment at the end of the second year.

Suppose when you received the first coupon payment you immediately invested at 4 percent for 1 year. That coupon payment will be worth \$65 × 1.04, or \$67.6, 1 year later. At the end of the 2 years, the total value of coupon income received is \$67.6 + \$65, or \$132.6. The price change on the bond is a capital loss: \$1,015.25 – \$1,038.05, or –\$22.8. The rate of return on the investment is

$$\text{Rate of return} = \frac{\$132.6 - \$22.8}{\$1{,}038.05} = .10578, \text{ or } 10.58\%$$

Did you notice that this is a *two-year* rate of return? The effective annual equivalent is $(1.1058)^{1/2} - 1$, or 5.2 percent.

How do you know the rate at which the intermediate coupons payments are invested? You can use the actual rates available at the time you received the coupons. Another approach is to use a variation on the yield-to-maturity calculation. Using this method, your rate of return is the discount rate, that equates the purchase price to the present value of the coupons and the price you receive when you sell the bond. This assumes that all of the coupons are invested at that discount rate for the remaining time you own the bond. You can use this approach to calculate the after-tax rate of return too—just use the after-tax cash flows. We will see this approach to calculating rates of return again in Chapter 6, but there we will call it the *internal rate of return*.

▸ EXAMPLE 4.5 *Calculating the Rate of Return on a Two-Year Bond Investment*

You buy a 6.5 percent bond for $1,038.05 and sell it for $1,015.25 2 years later. What is the rate of return on your investment if you use the yield-to-maturity approach? Using a calculator, enter PV of –$1,038.05, PMT of $65, FV of $1,015.25, and $n = 2$. Now compute the interest rate, which is your rate of return. You should get 5.19 percent.

INTEREST RATE RISK

interest rate risk The risk in bond prices due to fluctuations in interest rates.

We have seen that bond prices fluctuate as interest rates change. In other words, bonds exhibit **interest rate risk.** Bond investors cross their fingers that market interest rates will fall, so that the price of their bond will rise. If they are unlucky and the market interest rate rises, the value of their investment falls.

But all bonds are not equally affected by changing interest rates. Compare the two curves in Figure 4.6. The green line shows how the value of the 3-year, 6.5 percent coupon bond varies with the level of the interest rate. The blue line shows how the price of a 30-year, 6.5 percent bond varies with the level of interest rates. You can see that the 30-year bond is more sensitive to interest rate fluctuations than the 3-year bond. This should not surprise you. If you buy a 3-year bond when the interest rate is 5.1 percent, and rates then rise, you will be stuck with a bad deal—you have just loaned your money at a lower interest rate than if you had waited. However, think how much worse it would be if the loan had been for 30 years, rather than 3 years. The longer the period of the loan, the more income you have lost by accepting what turns out to be a low coupon rate. This shows that the price of the longer-term bond had a greater decline. Of course, there is a flip side to this effect, which you can also see from Figure 4.6. When interest rates fall, the longer-term bond responds with a greater increase in price.

☑ CHECK POINT 4.7

Suppose that the interest rate rises overnight from 5.1 percent to 10 percent. Calculate the present values of the 6.5 percent, 3-year bond and of the 6.5 percent, 30-year bond both before and after this change in interest rates. Confirm that your answers correspond with Figure 4.6. Use your financial calculator.

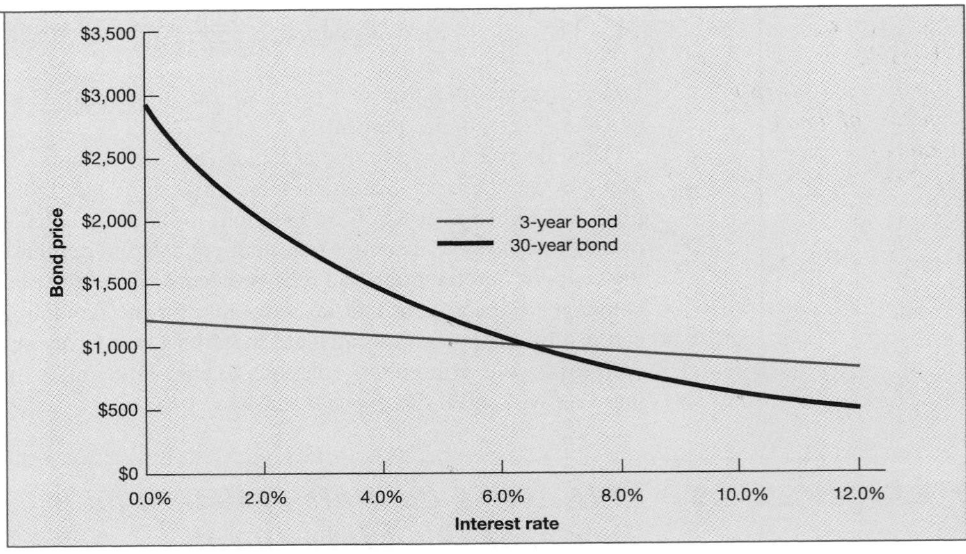

FIGURE 4.6
Plots of bond prices as a function of the interest rate. Long-term bond prices are more sensitive to the interest rate than prices of short-term bonds.

THE YIELD CURVE

Look back for a moment to Figure 4.2. The Canada bonds are arranged in order of their maturity. Notice that the longer the maturity, the higher the yield. This is usually the case, though sometimes long-term bonds offer *lower* yields.

yield curve Graph of the relationship between time to maturity and yield to maturity.

In addition to showing the yields on individual bonds, the *Globe and Mail* also shows a plot of the relationship between bond yields and maturity. This is known as the **yield curve.** You can see from the yield curve in Figure 4.7 that bonds with 3 months to maturity offered a yield of about 4.25 percent; those with more than 10 years of maturity offered a yield of almost 6 percent.

Why didn't everyone buy long-maturity bonds and earn the extra 1.75 percentage points? Who were those investors who put their money into short-term Canada bonds at only 4.25 percent?

Even when the yield curve is upward sloping, investors might rationally stay away from long-term bonds for two reasons. First, the prices of long-term bonds fluctuate much more than prices of short-term bonds. Figure 4.6 illustrates that long-term bond prices are more sensitive to shifting interest rates. A sharp increase in interest rates could easily knock 20 or 30 percent off long-term bond prices. If investors don't like price fluctuations, they will invest their funds in short-term bonds unless they receive a higher yield to maturity on long-term bonds.

Second, short-term investors can profit if interest rates rise. Suppose you hold a 1-year bond. A year from now when the bond matures you can reinvest the proceeds and enjoy whatever rates the bond market offers then. Rates may be high enough to offset the first year's relatively low yield on the 1-year bond. Thus you often see an upward-sloping yield curve when future interest rates are expected to rise. We return to this issue in Chapter 12.

NOMINAL AND REAL RATES OF INTEREST

In Chapter 3 we drew a distinction between nominal and real rates of interest. The cash flows on the 6.5 percent Canada bonds are fixed in nominal terms. Investors are sure to receive an interest payment of $65 each year, but they do not know what that money will buy them. The *real* interest rate on the bonds depends on the rate of inflation. For example, if

FIGURE 4.7
The yield curve. A plot of yield to maturity as a function of time to maturity for Government of Canada bonds, reported June 1, 2001.

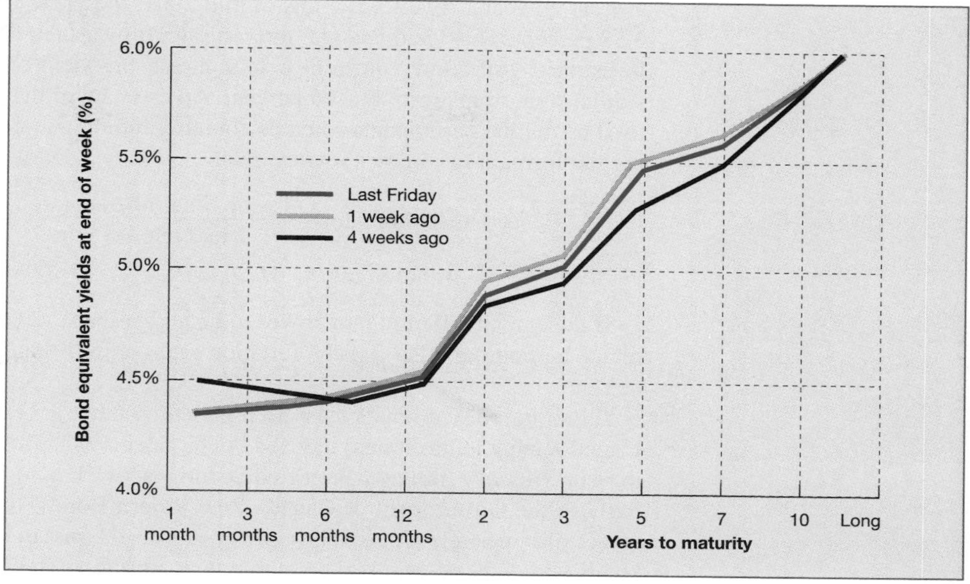

Source: RBC Capital Market, Fixed Income.

the nominal rate of interest is 5.1 percent and the inflation rate is 3 percent, then the real interest rate is calculated as follows:

$$(1 + \text{real interest rate}) = \frac{1 + \text{nominal interest rate}}{1 + \text{inflation rate}} = \frac{1.051}{1.03} = 1.0204$$

$$\text{Real interest rate} = .0204, \text{ or } 2.04\%$$

Since the inflation rate is uncertain, so is the real rate of interest on the bonds.

real return bonds
Bonds with a nominal coupon payment, determined by a fixed real coupon payment and the inflation rate.

You *can* nail down a real rate of interest by buying an indexed or **real return bond**, whose payments are linked to inflation. The Government of Canada began issuing inflation-indexed or real return bonds, RRBs, in 1991. The real cash flows are fixed, but the nominal cash flows (coupon payments and principal) are increased as the consumer price index increases. For example, the 4.25 percent RRB due December 1, 2021, pays annual real coupons of $42.50. In Figure 4.2, prices and yields of the three issues of Government of Canada real return bonds are seen at the bottom of the third column.

To see how the nominal coupon is calculated, suppose the Government of Canada issues a 3 percent, 2-year real return bond. The real cash flows are fixed but the nominal cash flows will depend on the increase in the consumer price index. Suppose inflation turns out to be 5 percent in Year 1 and a further 4 percent in Year 2. The real and nominal cash flows of the bonds would be

	Year 1	Year 2
Real cash flows	$30	$1030
Nominal cash flows	$30 × 1.05 = $31.50	$1030 × 1.05 × 1.04 = $1,124.76

For the 4.25 percent RRB, the nominal value of each coupon is calculated when the coupon payment is due and reflects the inflation that has occurred since the issue of the bond. We won't know the nominal value of the principal until just before the bond matures in 2021.

Currently, all real return bond issues of the Government of Canada have maturities of at least 20 years. As we write this in mid-2001, the yield to maturity on Canada RRBs is 3.58 percent. This yield is a real interest rate. It measures the amount of extra goods your investment will allow you to buy. In contrast, the yield on nominal Canada bonds with similar term to maturity is 5.95 percent. An estimate of the expected annual inflation rate used by market participants when discounting future cash flows can be found by rearranging the formula for the real interest rate:

$$(1 + \text{inflation rate}) = \frac{1 + \text{nominal interest rate}}{1 + \text{real interest rate}} = \frac{1.0595}{1.0358} = 1.0229$$

$$\text{Inflation rate} = .0229, \text{ or } 2.29\%$$

If the annual inflation rate proves to be higher than 2.29 percent, you will earn a higher return by holding RRBs, if the inflation rate is lower than 2.29 percent, the reverse will be true.

Inflation-indexed bonds have been issued by other governments and corporations. The United Kingdom has issued indexed bonds since 1982. The United States Treasury began to issue Treasury Inflation-Protected Securities, or TIPs, in 1997 and structured them similarly to the Government of Canada Real Return Bonds. In 2000, 407 International Inc., owner of largest electronic toll highway in Canada, just north of Toronto, sold real return bonds with 5.29 percent real coupon rate, maturing in 2039.

Real interest rates depend on the supply of savings and the demand for new investment. As this supply-demand balance changes, real interest rates change. But they do so gradually. The green line in Figure 4.8 shows that the real interest rate on the Government of Canada Real Return Bonds has fluctuated within a relatively narrow range.

Suppose that investors upwardly revise their forecast of inflation by 1 percent. How will this affect interest rates? If investors are concerned about the purchasing power of their money, the changed forecast should not affect the real rate of interest. The *nominal* interest rate must therefore rise by 1 percent to compensate investors for the higher inflation prospects.

The blue line in Figure 4.8 shows the nominal rate of interest in Canada since 1991. You can see that the nominal rate is much more variable than the real rate. In 1991, the nominal interest rate was almost 5 percent above the real rate. You can clearly see the impact of steady decline in inflation through most of the 1990s, causing nominal yields to fall.

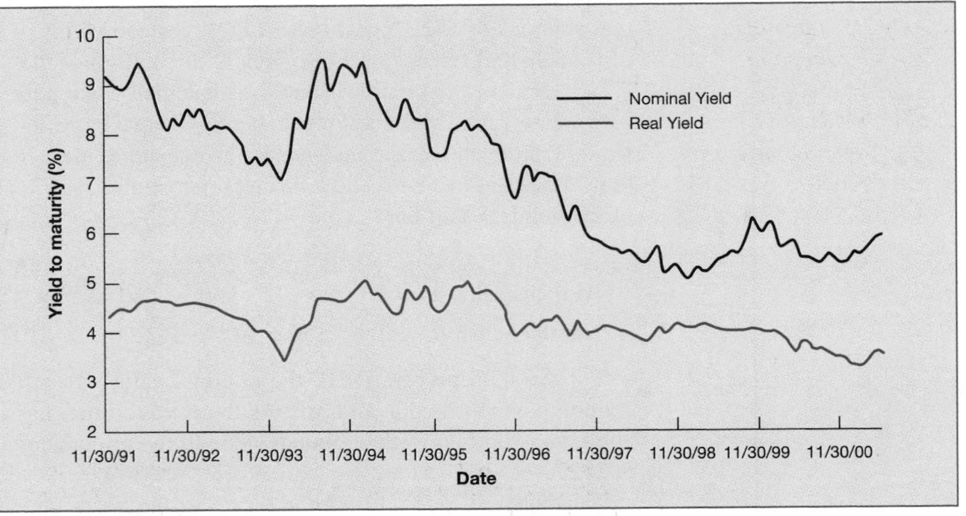

FIGURE 4.8
Real and nominal yields to maturity on the Government of Canada's real return and nominal bonds

DEFAULT RISK

Our focus so far has been on Government of Canada bonds. But the federal government is not the only issuer of bonds. Provincial and municipal governments borrow by selling bonds. So do corporations. Canadian governments and corporations also borrow in the United States and in other countries. The bonds may be denominated in Canadian dollars, U.S. dollars and sometimes in another currency, such as the British pound or Japanese yen.

There is an important distinction between bonds issued by corporations and those issued by the Government of Canada. National governments don't go bankrupt—they just print more money.[5] So investors do not worry that the Canadian government will *default* on its bonds. However, there is some chance that corporations may get into financial difficulties and may default on their bonds. Thus the payments promised to corporate bondholders represent a best case scenario: The firm will never pay more than the promised cash flows, but in hard times it may pay less.

default (or credit) risk The risk that a bond issuer may default on its bonds.

The risk that a bond issuer may default on its obligations is called **default risk** (or **credit risk**). It should be no surprise to find that to compensate for this default risk companies need to promise a higher rate of interest than the Canadian government when borrowing money. The difference between the promised yield on a corporate bond and the yield on a Canada bond with the same coupon and maturity is called the **default premium**, or **credit spread**. The greater the chance that the company will get into trouble, the higher the default premium demanded by investors.

default premium or credit spread The additional yield on a bond investors require for bearing credit risk.

The safety of most corporate bonds can be judged from bond ratings provided by the Dominion Bond Rating Service (DBRS), Moody's, Standard & Poor's, or other bond-rating firms. Table 4.1 lists the possible bond ratings in declining order of quality. For example, the bonds that receive the highest rating are known as AAA, or triple A bonds. Then come AA, or double A, A bonds, BBB bonds, and so on. Bonds rated BBB and above are called **investment grade,** while those with a rating of BB or below are referred to as *speculative grade, high-yield,* or **junk bonds.**

investment grade Bonds rated Baa or above by Moody's or BBB, or above by Standard & Poor's or DBRS.

junk bond Bond with a rating below Baa or BBB.

It is rare for highly rated bonds to default. For example, since 1971 fewer than one in a thousand triple A bonds have defaulted within 10 years of issue. On the other hand, almost half of the bonds that were rated CCC by Standard & Poor's at issue have defaulted within 10 years. Of course, bonds rarely fall suddenly from grace. As time passes and the

TABLE 4.1
Key to DBRS, S&P, and Moody's bond ratings. (Moody's ratings in brackets.) The highest quality bonds are rated triple A, then come double A bonds, and so on.

Bond Rating	Safety
AAA, (Aaa)	The strongest rating; ability to repay interest and principal is very strong.
AA, (Aa)	Very strong likelihood that interest and principal will be repaid.
A, (A)	Strong ability to repay, but some vulnerability to change in circumstances.
BBB, (Baa)	Adequate capacity to repay; more vulnerability to changes in economic circumstances.
BB, (Ba)	Considerable uncertainty about ability to repay.
B, (B)	Likelihood of interest and principal payments over sustained periods is questionable.
CCC, (Caa) CC, (Ca)	Bonds in the CCC and CC classes may already be in default or in danger of imminent default.
C, (C)	Little prospect for interest or principal on the debt ever to be repaid.

[5] But they can't print money of other countries. Therefore when a government borrows in a foreign currency, investors worry that in some future crisis the government may not be able to come up with enough of the foreign currency to repay the debt. This worry shows up in the yield that investors demand on such debt. For example, during the Asian financial crisis in 1998, yields on the U.S. dollar bonds issued by the Indonesian government rose to 18 percentage points above the yields on comparable U.S. Treasury issues.

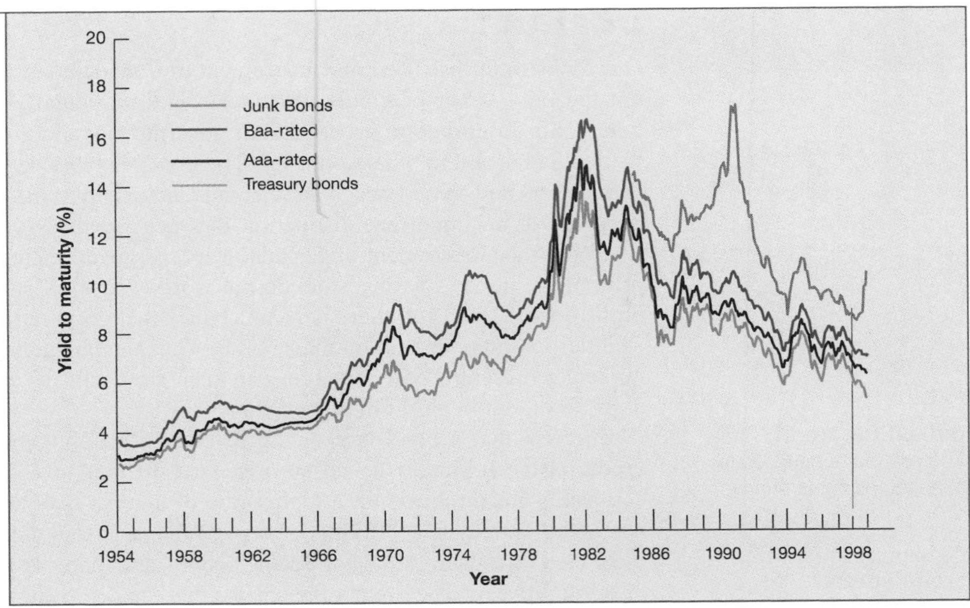

FIGURE 4.9
Yields on U.S. long-term bonds. Bonds with greater credit risk promise higher yields to maturity.

company becomes progressively more shaky, the agencies revise the bond's rating downward to reflect the increasing probability of default.

As you would expect, the yield on corporate bonds varies with the bond rating. Figure 4.9 presents the yields on default-free long-term U.S. Treasury (government) bonds, AAA-rated corporate bonds, and BBB-rated bonds since 1954. It also shows junk bond yields starting in November 1984. You can see that yields on the four groups of bonds track each other closely. However, promised yields go up as safety falls off. Although these data are for U.S. bonds, the picture would look much the same for Canadian bonds. One notable difference would be the much later start for Canadian junk bond yield data as this market developed much later than in the U.S.

▸ EXAMPLE 4.6 *Promised versus Expected Yield to Maturity*

Bad Bet Inc. issued bonds several years ago with a coupon rate (paid annually) of 10 percent and face value of $1,000. The bonds are due to mature in 6 years. However, the firm is currently in bankruptcy proceedings, the firm has ceased to pay interest, and the bonds sell for only $200. Based on *promised* cash flow, the yield to maturity on the bond is 63.9 percent. (On your calculator, set PV = –200, FV = 1,000, PMT = 100, n = 6, and compute i.) But this calculation is based on the very unlikely possibility that the firm will resume paying interest and come out of bankruptcy. Suppose that the most likely outcome is that after 3 years of litigation, during which no interest will be paid, debtholders will receive $.27 on the dollar—that is, they will receive $270 for each bond with $1,000 face value. In this case the expected return on the bond is 10.5 percent. (On your calculator, set PV = –200, FV = 270, PMT = 0, n = 3, and compute i.) When default is a real possibility, the promised yield can depart considerably from the expected return. In this example, the default premium is greater than 50 percent.

VARIATIONS IN CORPORATE BONDS

Most corporate bonds are similar to the 6.5 percent Canada bonds that we examined earlier in the chapter. In other words, they promise to make a fixed nominal coupon payment for each year until maturity, at which point they also promise to repay the face value. However, you will find that there is greater variety in the design of corporate bonds. We will return to this issue in Chapter 13, but here are a few types of corporate bonds that you may encounter.

Zero-Coupon Bonds. Corporations sometimes issue zero-coupon bonds. In this case, investors receive $1,000 face value at the maturity date but do not receive a regular coupon payment. In other words, the bond has a coupon rate of zero. You learned how to value such bonds in Chapter 3. These bonds are issued at prices considerably below face value, and the investor's return comes from the difference between the purchase price and the payment of face value at maturity.

Floating-Rate Bonds. Sometimes the coupon rate can change over time. For example, floating-rate bonds make coupon payments that are tied to some measure of current market rates. The rate might be reset once a year to the current Treasury bill rate plus 2 percent. So if the Treasury bill rate at the start of the year is 6 percent, the bond's coupon rate over the next year would set at 8 percent. This arrangement means that the bond's coupon rate always approximates current market interest rates.

Convertible Bonds. If you buy a convertible bond, you can choose later to exchange it for a specified number of shares of common stock. For example, a convertible bond that is issued at par value of $1,000 may be convertible into 50 shares of the firm's stock. Because convertible bonds offer the opportunity to participate in any price appreciation of the company's stock, investors will accept lower interest rates on convertible bonds.

4.3 Summary

1. **What are the differences between the bond's coupon rate, current yield, and yield to maturity?**

   A bond is a long-term debt of a government or corporation. When you own a bond, you receive a fixed interest payment each year until the bond matures. This payment is known as the coupon. The **coupon rate** is the annual coupon payment expressed as a fraction of the bond's **face value.** At maturity the bond's face value is repaid. In Canada most bonds have a face value of $1,000. The **current yield** is the annual coupon payment expressed as a fraction of the bond's price. The **yield to maturity** measures the average rate of return to an investor who purchases the bond and holds it until maturity, accounting for coupon income as well as the difference between purchase price and face value.

2. **How can one find the market price of a bond given its yield to maturity and find a bond's yield given its price? Why do prices and yields vary inversely?**

   Bonds are valued by discounting the coupon payments and the final repayment by the yield to maturity on comparable bonds. The bond payments discounted at the bond's yield to maturity equal the bond price. You may also start with the bond price and ask what interest rate the bond offers. This interest rate that equates the present value of bond payments to the bond price is the yield to maturity. Because present values are lower when discount rates are higher, price and yield to maturity vary inversely.

3. **Why do bonds exhibit interest rate risk?**

   Bond prices are subject to interest rate risk, rising when market interest rates fall and falling when market rates rise. Long-term bonds exhibit greater **interest rate risk** than short-term bonds.

4. **Why do investors pay attention to bond ratings and demand a higher interest rate for bonds with low ratings?**

   Investors demand higher promised yields if there is a high probability that the borrower will run into trouble and default. **Credit risk** implies that the promised yield to maturity on the bond is higher than the expected yield. The additional yield investors require for bearing credit risk is called the **default premium.** Bond ratings measure the bond's credit risk.

RELATED WEB LINKS

www.finpipe.com The Financial Pipeline is an Internet site dedicated to financial education; see the page on bonds

www.investinginbonds.com All about bond pricing

www.bloomberg.com/markets/C13.html A look at the U.S. yield curve, updated daily

www.bondmarkets.com/publications/IGCORP/what.htm A guide to corporate bonds

www.moodys.com The website of the bond rating agency

www.standardandpoors.com/ratings Standard & Poor's provides information on how it rates securities

www.rbcds.com RBC Capital Markets, one of Canada's largest bond dealers

www.tdwaterhouse.com Online brokerage service

www.bankofcanada.ca For yield-to-maturity data

www.bondsonline.com/asp/corp/spreadbank.html Yields to maturity for corporate bonds

www.ebond.ca Current Canadian federal and provincial bond prices

KEY TERMS

bond	113	current yield	118	real return bonds	127
coupon	113	yield to maturity	119	default (or credit) risk	129
face value, par value, maturity value, principal	113	rate of return	121	default premium	129
		interest rate risk	125	investment grade	129
coupon rate	113	yield curve	126	junk bond	129

QUESTIONS AND PROBLEMS

*Answers in Appendix B

BASIC

*1. **Bond Yields.** A 30-year Canada bond is issued with par value of $1,000, paying interest of $80 per year. If market yields increase shortly after the bond is issued, what happens to the bond's

a. coupon rate
b. price
c. yield to maturity
d. current yield

2. **Bond Yields.** If a bond with par value of $1,000 and a coupon rate of 8 percent is selling at a price of $970, is the bond's yield to maturity more or less than 8 percent? What about the current yield?

*3. **Bond Yields.** A bond with par value $1,000 has a current yield of 7.5 percent and a coupon rate of 8 percent. What is the bond's price?

*4. **Bond Pricing.** A 6-year Circular File bond pays interest of $80 annually and sells for $950. What is its coupon rate, current yield, and yield to maturity?

5. **Bond Pricing.** If Circular File (see question 4) wants to issue a new 6-year bond at face value, what coupon rate must the bond offer?

6. **Bond Yields.** A BCE bond has 10 years until maturity, a coupon rate of 8 percent, and sells for $1,050.

a. What is the current yield on the bond?
b. What is the yield to maturity?

7. **Coupon Rate.** General Matter's outstanding bond issue has a coupon rate of 10 percent and a current yield of 9.6 percent, and it sells at a yield to maturity of 9.25 percent. The firm wishes to issue additional bonds to the public at par value. What coupon rate must the new bonds offer in order to sell at par?

8. **Financial Pages.** Turn back to Figure 4.2. What is the current yield of the 8.75 percent, December 1, 2005 maturity? What was the closing bid price of the bond on the previous day?

*9. **Rate of Return.** You bought a 10-year, 5 percent coupon bond for $1,000 and sold it 1 year later for $1,100. What is the rate of return on your investment if the bond pays interest annually?

*10. **After-Tax Rate of Return.** Refer to problem 9. If your marginal tax rate is 30 percent, what is the after-tax rate of return on your bond investment?

PRACTICE

*11. **Bond Prices and Returns.** One bond has a coupon rate of 8 percent, another a coupon rate of 12 percent. Both bonds have 10-year maturities and sell at a yield to maturity of 10 percent. If their yields to maturity next year are still 10 percent, what is the rate of return on each bond? Does the higher coupon bond give a higher rate of return?

*12. **Bond Returns.**

a. If the BCE bond in problem 6 has a yield to maturity of 8 percent 1 year from now, what will its price be?

b. What will be your rate of return if you buy it today and sell it in 1 year?

c. If the inflation rate during the year is 3 percent, what is the real rate of return on the bond?

*13. **Bond Pricing.** A Stelco bond carries a coupon rate of 8 percent, has 9 years until maturity, and sells at a yield to maturity of 9 percent.

a. What interest payments do bondholders receive each year?

b. At what price does the bond sell? (Assume annual interest payments.)

c. What will happen to the bond price if the yield to maturity falls to 7 percent?

*14. **Bond Pricing.** A 30-year maturity bond with $1,000 face value makes annual coupon payments and has a coupon rate of 8 percent. What is the bond's yield to maturity if the bond is selling for

a. $900

b. $1,000

c. $1,100

15. **Bond Pricing.** Repeat the previous problem if the bond makes semiannual coupon payments.

16. **Bond Pricing.** Fill in the table below for the following zero-coupon bonds. The face value of each bond is $1,000.

Price	Maturity (Years)	Yield to Maturity
$300	30	—
$300	—	8%
—	10	10%

17. **Consol Bonds.** Perpetual Life Corp. has issued consol bonds with coupon payments of $80. (Consols pay interest forever and never mature. They are perpetuities.) If the required rate of return on these bonds at the time they were issued was 8 percent, at what price were they sold to the public? If the required return today is 12 percent, at what price do the consols sell?

*18. **Bond Pricing.** Sure Tea Co. has issued 9 percent annual coupon bonds, which are now selling at a yield to maturity of 10 percent and current yield of 9.8375 percent. What is the remaining maturity of these bonds?

19. **Bond Pricing.** Large Industries bonds sell for $1,065.15. The bond life is 9 years, and the yield to maturity is 7 percent. What must be the coupon rate on the bonds?

*20. **Bond Prices and Yields.**

a. Several years ago, Castles in the Sand, Inc., issued bonds at face value at a yield to maturity of 8 percent. Now, with 8 years left until the maturity of the bonds, the company has run into hard times, and the yield to maturity on the bonds has increased to 14 percent. What has happened to the price of the bond?

b. Suppose that investors believe that Castles can make good on the promised coupon payments, but that the company will go bankrupt when the bond matures and the principal comes due. The expectation is that investors will receive only 80 percent of face value at maturity. If they buy the bond today, what yield to maturity do they expect to receive?

*21. **Bond Returns.** You buy an 8 percent coupon, 10-year maturity bond for $980. A year later, the bond price is $1,050.

a. What is the new yield to maturity on the bond?
b. What is your rate of return over the year?

22. **Bond Returns.** You buy an 8 percent coupon, 10-year maturity bond when its yield to maturity is 9 percent. A year later, the yield to maturity is 10 percent. What is your rate of return over the year?

23. **Interest Rate Risk.** Consider three bonds with 8 percent coupon rates, all selling at face value. The short-term bond has a maturity of 4 years, the intermediate-term bond has maturity of 8 years, and the long-term bond has maturity of 30 years.

a. What will happen to the price of each bond if their yields increase to 9 percent?
b. What will happen to the price of each bond if their yields decrease to 7 percent?
c. What do you conclude about the relationship between time to maturity and the sensitivity of bond prices to interest rates?

*24. **Rate of Return.** A 2-year maturity bond with $1,000 face value makes annual coupon payments of $80 and is selling at face value. What will be the rate of return on the bond if its yield to maturity at the end of the year is

a. 6 percent
b. 8 percent
c. 10 percent

25. **Rate of Return.** A bond that pays coupons annually is issued with a coupon rate of 4 percent, maturity of 30 years, and a yield to maturity of 8 percent. What rate of return will be earned by an investor who purchases the bond and holds it for 1 year if the bond's yield to maturity at the end of the year is 9 percent?

*26. **Rate of Return.** Five years ago you purchased an 8 percent coupon bond for $975. Today you sold the bond for $1,000. What is your rate of return on the bond in each of the following situations:

a. All coupons were immediately spent when received.
b. All coupons were reinvested in your bank account, which pays 1 percent interest until the bond is sold.
c. All coupons were reinvested at 8.64 percent until the bond is sold.

*27. **Rate of Return.** Looking back at the previous question, use the yield-to-maturity method to compute the rate of return on your bond investment.

*28. **Bond Risk.** A bond's credit rating provides a guide to its risk. Long-term bonds rated AA currently offer yields to maturity of 8.5 percent EAR. A-rated bonds sell at yields of 8.8 percent EAR. If a 10-year bond with a coupon rate of 8 percent, paid semiannually, is downgraded by DBRS from AA to A rating, what is the likely effect on the bond price?

*29. **Real Returns.** Suppose that you buy a 1-year maturity bond for $1,000 that will pay you $1,000 plus a coupon payment of $60 at the end of the year. What real rate of return will you earn if the inflation rate is

a. 2 percent
b. 4 percent
c. 6 percent
d. 8 percent

30. **Real Returns.** Now suppose that the bond in the previous problem is a real return bond with a coupon rate of 4 percent. What will the cash flow provided by the bond be for each of the four inflation rates? What will be the real and nominal rates of return on the bond in each scenario?
31. **Real Returns.** Now suppose the real return bond in the previous problem is a 2-year maturity bond. What will be the bondholder's cash flows in each year in each of the inflation scenarios?

CHALLENGE

32. **Interest Rate Risk.** Suppose interest rates increase from 8 percent to 9 percent. Which bond will suffer the greater percentage decline in price: a 30-year bond paying annual coupons of 8 percent, or a 30-year zero coupon bond? Can you explain intuitively why the zero exhibits greater interest rate risk even though it has the same maturity as the coupon bond?

*33. **After-Tax Rate of Return.** Using the information in problem 26, calculate your after-tax rate of return on your bond investment assuming that your marginal tax rate is 35 percent. You pay tax on the interest when it is received.

34. **Bond Prices and Yields.** Big Time Company is planning to raise $15 million by selling 10-year bonds. The bond rating agency has advised the company that the bonds will have an A rating. Currently, the difference between the yield to maturity of A-rated corporate bonds over similar maturity Government of Canada bonds is 150 basis points (which is called the credit spread). If 10-year Canada bonds are currently priced to yield 5 percent, how many bonds will Big Time have to sell to raise the needed funds? Note that the convention is to set the coupon rate on the corporate bond issue so that the new bonds will sell at par value.

INTERNET PROBLEMS

1. Use historical yield-to-maturity data from the Bank of Canada website at www.bankofcanada.ca to look at bonds of different types. From the main page, click on "Bonds and Securities" on the left side of the main page and then select "Historic Bond Yields" (www.bankofcanada.ca/en/bond-look.htm). Follow the instructions and download 60 months of yield-to-maturity data for long-term corporate bonds (series B14048), long-term provincial bonds (B14047) and long-term Canada bonds (series B14013) and put the data into a spreadsheet. Calculate the average spreads of the corporate and provincial bonds over the Canada bonds. Graph the yields to maturity over time. What do you see? Does it make sense?
2. It is difficult to get online yield-to-maturity and credit spread data for Canadian corporate bonds with different debt ratings. Currently, www.ebond.ca is not providing bond data but may do so in the future. However, U.S. data is available. Go to www.bondsonline.com/asp/corp/spreadbank.html. You will see a table showing current extra yields to maturity (credit spreads) of corporate bonds of different risk over comparable term U.S. government bonds. Spreads are provided for different industries. Select "Industrials" (at the bottom of the page). Using the data in the table, estimate the required rate of return on a 10-year debt issue by a U.S. company with A1 or A-rated debt. What if its debt had a B1 or B rating? The current yield to maturity on U.S. government bonds is at www.bondsonline.com/asp/news/composites.html. To learn more about bonds and credit spreads, check out www.finpipe.com then click on "Bonds." Select "Bond Spreads" and read about the factors affecting spreads.
3. From either the *Globe and Mail* or the *National Post*, find five different corporate bonds. Go to one of the bond rating agencies such as www.dbrs.com or www.standardpoor.com/RatingsActions/RatingsLists/CanadianIssuers/index.html and look up the bonds' ratings. Compare the bonds' yields to maturity to comparable term Government of Canada bonds. Do the yields make sense relative to their bond ratings?

SOLUTIONS TO CHECK POINTS

4.1 a. The bid price, your selling price, is 99.1 percent of face value, or \$991.

b. To buy the bond, you pay a higher price. The dealer sets a spread to cover her costs of holding inventory of bonds. She buys the bond from you at a lower price than she is willing to sell to you.

c. The bond price increased by .03 percent of face value, or \$0.3.

d. The annual coupon is 5.5 percent of face value, or \$55, paid in two semiannual installments.

e. The yield to maturity, based on the bid price, is 5.63 percent.

4.2 The coupon is 9 percent of \$1,000, or \$90, a year. First value the 6-year annuity of coupons:

$$\begin{aligned} PV &= \$90 \times (\text{6-year annuity factor}) \\ &= \$90 \times \left[\frac{1}{.12} - \frac{1}{.12(1.12)^6}\right] \\ &= \$90 \times 4.11 = \$370.03 \end{aligned}$$

Then value the final payment and add up:

$$PV = \frac{\$1,000}{(1.12)^6} = \$506.63$$

$$\text{PV of bond} = \$370.03 + \$506.63 = \$876.66$$

4.3 The yield to maturity is about 8 percent because the present value of the bond's cash returns is \$1,199 when discounted at 8 percent:

$$\begin{aligned} PV &= PV\ (\text{coupons}) + PV\ (\text{final payment}) \\ &= (\text{coupon} \times \text{annuity factor}) + (\text{face value} \times \text{discount factor}) \\ &= \$140 \times \left[\frac{1}{.08} - \frac{1}{.08(1.08)^4}\right] + \$1,000 \times \frac{1}{1.08^4} \\ &= \$463.70 + \$735.03 = \$1,199 \end{aligned}$$

4.4 The 6.5 percent coupon bond with maturity 2004 starts with 3 years left until maturity and sells for \$1,038.05. At the end of the year, the bond has only 2 years to maturity and investors demand an interest rate of 7 percent. Therefore, the value of the bond becomes

$$\text{PV at 7\%} = \frac{\$65}{(1.07)} + \frac{\$1,065}{(1.07)^2} = \$990.06$$

You invested \$1,038.05. At the end of the year you receive a coupon payment of \$65 and have a bond worth \$990.96. Your rate of return is therefore

$$\text{Rate of return} = \frac{\$65 + (\$990.96 - \$1,038.05)}{\$1,038.05} = .0173, \text{ or } 1.73\%$$

The yield to maturity at the start of the year was 7.14 percent. However, because interest rates rose during the year, the bond price fell and the rate of return was below the yield to maturity.

4.5 By the end of this year, the bond will have only 1 year left until maturity. It will make only one more payment of coupon plus face value, so its price will be \$1,065/1.051 = \$1,013.32. The rate of return is therefore

$$\frac{\$65 + (\$1,013.32 - \$1,025.99)}{\$1,025.99} = .051, \text{ or } 5.1\%$$

4.6 The coupon payment is .08 x \$1,000, or \$80, before tax. The tax on the coupon interest is .4 x \$80, or \$32. A capital loss of \$1,150 – \$1,200 = \$50 is made. The capital loss can only be used to reduce taxable capital gain. You must have had a capital gain of at least \$50 to use the loss to reduce your capital gains tax. The tax savings from the loss is .5 × .4 × \$50, or \$10. The before tax rate of return is

$$\frac{\$80 + (\$1,150 - \$1,200)}{\$1,200} = .025, \text{ or } 2.5\%$$

The after-tax rate of return is

$$\frac{\$80 - \$32 + (\$1{,}150 - \$1{,}200) + \$10}{\$1{,}200} = .0067, \text{ or } 0.67\%$$

If you had no capital gains to use up the loss, your after-tax return would be worse: – .167%!

4.7 At an interest rate of 5.1 percent, the 3-year bond sells for $1,038.05. If the interest rate jumps to 10 percent, the bond price falls to $912.96, a decline of 12.1 percent. The 30-year bond sells for $1,212.78 when the interest rate is 5.1 percent, but its price falls to $670.06 at an interest rate of 10 percent, a much larger percentage decline of 44.8 percent.

CHAPTER 5

Valuing Stocks

5.1 Stocks and the Stock Market

5.2 Book Values, Liquidation Values, and Market Values

5.3 Valuing Common Stocks

5.4 Simplifying the Dividend Discount Model

5.5 Growth Stocks and Income Stocks

5.6 Summary

Instead of borrowing cash to pay for its investments, a firm can sell new shares of common stock to investors. Whereas bond issues commit the firm to make a series of specified interest payments to the lenders, stock issues are more like taking on new partners. The shareholders all share in the fortunes of the firm according to the number of shares they hold. In this chapter, we will take a first look at stocks, the stock market, and principles of stock valuation.

We start by looking at how stocks are bought and sold. Then we look at what determines stock prices and how stock valuation formulas can be used to infer the rate of return that investors are expecting. We will see how the firm's investment opportunities are reflected in the stock price and why stock market analysts focus so much attention on the price earnings, or P/E ratio, of the company.

Why should you care how stocks are valued? After all, if you want to know the value of a firm's stock, you can look up the stock price in a business newspaper or with its online service, such as the *Globe and Mail*'s www.globeandmail.com and the *National Post*'s www.nationalpost.com. But you need to know what determines prices for at least two reasons. First, you may wish to check that any shares that you own are fairly priced and to gauge your beliefs against the rest of the market. Second, corporations need to have some understanding of how the market values firms in order to make decisions about good capital budgeting. A project is attractive if it increases shareholder wealth. But you can't judge that unless you know how shares are valued.

After studying this chapter you should be able to

- Understand the stock trading reports in the financial pages of newspapers.
- Calculate the present value of a stock given forecasts of future dividends and future stock price.
- Use stock valuation formulas to infer the expected rate of return on a common stock.
- Interpret price-earnings ratios.

5.1 Stocks and the Stock Market

A shareholder is part-owner of a firm who is entitled to the firm's residual cash flow, the remaining cash flow after all other suppliers, lenders, and the government have been paid. Common shareholders are also entitled to elect the board of directors and to cast one vote per share owned at shareholders' meetings. Some firms in Canada, the United States, and in many European countries also issue shares that are entitled to the residual cash flow, but do not have full voting rights. For example, Molson, Inc., has two classes of equity, Class A non-voting shares and Class B common shares. Although the Class A shares do not usually vote at shareholders' meetings, they do elect three members of the board of directors.[1] The Class B shareholders have one vote per share. There were 47.7 million Class A shares outstanding on March 31, 2001, but only 12 million Class B shares. The Class A shares are entitled to $.067 of dividends each year before the Class B shares are paid the same amount. However, both classes share equally in any further dividends paid. Recently both shares have received the same dividends of $.72 per share.

common stock Ownership shares in a publicly held corporation.

Firms issue shares of **common stock** to the public when they need to raise money.[2] They typically engage investment dealers such as RBC Capital Markets or BMO Nesbitt Burns to help them market these shares. Sales of new stock by the firm are said to occur in the **primary market.** There are two types of primary market issues. In an **initial public offering,** or **IPO,** a company that has been privately owned sells stock to the public for the first time. Some IPOs have proved very popular with investors. For example, a star performer in 2000 was 724 Solutions. Its shares were sold to investors at $37.31 each, and by the end of the first day, they had reached $103.50, a gain of over 277 percent. Within one month, the 724 stock price reached over $330!

primary market Market for newly issued securities, sold by the company to raise cash.

initial public offering (IPO) First offering of stock to the general public.

Established firms that already have issued stock to the public also may decide to raise money from time to time by issuing additional shares. Sales of new shares by such firms are also primary market issues and are called *seasoned offerings.* When a firm issues new shares to the public, the previous owners share their ownership of the company with additional shareholders. In this sense, issuing new shares is like having new partners buy into the firm.

Shares of stock can be risky investments. For example, the shares of 360networks were first issued to the public in April 2000 at $21 a share. In September 2000, 360networks' shares hit $35.90; less than a year later, the company failed to make a required $11 million (US) interest payment, and its stock price had fallen to $.34. You can understand why investors would be unhappy if forced to tie the knot with a particular company forever. So large companies usually arrange for their stocks to be listed on a stock exchange, which allows investors to trade existing stocks among themselves. Exchanges are really markets for secondhand stocks, but they prefer to describe themselves as **secondary markets,** which sounds more important.

secondary market Market in which already-issued securities are traded among investors.

The major stock exchange in Canada is the Toronto Stock Exchange, TSX, www.tsx.ca, listing shares of established, large companies. The TSX Venture Exchange, formerly the Canadian Venture Exchange, lists new, smaller companies, including those active in natural resource exploration, manufacturing, and technology. The TSX Venture Exchange was acquired by the TSX through a merger in 2001 and is a wholly owned subsidiary of the TSX. Merging the exchanges makes it easier for successful companies to move up to the

[1] Having the right to elect board members is not typical of Canadian non-voting shares. Most companies' non-voting shareholders are not entitled to vote on typical corporate matters, such as changes to the compensation of senior officers or electing members of the board. However, in special circumstances, such as the decision to wind-up the company, non-voting shareholders are entitled to vote.

[2] We use the terms "shares," "stock," and "common stock" interchangeably, as we do "shareholders" and "stockholders."

larger TSX. All Canadian markets are electronic *auction markets*. Each stock exchange maintains an electronic order book, showing offers to buy and sell with shares sold to the highest bidder.

The two major exchanges in the United States are the New York Stock Exchange (NYSE) and the Nasdaq market. The NYSE is also an auction market. By contrast, Nasdaq operates a *dealer market,* in which dealers use computer links to quote prices for shares they are willing to buy and sell. A broker must survey the prices quoted by different dealers to get a sense of where the best price is.

An important development in recent years has been the advent of electronic communication networks, or ECNs, which have captured ever-larger shares of trading volume. These are electronic auction houses that match up investors' orders to buy and sell shares. For example, TD Waterhouse offers after-hours trading: Trading continues after the stock exchanges have closed. TD offers this to its clients through an ECN and is operated by a group of U.S. brokerage firms.

Of course, there are stock exchanges in many other countries. As you can see from Figure 5.1, the major exchanges in cities such as London, Tokyo, and Frankfurt trade vast numbers of shares. But there are also literally hundreds of smaller exchanges throughout the world. For example, the Tanzanian stock exchange opens for just half an hour each week and trades shares in two companies.

READING THE STOCK MARKET LISTINGS

When you read the stock market pages in the newspaper, you are looking at the secondary market. Figure 5.2 is an excerpt from the *Globe and Mail* of TSX trading on June 27, 2001. The highlighted bar in the figure emphasizes the listing for Molson, Inc., Class A non-voting shares.[3] The two numbers to the left of Molson are the highest and lowest prices at which the stock has traded in the last 52 weeks, \$49.25 and \$27.40, respectively. That's a reminder of just how much stock prices fluctuate.

Skip to the column starting with "High," and you will see the prices at which the stock traded on June 26. The highest price at which the stock traded that day was \$47 per share,

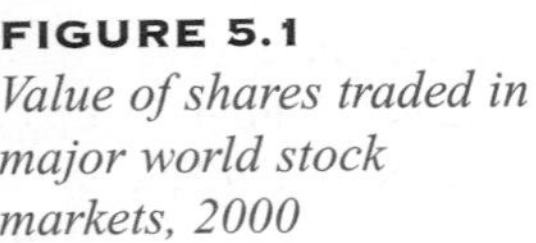

FIGURE 5.1
Value of shares traded in major world stock markets, 2000

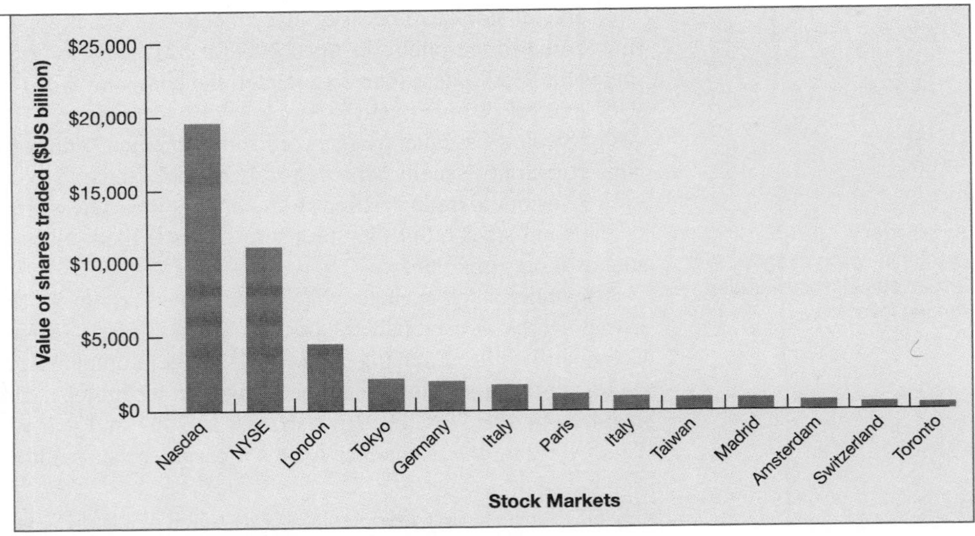

Source: International Federation of Stock Exchanges, www.fibv.com.

[3] The table shows not only the company's name, usually abbreviated, but also the symbol, or ticker, which is used to identify the company on the TSX price screens. The symbol for Molson, Inc. Class A non-voting shares is "MOL.A"; other companies' symbols are not so obvious.

FIGURE 5.2
TSX stock market listings from the Globe and Mail, *June 27, 2001*

TORONTO

365-day High	365-day Low	Stock	Sym	Div	High	Low	Close	Chg	Vol (100s)	Yield	P/E ratio
3.25	1.55	Marks Wk	MWW		3.10	3.00	3.00	+0.05	299		10.0
4.15	1.70	Marsulex	MLX		4.00	3.70	3.75		117		
1.80	1.30	Matco	MCO.B		1.55	1.55	1.55	–0.05	20		14.1
3.40	1.25	Matrikon	MTK		1.90	1.80	1.80	–0.09	43		
46.32	19.00	Maverick	MAV	0.20	26.35	24.65	25.90	+0.01	83	0.8	66.4
12.00	5.50	Maxxcom	MXX		5.55	5.55	5.55		4		12.9
0.80	0.48	Mazarin	MAZ		0.57	0.55	0.56	–0.01	150		
1.20	0.35	McCarvill	MCR		0.57	0.56	0.56	–0.04	125		
2.38	1.25	McCoy Br	MCB		2.00	1.95	2.00		70		
0.46	0.07	McWatter	MCW		0.15	0.15	0.15	–.015	96		
11.40	5.75	Mec Hldgs	MEH		11.00	10.55	10.55	–0.25	53		50.2
4.20	0.35	Med Net	MDT	0.45	0.70	0.45	0.45	+0.05	2		
8.25	2.30	Medcomsft	MSF		7.60	6.85	7.60	+0.45	962		16.5
2.95	1.12	MediSoluti	MSH		2.08	2.05	2.07	–0.01	383		11.5
3.44	1.15	Memotec	MCM		1.60	1.40	1.50	–0.10	294		
5.50	2.70	Meota Res	MRZ		4.30	4.25	4.30	+0.05	2139		6.5
14.20	7.25	MeridinGl	MNG		13.40	12.40	13.40	+0.90	1373		16.8
121.00	80.00	Merrill Lyn	MLC	.965	97.00	93.00	94.25	–7.85	161	10	14.3
33.00	24.00	Merrill Lyn	BUL		25.05	25.05	25.05		2		
1.30	0.18	Metallica	MR		1.09	1.13	1.03	–0.02	1350		
13.95	3.99	♣Methanx	MX		9.00	8.70	8.75	–0.35	1580		4.3
28.70	17.65	Metro	MRU.A	0.36	28.30	27.95	28.30	+0.20	425	1.3	12.7
0.85	0.41	Microbix Bi	MBX		.465	0.41	0.43	–0.05	144		
61.00	10.20	♣Microcll	MTI.B		13.10	11.91	12.32	–0.03	656		
8.60	0.40	Microforu	MCF		0.53	0.51	0.53	+0.01	571		
7.45	2.95	Micrologix	MBI		3.39	3.15	3.20	+0.10	202		
3.25	2.40	Middlefiel	MBN		3.10	3.10	3.10	+0.10	20		5.4
4.65	0.45	♣Minacs	MXW		4.40	4.40	4.40	+0.20	1		27.5
2.23	0.87	Minefinder	MFL		1.25	1.15	1.15	–0.05	710		
1.75	0.66	Min du Nd	MDN		0.90	0.82	0.82		180		
1.75	0.77	Miramar	MAE		1.30	1.26	1.30		854		
5.50	1.05	Mist	MIS		1.26	1.26	1.26	–0.24	3		31.5
5.95	1.90	Mitec Tele	MTM		4.50	4.30	4.30	–0.35	57		
37.65	10.22	Mitel	MLT		14.45	14.00	14.30	–0.55	5791		
26.00	24.50	Mitel	MTL.PR.A	2.00	25.00	25.00	25.00		7	8.0	
0.65	0.30M	Mobile Cli	MCC		0.50	0.47	0.50	+.015	115		6.2
2.70	0.27	Mobile Cm	MBL		0.39	0.36	.385	+.015	398		
49.25	27.40	♣Mol	MOL.A	0.72	47.00	46.45	46.45	–0.25	983	1.6	20.6
9.25	3.35	Moore	MCL	0.31	8.40	8.15	8.27	–0.13	1517	3.8	
7.10	0.43	Mortice Ke	MKK		1.35	1.25	1.34		3189		

Source: The *Globe and Mail*, June 27, 2001.

the lowest was $46.45, and the closing price was also $46.45, which was $.25 lower than the previous day's close.

dividend Periodic cash distribution from the firm to its shareholders.

The 0.72 value to the right of Molson is the annual **dividend** per share paid by the company.[4] In other words, investors in Molson shares currently receive an annual income of $.72 on each share. Of course Molson is not bound to keep that level of dividend in the future. You hope earnings and dividends will rise, but it's possible that profits will slump and Molson will cut its dividend.

The dividend yield, under the heading Yield, tells you how much dividend income you receive for each $100 that you invest in the stock. For Molson, the yield is $.72/$46.45 = .016, or 1.6 percent. Therefore, for every $100 invested in the stock, you would receive annual dividend income of $1.60. The dividend yield on the stock is like the current yield on a bond. Both look at the current income as a percentage of price. Both ignore prospective capital gains or losses and therefore do not correspond to total rates of return.

If you scan Figure 5.2, you will see that dividend yields vary widely across companies. Many of the shares are not receiving dividends and therefore have zero yields. Moore Corporation shows a dividend yield of 3.8 percent, based on its last dividend paid. However, the company announced in April 2001 that it would not be paying its normal July dividend. The records in the newspaper will be corrected after the July dividend is actually missed. Investors are content with a low or zero current yield as long as they can look to higher future dividends and rising share prices.

[4] Actually, it's the last quarterly dividend multiplied by 4.

price-earnings (P/E) multiple Ratio of stock price to earnings per share.

The **price-earnings (P/E) multiple** for Molson Class A is reported as 20.6. This is the ratio of the share price to earnings per share. The P/E ratio is a key tool of stock market analysts. For example, low P/E stocks are sometimes touted as good buys for investors. We will have more to say about P/E later in the chapter.

The column headed "Vol 100s" shows that the trading volume in Molson was 983 *round lots*. Each round lot is 100 shares, so 98,300 shares of Molson traded on this day. A trade of less than 100 shares is an *odd lot*.

Molson's Class B common shares are also listed for trading in the TSE—but trade infrequently. No Class B shares were traded on June 26. However, in the Toronto Bid/Ask section of the *Globe and Mail*, the bid price, your selling price, was $46.50, and the ask price, your buying price, was $47.25.[5]

CHECK POINT 5.1 Explain the entries for Mitel in Figure 5.2.

5.2 Book Values, Liquidation Values, and Market Values

Why is Molson Class A selling at $46.45 per share when the stock of Methanx, listed above Molson, is priced at $8.75? And why does it cost $20.60 to buy one dollar of Molson earnings, while Methanx is selling at 4.3 times earnings? Do these numbers imply that one stock is a better buy than the other?

Finding the value of Molson stock may sound like a simple problem. Each year Molson publishes a balance sheet that shows the value of the firm's assets and liabilities. The simplified balance sheet in Table 5.1 shows that the book value of all Molson's assets—plant and machinery, inventories of materials, cash in the bank, and so on—was $3,280.8 million on March 31, 2001. Molson's liabilities—money that it owes the banks, taxes that are due to be paid, and the like—amounted to $2,485.4 million. The difference between the value of the assets and the liabilities was $795.4 million. This was the **book value** of the firm's equity.[6] Book value records all the money that Molson has raised from its shareholders plus all the earnings that have been plowed back on its behalf.

book value Net worth of the firm according to the balance sheet.

Book value is a reassuringly definite number. Price WaterhouseCoopers, one of Canada's largest accounting firms, tells us:

> In our opinion, these consolidated financial statements fairly present, in all material respects, the financial position of the Corporation [Molson, Inc.] as at March 31, 2001, and 2000, and the results of its operations and cash flows for the years then ended in accordance with generally accepted accounting principles.

But does the stock price equal book value? Let's see. Molson has issued 59.7 million shares, so the balance sheet suggests that each share was worth $795/59.7 = $13.32.

[5] This use of the words "bid" and "ask" might appear to have opposite meanings. The words refer to the market-maker, or dealer, a special market participant who is always ready to buy or sell the stock. From the market-maker's perspective, the words make sense: The bid price is her buying price and the ask price is her selling price. The difference, or spread, is her compensation for holding inventory in the stock.

[6] "Equity" is yet another word for stock. Thus shareholders are often referred to as "equity investors."

TABLE 5.1
Balance sheet

BALANCE SHEET FOR MOLSON, INC., MARCH 31, 2001 (figures in millions of dollars)			
Assets		**Liabilities and Shareholders' Equity**	
Plant, equipment, and other assets	3,280.8	Liabilities	2,485.4
		Equity	795.4

But Molson shares were actually selling at $43.70 on March 31, 2001, more than three times their book value. This and the other cases shown in Table 5.2 tell us that investors in the stock market do *not* just buy and sell at book value per share.

Investors know that accountants don't even try to estimate market values. The value of the assets reported on the firm's balance sheet is equal to their original (or "historical") cost less an allowance for depreciation. But that may not be a good guide to what the firm would need to pay to buy the same assets today. For example, in 1970, United Airlines bought four new Boeing 747s for $128 million each. By the end of 1986 they had been fully depreciated and were carried in the company accounts at a residual book value of $200,000 each. But actual secondhand aircraft prices have often *appreciated,* not depreciated.[7] In fact, the planes could have been sold for upwards of $20 million each.

liquidation value Net proceeds that would be realized by selling the firm's assets and paying off its creditors.

Well, maybe stock price equals **liquidation value** per share, that is, the amount of cash per share a company could raise if it sold off all its assets in secondhand markets and paid off all its debts. Wrong again. A successful company ought to be worth more than liquidation value. That's the goal of bringing all those assets together in the first place.

The difference between a company's actual value and its book or liquidation value is often attributed to *going-concern value,* which refers to three factors:

1. *Extra earning power.* A company may have the ability to earn more than an adequate rate of return on assets. For example, if United can make better use of its planes than its competitors make of theirs, it will earn a higher rate of return. In this case the value of the planes to United will be higher than their book value or secondhand value.
2. *Intangible assets.* There are many assets that accountants don't put on the balance sheet. Some of these assets are extremely valuable to the companies owning or using

TABLE 5.2
Market versus book values based on stock price for June 27, 2001

Firm	Stock Price	Book Value per Share	Ratio: Price/Book Value
Air Canada	$ 8.57	$ 1.3	6.59
Aliant	29.51	10	2.95
BCE, Inc.	39.45	19.96	1.98
Biomira, Inc.	9.96	1.05	9.49
Bombardier	22.7	2.57	8.83
Canada Bread	13.2	10.99	1.20
Shaw Communications	35.51	7.33	4.84
Mitel	13.95	5.25	2.66
Microcell Telecommunications	12.24	–10	n/a
Westcoast Energy	35.75	22.76	1.57
Westjet	24	4.02	5.97

Source: Stock prices from www.globeinvestor.com, book value from *Financial Post*'s "Investor Reports."

[7] This is partly due to inflation. Book values for Canadian and U.S. corporations are not inflation-adjusted. Also, when the accountants set up the original depreciation schedule, nobody anticipated how long these aircraft would remain in service.

them but would be difficult to sell intact to other firms. Take Biomira, a biotechnology company developing drugs for treating cancer. As you can see from Table 5.2, it sells for about 9.5 times book value. Where did all that extra value come from? Largely, it resulted from the expected success of its extensive research and development (R&D) program. Canadian accountants don't recognize R&D as an investment and don't put it on the company's balance sheet. Successful R&D and the expectation of successful R&D do show up in stock prices, however.

3. *Value of future investments.* If investors believe a company will have the opportunity to make exceedingly profitable investments in the future, they will pay more for the company's stock today. When 360networks, Inc., a provider of fibre-optic communications products and services, first sold its stock to investors on April 20, 2000, the book value of shareholders' equity was about $1.58 per share; yet, investors paid $21 per share in the IPO. Within a month, the shares were trading at $330—far exceeding the book value. 360networks, Inc., was a *growth company*. In large part, the high market value reflected the value of future investments in fibre-optic networks and the accompanying revenues to be collected from companies using the networks.

Market price need not, and generally does not, equal either book value or liquidation value. Unlike market value, neither book value nor liquidation value treats the firm as a going concern.

It is not surprising that stocks virtually never sell at book or liquidation values. Investors buy shares based on present and *future* earning power. Two key features determine the profits the firm will be able to produce: first, the earnings that can be generated by the firm's current tangible and intangible assets, and second, the opportunities the firm has to invest in lucrative projects that will increase future earnings.

▶ EXAMPLE 5.1 *Pacific Northern Gas and Nortel Networks*

Pacific Northern Gas, a gas pipeline utility servicing northern British Columbia, is not a growth company, its market is limited to the geographic area it services. More importantly, it is a regulated utility so its profits on present and future investment are limited.

In contrast, Nortel Networks, a telecommunications equipment manufacturer, is a growth company. Despite the fact that Nortel had negative net income in 1998, 1999, and 2000, the stock price grew exponentially, hitting a high of $123.10 in July 2000. The value came from Nortel's market position, its highly regarded products, and the promise of product innovations and future sales that would presumably lead to future earnings. Nortel is a growth firm because much of its market value depended on intangible assets and the profitability of future investments. It is not surprising then that in July 2000, Pacific Northern Gas shares sold for less than book value while Nortel sold for about 40 times book value.

Subsequently, however, Nortel experienced a colossal drop in share price, largely the result of unexpected decreases in current and expected future sales. Between its high in July 2000 and March 2002, the stock price fell from $115 to about $7.50, almost a 94 percent loss in value. As of March 2002, Nortel's shares sold for about 3.7 times book value. Pacific Northern Gas still traded below book value.

Future investment opportunities are great sources of market value but vulnerable to rapid loss when expectations for the future change. In contrast, earnings from current assets are much more stable. Companies with significant value from growth, such as Nortel, experience wider price swings than those with less value from growth, such as Pacific Northern Gas.

market-value balance sheet Financial statement that uses the market value of all assets and liabilities.

Financial executives are not bound by generally accepted accounting principles, and they sometimes construct a firm's **market-value balance sheet.** Such a balance sheet helps them to think about and evaluate the sources of firm value. Take a look at Table 5.3. A market-value balance sheet contains two classes of assets: (1) assets already in place (a) tangible and (b) intangible, and (2) opportunities to invest in attractive future ventures. Pacific Northern Gas's stock market value is dominated by tangible assets in place; Nortel's by the value of future investment opportunities.

Other firms, like Microsoft, have it all. Microsoft earns plenty from its current products. These earnings are part of what makes the stock attractive to investors. In addition, investors are willing to pay for the company's ability to invest profitably in new ventures that will increase future earnings.

Let's summarize. Just remember:

- *Book value* records what a company has paid for its assets with a simple and often unrealistic deduction for depreciation and no adjustment for inflation. It does not capture the true value of a business.
- *Liquidation value* is what the company could net by selling its assets and repaying its debts. It does not capture the value of a successful "going concern."
- *Market value* is the amount that investors are willing to pay for the shares of the firm. This depends on the earning power of *today's* assets and the expected profitability of *future* investments.

The next question is: What determines market value?

CHECK POINT 5.2

In the 1970s, the computer industry was dominated by IBM and was growing rapidly. In the 1980s, many new competitors entered the market, and computer prices fell. Computer makers in the 1990s, including IBM, struggled with thinning profit margins and intense competition. How has IBM's market-value balance sheet changed over time? Have assets in place become proportionately more or less important? Do you think this progression is unique to the computer industry?

5.3 Valuing Common Stocks

TODAY'S PRICE AND TOMORROW'S PRICE

The cash payoff to owners of common stocks comes in two forms: (1) cash dividends, and (2) capital gains or losses. Usually investors expect to get some of each. Suppose that the current price of a share is P_0, that the expected price a year from now is P_1, and that the expected dividend per share is DIV_1. The subscript on P_0 denotes "time zero," which is today; the subscript on P_1 denotes "time 1," which is 1 year hence. We simplify by assuming that dividends are paid only once a year and that the next dividend will come in

TABLE 5.3 *Market-value balance sheet*

A MARKET-VALUE BALANCE SHEET	
Assets	**Liabilities and Shareholders' Equity**
Assets in place	Market value of debt and other obligations
Investment opportunities	Market value of shareholders' equity

1 year. The rate of return that investors expect from this share over the next year is the expected dividend per share DIV_1 plus the expected increase in price $P_1 - P_0$, all divided by the price at the start of the year P_0:

$$\textbf{Expected return} = r = \frac{\mathbf{DIV_1 + P_1 - P_0}}{\mathbf{P_0}} \tag{5.1}$$

Let us now look at how our formula works. Suppose Blue Skies' stock is selling for $75 a share ($P_0$ = $75). Investors expect a $3 cash dividend over the next year (DIV_1 = $3). They also expect the stock to sell for $81 a year hence ($P_1$ = $81). Then the expected return to shareholders is 12 percent:

$$r = \frac{\$3 + \$81 - \$75}{\$75} = .12\text{, or } 12\%$$

Notice that this expected return comes in two parts, the dividend and capital gain:

$$\begin{aligned}\text{Expected rate of return} &= \text{expected dividend yield} + \text{expected capital gain}\\ &= \frac{DIV_1}{P_0} + \frac{P_1 - P_0}{P_0}\\ &= \frac{\$3}{\$75} + \frac{\$81 - \$75}{\$75}\\ &= .04 + .08 = .12\text{, or } 12\%\end{aligned}$$

Of course, the *actual* return for Blue Skies may turn out to be more or less than investors expect. Actual stock returns were negative for many companies in 2001. For example, Nortel's share price on June 27, 2000, was $101.50. One year later, it was $12.83. During the year, dividends of $0.075 were paid, providing an actual rate of return of ($.075 + $12.83 – $101.50)/$101.50 = –.873, or – 87.3 percent!

This figure is almost certainly well below investor expectations. At the other extreme, the share price of Zenon Environmental, developer of water purification systems, increased from $6.75 on June 27, 2000, to $15.50 1 year later. Since it did not pay a dividend, investors earned an actual return of ($0 + $15.50 – $6.75)/$6.75 = 1.30, or 130 percent—well above expectations. Never confuse the actual outcome with the expected outcome.

When you take taxes into account, your rate of return will be lower since both dividend income and capital gains are taxable. To calculate the after-tax rate of return on your stock investment, first determine the taxes on dividends and capital gains, and then use the after-tax cash flows in the return calculation. For example, suppose you bought shares of Big Time Toys for $15, received a dividend of $1, and sold the shares a year later for $17. Your before-tax rate of return is ($1 + $17 – $15)/$15 = .2, or 20 percent. Suppose your marginal personal tax rate is 35 percent. However, only 50 percent of capital gains are subject to tax, and the tax on dividends is reduced by both the federal and provincial dividend tax credits.[8] To simplify, assume that the dividend tax rate is 20 percent; thus, the tax on dividends is .2 × $1 or $.20. The tax on the capital gain is .5 × .35 × ($17 – $15), or $.35. The after-tax rate of return is ($1 – $.2 + $17 – $15 – $.35)/$15 = .1633, or 16.33 percent.

We saw how to work out the expected return on Blue Skies stock given today's stock price and forecasts of next year's stock price and dividends. You can also explain the

[8] Go back to Chapter 2 for details on the taxation of dividend income.

market value of the stock in terms of investors' forecasts of dividends and price, and the expected return offered by other equally risky stocks. This is just the present value of the cash flows the stock will provide to its owner:

$$\text{Price today} = P_0 = \frac{\text{DIV}_1 + P_1}{1 + r}$$

For Blue Skies $\text{DIV}_1 = \$3$ and $P_1 = \$81$. If stocks of similar risk offer an expected return of $r = 12$ percent, then today's price for Blue Skies should be \$75:

$$P_0 = \frac{\$3 + \$81}{1.12} = \$75$$

How do we know that \$75 is the right price? Because no other price could survive in competitive markets. What if P_0 were above \$75? Then the expected rate of return on Blue Skies stock would be *lower* than on other securities of equivalent risk. Investors would bail out of Blue Skies stock and substitute the other securities. In the process they would force down the price of Blue Skies stock. If P_0 were less than \$75, Blue Skies stock would offer a *higher* expected rate of return than equivalent-risk securities. Everyone would rush to buy, forcing the price up to \$75. When the stock is priced correctly (that is, price equals present value), the *expected* rate of return on Blue Skies stock is also the rate of return that investors *require* to hold the stock.

At each point in time all securities of the same risk are priced to offer the same expected rate of return. This is a fundamental characteristic of prices in well-functioning markets. It is also common sense.

CHECK POINT 5.3

Androscoggin Copper is increasing next year's dividend to \$5 per share. The forecast stock price next year is \$105. Equally risky stocks of other companies offer expected rates of return of 10 percent. What should Androscoggin common stock sell for?

THE DIVIDEND DISCOUNT MODEL

We have managed to explain today's stock price P_0 in terms of the dividend DIV_1 and the expected stock price next year P_1. But future stock prices are not easy to forecast directly, though you may encounter individuals who claim to be able to do so. A formula that requires tomorrow's stock price to explain today's stock price is not generally helpful.

As it turns out, we can express a stock's value as the present value of all the forecast future dividends paid by the company to its shareholders without referring to the future stock price. This is the **dividend discount model**:

dividend discount model Discounted cash-flow model of today's stock price which states that share value equals the present value of all expected future dividends.

$$P_0 = \text{present value of } (\text{DIV}_1, \text{DIV}_2, \text{DIV}_3, \ldots, \text{DIV}_t, \ldots)$$

$$= \frac{\text{DIV}_1}{1+r} + \frac{\text{DIV}_2}{(1+r)^2} + \frac{\text{DIV}_3}{(1+r)^3} + \cdots + \frac{\text{DIV}_t}{(1+r)^t} + \cdots$$

How far out in the future could we look? In principle, 40, 60, or 100 years or more—corporations are potentially immortal. However, far-distant dividends will not have significant present values. For example, the present value of \$1 received in 30 years using a 10 percent discount rate is only \$.057. Most of the value of established companies comes from dividends to be paid within a person's working lifetime.

How do we get from the one-period formula $P_0 = (\text{DIV}_1 + P_1)/(1 + r)$ to the dividend discount model? We look at increasingly long investment horizons.

Let's consider investors with different investment horizons. Each investor will value the share of stock as the present value of the dividends that she expects to receive plus the present value of the price at which the stock is eventually sold. Unlike bonds, however, the final horizon date for stocks is not specified—stocks do not "mature." Moreover, both dividends and final sales price can only be estimated. But the general valuation approach is the same. For a one-period investor, the valuation formula looks like this:

$$P_0 = \frac{\text{DIV}_1 + P_1}{1 + r}$$

A 2-year investor would value the stock as

$$P_0 = \frac{\text{DIV}_1}{1 + r} + \frac{\text{DIV}_2 + P_2}{(1 + r)^2}$$

and a 3-year investor would use the formula

$$P_0 = \frac{\text{DIV}_1}{1 + r} + \frac{\text{DIV}_2}{(1 + r)^2} + \frac{\text{DIV}_3 + P_3}{(1 + r)^3}$$

In fact we can look as far out into the future as we like. Suppose we call our horizon date H. Then the stock valuation formula would be

$$\mathbf{P_0 = \frac{DIV_1}{1 + r} + \frac{DIV_2}{(1 + r)^2} + \ldots + \frac{DIV_H + P_H}{(1 + r)^H}} \tag{5.2}$$

In words, the value of a stock is the present value of the dividends it will pay over the investor's horizon plus the present value of the expected stock price at the end of that horizon.

Does this mean that investors of different horizons will all come to different conclusions about the value of the stock? No! Regardless of the investment horizon, the stock value will be the same. This is because the stock price at the horizon date is determined by expectations of dividends from that date forward. Therefore, as long as the investors are consistent in their assessment of the prospects of the firm, they will arrive at the same present value. Let's confirm this with an example.

▸ EXAMPLE 5.2 *Valuing Blue Skies Stock*

Take Blue Skies. The firm is growing steadily and investors expect both the stock price and the dividend to increase at 8 percent per year. Now consider three investors: Erste, Zweiter, and Dritter. Erste plans to hold Blue Skies for 1 year, Zweiter for 2, and Dritter for 3. Compare their payoffs:

	Year 1	Year 2	Year 3
Erste	$\text{DIV}_1 = 3$ $P_1 = 81$		
Zweiter	$\text{DIV}_1 = 3$	$\text{DIV}_2 = 3.24$ $P_2 = 87.48$	
Dritter	$\text{DIV}_1 = 3$	$\text{DIV}_2 = 3.24$	$\text{DIV}_3 = 3.50$ $P_3 = 94.48$

Remember, we assumed that dividends and stock prices for Blue Skies are expected to grow at a steady 8 percent. Thus $DIV_2 = \$3 \times 1.08 = \$3.24$, $DIV_3 = \$3.24 \times 1.08 = \$3.50$, and so on.

Erste, Zweiter, and Dritter all require the same 12 percent expected return. So we can calculate present value over Erste's 1-year horizon:

$$PV = \frac{DIV_1 + P_1}{1+r} = \frac{\$3 + \$81}{1.12} = \$75$$

or Zweiter's 2-year horizon:

$$\begin{aligned} PV &= \frac{DIV_1}{1+r} + \frac{DIV_2 + P_2}{(1+r)^2} \\ &= \frac{\$3.00}{1.12} + \frac{\$3.24 + \$87.48}{(1.12)^2} \\ &= \$2.68 + \$72.32 = \$75 \end{aligned}$$

or Dritter's 3-year horizon:

$$\begin{aligned} PV &= \frac{DIV_1}{1+r} + \frac{DIV_2}{(1+r)^2} + \frac{DIV_3 + P_3}{(1+r)^3} \\ &= \frac{\$3}{1.12} + \frac{\$3.24}{(1.12)^2} + \frac{\$3.50 + \$94.48}{(1.12)^3} \\ &= \$2.68 + \$2.58 + \$69.74 = \$75 \end{aligned}$$

All agree the stock is worth \$75 per share. This illustrates our basic principle: The value of a common stock equals the present value of dividends received out to the investment horizon plus the present value of the forecast stock price at the horizon. Moreover, when you move the horizon date, the stock's present value should not change. The principle holds for horizons of 1, 3, 10, 20, and 50 years or more.

CHECK POINT 5.4

Refer to Check Point 5.3. Assume that Androscoggin Copper's dividend and share price are expected to grow at a constant 5 percent rate per year. Calculate the current value of Androscoggin stock with the dividend discount model using a 3-year horizon. You should get the same answer as in Check Point 5.3.

Look at Table 5.4, which continues the Blue Skies example for various time horizons, still assuming that the dividends are expected to increase at a steady 8 percent compound

TABLE 5.4
Value of Blue Skies' stock for various time horizons, given 8 percent growth of dividends

Horizon, Years	PV (Dividends)	+	PV (Terminal Price)	=	Value per Share
1	\$ 2.68		\$72.32		\$75.00
2	5.26		69.74		75.00
3	7.75		67.25		75.00
10	22.87		52.13		75.00
20	38.76		36.24		75.00
30	49.81		25.19		75.00
50	62.83		12.17		75.00
100	73.02		1.98		75.00

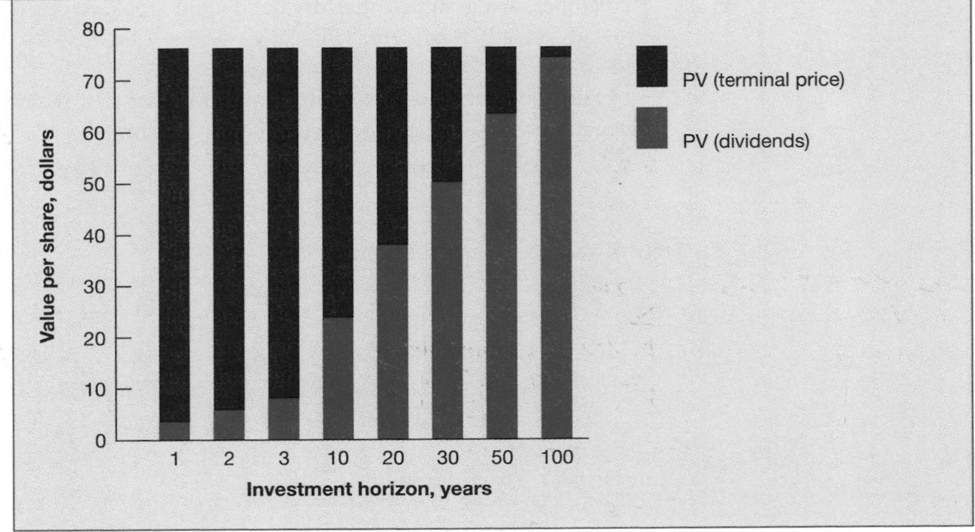

FIGURE 5.3
Value of Blue Skies for different horizons

rate. The expected price increases at the same 8 percent rate. Each row in the table represents a present value calculation for a different horizon year. Note that present value does not depend on the investment horizon. Figure 5.3 presents the same data in a graph. Each column shows the present value of the dividends up to the horizon and the present value of the price at the horizon. As the horizon recedes, the dividend stream accounts for an increasing proportion of present value, but the *total* present value of dividends plus terminal price always equals \$75.

If the horizon is infinitely far away, then we can forget about the final horizon price—it has almost no present value—and simply say

Stock price = PV (all future dividends per share) (5.3)

This is the dividend discount model.

5.4 Simplifying the Dividend Discount Model

THE DIVIDEND DISCOUNT MODEL WITH NO GROWTH

Consider a company that pays out all its earnings to its common shareholders. Such a company could not grow because it could not reinvest.[9] Stockholders might enjoy a generous immediate dividend, but they could forecast no increase in future dividends. The company's stock would offer a perpetual stream of equal cash payments, $\text{DIV}_1 = \text{DIV}_2 = \cdots = \text{DIV}_t = \cdots$.

The dividend discount model says that these no-growth shares should sell for the present value of a constant, perpetual stream of dividends. We learned how to do that calculation when we valued perpetuities in Chapter 3. Just divide the annual cash payment by the discount rate. The discount rate is the rate of return demanded by investors in other stocks of the same risk:

$$P_0 = \frac{\text{DIV}_1}{r}$$

[9] Assuming it does not raise money by issuing new shares.

Since our company pays out all its earnings as dividends, dividends and earnings are the same, and we could just as well calculate stock value by

$$\text{Value of a no-growth stock} = P_0 = \frac{\text{EPS}_1}{r}$$

where EPS_1 represents next year's earnings per share of stock. Thus some people loosely say, "Stock price is the present value of future earnings," and calculate value by this formula. Be careful—this is a special case. We'll return to the formula later in this chapter.

CHECK POINT 5.5

Moonshine Industries has produced a barrel per week for the past 20 years but cannot grow because of certain legal hazards. It earns \$25 per share per year and pays it all out to shareholders. The shareholders have alternative, equivalent-risk ventures yielding 20 percent per year on average. How much is one share of Moonshine worth? Assume the company can keep going indefinitely.

THE CONSTANT-GROWTH DIVIDEND DISCOUNT MODEL

The dividend discount model requires a forecast of dividends for every year into the future, which poses a bit of a problem for stocks with lives that are potentially infinite. Unless we want to spend a lifetime forecasting dividends, we must use simplifying assumptions to reduce the number of estimates. The easiest simplification assumes a no-growth perpetuity that works for no-growth common shares.

Here's another simplification that finds a good deal of practical use: Suppose forecast dividends grow at a constant rate into the indefinite future. If dividends grow at a steady rate, then instead of forecasting an infinite number of dividends, we need to forecast only the next dividend and the dividend growth rate.

Recall Blue Skies. It will pay a \$3 dividend in 1 year. If the dividend grows at a constant rate of $g = .08$ (8 percent) thereafter, then dividends in future years will be

$$\begin{aligned}
\text{DIV}_1 &= \$3 &&= \$3.00\\
\text{DIV}_2 &= \$3 \times (1+g) = \$3 \times 1.08 &&= \$3.24\\
\text{DIV}_3 &= \$3 \times (1+g)^2 = \$3 \times 1.08^2 &&= \$3.50
\end{aligned}$$

Plug these forecasts of future dividends into the dividend discount model:

$$\begin{aligned}
P_0 &= \frac{D_1}{1+r} + \frac{D_1(1+g)}{(1+r)^2} + \frac{D_1(1+g)^2}{(1+r)^3} + \frac{D_1(1+g)^3}{(1+r)^4} + \cdots\\
&= \frac{\$3}{1.12} + \frac{\$3.24}{1.12^2} + \frac{\$3.50}{1.12^3} + \frac{\$3.78}{1.12^4} + \cdots\\
&= \$2.68 + \$2.58 + \$2.49 + \$2.40 + \cdots
\end{aligned}$$

Although there is an infinite number of terms, each term is proportionately smaller than the preceding one as long as the dividend growth rate g is less than the discount rate r. Because the present value of far-distant dividends will always get closer to zero, the sum of all of these terms is finite despite the fact that an infinite number of dividends will be paid. The sum can be shown to equal

$$P_0 = \frac{\text{DIV}_1}{r-g}$$

This equation is called the **constant-growth dividend discount model,** or the *Gordon growth model*, after Myron Gordon, who popularized it.[10]

▶ EXAMPLE 5.3 *Blue Skies Valued by the Constant-Growth Model*

Let's apply the constant-growth model to Blue Skies. Assume a dividend has just been paid. The next dividend, to be paid in a year, is forecast at $DIV_1 = \$3$, the growth rate of dividends is $g = 8$ percent, and the discount rate is $r = 12$ percent. Therefore, we solve for the stock value as

$$P_0 = \frac{DIV_1}{r - g} = \frac{\$3}{.12 - .08} = \$75$$

constant-growth dividend discount model Version of the dividend discount model in which dividends grow at a constant rate.

The constant-growth formula is close to the formula for the present value of a perpetuity. Suppose you forecast no growth in dividends ($g = 0$). Then the dividend stream is a simple perpetuity, and the valuation formula is $P_0 = DIV_1/r$. This is precisely the formula you used in Check Point 5.5 to value Moonshine, a no-growth common stock.

The constant-growth model generalizes the perpetuity formula to allow for constant growth in dividends. Notice that as g increases, the stock price also rises. However, the constant-growth formula is valid only when g is less than r. If someone forecasts perpetual dividend growth at a rate greater than investors' required return r, then two things happen:

1. The formula explodes. It gives nutty answers. (Try a numerical example.)
2. You know the forecast is wrong because far-distant dividends would have incredibly high present values. (Again, try a numerical example. Calculate the present value of a dividend paid after 100 years, assuming $DIV_1 = \$3$, $r = .12$, but $g = .20$.)

ESTIMATING EXPECTED RATES OF RETURN

We argued earlier in Section 5.3 that in competitive markets common stocks with the same risk are priced to offer the same expected rate of return. But how do you figure out what that expected rate of return is?

It's not easy. Consensus estimates of future dividends, stock prices, or overall rates of return are not published in the *Globe and Mail* or reported by TV newscasters. Economists argue about which statistical models give the best estimates. There are nevertheless some useful rules of thumb that can give sensible numbers.

One rule of thumb is based on the constant-growth dividend discount model. Remember that it forecasts a constant growth rate g in both future dividends and stock prices. That means forecast capital gains equal g per year.

We can calculate the expected rate of return by rearranging the constant-growth formula as

$$\begin{aligned} r &= \frac{DIV_1}{P_0} + g \qquad (5.4) \\ &= \textbf{dividend yield + growth rate} \end{aligned}$$

[10] Notice that the first dividend is assumed to come at the *end* of the first period and is discounted for a full period. If the stock has just paid its dividend, then next year's dividend will be $(1 + g)$ times the dividend just paid. So another way to write the valuation formula is

$$P_0 = \frac{DIV_1}{r - g} = \frac{DIV_0 \times (1 + g)}{r - g}$$

For Blue Skies, the expected first-year dividend is \$3 and the growth rate 8 percent. With an initial stock price of \$75, the expected rate of return is

$$
\begin{aligned}
r &= \frac{\text{DIV}_1}{P_0} + g \\
&= \frac{\$3}{\$75} + .08 = .04 + .08 = .12, \text{ or } 12\%
\end{aligned}
$$

Suppose we found another stock with the same risk as Blue Skies. It ought to offer the same expected rate of return even if its immediate dividend or expected growth rate is very different. The required rate of return is not the unique property of Blue Skies or any other company; it is set in the worldwide market for common stocks. Blue Skies cannot change its value of r by paying higher or lower dividends, or by growing faster or slower, unless these changes also affect the risk of the stock. When we use the rule of thumb formula, $r = \text{DIV}_1/P_0 + g$, we are *not* saying that r, the expected rate of return, is *determined by* DIV_1 or g. It is determined by the rate of return offered by other equally risky stocks. That return determines how much investors are willing to pay for Blue Skies' forecast future dividends:

$$
\underbrace{\frac{\text{DIV}_1}{P_0}}_{\substack{\text{Given DIV}_1 \text{ and} \\ g\text{, investors set} \\ \text{the stock price}}} + g = r = \underbrace{\text{expected rate of return offered by other, equally risky stocks}}_{\substack{\text{so that Blue Skies offers an} \\ \text{adequate expected rate of} \\ \text{return, } r}}
$$

▸ EXAMPLE 5.4 *Blue Skies Gets a Windfall*

Blue Skies has won a lawsuit against its archrival, Nasty Manufacturing; the lawsuit forces Nasty Manufacturing to withdraw as a competitor in a key market. As a result Blue Skies is able to generate 9 percent per year future growth without sacrificing immediate dividends. Will that increase r, the expected rate of return?

This is very good news for Blue Skies shareholders. The stock price will jump to

$$
P_0 = \frac{\text{DIV}_1}{r - g} = \frac{\$3}{.12 - .09} = \$100
$$

But at the new price Blue Skies will offer the same 12 percent expected return:

$$
\begin{aligned}
r &= \frac{\text{DIV}_1}{P_0} + g \\
&= \frac{\$3}{\$100} + .09 = .12, \text{ or } 12\%
\end{aligned}
$$

Blue Skies' good news is reflected in a higher stock price today not in a higher expected rate of return in the future. The unchanged expected rate of return corresponds to Blue Skies' unchanged risk.

☑ CHECK POINT 5.6

Androscoggin Copper can grow at 5 percent per year indefinitely. It's selling at \$100, and next year's dividend is \$5. What is the expected rate of return from investing in Carrabasset Mining common stock? Carrabasset and Androscoggin shares are equally risky.

Few real companies are expected to grow in such a regular and convenient way as Blue Skies or Androscoggin Copper. Nevertheless, in some mature industries, growth is reasonably stable and the constant-growth model approximately valid. In such cases the model can be turned around to infer the rate of return expected by investors.

NONCONSTANT GROWTH

Many companies grow at rapid or irregular rates for several years before finally settling down. Obviously we can't use the constant-growth dividend discount model in such cases. However, we have already looked at an alternative approach. Set the *investment horizon* (Year H) at the future year by which you expect the company's growth to settle down. Calculate the present value of dividends from now to the horizon year. Forecast the stock price in that year and discount it also to present value. Then add it up to get the total present value of dividends plus the ending stock price. The formula is

$$P_0 = \underbrace{\frac{\text{DIV}_1}{1+r} + \frac{\text{DIV}_2}{(1+r)^2} + \cdots + \frac{\text{DIV}_H}{(1+r)^H}}_{\text{PV of dividends from Year 1 to horizon}} + \underbrace{\frac{P_H}{(1+r)^H}}_{\text{PV of stock price at horizon}} \qquad (5.5)$$

The stock price in the horizon year is often called *terminal value.*

▶ EXAMPLE 5.5 *Estimating the Value of United Bird Seed's Stock*

Ms. Dawn Chorus, founder and president of United Bird Seed, is wondering whether the company should make its first public sale of common stock, and if so, at what price.

The company's financial plan envisages rapid growth over the next 3 years but only moderate growth afterwards. Forecast earnings and dividends are as follows:

Year	1	2	3	4	5	6	7	8
Earnings per share	$2.45	3.11	3.78	5% growth thereafter				
Dividends per share	$1.00	1.20	1.44	5% growth thereafter				

Thus you have a forecast of the dividend stream for the next 3 years. The tricky part is to estimate the price in the Year 3 horizon. Ms. Chorus could look at stock prices for mature pet food companies whose scale, risk, and growth prospects today roughly match those projected for United Bird Seed in Year 3. Suppose further that these companies tend to sell at price-earnings ratios of about 8. Then you could reasonably guess that the P/E ratio of United will likewise be 8. That implies

$$P_3 = 8 \times \$3.78 = \$30.24$$

You are now in a position to determine the value of shares in United. If investors demand a return of $r = 10$ percent, then the price today should be

$$P_0 = \text{PV (dividends from Years 1 to 3)} + \text{PV (forecast stock price in Year 3)}$$

$$\text{PV (dividends)} = \frac{\$1.00}{1.10} + \frac{\$1.20}{1.10^2} + \frac{\$1.44}{1.10^3} = \$2.98$$

$$\text{PV}(P_H) = \frac{\$30.24}{(1.10)^3} = \$22.72$$

$$P_0 = \$2.98 + \$22.72 = \$25.70$$

Thus, the price today should be about \$25.70 per share.

United Bird Seed is looking forward to several years of very rapid growth, so you could not use the constant-growth formula to value United's stock today. But the formula may help you check your estimate of the terminal price in Year 3, when the company has settled down to a steady rate of growth. From then on dividends are forecast to grow at a constant rate of $g = .05$, or 5 percent. Thus the expected dividend in Year 4 is

$$\text{DIV}_4 = 1.05 \times \text{DIV}_3 = 1.05 \times \$1.44 = \$1.512$$

and the expected terminal price in Year 3 is

$$P_3 = \frac{\text{DIV}_4}{r - g} = \frac{\$1.512}{.10 - .05} = \$30.24$$

the same value we found when we used the P/E ratio to predict P_3. In this case our two approaches give the same estimate of P_3, though you shouldn't bet on that always being the case in practice.

CHECK POINT 5.7

Suppose that another stock market analyst predicts that United Bird Seed will not settle down to a constant 5 percent growth rate in dividends until after Year 4, and that dividends in Year 4 will be \$1.73 per share. What is the fair price for the stock according to this analyst?

5.5 Growth Stocks and Income Stocks

We often hear investors speak of *growth stocks* and *income stocks.* They seem to buy growth stocks primarily in the expectation of capital gains, and they are interested in the future growth of earnings rather than in next year's dividends. On the other hand, they buy income stocks principally for the cash dividends. Let us see whether these distinctions make sense.

Think back once more to Blue Skies. It is expected to pay a dividend next year of \$3 ($\text{DIV}_1 = 3$), and this dividend is expected to grow at a steady rate of 8 percent a year ($g = .08$). If investors require a return of 12 percent ($r = .12$), then the price of Blue Skies should be $\text{DIV}_1/(r - g) = \$3/(.12 - .08) = \$75$.

payout ratio Fraction of earnings paid out as dividends.

plowback ratio Fraction of earnings retained by the firm.

Suppose that Blue Skies' existing assets generate earnings per share of \$5. It pays out 60 percent of these earnings as a dividend. This **payout ratio** results in a dividend of .60 × \$5 = \$3. The remaining 40 percent of earnings, the **plowback ratio,** is retained by the firm and "plowed back" into a new plant and new equipment. (The plowback ratio is also called the earnings *retention ratio.*) On this new equity investment Blue Skies earns a return of 20 percent.

If *all* of these earnings were plowed back into the firm, Blue Skies would grow at 20 percent per year. Because a portion of earnings is not reinvested in the firm, the growth rate will be less than 20 percent. The higher the fraction of earnings plowed back into the company, the higher the growth rate. So assets, earnings, and dividends all grow by

$$\begin{aligned} g &= \textbf{return on equity} \times \textbf{plowback ratio} \\ &= .20 \times .40 = .08, \text{ or } 8\% \end{aligned}$$

What if Blue Skies did not plow back any of its earnings into a new plant and new equipment? In that case it would pay out all its earnings as dividends but would forgo any growth in dividends. So we could recalculate value with $\text{DIV}_1 = \$5$ and $g = 0$:

$$P_0 = \frac{\$5.00}{.12 - 0} = \$41.67$$

Thus if Blue Skies did not reinvest any of its earnings, its stock price would not be \$75 but \$41.67. The \$41.67 represents the value of earnings from the assets that are already in place. The rest of the stock price (\$75 – \$41.67 = \$33.33) is the net present value of the future investments that Blue Skies is expected to make. This is reflected in the market-value balance sheet, Table 5.5.

What if Blue Skies kept to its policy of reinvesting 40 percent of its profits, but the forecast return on this new investment was only 12 percent? In that case the expected growth in dividends would also be lower:

$$g = \text{return on equity} \times \text{plowback ratio}$$
$$= .12 \times .40 = .048, \text{ or } 4.8\%$$

If we plug this new value for g into our valuation formula, again we come up with a value of \$41.67 for Blue Skies stock:

$$P_0 = \frac{\text{DIV}_1}{r - g} = \frac{\$3.00}{.12 - .048} = \$41.67$$

Plowing earnings back into new investments may result in growth in earnings and dividends, but it does not add to the current stock price if that money is expected to earn only the return that investors require. Plowing earnings back *does* add to value if investors believe that the reinvested earnings will earn a higher rate of return than investors require.

present value of growth opportunities (PVGO) Net present value of a firm's future investments.

sustainable growth rate Steady rate at which a firm can grow; return on equity times plowback ratio.

To repeat, if Blue Skies did not plow back earnings or if it earned only the return that investors required on the new investment, its stock price would be \$41.67. The total value of Blue Skies stock is \$75. Of the \$75, \$41.67 is the value of the assets already in place, and the remaining \$33.33 is the present value of the superior returns on assets to be acquired in the future. The latter is called the **present value of growth opportunities,** or **PVGO.** (Remember that investors expected Blue Skies to earn 20 percent on its new investments, well above the 12 percent expected return necessary to attract investors.)

By the way, growth rates calculated as

$$g = \text{return on equity} \times \text{plowback ratio}$$

are often referred to as **sustainable growth rates.**

☑ CHECK POINT 5.8

Suppose that instead of plowing money back into lucrative ventures, Blue Skies' management is investing at an expected return on equity of 10 percent, which is *below* the return of 12 percent that investors could expect to get from comparable securities.

TABLE 5.5

MARKET-VALUE BALANCE SHEET FOR BLUE SKIES
(all quantities on a per-share basis)

Assets		Liabilities and Shareholders' Equity	
Assets in place	\$41.67	Shareholders' equity	\$75
Investment opportunities	33.33	Debt*	0

*We assume the firm is all-equity financed.

a. Find the sustainable growth rate of dividends and earnings in the above circumstances. Assume a 60 percent payout ratio.
b. Find the new value of its investment opportunities. Explain why this value is negative despite the positive growth rate of earnings and dividends.
c. If you were a corporate raider, would Blue Skies be a good candidate for an attempted takeover?

THE PRICE-EARNINGS RATIO

The superior prospects of Blue Skies are reflected in its price-earnings ratio. With a stock price of $75 and earnings of $5, the P/E ratio is $75/$5 = 15. If Blue Skies had no growth opportunities, its stock price would be only $41.67 and its P/E would be $41.67/$5 = 8.33. The P/E ratio, therefore, is an indicator of the prospects of the firm. To justify a high P/E, one must believe the firm is endowed with ample growth opportunities.

WHAT DO EARNINGS MEAN?

Be careful when you look at price-earnings ratios. In our discussion, "expected future earnings" refer to expected cash flow less the true depreciation in the value of the assets. What is "true" depreciation? It is the amount that the firm must reinvest simply to offset any deterioration in its assets. In practice, however, when accountants calculate the earnings that are reported in the company's income statement, they do not attempt to measure true depreciation. Instead reported earnings are based on generally accepted accounting principles, which use rough-and-ready rules of thumb to calculate the depreciation of the firm's assets. A switch in the depreciation method can dramatically change reported earnings without affecting the true profitability of the firm.

Other accounting choices that can affect reported earnings are the method for valuing inventories, the decision to treat research and development as a current expense rather than as an investment, and the way that tax liabilities are reported.

The dramatic appreciation in stock prices in the late 1990s was attributed by many investors to a "new paradigm," where the revolution in information technology would boost company profitability. Stephen Jarislowsky, a Montreal-based money manager, and Warren Buffett, an American money manager, were among others who argued that the price increases were based on groundless speculation. Others pointed out that distortions were created in the income statements of technology companies because large investments in research, development, software, and training had to be treated as expenses, which immediately reduced reported earnings. Had GAAP permitted them to be accounted as investments in intangible assets, the spending would have been gradually depreciated over time, reducing reported earnings more slowly. They argued that the unusually high P/E ratios were due in part to these accounting methods, which understate earnings—the stock market participants correctly gave high prices to the shares of these stocks.

We now know that the prices of the high-tech flyers have crashed back to earth, and many of the companies have or will go bankrupt. This raises tough questions about how to correctly value shares. We will discuss this topic further in Chapter 12.

VALUING ENTIRE BUSINESSES

Investors routinely buy and sell shares of common stock. Companies frequently buy and sell entire businesses. So it is natural to ask whether the formulas that we have presented in this chapter can also be used to value these businesses.

FINANCE IN ACTION

A Small Spat about $1.6 Billion

Company valuation is not a precise science. When two companies dispute the price that one should pay for the other, a battle between their investment bankers can be guaranteed.

AT&T bought McCaw Cellular in 1994. As a result it acquired McCaw's 52 percent stake in the shares of a cellular communications company, LIN Broadcasting, and assumed an obligation to buy the remaining 48 percent of the shares at their fair value. The process for determining fair value was laid down when McCaw acquired its initial stake in LIN. AT&T and LIN had 30 days to come up with an initial valuation of the shares and then a further 15 days to consider their final numbers. If the two companies' valuations were less than 10 percent apart, AT&T would be obliged to buy at the average of the two prices. If they were more than 10 percent apart, an independent arbitrator would be appointed. If the arbitrator decided that the true value was about midway between the two companies' valuations, then the arbitrator's valuation would be used. If it was close to AT&T's valuation, then the arbitrator's price and AT&T's price would be averaged, and LIN's valuation would be ignored. Conversely, if it was close to LIN's figure, then the arbitrator's price would be averaged in with LIN's valuation and AT&T's figure would be ignored.

Each company appointed an investment bank to prepare and argue its case. AT&T's case was presented by Morgan Stanley while LIN's case was prepared by Bear Stearns and Lehman Brothers. Each side faced a quandary. AT&T's advisers were tempted to go for a low figure, while LIN's advisers were tempted to come up with a high figure. But if the dispute went to arbitration, then an extreme valuation was more likely to be out of line with the arbitrator's figure, and therefore was more likely to be ignored. It seemed to make sense to take an extreme position only if each could be sure that the other side would do so also. Conversely, a more middle-of-the-road posture made sense if each could be confident that the other would provide a middle-of-the-road valuation.

When the two parties met at Morgan Stanley's offices to examine each other's valuations, there was a stunned silence, and then Bear Stearns' team began to laugh. Morgan Stanley's valuation was $100 a share, while Lehman Brothers and Bear Stearns came up with a figure of $162 a share. Since AT&T was proposing to buy 25 million LIN shares, the disagreement amounted to a thumping $1.6 billion.

Fifteen days later the two sides met again to exchange their final valuations. There was an air of shock in the room; despite hearing the other side's arguments, the difference in their valuations had barely narrowed. It seemed that an independent arbitrator was required, and so another investment bank, Wasserstein Perella, was called in to provide an independent valuation.

Some weeks later a herd of about 50 investment bankers and lawyers crowded into the offices of Wasserstein Perella to defend their estimates of the value of LIN. Comparisons were made with the value of other cellular communications companies. Each side presented projections of LIN's future profits and dividends. There were also arguments about the rate at which these future dividends should be discounted. For example, each side argued that the other had failed to properly measure the risk of the stock.

The final upshot: After hearing the arguments from both sides, Wasserstein Perella placed a value of $127.50 on each share of LIN. This meant that the total cost of the shares to AT&T was about $3.3 billion.

Source: The story of the valuation of LIN Broadcasting is set out in S. Neish, "Wrong Number," *Global M&A* (Summer 1995).

Sure! Take the case of Blue Skies. Suppose that it has 2 million shares outstanding. It plans to pay a dividend of DIV_1 = $3 a share. So the *total* dividend payment is 2 million × $3 = $6 million. Investors expect a steady dividend growth of 8 percent a year and require a return of 12 percent. So the total value of Blue Skies is

$$PV = \frac{\$6 \text{ million}}{.12 - .08} = \$150 \text{ million}$$

Alternatively, we could say that the total value of the company is the number of shares times the value per share:

$$PV = 2 \text{ million} \times \$75 = \$150 \text{ million}$$

Of course things are always harder in practice than in principle. Forecasting cash flows and settling on an appropriate discount rate require skill and judgment. As the above Finance in Action box shows, there can be plenty of room for disagreement.

5.6 Summary

1. **What information about company stocks is regularly reported in the financial pages of newspapers and online financial services?**

Firms that wish to raise new capital may either borrow money or bring new "partners" into the business by selling shares of **common stock.** Large companies usually arrange for their stocks to be traded on a stock exchange. The stock listings report the stock's **dividend yield,** price, and trading volume.

2. **How can one calculate the present value of a stock given forecasts of future dividends and future stock price?**

Shareholders generally expect to receive (1) cash **dividends,** and (2) capital gains or losses. The rate of return that they expect over the next year is defined as the expected dividend per share DIV_1 plus the expected increase in price $P_1 - P_0$, all divided by the price at the start of the year P_0.

Unlike the fixed interest payments that the firm promises to bondholders, the dividends that are paid to shareholders depend on the fortunes of the firm. That's why a company's common stock is riskier than its debt. The return that investors expect on any one stock is also the return that they demand on all stocks subject to the same degree of risk. The present value of a stock equals the present value of the forecast future dividends and future stock price, using that expected return as the discount rate.

3. **How can stock valuation formulas be used to infer the expected rate of return on a common stock?**

The present value of a share is equal to the stream of expected dividends per share up to some horizon date plus the expected price at this date, all discounted at the return that investors require. If the horizon date is far away, we simply say that stock price equals the present value of all future dividends per share. This is the **dividend discount model.**

If dividends are expected to grow forever at a constant rate g, then the expected return on the stock is equal to the dividend yield (DIV_1/P_0) plus the expected rate of dividend growth. The value of the stock according to this **constant-growth dividend discount model** is $P_0 = \text{DIV}_1/(r - g)$.

4. **How should investors interpret price-earnings ratios?**

You can think of a share's value as the sum of two parts—the value of the assets in place and the **present value of growth opportunities,** that is, of future opportunities for the firm to invest in high-return projects. The **price-earnings (P/E) ratio** reflects the market's assessment of the firm's growth opportunities.

RELATED WEB LINKS

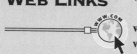

www.ganesha.org/invest/index.html Links to information useful for valuing securities
www.tsx.ca Information about stocks trading on the Toronto Stock Exchange and the TSX Venture Exchange
www.nasdaq.com Information about Nasdaq and Amex-traded stocks
www.nyse.com Information about stocks and trading on the New York Stock Exchange
www.fool.com/School/HowtoValueStocks.htm How investors value firms
www.zacks.com Information and analyses from Zacks Investment Research
www.investools.com Investing tools, links to research reports on public companies and investment newsletters
www.brill.com Information on mutual funds, as well as articles and other educational resources
www.nationalpost.com Look up stock prices
www.globeinvestor.com Information about companies and their common share prices

Key Terms

common stock 139
primary market 139
initial public offering (IPO) 139
secondary market 139
dividend 141
price-earnings (P/E) multiple 142
book value 142
liquidation value 143
market-value balance sheet 145
dividend discount model 147
constant-growth dividend discount model 152
payout ratio 155
plowback ratio 155
present value of growth opportunities (PVGO) 156
sustainable growth rate 156

Questions and Problems

*Answers in Appendix B

Basic

1. **Dividend Discount Model.** Corus Entertainment has never paid a dividend, but its share price is $35 and the market value of its stock is $1,488 million. Does this invalidate the dividend discount model?
2. **Dividend Yield.** Favoured stock will pay a dividend this year of $2.40 per share. Its dividend yield is 8 percent. At what price is the stock selling?

*3. **Preferred Stock.** Preferred Products has issued preferred stock with a $7 annual dividend that will be paid in perpetuity.
   a. If the discount rate is 12 percent, at what price should the preferred sell?
   b. At what price should the stock sell 1 year from now?
   c. What is the dividend yield, the capital gains yield, and the expected rate of return of the stock?

4. **Constant-Growth Model.** Waterworks has a dividend yield of 8 percent. If its dividend is expected to grow at a constant rate of 5 percent, what must be the expected rate of return on the company's stock?
5. **Dividend Discount Model.** How can we say that price equals the present value of all future dividends when many actual investors may be seeking capital gains and planning to hold their shares for only a year or two? Explain.

*6. **Rate of Return.** Steady As She Goes, Inc. will pay a year-end dividend of $2.50 per share. Investors expect the dividend to grow at a rate of 4 percent indefinitely.
   a. If the stock currently sells for $25 per share, what is the expected rate of return on the stock?
   b. If the expected rate of return on the stock is 16.5 percent, what is the stock price?

7. **Dividend Yield.** BMM Industries pays a dividend of $2 per quarter. The dividend yield on its stock is reported at 4.8 percent. What price is the stock selling at?

Practice

*8. **Stock Values.** Integrated Potato Chips paid a $1 per share dividend *yesterday*. You expect the dividend to grow steadily at a rate of 4 percent per year.
   a. What is the expected dividend in each of the next 3 years?
   b. If the discount rate for the stock is 12 percent, at what price will the stock sell?
   c. What is the expected stock price 3 years from now?
   d. If you buy the stock and plan to hold it for 3 years, what payments will you receive? What is the present value of those payments? Compare your answer to part (b).

9. **Constant-Growth Model.** A stock sells for $40. The next dividend will be $4 per share. If the rate of return earned on reinvested funds is 15 percent and the company reinvests 40 percent of earnings in the firm, what must be the discount rate?

*10. **Constant-Growth Model.** Gentleman Gym just paid its annual dividend of $2 per share, and it is widely expected that the dividend will increase by 5 percent per year indefinitely.
   a. What price should the stock sell at? The discount rate is 15 percent.
   b. How would your answer change if the discount rate were only 12 percent? Why does the answer change?

11. **Constant-Growth Model.** Arts and Crafts, Inc. will pay a dividend of $5 per share in 1 year. It sells at $50 a share, and firms in the same industry provide an expected rate of return of 14 percent. What must be the expected growth rate of the company's dividends?

*12. **Constant-Growth Model.** Eastern Electric currently pays a dividend of about $1.64 per share and sells for $27 a share.

a. If investors believe the growth rate of dividends is 3 percent per year, what rate of return do they expect to earn on the stock?

b. If investors' required rate of return is 10 percent, what must be the growth rate they expect of the firm?

c. If the sustainable growth rate is 5 percent and the plowback ratio is .4, what must be the rate of return earned by the firm on its new investments?

13. **Constant-Growth Model.** You believe that the Non-Stick Gum Factory will pay a dividend of $2 on its common stock next year. Thereafter, you expect dividends to grow at a rate of 6 percent a year in perpetuity. If you require a return of 12 percent on your investment, how much should you be prepared to pay for the stock?

14. **Negative Growth.** Horse and Buggy Inc. is in a declining industry. Sales, earnings, and dividends are all shrinking at a rate of 10 percent per year.

a. If r = 15 percent and DIV_1 = $3, what is the value of a share?

b. What price do you forecast for the stock next year?

c. What is the expected rate of return on the stock?

d. Can you distinguish between "bad stocks" and "bad companies"? Does the fact that the industry is declining mean that the stock is a bad buy?

*15. **Constant-Growth Model.** Metatrend's stock will generate earnings of $5 per share this year. The discount rate for the stock is 15 percent and the rate of return on reinvested earnings is also 15 percent.

a. Find both the growth rate of dividends and the price of the stock if the company reinvests the following fraction of its earnings in the firm: (1) 0 percent (2) 40 percent (3) 60 percent.

b. Redo part (a) now assuming that the rate of return on reinvested earnings is 20 percent. What is the present value of growth opportunities for each reinvestment rate?

c. Considering your answers to parts (a) and (b), can you briefly state the difference between companies experiencing growth versus companies with growth opportunities?

*16. **Nonconstant Growth.** You expect a share of stock to pay dividends of $1, $1.25, and $1.50 in each of the next 3 years. You believe the stock will sell for $20 at the end of the third year.

a. What is the stock price if the discount rate for the stock is 10 percent?

b. What is the dividend yield?

17. **Constant-Growth Model.** Here are recent data on two stocks, both of which have discount rates of 15 percent:

	Stock A	Stock B
Return on equity	15%	10%
Earnings per share	$2.00	$1.50
Dividends per share	$1.00	$1.00

a. What are the dividend payout ratios for each firm?

b. What are the expected dividend growth rates for each firm?

c. What is the proper stock price for each firm?

*18. **P/E Ratios.** Web Cites Research projects a rate of return of 20 percent on new projects. Management plans to plow back 30 percent of all earnings into the firm. Earnings this year will be $2 per share, and investors expect a 12 percent rate of return on the stock.

a. What is the sustainable growth rate?
b. What is the stock price?
c. What is the present value of growth opportunities?
d. What is the P/E ratio?
e. What would the price and P/E ratio be if the firm paid out all earnings as dividends?
f. What do you conclude about the relationship between growth opportunities and P/E ratios?

19. **Constant-Growth Model.** Fincorp will pay a year-end dividend of $4.80 per share, which is expected to grow at a 4 percent rate indefinitely. The discount rate is 12 percent.
    a. What is the stock selling for?
    b. If earnings are $6.20 a share, what is the implied value of the firm's growth opportunities?

*20. **P/E Ratios.** No-Growth Industries pays out all of its earnings as dividends. It will pay its next $4 per share dividend in a year. The discount rate is 12 percent.
    a. What is the price-earnings ratio of the company?
    b. What would the P/E ratio be if the discount rate were 10 percent?

21. **Growth Opportunities.** Stormy Weather has no attractive investment opportunities. Its return on equity equals the discount rate, which is 10 percent. Its expected earnings this year are $3 per share. Find the stock price, P/E ratio, and growth rate of dividends for plowback ratios of
    a. zero
    b. .40
    c. .80

*22. **Growth Opportunities.** Trend-line Inc. has been growing at a rate of 6 percent per year and is expected to continue to do so indefinitely. The next dividend is expected to be $5 per share.
    a. If the market expects a 10 percent rate of return on Trend-line, at what price must it be selling?
    b. If Trend-line's earnings per share will be $8, what part of Trend-line's value is due to assets in place, and what part to growth opportunities?

23. **P/E Ratios.** Castles in the Sand generates a rate of return of 20 percent on its investments and maintains a plowback ratio of .30. Its earnings this year will be $2 per share. Investors expect a 12 percent rate of return on the stock.
    a. Find the price and P/E ratio of the firm.
    b. What happens to the P/E ratio if the plowback ratio is reduced to .20? Why?
    c. Show that if plowback equals zero, the earnings-price ratio, E/P, falls to the expected rate of return on the stock.

24. **Dividend Growth.** Grandiose Growth has a dividend growth rate of 20 percent. The discount rate is 10 percent. The end-of-year dividend will be $2 per share.
    a. What is the present value of the dividend to be paid in Year 1? Year 2? Year 3?
    b. Could anyone rationally expect this growth rate to continue indefinitely?

*25. **Stock Valuation.** Start-up Industries is a new firm, which has raised $100 million by selling shares of stock. Management plans to earn a 24 percent rate of return on equity, which is more than the 15 percent rate of return available on comparable-risk investments. Half of all earnings will be reinvested in the firm.
    a. What will be Start-up's ratio of market value to book value?
    b. How would that ratio change if the firm can earn only a 10 percent rate of return on its investments?

26. **Nonconstant Growth.** Planned Obsolescence has a product that will be in vogue for 3 years, at which point the firm will close up shop and liquidate the assets. As a result, forecast dividends are DIV_1 = $2, DIV_2 = $2.50, and DIV_3 = $18. What is the stock price if the discount rate is 12 percent?

*27. **Nonconstant Growth.** Tattletale News Corp. has been growing at a rate of 20 percent per year, and you expect this growth rate in earnings and dividends to continue for another 3 years.

a. If the last dividend paid was $2, what will the next dividend be?

b. If the discount rate is 15 percent and the steady growth rate after 3 years is 4 percent, what should the stock price be today?

28. **Nonconstant Growth.** Reconsider Tattletale News from the previous problem.

a. What is your prediction for the stock price in 1 year?

b. Show that the expected rate of return equals the discount rate.

*29. **After-Tax Rate of Return.** One year ago you purchased 100 shares of Dog Bites common stock for $25. You received dividends of $.70 per share and just sold the shares for $26.25 each. What are your before- and after-tax rates of return? Your marginal personal tax rate is 40 percent, your dividend tax rate is 30 percent, and capital gains are taxed at 50 percent of your personal rate.

CHALLENGE

30. **Sustainable Growth.** Computer Corp. reinvests 60 percent of its earnings in the firm. The stock sells for $50, and the next dividend will be $2.50 per share. The discount rate is 15 percent. What is the rate of return on the company's reinvested funds?

31. **Nonconstant Growth.** A company will pay a $1 per share dividend in 1 year. The dividend in 2 years will be $2 per share, and it is expected that dividends will grow at 5 percent per year thereafter. The expected rate of return on the stock is 12 percent.

a. What is the current price of the stock?

b. What is the expected price of the stock in a year?

c. Show that the expected return, 12 percent, equals dividend yield plus capital appreciation.

32. **Nonconstant Growth.** Phoenix Industries has pulled off a miraculous recovery. Four years ago it was near bankruptcy. Today, it announced a $1 per share dividend to be paid a year from now, the first dividend since the crisis. Analysts expect dividends to increase by $1 a year for another 2 years. After the third year (in which dividends are $3 per share), dividend growth is expected to settle down to a more moderate long-term growth rate of 6 percent. If the firm's investors expect to earn a return of 14 percent on this stock, what must be its price?

*33. **Nonconstant Growth.** Compost Science, Inc. (CSI) is in the business of converting Boston's sewage sludge into fertilizer. The business is not in itself very profitable. However, to induce CSI to remain in business, the Metropolitan District Commission (MDC) has agreed to pay whatever amount is necessary to yield CSI a 10 percent return on investment. At the end of the year, CSI is expected to pay a $4 dividend. It has been reinvesting 40 percent of earnings and growing at 4 percent a year.

a. Suppose CSI continues on this growth trend. What is the expected rate of return from purchasing the stock at $100?

b. What part of the $100 price is attributable to the present value of growth opportunities?

c. Now the MDC announces a plan for CSI to treat Cambridge sewage. CSI's plant will therefore be expanded gradually over 5 years. This means that CSI will have to reinvest 80 percent of its earnings for 5 years. Starting in Year 6, however, it will again be able to pay out 60 percent of earnings. What will be CSI's stock price once this announcement is made and its consequences for CSI are known?

34. **Nonconstant Growth.** Better Mousetraps has come out with an improved product, and the world is beating a path to its door. As a result, the firm projects growth of 20 percent per year for 4 years. By then, other firms will have copycat technology, competition will drive down profit margins, and the sustainable growth rate will fall to 5 percent. The most recent annual dividend was DIV_0 = $1.00 per share.

a. What are the expected values of DIV_1, DIV_2, DIV_3, and DIV_4?
b. What is the expected stock price 4 years from now? The discount rate is 10 percent.
c. What is the stock price today?
d. Find the dividend yield, DIV_1/P_0.
e. What will next year's stock price, P_1, be?
f. What is the expected rate of return to an investor who buys the stock now and sells it in 1 year?

35. **After-Tax Rate of Return.** You live in B.C. and your marginal federal tax rate is 22 percent, your marginal provincial tax rate is 11.9 percent, the dividend gross-up factor is 125 percent, the federal dividend tax credit is 13.33 percent of grossed-up dividends, and the provincial dividend tax credit is 6.6 percent of grossed-up dividends. If you bought shares of Mighty Mixer for $50, received dividends of $2, and sold the shares for $53 1 year after you bought them, what are your before- and after-tax rates of return?

36. **After-Tax Rate of Return.** Refer back to problem 35. Suppose you bought the shares of Mighty Mixer for $50, received annual dividends of $2, and sold the shares for $55, 3 years after you bought them. What are your before- and after-tax rates of return on your investment? *Hint:* You will need to make an assumption about what happens to the $2 dividends received in Year 1 and Year 2.

37. **After-Tax Rate of Return.** You have $10,000 to invest and are considering either a consol (a perpetual bond) or preferred shares of Canada Leasing. The consol has a $1,000 par value, an annual coupon rate of 4 percent, and never matures. The preferred share pays fixed dividends of $6 and is expected to continue indefinitely. Currently, the consol is selling for $800 and the preferred share for $120.
    a. What is the before-tax expected rate of return on each of the investments?
    b. If your personal tax rate is 35 percent, your dividend tax rate is 29 percent, and capital gains are taxed at 50 percent of the personal tax rate, what is the after-tax expected rate of return on each investment?
    c. What is the expected rate of return on each investment to a Canadian corporation with a corporate tax rate of 35 percent?
    d. Why do you think that many of the preferred shares sold by Canadian corporations are purchased by other Canadian corporations?

38. **Nonconstant Growth.** Skyward Ideas currently pays no dividends but invests all of its earnings into the company. Analysts expect that in 3 years from today, the company will pay its first annual dividend of $.50 and dividends will grow at 6 percent thereafter. If the discount rate is 10 percent, at what price should the stock sell today?

39. **Nonconstant Growth.** City Garden Suppliers paid a $1 dividend yesterday. It is expected that the dividend will grow at 10 percent per year for 4 years, 8 percent per year for 10 years, and then grow at 5 percent per year thereafter. If the investors' expected rate of return is 12 percent, what is the stock worth today? *Hint:* Use the present value formula for a growing annuity from Chapter 3.

40. **Nonconstant Growth.** Golddigger, a gold exploration and development company, currently pays no dividends. Using the company's assay reports, analysts have determined the following possible outcomes of Goldigger's exploration efforts in 1 year:

Event	Probability	Annual Dividend per Share
High-quality gold vein	40%	$8
Medium-quality gold vein	50	2
No gold	10	0

If gold is found, the mine is expected to operate for 20 years and then be exhausted. If investors expect to earn 9 percent on gold mining stocks, what will be the price of the stock today?

41. **Nonconstant Growth.** ABC Manufacturing pays dividends annually. Today is May 1, 2003. Its next dividend, to be paid in 1 year from today, will be $1.20 per share. The company is involved in a research and development (R&D) program to develop a new widget. The results are expected in 1 year. The discount rate is 10 percent.

   a. It is May 1, 2004. The new widget is a great success, and ABC pays its previously announced $1.20 dividend and announces the 2005 dividend will be $2.50 per share. What will be the stock price on May 1, 2004, if dividends are expected to grow at 6 percent in perpetuity?

   b. Suppose, instead, it is May 1, 2004, and the company announces that the widget program has ended and that the next annual dividend will be $1.248, 4 percent larger than the dividend it just paid. What is the stock price May 1, 2004?

   c. If the probability of success of the R&D is 30 percent, what price would you expect the stock to be today?

   d. Suppose you bought the stock for the price you calculated in part (c) and the research and development program is successful, what will be the 1-year rate of return on your investment? What will be the 1-year rate of return on your investment if the R&D is not successful? What is the expected rate of return?

Internet Problems

1. Information about companies and their shares abounds on the web. Visit www.globeinvestor.com and http://ca.finance.yahoo.com. Click on "Symbol Lookup" to find Molson Class A stock price history. What other types of information are reported on these websites?
2. Visit the Toronto Stock Exchange website at www.tsx.ca, click on "Listed Companies." Find Molson's information and compare it to what is found on www.globeinvestor.com or http://ca.finance.yahoo.com.
3. Pick two Canadian companies listed on either the TSX or the Venture Exchange and compare their stock price data and dividend payments. Go to each company's website and assess which one is doing a better job of providing information to shareholders.
4. Create a list of preferred shares traded on the Toronto Stock Exchange by using the "Filter" function on Globeinvestor.com. Select "Preferred" from the pull-down menu labelled "Security." Look at BCE.PR.P-T, which pays a fixed annual dividend of $1.60 per share. Use the current price of the preferred share to calculate the expected rate of return on the preferred share. If your personal tax rate is 35 percent and your dividend tax rate is 20 percent, what is the expected after-tax rate of return on these preferred shares?
5. It is difficult to get detailed information about companies' preferred shares from the web. Royal Bank, however, provides one exception. Look at www.rbc.com/investorrelations/preferred.html to learn about the specific features of the various classes of preferred shares they sell. Find the current yield on each class and compare them to each other. What conclusions can you draw about the market's assessment of these securities?

Solutions to Check Points

5.1 Methanx's (stock symbol MX) high and low prices over the past 52 weeks have been $13.95 and $3.99 per share. It pays no dividends. The highest price at which the shares traded during the day was $9, the lowest was $8.70, and the closing price was $8.75, which was $.35 higher than the previous day's close. Trading volume was 158,000 shares. The ratio of stock price to earnings per share, the P/E ratio, was 4.3.

5.2 IBM's forecast future profitability has fallen. Thus the value of future investment opportunities has fallen relative to the value of assets in place. This happens in all growth industries sooner or later, as competition increases and profitable new investment opportunities shrink.

5.3 $P_0 = \dfrac{\text{DIV}_1 + P_1}{1 + r} = \dfrac{\$5 + \$105}{1.10} = \$100$

5.4 Since dividends and share price grow at 5 percent,

$$\text{DIV}_2 = \$5 \times 1.05 = \$5.25,\ \text{DIV}_3 = \$5 \times 1.05^2 = \$5.51$$

$$P_3 = \$100 \times 1.05^3 = \$115.76$$

$$P_0 = \frac{\text{DIV}_1}{1 + r} + \frac{\text{DIV}_2}{(1 + r)^2} + \frac{\text{DIV}_3 + P_3}{(1 + r)^3}$$

$$= \frac{\$5.00}{1.10} + \frac{\$5.25}{1.10^2} + \frac{\$5.51 + \$115.76}{1.10^3} = \$100$$

5.5 $P_0 = \dfrac{\text{DIV}}{r} = \dfrac{\$25}{.20} = \$125$

5.6 The two firms have equal risk, so we can use the data for Androscoggin to find the expected return on either stock:

$$r = \frac{\text{DIV}_1}{P_0} + g = \frac{\$5}{\$100} + .05 = .10, \text{ or } 10\%$$

5.7 We've already calculated the present value of dividends through Year 3 as \$2.98. We can also forecast stock price in Year 4 as

$$P_4 = \frac{\$1.73 \times 1.05}{.10 - .05} = \$36.33$$

$$P_0 = \text{PV (dividends through Year 3)} + \text{PV}(\text{DIV}_4) + \text{PV}(P_4)$$

$$= \$2.98 + \frac{\$1.73}{1.10^4} + \frac{\$36.33}{1.10^4}$$

$$= \$2.98 + \$1.18 + \$24.81 = \$28.97$$

5.8 a. The sustainable growth rate is

$$g = \text{return on equity} \times \text{plowback ratio}$$

$$= .10 \times .40 = .04, \text{ or } 4\%$$

b. First value the company. At a 60 percent payout ratio, DIV_1 = \$3.00 as before. Using the constant-growth model,

$$P_0 = \frac{\$3}{.12 - .04} = \$37.50$$

which is \$4.17 per share less than the company's no-growth value of \$41.67. In this example Blue Skies is throwing away \$4.17 of potential value by investing in projects with unattractive rates of return.

c. Sure. A raider could take over the company and generate a profit of \$4.17 per share just by halting all investments offering less than the 12 percent rate of return demanded by investors. This assumes the raider could buy the shares for \$37.50.

MINICASE

Terence Breezeway, the CEO of Prairie Home Stores, wondered what retirement would be like. It was almost 20 years to the day since his uncle Jacob Breezeway, Prairie Home's founder, had asked him to take responsibility for managing the company. Now it was time to spend more time riding and fishing on the old Lazy Beta Ranch.

Under Mr. Breezeway's leadership Prairie Home had grown slowly but steadily and was solidly profitable. (Table 5.6 shows earnings, dividends, and book asset values for the last 5 years.) Most of the company's supermarkets had been modernized and its brand name was well-known.

Mr. Breezeway was proud of this record, although he wished that Prairie Home could have grown more rapidly. He had passed up several opportunities to build new stores in adjacent counties. Prairie Home was still just a family company. Its common stock was distributed among 15 grandchildren and nephews of Jacob Breezeway, most of whom had come to depend on generous regular dividends. The commitment to high-dividend payout had reduced the earnings available for reinvestment and thereby constrained growth.

Mr. Breezeway believed the time had come to take Prairie Home public. Once its shares were traded in the public market, the Breezeway descendants who needed (or just wanted) more cash to spend could sell off part of their holdings. Others with more interest in the business could hold on to their shares and be rewarded by higher future earnings and stock prices.

But if Prairie Home did go public, what should its shares sell for? Mr. Breezeway worried that shares would be sold, either by Breezeway family members or by the company itself, at too low a price. One relative was about to accept a private offer for $200, the current book value per share, but Mr. Breezeway had intervened and convinced the would-be seller to wait.

Prairie Home's value did not just depend on its current book value or earnings, but on its future prospects, which were good. One financial projection (shown in the top panel of Table 5.7) called for growth in earnings of over 100 percent by 2013. Unfortunately this plan would require reinvestment of all Prairie Home's earnings from 2008 to 2012. After that the company could resume its normal dividend payout and growth rate. Mr. Breezeway believed this plan was feasible.

He was determined to step aside for the next generation of top management. But before retiring he had to decide whether to recommend that Prairie Home Stores "go public"—and before that decision, he had to know what the company was worth.

Full of thought, he rode to work the next morning. He left his horse at the south corral and ambled down the dusty street to Mike Gordon's Saloon, where Francine Firewater, the company's CFO, was having her usual steak-and-beans breakfast. He asked Ms. Firewater to prepare a formal report to Prairie Home shareholders, valuing the company on the assumption that its shares were publicly traded.

Ms. Firewater asked two questions immediately: First, what should she assume about investment and growth? Mr. Breezeway suggested two valuations: one assuming more rapid expansion (as in the top panel of Table 5.7) and another just projecting past growth (as in the bottom panel of Table 5.7).

Second, what rate of return should she use? Mr. Breezeway said that 15 percent, Prairie Home's usual return on book equity, sounded right to him, but he referred her to an article in the *Journal of Finance* indicating that investors in rural supermarket chains, with risks similar to Prairie Home Stores, expected to earn about 11 percent on average.

TABLE 5.6
Financial data for Prairie Home Stores, 2002–2006 (figures in millions)

	2002	2003	2004	2005	2006
Book value, start of year	$62.7	66.1	69.0	73.9	76.5
Earnings	$9.7	9.5	11.8	11.0	11.2
Dividends	$6.3	6.6	6.9	7.4	7.7
Addition to retained earnings	$3.4	2.9	4.9	2.6	3.5
Book value, end of year	$66.1	69.0	73.9	76.5	80.0

Notes:
1. Prairie Home Stores has 400,000 common shares.
2. The company's policy is to pay cash dividends equal to 10 percent of start-of-year book value.

TABLE 5.7
Financial projections for Prairie Home Stores, 2007–2012 (figures in millions)

	2007	2008	2009	2010	2011	2012
Rapid-Growth Scenario						
Book value, start of year	80	92	105.8	121.7	139.9	146.9
Earnings	12	13.8	15.9	18.3	21.0	22.0
Dividends	0	0	0	0	14	14.7
Addition to retained earnings	12	13.8	15.9	18.3	7.0	7.4
Book value, end of year	92	105.8	121.7	140.0	146.9	154.3
Constant-Growth Scenario						
Book value, start of year	80	84	88.2	92.6	97.2	102.1
Earnings	12	12.6	13.2	13.9	14.6	15.3
Dividends	8	8.4	8.8	9.3	9.7	10.2
Addition to retained earnings	4	4.2	4.4	4.6	4.9	5.1
Book value, end of year	84	88.2	92.6	97.2	102.1	107.2

Notes:

1. Both panels assume earnings equal to 15 percent of start-of-year book value. This profitability rate is constant.
2. The top panel assumes all earnings are reinvested from the start of 2008 to the end of 2011. At the end of 2012 and later years, two-thirds of earnings are paid out as dividends and one-third reinvested.
3. The bottom panel assumes two-thirds of earnings are paid out as dividends in all years.
4. Columns may not add up because of rounding.

CHAPTER 6

Net Present Value and Other Investment Criteria

6.1 Net Present Value

6.2 Other Investment Criteria

6.3 Investment Criteria When Projects Interact

6.4 Capital Rationing

6.5 Summary

P. 169-181, 188-191.

The investment decision, also known as *capital budgeting,* is central to the success of the company. We have already seen that capital investments sometimes absorb substantial amounts of cash; they also have very long-term consequences. The assets you buy today may determine the business you are in many years hence.

For some investment projects "substantial" is an understatement. Consider the following examples:

- Construction of the Channel Tunnel linking England and France cost about $15 billion (US) from 1986 to 1994.
- The cost of bringing one new prescription drug to market was estimated to be at least $300 million (US).
- The development cost of Ford's "world car," the Mondeo, was about $6 billion (US).
- Production and merchandising costs for three new *Star Wars* movies are estimated at about $3 billion (US).
- The future development cost of a super-jumbo jet airliner, seating 600 to 800 passengers, has been estimated at over $10 billion (US).
- The 13-kilometre-long Confederation Bridge linking New Brunswick and Prince Edward Island cost $1 billion.
- The Sable Island Offshore Energy Project, which will bring natural gas to the Atlantic Provinces and northeastern United States through hundreds of kilometres of pipelines, is estimated to cost over $2 billion (US).

Notice from these examples of big capital projects that many projects require heavy investment in intangible assets. The costs of drug development are almost all research and testing, for example, and much of the development cost of Ford's Mondeo went into design and testing. Any expenditure made in the hope of generating more cash later can be called a *capital investment project,* regardless of whether the cash outlay goes to tangible or intangible assets.

A company's shareholders prefer to be rich rather than poor. Therefore, they want the firm to invest in every project that is worth more than it costs. The difference between a project's value and its cost is termed the *net present value.* Companies can best help their shareholders by investing in projects with a *positive* net present value.

We start this chapter by showing how to calculate the net present value of a simple investment project. We also examine other criteria that companies sometimes consider when evaluating investments, such as the project's payback period or book rate of return. We will see that these are little better than rules of thumb. Although there is a place for rules of thumb in this world, an engineer needs something more accurate when designing a 100-storey building, and a financial manager needs more than a rule of thumb when making a substantial capital investment decision.

Instead of calculating a project's net present value, companies sometimes compare the expected rate of return from investing in a project with the return that shareholders could earn on equivalent-risk investments in the capital market. Companies accept only those projects that provide a higher return than shareholders could earn for themselves. This rate of return rule generally gives the same answers as the net present value rule, but as we shall see, it has some pitfalls.

We then turn to more complex issues such as project interactions. These occur when a company is obliged to *choose* between two or more competing proposals; if it accepts one proposal, it cannot take the other. For example, a company may need to choose between buying an expensive, durable machine or a cheap and short-lived one. We will show how the net present value criterion can be used to make such choices.

Sometimes the firm may be forced to make choices because it does not have enough money to take on every project that it would like. We will explain how to maximize shareholder wealth when capital is rationed. It turns out that the solution is to pick the projects that have the highest net present value per dollar invested. This measure is known as the *profitability index.*

After studying this chapter you should be able to

- Calculate the net present value of an investment.
- Calculate the internal rate of return of a project and know what to look out for when using the internal rate of return rule.
- Explain why the payback and discounted payback rules and book rate of return rule *don't* always make shareholders better off.
- Use the net present value rule to analyze three common problems that involve competing projects: (a) when to postpone an investment expenditure, (b) how to choose between projects with equal lives, and (c) when to replace equipment.
- Calculate the profitability index and use it to choose between projects when funds are limited.

6.1 Net Present Value

In Chapter 3 you learned how to discount future cash payments to find their present value. We now apply these ideas to evaluate a simple investment proposal.

Suppose that you are in the real estate business. You are considering construction of an office block. The land would cost $50,000 and construction would cost a further $300,000. You foresee a shortage of office space and predict that a year from now you will be able to sell the building for $400,000. Thus you would be investing $350,000 now in the expectation of realizing $400,000 at the end of the year. You should go ahead if the present value of the $400,000 payoff is greater than the investment of $350,000.

Assume for the moment that the $400,000 payoff is a sure thing. The office building is not the only way to obtain $400,000 a year from now. You could invest in a 1-year Treasury bill. Suppose the T-bill offers interest of 7 percent. How much would you have to invest in it in order to receive $400,000 at the end of the year? That's easy: you would have to invest

$$\$400{,}000 \times \frac{1}{1.07} = \$400{,}000 \times .935 = \$373{,}832$$

Therefore, at an interest rate of 7 percent, the present value of the $400,000 payoff from the office building is $373,832.

Let's assume that as soon as you have purchased the land and laid out the money for construction, you decide to cash in on your project. How much could you sell it for? Since the property will be worth \$400,000 in a year, investors would be willing to pay at most \$373,832 for it now. That's all it would cost them to get the same \$400,000 payoff by investing in a government security. Of course you could always sell your property for less, but why sell for less than the market will bear?

The \$373,832 present value is the only price that satisfies both buyer and seller. In general, the present value is the only feasible price, and the present value of the property is also its *market price* or *market value.*

To calculate present value, we discounted the expected future payoff by the rate of return offered by comparable investment alternatives. The discount rate—7 percent in our example—is often known as the **opportunity cost of capital.** It is called the opportunity cost because it is the return that is being given up by investing in the project.

opportunity cost of capital Expected rate of return given up by investing in a project.

The building is worth \$373,832, but this does not mean that you are \$373,832 better off. You committed \$350,000, and therefore your **net present value (NPV)** is \$23,832. Net present value is found by subtracting the required initial investment from the present value of the project cash flows:

net present value (NPV) Present value of cash flows minus initial investment.

$$\textbf{NPV} = \textbf{PV} - \textbf{required investment} \qquad (6.1)$$
$$= \$373{,}832 - \$350{,}000 = \$23{,}832$$

In other words, your office development is worth more than it costs—it makes a *net* contribution to value.

The net present value *rule* states that managers increase shareholders' wealth by accepting all projects that are worth more than they cost. Therefore, they should accept all projects with a positive net present value.

A COMMENT ON RISK AND PRESENT VALUE

In our discussion of the office development we assumed we knew the value of the completed project. Of course, you will never be *certain* about the future values of office buildings. The \$400,000 represents the best *forecast,* but it is not a sure thing.

Therefore, our initial conclusion about how much investors would pay for the building is wrong. Since they could achieve \$400,000 risk-free by investing in \$373,832 worth of Treasury bills, they would not buy your building for that amount. You would have to cut your asking price to attract investors' interest.

Here we can invoke a basic financial principle:

A risky dollar is worth less than a safe one.

Most investors avoid risk when they can do so without sacrificing return. However, the concepts of present value and the opportunity cost of capital still apply to risky investments. It is still proper to discount the payoff by the rate of return offered by a comparable investment. But we have to think of *expected* payoffs and the *expected* rates of return on other investments.

Not all investments are equally risky. The office development is riskier than a Treasury bill, but is probably less risky than investing in a start-up biotech company. Suppose you believe the office development is as risky as an investment in the stock market and that you forecast a 12 percent rate of return for stock market investments. Then 12 percent would be the appropriate opportunity cost of capital. That is what you are giving up by not investing in comparable securities. You can now recompute NPV:

$$\text{PV} = \$400{,}000 \times \frac{1}{1.12} = \$400{,}000 \times .893 = \$357{,}143$$

$$\text{NPV} = \text{PV} - \$350{,}000 = \$7{,}143$$

If other investors agree with your forecast of a \$400,000 payoff and with your assessment of a 12 percent opportunity cost of capital, then the property ought to be worth \$357,143 once construction is under way. If you tried to sell for more than that, there would be no takers because the property would then offer a lower expected rate of return than the 12 percent available in the stock market. The office building still makes a net contribution to value, but it is much smaller than our earlier calculations indicated.

CHECK POINT 6.1

What is the office development's NPV if construction costs increase to \$355,000? Assume the opportunity cost of capital is 12 percent. Is the development still a worthwhile investment? How high can development costs be before the project is no longer attractive? Now suppose that the opportunity cost of capital is 20 percent with construction costs of \$355,000. Why is the office development no longer an attractive investment?

VALUING LONG-LIVED PROJECTS

The net present value rule works for projects of any length. For example, suppose that you have identified a possible tenant who would be prepared to rent your office block for 3 years at a fixed annual rent of \$16,000. You forecast that after you have collected the third year's rent the building could be sold for \$450,000. Thus the cash flow in the first year is C_1 = \$16,000, in the second year it is C_2 = \$16,000, and in the third year it is C_3 = \$466,000. For simplicity, we will again assume that these cash flows are certain and that the opportunity cost of capital is $r = 7$ percent.

Figure 6.1 shows a time line of these cash flows and their present values. To find the present values, we discount the future cash flows at the 7 percent opportunity cost of capital:

$$\text{PV} = \frac{C_1}{1+r} + \frac{C_2}{(1+r)^2} + \frac{C_3}{(1+r)^3}$$

$$= \frac{\$16{,}000}{1.07} + \frac{\$16{,}000}{(1.07)^2} + \frac{\$466{,}000}{(1.07)^3} = \$409{,}323$$

The net present value of the revised project is NPV = \$409,323 – \$350,000 = \$59,323. Constructing the office block and renting it for 3 years makes a greater addition to your wealth than selling the office block at the end of the first year.

Of course, rather than subtracting the initial investment from the project's present value, you could calculate NPV directly, as in the following equation, where C_0 denotes the initial cash outflow required to build the office block. (Notice that C_0 is negative, reflecting the fact that it is a cash outflow.)

$$\text{NPV} = C_0 + \frac{C_1}{1+r} + \frac{C_2}{(1+r)^2} + \frac{C_3}{(1+r)^3}$$

$$= -\$350{,}000 + \frac{\$16{,}000}{1.07} + \frac{\$16{,}000}{(1.07)^2} + \frac{\$466{,}000}{(1.07)^3} = \$59{,}323$$

Let's check that the owners of this project really are better off. Suppose you put up \$350,000 of your own money, commit to build the office building, and sign a lease that will bring in \$16,000 a year for 3 years. Now you can cash in by selling the project to someone else.

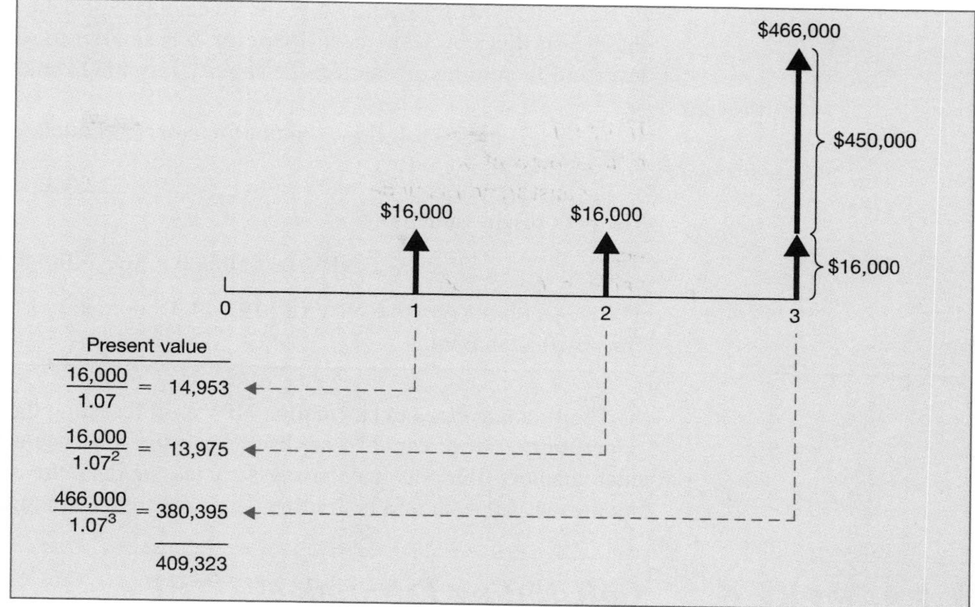

FIGURE 6.1
Cash flows and their present values for the office block project. Final cash flow of $466,000 is the sum of the rental income in Year 3 plus the forecast sales price for the building

Suppose you sell 1,000 shares in the project. Each share represents a claim to 1/1,000 of the future cash flows. Since the cash flows are sure things, and the interest rate offered by other sure things is 7 percent, investors will value the shares for

$$\text{Price per share} = P = \frac{\$16}{1.07} + \frac{\$16}{(1.07)^2} + \frac{\$466}{(1.07)^3} = \$40.93$$

Thus you can sell the project to outside investors for 1,000 × $40.93 = $409,300, which, save for rounding, is exactly the present value we calculated earlier. Your net gain is

$$\text{Net gain} = \$409,300 - \$350,000 = \$59,300$$

which is the project's NPV. This equivalence should be no surprise, since the present value calculation is *designed* to calculate the value of future cash flows to investors in the capital markets.

Notice that in principle there could be a different opportunity cost of capital for each period's cash flow. In that case, we would discount C_1 by r_1, the discount rate for 1-year cash flows; C_2 would be discounted by r_2; and so on. Here we assume that the cost of capital is the same regardless of the date of the cash flow. We do this for one reason only—simplicity. But we are in good company: with only rare exceptions, firms decide on an appropriate discount rate and then use it to discount all project cash flows.

▶ EXAMPLE 6.1 *Valuing a New Computer System*

Obsolete Technologies is considering the purchase of a new computer system to help handle its warehouse inventories. The system costs $50,000, is expected to last 4 years, and should reduce the cost of managing inventories by $22,000 a year. The opportunity cost of capital is 10 percent. Should Obsolete go ahead?

Don't be put off by the fact that the computer system does not generate any sales. If the expected cost savings are realized, the company's cash flows will be $22,000 a year higher as a result of buying the computer. Thus we can say that the computer increases cash flows by \$22,000 a year for each of 4 years. To calculate present value, you can discount each of these cash flows by 10 percent. However, it is smarter to recognize that the cash flows are level and therefore you can use the annuity formula to calculate the present value:

$$\begin{aligned} \text{PV} = \text{cash flow} \times \text{annuity factor} &= \$22{,}000 \times \left[\frac{1}{.10} - \frac{1}{.10(1.10)^4}\right] \\ &= \$22{,}000 \times 3.170 = \$69{,}740 \end{aligned}$$

The net present value is

$$\text{NPV} = -\$50{,}000 + \$69{,}740 = \$19{,}740$$

The project has a positive NPV of \$19,740. Undertaking it would increase the value of the firm by that amount.

The first two steps in calculating NPVs—forecasting the cash flows and estimating the opportunity cost of capital—are tricky, and we will have a lot more to say about them in later chapters. But once you have assembled the data, the calculation of present value and net present value should be routine. Here is another example.

EXAMPLE 6.2 *Calculating Eurotunnel's NPV*

One of the world's largest commercial investment projects was construction of the Channel Tunnel by the Anglo-French company Eurotunnel. Here is a chance to put yourself in the shoes of Eurotunnel's financial manager and find out whether the project looked like a good deal for shareholders. The figures in the column headed *cash flow* in Table 6.1 are based on the forecasts of construction costs and revenues that the company provided to investors in 1986.

The Channel Tunnel project was not a safe investment. Indeed the prospectus to the Channel Tunnel share issue cautioned investors that the project "involves significant risk and should be regarded at this stage as speculative. If for any reason the Project is abandoned or Eurotunnel is unable to raise the necessary finance, it is likely that equity investors will lose some or all of their money."

To induce them to invest in the project, investors needed a higher prospective rate of return than they could get on safe government bonds. Suppose investors expected a return of 13 percent from investments in the capital market that had a degree of risk similar to that of the Channel Tunnel. That was what investors were giving up when they provided the capital for the tunnel. To find the project's NPV, we therefore discount the cash flows in Table 6.1 at 13 percent.

Since the tunnel was expected to take about 7 years to build, there are 7 years of negative cash flows in Table 6.1. To calculate NPV you just discount all the cash flows, positive and negative, at 13 percent and sum the results. Call 1986 Year 0, 1987 Year 1, and so on. Then

$$\begin{aligned} \text{NPV} &= C_0 + \frac{C_1}{1+r} + \frac{C_2}{(1+r)^2} + \cdots \\ &= -£457 + \frac{-£476}{1.13} + \frac{-£497}{(1.13)^2} + \cdots + \frac{£17{,}781}{(1.13)^{24}} = £251 \text{ million} \end{aligned}$$

Net present value of the forecast cash flows is £251 million, making the tunnel a worthwhile project, though not by a wide margin, considering the planned investment of nearly £4 billion.

TABLE 6.1
Forecast cash flows and present values in 1986 for the Channel Tunnel. The investment apparently had a small positive NPV of £251 million (figures in millions of pounds).

Year	Cash Flow	PV at 13 Percent
1986	–£457	–£457
1987	–476	–421
1988	–497	–389
1989	–522	–362
1990	–551	–338
1991	–584	–317
1992	–619	–297
1993	211	90
1994	489	184
1995	455	152
1996	502	148
1997	530	138
1998	544	126
1999	636	130
2000	594	107
2001	689	110
2002	729	103
2003	796	100
2004	859	95
2005	923	90
2006	983	86
2007	1,050	81
2008	1,113	76
2009	1,177	71
2010	17,781	946
Total		+£251
	NPV = total = £251 million	

Note: Cash flow for 2010 includes the value in 2010 of forecast cash flows in all subsequent years.
Source: Eurotunnel Equity II Prospectus, October 1986. Used by permission. Some of these figures involve guesswork because the prospectus reported accumulated construction costs including interest expenses.

Of course, NPV calculations are only as good as the underlying cash-flow forecasts. The well-known Pentagon Law of Large Projects states that anything big takes longer and costs more than you were originally led to believe. As the law predicted, the tunnel proved much more expensive to build than anticipated in 1986, and the opening was delayed by more than a year. Revenues also have been below forecast, and Eurotunnel has not even generated enough profits to pay the interest on its debt. Thus, with hindsight, the tunnel was a negative-NPV venture.

6.2 Other Investment Criteria

Use of the net present value rule as a criterion for accepting or rejecting investment projects will maximize the value of the firm's shares. However, other criteria are sometimes also considered by firms when evaluating investment opportunities. Some of these rules are liable to give wrong answers; others simply need to be used with care. In this section, we introduce four of these alternative investment criteria: internal rate of return, payback and discounted payback periods, and book rate of return.

INTERNAL RATE OF RETURN

Instead of calculating a project's net present value, companies often prefer to ask whether the project's return is higher or lower than the opportunity cost of capital. For example, think back to the original proposal to build the office block. You planned to invest \$350,000 to get back a cash flow of C_1 = \$400,000 in 1 year. Therefore, you forecast a profit on the venture of \$400,000 – \$350,000 = \$50,000, and a rate of return of

$$\text{Rate of return} = \frac{\text{profit}}{\text{investment}} = \frac{C_1 - \text{investment}}{\text{investment}} = \frac{\$400{,}000 - \$350{,}000}{\$350{,}000}$$

$$= .1429, \text{ or about } 14.3\%$$

The alternative of investing in a Treasury bill would provide a return of only 7 percent. Thus the return on your office building is higher than the opportunity cost of capital.[1]

This suggests two rules for deciding whether to go ahead with an investment project:

1. *The NPV rule.* Invest in any project that has a positive NPV when its cash flows are discounted at the opportunity cost of capital.
2. *The rate of return rule.* Invest in any project offering a rate of return that is higher than the opportunity cost of capital.

Both rules set the same cutoff point. An investment that is on the knife edge with an NPV of zero will also have a rate of return that is just equal to the cost of capital.

Suppose that the rate of interest on Treasury bills is not 7 percent but 14.3 percent. Since your office project also offers a return of 14.3 percent, the rate of return rule suggests that there is now nothing to choose between taking the project and leaving your money in Treasury bills.

The NPV rule also tells you that if the interest rate is 14.3 percent, the project is evenly balanced with an NPV of zero:[2]

$$\text{NPV} = C_0 + \frac{C_1}{1+r} = -\$350{,}000 + \frac{\$400{,}000}{1.143} = 0$$

The project would make you neither richer nor poorer; it is worth what it costs. Thus the NPV rule and the rate of return rule both give the same decision on accepting the project.

A CLOSER LOOK AT THE RATE OF RETURN RULE

We know that if the office project's cash flows are discounted at a rate of 7 percent the project has a net present value of \$23,832. If they are discounted at a rate of 14.3 percent, it has an NPV of zero. In Figure 6.2 the project's NPV for a variety of discount rates is plotted. This is often called the *NPV profile* of the project. Notice two important things about Figure 6.2:

1. The project rate of return (in our example, 14.3 percent) is also the discount rate which would give the project a zero NPV. This gives us a useful definition: *the rate of return is the discount rate at which NPV equals zero.*[3]

[1] Recall that we are assuming the profit on the office building is risk-free. Therefore, the opportunity cost of capital is the rate of return on other risk-free investments.

[2] Notice that the initial cash flow C_0 is negative. The *investment* in the project is therefore $-C_0 = -(-\$350{,}000)$, or \$350,000.

[3] Check it for yourself. If NPV = $C_0 + C_1/(1 + r) = 0$, then rate of return = $(C_1 + C_0)/-C_0 = r$.

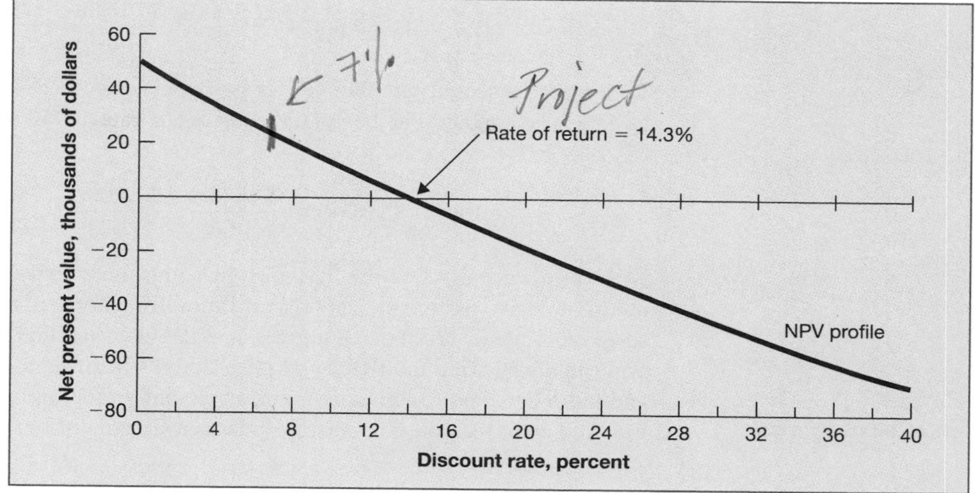

FIGURE 6.2
The value of the office project is lower when the discount rate is higher. The project has positive NPV if the discount rate is less than 14.3 percent.

2. If the opportunity cost of capital is less than the project rate of return, then the NPV of your project is positive. If the cost of capital is greater than the project rate of return, then NPV is negative. Thus the rate of return rule and the NPV rule are equivalent.

CALCULATING THE RATE OF RETURN FOR LONG-LIVED PROJECTS

There is no ambiguity in calculating the rate of return for an investment that generates a single payoff after one period. Remember that C_0, the time 0 cash flow corresponding to the initial investment, is negative. Thus

$$\text{Rate of return} = \frac{\text{profit}}{\text{investment}} = \frac{C_1 - \text{investment}}{\text{investment}} = \frac{C_1 + C_0}{-C_0}$$

But how do we calculate return when the project generates cash flows in several periods? Go back to the definition that we just introduced—*the project rate of return is also the discount rate which gives the project a zero NPV.* Managers usually refer to this figure as the project's **internal rate of return,** or **IRR.**[4] It is also known as the *discounted cash flow (DCF) rate of return.*

internal rate of return (IRR) Discount rate at which project NPV = 0.

Let's calculate the IRR for the revised office project. If you rent out the office block for 3 years, the cash flows are as follows:

Year	0	1	2	3
Cash flows	–$350,000	+16,000	+16,000	+466,000

The IRR is the discount rate at which these cash flows would have zero NPV. Thus

$$\text{NPV} = -\$350{,}000 + \frac{\$16{,}000}{1 + \text{IRR}} + \frac{\$16{,}000}{(1 + \text{IRR})^2} + \frac{\$466{,}000}{(1 + \text{IRR})^3} = 0$$

There is no simple general method for solving this equation. You have to rely on a little trial and error. Let us arbitrarily try a zero discount rate. This gives an NPV of $148,000:

[4] In Chapter 4 you learned how to calculate the yield to maturity on a bond. A bond's yield to maturity is just its internal rate of return.

$$NPV = -\$350{,}000 + \frac{\$16{,}000}{1.0} + \frac{\$16{,}000}{(1.0)^2} + \frac{\$466{,}000}{(1.0)^3} = \$148{,}000$$

With a zero discount rate the NPV is positive. So the IRR must be greater than zero.

The next step might be to try a discount rate of 50 percent. In this case NPV is –\$194,000:

$$NPV = -\$350{,}000 + \frac{\$16{,}000}{1.50} + \frac{\$16{,}000}{(1.50)^2} + \frac{\$466{,}000}{(1.50)^3} = -\$194{,}000$$

NPV is now negative. So the IRR must lie somewhere between zero and 50 percent. In Figure 6.3 we have plotted the net present values for a range of discount rates. You can see that a discount rate of 12.96 percent gives an NPV of zero. Therefore, the IRR is 12.96 percent. You can always find the IRR by plotting an NPV profile, as in Figure 6.3, but it is quicker and more accurate to let a computer or specially programmed financial calculator do the trial and error for you. The nearby Financial Calculator box illustrates how to do so.

The rate of return rule tells you to accept a project if the rate of return exceeds the opportunity cost of capital.

You can see from Figure 6.3 why this makes sense. Because the NPV profile is downward sloping, the project has a positive NPV as long as the opportunity cost of capital is less than the project's 12.96 percent IRR. If the opportunity cost of capital is higher than the 12.96 percent IRR, NPV is negative. Therefore, when we compare the project IRR with the opportunity cost of capital, we are effectively asking whether the project has a positive NPV. This was true for our one-period office project. It is also true for our three-period office project. We conclude that

The rate of return rule will give the same answer as the NPV rule *as long as the NPV of a project declines smoothly as the discount rate increases.*

The usual agreement between the net present value and internal rate of return rules should not be a surprise. Both are *discounted cash flow* methods of choosing between projects. Both are concerned with identifying those projects that make shareholders better off

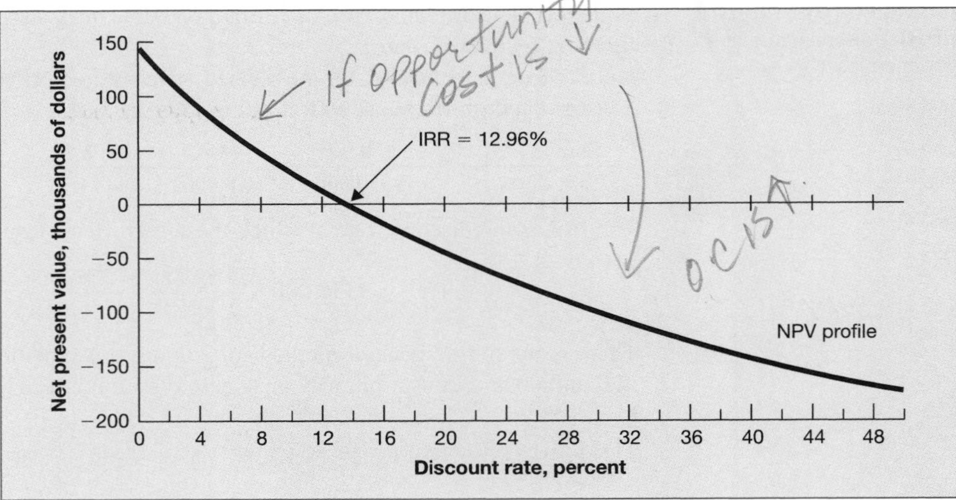

FIGURE 6.3
The internal rate of return is the discount rate for which NPV equals zero.

Using Financial Calculators to Find NPV and IRR

We saw in Chapter 3 that the formulas for the present and future values of level annuities and one-time cash flows are built into financial calculators. However, as the example of the office block illustrates, most investment projects entail multiple cash flows that cannot be expected to remain level over time. Fortunately, many calculators are equipped to handle problems involving a sequence of uneven cash flows. In general, the procedure is quite simple. You enter the cash flows one by one into the calculator, and then you press the IRR key to find the project's internal rate of return. The first cash flow you enter is interpreted as coming immediately, the next cash flow is interpreted as coming at the end of one period, and so on. We can illustrate using the office block as an example. To find the project IRR, you would use the following sequence of keystrokes:

Hewlett-Packard HP-10B	Sharpe EL-733A	Texas Instruments BA II Plus
–350,000 [CFj]	–350,000 [CFi]	[CF]
16,000 [CFj]	16,000 [CFi]	[2nd] [{CLR Work}]
16,000 [CFj]	16,000 [CFi]	–350,000 [ENTER] [↓]
466,000 [CFj]	466,000 [CFi]	16,000 [ENTER] [↓]
		16,000 [ENTER] [↓]
		466,000 [ENTER] [↓]
[ ] [{IRR/YR}]	[IRR]	[IRR]
		[CPT]

The calculator should display the value 12.96, the project's internal rate of return.

To calculate project NPV, the procedure is similar. You need to enter the discount rate in addition to the project cash flows, and then simply press the NPV key. Here is the specific sequence of keystrokes, assuming that the opportunity cost of capital is 7 percent:

Hewlett-Packard HP-10B	Sharpe EL-733A	Texas Instruments BA II Plus
–350,000 [CFj]	–350,000 [CFi]	[CF]
16,000 [CFj]	16,000 [CFi]	[2nd] [{CLR Work}]
16,000 [CFj]	16,000 [CFi]	–350,000 [ENTER] [↓]
466,000 [CFj]	466,000 [CFi]	16,000 [ENTER] [↓]
7 [I/YR]	7 [i]	16,000 [ENTER] [↓]
		466,000 [ENTER] [↓]
[ ] [{NPV}]	[NPV]	[NPV]
		7 [ENTER]
		[↓] [CPT]

The calculator should display the value 59,323, the project's NPV when the discount rate is 7 percent.

By the way, you can check the accuracy of our earlier calculations using your calculator. Enter 50 percent for the discount rate (press 50, then press *i*) and then press the NPV key to find that NPV = –194,148. Enter 12.96 (the project's IRR) as the discount rate and you will find that NPV is just about zero (it is not exactly zero, because we are rounding off the IRR to only two decimal places).

and both recognize that companies always have a choice: they can invest in a project or, if the project is not sufficiently attractive, they can give the money back to shareholders and let them invest it for themselves in the capital market.

CHECK POINT 6.2

Suppose the cash flow in Year 3 is only $416,000. Redraw Figure 6.3. How would the IRR change?

A WORD OF CAUTION

Some people confuse the internal rate of return on a project with the opportunity cost of capital. Remember that the project IRR measures the profitability of the project. It is an *internal* rate of return in the sense that it depends only on the project's own cash flows. The opportunity cost of capital is the standard for deciding whether to accept the project. It is equal to the return offered by equivalent-risk investments in the capital market.

PAYBACK

These days almost all large companies use discounted cash flow in some form, but sometimes they use it in combination with other theoretically inappropriate measures of performance. We next examine three of these measures: the payback period, the discounted payback period, and the book rate of return.

We suspect that you have often heard conversations that go something like this: "A washing machine costs about $400. But we are currently spending $3 a week, or around $150 a year, at the laundromat. So the washing machine should pay for itself in less than 3 years." You have just encountered the payback rule.

payback period Time until cash flows recover the initial investment of the project.

A project's **payback period** is the length of time before you recover your initial investment. For the washing machine the payback period was just under 3 years.

The payback rule states that a project should be accepted if its payback period is less than a specified cutoff period.

For example, if the cutoff period is 4 years, the washing machine makes the grade; if the cutoff is 2 years, it doesn't.

As a rough rule of thumb the payback rule may be adequate, but it is easy to see that it can lead to nonsensical decisions. For example, compare projects A and B. Project A has a 2-year payback and a large positive NPV. Project B also has a 2-year payback but a negative NPV. Project A is clearly superior but the payback rule ranks both equally. This is because payback does not consider any cash flows that arrive after the payback period. A firm that uses the payback criterion with a cutoff of 2 or more years would accept both A and B despite the fact that only A would increase shareholder wealth.

	Cash Flows, Dollars				Payback	
Project	C_0	C_1	C_2	C_3	**Period, Years**	**NPV at 10%**
A	–2,000	+1,000	+1,000	+10,000	2	$7,249
B	–2,000	+1,000	+1,000	0	2	–264
C	–2,000	0	+2,000	0	2	–347

A second problem with payback is that it gives equal weight to all cash flows arriving *before* the cutoff period despite the fact that the more distant flows are less valuable. For example, look at Project C. It also has a payback period of 2 years but it has an even lower NPV than Project B. Why? Because its cash flows arrive later within the payback period.

To use the payback rule a firm has to decide on an appropriate cutoff period. If it uses the same cutoff regardless of project life, it will tend to accept too many short-lived projects and reject too many long-lived ones. The payback rule will bias the firm against accepting long-term projects because cash flows that arrive after the payback period are ignored.

Earlier in the chapter we evaluated the Channel Tunnel project. Large construction projects of this kind inevitably have long payback periods. The cash flows that we presented in Table 6.1 implied a payback period of just over 14 years. But most firms that employ the payback rule use a much shorter cutoff period than this. If they used the payback rule mechanically, long-lived projects like the Channel Tunnel wouldn't have a chance.

In our example, the payback works out to be exactly 2 years for all three projects. Suppose the numbers don't work out exactly, as in Project D below:

	Project D Cash Flow, Dollars				Payback Period,
Year	**0**	**1**	**2**	**3**	**Years**
Cash Flow	–2,000	+1,000	+500	+1,000	
Cumulative Cash Flow	–2,000	–1,000	–500	+500	$2\frac{1}{2}$

We see that the initial investment is $2,000, whereas the cash inflows over years 1 to 3 are $2,500. The cumulative cash flows are negative until Year 2 but they become positive by Year 3. This means that the project pays back sometime in the third year. If we assume that cash inflows occur uniformly across time, we can figure out the fractional year. We see that out of the total cash flow of $1,000 in Year 3, the first $500 comes in by 500/1,000 = 0.5 years. The payback is therefore 2.5 years.

The primary attraction of the payback criterion is its simplicity. But remember that the hard part of project evaluation is forecasting the cash flows, not doing the arithmetic. Today's spreadsheets make discounting a trivial exercise. Therefore, the payback rule saves you only the easy part of the analysis.

We have had little good to say about payback. So why do many large companies continue to use it? Senior managers don't truly believe that all cash flows after the payback period are irrelevant. It seems more likely (and more charitable to those managers) that payback survives because the deficiencies are relatively unimportant or because there are some offsetting benefits. Thus managers may point out that payback is the simplest way to *communicate* an idea of project desirability. Investment decisions require discussion and negotiation between people from all parts of the firm and it is important to have a measure that everyone can understand. Perhaps, also, managers favour quick payback projects even when they have lower NPVs, because they believe that quicker profits mean quicker promotion. That takes us back to Chapter 1 where we discussed the need to align the objectives of managers with those of the shareholders.

In practice, payback is most commonly used when the capital investment is small or when the merits of the project are so obvious that more formal analysis is unnecessary. For example, if a project is expected to produce constant cash flows for 10 years and the payback period is only 2 years, the project in all likelihood has a positive NPV.

DISCOUNTED PAYBACK

discounted payback period The time until discounted cash flows recover the initial investment in the project.

Sometimes managers calculate the **discounted payback period**. This is the number of periods before the present value of prospective cash flows equals or exceeds the initial investment.

The discounted payback rule asks: How long must the project last in order to offer a positive net present value?

This surmounts the objection that equal weight is given to all cash flows *before* the cutoff date. However, the discounted payback rule still takes no account of cash flows *after* the cutoff date.

Project A

Year	Cash Flows, Dollars	Discounted Cash Flows at 10 percent, Dollars	Cumulative Discounted Cash Flows, Dollars
0	–2,000	–2,000	–2,000
1	+1,000	909	–1,091
2	+1,000	827	–264
3	+10,000	7,513	+7,249
		NPV = 7,249	

To show how this would work suppose we look at the cash flows for Project A once again. These cash flows are discounted at 10 percent, the total discounted cash flows represent the project's NPV of $7249. The cumulative discounted cash flows are negative until

Year 2 but sizably positive by Year 3. This means the project pays back sometime in the third year. Once again, assuming uniform cash inflows across time, we can figure out the fractional year. We see that out of the total discounted cash flow of $7,513 in Year 3, the first $264 comes in by 264/7,513 = 0.04 years. The discounted payback is therefore 2.04 years.

The discounted payback does offer one important advantage over the normal payback criterion. If a project meets a discounted payback cutoff, it must have a positive NPV because the cash flows that accrue up to the discounted payback period are (by definition) just sufficient to provide a present value equal to the initial investment. Any cash flows after that date tip the balance and ensure positive NPV.

Despite this advantage, the discounted payback rule has little to recommend it. It still ignores all cash flows occurring after the arbitrary cutoff date, and therefore, will incorrectly reject some positive NPV opportunities. It is no easier to use than the NPV rule because both project cash flows and an appropriate discount rate must be determined. The best that can be said is it is a better criterion than the (even more unsatisfactory) payback rule.

CHECK POINT 6.3

A project costs $3,000 and will generate annual cash flows of $660 for 7 years. What is the payback period? If the interest rate is 6 percent, what is (a) the discounted payback period, and (b) the project NPV? Should the project be accepted?

BOOK RATE OF RETURN

We pointed out that net present value and internal rate of return are both discounted cash-flow measures. In other words, each measure depends only on the project's cash flows and the opportunity cost of capital. But when companies report to shareholders on their performance, they do not show simply the cash flows. Instead they report the firm's book income and book assets.

book rate of return Accounting income divided by book value. Also called accounting rate of return.

Shareholders and financial managers sometimes use these accounting numbers to calculate a **book rate of return** (also called the *accounting rate of return*). In other words, they look at the company's book income (i.e., accounting profits) as a proportion of the book value of the assets:

$$\textbf{Book rate of return} = \frac{\textbf{book income}}{\textbf{book assets}} \tag{6.2}$$

EXAMPLE 6.3 *Book Rate of Return*

Salad Daze invests $90,000 in a vegetable washing machine. The machine will increase cash flows by $50,000 a year for 3 years, when it will need to be replaced. The contribution to accounting profits equals this cash flow less an allowance for depreciation of $30,000 a year. (We ignore taxes to keep things simple.) The book return on this project in each year can be calculated as follows:

Book Value, Start of Year ($ thousands)	Net Income during Year ($ thousands)	Book Value, End of Year ($ thousands)	Book Rate of Return = Income/Book Value at Start of Year
90	50 – 30 = 20	60	20/90 = .222 = 22.2%
60	50 – 30 = 20	30	20/60 = .333 = 33.3%
30	50 – 30 = 20	0	20/30 = .667 = 66.7%

We have already seen that cash flows and accounting income may be very different. For example, the accountant labels some cash outflows as *capital investments* and others as *operating expenses.* The operating expenses are deducted immediately from each year's income, while the capital investment is depreciated over a number of years. Thus the book rate of return depends on which items the accountant chooses to treat as capital investments and how rapidly they are depreciated. Book rate of return is not generally the same as the internal rate of return and, as you can see in Check Point 6.4, the difference between the two can be considerable. Book rate of return therefore can easily give a misleading impression of the attractiveness of a project.

Managers seldom make investment decisions nowadays on the basis of accounting numbers. But they know that the company's shareholders pay considerable attention to book measures of profitability, and therefore, naturally, they look at how major projects would affect the company's book rate of return.

CHECK POINT 6.4

Suppose that a company invests $60,000 in a project. The project generates a cash inflow of $30,000 a year for each of 3 years and nothing thereafter. Book income in each year is equal to this cash flow *less* an allowance for depreciation of $20,000 a year. For simplicity, we assume there are no taxes.

a. Calculate the project's internal rate of return. (If you do not have a financial calculator or spreadsheet program, this will require a little trial and error.)
b. Now calculate the book rate of return in each year by dividing the book income for that year by the book value of the assets at the start of the year.

6.3 Investment Criteria When Projects Interact

Let's pause for a moment to review. We have seen that the NPV rule is the most reliable criterion for project evaluation. NPV is reliable because it measures the difference between the *cost* of a project and the *value* of the project. That difference—the *net* present value—is the amount by which the project would increase the value of the firm. Other rules such as payback period or book return at best may be viewed as rough proxies for the attractiveness of a proposed project. Because they are not based on value, they can easily lead to incorrect investment decisions. Of the alternatives to the NPV rule, IRR is clearly the best choice in that it usually results in the same accept-or-reject decision as the NPV rule, but like the alternatives, it does not quantify the contribution to the firm's value. We will see shortly that this can cause problems when managers have to choose among competing projects.

We are now ready to extend our discussion of investment criteria to encompass some of the issues encountered when managers must choose among projects that interact—that is, when acceptance of one project affects another one. The NPV rule can be adapted to these new problems with only a bit of extra effort. But unless you are careful, the IRR rule may lead you astray.

MUTUALLY EXCLUSIVE PROJECTS

Most of the projects we have considered so far involve take-it-or-leave-it decisions. But almost all real-world decisions about capital expenditures involve either–or choices. You could build an apartment block on that vacant site rather than build an office block. You could build a 5-storey office block or a 50-storey one. You could heat it with oil or with natural gas. You could build it today, or wait a year to start construction. Such choices are said to be **mutually exclusive.**

mutually exclusive projects Two or more projects that cannot be pursued simultaneously.

When you need to choose between mutually exclusive projects, the decision rule is simple. Calculate the NPV of each project and, from those options that have a positive NPV, choose the one whose NPV is highest.

EXAMPLE 6.4 *Choosing between Two Projects*

It has been several years since your office last upgraded its office networking software. Two competing systems have been proposed. Both have an expected useful life of 3 years, at which point it will be time for another upgrade. One proposal is for an expensive cutting-edge system, which will cost $800,000 and increase firm cash flows by $350,000 a year through increased productivity. The other proposal is for a cheaper, somewhat slower system. This system would cost only $700,000 but would increase cash flows by only $300,000 a year. If the cost of capital is 7 percent, which is the better option?

The following table summarizes the cash flows and the NPVs of the two proposals:

	Cash Flows, Thousands of Dollars				
System	C_0	C_1	C_2	C_3	**NPV at 7%**
Faster	–800	+350	+350	+350	+118.5
Slower	–700	+300	+300	+300	+ 87.3

In both cases, the software systems are worth more than they cost, but the faster system would make the greater contribution to value and therefore should be your preferred choice.

Mutually exclusive projects, such as our two proposals to update the networking system, involve a *project interaction,* since taking one project forecloses the other. Unfortunately, not every project interaction is as simple to evaluate as the choice between the two networking projects, but we will explain how to tackle three important decisions:

- *The investment timing decision.* Should you buy a computer now or wait and think again next year? (Here today's investment is competing with possible future investments.)
- *The choice between long- and short-lived equipment.* Should the company save money today by installing cheaper machinery that will not last as long? (Here today's decision would accelerate a later investment in machine replacement.)
- *The replacement decision.* When should existing machinery be replaced? (Using it another year could delay investment in machine replacement.)

INVESTMENT TIMING

Let us return to Example 6.1, where Obsolete Technologies was contemplating the purchase of a new computer system. The proposed investment has a net present value of almost $20,000, so it appears that the cost savings would easily justify the expense of the system. However, the financial manager is not persuaded. She reasons that the price of computers is continually falling and therefore proposes postponing the purchase, arguing that the NPV of the system will be even higher if the firm waits until the following year. Unfortunately, she has been making the same argument for 10 years and the company is steadily losing business to competitors with more efficient systems. Is there a flaw in her reasoning?

This is a problem in investment timing. When is it best to commit to a positive-NPV investment? Investment timing problems all involve choices among mutually exclusive investments. You can either proceed with the project now, or you can do so later. You can't do both.

Table 6.2 lays out the basic data for Obsolete. You can see that the cost of the computer is expected to decline from $50,000 today to $45,000 next year, and so on. The new computer system is expected to last for 4 years from the time it is installed. The present value of the savings *at the time of installation* is expected to be $70,000. Thus if Obsolete invests today, it achieves an NPV of $70,000 – $50,000 = $20,000; if it invests next year, it will have an NPV of $70,000 – $45,000 = $25,000.

Isn't a gain of $25,000 better than one of $20,000? Well, not necessarily—you may prefer to be $20,000 richer *today* rather than $25,000 richer *next year.* The better choice depends on the cost of capital. The fourth column of Table 6.2 shows the value today (Year 0) of those net present values at a 10 percent cost of capital. For example, you can see that the discounted value of that $25,000 gain is $25,000/1.10 = $22,700. The financial manager has a point. It is worth postponing investment in the computer, but it should not be postponed indefinitely. You maximize net present value today by buying the computer in Year 3.

TABLE 6.2

Obsolete Technologies: the gain from purchase of a computer is rising, but the NPV today is highest if the computer is purchased in Year 3 (figures in thousands of dollars).

Year of Purchase	Cost of Computer	PV Savings	NPV at Year of Purchase (r = 10%)	NPV Today	
0	$50	$70	$20	$20.0	
1	45	70	25	22.7	
2	40	70	30	24.8	
3	36	70	34	25.5	← optimal purchase date
4	33	70	37	25.3	
5	31	70	39	24.2	

Notice that you are involved in a trade-off. The sooner you can capture the $70,000 savings the better, but if it costs you less to realize those savings by postponing the investment, it may pay you to do so. If you postpone the purchase by 1 year, the gain from buying a computer rises from $20,000 to $25,000, an increase of 25 percent. Since the cost of capital is only 10 percent, it pays to postpone at least until Year 1. If you postpone from Year 3 to Year 4, the gain rises from $34,000 to $37,000, a rise of just under 9 percent. Since this is less than the cost of capital, it is not worth waiting any longer.

The decision rule for investment timing is to choose the investment date that results in the highest net present value *today*.

CHECK POINT 6.5

Unfortunately Obsolete Technology's business is shrinking as the company dithers and dawdles. Its chief financial officer realizes that the savings from installing the new computer will likewise shrink by $4,000 per year, from a present value of $70,000 now to $66,000 next year, then to $62,000, and so on. Redo Table 6.2 with this new information. When should Obsolete buy the new computer?

LONG- VERSUS SHORT-LIVED EQUIPMENT

Suppose the firm is forced to choose between two machines, D and E. The two machines are designed differently but have identical capacity and do exactly the same job. Machine D costs $15,000 and will last 3 years. It costs $4,000 per year to run. Machine E is an "economy" model, costing only $10,000, but it will last only 2 years and costs $6,000 per year to run.

Because the two machines produce exactly the same product, the only way to choose between them is on the basis of cost. Suppose we compute the present value of the costs:

	Costs, Thousands of Dollars				
Year:	**0**	**1**	**2**	**3**	**PV at 6%**
Machine D	15	4	4	4	25.69
Machine E	10	6	6	—	21.00

Should we take machine E, the one with the lower present value of costs? Not necessarily. All we have shown is that machine E offers 2 years of service for a lower cost than 3 years of service from machine D. But is the *annual* cost of using E lower than that of D?

Suppose the financial manager agrees to buy machine D and pay for its operating costs out of her budget. She then charges the plant manager an annual amount for use of the machine. There will be three equal payments starting in Year 1. Obviously, the financial manager has to make sure that the present value of these payments equals the present value of the costs of machine D, $25,690. The payment stream with such a present value when the discount rate is 6 percent turns out to be $9,610 a year. In other words, the cost of buying and operating machine D is equivalent to an annual charge of $9,610 a year for 3 years. This figure is therefore termed the **equivalent annual cost** of machine D.

equivalent annual cost The cost per period with the same present value as the cost of buying and operating a machine.

	Costs, Thousands of Dollars				
Year:	**0**	**1**	**2**	**3**	**PV at 6%**
Machine D	15	4	4	4	25.69
Equivalent annual cost		9.61	9.61	9.61	25.69

How did we know that an annual charge of $9,610 has a present value of $25,690? The annual charge is a 3-year annuity. So we calculate the value of this annuity and set it equal to $25,690:

$$\text{Equivalent annual cost} \times \text{3-year annuity factor} = \text{PV cost of D} = \$25{,}690$$

If the cost of capital is 6 percent, the 3-year annuity factor is 2.673. So

$$\textbf{Equivalent annual cost} = \frac{\textbf{present value of costs}}{\textbf{annuity factor}} \tag{6.3}$$

$$= \frac{\$25{,}690}{\text{3-year annuity factor}} = \frac{\$25{,}690}{2.673} = \$9{,}610$$

If we make a similar calculation of costs for machine E, we get:

	Costs, Thousands of Dollars			
Year:	**0**	**1**	**2**	**PV at 6%**
Machine E	10	6	6	21.00
Equivalent 2-year annuity		11.45	11.45	21.00

We see now that machine D is better, because its equivalent annual cost is less ($9,610 for D versus $11,450 for E). In other words, the financial manager could afford to set a lower *annual* charge for the use of D.

We thus have a rule for comparing assets of different lives: *Select the machine that has the lowest equivalent annual cost.*

Think of the equivalent annual cost as the level annual charge[5] necessary to recover the present value of investment outlays and operating costs. The annual charge continues for the life of the equipment. Calculate equivalent annual cost by dividing the appropriate present value by the annuity factor.

EXAMPLE 6.5 *Equivalent Annual Cost*

You need a new car. You can either purchase one outright for $15,000 or lease one for 7 years for $3,000 a year. If you buy the car, it will be worth $500 to you in 7 years. The discount rate is 10 percent. Should you buy or lease? What is the maximum lease you would be willing to pay?

The present value of the cost of purchasing is

$$\text{PV} = \$15{,}000 - \frac{\$500}{(1.10)^7} = \$14{,}743$$

The equivalent annual cost of purchasing the car is therefore the annuity with this present value:

$$\text{Equivalent annual cost} \times \begin{array}{c}\text{7-year annuity}\\ \text{factor at 10\%}\end{array} = \begin{array}{c}\text{PV cost}\\ \text{of buying}\end{array} = \$14{,}743$$

$$\text{Equivalent annual cost} = \frac{\$14{,}743}{\text{7-year annuity factor}} = \frac{\$14{,}743}{4.8684} = \$3{,}028$$

Therefore, the annual lease payment of $3,000 is less than the equivalent annual cost of buying the car. You should be willing to pay up to $3,028 annually to lease.

REPLACING AN OLD MACHINE

The previous example took the life of each machine as fixed. In practice, the point at which equipment is replaced reflects economics, not physical collapse. *We* usually decide when to replace. The machine will rarely decide for us.

Here is a common problem. You are operating an old machine that will last 2 more years before it gives up the ghost. It costs $12,000 per year to operate. You can replace it now with a new machine, which costs $25,000 but is much more efficient ($8,000 per year in operating costs) and will last for 5 years. Should you replace it now or wait a year? The opportunity cost of capital is 6 percent.

We can calculate the NPV of the new machine and its equivalent annual cost, that is, the 5-year annuity that has the same present value.

[5] This introduction to equivalent annual cost is somewhat simplified. For example, equivalent annual costs should be escalated with inflation when inflation is significant and the equipment long-lived. This would require us to equate equipment cost to the present value of a *growing* annuity.

Year:	0	1	2	3	4	5	PV at 6%
	Costs, Thousands of Dollars						
New machine	25	8	8	8	8	8	58.70
Equivalent 5-year annuity		13.93	13.93	13.93	13.93	13.93	58.70

The cash flows of the new machine are equivalent to an annuity of $13,930 per year. So we can equally well ask at what point we would want to replace our old machine, which costs $12,000 a year to run, with a new one costing $13,930 a year. When the question is posed this way, the answer is obvious. As long as your old machine costs only $12,000 a year, why replace it with a new machine that costs $1,930 more?

CHECK POINT 6.6

Machines F and G are mutually exclusive and have the following investment and operating costs. Note that machine F lasts for only 2 years:

Year:	0	1	2	3
F	10,000	1,100	1,200	—
G	12,000	1,100	1,200	1,300

Calculate the equivalent annual cost of each investment using a discount rate of 10 percent. Which machine is the better buy?

Now suppose you have an existing machine. You can keep it going for only one more year, but it will cost $2,500 in repairs and $1,800 in operating costs. Is it worth replacing now with either F or G?

MUTUALLY EXCLUSIVE PROJECTS AND THE IRR RULE

Whereas the NPV rule deals easily with mutually exclusive projects, the IRR rule does not. Because of the potential pitfalls in the use of the IRR rule, our advice is always to base your final decision on the project's net present value.[6]

Pitfall 1: Mutually Exclusive Projects. We have seen that firms are seldom faced with take-it-or-leave-it projects. Usually they need to choose from a number of mutually exclusive alternatives. Given a choice between competing projects, you should accept the one that adds most to shareholder wealth. This is the one with the higher NPV. However, it won't necessarily be the project with the higher internal rate of return. So the IRR rule can lead you astray when choosing between projects.

Think once more about the two office-block proposals from Section 6.1. You initially intended to invest $350,000 in the building and then sell it at the end of the year for $400,000. Under the revised proposal, you plan to rent out the offices for 3 years at a fixed annual rent of $16,000 and then sell the building for $450,000. Here are the cash flows, their IRRs, and their NPVs:

[6] The other rules we've considered, such as payback or book rate of return, give poor guidance even in the much simpler case of the accept/reject decision of a project considered in isolation. They are of no help in choosing among mutually exclusive projects.

Project	**Cash Flows, Thousands of Dollars** C_0	C_1	C_2	C_3	**IRR**	**NPV at 7%**
H: Initial proposal	−350	+400			+14.29	+\$24,000
I: Revised proposal	−350	+16	+16	+466	+12.96	+\$59,000

Both projects are good investments; both offer a positive NPV. But the revised proposal has the higher net present value and therefore is the better choice. Unfortunately, the superiority of the revised proposal doesn't show up as a higher rate of return. The IRR rule seems to say you should go for the initial proposal because it has the higher IRR. If you follow the IRR rule, you have the satisfaction of earning a 14.29 percent rate of return; if you use NPV, you are \$59,000 richer.

Figure 6.4 shows why the IRR rule gives the wrong signal. The figure plots the NPV of each project as a function of the discount rate. These two NPV profiles cross at an interest rate of 12.26 percent. So if the opportunity cost of capital is higher than 12.26 percent, the initial proposal, with its rapid cash inflow, is the superior investment. If the cost of capital is lower than 12.26 percent, then the revised proposal dominates. Depending on the discount rate, either proposal may be superior. For the 7 percent cost of capital that we have assumed, the revised proposal is the better choice.

Now consider the IRR of each proposal. The IRR is simply the discount rate at which NPV equals zero, that is, the discount rate at which the NPV profile crosses the horizontal axis in Figure 6.4. As noted, these rates are 14.29 percent for the initial proposal and 12.96 percent for the revised proposal. However, as you can see from Figure 6.4, the higher IRR for the initial proposal does not mean that it has a higher NPV.

In our example both projects involved the same outlay, but the revised proposal had the longer life. The IRR rule mistakenly favoured the quick-payback project, with the high percentage return but the lower NPV.

Remember, a high IRR is not an end in itself. You want projects that increase the value of the firm. Projects that earn a good rate of return for a long time often have higher NPVs than those that offer high percentage rates of return but die young.

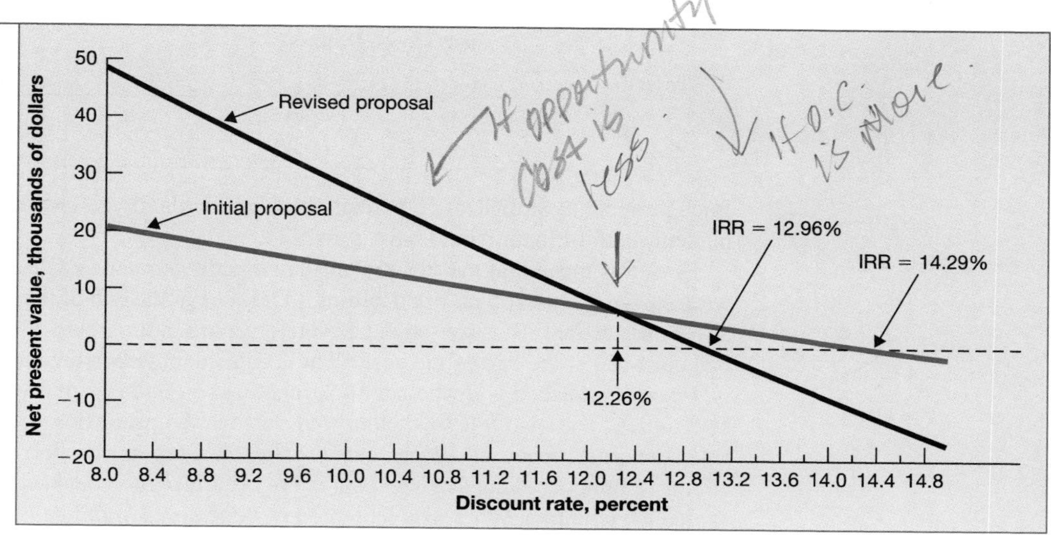

FIGURE 6.4
The initial proposal offers a higher IRR than the revised proposal, but its NPV is lower if the discount rate is less than 12.26 percent.

CHECK POINT 6.7

A rich, friendly, and probably slightly unbalanced benefactor offers you the opportunity to invest $1 million in two mutually exclusive ways. The payoffs are:

a. $2 million after 1 year, a 100 percent return.
b. $300,000 a year forever.

Neither investment is risky, and safe securities are yielding 7.5 percent. Which investment will you take? You can't take both, so the choices are mutually exclusive. Do you want to earn a high percentage return or do you want to be rich? By the way, if you really had this investment opportunity, you'd have no trouble borrowing the money to undertake it.

Pitfall 1a: Mutually Exclusive Projects Involving Different Outlays. A similar misranking also may occur when comparing projects with the same lives but different outlays. In this case the IRR may mistakenly favour small projects with high rates of return but low NPVs.

CHECK POINT 6.8

Your wacky benefactor now offers you the choice of two opportunities:

a. Invest $1,000 today and quadruple your money—a 300 percent return—in 1 year, with no risk.
b. Invest $1 million for 1 year at a guaranteed 50 percent return.

Which will you take? Do you want to earn a wonderful rate of return (300 percent) or do you want to be rich?

OTHER PITFALLS OF THE IRR RULE

The IRR rule is subject to problems beyond those associated with mutually exclusive investments. Here are a few more pitfalls to avoid.

Pitfall 2: Lending or Borrowing? Remember our condition for the IRR rule to work: the project's NPV must fall as the discount rate increases. Now consider the following projects:

	Cash Flows, Dollars			
Project	C_0	C_1	**IRR, %**	**NPV at 10%**
J	–100	+150	+50	+$36.4
K	+100	–150	+50	–$36.4

Each project has an IRR of 50 percent. In other words, if you discount the cash flows at 50 percent, both of them would have zero NPV.

Does this mean that the two projects are equally attractive? Clearly not. In the case of J we are paying out $100 now and getting $150 back at the end of the year. That is better than any bank account. But what about K? Here we are getting paid $100 now but we have to pay out $150 at the end of the year. That is equivalent to borrowing money at 50 percent.

If someone asked you whether 50 percent was a good rate of interest, you could not answer unless you also knew whether that person was proposing to lend or borrow at that rate. Lending money at 50 percent is great (as long as the borrower does not flee the country), but borrowing at 50 percent is not usually a good deal (unless of course you plan to flee the country). When you lend money, you want a *high* rate of return; when you borrow, you want a *low* rate of return.

If you plot a graph like Figure 6.2 for Project K, you will find the NPV increases as the discount rate increases. (Try it!) Obviously, the rate of return rule will not work in this case.

Project K is a fairly obvious trap, but if you want to make sure you don't fall into it, calculate the project's NPV. For example, suppose that the cost of capital is 10 percent. Then the NPV of Project J is +\$36.4 and the NPV of Project K is –\$36.4. The NPV rule correctly warns us away from a project that is equivalent to borrowing money at 50 percent.

When NPV rises as the interest rate rises, the rate of return rule is reversed:

When NPV is higher as the discount rate increases, a project is acceptable only if its internal rate of return is *less* than the opportunity cost of capital.

Pitfall 3: Multiple Rates of Return. Here is a trickier problem. King Coal Corporation is considering a project to strip-mine coal. The project requires an investment of \$22 million and is expected to produce a cash inflow of \$15 million in each of years 1 through 4. However, the company is obliged in Year 5 to reclaim the land at a cost of \$40 million. At a 10 percent opportunity cost of capital the project has an NPV of \$.7 million.

To find the IRR, we have calculated the NPV for various discount rates and plotted the results in Figure 6.5. You can see that there are *two* discount rates at which NPV = 0. That is, *each* of the following statements holds:

$$\text{NPV} = -22 + \frac{15}{1.06} + \frac{15}{1.06^2} + \frac{15}{1.06^3} + \frac{15}{1.06^4} - \frac{40}{1.06^5} = 0$$

and

$$\text{NPV} = -22 + \frac{15}{1.28} + \frac{15}{1.28^2} + \frac{15}{1.28^3} + \frac{15}{1.28^4} - \frac{40}{1.28^5} = 0$$

In other words, the investment has an IRR of both 6 *and* 28 percent. The reason for this is the double change in the sign of the cash flows. There can be as many different internal rates of return as there are changes in the sign of the cash-flow stream.[7]

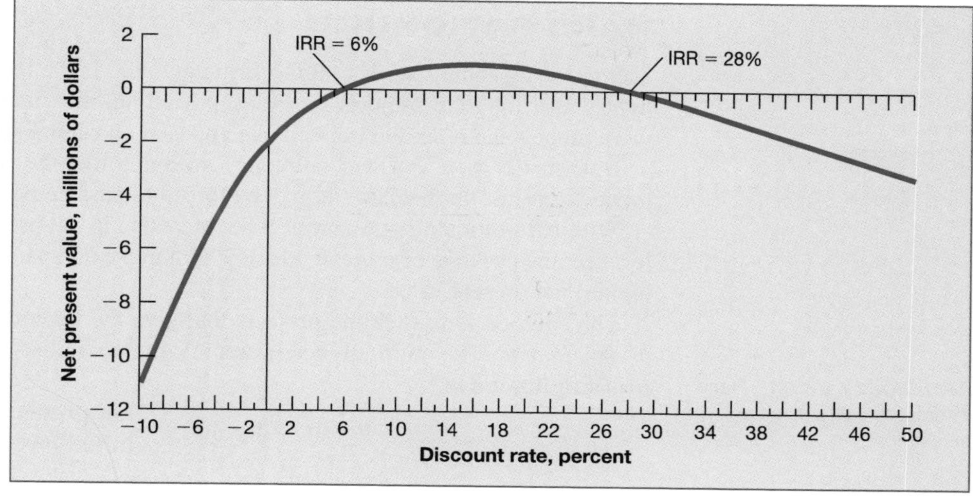

FIGURE 6.5
King Coal's project has two internal rates of return. NPV = 0 when the discount rate is either 6 percent or 28 percent

[7] There may be *fewer* IRRs than the number of sign changes. You may even encounter projects for which there is *no* IRR. For example, there is no IRR for a project that has cash flows of +\$1,000 in Year 0, –\$3,000 in Year 1, and +\$2,500 in Year 2. If you don't believe us, try plotting NPV for different discount rates. Can such a project ever have a negative NPV?

Is the coal mine worth developing? The simple IRR rule—accept if the IRR is greater than the cost of capital—won't help. For example, you can see from Figure 6.5 that with a low cost of capital (less than 6 percent) the project has a negative NPV. It has a positive NPV only if the cost of capital is between 6 percent and 28 percent.

When there are multiple changes in the sign of the cash flows, the IRR rule does not work, but the NPV rule always does.

6.4

Capital Rationing

A firm maximizes its shareholders' wealth by accepting every project that has a positive net present value. But this assumes that the firm can raise the funds needed to pay for these investments. This is usually a good assumption, particularly for major firms which can raise very large sums of money on fair terms and short notice. Why then does top management sometimes tell subordinates that capital is limited and that they may not exceed a specified amount of capital spending? There are two reasons.

SOFT RATIONING

capital rationing Limit set on the amount of funds available for investment.

For many firms the limits on capital funds are "soft." By this we mean that the **capital rationing** is not imposed by investors. Instead the limits are imposed by top management. For example, suppose that you are an ambitious, upwardly mobile junior manager. You are keen to expand your part of the business, and as a result, you tend to overstate the investment opportunities. Rather than trying to determine which of your many bright ideas really are worthwhile, upper management may find it simpler to impose a limit on the amount that you and other junior managers can spend. This limit forces you to set your own priorities.

Even if capital is not rationed, other resources may be. For example, very rapid growth can place considerable strains on management and the organization. A somewhat rough-and-ready response to this problem is to ration the amount of capital that the firm spends.

HARD RATIONING

Soft rationing should never cost the firm anything. If the limits on investment become so tight that truly good projects are being passed up, then upper management should raise more money and relax the limits it has imposed on capital spending.

But what if there is "hard rationing," meaning that the firm actually cannot raise the money it needs? In that case, it may be forced to pass up positive-NPV projects.

With hard rationing you may still be interested in net present value, but you now need to select the package of projects which is within the company's resources and yet gives the highest net present value.

profitability index Ratio of present value to initial investment.

The solution is to pick the projects that give the highest net present value *per dollar of investment.* The ratio of net present value to initial investment is known as the **profitability index.**[8]

$$\textbf{Profitability index} = \frac{\textbf{net present value}}{\textbf{initial investment}} \qquad (6.4)$$

[8] Sometimes the profitability index is defined as the ratio of present value to required investment. By this definition, all the profitability indexes calculated below are increased by 1.0. For example, Project L's index would be PV/investment = 4/3 = 1.33. Note that project rankings under either definition are identical.

Let us illustrate. Suppose that the opportunity cost of capital is 10 percent, that the company has total resources of $20 million, and it is presented with the following project proposals:

	Cash Flows, Millions of Dollars				
Project	C_0	C_1	C_2	**PV at 10%**	**NPV**
L	–3	+2.2	+2.42	$ 4	$1
M	–5	+2.2	+4.84	6	1
N	–7	+6.6	+4.84	10	3
O	–6	+3.3	+6.05	8	2
P	–4	+1.1	+4.84	5	1

All five projects have a positive NPV. Therefore, if there were no shortage of capital, the firm would like to accept all five proposals. But with only $20 million available, the firm needs to find the package that gives the highest possible NPV within the budget.

For our five projects the profitability index is calculated as follows:

Project	PV	Investment	NPV	Profitability Index
L	$ 4	$3	1	1/3 = 0.33
M	6	5	1	1/5 = 0.20
N	10	7	3	3/7 = 0.43
O	8	6	2	2/6 = 0.33
P	5	4	1	1/4 = 0.25

Project N offers the highest ratio of net present value to investment (0.43) and therefore N is picked first. Next come projects L and O, which tie with a ratio of 0.33, and after them comes P. These four projects use up exactly the $20 million budget. Between them they offer shareholders the highest attainable gain in wealth.[9]

CHECK POINT 6.9 Which projects should the firm accept if its capital budget is only $10 million?

PITFALLS OF THE PROFITABILITY INDEX

The profitability index is sometimes used to rank projects even when there is no soft or hard capital rationing. In this case the unwary user may be led to favour small projects over larger projects with higher NPVs. The profitability index was designed to select the projects with the most bang per buck—the greatest NPV per dollar spent. That's the right objective when bucks are limited. When they are not, a bigger bang is always better than a smaller one, even when more bucks are spent. Check Point 6.10 is a numerical example.

CHECK POINT 6.10 Calculate the profitability indexes of the two pairs of mutually exclusive investments in Check Points 6.7 and 6.8. Use a 7.5 percent discount rate. Does the profitability index give the right ranking in each case?

[9] Unfortunately, when capital is rationed in more than one period, or when personnel, production capacity, or other resources are rationed in addition to capital, it isn't always possible to get the NPV-maximizing package just by ranking projects on their profitability index. Tedious trial and error may be called for, or linear programming methods may be used.

Summary

1. **What is the net present value of an investment, and how do you calculate it?**

   The **net present value** of a project measures the difference between its value and cost. NPV is therefore the amount that the project will add to shareholder wealth. A company maximizes shareholder wealth by accepting all projects that have a positive NPV.

2. **How is the internal rate of return of a project calculated and what must one look out for when using the internal rate of return rule?**

   Instead of asking whether a project has a positive NPV, many businesses prefer to ask whether it offers a higher return than shareholders could expect to get by investing in the capital market. Return is usually defined as the discount rate that would result in a zero NPV. This is known as the **internal rate of return,** or IRR. The project is attractive if the IRR exceeds the **opportunity cost of capital.**

   There are some pitfalls in using the internal rate of return rule. Be careful about using the IRR when (1) the early cash flows are positive, (2) there is more than one change in the sign of the cash flows, or (3) you need to choose between two **mutually exclusive projects.**

3. **Why don't the payback and discounted payback rules and the book rate of return rule always make shareholders better off?**

   The net present value rule and the rate of return rule both properly reflect the time value of money. But companies sometimes use rules of thumb to judge projects. One is the **payback rule,** which states that a project is acceptable if you get your money back within a specified period. The payback rule takes no account of any cash flows that arrive after the payback period and fails to discount cash flows within the payback period.

   The **discounted payback rule** improves upon the payback rule by examining discounted cash flows. It states that a project is acceptable if the discounted cash flows recover your initial investment within a specified period.

   Book (or accounting) rate of return is the income of a project divided by the book value. Unlike the internal rate of return, book rate of return does not depend just on the project's cash flows. It also depends on which cash flows are classified as capital investments and which as operating expenses. Managers often keep an eye on how projects would affect book rate of return.

4. **How can the net present value rule be used to analyze three common problems that involve competing projects: when to postpone an investment expenditure; how to choose between projects with equal lives; and when to replace equipment?**

   Sometimes a project may have a positive NPV if undertaken today but an even higher NPV if the investment is delayed. Choose between these alternatives by comparing their NPVs *today.*

   When you have to choose between projects with different lives, you should put them on an equal footing by comparing the **equivalent annual cost** or benefit of the two projects. When you are considering whether to replace an aging machine with a new one, you should compare the cost of operating the old one with the equivalent annual cost of the new one.

5. **How is the profitability index calculated, and how can it be used to choose between projects when funds are limited?**

   If there is a shortage of capital, companies need to choose projects that offer the highest net present value per dollar of investment. This measure is known as the **profitability index.**

Related Web Links

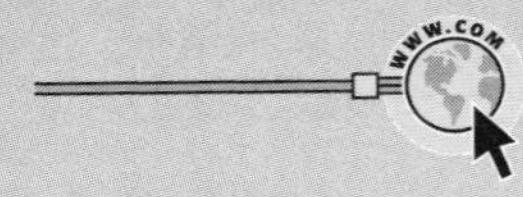

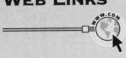

www.nacubo.org/website/members/bomag/cbg396.html A good article showing how capital budgeting is used in decision making

http://asbdc.ualr.edu/fod/1518.htm How net present value analysis helps answer business questions

www.channeltunnel.co.uk

Key Terms

Term	Page
opportunity cost of capital	171
net present value (NPV)	171
internal rate of return (IRR)	177
payback period	180
discounted payback period	181
book rate of return (accounting rate of return)	182
mutually exclusive projects	184
equivalent annual cost	186
capital rationing	192
profitability index	192

QUESTIONS AND PROBLEMS

*Answers in Appendix B

Problems 1–10 refer to two projects with the following cash flows:

Year	Project A	Project B
0	–$100	–$100
1	40	50
2	40	50
3	40	50
4	40	

BASIC

*1. **IRR/NPV.** If the opportunity cost of capital is 11 percent, which of these projects is worth pursuing?

2. **Mutually Exclusive Investments.** Suppose that you can choose only one of these projects. Which would you choose? The discount rate is still 11 percent.

*3. **IRR/NPV.** Which project would you choose if the opportunity cost of capital were 16 percent?

4. **IRR.** What are the internal rates of return on projects A and B?

*5. **Investment Criteria.** In light of your answers to problems 2 to 4, is there any reason to believe that the project with the higher IRR is the better project?

6. **Profitability Index.** If the opportunity cost of capital is 11 percent, what is the profitability index for each project? Does the profitability index rank the projects correctly?

*7. **Payback.** What is the payback period of each project?

8. **Discounted Payback.** What is the discounted payback for each project if the opportunity cost of capital is 11 percent?

9. **Investment Criteria.** Considering your answers to problems 2, 3, and 7, is there any reason to believe that the project with the lower payback period is the better project?

*10. **Book Rate of Return.** Accountants have set up the following depreciation schedules for the two projects:

Year:	1	2	3	4
Project A	$25	$25	$25	$25
Project B	33.33	33.33	33.34	

Calculate book rates of return for each year. Are these book returns the same as the IRR?

11. **NPV and IRR.** A project that costs $3,000 to install will provide annual cash flows of $800 for each of the next 6 years. Is this project worth pursuing if the discount rate is 10 percent? How high can the discount rate be before you would reject the project?

12. **Payback.** A project that costs $2,500 to install will provide annual cash flows of $600 for the next 6 years. The firm accepts projects with payback periods of less than 5 years. Will the project be accepted?

*13. **Profitability Index.** What is the profitability index of a project that costs $10,000 and provides cash flows of $3,000 in years 1 and 2 and $5,000 in years 3 and 4? The discount rate is 10 percent.

14. **Discounted Payback.** A project that costs $3,000 to install will provide annual cash flows of $800 for each of the next 6 years. The firm accepts projects with a discounted payback of 5 years or less. Should this project be pursued if the discount rate is 2 percent? What if the discount rate is 12 percent? Will the firm's decision change as the discount rate changes?

15. **NPV.** A proposed nuclear power plant will cost $2.2 billion to build and then will produce cash flows of $300 million a year for 15 years. After that period (in Year 15), it must be decommissioned at a cost of $900 million. What is project NPV if the discount rate is 6 percent? What if it is 16 percent?

PRACTICE

*16. **NPV/IRR.** Consider projects A and B:

	Cash Flows, Dollars			
Project	C_0	C_1	C_2	NPV at 10%
A	–30,000	21,000	21,000	+$6,446
B	–50,000	33,000	33,000	+$7,273

Calculate IRRs for A and B. Which project does the IRR rule suggest is best? Which project is really best?

*17. IRR. You have the chance to participate in a project that produces the following cash flows:

C_0	C_1	C_2
+$5,000	+$4,000	–$11,000

The internal rate of return is 13.6 percent. If the opportunity cost of capital is 12 percent, would you accept the offer?

*18. **NPV/IRR.**

a. Calculate the net present value of the following project for discount rates of 0, 50, and 100 percent:

C_0	C_1	C_2
–$6,750	+$4,500	+$18,000

b. What is the IRR of the project?

19. **IRR.** Marielle Machinery Works forecasts the following cash flows on a project under consideration. It uses the internal rate of return rule to accept or reject projects. Should this project be accepted if the required return is 12 percent?

C_0	C_1	C_2	C_3
–$10,000	0	+$7,500	+$8,500

*20. **NPV/IRR.** A new computer system will require an initial outlay of $20,000 but it will increase the firm's cash flows by $4,000 a year for each of the next 8 years. Is the system worth installing if the required rate of return is 9 percent? What if it is 14 percent? How high can the discount rate be before you would reject the project?

21. **Investment Criteria.** If you insulate your office for $1,000, you will save $100 a year in heating expenses. These savings will last forever.

a. What is the NPV of the investment when the cost of capital is 8 percent? 10 percent?
b. What is the IRR of the investment?
c. What is the payback period on this investment?
d. What is the discounted payback period on this investment when the cost of capital is 8 percent? 10 percent?

22. **NPV versus IRR.** Here are the cash flows for two mutually exclusive projects:

Project	C_0	C_1	C_2	C_3
A	–$20,000	+$8,000	+$8,000	+$8,000
B	–$20,000	0	0	+$25,000

a. At what interest rates would you prefer project A to B? *Hint*: Try drawing the NPV profile of each project.
b. What is the IRR of each project?

*23. **Payback and NPV.** A project has a life of 10 years and a payback period of 10 years. What must be true of project NPV?

24. **IRR/NPV.** Consider this project with an internal rate of return of 13.1 percent. Should you accept or reject the project if the discount rate is 12 percent?

Year	Cash Flow
0	+$100
1	–60
2	–60

*25. **Payback, Discounted Payback, and NPV.** A firm is considering the following projects. Its opportunity cost of capital is 10 percent.

		Cash Flows, Dollars			
Project	**Time: 0**	**1**	**2**	**3**	**4**
A	–5,000	+1,000	+1,000	+3,000	0
B	–1,000	0	+1,000	+2,000	+3,000
C	–5,000	+1,000	+1,000	+3,000	+5,000

a. What are the payback period and discounted payback period on each project?
b. Given that you wish to use the payback rule with a cutoff period of 2 years, which projects would you accept?
c. If you use a cutoff period of 3 years with the discounted payback rule, which projects would you accept?
d. Which projects have positive NPVs?
e. "Payback gives too much weight to cash flows that occur after the cutoff date." True or false?

26. **Book Rate of Return.** Consider these data on a proposed project:
Original investment = $200
Straight-line depreciation of $50 a year for 4 years
Project life = 4 years

Year:	**0**	**1**	**2**	**3**	**4**
Book value	$200	—	—	—	—
Sales		100	110	120	130
Costs		30	35	40	45
Depreciation		—	—	—	—
Net income		—	—	—	—

a. Fill in the blanks in the table.
b. Find the book rate of return of this project in each year.
c. Find project NPV if the discount rate is 20 percent.

27. **Book Rate of Return.** A machine costs $8,000 and is expected to produce profit before depreciation of $2,500 in each of years 1 and 2 and $3,500 in each of years 3 and 4. Assuming that the machine is depreciated at a constant rate of $2,000 a year and that there are no taxes, what is the average return on book?

*28. **Book Rate of Return.** A project requires an initial investment of $10,000, and over its 5-year life it will generate annual cash revenues of $5,000 and cash expenses of $2,000. The firm will use straight-line depreciation, but it does not pay taxes.

a. Find the book rates of return on the project for each year.
b. Is the project worth pursuing if the opportunity cost of capital is 8 percent?
c. What would happen to the book rates of return if half the initial $10,000 outlay were treated as an expense instead of a capital investment? *Hint:* Instead of depreciating all of the $10,000, treat $5,000 as an expense in the first year.
d. Does NPV change as a result of the different accounting treatment proposed in (c)?

29. **Profitability Index.** Consider the following projects:

Project	C_0	C_1	C_2
A	–$2,100	+$2,000	+$1,200
B	– 2,100	+ 1,440	+ 1,728

a. Calculate the profitability index for A and B assuming a 20 percent opportunity cost of capital.
b. Use the profitability index rule to determine which project(s) you should accept (i) if you could undertake both and (ii) if you could undertake only one.

30. **Capital Rationing.** You are a manager with an investment budget of $8 million. You may invest in the following projects. Investment and cash-flow figures are in millions of dollars.

Project	Discount Rate, %	Investment	Annual Cash Flow	Project Life, Years
A	10	3	1	5
B	12	4	1	8
C	8	5	2	4
D	8	3	1.5	3
E	12	3	1	6

a. Why might these projects have different discount rates?
b. Which projects should the manager choose?
c. Which projects will be chosen if there is no capital rationing?

31. **Profitability Index versus NPV.** Consider these two projects:

Project	C_0	C_1	C_2	C_3
A	–$18	+$10	+$10	+$10
B	–$50	+$25	+$25	+$25

a. Which project has the higher NPV if the discount rate is 10 percent?
b. Which has the higher profitability index?
c. Which project is most attractive to a firm that can raise an unlimited amount of funds to pay for its investment projects? Which project is most attractive to a firm that is limited in the funds it can raise?

*32. **Mutually Exclusive Investments.** Here are the cash flow forecasts for two *mutually exclusive* projects:

	Cash Flows, Dollars	
Year	Project A	Project B
0	–$100	–$100
1	30	49
2	50	49
3	70	49

a. Which project would you choose if the opportunity cost of capital is 2 percent?
b. Which would you choose if the opportunity cost of capital is 12 percent?
c. Why does your answer change?

33. **Investment Criteria.** Elm City Electronics is considering two mutually exclusive projects that differ greatly on the required investment and projected cash flows. The initial investment required for Project I is $250,000 while for Project II it is $25,000. Projected after-tax cash flows are shown below:

	Cash Flows, Dollars	
Year	**Project I**	**Project II**
1	12,000	15,000
2	18,000	8,000
3	18,000	6,000
4	30,000	6,000
5	250,000	500

The opportunity cost of capital for Elm City is 6 percent.

a. Decide which project you would choose by applying each of the following decision criteria separately. Explain your reasoning in each case: (a) payback period, (b) discounted payback period, (c) NPV, (d) IRR, and (e) profitability index.

b. Which project would you eventually choose? Explain your answer.

*34. **Equivalent Annual Cost.** A precision lathe costs $10,000 and will cost $20,000 a year to operate and maintain. If the discount rate is 12 percent and the lathe will last for 5 years, what is the equivalent annual cost of the tool?

35. **Equivalent Annual Cost.** A firm can lease a truck for 4 years at a cost of $30,000 annually. It can instead buy a truck at a cost of $80,000, with annual maintenance expenses of $10,000. The truck will be sold at the end of 4 years for $20,000. Which is the better option if the discount rate is 12 percent?

*36. **Multiple IRR.** Consider the following cash flows:

C_0	C_1	C_2	C_3	C_4
–22	+20	+20	+20	–40

a. Confirm that one internal rate of return on this project is (a shade above) 7 percent, and that the other is (a shade below) 34 percent.

b. Is the project attractive if the discount rate is 5 percent?

c. What if it is 20 percent? 40 percent?

d. Why is the project attractive at midrange discount rates but not at very high or very low rates?

*37. **Equivalent Annual Cost.** Econo-cool air conditioners cost $300 to purchase, result in electricity bills of $150 per year, and last for 5 years. Luxury Air models cost $500, result in electricity bills of $100 per year, and last for 8 years. The discount rate is 21 percent.

a. What are the equivalent annual costs of the Econo-cool and Luxury Air models?

b. Which model is more cost effective?

c. Now you remember that the inflation rate is expected to be 10 percent per year for the foreseeable future. Redo parts (a) and (b).

38. **Investment Timing.** You can purchase an optical scanner today for $400. The scanner provides benefits worth $60 a year. The expected life of the scanner is 10 years. Scanners are expected to decrease in price by 20 percent per year. Suppose the discount rate is 10 percent. Should you purchase the scanner today or wait to purchase? When is the best purchase time?

39. **Replacement Decision.** You are operating an old machine that is expected to produce a cash inflow of $5,000 in each of the next 3 years before it fails. You can replace it now with a new machine that costs $20,000 but is much more efficient and will provide a cash flow of $10,000 a year for 4 years. Should you replace your equipment now? The discount rate is 15 percent.

*40. **Replacement Decision.** A forklift will last for only 2 more years. It costs $5,000 a year to maintain. For $20,000 you can buy a new lift which can last for 10 years and should require maintenance costs of only $2,000 a year.

a. If the discount rate is 5 percent per year, should you replace the forklift?

b. If the discount rate is 10 percent per year? Why does your answer change?

CHALLENGE

41. **NPV/IRR.** Growth Enterprises believes its latest project, which will cost $80,000 to install, will generate a perpetual growing stream of cash flows. Cash flow at the end of this year will be $5,000, and cash flows in future years are expected to grow indefinitely at an annual rate of 5 percent.

a. If the discount rate for this project is 10 percent, what is the project NPV?

b. What is the project IRR?

42. **Investment Timing.** A classic problem in management of forests is determining when it is most economically advantageous to cut a tree for lumber. When the tree is young, it grows very rapidly. As it ages, its growth slows down. Why is the NPV-maximizing rule to cut the tree when its growth rate equals the discount rate?

43. **Multiple IRRs.** Strip Mining, Inc., can develop a new mine at an initial cost of $5 million. The mine will provide a cash flow of $30 million in 1 year. The land then must be reclaimed at a cost of $28 million in the second year.

a. What are the IRRs of this project?

b. Should the firm develop the mine if the discount rate is 10 percent? 20 percent? 350 percent? 400 percent?

SOLUTIONS TO CHECK POINTS

6.1 Even if construction costs are $355,000, NPV is still positive:

$$\text{NPV} = \text{PV} - \$355{,}000 = \$357{,}143 - \$355{,}000 = \$2{,}143$$

Therefore, the project is still worth pursuing. The project is viable as long as construction costs are less than the PV of the future cash flow, that is, as long as construction costs are less than $357,143. However, if the opportunity cost of capital is 20 percent, the PV of the $400,000 sales price is lower and NPV is negative:

$$\text{PV} = \$400{,}000 \times \frac{1}{1.20} = \$333{,}333$$

$$\text{NPV} = \text{PV} - \$355{,}000 = -\$21{,}667$$

The present value of the future cash flow is not as high when the opportunity cost of capital is higher. The project would need to provide a higher payoff in order to be viable in the face of the higher opportunity cost of capital.

6.2 The IRR is now about 8.9 percent because

$$\text{NPV} = -\$350{,}000 + \frac{\$16{,}000}{1.089} + \frac{\$16{,}000}{(1.089)^2} + \frac{\$416{,}000}{(1.089)^3} = 0$$

Note in Figure 6.6 that NPV falls to zero as the discount rate reaches 8.9 percent.

6.3 The payback period is \$3,000/\$660 = 4.6 years. We find the discounted payback period and NPV as follows:

Year	Cash Flows	Discount Factor	Discounted Cash Flows	Cumulative Discounted Cash Flows
0	–3,000	1.0000	–3,000	
1	660	0.9434	623	–2,377
2	660	0.8900	587	–1,790
3	660	0.8396	554	–1,236
4	660	0.7921	523	–713
5	660	0.7473	493	–220
6	660	0.7050	465	245
7	660	0.6651	439	**684**
				↓ NPV

Notice the cumulative discounted cash flows are negative until Year 5 and positive from Year 6. This means that the discounted payback period = 5 years + 220/465 = 5.5 years. The cumulative discounted cash flow for Year 7 is also the NPV, \$684.

You can also calculate NPV by taking the present value of a \$660 annuity for 7 years at 6 percent:

PV annuity = \$3,684
NPV = –\$3,000 + \$3,684 = \$684

The project should be accepted.

6.4 a. IRR = 23% (i.e., $-60 + 30/1.23 + 30/1.23^2 + 30/1.23^3 = 0$)

b. Year 1: Income/book value at start of Year 1 = (30 – 20)/60 = .17, or 17%
Year 2: Income/book value at start of Year 2 = (30 – 20)/40 = .25, or 25%
Year 3: Income/book value at start of Year 3 = (30 – 20)/20 = .50, or 50%

FIGURE 6.6
NPV falls to zero at an interest rate of 8.9 percent.

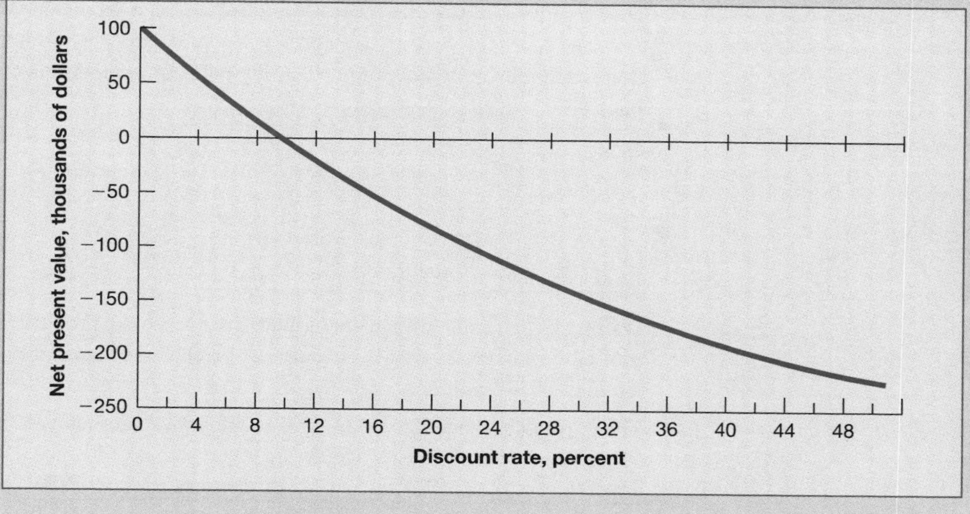

6.5

Year of Purchase	Cost of Computer	PV Savings	NPV at Year of Purchase	NPV Today
0	50	70	20	20
1	45	66	21	19.1
2	40	62	22	18.2
3	36	58	22	16.5
4	33	54	21	14.3
5	31	50	19	11.8

Purchase the new computer now.

6.6

Year:	0	1	2	3	PV of Costs
F. Cash flows	10,000	1,100	1,200		11,992
Equivalent annual cost		6,910	6,910		11,992
G. Cash flows	12,000	1,100	1,200	1,300	14,968
Equivalent annual cost		6,019	6,019	6,019	14,968

Machine G is the better buy. However, it's still better to keep the old machine going one more year. That costs $4,300, which is less than G's equivalent annual cost, $6,019.

6.7 You want to be rich. The NPV of the long-lived investment is much larger.

$$\text{Short: NPV} = -\$1 + \frac{\$2}{1.075} = +\$.8605 \text{ million}$$

$$\text{Long: NPV} = -\$1 + \frac{\$.3}{.075} = +\$3 \text{ million}$$

6.8 You want to be richer. The second alternative generates greater value at any reasonable discount rate. For example, suppose other risk-free investments offer 8 percent. Then

$$\text{NPV} = -\$1,000 + \frac{\$4,000}{1.08} = +\$2,703$$

$$\text{NPV} = -\$1,000,000 + \frac{\$1,500,000}{1.08} = +\$388,888$$

6.9 Rank each project in order of profitability index as in the following table:

Project	Profitability Index	Investment
N	0.43	$7
L	0.33	3
O	0.33	6
P	0.25	4
M	0.20	5

Starting from the top, we run out of funds after accepting projects N and L. While L and O have equal profitability indexes, project O could not be chosen because it would force total investment above the limit of $10 million.

6.10 The profitability index gives the wrong ranking for the first pair, the correct ranking for the second:

Project	PV	Investment	NPV	Profitability Index (NPV/Investment)
Short	$1,860,000	$1,000,000	$ 860,000	0.86
Long	4,000,000	1,000,000	3,000,000	3.0
Small	$ 3,703	$ 1,000	$ 2,703	2.7
Large	1,388,888	1,000,000	388,888	0.39

CHAPTER 7

Using Discounted Cash-Flow Analysis to Make Investment Decisions

7.1 Discount Cash Flows, Not Profits

7.2 Discount Incremental Cash Flows

7.3 Discount Nominal Cash Flows by the Nominal Cost of Capital

7.4 Separate Investment and Financing Decisions

7.5 Calculating Cash Flow

7.6 Business Taxes in Canada and the Capital Budgeting Decision

7.7 Example: Blooper Industries

7.8 Summary

Appendix 7A: Deriving the CCA Tax Shield

Think of the problems that General Motors faces when considering whether to introduce a new model. How much will we need to invest in new plant and equipment? What will it cost to market and promote the new car? How soon can we get the car into production? What is the projected production cost? What do we need in the way of inventories of raw materials and finished cars? How many cars can we expect to sell each year and at what price? What credit arrangements will we need to give our dealers? How long will the model stay in production? What happens at the end of that time? Can we use the plant and equipment elsewhere in the company? All of these issues affect the level and timing of project cash flows. In this chapter we continue our analysis of the capital budgeting decision by turning our focus to how the financial manager should prepare cash-flow estimates for use in net present value analysis.

In Chapter 6 we used the net present value rule to make a simple capital budgeting decision. You tackled the problem in four steps:

Step 1: Forecast the project cash flows.

Step 2: Estimate the opportunity cost of capital—that is, the rate of return that your shareholders could expect to earn if they invested their money in the capital market.

Step 3: Use the opportunity cost of capital to discount the future cash flows. The project's present value (PV) is equal to the sum of the discounted future cash flows.

Step 4: Net present value (NPV) measures whether the project is worth more than it costs. To calculate NPV you need to subtract the required investment from the present value of the future payoffs:

$$\text{NPV} = \text{PV} - \text{required investment}$$

You should go ahead with the project if it has a positive NPV.

We now need to consider how to apply the net present value rule to practical investment problems. The first step is to decide what to discount. We know the answer in principle: discount cash flows. This is why capital budgeting is often referred to as *discounted cash flow,* or *DCF,* analysis. But useful forecasts of cash flows do not arrive on a silver platter. Often the financial manager has to make do with raw data supplied by specialists in product design, production, marketing, and so on, and must adjust such data before they are useful. In addition, most financial forecasts are prepared in accordance with accounting principles that do not necessarily recognize cash flows when they occur. These data must also be adjusted.

We start this chapter with a discussion of the principles governing the cash flows that are relevant for discounting. We then present an example designed to show how standard accounting information can be used to compute those cash flows and why cash flows and accounting income usually differ. The example will lead us to various further points, including the links between depreciation and taxes and the importance of tracking investments in working capital.

After studying this chapter you should be able to

- Identify the cash flows properly attributable to a proposed new project.
- Calculate the cash flows of a project from standard financial statements.
- Understand how the company's tax bill is affected by depreciation and how this affects project value.
- Understand how changes in working capital affect project cash flows.

7.1 Discount Cash Flows, Not Profits

Up to this point we have been concerned mainly with the mechanics of discounting and with the various methods of project appraisal. We have had almost nothing to say about the problem of *what* you should discount. The first and most important point is this: to calculate net present value you need to discount cash flows, *not* accounting profits.

We stressed the difference between cash flows and profits in Chapter 2. Here we stress it again. Income statements are intended to show how well the firm has performed. They do not track cash flows.

If the firm lays out a large amount of money on a big capital project, you would not conclude that the firm performed poorly that year, even though a lot of cash is going out the door. Therefore, the accountant does not deduct capital expenditure when calculating the year's income but instead depreciates it over several years.

That is fine for computing year-by-year profits, but it could get you into trouble when working out net present value. For example, suppose that you are analyzing an investment proposal. It costs \$2,000 and is expected to bring in a cash flow of \$1,500 in the first year and \$500 in the second. You think that the opportunity cost of capital is 10 percent and so calculate the present value of the cash flows as follows:

$$PV = \frac{\$1,500}{1.10} + \frac{\$500}{(1.10)^2} = \$1,776.86$$

The project is worth less than it costs; it has a negative NPV:

$$NPV = \$1,776.86 - \$2,000 = -\$223.14$$

The project costs \$2,000 today, but accountants would not treat that outlay as an immediate expense. They would depreciate that \$2,000 over 2 years and deduct the depreciation from the cash flow to obtain accounting income:

	Year 1	Year 2
Cash inflow	+ \$1,500	+ \$ 500
Less depreciation	− 1,000	− 1,000
Accounting income	+ 500	− 500

Thus an accountant would forecast income of $500 in Year 1 and an accounting loss of $500 in Year 2.

Suppose you were given this forecast income and loss and naively discounted them. Now NPV *looks* positive:

$$\text{Apparent NPV} = \frac{\$500}{1.10} + \frac{-\$500}{(1.10)^2} = \$41.32$$

Of course we know that this is nonsense. The project is obviously a loser; we are spending money today ($2,000 cash outflow) and we are simply getting our money back ($1,500 in Year 1 and $500 in Year 2). We are earning a zero return when we could get a 10 percent return by investing our money in the capital market.

The message of the example is this:

When calculating NPV, recognize investment expenditures when they occur, not later when they show up as depreciation. Projects are financially attractive because of the cash they generate, either for distribution to shareholders or for reinvestment in the firm. Therefore, the focus of capital budgeting must be on cash flow, not profits.

Here is another example of the distinction between cash flow and accounting profits. Accountants try to show profit as it is earned, rather than when the company and the customer get around to paying their bills. For example, an income statement will recognize revenue when the sale is made, even if the bill is not paid for months. This practice also results in a difference between accounting profits and cash flow. The sale generates immediate profits, but the cash flow comes later.

▶ EXAMPLE 7.1 *Sales before Cash*

Reggie Hotspur, ace computer salesperson, closed a $500,000 sale on December 15, just in time to count it toward his annual bonus. How did he do it? Well, for one thing he gave the customer 180 days to pay. The income statement will recognize Hotspur's sale in December, even though cash will not arrive until June. But a financial analyst tracking cash flows would concentrate on the latter event.

The accountant takes care of the timing difference by adding $500,000 to accounts receivable in December, then reducing accounts receivable when the money arrives in June. (The total of accounts receivable is just the sum of all cash due from customers.)

You can think of the increase in accounts receivable as an investment—it's effectively a 180-day loan to the customer—and therefore a cash outflow. That investment is recovered when the customer pays. Thus financial analysts often find it convenient to calculate cash flow as follows:

December		**June**	
Sales	$500,000	Sales	0
Less investment in accounts receivable	–$500,000	Plus recovery of accounts receivable	+$500,000
Cash flow	0	Cash flow	$500,000

Note that this procedure gives the correct cash flow of $500,000 in June.

It is not always easy to translate accounting data back into actual dollars. If you are in doubt about what is a cash flow, simply count the dollars coming in and take away the dollars going out.

CHECK POINT 7.1

A regional supermarket chain is deciding whether to install a tewgit machine in each of its stores. Each machine costs $250,000. Projected income per machine is as follows:

Year:	1	2	3	4	5
Sales	$250,000	$300,000	$300,000	$250,000	$250,000
Operating expenses	200,000	200,000	200,000	200,000	200,000
Depreciation	50,000	50,000	50,000	50,000	50,000
Accounting income	0	50,000	50,000	0	0

Why would the stores continue to operate a machine in years 4 and 5 if it produces no profits? What are the cash flows from investing in a machine? Assume each tewgit machine is completely depreciated and has no salvage value at the end of its 5-year life.

7.2 Discount Incremental Cash Flows

A project's present value depends on the *extra* cash flows that it produces. Forecast the firm's cash flows first if you go ahead with the project. Then forecast the cash flows if you *don't* accept the project. Take the difference and you have the extra (or *incremental*) cash flows produced by the project:

$$\textbf{Incremental cash flow} = \textbf{cash flow with project} - \textbf{cash flow without project} \tag{7.1}$$

EXAMPLE 7.2 *Launching a New Product*

Consider the decision by Intel to launch its Pentium III microprocessor. A successful launch could mean sales of 50 million processors a year and several billion dollars in profits.

But are these profits all incremental cash flows? Certainly not. Our with-versus-without principle reminds us that we also need to think about what the cash flows would be *without* the new processor. Intel recognized that if it went ahead with the Pentium III, demand for its older Pentium II processors would be reduced. The incremental cash flows are therefore

Cash flow with Pentium III (including lower cash flow from Pentium II processors) − Cash flow without Pentium III (with higher cash flow from Pentium II processors)

The trick in capital budgeting is to trace all the incremental flows from a proposed project. Here are some things to look out for.

INCLUDE ALL INDIRECT EFFECTS

Intel's new processor illustrates a common indirect effect. New products often damage sales of an existing product. Of course, companies frequently introduce new products anyway, usually because they believe that their existing product line is under threat from competition.

Even if you don't go ahead with a new product, there is no guarantee that sales of the existing product line will continue at their present level. Sooner or later they will decline.

Sometimes a new project will *help* the firm's existing business. Suppose that you are the financial manager of an airline that is considering opening a new short-haul route from Prince George, B.C. to Vancouver's International Airport. When considered in isolation, the new route may have a negative NPV. But once you allow for the additional business that the new route brings to your other traffic out of Vancouver, it may be a very worthwhile investment.

To forecast incremental cash flow, you must trace out all indirect effects of accepting the project.

Some capital investments have very long lives once all indirect effects are recognized. Consider the introduction of a new jet engine. Engine manufacturers often offer attractive pricing to achieve early sales, because once an engine is installed, 15 years' sales of replacement parts are almost assured. Also, since airlines prefer to reduce the number of different engines in their fleet, selling jet engines today improves sales tomorrow as well. Later sales will generate further demands for replacement parts. Thus the string of incremental effects from the first sales of a new model engine can run out 20 years or more.

FORGET SUNK COSTS

Sunk costs are like spilled milk: they are past and irreversible outflows.

Sunk costs remain the same whether or not you accept the project. Therefore, they do not affect project NPV.

Unfortunately, often managers are influenced by sunk costs. For example, in 1971 Lockheed sought a federal guarantee for a bank loan to continue development of the Tristar airplane. Lockheed and its supporters argued that it would be foolish to abandon a project on which nearly $1 billion had already been spent. This was a poor argument, however, because the $1 billion was sunk. The relevant questions were how much more needed to be invested and whether the finished product warranted the *incremental* investment.

Lockheed's supporters were not the only ones to appeal to sunk costs. Some of its critics claimed that it would be foolish to continue with a project that offered no prospect of a satisfactory return on that $1 billion. This argument too was faulty. The $1 billion was gone, and the decision to continue with the project should have depended only on the return on the incremental investment.

INCLUDE OPPORTUNITY COSTS

Resources are almost never free, even when no cash changes hands. For example, suppose a new manufacturing operation uses land that could otherwise be sold for $100,000. This resource is costly; by using the land you pass up the opportunity to sell it. There is no out-of-pocket cost but there is an **opportunity cost,** that is, the value of the forgone alternative use of the land.

opportunity cost Benefit or cash flow forgone as a result of an action.

This example prompts us to warn you against judging projects "before versus after" rather than "with versus without." A manager comparing before versus after might not assign any value to the land because the firm owns it both before and after:

Before	Take Project	After	Cash Flow, Before versus After
Firm owns land	⟶	Firm still owns land	0

The proper comparison, *with versus without*, is as follows:

Before	Take Project	After	Cash Flow, with Project
Firm owns land	⟶	Firm still owns land	0

Before	Do Not Take Project	After	Cash Flow, without Project
Firm owns land	⟶	Firm sells land for $100,000	$100,000

Comparing the cash flows with and without the project, we see that $100,000 is given up by undertaking the project. The original cost of purchasing the land is irrelevant—that cost is sunk.

The opportunity cost equals the cash that could be realized from selling the land now, and therefore is a relevant cash flow for project evaluation.

When the resource can be freely traded, its opportunity cost is simply the market price.[1] However, sometimes opportunity costs are difficult to estimate. Suppose that you go ahead with a project to develop Computer Nouveau, pulling your software team off their work on a new operating system that some existing customers are not-so-patiently awaiting. The exact cost of infuriating those customers may be impossible to calculate, but you'll think twice about the opportunity cost of moving the software team to Computer Nouveau.

RECOGNIZE THE INVESTMENT IN WORKING CAPITAL

net working capital Current assets minus current liabilities.

Net working capital (often referred to simply as *working capital*) is the difference between a company's short-term assets and liabilities. The principal short-term assets are cash, accounts receivable (customers' unpaid bills), and inventories of raw materials and finished goods. The principal short-term liabilities are accounts payable (bills that *you* have not paid), notes payable, and accruals (liabilities for items such as wages or taxes that have recently been incurred but have not yet been paid).

Most projects entail an additional investment in working capital. For example, before you can start production, you need to invest in inventories of raw materials. Then, when you deliver the finished product, customers may be slow to pay and accounts receivable will increase. (Remember Reggie Hotspur's computer sale, described in Example 7.1. It required a $500,000, 6-month investment in accounts receivable.) Next year, as business builds up, you may need a larger stock of raw materials and you may have even more unpaid bills.

Investments in working capital, just like investments in plant and equipment, result in cash outflows.

[1] If the value of the land to the firm were less than the market price, the firm would sell it. On the other hand, the opportunity cost of using land in a particular project cannot exceed the cost of buying an equivalent parcel to replace it.

We find that working capital is one of the most common sources of confusion in forecasting project cash flows.[2] Here are the most common mistakes:

1. *Forgetting about working capital entirely.* We hope that you never fall into that trap.
2. *Forgetting that working capital may change during the life of the project.* Imagine that you sell $100,000 of goods per year and customers pay on average 6 months late. You will therefore have $50,000 of unpaid bills. Now you increase prices by 10 percent, so that revenues increase to $110,000. If customers continue to pay 6 months late, unpaid bills increase to $55,000, and therefore, you need to make an *additional* investment in working capital of $5,000.
3. *Forgetting that working capital is recovered at the end of the project.* When the project comes to an end, inventories are run down, any unpaid bills are (you hope) paid off, and you can recover your investment in working capital. This generates a cash *inflow.*

BEWARE OF ALLOCATED OVERHEAD COSTS

We have already mentioned that the accountant's objective in gathering data is not always the same as the investment analyst's. A case in point is the allocation of overhead costs such as rent, heat, or electricity. These overhead costs may not be related to a particular project, but they must be paid for nevertheless. Therefore, when the accountant assigns costs to the firm's projects, a charge for overhead is usually made. But our principle of incremental cash flows says that in investment appraisal we should include only the *extra* expenses that would result from the project.

A project may generate extra overhead costs, but then again, it may not. We should be cautious about assuming that the accountant's allocation of overhead costs represents the *incremental* cash flow that would be incurred by accepting the project.

CHECK POINT 7.2

A firm is considering an investment in a new manufacturing plant. The site is already owned by the company, but existing buildings would need to be demolished. Which of the following should be treated as incremental cash flows?

a. The market value of the site.
b. The market value of the existing buildings.
c. Demolition costs and site clearance.
d. The cost of a new access road put in last year.
e. Lost cash flows on other projects due to executive time spent on the new facility.
f. Future depreciation of the new plant.

7.3 Discount Nominal Cash Flows by the Nominal Cost of Capital

The distinction between nominal and real cash flows and interest rates is crucial in capital budgeting. Interest rates are usually quoted in *nominal* terms. If you invest $100 in a bank deposit offering 6 percent interest, then the bank promises to pay you $106 at the end of

[2] If you are not clear why working capital affects cash flow, look back to Chapter 2, where we gave a primer on working capital and a couple of simple examples.

the year. It makes no promises about what that \$106 will buy. The real rate of interest on the bank deposit depends on inflation. If inflation is 2 percent, that \$106 will buy you only 4 percent more goods at the end of the year than your \$100 could buy today. The *real* rate of interest is therefore about 4 percent.[3]

If the discount rate is nominal, consistency requires that cash flows be estimated in nominal terms as well, taking into account trends in selling price, labour and materials costs, and so on. This calls for more than simply applying a single assumed inflation rate to all components of cash flow. Some costs or prices increase faster than inflation, some slower. For example, perhaps you have entered into a 5-year fixed-price contract with a supplier. No matter what happens to inflation over this period, this part of your costs is fixed in nominal terms.

Of course, there is nothing wrong with discounting real cash flows at the real interest rate, although this is not commonly done. We saw in Chapter 3 that real cash flows discounted at the real discount rate give exactly the same present values as nominal cash flows discounted at the nominal rate.

It should go without saying that you cannot mix and match real and nominal quantities. Real cash flows must be discounted at a real discount rate, nominal cash flows at a nominal rate. Discounting real cash flows at a nominal rate is a *big* mistake.

While the need to maintain consistency may seem like an obvious point, analysts sometimes forget to account for the effects of inflation when forecasting future cash flows. As a result, they end up discounting real cash flows at a nominal interest rate. This can grossly understate project values.

▶ EXAMPLE 7.3 *Cash Flows and Inflation*

City Consulting Services is considering moving into a new office building. The cost of a 1-year lease is \$8,000, but this cost will increase in future years at the annual inflation rate of 3 percent. The firm believes that it will remain in the building for 4 years. What is the present value of its rental costs if the discount rate is 10 percent?

The present value can be obtained by discounting the nominal cash flows at the 10 percent discount rate as follows:

Year	Cash Flow	Present Value at 10% Discount Rate	
1	8,000	8,000/1.10 =	7,272.73
2	8,000 × 1.03 = 8,240	8,240/1.10^2 =	6,809.92
3	8,000 × 1.03^2 = 8,487.20	8,487.20/1.10^3 =	6,376.56
4	8,000 × 1.03^3 = 8,741.82	8,741.82/1.10^4 =	5,970.78
			\$26,429.99

[3] Remember from Chapter 3,

$$\text{Real rate of interest} \approx \text{nominal rate of interest} - \text{inflation rate}$$

The exact formula is

$$1 + \text{real rate of interest} = \frac{1 + \text{nominal rate of interest}}{1 + \text{inflation rate}}$$

$$= \frac{1.06}{1.02} = 1.0392$$

Therefore, the real interest rate is .0392, or 3.92 percent.

Alternatively, the real discount rate can be calculated as 1.10/1.03 – 1 = .067961 = 6.7961%. The present value of the cash flows can also be computed by discounting the real cash flows at the real discount rate as follows:

Year	Real Cash Flow	Present Value at 6.7961% Discount Rate
1	$8{,}000/1.03 = 7{,}766.99$	$7{,}766.99/1.067961 = 7{,}272.73$
2	$8{,}240/1.03^2 = 7{,}766.99$	$7{,}766.99/1.067961^2 = 6{,}809.92$
3	$8{,}487.20/1.03^3 = 7{,}766.99$	$7{,}766.99/1.067961^3 = 6{,}376.56$
4	$8{,}741.82/1.03^4 = 7{,}766.99$	$7{,}766.99/1.067961^4 = 5{,}970.78$
		\$26,429.99

Notice the real cash flow is a constant, since the lease payment increases at the rate of inflation. The present value of *each* cash flow is the same regardless of the method used to discount. The sum of the present values is also identical, of course.

☑ CHECK POINT 7.3

Nasty Industries is closing down an outmoded factory and throwing all of its workers out on the street. Nasty's CEO, Cruella DeLuxe, is enraged to learn that it must continue to pay for workers' health insurance for 4 years. The cost per worker next year will be \$2,400 per year, but the inflation rate is 4 percent, and health costs have been increasing at three percentage points faster than inflation. What is the present value of this obligation? The (nominal) discount rate is 10 percent.

7.4 Separate Investment and Financing Decisions

When we calculate the cash flows from a project, we ignore how that project is financed. The company may decide to finance partly by debt, but even if it did, we would *neither* subtract the debt proceeds from the required investment *nor* recognize the interest and principal payments as cash outflows. Regardless of the actual financing, we should view the project as if it were all-equity financed, treating all cash outflows required for the project as coming from shareholders and all cash inflows as going to them.

We do this to separate the analysis of the investment decision from the financing decision. We first measure whether the project has a positive net present value, assuming all-equity financing. Then we can undertake a separate analysis of the financing decision. We discuss financing decisions later in the book.

7.5 Calculating Cash Flow

A project cash flow is the sum of three components: investment in fixed assets such as plant and equipment, investment in working capital, and cash flow from operations:

$$\textbf{Total cash flow} = \textbf{cash flow from investment in plant and equipment} + \textbf{cash flow from investment in working capital} + \textbf{cash flow from operations} \quad (7.2)$$

Let's examine each of these in turn.

CAPITAL INVESTMENT

To get a project off the ground, a company will typically need to make considerable up-front investments in plant, equipment, research, marketing, and so on. For example, Gillette spent about $750 million to develop and build the production line for its Mach3 razor cartridge and an additional $300 million in its initial marketing campaign, largely before a single razor was sold. These expenditures are negative cash flows—negative because they represent a cash outflow from the firm.

Conversely, if a piece of machinery can be sold when the project winds down, the sales price (net of any taxes on the sale) represents a positive cash flow to the firm.

▶ EXAMPLE 7.4 *Cash Flow from Investments*

Gillette's competitor, Slick, invests $800 million to develop the Mock4 razor blade. The specialized blade factory will run for 7 years, until it is replaced by more advanced technology. At that point, the machinery will be sold for scrap metal, for a price of $50 million. Taxes of $10 million will be assessed on the sale.

Therefore, the initial cash flow from investment is –$800 million, and in 7 years, the cash flow from the disinvestment in the production line will be $50 million – $10 million = $40 million.

INVESTMENT IN WORKING CAPITAL

We pointed out earlier in the chapter that when a company builds up inventories of raw materials or finished product, the company's cash is reduced; the reduction in cash reflects the firm's investment in inventories. Similarly, cash is reduced when customers are slow to pay their bills—in this case, the firm makes an investment in accounts receivable. Investment in working capital, just like investment in plant and equipment, represents a negative cash flow. On the other hand, later in the life of a project, when inventories are sold off and accounts receivable are collected, the firm's investment in working capital is reduced as it converts these assets into cash.

▶ EXAMPLE 7.5 *Cash Flow from Investments in Working Capital*

Slick makes an initial (Year 0) investment of $10 million in inventories of plastic and steel for its blade plant. Then in Year 1 it accumulates an additional $20 million of raw materials. The total level of inventories is now $10 million + $20 million = $30 million, but the cash expenditure in Year 1 is simply the $20 million addition to inventory. The $20 million investment in additional inventory results in a cash flow of –$20 million.

Later on, say in Year 5, the company begins planning for the next-generation blade. At this point, it decides to reduce its inventory of raw material from $20 million to $15 million. This reduction in inventory investment frees up $5 million of cash, which is a positive cash flow. Therefore, the cash flows from inventory investment are –$10 million in Year 0, –$20 million in Year 1, and +$5 million in Year 5.

In general,

> **An *increase* in working capital implies a *negative* cash flow; a decrease implies a positive cash flow. The cash flow is measured by the *change* in working capital, not the *level* of working capital.**

CASH FLOW FROM OPERATIONS

The third component of project cash flow is cash flow from operations. There are several ways to work out this component.

Method 1. Take only the items from the income statement that represent cash flows. We start with cash revenues and subtract cash expenses and taxes paid. We do not, however, subtract a charge for depreciation because depreciation is an accounting entry not a cash expense. Thus

$$\text{Cash flow from operations} = \text{revenues} - \text{cash expenses} - \text{taxes paid}$$

Method 2. Alternatively, you can start with accounting profits and add back any deductions that were made for noncash expenses such as depreciation. (Remember from our earlier discussion that you want to discount cash flows, not profits.) By this reasoning,

$$\text{Cash flow from operations} = \text{net profit} + \text{depreciation}$$

Method 3. Although the depreciation deduction is *not* a cash expense, it does affect net profits and therefore taxes paid, which *is* a cash item.[4] For example, if the firm's tax bracket is 35 percent, each additional dollar of depreciation reduces taxable income by $1. Tax payments therefore fall by $.35, and cash flow increases by the same amount. The total **depreciation tax shield** equals the product of depreciation and the tax rate:

depreciation tax shield Reduction in taxes attributable to the depreciation allowance.

$$\textbf{Depreciation tax shield} = \textbf{depreciation} \times \textbf{tax rate} \qquad (7.3)$$

This suggests a third way to calculate cash flow from operations. First, calculate net profit *assuming* zero depreciation. This item would be (revenues – cash expenses) × (1 – tax rate). Now add back the tax shield created by depreciation. We then calculate operating cash flow as follows:

$$\begin{aligned}\text{Cash flow from operations} = {} & (\text{revenues} - \text{cash expenses}) \times (1 - \text{tax rate}) \\ & + (\text{depreciation} \times \text{tax rate})\end{aligned}$$

The following example confirms that the three methods for estimating cash flow from operations all give the same answer.

▸ EXAMPLE 7.6 *Cash Flow from Operations*

A project generates revenues of $1,000, cash expenses of $600, and depreciation charges of $200 in a particular year. The firm's tax bracket is 35 percent. Net income is calculated as follows:

	Revenues	$1,000
–	Cash expenses	600
–	Depreciation expense	200
=	Profit before tax	200
–	Tax at 35%	70
=	Net income	130

Methods 1, 2, and 3 all show that cash flow from operations is $330:

Method 1: Cash flow from operations = revenues – cash expenses – taxes
= 1,000 – 600 – 70 = 330

[4] The discussion here is general, without reference to the tax laws of any country. In Section 7.6 we will examine the treatment of depreciation in Canadian tax law.

Method 2: Cash flow from operations = net profit + depreciation
= 130 + 200 = 330

Method 3: Cash flow from operations = (revenues – cash expenses) × (1 – tax rate)
+ (depreciation × tax rate)
= (1,000 – 600) × (1 – .35) + (200 × .35) = 330

CHECK POINT 7.4

A project generates revenues of $600, expenses of $300, and depreciation charges of $200 in a particular year. The firm's tax bracket is 35 percent. Find the operating cash flow of the project using all three approaches.

In many cases, a project will seek to improve efficiency or cut costs. A new computer system may provide labour savings. A new heating system may be more energy efficient than the one it replaces. These projects also contribute to the operating cash flow of the firm—not by increasing revenue, but by reducing costs. As the next example illustrates, we calculate the addition to operating cash flow on cost-cutting projects just as we would for projects that increase revenues.

EXAMPLE 7.7 *Operating Cash Flow on Cost-Cutting Projects*

Suppose the new heating system costs $100,000 but reduces heating expenditures by $30,000 a year. The system will be depreciated straight-line over a 5-year period, so the annual depreciation charge will be $20,000. The firm's tax rate is 35 percent. We calculate the *incremental* effects on revenues, expenses, and depreciation charges as follows. Notice that the reduction in expenses increases revenues minus cash expenses.

Increase in (revenues minus expenses)	$30,000
– Additional depreciation expense	– 20,000
= Incremental profit before tax	= 10,000
– Incremental tax at 35%	– 3,500
= Change in net income	= 6,500

Therefore, the increment to operating cash flow can be calculated by *method 1* as

Increase in (revenues – cash expenses) – additional taxes
= $30,000 – $3,500
= $26,500

or by *method 2:*

Increase in net profit + additional depreciation
= $6,500 + $20,000
= $26,500

or by *method 3:*

Increase in (revenues – cash expenses) × (1 – tax rate) + (additional depreciation × tax rate)
= $30,000 × (1 – .35) + ($20,000 × .35)
= $26,500

Business Taxes in Canada and the Capital Budgeting Decision

DEPRECIATION AND CAPITAL COST ALLOWANCE

capital cost allowance The amount of write-off on depreciable assets allowed by Canada Customs and Revenue Agency (CCRA) against taxable income.

undepreciated capital cost (UCC) The balance remaining in an asset class that has not yet been depreciated in that year.

CCA tax shield Tax savings arising from the capital cost allowance charge.

While calculating profit before tax, or taxable income, the business is allowed to deduct an amount for depreciation on its depreciable assets. This deduction, called the **capital cost allowance (CCA)** in Canada, enables the business to recover the original amount invested in the asset over a period of time, free of tax. In a general sense,

$$\textbf{Taxable income} = \textbf{revenues} - \textbf{expenses} - \textbf{CCA} \tag{7.4}$$

The CCA for each year is calculated by multiplying the balance on the asset, called the **undepreciated capital cost (UCC)**, by the appropriate tax rate.[5] Although the CCA itself is a noncash charge, it does affect cash flow to the extent that it reduces the taxes paid. This tax saving, called the **CCA tax shield**, or sometimes, the *depreciation tax shield*, is discussed in more detail later in the chapter.

It is important to remember that although the terms depreciation and CCA are often used interchangeably, they are not necessarily the same. In fact, the depreciation figure shown in a company's income statement is often calculated in a different manner than the CCA it reports to Canada Customs and Revenue Agency (CCRA). We should note that only the CCA amount has an effect on the company's cash flows since it determines its tax bill.

THE ASSET CLASS SYSTEM

asset class Eligible depreciable assets are grouped into specified asset classes by CCRA. Each asset class has a prescribed CCA rate.

straight-line depreciation Constant depreciation for each year of the asset's accounting life.

declining balance depreciation This is computed by applying the depreciation rate to the asset balance for each year.

half-year rule Only one-half of the purchase cost of the asset is added to the asset class and used to compute CCA in the year of purchase.

All eligible depreciable assets are grouped into one of over 30 CCA **asset classes**. Each asset class has been assigned a CCA rate by CCRA. Table 7.1 provides details regarding some of the asset classes. We note that buildings are generally included in asset classes 1 and 3 and allowed a lower CCA rate. For instance, most buildings acquired after 1987 would fall in Class 1, and a firm that owned such buildings would be entitled to a CCA amount equal to 4 percent of the value of this class. At the other extreme, chinaware, cutlery, most computer software, and videotape cassettes used for rental purposes fall into asset class 12, which is allowed a 100 percent CCA rate. For most assets, CCA is calculated by applying the appropriate asset class rate against the declining asset balance (UCC amount). Intangible assets such as leasehold improvements (a Class 13 asset) or patents (a Class 14 asset) follow the **straight-line depreciation** method for computing CCA. For such assets, CCA essentially represents an annuity series.

Under the asset class system, all assets within a particular CCA class are depreciated for tax purposes as if they were a single asset. To understand how the asset class system works, suppose that you have started a business as a tourbus operator and have invested \$100,000 in a new bus. This would be a Class 10 asset for which the CCA is computed using a **declining balance depreciation** method and the applicable CCA rate is 30 percent. Suppose, in the second year, you decide to expand your business and buy another bus for \$100,000. To keep things simple, let us ignore the **half-year rule** for now.[6] Your CCA claims at the end of the first and second years are provided in Table 7.2.

[5] We can define UCC as the total cost of all assets in an asset class minus the accumulated CCA in that class. It is similar to the concept of "net fixed assets" under GAAP.

[6] The half-year rule will allow your firm to include one-half of the purchase cost of the asset for calculating the year's CCA in that asset class in the year the asset is purchased. This is the case regardless of what part of the year the asset is purchased. The remaining half of the purchase cost is added to the asset class in the next year.

TABLE 7.1
CCA rates and classes

The following is a partial list describing the most common capital cost allowance (CCA) classes.

Class number	Description	CCA rate
1	Most buildings made of brick, stone, or cement acquired after 1987, including their component parts such as electric wiring, lighting fixtures, plumbing, heating and cooling equipment, elevators, and escalators	4%
3	Most buildings made of brick, stone, or cement acquired before 1988, including their component parts as listed in Class 1 above	5%
7	Canoes, boats, and most other vessels, including their furniture, fittings, or equipment	15%
9	Aircraft, including furniture, fittings, or equipment attached, and their spare parts	25%
10	Automobiles (except taxis and those used for lease or rent), vans, wagons, trucks, buses, tractors, trailers, drive-in theatres, general-purpose electronic data-processing equipment (e.g., personal computers) and systems software, and timber-cutting and -removing equipment	30%
12	Chinaware, cutlery, linen, uniforms, dies, jigs, moulds or lasts, computer software (except systems software), cutting or shaping parts of a machine, certain production costs associated with making a motion picture film, such as apparel or costumes, videotape cassettes, ...	100%
13	Property that is leasehold interest (the maximum CCA rate depends on the type of the leasehold and the terms of the lease)	N/A
38	Most power-operated movable equipment acquired after 1987 used for moving, excavating, placing, or compacting earth, rock, concrete, or asphalt	30%
39	Machinery and equipment acquired after 1987 that is used in Canada primarily to manufacture and process goods for sale or lease	25%
43	Manufacturing and processing machinery and equipment acquired after February 25, 1992, described in Class 39 above	30%

Source: "CCA Rates and Classes," Canada Customs and Revenue Agency website, www.ccra-adrc.gc.ca.

You would reduce your taxable income in the first year by $30,000. You begin the next year with an undepreciated balance (the *undepreciated capital cost, UCC*) of $70,000 to which you would add the purchase cost of the second bus of $100,000 for a total UCC amounting to $170,000. In the second year you would be entitled to a CCA deduction from your taxable income of $51,000. The UCC remaining at the end of the second year is $119,000.

Let us now introduce the half-year rule for the illustration above. As shown in Table 7.3, the CCA for asset Class 10 is $15,000 in Year 1 and $40,500 in Year 2. Taxable income is reduced by these amounts in the 2 years. In the first year, CCA is calculated on one-half of the purchase cost of the asset or .5 × $100,000 × .30. In the second year, the total CCA

TABLE 7.2
Undepreciated capital cost (UCC) and capital cost allowance (CCA) (without the half-year rule)

Year	Cost of Buses	Beginning of Year UCC	CCA	End of Year UCC
1	$100,000	$100,000	$30,000[1]	$ 70,000
2	$100,000	$170,000	$51,000	$119,000

[1] $100,000 × .30.

TABLE 7.3
Undepreciated capital cost (UCC) and capital cost allowance (CCA) (with the half-year rule)

Year	Cost of Buses	Beginning of Year UCC	CCA	End of Year UCC
1	$100,000	$100,000	$15,000	$85,000
2	$100,000	$185,000	$40,500	$144,500

of $40,500 for the asset class is calculated as follows: for the asset purchased in the first year, CCA computed on the UCC balance is $85,000 × .30, or $25,500, whereas the half-year rule applies to the second year's purchase, and the eligible CCA is .5 × $100,000 × .30, or $15,000. Notice that, for Year 3, if you do not make any further additions to this asset class, CCA will be calculated on the UCC balance of $144,500 at the applicable rate of 30 percent.

SALE OF ASSETS

A company is entitled to a CCA as long as it owns at least one asset in the asset class. When a depreciable asset is sold, the undepreciated capital cost of its asset class is reduced by either the asset's sale price or its initial cost, whichever is less. The result is called the *adjusted cost of disposal*. In the example in Table 7.3, if the bus purchased in Year 1 for $100,000 is sold in Year 3 for $80,000, the adjusted cost of disposal is $80,000 and gets deducted from the UCC of Class 10 in Year 3.

In any given year, the company may buy new assets and sell old assets from within the same asset class. In this case, we would apply the *net acquisitions rule*. That is, we would determine the total cost of all additions to an asset class and then subtract the adjusted cost of disposal of all assets in that class. If the net acquisition is positive, we would apply the half-year rule and calculate CCA as shown earlier. Continuing with our tourbus operator example, suppose in Year 3, in addition to selling the bus bought in Year 1 for $80,000, we buy another luxury coach for $150,000. Our net acquisition in Year 3 will be $150,000 – $80,000, or $70,000. To calculate CCA for Year 3, we will apply the half-year rule on $70,000. This result will be added to the CCA computed on the UCC balance of $144,500 to get the overall CCA for Year 3. If, on the other hand, the net acquisition is negative, we do not adjust for the half-year rule. Instead, we will subtract the negative net acquisition amount from the beginning UCC balance of the asset class. CCA for the year will be calculated by applying the CCA rate on this net amount.

CHECK POINT 7.5

In Year 1 of your new business as a boat rental company, you have bought a motorboat for $100,000 and a sailboat for $80,000. In Year 2, you sell the motorboat for $100,000 and the sailboat for $75,000. You also buy a speedboat in Year 2 for $150,000. For CCA purposes, the boats are grouped in Class 7, which carries a 15 percent CCA rate. Calculate the CCA for years 1 and 2. What is the UCC balance at the end of Year 2?

TERMINATION OF ASSET POOL

What happens if the company disposes of its entire pool of assets in an asset class? Once again, we determine the adjusted cost of disposal (as the lower of the sale proceeds or the initial cost of this pool of assets) and subtract this amount from the undepreciated capital cost of the asset class. If this leaves a positive balance in the asset class and there are *no*

terminal loss When an asset class has a positive balance following the disposal of all assets in the class, this balance is called terminal loss. The UCC of the asset class is set to zero after a terminal loss is recognized.

other assets remaining in the class, this remaining balance is called a **terminal loss** and is deducted from taxable income. Also, the UCC then becomes zero, and the asset class ceases to generate CCA tax shields.[7]

If, on the other hand, we arrive at a negative balance after deducting the adjusted cost of disposal from the UCC of the asset class, this amount is called **recaptured depreciation** and is added back to taxable income. Once again, the undepreciated capital cost of the asset class becomes zero.

When an asset is sold for more than its initial cost, the difference between the sale price and initial cost is called a capital gain. Presently capital gains, net of any capital losses, are taxed at 50 percent of the firm's applicable marginal tax rate.

▶ EXAMPLE 7.8 *Recaptured Depreciation*

recaptured depreciation If the sale of an asset causes a negative balance in an asset class, the amount of the negative balance is known as recaptured depreciation and is added to taxable income.

Remember our example where you bought two buses in years 1 and 2, respectively, each costing $100,000. To calculate CCA, the buses fall into Class 10 and are eligible for a 30 percent CCA rate. From Table 7.3, we saw that after taking 2 years of CCA, the undepreciated capital cost in the asset class is $144,500. Suppose you now decide to end your career as a tourbus operator and terminate the pool of assets in this class by selling both buses. You sell each bus for $120,000 for a total sale value of $240,000. Notice that because the sale price of the buses exceeds their purchase cost, they have actually appreciated in value instead of depreciating. The adjusted cost of disposal is their total purchase cost of $200,000. In such a situation, CCRA will determine that you have taken $200,000 – $144,500 = $55,500 depreciation that did not reflect the economic depreciation on the assets. Therefore, this amount ($55,500) will be "recaptured" and added to your income to calculate tax. In addition, you have a capital gain of $240,000 – $200,000 = $40,000. The capital gain will be taxed at 50 percent of your firm's applicable marginal tax rate.

Suppose that instead of selling the two buses, you sell only one bus for $120,000 and continue running your business using the other bus. Notice that because one bus still remains in the asset class, the asset pool is not terminated. The UCC of $144,500 gets reduced by the adjusted cost of disposal of $100,000[8] but is still a positive amount of $44,500 and so there is no recaptured depreciation. You have also made a capital gain on the sale of $120,000 – $100,000 = $20,000.

CHECK POINT 7.6

Think again about Example 7.8. Suppose that instead of selling the two buses for $120,000 each, you sell the bus bought in Year 1 for $65,000 and the one bought in Year 2 for $70,000. What are the tax consequences of this transaction, assuming that the firm has no other Class 10 assets?

PRESENT VALUES OF CCA TAX SHIELDS

Suppose we start a new asset class by buying an asset. We'll use the following notation for our subsequent discussion:

[7] We should note that if the asset pool is not completely terminated—that is, there are other assets remaining in the asset class—then a positive balance would simply become the UCC of the class and continue to generate CCA tax shields.

[8] This amount, representing the initial purchase cost, is lower than the sale price of $120,000.

C	=	capital cost of an asset acquired at the beginning of Year 1
d	=	CCA rate for the asset class to which the asset belongs
UCC_t	=	undepreciated capital cost in Year t after deducting CCA for the year
T_c	=	the firm's tax rate
r	=	discount rate
S	=	salvage amount from the sale of the asset at the end of Year t

To properly evaluate a project and calculate its present value, we need to compute the present value of the CCA tax shields accruing from capital investments in the project. As we show later in our discussion of Example 7.9, an asset can continue to generate CCA tax shields for the firm even after it is sold, provided there are other assets remaining in its class and the total UCC balance for the asset class is positive. This suggests that the CCA tax shield from investing in an asset can continue in perpetuity, since we are essentially deducting a fraction of the remaining UCC balance over an infinite period. Equation 1 below can be used to compute the present value of a perpetual tax shield.[9]

$$\frac{CdT_c}{r+d}\left[\frac{1+.5r}{1+r}\right] \tag{1}$$

Let us now introduce a residual or salvage value arising from the sale of an asset into the discussion. We would deduct this salvage value from the UCC of the asset class, and thereby reduce the CCA deductions and CCA tax shields for later years. Let us assume that other assets remain in the asset class and the total UCC exceeds the salvage value.[10] If the asset is sold at the end of Year t for a salvage amount, S, then the total tax shield lost is a perpetuity with a present value at the end of Year t of

$$\frac{SdT_c}{d+r}$$

When we discount this back to the present, we get the present value of lost CCA tax shields due to salvage value:

$$\left[\frac{SdT_c}{d+r}\right]\left[\frac{1}{(1+r)^t}\right] \tag{2}$$

Combining equations 1 and 2 enables us to provide a general formula for the present value of the CCA tax shield:

Present value of CCA tax shield =

$$\left[\frac{CdT_c}{r+d}\right]\left[\frac{1+.5r}{1+r}\right]-\left[\frac{SdT_c}{d+r}\right]\left[\frac{1}{(1+r)^t}\right] \tag{3}$$

We can now look at an example on how to get the present value of the tax shields. Keep in mind that we are looking for incremental changes in CCA and UCC that arise because of the purchase (or sale) of assets for the project. From Chapter 2, we know that the combined federal and provincial tax rate varies from province to province. Also, the tax rate could be different depending on whether the firm is a large corporation or a small business, and also, whether it is in manufacturing and processing or some other industry. To illustrate the calculation of taxes, we will assume that the company pays a total of 35 percent of its taxable income to the federal and provincial government.

[9] A detailed discussion of how this equation is obtained follows in Appendix 7A.

[10] Notice that, otherwise, we may have to consider recapture of CCA and capital gains or terminal losses.

▶ EXAMPLE 7.9 *PV of CCA Tax Shields*

Suppose that in Year 1 you buy heavy equipment for your factory for an amount C of \$250,000. The equipment belongs to asset class 39 with a CCA rate $d = .25$. You intend to sell the equipment in Year 8 for a salvage value, S, of \$8,000. At the time of sale, you still anticipate having other assets in the class and a UCC that exceeds the salvage value of the asset, so you will not have to deal with recaptured CCA or a terminal loss. Your tax rate is 35 percent and your discount rate is 12 percent. You want to know the present value of the incremental tax shields generated from owning and eventually selling the asset.

To calculate the present value of such incremental tax shields, we would have to reduce the present value of CCA tax shields by the present value of the tax shields lost due to the sale of the asset in Year 8.

$$\text{PV of CCA tax shields} = \begin{array}{c}\text{PV of perpetual tax}\\ \text{shield on asset acquired}\\ \text{in Year 1}\end{array} - \begin{array}{c}\text{PV of perpetual tax}\\ \text{shield on salvage}\\ \text{value in Year 8}\end{array}$$

$$= \left[\frac{CdT_c}{r+d}\right]\left[\frac{1+.5r}{1+r}\right] - \left[\frac{SdT_c}{d+r}\right]\left[\frac{1}{(1+r)^t}\right]$$

$$= \left[\frac{250{,}000 \times .25 \times .35}{.12 + .25}\right]\left[\frac{1 + (.5 \times .12)}{1 + .12}\right]$$

$$- \left[\frac{8{,}000 \times .25 \times .35}{.25 + .12}\right]\left[\frac{1}{(1 + .12)^8}\right]$$

$$= \left[\frac{21{,}875}{.37}\right]\left[\frac{1.06}{1.12}\right] - \left[\frac{700}{.37}\right]\left[\frac{1}{2.48}\right]$$

$$= 55{,}954 - 763 = 55{,}191$$

From Table 7.4, note that the UCC generated by the machinery after 8 years of CCA tax shields is \$29,200. Even *after* selling the equipment in Year 8, you will continue to depreciate \$29,200 – \$8,000 = \$21,200 over future years. This example shows us a unique feature of Canadian tax law, that it is possible for an asset to generate CCA tax shields for the firm even after it is sold. Notice that two basic conditions have to be met for this to happen: (1) there are other assets remaining in its class and (2) the proceeds from disposing of any such assets are less than the total UCC for the asset class.

☑ CHECK POINT 7.7

You are evaluating a project that requires an investment of \$5,000 and generates revenues of \$3,000 and expenses of \$1,500. CCA on the project will be based on a declining balance system with an applicable rate of 15 percent. The project will last for 5 years, at which time the machinery will be worthless and the firm will no longer produce cash flows. The firm's tax bracket is 35 percent.

a. Find the relevant cash flows for the first 5 years.
b. Assume that depreciation is on a straight-line basis over 5 years. What is the yearly depreciation charge? How would this change the cash flows for the first 5 years?

TABLE 7.4
CCA and UCC generated by the heavy equipment till Year 8

Year	1	2	3	4	5	6	7	8
C	250,000							
CCA	31,250	54,688	41,016	30,762	23,071	17,303	12,978	9,732
UCC	218,750	164,062	123,046	92,284	69,213	51,910	38,932	29,200

Example: Blooper Industries

Now that we have examined many of the pieces of a cash-flow analysis, let's try to put them together into a coherent whole. As the newly appointed financial manager of Blooper Industries, you are about to analyze a proposal for mining and selling a small deposit of high-grade magnoosium ore.[11] You are given the forecasts shown in Table 7.5. We will walk through the lines in the table.

Capital Investment (line 1). The project requires an investment of $10 million in mining machinery. At the end of 5 years the machinery has no further value. The machinery falls into asset class 38, which has a CCA rate of 30 percent. The company owns other assets that also fall into this asset class. These other assets will remain in the asset class even after the magnoosium project ceases to exist after 5 years.

Working Capital (lines 2 and 3). Line 2 shows the level of working capital. As the project gears up in the early years, working capital increases, but later in the project's life, the investment in working capital is recovered.

Line 3 shows the *change* in working capital from year to year. Notice that in years 1 to 4 the change is positive; in these years the project requires a continuing investment in

TABLE 7.5
Financial projections for Blooper's magnoosium mine (figures in thousands of dollars)

Year:	0	1	2	3	4	5	6
1. Capital investment	10,000						
2. Working capital	1,500	4,075	4,279	4,493	4,717	3,039	0
3. Change in working capital	1,500	2,575	204	214	225	−1,678	−3,039
4. Revenues		15,000	15,750	16,538	17,364	18,233	
5. Expenses		10,000	10,500	11,025	11,576	12,155	
6. CCA of mining equipment (asset class 38, d = 30%)		1,500[1]	2,550	1,785	1,250	875	612 ...
7. Pretax profit		3,500	2,700	3,728	4,538	5,203	
8. Tax (35%)		1,225	945	1,305	1,588	1,821	
9. Profit after tax		2,275	1,755	2,423	2,950	3,382	

[1]In the first year, CCA is computed using the half-year rule.
Note: Some entries are subject to rounding error.

[11] Readers have inquired whether magnoosium is a real substance. Here, now, are the facts. Magnoosium was created in the early days of TV, when a splendid-sounding announcer closed a variety show by saying, "This program has been brought to you by Blooper Industries, proud producer of aleemium, magnoosium, and stool." We forget the company, but the blooper really happened.

working capital. Starting in Year 5 the change is negative; there is a disinvestment as working capital is recovered.

Revenues (line 4). The company expects to be able to sell 750,000 kilograms of magnoosium a year at a price of $20 a kilogram in Year 1. That points to initial revenues of 750,000 × 20 = $15,000,000. But be careful: inflation is running at about 5 percent a year. If magnoosium prices keep pace with inflation, you should up your forecast of the second-year revenues by 5 percent. Third-year revenues should increase by a further 5 percent, and so on. Line 4 in Table 7.5 shows revenues rising in line with inflation.

The sales forecasts in Table 7.5 are cut off after 5 years. That makes sense if the ore deposit will run out at that time. But if Blooper could make sales for Year 6, you should include them in your forecasts. We have sometimes encountered financial managers who assume a project life of (say) 5 years, even when they confidently expect revenues for 10 years or more. When asked the reason, they explain that forecasting beyond 5 years is too hazardous. We sympathize, but you just have to do your best. Do not arbitrarily truncate a project's life.

Expenses (line 5). We assume that the expenses of mining and refining also increase in line with inflation at 5 percent per year.

CCA (line 6). Mining equipment falls in asset class 38, which has a CCA rate of 30 percent. We compute CCA using the declining balance method which is prescribed by CCRA for this asset class. Notice from Table 7.6, that even though the magnoosium mine stops producing in Year 5, an undepreciated capital cost (UCC) balance of $2.04 million remains at the end of Year 5. This suggests that the initial investment has not been completely depreciated. In fact, computing with the declining balance system will continue to provide smaller CCA values each year over an infinite period. To get around this problem, we will use a method of computing the present value of the CCA tax shields under the declining balance system we described with equation 3, page 219. Even after the magnoosium mine shuts its operations in Year 5, we assume that the company has other assets in Class 38 and that the asset pool will not be terminated.

Pretax Profits (line 7). Profit after depreciation equals (revenues – expenses – CCA).

Tax (line 8). Company taxes are 35 percent of pretax profits. For example, in Year 1,

$$\text{Tax} = .35 \times 3{,}500 = 1{,}225, \text{ or } \$1{,}225{,}000$$

Profit after Tax (line 9). Profit after tax is simply equal to pretax profit less taxes.

TABLE 7.6
Computation of CCA and UCC balances for Blooper's magnoosium mine (figures in thousands of dollars)

Year	Capital Investment UCC	CCA	End of Year (UCC)
1	10,000	1,500	8,500
2	8,500	2,550	5,950
3	5,950	1,785	4,165
4	4,165	1,250	2,915
5	2,915	875	2,040
6	2,040	612	1,428

CALCULATING BLOOPER'S PROJECT CASH FLOWS

Table 7.5 provides most of the information you need to figure out the cash flows on the magnoosium project. These cash flows are the sum of three broad components: investment in plant and equipment, investment in working capital, and cash flows from operations. In turn, cash flows from operations comprise (1) operating cash flows excluding depreciation (CCA) and (2) the CCA tax shield.

Cash flow from investment in plant and equipment
\+ Cash flow from investment in working capital
\+ Cash flow from operations, including
- Operating cash flows
- CCA tax shield

= Total project cash flows

Table 7.7 provides calculations for yearly operating cash flows excluding CCA tax shields, Table 7.8 sets out the project cash flows excluding the CCA tax shield, and Table 7.9 provides details by year regarding the CCA tax shield. First, let's see where these figures come from.

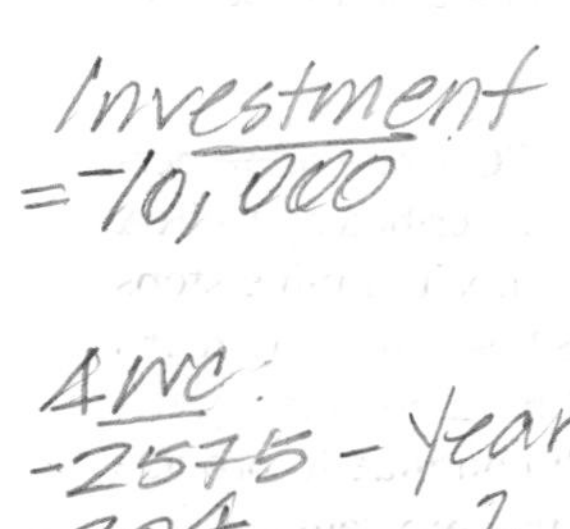

Capital Investment. Investment in plant and equipment is taken from line 1 of Table 7.5. Blooper's initial investment is a negative cash flow of –$10 million shown in line 1 of Table 7.8.

Investment in Working Capital. We've seen that investment in working capital, just like investment in plant and equipment, produces a negative cash flow. For instance, when the company builds up inventories of refined magnoosium, the company's cash is reduced, or when customers are slow to pay their bills, cash is reduced. An increase in working capital implies a negative cash flow; a decrease implies a positive cash flow.

The numbers required for these calculations come from lines 2 and 3 of Table 7.5. Line 2 shows the amount or level of working capital whereas line 3 shows the change in working capital. Notice the cash flow is measured by the *change* in working capital not the level of working capital. For instance, from Table 7.5, line 2, we see that Blooper makes an initial (Year 0) investment of $1,500,000 in working capital, which goes up to $4,075,000 in Year 1. This *total* level of working capital in Year 1 is arrived at by an additional investment in working capital of $2,575,000 in Year 1 to Year 0's investment, that is, $1,500,000 + $2,575,000 = $4,075,000. The additional investment in Year 1 of $2,575,000 is shown in line 3, Table 7.5, and results in a negative cash flow by this amount (line 2, Table 7.8).

TABLE 7.7
Operating cash flows excluding CCA tax shields for Blooper's magnoosium mine (figures in thousands of dollars)

Year:	0	1	2	3	4	5	6
Revenues		15,000	15,750	16,538	17,364	18,233	
– Expenses		10,000	10,500	11,025	11,576	12,155	
= Profit before tax		5,000	5,250	5,513	5,788	6,078	
– Tax at 35%		1,750	1,838	1,930	2,026	2,127	
= Operating cash flows (excluding CCA tax shield)		3,250	3,412	3,583	3,762	3,951	

TABLE 7.8
Cash flows for Blooper's magnoosium mine (figures in thousands of dollars)

Year:	0	1	2	3	4	5	6
1. Capital investment	–10,000						
2. Change in working capital	–1,500	–2,575	–204	–214	–225	1,678	3,039
3. Cash flows from operations (excluding CCA tax shield)		3,250	3,412	3,583	3,762	3,951	
4. Total cash flows (excluding CCA tax shield)	–11,500	675	3,208	3,369	3,537	5,629	3,039

Cash Flows from Operations. The third component of project cash flows is cash flow from operations. As we have discussed earlier, we can segregate this component into two parts: (1) operating cash flows, excluding CCA, and (2) the CCA tax shield. Let us discuss these one by one.

Operating cash flows, excluding CCA: Table 7.5 has the necessary data to calculate such operating cash flows. The details, in thousands of dollars, are provided in Table 7.7.

The cash flow amounts for Blooper's magnoosium mine are in line 3 of Table 7.8. Line 4 provides the yearly total cash flows excluding the CCA tax shield. Notice that the table does not fully capture the entire amount of cash flows for the project since the CCA tax shield is not included. Let us now examine the CCA tax shield.

CCA Tax Shield: In Section 7.6, we saw that CCA has an important effect on cash flows because it reduces taxable income and the firm's tax bill. For any year, this *tax shield* is calculated as the product of the CCA and tax rate.

$$\textbf{CCA tax shield} = \textbf{CCA} \times \textbf{tax rate} \tag{7.5}$$

For Blooper, which pays tax at a rate of 35 percent, this means that each additional dollar of CCA reduces taxable income by \$1 and taxes owed by 35 cents. Table 7.9 provides details regarding the CCA tax shields for Blooper. Notice that both the CCA and the CCA tax shield increase between years 1 and 2, but thereafter, are represented by a series of declining balances. This is because in Year 1 when Blooper purchases the machine, the half-year rule applies, but all subsequent CCA tax shield calculations use a declining balance system. Also, CCA tax shields from the project will continue to be generated beyond Year 5, assuming that Blooper will have other assets in Class 38 after the magnoosium mine is shut down.

TABLE 7.9
Computation by year of CCA tax shields for Blooper's magnoosium mine (figures in thousands of dollars)

Year:	0	1	2	3	4	5	6
CCA		1,500	2,550	1,785	1,250	875	612
× Tax Rate		.35	.35	.35	.35	.35	.35
= CCA Tax Shield		525	893	625	438	306	214

CALCULATING THE NPV OF BLOOPER'S PROJECT

Table 7.10 sets out the calculations for the total present value of cash flows excluding the CCA tax shield. Assume that investors expect a return of 12 percent from investments in the capital market with the same risk as the magnoosium project. This is the opportunity cost of the shareholders' money that Blooper is proposing to invest in the project. Therefore, to calculate NPV you need to discount the cash flows at 12 percent. Remember that to calculate the present value of a cash flow in Year t you can divide the cash flow by $(1 + r)^t$ or you can multiply by a discount factor which is equal to $1/(1 + r)^t$.

The total present value in Table 7.10 is not the net present value of the project because we still have to deal with the CCA tax shield. We deal with the tax shields separately because even though the magnoosium project terminates in Year 5 and we have computed cash flows till Year 6, from Table 7.6 we have noted that there is still a UCC balance at the end of Year 6 on which CCA can be computed for future years.[12] To compute the present value of the CCA tax shield, we use equation 3 (page 219). Notice that in the example we have assumed a zero salvage value, S, at the end of the project's life.

$$\text{PV of CCA tax shield} = \left[\frac{CdT_c}{r + d}\right]\left[\frac{1 + .5r}{1 + r}\right] - \left[\frac{SdT_c}{d + r}\right] \times \left[\frac{1}{(1 + r)^t}\right]$$

$$= \left[\frac{10{,}000 \times .3 \times .35}{.12 + .3}\right]\left[\frac{1 + (.5 \times .12)}{1 + .12}\right]$$

$$- \left[\frac{0 \times .3 \times .35}{.3 + .12}\right]\left[\frac{1}{(1 + .12)^6}\right]$$

$$= \$2{,}366$$

We now have all the necessary information to determine the net present value of Blooper's magnoosium project. It is the sum of the total present value excluding CCA tax shields in Table 7.10 and the present value of the CCA tax shield, that is

$$\begin{aligned} \text{NPV} &= \text{total PV excluding CCA tax shields} + \text{PV of CCA tax shield} \\ &= \$1{,}040 + \$2{,}366 = \$3{,}406 \end{aligned}$$

We see that when all cash flows are discounted and added up, the magnoosium project offers a positive net present value of about $3.4 million.

TABLE 7.10
Cash flows and total present value of Blooper's project excluding the CCA tax shield (figures in thousands of dollars)

Year:	0	1	2	3	4	5	6
Total cash flow excluding tax shields	−11,500	675	3,208	3,369	3,537	5,629	3,039
Discount factor	1.0000	.8929	.7972	.7118	.6355	.5674	.5066
Present value (excluding CCA tax shields	−11,500	603	2,557	2,398	2,248	3,194	1,540
Total present value (excluding CCA tax shields	1,040						

[12] Of course, this assumes that the firm has other assets in the asset class.

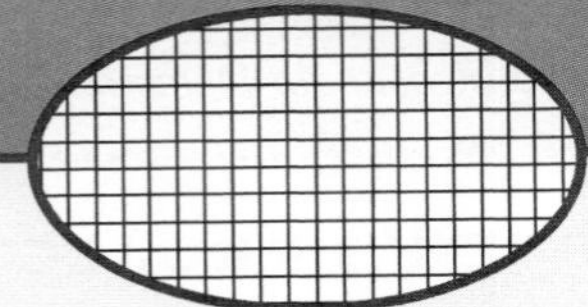

A SPREADSHEET MODEL FOR BLOOPER (FORMULA INSERTS)

	A	B	C	D	E	F	G	H
1	Year:	0	1	2	3	4	5	6
2	Capital investment	10,000						
3	Working capital	=0.15*C6+2/12*B5	=0.15*D6+2/12*C5	=0.15*E6+2/12*D5	=0.15*F6+2/12*E5	=0.15*G6+2/12*F5	=0.15*H6+2/12*G5	=0.15*I6+2/12*H5
4	Change in working capital	=B3	=C3-B3	=D3-C3	=E3-D3	=F3-E3	=G3-F3	=H3-G3
5	Revenues		15000	=C5*1.05	=D5*1.05	=E5*1.05	=F5*1.05	
6	Expenses		10000	=C6*1.05	=D6*1.05	=E6*1.05	=F6*1.05	
7	Profit before tax (excluding CCA tax shield)		=C5-C6	=D5-D6	=E5-E6	=F5-F6	=G5-G6	
8	Tax (35%)		=C7*0.35	=D7*0.35	=E7*0.35	=F7*0.35	=G7*0.35	
9	Operating cash flows (excluding CCA tax shield)		=C7-C8	=D7-D8	=E7-E8	=F7-F8	=G7-G8	
10	Salvage value							0
11	Total cash flow (excluding CCA tax shield)	=-B2-B4	=C2-C4+C9	=D2-D4+D9	=E2-E4+E9	=F2-F4+F9	=G2-G4+G9	=H2-H4+H9+H10
12	PV of cash flow (excluding CCA tax shield)	=B11/(1.12)^B1	=C11/(1.12)^C1	=D11/(1.12)^D1	=E11/(1.12)^E1	=F11/(1.12)^F1	=G11/(1.12)^G1	=H11/(1.12)^H1
13	Total present value (excluding CCA tax shield) (A)	=SUM(B12:H12)						
14	CCA		=0.5*B2*0.3	=(B2-C14)*0.3	=D14*0.7	=E14*0.7	=F14*0.7	=G14*0.7
15	CCA tax shield		=10000*0.3/2*0.35	=8500*0.3*0.35	=5950*0.3*0.35	=4165*0.3*0.35	=2916*0.3*0.35	=2041*0.3*0.35
16	PV of CCA tax shield (B)	=(B2*0.3*0.35/(0.12+0.3))*((1+(0.5*0.12))/(1+0.12))-(H10*0.3*0.35/(0.3+0.12)*(1/(1+0.12)^H1))						
17	Total net present value (A) + (B)	=(B13+B16)						

You might have guessed that discounted cash-flow analysis such as that of the Blooper case is tailor-made for spreadsheets. The worksheet directly above shows the formulas from the Excel spreadsheet that we used to generate the Blooper example. The first spreadsheet on the facing page shows the resulting values, which appear in the text in tables 7.5 through 7.10. This model assume that there is no salvage value on Blooper's equipment. We have also included a spreadsheet model in which we assume a salvage value of $1.5 million in Year 6.

The assumed values are the capital investment (cell B2), the initial level of revenues (cell C5), and expenses (cell C6). Rows 5 and 6 show that each entry for revenues and expenses equals the previous value times (1 + inflation rate), or 1.05. Row 3, which is the amount of working capital, is the sum of inventories and accounts receivable. To capture the fact that inventories tend to rise with production, we set working capital equal to .15 times the following year's expenses. Similarly, accounts receivable rise with sales, so we assumed that accounts receivable would be 1/6 times the current year's revenues. Each entry in row 3 is the sum of these two quantities.[13] Net investment in working capital (row 4) is the increase in working capital from one year to the next. Total cash flow excluding the CCA tax shield (row 11) is capital investment plus change in working capital plus profit after tax, which we have called operating cash flows. Cell H10 includes a provision for salvage value in Year 6 which is set at zero in the first spreadsheet model and $1.5 million in the second model. In row 12, we discount the cash flow amounts at a 12 percent discount rate and in cell B13 we add the present value of each cash flow to find the total present value excluding the CCA tax shield. Row 14 includes CCA values. Notice that the first year's CCA in cell C14 is computed using the half-year rule, whereas the subsequent CCA amounts follow the declining balance system. Row 15 includes the yearly CCA tax shields and row 16 incorporates the present value of the CCA tax shield. The project's net present value is provided in cell B17 as the sum of the total present value excluding the CCA tax shield (cell B13) and the present value of the CCA tax shield (cell B16).

Once the spreadsheet is up and running it is easy to do various sorts of "what if" analysis. Here are a few questions to try your hand.

Questions (Answers on page 234)

1. Suppose the firm can economize on working capital by managing inventories more efficiently. If the firm can reduce inventories from 15 percent to 10 percent of next year's cost of goods sold, what will be the effect on project NPV?
2. What happens to NPV if the inflation rate falls from 5 percent to zero and the discount rate falls from 12 percent to 7 percent? Given that the real discount rate is almost unchanged, why does project NPV increase?
3. Suppose that Blooper's mining equipment could be depreciated on a 5-year, straight-line basis. What is the present value of the depreciation tax shield? What happens to cash flow in each year and to the project NPV?

[13] For convenience we assume that Blooper pays all its bills immediately and therefore accounts payable equals zero. If it didn't, working capital would be reduced by the amount of the payables.

A SPREADSHEET MODEL FOR BLOOPER (WITHOUT SALVAGE VALUE)[1]

	A	B	C	D	E	F	G	H	I
1	Year:	0	1	2	3	4	5	6	…∞
2	Capital investment	10,000							
3	Working capital	1,500	4,075	4,279	4,493	4,717	3,039	0	
4	Change in working capital	1,500	2,575	204	214	225	−1,679	−3,039	
5	Revenues		15,000	15,750	16,538	17,364	18,233		
6	Expenses		10,000	10,500	11,025	11,576	12,155		
7	Profit before tax (excluding CCA tax shield)		5,000	5,250	5,513	5,788	6,078		
8	Tax (35%)		1,750	1,838	1,930	2,026	2,127		
9	Operating cash flows (excluding CCA tax shield)		3,250	3,412	3,583	3,762	3,950		
10	Salvage value							0	
11	Total cash flow (excluding CCA tax shield)	−11,500	675	3,208	3,369	3,538	5,629	3,039	
12	PV of cash flow (excluding CCA tax shield)	−11,500	603	2,558	2,398	2,248	3,194	1,540	
13	Total present value (excluding CCA tax shield) (A)	1,041							
14	CCA[2]		1,500	2,550	1,785	1,250	875	612	→ 0
15	CCA tax shield[2]		525	893	625	437	306	214	→ 0
16	PV of CCA tax shield[2] (B)	2,366							
17	Total net present value (A) + (B)	3,407							

Notes: [1] Some entries in this table may differ from those in tables 7.5 to 7.10 due to rounding error.
[2] The CCA and the CCA tax shield (lines 14 and 15) will continue even after Year 6. The PV of the CCA tax shield (line 16) has been calculated assuming that the CCA and the CCA tax shield will continue in perpetuity.

A SPREADSHEET MODEL FOR BLOOPER (WITH SALVAGE VALUE)[1]

	A	B	C	D	E	F	G	H	I
1	Year:	0	1	2	3	4	5	6	…∞
2	Capital investment	10,000							
3	Working capital	1,500	4,075	4,279	4,493	4,717	3,039	0	
4	Change in working capital	1,500	2,575	204	214	225	−1,679	−3,039	
5	Revenues		15,000	15,750	16,538	17,364	18,233		
6	Expenses		10,000	10,500	11,025	11,576	12,155		
7	Profit before tax (excluding CCA tax shield)		5,000	5,250	5,513	5,788	6,078		
8	Tax (35%)		1,750	1,838	1,930	2,026	2,127		
9	Operating cash flows (excluding CCA tax shield)		3,250	3,412	3,583	3,762	3,950		
10	Salvage value							1,500	
11	Total cash flow (excluding CCA tax shield)	−11,500	675	3,208	3,369	3,538	5,629	4,539	
12	PV of cash flow (excluding CCA tax shield)	−11,500	603	2,558	2,398	2,248	3,194	2,299	
13	Total present value (excluding CCA tax shield) (A)	1,801							
14	CCA[2]		1,500	2,550	1,785	1,250	875	612	→ 0
15	CCA tax shield[2]		525	893	625	437	306	214	→ 0
16	PV of CCA tax shield[2] (B)	2,176							
17	Total net present value (A) + (B)	3,977							

Notes: [1] Some entries in this table may differ from those in tables 7.5 to 7.10 due to rounding error.
[2] The CCA and the CCA tax shield (lines 14 and 15) will continue even after Year 6. The PV of the CCA tax shield (line 16) has been calculated assuming that the CCA and the CCA tax shield will continue in perpetuity.

Now let's consider a small point that often causes confusion. To calculate the present value of the first year's cash flow, we divide by $(1 + r) = 1.12$. Strictly speaking, this makes sense only if all the sales and all the costs occur exactly 365 days, 0 hours, and 0 minutes from now. But, of course, the year's sales don't all take place on the stroke of midnight December 31. However, when making capital budgeting decisions, companies are usually happy to pretend that all cash flows occur at 1-year intervals—for one reason only—simplicity. When sales forecasts are sometimes little more than intelligent guesses, it may be pointless to inquire how the sales are likely to be spread out during the year.[14]

FURTHER NOTES AND WRINKLES ARISING FROM BLOOPER'S PROJECT

Before we leave Blooper and its magnoosium project, we should cover a few extra wrinkles.

How to Deal with Salvage Value. So far, we have assumed that Blooper will not receive any salvage value from the mining equipment when the magnoosium mine is closed. But suppose Blooper forecasts that the equipment can be sold for $1.5 million in Year 6.

You recorded the initial $10 million investment as a negative cash flow. Now, in Year 6, you have a forecast return of $1.5 million of that investment. That is a positive cash flow estimate, which has a present value of

$$\frac{S}{(1+r)^6} = \frac{1.5}{(1.12)^6} = .76$$

The salvage value will also reduce future tax shields, and therefore, the present value of the CCA tax shield as follows:[15]

$$\frac{1}{(1+r)^6} \times \frac{SdT_c}{(r+d)} = \frac{1}{(1.12)^6} \times \frac{1.5 \times .3 \times .35}{(.12 + .3)} = .19$$

So we see that while the sale of the mining equipment increases the net present value of the project by $760,000, the present value of the lost tax shield from the salvage will reduce net present value by $190,000. Overall, net present value of the project will increase by $760,000 – $190,000 = $570,000.

A Further Note on CCA. We warned you earlier not to assume that all cash flows are likely to increase with inflation. The CCA tax shield is a case in point because CCRA lets companies depreciate only the amount of the original investment. For example, if you go back to CCRA to explain that inflation mushroomed since you made the investment and you should be allowed to depreciate more, CCRA won't listen. The *nominal* amount of CCA is fixed, and therefore, the higher the rate of inflation, the lower the *real* value of the CCA that you can claim.

[14] Financial managers sometimes assume cash flows arrive in the middle of the calendar year, that is, the end of June. This also makes NPV a midyear number. If you are standing at the start of the year, the NPV must be discounted for a further half-year. To do this, divide the midyear NPV by the square root of (1 + r). This midyear convention is roughly equivalent to assuming cash flows are distributed evenly throughout the year. This is a bad assumption for some industries. In retailing, for example, most of the cash flow comes late in the year as the holiday season approaches.

[15] Remember that we have assumed that Blooper has other machines in this asset class so the sale will not close out the asset class.

7.8 Summary

1. How should the cash flows properly attributable to a proposed new project be calculated?

Here is a checklist to bear in mind when forecasting a project's cash flows:

- Discount cash flows, not profits.
- Estimate the project's incremental cash flows—that is, the difference between the cash flows *with* the project and those *without* the project.
- Include all indirect effects of the project, such as its impact on the sales of the firm's other products.
- Forget sunk costs.
- Include **opportunity costs**, such as the value of land which you could otherwise sell.
- Beware of allocated overhead charges for heat, light, and so on. These may not reflect the incremental effects of the project on these costs.
- Remember the investment in working capital. As sales increase, the firm may need to make additional investments in working capital and, as the project finally comes to an end, it will recover these investments.
- Do not include debt interest or the cost of repaying a loan. When calculating NPV, assume that the project is financed entirely by the shareholders and that they receive all the cash flows. This isolates the investment decision from the financing decision.

2. How can the cash flows of a project be computed from standard financial statements?

Project cash flow does not equal profit. You must allow for changes in working capital as well as noncash expenses such as depreciation. Also, if you use a nominal cost of capital, consistency requires that you forecast *nominal* cash flows—that is, cash flows that recognize the effect of inflation.

3. How is the company's tax bill affected by capital cost allowance (CCA) and how does this affect project value?

CCA is not a cash flow. However, because CCA reduces taxable income, it reduces taxes. This tax reduction is called the **CCA tax shield**. For computing tax depreciation in Canada, assets are assigned into different **asset classes**, which have specified CCA rates. Most asset classes follow a declining balance system for computing CCA, and therefore, most assets continue to generate CCA tax shields over an infinite time frame. Because of this, we find the present value of operating cash flows separately from the present value of the CCA tax shields to determine the net present value of a project.

4. How do changes in working capital affect project cash flows?

Increases in **net working capital**, such as accounts receivable or inventory, are investments, and therefore, use cash. That is, they reduce the net cash flow provided by the project in that period. When working capital is run down, cash is freed up, so cash flow increases.

Related Web Links

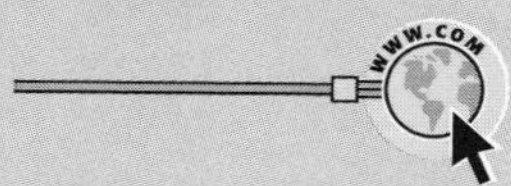

www-ec.njit.edu/~mathis/interactive/FCCalcBase4.html A net present value calculator from Professor Roswell Mathis

www.4pm.com/articles/palette.html Try the online demonstration here to see how good business judgment is used to formulate cash-flow projections

www.irs.ustreas.gov/prod/bus_info/index.html Tax rules affecting project cash flows can be found here

Key Terms

Term	Page
opportunity cost	207
net working capital	208
depreciation tax shield	213
capital cost allowance (CCA)	215
undepreciated capital cost (UCC)	215
CCA tax shield	215
asset class	215
straight-line depreciation	215
declining balance depreciation	215
half-year rule	215
terminal loss	218
recaptured depreciation	218

QUESTIONS AND PROBLEMS

*Answers in Appendix B

BASIC

1. **Cash Flows.** A new project will generate sales of $74 million, costs of $42 million, and depreciation expense of $10 million in the coming year. The firm's tax rate is 35 percent. Calculate cash flows for the year using all three methods discussed in the chapter and confirm that they are equal.

2. **Cash Flows.** Canyon Tours showed the following components of working capital last year:

	Beginning	End of Year
Accounts receivable	$24,000	$22,500
Inventory	12,000	13,000
Accounts payable	14,500	16,500

   a. What was the change in net working capital during the year?
   b. If sales were $36,000 and costs were $24,000, what was cash flow for the year? Ignore taxes.

*3. **Cash Flows.** Tubby Toys estimates that its new line of rubber ducks will generate sales of $7 million, operating costs of $4 million, and a depreciation expense of $1 million. If the tax rate is 40 percent, what is the firm's operating cash flow? Show that you get the same answer using all three methods to calculate operating cash flow.

4. **Cash Flows.** We've emphasized that the firm should pay attention only to cash flows when assessing the net present value of proposed projects. Depreciation is a noncash expense. Why then does it matter whether we assume straight-line depreciation or declining balance CCA depreciation when we assess project NPV?

*5. **Proper Cash Flows.** Quick Computing currently sells 10 million computer chips each year at a price of $20 per chip. It is about to introduce a new chip, and it forecasts annual sales of 12 million of these improved chips at a price of $25 each. However, demand for the old chip will decrease, and sales of the old chip are expected to fall to 3 million per year. The old chip costs $6 each to manufacture, and the new ones will cost $8 each. What is the proper cash flow to use to evaluate the present value of the introduction of the new chip?

*6. **Calculating Net Income.** The owner of a bicycle repair shop forecasts revenues of $160,000 a year. Variable costs will be $45,000, and rental costs for the shop are $35,000 a year. Depreciation on the repair tools will be $10,000. Prepare an income statement for the shop based on these estimates. The tax rate is 35 percent.

7. **Cash Flows.** Calculate the operating cash flow for the repair shop in the previous problem using all three methods suggested in the chapter: (a) net income plus depreciation; (b) cash inflow/cash outflow analysis; and (c) the depreciation tax shield approach. Confirm that all three approaches result in the same value for cash flow.

*8. **Cash Flows and Working Capital.** A house painting business had revenues of $16,000 and expenses of $9,000. There were no depreciation expenses. However, the business reported the following changes in various components of working capital:

	Beginning	End
Accounts receivable	$1,200	$4,500
Accounts payable	600	200

   Calculate net cash flow for the business for this period.

9. Incremental Cash Flows. A corporation donates a valuable painting from its private collection to an art museum. Which of the following are incremental cash flows associated with the donation?
   a. The price the firm paid for the painting.
   b. The current market value of the painting.
   c. The deduction from income that it declares for its charitable gift.
   d. The reduction in taxes due to its declared tax deduction.

*10. **Operating Cash Flows.** Laurel's Lawn Care, Ltd., has a new mower line that can generate revenues of $120,000 per year. Direct production costs are $40,000 and the fixed costs of maintaining the lawn mower factory are $15,000 a year. The factory originally cost $1 million and is included in an asset class with a CCA rate of 5 percent. Calculate the operating cash flows of the project for the next 6 years if the firm's tax bracket is 35 percent.

PRACTICE

*11. **Operating Cash Flows.** Talia's Tutus bought a new sewing machine for $40,000 that will be depreciated in asset class 39 which has a CCA rate of 30 percent. This firm's tax bracket is 35 percent.

a. Find the CCA amount each year for the next 3 years.

b. If the sewing machine is sold after 3 years for $20,000, what will be the after-tax proceeds on the sale if the firm's tax bracket is 35 percent? Assume that Talia's Tutus has other assets in class 39.

c. Now rework your calculations assuming that Talia's Tutus has no other assets in Class 39 and the asset class will be terminated upon the sale of the sewing machine in Year 3.

12. **Proper Cash Flows.** Conference Services Inc. has leased a large office building for $4 million per year. The building is larger than the company needs: two of the building's eight storeys are almost empty. A manager wants to expand one of her projects, but this will require using one of the empty floors. In calculating the net present value of the proposed expansion, upper management allocates one-eighth of $4 million of building rental costs (i.e., $.5 million) to the project expansion, reasoning that the project will use one-eighth of the building's capacity.

a. Is this a reasonable procedure for the purposes of calculating NPV?

b. Can you suggest a better way to assess the cost of the office space used by the project?

13. **Cash Flows and Working Capital.** A firm had net income last year of $1.2 million. Its depreciation expenses were $.5 million, and its total cash flow was $1.2 million. What happened to net working capital during the year?

14. **Cash Flows and Working Capital.** The only capital investment required for a small project is investment in inventory. Profits this year were $10,000, and inventory increased from $4,000 to $5,000. What was the cash flow from the project?

15. **Cash Flows and Working Capital.** A firm's balance sheets for year-ends 2000 and 2001 contain the following data. What happened to investment in net working capital during 2001? All items are in millions of dollars.

	Dec. 31, 2000	Dec. 31, 2001
Accounts receivable	32	35
Inventories	25	30
Accounts payable	12	25

*16. **Salvage Value.** Quick Computing (from problem 5) installed its previous generation of computer chip manufacturing equipment 3 years ago. Some of that older equipment will become unnecessary when the company goes into production of its new product. The obsolete equipment, which originally cost $40 million, has been depreciated straight-line over an assumed tax life of 5 years, but it can now be sold for $18 million. The firm's tax rate is 35 percent. What is the after-tax cash flow from the sale of the equipment?

17. **Salvage Value.** Your firm purchased machinery for $10 million. The machinery falls into asset class 38, which has a CCA rate of 25 percent. The project will end after 5 years. If the equipment can be sold for $4 million at the completion of the project and your firm's tax rate is 35 percent, what is the after-tax cash flow from the sale of the machinery? Assume that the firm has no other assets in Class 38 and the asset class will be terminated upon the sale of the machinery.

*18. **CCA, Depreciation, and Project Value.** Bottoms Up Diaper Service is considering the purchase of a new industrial washer. It can purchase the washer for $6,000 and sell its old washer for $2,000. The new washer will last for 6 years and save $1,500 a year in expenses. If the old washer is retained, it will also last for 6 more years after which it will have to be junked. The washers fall into an asset class with a CCA rate of 30 percent. Bottoms Up owns other washing machines that also fall into this asset class. The opportunity cost of capital is 15 percent and the firm's tax rate is 40 percent.

a. If the salvage value of the washer is expected to be zero at the end of its 6-year life, what are the cash flows of the project in years 0 to 6?
b. What is the project NPV?
c. What will the NPV and IRR be if the firm uses straight-line depreciation with a 6-year tax life?

19. **Equivalent Annual Cost.** What is the equivalent annual cost of the washer in the previous problem if the firm uses straight-line depreciation?

20. **Cash Flows and NPV.** Johnny's Lunches is considering purchasing a new, energy-efficient grill. The grill will cost $20,000 and will be depreciated in an asset class which carries a CCA rate of 30 percent. It will be sold for scrap metal after 3 years for $5,000. The grill will have no effect on revenues but will save Johnny's $10,000 in energy expenses. The firm has other assets in this asset class. The tax rate is 35 percent.

a. What are the operating cash flows in years 1 to 3?
b. What are total cash flows in years 1 to 3?
c. If the discount rate is 12 percent, should the grill be purchased?

*21. **Project Evaluation.** Revenues generated by a new fad product are forecast as follows:

Year	Revenues
1	$40,000
2	30,000
3	20,000
4	10,000
Thereafter	0

Expenses are expected to be 40 percent of revenues, and working capital required in each year is expected to be 20 percent of revenues in the following year. The product requires an immediate investment of $50,000 in plant and equipment.

a. What is the initial investment in the product? Remember working capital.
b. If the plant and equipment are in an asset class which has a CCA rate of 25 percent, and the firm's tax rate is 40 percent, what are the project cash flows in each year?
c. If the opportunity cost of capital is 10 percent, what is the project NPV?

22. **Buy versus Lease.** You can buy a car for $25,000 and sell it in 5 years for $5,000. Or you can lease the car for 5 years for $5,000 a year. The discount rate is 10 percent per year.

a. Which option do you prefer?
b. What is the maximum amount you should be willing to pay to lease rather than buy the car?

*23. **Project Evaluation.** Kinky Copies may buy a high-volume copier. The machine costs $100,000 and will be depreciated straight-line over 5 years to a salvage value of $20,000. Kinky anticipates that the machine can be sold in 5 years for $30,000. The machine will save $20,000 a year in labour costs but will require an increase in working capital, mainly paper supplies, of $10,000. The firm's marginal tax rate is 35 percent. Ignore the CCA system and assume that the straight-line depreciation method adopted by Kinky Copies will suffice for tax purposes. Should Kinky buy the machine? The discount rate is 8 percent.

24. **Project Evaluation.** Fireplaces Etc. is about to launch a new range of wood stoves, priced at $110 per unit. The unit cost of the wood stoves is $65. The firm expects to sell the wood stoves over the next

5 years. The venture will require an initial investment in plant and equipment of $25,000. Assume that the investment will be in an asset class with a CCA rate of 15 percent. At the end of 5 years, the plant and equipment will have a zero salvage value but Fireplaces Etc. will continue to have other assets in this asset class. Sales projections for the wood stoves are as follows:

Year	Unit Sales
1	300
2	350
3	400
4	500
5	500

The net working capital requirement (including the initial working capital needed in Year 0) is expected to be 20 percent of the following year's sales. The firm's tax rate is 35 percent. Using a discount rate of 15 percent, calculate the net present value of the project.

*25. **Project Evaluation.** Blooper Industries must replace its magnoosium purification system. Quick & Dirty Systems sells a relatively cheap purification system for $10 million. The system will last 5 years. Do-It-Right sells a sturdier but more expensive system for $12 million; it will last for 8 years. Both systems entail $1 million in operating costs; both will be depreciated in an asset class which has a CCA rate of 30 percent; neither will have any salvage value at the end of its life. The firm's tax rate is 35 percent, and the discount rate is 12 percent. Which system should Blooper install?

26. **Project Evaluation.** The following table presents sales forecasts for Golden Gelt Giftware. The unit price is $40. The unit cost of the giftware is $25.

Year	Unit Sales
1	22,000
2	30,000
3	14,000
4	5,000
Thereafter	0

It is expected that net working capital will amount to 25 percent of sales in the following year. For example, the store will need an initial (Year 0) investment in working capital of $.25 \times 22{,}000 \times \$40 = \$220{,}000$. Plant and equipment necessary to establish the giftware business will require an additional investment of $200,000. This investment will be depreciated in an asset class with a CCA rate of 25 percent. We will assume that the firm has other assets in this asset class. After 4 years, the equipment will have an economic and book value of zero. The firm's tax rate is 35 percent. The discount rate is 20 percent. What is the net present value of the project?

*27. **Project Evaluation.** Ilana Industries, Inc., needs a new lathe. It can buy a new high-speed lathe for $1 million. The lathe will cost $35,000 to run, will save the firm $125,000 in labour costs, and will be useful for 10 years. Suppose that for tax purposes, the lathe will be in an asset class with a CCA rate of 25 percent. Ilana has many other assets in this asset class. The lathe is expected to have a 10-year life with a salvage value of $100,000. The actual market value of the lathe at that time will also be $100,000. The discount rate is 10 percent and the corporate tax rate is 35 percent. What is the NPV of buying the new lathe?

CHALLENGE

28. **Project Evaluation.** The efficiency gains resulting from a just-in-time inventory management system will allow a firm to reduce its level of inventories permanently by $250,000. What is the most the firm should be willing to pay for installing the system?

*29. **Project Evaluation.** Better Mousetraps has developed a new trap. It can go into production for an initial investment in equipment of $6 million. The equipment will be depreciated straight-line over 5 years to a value of zero, but in fact it can be sold after 5 years for $500,000. The firm believes that working capital at each date must be maintained at a level of 10 percent of next year's forecast sales. The firm estimates production costs equal to $1.50 per trap and believes that the traps can be sold for $4 each. Sales forecasts are given in the following table. The project will come to an end in 5 years, when the trap becomes technologically obsolete. The firm's tax bracket is 35 percent, and the required rate of return on the project is 12 percent. What is project NPV?

Year:	**0**	**1**	**2**	**3**	**4**	**5**	**Thereafter**
Sales (millions of traps)	0	.5	.6	1.0	1.0	.6	0

30. **Working Capital Management.** Return to the previous problem. Suppose the firm can cut its requirements for working capital in half by using better inventory control systems. By how much will this increase project NPV?

*31. **Project Evaluation.** PC Shopping Network may upgrade its modem pool. It last upgraded 2 years ago, when it spent $115 million on equipment with an assumed life of 5 years and an assumed salvage value of $15 million for tax purposes. The firm uses straight-line depreciation. The old equipment can be sold today for $80 million. A new modem pool can be installed today for $150 million. This will have a 3-year life, and will be depreciated to zero using straight-line depreciation. The new equipment will enable the firm to increase sales by $25 million per year and decrease operating costs by $10 million per year. At the end of 3 years, the new equipment will be worthless. Assume the firm's tax rate is 35 percent and the discount rate for projects of this sort is 12 percent.

a. What is the net cash flow at time 0 if the old equipment is replaced?
b. What are the incremental cash flows in Years 1, 2, and 3?
c. What are the NPV and IRR of the replacement project?
d. Now ignore straight-line depreciation and assume that both new and old equipment are in an asset class with a CCA rate of 30 percent. PC Shopping Network has other assets in this asset class. What is the NPV of the replacement project? For this part, assume that the new equipment will have a salvage value of $30 million at the end of 3 years.

Solutions to Excel Spreadsheet Model Questions

1.

Year:	0	1	2	3	4	5	6	...∞
Capital investment	10,000							
Working capital	1,000	3,550	3,728	3,914	4,110	3,039	0	
Change in working capital	1,000	2,550	178	186	196	−1,071	−3,039	
Revenues		15,000	15,750	16,538	17,364	18,233		
Expenses		10,000	10,500	11,025	11,576	12,155		
Profit before tax (excluding CCA tax shield)		5,000	5,250	5,513	5,788	6,078		
Tax (35%)		1,750	1,838	1,929	2,026	2,127		
Operating cash flows (excluding CCA tax shield)		3,250	3,413	3,583	3,762	3,950		
Salvage value							0	
Total cash flow (excluding CCA tax shield)	−11,000	700	3,235	3,397	3,567	5,021	3,039	
PV of cash flow (excluding CCA tax shield)	−11,000	625	2,579	2,418	2,267	2,849	1,540	
Present value (excluding CCA tax shield) (A)	1,277							
CCA[1]		1,500	2,550	1,785	1,250	875	612	→ 0
CCA tax shield[1]		525	893	625	437	306	214	→ 0
PV of CCA tax shield[1] (B)	2,366							
Net present value (A) + (B)	3,643							

Notes: [1] The CCA and the CCA tax shield will continue even after Year 6. The PV of the CCA tax shield has been calculated assuming that the CCA and the CCA tax shield will continue in perpetuity.

2.

Year:	0	1	2	3	4	5	6	...∞
Capital investment	10,000							
Working capital	1,500	4,000	4,000	4,000	4,000	2,500	0	
Change in working capital	1,500	2,500	0	0	0	−1,500	−2,500	
Revenues		15,000	15,000	15,000	15,000	15,000		
Expenses		10,000	10,000	10,000	10,000	10,000		
Profit before tax (excluding CCA tax shield)		5,000	5,000	5,000	5,000	5,000		
Tax (35%)		1,750	1,750	1,750	1,750	1,750		
Operating cash flows (excluding CCA tax shield)		3,250	3,250	3,250	3,250	3,250		
Salvage value							0	
Total cash flow (excluding CCA tax shield)	−11,500	750	3,250	3,250	3,250	4,750	2,500	
PV of cash flow (excluding CCA tax shield)	−11,500	701	2,839	2,653	2,479	3,387	1,666	
Present value (excluding CCA tax shield) (A)	2,225							
CCA[1]		1,500	2,550	1,785	1,250	875	612	→ 0
CCA tax shield[1]		525	893	625	437	306	214	→ 0
PV of CCA tax shield[1] (B)	2,745							
Net present value (A) + (B)	4,970							

Notes: [1] The CCA and the CCA tax shield will continue even after Year 6. The PV of the CCA tax shield has been calculated assuming that the CCA and the CCA tax shield will continue in perpetuity.

Although the real discount rate is barely affected by the change in inflation, the real value of CCA and the present value of the CCA tax shield increase, which increases project NPV.

3.

Year:	0	1	2	3	4	5	6
Capital investment	10,000						
Working capital	1,500	4,075	4,279	4,493	4,717	3,039	0
Change in working capital	1,500	2,575	204	214	225	−1,679	−3,039
Revenues		15,000	15,750	16,538	17,364	18,233	
Expenses		10,000	10,500	11,015	11,576	12,155	
Profit before tax (excluding depreciation tax shield)		5,000	5,250	5,513	5,788	6,078	
Tax (35%)		1,750	1,838	1,930	2,026	2,127	
Operating cash flows (excluding depreciation tax shield)		3,250	3,412	3,583	3,762	3,950	
Salvage value							0
Total cash flow (excluding depreciation tax shield)	−11,500	675	3,209	3,369	3,538	5,629	3,039
PV of cash flow (excluding depreciation tax shield)	−11,500	603	2,558	2,398	2,248	3,194	1,540
Present value (excluding depreciation tax shield) (A)	1,041						
Depreciation		2,000	2,000	2,000	2,000	2,000	
Depreciation tax shield	0	700	700	700	700	700	0
PV of depreciation tax shield	0	625	558	498	445	396	0
Total present value of depreciation tax shield (B)	2,523						
Net present value (A) + (B)	3,564						

It is worthwhile noting that often large corporations keep two sets of books, one for shareholders and one for Canada Customs and Revenue Agency (CCRA). It is common to use straight-line depreciation on the shareholder books and the CCA system on the tax books. Only the CCA recorded in the tax books is relevant in capital budgeting.

Solutions to Check Points

7.1 Remember, discount cash flows, not profits. Each tewgit machine costs $250,000 right away; recognize that outlay, but forget accounting depreciation. Cash flows per machine are

Year:	0	1	2	3	4	5
Investment (outflow)	–250,000					
Sales		250,000	300,000	300,000	250,000	250,000
Operating expenses		–200,000	–200,000	–200,000	–200,000	–200,000
Cash flow	–250,000	+ 50,000	+100,000	+100,000	+ 50,000	+ 50,000

Each machine is forecast to generate $50,000 of cash flow in years 4 and 5. Thus it makes sense to keep operating for 5 years.

7.2 a., b. The site and buildings could have been sold or put to another use. Their values are opportunity costs, which should be treated as incremental cash outflows.

c. Demolition costs are incremental cash outflows.

d. The cost of the access road is sunk and not incremental.

e. Lost cash flows from other projects are incremental cash outflows.

f. Depreciation is not a cash expense and should not be included, except as it affects taxes. (Taxes are discussed later in this chapter.)

7.3 Actual health costs will be increasing at about 7 percent a year.

Year:	1	2	3	4
Cost per worker	$2,400	$2,568	$2,748	$2,940

The present value at 10 percent is $9,214 if the first payment is made immediately. If it is delayed a year, present value falls to $8,377.

7.4 The tax rate is T = 35 percent. Taxes paid will be

$$T \times (\text{revenue} - \text{expenses} - \text{depreciation}) = .35 \times (600 - 300 - 200) = \$35$$

Operating cash flow can be calculated as follows.

a. Revenue – expenses – taxes = 600 – 300 – 35 = $265

b. Net profit + depreciation = (600 – 300 – 200 – 35) + 200
= 65 + 200 = 265

c. (Revenues – cash expenses) × (1 – tax rate) + (depreciation × tax rate)
= (600 – 300) × (1 – .35) + (200 × .35) = 265

7.5

	Year 1	Year 2
Beginning UCC	—	$166,500
Net Acquisition	$180,000	(25,000)
CCA	13,500	21,225
Ending UCC	166,500	120,275

Calculations:

Year 1: CCA = $180, 000 × .5 × .15 = $13,500

Year 2: Adjusted cost of disposal = $100,000 + 75,000 = $175,000

Net acquisition = Total cost of additions – Adjusted cost of disposal
= $150,000 – $175,000 = –$25,000

CCA = $141,500 × .15 = $21,225

Ending UCC = $141,500 – $21,225 = $120,275

7.6 Adjusted cost of disposal = $65,000 + $70,000 = $135,000
UCC is reduced by this amount to $144,500 – $135,000 = $9,500.

If the firm has no other assets in Class 10, then the asset pool will be terminated, and the amount of $9,500 will be treated as a terminal loss.

7.7 a.

	All figures in dollars					
Year:	**0**	**1**	**2**	**3**	**4**	**5**
1. Capital investment	–5,000					
2. Revenues		3,000	3,000	3,000	3,000	3,000
3. Expenses		1,500	1,500	1,500	1,500	1,500
4. Profit before tax (2 – 3)		1,500	1,500	1,500	1,500	1,500
5. Tax at 35%		525	525	525	525	525
6. Operating cash flow excluding CCA tax shield (4 – 5)		975	975	975	975	975
7. UCC		4,625	3,931	3,341	2,840	2,414
8. CCA		375	694	590	501	426
9. CCA tax shield (.35 × 8)		131	243	207	175	149
10. Total yearly cash flows including CCA tax shield (1 + 6 + 9)	5,000	1,106	1,218	1,182	1,150	1,124

Notice that the amounts in row 10 do not reflect *all* cash flows, since there remains a UCC balance of $2,414 in Year 5, which should continue to provide CCA tax shields beyond Year 5 if there are other assets in the asset class.

b. If depreciation is on a staight-line basis over 5 years, we would change items 8, 9, and 10 of the table in part (a) above as follows:

	All figures in dollars					
Year:	**0**	**1**	**2**	**3**	**4**	**5**
8. Depreciation		1,000	1,000	1,000	1,000	1,000
9. Depreciation tax shield (.35 × 8)		350	350	350	350	350
10. Total yearly cash flows including depreciation tax shield (1 + 6 + 9)	–5,000	1,325	1,325	1,325	1,325	1,325

MINICASE

Jack Tar, CFO of Sheetbend & Halyard, Inc., opened the company confidential envelope. It contained a draft of a competitive bid for a contract to supply duffel canvas to the Canadian Armed Forces. The cover memo from Sheetbend's CEO asked Mr. Tar to review the bid before it was submitted.

The bid and its supporting documents had been prepared by Sheetbend's sales staff. It called for Sheetbend to supply 100,000 yards of duffel canvas per year for 5 years. The proposed selling price was fixed at $30 per yard.

Mr. Tar was not usually involved in sales, but this bid was unusual in at least two respects. First, if accepted by the navy, it would commit Sheetbend to a fixed price, long-term contract. Second, producing the duffel canvas would require an investment of $1.5 million to purchase machinery and to refurbish Sheetbend's plant in Saint John, New Brunswick.

Mr. Tar set to work and by the end of the week had collected the following facts and assumptions:

- The plant in Saint John was built in the early 1900s and is now idle. The plant was fully depreciated on Sheetbend's books, except for the purchase cost of the land (in 1947) of $10,000.
- Now that the land was valuable shorefront property, Mr. Tar thought the land and the idle plant could be sold, immediately or in the future, for $600,000.
- Refurbishing the plant would cost $500,000. This investment would be depreciated for tax purposes in an asset class that has a CCA rate of 5 percent.
- The new machinery would cost $1 million. This investment could be depreciated in an asset class that has a CCA rate of 30 percent.
- The refurbished plant and new machinery would last for many years. However, the remaining market for duffel canvas was small, and it was not clear that additional orders could be obtained once the Forces contract was finished. The machinery was custom built and could be used only for duffel canvas. Its second-hand value at the end of 5 years was probably zero.
- Table 7.11 shows the sales staff's forecasts of income from the navy contract. Mr. Tar reviewed this forecast and decided that its assumptions were reasonable, except that the forecast used book, not tax, depreciation.
- But the forecast income statement contained no mention of working capital. Mr. Tar thought that working capital would average about 10 percent of sales.

Armed with this information, Mr. Tar constructed a spreadsheet to calculate the NPV of the duffel canvas project, assuming that Sheetbend's bid would be accepted by the Forces.

He had just finished debugging the spreadsheet when another confidential envelope arrived from Sheetbend's CEO. It contained a firm offer from a New Brunswick real estate developer to purchase Sheetbend's Saint John land and plant for $1.5 million in cash.

Should Mr. Tar recommend submitting the bid to the Forces at the proposed price of $30 per yard? The discount rate for this project is 12 percent.

TABLE 7.11
Forecast income statement for the navy duffel canvas project (dollar figures in thousands, except price per yard)

Year	1	2	3	4	5
1. Yards sold	100.00	100.00	100.00	100.00	100.00
2. Price per yard	30.00	30.00	30.00	30.00	30.00
3. Revenue (1 × 2)	3,000.00	3,000.00	3,000.00	3,000.00	3,000.00
4. Cost of goods sold	2,100.00	2,184.00	2,271.36	2,362.21	2,456.70
5. Operating cash flow (3 – 4)	900.00	816.00	728.64	637.79	543.30
6. Depreciation	250.00	250.00	250.00	250.00	250.00
7. Income (5 – 6)	650.00	566.00	478.64	387.79	293.30
8. Tax at 35%	227.50	198.10	167.52	135.72	102.65
9. Net income (7 – 8)	$422.50	$367.90	$311.12	$252.06	$190.64

Notes:

1. Yards sold and price per yard would be fixed by contract.
2. Cost of goods includes fixed cost of $300,000 per year plus variable costs of $18 per yard. Costs are expected to increase at the inflation rate of 4 percent per year.
3. Depreciation: A $1 million investment in machinery is depreciated straight-line over 5 years ($200,000 per year). The $500,000 cost of refurbishing the Saint John plant is depreciated straight-line over 10 years ($50,000 per year).

Appendix 7A: Deriving the CCA Tax Shield

Earlier, in Section 7.6, we saw that under Canada's CCA system, the tax shield from investing in an asset can continue in perpetuity. Equation 1 (page 219) provided a formula to compute the present value of this perpetual tax shield. In the following discussion, we will explain how equation 1 was arrived at. We will continue with the notation used earlier; that is,

C	=	capital cost of an asset acquired at the beginning of Year 1
d	=	CCA rate for the asset class to which the asset belongs
UCC_t	=	undepreciated capital cost in Year t after deducting CCA for the year
T_c	=	the firm's tax rate
r	=	discount rate
S	=	salvage amount from the sale of the asset at the end of Year t

We begin by making two simplifying assumptions, which will be relaxed later in the discussion. The assumptions are to ignore the half-year rule and the rules governing the disposal of assets. Suppose you start a new asset class by buying an asset. Our assumptions will enable you to get your first CCA tax shield from the asset in Year 1. The UCC of the class starts out at the beginning of Year 1 and is denoted $UCC_0 = C$.

Table 7.12 provides details regarding yearly beginning and ending UCC balances and the CCA, which is obtained as the product of the beginning UCC and the CCA rate, d. So, for instance, the CCA in Year 1 (CCA_1) is $d \times UCC_0 = Cd$.

After deducting CCA_1, the UCC at the end of year Year 1 becomes

$$\begin{aligned} UCC_1 &= UCC_0 - CCA \\ &= C - Cd \\ &= C(1 - d) \end{aligned}$$

Suppose C is \$200,000 and d is 10 percent, then CCA_1 is \$200,000 × .1 = \$20,000 and UCC_1 is \$200,000 × (1 – .1) = \$180,000. Similarly, the CCA for Year 2 is

$$CCA_2 = d \times UCC_1 = Cd(1 - d),$$

which is

$$\$20{,}000 \times (1 - .1) = \$200{,}000 \times .1 \times (1 - .1) = \$18{,}000$$

for our example. In Year t, you will have taken $t - 1$ previous CCA tax shields, so the UCC at the start of the year is $UCC_{t-1} = C(1 - d)^{t-1}$. The CCA for Year t will be

$$d \times UCC_{t-1} = Cd(1 - d)^{t-1}$$

For instance, if you take t to be 15 years, then, not surprisingly, the UCC balance in Year 15 will be quite small at

$$\$200{,}000 \times .1 \times (1 - .1)^{14} = \$4{,}575.36$$

TABLE 7.12
UCC and CCA

Year	Beginning of Year UCC	CCA	End of Year UCC
1	UCC_0	Cd	$UCC_1 = C(1 - d)$
2	UCC_1	$Cd(1 - d)$	$UCC_2 = C(1 - d)^2$
3	UCC_2	$Cd(1 - d)^2$	$UCC_3 = C(1 - d)^3$
–			
t	UCC_t	$Cd(1 - d)^{t-1}$	$UCC_t = C(1 - d)^t$

Until now, given the simplifying assumptions, we show that in a declining balance system, each asset will generate a stream of CCA amounts that will continue in perpetuity. Our algebraic expression also enables us to calculate the CCA and UCC amounts for any given year. Earlier we established that the CCA adds value to a capital investment project by reducing the firm's tax bill. A CCA stream in perpetuity will generate an infinite stream of tax savings. We now need to calculate the present value of this infinite stream of tax savings—that is, the PV of the CCA tax shield. For a given year, the CCA tax shield is simply the product of the year's CCA and the firm's tax rate, or CCA × T_c. A project will therefore generate the following CCA tax shields for years 1 through t:

Year:	1	2	3	—	t	—
CCA tax shield = CCA × T_c	CdT_c	$CdT_c(1-d)$	$CdT_c(1-d)^2$	—	$CdT_c(1-d)^{t-1}$	—

The CCA tax shield forms a perpetuity that is growing at the rate $-d$; which means, in effect, it is declining at this rate. Conceptually, this is like the constant growth dividend we looked at in Section 5.4. Remember, when the dividend grows at a constant rate g, we arrive at the stock price as the present value of expected future dividends as follows:

$$\text{Stock price} = \frac{DIV_1}{(r-g)}$$

Similar to the stock value, the CCA tax shield has the following present value:

$$\text{PV of CCA tax shield} = \frac{CdT_c}{(r+d)}$$

To determine the value added to an investment project by the tax savings generated by CCA, we can add the present value of the perpetual tax shield to the present value of the "after-tax" revenues and expenses to get the overall present value of the project.

Let us now relax our two simplifying assumptions. Until now, we had ignored the half-year rule feature of Canadian tax law requiring that, in the year of purchase of a depreciable asset, only half of the asset's value is added to the asset class balance. The remaining half is added in the following year. When we consider the half-year rule, the present value of the CCA tax shield has to be computed for the two halves separately and then added up. To see how this is done, let us find the CCA stream on the two halves of the asset value, as follows:

Year:	1	2	3	...	t	...
CCA on first half of asset value	$Cd/2$	$Cd(1-d)/2$	$Cd(1-d)^2/2$	...	$Cd(1-d)^t/2$	...
CCA on second half of asset value	0	$Cd/2$	$Cd(1-d)/2$	...	$Cd(1-d)^{t-1}/2$	...

If we multiply by T_c then the PV of perpetual CCA tax shields for the first half becomes

$$\frac{1}{2}\left[\frac{CdT_c}{1+r} + \frac{CdT_c(1-d)}{(1+r)^2} + \frac{CdT_c(1-d)^2}{(1+r)^3} + \frac{CdT_c(1-d)^{t-1}}{(1+r)^t}\right] = \frac{1}{2}\left[\frac{CdT_c}{r+d}\right]$$

Notice that in the second half below, the same CCA stream (and CCA tax shields) are deferred 1 year.

$$\frac{1}{2}\left[\frac{CdT_c}{(1+r)^2} + \frac{CdT_c(1-d)}{(1+r)^3} + \frac{CdT_c(1-d)^2}{(1+r)^4} \cdots \frac{CdT_c(1-d)^{t-2}}{(1+r)^t}\right]$$

To find the present value of the second half, we have to discount the CCA tax shields back to time 0:

$$\frac{1}{2}\left[\frac{CdT_c}{r+d}\right]\left[\frac{1}{1+r}\right]$$

When we add up the two present values we get the total present value of the CCA tax shield under the half-year rule:

$$\frac{1}{2}\left[\frac{CdT_c}{r+d}\right] + \frac{1}{2}\left[\frac{CdT_c}{r+d}\right]\left[\frac{1}{1+r}\right]$$

Using a bit of algebra, this formula can be simplified to provide equation 1, which we discussed earlier:

$$= \frac{1}{2}\left[\frac{CdT_c}{r+d}\right]\left[1 + \frac{1}{1+r}\right]$$

$$= \frac{1}{2}\left[\frac{CdT_c}{r+d}\right]\left[\frac{1+r+1}{1+r}\right]$$

$$= \frac{CdT_c}{r+d}\left[\frac{1+.5r}{1+r}\right]$$

This general formula enables us to compute the present value of the tax shield on CCA under the half-year rule. Relaxing our second assumption, when a residual or salvage value arising from the sale of an asset is introduced into the discussion, we get the present value of lost CCA tax shields due to salvage value, as discussed in Section 7.6 and shown as equation 2 (page 219).

When we combine equations 1 and 2, we get a general formula for the present value of the CCA tax shield, which we presented earlier as equation 3:

Present value of CCA tax shield =

$$\left[\frac{CdT_c}{r+d}\right]\left[\frac{1+.5r}{1+r}\right] - \left[\frac{SdT_c}{(d+r)}\right]\left[\frac{1}{(1+r)^t}\right]$$

CHAPTER 8

Project Analysis

8.1 How Firms Organize the Investment Process

8.2 Some "What If" Questions

8.3 Break-Even Analysis

8.4 Flexibility in Capital Budgeting

8.5 Capital Budgeting Practices in Canadian Firms

8.6 Summary

It helps to use discounted cash-flow techniques to value new projects but good investment decisions also require good data. Therefore, we start this chapter by thinking about how firms organize the capital budgeting operation to get the kind of information they need. In addition, we look at how they try to ensure that everyone involved works together toward a common goal.

Project evaluation should never be a mechanical exercise in which the financial manager takes a set of cash-flow forecasts and cranks out a net present value. Cash-flow estimates are just that—estimates. Financial managers need to look behind the forecasts to try to understand what makes the project tick and what could go wrong with it. A number of techniques have been developed to help managers identify the key assumptions in their analysis. These techniques involve asking a number of "what if" questions. What if your market share turns out to be higher or lower than you forecast? What if interest rates rise during the life of the project? In the second part of this chapter we show how managers use the techniques of sensitivity analysis, scenario analysis, and break-even analysis to help answer these what-if questions.

Books about capital budgeting sometimes create the impression that once the manager has made an investment decision, there is nothing to do but sit back and watch the cash flows develop. But since cash flows rarely proceed as anticipated, companies constantly need to modify their operations. If cash flows are better than anticipated, the project may be expanded; if they are worse, it may be scaled back or abandoned altogether. In the third section of this chapter we describe how good managers take account of these options when they analyze a project and why they are willing to pay money today to build in future flexibility.

After studying this chapter you should be able to

- Appreciate the practical problems of capital budgeting in large corporations.
- Use sensitivity, scenario, and break-even analyses to see how project profitability would be affected by an error in your forecasts and understand why an overestimate of sales is more serious for projects with high operating leverage.
- Recognize the importance of managerial flexibility in capital budgeting.

How Firms Organize the Investment Process

For most sizable firms, investments are evaluated in two separate stages.

STAGE 1: THE CAPITAL BUDGET

capital budget List of planned investment projects.

Once a year, the head office generally asks each of its divisions and plants to provide a list of the investments that they would like to make.[1] These are gathered together into a proposed **capital budget.**

This budget is then reviewed and pruned by senior management and other staff specializing in planning and financial analysis. Usually there are negotiations between the firm's senior management and its divisional management, and there may also be special analyses of major outlays or ventures into new areas. Once the budget has been approved, it generally remains the basis for planning over the ensuing year.

Many investment proposals bubble up from the bottom of the organization. But sometimes the ideas are likely to come from higher up. For example, the managers of plants A and B cannot be expected to see the potential benefits of closing their plants and consolidating production at a new plant C. We expect divisional management to propose plant C. Similarly, divisions 1 and 2 may not be eager to give up their own data processing operations to a large central computer. That proposal would come from senior management.

Senior management's concern is to see that the capital budget matches the firm's strategic plans. It needs to ensure that the firm is concentrating its efforts in areas where it has a real competitive advantage. As part of this effort, management must also identify declining businesses that should be sold or allowed to run down.

The firm's capital investment choices should reflect both "bottom-up" and "top-down" processes—capital budgeting and strategic planning, respectively. The two processes should complement each other. Plant and division managers, who do most of the work in bottom-up capital budgeting, may not see the forest for the trees. Strategic planners may have a mistaken view of the forest because they do not look at the trees.

STAGE 2: PROJECT AUTHORIZATIONS

The annual budget is important because it allows everybody to exchange ideas before attitudes have hardened and personal commitments have been made. However, the fact that your pet project has been included in the annual budget doesn't mean you have permission to go ahead with it. At a later stage you will need to draw up a detailed proposal describing particulars of the project, engineering analyses, cash-flow forecasts, and present value calculations. If your project is large, this proposal may have to pass a number of hurdles before it is finally approved.

The type of backup information that you need to provide depends on the project category. For example, some firms use a fourfold breakdown:

1. Outlays required by law or company policy; for example, for pollution control equipment. These outlays do not need to be justified on financial grounds. The main issue is whether requirements are satisfied at the lowest possible cost. The decision is therefore likely to hinge on engineering analyses of alternative technologies.
2. Maintenance or cost reduction, such as machine replacement. Engineering analysis is

[1] Large firms may be divided into several divisions. For example, International Paper has divisions that specialize in printing paper, packaging, specialty products, and forest products. Each of these divisions may be responsible for a number of plants.

also important in machine replacement, but new machines have to pay their own way. In this category of the proposal the firm faces the classical capital budgeting problems described in chapters 6 and 7.

3. Capacity expansion in existing businesses. Projects in this category are less straightforward; these decisions may hinge on forecasts of demand, possible shifts in technology, and the reactions of competitors.
4. Investment for new products. Projects in this category are most likely to depend on strategic decisions. The first projects in a new area may not have positive NPVs if considered in isolation, but they may give the firm a valuable option to undertake follow-up projects. More about this later in the chapter.

PROBLEMS AND SOME SOLUTIONS

Valuing capital investment opportunities is hard enough when you can do the entire job yourself. In most firms, however, capital budgeting is a cooperative effort, and this brings with it some challenges.

Ensuring that Forecasts Are Consistent. Inconsistent assumptions often creep into investment proposals. For example, suppose that the manager of the furniture division is bullish (optimistic) on housing starts but the manager of the appliance division is bearish (pessimistic). This inconsistency makes the projects proposed by the furniture division look more attractive than those of the appliance division.

To ensure consistency, many firms begin the capital budgeting process by establishing forecasts of economic indicators, such as inflation and the growth in national income, as well as forecasts of particular items that are important to the firm's business, such as housing starts or the price of raw materials. These forecasts can then be used as the basis for all project analyses.

Eliminating Conflicts of Interest. In Chapter 1 we pointed out that while managers want to do a good job, they are also concerned about their own futures. If the interests of managers conflict with those of shareholders, the result is likely to be poor investment decisions. For example, new plant managers naturally want to demonstrate good performance right away. To this end, they might propose quick-payback projects even if NPV is sacrificed. Unfortunately, many firms measure performance and reward managers in ways that encourage such behaviour. If the firm always demands quick results, it is unlikely that plant managers will concentrate only on NPV.

Reducing Forecast Bias. Someone who is keen to get a project proposal accepted is also likely to look on the bright side when forecasting the project's cash flows. Such overriding optimism is a common feature in financial forecasts. For example, think of large public expenditure proposals. How often have you heard of a new missile, dam, or highway that actually cost *less* than was originally forecast? Think back to the Eurotunnel project introduced in Chapter 6. The final cost of the project was about 50 percent higher than initial forecasts. It is probably impossible to ever eliminate bias completely, but if senior management is aware of why bias occurs, it is at least partway to solving the problem.

Project sponsors are likely to overstate their case deliberately only if the head office encourages them to do so. For example, if middle managers believe that success depends on having the largest division rather than the most profitable one, they will propose large expansion projects that they do not believe have the largest possible net present value. Or if divisions must compete for limited resources, they will try to outbid each other for those resources. The fault in such cases is with top management—if lower level managers are not rewarded based on net present value and contribution to firm value, it should not be surprising that they focus their efforts elsewhere.

Other problems stem from sponsors' eagerness to obtain approval for their favourite projects. As the proposal travels up the organization, alliances are formed. Thus once a division has screened its own plants' proposals, the plants in that division unite in competing against outsiders. The result is that the head office may receive several thousand investment proposals each year, all essentially sales documents presented by united fronts and designed to persuade. The forecasts have been doctored to ensure that NPV appears positive.

Since it is difficult for senior management to evaluate each specific assumption in an investment proposal, capital investment decisions are effectively decentralized whatever the rules say. Some firms accept this; others rely on head office staff to check capital investment proposals.

Sorting the Wheat from the Chaff. Senior managers are continually bombarded with requests for funds for capital expenditures. All these requests are supported with detailed analyses showing that the projects have positive NPVs. How then can managers ensure that only worthwhile projects make the grade? One response of senior managers to the problem of poor information is to impose rigid expenditure limits on individual plants or divisions. These limits force the subunits to choose among projects. The firm ends up using capital rationing not because capital is unobtainable but as a way of decentralizing decisions.[2]

Senior managers might also ask some searching questions about why the project has a positive NPV. After all, if the project is so attractive, why hasn't someone already undertaken it? Will others copy your idea if it is so profitable? Positive NPVs are plausible only if your company has some competitive advantage.

Such an advantage can arise in several ways. You may be smart enough or lucky enough to be the first to the market with a new or improved product for which customers will pay premium prices. Your competitors eventually will enter the market and squeeze out excess profits, but it may take them several years to do so. Or you may have a proprietary technology or production cost advantage that competitors cannot easily match. You may have a contractual advantage such as the distributorship for a particular region. Or your advantage may be as simple as a good reputation and an established customer list.

Analyzing competitive advantage can also help ferret out projects that incorrectly appear to have a negative NPV. If you are the lowest cost producer of a profitable product in a growing market, then you should invest to expand along with the market. If your calculations show a negative NPV for such an expansion, then you have probably made a mistake.

8.2 Some "What If" Questions

SENSITIVITY ANALYSIS

sensitivity analysis Analysis of the effects of changes in sales, costs, and so on, on project profitability.

Uncertainty means that more things *can* happen than *will* happen. Therefore, whenever managers are given a cash-flow forecast, they try to determine what else might happen and the implications of those possible events. This is called **sensitivity analysis.**

Put yourself in the well-heeled shoes of the financial manager of the Finefodder supermarket chain. Finefodder is considering opening a new superstore in Gravenstein and your staff members have prepared the figures shown in Table 8.1. The figures are fairly typical for a new supermarket, except that to keep the example simple we have assumed no inflation. We have also assumed that the entire investment can be depreciated straight-line for

[2] We discussed capital rationing in Chapter 6.

TABLE 8.1
Cash-flow forecasts for Finefodder's new superstore

	Year 0	Years 1–12
Investment	–$5,400,000	
1. Sales		$16,000,000
2. Variable costs		13,000,000
3. Fixed costs		2,000,000
4. Depreciation		450,000
5. Pretax profit (1 – 2 – 3 – 4)		550,000
6. Taxes (at 40%)		220,000
7. Profit after tax		330,000
8. Cash flow from operations (4 + 7)		780,000
Net cash flow	–$5,400,000	$ 780,000

tax purposes, we have neglected the working capital requirement, and we have ignored the fact that at the end of the 12 years you could sell off the land and buildings.

As an experienced financial manager, you recognize immediately that these cash flows constitute an annuity, and therefore, you calculate present value by multiplying the $780,000 cash flow by the 12-year annuity factor. If the cost of capital is 8 percent, present value is

$$\begin{aligned} PV &= \$780{,}000 \times \text{12-year annuity factor} \\ &= \$780{,}000 \times 7.536 = \$5.878 \text{ million} \end{aligned}$$

Subtract the initial investment of $5.4 million and you obtain a net present value of $478,000:

$$\begin{aligned} NPV &= PV - \text{investment} \\ &= \$5.878 \text{ million} - \$5.4 \text{ million} = \$478{,}000 \end{aligned}$$

Before you agree to accept the project, however, you want to delve behind these forecasts and identify the key variables that will determine whether the project succeeds or fails.

Some of the costs of running a supermarket are fixed. For example, regardless of the level of output, you still have to heat and light the store and pay the store manager. These **fixed costs** are forecast to be $2 million per year.

fixed costs Costs that do not depend on the level of output.

Other costs vary with the level of sales. In particular, the lower the sales, the less food you need to buy. Also, if sales are lower than forecast, you can operate a lower number of checkouts and reduce the staff needed to restock the shelves. The new superstore's variable costs are estimated at 81.25 percent of sales. Thus **variable costs** = .8125 × $16 million = $13 million.

variable costs Costs that change as the level of output changes.

The initial investment of $5.4 million will be depreciated on a straight-line basis over the 12-year period, resulting in annual depreciation of $450,000. Profits are taxed at a rate of 40 percent.

These seem to be the important things you need to know, but look out for things that may have been forgotten. Perhaps there will be delays in obtaining planning permission, or perhaps you will need to undertake costly landscaping. The greatest dangers often lie in these *unknown* unknowns, or "unk-unks," as scientists call them.

Having found no unk-unks (no doubt you'll find them later), you look at how NPV may be affected if you have made a wrong forecast of sales, costs, and so on. To do this, you first obtain optimistic and pessimistic estimates for the underlying variables. These are set out in the left-hand columns of Table 8.2.

Next you see what happens to NPV under the optimistic or pessimistic forecasts for

TABLE 8.2
Sensitivity analysis for superstore project

Variable	Range			NPV		
	Pessimistic	Expected	Optimistic	Pessimistic	Expected	Optimistic
Investment (in dollars)	6,200,000	5,400,000	5,000,000	–121,000	+478,000	+778,000
Sales (in dollars)	14,000,000	16,000,000	18,000,000	–1,218,000	+478,000	+2,174,000
Variable cost as percent of sales (Range: %; NPV: $)	83	81.25	80	–788,000	+478,000	+1,382,000
Fixed cost (in dollars)	2,100,000	2,000,000	1,900,000	+26,000	+478,000	+930,000

each of these variables. You recalculate project NPV under these various forecasts to determine which variables are most critical to NPV.

EXAMPLE 8.1 *Sensitivity Analysis*

The right-hand side of Table 8.2 shows the project's net present value if the variables are set *one at a time* to their optimistic and pessimistic values. For example, if fixed costs are \$1.9 million rather than the forecast \$2.0 million, annual cash flows are increased by (1 – tax rate) × (\$2.0 million – \$1.9 million) = .6 × \$100,000 = \$60,000. If the cash flow increases by \$60,000 a year for 12 years, then the project's present value increases by \$60,000 times the 12-year annuity factor, or \$60,000 × 7.536 = \$452,000. Therefore, NPV increases from the expected value of \$478,000 to \$478,000 + \$452,000 = \$930,000, as shown in the bottom right corner of the table. The other entries in the three columns on the right in Table 8.2 similarly show how the NPV of the project changes when each input is changed.

Your project is by no means a sure thing. The principal uncertainties appear to be sales and variable costs. For example, if sales are only \$14 million rather than the forecast \$16 million (and all other forecasts are unchanged), then the project has an NPV of –\$1.218 million. If variable costs are 83 percent of sales (and all other forecasts are unchanged), then the project has an NPV of –\$788,000.

CHECK POINT 8.1

Recalculate cash flow as in Table 8.1 if variable costs are 83 percent of sales. Confirm that NPV will be –\$788,000.

Value of Information. Now that you know the project could be thrown badly off course by a poor estimate of sales, you might like to see whether it is possible to resolve some of this uncertainty. Perhaps your worry is that the store will fail to attract sufficient shoppers from neighbouring towns. In that case, additional survey data and more careful analysis of travel times may be worthwhile.

On the other hand, there is less value to gathering additional information about fixed costs. Because the project is marginally profitable even under pessimistic assumptions about fixed costs, you are unlikely to be in trouble if you have estimated that variable incorrectly.

Limits to Sensitivity Analysis. Your analysis of the forecasts for Finefodder's new superstore is known as a *sensitivity analysis.* Sensitivity analysis expresses cash flows in terms of unknown variables and then calculates the consequences of incorrectly estimating those variables. It forces the manager to identify the underlying factors, indicates where additional information would be most useful, and helps to expose confused or inappropriate forecasts.

Of course, there is no law stating which variables you should consider in your sensitivity analysis. For example, you may wish to look separately at labour costs and the costs of the goods sold. Or, if you are concerned about a possible change in the corporate tax rate, you may wish to look at the effect of such a change on the project's NPV.

One drawback to sensitivity analysis is that it gives somewhat ambiguous results. For example, what exactly do *optimistic* and *pessimistic* mean? One department may be interpreting the terms in a different way from another. Ten years from now, after hundreds of projects, hindsight may show that one department's pessimistic limit was exceeded twice as often as the other's; but hindsight won't help you now while you're making the investment decision.

Another problem with sensitivity analysis is that the underlying variables are likely to be interrelated. For example, if sales exceed expectations, demand will likely be stronger than you anticipated and your profit margins will be wider. Or, if wages are higher than your forecast, both variable costs and fixed costs are likely to be at the upper end of your range.

Because of these connections, you cannot push *one-at-a-time* sensitivity analysis too far. It is impossible to obtain expected, optimistic, and pessimistic values for total *project* cash flows from the information in Table 8.2. Still, it does give a sense of which variables should be most closely monitored.

SCENARIO ANALYSIS

scenario analysis Project analysis given a particular combination of assumptions.

When variables are interrelated, managers often find it helpful to look at how their project would fare under different scenarios. **Scenario analysis** allows them to look at different but *consistent* combinations of variables. Forecasters generally prefer to give an estimate of revenues or costs under a particular scenario rather than giving some absolute optimistic or pessimistic value.

▶ EXAMPLE 8.2 *Scenario Analysis*

You are worried that Stop and Scoff may decide to build a new store in nearby Salome. That would reduce sales in your Gravenstein store by 15 percent and you might be forced into a price war to keep the remaining business. Prices might be reduced to the point that variable costs equal 82 percent of revenue. Table 8.3 shows that under this scenario of lower sales and smaller margins your new venture would no longer be worthwhile.

simulation analysis Estimation of the probabilities of different possible outcomes, e.g., from an investment project.

An extension of scenario analysis is called **simulation analysis.** Here, instead of specifying a relatively small number of scenarios, a computer generates several hundred or thousand possible combinations of variables according to probability distributions specified by the analyst. Each combination of variables corresponds to one scenario. Project NPV and other outcomes of interest can be calculated for each combination of variables, and the entire probability distribution of outcomes can be constructed from the simulation results.

TABLE 8.3
Scenario analysis, NPV of Finefodder's Gravenstein superstore with scenario of new competing store in nearby Salome

	Cash Flows Years 1–12	
	Base Case	**Competing Store Scenario**[a]
1. Sales	$16,000,000	$13,600,000
2. Variable costs	13,000,000	11,152,000
3. Fixed costs	2,000,000	2,000,000
4. Depreciation	450,000	450,000
5. Pretax profit (1 – 2 – 3 – 4)	550,000	–2,000
6. Taxes (40%)	220,000	–800
7. Profit after tax	330,000	–1,200
8. Cash flow from operations (4 + 7)	780,000	448,800
Present value of cash flows	5,878,000	3,382,000
NPV	478,000	–2,018,000

[a] *Assumptions:* Competing store causes (1) a 15 percent reduction in sales and (2) variable costs to increase to 82 percent of sales.

CHECK POINT 8.2 What is the basic difference between sensitivity analysis and scenario analysis?

Break-Even Analysis

break-even analysis Analysis of the level of sales at which the company breaks even.

When we undertake a sensitivity analysis of a project or when we look at alternative scenarios, we are asking how serious it would be if we misestimated sales or costs. Managers sometimes prefer to rephrase this question and ask how far off the estimates could be before the project begins to lose money. This exercise is known as **break-even analysis.**

For many projects, the make-or-break variable is sales volume. Therefore, managers most often focus on the break-even level of sales. However, you might also look at other variables, for example, at how high costs could be before the project goes into the red.

As it turns out, "losing money" can be defined in more than one way. Most often, the break-even condition is defined in terms of accounting profits. More properly, however, it should be defined in terms of net present value. We will start with accounting break-even, show that it can lead you astray, and then show how NPV break-even can be used as an alternative.

ACCOUNTING BREAK-EVEN ANALYSIS

The *accounting break-even* point is the level of sales at which profits are zero, or equivalently, at which total revenues equal total costs. As we have seen, some costs are fixed regardless of the level of output. Other costs vary with the level of output.

When you first analyzed the superstore project, you came up with the following estimates:

Sales	$16	million
Variable cost	13	million
Fixed costs	2	million
Depreciation	0.45	million

Notice that variable costs are 81.25 percent of sales. So, for each additional dollar of sales, costs increase by only \$.8125. We can easily determine how much business the superstore needs to attract to avoid losses. If the store sells nothing, the income statement will show fixed costs of \$2 million and depreciation of \$450,000. Thus there will be a *loss* of \$2.45 million. Each dollar of sales reduces this loss by \$1.00 – \$.8125 = \$.1875. Therefore, to cover fixed costs plus depreciation, you need sales of 2.45 million/.1875 = \$13.067 million. At this sales level, the firm will break even. More generally,

$$\textbf{Break-even level of revenues} = \frac{\textbf{fixed costs including depreciation}}{\textbf{additional profit from each additional dollar of sales}} \qquad (8.1)$$

Table 8.4 shows how the income statement looks with only \$13.067 million of sales.

Figure 8.1 shows how the break-even point is determined. The 45-degree line shows accounting revenues. The cost line shows how costs vary with sales. If the store doesn't sell a cent, it still incurs fixed costs and depreciation amounting to \$2.45 million. Each extra dollar of sales adds \$.8125 to these costs. When sales are \$13.067 million, the two lines cross, indicating that costs equal revenues. For lower sales, revenues are less than costs and the project is in the red; for higher sales, revenues exceed costs and the project moves into the black.

Is a project that breaks even in accounting terms an acceptable investment? If you are not sure about the answer, this may be an easier question: Would you be happy about an investment in a stock that after 5 years gave you a total rate of return of zero? We hope not. You might break even on such a stock but a zero return does not compensate you for the time value of money or the risk that you have taken.

A project that simply breaks even on an accounting basis gives you your money back but does not cover the opportunity cost of the capital tied up in the project. A project that breaks even in accounting terms will surely have a negative NPV.

Let's check this with the superstore project. Suppose that in each year the store has sales of \$13.067 million—just enough to break even on an accounting basis. What would be the cash flow from operations?

$$\begin{aligned}\text{Cash flow from operations} &= \text{profit after tax} + \text{depreciation}\\ &= 0 + \$450{,}000 = \$450{,}000\end{aligned}$$

TABLE 8.4
Income statement, break-even sales volume

Item	$ Thousands	
Revenues	13,067	
Variable costs	10,617	(81.25 percent of sales)
Fixed costs	2,000	
Depreciation	450	
Pretax profit	0	
Taxes	0	
Profit after tax	0	

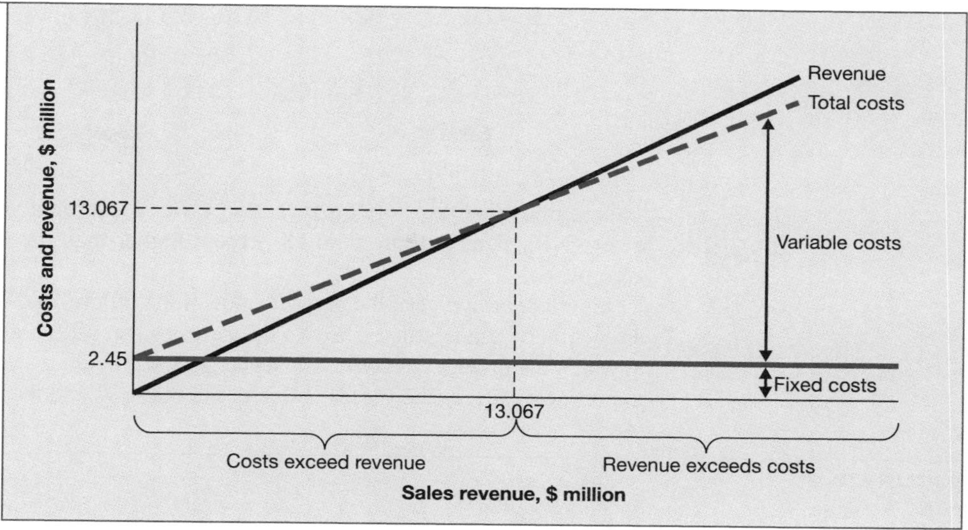

FIGURE 8.1
The financial managers in large corporations

The initial investment is $5.4 million. In each of the next 12 years, the firm receives a cash flow of $450,000. So the firm gets its money back:

$$\text{Total cash flow from operations} = \text{initial investment}$$
$$12 \times \$450{,}000 = \$5.4 \text{ million}$$

But revenues are *not* sufficient to repay the *opportunity cost* of that $5.4 million investment. NPV is negative.

NPV BREAK-EVEN ANALYSIS

Instead of asking how bad sales can get before the project makes an accounting loss, it is more useful to focus on the point at which NPV switches from positive to negative.

The cash flows of the project in each year will depend on sales as follows:

1. Variable costs	81.25 percent of sales
2. Fixed costs	$2 million
3. Depreciation	$450,000
4. Pretax profit	(.1875 × sales) – $2.45 million
5. Tax (at 40%)	.40 × (.1875 × sales – $2.45 million)
6. Profit after tax	.60 × (.1875 × sales – $2.45 million)
7. Cash flow (3 + 6)	$450,000 + .60 × (.1875 × sales – $2.45 million) = .1125 × sales – $1.02 million

This cash flow will last for 12 years. So to find its present value we multiply by the 12-year annuity factor. With a discount rate of 8 percent, the present value of $1 a year for each of 12 years is $7.536. Thus the present value of the cash flows is

$$\text{PV (cash flows)} = 7.536 \times (.1125 \times \text{sales} - \$1.02 \text{ million})$$

The project breaks even in present value terms (that is, has a zero NPV) if the present value of these cash flows is equal to the initial $5.4 million investment. Therefore, break-even occurs when

$$\text{PV (cash flows)} = \text{investment}$$
$$7.536 \times (.1125 \times \text{sales} - \$1.02 \text{ million}) = \$5.4 \text{ million}$$
$$-\$7.69 \text{ million} + .8478 \times \text{sales} = \$5.4 \text{ million}$$
$$\text{sales} = \frac{5.4 + 7.69}{.8478} = \$15.4 \text{ million}$$

This implies that the store needs sales of $15.4 million a year for the investment to have a zero NPV. This is more than 18 percent higher than the point at which the project has zero profit.

Figure 8.2 is a plot of the present value of the inflows and outflows from the superstore as a function of annual sales. The two lines cross when sales are $15.4 million. This is the point at which the project has zero NPV. As long as sales are greater than this, the present value of the inflows exceeds the present value of the outflows and the project has a positive NPV.

FIGURE 8.2
NPV break-even analysis

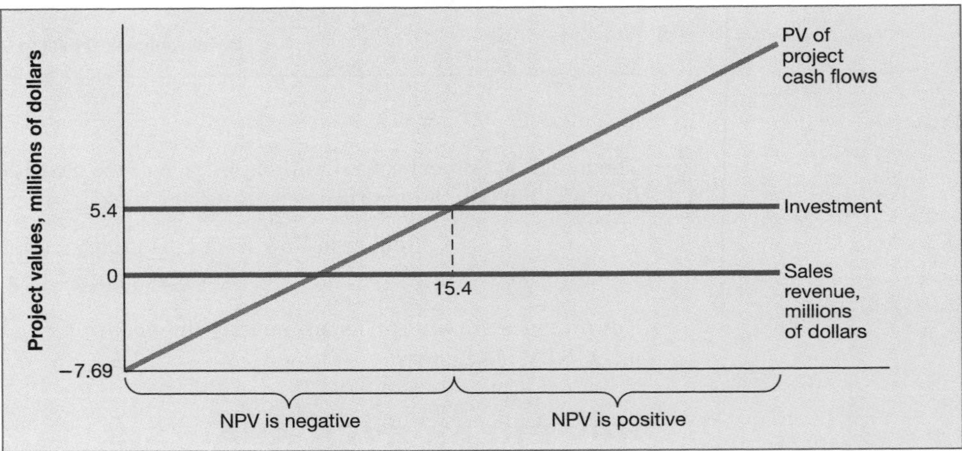

CHECK POINT 8.3

What would be the NPV break-even level of sales if the capital investment was only $5 million?

EXAMPLE 8.3 *Break-Even Analysis*

We have said that projects that break even on an accounting basis are really making a loss—they are losing the opportunity cost of their investment. Here is a dramatic example. Lophead Aviation is contemplating investment in a new passenger aircraft, code-named the Trinova. Lophead's financial staff has gathered together the following estimates:

1. The cost of developing the Trinova is forecast at $900 million, and this investment can be depreciated in six equal annual amounts.
2. Production of the plane is expected to take place at a steady annual rate over the following 6 years.
3. The average price of the Trinova is expected to be $15.5 million.
4. Fixed costs are forecast at $175 million a year.
5. Variable costs are forecast at $8.5 million a plane.

6. The tax rate is 50 percent.
7. The cost of capital is 10 percent.

How many aircraft does Lophead need to sell to break even in accounting terms? And how many does it need to sell to break even on the basis of NPV? (Notice that the break-even point is defined here in terms of number of aircraft, rather than revenue. But since revenue is proportional to planes sold, these two break-even concepts are interchangeable.)

To answer the first question, we set out the profits from the Trinova program in rows 1 to 7 of Table 8.5 (ignore row 8 for a moment).

In accounting terms the venture breaks even when pretax profit (and therefore net profit) is zero. In this case,

$$(7 \times \text{planes sold}) - 325 = 0$$

$$\text{Planes sold} = \frac{325}{7} = 46$$

Thus Lophead needs to sell about 46 planes a year, or a total of about 280 planes over the 6 years to show a profit.

Notice that we obtain the same result if we attack the problem in terms of the break-even level of revenue. The variable cost of each plane is \$8.5 million, which is 54.8 percent of the \$15.5 million price. Therefore, each dollar of sales increases pretax profits by \$1 – \$.548 = \$.452. So

$$\text{Break-even revenue} = \frac{\text{fixed costs including depreciation}}{\text{additional profit from each additional dollar of sales}}$$

$$= \frac{\$325 \text{ million}}{.452} = \$719 \text{ million}$$

Since each plane cost \$15.5 million, this revenue level implies sales of 719/15.5 = 46 planes per year.

Now let us look at what sales are needed before the project has a zero NPV. Development of the Trinova costs \$900 million. For each of the next 6 years the company expects a cash flow of \$3.5 million × planes sold – \$12.5 million (see row 8 of Table 8.5). If the cost of capital is 10 percent, the 6-year annuity factor is 4.355. So

$$\text{NPV} = -900 + 4.355(3.5 \times \text{planes sold} - 12.5)$$
$$= 15.24 \times \text{planes sold} - 954.44$$

TABLE 8.5

Forecast profitability for production of the Trinova airliner (figures in millions of dollars)

	Year 0	Years 1–6
Investment	\$900	
1. Sales		15.5 × planes sold
2. Variable costs		8.5 × planes sold
3. Fixed costs		175
4. Depreciation		900/6 = 150
5. Pretax profit (1 – 2 – 3 – 4)		(7 × planes sold) – 325
6. Taxes (at 50%)		(3.5 × planes sold) – 162.5
7. Net profit (5 – 6)		(3.5 × planes sold) – 162.5
8. Net cash flow (4 + 7)	–\$900	(3.5 × planes sold) – 12.5

If the project has a zero NPV,

$$0 = 15.24 \text{ planes sold} - 954.44$$

$$\text{planes sold} = 63$$

Thus Lophead can recover its initial investment with sales of 46 planes a year (about 280 in total), but it needs to sell 63 a year (or about 375 in total) to earn a return on this investment equal to the opportunity cost of capital.

Our example may seem fanciful but it is based loosely on reality. In 1971 Lockheed was in the middle of a major program to bring out the L-1011 TriStar airliner. This program was to bring Lockheed to the brink of failure and it tipped Rolls-Royce (supplier of the TriStar engine) over the brink. In giving evidence to the U.S. Congress, Lockheed argued that the TriStar program was commercially attractive and that sales would eventually exceed the break-even point of about 200 aircraft. But in calculating this break-even point Lockheed appears to have ignored the opportunity cost of the huge capital investment in the project. Lockheed probably needed to sell about 500 aircraft to reach a zero net present value.[3]

CHECK POINT 8.4

What is the basic difference between sensitivity analysis and break-even analysis?

OPERATING LEVERAGE

A project's break-even point depends on both its *fixed costs,* which do not vary with sales, and the profit on each extra sale. Managers often face a trade-off between these variables. For example, we typically think of rental expenses as fixed costs. But supermarket companies sometimes rent stores with contingent rent agreements. This means that the amount of rent the company pays is tied to the level of sales from the store. Rent rises and falls along with sales. The store thus replaces a fixed cost with a *variable cost* that rises along with sales. Because a greater proportion of the company's expenses will fall when its sales fall, its break-even point is reduced.

Of course, a high proportion of fixed costs is not all bad. The firm whose costs are largely fixed fares poorly when demand is low, but it may make a killing during a boom. Let us illustrate.

Finefodder has a policy of hiring long-term employees who will not be laid off except in the most dire circumstances. For all intents and purposes, these salaries are fixed costs. Its rival, Stop and Scoff, has a much smaller permanent labour force and uses expensive temporary help whenever demand for its product requires extra staff. A greater proportion of its labour expenses are therefore variable costs.

Suppose that if Finefodder adopted its rival's policy, fixed costs in its new superstore would fall from $2 million to $1.56 million but variable costs would rise from 81.25 to 84 percent of sales. Table 8.6 shows that with the normal level of sales, the two policies fare

[3] The true break-even point for the TriStar program is estimated in U. E. Reinhardt, "Break-Even Analysis for Lockheed's TriStar: An Application of Financial Theory," *Journal of Finance* 28 (September 1973), pp. 821–838.

equally. In a slump a store that relies on temporary labour does better since its costs fall along with revenue. In a boom the reverse is true and the store with the higher proportion of fixed costs has the advantage.

operating leverage Degree to which costs are fixed.

degree of operating leverage (DOL) Percentage change in profits given a 1 percent change in sales.

If Finefodder follows its normal policy of hiring long-term employees, each extra dollar of sales results in a change of \$1.00 – \$.8125 = \$.1875 in pretax profits. If it uses temporary labour, an extra dollar of sales leads to a change of only \$1.00 – \$.84 = \$.16 in profits. As a result, a store with high fixed costs is said to have high **operating leverage.** High operating leverage magnifies the effect on profits of a fluctuation in sales.

We can measure a business's operating leverage by asking how much pretax profits, or EBIT, change for each 1 percent change in sales. The **degree of operating leverage,** often abbreviated as **DOL,** is this measure.

$$\mathbf{DOL} = \frac{\textbf{percentage change in profits}}{\textbf{percentage change in sales}} \tag{8.2}$$

For example, Table 8.6 shows that as the store moves from normal conditions to boom, sales increase from \$16 million to \$19 million, a rise of 18.75 percent. For the policy with high fixed costs, profits increase from \$550,000 to \$1,112,000, a rise of 102.2 percent. Therefore,

$$\text{DOL} = \frac{102.2}{18.75} = 5.45$$

The percentage change in sales is magnified more than fivefold in terms of the percentage impact on profits.

Now look at the operating leverage of the store if it uses the policy with low fixed costs but high variable costs. As the store moves from normal times to boom, profits increase from \$550,000 to \$1,030,000, a rise of 87.3 percent. Therefore,

$$\text{DOL} = \frac{87.3}{18.75} = 4.65$$

Because some costs remain fixed, a change in sales continues to have a magnified effect on profits but the degree of operating leverage is lower.

In fact, one can show that degree of operating leverage depends on fixed charges (including depreciation) in the following manner:[4]

$$\mathbf{DOL} = 1 + \frac{\textbf{fixed costs}}{\textbf{profits}} \tag{8.3}$$

This relationship makes it clear that operating leverage increases with fixed costs.

[4] This formula for DOL can be derived as follows. If sales increase by 1 percent, then variable costs also should increase by 1 percent, and profits will increase by .01 × (sales – variable costs) = .01 × (profits + fixed costs). Now recall the definition of DOL:

$$\begin{aligned}\text{DOL} &= \frac{\text{percentage change in profits}}{\text{percentage change in sales}} = \frac{\text{change in profits/level of profits}}{.01}\\ &= 100 \times \frac{\text{change in profits}}{\text{level of profits}} = 100 \times \frac{.01 \times (\text{profits} + \text{fixed costs})}{\text{level of profits}}\\ &= 1 + \frac{\text{fixed costs}}{\text{profits}}\end{aligned}$$

TABLE 8.6
A store with high operating leverage performs relatively badly in a slump but flourishes in a boom (figures in thousands of dollars)

	High Fixed Costs			High Variable Costs		
	Slump	**Normal**	**Boom**	**Slump**	**Normal**	**Boom**
Sales	13,000	16,000	19,000	13,000	16,000	19,000
– Variable costs	10,563	13,000	15,438	10,920	13,440	15,960
– Fixed costs	2,000	2,000	2,000	1,560	1,560	1,560
– Depreciation	450	450	450	450	450	450
= Pretax profit	–13	550	1,112	70	550	1,030

▸ EXAMPLE 8.4 *Operating Leverage*

Suppose the firm adopts the high-fixed-cost policy. Then fixed costs including depreciation will be 2.00 + .45 = \$2.45 million. Since the store produces profits of \$.55 million at a normal level of sales, DOL should be

$$\text{DOL} = 1 + \frac{\text{fixed costs}}{\text{profits}} = 1 + \frac{2.00 + .45}{.55} = 5.45$$

This value matches the one we obtained by comparing the actual percentage changes in sales and profits.

You can see from this example that the risk of a project is affected by the degree of operating leverage. If a large proportion of the costs is fixed, a shortfall in sales has a magnified effect on profits.

We will have more to say about risk in the next three chapters.

☑ CHECK POINT 8.5

Suppose that sales increase by 10 percent from the values in the normal scenario. Compute the percentage change in pretax profits from the normal level for both policies in Table 8.6. Compare your answers to the values predicted by the DOL formula.

8.4 Flexibility in Capital Budgeting

Sensitivity analysis and break-even analysis help managers understand why a venture might fail. Once you know this you can decide whether it is worth investing more time and effort in trying to resolve the uncertainty.

Of course, it is impossible to clear up all doubts about the future. Therefore, managers also try to build flexibility into a project and they value more highly the project that allows them to mitigate the effect of unpleasant surprises and capitalize on pleasant ones.

DECISION TREES

The scientists of MacCaugh have developed a diet whiskey and the firm is ready to go ahead with pilot production and test marketing. The preliminary phase will take a year and cost \$200,000. Management feels that there is only a 50-50 chance that the pilot production and market tests will be successful. If they are, then MacCaugh will build a \$2 million plant which will generate an expected annual cash flow in perpetuity of \$480,000 a year after taxes. Given an opportunity cost of capital of 12 percent, project NPV in this case will be –\$2 million + \$480,000/.12 = \$2 million. If the tests are not successful, MacCaugh will discontinue the project and the cost of the pilot production will be wasted. How can MacCaugh decide whether to spend the money on the pilot program?

Notice that the only decision MacCaugh needs to make now is whether to go ahead with the preliminary phase. Depending on how that works out, it may choose to go ahead with full-scale production.

decision tree Diagram of sequential decisions and possible outcomes.

When faced with projects like this that involve sequential decisions, it is often helpful to draw a **decision tree,** as in Figure 8.3. You can think of the problem as a game between MacCaugh and fate. The square represents a decision point for MacCaugh and the circle represents a decision point for fate. MacCaugh starts the play at the left-hand box. If MacCaugh decides to test, then fate will cast the enchanted dice and decide the result of the tests. Given the test results, the firm faces a second decision: Should it invest \$2 million and start full-scale production?

The second-stage decision is obvious: *Invest if the tests indicate that NPV is positive, and stop if they indicate that NPV would be negative.* Now the firm can easily decide between paying for the test program or stopping immediately. The net present value of stopping is zero, so the first-stage decision boils down to a simple problem: Should MacCaugh invest \$200,000 now to obtain a 50 percent chance of a project with an NPV of \$2 million a year later? If payoffs of zero and \$2 million are equally likely, the *expected* payoff is (.5 × 0) + (.5 × 2 million) = \$1 million. Thus the pilot project offers an expected payoff of \$1 million on an investment of \$200,000. At any reasonable cost of capital, this is a good deal.

✔ CHECK POINT 8.6

Goody Foods has developed choc-o-spice cookies with a distinct flavour it believes will be popular with young people. The product will be test-marketed in Atlantic Canada for 2 years. It requires an initial investment of \$2 million, and because of heavy promotional expenses, it is not expected to generate any positive cash flows after tax (CFAT) during the first 2 years. There is a 60 percent chance that demand for the choc-o-spice cookies

FIGURE 8.3
Decision tree

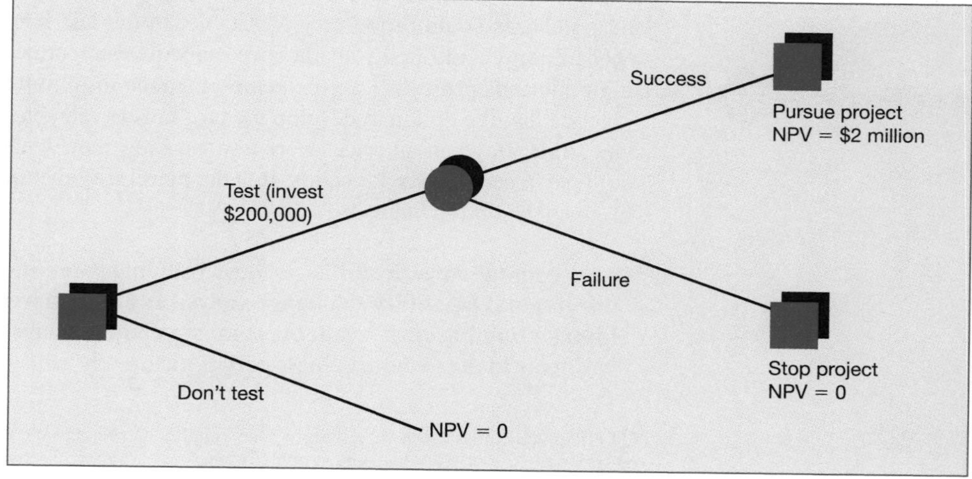

will be satisfactory; if that is so, a further investment cost of $5 million will be incurred in Year 2 to market the cookies nationwide. The subsequent CFATs expected are $4 million, $7 million, and $6 million, in years 3, 4, and 5, respectively. The cookies will be withdrawn from the market if the test-market results are unfavourable (a 40 percent chance) in Year 2.

Goody Foods considers the project to be of average risk, with a 15 percent opportunity cost of capital. The company intends to use net present value analysis to determine whether it will be worthwhile to go forward with the project. What decision should the company make?

THE OPTION TO EXPAND

Notice that MacCaugh's expenditure on the pilot program buys a valuable managerial option. The firm has the *option* to produce the new product depending on the outcome of the tests. If the pilot program turns up disappointing results, the firm can walk away from the project without incurring additional costs.

The option to walk away once the results are revealed introduces a valuable asymmetry. Good outcomes can be exploited, while bad outcomes can be limited by cancelling the project.

MacCaugh was not obliged to have a pilot program. Instead, it could have gone directly into full-scale whiskey production. After all, if diet whiskey is a success, the sooner MacCaugh can clean up the market the better. But it is possible that the product will *not* take off; in which case the expenditure on the pilot operation may help the firm avoid a costly mistake. When it proposed a pilot project, MacCaugh's management was simply following the fundamental rule of swimmers: If you know the water temperature (and depth), dive in; if you don't, try putting a toe in first.

Here is another example of an apparently unprofitable investment that has value because of the flexibility it gives to make further follow-on investments. Some of the world's largest oil reserves are found in the Athabasca tar sands of Alberta. Until recently, the cost of extracting oil from the sands was substantially higher than the current market price, and almost certainly higher than most people's estimate of the likely price in the future. Yet oil companies were prepared to pay considerable sums for these tracts of barren land. Why?

The answer is that ownership of these tracts gives the companies an option. They are not obliged to extract the oil. If oil prices remain below the cost of extraction, the Athabasca sands remain undeveloped. But if prices rise above the cost of extraction, those land purchases could prove very profitable. In the last few years, oil companies such as Suncor Energy and Shell Canada have made investment commitments of billions of dollars in oil sands projects, (see the nearby Finance in Action box).

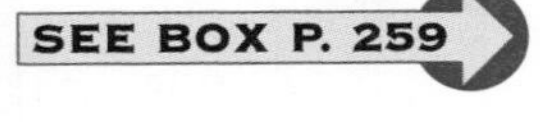

Notice that the option to develop the tar sands is valuable because the future price of oil is uncertain. If, when oil prices were low, we *knew* they would remain at that level, nobody would pay a cent for the tar sands. It is the possibility that oil prices will fluctuate sharply that gives the option value.[5]

As a general rule, flexibility is most valuable when the future is most uncertain. The ability to change course as events develop and new information becomes available is most valuable when it is hard to predict with confidence what the best action ultimately will turn out to be.

[5] Oil prices sometimes move very sharply. They roughly halved between the beginning of 1997 and the end of 1998. By early 2000, they had almost trebled.

FINANCE IN ACTION

Syncrude Consortium's Staged Investment in Alberta's Oil Sands Operations

Buoyed by market and political momentum, Syncrude Canada Ltd., the consortium that runs northern Alberta's largest oil sands operation, will seek owner approval by July for the next and largest stage of its $8 billion expansion.

The Imperial Oil–led plant has also begun work on Stage 4, the final stage of its Syncrude 21 suite of projects, which may be larger than originally planned, Eric Newell, chairperson and chief executive, said in an interview.

"We continue at Syncrude to spend between $30 million and $40 million a year on research and development and we are continuing to find better ways. And who knows, you may see that investment even larger," he said. "The oil sands has a tremendous future and Syncrude is going to continue to be a major player."

Under current estimates, Stage 4 calls for investment of about $2.3 billion to boost production by about 100,000 barrels a day to raise Syncrude's output to 465,000 barrels a day, or 25 percent of Canada's crude oil requirements, upon the project's completion at the end of the decade.

Shell Canada Ltd.'s own expansion, which peaks this year, was scheduled to be near completion by mid-2002, while Suncor Energy, Inc.'s is already past its peak and wrapping up this year.

Shell has said the cost of its $3.5 billion Athabasca oil sands project could escalate by about 15 percent because of a tight market for skilled labour. Suncor suggested similar cost pressures could further increase its expansion costs, which have already jumped to $2.8 billion from original estimates of about $2 billion.

Newell said he is encouraged by political attention but said new development must wait until those projects already underway were completed.

"In 1995, we didn't have any projects going ahead, and now we have $51 billion in terms of announced projects," he said. "It's hard for me to imagine that we could entertain more right now." He added that the oil sands reserves, which rival those of Saudi Arabia, offer opportunities for more expansion as long as governments stand aside and let the market work.

Source: Excerpted from Claudia Cattaneo, "Syncrude Staged for $8 Billion Expansion: Consortium to Seek Approval for Go-Ahead in July," *The National Post*, March 25, 2002, p. C7.

You can probably think of many other investments that take on added value because of the further opportunities that they may open up. For example, when designing a factory, it may make sense to provide for the possibility in the future of an additional production line; when building a four-lane highway, it may pay to build six-lane bridges so that the road can be converted later to six lanes if traffic volume turns out to be higher than expected.

ABANDONMENT OPTIONS

If the option to expand has value, what about the option to bail out? Projects don't just go on until the equipment disintegrates. The decision to terminate a project is usually taken by management, not by nature. Once the project is no longer profitable, the company will cut its losses and exercise its option to abandon the project.

Some assets are easier to bail out of than others. Tangible assets are usually easier to sell than intangible ones. It helps to have active secondhand markets, which really exist only for standardized, widely used items. Real estate, airplanes, trucks, and certain machine tools are likely to be relatively easy to sell. On the other hand, the knowledge accumulated by a drug company's research and development program is a specialized intangible asset and probably would not have significant abandonment value. Some assets, such as old mattresses, even have negative abandonment value; you have to pay to get rid of them. It is very costly to decommission nuclear power plants or to reclaim land that has been strip-mined. Managers recognize the option to abandon when they make the initial investment.

▸ EXAMPLE 8.5 *Abandonment Option*

Suppose that the Wigeon Company must choose between two technologies for the manufacture of a new product, a Wankel engine outboard motor:

1. Technology A uses custom-designed machinery to produce the complex shapes required for Wankel engines at low cost. But if the Wankel engine doesn't sell, this equipment will be worthless.
2. Technology B uses standard machine tools. Labour costs are much higher, but the tools can easily be sold if the motor doesn't sell.

Technology A looks better in an NPV analysis of the new product, because it was designed to have the lowest possible cost at the planned production volume. Yet you can sense the advantage of technology B's flexibility if you are unsure whether the new outboard will sink or swim in the marketplace.

When you are unsure about the success of a venture, you may wish to choose a flexible technology with a good resale market to preserve the option to abandon the project at low cost.

CHECK POINT 8.7

Consider a firm operating a copper mine that incurs both variable and fixed costs of production. Suppose the mine can be shut down temporarily if copper prices fall below the variable cost of mining copper. Why is this a valuable operating option? How does it increase the NPV of the mine to the operator?

FLEXIBLE PRODUCTION FACILITIES

Companies try to avoid becoming dependent on a single source of raw materials, building flexibility into their production facilities whenever possible. For example, at current prices gas-fired industrial boilers are cheaper to operate than oil-fired ones. Yet most companies prefer to buy boilers that can use *either* oil *or* natural gas, even though these dual-fired boilers cost more than a gas-fired boiler.[6] The reason is obvious. If gas prices rise relative to oil prices, the dual-fired boiler gives the company a valuable option to switch to low-cost oil. In effect the company has the option to exchange one asset (an oil-fired boiler) for another (a gas-fired boiler).

If the firm is uncertain about the future demand for its products, it may also build in the option to vary the output mix. For example, in recent years automobile manufacturers have made major investments in flexible production facilities that allow them to change their output rapidly in response to consumer demand.

INVESTMENT TIMING OPTIONS

Suppose that you have a project that might be a big winner or a big loser. The project's upside potential outweighs its downside potential, and it has a positive NPV if undertaken

[6] See N. Kulatilaka, "The Value of Flexibility: The Case of a Dual-Fuel Industrial Steam Boiler," *Financial Management* 22 (Autumn 1993), pp. 271–280.

today. However, the project is not "now-or-never." Should you invest right away or wait? It's hard to say. If the project truly is a winner, waiting means loss or deferral of its early cash flows. But if it turns out to be a loser, it may pay to wait and get a better fix on the likely demand.

You can think of any project proposal as giving you the *option* to invest today. You don't have to exercise that option immediately. Instead you need to weigh the value of the cash flows lost by delaying against the possibility that you will pick up some valuable information.

Think again of those tar sands in Athabasca. Suppose that the price of oil is at 10 cents a barrel above your cost of production. You can extract the oil profitably at this price, and the required investment has a small positive NPV if the price stays where it is. But it still might be worth delaying production. After all, if the price plummets, you will by waiting avoid a costly mistake. If it rises further, however, you can invest and make a killing.

We repeat, it is because the future is so uncertain that managers value flexibility. Ideally, a project will give the firm an option to expand if things go well and to bail out or switch production if they don't. In addition, it may pay the firm to postpone the project.

Some managers treat capital investment decisions as black boxes; they are handed cash-flow forecasts and they churn out present values without looking inside the black box. But successful firms ask not only what could be wrong with the forecasts but whether there are opportunities to respond to surprises. In other words, they recognize the value of flexibility.

CHECK POINT 8.8

Investments in new products or production capacity often include an option to expand. What are the other major types of options encountered in capital investment decisions?

8.5 Capital Budgeting Practices in Canadian Firms

How do Canadian firms make their capital budgeting decisions? Over the years, several studies have attempted to answer this question. A survey of the capital budgeting practices of large Canadian firms and foreign firms operating in Canada in the 1990s concluded that most firms used multiple capital budgeting methods to assess capital investments.[7] Table 8.7 provides partial results from the survey.

The study notes that discounted cash flow (DCF) methods, including NPV and IRR techniques, were used by more than 75 percent of respondents to evaluate different types of projects, such as expansion of existing operations, expansion into new operations, foreign operations, and leasing. The propensity to use DCF techniques increased with the complexity of the project decision. Of the DCF methods, IRR was used more frequently than NPV in every instance except leasing. The payback method was also common; and noticeably more frequent when it was employed in conjunction with DCF methods as part of a multiple criteria evaluation.

For purposes of cash-flow forecasting, quantitative methods—particularly sensitivity analysis—were used by 39.5 percent of respondents. This may reflect the popularity among firms of PC-based spreadsheet programs. Most of these respondents also indicated

[7] See V. M. Jog and A. K. Srivastava, "Capital Budgeting Practices in Corporate Canada," *Financial Practice and Education* 5 (Fall/Winter 1995), pp. 37–43.

TABLE 8.7
Propensity to use various capital budgeting techniques[1]

Models Used	Replacement Projects (%)	Expansion—Existing Operations (%)	Expansion—New Operations (%)	Foreign Operations (%)	Abandonment (%)	Leasing (%)
ARR/Book Rate of Return	14.9	17.5	19.9	14.6	15.2	9.3
IRR	51.2	64.3	65.1	67.0	28.3	44.9
NPV	38.0	42.9	47.6	47.6	41.3	53.3
Payback	53.7	52.4	50.0	50.0	21.7	17.8
DCF Methods	66.1	80.9	84.9	80.5	53.3	77.6

[1] The numbers indicate the percentage of respondents citing the use of a particular technique either alone or in combination with other techniques.

Source: V. M. Jog and A. K. Srivastava, "Capital Budgeting Practices in Corporate Canada," *Financial Practice and Education* 5 (Fall/Winter 1995), pp. 37–43.

that they used quantitative methods together with qualitative methods, such as management's subjective estimates, which suggests the importance of strategic considerations in capital budgeting decisions. Surprisingly, 18 percent of the respondents did not use any quantitative methods at all, and at least one-quarter of the respondents did not have a formal risk analysis technique in use.

8.6 Summary

1. **What are some of the practical problems of capital budgeting in large corporations?**

For most large corporations there are two stages in the investment process: the preparation of the **capital budget,** which is a list of planned investments, and the authorization process for individual projects. This process is usually a cooperative effort.

Investment projects should never be selected through a purely mechanical process. Managers need to ask why a project should have a positive NPV. A positive NPV is plausible only if the company has some competitive advantage that prevents its rivals from stealing most of the gains.

2. **How are sensitivity, scenario, and break-even analyses used to see the effects of forecasting errors on project profitability? Why is an overestimate of sales more serious for projects with high operating leverage?**

Good managers realize that the forecasts behind NPV calculations are imperfect. Therefore, they explore the consequences of a poor forecast and check whether it is worth doing some more homework. They use the following principal tools to answer these what-if questions:

- **Sensitivity analysis,** where one variable at a time is changed.
- **Scenario analysis,** where the manager looks at the project under alternative scenarios.
- **Simulation analysis,** an extension of scenario analysis in which a computer generates hundreds or thousands of possible combinations of variables.
- **Break-even analysis,** where the focus is on how far sales could fall before the project begins to lose money. Often the phrase "lose money" is defined in terms of accounting losses, but it makes more sense to define it as "failing to cover the opportunity cost of capital"—in other words, as a negative NPV.
- **Operating leverage,** the degree to which costs are fixed. A project's break-even point will be affected by the extent to which costs can be reduced as sales decline. If the project has mostly **fixed costs,** it is said to have *high operating leverage.* High operating leverage implies that profits are more sensitive to changes in sales.

3. **Why is managerial flexibility important in capital budgeting?**

Some projects may take on added value because they give the firm the option to bail out if things go wrong or to capitalize on success by expanding. We showed how **decision trees** may be used to analyze such flexibility.

4. **How do Canadian firms make their capital budgeting decisions?**

A survey reports that most firms use multiple capital budgeting methods to assess capital investments, including the NPV, IRR, and payback rules. For purposes of cash-flow forecasting, firms use quantitative methods, such as sensitivity analysis, as well as qualitative methods, such as management's subjective estimates. Strategic considerations are very important in capital budgeting decisions.

RELATED WEB LINKS

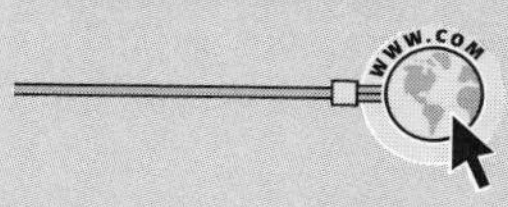

www.windpower.dk/tour/econ/econ.htm Evaluation of a sample energy-saving project
www.palisade.com Software for Monte Carlo analysis
www.suncor.com
www.lockheedmartin.com

KEY TERMS

capital budget	243	scenario analysis	248	degree of operating leverage (DOL)	255
sensitivity analysis	245	simulation analysis	248	decision tree	257
fixed costs	246	break-even analysis	249		
variable costs	246	operating leverage	255		

QUESTIONS AND PROBLEMS

*Answers in Appendix B

BASIC

*1. **Fixed and Variable Costs.** In a slow year, Wimpy's Burgers will produce 1 million hamburgers at a total cost of $1.75 million. In a good year, it can produce 2 million hamburgers at a total cost of $2.25 million. What are the fixed and variable costs of hamburger production?

2. **Average Cost.** Reconsider Wimpy's Burgers from problem 1.
   a. What is the average cost per burger when the firm produces 1 million hamburgers?
   b. What is average cost when the firm produces 2 million hamburgers?
   c. Why is average cost lower when more burgers are produced?

3. **Sensitivity Analysis.** A project currently generates sales of $10 million, variable costs equal to 50 percent of sales, and fixed costs of $2 million. The firm's tax rate is 35 percent. What are the effects of the following changes on after-tax profits and cash flows?
   a. Sales increase from $10 million to $11 million.
   b. Variable costs increase to 60 percent of sales.

PRACTICE

*4. **Sensitivity Analysis.** The project in the preceding problem will last for 10 years. The discount rate is 12 percent.
   a. What is the effect on project NPV of each of the changes considered in the problem?
   b. If project NPV under the base-case scenario is $2 million, how much can fixed costs increase before NPV turns negative?
   c. How much can fixed costs increase before accounting profits turn negative?

*5. **Sensitivity Analysis.** Emperor's Clothes Fashions can invest $5 million in a new plant for producing invisible makeup. The plant has an expected life of 5 years, and expected sales are 6 million jars of makeup a year. Fixed costs are $2 million a year, and variable costs are $1 per jar. The product will be priced at $2 per jar. The plant will be depreciated straight-line over 5 years to a salvage value of zero. The opportunity cost of capital is 12 percent, and the tax rate is 40 percent.
   a. What is project NPV under these base-case assumptions?
   b. What is NPV if variable costs turn out to be $1.20 per jar?
   c. What is NPV if fixed costs turn out to be $1.5 million per year?
   d. At what price per jar would the project NPV equal zero?

6. **Scenario Analysis.** The most likely outcomes for a particular project are estimated as follows:

Unit price:	$50
Variable cost:	$30
Fixed cost:	$300,000
Expected sales:	30,000 units per year

However, you recognize that some of these estimates are subject to error. Suppose that each variable may turn out to be either 10 percent higher or 10 percent lower than the initial estimate. The project will last for 10 years and requires an initial investment of $1 million, which will be depreciated straight-line over the project life to a final value of zero. The firm's tax rate is 35 percent and the required rate of return is 14 percent. What is project NPV in the "best-case" scenario, that is, assuming all variables take on the best possible value? What about the "worst-case" scenario?

7. **Scenario Analysis.** Reconsider the best- and worst-case scenarios in the previous problem. In terms of the combination of variables, do the best- and worst-case outcomes seem reasonable when each variable is treated independently? For example, if price is higher than predicted, is it more or less likely that cost is higher than predicted? What other relationships may exist among the variables?

8. **Break-Even.** The following estimates have been prepared for a project under consideration:

Fixed costs:	$20,000
Depreciation:	$10,000
Price:	$2
Accounting break-even:	60,000 units

What must be the variable cost per unit?

*9. **Break-Even.** Dime a Dozen Diamonds makes synthetic diamonds by treating carbon. Each diamond can be sold for $100. The materials cost for a standard diamond is $30. The fixed costs incurred each year for factory upkeep and administrative expenses are $200,000. The machinery costs $1 million and is depreciated straight-line over 10 years to a salvage value of zero.

a. What is the accounting break-even level of sales in terms of number of diamonds sold?
b. What is the NPV break-even level of sales assuming a tax rate of 35 percent, a 10-year project life, and a discount rate of 12 percent?

10. **Break-Even.** Turn back to problem 9.

a. Would the accounting break-even point in the first year of operation increase or decrease if the machinery were depreciated over a 5-year period?
b. Would the NPV break-even point increase or decrease if the machinery were depreciated over a 5-year period?

*11. **Break-Even.** You are evaluating a project that will require an investment of $10 million that will be depreciated over a period of 7 years. You are concerned that the corporate tax rate will increase during the life of the project. Would such an increase affect the accounting break-even point? Would it affect the NPV break-even point?

*12. **Break-Even.** Define the *cash-flow break-even point* as the sales volume (in dollars) at which cash flow equals zero. Is the cash-flow break-even level of sales higher or lower than the zero-profit break-even point?

13. **Break-Even and NPV.** If a project operates at cash-flow break-even (see problem 12) for its entire life, what must be true of the project's NPV?

*14. **Break-Even.** Modern Artifacts can produce keepsakes that will be sold for $80 each. Nondepreciated fixed costs are $1,000 per year and variable costs are $60 per unit.

a. If the project requires an initial investment of $3,000 and is expected to last for 5 years and the firm pays no taxes, what are the accounting and NPV break-even levels of sales? The initial investment will be depreciated straight-line over 5 years to a final value of zero, and the discount rate is 10 percent.

b. How do your answers change if the firm's tax rate is 40 percent?

*15. **Break-Even.** A financial analyst based in the United States has computed both accounting and NPV break-even sales levels for a project under consideration using straight-line depreciation over a 6-year period. The project manager wants to know what will happen to these estimates if the firm uses depreciation calculated on the basis of the Modified Accelerated Cost Recovery System (MACRS). Firms in the United States are allowed by the Internal Revenue Service to depreciate their equipment for tax purposes using this system. The capital investment will be in a 5-year recovery period class under MACRS rules. Under the rules, applicable percentage depreciation rates over years 1 to 6 will be 20, 32, 19.20, 11.52, 11.52 and 5.76, so the firm will be able to use higher rates in earlier years. The firm is in a 35 percent tax bracket.

a. What (qualitatively) will happen to the accounting break-even level of sales in the first years of the project?

b. What (qualitatively) will happen to the NPV break-even level of sales?

c. If you were advising the analyst, would the answer to (a) or (b) be important to you? Specifically, would you say that the switch to MACRS makes the project more or less attractive?

16. **Break-Even.** Reconsider Finefodder's new superstore. Suppose that by initially investing an additional $600,000 in more efficient checkout equipment, Finefodder could reduce variable costs to 80 percent of sales.

a. Using the base-case assumptions (Table 8.1), find the NPV of this alternative scheme. *Hint:* Remember to focus on the *incremental* cash flows from the project.

b. At what level of sales will accounting profits be unchanged if the firm invests in the new equipment? Assume the equipment receives the same 12-year straight-line depreciation treatment as in the original example. *Hint:* Focus on the project's incremental effects on fixed and variable costs.

c. What is the NPV break-even point?

*17. **Break-Even and NPV.** If the superstore project (see the previous problem) operates at accounting break-even, will net present value be positive or negative?

18. **Operating Leverage.** You estimate that your cattle farm will generate $1 million of profits on sales of $4 million under normal economic conditions, and that the degree of operating leverage is 7.5. What will profits be if sales turn out to be $3.5 million? What if they are $4.5 million?

19. **Operating Leverage.**

a. What is the degree of operating leverage of Modern Artifacts (in problem 14) when sales are $8,000?

b. What is the degree of operating leverage when sales are $10,000?

c. Why is operating leverage different at these two levels of sales?

*20. **Operating Leverage.** What is the lowest possible value for the degree of operating leverage for a profitable firm? Show with a numerical example that if Modern Artifacts (see problem 14*a*) has zero fixed costs, then DOL = 1, and in fact, sales and profits are directly proportional so that a 1 percent change in sales results in a 1 percent change in profits.

21. **Operating Leverage.** A project has fixed costs of $1,000 per year, depreciation charges of $500 a year, revenue of $6,000 a year, and variable costs equal to two-thirds of revenues.

a. If sales increase by 5 percent, what will be the increase in pretax profits?

b. What is the degree of operating leverage of this project?

c. Confirm that the percentage change in profits equals DOL times the percentage change in sales.

22. **Project Options.** Your midrange guess as to the amount of oil in a prospective field is 10 million barrels, but in fact there is a 50 percent chance that the amount of oil is 15 million barrels, and a 50 per-

cent chance of 5 million barrels. If the actual amount of oil is 15 million barrels, the present value of the cash flows from drilling will be $8 million. If the amount is only 5 million barrels, the present value will be only $2 million. It costs $3 million to drill the well. Suppose that a seismic test that costs $100,000 can verify the amount of oil under the ground. Is it worth paying for the test? Use a decision tree to justify your answer.

*23. **Project Options.** A silver mine can yield 10,000 ounces of copper at a variable cost of $8 per ounce. The fixed costs of operating the mine are $10,000 per year. In half the years, silver can be sold for $12 per ounce; in the other years, silver can be sold for only $6 per ounce. Ignore taxes.

a. What is the average cash flow you will receive from the mine if it is always kept in operation and the silver is always sold in the year it is mined?
b. Now suppose you can shut down the mine in years of low silver prices. What happens to the average cash flow from the mine?

24. **Project Options.** An auto plant that costs $100 million to build can produce a new line of cars that will produce cash flows with a present value of $140 million if the line is successful, but only $50 million if it is unsuccessful. You believe that the probability of success is only about 50 percent.

a. Would you build the plant?
b. Suppose that the plant can be sold for $90 million to another automaker if the auto line is not successful. Now would you build the plant?
c. Illustrate the option to abandon in (b) using a decision tree.

25. **Production Options.** Explain why options to expand or contract production are most valuable when forecasts about future business conditions are most uncertain.

CHALLENGE

26. **Decision Tree.** Zoom Technologies, Inc., is considering expanding its operations into digital music devices. Zoom anticipates an initial investment of $1.3 million and, at best, an operational life of 3 years for the project. Zoom's management team has considered several probable outcomes over the life of the project, which it has labelled as either "successes" or "failures." Accordingly, Zoom anticipates that in the first year of operations there is a 65 percent chance of "success," with after-tax cash flow of $800,000, or a 35 percent chance of "failure," with a meagre $1,000 cash flow after tax.

If the project "succeeds" in the first year, Zoom expects three probable outcomes regarding net cash flows after tax in the second year. These outcomes are $2.2 million, $1.8 million, or $1.5 million, with probabilities of 0.3, 0.5, and 0.2, respectively. In the third and final year of operation, the net cash flows after tax are expected to be either $35,000 more or $55,000 less than they were in Year 2, with an equal chance of occurrence.

If, on the other hand, the project "fails" in Year 1, there is a 60 percent chance that it will produce net cash flows after tax of only $1,500 in years 2 and 3. There is also a 40 percent chance that it will really fail, Zoom will earn nothing in Year 2, and will get out of this line of business, terminating the project and resulting in no net cash flows after tax in Year 3.

The opportunity cost of capital for Zoom Technologies is 10 percent.

a. Construct a decision tree representing the possible outcomes.
b. Determine the joint probability of each possible sequence of events.
c. What is the project's expected NPV?

*27. **Abandonment Option.** Hit or Miss Sports is introducing a new product this year. If its see-at-night soccer balls are a hit, the firm expects to be able to sell 50,000 units a year at a price of $60 each. If the new product is a bust, only 30,000 units can be sold at a price of $55. The variable cost of each ball is $30 and fixed costs are zero. The cost of the manufacturing equipment is $6 million, and the project life is estimated at 10 years. The firm will use straight-line depreciation over the 10-year life of the project. The firm's tax rate is 35 percent and the discount rate is 12 percent.

a. If each outcome is equally likely, what is the expected NPV? Will the firm accept the project?
b. Suppose now that the firm can abandon the project and sell off the manufacturing equipment for $5.4 million if demand for the balls turns out to be weak. The firm will make the decision to continue or abandon after the first year of sales. Does the option to abandon change the firm's decision to accept the project?

28. **Expansion Option.** Now suppose that Hit or Miss Sports from the previous problem can expand production if the project is successful. By paying its workers overtime, it can increase production by 20,000 units; the variable cost of each ball will be higher, equal to $35 per unit. By how much does this option to expand production increase the NPV of the project?

SOLUTIONS TO CHECK POINTS

8.1 Cash flow forecasts for Finefodder's new superstore:

	Year 0	Years 1–12
Investment		–5,400,000
1. Sales		16,000,000
2. Variable costs		13,280,000
3. Fixed costs		2,000,000
4. Depreciation		450,000
5. Pretax profit (1 – 2 – 3 – 4)		270,000
6. Taxes (at 40%)		108,000
7. Profit after tax		162,000
8. Cash flow from operations (4 + 7)		612,000
Net cash flow	–5,400,000	612,000

NPV = –$5.4 million + (7.536 × $612,000) = –$788,000

8.2 Both calculate how NPV depends on input assumptions. Sensitivity analysis changes inputs one at a time, whereas scenario analysis changes several variables at once. The changes should add up to a consistent scenario for the project as a whole.

8.3 With the lower initial investment, depreciation is also lower; it now equals $417,000 per year. Cash flow is now as follows:

1. Variable costs	81.25 percent of sales
2. Fixed costs	$2 million
3. Depreciation	$417,000
4. Pretax profit	(.1875 × sales) – $2.417 million
5. Tax (at 40%)	.4 × (.1875 × sales – $2.417 million)
6. Profit after tax	.6 × (.1875 × sales – $2.417 million)
7. Cash flow (3 + 6)	.6 × (.1875 × sales – $2.417 million) + $417,000 = .1125 × sales – $1.033 million

Break-even occurs when

PV (cash inflows) = investment
7.536 × (.1125 × sales – $1.033 million) = $5.0 million
and sales = $15.08 million

8.4 Break-even analysis finds the level of sales or revenue at which NPV = 0. Sensitivity analysis changes these and other input variables to optimistic and pessimistic values and recalculates NPV.

8.5 Reworking Table 8.6 for the normal level of sales and 10 percent higher sales gives the following:

	High Fixed Costs		High Variable Costs	
	Normal	10% Higher Sales	Normal	10% Higher Sales
Sales	16,000	17,600	16,000	17,600
– Variable costs	13,000	14,300	13,440	14,784
– Fixed costs	2,000	2,000	1,560	1,560
– Depreciation	450	450	450	450
= Pretax profit	550	850	550	806

For the high-fixed-cost policy, profits increase by 54.5 percent, from $550,000 to $850,000. For the low-fixed-cost policy, profits increase by 46.5 percent. In both cases the percentage increase in profits equals DOL times the percentage increase in sales. This illustrates that DOL measures the sensitivity of profits to changes in sales.

8.6 A decision tree model for Goody Foods' choc-o-spice cookie project is provided below:

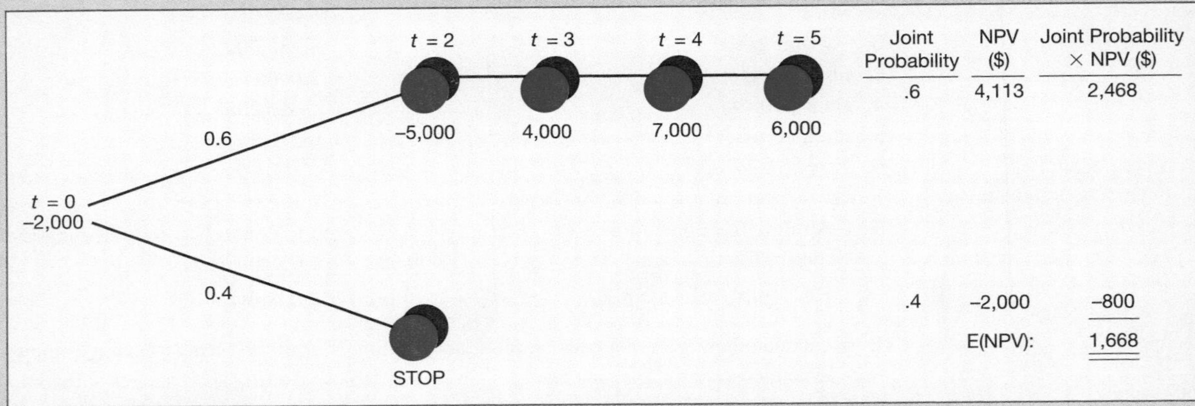

NPV analysis for satisfactory outcome (figure in thousands of dollars)

Year	Cash Flows ($)	Present Value = $1/(1.14)^t$	Discounted Cash Flows ($)
0	–2,000	1.0000	–2,000
1	—	.8772	
2	–5,000	.7695	–3,848
3	4,000	.6750	2,700
4	7,000	.5921	4,145
5	6,000	.5194	3,116
		NPV	4,113

8.7 The option to shut down is valuable because the mine operator can avoid incurring losses when copper prices are low. If the shut-down option were not available, cash flow in the low-price periods would be negative. With the option, the worst cash flow is zero. By allowing managers to respond to market conditions, the option makes the worst-case cash flow better than it would be otherwise. The average cash flow (that is, averaging over all possible scenarios) therefore must improve, which increases project NPV.

8.8 Abandonment options, options due to flexible production facilities, and investment timing options.

MINICASE

Maxine Peru, the CEO of Peru Resources, hardly noticed the plate of savoury quenelles de brochet and the glass of Corton Charlemagne '94 on the table before her. She was absorbed by the engineering report handed to her just as she entered the executive dining room.

The report described a proposed new mine on the North Ridge of Mt. Zircon. A vein of transcendental zirconium ore had been discovered there on land owned by Peru's company. Test borings indicated sufficient reserves to produce 340 tons per year of transcendental zirconium over a 7-year period.

The vein probably also contained hydrated zircon gemstones. The amount and quality of these zircons were hard to predict, since they tended to occur in "pockets." The new mine might come across one, two, or dozens of pockets. The mining engineer guessed that 150 pounds per year might be found. The current price for high-quality hydrated zircon gemstones was $3,300 per pound.

Peru Resources was a family-owned business with total assets of $45 million, including cash reserves of $4 million. The outlay required for the new mine would be a major commitment. Fortunately, Peru Resources was conservatively financed, and CEO Peru believed that the company could borrow up to $9 million at an interest rate of about 8 percent.

The mine's operating costs were projected at $900,000 per year, including $400,000 of fixed costs and $500,000 of variable costs. Peru thought these forecasts were accurate. The big question marks seemed to be the initial cost of the mine and the selling price of transcendental zirconium.

Opening the mine, and providing the necessary machinery and ore-crunching facilities, was supposed to cost $10 million, but cost overruns of 10 percent or 15 percent were common in the mining business. In addition, new environmental regulations, if enacted, could increase the cost of the mine by $1.5 million.

There was a cheaper design for the mine, which would reduce its cost by $1.7 million and eliminate much of the uncertainty about cost overruns. Unfortunately, this design would require much higher fixed operating costs. Fixed costs would increase to $850,000 per year at planned production levels.

The current price of transcendental zirconium was $10,000 per ton, but there was no consensus about future prices.[1] Some experts were projecting rapid price increases to as much as $14,000 per ton. On the other hand, there were pessimists saying that prices could be as low as $7,500 per ton. Peru did not have strong views either way: her best guess was that price would just increase with inflation at about 3.5 percent per year. (Mine operating costs would also increase with inflation.)

Peru had wide experience in the mining business, and she knew that investors in similar projects usually wanted a forecast nominal rate of return of at least 14 percent.

You have been asked to assist Peru in evaluating this project. Lay out the base-case NPV analysis and undertake sensitivity, scenario, or break-even analyses as appropriate. Assume that Peru Resources pays tax at a 35 percent rate. For simplicity, also assume that the investment in the mine could be depreciated for tax purposes straight-line over 7 years.

What forecasts or scenarios should worry Peru the most? Where would additional information be most helpful? Is there a case for delaying construction of the new mine?

[1] There were no traded forward or futures contracts on transcendental zirconium. See Chapter 26.

PART THREE

Risk

9 Introduction to Risk, Return, and the Opportunity Cost of Capital

10 Risk, Return, and Capital Budgeting

11 The Cost of Capital

CHAPTER 9

Introduction to Risk, Return, and the Opportunity Cost of Capital

9.1 Rates of Return: A Review

9.2 Seventy-Five Years of Capital Market History

9.3 Measuring Risk

9.4 Risk and Diversification

9.5 Thinking about Risk

9.6 Summary

We have thus far skirted the issue of project risk; now it is time to confront it head-on. We can no longer be satisfied with vague statements like "The opportunity cost of capital depends on the risk of the project." We need to know how to measure risk and we need to understand the relationship between risk and the cost of capital. These are the topics of the next two chapters.

Think for a moment what the cost of capital for a project means. It is the rate of return that shareholders could expect to earn if they invested in equally risky securities. So one way to estimate the cost of capital is to find securities that have the same risk as the project and then estimate the expected rate of return on these securities.

We start our analysis by looking at the rates of return earned in the past from different investments, concentrating on the *extra* return that investors have received for investing in risky rather than safe securities. We then show how to measure the risk of a portfolio by calculating its standard deviation and we look again at past history to find out how risky it is to invest in the stock market.

Finally, we explore the concept of diversification. Most investors do not put all their eggs into one basket—they diversify. Thus investors are not concerned with the risk of each security in isolation; instead they are concerned with how much it contributes to the risk of a diversified portfolio. We therefore need to distinguish between the risk that can be eliminated by diversification and the risk that cannot be eliminated.

After studying this chapter you should be able to

- Estimate the opportunity cost of capital for an "average risk" project.
- Calculate the standard deviation of returns for individual common stocks or for a stock portfolio.
- Understand why diversification reduces risk.
- Distinguish between unique risk, which can be diversified away, and market risk, which cannot.

9.1 Rates of Return: A Review

When investors buy a stock or a bond, their return comes in two forms: (1) a dividend or interest payment, and (2) a capital gain or a capital loss. For example, suppose you were lucky enough to buy the stock of Canadian Pacific at the beginning of 2000 when its price was about \$31 a share. By the end of the year the value of that investment had appreciated to \$42.75, giving a capital gain of \$42.75 – 31 = \$11.75. In addition, in 2000 Canadian Pacific paid a dividend of \$.56 a share.

The *percentage* return on your investment was therefore

$$\textbf{Percentage return} = \frac{\textbf{capital gain + dividend}}{\textbf{initial share price}} \tag{9.1}$$

$$= \frac{\$11.75 + \$.56}{\$31} = .397, \text{ or } 39.7\%$$

The percentage return can also be expressed as the sum of the *dividend yield* and *percentage capital gain.* The dividend yield is the dividend expressed as a percentage of the stock price at the beginning of the year:

$$\textbf{Dividend yield} = \frac{\textbf{dividend}}{\textbf{initial share price}} \tag{9.2}$$

$$= \frac{\$.56}{\$31} = .018, \text{ or } 1.8\%$$

Similarly, the percentage capital gain is

$$\textbf{Percentage capital gain} = \frac{\textbf{capital gain}}{\textbf{initial share price}} \tag{9.3}$$

$$= \frac{\$11.75}{\$31} = .379, \text{ or } 37.9\%$$

Thus the total return is the sum of 1.8% + 37.9% = 39.7%.

EXAMPLE 9.1 *Equivalent Annual Rate of Return*

Although a rate of return can be calculated over any time period—a day, a month, 5 years—the convention is to report annual rates of return. As we saw in Chapter 3, we need to calculate the equivalent annual rate. For example, suppose you bought a share of Canadian Pacific at the end of 2000 and sold it at the end of July, 2001, when the stock was at \$56.55 per share. The capital gain was \$56.55 – \$42.75 or \$13.8. Two dividends of \$0.14 each were also paid. The percentage rate of return was (\$13.8 + \$.28)/\$42.75 or 32.9 percent. Was this better than the 39.7 percent return earned in 2000? To compare, convert the 7-month return to its annual equivalent. One way to do this is to work out the *monthly* equivalent to 32.9 percent in 7 months, and then, convert the monthly rate to an annual rate. The monthly equivalent rate is $(1 + \text{7-month rate})^{1/7} - 1 = (1.329)^{1/7} - 1 = .04147$ or 4.147 percent per month. The annual equivalent rate of the monthly rate is $(1 + \text{1-month rate})^{12} - 1 = (1.04147)^{12} - 1 = .628$, or 62.8 percent per year.[1]

---

[1] We could have jumped directly to the annual equivalent rate by recognizing that a year is 12/7 of a 7-month period, making the annual equivalent rate equal to $(1.329)^{12/7} - 1$, or 62.8 percent.

Remember that in Chapter 3 we made a distinction between the *nominal* rate of return and the *real* rate of return. The nominal return measures how much more money you will have at the end of the year if you invest today. The 2000 return that we just calculated for Canadian Pacific stock is therefore a nominal return. The real rate of return tells you how much more you will be able to *buy* with your money at the end of the year. To convert from a nominal to a real rate of return, we use the following relationship:

$$\mathbf{1 + real\ rate\ of\ return = \frac{1 + nominal\ rate\ of\ return}{1 + inflation\ rate}} \tag{9.4}$$

In 2000, inflation was 3.2 percent. So we calculate the real rate of return on Canadian Pacific stock as follows:

$$1 + \text{real rate of return} = \frac{1.397}{1.032} = 1.354$$

Therefore, the real rate of return equals .354, or 35.4 percent. Fortunately, inflation in 2000 was moderate; the real return was only slightly less than the nominal return.

CHECK POINT 9.1

Suppose you buy a bond for $1,020 with a 15-year maturity paying an annual coupon of $80. A year later interest rates have dropped and the bond's price has increased to $1,050. What are your nominal and real rates of return? Assume the inflation rate is 4 percent.

9.2 Seventy-Five Years of Capital Market History

When you invest in a stock, you can't be sure that your annual return is going to be as high as that of Canadian Pacific in 2000 or 2001. But by looking at the history of security returns, you can get some idea of the return that investors might reasonably expect from investments in different types of securities and of the risks that they face. Let us look, therefore, at the risks and returns that investors have experienced in the past.

MARKET INDEXES

Investors can choose from an enormous number of different securities. Currently, about 1,550 common stocks trade on the Toronto Stock Exchange (TSX; www.tsx.ca), which list shares of large, established companies, and about 2,340 trade on the TSX Venture Exchange (also at www.tsx.ca), which lists new and smaller firms.[2] In addition, Canadian investors are free to cross-border shop in the U.S. and overseas markets. The New York Stock Exchange (NYSE), the major U.S. stock exchange, lists about 3,100 common stocks. Over 5,000 common stocks are traded through Nasdaq, a network of dealers linked by computer terminals and telephones. The London Stock Exchange lists common shares of more than 2,920 companies; it is Europe's largest stock exchange.

market index Measure of the investment performance of the overall market.

Financial analysts can't track every stock, so they rely on **market indexes** to summarize the return on different classes of securities. The primary stock market index in Canada

[2] The TSX Venture Exchange, formerly the Canadian Venture Exchange, CDNX, which was created through the merger of the Vancouver and Alberta Stock Exchanges, is owned by the TSX Group but maintains separate listing requirements. The Bourse de Montréal, formerly known as the Montreal Exchange, no longer lists stocks (it once listed over 800 common shares), but has become Canada's exclusive derivative securities market.

S&P/TSX Composite Index Index of the investment performance of a portfolio of the major stocks listed on the Toronto Stock Exchange. Also called the TSX. Formerly called the TSE 300.

TSX Total Return Index Value (TRIV) Measure of the composite index based on the prices plus dividends paid by the stocks in the S&P/TSX Composite Index. Formerly the TSE 300 Total Return Index.

S&P/TSX Capped Composite Index Index based on the prices of the TSX stocks, with no stock weighted more than 10 percent. Formerly the TSE 300 Capped Index.

Dow Jones Industrial Average U.S. index of the investment performance of a portfolio of 30 "blue-chip" stocks.

Standard & Poor's Composite Index U.S. index of the investment performance of a portfolio of 500 large stocks. Also called the S&P 500.

is the **S&P/TSX Composite Index**, based on a portfolio of the largest TSX stocks.[3] It is a value-weighted index, measuring the performance of a portfolio that holds shares in each firm in proportion to the number of shares that have been issued to investors. Thus the TSX shows the *average* performance of investors in the stocks. The index is calculated by multiplying the current share prices by the number outstanding shares. The number is then divided by the original value of the index, arbitrarily taken from January 1975, and multiplied by 1,000. An index value of 8,000 says that the TSX stocks have increased 8 times from their 1975 value. If the index rises by 80 points to end the day at 8,080, the portfolio makes a capital gain of 80/8,000 = .01, or 1 percent.[4]

To know the total rate of return (capital gains plus dividends) on the TSX stocks, you must use the **TSX Total Return Index Value**, which includes dividends paid to stocks in the index. For example, in May 2001, the S&P/TSX Composite Index increased from 7,946.6 to 8,161.9 points, or a 2.71 percent capital gain. Over the same period, the TSX Total Return Index Value increased from 17,246.49 to 17,734.7 points, for a total return of 2.83 percent. The higher rate of return on the TRIV comes from dividends earned during the month. Use the TRIV rate of return to compare the total rate of return on a stock to the market's return.

The fact that the TSX index is value-weighted created interesting situations in 1999 and 2000 when the market value of one of its stocks, Nortel Networks, soared. At one point, Nortel accounted for more than 30 percent of the index's value. Since the index is used to assess the performance of investment portfolios, portfolio managers, especially those legally restricted to not hold more than 10 percent of their portfolio in any one company, argued that the TSX was an inappropriate benchmark. Consequently, the **S&P/TSX Capped Composite Index** was created and limited the weight on any one company to less than 10 percent. Now that Nortel's share price has fallen, it accounts for about 10 percent of the TSX and interest in the TSX Capped Index has waned.

The best-known stock market index in the United States is the **Dow Jones Industrial Average,** generally known as *the Dow.* The Dow tracks the performance of a portfolio that holds one share in each of 30 large firms.

However, it is far from the best measure of the performance of the U.S. stock market. First, with only 30 large industrial stocks, it is not representative of the performance of stocks generally. Second, investors don't usually hold an equal number of shares in each company. For example, in 1999 there were 3.3 billion shares in General Electric and only 1.1 billion in DuPont. So on average investors did *not* hold the same number of shares in the two firms. Instead, they held three times as many shares in General Electric as in DuPont. It doesn't make sense, therefore, to look at an index that measures the performance of a portfolio with an equal number of shares in the two firms.

The **Standard & Poor's Composite Index,** better known as the *S&P 500,* includes the stocks of 500 major U.S. companies and is therefore a more comprehensive index than the Dow. Like the TSE 300, it measures the performance of a portfolio that holds shares in each firm in proportion to the number of shares that have been issued to investors. For

[3] In 2002, the TSX index replaced the *TSE 300 Composite Index*, which consisted of exactly 300 stocks. The transition from the TSE 300 to the TSX was scheduled for completion by December 31, 2002. Companies must be of a minimum size and liquidity to be included in the TSX index, and it is anticipated that the TSX will list about 225 stocks once those that are too small and those that do not trade with sufficient frequency are dropped. All former TSE indexes have been relabelled TSX indexes.

[4] In a typical value-weighted index, the weight of each stock is based on the total number of shares outstanding. However the weights for TSX stocks are based on the number of shares outstanding minus the number of shares held in *control blocks.* The TSX defines a control block as a group of shares owned by one investor representing more than 20 percent of the outstanding shares. Shares held in control blocks are not included on the grounds that they tend to trade infrequently.

example, the S&P portfolio would hold three times as many shares in General Electric as DuPont. Thus the S&P 500 shows the *average* performance of investors in the 500 firms.

Only a small proportion of the thousands of publicly traded companies are represented in the TSX or the S&P 500. However, these firms are among the largest in Canada and the United States, respectively, and they account for roughly 70 percent of the stocks traded. Therefore, success for professional investors usually means "beating the TSX" or "beating the S&P."

Market indexes track performance of stock markets around the world. The main index of the London Stock Exchange, the world's third largest stock market after the NYSE and Nasdaq, is the Financial Times Stock Exchange Index, FTSE 100, or the "footsie." The Tokyo Stock Exchange market index is the Nikkei 225. Many other indexes have been created to measure performance of special groups of stock, such as the S&P/TSX Canadian SmallCap Index based on smaller companies listed on the TSX. Morgan Stanley Capital International (MSCI) even computes a world stock market index and Standard & Poor's produces many indexes for markets around the world. You can visit their website at www.spglobal.com for more information.

THE HISTORICAL RECORD

The historical returns of stock or bond market indexes can give us an idea of the typical performance of different investments. The most recent study of the Canadian Institute of Actuaries, *Report on Canadian Economic Statistics 1924–2000*, augmented by data from Scotia Capital's publication *Investment Returns 2000* and CANSIM, provides historical information on Canadian market indexes. From the information sources, we can measure the historical performance of the following portfolios:

1. A portfolio of 91-day government securities, known as Treasury bills.[5]
2. A portfolio of long-term Canadian government bonds.
3. A portfolio of stocks of large companies.[6]

These portfolios are not equally risky. Treasury bills are about as safe an investment as you can make. Because they are issued by the government, you can be sure that you will get your money back. Their short-term maturity means that their prices are relatively stable. In fact, investors who wish to lend money for 3 months can achieve a certain payoff by buying 3-month Treasury bills. Of course, they can't be sure what that money will buy; there is still some uncertainty about inflation.

Long-term government bonds are also certain to be repaid when they mature, but the prices of these bonds fluctuate more as interest rates vary. When interest rates fall, the value of long-term bonds rises; when rates rise, the value of the bonds falls.

Common stocks are the riskiest of the three groups of securities. When you invest in common stocks, there is no promise that you will get your money back. As a part-owner of the corporation, you receive whatever is left over after the bonds and any other debts have been repaid.

Figure 9.1 illustrates the investment performance of Canadian stocks, bonds, and bills since 1926. The figure shows how much one dollar invested at the start of 1926 would have

[5] Canada did not have Treasury bills until 1934. We used U.S. Treasury bill data from Ibbotson Associates adjusted for the U.S.-Canada exchange rate for the years 1926 to 1933.

[6] Data for the TSE 300 index are only available from 1956 onward. The TSE Industrial Index is used for 1935 to 1956, and an index by Urquhart and Buckley for 1926 to 1934. See M. C. Urquhart and K. A. H. Buckley, *Historical Statistics of Canada* (Toronto: Macmillan, 1965). This raises questions as to whether these three stock indexes are really comparable in terms of risk. Of course, the companies in the S&P index have changed over time as well. For convenience we will refer to all the stock price data as the TSX.

FIGURE 9.1
The value to which a $1 investment made in 1926 would have grown by the end of 2000

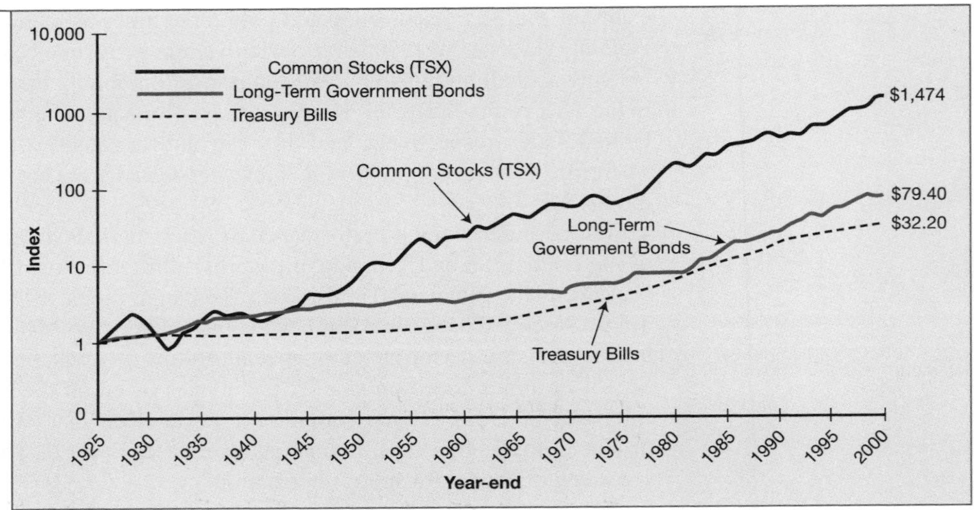

Source: Canadian Institute of Actuaries, *Report on Canadian Economic Statistics 1924–2000.* Used with permission.

grown to by the end of 2000, assuming that all dividend or interest income had been reinvested in the portfolio.

You can see that the performance of the portfolios fits our intuitive risk ranking. Common stocks were the riskiest investment but they also offered the greatest gains. One dollar invested in 1926 in a portfolio of common stocks would have grown to $1,474 by 2000. At the other end of the spectrum, an investment of $1 in a Treasury bill would have accumulated to only $32.

With the historical data, rates of return are calculated for each of these portfolios for each year from 1926 to 2000. These rates of return are comparable to the figure that we calculated for Canadian Pacific. In other words, they include (1) dividends or interest and (2) any capital gains or losses. The averages of the 75 rates of return are shown in Table 9.1.

maturity premium Extra average return from investing in long-term bonds versus short-term Treasury securities.

risk premium Expected return in excess of risk-free return as compensation for risk.

The safest investment, Treasury bills, had the lowest rates of return—they averaged 4.8 percent a year. Long-term government bonds gave slightly higher returns than Treasury bills. This difference is called the **maturity premium.** Common stocks were in a class by themselves. Investors who accepted the risk of common stocks received on average an extra return of 7.0 percent a year over the return on Treasury bills. This compensation for taking on the risk of common stock ownership is known as the **market risk premium:**

$$\text{Rate of return on common stocks} = \text{interest rate on Treasury bills} + \text{market risk premium}$$

The historical record shows that investors have received a risk premium for holding risky assets. Average returns on high-risk assets are higher than those on low-risk assets.

You may ask why we look back over such a long period to measure average rates of return. The reason is that annual rates of return for common stocks fluctuate so much that averages taken over short periods are extremely unreliable. In some years investors in common stocks had a disagreeable shock and received a substantially lower return than they expected. In other years they had a pleasant surprise and received a higher-than-expected

TABLE 9.1
Average rates of return on Treasury bills, government bonds, and common stocks, 1926–2000 (figures in percent per year)

Portfolio	Average Annual Rate of Return	Average Risk Premium (Extra Return versus Treasury Bills)
Treasury bills	4.8	
Long-term government bonds	6.4	1.6
Common stocks	11.8	7.0

return. By averaging the returns across both the rough years and the smooth ones, we should get a fair idea of the typical return that investors might justifiably expect.

While common stocks have offered the highest average returns, they have also been riskier investments. Figure 9.2 shows the 75 annual rates of return for the three portfolios. The fluctuations in year-to-year returns on common stocks are remarkably wide. There were 2 years (1933 and 1950) when investors earned a return of more than 50 percent. However, Figure 9.2 shows that you can also lose money by investing in the stock market. The most dramatic case was the world stock market crash of 1929/1932. Shortly after U.S. President Coolidge joyfully had observed that stocks were "cheap at current prices," stocks rapidly became even cheaper. Between 1929 and 1932, the Canadian and U.S. stock markets fell 64 percent.

Another major market crash, that of Monday, October 19, 1987, does not show up in Figure 9.2. On that day the TSX fell by 11 percent and the S&P 500 fell by 23 percent, their largest one-day falls in history. However, Black Monday came after a prolonged rise in stock prices, so that over 1987 as a whole investors in common stocks earned a return of 5.2 percent. This was not a terrible return, but many investors who rode the 1987 roller coaster feel that it is not a year they would care to repeat.

The period between 1999 and 2001 is another period of extreme volatility. With massive business investment in new information-based technologies, the value of telecommunications, technology, and dot-com stocks boomed. This fuelled double-digit increases in prices on world stock markets between 1999 and mid-2000. S&P/TSX Composite Index started 1999 at only 6,495.94 and ended the year at 8,413.75, an increase of almost

FIGURE 9.2
Rates of return, 1926–2000

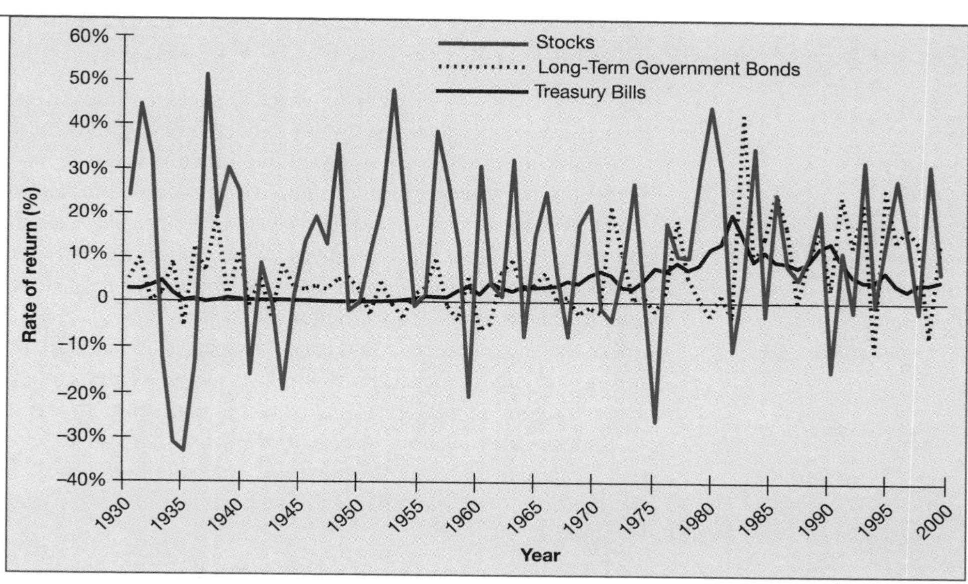

Source: Canadian Institute of Actuaries, *Report on Canadian Economic Statistics 1924–2000*. Used with permission.

30 percent. By September 1, 2000, it had reached an all-time high of 11,388.82, producing more than a 35 percent return for the first 8 months of 2000, or 57.5 percent on an equivalent annual basis. Even more dramatically, the U.S. Nasdaq Composite Index, with a heavier concentration of technology and dot-com stocks, increased nearly 86 percent in 1999. At its peak in March 2000, the Nasdaq index hit 5048.62, 103 percent higher than where it started in 1999. The S&P 500, with a broader mix of both old and new economy stocks, experienced less stellar increases. Its 1999 return was 19.5 percent, and at its peak in March 2000 was a 24 percent increase from the beginning of 1999.

Unfortunately the boom in stock prices was followed by a bust. Between mid-2000 and the following year, a general economic slowdown led to the crash of technology and telecommunications stocks and produced significant market losses. From its all-time highest value in September 2000, the TSX had fallen 33 percent by the end of August 2001. From its peak in March 2000, the Nasdaq had fallen 62 percent by the end of August 2001. The stock price gains of the technology stocks were largely wiped out by the more recent price falls. The broader S&P 500 didn't fall as far but still experienced negative rates of return in 2001. Not as quick a decline as the crash of 1987, the decline was nonetheless dramatic. With the horrific terrorist attacks of September 2001, the already faltering economy and stock market declined further. The 2001 rate of return was –13.9 percent for the TSX, –13 percent for the S&P 500, and –21.1 percent on the Nasdaq.

CHECK POINT 9.2

Here are the average rates of return for the postwar period 1950 to 2000:

Stocks	12.8%
Government bonds	7.1
Treasury bills	6.5

What were the risk premium on stocks and the maturity premium on government bonds for this period?

USING HISTORICAL EVIDENCE TO ESTIMATE TODAY'S COST OF CAPITAL

Think back now to Chapter 6, where we showed how firms calculate the present value of a new project by discounting the expected cash flows by the opportunity cost of capital. The opportunity cost of capital is the return that the firm's shareholders are giving up by investing in the project rather than in comparable risk alternatives.

Measuring the cost of capital is easy if the project is a sure thing. Since shareholders can obtain a sure-fire payoff by investing in a Government of Canada Treasury bill, the firm should invest in a risk-free project only if it can at least match the rate of interest on such a loan. If the project is risky—and most projects are—then the firm needs to at least match the return that shareholders could expect to earn if they invested in securities of similar risk. It is not easy to put a precise figure on this, but our skim through history provides an idea of the average return an investor might expect to earn from an investment in risky common stocks.

Suppose there is an investment project which you *know*—don't ask how—has the same risk as an investment in the portfolio of stocks in the S&P/TSX Composite Index. We will say that it has the same degree of risk as the *market portfolio* of common stocks.[7]

[7] This is speaking a bit loosely, because the TSX does not include all stocks traded in Canada, much less in world markets. When the TSX is finalized, the index will have even fewer stocks.

Instead of investing in the project, your shareholders could invest directly in this market portfolio of common stocks. Therefore, the opportunity cost of capital for your project is the return that the shareholders could expect to earn on the market portfolio. This is what they are giving up by investing money in your project.

The problem of estimating the project cost of capital boils down to estimating the currently expected rate of return on the market portfolio. One way to estimate the expected market return is to assume that the future will be like the past and that today's investors expect to receive the average rates of return shown in Table 9.1. In this case, you would judge that the expected market return today is 11.8 percent, the average of past market returns.

Unfortunately, this is *not* the way to do it. Investors are not likely to demand the same return each year on an investment in common stocks. For example, we know that the interest rate on safe Treasury bills varies over time. At their peak in 1981, Treasury bills offered a return of 20 percent, more than 15 percentage points above the 4.8 percent average return on bills shown in Table 9.1.

What if you were called upon to estimate the expected return on common stocks in 1981? Would you have said 11.8 percent? That doesn't make sense. Who would invest in the risky stock market for an expected return of 11.8 percent when you could get a safe 20 percent from Treasury bills?

A better procedure is to take the *current* interest rate on Treasury bills plus 7 percent, the average *risk premium* shown in Table 9.1. In 1981, when the rate on Treasury bills was 20 percent, that would have given

$$\begin{aligned}\text{Expected market return (1981)} &= \text{interest rate on Treasury bills (1981)} + \text{normal risk premium} \\ &= 20\% + 7\% = 27\%\end{aligned}$$

The first term on the right-hand side tells us the time value of money in 1981; the second term measures the compensation for risk.

The expected return on an investment provides compensation to investors both for waiting (the time value of money) and for worrying (the risk of the particular asset).

What about today? As we write this in mid-2001, Treasury bills offer a return of only 4.2 percent. This suggests that investors in common stocks are looking for a return of just over 11 percent:[8]

$$\begin{aligned}\text{Expected market return (2001)} &= \text{interest rate on Treasury bills (2001)} + \text{normal risk premium} \\ &= 4.2\% + 7\% = 11.2\%\end{aligned}$$

These calculations assume that there is a normal, stable risk premium on the market portfolio, so that the expected *future* risk premium can be measured by the average past risk premium. But even with 75 years of data, we cannot estimate the market risk premium exactly; moreover, we cannot be sure that investors today are demanding the same reward for risk that they were in the 1940s or 1960s. All this leaves plenty of room for argument about what the risk premium *really* is. Many financial managers and economists believe

[8] In practice, things might be a bit more complicated. We've mentioned the yield curve, the relationship between bond maturity and yield. When firms consider investments in long-lived projects, they usually think about risk premiums relative to long-term bonds. In this case, the risk-free rate would be taken as the current long-term bond yield less the average maturity premium on such bonds.

that long-run historical returns are the best measure available and therefore settle on a risk premium of about 7 percent. Others have a gut instinct that investors don't need such a large risk premium to persuade them to hold common stocks and so shade downward their estimate of the expected future risk premium.

9.3

Measuring Risk

You now have some benchmarks. You know that the opportunity cost of capital for safe projects must be the rate of return offered by safe Treasury bills and you know that the opportunity cost of capital for "average risk" projects must be the expected return on the market portfolio. But you *don't* know how to estimate the cost of capital for projects that do not fit these two simple cases. Before you can do this you need to understand more about investment risk.

The average fuse time for army hand grenades is 7 seconds, but that average hides a lot of potentially relevant information. If you are in the business of throwing grenades, you need some measure of the variation around the average fuse time.[9] Similarly, if you are in the business of investing in securities, you need some measure of how far the returns may differ from the average.

Figure 9.2 showed the year-by-year returns for several investments from 1926 to 2000. Another way of presenting these data is by histograms such as Figure 9.3. Each bar shows the number of years that the market return fell within a specific range. For example, you can see that in 5 of the 75 years the return on common stocks was between +15 percent and +20 percent. The risk shows up in the wide spread of outcomes. In 1 year the return was between +50 percent and +55 percent but there were also 2 years in which it was between –30 percent and –35 percent.

VARIANCE AND STANDARD DEVIATION

The third histogram in Figure 9.3 shows the variation in common stock returns. The returns on common stock have been more variable than returns on bonds and Treasury bills. Common stocks have been risky investments. They will almost certainly continue to be risky investments.

Investment risk depends on the dispersion or spread of possible outcomes. Sometimes a picture like Figure 9.3 tells you all you need to know about (past) dispersion. But in general, pictures do not suffice. The financial manager needs a numerical measure of dispersion. The standard measures are **variance** and **standard deviation.** More variable returns imply greater investment risk. This suggests that some measure of dispersion will provide a reasonable measure of risk, and dispersion is precisely what is measured by variance and standard deviation.

variance Average value of squared deviations from mean. A measure of volatility.

standard deviation Square root of variance. Another measure of volatility.

Here is a very simple example showing how variance and standard deviation are calculated. Suppose that you are offered the chance to play the following game. You start by investing \$100. Then two coins are flipped. For each head that comes up your starting balance will be *increased* by 20 percent, and for each tail that comes up your starting balance will be *reduced* by 10 percent. There are four equally likely outcomes:

- Head + head: You make 20 + 20 = 40%
- Head + tail: You make 20 – 10 = 10%
- Tail + head: You make –10 + 20 = 10%
- Tail + tail: You make –10 – 10 = –20%

[9] We can reassure you; the variation around the standard fuse time is very small.

FIGURE 9.3

Historical returns on major asset classes, 1926–2000

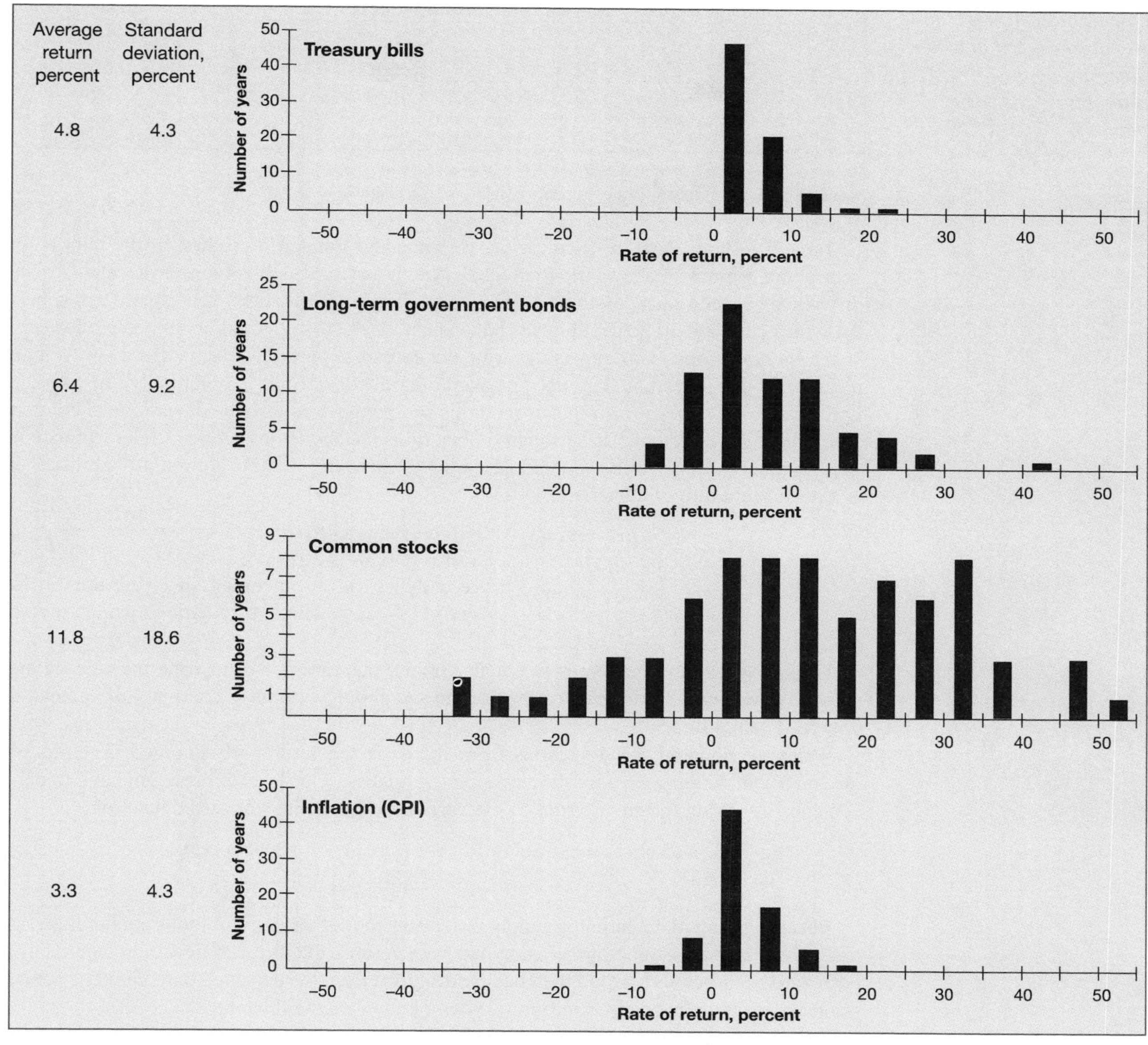

Source: Canadian Institute of Actuaries, *Report on Canadian Economic Statistics 1924–2000.* Used with permission.

There is a chance of 1 in 4, or .25, that you will make 40 percent; a chance of 2 in 4, or .5, that you will make 10 percent; and a chance of 1 in 4, or .25, that you will lose 20 percent. The game's expected return is therefore a weighted average of the possible outcomes:

$$\begin{aligned}\text{Expected return} &= \text{probability-weighted average of possible outcomes}\\ &= (.25 \times 40) + (.5 \times 10) + (.25 \times -20) = +10\%\end{aligned}$$

If you play the game a very large number of times, your average return should be 10 percent.

TABLE 9.2
The coin-toss game: calculating variance and standard deviation when there are equal probabilities of each outcome

(1) Percent Rate of Return	(2) Deviation from Expected Return	(3) Squared Deviation
+40	+30	900
+10	0	0
+10	0	0
−20	−30	900

Variance = average of squared deviations = 1,800/4 = 450
Standard deviation = square root of variance = $\sqrt{450}$ = 21.2, about 21%

Table 9.2 shows how to calculate the variance and standard deviation of the returns on your game. Column 1 shows the four equally likely outcomes. In column 2 we calculate the difference between each possible outcome and the expected outcome. You can see that at best the return could be 30 percent higher than expected; at worst it could be 30 percent lower.

These deviations in column 2 illustrate the spread of possible returns. But if we want a measure of this spread, it is no use just averaging the deviations in column 2—the average is always going to be zero. To get around this problem, we *square* the deviations in column 2 before averaging them. These squared deviations are shown in column 3. The variance is the weighted average of the squared deviations, where the weights are the probabilities. It is a useful measure of dispersion.

$$\textbf{Variance} = \textbf{probability-weighted average of squared deviations around the expected return} \quad (9.5)$$
$$= (.25 \times 900) + (.25 \times 0) + (.25 \times 0) + (.25 \times 900)$$
$$= 450$$

When each of the outcomes is equally likely, the variance is just the average of the squared deviations. Taking the average of the squared deviations in column 4 of Table 9.2, you get 1,800/4 or 450.

When we squared the deviations from the expected return, we changed the units of measurement from *percentages* to *percentages squared.* Our last step is to get back to percentages by taking the square root of the variance. This is the standard deviation:

$$\textbf{Standard deviation} = \textbf{square root of variance} \quad (9.6)$$
$$= \sqrt{450} = 21\%$$

Because standard deviation is simply the square root of variance, it too is a natural measure of risk. If the outcome of the game had been certain, the standard deviation would have been zero because there would then be no deviations from the expected outcome. The actual standard deviation is positive because we *don't* know what will happen.

When we calculated variance in Table 9.2 we recorded each of the four possible outcomes separately. An alternative would have been to recognize that in two of the cases the outcomes were the same. Thus there was a 50 percent chance of a 10 percent return from the game, a 25 percent chance of a 40 percent return, and a 25 percent chance of a –20 percent return. We calculate variance by weighting each squared deviation by the probability and then summing the results. Table 9.3 confirms that this method gives the same answer.

Now think of a second game. It is the same as the first except that each head means a 35 percent gain and each tail means a 25 percent loss. Again there are four equally likely outcomes:

- Head + head: You gain 70%
- Head + tail: You gain 10%

TABLE 9.3
The coin-toss game: calculating variance and standard deviation when there are different probabilities of each outcome

(1) Percent Rate of Return	(2) Probability of Return	(3) Deviation from Expected Return	(4) Probability × Squared Deviation
+40	.25	+30	.25 × 900 = 225
+10	.50	0	.50 × 0 = 0
–20	.25	–30	.25 × 900 = 225

Variance = sum of squared deviations weighted by probabilities = 225 + 0 + 225 = 450
Standard deviation = square root of variance = $\sqrt{450}$ = 21.2, about 21%

- Tail + head: You gain 10%
- Tail + tail: You lose 50%

For this game, the expected return is 10 percent, the same as that of the first game, but it is more risky. For example, in the first game, the worst possible outcome is a loss of 20 percent, which is 30 percent worse than the expected outcome. In the second game the downside is a loss of 50 percent, or 60 percent below the expected return. This increased spread of outcomes shows up in the standard deviation, which is double that of the first game, 42 percent versus 21 percent. By this measure the second game is twice as risky as the first.

CHECK POINT 9.3

Calculate the expected return, the variance, and the standard deviation of this second coin-toss game in the same formats as tables 9.2 and 9.3.

MEASURING THE VARIATION IN STOCK RETURNS

When estimating the spread of possible outcomes from investing in the stock market, most financial analysts start by assuming that the spread of returns in the past is a reasonable indication of what could happen in the future. Therefore, they calculate the variance and standard deviation of past returns. However, this situation is not the same as the previous coin-toss example, where the probability of each possible outcome was known, and variance was calculated as the probability-weighted average of the squared deviations. In the coin-toss example, we calculated the *population* variance and the *population* standard deviation. Here we have a sample of observed rates of return and the probability of each possible return is unknown.[10] Using a sample of observations, we calculate the *sample* variance. As before, the squared deviations from the average rate of return are calculated. The sample variance is the sum of the squared deviations around the estimated average rate of return, divided by the number of observations minus one:

$$\text{Variance based on a sample of observations} = \frac{\text{sum of the squared deviations around the average}}{\text{number of observations} - 1}$$

The sample standard deviation is the square root of the sample variance.

Although there are two different definitions of variance, people often call them both variance. However, you can always tell which variance is being used. If you know the probability of each possible value, you have the population variance, as in the coin-toss

[10] In terms of statistics, we are drawing a distinction between calculating the variance of a population, where you know the probability of every possible outcome (the coin-toss example), and estimating the variance of a population with a sample of observations. We use the sample variance to infer what is the true but unknown variance of the population. That is why the sample variance is also called the *estimated* variance of the population.

TABLE 9.4
The average return and standard deviation of stock market returns, 1995–2000

Year	Rate of Return	Deviation from Average Return	Squared Deviation
1995	14.5	–1.4	1.9
1996	28.3	12.4	154.9
1997	15.0	–0.9	0.8
1998	–1.6	–17.5	305.6
1999	31.7	15.8	250.1
2000	7.4	–8.5	72.1
Total	95.45		785.5

Average rate of return = 95.4/6 = 15.9%
Variance = sum of squared deviations/(number of observations – 1) = 785.5/(6 – 1) = 157.1
Standard deviation = square root of variance $\sqrt{157.1}$ = 12.5%

Source: Canadian Institute of Actuaries, *Report on Canadian Economic Statistics 1924–2000*. Used with permission.

example. If you have a group of observed values, the sample variance is calculated using the formula on the previous page.

To illustrate, suppose that you were presented with the data for stock market returns shown in Table 9.4. The average return over the 6 years from 1995 to 2000 was 15.9 percent. This is just the sum of the returns over the 6 years divided by 6 (95.4/6 = 15.9 percent).

Column 2 in Table 9.4 shows the difference between each year's return and the average return. For example, in 1995 the return of 14.5 percent on common stocks was below the 6-year average by 1.4 percent (14.5 – 15.9 = 1.4 percent). In column 3 we square these deviations from the average. The variance is the sum of these squared deviations divided by the number of observations minus one:

$$\textbf{Variance} = \textbf{sum of squared deviations/(number of observations} - \textbf{1)} \qquad (9.7)$$

$$= \frac{785.5}{6-1} = 157.1$$

Since standard deviation is the square root of the variance,

$$\textbf{Standard deviation} = \textbf{square root of variance} \qquad (9.8)$$

$$= \sqrt{157.1} = 12.5\%$$

It is difficult to measure the risk of securities on the basis of just six past outcomes. Therefore, Table 9.5 lists the annual standard deviations for our three portfolios of securities over the period from 1926 to 2000. As expected, Treasury bills were the least variable security, and common stocks were the most variable. Long-term government bonds hold the middle ground.

Of course, there is no reason to believe that the market's variability should stay the same over many years. Indeed many people believe that in recent years the stock market has become more volatile due to irresponsible speculation by . . . (fill in the name of your preferred guilty party). Figure 9.4 provides a chart of the volatility of the Canadian and United

TABLE 9.5
Standard deviation of rates of return, 1926–2000

Portfolio	Standard Deviation, %
Treasury bills	4.3
Long-term government bonds	9.2
Common stocks	18.6

Source: Canadian Institute of Actuaries, *Report on Canadian Economic Statistics 1924–2000*. Used with permission.

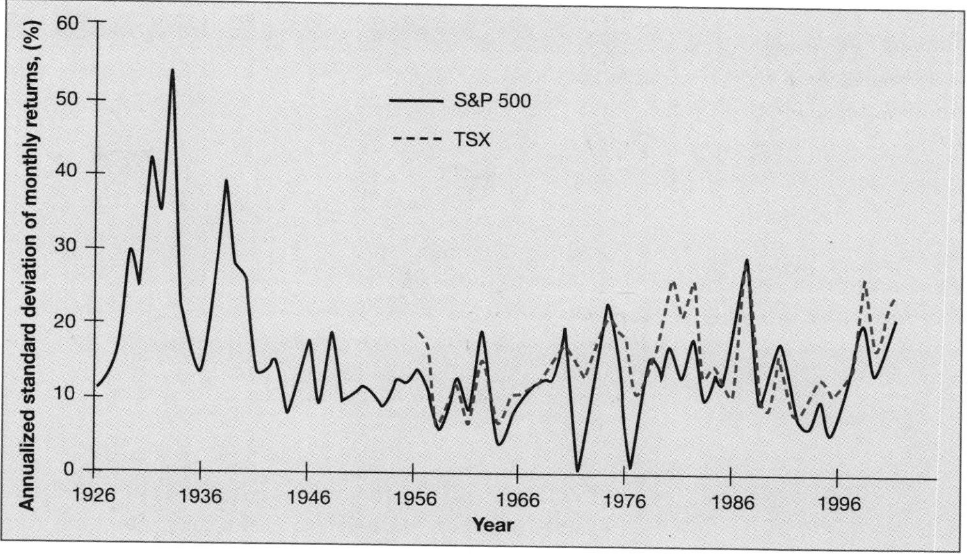

FIGURE 9.4
Canadian and U.S. stock market volatility, 1926–2000

States stock markets for each year from 1926 to 2001.[11] You can see that there are periods of unusually high variability, but there is no long-term upward trend.

Risk and Diversification

DIVERSIFICATION

We can calculate our measures of variability equally well for individual securities and portfolios of securities. Of course, the level of variability over 75 years is less interesting for specific companies than for the market portfolio because it is a rare company that faces the same business risks today as it did in 1926.

Table 9.6 presents estimated standard deviations for 13 well-known common stocks for a recent 5-year period.[12] Do these standard deviations look high to you? They should. Remember that the market portfolio's standard deviation was about 19 percent over the entire 1926 to 2000 period. Of our individual stocks, only Westcoast Energy had a standard deviation of less than 19 percent. Most stocks are substantially more variable than the market portfolio; only a handful are less variable.

This raises an important question: The market portfolio is made up of individual stocks, so why isn't its variability equal to the average variability of its components? The answer is that **diversification** reduces variability.

diversification Strategy designed to reduce risk by spreading the portfolio across many investments.

Selling umbrellas is a risky business; you may make a killing when it rains but you are likely to lose your shirt in a heat wave. Selling ice cream is no safer; you do well in a heat wave but business is poor in the rain. Suppose, however, that you invest in both an umbrella shop and an ice cream shop. By diversifying your investment across the two businesses you make an average level of profit come rain or shine.

[11] We converted the monthly variance to an annual variance by multiplying by 12. In other words, the variance of annual returns is 12 times that of monthly returns. The longer you hold a security, the more risk you have to bear.

[12] We pointed out earlier that six annual observations are insufficient to give a reliable estimate of variability. Therefore, these estimates are derived from 60 monthly rates of return and then the monthly variance is multiplied by 12.

TABLE 9.6
Standard deviations for selected common stocks, January 1995–December 1999

Stock	Standard Deviation, %
Agrium	35.2
Alcan Aluminum	30.4
BCE	30.8
Biomira	76.4
Cameco	29.8
Canadian Pacific	23.7
CanWest Global	36.8
CN Rail	30.4
Four Seasons Hotel	41.3
Inco	42.9
Magna International	25.0
Royal Bank	25.7
Westcoast Energy	16.4

Portfolio diversification works because prices of different stocks do not move exactly together. Statisticians make the same point when they say that stock price changes are less than perfectly correlated. Diversification works best when the returns are negatively correlated, as is the case for our umbrella and ice cream businesses. When one business does well, the other does badly. Unfortunately, in practice, stocks that are negatively correlated are extremely rare.

ASSET VERSUS PORTFOLIO RISK

The history of returns on different asset classes provides compelling evidence of a risk–return trade-off and suggests that the variability of the rates of return on each asset class is a useful measure of risk. However, volatility of returns can be a misleading measure of risk for an individual asset held as part of a portfolio. To see why, consider the following example.

Suppose there are three equally likely outcomes, or *scenarios,* for the economy: a recession, normal growth, and a boom. An investment in an auto stock will have a rate of return of –8 percent in a recession, 5 percent in a normal period, and 18 percent in a boom. Auto firms are *cyclical*: they do well when the economy does well. In contrast, gold firms are often said to be *countercyclical,* meaning that they do well when other firms do poorly. Suppose that stock in a gold mining firm will provide a rate of return of 20 percent in a recession, 3 percent in a normal period, and –20 percent in a boom. These assumptions are summarized in Table 9.7.

It appears that gold is the more volatile investment. The difference in return across the boom and bust scenarios is 40 percent (–20 percent in a boom versus +20 percent in a recession) compared to a spread of only 26 percent for the auto stock. In fact, we can confirm the higher volatility by measuring the variance or standard deviation of returns of the two assets. The calculations are set out in Table 9.8.

Since all three scenarios are equally likely, the expected return on each stock is simply the average of the three possible outcomes.[13] For the auto stock the expected return is 5 percent; for the gold stock it is 1 percent. The variance is the average of the squared deviations from the expected return, and the standard deviation is the square root of the variance.

[13] If the probabilities were not equal, we would need to weight each outcome by its probability in calculating the expected outcome and the variance.

TABLE 9.7
Rate of return assumptions for two stocks

		Rate of Return, %	
Scenario	**Probability**	**Auto Stock**	**Gold Stock**
Recession	1/3	−8	+20
Normal	1/3	+5	+3
Boom	1/3	+18	−20

CHECK POINT 9.4

Suppose the probabilities of the recession or boom are .30, while the probability of a normal period is .40. Would you expect the variance of returns on these two investments to be higher or lower? Why? Confirm by calculating the standard deviation of the auto stock.

The gold mining stock offers a lower expected rate of return than the auto stock, and *more* volatility—a loser on both counts, right? Would anyone be willing to hold gold mining stocks in an investment portfolio? The answer is a resounding Yes.

To see why, suppose you do believe that gold is a lousy asset, and therefore, hold your entire portfolio in the auto stock. Your expected return is 5 percent and your standard deviation is 10.6 percent. We'll compare that portfolio to a partially diversified one, invested 75 percent in autos and 25 percent in gold. For example, if you have a $10,000 portfolio, you could put $7,500 in autos and $2,500 in gold.

First, we need to calculate the return on this portfolio in each scenario. The portfolio return is the weighted average of returns on the individual assets with weights equal to the proportion of the portfolio invested in each asset. For a portfolio formed from only two assets,

$$\text{Portfolio rate of return} = \left(\begin{array}{c}\text{fraction of portfolio}\\ \text{in first asset}\end{array}\right) \times \left(\begin{array}{c}\text{rate of return}\\ \text{on first asset}\end{array}\right) + \left(\begin{array}{c}\text{fraction of portfolio}\\ \text{in second asset}\end{array}\right) \times \left(\begin{array}{c}\text{rate of return}\\ \text{on second asset}\end{array}\right) \tag{9.9}$$

TABLE 9.8
Expected return and volatility for two stocks

	Auto Stock			Gold Stock		
Scenario	**Rate of Return, %**	**Deviation from Expected Return, %**	**Squared Deviation**	**Rate of Return, %**	**Deviation from Expected Return, %**	**Squared Deviation**
Recession	−8	−13	169	+20	+19	361
Normal	+5	0	0	+3	+2	4
Boom	+18	+13	169	−20	−21	441
Expected return	$\frac{1}{3}(-8+5+18)=5\%$			$\frac{1}{3}(+20+3-20)=1\%$		
Variance[a]	$\frac{1}{3}(169+0+169)=112.7$			$\frac{1}{3}(361+4+441)=268.7$		
Standard deviation ($=\sqrt{\text{variance}}$)	$\sqrt{112.7}=10.6\%$			$\sqrt{268.7}=16.4\%$		

[a] Variance = probability-weighted average of squared deviations from the expected value

TABLE 9.9
Rates of return for two stocks and a portfolio

Scenario	Probability	Rate of Return, % Auto Stock	Gold Stock	Portfolio Return, %[a]
Recession	1/3	−8	+20	−1%
Normal	1/3	+5	+3	+4.5
Boom	1/3	+18	−20	+8.5
Expected return		5%	1%	4%
Variance		112.7	268.7	15.2
Standard deviation		10.6%	16.4%	3.9%

[a] Portfolio return = (.75 × auto stock return) + (.25 × gold stock return).

For example, autos have a weight of .75 and a rate of return of −8 percent in the recession, and gold has a weight of .25 and a return of 20 percent in a recession. Therefore, the portfolio return in the recession is the following weighted average:[14]

$$\text{Portfolio return in recession} = [.75 \times (-8\%)] + [.25 \times 20\%] = -1\%$$

Table 9.9 expands Table 9.7 to include the portfolio of the auto and gold mining stocks. The expected returns and volatility measures are summarized at the bottom of the table. The surprising finding is this: When you shift funds from the auto stock to the more volatile gold mining stock, your portfolio variability actually *decreases.* In fact, the volatility of the auto-plus-gold stock portfolio is considerably less than the volatility of *either* stock separately. This is the payoff to diversification.

We can understand this more clearly by focusing on asset returns in the two extreme scenarios, boom and recession. In the boom, when auto stocks do best, the poor return on gold reduces the performance of the overall portfolio. However, when auto stocks are stalling in a recession, gold shines, providing a substantial positive return that boosts portfolio performance. The gold stock offsets the swings in the performance of the auto stock, reducing the best-case return but improving the worst-case return. The inverse relationship between the returns on the two stocks means that the addition of the gold mining stock to an all-auto portfolio stabilizes returns.

A gold stock is really a *negative-risk* asset to an investor starting with an all-auto portfolio. Adding it to the portfolio reduces the volatility of returns. The *incremental* risk of the gold stock (that is, the *change* in overall risk when gold is added to the portfolio) is *negative* despite the fact that gold returns are highly volatile.

In general, the incremental risk of a stock depends on whether its returns tend to vary with or against the returns of the other assets in the portfolio. Incremental risk does not just depend on a stock's volatility. If returns do not move closely with those of the rest of the portfolio, the stock will reduce the volatility of portfolio returns.

We can summarize as follows:

> **1. Investors care about the expected return and risk of their *portfolio* of assets. The risk of the overall portfolio can be measured by the volatility of returns, that is, the variance or standard deviation.**

[14] Let's confirm this. Suppose you invest \$7,500 in autos and \$2,500 in gold. If the recession hits, the rate of return on autos will be −8 percent, and the value of the auto investment will fall by 8 percent to \$6,900. The rate of return on gold will be 20 percent, and the value of the gold investment will rise 20 percent to \$3,000. The value of the total portfolio falls from its original value of \$10,000 to \$6,900 + \$3,000 = \$9,900, which is a rate of return of −1 percent. This matches the rate of return given by the formula for the weighted average.

2. The standard deviation of the returns of an individual security measures how risky that security would be if held in isolation. But an investor who holds a portfolio of securities is interested only in how each security affects the risk of the entire portfolio. The contribution of a security to the risk of the portfolio depends on how the security's returns vary with the investor's other holdings. Thus a security that is risky if held in isolation may nevertheless serve to reduce the variability of the portfolio, as long as its returns vary inversely with those of the rest of the portfolio.

CORRELATION AND PORTFOLIO DIVERSIFICATION

We have given you an intuitive idea of how diversification reduces risk: Combining assets into a portfolio reduces risk because the assets' prices do not move in exact lockstep. When one stock is doing poorly, another may be doing well, helping to offset the negative impact of the stock with the poorer performance on the portfolio return. However, to understand portfolio diversification more fully we need to look in more detail at *correlation*.

correlation coefficient Measure of how closely two variables move together.

The **correlation coefficient**—always a number between –1 and 1—measures the degree to which two variables move together. If the correlation coefficient is greater than zero, the two variables tend to move in the same direction; they are *positively* correlated. The higher the correlation coefficient the stronger the relationship is between the two variables. When the correlation coefficient equals 1, the variables are perfectly positively correlated and the variables move in lockstep. On the other hand, if the correlation coefficient is less than zero, the two variables tend to move in the opposite direction; they are *negatively* correlated. With a correlation coefficient equal to –1, the variables are perfectly negatively correlated. If the correlation coefficient equals zero, a change in one variable does not tell you anything about the likely change in the other; the variables are said to be *uncorrelated*.

CHECK POINT 9.5

Are each of the following pairs of variables likely to be positively correlated, negatively correlated, or uncorrelated? Briefly explain why.

a. The number of hours of sunshine per day and the average daily air temperature.
b. The number of hours of television you watch per day and your grade on your finance final.
c. The flying time from Vancouver to St. John's and the quality of the in-flight movie.
d. The level of interest rates in the United States and the level of interest rates in Canada.

Correlation is a useful concept for measuring how stocks move relative to each other. In the previous example, we said that auto firms were cyclical: they tend to do well when the economy is doing well. In other words, the return on auto stocks is positively correlated with the economy. On the other hand, gold stocks were said to be countercyclical, tending to do well when the economy is doing poorly. Thus the return on gold stocks tends to have low correlation with the economy.

The degree of correlation among assets determines the extent to which risk is reduced through portfolio diversification. To illustrate, we will create a portfolio of two stocks, Steelco (S), manufacturer of construction steel, and Gold Bear (G), a goldmine and refinery. We know that the expected return on Steelco shares, r_S, is 15 percent, and the expected return on Gold Bear shares, r_G, is 9 percent. The standard deviation of return on Steelco is

12% and the standard deviation of return on Gold Bear is 18%. What are the expected return and standard deviation of return for a portfolio of these two stocks?

The expected return on the portfolio of Steelco and Gold Bear stocks will depend on the fraction of funds invested in each. Let x_S be the fraction of the total funds invested in shares of Steelco and x_G be the fraction invested in shares of Gold Bear Mine. The expected return on the portfolio is the weighted average of the expected returns on the two stocks, where the weights equal the fraction invested in each, so

$$r_p = x_S\,(15\%) + x_G\,(9\%)$$

If 100% of the funds are invested in Steelco, $x_S = 1$ and $x_G = 0$, the portfolio expected return is 15%, the expected return on Steelco. If 25% of the funds are invested in Steelco ($x_S = .25$) and 75% are invested in Gold Bear ($x_G = .75$), the expected portfolio return is

$$r_p = .25(15\%) + .75\,(9\%) = 10.5\%$$

The general formula for expected return of a portfolio is simply the weighted average of the expected return on the assets in the portfolio, where the weights are the fractions invested in each stock:

$$\text{Portfolio expected return} = r_p = x_S\,r_S + x_G\,x_G$$

Is the portfolio standard deviation equal to the weighted average of the standard deviations of assets in the portfolio? The answer depends on the correlation between the assets in the portfolio. If the assets' returns are perfectly positively correlated, there is no benefit from diversification and the portfolio standard deviation is simply the weighted average of the individual stocks' standard deviations. However, if the stocks are less than perfectly correlated, diversification reduces portfolio risk—the portfolio standard deviation will be less than the weighted average of the assets' standard deviations.

To show you how this works, we need a bit of notation. The commonly used symbol for standard deviation is the Greek letter σ ("sigma"). Thus the standard deviation of the return on Steelco is σ_S, and for Gold Bear, σ_G. We use the Greek letter ρ ("rho") to represent the correlation coefficient. Thus ρ_{SG} is the correlation coefficient for Steelco and Big Bear. The expression for the standard deviation of a portfolio with two stocks is

$$\text{Portfolio standard deviation} = \sigma_p = \sqrt{x_S^2\sigma_S^2 + x_G^2\sigma_G^2 + 2x_Sx_G\rho_{SG}\sigma_S\sigma_G}$$

Notice that the portfolio standard deviation depends on the individual stocks' standard deviations and also on their correlation to one another.

To see how different values of the correlation coefficient affect the portfolio standard deviation, consider a portfolio with 25 percent invested in Steelco ($x_S = .25$) and 75 percent invested in Gold Bear Mine ($x_G = .75$). If the returns on Steelco and Gold Bear are perfectly positively correlated, $\rho_{SG} = 1$, the portfolio standard deviation is

$$\sigma_p = \sqrt{(.25)^2(.12)^2 + (.75)^2(.18)^2 + 2(.25)(.75)(1)(.12)(.18)} = .165$$

This is also the weighted average of Steelco's and Gold Bear's standard deviations: (.25)(.12) + (.75)(.18) = .165. Only if the stocks are perfectly positively correlated, $\rho_{SG} = 1$, will there be no benefit from diversification. Table 9.10 shows portfolio standard deviation for possible correlation coefficients. See how as the correlation gets lower, the benefit from diversification increases.

Can portfolio risk (portfolio standard deviation) be reduced to zero through diversification? If some assets are negatively correlated with the others, it is mathematically possible to reduce the portfolio risk to zero. In our example, if the correlation coefficient was

TABLE 9.10
Relationship between correlation and portfolio standard deviation

Correlation Coefficient, ρ_{SG}	Portfolio Standard Deviation $= \sigma_p = \sqrt{x_S^2\sigma_S^2 + x_G^2\sigma_G^2 + 2x_Sx_G\rho_{SG}\sigma_S\sigma_G}$ $= \sqrt{(.25)^2(.12)^2 + (.75)^2(.18)^2 + 2(.25)(.75)\rho_{SG}(.12)(.18)}$
1	.165
.8	.160
.2	.144
0	.138
−.3	.129
−.7	.116
−1	.105

−.3, and you invested about 65 percent in Steelco and 35 percent in Gold Bear, the portfolio standard deviation would be close to zero.

Unfortunately, assets with negative correlation with the economy are hard to find. Although some assets have low correlation with other assets (gold, for instance), all assets' returns tend to be positively correlated. Portfolio diversification can reduce risk up to a point but cannot remove all risks.[15]

CHECK POINT 9.6

Go back to Table 9.9 for the auto and gold stock example. Use the formula for portfolio variance to show that the returns on auto and gold stocks are almost perfectly negatively correlated.

EXAMPLE 9.2

Alcan Aluminum and BCE

Let's look at a more realistic example of the effect of diversification. Figure 9.5*a* shows the monthly returns of Alcan Aluminum stock from 1994 to 1999. The average *monthly* return was 1.4 percent but you can see that there was considerable variation around that average. The standard deviation of *monthly* returns was 8.8 percent. As a rule of thumb, in roughly one-third of the months, the return is likely to be more than one standard deviation above or below the average return.[16] The figure shows that the return did indeed differ by more than 8.8 percent from the average on about a third of the occasions.

Figure 9.5*b* shows the monthly returns of BCE. The average *monthly* return on BCE was 3.6 percent and the standard deviation was 8.9 percent, about the same as that of Alcan. Again you can see that in about one-third of the cases the return differed from the average by more than one standard deviation.

An investment in *either* Alcan or BCE would have been very variable. But the fortunes of the two stocks were not perfectly related. There were many occasions when a decline in the value of one stock was cancelled by a rise in the price of the other. Because the two stocks did not move in exact lockstep, there was an opportunity to reduce variability by spreading one's investment between them. For example, Figure 9.5*c* shows the returns on a portfolio that was equally divided between the stocks. The monthly standard deviation of this portfolio would have been only 7.3 percent—that is, about 82 percent of the variability of the individual stocks.

[15] The mathematical definition of correlation between two variables is their covariance divided by the product of their standard deviations. See page 307 for the formula. Covariance is another way to measure the co-movement of variables and is the probability-weighted average of the product of each variable's difference from its mean, for each possible future event. Using the data for Auto and Gold Stock, Table 9.8, the covariance is 1/3 × (−8 − 5) × (20 − 1) + 1/3 × (5 − 5) × (3 − 1) + 1/3 (18 − 5) × (−20 − 1) = −173.3. See a basic statistics text for more information.

[16] For any normal distribution, approximately one-third of the observations lie more than one standard deviation above or below the average. Over short intervals, stock returns are roughly normally distributed.

☑ CHECK POINT 9.7

An investor is currently fully invested in gold mining stocks. Which action would do more to reduce portfolio risk: diversification into silver mining stocks or automotive stocks? Why?

FIGURE 9.5

Monthly rates of return for Alcan, BCE, and a portfolio invested 50% in each stock, 1994–1999. The variability of a portfolio with equal holdings in Alcan and BCE would have been only 82 percent of the variability of the individual stocks.

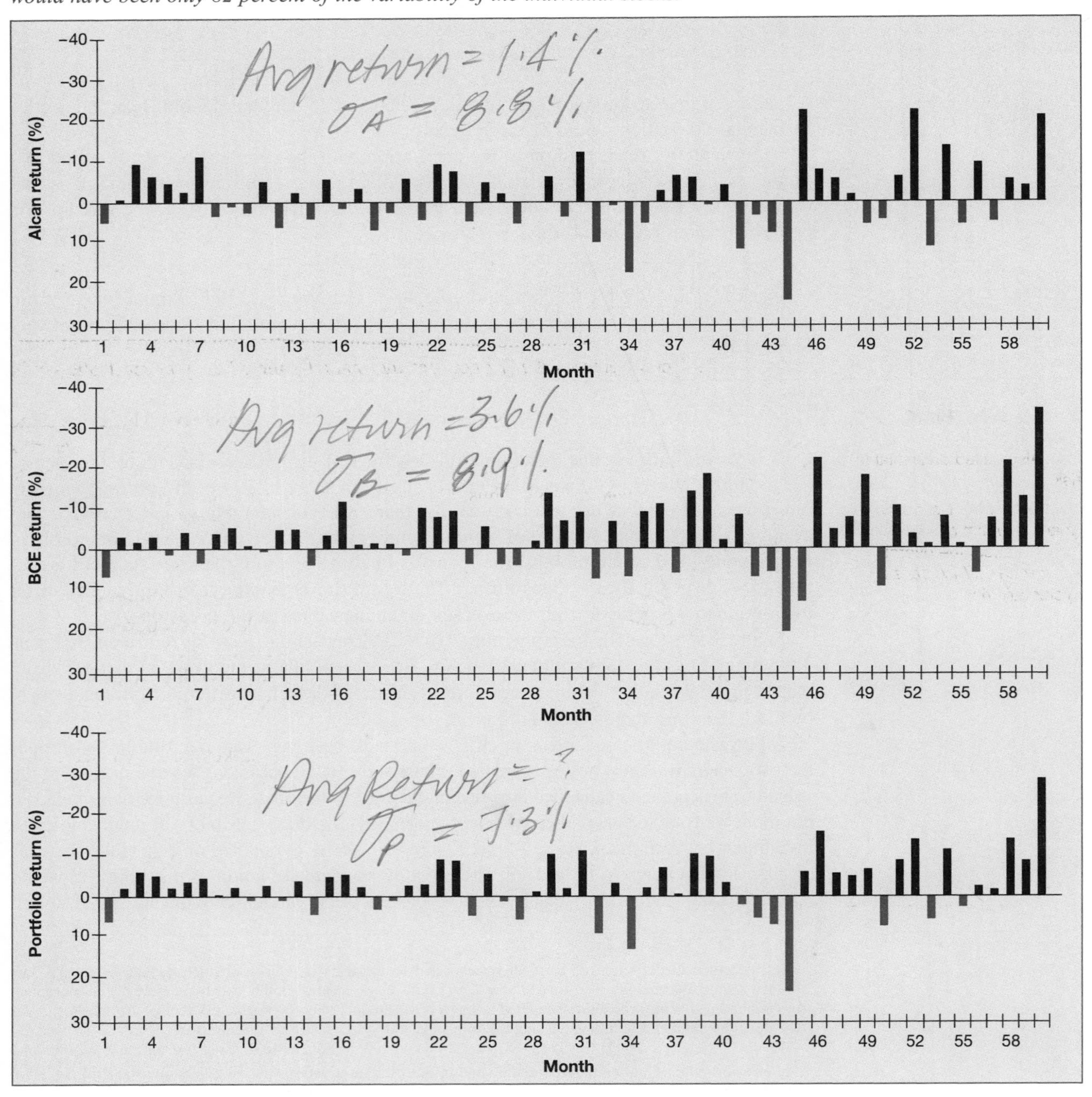

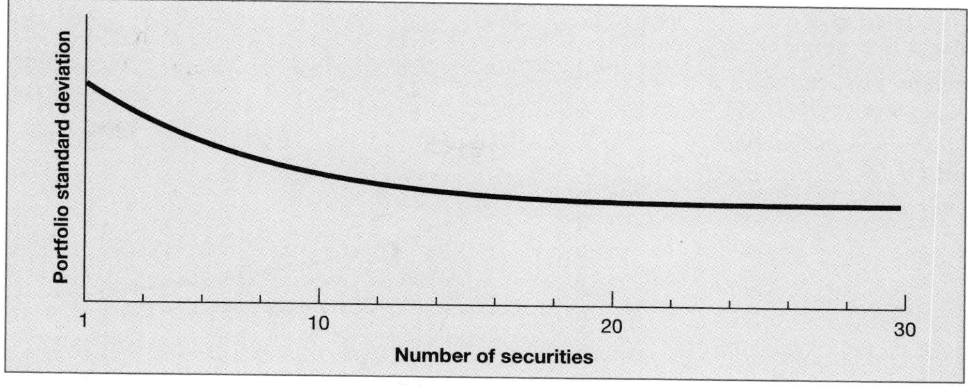

FIGURE 9.6
Diversification reduces risk (standard deviation) rapidly at first, then more slowly.

MARKET RISK VERSUS UNIQUE RISK

Our examples illustrate that even a little diversification can provide a substantial reduction in variability. Suppose you calculate and compare the standard deviations of randomly chosen one-stock portfolios, two-stock portfolios, five-stock portfolios, and so on. You can see from Figure 9.6 that diversification can cut the variability of returns by about half. But you can get most of this benefit with relatively few stocks: the improvement is slight when the number of stocks is increased beyond, say, 15.

Figure 9.6 also illustrates that no matter how many securities you hold, you cannot eliminate all risk. There remains the danger that the market—including your portfolio—will plummet.

unique risk Risk factors affecting only the particular firm. Also called diversifiable risk.

market risk Economywide (macroeconomic) sources of risk that affect the overall stock market. Also called systematic risk.

The risk that can be eliminated by diversification is called **unique risk.** This is the same as saying that stock returns tend to be less than perfectly positively correlated. The risk that you can't avoid—regardless of how much you diversify—is generally known as **market risk**, or *systematic risk.* Thus, although stocks are less than perfectly positively correlated, they are nonetheless positively correlated, and portfolio standard deviation cannot be reduced to zero.

***Unique risk* arises because many of the perils that surround an individual company are peculiar to that company and perhaps its direct competitors. *Market risk* stems from economywide perils that threaten all businesses. Market risk explains why stocks have a tendency to move together, so that even well-diversified portfolios are exposed to market movements.**

Figure 9.7 divides risk into its two parts—unique risk and market risk. If you have only a single stock, unique risk is very important; but once you have a portfolio of 30 or more stocks, diversification has done most of what it can to eliminate risk.

For a reasonably well-diversified portfolio, only market risk matters.

EXAMPLE 9.3 *International Portfolio Diversification*

If holding a portfolio of Canadian stocks reduces investors' risk without sacrificing return, holding a portfolio of Canadian and foreign stocks should further reduce risk. Investing internationally yields benefits to investors from increased diversification; that is, the decreased portfolio standard deviation which results from including an international

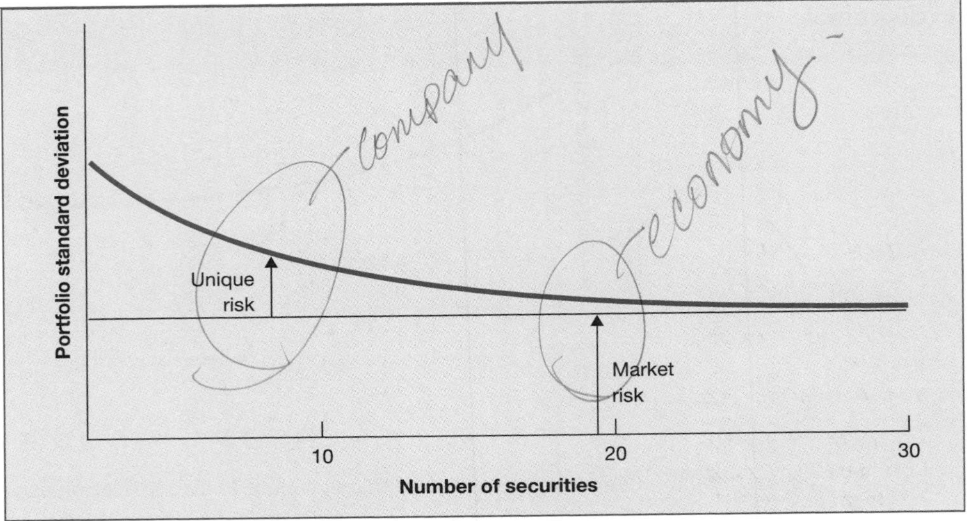

FIGURE 9.7
Diversification eliminates unique risk. But there is some risk that diversification cannot eliminate. This is called market risk.

component within their portfolios. The ability to reduce risk without sacrificing return arises because not all markets move up or down at the same time. Due to this less than perfect positive correlation between the Canadian financial markets and financial markets in other countries, losses in the domestic market can often be offset by gains in those foreign markets that have a low correlation to our markets. By diversifying internationally, the investor hopes to have international investments that are doing well when the Canadian portion of the portfolio is not, and vice versa.

Look back at Figure 9.4. You will see that the standard deviations of the TSX and the S&P 500 tend to move together but not perfectly. The correlation coefficient between the annual rates of return of the two market indexes over the period 1956 to 2000 is about 69 percent. By holding both stock indexes, you can reduce portfolio risk, since the markets are not perfectly correlated. But the high degree of integration between the U.S. and Canadian economies and stock markets means that the correlation coefficient is far from zero, reflecting the common market risk.

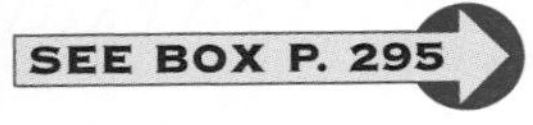
SEE BOX P. 295

You can add stocks from other countries to further reduce the portfolio risk provided that their returns are less than perfectly correlated with the U.S. and Canadian markets. See the nearby Finance in Action box for a discussion of globalization and the opportunities for international portfolio diversification.

9.5 Thinking about Risk

How can you tell which risks are unique and diversifiable? Where do market risks come from? Here are three messages to help you think clearly about risk.

MESSAGE 1: SOME RISKS LOOK BIG AND DANGEROUS BUT REALLY ARE DIVERSIFIABLE

Managers confront risks "up close and personal." They must make decisions about particular investments. The failure of such an investment could cost a promotion, bonus, or a steady job. Yet that same investment may not seem risky to an investor who can stand back and combine it in a diversified portfolio with many other assets or securities.

FINANCE IN ACTION

A Small World After All

Academic researchers and investment advisers have been strongly recommending that investors diversify their portfolios by investing in international equities. Supported by extensive academic research that has proclaimed the risk reduction advantages of international diversification, increasing numbers of investors look for international equity components within the asset allocation of their portfolios. Here are some thoughts on opportunities for international diversification from a well-known financial economist, Burton Malkiel, as reported in Benefits Canada, *a trade journal for pension fund managers.*

The importance of international diversification is critical for institutional investors in Canada. This country represents less than 3 percent of the global economy for heaven's sake. Too significant a reliance on domestic stocks and bonds is a recipe for disaster.

Canadian pension fund executives have understood this for years. The assets of Canada's top 100 pension funds have never been as internationally diversified as they are now. The global equity holdings held by the country's 100 largest funds jumped almost $9 billion in 2000 alone.

But while the importance of international diversification is understood, its effectiveness has to be seen within the context of this emerging global economy. Just as globalization helps Canadian pension fund managers develop international investment portfolios, it may also reduce the diversification benefits those portfolios offer.

That warning comes from one of the world's most influential economists. Burton Malkiel, the Chemical Bank chairperson, professor of economics at Princeton University, and author of *A Random Walk Down Wall Street*, says it is time to reexamine the assumption that international markets don't move in lockstep.

"Our global markets are much more closely tied and the correlations among markets are much higher than they have been in the past," says Malkiel. He made his comments during an interview with *Benefits Canada* last month. "The diversification benefits are likely to be a little less."

Malkiel isn't suggesting Canadian pension asset managers buck the international investment trend. In fact he describes himself as a "big believer in globalization." But Malkiel warns you can't assume a level of diversification that isn't there.

Globalization lends stability to international markets—it encourages higher correlations. For example, we need look only as far as British Columbia to understand the international impact of a financial crisis in Asia.

What is Malkiel's recommendation? There's more to investing than geography.

"There are three asset classes where correlations have not increased," he says. "One is real estate—global real estate as well. The second is bonds. I consider high yield bonds to be an equity type of asset. You're really getting paid to take those risks in the bond market, and the correlations don't seem to have gone up. Third, I think the risk of inflation is going to be a worldwide phenomenon. One asset class that is uncorrelated with both equities and real estate are inflation-protection securities such as are issued by the U.S. and Canadian federal governments."

Adapted from "A Small World after All," Kevin Press, kpress@rmpublishing.com.

Source: *Benefits Canada* 25/5 (May 2001), p.7.

EXAMPLE 9.4 *Wildcat Oil Wells*

You have just been promoted to director of exploration, Western Hemisphere, of MPS Oil. The manager of your exploration team in far-off Costaguana has appealed for $20 million extra to drill in an even steamier part of the Costaguanan jungle. The manager thinks there may be an "elephant" field worth $500 million or more hidden there. But the chance of finding it is at best one in 10, and yesterday, MPS's CEO sourly commented on the $100 million already "wasted" on Costaguanan exploration.

Is this a risky investment? For you it probably is; you may be a hero if oil is found, and a goat otherwise. But MPS drills hundreds of wells worldwide; for the company as a whole, it's the *average* success rate that matters. Geologic risks (is there oil or not?) should average out. The risk of a worldwide drilling program is much less than the apparent risk of any single wildcat well.

Back up one step and think of the investors who buy MPS stock. The investors may hold other oil companies, too, as well as companies producing steel, computers, clothing, cement, and breakfast cereal. They naturally—and realistically—assume that your successes and failures in drilling oil wells will average out with the thousands of independent bets made by the companies in their portfolio.

Therefore, the risks you face in Costaguana do not affect the rate of return they demand for investing in MPS Oil. Diversified investors in MPS stock will be happy if you find that elephant field, but they are unlikely to notice if you fail and lose your job. In any case, they will not demand a higher *average* rate of return for worrying about geologic risks in Costaguana.

▶ EXAMPLE 9.5 *Fire Insurance*

Would you be willing to write a $100,000 fire insurance policy on your neighbour's house? The neighbour is willing to pay you $100 for a year's protection, and experience shows that the chance of fire damage in a given year is substantially less than one in a thousand. But if your neighbour's house is damaged by fire, you would have to pay up.

Few of us have deep enough pockets to insure our neighbours, even if the odds of fire damage are very low. Insurance seems a risky business if you think policy by policy. But a large insurance company, which may issue a million policies, is concerned only with average losses, which can be predicted with excellent accuracy.

☑ CHECK POINT 9.8

Imagine a laboratory at IBM, late at night. One scientist speaks to another.

"You're right, Watson, I admit this experiment will consume all the rest of this year's budget. I don't know what we'll do if it fails. But if this yttrium–magnoosium alloy superconducts, the patents will be worth millions."

Would this be a good or bad investment for IBM? Can't say. But from the ultimate investors' viewpoint this is *not* a risky investment. Explain why.

MESSAGE 2: MARKET RISKS ARE MACRO RISKS

We have seen that diversified portfolios are not exposed to the unique risks of individual stocks but are exposed to the uncertain events that affect the entire securities market and the entire economy. These are macroeconomic, or "macro," factors such as changes in interest rates, industrial production, inflation, foreign exchange rates, and energy costs. These factors affect most firms' earnings and stock prices. When the relevant macro risks turn generally favourable, stock prices rise and investors do well; when the same variables go the other way, investors suffer.

You can often assess relative market risks just by thinking through exposures to the business cycle and other macro variables. The following businesses have substantial macro and market risks:

- *Airlines.* Because business travel falls during a recession, and individuals postpone vacations and other discretionary travel, the airline industry is subject to the swings of the business cycle. On the positive side, airline profits really take off when business is booming and personal incomes are rising.
- *Machine tool manufacturers.* These businesses are especially exposed to the business cycle. Manufacturing companies that have excess capacity rarely buy new machine tools to expand. During recessions, excess capacity can be quite high.

Here, on the other hand, are two industries with less than average macro exposures:

- *Food companies.* Companies selling staples, such as breakfast cereal, flour, and dog food, find that demand for their products is relatively stable in good times and bad.

- *Electric utilities.* Business demand for electric power varies somewhat across the business cycle, but by much less than demand for air travel or machine tools. Also, many electric utilities' profits are regulated. Regulation cuts off upside profit potential but also gives the utilities the opportunity to increase prices when demand is slack.

Remember, investors holding diversified portfolios are mostly concerned with macroeconomic risks. They do not worry about microeconomic risks peculiar to a particular company or investment project. Micro risks wash out in diversified portfolios. Company managers may worry about both macro and micro risks, but only the former affect the cost of capital.

CHECK POINT 9.9

Which company of each of the following pairs would you expect to be more exposed to macro risks?

a. A luxury Montreal restaurant or an established Burger Queen franchise?
b. A paint company that sells through small paint and hardware stores to do-it-yourselfers, or a paint company that sells in large volumes to Ford, GM, and Honda?

MESSAGE 3: RISK CAN BE MEASURED

Air Canada clearly has more exposure to macro risks than food companies such as Westons or Kraft. These are easy cases. But is IBM stock a riskier investment than Imperial Oil? That's not an easy question to reason through. We can, however, *measure* the risk of IBM and Imperial Oil by looking at how their stock prices fluctuate.

We've already hinted at how to do this. Remember that diversified investors are concerned with market risks. The movements of the stock market sum up the net effects of all relevant macroeconomic uncertainties. If the market portfolio of all traded stocks is up in a particular month, we conclude that the net effect of macroeconomic news is positive. Remember, the performance of the market is barely affected by a firm-specific event. These cancel out across thousands of stocks in the market.

How do we measure the risk of a single stock, like IBM or Imperial Oil? We do not look at the stocks in isolation, because the risks that loom when you're up close to a single company are often diversifiable. Instead we measure the individual stock's sensitivity to the fluctuations of the overall stock market. We will show you how this works in the next chapter.

9.6 Summary

1. How can one estimate the opportunity cost of capital for an "average risk" project?

Over the past 75 years the calculated return on the **TSX Total Return Index Value** of common stocks has averaged about 7 percent a year higher than the return on safe Treasury bills. This is the **risk premium** that investors have received for taking on the risk of investing in stocks. Long-term bonds have offered a higher return than Treasury bills but less than stocks.

If the risk premium in the past is a guide to the future, we can estimate the expected return on the market today by adding that 7 percent expected risk premium to today's interest rate on Treasury bills. This would be the opportunity cost of capital for an average-risk project, that is, one with the same risk as a typical share of common stock.

2. How is the standard deviation of returns for individual common stocks or a stock portfolio calculated?

The spread of outcomes on different investments is commonly measured by the **variance** or **standard deviation** of the possible outcomes. The variance is the average of the squared deviations around the average outcome, and the standard deviation is the square root of the variance. The standard deviation of the returns on a market portfolio of common stocks has averaged about 19 percent per year.

3. **Why does diversification reduce risk?**

The standard deviation of returns is generally higher on individual stocks than it is on the market. Because individual stocks do not move in exact lockstep, much of their risk can be diversified away. By spreading your portfolio across many investments you smooth out the risk of your overall position. The risk that can be eliminated through diversification is known as **unique risk.**

4. **What is the difference between unique risk, which can be diversified away, and market risk, which cannot?**

Even if you hold a well-diversified portfolio, you will not eliminate all risk. You will still be exposed to macroeconomic changes that affect most stocks and the overall stock market. These macro risks combine to create **market risk**—that is, the risk that the market as a whole will slump.

Stocks are not all equally risky. But what do we mean by a "high risk" stock? We don't mean a stock that is risky if held in isolation; we mean a stock that makes an above-average contribution to the risk of a diversified portfolio. In other words, investors don't need to worry much about the risk that they can diversify away; they *do* need to worry about risk that can't be diversified. This depends on the stock's sensitivity to macroeconomic conditions.

Related Web Links

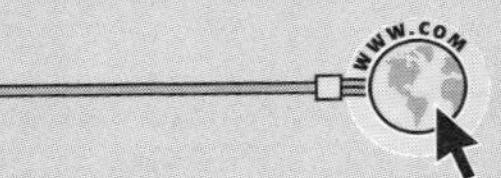

www.financialengines.com Some good introductory material on risk, return, and inflation

www.stern.nyu.edu/~adamodar This New York University site contains some historical data on market risk and return

www.tsx.ca Toronto Stock Exchange and TSX Venture Exchange

www.nyse.com New York Stock Exchange

www.spglobal.com Standard & Poor's indexes, including S&P/TSX Composite Index

Key Terms

market index	273	Dow Jones Industrial Average	274	variance	280
S&P/TSX Composite Index	274	Standard & Poor's Composite Index	274	standard deviation	280
S&P/TSX Total Return Index	274	maturity premium	276	diversification	285
S&P/TSX Capped Composite Index	274	risk premium	276	correlation coefficient	289
				unique risk	293
				market risk	293

Questions and Problems

*Answers in Appendix B

Basic

*1. **Rate of Return.** A stock is selling today for $40 per share. At the end of the year, it pays a dividend of $2 per share and sells for $44. What is the total rate of return on the stock? What are the dividend yield and capital gains yield?

2. **Rate of Return.** Return to problem 1. Suppose the year-end stock price after the dividend is paid is $36. What are the dividend yield and capital gains yield in this case? Why is the dividend yield unaffected?

*3. **Real versus Nominal Returns.** You purchase 100 shares of stock for $40 a share. The stock pays a $2 per share dividend at year-end. What is the rate of return on your investment for these end-of-year stock prices? What is your real (inflation-adjusted) rate of return? Assume an inflation rate of 5 percent.

a. $38
b. $40
c. $42

4. **Real versus Nominal Returns.** The Costaguanan stock market provided a rate of return of 95 percent. The inflation rate in Costaguana during the year was 80 percent. In Canada, in contrast, the stock mar-

ket return was only 14 percent, but the inflation rate was only 3 percent. Which country's stock market provided the higher real rate of return?

*5. **Real versus Nominal Returns.** The inflation rate in Canada between 1950 and 2000 averaged 4.4 percent. What was the average real rate of return on Treasury bills, government bonds, and common stocks in that period? Use the data in Check Point 9.2.

6. **Real versus Nominal Returns.** Do you think it is possible for risk-free Treasury bills to offer a negative nominal interest rate? Might they offer a negative *real* expected rate of return?

*7. **Market Indexes.** The accompanying table shows the complete history of stock prices on the Polish stock exchange for 9 weeks in 1991. At that time only five stocks were traded. Construct two stock market indexes, one using equal weights, the other using value weights.

Prices (in zlotys) for the first 9 weeks of trading on the Warsaw Stock Exchange, beginning in April 1991. There was one trading session per week. Only five stocks were listed in the first 9 weeks.

	Stock				
Week	**Tonsil (Electronics) 1,500***	**Prochnik (Garments) 1,500***	**Krosno (Glass) 2,200***	**Exbud (Construction) 1,000***	**Kable (Electronics) 1,000***
1	85	56	59.5	149	80
2	76.5	51	53.5	164	80
3	69	46	49	180	80
4	62.5	41.5	47	198	79.5
5	56.5	38	51.5	217	80
6	56	41.5	56.5	196	80
7	61.5	45.5	62	177	80
8	67.5	50	60	160	80.5
9	61	45.5	54	160	72.5

* Number of shares outstanding.
Source: We are indebted to Professor Mary M. Cutler for providing these data.

8. **Stock Market History.** Using the data in problem 7, calculate the average rate of return and standard deviation of return for each stock as well as for an equal-weighted portfolio of all the stocks. Do you observe any benefits from diversification?

PRACTICE

*9. **Risk Premiums.** Here are annual stock market, bond and bill percentage returns between 1996 and 2001:

Year	TSX Return	T-Bill Return	Long Bond Return
1996	28.35	4.49	14.29
1997	14.98	3.30	17.45
1998	–1.58	4.81	14.13
1999	31.71	4.83	–7.15
2000	7.41	5.49	13.64

a. What were the risk premiums on the TSX and on long-term government bonds in each year?
b. What were the average risk premiums for the TSX and long-term government bonds?
c. What was the standard deviation of each risk premium? Do they make sense?

10. **Market Indexes.** In 1990, the Dow Jones Industrial Average was at a level of about 2,600. In mid-2001, it was about 10,000. Would you expect the Dow in 2001 to be more or less likely to move up or down by more than 40 points in a day than in 1990? Does this mean the market was riskier in 2001 than it was in 1990?

11. **Maturity Premiums.** Investments in long-term government bonds produced a negative average return during the period 1977–1981. How should we interpret this? Did bond investors in 1977 expect to earn a negative maturity premium? What do these 5 years of bond returns tell us about the normal future maturity premium?

12. **Risk Premiums.** What will happen to the opportunity cost of capital if investors suddenly become especially conservative and less willing to bear investment risk?

13. **Risk Premiums and Discount Rates.** You believe that a stock with the same market risk as the TSX will sell at year-end at a price of $50. The stock will pay a dividend at year-end of $2. What price will you be willing to pay for the stock today? *Hint:* Start by checking today's 3-month Treasury bill rate.

*14. **Scenario Analysis.** The common stock of Leaning Tower of Pita, Inc., a restaurant chain, will generate the following payoffs to investors next year:

	Probability	Dividend	Stock Price
Boom	.3	$5	$195
Normal economy	.5	2	100
Recession	.2	0	0

The company goes out of business if a recession hits. Calculate the expected rate of return and standard deviation of return to Leaning Tower of Pita shareholders. The stock is selling today for $90.

*15. **Portfolio Risk.** Who would view the stock of Leaning Tower of Pita (see problem 14) as a risk-reducing investment—the owner of a gambling casino or a successful bankruptcy lawyer? Explain.

16. **Scenario Analysis.** The common stock of Escapist Films sells for $25 a share and offers the following payoffs next year:

	Probability	Dividend	Stock Price
Boom	.3	$0	$18
Normal economy	.5	1	26
Recession	.2	3	34

Calculate the expected return and standard deviation of Escapist. Then calculate the expected return and standard deviation of a portfolio half invested in Escapist and half in Leaning Tower of Pita (from problem 14). Show that the portfolio standard deviation is lower than either stock's. Explain why this happens.

*17. **Scenario Analysis.** Consider the following scenario analysis:

		Rate of Return	
Scenario	**Probability**	**Stocks**	**Bonds**
Recession	.2	–5%	+14%
Normal economy	.6	+15	+8
Boom	.2	+25	+4

a. Is it reasonable to assume that bonds will provide higher returns in recessions than in booms?
b. Calculate the expected rate of return and standard deviation for each investment.
c. Which investment would you prefer?

18. **Portfolio Analysis.** Use the data in the previous problem and consider a portfolio with weights of .60 in stocks and .40 in bonds.

a. What is the rate of return on the portfolio in each scenario?
b. What is the expected rate of return and standard deviation of the portfolio?
c. Would you prefer to invest in the portfolio, in stocks only, or in bonds only?
d. Calculate the correlation coefficient for the bond and stock returns.

*19. **Risk Premium.** If the stock market return in 2008 turns out to be –20 percent, what will happen to our estimate of the "normal" risk premium? Does this make sense?

20. **Diversification.** In which of the following situations would you get the largest reduction in risk by spreading your portfolio across two stocks?

    a. The stock returns vary with each other.
    b. The stock returns are independent.
    c. The stock returns vary against each other.

*21. **Market Risk.** Which firm from each pair would you expect to have greater market risk?

    a. General Steel or General Food Supplies.
    b. Club Med or General Cinemas.

22. **Risk and Return.** A stock will provide a rate of return of either –20 percent or +30 percent.

    a. If both possibilities are equally likely, calculate the expected return and standard deviation.
    b. If Treasury bills yield 5 percent, and investors believe that the stock offers a satisfactory expected return, what must be the market risk of the stock?

*23. **Unique versus Market Risk.** Sassafras Oil is staking all its remaining capital on wildcat exploration off the Côte d'Huile. There is a 10 percent chance of discovering a field with reserves of 50 million barrels. If it finds oil, it will immediately sell the reserves to Big Oil, at a price depending on the state of the economy. Thus the possible payoffs are as follows:

	Value of Reserves, per Barrel	Value of Reserves, 50 Million Barrels	Value of Dryholes
Boom	$4.00	$200,000,000	0
Normal economy	$5.00	$250,000,000	0
Recession	$6.00	$300,000,000	0

Is Sassafras Oil a risky investment for a diversified investor in the stock market—compared, say, to the stock of Leaning Tower of Pita, described in problem 14? Explain.

24. **Portfolio Risk and Return.** The expected return on Big Time Toys is 9 percent and its standard deviation is 20 percent. The expected return on Chemical Industries is 8 percent and its standard deviation is 25 percent.

    a. Suppose the correlation coefficient for the two stocks' returns is .2. What is the expected return and standard deviation of a portfolio with 30 percent invested in Big Time Toys and the rest in Chemical Industries?
    b. If the correlation coefficient is .7, recalculate the portfolio expected return and standard deviation, assuming the portfolio weights are unchanged.
    c. Explain the difference between your answers to (a) and (b).

*25. **Portfolio Risk and Return.** Using the data in problem 9,

    a. Calculate the average rate of return and standard deviation of return for the TSX, government bonds, and T-bills between 1996 and 2000.
    b. Form a portfolio with one-third in each of the three securities and calculate its average rate of return and standard deviation. Can you see any benefit from diversification?

INTERNET PROBLEMS

1. **U.S. market data.** Go to www.stern.nyu.edu/~adamodar, a website of New York University finance professor Aswath Damodaran. Spend some time exploring and you will find a lot of interesting spreadsheets and information. While there, click on "Updated Data," find "Historical Returns on Stocks, Bonds, and Bills – United States," and select "Download." The data should now be in a spreadsheet. Compute the arithmetic average for the annual return for stocks, T-bills, and T-bonds for the last 30

years of data. Compute the standard deviation for each set of returns. Do the values make sense? Repeat using only the last 5 years of data. Do the values still make sense?

2. **Canadian market data.** Go to the website of the Institute of Canadian Actuaries at www.actuaries.ca/publications/index2001_e.html and find the *Report on Canadian Economic Statistics 1924–2000.* Click on "Tables" and then look at Table 1-A, which contains the annual rates of return for various financial indexes. Using the data, calculate the arithmetic average for the annual return and standard deviation for stocks, Canada long-term bonds, mortgages, and T-bills from 1952. For each index, calculate its excess return over T-bills. Also, adjust each series by inflation to calculate the real rates of return. Do the average returns, standard deviations, and spreads over T-bills make sense? Repeat using only the last 5 years of data. Do the calculated values still make sense? Why might using only a few years of data not be a smart idea when estimating the market risk premium?

SOLUTIONS TO CHECK POINTS

9.1 The bond price at the end of the year is \$1,050. Therefore, the capital gain on each bond is \$1,050 – \$1,020 = \$30. Your dollar return is the sum of the income from the bond, \$80, plus the capital gain, \$30, or \$110. The rate of return is

$$\frac{\text{Income plus capital gain}}{\text{Original price}} = \frac{80 + 30}{1{,}020} = .108, \text{ or } 10.8\%$$

Real rate of return is

$$\frac{1 + \text{nominal return}}{1 + \text{inflation rate}} - 1 = \frac{1.108}{1.04} - 1 = .065, \text{ or } 6.5\%$$

9.2 The risk premium on stocks is the average return in excess of Treasury bills. This was 12.8 – 6.5 = 6.3%. The maturity premium is the average return on Canada long bonds minus the return on Treasury bills. It was 7.1 – 6.5 = .6%.

9.3 Expected return = (.25 x 70) + (.5 x 10) + (.25 x –50) = +10%
Variance and standard deviation calculation with equal probabilities:

Rate of Return	Deviation	Squared Deviation
+70%	+60%	3,600
+10	0	0
+10	0	0
–50	–60	3,600

Variance = average of squared deviations = 7,200/4 = 1,800
Standard deviation = square root of variance = $\sqrt{1{,}800}$ = 42.4, or about 42%

Variance and standard deviation calculation with unequal probabilities:

(1) Rate of Return (%)	(2) Probability of Return	(3) Deviations from Expected Return (%)	(4) Probability × Squared Deviation
+70	.25	+60	.25 × 3600 = 900
+10	.50	0	.50 × 0 = 0
–50	.25	–60	.25 × 3600 = 900

Variance = sum of squared deviations weighted by probabilities = 900 + 0 + 900 = 1,800
Standard deviation = square root of variance = $\sqrt{1{,}800}$ = 42.4, or about 42%

9.4 The standard deviation should decrease because there is now a lower probability of the more extreme outcomes. The expected rate of return on the auto stock is now

$$[.3 \times (-8\%)] + [.4 \times 5\%] + [.3 \times 18\%] = 5\%$$

The variance is

$$[.3 \times (-8 - 5)^2] + [.4 \times (5 - 5)^2] + [.3 \times (18 - 5)^2] = 101.4$$

The standard deviation is $\sqrt{101.4} = 10.07$ percent, which is lower than the value assuming equal probabilities of each scenario.

9.5 a. Since sunshine heats the air, the number of hours of sunshine per day and average daily temperature will be positively correlated. However, they will not be perfectly positively correlated because other factors affect air temperature such as latitude, altitude, and season.

b. The more television watched, the less time you have to study and the lower will be your grade in finance. Thus these two variables will be negatively correlated.

c. The quality of the in-flight movie has no relationship with the flying time. Thus these two variables are uncorrelated. Of course, if the movie is boring, the trip will *seem* to take longer!

d. The connectedness of the Canadian and U.S. economies and financial markets leads to a positive correlation between interest rates in Canada and the United States.

9.6 Let the auto stock be stock 1 and the gold stock be stock 2. Portfolio standard deviation formula for stocks 1 and 2 is

$$\sigma_p = \sqrt{x_1^2\sigma_1^2 + x_2^2\sigma_2^2 + 2x_1x_2\rho_{12}\sigma_1\sigma_2}$$

The known values are $x_1 = .75$, $x_2 = .25$, $\sigma_1 = .106$, $\sigma_2 = .164$, and $\sigma_P = .039$. The unknown is the correlation coefficient, ρ_{12}.

Substitute in all of the known values and solve for ρ_{12}:

$$\rho_{12} = [(.039)^2 - (.75)^2(.106)^2 - (.25)^2(.164)^2]/[(2)(.75)(.25)(.106)(.164)] = -.994$$

9.7 The gold mining stock's returns are more highly correlated with the silver mining company than with a car company. As a result, the automotive firm will offer a greater diversification benefit. The power of diversification is lowest when rates of return are highly correlated, performing well or poorly in tandem. Shifting the portfolio from one such firm to another has little impact on overall risk.

9.8 The success of this project depends on the experiment. Success does *not* depend on the performance of the overall economy. The experiment creates a diversifiable risk. A portfolio of many stocks will embody "bets" on many such unique risks. Some bets will work out and some will fail. Because the outcomes of these risks do not depend on common factors, such as the overall state of the economy, the risks will tend to cancel out in a well-diversified portfolio.

9.9 a. The luxury restaurant will be more sensitive to the state of the economy because expense account meals will be curtailed in a recession. Burger Queen meals should be relatively recession-proof.

b. The paint company that sells to the auto producers will be more sensitive to the state of the economy. In a downturn, auto sales fall dramatically as consumers stretch the lives of their cars. In contrast, in a recession, more people "do it themselves," which makes paint sales through small stores more stable and less sensitive to the economy.

CHAPTER 10

Risk, Return, and Capital Budgeting

10.1 Measuring Market Risk

10.2 Risk and Return

10.3 Capital Budgeting and Project Risk

10.4 Summary

In Chapter 9 we began to come to grips with the topic of risk. We made the distinction between *unique* risk and macro, or *market,* risk. Unique risk arises from events that affect only the individual firm or its immediate competitors; it can be eliminated by diversification. But regardless of how much you diversify, you cannot avoid the macroeconomic events that create market risk. This is why investors do not require a higher rate of return to compensate for unique risk but do need a higher return to persuade them to take on market risk.

How can you measure the market risk of a security or a project? We will see that market risk is usually measured by the sensitivity of the investment's returns to fluctuations in the market. We will also see that the risk premium investors demand should be proportional to this sensitivity. This relationship between risk and return is a useful way to estimate the return that investors expect from investing in common stocks.

Finally, we will distinguish between the risk of the company's securities and the risk of an individual project. We will also consider what managers should do when the risk of the project is different from that of the company's existing business.

After studying this chapter you should be able to

- Measure and interpret the market risk, or beta, of a security.
- Relate the market risk of a security to the rate of return that investors demand.
- Calculate the opportunity cost of capital for a project.

Measuring Market Risk

market portfolio Portfolio of all assets in the economy. In practice a broad stock market index, such as the S&P/TSX or S&P 500 Composite Index, is used to represent the market.

Changes in interest rates, government spending, monetary policy, oil prices, foreign exchange rates, and other macroeconomic events affect almost all companies and the returns on almost all stocks. We can therefore assess the impact of "macro" news by tracking the rate of return on a **market portfolio** of all securities. If the market is up on a particular day, then the net impact of macroeconomic changes must be positive. We know the performance of the market reflects only macro events, because firm-specific events—that is, unique risks—average out when we look at the combined performance of thousands of companies and securities.

In principle, the market portfolio should contain all assets in the world economy—not just stocks, but bonds, foreign securities, real estate, and so on. In practice, however, financial analysts make do with indexes of the stock market, such as the S&P/TSX Composite Index (TSX) or the Standard & Poor's Composite Index (the S&P 500).[1]

beta Sensitivity of a stock's return to the return on the market portfolio.

Our task here is to define and measure the risk of *individual* common stocks. You can probably see where we are headed. Risk depends on exposure to macroeconomic events and can be measured as the sensitivity of a stock's returns to fluctuations in returns on the market portfolio. This sensitivity is called the stock's **beta.** Beta is often written as the Greek letter β.

MEASURING BETA

In the last chapter we looked at the variability of individual securities. Biomira had the highest standard deviation and Westcoast Energy the lowest. If you had held Biomira on its own, your returns would have varied almost five times as much as if you had held Westcoast Energy. But wise investors don't put all their eggs in just one basket: they reduce their risk by diversification. An investor with a diversified portfolio will be interested in the effect each stock has on the risk of the entire portfolio.

Diversification can eliminate the risk that is unique to individual stocks, but not the risk that the market as a whole may decline, carrying your stocks with it.

Some stocks are less affected than others by market fluctuations. Investment managers talk about "defensive" and "aggressive" stocks. Defensive stocks are not very sensitive to market fluctuations. In contrast, aggressive stocks amplify any market movements. If the market goes up, it is good to be in aggressive stocks; if it goes down, it is better to be in defensive stocks (and better still to have your money in the bank).

Aggressive stocks have high betas, betas greater than 1.0, meaning that their returns tend to respond more than one-for-one to changes in the return of the overall market. The betas of defensive stocks are less than 1.0. The returns of these stocks vary less than one-for-one with market returns. The average beta of all stocks is—no surprises here—1.0 exactly.

Now we'll show you how betas are measured.

▶ EXAMPLE 10.1 *Measuring Beta for Turbot-Charged Seafoods*

Suppose we look back at the trading history of Turbot-Charged Seafoods and pick out 6 months when the return on the market portfolio was plus or minus 1 percent.

[1] We discussed the most popular stock market indexes in Section 9.2.

Month	Market Return, %	Turbot-Charged Seafood's Return, %	
1	+1	+ .8	
2	+1	+ 1.8	Average = +.8%
3	+1	− .2	
4	−1	− 1.8	
5	−1	+ .2	Average = −.8%
6	−1	− .8	

Look at Figure 10.1, where these observations are plotted. We've drawn a line through the average performance of Turbot when the market is up or down by 1 percent. *The slope of this line is Turbot's beta.* You can see right away that the beta is .8, because on average Turbot stock gains or loses .8 percent when the market is up or down by 1 percent. Notice that a 2-percentage-point difference in the market return (−1 to +1) generates on average a 1.6-percentage-point difference for Turbot shareholders (−.8 to +.8). The ratio, 1.6/2 = .8, is beta.

In 4 months, Turbot's returns lie above or below the line in Figure 10.1. The distance from the line shows the response of Turbot's stock returns to news or events that affected Turbot but did *not* affect the overall market. For example, in Month 2, investors in Turbot stock benefited from good macroeconomic news (the market was up 1 percent) and also from some favourable news specific to Turbot. The market rise gave a boost of .8 percent to Turbot stock (beta of .8 times the 1 percent market return). Then firm-specific news gave Turbot shareholders an extra 1 percent return, for a total return that month of 1.8 percent.

As this example illustrates, we can break down common stock returns into two parts: the part explained by market returns and the firm's beta, and the part due to news that is specific to the firm. Fluctuations in the first part reflect market risk; fluctuations in the second part reflect unique risk.

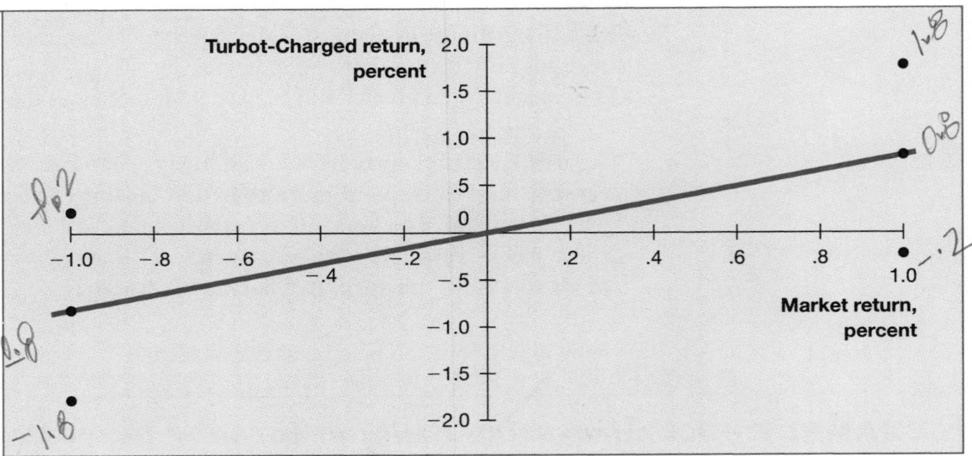

FIGURE 10.1
This figure is a plot of the data presented in the table from Example 10.1. Each point shows the performance of Turbot-Charged Seafoods stock when the overall market is either up or down by 1 percent. On average, Turbot-Charged moves in the same direction as the market, but not as far. Therefore, Turbot-Charged's beta is less than 1.0. We can measure beta by the slope of a line fitted to the points in the figure. In this case it is .8.

Of course diversification can get rid of the unique risks. That's why wise investors, who don't put all their eggs in one basket, will look to Turbot's less-than-average beta and call its stock "defensive."

CHECK POINT 10.1

Here are 6 months' returns to shareholders in the Anchovy Queen restaurant chain:

Month	Market Return, %	Anchovy Queen Return, %
1	+1	+2
2	+1	+0
3	+1	+1
4	−1	−1
5	−1	+0
6	−1	−2

Draw a figure like Figure 10.1 and check the slope of the fitted line. What is Anchovy Queen's beta?

Real life doesn't serve up numbers quite as convenient as those in our examples so far. However, the procedure for measuring real companies' betas is exactly the same:

1. Observe rates of return, usually monthly, for the stock and the market.
2. Plot the observations as in Figure 10.1.
3. Fit a line showing the average return to the stock at different market returns.

Beta is the slope of the fitted line.

This may sound like a lot of work but in practice computers do it for you. In Excel, the Slope function will give you the slope of a fitted line. Suppose you have 60 monthly rates of return for a stock and for the TSX. If the stock returns are in cells A1 to A60 and the market returns are in cells B1 to B60, the beta of the stock is Slope(A1:A60,B1:B60).

You can also calculate the beta of a stock if you know the correlation of the stock's return with the market's return, and the standard deviations of the stock and market returns. Using the notation from Chapter 9, let $\rho_{j,m}$ be the correlation coefficient for the return on stock j with the market; σ_j, the standard deviation of the return on stock j; and σ_m, the standard deviation of the return on the market. The beta of stock j is the correlation coefficient times the stock's standard deviation, divided by the market's standard deviation:

$$\text{Beta of stock j, } \beta_j = \frac{\rho_{j,m}\sigma_j}{\sigma_m}$$

For example, if a stock has a correlation coefficient with the market equal to .7 and the stock return's standard deviation is 30 percent and the market return's standard deviation is 20 percent, the beta of the stock is .7 × .3/.2 = 1.05. If the stock's correlation with the market is only .3, its beta will be much lower: .3 × .3/.2 = .45.

Another way to measure the relatedness of changes in one random variable with another is *covariance*. The correlation between two variables equals their covariance divided by the product of their standard deviations: $\rho_{j,m} = \text{cov}(r_j, r_m)/\sigma_j\sigma_m$. If we replace correlation with this expression, we get another expression for beta: covariance between the return on the stock and the market, divided by the variance of the market return, σ_m^2:

$$\text{Beta of stock j, } \beta_j = \frac{\text{cov}(r_j, r_m)}{\sigma_m^2}$$

This formula for beta is consistent with our estimation of beta as the slope of the fitted line. Consult any basic statistics text and you will see that the slope of a fitted line can be expressed in terms of covariance and variance.

Here are two real examples of how to estimate stock betas.

BETAS FOR INCO AND WESTCOAST ENERGY

Each point in Figure 10.2*a* shows the return on Inco stock and the return on the market index in a different month. For example, the circled point shows that in the month of June 1999 Inco stock price rose by 26 percent, whereas the market index rose by 5.1 percent. Notice that more often than not Inco outperformed the market when the index rose and underperformed the market when the index fell. Thus Inco was a relatively aggressive, high-beta stock.

We have drawn a line of best fit through the points in the figure.[2] The slope of this line is 1.33. For each extra 1 percent rise in the market, Inco stock price moved on average an extra 1.33 percent. For each extra 1 percent fall in the market, Inco stock price fell an extra 1.33 percent. Thus Inco's beta was 1.33.

Of course, Inco's stock returns are not perfectly related to market returns. The company was also subject to unique risk, which shows up in the scatter of points around the line. Sometimes Inco flew south while the market went north, or vice versa.

Figure 10.2*b* shows a similar plot of the monthly returns for Westcoast Energy. In contrast to Inco, Westcoast Energy was a defensive, low-beta stock. It was not highly sensitive to market movements, usually lagging when the market rose and yet doing better (or not as badly) when the market fell. The slope of the line of best fit shows that on average an extra 1 percent change in the index resulted in an extra .48 percent change in the price of Westcoast Energy stock. Thus Westcoast Energy's beta was .48.

You may find it interesting to look at Table 10.1, which shows how past market movements have affected several well-known stocks. Westcoast Energy had the lowest beta: its stock return was .48 times as sensitive as the average stock to market movements. Alcan Aluminum was at the other extreme: its return was 1.50 times as sensitive as the average stock to market movements.

TABLE 10.1
Betas for selected common stocks, January 1995–December 1999

Stock	Beta
Agrium	.79
Alcan Aluminum	1.50
BCE	1.36
Biomira	1.25
Cameco	.79
Canadian Pacific	.94
CanWest Global Communications	.76
CN Rail	.98
Four Seasons Hotel	1.44
Inco	1.33
Magna International	.68
Royal Bank	1.13
Westcoast Energy	.48

Note: Betas are calculated with 5 years of monthly returns.

[2] The line of best fit is usually known as a *regression* line. The slope of the line can be calculated using *ordinary least squares* regression. The dependent variable is the return on the stock (Inco). The independent variable is the return on the market index, in this case, a value-weighted market index from the Center for Research in Security Prices (CRSP). We chose not to use the TSX Total Return Index Value because in 1999 and 2000 it became heavily weighted in Nortel stocks and did not reflect a widely diversified portfolio.

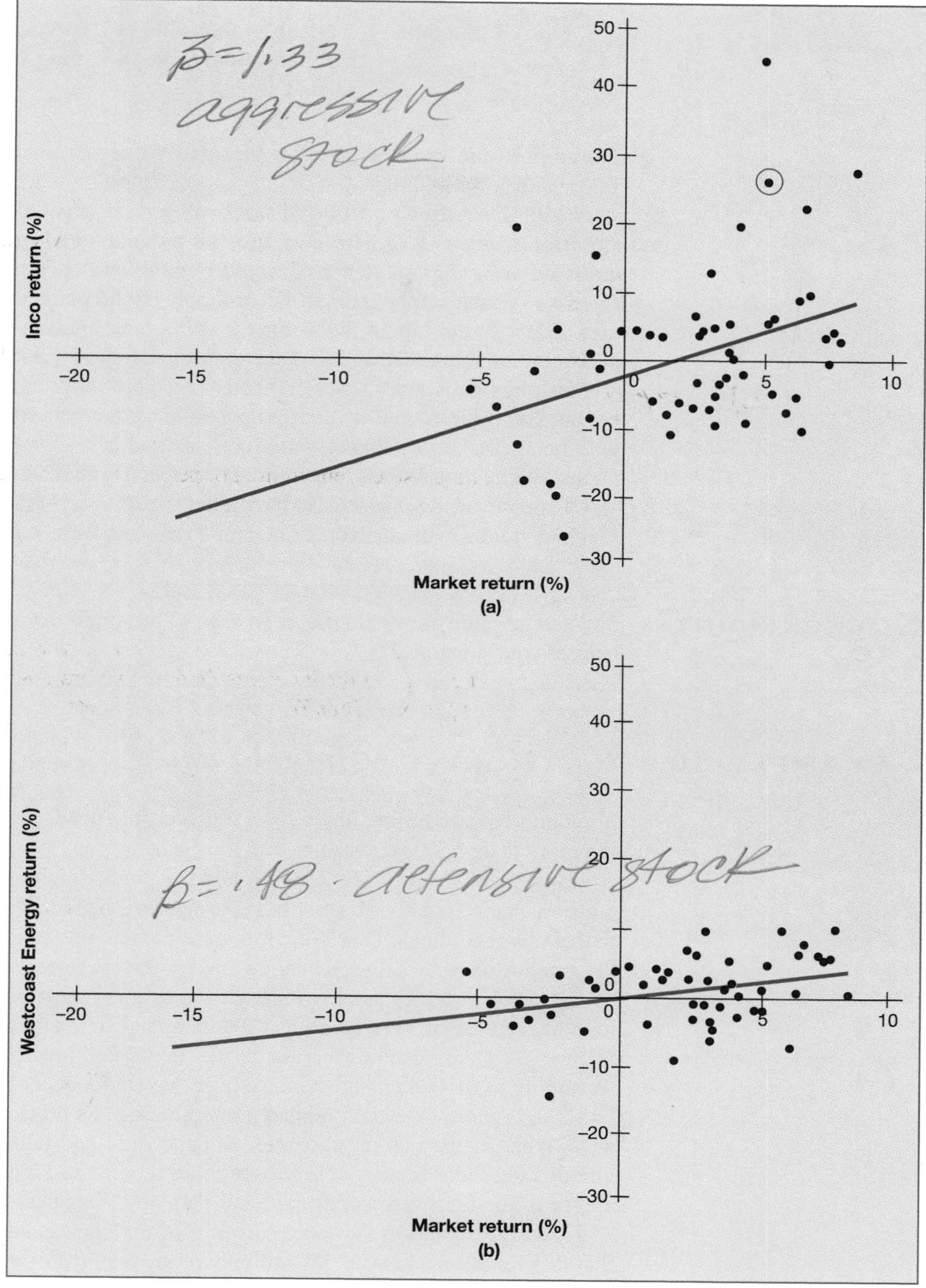

FIGURE 10.2
(a) Each point in this figure shows the returns on Inco common stock and the overall market in a particular month. Sixty months are plotted in all. Inco's beta is the slope of the line fitted to these points. Inco has a relatively high beta of 1.33.
(b) In this plot of 60 months' returns for Westcoast Energy and the overall market, the slope of the fitted line is much less than Inco's beta in (a). Westcoast Energy has a relatively low beta of .48.

PORTFOLIO BETAS

Diversification decreases variability from unique risk but not from market risk. The beta of a portfolio is just an average of the betas of the securities in the portfolio, weighted by the investment in each security. For example, a portfolio comprising only two stocks would have a beta as follows:

Beta of portfolio = (fraction of portfolio in first stock × beta of first stock) + (fraction of portfolio in second stock × beta of second stock)

Thus a portfolio invested 50-50 in Inco and Westcoast Energy would have a beta of (.5 × 1.33) + (.5 × .48) = .905.

A well-diversified portfolio of stocks all with betas of 1.33, like Inco, would still have a portfolio beta of 1.33. However, most of the individual stocks' unique risk would be diversified away. The market risk would remain, and such a portfolio would end up 1.33 times as variable as the market. For example, if the market has an annual standard deviation of 19 percent (about the historical average reported in Chapter 9), a fully diversified portfolio with beta of 1.33 has a standard deviation of 1.33 × 19 = 25.3 percent.

Portfolios with betas between 0 and 1.0 tend to move in the same direction as the market but not as far. A well-diversified portfolio of low-beta stocks like Westcoast Energy, all with betas of .48, has almost no unique risk and is relatively unaffected by market movements. Such a portfolio is .48 times as variable as the market.

Of course, on average, stocks have a beta of 1. A well-diversified portfolio including all kinds of stocks, with an average beta of 1, has the same variability as the market index.

CHECK POINT 10.2

Say you invested an equal amount in each of the stocks shown in Table 10.1. Calculate the beta of your portfolio.

▸ EXAMPLE 10.2 *How Risky Are Mutual Funds?*

You don't have to be wealthy to own a diversified portfolio. You can buy shares in one of the more than 4,500 mutual funds in the Canada.

Investors buy shares of the funds, and the funds use the money to buy portfolios of securities. The returns on the portfolios are passed back to the funds' owners in proportion to their shareholdings. Therefore, the funds act like investment cooperatives, offering even the smallest investors diversification and professional management at low cost.

Let's look at the betas of two mutual funds that invest in stocks. Figure 10.3*a* plots the monthly returns of TD's Precious Metals mutual fund and the TSX index from July 1998 to June 2001. You can see that the stocks in the Precious Metals fund had below average sensitivity to market changes: on average they had a beta of .48.

If the Precious Metals fund had no unique risk, its portfolio would have been .48 times as variable as the market portfolio. But the fund had not diversified away quite all the unique risk; there is still some scatter about the line in Figure 10.3*a*. As a result, the variability of the fund was somewhat more than .48 times that of the market.

Figure 10.3*b* shows the same sort of plot for TD Canadian Index mutual fund. Notice that this fund has a beta of .99 and only a tiny residual of unique risk—the fitted line fits almost exactly because an *index fund* is designed to track the market as closely as possible. The managers of the fund do not attempt to pick good stocks but just work to achieve full diversification at very low cost. (The TD Canadian Index fund takes investments of as little as $1,000 outside an RRSP and $100 inside one, and manages the fund for an annual fee of .85 percent of the fund's assets.) The index fund is *fully diversified.* Investors in this fund buy the market as a whole and don't have to worry at all about unique risk.

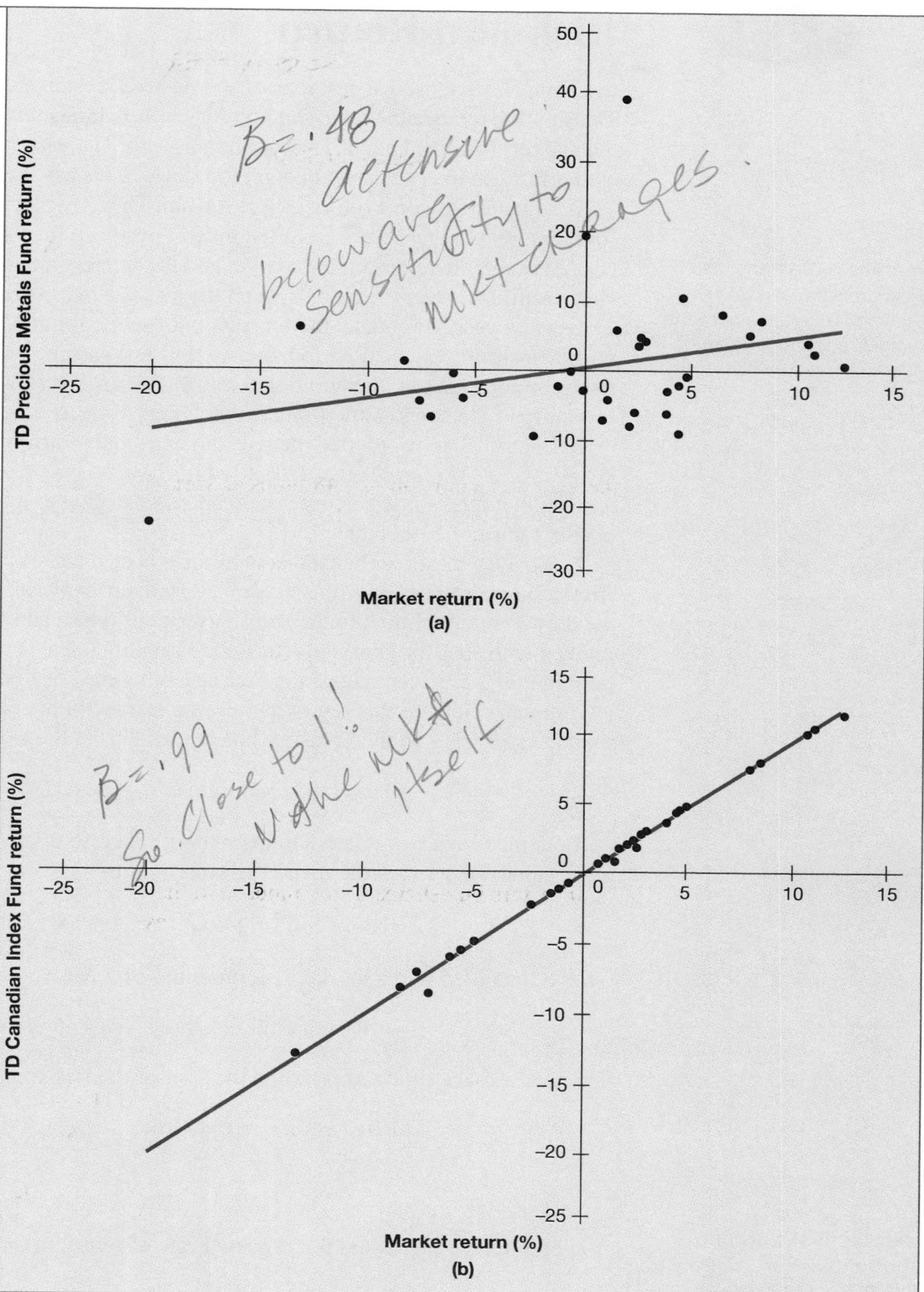

FIGURE 10.3
(a) The slope of the fitted line shows that investors in the TD Precious Metals mutual fund bore market risk less than that of the TSX portfolio. TD Precious Metals' beta was .48. This was the average beta of the individual common stocks held by the fund. They also bore some unique risk, however: note the scatter of TD Precious Metals' returns above and below the fitted line.
(b) The TD Canadian Index Fund is a fully diversified index fund designed to track the performance of the market. Note the fund's beta (.99) and the absence of unique risk. The fund's returns lie almost precisely on the fitted line, relating its returns to those of the TSX portfolio.

☑ CHECK POINT 10.3

Suppose you could achieve full diversification in a portfolio constructed from stocks with an average beta of .5. If the standard deviation of the market is 20 percent per year, what is the standard deviation of the portfolio return?

10.2 Risk and Return

In Chapter 9 we looked at past returns on selected investments. The least risky investment was Treasury bills. Since the return on Treasury bills is fixed, it is unaffected by what happens to the market. Thus the beta of Treasury bills is zero. The *most* risky investment that we considered was the market portfolio of common stocks. This has average market risk: its beta is 1.0.

market risk premium Risk premium of market portfolio. Difference between market return and return on risk-free Treasury bills.

Wise investors don't run risks just for fun. They are playing with real money and therefore require a higher return from the market portfolio than from Treasury bills. The difference between the return on the market and the interest rate on T-bills is termed the **market risk premium.** Over the past 75 years the average market risk premium has been just over 7 percent a year. Of course, there is plenty of scope for argument as to whether the past 75 years constitute a typical period, but we will just assume here that 7 percent is the normal risk premium; that is, the additional return that an investor could reasonably expect from investing in the stock market rather than Treasury bills.

In Figure 10.4*a* we plotted the risk and expected return from Treasury bills and the market portfolio. You can see that Treasury bills have a beta of zero and a risk-free return; we'll assume that return is 4 percent. The market portfolio has a beta of 1.0 and an assumed expected return of 11 percent.[3]

Now, given these two benchmarks, what expected rate of return should an investor require from a stock or portfolio with a beta of .5? Halfway between, of course. Thus in Figure 10.4*b* we drew a straight line through the Treasury bill return and the expected market return and marked with an *X* the expected return for a beta of .5, that is, 7.5 percent. This includes a risk premium of 3.5 percent above the Treasury bill return of 4 percent.

You can calculate this return as follows: start with the difference between the expected market return r_m and the Treasury bill rate r_f. This is the expected market risk premium.

$$\text{Market risk premium} = r_m - r_f = 11\% - 4\% = 7\%$$

Beta measures risk relative to the market. Therefore, the expected risk premium on any asset equals beta times the market risk premium:

$$\textbf{Risk premium on any asset} = \boldsymbol{r - r_f = \beta(r_m - r_f)} \tag{10.1}$$

With a beta of .5 and a market risk premium of 7 percent,

$$\text{Risk premium} = \beta(r_m - r_f) = .5 \times 7 = 3.5\%$$

The total expected rate of return is the sum of the risk-free rate and the risk premium:

$$\textbf{Expected return} = \textbf{risk-free rate} + \textbf{risk premium} \tag{10.2}$$

$$\begin{aligned} r &= r_f + \beta(r_m - r_f) \\ &= 4\% + 3.5\% = 7.5\% \end{aligned}$$

capital asset pricing model (CAPM) Theory of the relationship between risk and return which states that the expected risk premium on any security equals its beta times the market risk premium.

You could have calculated the expected rate of return in one step from this formula:

$$\begin{aligned} \text{Expected return} = r &= r_f + \beta(r_m - r_f) \\ &= 4\% + (.5 \times 7\%) = 7.5\% \end{aligned}$$

This formula states the basic risk–return relationship called the **capital asset pricing model,** or **CAPM.** The CAPM has a simple interpretation:

[3] On past evidence the risk premium on the market is 7 percent. With a 4 percent Treasury bill rate, the expected market return would be 4 + 7 = 11 percent.

FIGURE 10.4
(a) Here we begin the plot of expected rate of return against beta. The first benchmarks are Treasury bills (beta = 0) and the market portfolio (beta = 1.0). We assume a Treasury bill rate of 4 percent and a market return of 11 percent. The market risk premium is 11 – 4 = 7 percent.
(b) A portfolio split evenly between Treasury bills and the market will have beta = .5 and an expected return of 7.5 percent (point X). A portfolio invested 80 percent in the market and 20 percent in Treasury bills has beta = .8 and an expected rate of return of 9.6 percent (point Y). Note that the expected rate of return on any portfolio mixing Treasury bills and the market lies on a straight line. The risk premium is proportional to the portfolio beta.

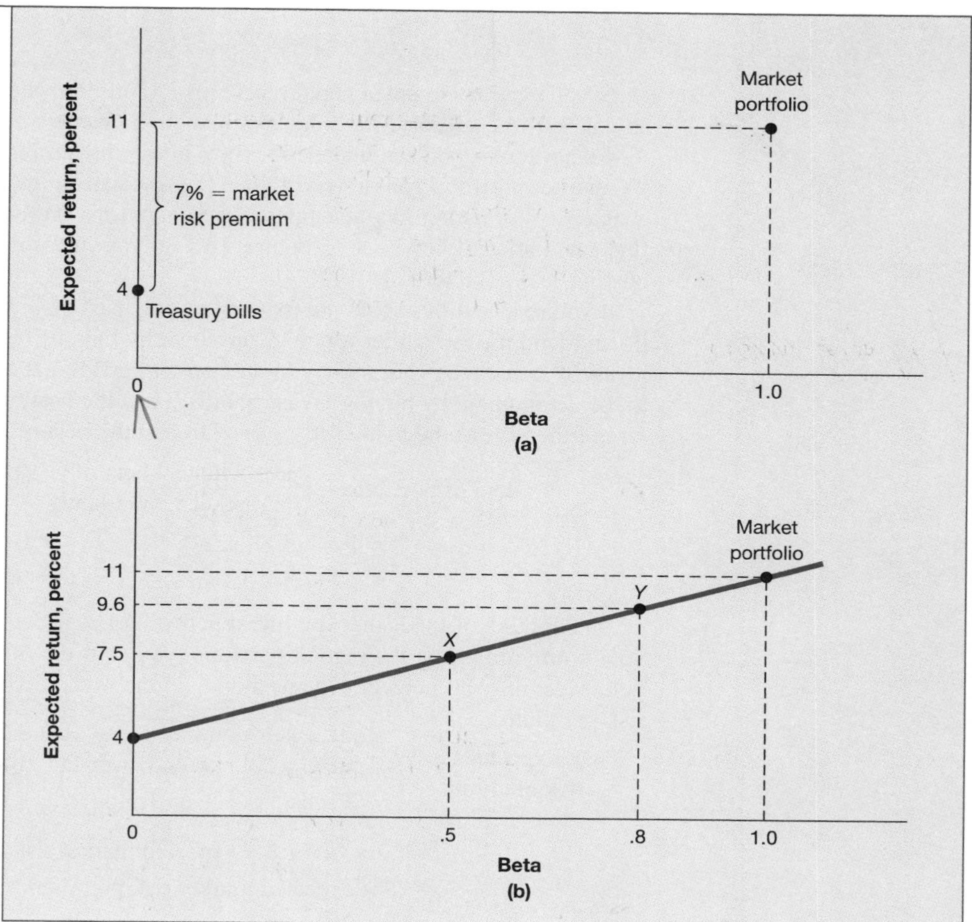

The expected rates of return demanded by investors depend on two things: (1) compensation for the time value of money (the risk-free rate, r_f) and (2) a risk premium, which depends on beta and the market risk premium.

Note that the expected rate of return on an asset with $\beta = 1$ is just the market return. With a risk-free rate of 4 percent and market risk premium of 7 percent,

$$r = r_f + \beta(r_m - r_f)$$
$$= 4\% + (1 \times 7\%) = 11\%$$

r=6+(1.5×7)=16.5%

CHECK POINT 10.4

What are the risk premium expected rate of return on a stock with $\beta = 1.5$? Assume a Treasury bill rate of 6 percent and a market risk premium of 7 percent.

WHY THE CAPM WORKS

The CAPM assumes that the stock market is dominated by well-diversified investors who are concerned only with market risk. That makes sense in a stock market where trading is dominated by large institutions and even small fry can diversify at very low cost.

▸ EXAMPLE 10.3 *How Would You Invest $1 Million?*

Have you ever daydreamed about receiving a $1 million cheque, no strings attached, from an unknown benefactor? Let's daydream about how you would invest it.

We have two good candidates: Treasury bills, which offer an absolutely safe return, and the market portfolio (possibly via the TD Canadian Index fund discussed earlier in this chapter). The market has generated superior returns on average, but those returns have fluctuated a lot. (Look back to Figure 9.3.) So your investment policy is going to depend on your tolerance for risk.

If you're a cautious soul, you may invest only part of your money in the market portfolio and lend the remainder to the government by buying Treasury bills. Suppose that you invest 80 percent of your money in the market portfolio and lend out the other 20 percent to the government by buying Treasury bills. Then the beta of your portfolio will be a mixture of the beta of the market ($\beta_{\text{market}} = 1.0$) and the beta of the T-bills ($\beta_{\text{T-bills}} = 0$):

$$\text{Beta of portfolio} = \left(\begin{matrix}\text{proportion}\\ \text{in market}\end{matrix} \times \begin{matrix}\text{beta of}\\ \text{market}\end{matrix}\right) + \left(\begin{matrix}\text{proportion}\\ \text{in T-bills}\end{matrix} \times \begin{matrix}\text{beta of}\\ \text{T-bills}\end{matrix}\right)$$

$$\begin{aligned}\beta &= (.8 \times \beta_{\text{market}}) + (.2 \times \beta_{\text{T-bills}})\\ &= (.8 \times 1.0) + (.2 \times 0) = .80\end{aligned}$$

The fraction of funds that you invest in the market also affects your return. If you invest your entire million in the market portfolio, you earn the full market risk premium. But if you invest only 80 percent of your money in the market, you earn only 80 percent of the risk premium.

$$\begin{matrix}\text{Expected}\\ \text{risk premium}\\ \text{on portfolio}\end{matrix} = \left(\begin{matrix}\text{proportion in}\\ \text{T-bills}\end{matrix} \times \begin{matrix}\text{risk premium}\\ \text{on T-bills}\end{matrix}\right) + \left(\begin{matrix}\text{proportion in}\\ \text{market}\end{matrix} \times \begin{matrix}\text{market risk}\\ \text{premium}\end{matrix}\right)$$

$$\begin{aligned}&= (.2 \times 0) + (.8 \times \text{expected market risk premium})\\ &= .8 \times \text{expected market risk premium}\\ &= .8 \times 7 = 5.6\%\end{aligned}$$

The expected return on your portfolio is equal to the risk-free interest rate plus the expected risk premium:

$$\text{Expected portfolio return} = r_{\text{portfolio}} = 4 + 5.6 = 9.6\%$$

In Figure 10.4*b* we show the beta and expected return on this portfolio by the letter *Y*.

THE SECURITY MARKET LINE

Example 10.3 illustrates a general point: by investing some proportion of your money in the market portfolio and lending (or borrowing)[4] the balance, you can obtain any

[4] Notice that the security market line extends above the market return at $\beta = 1$. How would you generate a portfolio with, say, $\beta = 2$? It's easy, but it's risky. Suppose you borrow $1 million and invest the loan plus $1 million in the market portfolio. That gives you $2 million invested and a $1 million liability. Your portfolio now has a beta of 2:

$$\text{Beta of portfolio} = (\text{proportion in market} \times \text{beta of market}) + (\text{proportion in loan} \times \text{beta of loan})$$

$$\begin{aligned}\beta &= (2 \times \beta_{\text{market}}) + (-1 \times \beta_{\text{loan}})\\ &= (2 \times 1.0) + (-1 \times 0) = 2\end{aligned}$$

Notice that the proportion in the loan is negative because you are borrowing, not lending, money.

By the way, borrowing from a bank or stockbroker would not be difficult or unduly expensive as long as you put up your $2 million stock portfolio as security for the loan.

Can you calculate the risk premium and the expected rate of return on this borrow-and-invest strategy?

security market line Relationship between expected return and beta.

combination of risk and expected return along the sloping line in Figure 10.5. This line is generally known as the **security market line.**

CHECK POINT 10.5

How would you construct a portfolio with a beta of .25? What is the expected return to this strategy? Assume Treasury bills yield 6 percent and the market risk premium is 7 percent.

The security market line describes the expected returns and risks from investing different fractions of your funds in the market. It also sets a standard for other investments. Investors will be willing to hold other investments only if they offer equally good prospects. Thus the required risk premium for *any* investment is given by the security market line:

Risk premium on investment = beta × expected market risk premium

Look back to Figure 10.4*b,* which asserts that an individual common stock with $\beta = .5$ must offer a 7.5 percent expected rate of return when Treasury bills yield 4 percent and the market risk premium is 7 percent. You can now see why this has to be so. If that stock offered a lower rate of return, nobody would buy even a little of it—they could get 7.5 percent just by investing 50-50 in Treasury bills and the market. And if nobody wants to hold the stock, its price has to drop. A lower price means a better buy for investors, that is, a higher rate of return. The price will fall until the stock's expected rate of return is pushed up to 7.5 percent. At that price and expected return the CAPM holds.

If, on the other hand, our stock offered more than 7.5 percent, diversified investors would want to buy more of it. That would push the price up and the expected return down to the levels predicted by the CAPM.

This reasoning holds for stocks with any beta. That's why the CAPM makes sense, and why the expected risk premium on an investment should be proportional to its beta.

CHECK POINT 10.6

Suppose you invest $400,000 in Treasury bills and $600,000 in the market portfolio. What is the return on your portfolio if T-bills yield 6 percent and the expected return on the market is 15 percent? What does the return on this portfolio imply for the expected return on individual stocks with betas of .6?

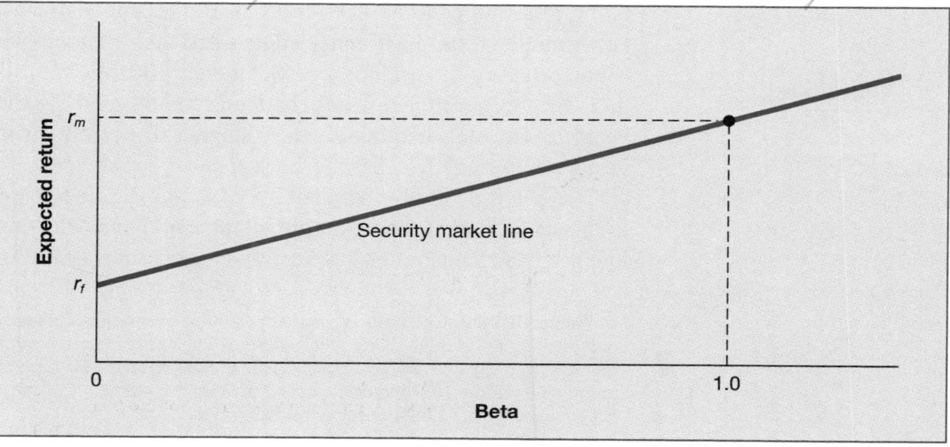

FIGURE 10.5
The security market line shows how expected rate of return depends on beta. According to the capital asset pricing model, expected rates of return for all securities and all portfolios lie on this line.

HOW WELL DOES THE CAPM WORK?

The basic idea behind the capital asset pricing model is that investors expect a reward for both waiting and worrying. The greater the worry, the greater the expected return. If you invest in a risk-free Treasury bill, you just receive the rate of interest. That's the reward for waiting. When you invest in risky stocks, you can expect an extra return or risk premium for worrying. The capital asset pricing model states that this risk premium is equal to the stock's beta times the market risk premium. Therefore,

$$\text{Expected return on stock} = \text{risk-free interest rate} + (\text{beta} \times \text{market risk premium})$$

$$r = r_f + \beta(r_m - r_f)$$

How well does the CAPM work in practice? Do the returns on stocks with betas of .5 on average lie halfway between the return on the market portfolio and the interest rate on Treasury bills? Unfortunately, the evidence is conflicting. Let's look back to the actual returns earned by investors in low-beta stocks and in high-beta stocks.

Imagine that in 1931 ten investors gathered in a Wall Street bar to discuss their portfolios. Each agreed to follow a different strategy. Each year investor 1 opted to buy the 10 percent of New York Stock Exchange stocks with the lowest betas; investor 2 chose the 10 percent with the next-lowest betas; and so on, up to investor 10, who agreed to buy the stocks with the highest betas. They also agreed that they would return 60 years later to compare results, and so they parted with much cordiality and good wishes.

In 1991 the same 10 investors, now much older and wealthier, met again in the same bar. Figure 10.6 shows how they fared. Investor 1's portfolio turned out to be much less risky than the market; its beta was only .49. However, investor 1 also realized the lowest return, 9 percent above the risk-free rate of interest. At the other extreme, the beta of investor 10's portfolio was 1.52, about three times that of investor 1's portfolio. But investor 10 was rewarded with the highest return, averaging 17 percent above the interest rate. So over this 60-year period, returns did indeed increase with beta.

As you can see from Figure 10.6, the market portfolio over the same 60-year period provides an average return of 14 percent above the interest rate[5] and (of course) had a beta of 1.0. The CAPM predicts that the risk premium should lie on the upward-sloping security market line in Figure 10.6. Since the market provided a risk premium of 14 percent, investor 1's portfolio, with a beta of .49, should have provided a risk premium of a shade under 7 percent, and investor 10's portfolio, with a beta of 1.52, should have given a premium of a shade over 21 percent. You can see that while high-beta stocks performed better than low-beta stocks, the difference was not as great as the CAPM predicts.

Figure 10.6 provides broad support for the CAPM, though it suggests that the line relating return to beta has been too flat. But recent years have been less kind to the CAPM. For example, if the 10 friends had invested their cash in 1966 rather than 1931, there would have been very little relation between their portfolio returns and beta. Does this imply that there has been a fundamental change in the relation between risk and return in the last 30 years or did high-beta stocks just happen to perform worse during these years than investors expected? It is hard to be sure.

There is little doubt that the CAPM is too simple to capture everything that is going on in the stock market. For example, it appears that stocks of small companies or stocks with low price-earnings ratios have offered higher rates of return than the CAPM predicts. This

[5] In Figure 10.6 the stocks in the "market portfolio" are weighted equally. Since the stocks of small firms have provided higher average returns than those of large firms, the risk premium on an equally weighted index is higher than on a value-weighted index. This is one reason for the difference between the 14 percent market risk premium in Figure 10.6 and the 7 percent premium reported in Table 9.1. Also, this study is based on U.S. market data and covers a different time period than we used in Chapter 9.

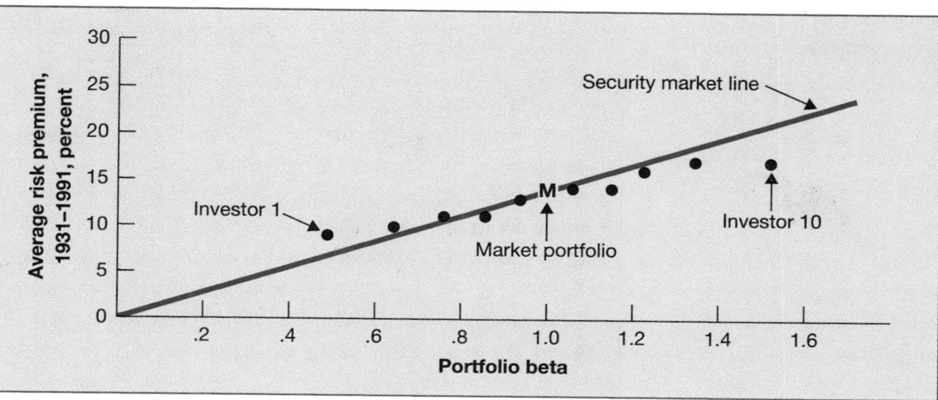

FIGURE 10.6
The capital asset pricing model states that the expected risk premium from any investment should lie on the security market line. The dots show the actual average risk premiums from portfolios with different betas. The high-beta portfolios generated higher average returns, just as predicted by the CAPM. But the high-beta portfolios plotted below the security market line, and four of the five low-beta portfolios plotted above. A line fitted to the 10 portfolio returns would be flatter than the market line.

Source: F. Black, "Beta and Return," *Journal of Portfolio Management* 20 (Fall 1993) pp. 8–18. © 1993. Used by permission of Institutional Investor, Inc.

has prompted headlines like "Is Beta Dead?" in the business press.[6] It is not the first time that beta has been declared dead, but the CAPM is still being used. Only strong theories can have more than one funeral.

The CAPM is not the only model of risk and return. It has several brothers and sisters as well as second cousins. These other models, including the multi-factor CAPM and Arbitrage Pricing Theory (APT), argue that the risk of a stock depends on more than its correlation with the market index. Although much of a stock's risk does depend on the general movement of the market, stock risk may also be affected by the growth rate of GDP, the yield spread between long- and short-term bonds, and relative firm size.[7] Researchers have examined these other factors and some believe that beta and the CAPM is not enough to capture all the systematic (non-diversifiable) risks.[8] However, the CAPM captures two fundamental ideas in a simple way. First, almost everyone agrees that investors require some extra return for taking on risk. Second, investors appear to be concerned principally with the market risk that they cannot eliminate by diversification. That is why financial managers rely on the capital asset pricing model as a good rule of thumb.

USING THE CAPM TO ESTIMATE EXPECTED RETURNS

To calculate the returns that investors are expecting from particular stocks, we need three numbers—the risk-free interest rate, the expected market risk premium, and the beta. In August 2001, the interest rate on Treasury bills was about 4 percent. Assume that the market risk premium is about 7 percent. Finally, look back to Table 10.1, where we gave you betas of several stocks. Table 10.2 puts these numbers together to give an estimate of the expected return from each stock. Let's take Agrium as an example:

$$\text{Expected return on Agrium} = \text{risk-free interest rate} + \left(\text{beta} \times \begin{matrix}\text{expected market}\\ \text{risk premium}\end{matrix}\right)$$

$$r = 4.0\% + (.79 \times 7\%)$$

$$= 9.53\%$$

[6] A. Wallace, "Is Beta Dead?" *Institutional Investor* 14 (July 1980), pp. 22–30.

[7] To learn more about models of stock returns, see Z. Bodie, A. Kane, and A. J. Marcus, *Investments* (3rd ed.) (Toronto: McGraw-Hill Ryerson, 2000).

[8] Visit www.ibbotson.com, the website of Ibbotson Associates, to see how one company estimates and sells CAPM betas and other risk measures. Click on "Cost of Capital Center." Another company known for its risk measurements, including beta calculations is Barra, www.barra.com.

TABLE 10.2
Expected rates of return

Stock	Expected return, %
Agrium	9.53
Alcan Aluminum	14.5
BCE	13.52
Biomira	12.75
Cameco	9.53
Canadian Pacific	10.58
CanWest Global Communications	9.32
CN Rail	10.86
Four Seasons Hotel	14.08
Inco	13.31
Magna International	8.76
Royal Bank	11.91
Westcoast Energy	7.36

Note: Expected return $= r = r_f + \beta(r_m - r_f) = 4\% + (\beta \times 7\%)$.

You can also use the capital asset pricing model to find the discount rate for a new capital investment. For example, suppose you are asked to analyze a proposal by Biomira to expand its operations. At what rate should you discount the forecast cash flows? According to Table 10.2 investors are looking for a return of 12.75 percent from investments with the risk of Biomira stock. That is the opportunity cost of capital for Biomira's expansion project.

In practice, choosing a discount rate is seldom this easy. (After all, you can't expect to become a captain of finance simply by plugging numbers into a formula.) For example, you must learn how to estimate the return demanded by the company's investors when the company has issued both equity and debt securities. We could ignore this complication in the case of Biomira because it is financed almost entirely by common equity. Therefore, the risk of its assets equals the risk of its equity. Most companies, however, finance themselves with a mix of debt and equity. We will come to such refinements later.

EXAMPLE 10.4 *Comparing Project Returns and the Opportunity Cost of Capital*

You have forecast the cash flows on a project and calculated that its internal rate of return is 12 percent. Suppose that Treasury bills offer a return of 4 percent and the expected market risk premium is 7 percent. Should you go ahead with the project?

To answer this question you need to figure out the opportunity cost of capital r. This depends on the project's beta. For example, if the project is a sure thing, the beta is zero and the cost of capital equals the interest rate on Treasury bills:

$$r = 4 + (0 \times 7) = 4\%$$

If your project offers a return of 12 percent when the cost of capital is 4 percent, you should obviously go ahead.[9]

Sure-fire projects rarely occur outside finance texts. So let's think about the cost of capital if the project has the same risk as the market portfolio. In this case beta is 1 and the cost of capital is the expected return on the market:

$$r = 4 + (1 \times 7) = 11\%$$

[9] In Chapter 6 we described some special cases where you should prefer projects that offer a *lower* internal rate of return than the cost of capital. We assume here that your project is a "normal" one, and that you prefer high IRRs to low ones.

FIGURE 10.7
The expected return of this project is less than the expected return one could earn on stock market investments with the same market risk (beta). Therefore, the project's expected return–risk combination lies below the security market line, and the project should be rejected.

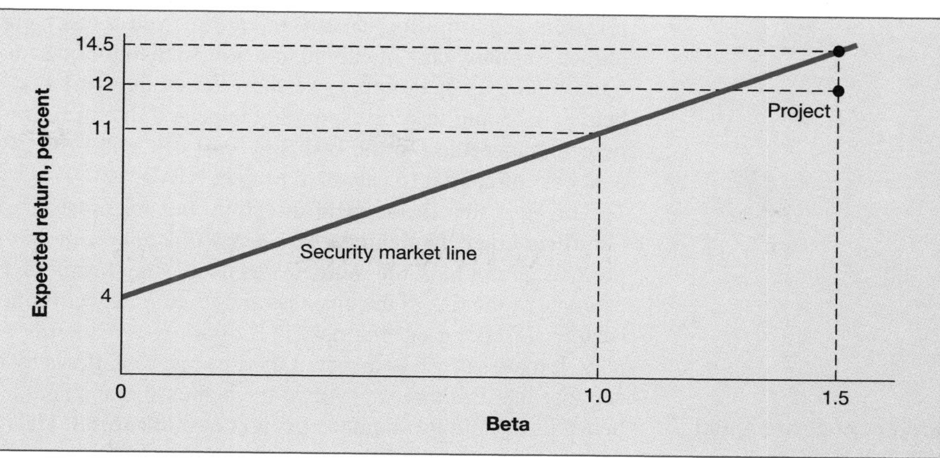

The project appears less attractive than before, but still worth doing.

What if the project has even higher risk? Suppose, for example, that it has a beta of 1.5. What is the cost of capital in this case? To find the answer, we plug a beta of 1.5 into our formula for r:

$$r = 4 + (1.5 \times 7) = 14.5\%$$

A project this risky would need a return of at least 14.5 percent to justify going ahead. The 12 percent project should be rejected.

This rejection occurs because, as Figure 10.7 shows, the project's expected rate of return plots below the security market line. The project offers a lower return than investors can get elsewhere, so it is a negative-NPV investment.

The security market line provides a standard for project acceptance. If the project's return lies above the security market line, then the return is higher than investors could expect to get by investing their funds in the capital market, and therefore, is an attractive investment opportunity.

☑ CHECK POINT 10.7

Suppose that Biomira's expansion project is forecast to produce cash flows of $50 million a year for each of 10 years. What is its present value? Use data from Table 10.2. What would the present value be if the beta of the investment were .7?

10.3 Capital Budgeting and Project Risk

COMPANY VERSUS PROJECT RISK

company cost of capital Expected rate of return demanded by investors in a company, determined by the average risk of the company's assets and operations.

Long before the development of modern theories linking risk and return, smart financial managers adjusted for risk in capital budgeting. They realized intuitively that, other things being equal, risky projects are less desirable than safe ones and must provide higher rates of return.

Many companies estimate the rate of return required by investors in their securities and use this **company cost of capital** to discount the cash flows on all new projects. Since investors require a higher rate of return from a risky company, risky firms will have a higher company cost of capital and will set a higher discount rate for their new investment opportunities. For example, we showed in Table 10.1 that on past evidence Biomira has a beta of 1.25 and the corresponding expected rate of return (see Table 10.2) is about 12.75 percent. According to the company cost of capital rule, Biomira should use a 12.75 percent cost of capital to calculate project NPVs.

This is a step in the right direction, but we must take care when the firm has issued securities other than equity. Moreover, this approach can get a firm in trouble if its new projects do not have the same risk as its existing business. Biomira's beta reflects investors' estimate of the risk of the business and its company cost of capital is the return that investors require for taking on this risk. If Biomira is considering an expansion of its regular business, it makes sense to discount the forecast cash flows by the company cost of capital. But suppose that Biomira is wondering whether to branch out into the broadcasting business. Its beta tells us nothing about the **project cost of capital.** That depends on the risk of the broadcasting business and the return that shareholders require from investing in such a business.

project cost of capital
Minimum acceptable expected rate of return on a project given its risk.

The concept of measuring the project's cost of capital on the basis of the project's risk seems straightforward to us. However, sometimes managers seriously miscalculate a project's required rate of return because they ignore the fact that the project's risk is very different than the firm's overall risk. To avoid that mistake, ask yourself: If this project were a mini-firm, separate from our company, what rate of return would investors require to be willing to invest in it? When a firm evaluates an investment, it must use a required rate of return that corresponds to the risk of the investment.

The principle of assessing the required rate of return on the basis of the risk of the investment applies to your own investment activities. Suppose you take money from your savings account, which is currently paying 1 percent annual interest, and invest in shares of Inco. You would not be happy if your expected return on the Inco shares was only 1 percent. You would expect to earn a higher rate of return to compensate for the substantially higher market risk associated with Inco, right? The same applies to a firm's investment decisions: the project's required rate of return depends on the project's risk.

The project cost of capital depends on the use to which that capital is put. Therefore, it depends on the risk of the project and not on the risk of the company. If a company invests in a low-risk project, it should discount the cash flows at a correspondingly low cost of capital. If it invests in a high-risk project, those cash flows should be discounted at a high cost of capital.

SEE BOX P. 321

The nearby Finance in Action box discusses how companies decide on the discount rate. It notes, for example, that Siemens, a German industrial giant, uses 16 different discount rates, depending on the riskiness of each line of its business.

CHECK POINT 10.8

The company cost of capital for Biomira is about 12.75 percent (see Table 10.2); for CanWest Global Communications it is about 9.3 percent. What would be the more reasonable discount rate for Biomira to use for its proposed broadcasting division? Why?

DETERMINANTS OF PROJECT RISK

We have seen that the company cost of capital is the correct discount rate for projects that have the same risk as the company's existing business, but *not* for those projects that are

FINANCE IN ACTION

How High a Hurdle?

It did raise some eyebrows at first. Two months ago, when Aegon, a Dutch life insurer known for taking care of its shareholders, bought Transamerica, a San Francisco–based insurer, Aegon said it was expecting a return of only 9% from the deal, well below the 11% "hurdle rate" it once proclaimed as its benchmark. Had this darling of the stock market betrayed its devoted investors for the sake of an eye-catching deal?

Not at all. Years of falling interest rates and rising equity valuations have shrunk the cost of capital for firms such as Aegon. So companies that regularly adjust the hurdle rates they use to evaluate potential investment projects and acquisitions are not cheating their shareholders. Far from it: they are doing their investors a service. Unfortunately, such firms are rare in Europe. "I don't know many companies at all who lowered their hurdle rates in line with interest rates, so they're all underinvesting," says Greg Milano, a partner at Stern Stewart, a consultancy that helps companies estimate their cost of capital.

This has a huge impact on corporate strategy. Companies generally make their investment decisions by discounting the net cash flows a project is estimated to generate to their present value. If the net present value is positive, the project should make shareholders better off.

Generally speaking, says Paul Gibbs, an analyst at J.P. Morgan, an American bank, finance directors in America often review their hurdle rates; in continental Europe they do so sometimes, and in Britain, rarely. As a result, the Confederation of British Industry, a big-business lobby, worries about underinvestment, and officials at the Bank of England grumble about firms' reluctance to lower hurdles. This reluctance seems surprising, since companies with high hurdle rates will tend to lose out in bidding for business assets or firms. The hurdle rate should reflect not only interest rates but also the riskiness of each individual project. For instance, Siemens, a German industrial giant, last year started assigning a different hurdle rate to each of its 16 businesses, ranging from household appliances to medical equipment and semiconductors. The hurdle rates—from 8% to 11%—are based on the volatility of shares in rival companies in the relevant industry, and are under constant review.

Source: "How High a Hurdle?" *The Economist,* May 8, 1999, p. 82.

safer or riskier than the company's average. How do we know whether a project is unusually risky? Estimating project risk is never going to be an exact science, but here are a few things to bear in mind.

First, we saw in Chapter 8 that operating leverage increases the risk of a project. When a large fraction of your costs is fixed, any change in revenues can have a dramatic effect on earnings. Therefore, projects that involve high fixed costs tend to have higher betas.

Second, many people intuitively associate risk with the variability of earnings. But much of this variability reflects diversifiable risk. Lone prospectors in search of gold look forward to extremely uncertain future earnings, but whether they strike it rich is not likely to depend on the performance of the rest of the economy. These investments have a high standard deviation but a low beta.

pure play approach Estimating project cost of capital using the cost of capital of another company involved exclusively in the same type of project.

Third, look at the risk and required rate of return of a similar risk project outside of the firm. (We saw this in Check Point 10.8). Biomira uses the required rate of return of a company already in the broadcasting industry—CanWest Global—to assess its investment in a broadcasting division. Using CanWest's cost of capital is an application of the **pure play approach** to determine project risk. *Pure play* is a term used by investors to refer to companies exclusively involved in a single line of business. If you wanted a pure play in silver, you would invest in a silver mining company and not in diversified company that owns a silver mine.

The key to the pure play approach is finding the beta and market-required rate of return of company exclusively involved in the type of project under consideration. If the comparable company is publicly traded, its beta may be available from a company specializing in financial analysis such as Barra or Bloomberg. You can also estimate the beta yourself using the stock's monthly rates of return, like we did for Figure 10.2. If the comparable company is not publicly traded, you may wish to estimate its beta with rates of return based on accounting earnings or cash flow.[10]

It may be difficult to find a suitable pure play for comparison. Many companies are involved in several different businesses and hence their betas reflect the risks of all of the businesses. Like any portfolio, the beta of a company is the sum of the betas of its businesses, each weighted by their fraction of the firm's total value. Even if a comparable company is found, determining the appropriate risk and discount rate may be complicated by a different capital structure. We will have more to say about this in Chapter 11.

You cannot hope to measure the systematic risk of a project with any precision, but good managers examine any project from a variety of angles and look for clues to its riskiness. They know that high market risk is a characteristic of cyclical ventures and of ventures with high fixed costs. They think about the major uncertainties affecting the economy and how projects are affected by these uncertainties. Experience at assessing risks plays an important role too. Regrettably, we have no magic formula for determining a project's risk. On the other hand, if such a formula existed, no one would pay financial managers handsomely for their expertise.

What matters is the strength of the relationship between the firm's earnings and the aggregate earnings of all firms. Thus cyclical businesses, whose revenues and earnings are strongly dependent on the state of the economy, tend to have high betas and a high cost of capital. By contrast, businesses that produce essentials, such as food, beer, and cosmetics, are less affected by the state of the economy. They tend to have low betas and a low cost of capital.

DON'T ADD FUDGE FACTORS TO DISCOUNT RATES

Risk to an investor arises because an investment adds to the spread of possible portfolio returns. To a diversified investor, risk is predominantly market risk. But in everyday usage *risk* simply means "bad outcome." People think of the "risks" of a project as the things that can go wrong. For example,

- A geologist looking for oil worries about the risk of a dry hole.
- A pharmaceutical manufacturer worries about the risk that a new drug which reverses balding may not be approved by Health Canada.
- The owner of a hotel in a politically unstable part of the world worries about the political risk of expropriation.

Managers sometimes add fudge factors to discount rates to account for worries such as these.

This sort of adjustment makes us nervous. First, the bad outcomes we cited appear to reflect diversifiable risks which would not affect the expected rate of return demanded by investors. Second, the need for an adjustment in the discount rate usually arises because managers fail to give bad outcomes their due weight in cash-flow forecasts. They then try to offset that mistake by adding a fudge factor to the discount rate. For example, if a manager is worried about the possibility of a bad outcome, such as a dry hole in oil exploration,

[10] For example, see W. H. Beaver and J. Manegold, "The Association between Market-Determined and Accounting-Determined Measures of Systematic Risk: Some Further Evidence," *Journal of Financial and Quantitative Analysis*, 10 (June 1975), pp. 231–284.

he or she may reduce the value of the project by using a higher discount rate. This approach is unsound, however. Instead, the possibility of the dry hole should be included in the calculation of the expected cash flows to be derived from the well. Suppose that there is a 50 percent chance of a dry hole and a 50 percent chance that the well will produce oil worth $20 million. Then the *expected* cash flow is not $20 million but $(.5 \times 0) + (.5 \times 20) = \$10$ million. You should discount the $10 million expected cash flow at the opportunity cost of capital: it does not make sense to discount the $20 million using a fudged discount rate.

Expected cash-flow forecasts should already reflect the probabilities of *all* possible outcomes, good and bad. If the cash-flow forecasts are prepared properly, the discount rate should reflect only the market risk of the project. It should not have to be fudged to offset errors or biases in the cash-flow forecast.

10.4 Summary

1. **How can you measure and interpret the market risk, or beta, of a security?**

The contribution of a security to the risk of a diversified portfolio depends on its market risk. But not all securities are equally affected by fluctuations in the market. The sensitivity of a stock to market movement is known as **beta.** Stocks with a beta greater than 1.0 are particularly sensitive to market fluctuations. Those with a beta of less than 1.0 are not so sensitive to such movements. The average beta of all stocks is 1.0.

2. **What is the relationship between the market risk of a security and the rate of return that investors demand of that security?**

The extra return that investors require for taking risk is known as the risk premium. The **market risk premium**—that is, the risk premium on the **market portfolio**—averaged 7 percent between 1926 and 2000. The **capital asset pricing model** states that the expected risk premium of an investment should be proportional to both its beta and the market risk premium. The expected rate of return from any investment is equal to the risk-free interest rate plus the risk premium, so the **CAPM** boils down to

$$r = r_f + \beta(r_m - r_f)$$

The **security market line** is the graphical representation of the CAPM equation. The security market line relates the expected return investors demand of a security to the beta.

3. **How can a manager calculate the opportunity cost of capital for a project?**

The opportunity cost of capital is the return that investors give up by investing in the project rather than in securities of equivalent risk. Financial managers use the capital asset pricing model to estimate the opportunity cost of capital. The **company cost of capital** is the expected rate of return demanded by investors in a company, determined by the *average* risk of the company's assets and operations.

The opportunity cost of capital depends on the use to which the capital is put. Therefore, required rates of return are determined by the risk of the project, not by the risk of the firm's existing business. The **project cost of capital** is the minimum acceptable expected rate of return on a project given its risk.

Your cash-flow forecasts should already factor in the chances of pleasant and unpleasant surprises. Potential bad outcomes should be reflected in the discount rate only to the extent that they affect beta.

Related Web Links

www.stanford.edu/~wfsharpe/ws/wksheets.htm William Sharpe's site contains "portfolio optimizers," spreadsheets that can be used to construct efficiently diversified portfolios

www.riskmetrics.com RiskMetrics® Group maintains this site, which uses modern portfolio theory to help manage risk; some of the content at this site, including educational and demonstration materials, is free

www.finance.yahoo.com You can find stock betas as well as other risk measures and company profiles here

KEY TERMS

market portfolio	305	capital asset pricing model (CAPM)	312	company cost of capital	319
beta	305	security market line	315	project cost of capital	320
market risk premium	312			pure play approach	321

QUESTIONS AND PROBLEMS

*Answers in Appendix B

BASIC

*1. **Risk and Return.** True or false? Explain or qualify as necessary.

a. Investors demand higher expected rates of return on stocks with more variable rates of return.

b. The capital asset pricing model predicts that a security with a beta of zero will provide an expected return of zero.

c. An investor who puts $10,000 in Treasury bills and $20,000 in the market portfolio will have a portfolio beta of 2.

d. Investors demand higher expected rates of return from stocks with returns that are highly exposed to macroeconomic changes.

e. Investors demand higher expected rates of return from stocks with returns that are very sensitive to fluctuations in the stock market.

2. **Diversifiable Risk.** In light of what you've learned about market versus diversifiable (unique) risks, explain why an insurance company has no problem in selling life insurance to individuals but is reluctant to issue policies insuring against flood damage to residents of coastal areas. Why don't the insurance companies simply charge coastal residents a premium that reflects the actuarial probability of damage from hurricanes and other storms?

*3. **Unique vs. Market Risk.** Figure 10.8 plots monthly rates of return from 1997 to 2003 for the Snake Oil mutual fund. Was this fund well-diversified? Explain.

4. **Risk and Return.** Suppose that the risk premium on stocks and other securities did in fact rise with total risk (that is, the variability of returns) rather than just market risk. Explain how investors could exploit the situation to create portfolios with high expected rates of return but low levels of risk.

5. **CAPM and Hurdle Rates.** A project under consideration has an internal rate of return of 14 percent and a beta of .6. The risk-free rate is 4 percent and the expected rate of return on the market portfolio is 11 percent.

a. Should the project be accepted?

b. Should the project be accepted if its beta is 1.6?

c. Why does your answer change?

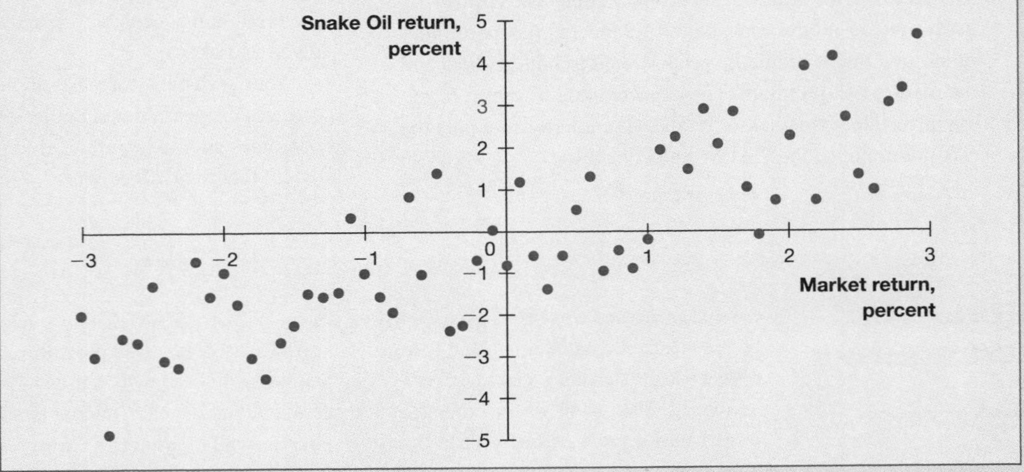

FIGURE 10.8
Monthly rates of return for the Snake Oil mutual fund and the S&P/TSX Composite Index (See problem 3)

PRACTICE

6. **CAPM and Valuation.** You are considering acquiring a firm that you believe can generate expected cash flows of $10,000 a year forever. However, you recognize that those cash flows are uncertain.
   a. Suppose you believe that the beta of the firm is .4. How much is the firm worth if the risk-free rate is 5 percent and the expected rate of return on the market portfolio is 15 percent?
   b. By how much will you overvalue the firm if its beta is actually .6?

*7. **CAPM and Expected Return.** If the risk-free rate is 6 percent and the expected rate of return on the market portfolio is 14 percent, is a security with a beta of 1.25 and an expected rate of return of 14 percent overpriced or underpriced?

8. **Using Beta.** Investors expect the market rate of return this year to be 14 percent. A stock with a beta of .8 has an expected rate of return of 12 percent. If the market return this year turns out to be 10 percent, what is your best guess as to the rate of return on the stock?

*9. **Unique vs. Market Risk.** Figure 10.9 shows plots of monthly rates of return on three stocks versus the stock market index. The beta and standard deviation of each stock is given beside its plot.
   a. Which stock is riskiest to a diversified investor?
   b. Which stock is riskiest to an undiversified investor who puts all her funds in one of these stocks?
   c. Consider a portfolio with equal investments in each stock. What would this portfolio's beta have been?
   d. Consider a well-diversified portfolio made up of stocks with the same beta as Exxon. What are the beta and standard deviation of this portfolio's return? The standard deviation of the market portfolio's return is 20 percent.
   e. What is the expected rate of return on each stock? Use the capital asset pricing model with a market risk premium of 8 percent. The risk-free rate of interest is 4 percent.

10. **Calculating Beta.** Following are several months' rates of return for Tumblehome Canoe Company. Prepare a plot like Figure 10.1. What is Tumblehome's beta?

Month	Market Return, %	Tumblehome Return, %
1	0	+1
2	0	–1
3	–1	–2.5
4	–1	–0.5
5	+1	+2
6	+1	+1
7	+2	+4
8	+2	+2
9	–2	–2
10	–2	–4

*11. **Expected Returns.** Consider the following two scenarios for the economy, and the returns in each scenario for the market portfolio, an aggressive stock A, and a defensive stock D.

	Rate of Return		
Scenario	**Market**	**Aggressive Stock A**	**Defensive Stock D**
Bust	–8%	–10%	–6%
Boom	32	38	24

   a. Find the beta of each stock. In what way is stock D defensive?
   b. If each scenario is equally likely, find the expected rate of return on the market portfolio and on each stock.
   c. If the T-bill rate is 4 percent, what does the CAPM say about the fair expected rate of return on the two stocks?
   d. Which stock seems to be a better buy based on your answers to (a) through (c)?

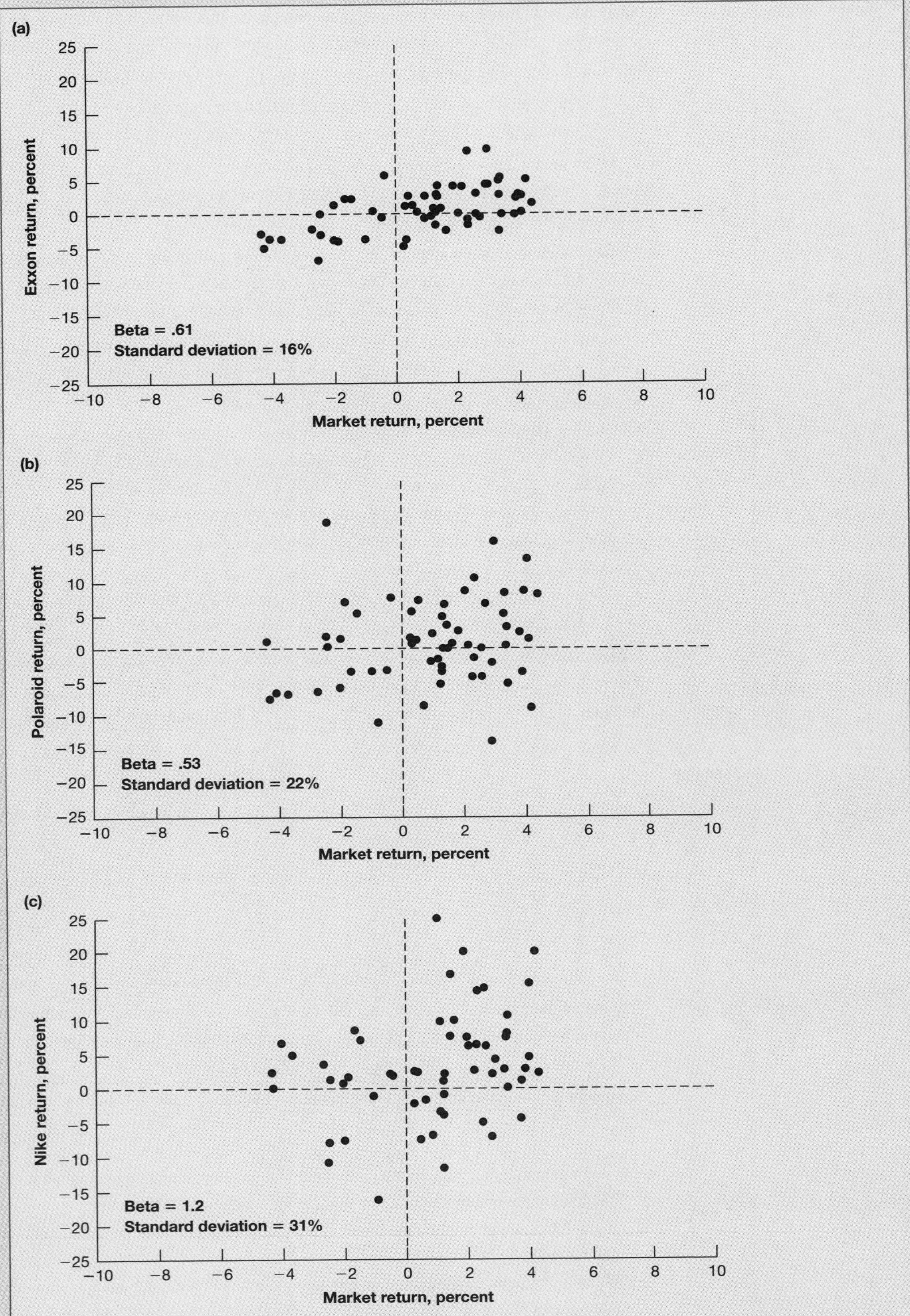

FIGURE 10.9
These plots show monthly rates of return for (a) Exxon, (b) Polaroid, (c) Nike, and the market portfolio. See problem 9.

12. **CAPM and Cost of Capital.** Draw the security market line when the Treasury bill rate is 10 percent and the market risk premium is 8 percent. What are the project costs of capital for new ventures with betas of .75 and 1.75? Which of the following capital investments have positive NPVs?

Project	Beta	Internal Rate of Return, %
P	1.0	20
Q	0.0	10
R	2.0	25
S	0.4	16
T	1.6	25

*13. **CAPM and Valuation.** You are a consultant to a firm evaluating an expansion of its current business. The annual cash-flow forecasts (in millions of dollars) for the project are:

Years	Annual Cash Flow
0	−100
1–10	+ 15

Based on the behaviour of the firm's stock, you believe that the beta of the firm is 1.4. Assuming that the rate of return available on risk-free investments is 5 percent and that the expected rate of return on the market portfolio is 15 percent, what is the net present value of the project?

14. **CAPM and Cost of Capital.** Reconsider the project in the preceding problem. What is the project IRR? What is the cost of capital for the project? Does the accept–reject decision using IRR agree with the decision using NPV?

*15. **CAPM and Valuation.** A share of stock with a beta of .75 now sells for $50. Investors expect the stock to pay a year-end dividend of $2. The T-bill rate is 4 percent, and the market risk premium is 8 percent. If the stock is perceived to be fairly priced today, what must be investors' expectation for the price of the stock at the end of the year?

16. **CAPM and Expected Return.** Reconsider the stock in the preceding problem. Suppose investors actually believe the stock will sell for $54 at year-end. Is the stock a good or bad buy? What will investors do? At what point will the stock reach an "equilibrium" at which it again is perceived as fairly priced?

17. **Portfolio Risk and Return.** Suppose that the TSX, with a beta of 1.0, has an expected return of 13 percent and T-bills provide a risk-free return of 5 percent.
    a. What would be the expected return and beta of portfolios constructed from these two assets with weights in the TSX of (1) 0; (2) .25; (3) .5; (4) .75; (5) 1.0?
    b. Based on your answer to (a), what is the trade-off between risk and return, that is, how does expected return vary with beta?
    c. What does your answer to (b) have to do with the security market line relationship?

18. **Portfolio Risk and Return.** Suppose that the TSX, with a beta of 1.0, has an expected return of 15 percent and T-bills provide a risk-free return of 5 percent.
    a. How would you construct a portfolio from these two assets with an expected return of 12 percent?
    b. How would you construct a portfolio from these two assets with a beta of .4?
    c. Show that the risk premiums of the portfolios in (a) and (b) are proportional to their betas.

*19. **CAPM and Valuation.** You are considering the purchase of real estate which will provide perpetual income that should average $50,000 per year. How much will you pay for the property if you believe its market risk is the same as the market portfolio's? The T-bill rate is 5 percent, and the expected market return is 12.5 percent.

20. **Risk and Return.** According to the CAPM, would the expected rate of return on a security with a beta less than zero be more or less than the risk-free interest rate? Why would investors be willing to invest in such a security? *Hint:* Look back to the auto and gold example in Chapter 9.

*21. **CAPM and Expected Return.** The following table shows betas for several companies. Calculate each stock's expected rate of return using the CAPM. Assume the risk-free rate of interest is 4 percent. Use a 7 percent risk premium for the market portfolio.

Company	Beta
Alliance Atlantis Communications	.69
Big Rock Brewery	.48
Intrawest Corp.	.95
Nortel Networks	2.25

22. **CAPM and Expected Return.** Stock A has a beta of .5 and investors expect it to return 5 percent. Stock B has a beta of 1.5 and investors expect it to return 13 percent. Use the CAPM to find the market risk premium and the expected rate of return on the market.

*23. **CAPM and Expected Return.** If the expected rate of return on the market portfolio is 14 percent and T-bills yield 6 percent, what must be the beta of a stock that investors expect to return 10 percent?

24. **Project Cost of Capital.** Suppose Intrawest Corporation, owner and operator of ski resorts and golf courses, is considering a new investment in the common stock of a brewery. Which of the betas shown in the table in problem 21 is most relevant in determining the required rate of return for this venture? Explain why the expected return to Intrawest stock is *not* the appropriate required return.

*25. **Risk and Return.** True or false? Explain or qualify as necessary.

a. The expected rate of return on an investment with a beta of 2 is twice as high as the expected rate of return of the market portfolio.
b. The contribution of a stock to the risk of a diversified portfolio depends on the market risk of the stock.
c. If a stock's expected rate of return plots below the security market line, it is underpriced.
d. A diversified portfolio with a beta of 2 is twice as volatile as the market portfolio.
e. An undiversified portfolio with a beta of 2 is twice as volatile as the market portfolio.

*26. **CAPM and Expected Return.** A mutual fund manager expects her portfolio to earn a rate of return of 9 percent this year. The beta of her portfolio is .8. If the rate of return available on risk-free assets is 4 percent and you expect the rate of return on the market portfolio to be 11 percent, should you invest in this mutual fund?

27. **Required Rate of Return.** Reconsider the mutual fund manager in the previous problem. Explain how you would use a stock index mutual fund and a risk-free position in Treasury bills (or a money-market mutual fund) to create a portfolio with the same risk as the manager's but with a higher expected rate of return. What is the rate of return on that portfolio?

28. **Required Rate of Return.** In view of your answer to the preceding problem, explain why a mutual fund must be able to provide an expected rate of return in excess of that predicted by the security market line for investors to consider the fund an attractive investment opportunity.

29. **CAPM.** We Do Bankruptcies is a law firm that specializes in providing advice to firms in financial distress. It prospers in recessions when other firms are struggling. Consequently, its beta is negative, –0.2.

a. If the interest rate on Treasury bills is 5 percent and the expected return on the market portfolio is 15 percent, what is the expected return on the shares of the law firm according to the CAPM?
b. Suppose you invested 90 percent of your wealth in the market portfolio and the remainder of your wealth in the shares in the law firm. What would be the beta of your portfolio?

CHALLENGE

30. **Leverage and Portfolio Risk.** Footnote 4 in the chapter asks you to consider a borrow-and-invest strategy in which you use $1 million of your own money and borrow another $1 million to invest $2 million in a market index fund. If the risk-free interest rate is 4 percent and the expected rate of return on the market index fund is 12 percent, what is the risk premium and expected rate of return on the borrow-and-invest strategy? Why is the risk of this strategy twice that of simply investing your $1 million in the market index fund?

31. **CAPM and Valuation.** BigCo has a market value of $1 billion and a beta of .9. It has three divisions: chemical processing, oil and gas distribution, and plastic products. The company is thinking about buying another chemical producer, ChemCo. ChemCo is expected to earn cash flows of $9 million this year and cash flows are expected to grow 4 percent per year thereafter. The beta of ChemCo is 1.4. Currently, the risk-free rate is 4 percent and the expected rate of return on the market portfolio is 11 percent.
    a. What is the expected rate of return for BigCo?
    b. What discount rate should BigCo use to evaluate ChemCo and why?
    c. How much is ChemCo worth?
    d. Suppose BigCo acquires ChemCo for the price in (c). What will be BigCo's new beta after adding ChemCo?

32. **CAPM and Valuation.** Food Express is a well-established grocery chain. Computer Power is an up and coming computer software developer for business. Bridge Steel is an integrated steel producer, focusing on steel for buildings and bridges. Some information about the companies was provided by an investment banking company:

Firm	Beta	Expected Cash Flow Year 1	Expected Cash Flow Growth Rate Years 2 to 5	Expected Cash Flow Growth Rate Year 6 and on
Food Express	.85	7 million	3%	3%
Computer Power	.95	2 million	8%	4%
Bridge Steel	1.3	10 million	2%	3%

    a. If the risk-free rate is 4 percent and the expected return on the market portfolio is 10 percent, what is each firm worth?
    b. If you owned all three companies, what would be the beta of your stock portfolio?

33. **Calculating Beta.** Conglomerated Industries has four divisions, each worth about one-quarter of the firm's market value. The following chart summarizes the possible returns on the divisions as well as on the market portfolio.

State of the Economy	Probability	Division Internal Rates of Return				Market Portfolio
		A	B	C	D	
Recession	.20	8%	–10%	–1%	–4%	–3%
Normal	.60	8%	15%	7%	15%	11%
Boom	.20	9%	30%	10%	20%	22%
Correlation with the market portfolio		0.730	0.995	0.970	0.945	1

    a. Calculate the expected rate of return and standard deviation of return for each division, the firm, and the market.
    b. What is the beta of the divisions, the firm, and the market?
    c. According to the CAPM, what rate of return do investors require for each division?
    d. If the company was thinking of selling the underperforming divisions, which one(s) should it consider selling? Explain your answer.

INTERNET PROBLEMS

1. **Calculating required rates of return.** It is difficult to find betas of Canadian companies from Canadian websites. However, you can find betas at http://finance.yahoo.com for Canadian stocks listed for trading in the United States on the NYSE, ASE, or Nasdaq. For example, Rogers Wireless Communications, Inc., RCN, is listed on the NYSE. To find its beta, first get to the RCN "Basic" page and then click on "Profile." Go down the page until you find the beta estimate.

   To find Canadian stocks listed on the NYSE, go to www.nyse.com, click on "Listed Companies," and select the "Geography" tab and select Canada. For Canadian stock on Nasdaq, go to www.nasdaq.com/asp/NonUSoutput.asp?page=C.

   Find the beta estimates for five different Canadian stocks and estimate their required rates of return. Get current Treasury bill rates from any bank, such as Royal Bank, www.royalbank.ca/rates/treasbil.html, and use the historical market risk premium of 7 percent.

SOLUTIONS TO CHECK POINTS

10.1 See Figure 10.10. Anchovy Queen's beta is 1.

10.2 A portfolio's beta is just a weighted average of the betas of the securities in the portfolio. In this case the weights are equal, since an equal amount is assumed invested in each of the stocks in Table 10.1. The average beta of these stocks is (.79 + 1.5 + 1.36+ 1.25 + .79 + .94 + .76 + .98 + 1.44 + 1.33 + .68 + 1.13 + .48)/13 = 1.03.

10.3 The standard deviation of a fully diversified portfolio's return is proportional to its beta. The standard deviation in this case is .5 × 20 = 10 percent.

10.4 $r = r_f + \beta(r_m - r_f)$
$= 6 + (1.5 \times 7) = 16.5\%$

10.5 Put 25 percent of your money in the market portfolio and the rest in Treasury bills. The expected market return is 6% + 1 × 7% = 13%. The portfolio's beta is .25 and its expected return is

$$r_{\text{portfolio}} = (.75 \times 6) + (.25 \times 13) = 7.75\%$$

10.6 $r_{\text{portfolio}} = (.4 \times 6) + (.6 \times 15) = 11.4\%$

This portfolio's beta is .6, since $600,000, which is 60 percent of the investment, is in the market portfolio. Investors would not buy a stock with a beta of .6 it unless it also offered a rate of return of 11.4 percent, and would rush to buy if it offered more. The stock price would adjust until the stock's expected rate of return was 11.4 percent.

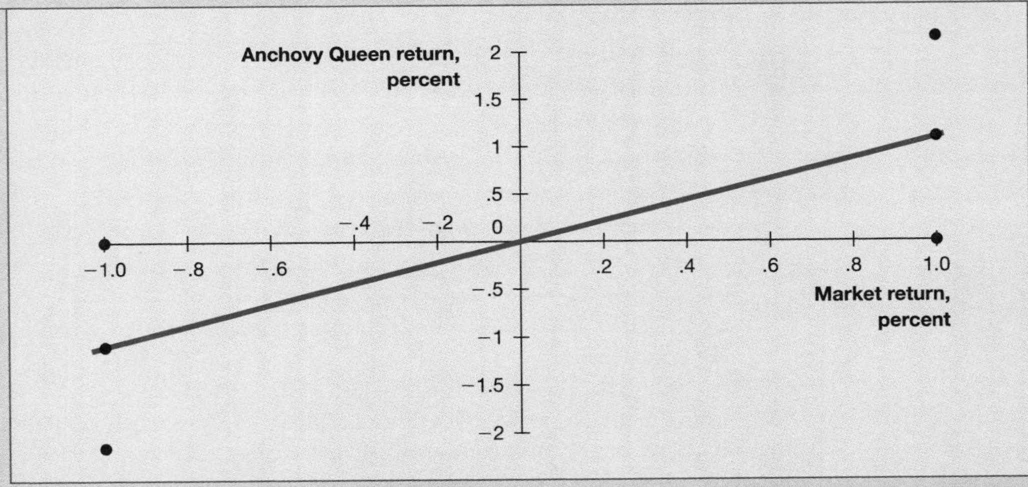

FIGURE 10.10
Each point shows the performance of Anchovy Queen stock when the market is up or down by 1 percent. On average, Anchovy Queen stock follows the market; it has a beta of 1.

10.7 Present value = \$50 million × 10-year annuity factor at 12.75%

= \$274.04 million

If $\beta = .7$, then the cost of capital falls to

$$r = 4\% + (.7 \times 7\%) = 8.9\%$$

and the value of the 10-year annuity increases to \$322.30 million.

10.8 Biomira should use CanWest's cost of capital. Biomira's cost of capital tells us what expected rate of return investors demand from the biotechnology business. This is not the appropriate project cost of capital for Biomira's venture into broadcasting. Note that we have ignored the fact that CanWest is financed with a mix of debt and equity. And we have not considered whether Biomira's proposed new venture makes any business sense. We shall deal with these issues in due course.

CHAPTER 11

The Cost of Capital

11.1 Geothermal's Cost of Capital

11.2 Calculating the Weighted-Average Cost of Capital

11.3 Measuring Capital Structure

11.4 Calculating Required Rates of Return

11.5 Big Oil's Weighted-Average Cost of Capital

11.6 Interpreting the Weighted-Average Cost of Capital

11.7 Flotation Costs and the Cost of Capital

11.8 Summary

In the last chapter you learned how to use the capital asset pricing model to estimate the expected return on a company's common stock. If the firm is financed wholly by common stock, then the shareholders own all the firm's assets and are entitled to all the cash flows. In this case, the expected return required by investors in the common stock equals the company cost of capital.[1]

Most companies, however, are financed by a mixture of securities, including common stock, bonds, and often preferred stock or other securities. Each of these securities has different risks and therefore people who invest in them look for different rates of return. In these circumstances, the company cost of capital is no longer the same as the expected return on the common stock. It depends on the expected return from all the securities that the company has issued. It also depends on taxes because interest payments made by a corporation are tax-deductible expenses.

Therefore, the company cost of capital is usually calculated as a weighted average of the *after-tax* interest cost of debt financing and the "cost of equity"; that is, the expected rate of return on the firm's common stock. The weights are the fractions of debt and equity in the firm's capital structure. Managers refer to the firm's *weighted-average cost of capital*, or *WACC* (rhymes with "quack").

Managers use the weighted-average cost of capital to evaluate average-risk capital investment projects. "Average risk" means that the project's risk matches the risk of the firm's existing assets and operations. This chapter explains how the weighted-average cost of capital is calculated in practice.

After studying this chapter you should be able to

- Calculate a firm's capital structure.
- Estimate the required rates of return on the securities issued by the firm.
- Calculate the weighted-average cost of capital.
- Understand when the weighted-average cost of capital is—or isn't—the appropriate discount rate for a new project.

Managers calculating WACC can get bogged down in formulas. We want you to understand *why* WACC works, not just how to calculate it. Let's start with "why?" We'll listen in as a young financial manager struggles to recall the rationale for project discount rates.

[1] Investors will invest in the firm's securities only if they offer the same expected return as that of other equally risky securities. When securities are properly priced, the return that investors can *expect* from their investments is therefore also the return that they *require*.

Geothermal's Cost of Capital

Jo Ann Cox, a recent graduate of a prestigious Canadian bus
cup of black coffee and tried again to remember what she onc
rates. Why hadn't she paid more attention in Finance 101? W
text the day after passing the finance final?

Costas Thermopolis, her boss and CEO of Geothermal Corporation, had told her to prepare a financial evaluation of a proposed expansion of Geothermal's production. She was to report at 9 o'clock Monday morning. Thermopolis, whose background was geophysics not finance, not only expected a numerical analysis, he expected her to explain it to him.

Thermopolis had founded Geothermal in 1993 to produce electricity from geothermal energy trapped deep under Alberta. The company had pioneered this business and had been able to obtain perpetual production rights for a large tract on favourable terms from the Canadian government. When the 2002 oil shock drove up energy prices worldwide, Geothermal became an exceptionally profitable company. It was currently reporting a rate of return on book assets of 25 percent per year.

Now, in 2004, production rights are no longer cheap. The proposed expansion would cost \$30 million and should generate a perpetual after-tax cash flow of \$4.5 million annually. The projected rate of return is 4.5/30 = .15, or 15 percent, much less than the profitability of Geothermal's existing assets. However, once the new project is up and running, it will be no riskier than Geothermal's existing business.

Jo Ann realized that 15 percent is not necessarily a bad return—though, of course, 25 percent would have been better. Fifteen percent might still exceed Geothermal's cost of capital, that is, exceed the expected rate of return that outside investors would demand to invest money in the project. If the cost of capital was less than the 15 percent expected return, expansion would be a good deal and would generate net value for Geothermal and its shareholders.

Jo Ann remembered how to calculate the cost of capital for companies which use only common stock financing. Briefly she sketched the argument.

"I need the expected rate of return investors would require from Geothermal's real assets—the wells, pumps, generators, etc. That rate of return depends on the assets' risk. However, the assets aren't traded in the stock market, so I can't observe how risky they have been. I can only observe the risk of Geothermal's common stock.

"But if Geothermal issues only stock—no debt—then owning the stock means owning the assets, and the expected return demanded by investors in the stock must also be the cost of capital for the assets." She jotted down the following identities:

Value of business = value of stock

Risk of business = risk of stock

Rate of return on business = rate of return on stock

Investors' required return from business = investors' required return from stock

Unfortunately, Geothermal had borrowed a substantial amount of money; its shareholders did *not* have unencumbered ownership of Geothermal's assets. The expansion project would also justify some extra debt finance. Jo Ann realized that she would have to look at Geothermal's **capital structure**—its mix of debt and equity financing—and consider the required rates of return of debt as well as equity investors.

capital structure A firm's mix of long-term financing.

Geothermal had issued 22.65 million shares, now trading at \$20 each. Thus shareholders valued Geothermal's equity at \$20 × 22.65 million = \$453 million. In addition, the company had issued bonds with a market value of \$194 million. The market value of the company's debt and equity was therefore \$194 + \$453 = \$647 million. Debt was 194/647 = .3, or 30 percent of the total.

"Geothermal's worth more to investors than either its debt or its equity," Jo Ann mused. "But I ought to be able to find the overall value of Geothermal's business by adding up the debt and equity." She sketched a rough balance sheet:

Assets		Liabilities and Shareholders' Equity		
Market value of assets = value of Geothermal's existing business	\$647	Market value of debt	\$194	(30%)
		Market value of equity	\$453	(70%)
Total value	\$647	Total value	\$647	(100%)

"Holy Toledo, I've got it!" Jo Ann exclaimed. "If I bought *all* the securities issued by Geothermal, debt as well as equity, I'd own the entire business. That means. . . ." She jotted again:

Value of business = value of portfolio of all the firm's debt and equity securities (11.1)

Risk of business = risk of portfolio (11.2)

Rate of return on business = rate of return on portfolio (11.3)

Investors' required return on business (company cost of capital) = investors' required return on portfolio (11.4)

"All I have to do is calculate the expected rate of return on a portfolio of all the firm's securities. That's easy. The debt's yielding 8 percent, and Fred, that nerdy banker, says that equity investors want 14 percent. Suppose he's right. The portfolio would contain 30 percent debt and 70 percent equity, so. . . ."

$$\text{Portfolio return} = (.3 \times 8\%) + (.7 \times 14\%) = 12.2\%$$

It was all coming back to her now. The company cost of capital is just a weighted average of returns on debt and equity, with weights depending on relative market values of the two securities.

"But there's one more thing. Interest is tax-deductible. If Geothermal pays \$1 of interest, taxable income is reduced by \$1, and the firm's tax bill drops by 35 cents (assuming a 35 percent tax rate). The net cost is only 65 cents. So the cost of debt is not 8 percent, but .65 × 8 = 5.2 percent.

"Now I can finally calculate the weighted-average cost of capital:

$$\text{WACC} = (.3 \times 5.2\%) + (.7 \times 14\%) = 11.4\%$$

"Looks like the expansion's a good deal. Fifteen's better than 11.4. But I sure need a break."

Calculating the Weighted-Average Cost of Capital

Jo Ann's conclusions were important. It should be obvious by now that the choice of the discount rate can be crucial, especially when the project involves large capital expenditures or is long-lived. The nearby Finance in Action box describes how a major investment in a

FINANCE IN ACTION

Choosing the Discount Rate

Shortly before the British government began to sell off the electricity industry to private investors, controversy erupted over the industry's proposal to build a 1,200-megawatt nuclear power station known as Hinkley Point C. The government argued that a nuclear station would both diversify the sources of electricity generation and reduce sulphur dioxide and carbon dioxide emissions. Protesters emphasized the dangers of nuclear accidents and attacked the proposal as "bizarre, dated and irrelevant."

At the public inquiry held to consider the proposal, opponents produced some powerful evidence that the nuclear station was also a very high cost option. Their principal witness, Professor Elroy Dimson, argued that the government-owned power company had employed an unrealistically low figure for the opportunity cost of capital. Had the government-owned industry used a more plausible figure, the cost of building and operating the nuclear station would have been higher than that of a comparable station based on fossil fuels.

The reason why the choice of discount rate was so important was that nuclear stations are expensive to build but cheap to operate. If capital is cheap (i.e., the discount rate is low), then the high up-front cost is less serious. But if the cost of capital is high, then the high initial cost of nuclear stations made them uneconomic.

Evidence produced at the inquiry suggested that the construction cost of a nuclear station was £1,527 million (or about $2.3 billion), while the cost of a comparable non-nuclear station was only £895 million. However, power stations last about 40 years and, once built, nuclear stations cost much less to operate than non-nuclear stations. If operated at 75 percent of theoretical capacity, the running costs of the nuclear station would be about £63 million a year, compared with running costs of £168 million a year for the non-nuclear station.

The following table shows the cost advantage of the nuclear power station at different (real) discount rates. At a 5 percent discount rate, which was the figure used by the government, the present value of the costs of the nuclear option was nearly £1 billion lower than that of a station based on fossil fuels. But with a discount rate of 16 percent, which was the figure favoured by Professor Dimson, the position was almost exactly reversed, so that the government could save nearly £1 billion by refusing the power company permission to build Hinkley Point C and relying instead on new fossil-fuel power stations.

Thirteen years after the inquiry, the proposal to construct Hinkley Point C has not been implemented.However, British Energy, the privatized electric utility, has suggested that it is time to build new nuclear power stations. To do so, they need the approval of the British government—and more hearings may take place—which means discussion may well resume about the appropriate discount rate for the project.

Present value of the cost advantage to a nuclear rather than a fossil-fuel station (figures in billions of pounds)

Real Discount Rate	Present Value of the Cost Advantage of the Nuclear Station
5%	0.9
8	0.2
10	–0.1
12	–0.4
14	–0.7
16	–0.9
18	–1.2

Technical Notes:

1. Present values are measured at the date that the power station comes into operation.
2. The above table assumes for simplicity that construction costs for nuclear stations are spread evenly over the 8 years before the station comes into operation, while the costs for fossil-fuel stations are assumed to be spread evenly over the 4 years before operation. As a result, the present value of the costs of the two stations may differ slightly from the more precise estimates produced by Professor Dimson.

Source: Adapted with permission from *Energy Economics*, July 1989, E. Dimson, "The Discount Rate for a Power Station," 1989, Elsevier Science Ltd., Oxford, England.

power station—an investment with both a large capital expenditure and very long life—turned on the choice of the discount rate.

Think again what the company cost of capital is, and what it is used for. We *define* it as the opportunity cost of capital for the firm's existing assets; we *use* it to value new assets that have the same risk as the old ones. The weighted-average cost of capital is a way of estimating the company cost of capital; it also incorporates an adjustment for the taxes a company saves when it borrows.

CALCULATING COMPANY COST OF CAPITAL AS A WEIGHTED AVERAGE

Calculating the company cost of capital is straightforward, though not always easy, when only common stock is outstanding. For example, a financial manager could estimate beta and calculate shareholders' required rate of return using the capital asset pricing model (CAPM). This would be the expected rate of return investors require on the company's existing assets and operations and also the expected return they will require on new investments that do not change the company's market risk.

But most companies issue debt as well as equity.

The company cost of capital is a *weighted average* of the returns demanded by debt and equity investors. The weighted average is the expected rate of return investors would demand on a portfolio of all the firm's outstanding securities.

Let's review Jo Ann Cox's calculations for Geothermal. To avoid complications, we'll ignore taxes for the next couple of pages. The total market value of Geothermal, which we denote as V, is the sum of the values of the outstanding debt D and the equity E. Thus firm value is $V = D + E$ = \$194 million + \$453 million = \$647 million. Debt accounts for 30 percent of the value and equity accounts for the remaining 70 percent. If you held all the shares and all the debt, your investment in Geothermal would be V = \$647 million. Between them, the debt and equity holders own *all* the firm's assets. So V is also the value of these assets—the value of Geothermal's existing business.

Suppose that Geothermal's equity investors require a 14 percent rate of return on their investment in the stock. What rate of return must a new project provide in order that all investors—both debtholders and shareholders—earn a fair rate of return? The debtholders require a rate of return of r_{debt} = 8 percent. So each year the firm will need to pay interest of $r_{\text{debt}} \times D = .08 \times \$194$ million = \$15.52 million. The shareholders, who have invested in a riskier security, require a return of r_{equity} = 14 percent on their investment of \$453 million. Thus in order to keep shareholders happy, the company needs additional income of $r_{\text{equity}} \times E = .14 \times \$453$ million = \$63.42 million. To satisfy both the debtholders and the shareholders, Geothermal needs to earn \$15.52 million + \$63.42 million = \$78.94 million. This is equivalent to earning a return of $r_{\text{assets}} = 78.94/647 = .122$, or 12.2 percent.

Figure 11.1 illustrates the reasoning behind our calculations. The figure shows the amount of income needed to satisfy the debt and equity investors. Notice that debtholders account for 30 percent of Geothermal's capital structure but receive less than 30 percent of its expected income. On the other hand, they bear less than a 30 percent share of risk, since they have first cut at the company's income, and also first claim on its assets if the company gets in trouble. Shareholders expect a return of more than 70 percent of Geothermal's income because they bear correspondingly more risk.

However, if you buy *all* Geothermal's debt and equity, you own its assets lock, stock, and barrel. You receive all the income and bear all the risks. The expected rate of return you would require on this portfolio of securities is the same return you would require from unencumbered ownership of the business. This rate of return—12.2 percent, ignoring taxes—is therefore the company cost of capital and the required rate of return from an equal-risk expansion of the business.

The bottom line (still ignoring taxes) is

Company cost of capital = weighted average of debt and equity returns (11.5)

The underlying algebra is simple. Debtholders need income of ($r_{\text{debt}} \times D$) and the equity

FIGURE 11.1
Geothermal's debtholders account for 30 percent of the company's capital structure, but they get a smaller share of income because their return is guaranteed by the company. Geothermal's shareholders bear more risk and receive, on average, greater return. Of course if you buy all the debt and all the equity, you get all the income.

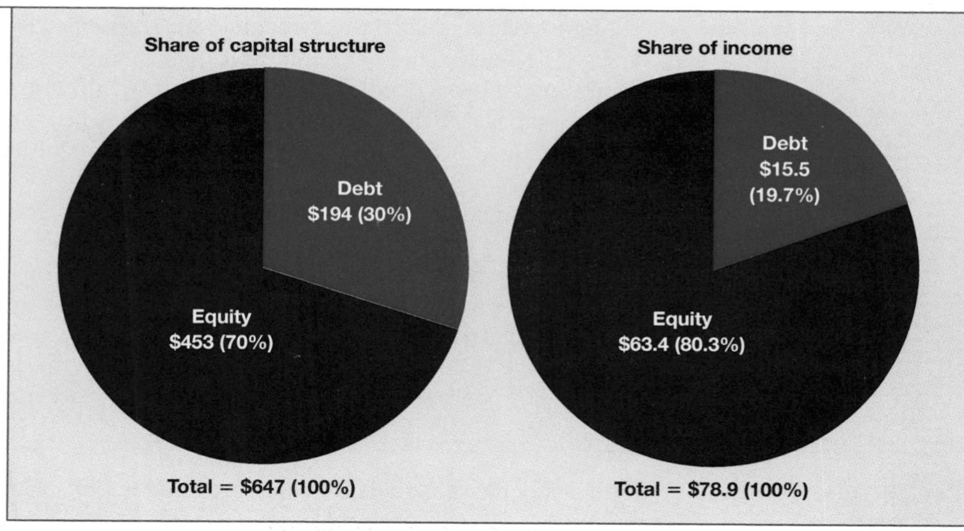

investors need income of ($r_{\text{equity}} \times E$). The *total* income that is needed is ($r_{\text{debt}} \times D$) + ($r_{\text{equity}} \times E$). The amount of their combined existing investment in the company is V. So to calculate the return that is needed on the assets, we simply divide the income by the investment:

$$r_{\text{assets}} = \frac{\textbf{total income}}{\textbf{value of investment}} \tag{11.6}$$

$$= \frac{(D \times r_{\text{debt}}) + (E \times r_{\text{equity}})}{V} = \left(\frac{D}{V} \times r_{\text{debt}}\right) + \left(\frac{E}{V} \times r_{\text{equity}}\right)$$

For Geothermal,

$$r_{\text{assets}} = (.30 \times 8\%) + (.70 \times 14\%) = 12.2\%$$

This figure is the expected return demanded by investors in the firm's assets.

CHECK POINT 11.1

Hot Rocks Corp., one of Geothermal's competitors, has issued long-term bonds with a market value of $50 million and an expected return of 9 percent. It has 4 million shares outstanding trading for $10 each. At this price the shares offer an expected return of 17 percent. What is the weighted-average cost of capital for Hot Rocks' assets and operations? Assume Hot Rocks pays no taxes.

MARKET VERSUS BOOK WEIGHTS

The company cost of capital is the expected rate of return that investors demand from the company's assets and operations.

The cost of capital must be based on what investors are actually willing to pay for the company's outstanding securities—that is, based on the securities' *market* values.

Market values usually differ from the values recorded by accountants in the company's books. The book value of Geothermal's equity reflects money raised in the past from shareholders or reinvested by the firm on their behalf. If investors recognize Geothermal's excellent prospects, the market value of equity may be much higher than book value, and the debt ratio will be lower when measured in terms of market values rather than book values.

Financial managers use book debt-to-value ratios for various other purposes, and sometimes they unthinkingly look to the book ratios when calculating weights for the company cost of capital. That's a mistake, because the company cost of capital measures what investors want from the company, and it depends on how *they* value the company's securities. That value depends on future profits and cash flows, not on accounting history. Book values, while useful for many other purposes, only measure net cumulative historical outlays; they don't generally measure market values accurately.

CHECK POINT 11.2

Here is a book-value balance sheet for Rhodes Construction Company. Figures are in millions.

Assets		Liabilities and Shareholders' Equity	
Assets (book value)	$75	Debt	$25
		Equity	50
	$75		$75

Unfortunately, the company has fallen on hard times. The 6 million shares are trading for only $4 apiece, and the market value of its debt securities is 20 percent below the face (book) value. Because of the company's large cumulative losses, it will pay no taxes on future income.

Suppose shareholders now demand a 20 percent expected rate of return. The bonds are now yielding 14 percent. What is the weighted-average cost of capital?

TAXES AND THE WEIGHTED-AVERAGE COST OF CAPITAL

Thus far in this section our examples have ignored taxes. Taxes are important because interest payments are deducted from income before tax is calculated. Therefore, the cost to the company of an interest payment is reduced by the amount of this tax saving.

The interest rate on Geothermal's debt is $r_{\text{debt}} = 8$ percent. However, with a corporate tax rate of $T_c = .35$, the government bears 35 percent of the cost of the interest payments. The government doesn't send the firm a cheque for this amount, but the income tax that the firm pays is reduced by 35 percent of its interest expense.

Therefore, Geothermal's after-tax cost of debt is only 100 – 35 = 65 percent of the 8 percent pretax cost:

$$\begin{aligned} \textbf{After-tax cost of debt} &= \textbf{pretax cost} \times \textbf{(1 – tax rate)} \\ &= r_{\text{debt}} \times (1 - T_c) \\ &= 8\% \times (1 - .35) = 5.2\% \end{aligned} \tag{11.7}$$

We can now adjust our calculation of Geothermal's cost of capital to recognize the tax saving associated with interest payments:

$$\text{Company cost of capital, after-tax} = (.3 \times 5.2\%) + (.7 \times 14\%) = 11.4\%$$

CHECK POINT 11.3

Criss-cross Industries has earnings before interest and taxes (EBIT) of $10 million. Interest payments are $2 million and the corporate tax rate is 35 percent. Construct a simple income statement to show that the debt interest reduces the taxes the firm owes to the government. How much more tax would Criss-cross pay if it were financed solely by equity?

weighted-average cost of capital (WACC) Expected rate of return on a portfolio of all the firm's securities, adjusted for tax savings due to interest payments.

Now we're back to the **weighted-average cost of capital,** or **WACC.** The general formula is

$$\text{WACC} = \left[\frac{D}{V} \times (1 - T_c)r_{\text{debt}}\right] + \left(\frac{E}{V} \times r_{\text{equity}}\right) \tag{11.8}$$

CHECK POINT 11.4

Calculate WACC for Hot Rocks (Check Point 11.1) and Rhodes Construction (Check Point 11.2) assuming the companies face a 35 percent corporate income tax rate.

WHAT IF THERE ARE THREE (OR MORE) SOURCES OF FINANCING?

We have simplified our discussion of the cost of capital by assuming the firm has only two classes of securities: debt and equity. Even if the firm has issued other classes of securities, our general approach to calculating WACC remains unchanged. You simply calculate the weighted-average after-tax return of each security type.

For example, suppose the firm also has outstanding preferred stock. Preferred stock has some of the characteristics of both common stock and fixed-income securities. Like bonds, preferred stock promises to pay a given, usually level, stream of dividends. Unlike bonds, however, there is no maturity date for the preferred stock. The promised dividends constitute a perpetuity as long as the firm stays in business. Moreover, a failure to come up with the cash to pay the dividends does not push the firm into bankruptcy. Instead, dividends owed simply cumulate; the common shareholders do not receive dividends until the accumulated preferred dividends have been paid. Finally, unlike interest payments, preferred stock dividends are not considered tax-deductible expenses.

How would we calculate WACC for a firm with preferred stock as well as common stock and bonds outstanding? Using P to denote preferred stock, we simply generalize the formula for WACC as follows:

$$\text{WACC} = \left[\frac{D}{V} \times (1 - T_c)r_{\text{debt}}\right] + \left(\frac{P}{V} \times r_{\text{preferred}}\right) + \left(\frac{E}{V} \times r_{\text{equity}}\right) \tag{11.9}$$

Let's try an example to make this concrete.

EXAMPLE 11.1 *Weighted-Average Cost of Capital for Executive Fruit*

Unlike Geothermal, Executive Fruit has issued three types of securities—debt, preferred stock, and common stock. The debtholders require a return of 6 percent, the preferred shareholders require an expected return of 12 percent, and the common shareholders require 18 percent. The debt is valued at $4 million ($D$ = 4), the preferred stock at $2 million ($P$ = 2), and the common stock at $6 million ($E$ = 6). The corporate tax rate is 35 percent. What is Executive's weighted-average cost of capital?

Don't be put off by the third security, preferred stock. We simply work through the following three steps.

Step 1. Calculate the value of each security as a proportion of the firm's value. Firm value is $V = D + P + E = 4 + 2 + 6 = \$12$ million. So $D/V = 4/12 = .33$; $P/V = 2/12 = .17$; and $E/V = 6/12 = .5$.

Step 2. Determine the required rate of return on each security. We have already given you the answers: $r_{\text{debt}} = 6\%$, $r_{\text{preferred}} = 12\%$, and $r_{\text{equity}} = 18\%$[2]

Step 3. Calculate a weighted average of the cost of the after-tax return on debt and the return on the preferred and common stock:

$$\text{Weighted-average cost of capital} = \left[\frac{D}{V} \times (1 - T_c) r_{\text{debt}}\right] + \left(\frac{P}{V} \times r_{\text{preferred}}\right) = \left(\frac{E}{V} \times r_{\text{equity}}\right)$$

$$= [.33 \times (1 - .35)\ 6\%] + (.17 \times 12\%) + (.5 \times 18\%)$$

$$= 12.3\%$$

WRAPPING UP GEOTHERMAL

We now turn one last time to Jo Ann Cox and Geothermal's proposed expansion. We want to make sure that she—and you—know how to *use* the weighted-average cost of capital.

Remember that the proposed expansion cost \$30 million and should generate a perpetual cash flow of \$4.5 million per year. A simple cash-flow worksheet might look like this:[3]

Revenue	\$10.0 million
– Operating expenses	– 3.08
= Pretax operating cash flow	6.92
– Tax at 35%	– 2.42
After-tax cash flow	\$ 4.5 million

Note that these cash flows do not include the tax benefits of using debt.

Geothermal's managers and engineers forecast revenues, costs, and taxes as if the project was to be all-equity financed. The interest tax shields generated by the project's actual debt financing are not forgotten, however. They are accounted for by using the *after-tax* cost of debt in the weighted-average cost of capital.

Project net present value is calculated by discounting the cash flow (which is a perpetuity) at Geothermal's 11.4 percent weighted-average cost of capital:

$$\text{NPV} = -30 + \frac{4.5}{.114} = +\$9.5 \text{ million}$$

Expansion will thus add \$9.5 million to the net wealth of Geothermal's owners.

CHECKING OUR LOGIC

Any project offering a rate of return more than 11.4 percent will have a positive NPV, assuming that the project has the same risk and financing as Geothermal's business. A project offering exactly 11.4 percent would be just break-even; it would generate just enough cash to satisfy both debtholders and shareholders.

[2] Financial managers often use "equity" to refer to *common* stock, even though a firm's equity strictly includes both common and preferred stocks. We continue to use r_{equity} to refer specifically to the expected return on the common stock.

[3] For this example we ignore depreciation, a noncash but tax-deductible expense. (If the project were really perpetual, why depreciate?)

Let's check that out. Suppose the proposed expansion had revenues of only \$8.34 million and after-tax cash flows of \$3.42 million:

	Revenue	\$8.34 million
–	Operating costs	– 3.08
=	Pretax operating cash flow	5.26
–	Tax at 35%	– 1.84
	After-tax cash flow	\$3.42 million

With an investment of \$30 million, the internal rate of return on this perpetuity is exactly 11.4 percent:

$$\text{Rate of return} = \frac{3.42}{30} = .114, \text{ or } 11.4\%$$

NPV is exactly zero:

$$\text{NPV} = -30 + \frac{3.42}{.114} = 0$$

When we calculated Geothermal's weighted-average cost of capital, we recognized that the company's debt ratio was 30 percent. When Geothermal's analysts use the weighted-average cost of capital to evaluate the new project, they are *assuming* that the \$30 million additional investment would support the issue of additional debt equal to 30 percent of the investment, or \$9 million. The remaining \$21 million is provided by the shareholders.

The following table shows how the cash flows would be shared between the debtholders and shareholders. We start with the pretax operating cash flow of \$5.26 million:

	Cash flow before tax and interest	\$5.26 million
–	Interest payment (.08 × \$9 million)	– .72
=	Pretax cash flow	4.54
–	Tax at 35%	– 1.59
	Cash flow after tax	\$2.95 million

Project cash flows before tax and interest are forecast to be \$5.26 million. Out of this figure, Geothermal needs to pay interest of 8 percent of \$9 million, which comes to \$.72 million. This leaves a pretax cash flow of \$4.54 million, on which the company must pay tax. Taxes equal .35 × 4.54 = \$1.59 million. Shareholders are left with \$2.95 million, just enough to give them the 14 percent return that they need on their \$21 million investment. (Note that 2.95/21 = .14, or 14 percent.) Therefore, everything checks out.

If a project has zero NPV when the expected cash flows are discounted at the weighted-average cost of capital, then the project's cash flows are just sufficient to give debtholders and shareholders the returns they require.

11.3 Measuring Capital Structure

We have explained the formula for calculating the weighted-average cost of capital. We will now look at some of the practical problems in applying that formula. Suppose that the financial manager of Big Oil has asked you to estimate the firm's weighted-average cost of capital. Your first step is to work out Big Oil's capital structure. But where do you get the data?

Financial managers usually start with the company's accounts, which show the *book* value of debt and equity, whereas the weighted-average cost of capital formula calls for their *market* values. A little work and a dash of judgment are needed to go from one to the other.

Table 11.1 shows the debt and equity issued by Big Oil. The firm has borrowed \$200 million from banks and has issued a further \$200 million of long-term bonds. These bonds have a coupon rate of 8 percent and mature at the end of 12 years. Finally, there are 100 million shares of common stock outstanding, each with a par value of \$1.00. But the accounts also recognize that Big Oil has in past years plowed back into the firm \$300 million of retained earnings. The total book value of the equity shown in the accounts is \$100 million + \$300 million = \$400 million.

The figures shown in Table 11.1 are taken from Big Oil's annual accounts and are therefore book values. Sometimes the differences between book values and market values are negligible. For example, consider the \$200 million that Big Oil owes the bank. The interest rate on bank loans is usually linked to the general level of interest rates. Thus if interest rates rise, the rate charged on Big Oil's loan also rises to maintain the loan's value. As long as Big Oil is reasonably sure to repay the loan, the loan is worth close to \$200 million. Most financial managers most of the time are willing to accept the book value of bank debt as a fair approximation of its market value.

What about Big Oil's long-term bonds? Since the bonds were originally issued, long-term interest rates have risen to 9 percent.[4] We can calculate the value today of each bond as follows.[5] There are 12 coupon payments of .08 × 200 = \$16 million, and then repayment of face value 12 years out. Thus the final cash payment to the bondholders is \$216 million. All the bond's cash flows are discounted back at the *current* interest rate of 9 percent.

$$\text{PV} = \frac{16}{1.09} + \frac{16}{(1.09)^2} + \frac{16}{(1.09)^3} + \cdots + \frac{216}{(1.09)^{12}} = \$185.7$$

Therefore, the bonds are worth only \$185.7 million, 92.8 percent of their face value.

If you used the book value of Big Oil's long-term debt rather than its market value, you would be a little bit off in your calculation of the weighted-average cost of capital, but probably not seriously so.

The really big errors are likely to arise if you use the book value of equity rather than its market value. The \$400 million book value of Big Oil's equity measures the total amount of cash that the firm has raised from shareholders in the past or has retained and invested on their behalf. But perhaps Big Oil has been able to find projects that were worth

TABLE 11.1
The book value of Big Oil's debt and equity (dollar figures in millions)

Bank debt	\$200	25.0%
Long-term bonds (12-year maturity, 8% coupon)	200	25.0
Common stock (100 million shares, par value \$1)	100	12.5
Retained earnings	300	37.5
Total	\$800	100.0%

[4] If Big Oil's bonds are traded, you can simply look up their price. But many bonds are not traded regularly, and in such cases you need to infer their price by calculating the bond's value using the rate of interest offered by similar bonds.

[5] We assume that coupon payments are annual. Most bonds in Canada and the United States actually pay interest twice a year.

TABLE 11.2
The market value of Big Oil's debt and equity (dollar figures in millions)

Bank debt	$ 200	12.6%
Long-term bonds	185.7	11.7
Total debt	385.7	24.3
Common stock, 100 million shares at $12	1,200	75.7
Total	$1,585.7	100%

more than they originally cost or perhaps the value of the assets has increased with inflation. Perhaps investors see great future investment opportunities for the company. All these considerations determine what investors are willing to pay for Big Oil's common stock.

If in September 2003 Big Oil stock was $12 a share, the total *market value* of the stock would be

$$\text{Number of shares} \times \text{share price} = 100 \text{ million} \times \$12 = \$1{,}200 \text{ million}$$

In Table 11.2 we show the market value of Big Oil's debt and equity. You can see that debt accounts for 24.3 percent of company value ($D/V = .243$) and equity accounts for 75.7 percent ($E/V = .757$). These are the proportions to use when calculating the weighted-average cost of capital. Notice that if you looked only at the book values shown in the company accounts, you would mistakenly conclude that debt and equity each accounted for 50 percent of value.

CHECK POINT 11.5

Here is the capital structure shown in Executive Fruit's *book* balance sheet:

Debt	$4.1 million	45 %
Preferred stock	2.2	24.2
Common stock	2.8	30.8
Total	$9.1 million	100 %

Explain why the percentage weights given above should *not* be used in calculating Executive Fruit's WACC.

11.4 Calculating Required Rates of Return

To calculate Big Oil's weighted-average cost of capital, you also need the rate of return that investors require from each security.

THE EXPECTED RETURN ON BONDS

We know that Big Oil's bonds offer a yield to maturity of 9 percent. As long as the company does not go belly-up, that is the rate of return investors can expect to earn from holding Big Oil's bonds. If there is any chance that the firm may be unable to repay the debt, however, the yield to maturity of 9 percent represents the most favourable outcome and the *expected* return is lower than 9 percent.

For most large and healthy firms, the probability of bankruptcy is sufficiently low that financial managers are content to take the promised yield to maturity on the bonds as a measure of the expected return. But beware of assuming that the yield offered on the bonds of Fly-by-Night Corporation is the return that investors could *expect* to receive.

THE EXPECTED RETURN ON COMMON STOCK

Estimates Based on the Capital Asset Pricing Model. In the last chapter we showed you how to use the capital asset pricing model to estimate the expected rate of return on common stock. The capital asset pricing model tells us that investors demand a higher rate of return from stocks with high betas. The formula is

$$\begin{matrix}\text{Expected return} \\ \text{on stock}\end{matrix} = \begin{matrix}\text{risk-free} \\ \text{interest rate}\end{matrix} + \left(\begin{matrix}\text{stock's} \\ \text{beta}\end{matrix} \times \begin{matrix}\text{expected market} \\ \text{risk premium}\end{matrix}\right)$$

Financial managers and economists measure the risk-free rate of interest by the yield on Treasury bills. To measure the expected market risk premium, they usually look back at capital market history, which suggests that investors have received an extra 7 to 9 percent a year from investing in common stocks rather than Treasury bills. Yet wise financial managers use this evidence with considerable humility, for who is to say whether investors in the past received more or less than they expected, or whether investors today require a higher or lower reward for risk than their parents did?

Let's suppose Big Oil's common stock beta is estimated at .85, the risk-free interest rate of r_f is 6 percent, and the expected market risk premium $(r_m - r_f)$ is 9 percent. Then the CAPM would put Big Oil's cost of equity at

$$\begin{aligned}\text{Cost of equity} = r_{\text{equity}} &= r_f + \beta(r_m - r_f) \\ &= 6\% + .85(9\%) = 13.65\%\end{aligned}$$

Of course no one can estimate expected rates of return to two decimal places, so we'll just round to 13.5 percent.

CHECK POINT 11.6

Jo Ann Cox decides to check whether Fred, the nerdy banker, was correct in claiming that Geothermal's cost of equity is 14 percent. She estimates Geothermal's beta at 1.2. The risk-free interest rate in 2004 is 6 percent, and the long-run average market risk premium is 9 percent. What is the expected rate of return on Geothermal's common stock, assuming of course that the CAPM is true? Recalculate Geothermal's weighted-average cost of capital.

Dividend Discount Model Cost of Equity Estimates. Whenever you are given an estimate of the expected return on a common stock, always look for ways to check whether it is reasonable. One check on the estimates provided by the CAPM can be obtained from the dividend discount model (DDM). In Chapter 5 we showed you how to use the constant-growth DDM formula to estimate the return that investors expect from different common stocks. *Remember the formula*: If dividends are expected to grow indefinitely at a constant rate g, then the price of the stock is equal to

$$P_0 = \frac{\text{DIV}_1}{r_{\text{equity}} - g}$$

where P_0 is the current stock price, DIV_1 is the forecast dividend at the end of the year, and r_{equity} is the expected return from the stock. We can rearrange this formula to provide an estimate of r_{equity}:

$$r_{\text{equity}} = \frac{\text{DIV}_1}{P_0} + g$$

In other words, the expected return on equity is equal to the dividend yield (DIV_1/P_0) plus the expected perpetual growth rate in dividends (g).

This constant-growth dividend discount model is widely used in estimating expected rates of return on common stocks of public utilities. Utility stocks have a fairly stable growth pattern and are therefore tailor-made for the constant-growth formula.

Remember that the constant-growth formula will get you into trouble if you apply it to firms with very high current rates of growth. Such growth cannot be sustained indefinitely.

Using the formula in these circumstances will lead to an overestimate of the expected return.

Beware of False Precision. Do not expect estimates of the cost of equity to be precise. In practice you can't know whether the capital asset pricing model fully explains expected returns or whether the assumptions of the dividend discount model hold exactly. Even if your formulas were right, the required inputs would be noisy and subject to error. Thus a financial analyst who can confidently locate the cost of equity in a band of two or three percentage points is doing pretty well. In this endeavour it is perfectly OK to conclude that the cost of equity is, say, "about 15 percent" or "somewhere between 14 and 16 percent."[6]

Sometimes accuracy can be improved by estimating the cost of equity or WACC for an industry or a group of comparable companies. This cuts down the "noise" that plagues single-company estimates. Suppose, for example, that Jo Ann Cox is able to identify three companies with investments and operations similar to Geothermal's. The average WACC for these three companies would be a valuable check on her estimate of WACC for Geothermal alone.

Or suppose that Geothermal is contemplating investment in oil refining. For this venture, Geothermal's existing WACC is probably not right; it needs a discount rate reflecting the risks of the refining business. It could therefore try to estimate WACC for a sample of oil refining companies. If too few "pure-play" refining companies were available—most oil companies invest in production and marketing as well as refining—an industry WACC for a sample of large oil companies could be a useful check or benchmark. (We report estimates of oil industry WACCs at the end of the next section.)

THE EXPECTED RETURN ON PREFERRED STOCK

Preferred stock that pays a fixed annual dividend can be valued from the perpetuity formula:

$$\text{Price of preferred} = \frac{\text{dividend}}{r_{\text{preferred}}}$$

where $r_{\text{preferred}}$ is the appropriate discount rate for the preferred stock. Therefore, we can infer the required rate of return on preferred stock by rearranging the valuation formula to

$$r_{\text{preferred}} = \frac{\textbf{dividend}}{\textbf{price of preferred}} \qquad (11.10)$$

For example, if a share of preferred stock sells for \$20 and pays a dividend of \$2 per share, the expected return on preferred stock is $r_{\text{preferred}} = \$2/\$20 = 10$ percent, which is simply the dividend yield.

[6] The calculations in this chapter have been done to one or two decimal places only to avoid confusion from rounding.

TABLE 11.3
Data needed to calculate Big Oil's weighted-average cost of capital (dollar figures in millions)

Security Type	Capital Structure		Required Rate of Return
Debt	D = \$ 385.7	D/V = .243	r_{debt} = .09, or 9%
Common stock	E = \$1,200	E/V = .757	r_{equity} = .135, or 13.5%
Total	V = \$1,585.7		

Note: Corporate tax rate = T_c = .35.

11.5 Big Oil's Weighted-Average Cost of Capital

Now that you have worked out Big Oil's capital structure and estimated the expected return on its securities, you need only simple arithmetic to calculate the weighted-average cost of capital. Table 11.3 summarizes the necessary data. Now all you need to do is plug the data from Table 11.3 into the weighted-average cost of capital formula:

$$\text{WACC} = \left[\frac{D}{V} \times (1 - T_c) r_{\text{debt}}\right] + \left(\frac{E}{V} \times r_{\text{equity}}\right)$$
$$= [.243 \times (1 - .35)\ 9\%] + (.757 \times 13.5\%) = 11.6\%$$

Suppose that Big Oil needed to evaluate a project with the same risk as its existing business that would also support a 24.3 percent debt ratio. The 11.6 percent weighted-average cost of capital is the appropriate discount rate for the cash flows.

REAL OIL COMPANY WACCS

Big Oil is entirely hypothetical—and not even very big compared to actual oil companies. Figure 11.2 shows estimated average costs of equity (r_{equity}) and WACCs for a sample of 10 to 12 large oil companies from 1965 to 1997. The latest estimates seem to fall below 10 percent, less than our hypothetical figure for Big Oil.

The WACC estimates in Figure 11.2 decline steadily since the early 1980s. Some of that decline can be attributed to a decline in interest rates over the 1980s and early 1990s. We have included a plot of the risk-free rate (r_f) in Figure 11.2 as a reference point. However, the

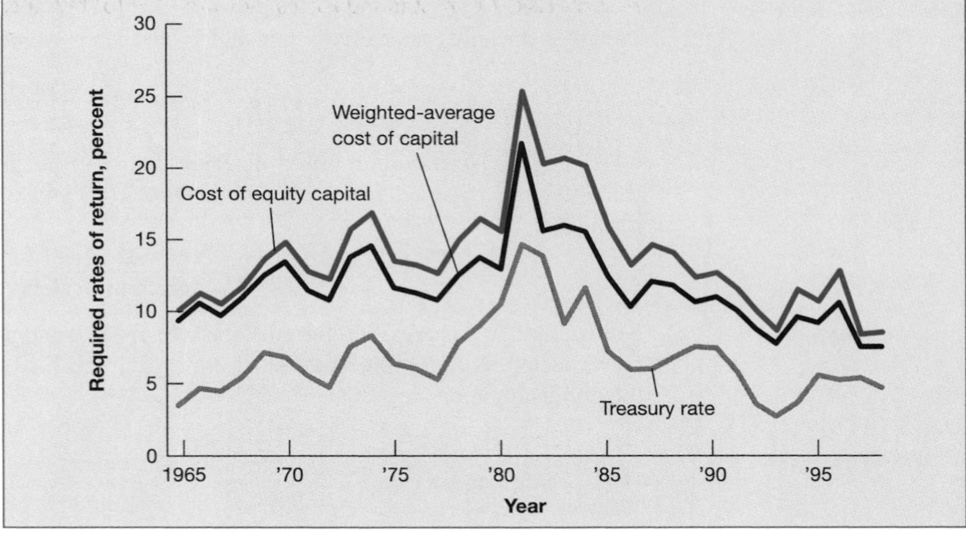

FIGURE 11.2
The middle line represents average weighted-average costs of capital for a sample of large oil companies. Average costs of equity (for the same sample) and the risk-free rate of interest are also plotted for comparison.

spread between the WACC estimates and these interest rates has also narrowed, suggesting that investors viewed the oil business as less risky in the early 1990s than a decade earlier.

Remember, the WACCs shown in Figure 11.2 are industry averages and therefore cover a wide range of activities. The large oil companies sampled are involved in some risky activities, such as exploration, and some relatively safe activities, such as franchising retail gas stations. The industry average will not be right for everything the industry does.

11.6 Interpreting the Weighted-Average Cost of Capital

WHEN YOU CAN AND CAN'T USE WACC

We first discussed the company cost of capital in Chapter 10, but at that stage we did not know how to measure the company cost of capital when the firm issues different types of securities or how to adjust for the tax-deductibility of interest payments. The weighted-average cost of capital formula solves those problems.

The weighted-average cost of capital is the rate of return that the firm must expect to earn on its average-risk investments in order to provide a fair expected return to all its security holders. We use it to value new assets that have the same risk as the old ones and that support the same ratio of debt. Strictly speaking, the weighted-average cost of capital is an appropriate discount rate only for a project that is a carbon copy of the firm's existing business. But often it is used as a companywide benchmark discount rate; the benchmark is adjusted upward for unusually risky projects and downward for unusually safe ones.

There is a good musical analogy here. Most of us, lacking perfect pitch, need a well-defined reference point, like middle C, before we can sing on key. But anyone who can carry a tune gets *relative* pitches right. Businesspeople have good intuition about *relative* risks (at least in industries they are used to) but not about absolute risk or required rates of return. Therefore, they set a company- or industrywide cost of capital as a benchmark. This is not the right hurdle rate for everything the company does, but good judgment adjustments can be used to make for more or less risky ventures.

SOME COMMON MISTAKES

One danger with the weighted-average formula is that it tempts people to make logical errors. Think back to your estimate of the cost of capital for Big Oil:

$$\begin{aligned}\text{WACC} &= \left[\frac{D}{V} \times (1 - T_c) r_{\text{debt}}\right] + \left(\frac{E}{V} \times r_{\text{equity}}\right) \\ &= [.243 \times (1 - .35)\ 9\%] + (.757 \times 13.5\%) = 11.6\%\end{aligned}$$

Now you might be tempted to say to yourself, "Aha! Big Oil has a good credit rating. It could easily push up its debt ratio to 50 percent. If the interest rate is 9 percent and the required return on equity is 13.5 percent, the weighted-average cost of capital would be

$$\text{WACC} = [.50 \times (1 - .35)\ 9\%] + (.50 \times 13.5\%) = 9.7\%\text{"}$$

"At a discount rate of 9.7 percent, we can justify a lot more investment."

That reasoning will get you into trouble. First, if Big Oil increased its borrowing, the lenders would almost certainly demand a higher rate of interest on the debt. Second, as the borrowing increased, the risk of the common stock would also increase and therefore the shareholders would demand a higher return.

There are actually two costs of debt finance. The explicit cost of debt is the rate of interest that bondholders demand. But there is also an implicit cost, because borrowing increases the required return to equity.

When you jumped to the conclusion that Big Oil could lower its weighted-average cost of capital to 9.7 percent by borrowing more, you were recognizing only the explicit cost of debt and not the implicit cost.

CHECK POINT 11.7

Jo Ann Cox's boss has pointed out that Geothermal proposes to finance its expansion entirely by borrowing at an interest rate of 8 percent. He argues that this is therefore the appropriate discount rate for the project's cash flows. Is he right?

HOW CHANGING CAPITAL STRUCTURE AFFECTS EXPECTED RETURNS

We will illustrate how changes in capital structure affect expected returns by focusing on the simplest possible case, where the corporate tax rate T_c is zero.

Think back to our earlier example of Geothermal. Geothermal, you may remember, has the following market-value balance sheet:

Assets		Liabilities and Shareholders' Equity		
Assets = value of Geothermal's existing business	$647	Debt	$194	(30%)
		Equity	$453	(70%)
Total value	$647	Value	$647	(100%)

Geothermal's debtholders require a return of 8 percent and the shareholders require a return of 14 percent. Since we assume here that Geothermal pays no corporate tax, its weighted-average cost of capital is simply the expected return on the firm's assets:

$$\text{WACC} = r_{\text{assets}} = (.3 \times 8\%) + (.7 \times 14\%) = 12.2\%$$

This is the return you would expect if you held all Geothermal's securities and therefore owned all its assets.

Now think what will happen if Geothermal borrows an additional $97 million and uses the cash to buy back and retire $97 million of its common stock. The revised market-value balance sheet is

Assets		Liabilities and Shareholders' Equity		
Assets = value of Geothermal's existing business	$647	Debt	$291	(45%)
		Equity	356	(55%)
Total value	$647	Value	$647	(100%)

If there are no corporate taxes, the change in capital structure does not affect the total cash that Geothermal pays out to its security holders and it does not affect the risk of those cash flows. Therefore, if investors require a return of 12.2 percent on the total package of debt and equity before the financing, they must require the same 12.2 percent return on the package afterward. The weighted-average cost of capital is therefore unaffected by the change in the capital structure. More on this topic appears in Chapter 15.

Although the required return on the *package* of the debt and equity is unaffected, the change in capital structure does affect the required return on the individual securities. Since the company has more debt than before, the debt is riskier and debtholders are likely to demand a higher return. Increasing the amount of debt also makes the equity riskier and increases the return that shareholders require.

WHAT HAPPENS IF CAPITAL STRUCTURE CHANGES AND THE CORPORATE TAX RATE IS NOT ZERO

We have shown that when there are no corporate taxes the weighted-average cost of capital is unaffected by a change in capital structure. Unfortunately, taxes can complicate the picture.[7] For the moment, just remember

- **The weighted-average cost of capital is the right discount rate for average-risk capital investment projects.**
- **The weighted-average cost of capital is the return the company needs to earn after tax in order to satisfy all its security holders.**
- **If the firm increases its debt ratio, both the debt and the equity will become more risky. The debtholders and equity holders require higher rates of return to compensate for the increased risk.**

REVISITING THE PROJECT COST OF CAPITAL

In Chapter 10 we introduced the project cost of capital: the minimum acceptable expected rate of return on a project, given its risks. When funds are invested in a project, the required rate of return on the investment depends on the project's *risk* not the source of funds. In Chapter 10 we discussed ways of finding a suitable estimate of a project's cost of capital. We now must extend that analysis to consider a project's weighted-average cost of capital.

We use the weighted-average cost of capital because, typically, firms are financed by a mix of securities. The weighted-average cost of capital depends on the expected return on all of the securities issued by the company. In our analysis so far, we have not answered an important question: Why are firms financed this way? We have shown that when there are no corporate taxes, a company's cost of capital is unaffected by how it is financed. With taxes, the analysis is more complex. We will deal with the details in Chapter 15. In the meantime we can say that a firm selects its capital structure to maximize the firm's or project's value. Consequently, the determination of the cost of capital appropriate for a

[7] There's nothing wrong with our formulas and examples, *provided* that the tax deductibility of interest payments doesn't change the aggregate risk of the debt and equity investors. However, if the tax savings from deducting interest are treated as safe cash flows, the formulas get more complicated. If you really want to dive into the tax-adjusted formulas showing how WACC changes with capital structure, we suggest Chapter 19 in R. A. Brealey and S. C. Myers, *Principles of Corporate Finance,* 6th ed. (New York: Irwin/McGraw-Hill, 2000).

project has two components. First, the risks of the project's cash flows must be assessed; that is, the project's asset beta must be determined. Second, the best financing mix must be selected. The project's weighted-average cost of capital will reflect the project's overall risk and the best securities mix for the project.

We now know that the pure play approach to assessing the project's risk is complicated by the choice of capital structure. As a first step, you may want to use the pure play company's weighted-average cost of capital as a proxy for the project's weighted-average cost of capital. This assumes that the pure play company's choice of financing mix is also the best mix of financing for the project. We caution that this simple approach may lead to poor investment decisions. You will want to be able to assess the appropriate capital structure for the project in question, the details of which are left for Chapter 15.

11.7 Flotation Costs and the Cost of Capital

To raise the necessary cash for a new project, the firm may need to issue stocks, bonds, or other securities. The costs of issuing these securities to the public can easily amount to 5 percent of funds raised. For example, a firm issuing $100 million in new equity may net only $95 million after incurring the costs of the issue. We will examine *flotation costs,* that is, the costs of "floating" new securities to the public, in Chapter 14.

Flotation costs involve real money. A new project is less attractive if the firm must spend large sums on issuing new securities. To illustrate, consider a project that will cost $900,000 to install and is expected to generate a level perpetual cash-flow stream of $90,000 a year. At a required rate of return of 10 percent, the project is just barely viable, with an NPV of zero: –$900,000 + $90,000/.10 = 0.

Now suppose that the firm needs to raise equity to pay for the project, and that flotation costs are 10 percent of funds raised. To raise $900,000, the firm actually must sell $1 million of equity. Since the installed project will be worth only $90,000/.10 = $900,000, NPV including flotation costs is actually –$1 million + $900,000 = –$100,000.

In our example, we recognized flotation costs as one of the incremental costs of undertaking the project. But instead of recognizing these costs explicitly, some companies attempt to cope with flotation costs by increasing the cost of capital used to discount project cash flows. By using a higher discount rate, project present value is reduced.

This procedure is flawed on practical as well as theoretical grounds. First, on a purely practical level, it is far easier to account for flotation costs as a negative cash flow than to search for an adjustment to the discount rate that will give the right NPV. Finding the necessary adjustment is easy only when cash flows are level or will grow indefinitely at a constant trend rate. This is almost never the case in practice, however. Of course, there always exists some discount rate that will give the right measure of the project's NPV, but this rate could no longer be interpreted as the rate of return available in the capital market for investments with the same risk as the project.

The cost of capital depends only on interest rates, taxes, and the risk of the project. Flotation costs should be treated as incremental (negative) cash flows; they do not increase the required rate of return.

11.8 Summary

1. **Why do firms compute weighted-average costs of capital?**

They need a standard discount rate for average-risk projects. An "average risk" project is one that has the same risk as the firm's existing assets and operations.

2. **What about projects that are not average?**

The **weighted-average cost of capital** can still be used as a benchmark. The benchmark is adjusted up for unusually risky projects and down for unusually safe ones.

3. **How do firms compute weighted-average costs of capital?**

Here's the WACC formula one more time:

$$\text{WACC} = r_{\text{debt}} \times (1 - T_c) \times D/V + r_{\text{equity}} \times E/V$$

The WACC is the expected rate of return on the portfolio of debt and equity securities issued by the firm. The required rate of return on each security is weighted by its proportion of the firm's total market value (not book value). Since interest payments reduce the firm's income tax bill, the required rate of return on debt is measured after tax, as $r_{\text{debt}} \times (1 - T_c)$.

This WACC formula is usually written assuming the firm's capital structure includes just two classes of securities, debt and equity. If there is another class, say preferred stock, the formula expands to include it. In other words, we would estimate $r_{\text{preferred}}$, the rate of return demanded by preferred shareholders, determine P/V, the fraction of market value accounted for by preferred, and add $r_{\text{preferred}} \times P/V$ to the equation. Of course the weights in the WACC formula always add up to 1.0. In this case, $D/V + P/V + E/V = 1.0$.

4. **How are the costs of debt and equity calculated?**

The cost of debt (r_{debt}) is the market interest rate demanded by bondholders. In other words, it is the rate that the company would pay on *new* debt issued to finance its investment projects. The cost of preferred ($r_{\text{preferred}}$) is just the preferred dividend divided by the market price of a preferred share.

The tricky part is estimating the cost of equity (r_{equity}), the expected rate of return on the firm's shares. Financial managers use the capital asset pricing model to estimate expected return. But for mature, steady-growth companies, it can also make sense to use the constant-growth dividend discount model. Remember, estimates of expected return are less reliable for a single firm's stock than for a sample of comparable-risk firms. Therefore, some managers also consider WACCs calculated for industries.

5. **What happens when capital structure changes?**

The rates of return on debt and equity will change. For example, increasing the debt ratio will increase the risk borne by both debt and equity investors and cause them to demand higher returns. However, this does *not* necessarily mean that the overall WACC will increase, because more weight is put on the cost of debt, which is less than the cost of equity. In fact, if we ignore taxes, the overall **cost of capital** will stay constant as the fractions of debt and equity change. This is discussed further in Chapter 15.

6. **Should WACC be adjusted for the costs of issuing securities to finance a project?**

No. If acceptance of a project would require the firm to issue securities, the flotation costs of the issue should be added to the investment required for the project. This reduces project NPV dollar for dollar. There is no need to adjust WACC.

Related Web Links

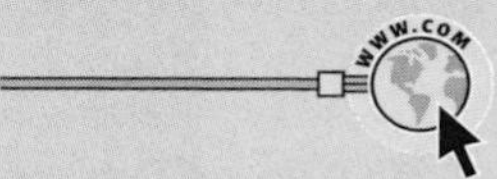

www.geocities.com/WallStreet/Market/1839/irates.html Incorporating risk premiums into the cost of capital

www.financeadvisor.com/coc.htm Another approach to calculating cost of capital

Key Terms

capital structure	333	weighted-average cost of capital (WACC)	339

QUESTIONS AND PROBLEMS

*Answers in Appendix B

BASIC

*1. **Cost of Debt.** Micro Spinoffs, Inc., issued 20-year debt a year ago at par value, with a coupon rate of 9 percent paid annually. Today, the debt is selling at $1,050. If the firm's tax bracket is 35 percent, what is its after-tax cost of debt?

2. **Cost of Preferred Stock.** Micro Spinoffs also has preferred stock outstanding. The stock pays a dividend of $4 per share and the stock sells for $40. What is the cost of preferred stock?

*3. **Calculating WACC.** Suppose Micro Spinoffs's cost of equity is 12.5 percent. What is its WACC if equity is 50 percent, preferred stock is 20 percent, and debt is 30 percent of total capital?

*4. **Cost of Equity.** Reliable Electric is a regulated public utility, and it is expected to provide steady growth of dividends of 5 percent per year for the indefinite future. Its last dividend was $5 per share; the stock sold for $60 per share just after the dividend was paid. What is the company's cost of equity?

5. **Calculating WACC.** Reactive Industries has the following capital structure. Its corporate tax rate is 35 percent. What is its WACC?

Security	Market Value	Required Rate of Return
Debt	$20 million	8%
Preferred stock	$10 million	10%
Common stock	$50 million	15%

*6. **Company versus Project Discount Rates.** Geothermal's WACC is 11.4 percent. Executive Fruit's WACC is 12.3 percent. Now Executive Fruit is considering an investment in geothermal power production. Should it discount project cash flows at 12.3 percent? Why or why not?

7. **Flotation Costs.** A project costs $10 million and has NPV of +$2.5 million. The NPV is computed by discounting at a WACC of 15 percent. Unfortunately, the $10 million investment will have to be raised by a stock issue. The issue would incur flotation costs of $1.2 million. Should the project be undertaken?

PRACTICE

*8. **WACC.** The common stock of Buildwell Conservation & Construction, Inc., has a beta of .8. The Treasury bill rate is 4 percent and the market risk premium is estimated at 8 percent. BCCI's capital structure is 30 percent debt paying a 5 percent interest rate, and 70 percent equity. What is BCCI's cost of equity capital? Its WACC? Buildwell pays no taxes.

9. **WACC and NPV.** BCCI (see the previous problem) is evaluating a project with an internal rate of return of 12 percent. Should it accept the project? If the project will generate a cash flow of $100,000 per year for 7 years, what is the most BCCI should be willing to pay to initiate the project?

*10. **Calculating WACC.** Find the WACC of William Tell Computers. The total book value of the firm's equity is $10 million; book value per share is $20. The stock sells for a price of $30 per share, and the cost of equity is 15 percent. The firm's bonds have a par value of $5 million and sell at a price of 110 percent of par. The yield to maturity on the bonds is 9 percent, and the firm's tax rate is 40 percent.

11. **WACC.** Nodebt, Inc., is a firm with all-equity financing. Its equity beta is .8. The Treasury bill rate is 5 percent and the market risk premium is expected to be 10 percent. What is Nodebt's asset beta? What is Nodebt's weighted-average cost of capital? The firm is exempt from paying taxes.

12. **Cost of Capital.** A financial analyst at Dawn Chemical notes that the firm's total interest payments this year were $10 million while total debt outstanding was $80 million, and he concludes that the cost of debt was 12.5 percent. What is wrong with this conclusion?

13. **Cost of Equity.** Bunkhouse Electronics is a recently incorporated firm that makes electronic entertainment systems. Its earnings and dividends have been growing at a rate of 30 percent, and the current dividend yield is 2 percent. Its beta is 1.2, the market risk premium is 8 percent, and the risk-free rate is 4 percent.

a. Calculate two estimates of the firm's cost of equity.
b. Which estimate seems more reasonable to you? Why?

*14. **Cost of Debt.** Olympic Sports has two issues of debt outstanding. One is a 9 percent coupon bond with a face value of $20 million, a maturity of 10 years, and a yield to maturity of 10 percent. The coupons are paid annually. The other bond issue has a maturity of 15 years, with coupons also paid annually, and a coupon rate of 10 percent. The face value of the issue is $25 million, and the issue sells for 92.8 percent of par value. The firm's tax rate is 35 percent.

a. What is the before-tax cost of debt for Olympic?
b. What is Olympic's after-tax cost of debt?

*15. **Capital Structure.** Examine the following book-value balance sheet for University Products, Inc. What is the capital structure of the firm based on market values? The preferred stock currently sells for $15 per share and the common stock for $20 per share. There are one million common shares outstanding.

BOOK VALUE BALANCE SHEET
(all values in millions)

Assets		**Liabilities and Net Worth**	
Cash and short-term securities	$ 1	Bonds, coupon = 8%, paid annually (maturity = 10 years, current yield to maturity = 9%)	$10
Accounts receivable	3	Preferred stock (par value $20 per share)	2
Inventories	7	Common stock	10
Plant and equipment	21	Retained earnings	10
Total	$32	Total	$32

16. **Calculating WACC.** Turn back to University Products's balance sheet from the previous problem. If the preferred stock pays a dividend of $2 per share, the beta of the common stock is .8, the market risk premium is 10 percent, the risk-free rate is 6 percent, and the firm's tax rate is 40 percent, what is University's weighted-average cost of capital?

*17. **Project Discount Rate.** University Products is evaluating a new venture into home computer systems (see problems 15 and 16). The internal rate of return on the new venture is estimated at 13.4 percent. WACCs of firms in the personal computer industry tend to average around 14 percent. Should the new project be pursued? Will University Products make the correct decision if it discounts cash flows on the proposed venture at the firm's WACC?

*18. **Cost of Capital.** The total market value of Muskoka Real Estate Company is $6 million, and the total value of its debt is $2 million. The treasurer estimates that the beta of the stock is currently 1.5 and that the expected risk premium on the market is 10 percent. The Treasury bill rate is 4 percent.

a. What is the required rate of return on Muskoka stock?
b. What is the beta of the company's existing portfolio of assets? The debt is perceived to be virtually risk-free.
c. Estimate the weighted-average cost of capital assuming a tax rate of 40 percent.
d. Estimate the discount rate for an expansion of the company's present business.
e. Suppose the company wants to diversify into the manufacture of rose-coloured glasses. The beta of optical manufacturers with no debt outstanding is 1.2. What is the required rate of return on Muskoka's new venture?

CHALLENGE

19. **Changes in Capital Structure.** Look again at our calculation of Big Oil's WACC. Suppose Big Oil is excused from paying taxes. How would its WACC change? Now suppose Big Oil makes a large stock issue and uses the proceeds to pay off all its debt. How would the cost of equity change?

20. **Changes in Capital Structure.** Refer again to problem 19. Suppose Big Oil starts from the financing mix in Table 11.3, and then borrows an additional $200 million from the bank. It then pays out a special $200 million dividend, leaving its assets and operations unchanged. What happens to Big Oil's WACC, still assuming it pays no taxes? What happens to the cost of equity?
21. **WACC and Taxes.** "The after-tax cost of debt is lower when the firm's tax rate is higher; therefore, the WACC falls when the tax rate rises. Thus, with a lower discount rate, the firm must be worth more if its tax rate is higher." Explain why this argument is wrong.
22. **Cost of Capital.** An analyst at Dawn Chemical notes that its cost of debt is far below that of equity. He concludes that it is important for the firm to maintain the ability to increase its borrowing because if it cannot borrow, it will be forced to use more expensive equity to finance some projects. This might lead it to reject some projects that would have seemed attractive if evaluated at the lower cost of debt. Comment on this reasoning.

SOLUTIONS TO CHECK POINTS

11.1 Hot Rocks's 4 million common shares are worth $40 million. Its market value balance sheet is

Assets		**Liabilities and Shareholders' Equity**		
Assets	$90	Debt	$50	(56%)
		Equity	40	(44%)
Value	$90	Value	$90	

WACC = (.56 × 9%) + (.44 × 17%) = 12.5%

We use Hot Rocks' pretax return on debt because the company pays no taxes.

11.2 Rhodes' 6 million shares are now worth only 6 million × $4 = $24 million. The debt is selling for 80 percent of book, or $20 million. The market value balance sheet is

Assets		**Liabilities and Shareholders' Equity**		
Assets	$44	Debt	$20	(45%)
		Equity	24	(55%)
Value	$44	Value	$44	

WACC = (.45 × 14%) + (.55 × 20%) = 17.3%

Note that this question ignores taxes.

11.3 Compare the two income statements, one for Criss-cross Industries and the other for a firm with identical EBIT but no debt in its capital structure. (All figures in millions.)

	Criss-cross	**Firm with No Debt**
EBIT	$10.0	$10.0
Interest expense	2.0	0.0
Taxable income	8.0	10.0
Taxes owed	2.8	3.5
Net income	5.2	6.5
Total income accruing to debt and equity holders	7.2	6.5

Notice that Criss-cross pays $.7 million less in taxes than its debt-free counterpart. Accordingly, the total income available to debt and equity holders is $.7 million higher.

11.4 For Hot Rocks,

$$\text{WACC} = [.56 \times 9 \times (1 - .35)] + (.44 \times 17) = 10.76\%$$

For Rhodes Construction,

$$\text{WACC} = [.45 \times 14 \times (1 - .35)] + (.55 \times 20) = 15.1\%$$

11.5 WACC measures the expected rate of return demanded by debt and equity investors in the firm (plus a tax adjustment capturing the tax-deductibility of interest payments). Thus the calculation must be based on what investors are actually paying for the firm's debt and equity securities. In other words, it must be based on market values.

11.6 From the CAPM:

$$\begin{aligned} r_{\text{equity}} &= r_f + \beta_{\text{equity}}(r_m - r_f) \\ &= 6\% + 1.20(9\%) = 16.8\% \\ \text{WACC} &= .3(1 - .35)\ 8\% + .7(16.8\%) = 13.3\% \end{aligned}$$

11.7 Jo Ann's boss is wrong. The ability to borrow at 8 percent does not mean that the cost of capital is 8 percent. This analysis ignores the side effects of the borrowing; for example, that at the higher indebtedness of the firm the equity will be riskier, and therefore, the equityholders will demand a higher rate of return on their investment.

MINICASE

Bernice Mountaindog was glad to be back at Sea Shore Salt. Employees were treated well. When she had asked a year ago for a leave of absence to complete her degree in finance, top management promptly agreed. When she returned with an honours degree, she was promoted from administrative assistant (she had been secretary to Joe-Bob Brinepool, the president) to treasury analyst.

Bernice thought the company's prospects were good. Sure, table salt was a mature business, but Sea Shore Salt had grown steadily at the expense of its less well-known competitors. The company's brand name was an important advantage, despite the difficulty most customers had in pronouncing it rapidly.

Bernice started work on January 2, 2003. The first two weeks went smoothly. Then Mr. Brinepool's cost of capital memo (shown on page 357) assigned her to explain Sea Shore Salt's weighted-average cost of capital to other managers. The memo came as a surprise to Bernice, so she stayed late to prepare for the questions that would surely come the next day.

Bernice first examined Sea Shore Salt's most recent balance sheet, summarized in Table 11.4. Then she jotted down the following additional points:

- The company's bank charged interest at current market rates, and the long-term debt had just been issued. Book and market values could not differ by much.
- But the preferred stock had been issued 35 years ago, when interest rates were much lower. The preferred stock was now trading for only $70 per share.
- The common stock traded for $40 per share. Next year's earnings per share would be about $4.00, and dividends per share, probably $2.00. Sea Shore Salt had traditionally paid out 50 percent of earnings as dividends and plowed back the rest.
- Earnings and dividends had grown steadily at 6 to 7 percent per year, in line with the company's sustainable growth rate:

$$\begin{aligned} \text{Sustainable growth rate} &= \text{return on equity} \times \text{plowback ratio} \\ &= 4.00/30 \times .5 \\ &= .067, \text{ or } 6.7\% \end{aligned}$$

- Sea Shore Salt's beta had averaged about .5, which made sense, Bernice thought, for a stable, steady-growth business. She made a quick cost of equity calculation using the capital asset pricing model (CAPM). With current interest rates of about 7 percent, and a market risk premium of 8 percent,

$$\begin{aligned} \text{CAPM cost of equity} = r_E &= r_f + \beta(r_m - r_f) \\ &= 7\% + .5(8\%) = 11\% \end{aligned}$$

This cost of equity was significantly less than the 16 percent decreed in Mr. Brinepool's memo. Bernice scanned her notes apprehensively. What if Mr. Brinepool's cost of equity was wrong? Was there some other way to estimate the cost of equity as a check on the CAPM calculation? Could there be other errors in his calculations?

Bernice resolved to complete her analysis that night. If necessary, she would try to speak with Mr. Brinepool when he arrived at his office the next morning. Her job was not just finding the right number. She also had to figure out how to explain it all to Mr. Brinepool.

TABLE 11.4
Sea Shore Salt's balance sheet, taken from the company's 2002 balance sheet (figures in millions of dollars)

Assets		**Liabilities and Net Worth**	
Working capital	$200	Bank loan	$120
Plant and equipment	360	Long-term debt	80
Other assets	40	Preferred stock	100
		Common stock, including retained earnings	300
Total	$600	Total	$600

Notes:
1. At year-end 2002, Sea Shore Salt had 10 million common shares outstanding.
2. The company had also issued 1 million preferred shares with book value of $100 per share. Each share receives an annual dividend of $6.00.

Sea Shore Salt Company
Salt Spring Island, British Columbia

CONFIDENTIAL MEMORANDUM

DATE: January 15, 2003
TO: S.S.S. Management
FROM: Joe-Bob Brinepool, President
SUBJECT: Cost of Capital

This memo states and clarifies our company's long-standing policy regarding hurdle rates for capital investment decisions. There have been many recent questions, and some evident confusion, on this matter.

Sea Shore Salt evaluates replacement and expansion investments by discounted cash flow. The discount or hurdle rate is the company's after-tax weighted-average cost of capital.

The weighted-average cost of capital is simply a blend of the rates of return expected by investors in our company. These investors include banks, bondholders, and preferred stock investors in addition to common shareholders. Of course many of you are, or soon will be, shareholders of our company.

The following table summarizes the composition of Sea Shore Salt's financing:

	Amount (in millions)	Percent of Total	Rate of Return (%)
Bank loan	\$120	20%	8%
Bond issue	80	13.3	7.75
Preferred stock	100	16.7	6
Common stock	300	50	16
	\$600	100%	

The rates of return on the bank loan and bond issue are of course just the interest rates we pay. However, interest is tax-deductible, so the after-tax interest rates are lower than shown above. For example, the after-tax cost of our bank financing, given our 35% tax rate, is 8(1 – .35) = 5.2%.

The rate of return on preferred stock is 6%. Sea Shore Salt pays a \$6 dividend on each \$100 preferred share.

Our target rate of return on equity has been 16% for many years. I know that some newcomers think this target is too high for the safe and mature salt business. But we must all aspire to superior profitability.

Once this background is absorbed, the calculation of Sea Shore Salt's weighted-average cost of capital (WACC) is elementary:

$$WACC = 8(1 - .35)(.2) + 7.75(1 - .35)(.133) + 6(.167) + 16(.50) = 10.7\%$$

The official corporate hurdle rate is therefore 10.7%.

If you have further questions about these calculations, please direct them to our new treasury analyst, Bernice Mountaindog. It is a pleasure to have Bernice back at Sea Shore Salt after a year's leave of absence to complete her degree in finance.

PART FOUR

Financing

12 Corporate Financing and the Lessons of Market Efficiency

13 An Overview of Corporate Financing

14 How Corporations Issue Securities

CHAPTER 12

Corporate Financing and the Lessons of Market Efficiency

12.1 Differences between Investment and Financing Decisions

12.2 What Is an Efficient Market?

12.3 Lessons of Market Efficiency

12.4 Summary

Up to this point we have concentrated almost exclusively on the firm's capital expenditure decision. Now we move to the other side of the balance sheet to look at how the firm can finance those capital expenditures. To put it crudely, you've learned how to spend money—now it's time to learn how to raise it.

Therefore, in the next few chapters, we assume that the firm has already decided on which investment projects to accept, and we focus on the best way to finance these projects. In this chapter we begin with some general lessons about the capital markets, where firms raise new capital.

Economists often talk about "efficient capital markets." By this they don't mean that the filing is up-to-date and desktops are tidy. They mean that information is widely and cheaply available to investors and that all relevant and ascertainable information is already reflected in security prices. All stocks, bonds, and other securities are fairly priced in efficient markets and offer expected returns just sufficient to compensate for the securities' risks.

Why should a hard-nosed financial manager care about market efficiency? He or she just wants to raise financing at the lowest possible cost, right?

Right—but finding financing that's *truly* low-cost is not as easy as it sounds. You've got to know where to look—and where not to look. Capital markets are full of traps and mirages for the unwary or naive manager who believes that it is easy to spot mispriced securities. The wary and sophisticated financial manager, who understands the implications of capital market efficiency, is much less likely to make an expensive financing mistake.

Of course no human institution is perfect and no financial market is perfectly efficient. But we always advise financial managers to start by assuming efficient capital markets. From that vantage point they can look out for the specific inefficiencies or imperfections (possibly due to taxes or government regulations) that can be used to create advantageous financing strategies.

After studying this chapter you should be able to

- Show how competition among investors leads to efficient markets.
- Cite evidence that supports the hypothesis that security markets are efficient—as well as some that contradicts it.
- Understand the implications of market efficiency for a firm's financial decisions.

Differences between Investment and Financing Decisions

In some ways financing decisions are more complicated than investment decisions. You need to be aware of the major financial institutions that provide financing and of the wide variety of securities that can be issued.

There are also ways in which financing decisions are easier than investment decisions. First, financing decisions do not have the same degree of finality as investment decisions. They are easier to reverse. For example, Inco can issue a bond and buy it back later if they have second thoughts. It would be far more difficult for Inco to dismantle or sell a nickel smelter that is no longer needed.

Second, it's harder to make or lose money by smart or stupid financing strategies. It is difficult to make money—that is, to find cheap financing—because the investors who supply the financing demand fair terms. At the same time, it's harder to lose money because competition among investors prevents any of them from demanding *more* than fair terms.

Competition in financial markets is more intense than in most product markets. In product markets, companies regularly find competitive advantages that allow positive-NPV investments. For example, a company may have only a few competitors that specialize in the same line of business in the same geographical area. Or it may be able to capitalize on patents or technology, or on customer recognition and loyalty. All this opens up the opportunity to make superior profits and find projects with positive NPVs.

But there are few protected niches in *financial* markets. You can't patent the design of a new security. Moreover, in these markets you always face fast-moving competition, including all the other corporations seeking funds, to say nothing of the provincial or state, local, and federal governments, financial institutions, individuals, and foreign firms and governments that also go to Toronto, New York, London, or Tokyo for financing. The investors who supply financing are numerous, and they are smart—money attracts brains. Most likely, these investors can assess values of securities at least as well as you can.

A smart financing decision makes shareholders wealthier. For example, the firm might hope to sell a security for more than it is worth. But if selling that security is a good deal for your shareholders, it must be a bad deal for the buyers. So, what are the chances that your firm could consistently trick investors into overpaying for its securities? Pretty slim. In general, firms should assume that the securities they issue sell for their true values.

But what do we mean by *true value?* It is a potentially slippery phrase. True value does not mean ultimate *future* value—we do not expect investors to be fortunetellers. It means a price that incorporates all the information *currently* available to investors. That is our definition of **efficient capital markets.**

efficient capital markets Financial markets in which security prices rapidly reflect all relevant information about asset values.

If capital markets are efficient, all securities are fairly priced in light of the information available to investors. If securities are fairly priced, then financing at prevailing market terms is never a positive NPV transaction.

Does that sound like a sweeping statement? It is. That is why we devote the rest of this chapter to the history, logic, and tests of market efficiency.

You may ask why we start our discussion of financing issues with this conceptual point, before you have even the most basic knowledge about securities, issue procedures, and financial institutions. We do it this way because financing decisions seem overwhelmingly complex if you don't learn to ask the right questions. You need to understand the efficient-market hypothesis, not because it is *universally* true but because it leads you to ask the right questions.

What Is an Efficient Market?

A STARTLING DISCOVERY: PRICE CHANGES ARE RANDOM

As is so often the case with important ideas, the concept of efficient markets was a byproduct of a chance discovery. In 1953 the Royal Statistical Society met in London to discuss a rather unusual paper.[1] Its author, Maurice Kendall, was a distinguished statistician, and the subject was the behaviour of stock and commodity prices. Kendall had been looking for regular price cycles, but to his surprise, he could not find them. Prices seemed to wander randomly, just as likely to go up or go down, on any particular day, *regardless of what had occurred on previous days.* In other words, prices seemed to follow a **random walk.**

random walk Security prices change randomly without predictable trends or patterns.

If you are not sure what we mean by "random walk," consider the following example. You are given $100 to play a game. At the end of each week a coin is tossed. If it comes up heads, you win 3 percent of your investment, if it is tails, you lose 2.5 percent. Therefore, your capital at the end of the first week is either $103 or $97.50. At the end of the second week, the coin is tossed again. Now the possible outcomes are as follows:

Start	Week 1		Week 2	
$100	Heads	$103.00	Heads	$106.09
			Tails	$100.43
	Tails	$ 97.50	Heads	$100.43
			Tails	$ 95.06

This process is a random walk because successive changes in the value of your stake are independent. That is, the odds of making money each week are the same, regardless of the value at the start of the week or the pattern of heads or tails in the previous weeks.

If a stock's price follows a random walk, the odds of an increase or decrease during any day, month, or year do not depend *at all* on the stock's previous price moves. The historical path of prices reveals useless information about the future—just as a long series of recorded heads and tails gives no information about the next coin toss.

Some people find it difficult to believe that stock prices follow a random walk. If you are one of them, look at the two charts in Figure 12.1. One of these charts shows the outcome from playing our game for 5 years; the other shows the actual performance of the Standard & Poor's Index for a 5-year period. Can you tell which one is which?

Of course, you would need much more evidence than Figure 12.1 before you could be confident that stock prices do indeed follow a random walk. Researchers have therefore employed a battery of sophisticated statistical tests and have looked at the behaviour of many individual stocks as well as market indexes over many periods. With remarkable unanimity these researchers have concluded that the sequence of past price changes provides little information about future changes. As a result, many of the researchers have become famous. Few, if any, have become rich.

Of course, this doesn't mean that stock price changes are picked out of the hat by some whimsical gremlin. If the stock price of Establishment Industries (EI) jumps up today, you can't assume that it will do so again tomorrow. But there is usually a good reason for the jump. Perhaps EI just announced a big increase in earnings or the development of a new wonder-drug that will boost profits in the future.

[1] See M. G. Kendall, "The Analysis of Economic Time-Series, Part I. Prices," *Journal of the Royal Statistical Society* 96 (1953), pp. 11–25.

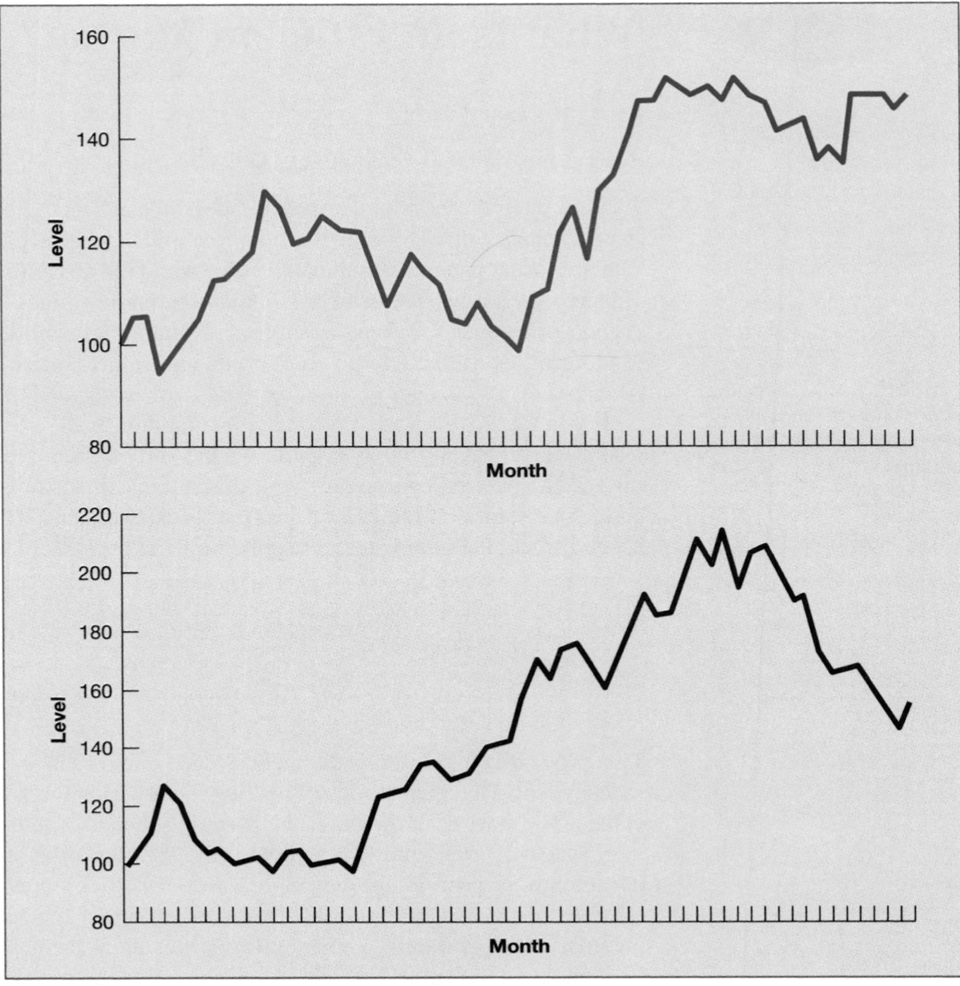

FIGURE 12.1
One of these charts shows the Standard & Poor's Index for a 5-year period. The other shows the results of playing our coin-toss game for 5 years. Can you tell which is which? (See page 374, problem 12 at the end of the chapter.)

CHECK POINT 12.1

If stock prices follow a random walk, are the following statements true or false?

a. Successive stock price changes are not related.
b. Stock prices fluctuate randomly above and below a normal long-run price.
c. The history of stock prices cannot be used to predict future returns to investors.
d. A historical plot of a stock's trading prices will show no apparent "peaks and valleys."

technical analysts Investors who attempt to identify over- or undervalued stocks by searching for patterns in past prices.

Some investors do try to spot patterns in stock prices. These investors are known as **technical analysts.** Some technical analysts are very successful investors, but we credit this to luck and good judgment, not to technical trading rules, because technical trading rules are useless when stock prices follow a random walk.

Technical analysts can help keep the market efficient, however. Their trading would extinguish any predictable patterns in stock prices. Suppose that there were a trend in some company's stock price. Then technical analysts could make superior profits, at least temporarily. For example, Figure 12.2 shows a hypothetical 2-month upswing for

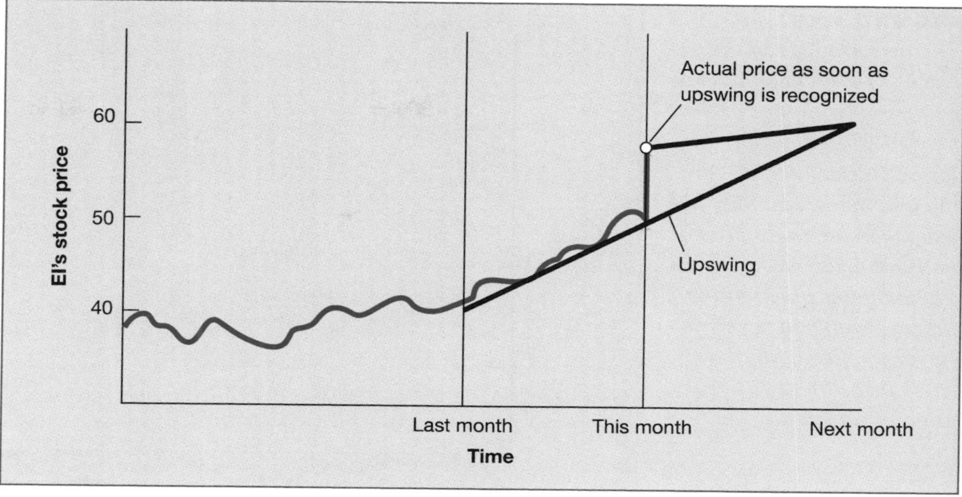

FIGURE 12.2
Cycles self-destruct as soon as they are recognized by investors. The stock price instantaneously jumps to the present value of the expected future price.

Establishment Industries (EI). The upswing started last month, when EI's stock price was $40, and it is expected to carry the stock price to $60 next month. What will happen when technicians perceive this bonanza? It will self-destruct. Since EI stock is a bargain at $50, investors will rush to buy. They will stop buying only when the stock offers a normal rate of return. Therefore, as soon as a price pattern becomes apparent to technical analysts, they immediately eliminate it by their trading.

THREE FORMS OF THE EFFICIENT-MARKET THEORY

weak-form efficiency Market prices rapidly reflect all information contained in the history of past prices.

fundamental analysts Analysts who attempt to find under- or overvalued securities by analyzing fundamental information, such as earnings, asset values, and business prospects.

If stock prices follow a random walk, you can't make superior profits just by studying past stock prices. Any information in those stock prices is already reflected in today's price. So the market is, at least, efficient in this sense. Such a market is called **weak-form efficient.**

But what about other kinds of publicly available information? Are they also immediately reflected in stock prices? After all, most investors don't just look at past stock prices. Instead they try to gauge a firm's business prospects by studying the financial and trade press, the company's financial accounts, the president's annual statement, the recommendations made by stockbrokers, and so on. These investors are **fundamental analysts,** in contrast to technical analysts, who examine past stock price movements.

Figure 12.3 illustrates how the release of relevant news is immediately reflected in security prices. The graph shows the price run-up of a sample of 194 firms that were targets of takeover attempts. In most takeovers, the acquiring firm is willing to pay a large premium over the current market price of the acquired firm; therefore, when a firm becomes a target of a takeover attempt, its stock price increases in anticipation of the takeover premium. Figure 12.3 shows that on the day the public becomes aware of a takeover attempt (Day 0 in the graph), the stock price of the typical target takes a big upward jump. The adjustment in stock price is immediate: After the big price move on the public announcement day, the run-up is over, and there is no further drift in the stock price, either upward or downward.[2] Within the day, the new stock prices apparently reflect (at least on average) the magnitude of the eventual takeover premium.

[2] However, prices on the days *before* the public announcement do show evidence of a sustained upward drift. This is evidence of a gradual "leakage" of information concerning the takeover attempt to insiders and their associates, who begin to purchase the target firm in anticipation of the public announcement. Consistent with efficient markets, however, once the information becomes public, it is reflected fully and immediately in stock prices.

FIGURE 12.3
The performance of the stocks of target companies compared with that of the market. The prices of target stocks jump up on the announcement day, but from then on, there are no unusual price movements. The announcement of the takeover attempt seems to be fully reflected in the stock price on the announcement day.

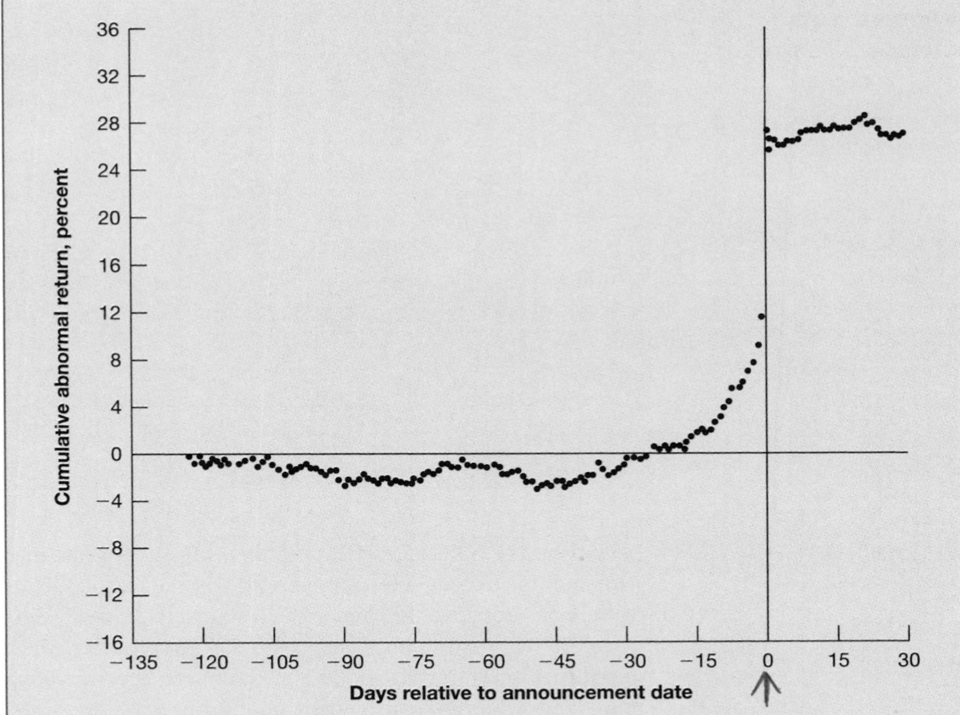

Source: A. Keown and J. Pinkerton, "Merger Announcements and Insider Trading Activity," *Journal of Finance 36* (September 1981). Copyright © 1981. Reprinted by permission of Blackwell Publishers.

Researchers have looked at the stock price reaction to many other types of news, for example, earnings and dividend announcements, plans to issue additional stock or to merge with another firm, or various sorts of macroeconomic news. Most of the information was rapidly and accurately reflected in the price of the stock; therefore, investors were not able to earn superior returns by buying or selling after the announcement. Such a market in which it is impossible to make superior returns from publicly available information is said to be **semi-strong-form efficient.**

semi-strong-form efficiency Market prices reflect all publicly available information.

strong-form efficiency Market prices rapidly reflect all information that is potentially available to determine true value.

Finally, there's **strong-form efficiency** in which prices reflect not just public information but *all* the information that can be acquired by painstaking analysis of the company and the economy. In such a market, prices would *always* be fair and *no* investor would be able to make consistently superior forecasts of stock prices.

Most tests of strong-form efficiency have analyzed the performance of professionally managed portfolios. Managers of such portfolios have every kind of published and unpublished information at their fingertips. If the market were not strong-form efficient, these managers ought to generate higher returns than ordinary investors. Yet no group of portfolio managers has been able to outperform the market consistently, after taking account of differences in risk.

Of course, it would be surprising if some managers were not smarter than others and could earn superior returns. But it seems to be difficult to spot the smart ones, and a top-performing manager one year has about an average chance of falling on his or her face the next year.

When evidence of the "only-average" performance of professional investment managers first appeared, it was greeted with skepticism—especially by the managers! But many investment managers are now convinced and indeed have given up the pursuit of superior performance. They simply "buy the index," which maximizes diversification and minimizes the costs of managing their portfolios. Corporate pension plans now invest over a quarter of their U.S. equity holdings in index funds.[3]

▶ EXAMPLE 12.1 *Performance of Money Managers*

Forbes Magazine, a widely read investment magazine, annually publishes an "honour roll" of the most consistently successful mutual funds. Suppose that each year starting in 1975 you invested an equal sum in each of these exceptional funds when *Forbes* announced its honour roll. You would have outperformed the market in only 5 of the following 16 years, and your average annual return before paying any initial fees would have been more than 1 percent below the return on the market.[4]

Indexing of professionally managed money makes sense if no manager can consistently get useful information ahead of the rest of the pack. When information does arrive, managers trade on it immediately, and stock prices respond right away. Such a market ends up strong-form efficient, even though the information moving stock prices is not readily available to the amateur investor.

The difficulty of "beating the market" has led some to suggest, partially in jest, that one might as well choose stocks by throwing darts at *The Wall Street Journal* as by making a "rational" selection. Actually, this view is far too simplistic *even if* markets are fully efficient, for it overlooks the importance of efficient diversification and the choice of an appropriate level of portfolio risk. Nevertheless, also partially in jest, *The Wall Street Journal* has initiated a series of overlapping 6-month investment contests between well-known stock market analysts and randomly selected stocks. The *Journal* publishes the results of the contest every month. The nearby Finance in Action box reports on a recent edition of this contest.

SEE BOX P. 366

☑ CHECK POINT 12.2

Technical analysts, fundamental analysts, and professional portfolio managers all try to earn superior returns in the stock market. Explain how each group's efforts help keep the market efficient.

NO THEORY IS PERFECT

We have seen that there are three forms of the efficient-market theory:

1. Weak form (the random walk theory)	Market prices reflect all information contained in past market prices
2. Semi-strong form	Market prices reflect all *publicly available* information
3. Strong form	Market prices reflect all known information

Few simple economic ideas are as well supported by the evidence as the efficient-market theory. But it would be wrong to pretend that there are no puzzles or apparent exceptions. For instance, company managers have made superior profits consistently when

[3] An index fund is designed to replicate the investment performance of a particular stock market index. The portfolio is invested in each stock in proportion to the stock's weight in the index. Individual investors can index, too. See Example 10.2 in Chapter 10.

[4] The classic study of fund performance is M. C. Jensen, "The Performance of Mutual Funds in the Period 1945–64," *Journal of Finance* 23 (May 1968), pp. 389–416. Recent studies include M. J. Gruber, "Another Puzzle: The Growth in Actively Managed Mutual Funds," *Journal of Finance* 51 (July 1996), pp. 783–810, and B. G. Malkiel, "Returns from Investing in Equity Mutual Funds 1971 to 1991," *Journal of Finance* 50 (June 1995), pp. 549–572. The performance of the *Forbes* "Honor Roll" funds was analyzed in Burton Malkiel's paper.

FINANCE IN ACTION

Darts Rout Pros in Latest Stock Contest

Maybe flinging darts at the stock tables isn't such a bad idea.

Four little-known small-capitalization stocks picked by tossing darts trounced the selections of four investment professionals in the latest round of this column's stock-picking competition.

The idea behind the contest is to determine whether stock markets are truly efficient. If they were, then all available information would be immediately taken into account by stock prices, and investment professionals wouldn't be able to predict today, based on what they know, what will happen to tomorrow's stock prices.

In his book *A Random Walk Down Wall Street,* Burton Malkiel took the idea to its logical conclusion. He suggested that in order to save on hefty broker and management fees, investors should entrust their stock market portfolio to a blindfolded monkey tossing darts at the financial pages of a newspaper.

Since 1990 *The Wall Street Journal*'s reporters have been testing the theory every month by tossing darts for the imaginary monkey. The portfolio then competes over six months against four stocks picked more scientifically by four investment professionals. Returns are calculated at the end of the six months.

The darts posted an average investment loss of about 21% in the period from February 14 through July 31, compared with an average 17.3% loss for the four pros. The Dow Jones Industrial Average, meanwhile, fell 2.5%.

Still, it was only the first victory for the forces of chance in six outings, and the pros remain comfortably ahead of the darts and the Dow industrials when results of all 134 six-month contests are tallied. As is the custom of this column, the pros who finished first and second have been invited to return for another round.

Results of the most recent contest put the score at 83 to 51 in favor of the pros over the darts in the 134 contests since current rules were adopted in 1990. Pitted against the Dow industrials, the pros are ahead 70 to 64. Meanwhile, the pros have racked up an average six-month investment gain of 11.2%, compared with 4.5% for the darts and 7.3% for the industrial average.

Source: Modified by permission of *The Wall Street Journal Europe*, © 1996 Dow Jones & Company, Inc., and *The Wall Street Journal*, August 8, 2001, © 2001 Dow Jones & Company, Inc. All Rights Reserved Worldwide.

they deal in their own company's stock.[5] This does not fit well with the strong form of the efficient-market theory. It implies that managers know more about their companies' prospects than even professional portfolio managers do.

It is not so surprising that insiders make superior profits, but there are other phenomena that need further explanation. For example, look at Figure 12.4, which shows the outcome of a $1 investment in the stocks of either small or large firms at the end of 1925. By the end of 1998, the $1 invested in small-firm stocks had appreciated to $5,117 while the investment in large firms was worth only $2,351. This superior performance of small-firm stocks took place over a relatively short period. Until the late 1950s, small-firm and large-firm stocks were neck and neck. A wide gap then opened up between 1957 and 1984. The value of small-firm stocks multiplied nearly 69 times; large-firm stocks rose just over 11 times. Unfortunately, almost as soon as most investors became aware of this bonanza, it was time for the stocks of large firms to start to catch up.[6]

Now the superior performance of small-firm stocks could mean one of three things. First, it could be that investors demanded a higher return from small firms to compensate for their extra risk. The difference between the betas of small and large firms is not nearly large enough to explain the differences in returns, but maybe small firms have extra risk that is not captured in their betas. Second, the higher returns of small firms could simply be a coincidence, a finding that stems from the efforts of many researchers to find interesting patterns in the data. The third possibility is that we have an important exception to

[5] See H. N. Seyhun, "Insiders' Profits, Costs of Trading, and Market Efficiency," *Journal of Financial Economics* 16 (June 1986), pp. 189–212.

[6] The first study to rigorously document the small-firm effect was not published until 1981. See R. N. Banz, "The Relationship between Return and Market Value of Common Stocks," *Journal of Financial Economics* 9 (1981), pp. 3–18.

FIGURE 12.4
$1 invested in a portfolio of small firms in 1926 would have grown to $5,117 by 1998. A $1 investment in large-firm stocks would have grown to $2,351. (Note that values are plotted on a log scale.)

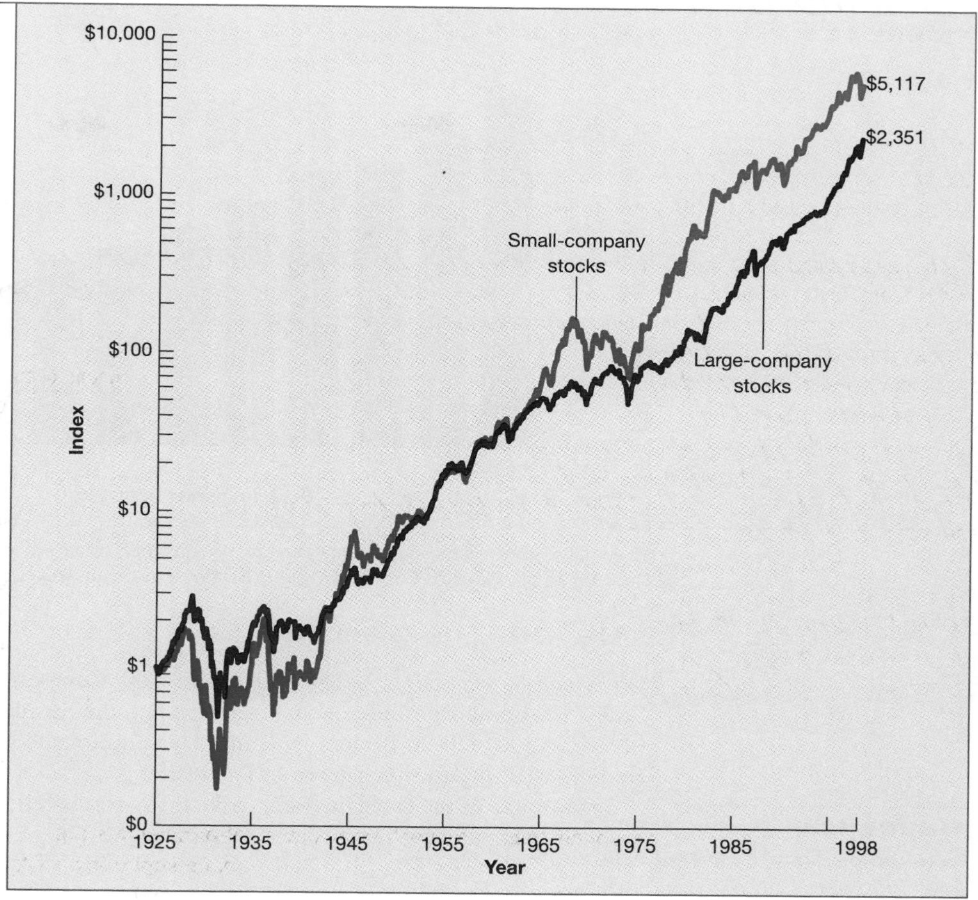

Source: Ibbotson Associates, Inc., *Stocks, Bonds, Bills and Inflation 1999 Yearbook,* Chicago: R. G. Ibbotson Associates, 1999.

the efficient-market theory, one that provided investors with the opportunity to predictably make superior profits over more than two decades.

The persistent performance of small-firm stocks is not the only puzzle. For example, stock returns also appear to have been related to the ratio of the book value of the equity shown in the firm's accounts to the market value of its shares. Figure 12.5 shows that between 1960 and 1990 the performance of those stocks with the highest book-to-market ratios outperformed those with the lowest ratios, by an average of about 11 percent a year. Unfortunately, no one can be sure whether this is one more example of an irrational and inefficient market or just another coincidence.

We believe that there is now widespread agreement that capital markets function well. So nowadays when economists come across instances where this apparently isn't true, they don't throw the efficient-market hypothesis onto the economic garbage heap. Instead they ask whether there is some missing ingredient that their theories ignore. Thus, despite the apparent superior performance of small-company stocks, few economists have, to our knowledge, been tempted to make a king-size investment in such stocks. Instead they have assumed that investors aren't stupid and have looked at whether small-firm stocks suffer from some other defect, such as a lack of easy marketability, which is not allowed for in our theories or tests.

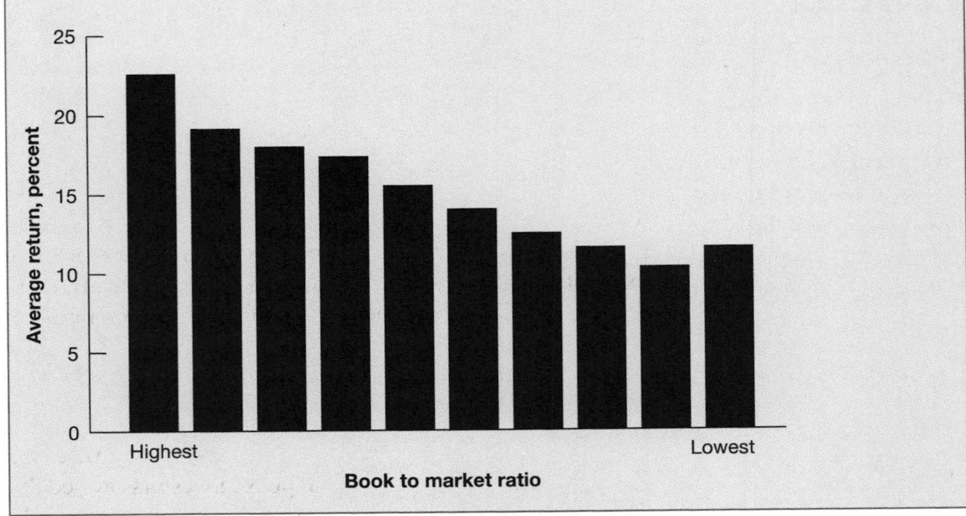

FIGURE 12.5
Between 1960 and 1990, stocks with high ratios of book value of equity to market value performed much better than stocks with low ratios of book to market.

Source: E. F. Fama and K. R. French, "The Cross Section of Expected Stock Returns," *Journal of Finance* 47 (June 1992), pp. 427–465. Copyright © 1991. Reprinted by permission of Blackwell Publishers.

THE CRASH OF 1987

On Monday, October 19, 1987, the TSE 300 Composite Index, predecessor to the S&P/TSX Composite Index, fell 11 percent and the Standard & Poor's Composite Index (the S&P 500) fell 20 percent in *1 day.* This crash came in the midst of 2 weeks of incredible volatility, as you can see in Figure 12.6.

In the wake of the crash, investors asked why prices fell so sharply. There was no obvious *new* information to justify such a sharp decline. The idea that market prices accurately

FIGURE 12.6
Daily rates of return on TSE 300 Index in 1987

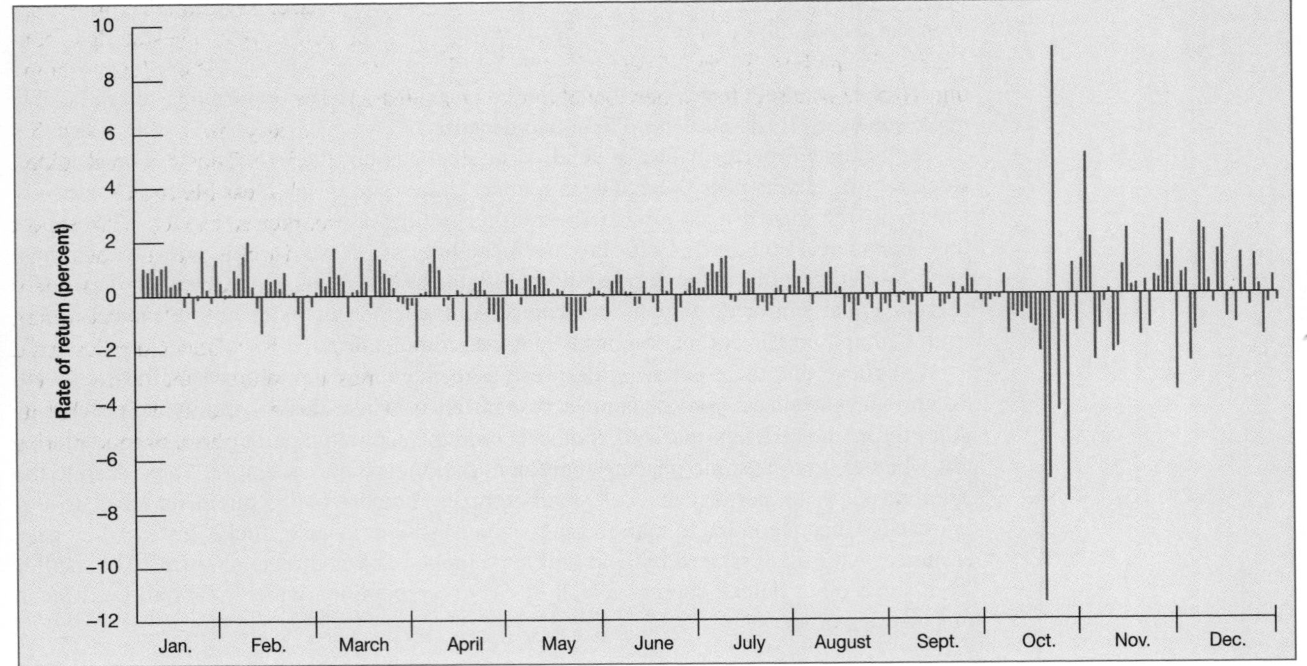

reflect all information available to investors, and thus are the best estimates of true values, seemed less compelling than before. It appears that prices were either irrationally high before Black Monday or irrationally low afterward. Could the theory of efficient markets be another casualty of the crash?

The crash reminds us of how exceptionally difficult it is to value common stocks from scratch. For example, suppose that in April 2002 you wanted to check whether common stocks were fairly valued. At least as a first stab, you might use the constant-growth formula that we introduced in Chapter 5. The annual dividend on the S&P/TSX Composite Index was about $123.[7] If this dividend was expected to grow at a steady rate of 8.42 percent a year and investors required an annual return of 10 percent a year from common stocks,[8] the constant-growth formula gives a value for the index of

$$\text{PV (index)} = \frac{\text{DIV}}{r - g} = \frac{123}{.1 - .0842} = 7784.8$$

which is close to the actual level of the index in April 2002. But how confident would you be about any of these figures? Suppose investors revised their assessment of the likely dividend growth rate to only 8.22 percent per year. This would produce a downward revision of 11 percent in your estimate of the correct level for the index, from 7782 to 6926:

$$\text{PV (index)} = \frac{\text{DIV}}{r - g} = \frac{123}{.1 - .0822} = 6926$$

In other words, an 11 percent price drop like the TSE 300's on Black Monday could have occurred in April 2002 if investors had suddenly become 0.2 percentage points less optimistic about future dividend growth.

The extreme difficulty of valuing common stocks from scratch has two important consequences. First, investors almost always price a common stock relative to yesterday's price or relative to today's price of comparable securities. In other words, they generally take yesterday's price as correct, and then adjust it upward or downward according to today's information. If information arrives smoothly, then as time passes investors become more and more confident that today's market level is correct. However, when investors lose confidence in the benchmark of yesterday's price, there may be a period of confused trading and volatile prices before a new benchmark is established.

Second, the idea that stock price *always* equals true value is nearly impossible to test, because it's so difficult to calculate value without referring to prices. Thus the crash didn't conclusively disprove the hypothesis, but many people now find it less plausible.

However, the crash does not undermine the evidence for market efficiency with respect to *relative* prices. Take Dow Chemical, for example, which sold for about $130 per share in September 2001. Could we *prove* that true value is $130? No, but we could be confident that Dow's price should be substantially greater than DuPont's (about $70 at the time), since the two companies were leaders in the same industry; however, Dow Chemical paid a higher dividend and had much higher forecast earnings per share. Moreover, if Dow Chemical announced unexpectedly higher earnings, we could be quite confident that its share price would respond instantly and without bias. In other words, the subsequent price would be set correctly relative to the prior price.

[7] The level of the index was about 7782 and its dividend yield was 1.58 percent. If you had invested 7782, spread out across all the stocks in the index, you would have received dividends of about $123 (= .0158 × $7782) per year.

[8] The Treasury bill rate was about 3 percent at the time. If we assume investors expected a 7 percent risk premium from investing in the stock market—the same as the historical average risk premium—then the total expected market return was 3 + 7 = 10 percent.

Most of the corporate finance lessons of the efficient-market hypothesis depend on these kinds of relative efficiencies. Let us now consider some of these lessons and at the same time briefly introduce some of the issues discussed in subsequent chapters.

CHECK POINT 12.3

Which of the following hypothetical "facts" would be violations of the efficient-market hypothesis? If inconsistent with market efficiency, which version of efficiency would be violated?

a. Stock returns tend to be more volatile in January than in other months.
b. Stocks that perform poorly in one week tend to outperform the rest of the market in the following week.
c. Roughly half of a group of professional portfolio managers "beat the market" in 1999.
d. Consistently superior returns are earned by buying a company's stock *the day after* an announcement of good news (for example, after an increase in earnings).

12.3 Lessons of Market Efficiency

MARKETS HAVE NO MEMORY

The weak form of the efficient-market theory states that the sequence of past price changes contains no information about future changes. Economists express the same idea more concisely when they say that "stock prices follow a random walk" or "the market has no memory." Sometimes financial managers seem to act as if this were not the case. For example, they are often reluctant to issue stock after a fall in price. They are inclined to wait for a rebound. Similarly, managers favour equity rather than debt financing after an abnormal price rise. The idea is to "catch the market while it's high." But we know that the market has no memory, and the cycles that financial managers seem to rely on do not exist.

Sometimes a financial manager will have inside information indicating that the firm's stock is overpriced or underpriced. Suppose, for example, that there is some good news that the market does not know, but managers do. The stock price will rise sharply when the news is revealed. Therefore, if the company sold shares at the current price, instead of waiting until the good news got out, it would be offering a bargain to new investors at the expense of present shareholders.

Naturally, managers are reluctant to sell new shares when they have favourable inside information. But such inside information has nothing to do with the history of the stock price. Your firm's stock could be selling now at half its price of a year ago, and yet, you could have special information suggesting that it is *still* grossly overvalued. Or it may still be undervalued at twice last year's price.

THERE ARE NO FINANCIAL ILLUSIONS

In an efficient market there are no financial illusions. Investors are unromantically concerned with the firm's cash flows and the portion of those cash flows to which they are entitled.

There are occasions, however, when managers seem to assume that investors suffer from financial illusions. For example, some firms devote enormous ingenuity to the task of manipulating earnings reported to shareholders. This is done by "creative accounting"—that is, by choosing accounting methods that stabilize and increase *reported* earnings without affecting the firm's cash flow. Presumably firms go to this trouble because management believes that shareholders take the earnings figures at face value. Some years ago, a leading accountant echoed this belief in the following complaint:

> Let us assume that you sincerely want to report the profits in the way you feel fairly presents the true results of your company's business. This is an admirable and objective motive; but when you do this, you find that your competitor shows a relatively more favorable profit result than you do. This creates a demand for the competitor's stock, while yours lags behind. You put your analyst to work, and you find that if your competitor followed the same accounting practices you do, your results would be better than his. You show this analysis to your complaining stockholders. Naturally, they ask, "If this is true, and if your competitor's accounting practices are generally accepted, too, why not change your accounting practices and thus improve your profits?" At that point you try to explain why your accounting is much more factual and reliable than your competitor's. Your stockholders listen, but nothing you can say will convince them that they should give up a 20 percent, 50 percent, or 100 percent possible increase in the market value just because you like certain accounting practices better than others.[9]

Was he right? Can the firm increase its market value by creative accounting? Researchers have tried to solve this question by looking at how the market reacts when companies change their accounting methods in order to boost their earnings. The results have suggested that investors are not easily fooled by such shenanigans and that the firm's shares are traded in an efficient, well-functioning market, where investors look to the face behind the mask.[10]

THERE ARE NO FREE LUNCHES ON WALL STREET OR BAY STREET

In an efficient market you can trust market prices. To put it another way, there are no free lunches on Wall Street or Bay Street. Here is an example:

Short-term interest rates are often different from long-term rates. For example, suppose that the interest rate on 1-year bonds is 4 percent, and the rate on 2-year bonds is 6 percent. Does this mean that investors should sell all their 1-year bonds and rush to take advantage of the high interest rates on the 2-year bonds? Could firms reduce the cost of their borrowing by issuing 1-year rather than 2-year bonds?

If you believe that markets are efficient, you should be suspicious of any simple rule that says one type of bond is cheap and another expensive. So what's the explanation? One possibility is that investors expect short-term interest rates to rise over the coming year. For example, suppose that the 1-year interest rate is expected to rise to 8 percent. Then investors who buy a 1-year bond now and reinvest the proceeds in another 1-year bond at the end of the year can expect to earn a total return over the 2 years of just over 12 percent—almost identical to the total return that you would get from buying the 2-year bond.[11] Conversely, companies could not expect to borrow any more cheaply by issuing two 1-year bonds in succession than by issuing a 2-year bond.

Thus when you see that short-term rates are different from long-term rates, there is probably a good reason for it—the market may be telling you that interest rates are expected to change.[12]

[9] L. Spacek, "Business Success Requires an Understanding of Unsolved Problems of Accounting and Financial Reporting," address to the financial accounting class, Graduate School of Business Administration, Harvard University, September 25, 1959.

[10] See, for example, R. S. Kaplan and R. Roll, "Investor Evaluation of Accounting Information: Some Empirical Evidence," *Journal of Business* 45 (April 1972), pp. 225–257, and R. W. Holthausen, "Evidence on the Effect of Bond Covenants and Management Compensation Contracts on the Choice of Accounting Technique: The Case of the Depreciation Switch-Back," *Journal of Accounting and Economics* 3 (1981), pp. 73–109.

[11] The total expected return on two 1-year bonds is $1.04 \times 1.08 - 1 = .1232$, or 12.32 percent. The total return on a 2-year bond is $1.06 \times 1.06 - 1 = .1236$, or 12.36 percent.

[12] Another explanation may be that the prices of long-term bonds fluctuate more than those of short-term bonds. A higher interest rate on long-term bonds is needed to compensate investors for this extra risk.

CHECK POINT 12.4

By 1999 average dividend yields on stocks had fallen to about 1.3 percent. Some investors in the stock market were upset at the meager immediate cash return on their money, and therefore, switched into high-dividend stocks. For example, they might sell a diversified mutual fund and buy stocks of electric and gas utilities, many of which offered dividend yields of over 4 percent. Such a shift could enhance the dividends received per dollar invested. But were these investors really better off? Would you expect their total returns (dividends plus capital gains) to increase?

12.4 Summary

1. How does competition among investors lead to efficient markets?

Competition between investors will tend to produce an **efficient capital market**—that is, a market in which prices rapidly reflect new information, and investors will have difficulty making consistently superior returns. We may indeed *hope* to beat the market, but in an efficient market all we can rationally *expect* is a return that is sufficient on average to compensate for the time value of money and for the risks we bear.

The efficient-market hypothesis comes in three different flavours. The **weak form** states that prices efficiently reflect all the information contained in the past series of stock prices. In this case it is impossible to earn superior returns simply by looking for patterns in stock prices; in other words, price changes are a random walk, and **technical analysis** will not help you to earn superior returns. The **semi-strong form** states that prices reflect all published information. This means it is impossible to make consistently superior returns just by reading the newspaper, looking at the company's annual accounts, and so on. This version of market efficiency implies that **fundamental analysis** will not help you to earn superior returns. The **strong form** states that stock prices effectively impound all available information. This form tells us that useful private information is hard to find, because in pursuing it you are in competition with thousands—perhaps millions—of active, intelligent, and greedy investors. The best you can do in this case is to assume that securities are fairly priced.

2. What evidence supports the hypothesis that security markets are efficient—and what evidence contradicts it?

The concept of an efficient market is astonishingly simple and remarkably well-supported by the facts. Among these facts are the rapid adjustment of security prices to public announcements of information about firms as well as the general inability of professionally managed portfolios to beat simple market indexes. Less than 30 years ago any suggestion that security investment is a fair game was generally regarded as bizarre. Today it is not only widely accepted in business schools, but it also permeates investment practice and government policy toward the security markets. On the other hand, there is some contradictory evidence. For example, small firms have tended to outperform large firms, even on a risk-adjusted basis. Similarly, firms with high ratios of book value to market value have outperformed other firms. These simple patterns would not be expected other than by chance in an efficient market.

3. What are some of the implications of market efficiency for a firm's financial decisions?

Sophisticated investors do not assume that superior returns come easy. Sophisticated financial managers do not assume that investors will willingly give them cheap financing. Both know that modern capital markets are highly competitive and efficient—and in particular, that prices of stocks, bonds, and other securities react quickly and accurately when new information arrives.

Although capital markets are not always 100 percent efficient, smart financial managers generally start by assuming efficient capital markets. Financial traps and mirages are most easily seen from that vantage point. Of course financial managers sometimes find opportunities in the wake of inefficiencies and imperfections. In that case they abandon the efficient-market vantage point and adapt financing strategy accordingly. But in general, because security prices are set fairly, it is easier to add value by smart investment decisions than by smart financing decisions.

An efficient market has no memory and offers no free lunches. Stock prices follow a random walk, in which the odds of a gain or loss tomorrow do not depend on past changes, so that managers cannot time security issues advantageously unless they have information the rest of the market does not. Moreover, because there are no financial illusions, managers cannot fool the market simply by manipulating accounting data.

Related Web Links

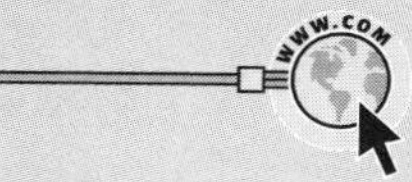

www.corporateinformation.com Information on corporations worldwide
www.wsrn.com Wall Street Research Net, offers information about many subjects and is also a gateway to other sites
www.stockinfo.standardpoor.com Extensive information about companies, industries, and markets
www.zacks.com Analysts' reports from Zacks Investment Research
www.vanguard.com Online educational brochures, including information on indexing in efficient markets, from the Vanguard Group

Key Terms

efficient capital markets	360	weak-form efficiency	363	semi-strong-form efficiency	364
random walk	361	fundamental analysts	363	strong-form efficiency	364
technical analysts	362				

Questions and Problems

*Answers in Appendix B

Basic

*1. **Forms of EMH.** Insert the missing words (below) from the following list: fundamental, semi-strong, strong, technical, weak.

There are three forms of the efficient-market hypothesis. Tests of randomness in stock prices provide evidence for the ______ form of the hypothesis. Tests of stock price reaction to well-publicized news provide evidence for the ______ form, and tests of the performance of professionally managed funds provide evidence for the ______ form. Market efficiency results from competition between investors. Many investors search for new information about the company's business that would help them to value the stock more accurately. This is known as ______ research. Such research helps to ensure that prices reflect all available information; in other words, it helps to keep the market efficient in the ______ form. Other investors study past stock prices for recurrent patterns that would allow them to make superior profits. This is known as ______ research. Such research helps to ensure that prices reflect all the information contained in past stock prices; in other words, it helps to keep the market efficient in the ______ form.

2. **Interpreting EMH.** True or false?

a. The efficient-market hypothesis asserts that investors have perfect forecasting ability.
b. The semi-strong form of the efficient-market hypothesis states that prices reflect all publicly available information.
c. In efficient markets the expected return on each stock is the same.
d. Fundamental analysis by security analysts and investors help keep markets efficient.
e. If the efficient-market hypothesis is correct, managers will not be able to increase stock prices by "creative accounting," which boosts reported earnings.

3. **Random Walks.** Here are actual rates of return for the Standard & Poor's 500 Index for a 60-month period. Figures are in percentages per month.

+2.0, +1.0, –.3, +4.0, +.6, +8.4, +6.2, –.3, +1.3, –2.8, +8.3, +1.5, –3.5, +4.1, +7.1, –.04, –5.9, +4.1, +5.3, –3.3, –4.4, +6.6, –.5, +3.7, –4.0, –2.6, +2.2, +3.9, +4.4, +.04, +1.3, –5.1, –6.0, –3.0, +2.3, –4.0, +4.5, –1.4, +3.3, +3.4, +2.1, +2.8, +4.5, +1.8, +5.0, +2.7, +2.8, +5.4, +.5, +.5, +.2, +4.0, +2.4, –.2, +3.6, –1.0, –4.4, +1.3, +1.9, +2.9

Now flip a coin 60 times and write down the returns that would be generated by the coin-toss game described at the start of Section 12.2. Calculate and plot the value of a $100 investment in the coin-toss game. Do the same calculation and plot for the actual market returns given above. See if your friends can tell which series is the real market.

*4. **Portfolio Management in Efficient Markets.** Even if markets are efficient, there still are important roles for professional money managers. What are some of these roles?

5. **Information and EMH.** "It's competition for information that makes securities markets efficient." Is this statement correct? Explain.

PRACTICE

6. **Forms of EMH.** Which of the following observations *appear* to violate market efficiency? Explain whether the inefficiency is weak, semi-strong, or strong.
   a. Managers make superior returns on their purchases of their company's stock.
   b. There is a positive relationship between the return on the market in one quarter and the change in aggregate corporate profits in the next quarter.
   c. Stocks of companies with unexpectedly high earnings appear to offer high returns for several months after the earnings announcement.
   d. Very risky stocks, on the average, give higher returns than safe stocks.
7. **Interpreting EMH.** How would you respond to the following comments?
   a. "Efficient market, my eye! I know of lots of investors who do crazy things."
   b. "Efficient market? Balderdash! I know at least a dozen people who have made a bundle in the stock market."
   c. "The trouble with the efficient-market theory is that it ignores investors' psychologies."
   d. "The business cycle is at least somewhat predictable, and stocks with positive betas respond to the state of the economy; therefore, stock prices must be predictable."

*8. **Real versus Financial Investments.** Why do investments in financial markets almost always have zero NPVs, whereas firms can find many investments in their product markets with positive NPVs?

9. **Indexing.** In an efficient market, it is hard to beat a simple indexing strategy. Does this mean that it is just as difficult to underperform that strategy, and therefore, is there any harm in trying? Explain why or why not.

10. **Investment Performance.** It seems that every month we read an article in the *Globe and Mail* or the *National Post* about a stockpicker with a marvelous track record. Do these examples mean that financial markets are really not efficient?

*11. **Implications of EMH.** The president of Good Fortunes, Inc. states at a press conference that the company has a 30-year history of ever-increasing dividend payments. Good Fortunes is widely regarded as one of the best-run firms in its industry. Does this make the stock of the firm a good buy? Explain.

12. **Trend Analysis.** The top graph in Figure 12.1 shows the actual performance of the Standard & Poor's 500 Index for a 5-year period. Two financial managers, Alpha and Beta, are contemplating this chart. Each manager's company needs to issue new shares of common stock sometime in the next year.

    Alpha: "My company's going to issue right away. The stock market cycle has obviously topped out, and the next move is almost surely down. Better to issue now and get a decent price for the shares."

    Beta: "You're too nervous—we're waiting. It's true that the market's been going nowhere for the past year or so, but the figure clearly shows a basic upward trend. The market's on the way up to a new plateau."

    What would you say to Alpha and Beta?

*13. **Implications of EMH.** "Long-term interest rates are at record highs. Most companies, therefore, find it cheaper to finance with common stock or relatively inexpensive short-term bank loans." Discuss.

*14. **Implications of EMH.** Suppose that a company *splits* its stock two-for-one, meaning that it doubles the number of shares outstanding. Each shareholder is given a new share for each one previously held, so that the number of shares held doubles. The split is not associated with any change in the firm's investment policy.
   a. Has the firm acquired any new assets as a result of the split?
   b. Has anything happened to the value of the firm's real assets (its projects)?
   c. What will happen to earnings per share?
   d. What should happen to the firm's stock price?
   e. What should happen to the dollar value of the shareholder's stock? Has investor wealth changed?

15. **Expectations and EMH.** Geothermal Corp. just announced good news: its earnings increased by 20 percent from last year's value. Most investors had anticipated an increase of 25 percent. Will Geothermal's stock price increase or decrease when the announcement is made?

CHALLENGE

*16. **Yield Curve and EMH.** If the yield curve is downward-sloping, meaning that long-term interest rates are lower than current short-term rates, what might investors believe about *future* short-term interest rates?

17. **Interpreting Price Changes.** In May 1987, Citicorp announced that it was bolstering its loan loss reserves by $3 billion in order to reflect its exposure to Third World borrowers. Consequently, second-quarter earnings were transformed from a $.5 billion profit to a $2.5 billion loss.

    In after-hours trading, the price of Citicorp stock fell sharply from its closing level of $50, but the next day when the market had had a chance to digest the news, the price recovered to $53. Other bank stocks fared less well and *The Wall Street Journal* reported that Citicorp's decision "triggered a big sell-off of international banking stocks that roiled stock markets around the world."

    Response to the Citicorp action varied. The bank's chairman claimed that "it significantly strengthens the institution," and analysts and bankers suggested that it was a notable step toward realism. For example, one argued that it was the recognition of the problem that made the difference, while another observed that the action "is merely recognizing what the stock market has been saying for several months: that the value of the sovereign debt of the big U.S. money centre banks is between 25 percent and 50 percent less than is carried in their books." The London *Financial Times* made the more cautionary comment that Citicorp had "simply rearranged its balance sheet, not strengthened its capital base," and the Lex column described the move as an "outsize piece of cosmetic self-indulgence rather than a great stride towards the reconstruction of Third World debt." A lead article in the same paper stated that "even if all this means that Citicorp shareholders are $3 billion poorer today, the group as a whole is better placed to absorb whatever shocks lie ahead."

    There was also considerable discussion of the implications for other banks. As one analyst summed up, "There's no question that the market will put higher confidence in those institutions that can reserve more fully."

    Discuss the general reaction to the Citicorp announcement. It is not often that a company announces a $2.5 billion loss in one quarter and its stock price rises. Do you think that the share price reaction was consistent with an efficient market?

INTERNET PROBLEMS

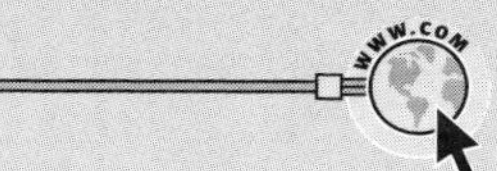

1. **Insider Trading.** Canadian corporate insiders are now required to post their trades on a new website, www.sedi.ca. Visit the website and look at the most recent report of insider trading. When did the insiders do their trading? Do you think this information might be valuable to you as an investor? Why?

2. **ETFs.** Many exchange-traded funds are now listed on the Toronto Stock Exchange. To see the list, go to www.globeinvestor.com, select "Filter," and pick "ETF." You will see all of the current ETFs. Pick four different ETFs and describe what index they are designed to mimic. Visit the websites of their sponsors and see if you can find out the fee investors pay for their ETF. Would you choose to invest in an ETF or an actively managed mutual fund? What role does market efficiency play in the choice of investing in ETFs versus actively managed mutual funds?

Solutions to Check Points

12.1 a. True.

b. False. There cannot be a long-run stock price. If there were, investors could make easy profits by investing in stocks when they are below the long-run price. This would be inconsistent with the notion that prices reflect all useful information about the firm.

c. True.

d. False. Note the *apparent* peaks and valleys in Figure 12.1.

12.2 Each looks for information about over- or undervalued securities. Technical analysts look for patterns in past prices, and fundamental analysts focus on published information. Portfolio managers may use both technical and fundamental information and also have in-house analysts who try to uncover hidden or superior information. When any of them find useful information, indicating, say, an undervalued stock, they buy aggressively, trying to beat other investors to the bargain. This trading moves the stock price up until the bargain disappears. Then the favourable information is fully incorporated in the stock price.

Of course the process works in reverse if unfavourable information is discovered. In either case, trading by informed investors moves the price until the information is fully reflected in it. This is the efficient-market outcome.

12.3 a. No violation. Even if volatility is predictable, this offers no way for investors to make excessive profits. It could simply be that more information is released in January. More news would generate higher volatility, but that does not imply that prices are incorrect.

b. Violation of weak-form efficiency. If stocks tended to reverse their performance from one week to the next, it would be easy for investors to make easy money; they would simply buy stocks of firms that performed poorly last week. The knowledge of a stock's price history would provide a route to easy profits.

c. No violation. This outcome is normal in a strong-form efficient market where portfolio managers cannot beat the market average. We expect roughly a half of these managers to get lucky in any particular year.

d. Violation of semi-strong efficiency. The good news ought to be fully incorporated in the stock price on the announcement day, leaving no superior profits for late buyers.

12.4 No and no. In an efficient market, investors are concerned with total return, including capital gains as well as dividends. Investors pursuing immediate dividend yield generally move into mature, low-growth companies and sacrifice the chance for substantial capital gains. Total return should depend on risk but not on the fraction of return received as dividends.

CHAPTER 13

An Overview of Corporate Financing

13.1 Common Stock

13.2 Preferred Stock

13.3 Corporate Debt

13.4 Convertible Securities

13.5 Patterns of Corporate Financing

13.6 Summary

13.7 Appendix 13A: The Bond Refunding Decision

This chapter begins our analysis of long-term financing decisions. In later chapters this will involve a careful look at some classic finance problems, such as how much firms should borrow and what dividends they should pay their shareholders. But before getting down to specifics, we will provide a brief overview of the types of long-term finance.

It is customary to classify sources of finance as debt or equity. When the firm borrows, it promises to repay the debt with interest. If it doesn't keep its promise, the debtholders may force the firm into bankruptcy. However, no such commitments are made to the equityholders. They are entitled to whatever is left over after the debtholders have been paid off. For this reason, equity is called a *residual claim* on the firm.

However, a simple division of sources of finance into debt and equity would miss the enormous *variety* of financing instruments that companies use today. For example, Table 13.1 shows the many securities issued by Canadian Pacific. Yet Canadian Pacific has not come close to exhausting the menu of possible securities.

This chapter introduces you to the principal families of securities and explains how they are used by corporations. We also draw attention to some of the interesting aspects of firms issuing these securities.

After studying this chapter you should be able to

- Describe the major classes of securities issued by firms to raise capital.
- Summarize recent trends in the use made by firms of different sources of finance.

TABLE 13.1
Large firms use many different kinds of securities. Look at the variety of securities issued by Canadian Pacific, Ltd.

Equity	Debt
Common stock	Debentures
Preferred stock	Medium-term notes
	Secured equipment loan
	Notes payable
	Equipment trust certificate
	Commercial paper
	Capital lease
	Bank loan

Source: Adapted from Canadian Pacific, Ltd., 2000 Annual Report at www.sedar.com.
Note: The website for the System for Electronic Document Analysis and Retrieval (SEDAR) provides a variety of information including annual reports and proxy forms for most publicly traded Canadian companies.

Common Stock

Most major corporations are far too large to be owned by one investor. For example, you would need to lay your hands on over $13 billion if you wanted to own all of Canadian Pacific, Ltd. (CP). (Since we wrote this chapter, CP has been broken up into separate companies. See nearby Finance in Action box.)

SEE BOX P. 388

CP is owned by about 34,000 different investors, each of whom holds a number of shares of common stock. These investors are therefore known as *shareholders* or *stockholders*. Altogether CP has outstanding 314 million shares of common stock. Thus if you were to buy one CP share, you would own 1/314,000,000, or about .00000003 percent of the company. Of course, a large pension fund, such as the Ontario Teachers' Pension Plan, might hold many thousands of CP shares.

issued shares Shares that have been issued by the company.

outstanding shares Shares that have been issued by the company and are held by investors.

authorized share capital Maximum number of shares that the company is permitted to issue as specified in the firm's articles of incorporation.

The 314 million shares held by investors at the end of 2000 represents the number of outstanding or **issued** and **outstanding shares** of CP. If CP wishes to raise more money, it can sell more shares. The maximum number of shares that can be issued is known as the **authorized share capital**, looking at Table 13.2, for CP, this is unlimited. However, many firms set a limit to their authorized share capital, which is specified in the firm's *articles of incorporation* and can be changed only with the permission of the shareholders. Votes on proposed changes to the articles of incorporation occur at shareholders' meetings.

par value Value of security shown on certificate.

additional paid-in capital Difference between issue price and par value of stock, also called capital surplus.

Table 13.2 shows how the investment by CP's stockholders is recorded in the company's books. The value of new shares issued by CP is shown in the common shares account. As of December 31, 2000, this is $1,695 million. In the past, a company issuing new shares would specify a monetary value, called **par value**, for such shares. The par value was an arbitrarily set number and almost always lower than the actual sale price of the new shares. The difference was recorded as **additional paid-in capital**, *paid-in surplus*, *capital surplus* or *contributed surplus*. The Canadian Business Corporations Act has since been changed to stop this practice, and today common shares mostly do not have a par value.[1] CP still retains a paid-in surplus account as a remnant of the old system.

retained earnings Earnings not paid out as dividends.

Besides buying new stock, shareholders also indirectly contribute new capital to the firm whenever profits that could be paid out as dividends are instead plowed back into the company. Table 13.2 shows that the cumulative amount of such **retained earnings** is about $7,274 million.

An amount of $138.6 million is shown in Table 13.2 for *foreign currency translation adjustments*, representing currency translation gains from CP's foreign operations. In this chapter we will ignore foreign exchange accounting.

[1] The practice of setting par value and using the additional paid-in capital account is still followed in the United States.

TABLE 13.2
Book value of common stockholders' equity of Canadian Pacific, Ltd., December 31, 2000 (Figures in millions)

Common shares	$1,695.0
Paid-in surplus	227.5
Retained earnings	7,274.4
Foreign currency translation adjustments	138.6
Net common equity	$9,335.5
Note:	
Authorized shares	unlimited
Issued shares	314

Source: Adapted from Canadian Pacific, Ltd., 2000 Annual Report at www.sedar.com.

The sum of common shares, paid-in surplus, retained earnings, and foreign currency translation adjustment gains is known as the *net common equity* of the firm. It equals the total amount contributed directly by shareholders when the firm issued new stock, and indirectly, when it plowed back part of its earnings.

During 2000, CP repurchased 12.9 million of its shares, which it had issued in the past.[2] In the United States, when a company repurchases some of its shares, it can continue to hold them as its own stock. These shares would appear in the balance sheet as treasury stock. In Canada treasury stock is not allowed. Instead, any shares repurchased must be cancelled. This is done by reducing the company's net equity account to the extent of the amount paid for any shares repurchased.[3] The common shares account is reduced by the average issue price. Any amount in excess of the average issue price is subtracted from retained earnings or, sometimes, from the paid-in surplus account. For example, suppose 1,000 shares are repurchased for $30 per share and the average issue price was $25 per share. To cancel the repurchased shares, the overall net equity account is reduced by $30 × $1,000 = $30,000. This is comprised of a reduction to the common shares account by $25 × $1,000 = $25,000 and a reduction to retained earnings by the remaining $5,000. The repurchase of the 12.9 million shares cost CP $438 million. It cancelled these shares by charging $69 million to its common shares account and about $369 million to its paid-in surplus account.

CHECK POINT 13.1

Generic Products has had one stock issue in which it sold 100,000 shares to the public at $15 per share. Can you fill in the following table?

Common shares	______
Retained earnings	______
Common equity	$3,000,000

BOOK VALUE VERSUS MARKET VALUE

We discussed the distinction between book and market value in Chapters 2 and 5, but it bears repeating.

Book value is a backward-looking measure. It tells us how much capital the firm has raised from shareholders in the past. It does not measure the value that investors place on those shares today. The market value of the firm is forward looking; it depends on the future dividends that shareholders expect to receive.

[2] We will look into why companies repurchase their shares in Chapter 16.

[3] For this reason, in Canada, the number of shares issued always equals the number outstanding.

CP's common equity has a book value of 9335.5 million. With 314 million shares outstanding, this translates to a book value of $9,335.5/314 = $29.73 per share. But in December 2000, CP shares were priced at about $42.75 each. So the total *market* value of the common stock was 314 million shares × $42.75 per share = $13.4 billion, nearly 45 percent more than the book value.

Market value is usually greater than book value. This is partly because inflation has driven the value of many assets above what they originally cost. Also, firms raise capital to invest in projects with present values that exceed initial cost. These positive-NPV projects made the shareholders better off. So we would expect the market value of the firm to be higher than the amount of money put up by the shareholders.

However, sometimes projects do go awry and companies fall on hard times. In this case, market value can fall below book value.

CHECK POINT 13.2

No-Name News can be established by investing $10 million in a printing press. The newspaper is expected to generate a cash flow of $2 million a year for 20 years. If the cost of capital is 10 percent, is the firm's market or book value greater? What if the cost of capital is 20 percent?

DIVIDENDS

Shareholders hope to receive a series of dividends on their investment. However, the company is not obliged to pay any dividends and the decision is up to the board of directors. In Chapter 16, we will discuss how that decision affects the value of the stock.

Because dividends are discretionary, they are not considered to be a business expense. Therefore, companies are not allowed to deduct dividend payments when they calculate their taxable income.

SHAREHOLDERS' RIGHTS

Ultimately, shareholders have control of the company's affairs. Occasionally companies need shareholder approval before they can take certain actions. For example, they need approval to increase the authorized capital or to merge with another company.

On most other matters, shareholder control boils down to the right to vote on appointments to the board of directors.

The board usually consists of the company's top management as well as *non-executive directors,* who are not employed by the firm. In principle, the board is elected as an agent of the shareholders. It appoints and oversees the management of the firm and meets to vote on such matters as new share issues. Most of the time the board will go along with the management, but in crisis situations it can be very independent. For example, when the management of RJR Nabisco, the giant American tobacco and food company, announced that it wanted to take over the company, the outside directors stepped in to make sure that the company was sold to the highest bidder. When serious accounting and managerial irregularities were found with Livent, the Toronto-based production company, which staged such hits as Phantom of the Opera, its board of directors fired the company's two co-founders and also filed a multimillion dollar civil suit against them.

VOTING PROCEDURES

majority voting Voting system in which each director is voted on separately.

cumulative voting Voting system in which all the votes one shareholder is allowed to cast can be cast for one candidate for the board of directors.

In most companies shareholders elect directors by a system of **majority voting.** In this case each director is voted on separately, and shareholders can cast one vote for each share they own. In some companies directors are elected by **cumulative voting.** The directors are then voted on jointly and the shareholders can, if they choose, cast all their votes for just one candidate. For example, suppose there are five directors to be elected and you own 100 shares. You therefore have a total of $5 \times 100 = 500$ votes. Under majority voting you can cast a maximum of 100 votes for any one candidate. With a cumulative voting system, you can cast all 500 votes for your favourite candidate. Cumulative voting makes it easier for a minority group of the shareholders to elect a director to represent their interests. That is why minority groups devote so much effort to campaigning for cumulative voting.

On many issues a simple majority of the votes cast is enough to carry the day, but there are some decisions that require a "supermajority" of between two-thirds and 80 percent of those eligible to vote. For example, a supermajority vote of two-thirds of the shareholders of record is usually needed to approve a merger. This requirement makes it difficult for the firm to be taken over and therefore helps to protect the incumbent management.

proxy contest Takeover attempt in which outsiders compete with management for shareholders' votes.

Shareholders can either vote in person or appoint a proxy to vote. The issues on which they are asked to vote are rarely contested, particularly in the case of large, publicly traded firms. Occasionally, however, there are **proxy contests** in which outsiders compete with the firm's existing management and directors for control of the corporation. But the odds are stacked against the outsiders because the insiders can get the firm to pay all the costs of presenting their case and obtaining votes.

In some special situations involving important corporate decisions such as mergers, or selling the firm's assets, the votes of most of the minority shareholders must be received. For example, the Ontario Securities Commission has introduced regulations that are intended to give the minority shareholders the opportunity to prevent majority shareholders and management from doing deals that reduce the value of the minority shareholders' shares. Sometimes powerful minority shareholders can successfully prevent takeover decisions made by the company's management or majority shareholders.

In 2000, a deal valued at \$5.7 billion was struck to sell the Montreal-based cable company Groupe Videotron Ltée to Rogers Communications, Inc., of Toronto. The powerful Caisse de dépôt et placement du Québec, Canada's biggest pension fund manager, which held a 10 percent minority voting stake in Videotron, opposed the deal because it wanted Videotron to remain in Québec. Caisse de dépôt broke ranks with the Chagnon family, which built Videotron into Québec's largest cable operator and held 71 percent of its votes. Instead, Caisse de dépôt engineered a competing bid with Montreal-based printing and publishing giant Quebecor, Inc., worth \$5.9 billion. Videotron was eventually acquired by Quebecor.

CLASSES OF STOCK

Many companies issue just one class of common stock. Sometimes, however, a firm may have two or more classes outstanding, which differ in their right to vote or receive dividends.[4] Suppose that a firm needs fresh capital but its present shareholders do not want to give up control of the firm. The existing shares could be labelled Class A, and then Class B shares could be issued to outside investors. The Class B shares could have limited voting rights, although they would probably sell for less as a result.

For instance, in May 2001, Bombardier had listed about 345 million Class A shares and

[4] In the United States, most companies issue one class of common stock and follow the practice of "one share, one vote."

over 1,022 million Class B shares on the Toronto Stock Exchange. The Class A shares carry 10 votes per share whereas the Class B shares carry only one vote per share. The Bombardier family controlled, through holding companies, over 81 percent of the Class A shares, or about 63 percent of the total voting rights of Bombardier.

Common shares without full voting rights are called *restricted shares*. There are various types of restricted shares. If the restricted shares have no votes, they are called *non-voting*. If the restricted shares have fewer votes per share than another class of common shares, they are called *subordinate voting*. You can also own *multiple voting* shares which carry multiple votes. As of October 2000, a total of 151 different classes of restricted shares were trading on the TSE. These included 57 classes of non-voting shares, 82 classes of subordinate voting shares, and one class of multiple voting shares. How do we figure out the type of class? If a share is denoted as Class B nv, *nv* stands for non-voting, if it is denoted as *sv*, it is subordinate voting, and *mv* stands for multiple voting. In addition to Bombardier, other large Canadian companies such as Power Corporation, Quebecor, Inc., and Magna International have also issued restricted voting shares. For instance, Power Corporation has issued subordinate voting shares, and Quebecor has Class A multiple voting shares as well as Class B subordinate voting shares.

Canadian securities regulators are also making it more difficult for a firm to convert an existing common share class into two share classes with different voting rights. In order to convert, most of the minority shareholders must approve. Also, the stock exchanges will not list a new class of non-voting or subordinate voting shares unless the shares have the right to participate in takeover bids. This right is called a *coattail provision*.

The following example illustrates how coattail provisions may be valuable.[5] In 1986 a group of independent dealers from Canadian Tire stores offered to purchase 49 percent of Canadian Tire common (voting) shares for $160.24 each, which were then trading at $40, while making no offer for the Class A non-voting stock, which traded at about $14.50. This offer, if accepted, would give them control of the firm since they already owned about 17 percent of the voting stock. However, the Class A non-voting stock had a coattail provision in place, which stated that in the event of a bid for all or substantially all of the voting common shares, the Class A shareholders would be entitled to tender their shares to the bidder as well. The Class A non-voting shareholders felt that a bid for 49 percent of the common stock meant "substantially all" of the voting shares, so the coattail provision should be triggered. Therefore, they took the view that they should also be allowed to sell their shares for $160.24 per share. The Ontario Securities Commission disallowed the transaction after holding a hearing. Their decision, in favour of the Class A non-voting shareholders, was later upheld by the court and the takeover bid was withdrawn.

CORPORATE GOVERNANCE IN CANADA AND ELSEWHERE

CP's shareholders own the company but they don't manage it. Management is delegated to a team of professional managers. Each shareholder owns only a small fraction of CP's shares and can exert little influence on the way the company is run. If shareholders do not like the policies the management team pursues, they can try to vote in another board of directors who will bring about a change in policy. But such attempts are rarely successful, and the shareholders' simplest solution is to sell the shares.

The separation between ownership and management in major Canadian corporations creates a potential conflict between shareholders (the principals who own the company)

[5] See also E. Maynes, C. Robinson, and A. White, "How Much Is a Share Vote Worth," *Canadian Investment Review* (Spring 1990), Volume III, pp. 49–55.

and managers (their agents who make the decisions). We noted in Chapter 2 several mechanisms that have evolved to mitigate this conflict:

- Shareholders elect a board of directors, which then appoints the managers, oversees them, and, on occasion, fires them.
- Managers' remuneration is tied to their performance.
- Poorly performing companies are taken over and the management is replaced by a new team.

These principles of corporate governance do not apply worldwide. Canada, the United States, Britain, Australia, and other English-speaking countries all have broadly similar systems, but other countries do not. In Japan industrial and financial companies are often linked together in a group called a *keiretsu.* For example, the Mitsubishi keiretsu contains 29 core companies, which includes two banks, two insurance companies, an automobile manufacturer, a steel producer, and a cement company. Members of the keiretsu are tied together in several ways. First, managers may sit on the boards of directors of other group companies, and a "president's council" of chief executives meets regularly. Second, each company in the group holds shares in many of the other companies. And third, companies generally borrow from the keiretsu's bank or from elsewhere within the group. These links may have several advantages. Companies can obtain funds from other members of the group without the need to reveal confidential information to the public, and if a member of the group runs into financial heavy weather, its problems can be worked out with other members of the group rather than in the bankruptcy court.

The more stable and concentrated shareholder base of large Japanese corporations may make it easier for them to resist pressures for short-term performance and allow them to focus on securing long-term advantages. But the Japanese system of corporate governance also has its disadvantages: The lack of market discipline can promote a life that's too cozy, and allow lagging or inefficient Japanese corporations to put off painful surgery.

Keiretsus are found only in Japan. Similar structures exist in other Asian countries; for instance, South Korea has large, powerful *chaebols.* Large companies in continental Europe are linked in some similar ways. For example, banks and other companies often own or control large blocks of shares and can push hard for changes in the management or strategy of poorly performing firms. (Banks in the United States are prohibited from large or permanent holdings of the stock of nonfinancial corporations.) Thus oversight and control are entrusted largely to banks and other corporations. Hostile takeovers of poorly performing companies are rare in Germany and virtually impossible in Japan.

preferred stock Stock that takes priority over common stock in regard to dividends.

net worth Book value of common shareholders' equity plus preferred stock.

For large corporations, separation of ownership and control is seen the world over. In Canada and the United States, control of large public companies is exercised through the board of directors and pressure from the stock market. In other countries the stock market is less important, and control shifts to major shareholders, typically banks and other companies.

13.2 Preferred Stock

Usually when investors talk about equity or stock, they are referring to common stock. But as of December 31, 2000, CP had also issued 8.8 million shares of 5.65 percent cumulative redeemable first preferred shares, Series A, for $220 million. The sum of CP's common equity and **preferred stock** is known as **net worth**. This amounts to $9,335.5 million + $220 million = $9,555.5 million.

For most companies preferred stock is much less important than common stock. However, it can be a useful method of financing in mergers and certain other special situations.

Like debt, most preferred stock promises a series of fixed payments to the investor and with relatively rare exceptions preferred dividends are paid in full and on time. For instance, CP promises a *fixed* annual dividend of $1.4125 on its preferred shares. This dollar amount can be obtained as the product of the fixed dividend rate of 5.65 percent and the value per share of $25. Nevertheless, preferred stock is legally an equity security. This is because payment of a preferred dividend is almost invariably within the discretion of the directors. The only obligation is that no dividends can be paid on the common stock until the preferred dividend has been paid.[6] If the company goes out of business, the preferred shareholders get in the queue after the debtholders but before the common shareholders.

Notice that CP's Series A preferred shares are *cumulative*. If the board of directors decides to skip a dividend payment on these shares, the unpaid dividend will be *in arrears*. In such a situation, the company may not pay dividends on common shares or redeem any preferred shares until all arrears are paid. If, on the other hand, a preferred share is *non-cumulative* then the investor is only entitled to payment of a dividend if the board of directors declares a dividend. Arrears do not accrue on non-cumulative preferred shares.

Like common stock, preferred stock usually does not have a final repayment However, a sizable number of issues tend to be *redeemable*. This means the company has the right to acquire the shares at a set amount known as the *call price*. CP's preferred shares are redeemable at $25 per share. Sometimes, preferred shares can also be *retractable*, in which case, the investor can force the company to buy back the share at a specified date.

Some preferred shares are *convertible*, which means that the shares can be converted into another class of shares—usually common shares—at a predetermined price (the exercise price) and for a certain period of time. For example, Bank of Montreal has issued Class B preferred shares, Series 3, which will be convertible into a specified number of common shares on or after August 25, 2004. To discourage investors from simply buying convertible preferred shares and immediately converting them, such shares usually trade at a premium. Investors like the convertibility option especially when the company's common stock has the potential for price appreciation, since investors will want to convert if the price of the common shares rise above the exercise price.

How do you tell whether a share is common or preferred? This is fairly easy to do because usually the stock symbols for preferred shares will have a special extension. For example, when preferred shares are listed on the TSE, the stock symbol ends in ".PR."

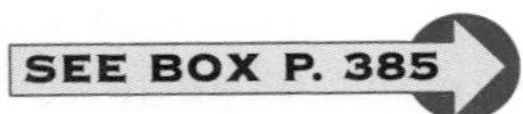
SEE BOX P. 385

Preferred stock rarely confers full voting privileges. This is an advantage to firms that want to raise new money without sharing control of the firm with the new shareholders. The nearby Finance in Action box suggests that many Canadian firms appear to issue preferred shares for this reason. However, if there is any matter that affects their place in the queue, preferred shareholders usually get to vote on it. Most issues also provide the holder with some voting power if the preferred dividend is skipped.

Companies cannot deduct preferred dividends when they calculate taxable income. However, dividend income is generally not taxed when received by Canadian corporations and is taxed at reduced rates when received by individuals who are eligible to a dividend tax credit.[7] Thus, in Canada, corporations tend to invest more in preferred shares than individual investors. Firms paying little or no tax could have a tax-based incentive to issue preferred shares rather than debt. For example, suppose XYZ Company pays no tax. The

[6] These days this obligation is usually cumulative. In other words, before the common shareholders get a cent, the firm must pay any preferred dividends that have been missed in the past.

[7] We discussed this issue in Chapter 2 and will also discuss it later in Chapter 16.

FINANCE IN ACTION

Is There Too Much Concentration of Power in Canadian Corporations?

Money managers and analysts are calling for an overhaul of investing laws to allow Canadians to invest more of their money in foreign firms in hopes of forcing uncompetitive and unaccountable domestic companies to respect the rights of minority shareholders.

As the Canadian market slowly loses its best companies to foreign takeovers, investors are being forced to choose from a slew of other stocks that are either controlled by family voting trusts, mired in various unrelated businesses, or drowning in red ink, analysts say.

Because Canadian investors can only invest up to 30 percent of their RRSP portfolio in foreign stocks and bonds, institutional investors must put 70 percent of their assets in Canadian securities if they want to sell to the retirement savings market. Despite this, Canada represents only about 2 percent of the world economy.

The laws were designed to protect Canadian industries and jobs from foreign competition and ensure most of Canada's wealth was kept within the country.

But investors and analysts say the rules have backfired, fostering an environment in which a small corporate elite can keep voting control of their companies while silencing common shareholders who have little choice but to invest in Canada.

Too many Canadian firms, such as Bombardier, Inc., Alliance Atlantis Communications, Inc., Chum, Ltd., and Shaw Communications, Inc., use preferred shares to let insiders control the majority of votes, although they may own just a fraction of the company's equity.

The restrictions are particularly onerous given the fact that such arrangements are almost unheard of in the United States.

What's more worrying is the fact that insider control and preferred voting structures are becoming more common, said Bill Mackenzie, president of Fairvest Proxy Monitor, which provides corporate governance advice to institutional shareholders.

In 1997, 23 percent of companies listed in the TSE 300 had a single shareholder holding more than half the voting shares. This year, that number rose to 30 percent, said Mr. Mackenzie.

Similarly in 1997, 17.7 percent of the companies in the index had preferred shares giving insiders with minority-equity stakes voting control. This year, that number jumped to 22.7 percent.

The laws ultimately hurt more than just big institutional investors, Mr. Mackenzie said. He argues that the concentration of power in Canada's corporate elite affects the entire Canadian market and every person with money invested in it.

Source: Excerpted from S. Maich, "Investing Rules Attacked: Pressure to Overhaul Foreign Content Laws," *The Financial Post* (August 16, 2001), pp. C1, C8.

company wishes to obtain financing from a bank which has offered it a loan at an 8 percent annual interest rate. If the bank's marginal tax rate is 35 percent, then after paying tax on the interest, the bank will receive a net return of $(1 - .35) \times 8\% = 5.2\%$. The bank can earn the same return by buying XYZ's preferred shares with a dividend yield of 5.2 percent, since the bank pays no tax on the preferred share dividends. Now consider XYZ's point of view. The company cannot use the interest deduction from the bank loan to reduce its tax since it pays no tax, so its before- and after-tax costs of the bank loan are 8 percent. On the other hand, if it sells preferred shares with a 5.2 percent dividend yield, it has reduced its cost of funds from 8 percent to 5.2 percent. It is much cheaper for XYZ to raise the needed money by selling preferred shares than by borrowing. The Government of Canada has made it more difficult for banks to buy preferred stock from other corporations. For instance, in 1987, the federal government introduced measures to reduce the tax loophole by requiring issuers of preferred shares to pay a 40 percent tax on preferred dividends.[8] The tax is refunded if the issuer is taxable.

Individual U.S. investors do not have the dividend tax credit of Canadian investors and must pay the full personal tax on dividend income. U.S. corporations enjoy some tax relief

[8] See I. Fooladi, P. A. McGraw, and G. S. Roberts, "Preferred Share Rule Freezes Out the Individual Investor," *CA Magazine* (April 11, 1988), pp. 38–41.

on dividend income. If one corporation buys another's stock, only 30 percent of the dividends it receives are taxed. This rule applies to both common and preferred stock but is most important for preferred for which returns are dominated by dividends rather than capital gains. Also, regulated American public utilities, which can take tax payments into account when negotiating the rates they charge to customers, can effectively pass the tax disadvantage of preferred stock on to the consumer. As a result, a large fraction of the dollar value of American offerings of nonconvertible preferred stock consists of issues by utilities. Overall, preferred share financing is used less in the United States than in Canada, due to lower tax incentives.

If you invest your firm's spare cash in a preferred stock, you will want to make sure that when it is time to sell the stock, it won't have plummeted in value. One problem with garden variety preferred stock that pays a fixed dividend is that the preferreds' market prices go up and down as interest rates change (because present values fall when rates rise). So one ingenious banker had an idea: Why not link the dividend on the preferred stock to interest rates so that it goes up when interest rates rise, and vice versa? The result is known as **floating-rate preferred.** If you own floating-rate preferred, the dividend rate could be tied to the prime rate of interest. You know that any change in interest rates will be counterbalanced by a change in the dividend payment, so the value of your investment is protected. For instance, Alcan Aluminum's preferred shares, Series C and E, carry floating dividend rates.

floating-rate preferred Preferred stock paying dividends that vary with short-term interest rates.

☑ CHECK POINT 13.3

A company in a 35 percent tax bracket can buy a bond yielding at 10 percent or a preferred stock of the same firm that is priced to yield 8 percent. Which will provide the higher after-tax yield? What if the purchaser is a private individual in a 35 percent tax bracket?

13.3 Corporate Debt

When companies borrow money, they promise to make regular interest payments and to repay the principal (that is, the original amount borrowed).

> **However, corporations have limited liability. By this we mean that the promise to repay the debt is not always kept. If the company gets into deep water, the company has the right to default on the debt and to hand over the company's assets to the lenders.**

Clearly the company will choose bankruptcy only if the value of the assets is less than the amount of the debt. In practice, when companies go bankrupt, this handover of assets is far from straightforward. For example, when Eaton's, the venerated department store, went into bankruptcy, there were a large number of creditors all jostling for a place in the queue. Some fashion companies reportedly sent their employees to the store locations to seize their merchandise. Sorting out these problems is left to the bankruptcy court.

Because lenders are not regarded as owners of the firm, they don't normally have any voting power. Also, the company's payments of interest are regarded as a cost and are therefore deducted from taxable income. Thus interest is paid out of *before-tax* income, whereas dividends on common and preferred stock are paid out of *after-tax* income. This means that the government provides a tax subsidy on the use of debt, which it does not provide on stock.

DEBT COMES IN MANY FORMS

An orderly scheme of classification is essential to cope with the almost endless variety of debt issues. We will walk you through the major distinguishing characteristics.

Interest Rate. The interest payment, or *coupon,* on most long-term loans is fixed at the time of issue. If a $1,000 bond is issued with a coupon of 10 percent, the firm continues to pay $100 a year regardless of how interest rates change. As we pointed out in chapters 3 and 4, you sometimes encounter zero-coupon bonds. In this case the firm does not make a regular interest payment. It just makes a single payment at maturity. Obviously, investors pay less for zero-coupon bonds.

prime rate Benchmark interest rate charged by banks.

Most loans from a bank and some long-term loans carry a *floating interest rate.* For example, your firm may be offered a loan at "1 percent over prime." The **prime rate** is the benchmark interest rate charged by banks to large customers with good to excellent credit. (But the largest and most creditworthy corporations can, and do, borrow at *less* than prime.) The prime rate is adjusted up and down with the general level of interest rates. When the prime rate changes, the interest on your floating-rate loan also changes.

Floating-rate loans are not always tied to the prime rate. Often they are tied to the rate at which international banks lend to one another. This is known as the *London Interbank Offered Rate,* or *LIBOR.*

CHECK POINT 13.4

Would you expect the price of a 10-year floating-rate bond to be more or less sensitive to changes in interest rates than the price of a 10-year maturity fixed-rate bond?

---

long-term debt Debt with more than 1 year remaining to maturity.

Maturity. **Long-term debt** is any debt repayable more than 1 year from the date of issue. Debt due in less than a year is termed *short-term* and is carried on the balance sheet as a current liability. Short-term debt is often described as unfunded debt, and long-term debt is described as funded, although it is clearly artificial to call a 364-day debt short-term and a 366-day debt long-term (except in leap years).

SEE BOX P. 388

There are corporate bonds of nearly every conceivable maturity. For example, Walt Disney Co. has issued bonds with a 100-year maturity. CP has issued perpetual debentures—that is, bonds which may survive forever (see the nearby Finance in Action box). At the other extreme we find firms borrowing literally overnight.

sinking fund Fund established to retire debt before maturity.

callable bond Bond that may be repurchased by firm before maturity at specified call price.

refunding When an old bond issue is replaced with a new one by the firm. Often, this is done when interest rates decline, and the firm can save on the interest cost of the new issue.

Repayment Provisions. Long-term loans are commonly repaid in a steady regular way, perhaps after an initial grace period. For bonds that are publicly traded, this is done by means of a **sinking fund.** Each year the firm puts aside a sum of cash into a sinking fund that is then used to buy back the bonds. When there is a sinking fund, investors are prepared to lend at a lower rate of interest. They know that they are more likely to be repaid if the company sets aside some cash each year than if the entire loan has to be repaid on a specific day.

Firms issuing debt to the public sometimes reserve the right to *call* the debt—that is, issuers of **callable bonds** may buy back the bonds before the final maturity date. The price at which the firm can call the bonds is set at the time that the bonds are issued. Call provisions usually come into effect after several years have elapsed since the bond issue. For instance, a bond issue may stipulate that it remain *call protected* during its first 5 years, in which case, the company may not issue a call during this time frame.

This option to call the bond is attractive to the issuer. If interest rates decline and bond prices rise, the issuer may repay the bonds at the specified call price and borrow the money back at a lower rate of interest. This would be a bond **refunding** decision by the company

FINANCE IN ACTION

CP Debenture Investors Want Vote

Investors holding Canadian Pacific, Ltd.'s historic consolidated debenture stock are asking for a right to vote on the company's breakup this fall, which is expected to create five separate companies.

Their application will be heard in court on July 9.

Calgary-based CP has scheduled a special shareholders' meeting for late September to approve the breakup, but it argues that investors holding the consolidated debenture stock shouldn't get a say.

The obscure bonds, which were issued late in the 19th century and early 20th century, are supposed to pay 4 percent interest in perpetuity in gold coin. But using gold coin to pay interest was outlawed in the 1930s in Canada and the United States, so holders are paid in cash.

Holders of the special stock were unsuccessful in a bid to overturn CP's previous restructuring in the 1990s. In that case, they argued that the debenture stock originally had first charge on all CP assets. But as a result of the earlier restructuring, the securities were backed only by the company's railway assets.

In February, CP ended years of speculation by announcing that it would break into separately traded companies in order to boost the overall value of those units.

When the transaction occurs, investors will be handed shares in five companies: Pan Canadian Petroleum, Ltd., Canadian Pacific Railway Co., Canadian Pacific Hotels & Resorts, Inc., Fording, Inc., and CP Ships Holdings, Inc.

As part of the plan, CP's preferred shareholders will be able to either tender their shares for $26 each or receive shares in a special fund scheduled for redemption in 2004.

Source: Excerpted from K. McArthur, "CP Debenture Investors Want Vote," the *Globe and Mail* (July 4, 2001), p. B3.

and would be made by looking at present values of the costs associated with calling the existing bond and the benefits associated with lower coupon payments on the new bond. The analysis would be conducted using a net present value framework. We will discuss the bond refunding decision later in Appendix 13A.

The call provision comes at the expense of bondholders because it limits investors' capital gain potential. If interest rates fall and bond prices rise, holders of callable bonds may find their bonds bought back by the firm for the call price.

CHECK POINT 13.5

Suppose CP is considering two issues of 20-year maturity coupon bonds; one issue will be callable, the other not. For a given coupon rate, will the callable or noncallable bond sell at the higher price? If both the bonds are to be sold to the public at par value, which bond must have the higher coupon rate?

subordinated debt Debt that may be repaid in bankruptcy only after senior debt is paid.

Seniority. Some debts are **subordinated.** In the event of default the subordinated lender gets in line behind the firm's general creditors. The subordinated lender holds a junior claim and is paid only after all senior creditors are satisfied.

When you lend money to a firm, you can assume that you hold a senior claim unless the debt agreement says otherwise. However, this does not always put you at the front of the line because the firm may have set aside some of its assets specifically for the protection of other lenders. This brings us to our next classification.

Security. When you borrow to buy your home, the bank or trust company will take out a mortgage on the house. The mortgage acts as security for the loan. If you default on the loan payments, the bank can seize your home.

secured debt Debt that has first claim on specified collateral in the event of default.

When companies borrow, they also may set aside certain assets as security for the loan. These assets are termed *collateral* and the debt is said to be **secured.** In the event of default, the secured lender has first claim on the collateral; unsecured lenders have a general claim on the rest of the firm's assets but only a junior claim on the collateral.

Default Risk. Seniority and security do not guarantee payment. A debt can be senior and secured but still as risky as a dizzy tightrope walker—it depends on the value and the risk of the firm's assets. In Chapter 4 we showed how the safety of most corporate bonds can be judged from bond ratings provided by Dominion Bond Rating Service, Moody's and Standard & Poor's. Bonds that are rated AAA or triple-A seldom default. At the other extreme, many speculative-grade bonds (or junk bonds) may be teetering on the brink.

As you would expect, investors demand a high return from low-rated bonds. We saw evidence of this in Chapter 4, where Figure 4.9 showed yields on default-free U.S. Treasury bonds as well as on corporate bonds in various rating classes. The lower rated bonds did, in fact, offer higher promised yields to maturity.

Country and Currency. These days capital markets know few national boundaries and many large firms, in particular, those with sizable foreign operations, borrow abroad. For example, a Canadian company may choose to finance a new plant in Switzerland by borrowing Swiss francs from a Swiss bank, or it may expand its Dutch operation by issuing a bond in Holland.

In addition to these national capital markets, there is also an international capital market centered mainly in London. There are about 500 banks in London from over 70 different countries, which include such giants as Citicorp, Union Bank of Switzerland, Deutsche Bank, Bank of Tokyo–Mitsubishi, Banque Nationale de Paris, and Barclays Bank. One reason they are there is to collect deposits in the major currencies. For example, suppose an Arab sheikh has just received payment in dollars for a large sale of oil to the United States. Rather than depositing the cheque in the United States, he may choose to open a U.S. dollar account with a bank in London. Dollars held in a bank outside the United States came to be known as **eurodollars.** Similarly, yen held outside Japan were termed *euroyen*, and so on). When the new European currency was named the euro, the term *eurodollars* became confusing. Doubtlessly, in time, bankers will dream up a new name for dollars held outside the United States; until they do, we'll just call them *international dollars.*

eurodollars Dollars held on deposit in a bank outside the United States.

The London bank branch that is holding the sheikh's U.S. dollar deposit may temporarily lend those dollars to a company in the same way that a bank in the United States may relend U.S. dollars that have been deposited with it. Thus a company can either borrow U.S. dollars from a bank in the United States or borrow U.S. dollars from a bank in London.[9]

If a firm wants to make an issue of long-term bonds, it can choose to do so in Canada. Alternatively, it can sell the bonds to investors in several countries. These bonds have traditionally been known as **eurobonds,** but *international bonds* may be a less misleading term. Although these bonds are sold to investors in different countries, they are typically denominated in the currency of the issuer. For example, a Canadian company could issue bonds denominated in Canadian dollars to investors in other countries. The payments on these bonds may be fixed in dollars, euros, or any other major currency. Companies usually sell these bonds to the London branches of the major international banks, which then resell them to investors throughout the world.

eurobond Bond that is denominated in the currency of one country but issued to investors in other countries.

Sometimes companies may issue **foreign bonds**, which are issued in another country and denominated in the currency of that country. For instance, Air Canada has long-term debt issues in several different currencies including the U.S. dollar, Swiss franc, and the deutsche mark.

foreign bond Bond issued in the currency of its country but the borrower is from another country.

[9] Because the Federal Reserve requires banks in the United States to keep interest-free reserves, there is a tax on U.S. dollar deposits in the United States. U.S. dollar deposits made overseas are free of this tax, and therefore, banks can afford to charge the borrower slightly lower interest rates.

private placement Sale of securities to a limited number of investors without a public offering.

Public versus Private Placements. Publicly issued bonds are sold to anyone who wishes to buy, and once they have been issued, they can be freely traded in the securities markets. In a **private placement,** the issue is sold directly to a small number of banks, insurance companies, or other investment institutions. Privately placed bonds generally cannot be resold to individuals in Canada but only to other qualified institutional investors. However, there is increasingly active trading among these investors.

There is more information about the difference between public issues and private placements in the next chapter.

protective covenant Restriction on a firm to protect bondholders.

Protective Covenants. When investors lend to a company, they know that they might not get their money back. But they expect that the company will use their money well and not take unreasonable risks. To help ensure this, lenders usually impose a number of conditions, or **protective covenants,** on companies that borrow from them. An honest firm is willing to accept these conditions because it knows that they enable the firm to borrow at a reasonable rate of interest.

Companies that borrow in moderation are less likely to get into difficulties than those that are up to the gunwales in debt. So lenders usually restrict the amount of extra debt that the firm can issue. Lenders are also eager to prevent others from pushing ahead of them in the queue if trouble occurs, so they will not allow the company to create new debt that is senior to them or to put aside assets for other lenders.

Another possible hazard for lenders is that the company will pay a bumper dividend to the shareholders, leaving no cash for the debtholders. Therefore, lenders sometimes limit the size of the dividends that can be paid.

SEE BOX P. 391

The story of Marriott in the nearby Finance in Action box shows what can happen when bondholders are not sufficiently careful about the conditions they impose. In the wake of the large losses suffered by Marriott bondholders, several observers predicted that investors would demand more restrictive bond covenants in future transactions.

CHECK POINT 13.6

In 1988, RJR Nabisco, the food and tobacco giant, had $5 billion (US) of A-rated debt outstanding. In that year the company was taken over, and $19 billion (US) of debt was issued and used to buy back equity. The debt ratio skyrocketed, and the debt was downgraded to a BB rating. The holders of the previously issued debt were furious, and one filed a lawsuit claiming that RJR had violated an implicit obligation not to undertake major financing changes at the expense of existing bondholders. Why did these bondholders believe they had been harmed by the massive issue of new debt? What type of explicit restriction would you have wanted if you had been one of the original bondholders?

A Debt by Any Other Name. The word *debt* sounds straightforward, but companies enter into a number of financial arrangements that look suspiciously like debt yet are treated differently in the accounts. Some of these obligations are easily identifiable. For example, accounts payable are simply obligations to pay for goods that have already been delivered and are therefore like short-term debt.

lease Long-term rental agreement.

Other arrangements are not so easy to spot. For example, instead of borrowing money to buy equipment, many companies **lease** or rent it on a long-term basis. In this case the firm promises to make a series of payments to the lessor (the owner of the equipment). This is just like the obligation to make payments on an outstanding loan. What if the firm can't make the payments? The lessor can then take back the equipment, which is precisely what would happen if the firm had *borrowed* money from the lessor, using the equipment as collateral for the loan. We will discuss the analysis of leasing in detail in Chapter 22.

FINANCE IN ACTION

Marriott Plan Enrages Holders of Its Bonds

Marriott Corp. has infuriated bond investors with a restructuring plan that may be a new way for companies to pull the rug out from under bondholders.

Prices of Marriott's existing bonds have plunged as much as 30 percent in the past two days in the wake of the hotel and food-services company's announcement that it plans to separate into two companies, one burdened with virtually all of Marriott's debt.

On Monday, Marriott said that it will divide its operations into two separate businesses. One, Marriott International, Inc., is a healthy company that will manage Marriott's vast hotel chain; it will get most of the old company's revenue, a larger share of the cash flow and will be nearly debt-free.

The second business, called Host Marriott Corp., is a debt-laden company that will own Marriott hotels along with other real estate and retain essentially all of the old Marriott's $3 billion of debt.

The announcement stunned and infuriated bondholders, who watched nervously as the value of their Marriott bonds tumbled and as Moody's Investors Service, Inc., downgraded the bond to the junk-bond category from investment grade.

Price Plunge

In trading, Marriott's 10 percent bonds that mature in 2012, which Marriott sold to investors just six months ago, were quoted yesterday at about $.80 on the dollar, down from $1.10 Friday. The price decline translates into a stunning loss of $300 for a bond with a $1,000 face amount.

Marriott officials concede that the company's spinoff plan penalizes bondholders. However, the company notes that, like all public corporations, its fiduciary duty is to stockholders not bondholders. Indeed, Marriott's stock jumped 12 percent Monday. (It fell a bit yesterday.)

Bond investors and analysts worry that if the Marriott spinoff goes through, other companies will soon follow suit by separating debt-laden units from the rest of the company. "Any company that fears it has underperforming divisions that are dragging down its stock price is a possible candidate" for such a restructuring, says Dorothy K. Lee, an assistant vice president at Moody's.

If the trend heats up, investors said, the Marriott restructuring could be the worst news for corporate bondholders since RJR Nabisco, Inc.'s managers shocked investors in 1987 by announcing they were taking the company private in a record $25 billion leveraged buy-out. The move, which loaded RJR with debt and tanked the value of RJR bonds, triggered a deep slump in prices of many investment-grade corporate bonds as investors backed away from the market.

Strong Covenants May Re-Emerge

Some analysts say the move by Marriott may trigger the re-emergence of strong covenants, or written protections, in future corporate bond issues to protect bondholders against such restructurings as the one being engineered by Marriott. In the wake of the RJR buy-out, many investors demanded stronger covenants in new corporate bond issues.

Some investors blame themselves for not demanding stronger covenants. "It's our own fault," said Robert Hickey, a bond fund manager at Van Kampen Merritt. In their rush to buy bonds in an effort to lock in yields, many investors have allowed companies to sell bonds with covenants that have been "slim to none," Mr. Hickey said.

Source: Reprinted by permission of *The Wall Street Journal* © 1992 Dow Jones & Company, Inc. All Rights Reserved Worldwide.

▸ EXAMPLE 13.1 *The Terms of Alcan's Bond Issue*

Now that you are familiar with some of the jargon, you might like to look at an example of a bond issue. Table 13.3 is a summary of the terms of a bond issue by Alcan. We have added some explanatory notes.

INNOVATION IN THE DEBT MARKET

We have discussed domestic bonds and eurobonds, fixed-rate and floating-rate loans, secured and unsecured loans, senior and junior loans, and much more. You might think that this gives you all the options you need. Yet almost every day, companies and their advisers dream up a new type of debt. Here are some examples of unusual bonds.

TABLE 13.3
Alcan's bond issue

Comments	Description of bond
1. A debenture is an unsecured bond.	**Alcan Aluminum, Ltd., 6.450% debentures, due 2011**
2. Coupon is 6.450 percent. Thus each bond makes an annual interest payment of .0645 × $1,000= $64.50	
3. Moody's bond rating is A2 and Standard and Poor's is A–.	**Rating: A2 and A–**
4. Alcan has issued and has outstanding $400 million (US) of the bonds.	Outstanding: $400,000,000 (US).
5. The bond was issued in March 2001 and is to be repaid in March 2011.	Dated: March 23, 2001. Due: March 15, 2011.
6. Interest is payable at six-month intervals on March and September 15.	Interest: March and September 15.
7. The bonds can be held in multiples of $1,000.	Denomination: $1,000 (US) and integral multiples thereof.
8. Unlike some bond issues, this issue does not give the company an option to call (i.e., repurchase) the bonds before maturity at specific prices. Thus the bond is not redeemable prior to maturity.	Early redemption: The debentures are not redeemable prior to maturity.
9. The bonds are not secured, that is, no assets have been set aside to protect the bondholders in the event of default.	Security: not secured.
10. The bonds were sold at a price of 99.748 percent of face value. The company will have to deduct the payment to the underwriters before it receives any money from the bond issue.	Offered: $400,000,000 (US) debenture offerings are priced at 99.748% of their principal amount to yield 6.485%. Morgan Stanley & Co. Inc., Credit Suisse First Boston Corporation, RBC Dominion Securities Corporation, Salomon Smith Barney, Inc., Scotia Capital (U.S.A.), Inc., CIBC World Markets Corp., and Toronto Dominion Securities (U.S.A.) are co-underwriters of the offerings, which are to be made by prospectus only.
11. A trustee is appointed to look after the bondholder's interest.	
12. The bonds are registered. The registrar keeps a record of who owns the bonds.	

Source: www.bondsonline.com; *Financial Post* Historical Reports at www.fpdata.finpost.com; www.alcan.com.

Indexed Bonds. We saw in Chapter 4 how the Canadian government has issued bonds whose payments rise in line with inflation. Occasionally borrowers have linked the payments on their bonds to the price of a particular commodity. For example, Mexico, which is a large oil producer, has issued billions of dollars worth of bonds that provide an extra payoff if oil prices rise. Mexico reasons that oil-linked bonds reduce its risk. If the price of oil is high, it can afford the higher payments on the bond. If oil prices are low, its interest payments will also be lower. The Swiss insurance company Winterthur has also issued an unusual bond with varying interest payments. The payments on the bonds are reduced if there is a hailstorm in Switzerland that damages at least 6,000 cars that have been insured by Winterthur.[10] The bondholders receive a higher interest rate but take on some of the company's risk.

Asset-Backed Bonds. The rock star David Bowie earns royalties from a number of successful albums such as *The Rise and Fall of Ziggy Stardust* and *Diamond Dogs*. But instead

[10] The Winterthur bond is an example of a *catastrophe* (or *CAT*) *bond*. Its payments are linked to the occurrence of a natural catastrophe. CAT bonds are discussed in M. S. Cantor, J. B. Cole, and R. L. Sandor, "Insurance Derivatives: A New Asset Class for the Capital Markets and a New Hedging Tool for the Insurance Industry," *Journal of Applied Corporate Finance* 10 (Fall 1997), pp. 69–83.

FINANCE IN ACTION

Canadian Tire Securitizes Credit Card Receivables in a Public Offering

Canadian Tire Corp. has joined the small but growing list of Canadian issuers that have securitized some of their credit card receivables in a public offering.

The issuer, along with Tim Hortons, is a defining symbol of Canada and raised $300 million from the offering of 5-year AAA-rated term notes and placed $15 million of subordinated notes.

Stan Pasternak, Canadian Tire treasurer, said the securities will be priced at 46 basis points over comparable Canada bonds.

Source: Excerpted from B. Critchley, "Canadian Tire Deal No Retread," *The Financial Post* (July 6, 2001), p. D3.

of waiting to receive these royalties, Bowie decided that he would prefer the money upfront. The solution was to issue $55 million 10-year bonds and to set aside the future royalty payments from the singer's albums to make the payments on these bonds. Such bonds are known as *asset-backed securities;* the borrower sets aside a group of assets and the income from these assets is then used to service the debt.

The Bowie bonds are an unusual example of an asset-backed security, but billions of dollars of house and commercial mortgages, credit card loans, personal lines of credit and receivables are packaged each year, or *securitized*, and resold as asset-backed bonds. According to a report issued by Dominion Bond Rating Service, Canada's outstanding asset-backed securities stood at about $79.4 billion at the end of 2000 compared with about $10 billion 5 years earlier. For the most part, these securities were comprised of assets financed by short-term unsecured debt such as commercial paper.[11] Securitization can be done through multiseller or single-seller programs that are typically offered by large investment dealers such as BMO Nesbitt Burns, TD Securities, or CIBC World Markets. For instance, a multiseller program that securitizes receivables may pool such receivables from a variety of providers and then finance those purchases by issuing commercial paper securities. In contrast, a single-seller program would involve a single provider. The above Finance in Action box describes a recent public offering by Canadian Tire through the securitization of some of their credit card receivables.

Similarly, commercial mortgage-backed securities can be securitized as single asset and multi-asset offerings, the former involving one building while the latter would involve several buildings. Recently, Brookfield Properties, a large Canadian real estate company, raised $432 (US) million from refinancing its One Liberty Plaza building in New York and a further $500 (US) million from refinancing another Manhattan building. In both deals, investors purchased securities known as *multi-class mortgage pass-through certificates*, which ranged from being AAA rated to just investment grade (BBB-).[12]

Reverse Floaters. Floating-rate bonds that pay a higher rate of interest when other interest rates fall and a lower rate when other rates rise are called *reverse floaters*. They are riskier than normal bonds. When interest rates rise, the prices of all bonds fall, but the prices of reverse floaters suffer a double whammy because the coupon payments on the bonds fall as the discount rate rises. In 1994, Orange County, California, learned this

[11] We will discuss commercial paper in more detail in Chapter 19.

[12] See also, B. Critchley, "Asset-Backed Market Soaring: Value of Securities up Eightfold from Five Years Ago," *Financial Post* (March 21, 2001), p. D3. See also, B. Critchley, "Brookfield Taps into U.S. MBS Market: Raises US$932 Million with New York Refinancings," *Financial Post* (March 19, 2001), p. C8. Following the tragic events of September 11, 2001, at New York's World Trade Center, the One Liberty Plaza complex had to be temporarily vacated. The building has since been reopened to tenants.

the hard way when it invested heavily in reverse floaters. Robert Citron, the treasurer, was betting that interest rates would fall. He was wrong; interest rates rose sharply and partly because of its investment in reverse floaters, the county lost $1.7 billion (US).

These three examples illustrate the great variety of potential security designs. As long as you can convince investors of its attractions, you can issue a callable, subordinated, floating-rate bond denominated in euros. Rather than combining features of existing securities, you may be able to create an entirely new one. We can imagine a copper mining company issuing preferred shares where the dividend fluctuates with the world copper price. We know of no such security, but it is perfectly legal to issue it and, who knows, it might generate considerable interest among investors.

Variety is intrinsically good. People have different tastes, levels of wealth, rates of tax, and so on. Why not offer them a choice? Of course the problem is the expense of designing and marketing new securities. But if you can think of a new security that will appeal to investors, you may be able to issue it on especially favourable terms, and thus, increase the value of your company.

13.4 Convertible Securities

warrant Right to buy shares from a company at a stipulated price before a set date.

We have seen that companies sometimes have the option to repay an issue of bonds before maturity. There are also cases in which *investors* have an option. The most dramatic case is provided by a **warrant,** which really is an option. Companies often issue warrants and bonds in a package.

EXAMPLE 13.2 *Warrants*

Macaw Bill wishes to make a bond issue, which could include some warrants as a "sweetener." Each warrant might allow you to purchase one share of Macaw stock at a price of $50 any time during the next 5 years. If Macaw's stock performs well, that option could turn out to be very valuable. For instance, if the stock price at the end of the 5 years is $80, then you pay the company $50 and receive in exchange a share worth $80. Of course, an investment in warrants also has its perils. If the price of Macaw stock fails to rise above $50, then the warrants expire and are worthless.

convertible bond Bond that the holder may exchange for a specified amount of another security.

A **convertible bond** gives its owner the option to exchange the bond for a predetermined number of common shares. The convertible bondholder hopes that the company's share price will zoom up so that the bond can be converted at a big profit. But if the shares zoom down, there is no obligation to convert; the bondholder remains just that. Not surprisingly, investors value this option to keep the bond or exchange it for shares, and therefore, a convertible bond sells at a higher price than a comparable bond that is not convertible.

The convertible is like a package of a bond and a warrant. But there is an important difference: When the owners of a convertible wish to exercise their options to buy shares, they do not pay cash—they just exchange the bond for shares of the stock.

Companies may also issue convertible preferred stock. In this case the investor receives preferred stock with fixed dividend payments but has the option to exchange this preferred stock for the company's common stock. The preferred stock issued by the Bank of Montreal is convertible into common stock.

These examples do not exhaust the options encountered by the financial manager. In fact once you read Chapter 25 and learn how to analyze options, you will find that they are all around you.

13.5 Patterns of Corporate Financing

We have now completed our tour of corporate securities. You may feel like the tourist who has just gone through 12 cathedrals in 5 days. But there will be plenty of time in later chapters for reflection and analysis. For now, let's look at how firms use these sources of finance.

Firms have two broad sources of cash: They can raise money from external sources by an issue of debt or equity, or they can plow back part of their profits. When the firm retains cash rather than paying the money out as dividends, it is increasing shareholders' investment in the firm.

internally generated funds Cash reinvested in the firm: depreciation plus earnings not paid out as dividends.

Figure 13.1 summarizes the sources of capital for Canadian corporations. The most striking aspect of this figure is the dominance of **internally generated funds,** defined as depreciation plus earnings that are not paid out as dividends.[13] For much of this period, over half of the total funding requirement of corporations was met from internally generated funds.

DO FIRMS RELY TOO HEAVILY ON INTERNAL FUNDS?

Gordon Donaldson, in a survey of corporate debt policies, encountered several firms which acknowledged "that it was their long-term objective to hold to a rate of growth which was consistent with their capacity to generate funds internally." A number of other firms appeared to think less about expenditure proposals that could be financed internally.[14]

At first glance, this behaviour doesn't make sense. As we have already noted, retained profits are additional capital invested by shareholders and represent, in effect, a compulsory issue of shares. A firm that retains $1 million could have paid out the cash as dividends and then sold new common shares to raise the same amount of additional capital. The opportunity cost of capital ought not to depend on whether the project is financed by retained profits or a new stock issue.

Why then do managers have an apparent preference for financing by retained earnings? Perhaps managers are simply taking the line of least resistance, dodging the discipline of the securities markets.

Think back to Chapter 1, where we pointed out that a firm is a team, consisting of managers, shareholders, debtholders, and so on. The shareholders and debtholders would like to monitor management to make sure that it is pulling its weight and truly maximizing market value. It is costly for individual investors to keep checks on management. However, large financial institutions are specialists in monitoring, so when the firm goes to the bank for a large loan or makes a public issue of stocks or bonds, managers know that they had better have all the answers. If they want a quiet life, they will avoid going to the

[13] Remember that depreciation is a noncash expense.

[14] See G. Donaldson, *Corporate Debt Capacity*, Division of Research, Graduate School of Business Administration, Harvard University, Boston, 1961, Chapter 3, especially pp. 51–56.

FIGURE 13.1
Sources of financing for nonfinancial Canadian firms

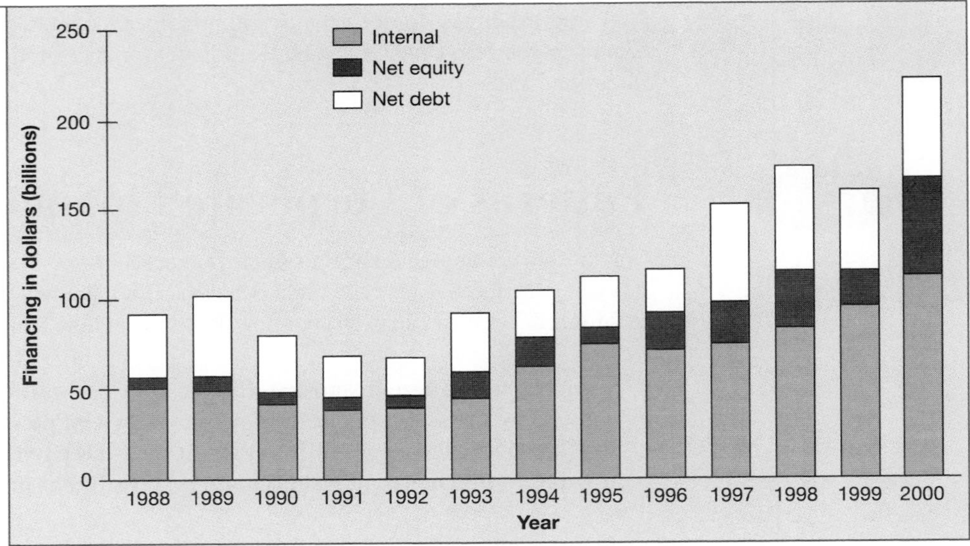

Source: Relevant data was compiled from CANSIM Matrix 0702, providing data series on financial flows for nonfinancial private corporations.

capital market to raise money, and they will retain sufficient earnings to be able to meet unanticipated demands for cash.

We do not mean to paint managers as loafers. There are also rational reasons for relying on internally generated funds. The costs of new securities are avoided, for example. Moreover, the announcement of a new equity issue is usually bad news for investors, who worry that the decision signals lower profits.[15] Raising equity capital from internal sources avoids the costs and the bad omens associated with equity issues.

CHECK POINT 13.7

"Since internal funds provide the bulk of industry's needs for capital, the securities markets serve little function." Does the speaker have a point?

EXTERNAL SOURCES OF CAPITAL

Of course firms don't rely exclusively on internal funds. They also issue securities and retire them, sometimes in big volume. For example, in the early 1990s, CP relied heavily on new debt by issuing considerable numbers of bonds. Between 1990 and 1991, its outstanding long-term debt increased by about 56 percent. After 1993, however, CP reduced its reliance on new debt financing, and its level of outstanding long-term debt stabilized. Despite this, the ratio of long-term debt to the book value of equity rose in the late 1990s and 2000. The ratio rose during this period because CP was buying back shares from the public. So, for instance, over the period between 1998 and 2000, CP had *negative* net stock issues.

Figure 13.2 shows the book value of CP's long-term debt to both the book value and market value of its equity. Notice that the ratio based on market value was higher than the ratio based on the book value in the beginning of the 1990s, but it has since stayed consistently lower. Also, the ratio of long-term debt to the *market* value of equity was, by

[15] Managers do have insiders' insights and naturally are tempted to issue stock when the stock price looks good to them, that is, when they are less optimistic than outside investors. The outside investors realize all this and will buy a new issue only at a discount from the preannouncement price. Stock issues are discussed further in the next chapter.

FIGURE 13.2
Long-term debt-to-equity ratios for Canadian Pacific, Ltd.

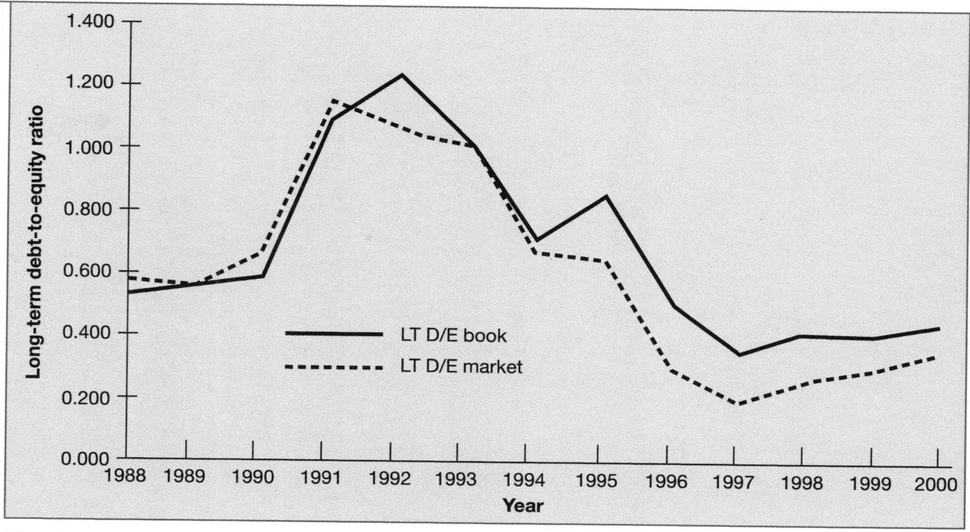

Note: LT D/E ratio (book) = Long-term debt/Shareholder's equity; LT D/E ratio (market) = Long-term debt/(Average number of common shares × average stock price).
Source: Financial Post Online, Historical Report at www.fpdata.finpost.com, April 2, 2001, and Canadian Pacific, Ltd., Annual Reports, Ten Year Summary, at www.cp.ca.

far, more stable. This reflects a general rise in stock market values in the 1990s, which allowed the market value of CP's equity to keep up with its issues of long-term debt.

CP was not alone in its use of share repurchases in the latter part of the 1990s. Other Canadian companies were repurchasing their shares as well during this period, often by making large issues of debt and using part of the money to buy back common stock. We see from Figure 13.1 that the proportion of net debt financing[16] by Canadian nonfinancial firms generally went up in the final years of the 1990s, but from Figure 13.3, their average debt-to-equity ratios actually came down in this period. The high profit levels during this period resulted in record-setting levels of internally generated funds. As a result, despite the share repurchases, common equity rose more than debt, resulting in lower debt-to-equity ratios.

However, share repurchase programs among Canadian and U.S. companies have recently been declining following the downturn in stock market prices. For instance, the number of share buyback programs in place for TSE-listed companies fell to 352 in July 2001 from 420 in July 2000. There has been a similar decline in share buyback programs among companies in the United States.

The net effect of these financing policies is shown in Figure 13.3, which confirms that debt-to-equity ratios for Canadian firms in the 1990s were relatively stable in book-value terms.

SEE BOX P. 399

Canadian corporations are carrying more debt than they did 30 years ago. The nearby Finance in Action box shows that Canadian companies have recently issued record levels of new bonds. Should we be worried? It is true that higher debt ratios mean that more companies are likely to fall into financial distress when a serious recession hits the economy. But all companies live with this risk to some degree, and it does not follow that less risk is better. Finding the optimal debt ratio is like finding the optimal speed limit: We can agree that accidents at 60 kilometres per hour are less dangerous, other things being equal, than accidents at 100 kilometres per hour, but we do not therefore set the national speed limit at 60. Speed has benefits as well as risks. So does debt, as we will see in Chapter 15.

[16] This includes long-term and short-term debt.

FIGURE 13.3
Average debt-to-equity ratios, Canadian non-financial enterprises

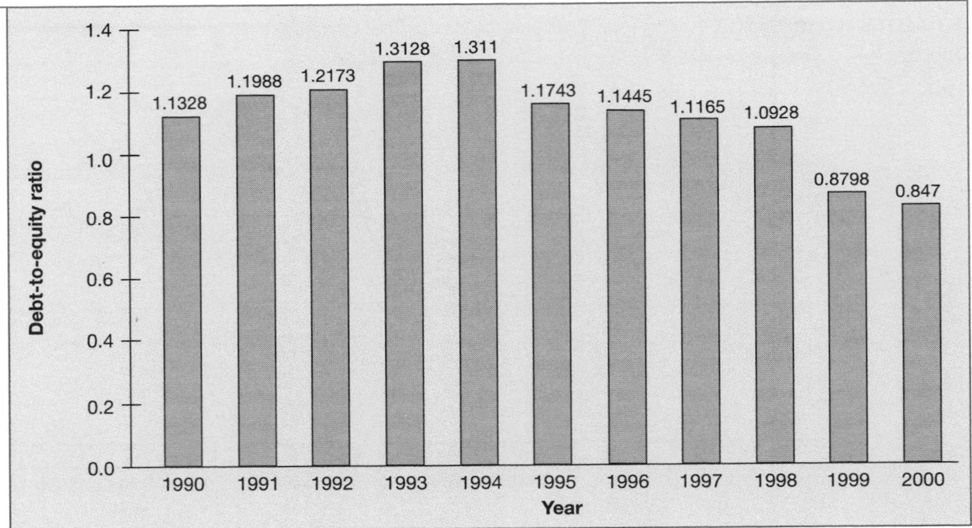

Note: The annual debt-to-equity ratios were calculated by taking the average of the quarterly debt-to-equity ratios reported for each year. Debt includes loans and accounts with affiliates plus borrowings. Equity is total equity.
Source: Statistics Canada, *Quarterly Financial Statistics for Enterprises,* Fourth Quarter, 1990–2000.

How do Canadian companies compare with firms in other countries with regard to the type of financing? Figure 13.4 provides information on long-term debt-to-equity ratios as well as total debt-to-equity ratios for the G-7 countries. Notice that Italy, Japan, France, and Germany tend to carry high debt levels. Much of the debt in these countries is carried by banks, which often tend to have close, long-term relationships with corporations. For instance, in Japan, such relationships have historically existed within the keiretsu system, which we described in Section 13.1. In recent years, the use of debt has increased in Canada while it has been falling in Japan. A number of Japanese companies have also been exploring public debt markets.

FIGURE 13.4
Long-term debt-to-equity ratios and total debt-to-equity ratios for non-financial enterprises for G-7 countries

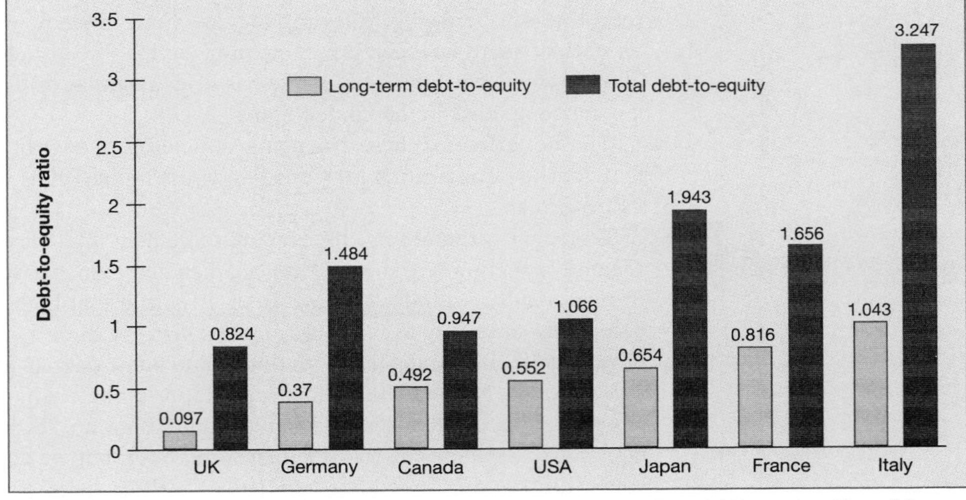

Source: Organization for Economic Cooperation and Development, "Non-Financial Enterprises Financial Statistics," 1996.

FINANCE IN ACTION

Are Canadian Companies on a Borrowing Binge?

Canadian companies issued a record level of new bonds last quarter, spurring the debt market...even as new stock offerings and corporate deals continue to slump.

Canadian corporate debt issues in the second quarter jumped to a record high of $24.2 billion in the gross amount of issues in the second quarter.

"There's been a lot of uncertainty about stocks. By comparison, corporate bonds have offered investors attractive spreads [in yields] relative to the government bond market," said Rob Palombi, a senior fixed-income analyst at Standard & Poor's MMS in Toronto.

Among the recent offerings galvanizing the market have been Quebecor, Inc.'s $1 billion bond issue and Hydro One, Inc.'s $550 million issue.

Telus Corp. solidified much of the bond market's recent enthusiasm with its mammoth and well-received $5 billion issue in late May.

The $24.2 billion in gross corporate debt issues in Canada in the second quarter surpassed the latest high of $21.2 billion in the second quarter of 1998, according to data from the Bank of Canada.

When taking into account the offsetting effect of $7.8 billion in corporate bonds that came due, and which companies therefore had to pay back to investors, total net bond issues were $16.4 billion in the last quarter. This was still a new record, beating the previous high of $15.6 billion in the second quarter of 1999.

As another example of the buoyant activity, net Canadian corporate debt in both the first and second quarter in this year was $26.8 billion, far stronger than the $12.7 billion in corporate debt issues in the first half of 2000.

Canadian debt also continued to attract a heavy level of foreign interest. While nearly $8.2 billion net corporate debt was issued in Canadian dollars in the second quarter, Canadian companies issued roughly the same amount in U.S. dollars and euros in the quarter.

As another comparison, Canadian corporations had issued only $2.4 billion in net foreign-denominated debt in the first six months of 2000. This year they issued $12.3 billion.

Falling interest rates have helped. Action by the Bank of Canada, and particularly, the U.S. Federal Reserve Board to spur the economy by lowering interest rates has led to a general decline in all bond yields across the board (and a consequential increase in bond prices, which automatically move in the opposite direction as yields do).

But even with corporate bond yields falling, they remain, as ever, higher than Government of Canada bond yields.

Corporate bonds with riskier ratings from debt-rating agencies, such as Telus's triple-B-plus rating from Standard & Poor's, and the accompanying higher yields these bonds have to offer are increasingly attracting investors.

With a wave of Government of Canada bonds recently coming due, investors have been looking for other bonds in which to put their money, helping to spark even more demand for corporate debt.

Source: Excerpted from G. Dixon, "Bond Issues Hit High in Second Quarter," the *Globe and Mail* (July 9, 2001), p. B1.

13.6 Summary

1. What are the major classes of securities issued by firms to raise capital?

Companies may raise money from shareholders by issuing more shares. They also raise money indirectly by plowing back cash that could otherwise have been paid out as dividends.

Preferred stock offers a fixed dividend but the company has the discretion not to pay it. It can't, however, then pay a dividend on the common stock. Despite its name, preferred stock is not a popular source of finance, but it is useful in special situations.

When companies issue debt, they promise to make a series of interest payments and to repay the principal. However, this liability is limited. Shareholders have the right to default on their obligation and to hand over the assets to the debtholders. Unlike dividends on common stock and preferred stock, the interest payments on debt are regarded as a cost and therefore they are paid out of before-tax income. Here are some forms of debt:

- *Fixed-rate* and *floating-rate* debt
- *Long-term* (funded) and *short-term* (unfunded) debt
- *Callable* and *sinking-fund* debt
- *Senior* and *subordinated* debt
- *Secured* and *unsecured* debt
- *Investment grade* and *junk* debt
- *Domestic* and *international* debt
- *Publicly traded* debt and *private placements*

The fourth source of finance consists of options and optionlike securities. The simplest option is a warrant, which gives its holder the right to buy a share from the firm at a set price by a set date. Warrants are often sold in combination with other securities. **Convertible bonds** give their holder the right to convert the bond to shares. They therefore resemble a package of straight debt and a warrant.

2. **What are recent trends in firms' use of different sources of finance?**

Internally generated cash is the principal source of company funds. Some people worry about that; they think that if management does not go to the trouble of raising money, it may be profligate in spending it.

In the late 1990s, net equity issues were *negative;* that is, companies repurchased more equity than they issued. At the same time companies issued large quantities of debt. However, large levels of **internally generated funds** in this period allowed book equity to increase despite the share repurchases, with the result that the ratio of long-term debt to book value of equity was fairly stable. Moreover, the stock market boom of the 1990s meant that the ratio of debt to the market value of equity actually fell considerably during this period.

Related Web Links

www.ashtonanalytics.com Information about the debt markets
www.finpipe.com See "Types of Bonds" for descriptions of many bond instruments
www.fcnbd.com/corporate/capital/mezzanine/index.html A menu of choices for corporations issuing different kinds of debt
www.hoovers.com Information about corporations and corporate financing
www.lacaisse.com La Caisse de dépot et placement du Québec
www.canadiantire.ca
www.cp.ca Canadian Pacific
www.osc.gov.on.ca Ontario Securities Commission
www.bondsonline.com Informative website on bonds

Key Terms

issued shares	378	net worth	383	eurodollars	389
outstanding shares	378	floating-rate preferred	386	eurobond	389
authorized share capital	378	prime rate	387	foreign bond	389
par value	378	long-term debt	387	private placement	390
additional paid-in capital	378	sinking fund	387	protective covenant	390
retained earnings	378	callable bond	387	lease	390
majority voting	381	refunding	387	warrant	394
cumulative voting	381	subordinated debt	388	convertible bond	394
proxy contest	381	secured debt	388	internally generated funds	395
preferred stock	383				

Questions and Problems

*Answers in Appendix B

Basic

*1. **Equity Accounts.** The authorized share capital of the Alfred Cake Company is 100,000 shares. Presently 20,000 shares are issued and outstanding. The equity is currently shown in the company's books as follows:

Common stock	$ 60,000
Retained earnings	30,000
Common equity	90,000

a. How many more shares can be issued without the approval of shareholders?
b. If the company issues 10,000 shares at $5 a share, show how this will appear in the company's books.

2. **Equity Accounts.** Look back at problem 1. What would happen to the company's books if instead it bought back 1,000 shares at $5 per share? The average issue price of these shares was $5.

*3. **Financing Terms.** Fill in the blanks by choosing the appropriate term from the following list: lease, funded, floating-rate, eurobond, convertible, subordinated, call, sinking fund, prime rate, private placement, public issue, senior, unfunded, eurodollar rate, warrant, debentures, term loan.

a. Debt maturing in more than 1 year is often called _________ debt.

b. An issue of bonds that is sold simultaneously in several countries is traditionally called a(n) _________.

c. If a lender ranks behind the firm's general creditors in the event of default, the loan is said to be _________.

d. In many cases a firm is obliged to make regular contributions to a(n) _________, which is then used to repurchase bonds.

e. Most bonds give the firm the right to repurchase or _________ the bonds at specified prices.

f. The benchmark interest rate that banks charge to their customers with good to excellent credit is generally termed the _________.

g. The interest rate on bank loans is often tied to short-term interest rates. These loans are usually called _________ loans.

h. Where there is a(n) _________, securities are sold directly to a small group of institutional investors. These securities cannot be resold to individual investors. In the case of a(n) _________, debt can be freely bought and sold by individual investors.

i. A long-term rental agreement is called a(n) _________.

j. A(n) _________ bond can be exchanged for shares of the issuing corporation.

k. A(n) _________ gives its owner the right to buy shares in the issuing company at a predetermined price.

4. **Financing Trends.** Are the following statements true or false? Explain.

a. In several recent years, nonfinancial corporations in Canada have repurchased more stock than they have issued.

b. A corporation pays tax on only 30 percent of the common or preferred dividends it receives from other corporations.

c. Because of the tax advantage, a large fraction of preferred shares is held by corporations.

5. **Preferred Stock.** In what ways is preferred stock like long-term debt? In what ways is it like common stock?

PRACTICE

*6. **Voting for Directors.** If there are 10 directors to be elected and a shareholder owns 90 shares, indicate the maximum number of votes that he or she can cast for a favourite candidate under

a. majority voting

b. cumulative voting

*7. **Voting for Directors.** The shareholders of the Pickwick Paper Company need to elect five directors. There are 400,000 shares outstanding. How many shares do you need to own to *ensure* that you can elect at least one director if the company has

a. majority voting

b. cumulative voting

Hint: How many votes in total will be cast? How many votes are required to ensure that at least a fifth of votes are cast for your choice?

8. **Equity Accounts.** Look back at Table 13.2.

a. Suppose that Canadian Pacific issues 10 million shares at $55 a share. Rework Table 13.2 to show the company's equity after the issue.

b. Suppose that Canadian Pacific *subsequently* repurchased 500,000 shares at $60 a share. Rework part (a) to show the effect of the further change. Take the average issue price of the shares to be $30.

9. **Protective Covenants.** Why might a bond agreement limit the amount of assets that the firm can lease?
10. **Bond Yields.** Other things being equal, will the following provisions increase or decrease the yield to maturity at which a firm can issue a bond?
    a. a call provision
    b. a restriction on further borrowing
    c. a provision of specific collateral for the bond
    d. an option to convert the bonds into shares

*11. **Income Bonds.** *Income bonds* are unusual. Interest payments on such bonds may be skipped or deferred if the firm's income is insufficient to make the payment. In what way are these bonds like preferred stock? Why might a firm choose to issue an income bond instead of preferred stock?

12. **Preferred Stock.** Preferred stock of financially strong firms sometimes sells at lower yields than the bonds of those firms. For weaker firms, the preferred stock has a higher yield. What might explain this pattern?

SOLUTIONS TO CHECK POINTS

13.1 The paid-in capital to the extent of common shares sold to the public is $15 × 100,000 shares = $1,500,000. Since book value is $3,000,000, retained earnings must be $1,500,000. Therefore, the accounts look like this:

Common shares:	
Paid-in capital	1,500,000
Retained earnings	1,500,000
Common equity	$3,000,000

13.2 Book value is $10 million. At a discount rate of 10 percent, the market value of the firm ought to be $2 million × 20-year annuity factor at 10% = $17 million, which exceeds book value. At a discount rate of 20 percent, market value falls to $9.7 million, which is below book value.

13.3 The corporation's after-tax yield on the bonds is 10% – (.35 × 10%) = 6.5%. The after-tax yield on the preferred is 8% – [.35 × (.30 × 8%)] = 7.16%. The preferred stock provides the higher after-tax rate despite its lower before-tax rate. For the individual, the tax rate on both the preferred and the bond is equal to 35 percent, so the investment with the higher before-tax rate also provides the higher after-tax rate.

13.4 Because the coupon on floating-rate debt adjusts periodically to current market conditions, the bondholder is less vulnerable to changes in market yields. The coupon rate paid by the bond is not locked in for as long a period of time. Therefore, prices of floaters should be less sensitive to changes in market interest rates.

13.5 The callable bond will sell at a lower price. Investors will not pay as much for the callable bond since they know that the firm may call it away from them if interest rates fall. Thus they know that their capital gains potential is limited, which makes the bond less valuable. If both bonds are to sell at par value, the callable bond must pay a higher coupon rate as compensation to the investor for the firm's right to call the bond.

13.6 The extra debt makes it more likely that the firm will not be able to make good on its promised payments to its creditors. If the new debt is not junior to the already-issued debt, then the original bondholders suffer a loss when their bonds become more susceptible to default risk. A protective covenant limiting the amount of new debt that the firm can issue would have prevented this problem. Investors, having witnessed the problems of the RJR bondholders, generally demanded the covenant on future debt issues.

13.7 Capital markets provide liquidity for investors. Because individual shareholders can always lay their hands on cash by selling shares, they are prepared to invest in companies that retain earnings rather than pay them out as dividends. Well-functioning capital markets allow the firm to serve all its shareholders simply by maximizing value. Capital markets also provide managers with information. Without this information, it would be very difficult to determine opportunity costs of capital or to assess financial performance.

Appendix 13A: The Bond Refunding Decision

We saw in Section 13.3 that corporate bonds often include a call provision that allows the company to pay back the debt early. If interest rates fall and bond prices rise, the option to buy back the bond at a fixed price can be very attractive to the company. The company can buy back the existing bond and issue a new one at a higher price and a lower interest rate.

The refunding decision would involve an analysis of whether it is profitable for the firm to replace an existing issue of higher-interest cost bonds with a new issue of lower-interest cost bonds.[17] The approach used is similar to the analysis done in a replacement capital-budgeting situation. This involves determining the net present value (NPV) of the proposed refunding after considering incremental after-tax cash flows from the new issue relative to the old issue. The analysis will typically be conducted for the period remaining until the maturity of the existing issue. A refunding project yielding a positive net present value would be taken up, while a negative net-present-value project will be rejected.

Let us examine the issues involved in a refunding project through the analysis conducted by the finance manager of Strike-a-Deal, Inc.

EXAMPLE 13.A The finance manager of Strike-a-Deal, Inc. has been closely watching interest rates with a view to refunding the company's 20-year, $100 million outstanding callable bonds, which were issued at par 5 years ago but still have 15 years remaining to maturity. The bonds carry a 10 percent coupon interest rate. Flotation costs of $3 million were incurred when the bonds were issued. The bonds carry a call premium of 10 percent. The finance manager feels that because of a drop in long-term interest rates, the firm can sell an additional $100 million of new 15-year bonds at a coupon interest rate of 7.7 percent. To ensure the availability of funds to refund the outstanding bonds, the new bonds will have to be sold one month before the old issue is called. The finance manager is well aware that interest will have to be paid on both issues for one month, but feels that the proceeds of the new issue can be invested for this period in money market funds to yield 5 percent annually. The estimated flotation cost on the new issue is $2.5 million. Strike-a-Deal's marginal tax rate is 35 percent. Should it refund its outstanding bonds?

As we have mentioned earlier, to determine the NPV of the proposed refunding, we would look at incremental after-tax cash flows from the new issue. To do this, we would compare, in present value terms, the net investment required to refund the bond issue with the incremental savings generated from lower interest payments on the new issue. To arrive at present values, we would discount all such after-tax cash flows by the after-tax cost of the new issue. This would be the appropriate discount rate. Refunding projects are of low risk to the firm since they only involve the replacement of one issue by another, so using the higher weighted average cost of capital rate would not be appropriate.

NET INVESTMENT COSTS ASSOCIATED WITH REFUNDING

Let us first look at the incremental investment required to refund the bond issue. For Strike-a-Deal, this will include the call premium to be paid on the old bonds, flotation

[17] The refunding decision can also be applied to preferred stock issues. For instance, a company may decide to replace an existing issue of preferred stock with a new issue carrying a lower dividend rate.

costs, and net additional interest costs for the overlapping month when both new and old bond issues are in place. Tax implications of such incremental costs will also have to be considered, so our objective will be to arrive at the overall *after-tax investment costs.*

Call Premium. This works out to 0 .1 × $100,000,000 = $10,000,000. The call premium is not a tax-deductible expense to the firm.

Flotation Costs. For tax purposes, flotation costs must be amortized over the life of the new bond or 5 years, whichever is less. The flotation cost on the old bond would have been amortized by now. However, the annual tax deduction on the flotation cost on the new bond issue will have to be computed.

So annual tax deduction on flotation cost of new issue = $2,500,000/5 = $500,000

Using Strike-a-Deal's marginal tax rate of 35 percent, the tax savings in each of the 5 years will be 0.35 × $500,000 = $175,000. This represents an annuity series over the 5-year period. The present value of these deductions will have to be computed. As discussed earlier, the appropriate discount rate here is the after-tax cost of the new debt issue:

$$\begin{aligned}\text{After-tax cost of new debt} &= 7.7\%\ (1 - \text{ tax rate})\\ &= 7.7\%\ (1 - 0.35)\\ &= 5.005\%\end{aligned}$$

We compute the present value of the tax saving by applying the annuity formula which we studied in Chapter 3:

$$\$175{,}000\left[\frac{1 - [1/(1.05005)^5]}{0.05005}\right] = \$757{,}554$$

When, from the gross flotation cost, we subtract the present value of the tax saving from amortizing such costs, we get the net after-tax flotation cost on the new issue:

Gross flotation costs on new issue	$2,500,000
Less: Present value of associated tax savings	– 757,554
Net after-tax flotation cost on new issue	$1,742,446

Additional Interest. The new bond issue will have to be sold one month before the old bonds are replaced, so for this month, Strike-a-Deal will have to incur interest costs on both issues. The additional cost during this month will be the interest that will have to be paid on the old issue. Because this interest is tax deductible, we will consider the after-tax interest cost on the old issue.

$$\begin{aligned}\text{Additional after-tax interest cost} &= \text{Dollar amount of old issue} \times\\ &\quad (1/12 \times \text{old interest rate})(1 - T)\\ &= \$100{,}000{,}000 \times (1/12 \times 0.1)(1 - 0.35)\\ &= \$541{,}667\end{aligned}$$

Keep in mind that the proceeds of the new issue can also be invested for a month. Strike-a-Deal has decided to invest in the money market for this period. Because any interest earned on this investment will incur tax, we compute the after-tax interest earned:

$$\begin{aligned}\text{After-tax interest earned} &= \text{Dollar amount of new issue} \times\\ &\quad (1/12 \times \text{new interest rate})(1 - T)\\ &= \$100{,}000{,}000 \times (1/12 \times 0.05)(1 - T)\\ &= \$270{,}833\end{aligned}$$

The net after-tax additional interest cost to Strike-a-Deal is the difference between the after-tax additional interest paid on the old issue and the after-tax interest earned on the new issue, or

$$\$541,667 - \$270,833 = \$270,834$$

Total After-Tax Investment Costs. We have now figured out the different after-tax component costs. When we add them up, we arrive at the total present value of net investments costs associated with the refunding decision.

Call premium	=	$10,000,000
Net after-tax flotation cost on new issue	=	$ 1,742,446
Net after-tax additional interest	=	$ 270,834
Total present value of net investment costs	=	$12,013,280

NET SAVINGS ASSOCIATED WITH REFUNDING

If Strike-a-Deal goes forward with the refunding, it will save every year on lower interest payments on the new issue. To determine the extent of the annual savings, we will have to take the difference between the yearly after-tax interest costs on the two issues. These savings will continue to be generated every year over the life of the new issue and can, therefore, be represented by a 15-year annuity.

The annual after-tax interest cost on the old issue is $100,000,000 × 0.10 × (1- 0.35) = $6,500,000. For the new issue, the annual after-tax interest cost is $100,000,000 × 0.077 × (1 – 0.35) = $5,005,000. So, the yearly interest savings from going forward with refunding is $6,500,000 – $5,005,000 = $1,495,000. To find the present value of this stream of yearly savings, we, once again, discount the annuity by the after-tax interest cost of the new issue:

$$\$1,495,000\left[\frac{1 - 1/(1.05005)^{15}}{0.05005}\right] = \$15,512,346$$

The present value of the net savings from refunding is, therefore, $15,512,346.

NET PRESENT VALUE ASSOCIATED WITH REFUNDING

Having figured out, in present value terms, the net savings and investment costs, we are now in a position to compute the NPV of the proposed refunding:

$$\begin{aligned}\text{NPV of refunding} &= \text{present value of net savings} - \text{net investment cost}\\ &= \$15,512,346 - \$12,013,280 = \$3,499,066\end{aligned}$$

Since NPV is positive, the finance manager of Strike-a-Deal concludes that it will be profitable for the company to refund the existing bond issue.

You may have noticed that the analysis of bond refunding is tailor-made for spreadsheets. The spreadsheet on page 407 recreates our analysis of Strike-a-Deal's proposed bond refunding. The worksheet that follows shows the formulas that were used to generate relevant values for the spreadsheet. Once we have the spreadsheet, we can try various sorts of "what-if analysis" to aid in our decision.

A Spreadsheet Model for Strike-a-Deal's Proposed Bond Refunding

	A	B	C	D
1		Rate	Time period (years)	Dollar amount ($)
2	Outstanding bond issue		0	100,000,000
3	Coupon interest rate on old issue	10%		
4	New bond issue		0	100,000,000
5	Coupon interest rate on new issue	7.7%		
6	After-tax coupon interest rate on new issue	5.0%		
7	Short-term money market investment yield	5.0%		
8	Marginal tax rate	35%		
9	**Present Value of Net Investment Costs**			
10	Call premium on outstanding bond issue	10%	0	10,000,000
11	Flotation cost on new issue		0	2,500,000
12	Flotation cost amortized for tax purposes		1–5	500,000
13	Annual tax savings on amortized flotation cost		1–5	175,000
14	PV of tax savings on flotation cost		0	757,554
15	Net after-tax flotation cost on new issue		0	1,742,446
16	Additional interest cost on old issue		0	541,667
17	Interest earned on short-term investment of new issue (after tax)		0	270,833
18	Net after-tax additional interest		0	270,833
19	Total PV of after-tax investment costs (D10 + D15 + D18)		0	12,013,280
20	**Net Savings from Refunding**			
21	Annual after-tax interest on old issue		1–15	6,500,000
22	Annual after-tax interest on new issue		1–15	5,005,000
23	Net annual savings in interest cost		1–15	1,495,000
24	PV of total interest cost savings over 15 years		0	15,512,346
25	**Net Present Value (NPV) from Bond Refunding** (D24 – D19)		0	**3,499,066**

Formula Inserts for Strike-a-Deal's Proposed Bond Refunding Spreadsheet Model

	A	B	C	D
1		Rate	Time period (years)	Dollar amount ($)
2	Outstanding bond issue		0	100,000,000
3	Coupon interest rate on old issue	0.1		
4	New bond issue		0	100,000,000
5	Coupon interest rate on new issue	0.077		
6	After-tax coupon interest rate on new issue	=B5*(1–B8)		
7	Short-term money market investment yield	0.05		
8	Marginal tax rate	0.35		
9	**Present Value of Net Investment Costs**			
10	Call premium on outstanding bond issue	0.1	0	=D2*B10
11	Flotation cost on new issue		0	2,500,000
12	Flotation cost amortized for tax purposes		1–5	=D11/5
13	Annual tax savings on amortized flotation cost		1–5	=D12*B8
14	PV of tax savings on flotation cost		0	=D13*(1–(1/(B6+1)^5))/B6
15	Net after-tax flotation cost on new issue		0	=D11–D14
16	Additional interest cost on old issue		0	=D2*(1/12*B3)(1–B8)
17	Interest earned on short-term investment of new issue (after tax)		0	=D4*(1/12*B7)(1–B8)
18	Net after-tax additional interest		0	=D16–D17
19	Total PV of after-tax investment costs (D10 + D15 + D18)		0	=D10 + D15 + D18
20	**Net Savings from Refunding**			
21	Annual after-tax interest on old issue		1–15	=D2*B3*(1–B8)
22	Annual after-tax interest on new issue		1–15	=D4*B5*(1–B8)
23	Net annual savings in interest cost		1–15	=D21–D22
24	PV of total interest cost savings over 15 years		0	=D23*(1–(1/(B6+1)^15))/B6
25	**Net Present Value (NPV) from Bond Refunding** (D24 – D19)		0	**=D24 – D19**

Practice Problems

1. **Bond Refunding.** E-Books.com currently has a 10-year $1 million bond issue outstanding (5 years remaining to maturity) with an 11 percent coupon interest rate and a $1000 par value. The call premium on these bonds is 5 percent. Because of a decline in interest rates, the firm would be able to refund the issue with a $1 million issue of 9 percent 5-year bonds. The flotation costs for refunding the issue are $25,000. The new bonds will have to be issued one month before the old bonds are called. The present return on short-term government securities is 5 percent annually. E-books has a marginal tax rate of 25 percent. Assume that there are no other costs associated with refunding. Should the firm refund the bond issue?
2. **Bond Refunding.** Food-Galore, Inc. has a $10 million outstanding bond issue, carrying a 12 percent coupon interest rate with 20 years remaining to maturity. This issue was sold 5 years ago and can be called by the company at a premium of 7 percent over its par value. Currently new 20-year bonds can be floated at a coupon interest rate of 9 percent. To ensure the availability of funds to pay off the old debt, the new bonds would be sold one month before the old issue is called, so for one month, interest would have to be paid on both issues. Flotation costs, comprised mainly of issuing and underwriting expenses, for the new debt would be $150,000. Currently, short-term interest rates are at 10 percent per annum. Food-Galore's marginal tax rate is 35 percent. Based on discounted cash flow analysis, should refunding take place?
3. **Bond Refunding.** Universal Heavy Equipment is looking into the possibility of refunding its 30-year $100 million outstanding bond issue, carrying a 14 percent coupon rate, which was sold 10 years ago. If the company goes ahead with the refunding, it can sell a new 20-year issue at a lower coupon rate of 10 percent, given current low interest rates in the economy. A call premium of 12 percent will have to be paid to retire the old bonds, while flotation costs on the new issue are expected to be $5 million. The company's marginal tax rate is 35 percent. The new bonds will have to be issued one month before the old bonds are called. Short-term government securities are presently providing a return of 6 percent annually. Universal's management is aware that the low interest rates may not last for very long and may, in fact, go up if the economy continues to grow very rapidly and creates inflationary pressures.
   1. Provide a complete bond refunding analysis and compute the NPV of the proposed refunding.
   2. Create a spreadsheet model of your analysis and also provide detailed formula inserts.

CHAPTER 14

How Corporations Issue Securities

14.1 Venture Capital

14.2 The Initial Public Offering

14.3 The Underwriters

14.4 Listing on the Stock Market

14.5 Rights Issues and General Cash Offers by Public Companies

14.6 The Private Placement

14.7 Summary

14.8 Appendix 14A: The Financing of New and Small Enterprises

14.9 Appendix 14B: Hotch Pot's New Issue Prospectus

Bill Gates and Paul Allen founded Microsoft in 1975 when they were both around 20. Eleven years later, Microsoft shares were sold to the public for $21 a share and immediately zoomed to $35. The largest shareholder was Bill Gates whose shares in Microsoft then were worth $350 million (US).

In 1976 two college dropouts, Steve Jobs and Steve Wozniak, sold their most valuable possessions: a van and a couple of calculators, and used the cash to start manufacturing computers in a garage. In 1980 when Apple Computer went public, the shares were offered to investors at $22 and jumped to $36. At that point, the shares owned by the company's two founders were worth $414 million (US).

In 1994 Marc Andreesen, a 24-year-old from the University of Illinois, joined with an investor, James Clark, and founded Netscape Communications. Just over a year later, Netscape stock was offered to the public at $28 a share and immediately leapt to $71. At this price James Clark's shares were worth $566 million (US), while Marc Andreesen's shares were worth $245 million (US).

Mike Lazardis quit his studies in electrical engineering at the University of Waterloo at 23. In 1984 he started Research In Motion (RIM) with two friends.[1] RIM went public in 1997, offering 13.8 million common shares at $7.25 each on the Toronto Stock Exchange. RIM's product, the BlackBerry e-mail pager-cum-computer, was such a success that by early 2000 its shares were trading at $260. Mike Lazardis became a billionaire, and recently shared an Academy Award for technical achievement with a co-worker for designing a device that quickened the pace of film editing.

Such stories illustrate that the most important asset of a new firm may be a good idea. But that is not all you need. To take an idea from the drawing board to a prototype and through to large-scale production requires ever greater amounts of capital.

[1] While it is true that some of these highly successful entrepreneurs dropped out of college or university, we do not want to give the impression that quitting school had anything to do with their success.

To get a new company off the ground, entrepreneurs may rely on their own savings and personal bank loans. But this is unlikely to be sufficient to build a successful enterprise. *Venture capital* firms specialize in providing new equity capital to help firms over the awkward adolescent period before they are large enough to "go public." In the first part of this chapter, we will explain how venture capital firms do this.

If the firm continues to be successful, there is likely to come a time when it needs to tap a wider source of capital. At this point it will make its first public issue of common stock. This is known as an *initial public offering,* or *IPO.* In the second section of the chapter we will describe what is involved in an IPO.

A company's initial public offering is seldom its last. In Chapter 13 we saw that internally generated cash is not usually sufficient to satisfy the firm's needs. Established companies make up the deficit by issuing more equity or debt. The remainder of this chapter looks at this process.

After studying this chapter you should be able to

- Understand how venture capital firms design successful deals.
- Understand how firms make initial public offerings and the costs of such offerings.
- Know what is involved when established firms make a general cash offer or a private placement of securities.
- Explain the role of the underwriter in an issue of securities.

14.1 Venture Capital

You have taken a big step. With a couple of friends, you have formed a corporation to open a number of fast food outlets, offering innovative combinations of international dishes such as sushi with sauerkraut, curry Bolognese, and chow mein with Yorkshire pudding. Breaking into the fast food business costs money, but after pooling your savings and borrowing to the hilt from the bank, you have raised $100,000 and purchased one million shares in the new company. At this *zero-stage* investment, your company's assets are $100,000 plus the *idea* for your new product.

That $100,000 is enough to get the business off the ground, but if the idea takes off, you will need more capital to pay for new restaurants. You therefore decide to look for an investor who is prepared to back an untried company in return for part of the profits. Equity capital in young businesses is known as **venture capital**, and it is provided by specialized venture capital firms, financial and investment institutions such as banks and pension funds, and government agencies. If you need very early stage financing for your new enterprise, you may seek financing from an **angel** investor. "Angels" are wealthy individual investors who can play a critical role in the creation of new ventures by making small-scale investments in local start-ups and early-stage ventures. They also bring a significant hands-on contribution to such business ventures. We will describe these venture capital providers in more detail in Appendix 14A.

venture capital Money invested to finance a new firm.

angel A wealthy individual investor in early-stage ventures.

Most entrepreneurs are able to spin a plausible yarn about their company. But it is as hard to convince a venture capitalist to invest in your business as it is to get a first novel published. Your first step is to prepare a *business plan.* This describes your product, the potential market, the production method, and the resources—time, money, employees, facilities, and equipment—needed for success. It helps if you can point out that you are prepared to put your money where your mouth is. By staking all your savings in the company, you *signal* your faith in the business.

The venture capital company knows that the success of a new business depends on the effort its managers put in. Therefore, it will try to structure a deal where you have a strong incentive to work hard. For example, if you agree to accept a modest salary (and look forward instead to increasing the value of your investment in the company's stock), the venture capital company knows you will be committed to working hard. However, if you insist on a watertight employment contract and a fat salary, you won't find it easy to raise venture capital.

You are unlikely to persuade a venture capitalist to give you as much money as you need all at once. Rather, the firm will probably give you enough to reach the first major checkpoint. Suppose you can convince the venture capital company to buy one million new shares for $.50 each. This means it owns half of the firm: It owns one million shares, and you and your friends also own one million shares. Because the venture capitalist is paying $500,000 for a claim to half your firm, it is placing a $1 million value on the business. After this *first-stage* financing, your company's balance sheet looks like this:

FIRST-STAGE MARKET-VALUE BALANCE SHEET
(Figures in millions)

Assets		**Liabilities and Shareholders' Equity**	
Cash from new equity	$ .5	New equity from venture capital	$ .5
Other assets	.5	Your original equity	.5
Value	$1.0	Value	$1.0

CHECK POINT 14.1

Why might the venture capital company prefer to put up only part of the funds upfront? Would this affect the amount of effort put in by you, the entrepreneur? Is your willingness to accept only part of the venture capital that will eventually be needed a good signal of the likely success of the venture?

Suppose that 2 years later your business has grown to the point where it needs a further injection of equity. This *second-stage* financing might involve the issue of another one million shares at $1 each. Some of these shares might be bought by the original backers and some by other venture capital firms. The balance sheet after the new financing would then be as follows:

SECOND-STAGE MARKET-VALUE BALANCE SHEET
(Figures in millions)

Assets		**Liabilities and Shareholders' Equity**	
Cash from new equity	$1.0	New equity from second-stage financing	$1.0
Other assets	2.0	Equity from first stage	1.0
		Your original equity	1.0
Value	$3.0	Value	$3.0

Notice that the value of the initial one million shares owned by you and your friends has now been marked up to $1 million. Is this beginning to sound like a money machine? It only works if you have made a success of the business and new investors are prepared to pay $1 to buy a share in the business. When you started out, it wasn't clear that sushi and sauerkraut would catch on. If it hadn't caught on, the venture capital firm could have refused to put up more funds.

You are not yet in a position to cash in on your investment, but your gain is real. The second-stage investors have paid $1 million for a one-third share in the company. (There are now three million shares outstanding, and the second-stage investors hold one million shares.) Therefore, at least these impartial observers—who are willing to back up their opinions with a large investment—must have decided that the company was worth at least $3 million. Your one-third share is therefore also worth $1 million.

For every 10 first-stage venture capital investments, only two or three may survive as successful, self-sufficient businesses, and only one may pay off big. From these statistics come two rules of success in venture capital investment: First, don't shy away from uncertainty; accept a low probability of success. But don't buy into a business unless you can see the *chance* of a big, public company in a profitable market. There's no sense taking a big risk unless the reward is big if you win. Second, cut your losses; identify losers early, and if you can't fix the problem—by replacing management, for example—don't throw good money after bad.

The same advice holds for any backer of a risky start-up business—after all, only a fraction of new businesses are funded by card-carrying venture capitalists. Some start-ups are funded directly by managers or by their friends and families. Some grow using bank loans and reinvested earnings. But if your start-up combines high risk, sophisticated technology, and substantial investment, you will probably try to find venture capital financing.

14.2 The Initial Public Offering

Very few new businesses make it big, but those that do can be very profitable. For example, an investor who provided $1,000 of first-stage financing for Intel would by mid-2000 have reaped $43 million (US). So venture capitalists and angel investors keep sane by reminding themselves of the success stories[2]—those who got in on the ground floor of firms like Intel, Lotus Development Corporation, and Research In Motion.[3] If a start-up is successful, the firm may need to raise a considerable amount of capital to gear up its production capacity. At this point, it needs more capital than can comfortably be provided by a small number of individuals or venture capitalists. The firm decides to sell shares to the public to raise the necessary funds.

initial public offering (IPO) First offering of stock to the general public.

A firm is said to *go public* when it sells its first issue of shares in a general offering to investors. This first sale of stock is called an *initial public offering*, or *IPO*.

An IPO is called a *primary* offering when new shares are sold to raise additional cash for the company. It is a *secondary* offering when the company's founders and the venture capitalist cash in on some of their gains by selling shares. A secondary offer, therefore, is no more than a sale of shares from the early investors to new investors, and the cash raised in a secondary offer does not flow to the company. Of course, IPOs can be and commonly are both primary and secondary: The firm raises new cash at the same time that some of the already-existing shares in the firm are sold to the public. Some of the biggest secondary offerings have involved governments selling off stock in nationalized enterprises. For example, the Japanese government raised $12.6 billion (US) by selling its stock in Nippon Telegraph and Telephone, and the British government took in $9 billion (US) from its sale of British Gas. The Canadian government received about $2.2 billion in 1996 in the biggest initial public offering in Canadian history—when 84 million shares of the newly privatized

[2] Fortunately, the successes have outweighed the failures. The National Venture Capital Association (NVCA) estimated that net returns on early-stage venture capital funds averaged 19 percent a year for the 10 years ending December 1998. With the recent decline in the price performance of Internet stocks, estimates of average 10-year returns of venture funds had declined to 12.8 percent by December 2000.

[3] The founder of Lotus took a class from one of the authors. Within 5 years the student had become a multimillionaire. Perhaps that will make you feel better about the cost of this book.

Canadian National Railway hit the stock market. The world's largest IPO took place in 1999 when the Italian government raised $19.3 billion (US) from the sale of shares in the state-owned electricity company, Enel.

ARRANGING A PUBLIC ISSUE

Once a firm decides to go public, the first task is to select the underwriters.

underwriter Firm that buys an issue of securities from a company and resells it to the public.

***Underwriters* are investment dealers that act as financial "midwives" to a new issue. Usually they play a triple role—first providing the company with procedural and financial advice, then buying the stock, and finally reselling it to the public.**

A small IPO may have only one underwriter, but larger issues usually require syndicate of underwriters who buy the issue and resell it. For example, the initial public offering by Microsoft involved a total of 114 underwriters.

spread Difference between public offer price and price paid by underwriter.

In the typical underwriting arrangement, called a *firm commitment,* the underwriters buy the securities from the firm and then resell them to the public. The underwriters receive payment in the form of a **spread**—that is, they are allowed to sell the shares at a slightly higher price than they paid for them. But the underwriters also accept the risk that they won't be able to sell the stock at the agreed offering price. If that happens, they will be stuck with unsold shares and must get the best price they can for them. In the more risky cases, the underwriter may not be willing to enter into a firm commitment and will handle the issue on a *best efforts* basis. In this case the underwriter agrees to sell as much of the issue as possible but does not guarantee the sale of the entire issue. Because fees tend to be less in a best efforts distribution, it might also be favoured by a high-quality issuer wishing to reduce issuing expenses.

Before any stock can be sold to the public, the company must satisfy the requirements of provincial securities laws and regulations.[4] Five provinces including Ontario, Québec, Alberta, Manitoba, and British Columbia have commissions while other provinces have securities acts. The stock may have to be registered with an appropriate securities commission. For instance, companies listed on the Toronto Stock Exchange (TSX) come under the purview of the Ontario Securities Commission (OSC), which administers the Ontario Securities Act. Generally, securities laws tend to be similar across provinces with the OSC playing a leadership role, given the overall importance of the TSX.

prospectus Formal summary that provides information on an issue of securities.

The first part of the registration statement is distributed to the public in the form of a preliminary **prospectus.** The preliminary prospectus contains some financial information that will also be included in the final prospectus, the company's history and its plans for the future, but it does not provide the price at which the security will be offered. It is sometimes called a *red herring* because it contains a printed disclaimer in red letters, which claims that it is not a final document and is subject to amendments because the securities commission has neither approved nor disapproved the registration statement.

One function of the prospectus is to warn investors about the risks involved in any investment in the firm. Some investors have joked that if they read prospectuses carefully, they would never dare buy a new issue. The appendix to this chapter is an example prospectus for your fast food business.

The securities commission, while reviewing the preliminary prospectus, may require it

[4] In contrast, in the U.S., all securities regulation is handled at the federal level by the Securities and Exchange Commission (SEC).

to be revised before approving it. Recent Canadian prospectuses can be found at the System for Electronic Documents and Retrieval (SEDAR) website (www.sedar.com).

The company and its underwriters also need to set the issue price. To gauge how much the stock is worth, they may undertake discounted cash-flow calculations like those described in Chapter 5. They also look at the price-earnings ratios of the shares of the firm's principal competitors.

Before settling on the issue price, the underwriters may arrange a "roadshow," which gives the underwriters and the company's management an opportunity to talk to potential investors. These investors may then offer their reaction to the issue, suggest what they think is a fair price, and indicate how much stock they would be prepared to buy. This allows the underwriters to build up a book of likely orders. Although investors are not bound by their indications, they know that if they want to remain in the underwriters' good books, they must be careful not to renege on their expressions of interest.

The managers of the firm are eager to secure the highest possible price for their stock, but the underwriters are likely to be cautious because they will be left with any unsold stock if they overestimate investor demand. As a result, underwriters typically try to underprice the initial public offering. **Underpricing,** they argue, is needed to tempt investors to buy stock and to reduce the cost of marketing the issue to customers.

underpricing Issuing securities at an offering price set below the true value of the security.

Underpricing represents a cost to the existing owners since the new investors are allowed to buy shares in the firm at a favourable price. The cost of underpricing may be very large.

It is common to see the stock price increase substantially from the issue price in the days following an issue. Such immediate price jumps indicate the amount by which the shares were underpriced compared to what investors were willing to pay for them. A study by Ibbotson, Sindelar, and Ritter of approximately 9,000 new issues from 1960 to 1987 found average underpricing of 16 percent.[5] Sometimes new issues are dramatically underpriced. In January 2000, for example, six million shares in 724 Solutions were sold in an IPO simultaneously on the Toronto and Nasdaq stock exchanges, priced at $37.29 and $26 (US), respectively, per share. When the issue opened, the stock started trading at $108 on the TSE and $73 (US) on Nasdaq. Greg Wolfond, the co-founder of 724 Solutions, owned eight million shares in the company and ended the day $828 million richer than when he woke up that morning. Unfortunately, the bonanza did not last. By July 2001, the stock price had fallen to a little over $10 on the TSX.

The nearby Finance in Action box reports on the phenomenal performance of Internet IPOs in the late 1990s.

EXAMPLE 14.1 *Underpricing of IPOs*

Suppose an IPO is a secondary issue, and the firm's founders sell part of their holding to investors. Clearly, if the shares are sold for less than their true worth, the founders will suffer an opportunity loss.

[5] R. G. Ibbotson, J. L. Sindelar, and J. R. Ritter, "Initial Public Offerings," *Journal of Applied Corporate Finance* 1 (Summer 1988), pp. 37–45. Note, however, that initial underpricing does not mean that IPOs are superior long-run investments. In fact, IPO returns over the first 3 years of trading have been less than a control sample of matching firms. See J. R. Ritter, "The Long-Run Performance of Initial Public Offerings," *Journal of Finance* 46 (March 1991), pp. 3–27.

FINANCE IN ACTION

Internet Shares: Loopy.com?

The tiny images are like demented postage stamps coming jerkily to life; the sound is prone to break up and at times could be coming from a bathroom plughole. Welcome to the Internet's live broadcasting experience. However, despite offering audio-visual quality that would have been unacceptable in the pioneering days of television, a small, loss-making company called Broadcast.com broke all previous records when it made its Wall Street debut on July 17th.

Shares in the Dallas-based company were offered at $18 and reached as high as $74 before closing at $62.75—a gain of nearly 250 percent on the day after a feeding frenzy in which 6.5 million shares changed hands. After the dust had settled, Broadcast.com was established as a $1 billion company, and its two 30-something founders, Mark Cuban and Todd Wagner, were worth nearly $500 million between them.

In its three years of existence, Broadcast.com, formerly known as AudioNet, has lost nearly $13 million, and its offer document frankly told potential investors that it had absolutely no idea when it might start to make money. So has Wall Street finally taken leave of its senses?

The value being placed on Broadcast.com is not obviously loopier than a number of other gravity-defying Internet stocks, particularly the currently fashionable "portals"—gateways to the Web—such as Yahoo! and America Online. Yahoo!, the Internet's leading content aggregator, has nearly doubled in value since June. On the back of revenue estimates of around $165 million, it has a market value of $8.7 billion.

Mark Hardie, an analyst with the high-tech consultancy Forrester Research, does not believe, in any case, that the enthusiasm for Broadcast.com has been overdone. He says, "There are no entrenched players in this space. The 'old' media are aware that the intelligence to exploit the Internet lies outside their organizations and are standing back waiting to see what happens. Broadcast.com is well-positioned to be a service intermediary for those companies and for other content owners." Persuaded?

Note: The dollar amounts are in U.S. currency.

Source:

But what if the IPO is a primary issue that raises new cash for the company? Do the founders care whether the shares are sold for less than their market value? The following example illustrates that they do care.

Suppose Cosmos.com has two million shares outstanding and now offers a further one million shares to investors at $50. On the first day of trading, the share price jumps to $80, so that the shares that the company sold for $50 million are now worth $80 million. The total market capitalization of the company is 3 million × $80 = $240 million.

The value of the founders' shares is equal to the total value of the company *less* the value of the shares that have been sold to the public—in other words, $240 – $80 = $160 million. The founders might justifiably rejoice at their good fortune. However, if the company had issued shares at a higher price, it would have needed to sell fewer shares to raise the $50 million that it needs, and the founders would have retained a larger share of the company. For example, suppose that the outside investors, who put up $50 million, received shares that were *worth* only $50 million. In that case the value of the founders' shares would be $240 – $50 = $190 million.

The effect of selling shares below their true value is to transfer $30 million of value from the founders to the investors who buy the new shares.

Unfortunately, underpricing does not mean that anyone can become wealthy by buying stock in IPOs. If an issue is underpriced, everybody will want to buy it and the underwriters will not have enough stock to go around. You are therefore likely to get only a small share of these hot issues. If it is overpriced, other investors are unlikely to want it, and the underwriter will be only too delighted to sell it to you. This phenomenon is known as the *winner's curse.*[6] It implies that, unless you can spot which issues are underpriced, you are likely to receive a small proportion of the cheap issues and a large proportion of the expensive ones. Since the dice are loaded against uninformed investors, they will play the game only if there is substantial underpricing on average.

EXAMPLE 14.2 *Underpricing of IPOs and Investor Returns*

Suppose that an investor will earn an immediate 10 percent return on underpriced IPOs and lose 5 percent on overpriced IPOs. But because of high demand, you may get only half the shares you bid for when the issue is underpriced. Suppose you bid for $1,000 of shares in two issues, one overpriced and the other underpriced. You are awarded the full $1,000 of the overpriced issue, but only $500 worth of shares in the underpriced issue. The net gain on your two investments is $(.10 \times \$500) - (.05 \times \$1{,}000) = 0$. Your net profit is zero, despite the fact that on average, IPOs are underpriced. You have suffered the winner's curse: You "win" a larger allotment of shares when they are overpriced.

CHECK POINT 14.2

What is the percentage profit earned by an investor who can identify the underpriced issues in Example 14.2? Who are such investors likely to be?

flotation costs The costs incurred when a firm issues new securities to the public.

The costs of a new issue are termed **flotation costs.** Underpricing is not the only flotation cost. In fact, when people talk about the cost of a new issue, they often think only of the *direct costs* of the issue. For example, preparation of the registration statement and prospectus involves management, legal counsel, and accountants, as well as underwriters and their advisers. There is also the underwriting spread. (Remember, underwriters make their profit by selling the issue at a higher price than they paid for it.)

According to the Toronto Stock Exchange, Canadian companies raised over $20 billion in new equity financing in the first 10 months of 2000, including about $8 billion through 43 initial public offerings. Figure 14.1 summarizes the results of a study that compared the direct costs of going public, expressed as a percentage of total proceeds for IPO's on the TSE, Nasdaq, and NYSE over the period of January 1, 1998, and September 30, 1999.[7] Direct costs include underwriting commissions, legal, accounting and other administrative costs. In general, larger IPO issues have lower direct costs as a percentage of total proceeds. For a small IPO of no more than $10 million, the underwriting spread and administrative costs are likely to absorb over 11 to 17 percent of the proceeds from the issue depending on the exchange. For the very largest IPOs, these direct costs may amount to only 3.5 percent of the proceeds.

Figure 14.2 details the extent of underpricing on the three exchanges for a sub-sample of the group of IPOs discussed above. This is estimated by calculating the percentage difference between the offer price of the share and its closing price after the first day of trading. For the TSE, the simple average of the underpricing was 10 percent while the

[6] The highest bidder in an auction is the participant who places the highest value on the auctioned object. Therefore, it is likely that the winning bidder has an overly optimistic assessment of true value. Winning the auction suggests that you have overpaid for the object—this is the winner's curse. In the case of IPOs, your ability to "win" an allotment of shares may signal that the stock is overpriced.

[7] For complete details of the study, see T. Shutt and H. Williams, "Going to Market: The Costs of IPOs in Canada and the United States." The Conference Board of Canada (June 2000), pp. 1–4.

FIGURE 14.1
Direct cost as a percent of total proceeds (by size category, figures in millions, U.S. dollars)

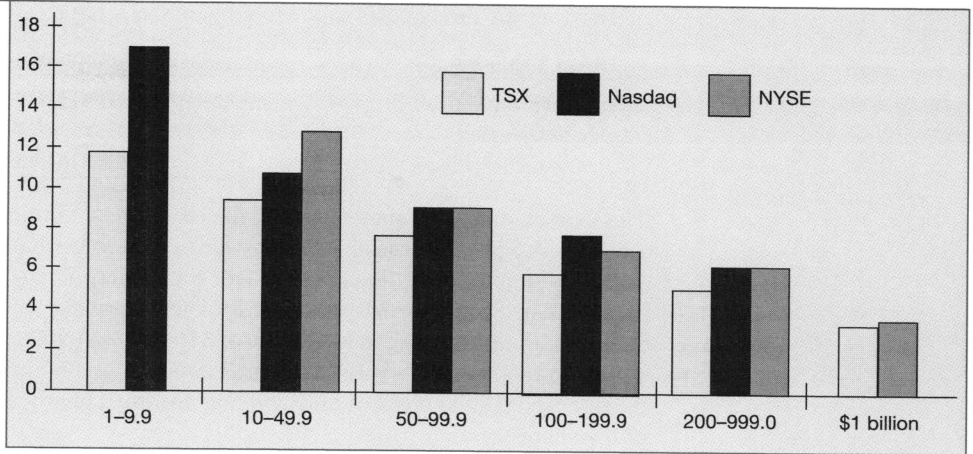

Source: Financial Post DataGroup, Securities Data Company. Excerpted from T. Shutt and H. Williams, "Going to Market: The Cost of IPOs in Canada and the United States," The Conference Board of Canada (June 2000), pp. 1–4.

weighted average was 5.8 percent. For the American exchanges, the numbers were found to be higher.

EXAMPLE 14.3 *Costs of an IPO*

When the American investment bank Goldman Sachs went public in 1999, the sale was partly a primary issue (the company sold new shares to raise cash) and partly a secondary one (two large existing shareholders cashed in some of their shares). The underwriters acquired a total of 69 million Goldman Sachs shares for $50.75 (US) each and sold them to the public at an offering price of $53.[8] The underwriters' spread was therefore $53 – $50.75 = $2.25. The firm and its shareholders also paid a total of $9.2 million in legal fees and other costs. By the end of the first day's trading, Goldman's stock price had risen to $70.

FIGURE 14.2
Degree of underpricing

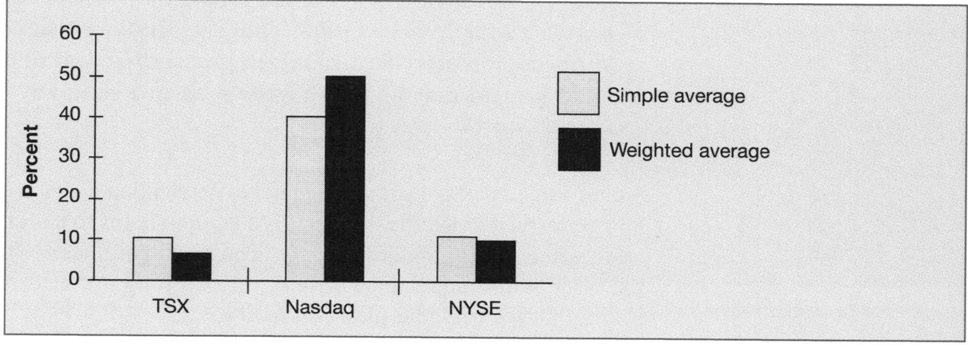

Source: Financial Post DataGroup, Securities Data Company. Excerpted from T. Shutt and H. Williams, "Going to Market: The Cost of IPOs in Canada and the United States," The Conference Board of Canada (June 2000), pp. 1–4.

[8] No prizes for guessing which investment bank acted as lead underwriter.

Here are the direct costs of the Goldman Sachs issue:

Direct Expenses	**(US$ in millions)**
Underwriting spread	69 million × \$2.25 = \$155.25
Other expenses	9.2
Total direct expenses	\$164.45

The total amount of money raised by the issue was 69 million × \$53 = \$3,657 million. Of this sum, 4.5 percent was absorbed by direct expenses (that is, 164.45/3,657 = .045).

In addition to these direct costs, there was underpricing. The market valued each share of Goldman Sachs at \$70, so the cost of underpricing was 69 million × (\$70 – \$53) = \$1,173 million, resulting in total costs of \$164.45 + \$1,173 = \$1,337.45 million. Therefore, while the total market value of the issued shares was 69 million × \$70 = \$4,830 million, direct costs and the costs of underpricing absorbed nearly 28 percent of the market value of the shares.

CHECK POINT 14.3

Suppose that the underwriters acquired Goldman Sachs shares for \$60 (US) and sold them to the public at an offering price of \$64. If all other features of the offer were unchanged (and investors still valued the stock at \$70 a share), what would have been the direct costs of the issue and the costs of underpricing? What would have been the total costs as a proportion of the market value of the shares?

14.3 The Underwriters

We have described underwriters as playing a triple role—providing advice, buying a new issue from the company, and reselling it to investors. Underwriters don't just help the company make its initial public offering; they are called in whenever a company wishes to raise cash by selling securities to the public.

Most companies raise capital only occasionally, but underwriters are in the business all the time. Established underwriters are careful of their reputation and will not handle a new issue unless they believe the facts have been presented fairly to investors. Thus, in addition to handling the sale of an issue, the underwriters, in effect, give it their seal of approval. This implied endorsement may be worth quite a bit to a company that is coming to the market for the first time.

For large issues, a group of underwriters called a *syndicate* or *banking group* will usually be formed to handle the sale. Syndication helps to market and distribute the issue more widely and also to spread its risks. The principal underwriter acts as the lead manager to the issue while other underwriters in the group are also responsible for buying and reselling the security, but play *non-lead* roles.

Underwriting is not always fun. On October 15, 1987, the British government finalized arrangements to sell its holding of British Petroleum (BP) shares at £3.30 a share. This huge issue involving more than \$12 billion was underwritten by an international group of underwriters and simultaneously marketed in a number of countries. Four days after the

TABLE 14.1
Canada's top underwriters for equity and debt, 2000 (dollar figures in millions)

Underwriter	No. as Lead	Value of Issues ($)	No. as Non-Lead	Value of Issues ($)	Total No. of Deals	Value of Issues ($)
RBC Dominion Securities	126	8,409	201	6,571	327	14,980
TD Securities	112	8,274	216	6,312	328	14,586
CIBC World Markets	110	6,627	212	6,750	322	13,376
BMO Nesbitt Burns	59	5,078	214	6,324	273	11,402
Scotia Capital	81	4,896	198	6,348	279	11,244
Merrill Lynch	45	4,552	144	4,633	189	9,184
National Bank Financial	58	2,689	172	3,433	230	6,122
Goldman Sachs	8	860	24	1,349	32	2,209
Credit Suisse First Boston	8	1,530	11	652	19	2,182
Saloman Smith Barney	13	1,502	6	281	19	1,783

Source: "The Dealmakers," the *National Post* (February 28, 2001), p. E4.

underwriting arrangement was finalized, the October stock market crash occurred and stock prices nose-dived. The underwriters appealed to the British government to cancel the issue but the government hardened its heart and pointed out that the underwriters knew the risks when they agreed to handle the sale.[9] By the closing date of the offer, the price of BP stock had fallen to £2.96, and the underwriters had lost more than $1 billion (US).

WHO ARE THE UNDERWRITERS?

Since underwriters play such a crucial role in new issues, we should look at who they are. Several hundred investment banks, security dealers, and brokers are, at least, sporadically involved in underwriting. However, the market for the larger issues is dominated by the major investment dealers, which specialize in underwriting new issues, dealing in securities, and arranging mergers. These firms enjoy great prestige, experience, and financial muscle.

Table 14.1 lists some of the largest Canadian firms, ranked by total value of issues in 2000. Notice that each of the firms has acted as a lead underwriter and also in a non-lead capacity within a syndicate. RBC Dominion Securities, the winner, raised a total of $14,980 million. Of course, only a small proportion of these issues was for companies that were coming to the market for the first time. Table 14.2 lists the top 10 Canadian corporate equity issues in 2000.

Some of the largest debt and equity issues are in the United States. In Chapter 13, we pointed out that instead of issuing bonds in Canada, corporations can issue eurobonds in London, which are then sold to investors outside Canada. In addition, new equity issues by large multinational companies are increasingly marketed to investors throughout the world. Since these securities are sold in a number of countries, many of the major international banks are involved in underwriting the issues. Have a look at Table 14.3. It shows the names of principal underwriters of global and U.S. debt and equity issues in 2000.

[9] The government's only concession was to put a floor on the underwriters' losses by giving them the option to resell their stock to the government at £2.80 a share. The BP offering is described and analyzed in C. Muscarella and M. Vetsuypens, "The British Petroleum Stock Offering: An Application of Option Pricing," *Journal of Applied Corporate Finance* 1 (1989), pp. 74–80.

TABLE 14.2
Top 10 corporate equity financing issues in 2000

Issuer	Total Proceeds in $*	Lead Underwriter
Sun Life Financial Services	2,064,291,888	RBC Dominion Securities
Celestica	1,519,840,000	RBC Dominion Securities
C-MAC Industries	1,081,000,000	Merrill Lynch
360networks	1,071,647,116	Goldman Sachs
Research In Motion	929,400,000	Merill Lynch
Canadian Hunter Exploration	618,844,339	CIBC World Markets
Royal Bank of Canada	575,874,000	RBC Dominion Securities
Pro-AMS U.S. Trust	570,518,825	RBC Dominion Securities
Ballard Power Systems	506,710,500	Morgan Stanley, Dean Witter
Biovail	434,520,000	Donaldson, Lufkin & Jenrette Securities

*Canadian equivalent

Source: "The Dealmakers," the *National Post* (February 28, 2001), p. E4.

TABLE 14.3
Top five underwriters of debt, equity and equity-related issues in 2000 (figures in millions, U.S. dollars)

Global			U.S.		
Underwriter	**Proceeds**	**No. of Issues**	**Underwriter**	**Proceeds**	**No. of Issues**
Merrill Lynch & Co., Inc.	380,366.6	3,148	Merril Lynch & Co., Inc.	289,887.7	2,736
Saloman Smith Barney	328,900.0	1,893	Salomon Smith Barney	251,704.2	1,514
Morgan Stanley Dean Witter	280,526.0	2,581	Credit Suisse First Boston	211,141.5	1,450
Credit Suisse First Boston	280,378.6	1,872	JP Morgan	207,172.6	1,305
JP Morgan	271,407.9	1,592	Morgan Stanley Dean Witter	194,656.8	2,131
Top 5 totals	1,541,579.1	11,086	**Top 5 totals**	1,154,562.8	9.136
Industry totals	3,042,185.3	20,427	**Industry totals**	1,957,895.1	15,686

Source: Thomson Financial website at www.tfsd.com.

14.4 Listing on the Stock Market

When a firm decides on an initial public offering of its stocks, it has to decide where its newly issued shares should be traded. As we have discussed in chapters 1 and 5, stock markets can be either organized exchanges with centralized physical locations or over-the-counter markets consisting of a network of security dealers who trade with each other over the phone and increasingly over electronic networks. Most trading in the shares of large Canadian corporations takes place on the Toronto Stock Exchange (TSX), while shares of smaller and emerging companies are traded through the Canadian Venture Exchange (CDNX). Electronic trading in shares can also be done through Nasdaq Canada, which recently launched operations in Montreal for the purpose of trading in shares listed on the Nasdaq stock market. Table 14.4 provides details regarding the trading activity for June 2001 of the Toronto Stock Exchange and the Canadian Venture Exchange.

In order to list its stock issue on a stock exchange, the firm will have to meet the exchange's listing requirements and pay the requisite listing fee. These tend to vary; generally, the larger and more prestigious stock exchanges also tend to have stricter listing requirements and higher listing fees. Table 14.5 summarizes major listing requirements of the TSX for profitable industrial companies.

TABLE 14.4
Trading activity on Canadian stock exchanges

	Trading Activity, June 2001	
Stock Exchange	**Value of Shares (Millions of Dollars)**	**Volume of Shares (Millions of Shares)**
Toronto Stock Exchange	$57,700	3,200
Canadian Venture Exchange	451	763

Source: The Toronto Stock Exchange website at www.tsx.com and the Canadian Venture Exchange website at www.cdnx.com.

TABLE 14.5
*Toronto Stock Exchange: major listing requirements for profitable industrial companies**

(i) *Assets:* Net tangible assets of $2,000,000.

(ii) *Earnings:* Earnings from ongoing operations of at least $200,000 before taxes and extraordinary items in the fiscal year immediately preceding the filing of the listing application.

(iii) *Cash Flow:* Pre-tax cash flow of $500,000 in the immediately preceding fiscal year.

(iv) *Working Capital and Capital Structure:* Adequate working capital to carry on the business and an appropriate capital structure.

(v) *Public Distribution:* At least 1,000,000 freely tradeable shares having an aggregate market value of $4,000,000 must be held by at least 300 public holders, each holding 100 or more shares. In circumstances where public distribution is achieved other than by way of a public offering, e.g., by way of a reverse take-over, share exchange offer, or other distribution, the Exchange may require evidence that a satisfactory market in the company's securities will develop. Prior trading on another market or sponsorship by a Participating Organization, which will assist in maintaining an orderly market, may satisfy this condition.

(vi) *Management:* Management (including the company's board of directors) should have adequate experience and technical expertise relevant to the company's business and industry and adequate public company experience. Companies will be required to have at least two Canadian directors unless they are foreign applicants that comply with all of the Minimum Listing Requirements for Foreign Companies.

* The requirements vary with the type of industrial companies, that is profitable companies, companies forecasting profitability, technology companies, or research and development companies. Different requirements also exist for mining, and oil and gas companies. Complete details regarding all listing requirements are provided on the TSX website at www.tsx.com.

14.5 Rights Issues and General Cash Offers by Public Companies

seasoned offering Sale of securities by a firm that is already publicly traded.

rights issue Issue of securities offered only to current shareholders.

After the initial public offering, a successful firm will continue to grow and from time to time it will need to raise more money by issuing stock or bonds. An issue of additional stock by a company whose stock already is publicly traded is called a **seasoned offering.** Any issue of securities needs to be formally approved by the firm's board of directors. If a stock issue requires an increase in the company's authorized capital, it also needs the consent of the shareholders.

Public companies can issue securities either by making a general cash offer to investors at large or by making a **rights issue,** which is limited to existing shareholders. Let us first concentrate on the mechanics of the rights issue.

RIGHTS ISSUES

In a rights issue, the company offers the shareholders the opportunity, or *right,* to buy more shares at an "attractive" subscription price. For example, if the current stock price is $100, the company might offer investors an additional share at $50 for each share they hold. Suppose that before the issue an investor has one share worth $100 and $50 in the bank. If the investor takes up the offer of a new share, that $50 of cash is transferred from the investor's bank account to the company's. The investor now has two shares that are a claim on the original assets worth $100 and on the $50 cash that the company has raised. So the two shares are worth a total of $150, or $75 each.

By directly offering a new share issue to existing shareholders, a company could hope to save on issuing and underwriting expenses. Also, shareholders do not run a risk of dilution of their proportional shareholding and are able to retain their voting position on the company's major business decisions. Of course, shareholders will have an incentive to exercise their rights only if the subscription price stays below the market price of the shares. Otherwise, if the share price falls, the full issue of new shares may not be taken up. To protect against this possibility, the firm may enter into a **standby underwriting agreement** with an investment dealer. Under this arrangement, the underwriter stands ready to purchase any unsold shares and receives a *standby fee* and possible additional amounts depending on the extent of unsold shares. Also, the company may give its shareholders an **oversubscription privilege** under which they will be able to purchase any unsold shares at the subscription price. Of course, a small proportion of shareholders may not exercise their rights, perhaps because they are away on vacation or for other personal reasons.

standby underwriting agreement The underwriter stands ready to purchase any unsold shares.

oversubscription privilege Given to shareholders in a rights issue, enabling them to purchase any unsold shares at the subscription price.

In some countries, rights issues are the most common or only method for issuing common stock. In Canada, they are less common. Sometimes, a preemptive right is contained in the firm's articles of incorporation, in which case, the firm has to offer any new issue of common stock to its existing shareholders.

In a rights offering, existing shareholders receive one right for each share of stock held. To take advantage of the rights offering, shareholders will have to exercise the right within a specified period of time by submitting a completed subscription form to the company's subscription agent. If rights are not exercised within the period stipulated, they will expire.

▸ EXAMPLE 14.4 *Rights Issues*

Easy Writer Word Processing Company has one million shares outstanding, selling at $20 a share. To finance the development of a new software package, it plans a rights issue, allowing one new share to be purchased for each 10 shares currently held. The purchase price will be $10 a share. How many shares will be issued? How much money will be raised? What will be the stock price after the rights issue?

The firm will issue one new share for every 10 old ones, or 100,000 shares. So shares outstanding will rise to 1.1 million. The firm will raise $10 × 100,000 = $1 million. Therefore, the total value of the firm will increase from $20 million to $21 million, and the stock price will fall to $21 million/1.1 million shares = $19.09 per share.

The standard procedure for issuing rights involves the firm announcing the issue and setting a **holder-of-record date**. This is the date on which existing shareholders, as listed in the company's records, are entitled to the stock rights. Actually, to comply with stock exchange rules, the stock will usually go *ex-rights* four trading days before the holder-of-record date. If the stock is sold before this date, the new owner will receive the rights, and so, its value will be *with rights*, *rights-on*, or *cum-rights*. If the stock is sold after the **ex-rights date**, the buyer will no longer be entitled to the rights.

holder-of-record date The date on which shareholders appearing on company records are entitled to receive the stock rights.

ex-rights date This date is usually four business days before the holder-of-record date.

Since rights offerings enable shareholders to buy shares at a favourable price, they clearly have value. How would you arrive at the value of a right? Notice that to buy one new share, the existing shareholder will have to use 10 rights and pay the purchase price of $10. However, the market price of the share after the rights issue, that is the ex-rights price, is $19.09. We can, therefore, formulate an equation that will give the theoretical value of a right.

$$\text{Value of one right} = \frac{\begin{array}{c}\text{Market value of}\\ \text{share, ex-rights}\end{array} - \text{subscription price}}{\begin{array}{c}\text{Number of rights required}\\ \text{to purchase a share}\end{array}}$$

$$= \frac{\$19.09 - \$10}{10} = \frac{\$9.09}{10} = \$0.91$$

You can also arrive at the theoretical value of a right by using the price of the stock during the cum-rights period.

$$\text{Value of one right} = \frac{\begin{array}{c}\text{Market value of}\\ \text{share, rights on}\end{array} - \text{subscription price}}{\begin{array}{c}\text{Number of rights required}\\ \text{to purchase a share}\end{array} + 1}$$

$$= \frac{\$20 - \$10}{10 + 1} = \frac{\$10}{11} = \$0.91$$

Suppose Easy Writer Word Processing Company announces the terms of its rights offering on May 31, stating that the rights would be mailed to shareholders of record as of July 15. In this case, the ex-rights date is July 11, and so shareholders who own the stock until July 10 are entitled to receive the rights. The rights-on price of the shares is $20 and it drops to the ex-rights price of $19.09. Notice that the share price drops by $.91, that is, to the extent of the value of a right.

GENERAL CASH OFFERS

general cash offer Sale of securities open to all investors by an already-public company.

When a public company makes a **general cash offer** of debt or equity, it essentially follows the same procedure used when it first went public. This means that it must first register the issue in compliance with the regulations of relevant provincial commissions. The issue is then sold to an underwriter under a firm-commitment arrangement or on a best-effort basis.[10] The underwriter (or syndicate of underwriters), in turn, offers the securities to the public.

bought deal The underwriter buys securities from the issuing company and sells them to investors.

Many underwriting agreements, including those involving firm commitments, may contain a *market-out clause*, which limits the underwriters' risk. This clause can enable the underwriter to terminate the underwriting agreement without penalty under extraordinary circumstances or even if the underwriter judges that the state of the financial market is not good for the security issue. In Canada, competition for lucrative underwriting deals and a dislike of the market-out clause among investors has created an environment for **bought deals,** which are often used by large, well-known companies for their seasoned equity issues. Here, the investment dealer buys the entire offering from the issuing company and then decides how to sell it to investors. This is advantageous to the company because it is

[10] A large issue will typically be handled by a syndicate of underwriters.

able to obtain a relatively quick and firm commitment on its securities. Bought deals are not commonly used in the United States.

prompt offering prospectus (POP) system Allows qualified firms quicker access to capital markets by enabling them to use a short-form filing process rather than a full prospectus.

Usually the large issuers in Canada who go for bought deals can also take advantage of the **Prompt Offering Prospectus (POP) system**, which allows short-form filing since much of the information contained in the regular prospectus is already expected to have been filed annually. Thus under the POP system, only material changes and financial statements have to be provided to regulators who are able to give their clearance within about five days—instead of several weeks required for a full prospectus. The investing public must still be provided with a regular prospectus. In the United States, companies can take advantage of **shelf registration**, which allows them to file a single registration statement covering financing plans for up to 2 years into the future. Within this time period, companies to not need to prepare a separate registration statement every time they issue new securities.

shelf registration A procedure followed in the U.S. that allows firms to file one registration statement for several issues of the same security.

COSTS OF THE GENERAL CASH OFFER

Whenever a firm makes a cash offer, it incurs substantial administrative costs. Also, the firm needs to compensate the underwriters by selling them securities below the price that they expect to receive from investors. Figure 14.3 shows the average underwriting spread and administrative costs for several types of security issues in the United States.[11]

The figure clearly shows the economies of scale in issuing securities. Costs may absorb 15 percent of a $1 million (US) seasoned equity issue but less than 4 percent of a $500 million issue. This occurs because a large part of the issue cost is fixed. The costs are similar in Canada.[12]

Figure 14.3 shows that issue costs are higher for equity than for debt securities—the costs for both types of securities, however, show the same economies of scale. Issue costs are higher for equity than for debt because administrative costs are somewhat higher, and also because underwriting stock is riskier than underwriting bonds. The underwriters demand additional compensation for the greater risk they take in buying and reselling equity.

☑ CHECK POINT 14.4

Use Figure 14.3 to compare the costs of 10 issues of $15 million (US) of stock in a seasoned offering versus one issue of $150 million (US).

MARKET REACTION TO STOCK ISSUES

Because stock issues usually throw a sizable number of new shares onto the market, it is widely believed that they must temporarily depress the stock price. If the proposed issue is very large, this price pressure may, it is thought, be so severe as to make it almost impossible to raise money.

This belief in price pressure implies that a new issue depresses the stock price temporarily below its true value. However, that view doesn't appear to fit very well with the

[11] These figures do not capture all administrative costs. For example, they do not include management time spent on the issue.

[12] A recent study finds that average Canadian underwriter fees for medium-sized IPOs ($10 to 50 million) average 6 percent, compared with a U.S. average of 7 percent. See L. Kryzanowski and I. Rakita "Is the U.S. 7 percent Solution Equivalent to the Canadian 6 percent Solution?" *Canadian Investment Review* (Fall 1999), Volume 2, pp. 27–34.

FIGURE 14.3

Total direct costs as a percentage of gross proceeds. The total direct costs for initial public offerings (IPOs), seasoned equity offerings (SEOs), convertible bonds, and straight bonds are composed of underwriter spreads and other direct expenses.

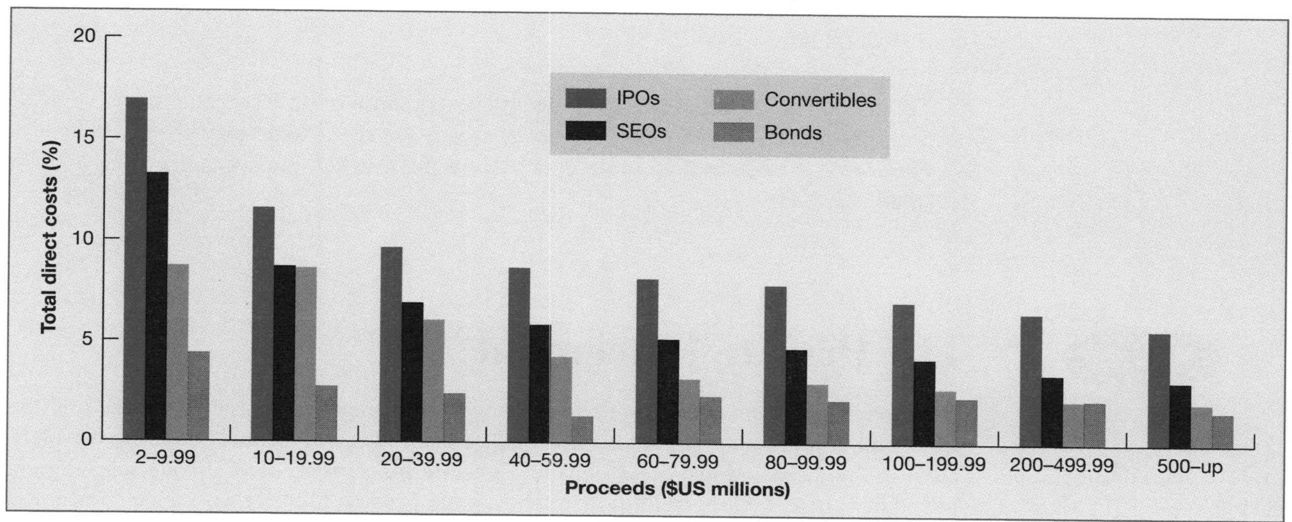

Source: I. Lee, S. Lochhead, J. Ritter, and Q. Zhao, "The Costs of Raising Capital," *Journal of Financial Research* 19 (Spring 1996), pp. 59–74. Copyright © 1996. Reprinted by permission.

notion of market efficiency. If the stock price falls solely because of increased supply, then that stock would offer a higher return than comparable stocks, and investors would be attracted to it like ants to a picnic.

Economists who have studied new issues of common stock have generally found that the announcement of the issue *does* result in a decline in the stock price. For industrial issues in the United States, this decline amounts to about 3 percent.[13] While this may not sound overwhelming, such a price drop can be a large fraction of the money raised. Suppose that a company with a market value of equity of $5 billion announces its intention to issue $500 million of additional equity and thereby causes the stock price to drop by 3 percent. The loss in value is .03 × $5 billion, or $150 million. That's 30 percent of the amount of money raised (.30 × $500 million = $150 million).

What's going on here? Is the price of the stock simply depressed by the prospect of the additional supply? Possibly, but here is an alternative explanation.

Suppose managers (who have better information about the firm than outside investors) know that their stock is undervalued. If the company sells new stock at this low price, it will give the new shareholders a good deal at the expense of the old shareholders. In these circumstances managers might be prepared to forgo the new investment rather than sell shares at too low a price.

If managers know that the stock is *overvalued,* the position is reversed. If the company

[13] See, for example, P. Asquith and D. W. Mullins, "Equity Issues and Offering Dilution," *Journal of Financial Economics* 15 (January–February 1986), pp. 61–90; R. W. Masulis and A. N. Korwar, "Seasoned Equity Offerings: An Empirical Investigation," *Journal of Financial Economics* 15 (January–February 1986), pp. 91–118; W. H. Mikkelson and M. M. Partch, "Valuation Effects of Security Offerings and the Issuance Process," *Journal of Financial Economics* 15 (January–February 1986), pp. 31–60. There appears to be a smaller price decline for utility issues. Also Marsh observed a smaller decline for rights issues in the United Kingdom; see P. R. Marsh, "Equity Rights Issues and the Efficiency of the UK Stock Market," *Journal of Finance* 34 (September 1979), pp. 839–862.

sells new shares at the high price, it will help its existing shareholders at the expense of the new ones. Managers might be prepared to issue stock even if the new cash were just put in the bank.

Of course investors are not stupid. They can predict that managers are more likely to issue stock when they think it is overvalued, and therefore, they mark the price of the stock down accordingly.

The tendency for stock prices to decline at the time of an issue may have nothing to do with increased supply. Instead, the stock issue may simply be a *signal* that well-informed managers believe the market has overpriced the stock.[14]

14.6 The Private Placement

private placement Sale of securities to a limited number of investors without a public offering.

Whenever a company makes a public offering, it must register the issue with the relevant provincial commission. It could avoid this costly process by selling the issue privately. There are no hard and fast definitions of a **private placement**. Most private sales of debt and equity are to exempt institutions such as large pension funds or insurance companies, which are considered to be knowledgeable buyers and will not require all the information provided in a regular prospectus. Presently, the minimum investment requirement for a private placement is $150,000, which effectively shuts out average investors, although some wealthy individuals do participate as buyers.

One disadvantage of a private placement is that the investor cannot easily resell the security. This is less important to institutions such as insurance companies, which invest huge sums of money in corporate debt for the long haul.

As you would expect, it costs less to arrange a private placement than to make a public issue. That might not be so important for the very large issues where costs are less significant, but it is a particular advantage for companies making smaller issues.

Another advantage of the private placement is that the debt contract can be custom-tailored for firms with special problems or opportunities. Also, if the firm wishes later to change the terms of the debt, it is much simpler to do this with a private placement where only a few investors are involved.

Therefore, it is not surprising that private placements occupy a particular niche in the corporate debt market, namely, loans to small- and medium-sized firms. These are the firms that face the highest costs in public issues, that require the most detailed investigation, and that may require specialized, flexible loan arrangements.

We do not mean that large, safe, and conventional firms should rule out private placements. Enormous amounts of capital are sometimes raised by this method. For example, Air Canada recently borrowed $400 million through a private placement of senior unsecured debt. Also, Rogers Sugar, Ltd., a large confectioner based in Western Canada, had a $100 million private placement offering managed by CIBC World Markets. Nevertheless, the advantages of private placement—avoiding registration costs and establishing a direct relationship with the lender—are generally more important to smaller firms.

[14] This explanation was developed in S. C. Myers and N. S. Mailuf's "Corporate Financing and Investment Decisions When Firms Have Information That Investors Do Not Have," *Journal of Financial Economics* 13 (1984), pp. 187–222.

Of course these advantages are not free. Lenders in private placements have to be compensated for the risks they face and for the costs of research and negotiation. They also have to be compensated for holding an asset that is not easily resold. All these factors are rolled into the interest rate paid by the firm. It is difficult to generalize about the differences in interest rates between private placements and public issues, but a typical yield differential could be on the order of half a percentage point.

14.7 Summary

1. **How do venture capital firms design successful deals?**

Infant companies raise **venture capital** to carry them through to the point where they can make their first public issue of stock. More established publicly traded companies can issue additional securities in a **general cash offer.**

Financing choices should be designed to avoid conflicts of interest. This is especially important in the case of a young company that is raising venture capital. If both managers and investors have an important equity stake in the company, they are likely to pull in the same direction. The willingness to take that stake also *signals* management's confidence in the new company's future. Therefore, most deals require that the entrepreneur maintain large stakes in the firm. In addition, most venture financing is done in stages that keep the firm on a short leash and force it to prove, at several crucial points, that it is worthy of additional investment.

2. **How do firms make initial public offerings and what are the costs of such offerings?**

The **initial public offering** is the first sale of shares in a general offering to investors. The sale of the securities is usually managed by an underwriting firm that buys the shares from the company and resells them to the public. The **underwriter** helps to prepare a **prospectus,** which describes the company and its prospects. The costs of an IPO include direct costs such as legal and administrative fees as well as the **underwriting spread**—the difference between the price the underwriter pays to acquire the shares from the firm and the price the public pays the underwriter for those shares. Another major implicit cost is the **underpricing** of the issue—that is, shares are typically sold to the public somewhat below the true value of the security. This discount is reflected in abnormally high average returns to new issues on the first day of trading.

3. **What are some of the significant issues that arise when established firms make a rights issue, a general cash offer, or a private placement of securities?**

There are always economies of scale in issuing securities. It is cheaper to go to the market once for $100 million than to make two trips for $50 million each. Consequently, firms "bunch" security issues. This may mean relying on short-term financing until a large issue is justified. Or it may mean issuing more than is needed at the moment to avoid another issue later.

A **seasoned offering** may depress the stock price. The extent of this price decline varies, but for issues of common stocks by industrial firms, the fall in the value of the existing stock may amount to a significant proportion of the money raised. The likely explanation for this pressure is the information the market reads into the company's decision to issue stock.

The **Prompt Offering Prospectus (POP) system** often makes sense for equity or debt issues by well-established companies. It allows short-form filing to regulators and, thereby, reduces the time taken to arrange a new issue.

Private placements are well-suited for small, risky, or unusual firms. Of course, established and conventional firms also often raise large sums of capital by this method. The special advantages of private placement stem from avoiding registration expenses and getting a more direct relationship with the lender.

4. **What is the role of the underwriter in an issue of securities?**

The underwriter manages the sale of the securities for the issuing company. The underwriting firms have expertise in such sales because they are in the business all the time, whereas the company raises capital only occasionally. Moreover, the underwriters may give an implicit seal of approval to the offering. Because the underwriters will not want to squander their reputation by misrepresenting facts to the public, the implied endorsement may be quite important to a firm coming to the market for the first time.

Related Web Links

www.FreeEDGAR.com Information on registration of new securities offerings in the United States
http://cbs.marketwatch.com/news/current/ipo_rep.htx?source=htx/http2_mw List of new IPOs
www.cob.ohio-state.edu/~fin/resources_education/credit.htm The changing mix of corporate financing
www.vnpartners.com/primer.htm Venture capital as a source of project financing
www.strategis.ic.gc.ca Industry Canada
www.bdc.ca Business Development Bank of Canada
www.venturedrive.com Early stage financing
www.rim.net Research In Motion
www.osc.gov.on.ca Ontario Securities Commission
www.sedar.com Information on document filings by Canadian companies including for new securities
www.724.com 724 Solutions
www.cvca.ca Canadian Venture Capital Association (CVCA)
www.canadavc.com Venture capital information
www.iclub.com/investorama.html Products and services targeted at investment clubs

Key Terms

venture capital	410	flotation costs	416	general cash offer	423
angel	410	seasoned offering	421	bought deal	423
initial public offering (IPO)	412	rights issue	421	prompt offering prospectus (POP) system	424
underwriter	413	standby underwriting agreement	422	shelf registration	424
spread	413	oversubscription privilege	422	private placement	426
prospectus	413	holder-of-record date	422		
underpricing	414	ex-rights date	422		

Questions and Problems

*Answers in Appendix B

Basic

*1. **Underwriting.**
   a. Is a rights issue more likely to be used for an initial public offering or for subsequent issues of stock?
   b. Is a private placement more likely to be used for issues of seasoned stock or seasoned bonds by an industrial company?
   c. Is the Prompt Offering Prospectus (POP) system more likely to be used for issues of unseasoned stocks or bonds by a large industrial company?

2. **Underwriting.** Each of the following terms is associated with one of the events beneath. Can you match them up?
   a. Red herring
   b. Firm commitment
   c. Rights issue
   A. The underwriter agrees to buy the issue from the company at a fixed price.
   B. The company offers to sell stock to existing stockholders.
   C. The company issues a preliminary prospectus for distribution to the public.

*3. **Underwriting Costs.** For each of the following pairs of issues state which of the two you would expect to involve the lower proportionate underwriting and administrative costs, other things being equal:
   a. a large issue/a small issue
   b. a bond issue/a common stock issue
   c. a small private placement of bonds/a small general cash offer of bonds

*4. **IPO Costs.** Why are the issue costs for debt issues generally less than those for equity issues?

5. **Venture Capital.** Why do venture capital companies prefer to advance money in stages?

6. **IPOs.** Your broker calls and says that you can get 500 shares of an imminent IPO at the offering price. Should you buy? Are you worried about the fact that your broker called *you?*

PRACTICE

*7. **IPO Underpricing.** Having heard about IPO underpricing, I put in an order to my broker for 1,000 shares of every IPO he can get for me. After 3 months, my investment record is as follows:

IPO	Shares Allocated to Me	Price per Share	Initial Return
A	500	$10	7%
B	200	20	12
C	1,000	8	–2
D	0	12	23

a. What is the average underpricing of this sample of IPOs?
b. What is the average initial return on my "portfolio" of shares purchased from the four IPOs I bid on? Calculate the average initial return, weighting by the amount of money invested in each issue.
c. Why have I performed so poorly relative to the average initial return on the full sample of IPOs? What lessons do you draw from my experience?

8. **IPO Costs.** Moonscape has just completed an initial public offering. The firm sold three million shares at an offer price of $8 per share. The underwriting spread was $.50 a share. The price of the stock closed at $11 per share at the end of the first day of trading. The firm incurred $100,000 in legal, administrative, and other costs. What were flotation costs as a fraction of funds raised?

9. **IPO Costs.** Look at the illustrative new-issue prospectus in Appendix 14B.

a. Is this issue a primary offering, a secondary offering, or both?
b. What are the direct costs of the issue as a percentage of the total proceeds? Are these more than the average for an issue of this size?
c. Suppose that on the first day of trading the price of Hotch Pot's stock is $15 a share. What are the *total* costs of the issue as a percentage of the market price?
d. After paying her share of the expenses, how much will the firm's president, Emma Lucullus, receive from the sale? What will be the value of the shares that she retains in the company?

*10. **Flotation Costs.** "For small issues of common stock, the costs of flotation amount to about 15 percent of the proceeds. This means that the opportunity cost of external equity capital is about 15 percentage points higher than that of retained earnings." Does this make sense?

11. **Flotation Costs.** When Microsoft went public, the company sold two million new shares (the primary issue). In addition, existing shareholders sold .8 million shares (the secondary issue) and kept 21.1 million shares. The new shares were offered to the public at $21, and the underwriters received a spread of $1.31 a share. At the end of the first day's trading, the market price was $35 a share.

a. How much money did the company receive before paying its portion of the direct costs?
b. How much did the existing shareholders receive from the sale before paying their portion of the direct costs?
c. If the issue had been sold to the underwriters for $30 a share, how many shares would the company have needed to sell to raise the same amount of cash?
d. How much better off would the existing shareholders have been?

*12. **Flotation Costs.** The market value of the marketing research firm Fax Facts is $600 million. The firm issues an additional $100 million of stock, but as a result the stock price falls by 2 percent. What is the cost of the price drop to existing shareholders as a fraction of the funds raised?

13. **Flotation Costs.** Young Corporation stock currently sells for $30 per share. There are one million shares currently outstanding. The company announces plans to raise $3 million by offering shares to the public at a price of $30 per share.
    a. If the underwriting spread is 8 percent, how many shares will the company need to issue in order to be left with net proceeds of $3 million?
    b. If other administrative costs are $60,000, what is the dollar value of the total direct costs of the issue?
    c. If the share price falls by 3 percent at the announcement of the plans to proceed with a seasoned offering, what is the dollar cost of the announcement effect?

*14. **Private Placements.** You need to choose between the following types of issues:

    A public issue of $10 million face value of 10-year debt. The interest rate on the debt would be 8.5 percent and the debt would be issued at face value. The underwriting spread would be 1.5 percent and other expenses would be $80,000.

    A private placement of $10 million face value of 10-year debt. The interest rate on the private placement would be 9 percent, but the total issuing expenses would be only $30,000.

    a. What is the difference in the proceeds to the company's net of expenses?
    b. Other things being equal, which is the better deal?
    c. What other factors beyond the interest rate and issue costs would you wish to consider before deciding between the two offers?

*15. **Rights.** In 2001, Pandora, Inc., makes a rights issue at a subscription price of $5 a share. One new share can be purchased for every four shares held. Before the issue there were 10 million shares outstanding, and the share price was $6.
    a. What is the total amount of new money raised?
    b. What is the expected stock price after the rights are issued?

16. **Rights.** Problem 15 contains details of a rights offering by Pandora. Suppose that the company had decided to issue the new stock at $4 instead of $5 a share. How many new shares would it have needed to raise the same sum of money? Recalculate the answers to problem 15. Show that Pandora's shareholders are just as well off if it issues the shares at $4 a share rather than $5, assumed in problem 15.

*17. **Rights.** Consolidated Jewels needs to raise $2 million to pay for its Diamonds in the Rough campaign. It will raise the funds by offering 200,000 rights, each of which entitles the owner to buy one new share. The company currently has one million shares outstanding priced at $20 each.
    a. What must be the subscription price on the rights the company plans to offer?
    b. What will be the share price after the rights issue?
    c. What is the value of a right to buy one share?
    d. How many rights would be issued to an investor who currently owns 1,000 shares?
    e. Show that the investor who currently holds 1,000 shares is unaffected by the rights issue. Specifically, show that the value of the rights plus the value of the 1,000 shares after the rights issue equals the value of the 1,000 shares before the rights issue.

18. **Rights.** Associated Breweries is planning to market unleaded beer. To finance the venture it proposes to make a rights issue with a subscription price of $10. One new share can be purchased for each two shares held. The company currently has 100,000 shares outstanding priced at $40 a share. Assuming that the new money is invested to earn a fair return, give values for the
    a. number of new shares
    b. amount of new investment
    c. total value of company after issue
    d. total number of shares after issue
    e. share price after the issue

CHALLENGE

19. **Venture Capital.** Here is a difficult question. Pickwick Electronics is a new high-tech company financed entirely by one million ordinary shares, all of which are owned by George Pickwick. The firm needs to raise $1 million now for stage one and, assuming all goes well, a further $1 million at the end of 5 years for stage two.

    First Cookham Venture Partners is considering two possible financing schemes:

    1. Buying two million shares now at their current valuation of $1.
    2. Buying one million shares at the current valuation and investing a further $1 million at the end of 5 years at whatever the shares are worth.

    The outlook for Pickwick is uncertain, but as long as the company can secure the additional financing for stage two, it will be worth either $2 million or $12 million after completing stage two. (The company will be valueless if it cannot raise the funds for stage two.) Show the possible payoffs for Mr. Pickwick and First Cookham and explain why one scheme might be preferred. Assume an interest rate of zero.

SOLUTIONS TO CHECK POINTS

14.1 Unless the firm can secure second-stage financing, it is unlikely to succeed. If the entrepreneur is going to reap any reward on his own investment, he needs to put in enough effort to get further financing. By accepting only part of the necessary venture capital, management increases its own risk and reduces that of the venture capitalist. This decision would be costly and foolish if management lacked confidence that the project would be successful enough to get past the first stage. A credible signal by management is one that only managers who are truly confident can afford to provide. However, words are cheap and there is little to be lost by *saying* that you are confident (although if you are proved wrong, you may find it difficult to raise money a second time).

14.2 If an investor can distinguish between overpriced and underpriced issues, she will bid only on the underpriced ones. In this case she will purchase only issues that provide a 10 percent gain. However, the ability to distinguish these issues requires considerable insight and research. The return to the informed IPO participant may be viewed as a return on the resources expended to become informed.

14.3 Direct expenses

	Figures in millions
Underwriting spread = 69 million × $4	$ 276.0
Other expenses	9.2
Total direct expenses	$ 285.2
Underpricing = 69 million × ($70 – $64)	$ 414.0
Total expenses	$ 699.2
Market value of issue = 69 million × $70	$4,830.0

Expenses as proportion of market value = 699.2/4,830 = .145 = 14.5%.

14.4 Ten issues of $15 million each will cost about 9 percent of proceeds, or .09 × $150 million = $13.5 million. One issue of $150 million will cost only 4 percent of $150 million, or $6 million.

MINICASE

Pet.Com was founded in 1997 by two graduates of the University of Wisconsin with help from Georgina Sloberg, who had built up an enviable reputation for backing new start-up businesses. Pet.Com's user-friendly system was designed to find buyers for unwanted pets. Within 3 years the company was generating revenues of $3.4 million a year, and despite racking up sizable losses, was regarded by investors as one of the hottest new e-commerce businesses. The news that the company was preparing to go public therefore generated considerable excitement.

The company's entire equity capital of 1.5 million shares was owned by the two founders and Ms. Sloberg. The initial public offering involved the sale of 500,000 shares by the three existing shareholders, together with the sale of a further 750,000 shares by the company in order to provide funds for expansion.

The company estimated that the issue would involve legal fees, auditing, printing, and other expenses of $1.3 million, which would be shared proportionately between the selling shareholders and the company. In addition, the company agreed to pay the underwriters a spread of $1.25 per share.

The roadshow had confirmed the high level of interest in the issue, and indications from investors suggested that the entire issue could be sold at a price of $24 a share. The underwriters, however, cautioned about being too greedy on price. They pointed out that indications from investors were not the same as firm orders. Also, they argued, it was much more important to have a successful issue than to have a group of disgruntled shareholders. They therefore suggested an issue price of $18 a share.

That evening Pet.Com's financial manager decided to run through some calculations. First she worked out the net receipts to the company and the existing shareholders, assuming that the stock was sold for $18 a share. Next she looked at the various costs of the IPO and tried to judge how they stacked up against the typical costs for similar IPOs. That brought her up against the question of underpricing. When she had raised the matter with the underwriters that morning, they had dismissed the notion that the initial day's return on an IPO should be considered part of the issue costs. One of the members of the underwriting team had asked: "The underwriters want to see a high return and a high stock price. Would Pet.Com prefer a low stock price? Would that make the issue less costly?" Pet.Com's financial manager was not convinced but felt that she should have a good answer. She wondered whether underpricing was only a problem because the existing shareholders were selling part of their holdings. Perhaps the issue price would not matter if they had not planned to sell.

Appendix 14A: The Financing of New and Small Enterprises

Venture Capital in Canada

We saw in Section 14.1 that venture capital is an important source of equity for start-up companies that have the potential to develop into significant economic contributors. Venture capitalists make risky investments with the expectation of earning high rewards if the young ventures become successful. Often, their investments pay off handsomely, as in the case of companies such as Microsoft, Intel, or Research In Motion, which are today established leaders in their respective industries. Of course, venture capitalists may seek to lessen the risk of venture investing in a number of ways. For instance, before making investment decisions, they try to carefully screen the technical and business merits of the proposed company, and usually end up investing in only a small percentage of the businesses they review. They also like to actively work with managements of companies they invest in by contributing their business knowledge and experience, gained from helping other companies with similar growth challenges. Often, they diversify their investments by developing a portfolio of young companies in a single venture fund. Many times they will co-invest with other professional venture capital firms in syndicated investment arrangements. In addition, many venture capitalists manage multiple funds together. Table 14.A1 lists some of the important attributes of classic venture capital investing.

TYPES OF VENTURE CAPITAL FUNDS

In Canada, venture capital activity has grown significantly over the last decade. For instance, in 1990 there were 34 venture funds with $3.3 billion worth of capital under management. By 2000, the number of funds had grown to 150. Together, these funds had over $18 billion worth of capital under management.

Canada's venture capital funds can be grouped into one of five categories: private independent, labour-sponsored, corporate, government and hybrid.[15] *Private independent firms* typically have no affiliations with any other financial institution. Some large private independent funds have been very active. For instance, in 2000, slightly more than $4 billion of new capital flowed into the industry across all fund types, with private independent funds attracting about 40 percent of this new capital. Another 40 percent went to labour-sponsored venture capital funds, which we will describe next.

Labour-sponsored funds are venture capital pools formed with the help of provincial and federal governments. These funds were mostly introduced in the late 1980s to facilitate business and economic growth. By 2000, these had about 50 percent of the money invested in the venture capital industry, mainly because of generous tax incentives given to investors in such funds. Presently, investors receive a 15 percent tax credit from both the federal government and participating provincial governments. Moreover, the investment is Registered Retirement Savings Plan (RRSP) eligible, and therefore, provides the investor with an additional tax benefit in the form of a tax deferral, but it depends on the investor's

TABLE 14.A1
Attributes of classic venture capital investing

1. Create new businesses or expand or revitalize existing ones.
2. The investor, usually the venture capital (VC) fund's general manager and associates, are involved in the management of their portfolio companies, providing a great deal of "value-added" to their companies.
3. The *potential* return from the investment is quite large due to investing in high risk/high reward situations.
4. Only a few investments are made each year after many candidates have been screened and a handful have been fully analyzed.
5. Negotiate appropriate financial structures using individualized investment instruments.
6. Take a long-term orientation towards their portfolio companies because of the illiquidity of their investments.
7. Try to maximize the growth of their funds since the VC receives as incentive, compensation as a percentage of the capital gains after return of capital.
8. Venture capitalists often diversify their risk by syndicating their investment with other VC funds.

Based on information in K. W. Rind, "The Role of Venture Capital in Corporate Development," *Strategic Management Journal* (April–June 1981), pp. 169–180.

Source: A. Best and D. Mitra, "The Venture Capital Industry in Canada," *Journal of Small Business Management* (April 1997), Vol. 35, No. 2, pp. 105–110.

[15] These classifications are used by the Canadian Venture Capital Association (CVCA) to provide periodic reports on venture capital activity. The reports are available on its website at www.cvca.ca. Data for these reports is often compiled by Macdonald and Associates, Ltd., which is the best-known data source of Canadian venture capital activity.

income level. Labour-sponsored funds are structured in a similar fashion to mutual funds. Individuals are able to buy shares in the fund, allowing investment by those who are not wealthy. The fund pools the money with the objective of investing in enterprises that have yet to go public, instead of purchasing stocks and bonds. Three large and active labour-sponsored funds are Working Ventures, sponsored by the Canadian Federation of Labour, Fonds de Solidarité des Travailleurs du Québec, and Triax Growth Fund.

A number of *Corporate Venture Capital Funds* also exist in Canada. These could include financial corporation funds, which tend to be venture capital affiliates or subsidiaries set up by large Canadian banks. For instance, Royal Bank Ventures, Inc. is a subsidiary of the Royal Bank Financial Group. The financial institution can provide a range of financial services to entrepreneurs and enhance their credibility with suppliers and customers. You could also have subsidiaries of large manufacturing companies such as Dow Chemical Venture Capital Group, or subsidiaries of utility and power corporations such as Hydro-Québec Capitech, Inc. Goals of corporate venture capital funds tend to be strategically tied to the parent organization; they often prefer to invest in ventures that will give them access to new technologies or provide a competitive advantage. For instance, recently, Ballard Power Systems, Westcoast Energy, and the multinational giant Royal Dutch/Shell Group announced the launch of Chrysalix Energy, a new multimillion dollar fund which will back new energy ventures, particularly in the area of fuel-cell technology.

Federal or provincial governments run *government funds* by employing professional venture capital fund managers. For instance, the federal Business Development Corporation (BDC) has an active venture capital division which, for the end of fiscal year March 2001, had a total commitment of venture capital investments of $296 million. The BDC has focused on using venture capital to generate growth in new economy industries such as biotechnology, medical/health-related, and information technology. Much of the financing goes to companies in early stages of development and considered to be high risk. Some crown corporations such as the Export Development Corporation have venture capital operations as well. Provincial governments have also sponsored their own funds with goals of nurturing small businesses and also providing financing to high-technology firms. Examples include Discovery Enterprises in British Columbia and the Alberta Opportunity Company.

Hybrid funds could be formed jointly by the government and private investors or in response to a government incentive. Halifax-based ACF Equity Atlantic, Inc. is an example of a hybrid fund. Government and hybrid funds have profit maximizing objectives similar to private and labour-sponsored funds.

Table 14.A2 lists some Canadian venture capital funds and describes their investment preferences.

STAGES OF DEVELOPMENT FINANCED BY CANADIAN VENTURE CAPITAL FIRMS

New enterprises can be at different stages of development. Described below are some of the stages firms may go through after they are started.

- *Seed Stage:* the very early stage when the new enterprise may seek to test a concept or build a product prototype and develop a product.
- *Start-Up Stage:* the enterprise may have a product being developed, but not yet marketed and sold commercially.
- *Expansion Stage:* the firm requires significant capital for plant expansion, marketing, and to initiate full commercial production and sales.

TABLE 14.A2

Some representative Canadian venture capital firms

Firm	Type of Firm	Capital under Management ($ millions)	Geographic Preference	Industry Preference
ACF Equity Atlantic, Inc.	Private hybrid	$ 30	Atlantic Canada	Information technology, life science, and marine technologies
Ventures West Management, Inc.	Private independent fund	$300	Within Canada	Biotechnology, communications, computer-related, electronic components and equipment
Working Ventures Canadian Fund, Inc.	Labour-sponsored investment fund	$700	New Brunswick, Nova Scotia, Ontario, P.E.I., Saskatchewan	All sectors *except* real estate
Hydro-Québec CapiTech, Inc.	100% owned by Hydro-Québec	$100	Province of Québec, North America, Europe	Energy technologies, or related or derived products sector
Scotia Merchant Capital Corporation	Merchant bank wholly owned by the Bank of Nova Scotia	Initial $250	Canada or USA	Businesses *excluded:* Real estate, mining, oil and gas

Source: Information compiled in July–August from the Canadian Venture Capital Association's website at www.cvca.ca.

TABLE 14.A3

Venture capital investment activity by stage of development in 2000

Stage	Amount $ (millions)	Percentage of Total
Early Stage	$2,841	45
Expansion	3,081	49
Acquisition/Buyout	191	3
Turnaround	78	1
Other	128	2
Total	**6,319**	**100**

Source: Canadian Venture Capital Association's website at www.cvca.ca.

- *Acquisition/Buyout Stage:* the management of the firm acquires a product line, a division, or a company.
- *Turnaround Stage:* the firm was once profitable but is now earning less than its cost of capital.

Generally the seed and start-up stages are considered to be the early stages of development. During their life cycle, all firms will go through the seed, start-up, and expansion stages, but not all will experience the buyout or turnaround stages. From Table 14.A3, we see that Canadian venture capital firms tend to finance enterprises across different stages of development. Over $2.8 billion, or roughly 47 percent of all investments, went to financing early-stage enterprises, including seed, start-up, and other early stage firms. Although, in 2000, compared with past years, there was more of an emphasis on new ventures or those in early stages of development; most of the capital invested still went to follow-on investments as opposed to first-time deals. In general, venture capitalists have tended to move away from funding very early-stage activity, preferring instead to get involved in later-stage activity involving large-sized investments.

RECENT VENTURE CAPITAL INVESTMENT ACTIVITY

Canada's venture capital firms have been very active in recent years with record investments of $6.3 billion in 2000, well over double the $2.7 billion invested in 1999.[16] Table 14.A4 provides sector-wise details regarding where the venture capital firms invested in 2000. We see that 89 percent of the investing has focused on large deals involving technology companies, particularly in communications, Internet, software, life sciences, and electronics. Topping the list were communications and networking companies, such as those in fibre-optics, telecommunications services or connectivity products, which absorbed $1.4 billion. Internet-based firms received over $1.2 billion. Life science companies captured in excess of $1.1 billion, while firms in computer products, particularly software, got $1 billion. Companies in traditional industries, such as manufacturing or consumer-related received only 15 percent of venture capital investments. The average size of financing was $4.4 million, up from $2.7 million in 1999. About $3 billion, or 47 percent of the total invested, went to Ontario-based technology-intensive firms, particularly in the Greater Toronto Area and the Ottawa Valley region. Québec-based companies captured the second largest portion of total spending—about 21 percent.

TABLE 14.A4
Venture capital investment activity by sector

	2000		1999	
Industry	**Amount $ (millions)**	**Percentage of Total**	**Amount $ (millions)**	**Percentage of Total**
Technology				
Biotechnology	684	11	316	12
Medical/health related	446	7	159	6
Communications	1,365	22	359	13
Computer related	1,037	16	982	36
Internet related	1,222	19	0	0
Electronics	555	9	262	10
Other technology	338	5	90	3
Total	**5,647**	**89**	**2,168**	**80**
Traditional				
Consumer related	237	4	126	5
Manufacturing	201	3	147	5
Miscellaneous	234	4	279	10
Total	**672**	**11**	**552**	**20**
TOTAL	**6,319**	**100**	**2,720**	**100**

Source: Canadian Venture Capital Association's website at www.cvca.ca.

ANGEL INVESTING

Although the organized venture capital industry plays an important role in the creation of new ventures, those seeking very early-stage financing for small and new enterprises often have to resort to informal financing sources. In this context, wealthy individual investors, known as *angels,* can play a critical role by making small-scale investments in local

[16] In comparison, the American venture capital industry also reported a record-breaking year in 2000, investing $103 billion (US). Canada's venture capital spending was about 4 percent of disbursements by the American industry, after adjusting for currency rates.

start-ups and early-stage ventures, and by bringing a significant hands-on contribution to such business ventures.

The angel investor, typically a millionaire or a multimillionaire, may invest on average between $100,000 and $250,000 in a start-up, and prefers to be involved with the project. According to some estimates, there are about 200,000 angel investors in Canada.[17] Angels can play either *active* or *passive* roles in the investee firms. "Active" angels are often highly motivated ex-entrepreneurs who are skilled at picking good management teams and good ideas. They help companies arrange additional financing, hire top management, and recruit knowledgeable board members. "Passive" angels provide only money and rarely monitor the firm closely; they are often part of an informal network led by one or more active angels who find deals and manage the investments. A number of organized services exist that are designed to match angel investors with entrepreneurs looking to fund their new ventures. These angel-network services include Ottawa Capital Network, VentureDrive.com, the Montreal-based InvestAngel Network, the Ottawa-based eValhalla.com, and the Toronto chapter of the International Angel Investors Group.

Other Sources of Small Business Financing

FINANCING UNDER THE CANADA SMALL BUSINESS FINANCING ACT[18]

These are term loans of up to 10 years available through all chartered banks, most credit unions and caisses populaires, and many trust and insurance companies, and are guaranteed by the federal government if taken for specific purposes and limits. The loans are available under the federal government's Canada Small Business Financing Act (CSBFA) to small businesses in Canada which have gross revenues of $5 million or less in the year of application for the loan. The loans can be used to finance up to 90 percent of the purchase or improvement of eligible assets such as land, premises, and equipment. The loans cannot be used to buy shares or provide working capital. CSBFA loans are made to small businesses in a variety of industries such as communication, construction, manufacturing, transportation, and wholesale trade. The loans are not available to farming, charitable, or religious enterprises.

BUSINESS DEVELOPMENT BANK OF CANADA

The Business Development Bank of Canada (BDC) is a Crown financial institution that specializes in providing financial and other support services to small- and medium-sized businesses in Canada. BDC's major activities include term lending, giving loan guarantees, and providing venture capital financing. It is also involved in lease financing and providing consultancy services. As of the end of fiscal year March 2001, BDC had 19,884 customers to whom the total financing committed exceeded $6.3 billion.[19] During the fiscal year ending on March 2001, total financing authorized had reached a record $1.65 billion. In recent years, BDC has targeted its investment focus on knowledge-based and export-oriented industries, with total financing authorized in fiscal 2001 increasing by 24 percent from the

[17] See, for instance, the *Globe and Mail* "Startups Angle for Angels" (June 29, 2000), p. T1.

[18] Details are available at the Industry Canada website, http://strategis.ic.gc.ca.

[19] BDC Annual Report 2001 at www.bdc.ca.

previous year to $834 million. It also plays an active role in the First Peoples' market and in supporting female entrepreneurs.

REGIONAL AND PROVINCIAL LENDING PROGRAMS

There are a number of regional agencies across Canada that have lending and other assistance programs, designed to nurture and grow small businesses. Some of the important regional agencies and initiatives include Atlantic Canada Opportunities Agency (ACOA), Federal Economic Development Initiative in Northern Ontario (FedNor); Canada Economic Development for Québec Regions: Financing; and Western Economic Diversification Canada: Financing. For descriptions of such agencies and details regarding the services provided by them, you can go to the Industry Canada website at http://strategis.ic.gc.ca.

INTERNET AND PRACTICE PROBLEMS

1. **Venture Capital and Angel Investing.** This chapter has provided website information for several venture capital sources and angel investing networks. Use the Internet to explore these websites. Also, see whether you can identify other interesting websites that will provide useful information on venture capital and angel investing activity.
2. **Venture Capital.** Based on your Internet research in question 1, can you answer the following?
   a. We described different types of venture capital funds that exist in Canada. What are the main differences in investment goals and characteristics between these funds? Do some types of funds appear to participate more in earlier stage financing than others?
   b. Do some venture capitalists appear to specialize by investing in only a few selected industries, while others are more diversified in their investment activity? Can you think of some good reasons for firms pursuing either of the two strategies?
   c. Venture capitalists have geographical preferences for their investment activity. Can you discern some common motivations for such preferences?
3. **Venture Capital and Angel Investing.** Venture capitalists and many angel investors are often actively involved with the ventures in which they invest. How does this benefit the entrepreneur? Does this benefit the venture capitalist and angel investor as well?

Appendix 14B: Hotch Pot's New Issue Prospectus[20]

PROSPECTUS

800,000 Shares
Hotch Pot, Inc.
Common Stock

Of the 800,000 shares of Common Stock offered hereby, 500,000 shares are being sold by the Company and 300,000 shares are being sold by the Selling Shareholders. See "Principal and Selling Shareholders." The Company will not receive any of the proceeds from the sale of shares by the Selling Shareholders.

Before this offering there has been no public market for the Common Stock. **These securities involve a high degree of risk. See "Certain Factors."**

THESE SECURITIES HAVE NOT BEEN APPROVED OR DISAPPROVED BY A SECURITIES COMMISSION NOR HAS ANY COMMISSION PASSED ON THE ACCURACY OR ADEQUACY OF THIS PROSPECTUS. ANY REPRESENTATION TO THE CONTRARY IS A CRIMINAL OFFENSE.

	Price to Public	Underwriting Discount	Proceeds to Company[1]	Proceeds to Selling Shareholders
Per share	$12.00	$1.30	$10.70	$10.70
Total	$9,600,000	$1,040,000	$5,350,000	$3,210,000

[1] Before deducting expenses payable by the Company estimated at $400,000, of which $250,000 will be paid by the Company and $150,000 by the Selling Stockholders.

The Common Shares are offered, subject to prior sale, when, as, and if delivered to and accepted by the Underwriters and subject to approval of certain legal matters by their counsel and by counsel for the Company and the Selling Shareholders. The Underwriters reserve the right to withdraw, cancel, or modify such offers and reject orders in whole or in part.

Silverman Pinch Inc. **April 1, 2000**

No person has been authorized to give any information or to make any representations, other than as contained therein, in connection with the offer contained in this Prospectus, and, if given or made, such information or representations must not be relied upon. This Prospectus does not constitute an offer of any securities other than the registered securities to which it relates or an offer to any person in any jurisdiction where such an offer would be unlawful. The delivery of this Prospectus at any time does not imply that information herein is correct as of any time subsequent to its date.

IN CONNECTION WITH THIS OFFERING, THE UNDERWRITER MAY OVER ALLOT OR EFFECT TRANSACTIONS WHICH STABILIZE OR MAINTAIN THE MARKET PRICE OF THE COMMON SHARES OF THE COMPANY AT A LEVEL ABOVE THAT WHICH MIGHT OTHERWISE PREVAIL IN THE OPEN MARKET. SUCH STABILIZING, IF COMMENCED, MAY BE DISCONTINUED AT ANY TIME.

[20] Most prospectuses have content similar to that of the Hotch Pot prospectus but go into considerably more detail. Also, we have omitted from the Hotch Pot prospectus the company's financial statements.

Prospectus Summary

The following summary information is qualified in its entirety by the detailed information and financial statements appearing elsewhere in this Prospectus.

The Company: Hotch Pot, Inc. operates a chain of 140 fast food outlets in Canada, offering unusual combinations of dishes.

The Offering: Common Shares offered by the Company 500,000 shares;
Common Shares offered by the Selling Shareholders 300,000 shares;
Common Shares to be outstanding after this offering 3,500,000 shares.

Use of Proceeds: For the construction of new restaurants and to provide working capital.

THE COMPANY

Hotch Pot, Inc. operates a chain of 140 fast food outlets in Ontario, Québec, and British Columbia. These restaurants specialize in offering an unusual combination of foreign dishes.

The Company was organized in Ontario in 1990.

USE OF PROCEEDS

The Company intends to use the net proceeds from the sale of 500,000 shares of Common Stock offered hereby, estimated at approximately $5 million, to open new outlets in the Atlantic provinces and to provide additional working capital. It has no immediate plans to use any of the net proceeds of the offering for any other specific investment.

DIVIDEND POLICY

The company has not paid cash dividends on its Common Stock and does not anticipate that dividends will be paid on the Common Stock in the foreseeable future.

CERTAIN FACTORS

Investment in the Common Stock involves a high degree of risk. The following factors should be carefully considered in evaluating the Company:

Substantial Capital Needs. The Company will require additional financing to continue its expansion policy. The Company believes that its relations with its lenders are good, but there can be no assurance that additional financing will be available in the future.

Competition. The Company is in competition with a number of restaurant chains supplying fast food. Many of these companies are substantially larger and better capitalized than the Company.

CAPITALIZATION

The following table sets forth the capitalization of the Company as of December 31, 1999, and is adjusted to reflect the sale of 500,000 shares of Common Stock by the Company.

	Actual	As Adjusted
	($ thousands)	
Long-term debt	$ —	$ —
Stockholders' equity		
Common shares: 3,000,000 shares outstanding, 3,500,000 shares outstanding, as adjusted	2,000	7,350
Retained earnings	3,200	3,200
Total shareholders' equity	5,200	10,550
Total capitalization	$5,200	$10,550

SELECTED FINANCIAL DATA

[*The Prospectus typically includes a summary income statement and balance sheet.*]

MANAGEMENT'S ANALYSIS OF RESULTS OF OPERATIONS AND FINANCIAL CONDITION

Revenue growth for the year ended December 31, 1999, resulted from the opening of 10 new restaurants in the Company's existing geographic area and from sales of a new range of desserts, notably crêpe suzette with custard. Sales per customer increased by 20% and this contributed to the improvement in margins.

During the year the Company borrowed $600,000 from its banks at an interest rate of 2% above the prime rate.

BUSINESS

Hotch Pot, Inc. operates a chain of 140 fast food outlets in Ontario, Québec, and British Columbia. These restaurants specialize in offering an unusual combination of international dishes. Fifty percent of the company's revenues were derived from the sale of two dishes, sushi and sauerkraut, and curry bolognese. All dishes are prepared in three regional centres and then frozen and distributed to the individual restaurants.

MANAGEMENT

The following table sets forth information regarding the Company's directors, executive officers, and key employees:

Name	Age	Position
Emma Lucullus	28	President, Chief Executive Officer, and Director
Ed Lucullus	33	Treasurer & Director

Emma Lucullus Emma Lucullus established the Company in 1990 and has been its Chief Executive Officer since that date.

Ed Lucullus Ed Lucullus has been employed by the Company since 1990.

EXECUTIVE COMPENSATION

The following table sets forth the cash compensation paid for services rendered for the year 1999 by the executive officers:

Name	Capacity	Cash Compensation
Emma Lucullus	President and Chief Executive Officer	$130,000
Ed Lucullus	Treasurer	$ 95,000

CERTAIN TRANSACTIONS

At various times between 1990 and 1999, First Cookham Venture Partners invested a total of $1.5 million in the Company. In connection with this investment, First Cookham Venture Partners was granted certain rights to registration under the Ontario Securities Act, including the right to have their shares of Common Stock registered at the Company's expense with the Ontario Securities Commission.

PRINCIPAL AND SELLING STOCKHOLDERS

The following table sets forth certain information regarding the beneficial ownership of the Company's voting Common Stock as of the date of this prospectus by (i) each person known by the Company to be the beneficial owner of more than 5% of its voting Common Stock, and (ii) each director of the Company who beneficially owns voting Common Stock. Unless otherwise indicated, each owner has sole voting and dispositive power over his or her shares.

Name of Beneficial Owner	Shares Beneficially Owned prior to Offering		Shares to Be Sold	Shares Beneficially Owned after Offering	
	Number	Percent		Number	Percent
Emma Lucullus	400,000	13.3	25,000	375,000	12.9
Ed Lucullus	400,000	13.3	25,000	375,000	12.9
First Cookham Venture Partners	1,700,000	66.7	250,000	1,450,000	50.0
Hermione Kraft	200,000	6.7	—	200,000	6.9

DESCRIPTION OF CAPITAL STOCK

The Company's authorized capital stock consists of 10,000,000 shares of voting Common Stock.

As of the date of this Prospectus, there are four holders of record of the Common Stock.

Under the terms of one of the Company's loan agreements, the Company may not pay cash dividends on Common Stock except from net profits without the written consent of the lender.

UNDERWRITING

Subject to the terms and conditions set forth in the Underwriting Agreement, the Underwriter, Silverman Pinch, Inc., has agreed to purchase from the Company and the Selling Stockholders 800,000 shares of Common Stock.

There is no public market for the Common Stock. The price to the public for the Common Stock was determined by negotiation between the Company and the Underwriter, and was based on, among other things, the Company's financial and operating history and condition, its prospects, and the prospects for its industry in general, the management of the Company, and the market prices of securities for companies in businesses similar to that of the Company.

LEGAL MATTERS

The validity of the shares of Common Stock offered by the Prospectus is being passed on for the Company by Blair, Kohl, and Chirac, and for the Underwriter by Chretien Howard.

LEGAL PROCEEDINGS

Hotch Pot was served in January 2000 with a summons and complaint in an action commenced by a customer who alleged that consumption of the Company's products caused severe nausea and loss of feeling in both feet. The Company believes that the complaint is without foundation.

EXPERTS

The consolidated financial statements of the Company have been so included in reliance on the reports of Hooper Firebrand, independent accountants, given on the authority of that firm as experts in auditing and accounting.

FINANCIAL STATEMENTS

[*Text and tables omitted.*]

PART FIVE

Capital Structure and Dividend Policy

15 THE CAPITAL STRUCTURE DECISION

16 DIVIDEND POLICY

CHAPTER 15

The Capital Structure Decision

15.1 How Borrowing Affects Value in a Tax-Free Economy

15.2 Capital Structure and Corporate Taxes

15.3 Costs of Financial Distress

15.4 Explaining Financing Choices

15.5 Summary

A firm's basic financial resource is the stream of cash flows produced by its assets and operations. When the firm is financed entirely by common stock, all those cash flows belong to the shareholders. When it issues both debt and equity, the firm splits the cash flows into two streams, a relatively safe stream that goes to the debtholders and a more risky one that goes to the shareholders.

The firm's mix of securities is known as its capital structure. Most high-tech firms, such as Ballard Power and Research In Motion, rely almost wholly on equity finance, so do most biotech, software, and Internet companies. At the other extreme, debt accounts for a substantial part of the market value of retailers, utilities, and banks. For instance, Loblaw's total debt is higher than its total equity.

Capital structure is not immutable. Firms change their capital structure, sometimes almost overnight. For instance, Alliance Atlantis Communications recently announced a $131.5 million offering of Class B nonvoting common shares that will be used to pay down some of the firm's debt. In the 1990s, DuPont Canada generated large amounts of cash flows and used the money to pay off its long-term debt. Later in the chapter you will see how an American company, Sealed Air Corporation, benefited from changing its capital structure.

Shareholders want management to choose the mix of securities that maximizes firm value. But does this optimal capital structure exist? We must consider the possibility that no combination has any greater appeal than any other. Perhaps the really important decisions concern the company's assets, and decisions about capital structure are mere details—matters to be attended to but not worried about.

In the first part of the chapter, we will look at examples in which capital structure *doesn't* matter. After that we will put back some of the things that *do* make a difference, such as taxes, bankruptcy, and the signals that your financing decisions may send to investors. At the end of the chapter, we will draw up a checklist for financial managers who need to decide on the firm's capital structure.

After studying this chapter you should be able to

- Analyze the effect of debt finance on the risk and required return of equityholders.
- Appreciate the advantages and disadvantages of debt finance.
- Cite the various costs of financial distress.
- Explain why the debt-equity mix varies across firms and across industries.

15.1 How Borrowing Affects Value in a Tax-Free Economy

It is after the ball game and the pizza man is delivering a pizza to Yogi Berra. "Should I cut it into four slices as usual, Yogi?" asks the pizza man. "No," replies Yogi, "Cut it into eight; I'm hungry tonight."

capital structure Firm's mix of financing.

If you understand why more slices won't sate Yogi's appetite, you will have no difficulty understanding why a company's choice of **capital structure** can't increase the underlying value of the cash flows generated by its real assets and operations.

Think of a simple balance sheet with all entries expressed as current market values:

Assets	Liabilities and Stockholders' Equity
Value of cash flows from the firm's real assets and operations	Market value of debt Market value of equity
Value of firm	Value of firm

The right- and left-hand sides of a balance sheet are always equal. (Balance sheets have to balance!) Therefore, if you add up the market value of all the firm's debt and equity securities, you can calculate the value of the future cash flows from the real assets and operations.

In fact the value of those cash flows *determines* the value of the firm and therefore determines the aggregate value of all the firm's outstanding debt and equity securities. If the firm changes its capital structure, say by using more debt and less equity financing, overall value should not change.

Think of the left-hand side of the balance sheet as the size of the pizza; the right-hand side determines how it is sliced. A company can slice its cash flow into as many parts as it likes, but the value of those parts will always sum back to the value of the unsliced cash flow. (Of course, we have to make sure that none of the cash-flow stream is lost in the slicing. We cannot say that the value of a pizza is independent of how it is sliced if the slicer is also a nibbler.)

The basic idea here (the value of a pizza does not depend on how it is sliced) has various applications. Yogi Berra got friendly chuckles for his misapplication. Franco Modigliani and Merton Miller received Nobel prizes for applying it to corporate financing. Modigliani and Miller, always referred to as "MM," showed in 1958 that the value of a firm does not depend on how its cash flows are "sliced." More precisely, they demonstrated the following proposition:

When there are no taxes and well-functioning capital markets exist, the market value of a company does not depend on its capital structure. In other words, financial managers cannot increase value by changing the mix of securities used to finance the company.

Of course this MM proposition rests on some important simplifying assumptions. For example, capital markets have to be "well functioning." That means that investors can trade securities without restrictions and can borrow or lend on the same terms as the firm. It also means that capital markets are efficient, so that securities are fairly priced given the information available to investors. (We discussed market efficiency in Chapter 12.) MM's proposition also assumes that there are no distorting taxes, and it ignores the costs encountered if a firm borrows too much and lands in financial distress.

The firm's capital structure decision can matter if these assumptions are not true or if other practical complications are encountered. But the best way to *start* thinking about capital structure is to work through MM's argument. To keep things as simple as possible, we will ignore taxes until further notice.

MM'S ARGUMENT

Cleo, the president of River Cruises, is reviewing the firm's capital structure with Antony, the financial manager. Table 15.1 shows the current position. The company has no debt and all its operating income is paid as dividends to the shareholders. The *expected* earnings and dividends per share are $1.25, but this figure is by no means certain—it could turn out to be more or less than $1.25. For example, earnings could fall to $.75 in a slump, or they could jump to $1.75 in a boom.

The price of each share is $10. The firm expects to produce a level stream of earnings and dividends in perpetuity. With no growth forecast, shareholders' expected return is equal to the dividend yield—that is, the expected dividend per share divided by the price, $1.25/$10 = .125, or 12.5 percent.

Cleo has come to the conclusion that shareholders would be better off if the company had equal proportions of debt and equity. She therefore proposes to issue $500,000 of debt at an interest rate of 10 percent and to use the proceeds to repurchase 50,000 shares. This is called a **restructuring.** Notice that the $500,000 raised by the new borrowing does not stay in the firm. It goes right out the door to shareholders in order to repurchase and retire 50,000 shares. Therefore, the assets and investment policy of the firm are not affected. Only the financing mix changes.

restructuring Process of changing the firm's capital structure without changing its assets.

What would MM say about this new capital structure? Suppose the change is made. Operating income is the same, so the value of the "pie" is fixed at $1 million. With $500,000 in new debt outstanding, the remaining common shares must be worth $500,000, that is, 50,000 shares at $10 per share. The total value of the debt and equity is still $1 million.

Since the value of the firm is the same, common shareholders are no better or worse off than before. River Cruises' shares still trade at $10 each. The overall value of River Cruises' equity falls from $1 million to $500,000, but shareholders have also received $500,000 in cash.

Antony points all this out. "The restructuring doesn't make our shareholders any richer or poorer, Cleo. Why bother? Capital structure doesn't matter."

TABLE 15.1 *River Cruises is entirely equity-financed. Although it expects to have an income of $125,000 in perpetuity, this income is not certain. This table shows the return to the shareholders under different assumptions about operating income. No taxes are assumed.*

Data			
Number of shares	100,000		
Price per share	$10		
Market value of shares	$1 million		
	State of the Economy		
	Slump	**Normal**	**Boom**
Operating income	$75,000	125,000	175,000
Earnings per share	$.75	1.25	1.75
Return on shares	7.5%	12.5%	17.5%
		Expected outcome	

✔ CHECK POINT 15.1

Suppose River Cruises issues $350,000 of new debt (rather than $500,000) and uses the proceeds to repurchase and retire common stock. How does this affect price per share? How many shares will be left outstanding?

HOW BORROWING AFFECTS EARNINGS PER SHARE

Cleo is unconvinced. She prepares Table 15.2 and Figure 15.1 to show how borrowing $500,000 could increase earnings per share. Comparison of tables 15.1 and 15.2 shows that "normal" earnings per share increase to $1.50 (versus $1.25) after the restructuring. Table 15.2 also shows more "upside" (earnings per share of $2.50 versus $1.75) and more "downside" ($.50 versus $.75).

The blue line in Figure 15.1 shows how earnings per share would vary with operating income under the firm's current all-equity financing. It is therefore simply a plot of the data in Table 15.1. The green line shows how earnings per share would vary if the company moves to equal proportions of debt and equity. It is therefore a plot of the data in Table 15.2.

Cleo reasons as follows: "It is clear that debt could either increase or reduce the return to the equityholder. In a slump the return to the equityholder is reduced by the use of debt, but otherwise it is *increased.* We could be heading for a recession, but it doesn't look likely. Maybe we could help our shareholders by going ahead with the debt issue."

As financial manager, Antony replies as follows: "I agree that borrowing will increase earnings per share as long as there's no slump. But we're not really doing anything for shareholders that they can't do on their own. Suppose River Cruises does *not* borrow. In that case an investor could go to the bank, borrow $10, and then invest $20 in two shares. Such an investor would put up only $10 of her own money. (Table 15.3 shows how the payoffs on this $10 investment vary with River Cruises' operating income.) You can see that these payoffs are exactly the same as the investor would get by buying one share in the company after the restructuring. (Compare the last two lines of tables 15.2 and 15.3.) It makes no difference whether shareholders borrow directly or whether River Cruises borrows on their behalf. Therefore, if River Cruises goes ahead and borrows, it will not allow

TABLE 15.2
River Cruises is wondering whether to issue $500,000 of debt at an interest rate of 10 percent and repurchase 50,000 shares. This table shows the return to the shareholder under different assumptions about operating income. Returns to shareholders are increased in normal and boom times but fall more in slumps.

Data			
Number of shares	50,000		
Price per share	$10		
Market value of shares	$500,000		
Market value of debt	$500,000		
Outcomes			
	State of the Economy		
	Slump	**Normal**	**Boom**
Operating income	$75,000	125,000	175,000
Interest	$50,000	50,000	50,000
Equity earnings	$25,000	75,000	125,000
Earnings per share	$.50	1.50	2.50
Return on shares	5%	15%	25%
		Expected outcome	

FIGURE 15.1
Borrowing increases River Cruises' earnings per share (EPS) when operating income is greater than $100,000 but reduces it when operating income is less than $100,000. Expected EPS rises from $1.25 to $1.50.

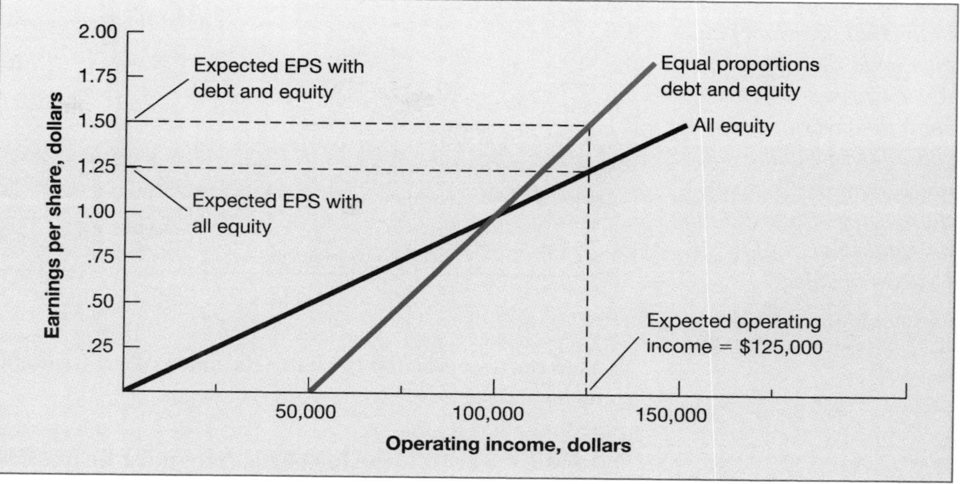

investors to do anything that they could not do already, and so it cannot increase the value of the firm."

"We can run the same argument in reverse and show that investors won't be *worse* off after the restructuring either. Imagine an investor who owns two shares in the company before the restructuring. If River Cruises borrows money, there is some chance that the return on the shares will be lower than before. If that possibility is not to our investor's taste, he can buy one share in the restructured company and also invest $10 in the firm's debt. (Table 15.4 shows how the payoff on this investment varies with River Cruises' operating income.) You can see that these payoffs are exactly the same as the investor got before the restructuring. (Compare the last lines of tables 15.1 and 15.4.) By lending half of his capital (by investing in River Cruises' debt), the investor offsets the company's borrowing exactly. So if River Cruises goes ahead and borrows, it won't *stop* investors from doing anything that they could previously do."

This recreates MM's original argument.[1] As long as investors can borrow or lend on their own account on the same terms as the firm, they are not going to pay more for a firm

TABLE 15.3
Individual investors can replicate River Cruises' borrowing by borrowing on their own. In this example, it is assumed that River Cruises has not restructured. However, the investor can put up $10 of her own money, borrow $10 more, and buy two shares at $10 apiece. This generates the same rates of return as in Table 15.2.

	State of the Economy		
	Slump	**Normal**	**Boom**
Earnings on two shares	$1.50	2.50	3.50
Less interest at 10%	$1.00	1.00	1.00
Net earnings on investment	$ .50	1.50	2.50
Return on $10 investment	5%	15%	25%
		Expected outcome	

[1] There are many more general—and technical—proofs of the MM proposition. We will not pursue them here.

TABLE 15.4
Individual investors can also undo the effects of River Cruises' borrowing. Here the investor buys one share for $10 and lends out $10 more. Compare these rates of return to the original returns of River Cruises in Table 15.1.

	State of the Economy		
	Slump	**Normal**	**Boom**
Earnings on one share	$ .50	1.50	2.50
Plus interest at 10%	$1.00	1.00	1.00
Net earnings on investment	$1.50	2.50	3.50
Return on $20 investment	7.5%	12.5%	17.5%
		Expected outcome	

that has borrowed on their behalf. The value of the firm after the restructuring must be the same as before.

In other words, the value of the firm must be unaffected by its capital structure.

MM's proposition I (debt irrelevance proposition) The value of a firm is unaffected by its capital structure.

This conclusion is widely known as **MM's proposition I**. It is also called the **MM debt irrelevance proposition**, because it shows that under ideal conditions the firm's debt policy shouldn't matter to shareholders.

CHECK POINT 15.2

Suppose that River Cruises had issued $750,000 of debt and uses the proceeds to buy back stock.

a. What would be the impact of a $50,000 change in operating income on earnings per share?
b. Show how a conservative investor could "undo" the change in River Cruises' capital structure by varying the investment strategy shown in Table 15.4. *Hint:* The investor will have to lend $3 for every dollar invested in River Cruises' stock.

HOW BORROWING AFFECTS RISK AND RETURN

Figure 15.2 summarizes the implications of MM's debt irrelevance proposition for River Cruises. The upper circles represent firm value, the lower circles expected, or "normal," operating income. Restructuring does not affect the size of the circles, because the amount and risk of operating income are unchanged. Thus if the firm raises $500,000 in debt and uses the proceeds to repurchase and retire shares, the remaining shares *must* be worth $500,000, and the total value of debt and equity *must* stay at $1 million.

The two bottom circles in Figure 15.2 are also the same size. But notice that the bottom right circle shows that shareholders can expect to earn more than half of River Cruises' normal operating income. They get more than half of the expected "income pie." Does that mean shareholders are better off? MM say no. Why not? The answer is that shareholders bear more risk.

operating risk, business risk Risk in firm's operating income.

Look again at tables 15.1 and 15.2. Restructuring does not affect operating income, regardless of the state of the economy. Therefore, debt financing does not affect the **operating risk** or, equivalently, the **business risk** of the firm. But with less equity outstanding, a change in operating income has a greater impact on earnings per share. Suppose operating income drops from $125,000 to $75,000. Under all-equity financing,

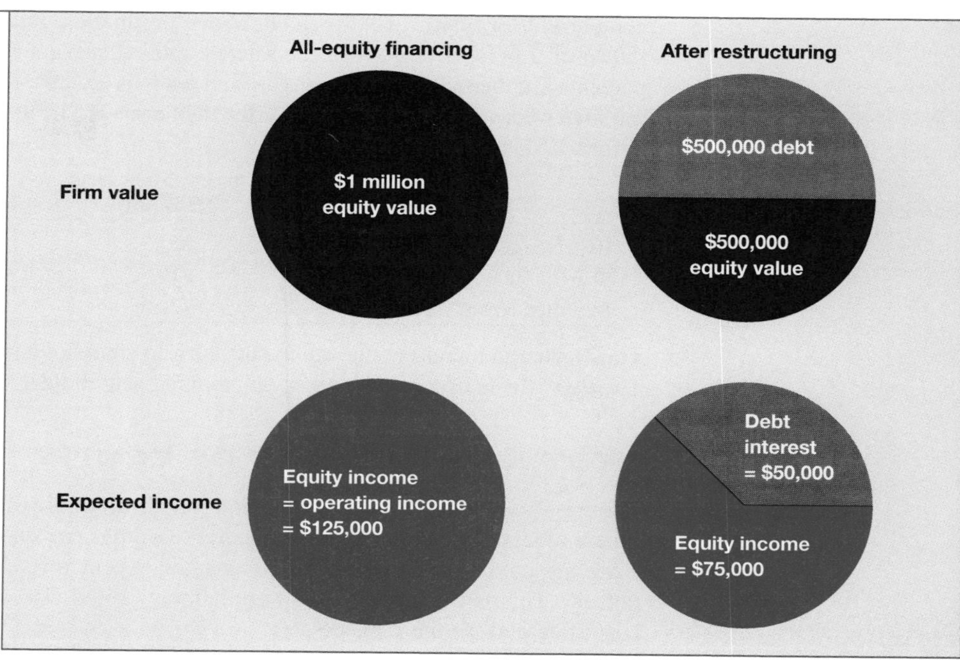

FIGURE 15.2 *"Slicing the pie" for River Cruises. The circles on the left assume the company has no debt. The circles on the right reflect the proposed restructuring. The restructuring splits firm value (top circles) 50-50. Shareholders get more than 50 percent of expected, or "normal," operating income (bottom circles), but only because they bear financial risk. Note that restructuring does* not *affect total firm value or operating income.*

there are 100,000 shares; so earnings per share fall by $.50. With 50 percent debt, there are only 50,000 shares outstanding; so the same drop in operating income reduces earnings per share by $1.

financial leverage Debt financing to amplify the effects of changes in operating income on the returns to stockholders.

You can see now why the use of debt finance is known as **financial leverage**, and a firm that has issued debt is described as a *levered firm.* The debt increases the uncertainty about percentage stock returns. If the firm is financed entirely by equity, a decline of $50,000 in operating income reduces the return on the shares by 5 percent. If the firm issues debt, then the same decline of $50,000 in operating income reduces the return on the shares by 10 percent. (Compare tables 15.1 and 15.2.) In other words, the effect of leverage is to double the magnitude of the upside and downside in the return on River Cruises' shares. Whatever the beta of the firm's shares before the restructuring, it would be twice as high afterward.

financial risk Risk to shareholders resulting from the use of debt.

Debt finance does not affect the operating risk but it does add *financial risk.* With only half the equity to absorb the same amount of operating risk, risk per share must double.[2]

Consider now the implications of MM's proposition I for the expected return on River Cruises' stock. Before the proposed debt issue, the expected stream of earnings and dividends per share is $1.25. Since investment in the shares is risky, the shareholders require a return of 12.5 percent, or 2.5 percent above the interest rate. So the share price (which for a perpetuity is equal to the expected dividends divided by the required return) is $1.25/.125 = $10. The good news is that after the debt issue, expected earnings and dividends rise to $1.50. The bad news is that the risk of the shares has now doubled. So instead of being

[2] Think back to Section 8.3, where we showed that fixed costs increase the variability in a firm's profits. These fixed costs are said to provide *operating leverage.* It is exactly the same with debt. Debt interest is a fixed cost and therefore debt magnifies the variability of profits after interest. These fixed interest charges create financial leverage.

content with a return of 2.5 percent above the interest rate, shareholders now demand a return of 5 percent more than the interest rate—that is, a required return of 10 + 5 = 15 percent. The benefit from the rise in dividends is exactly cancelled out by the rise in the required return. The share price after the debt issue is $1.50/.15 = $10—exactly the same as before.

	Current Structure: All Equity	**Proposed Structure: Equal Debt and Equity**
Expected earnings per share	$1.25	$1.50
Share price	$10	$10
Expected return on share	12.5%	15.0%

Thus leverage increases the expected return to shareholders but it also increases the risk. The two effects cancel each other out, leaving shareholder value unchanged.

DEBT AND THE COST OF EQUITY

What is River Cruises' cost of capital? With all-equity financing, the answer is easy. Shareholders pay $10 per share and expect earnings per share of $1.25. If the earnings per share are paid out in a perpetual stream, the expected return is $1.25/10 = .125, or 12.5 percent. This is the cost of equity capital, r_{equity}, and also, r_{assets}, the expected return and cost of capital for the firm's assets.

Since the restructuring does not change operating earnings or firm value, it should not change the cost of capital either. Suppose the restructuring takes place. Also, by a grand stroke of luck you simultaneously become an Internet billionaire. Flush with cash, you decide to buy *all* the outstanding debt and equity of River Cruises. What rate of return should you expect on this investment? The answer is 12.5 percent, because once you own all the debt and equity, you will effectively own all the assets and receive all the operating income.

You will indeed get 12.5 percent. Table 15.2 shows expected earnings per share of $1.50, and share price is still $10. Therefore, the expected return on equity is $1.50/10 = .15, or 15 percent ($r_{\text{equity}} = .15$). The return on debt is 10 percent ($r_{\text{debt}} = .10$). Your overall return is

$$(.5 \times .10) + (.5 \times .15) = .125 = r_{\text{assets}}$$

There is obviously a general principle here: The appropriate weighted average of r_{debt} and r_{equity} takes you to r_{assets}, the opportunity cost of capital for the company's assets. The formula is

$$r_{\text{assets}} = (r_{\text{debt}} \times D/V) + (r_{\text{equity}} \times E/V)$$

where D and E are the amounts of outstanding debt and equity and V equals overall firm value, the sum of D and E. Remember that D, E, and V are market values, not book values.

This formula does not match the weighted-average cost of capital (WACC) formula presented in Chapter 11.[3] Don't worry, we'll get to WACC in a moment. (Remember, we're still ignoring taxes.) First let's look at the implications of MM's debt irrelevance proposition for the cost of equity.

MM's proposition I states that the firm's choice of capital structure does not affect the firm's operating income or the value of its assets. So r_{assets}, the expected return on the package of debt and equity, is unaffected.

[3] See sections 11.1 and 11.2.

However, we have just seen that leverage does increase the risk of the equity and the return that shareholders demand. To see how the expected return on equity varies with leverage, we simply rearrange the formula for the company cost of capital as follows:

$$r_{\text{equity}} = r_{\text{assets}} + \frac{D}{E}\,(r_{\text{assets}} - r_{\text{debt}})$$

which in words says that

$$\begin{matrix}\textbf{Expected} \\ \textbf{return} \\ \textbf{on equity}\end{matrix} = \begin{matrix}\textbf{expected} \\ \textbf{return} \\ \textbf{on assets}\end{matrix} + \left[\begin{matrix}\textbf{debt-} \\ \textbf{equity} \\ \textbf{ratio}\end{matrix} \times \left(\begin{matrix}\textbf{expected} \\ \textbf{return on} \\ \textbf{assets}\end{matrix} - \begin{matrix}\textbf{expected} \\ \textbf{return on} \\ \textbf{debt}\end{matrix}\right)\right] \qquad (15.1)$$

MM's proposition II The required rate of return on equity increases as the firm's debt-equity ratio increases.

This is **MM's proposition II.** It states that the expected rate of return on the common stock of a leveraged firm increases in proportion to the debt-equity ratio (*D*/*E*), expressed in market values. Note that $r_{\text{equity}} = r_{\text{assets}}$ if the firm has no debt.

EXAMPLE 15.1 *River Cruises' Cost of Equity*

We can check out MM's proposition II for River Cruises. Before the decision to borrow

$$r_{\text{equity}} = r_{\text{assets}} = \frac{\text{expected operating income}}{\text{market value of all securities}}$$

$$= \frac{125{,}000}{1{,}000{,}000} = .125, \text{ or } 12.5\%$$

If the firm goes ahead with its plan to borrow, the expected return on assets, r_{assets}, is still 12.5 percent. So the expected return on equity is

$$\begin{aligned} r_{\text{equity}} &= r_{\text{assets}} + \frac{D}{E}\,(r_{\text{assets}} - r_{\text{debt}}) \\ &= .125 + \frac{500{,}000}{500{,}000}\,(.125 - .10) \\ &= .15, \text{ or } 15\% \end{aligned}$$

We pointed out in Chapter 11 that you can think of a debt issue as having an explicit cost and an implicit cost. The explicit cost is the rate of interest charged on the firm's debt.

Debt also increases financial risk and causes shareholders to demand a higher return on their investment. Once you recognize this implicit cost, debt is no cheaper than equity—the return that investors require on their assets is unaffected by the firm's borrowing decision.

CHECK POINT 15.3

When the firm issues debt, why does r_{assets}, the company cost of capital remain fixed, while the expected return on equity, r_{equity}, changes? Why is it not the other way around?

The implications of MM's proposition II are shown in Figure 15.3. No matter how much the firm borrows, the expected return on the package of debt and equity, r_{assets}, is

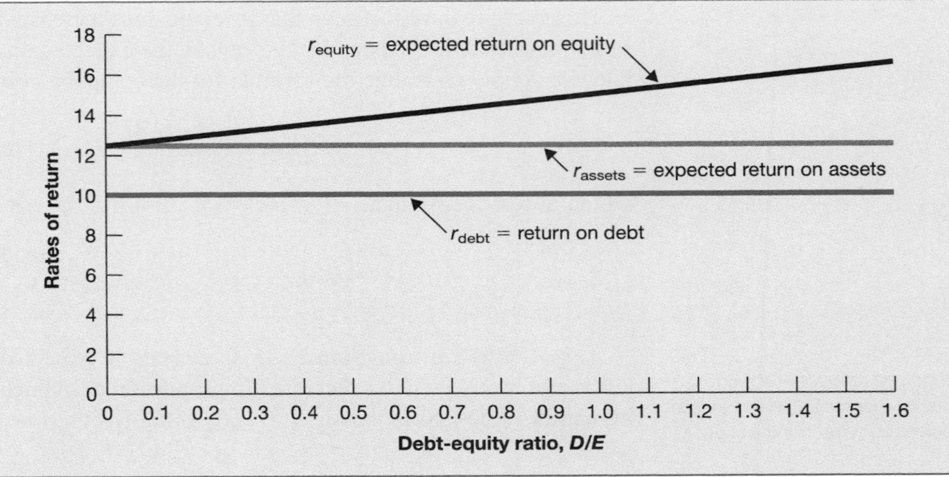

FIGURE 15.3
MM's proposition II with a fixed interest rate on debt. The expected return on River Cruises' equity rises in line with the debt-equity ratio. The weighted average of the expected returns on debt and equity is constant, equal to the expected return on assets.

unchanged, but the expected rate of return on the separate parts of the package does change. How is this possible? Because the proportions of debt and equity in the package are also changing. More debt means that the cost of equity increases, but at the same time the *amount* of equity is less.

In Figure 15.3 we have drawn the rate of interest on the debt as constant no matter how much the firm borrows. That is not wholly realistic. It is true that most large, conservative companies could borrow a little more or less without noticeably affecting the interest rate that they pay. But at higher debt levels lenders become concerned that they may not get their money back, and they demand higher rates of interest. Figure 15.4 modifies Figure 15.3 to take account of this. You can see that as the firm borrows more, the risk of default increases and the firm has to pay higher rates of interest. Proposition II continues to predict that the expected return on the package of debt and equity does not change. However, the slope of the r_{equity} line now tapers off as D/E increases. Why? Essentially because holders of risky debt begin to bear part of the firm's operating risk. As the firm borrows more, more of that risk is transferred from shareholders to bondholders.

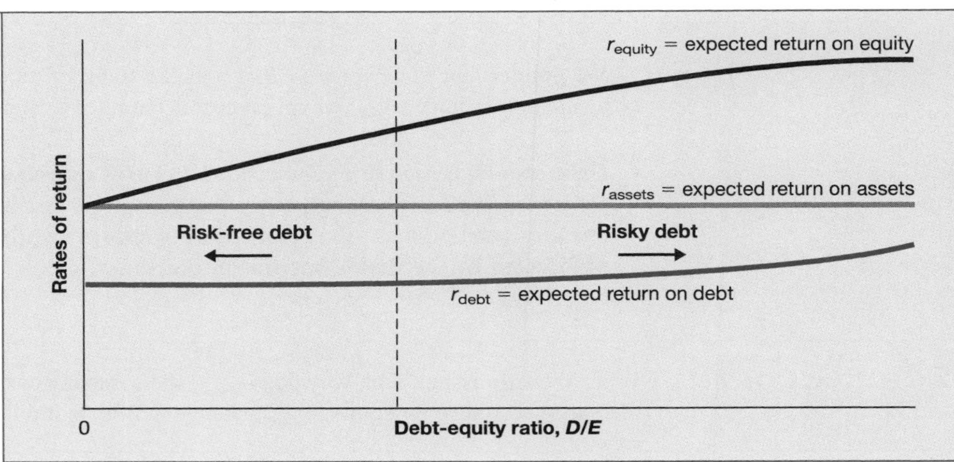

FIGURE 15.4
MM's proposition II, when debt is not risk-free. As the debt-equity ratio increases, debtholders demand a higher expected rate of return to compensate for the risk of default. The expected return on equity increases more slowly when debt is risky because the debtholders take on part of the risk. The expected return on the package of debt and equity, r_{assets}, remains constant.

Figures 15.3 and 15.4 wrap up our discussion of MM's leverage irrelevance proposition. Because overall firm value is constant, the average return on the firm's debt and equity securities is also constant, regardless of the fraction of debt financing. This result follows from MM's assumptions that capital markets are well-functioning and taxes are absent. Now it's time to put taxes back into the picture.

15.2 Capital Structure and Corporate Taxes

The MM propositions suggest that debt policy should not matter. Yet financial managers do worry about debt policy, and for good reasons. Now we are ready to see why.

If debt policy were *completely* irrelevant, actual debt ratios would vary randomly from firm to firm and from industry to industry. Yet almost all airlines, utilities, banks, and real estate development companies rely heavily on debt. And so do many firms in capital-intensive industries like steel, aluminum, chemicals, petroleum, and mining. On the other hand, it is rare to find a drug company or advertising agency that is not predominantly equity-financed. Glamorous growth companies seldom use much debt, despite rapid expansion and often heavy requirements for capital.

The explanation of these patterns lies partly in the things that we have so far left out of our discussion. Now we will put all these things back in, starting with taxes.

DEBT AND TAXES AT RIVER CRUISES

Debt financing has one important advantage. The interest that the company pays is a tax-deductible expense but equity income is subject to corporate tax.

To see the advantage of debt finance, let's look once again at River Cruises. Table 15.5 shows how expected income is reduced if profits are taxed at a rate of 35 percent. The left-hand column sets out the position if River Cruises is financed entirely by equity. The right-hand column shows what happens if the firm issues $500,000 of debt at an interest rate of 10 percent.

interest tax shield Tax savings resulting from deductibility of interest payments.

Notice that the combined income of the debtholders and equityholders is higher by $17,500 when the firm is levered. This is because the interest payments are tax-deductible. Thus every dollar of interest reduces taxes by $.35. The total amount of tax savings is simply .35 × interest payments. In the case of River Cruises, the **interest tax shield** is .35 × $50,000 = $17,500 each year. In other words, the "pie" of after-tax income to be shared by debt and equity investors increases by $17,500 relative to the zero-debt case. Since the debtholders receive no more than the going rate of interest, the benefit of this interest tax shield is captured by the shareholders.

The interest tax shield is a valuable asset. Let's see how much it could be worth. Suppose that River Cruises plans to replace its bonds when they mature and to keep "rolling over" the debt indefinitely. It therefore looks forward to a permanent stream of tax savings of $17,500 per year. These savings depend only on the corporate tax rate and on the ability of River Cruises to earn enough to cover interest payments. So the risk of the tax shield is likely to be small. Therefore, if we wish to compute the present value of all the future tax savings associated with permanent debt, we should discount the interest tax shields at a relatively low rate.

But what rate? The most common assumption is that the risk of the tax shields is the same as that of the interest payments generating them. Thus we discount at 10 percent, the expected rate of return demanded by investors who are holding the firm's debt. If the debt

TABLE 15.5
Since debt interest is tax-deductible, River Cruises' debtholders and equity-holders expect to receive a higher combined income when the firm is leveraged.

	Zero Debt	$500,000 of Debt
Expected operating income	$125,000	$125,000
Debt interest at 10%	0	50,000
Before-tax income	125,000	75,000
Tax at 35%	43,750	26,250
After-tax income	81,250	48,750
Combined debt and equity income (debt interest + after-tax income)	81,250	98,750

is permanent, then the firm can look forward to an annual savings of $17,500 in perpetuity. Their present value is

$$\text{PV tax shield} = \frac{\$17{,}500}{.10} = \$175{,}000$$

This is what the tax savings are worth to River Cruises.

How does company value change? We continue to assume that if the firm is all-equity financed, the shareholders will demand a 12.5 percent return, and therefore, the company will be valued at $81,250/.125 = $650,000.[4] But if River Cruises issues $500,000 of permanent debt, the package of all the firm's securities increases by the value of the tax shield to $650,000 + $175,000 = $825,000.

Let us generalize. The interest payment each year equals the rate of interest times the amount borrowed, or $r_{\text{debt}} \times D$. The annual tax savings is the corporate tax rate, T_c, times the interest payment. Therefore,

$$\begin{aligned}\text{Annual tax shield} &= \text{corporate tax rate} \times \text{interest payment} \\ &= T_c \times (r_{\text{debt}} \times D)\end{aligned}$$

If the tax shield is perpetual, we use the perpetuity formula to calculate its present value:

$$\textbf{PV tax shields} = \frac{\textbf{annual tax shield}}{r_{\textbf{debt}}} = \frac{T_c \times (r_{\textbf{debt}} \times D)}{r_{\textbf{debt}}} = T_c D \qquad (15.2)$$

Of course the present value of the tax shield is less if the firm does not plan to borrow permanently or if it may not be able to use the tax shields in the future.[5] This present value (T_cD) is actually the maximum possible value. However, we will continue to use this value in the rest of this chapter in order to keep the argument and illustrations simple.

CHECK POINT 15.4

In 2000, BCE, Inc. paid out $1,336 million as debt interest. How much more tax would BCE have paid if the firm was entirely equity-financed? What is the present value of BCE's interest tax shield if BCE planned to keep its borrowing permanently at the 2000 level? Assume an interest rate of 8 percent and a corporate tax rate of 35 percent.

---

[4] The firm was worth $1 million when the corporate tax rate was zero (see Table 15.1). It is worth only $650,000 when all-equity financed because 35 percent of income is lost to taxes.

[5] The value of the interest tax shield is also reduced if the future level of debt is not fixed, but it is increased when the firm does well and paid down when it does poorly. In this case the future interest tax shields are correlated with the firm's performance and are therefore risky.

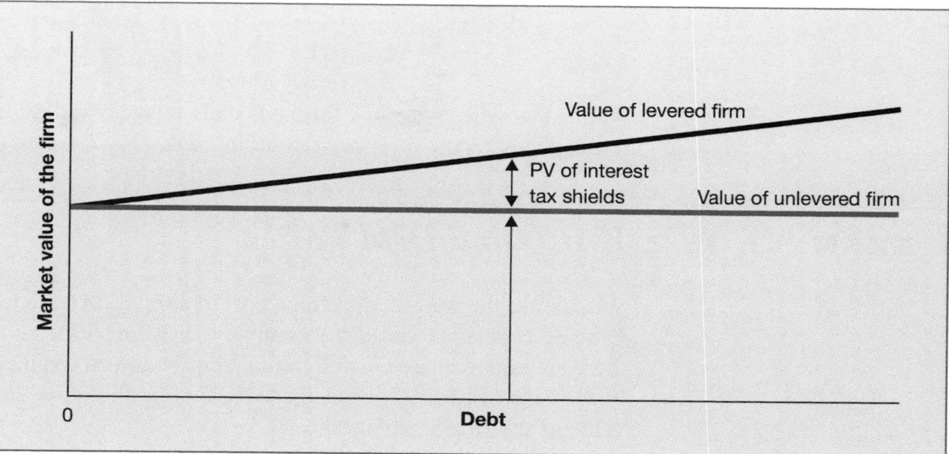

FIGURE 15.5
The heavy blue line shows how the availability of interest tax shields affects the market value of the firm. Additional borrowing decreases corporate income tax payments and increases the cash flows available to lenders and shareholders; thus, market value increases.

HOW INTEREST TAX SHIELDS CONTRIBUTE TO THE VALUE OF SHAREHOLDERS' EQUITY

MM's proposition I amounts to saying that "the value of the pizza does not depend on how it is sliced." The pizza is the firm's assets, and the slices are the debt and equity claims. If we hold the pizza constant, then a dollar more of debt means a dollar less of equity value.

But there is really a third slice—the government's. MM would still say that the value of the pizza—in this case the company value *before taxes*—is not changed by slicing. But anything the firm can do to reduce the size of the government's slice obviously leaves more for the others. One way to do this is to borrow money. This reduces the firm's tax bill and increases the cash payments to the investors. The value of their investment goes up by the present value of the tax savings.

In a no-tax world, MM's proposition I states that the value of the firm is unaffected by capital structure. But MM also modified proposition I to recognize corporate taxes:

Value of levered firm = value if all-equity financed + present value of tax shield

In the special case of permanent debt,

$$\textbf{Value of levered firm = value if all-equity financed} + T_c D$$

This "corrected" formula is illustrated in Figure 15.5. It implies that borrowing increases firm value and shareholders' wealth.

CORPORATE TAXES AND THE WEIGHTED-AVERAGE COST OF CAPITAL

We have shown that when there are corporate taxes, debt provides the company with a valuable tax shield. Few companies explicitly calculate the present value of interest tax shields associated with a particular borrowing policy. The tax shields are not forgotten however, because they show up in the discount rate used to evaluate capital investments.

Since debt interest is tax-deductible, the government in effect pays 35 percent of the interest cost. So to keep its investors happy, the firm has to earn the *after-tax* rate of interest on its debt and the return required by shareholders. Once we recognize the tax benefit of debt, the weighted-average cost of capital formula (see Chapter 11 for a review if you need one) becomes

$$\text{WACC} = (1 - T_c)\, r_{\text{debt}} \left(\frac{D}{D+E}\right) + r_{\text{equity}} \left(\frac{E}{D+E}\right) \tag{15.3}$$

Notice that when we allow for the tax advantage of debt, the weighted-average cost of capital depends on the *after-tax* rate of interest, $(1 - T_c) \times r_{\text{debt}}$.

▶ EXAMPLE 15.2 *WACC and Debt Policy*

We can use the weighted-average cost of capital formula to see how leverage affects River Cruises' cost of capital if the company pays corporate tax. When a company has no debt, the weighted-average cost of capital and the return required by shareholders are identical. In the case of River Cruises, the WACC with all-equity financing is 12.5 percent, and the value of the firm is $650,000.

Now let us calculate the weighted-average cost of capital if River Cruises issues $500,000 of permanent debt (D = $500,000). Company value increases by PV tax shield = $175,000, from $650,000 to $825,000 (meaning that $D + E$ = $825,000). Therefore the value of equity must be $825,000 – $500,000 = $325,000 ($E$ = $325,000).

To calculate River Cruises' weighted-average cost of capital, we would need to know its cost of equity after issuing debt. We can take some guidance from MM Proposition II with corporate taxes, which tells us that for a levered firm, the expected rate of return to shareholders, or the cost of equity should be

$$r_{\text{equity}} = r_{\text{assets}} + (D/E)(1 - T_c)(r_{\text{assets}} - r_{\text{debt}})$$

We get, $r_{\text{equity}} = .125 + (500{,}000/325{,}000)(1 - .35)(.125 - .10) = .15$.

Table 15.5 shows that when River Cruises borrows, the expected equity income is $48,750. So the expected return to shareholders is $48,750/$325,000 = 15 percent ($r_{\text{equity}} = .15$).[6] The interest rate is 10 percent ($r_{\text{debt}} = .10$) and the corporate tax rate is 35 percent ($T_c = .35$). This is all the information we need to see how leverage affects River Cruises' weighted-average cost of capital:

$$\text{WACC} = (1 - T_c) r_{\text{debt}} \left(\frac{D}{D+E}\right) + r_{\text{equity}} \left(\frac{E}{D+E}\right)$$

$$= (1 - .35)\ .10 \left(\frac{500{,}000}{825{,}000}\right) + .15 \left(\frac{325{,}000}{825{,}000}\right) = .0985, \text{ or } 9.85\%$$

We saw earlier that if there are no corporate taxes, the weighted-average cost of capital is unaffected by borrowing. But when there are corporate taxes, debt provides the company with a new benefit—the interest tax shield. In this case leverage reduces the weighted-average cost of capital (in River Cruises' case from 12.5 percent to 9.85 percent).

Figure 15.6 repeats Figure 15.3 except that now we have allowed for the effect of taxes on River Cruises' cost of capital. You can see that as the company borrows more, the expected return on equity rises, but the rise is less rapid than in the absence of taxes. The after-tax cost of debt is only 6.5 percent. As a result, the weighted-average cost of capital declines. For example, if the company has debt of $500,000, the equity is worth $325,000, and the debt-equity ratio (D/E) is $500,000/$325,000 = 1.54. Figure 15.6 shows that with

[6] This is consistent with our result obtained from using the equation based on MM Proposition II with corporate taxes.

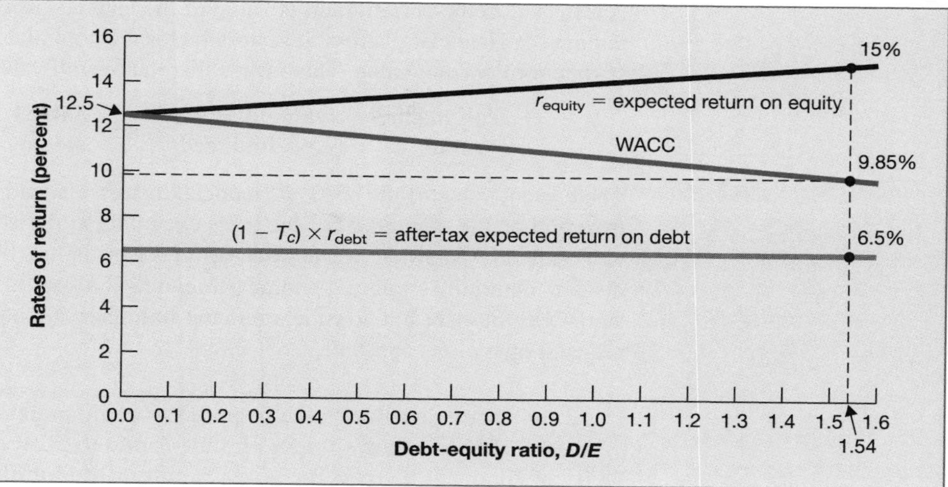

FIGURE 15.6
Changes in River Cruises' cost of capital with increased leverage, when there are corporate taxes. The after-tax cost of debt is assumed to be constant at (1 – .35)10 = 6.5 percent. With increased borrowing the cost of equity rises, but more slowly than in the no-tax case (see Figure 15.3). The weighted-average cost of capital (WACC) declines as the firm borrows more.

this amount of debt the weighted-average cost of capital is 9.85 percent, the same figure that we calculated above.

THE IMPLICATIONS OF CORPORATE TAXES FOR CAPITAL STRUCTURE

If borrowing provides an interest tax shield, the implied optimal debt policy appears to be embarrassingly extreme: All firms should borrow to the hilt. This maximizes firm value and minimizes the weighted-average cost of capital.

MM were not that fanatical about it. No one would expect the gains to apply at extreme debt ratios. For example, if a firm borrows heavily, all its operating income may go to pay interest, and therefore, there are no corporate taxes to be paid. There is no point in such firms borrowing any more.

There may also be some tax *disadvantages* to borrowing because bondholders have to pay personal income tax on any interest they receive. Shareholders, on the other hand, can get a tax break because some of their returns come as capital gains. Capital gains are not taxed until the stock is sold and currently, only 50 percent of such capital gains are taxed.[7]

All this suggests that there may come a point at which the tax savings from debt level off and may even decline. But it doesn't explain why highly profitable companies with large tax bills often thrive with little or no debt. There are clearly factors besides tax to consider.

15.3 Costs of Financial Distress

Financial distress occurs when promises to creditors are broken or honoured with difficulty. Sometimes financial distress leads to bankruptcy. Sometimes it only means skating on thin ice.

As we will see, financial distress is costly. Investors know that levered firms may run into financial difficulty, and they worry about the **costs of financial distress.** That worry

costs of financial distress Costs arising from bankruptcy or distorted business decisions before bankruptcy.

[7] Recall from Chapter 2 that combined federal and provincial tax rates on ordinary income can be close to 50 percent in most provinces. But, as we have just discussed, capital gains are taxed at one-half of the regular personal tax rate.

is reflected in the current market value of the levered firm's securities. Even if the firm is not now in financial distress, investors factor the potential for future distress into their assessment of current value. This means that the overall value of the firm is

$$\textbf{Overall market value} = \textbf{value if all-equity financed} + \textbf{PV tax shield} - \textbf{PV costs of financial distress} \quad (15.4)$$

The present value of the costs of financial distress depends both on the probability of distress and on the magnitude of the costs encountered if distress occurs.

Figure 15.7 shows how the trade-off between the tax benefits of debt and the costs of distress determines optimal capital structure. Think of a firm like River Cruises, which starts with no debt but considers moving to higher and higher debt levels, holding its assets and operations constant.

At moderate debt levels the probability of financial distress is trivial and therefore the tax advantages of debt dominate. But at some point the probability of financial distress increases rapidly with additional borrowing, and the potential costs of distress begin to take a substantial bite out of firm value. The theoretical optimum is reached when the present value of tax savings due to additional borrowing is just offset by increases in the present value of costs of distress.

trade-off theory Debt levels are chosen to balance interest tax shields against the costs of financial distress.

This is called the **trade-off theory** of optimal capital structure. The theory says that managers will try to increase debt levels to the point where the value of additional interest tax shields is offset by the additional costs of financial distress exactly.

An enterprise that maximizes firm value should also minimize its weighted-average cost of capital. It follows that a particular debt-to-equity ratio represents the *optimal capital structure* if it results in the lowest possible weighted-average cost of capital, keeping in mind the potential costs of financial distress and bankruptcy that can result from excessive debt. We see this in Figure 15.8.

Now let's take a closer look at financial distress.

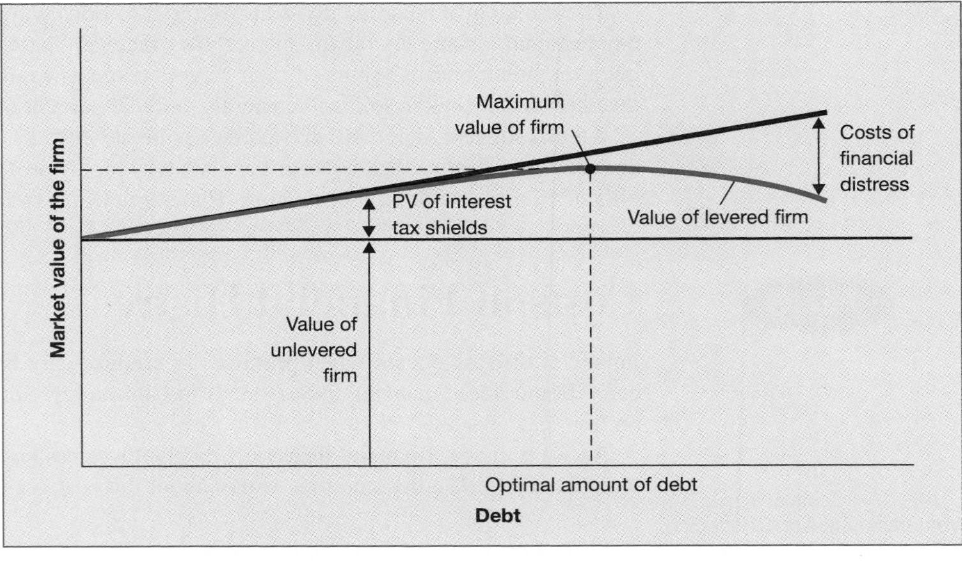

FIGURE 15.7
The trade-off theory of capital structure. The curved green line shows how the market value of the firm initially increases as the firm borrows but decreases as the costs of financial distress become more and more important. The optimal capital structure balances the costs of financial distress against the value of the interest tax shields generated by borrowing.

FIGURE 15.8
The figure shows that an optimum capital structure is consistent with a minimum WACC for the firm.

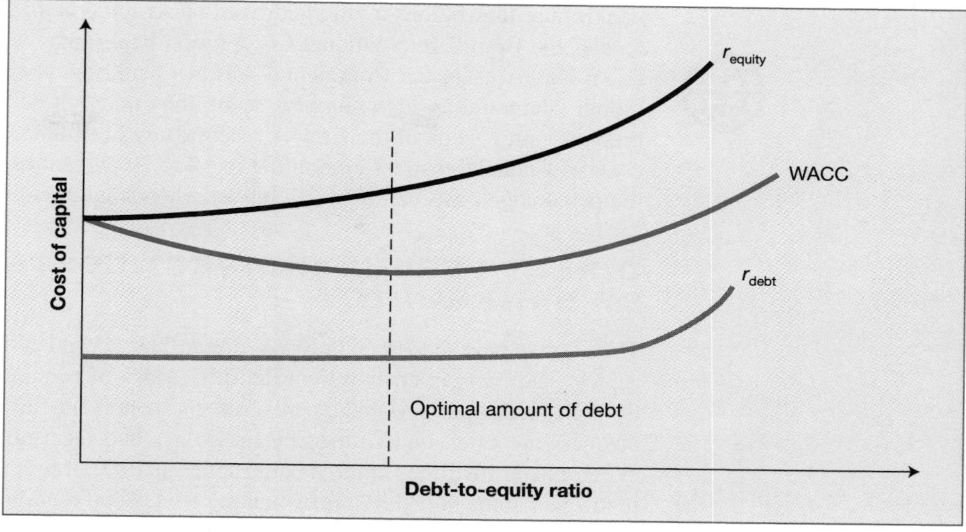

BANKRUPTCY COSTS

In principle, bankruptcy is merely a legal mechanism for allowing creditors (that is, lenders) to take over the firm when the decline in the value of its assets triggers a default on outstanding debt. If the company cannot pay its debts, the company is turned over to the creditors, who become the new owners; the old shareholders are left with nothing. Bankruptcy is not the *cause* of the decline in the value of the firm. It is the result.

In practice, of course, anything involving courts and lawyers cannot be free. The fees involved in a bankruptcy proceeding are paid out of the remaining value of the firm's assets. Creditors end up with only what is left after paying the lawyers and other court expenses. If there is a possibility of bankruptcy, the current market value of the firm is reduced by the present value of these potential costs.

It is easy to see how increased leverage affects the costs of financial distress. The more the firm owes, the higher the chance of default and therefore the greater the expected value of the associated costs. This reduces the current market value of the firm.

Creditors foresee the costs and realize that if default occurs, the bankruptcy costs will come out of the value of the firm. For this they demand compensation in advance in the form of a higher promised interest rate. This reduces the possible payoffs to shareholders and reduces the current market value of their shares.

CHECK POINT 15.5

Suppose investors foresee $2 million of legal costs if the firm defaults on its bonds. How does this affect the value of the firm's bonds if bankruptcy occurs? How does the possibility of default affect the interest rate demanded by bondholders today? How does this possibility affect today's value of the firm's common stock?

EVIDENCE ON BANKRUPTCY COSTS

Bankruptcy costs can add up fast. Manville, which declared bankruptcy in 1982 because of expected liability for asbestos-related health claims, spent $200 million (US) on

bankruptcy fees before it emerged from bankruptcy in 1988.[8] The legal and professional fees of the Braniff International Corporation bankruptcy were reported to be $12 million (US); legal fees in the Continental Airlines bankruptcy were running $2 million (US) a month. Daunting as such numbers seem, they may not be a large *percentage* of the total prebankruptcy value of the firm. A recent study of troubled, highly leveraged firms found costs of financial distress amounting to 10 to 20 percent of predistress market value.[9] But the percentage costs can be much higher when smaller companies get into trouble.

DIRECT VERSUS INDIRECT COSTS OF BANKRUPTCY

Thus far we have discussed only the *direct* (that is, legal and administrative) costs of bankruptcy. The *indirect* costs reflect the difficulties of running a company while it is going through bankruptcy. Management's efforts to prevent further deterioration in the firm's business are often undermined by the delays and legal tangles that go with bankruptcy. When Eastern Airlines entered bankruptcy in 1989, it was in severe financial trouble, but it still had some valuable, profit-making routes and readily saleable assets such as planes and terminal facilities. After nearly 2 years under the "protection" of a bankruptcy court, which allowed Eastern to continue loss-making operations, there was hardly anything of value left when it was finally forced to liquidate in 1991. Another illustration of the indirect costs of bankruptcy is provided in the nearby Finance in Action box, which describes the disruption to Penn Central Railroad's business.

SEE BOX P. 463

We don't know how much these indirect costs add to the expenses of bankruptcy. We suspect it is a significant number, particularly when bankruptcy proceedings are prolonged. Perhaps the best evidence is the reluctance of creditors to force a firm into bankruptcy. In principle, they would be better off to end the agony and seize the assets as soon as possible. But instead creditors often overlook defaults in the hope of nursing the firm over a difficult period. They do this in part to avoid the costs of bankruptcy. There is an old financial saying, "Borrow $1,000 and you've got a banker. Borrow $10,000,000 and you've got a partner."

FINANCIAL DISTRESS WITHOUT BANKRUPTCY

Not every firm that gets into trouble goes bankrupt. As long as the firm can scrape up enough cash to pay the interest on its debt, it may be able to postpone bankruptcy for many years. Eventually the firm may recover, pay off its debt, and escape bankruptcy altogether.

A narrow escape from bankruptcy does *not* mean that costs of financial distress are avoided. When a firm is in trouble, suppliers worry that they may not be paid, potential customers fear that the firm will not be able to honour its warranties, and employees start contemplating their next job. While all firms suffer in times of financial trouble, manufacturers of relatively expensive, durable products requiring regular after-sales service, such as automobile or computer companies, can have particularly high costs associated with financial distress. Similarly, the perception that an airline company is in financial trouble may scare away customers concerned about the maintenance and safety of the aircraft and its ability to honour frequent flyer programs. For instance, before Canadian Airlines was taken over by Air Canada, there were concerns about their growing financial difficulties, which caused business travellers to switch to other airlines.

[8] S. P. Sherman, "Bankruptcy's Spreading Blight," *Fortune* (June 3, 1991), pp. 123–132.

[9] G. Andrade and S. N. Kaplan, "How Costly Is Financial (Not Economic) Distress? Evidence from Highly Leveraged Transactions that Became Distressed," *Journal of Finance* 53 (October 1998), pp. 1443–1493.

FINANCE IN ACTION

Penn Central's Bankruptcy

The Penn Central Railroad went under in June 1970. It was the largest and most dramatic corporate failure up to that time. Four years later, with bankruptcy proceedings nowhere near completion, *Business Week* published an article called "Why the Penn Central Is Falling Apart." The article noted that

> although the railroad needed to invest huge sums of money to rebuild its facilities and continue operations, its creditors were more concerned with getting their own money back, even if that meant shutting down the railroad. In a chicken-and-egg type of problem, the capital necessary to make the railroad viable would not be forthcoming unless Penn Central could convince investors that it could be reorganized as a viable corporation.

Penn Central could have raised money by selling off some of its assets, but its creditors naturally opposed this. As the *Business Week* article put it:

> Agonizingly for everyone on the Penn Central, there is a tremendous source of capital that cannot be touched. For example, just about every abandoned mine branch in the Allegheny Mountains is chock full of old Penn Central cars destined for scrap. With today's scrap prices, they are a potential gold mine. But the creditors will not allow this asset to be turned into cash that will be reinvested in the estate, since that estate is eroding everyday.

Penn Central's problems show that some of the most important costs of bankruptcy are difficult to measure. The disruption of business activity is less visible but can be far more costly than the firm's legal bills.

Source: Quotations from *Business Week*, October 12, 1974.

The firm's bondholders and stockholders both want the company to recover, but in other respects their interests may be in conflict. In times of financial distress the security holders are like many political parties—united on generalities but threatened by squabbling on any particular issue.

Financial distress is costly when conflicts get in the way of running the business. Shareholders are tempted to forsake the usual objective of maximizing the overall market value of the firm; they pursue their self-interests instead. They are tempted to play games at the expense of their creditors. These games add to the costs of financial distress.

Think of a company—call it Double-R Nutting—which is teetering on the brink of bankruptcy. It has large debts and large losses. Double-R's assets have little value, and if its debts were due today, Double-R would default, leaving the firm bankrupt. The assets would then be sold off, the debtholders would perhaps receive a few cents on the dollar, and the shareholders would be left with nothing.

But suppose the debts are not due yet. That grace period explains why Double-R's shares still have value. There could be a stroke of luck that will rescue the firm and allow it to pay off its debts with something left over. That's a long shot—unless firm value increases sharply, the stock will be valueless. But the owners have a secret weapon: They control investment and operating strategy.

The First Game: Bet the Bank's Money. Suppose Double-R has the opportunity to take a wild gamble. If it can't pull it off, the shareholders will be no worse off, the company will probably go under anyway. But if the gamble does succeed, there will be more than enough assets to pay off the debt, and the surplus will go into the shareholders' pockets. You can see why management might want to take the chance. In taking the gamble, they are essentially betting the debtholders' money, but if Double-R does hit the jackpot, the equityholders get most of the loot.

One owner-manager of a small bankrupt company called KenDavis Industries put the point this way: "Everyone agrees there is no shareholder equity—so *we've* got *nothing* to lose. The *banks* have it all on the line now—not us." In another case, the managers of the failing firm took the incentive to gamble literally. They went to Las Vegas and bet the company's money, hoping to win enough to pay off the creditors. The effects of such distorted incentives to take on risk are usually not this blatant, but the results can be the same. For example, Sambo's Restaurants borrowed against unencumbered assets while in bankruptcy proceedings and used the funds to pay for a risky marketing initiative, changing the name and concept of its restaurants. When the gamble failed, unsecured creditors suffered most of the loss: They received only $.11 of each dollar owed to them.[10]

These kinds of warped capital investment strategies clearly are costly for the bondholders and for the firm as a whole. Why do we say they create costs of financial distress? Because the temptation to follow such strategies is strongest when the odds of default are high. A healthy firm would never invest in Double-R's negative-NPV gamble, since it would be gambling with its own money, not the bondholders'. A healthy firm's creditors would not be vulnerable to this type of game.

The Second Game: Don't Bet Your Own Money. We have just seen how shareholders, acting in self-interest, may take on risky, unprofitable projects. These are errors of commission. We will now illustrate how conflicts of interest may also lead to errors of omission.

Suppose Double-R uncovers a relatively safe project with a positive NPV. Unfortunately, the project requires a substantial investment. Double-R will need to raise this extra cash from its shareholders. Although the project has a positive NPV, the profits may not be sufficient to rescue the company from bankruptcy. If that is so, all the profits from the new project will be used to help pay off the company's debt, and the shareholders will get no return on the cash they put up. Although it is in the firm's interest to go ahead with the project, it is *not* in the owners' interest, and the project will be passed up.

Again, our example illustrates a general point. The value of any investment opportunity to the firm's *shareholders* is reduced because project benefits must be shared with the bondholders. Thus it may not be in the shareholders' interest to contribute fresh equity capital even if that means forgoing positive-NPV opportunities.

These two games illustrate potential conflicts of interest between shareholders and debtholders. These conflicts, which theoretically affect all levered firms, become much more serious when firms are staring bankruptcy in the face.

If the probability of default is high, managers and shareholders will be tempted to take excessively risky projects. At the same time, shareholders may refuse to contribute more equity capital even if the firm has safe, positive-NPV opportunities. Shareholders would rather take money out of the firm than put new money in.

The more the firm borrows, the greater the temptation to play such games. The increased odds of poor decisions in the future prompt investors to reduce today's assessment of the market value of the firm. Potential lenders, realizing that games may be played at their expense in the future, protect themselves by demanding better terms on the money they lend today. So the fall in value comes out of shareholders' pockets. This is the reason that it is ultimately in the shareholders' interest to avoid temptation. The easiest way to do this is to limit borrowing to levels at which the firm's debt is safe or close to it.

[10] These cases are cited in Lynn M. LoPucki, "The Trouble with Chapter 11," *Wisconsin Law Review* (1993), pp. 729–760.

Frequently, agreements between shareholders and bondholders, called *protective covenants*, are incorporated as part of the loan document. These covenants are designed to safeguard the interests of bondholders. While many covenants carry restrictive clauses that can reduce flexibility in managerial decision making, these agreements can also have the effect of lowering interest rates.

We do not mean to leave the impression that managers and shareholders always succumb to temptation unless restrained. Usually they refrain voluntarily, not only from a sense of fair play but also on pragmatic grounds: A firm or individual that makes a killing today at the expense of a creditor will be coldly received when the time comes to borrow again. Aggressive game playing is done only by out-and-out crooks and by firms in extreme financial distress. Firms limit borrowing precisely because they don't wish to be in distress and exposed to the temptation to play.

☑ CHECK POINT 15.6

We have described two games that might be played by firms in financial distress. Why are the games costly? How does the possibility that the game might be played at some point in the future affect today's capital structure decisions?

COSTS OF DISTRESS VARY WITH TYPE OF ASSET

Suppose your firm's only asset is a large downtown hotel, Heartbreak Hotel, mortgaged to the hilt. A recession hits, occupancy rates fall, and the mortgage payments cannot be met. The lender takes over and sells the hotel to a new owner and operator. The stock is worthless and you use the firm's stock certificates for wallpaper.

What is the cost of bankruptcy? In this example, probably very little. The value of the hotel is, of course, much less than you hoped, but that is due to the lack of guests not bankruptcy. Bankruptcy does not damage the hotel itself. The direct bankruptcy costs are restricted to items such as legal and court fees, real estate commissions, and the time the lender spends sorting things out.

Suppose we repeat the story of Heartbreak Hotel for Fledgling Electronics. Everything is the same, except for the underlying assets. Fledgling is a high-tech going concern and much of its value reflects investors' beliefs that its research team will come up with profitable ideas. Fledgling is a "people business"; its most important assets go down in the elevator and into the parking lot every night.

If Fledgling gets into trouble, the shareholders may be reluctant to put up money to cash in on those profitable ideas—why should they put up cash which will simply go to pay off the banks? Failure to invest is likely to be much more serious for Fledgling than for a company like Heartbreak Hotel.

If Fledgling finally defaults on its debt, the lender would find it much more difficult to cash in by selling off the assets. In fact, if trouble comes, many of those assets may drive into the sunset and never come back.

Some assets, like good commercial real estate, can pass through bankruptcy and reorganization largely unscathed; the values of other assets are likely to be considerably diminished. The losses are greatest for intangible assets that are linked to the continuing prosperity of the firm. An important determinant of debt capacity is the availability of collateral. When a firm faces financial distress, certain assets such as plants, land, and equipment are more readily valued and sold than patents, brand names, and other intangibles. That may be why debt ratios are low in the pharmaceutical industry, where company values depend on continued success in research and development. It may also explain the low debt ratios in many service companies, whose main asset is their skilled labour. On the other hand, capital-intensive manufacturing firms or wholesale and retail businesses with sizable tangible assets tend to have higher debt ratios. Table 15.6 provides debt-to-equity ratios for some representative Canadian firms in different industries as well as industry average debt-to-equity ratios. Notice the very low debt-to-equity ratio of the biotechnology and pharmaceuticals company, QLT, Inc., but the relatively high debt-to-equity ratio of Loblaw, the large grocery chain. The moral of these examples is

Do not think only about whether borrowing is likely to bring trouble. Think also of the value that may be lost if trouble comes.

CHECK POINT 15.7

For which of the following companies would the costs of financial distress be most serious? Why?

- A 3-year-old biotech company. So far the company has no products approved for sale, but its scientists are hard at work developing a breakthrough drug.
- An oil production company with 50 producing wells and 20 million barrels of existing oil reserves.

We have now completed our review of the building blocks of the trade-off theory of optimal capital structure. In the next section we will sum up that theory and briefly cover a competing "pecking order" theory.

15.4 Explaining Financing Choices

THE TRADE-OFF THEORY

Financial managers often think of the firm's debt-equity decision as a trade-off between interest tax shields and the costs of financial distress. Of course, there is controversy about how valuable interest tax shields are and what kinds of financial trouble are most threatening, but these disagreements are only variations on a theme. Thus Figure 15.7 illustrates the debt-equity trade-off.

This trade-off theory predicts that target debt ratios will vary from firm to firm. Companies with safe, tangible assets and plenty of taxable income to shield should have high target ratios. Unprofitable companies with risky, intangible assets should rely primarily on equity financing.

All in all, this trade-off theory of capital structure tells a comforting story. It avoids extreme predictions and rationalizes moderate debt ratios. But what are the facts? Can the trade-off theory of capital structure explain how companies actually behave?

The answer is yes and no. On the yes side, the trade-off theory successfully explains many industry differences in capital structure. For example, high-tech growth companies, whose assets are risky and mostly intangible, normally use relatively little debt. Utilities or retailers can and do borrow heavily because their assets are tangible and relatively safe. From Table 15.6, compare the low debt-to-equity ratio of the high-tech company, Research In Motion, with the much higher debt-to-equity ratio of the utility company, ATCO. Notice that in general, the company ratios are consistent with their respective industry averages.

TABLE 15.6
Debt-to-equity ratios for a sample of Canadian firms and industries in 2000

Firm	Debt-to-Equity Ratio	Industry	Industry Average Debt-to-Equity Ratio
Magna International, Inc.	0.18	Auto, parts and transportation equipment	0.95
QLT, Inc.	0.04	Biotechnology and pharmaceuticals	0.21
St. Lawrence Cement Group	0.42	Building materials	0.62
Rogers Communications, Inc.	7.60	Communications and media	2.67
Emco, Ltd.	1.38	Fabricating and engineering	0.95
Power Financial Corp.	0.18	Financial management	0.54
Maple Leaf Foods, Inc.	1.44	Food and beverage	1.12
Barrick Gold Corporation	0.22	Gold and precious metals	0.45
Extendicare, Inc.	2.27	Hospitality	2.89
Imperial Oil, Ltd.	0.30	Oil and gas	0.56
Abitibi-Consolidated, Inc.	1.22	Paper and forest products	1.41
Enbridge, Inc.	2.27	Pipelines	2.22
Stelco, Inc.	0.62	Steel	1.07
Research In Motion, Ltd.	0.02	Technology	0.28
ATCO, Ltd.	1.54	Telephone and utilities	2.28
Canadian National Railway Company	0.76	Transportation and environmental services	1.43
Loblaw Companies, Ltd.	1.05	Wholesale and retail	0.72

Source: Financial Post Online, FP Reports, Industry Reports and Investor Report 2001, at www.fpdata.finpost.com.

On the no side, there are other things the trade-off theory cannot explain. It cannot explain why some of the most successful companies thrive with little debt. Consider, for example, the large American pharmaceutical company Merck, which is basically all-equity financed. Granted, Merck's most valuable assets are intangible—the fruits of its research and development. We know that intangible assets and conservative capital structures should go together. But Merck also has a very large corporate income tax bill ($3 billion in 2000) and the highest possible credit rating. It could borrow enough to save tens of millions of tax dollars without raising a whisker of concern about possible financial distress.

Merck illustrates an odd fact about real-life capital structures: The most profitable companies generally borrow the least. Here the trade-off theory fails because it predicts exactly the reverse. Under the trade-off theory, high profits should mean more debt-servicing capacity and more taxable income to shield and therefore should give a *higher* debt ratio.

CHECK POINT 15.8

Rank these industries in order of predicted debt ratios under the trade-off theory of capital structure (1) Internet software, (2) auto manufacturing, and (3) regulated electric utilities.

A PECKING ORDER THEORY

There is an alternative theory that could explain why profitable companies borrow less. It is based on *asymmetric information*—managers know more than outside investors about the profitability and prospects of their firm. Thus investors may not be able to assess the true value of a new issue of securities by the firm. They may be especially reluctant to buy newly issued common stock, because they worry that the new shares will turn out to be overpriced.

Such worries can explain why the announcement of a stock issue can drive down the stock price.[11] If managers know more than outside investors, the manager will be tempted to time stock issues when their companies' stock is *overpriced*—in other words, when the managers are relatively pessimistic. On the other hand, optimistic managers will see their companies' shares as *underpriced* and decide *not* to issue. You can see why investors would learn to interpret the announcement of a stock issue as a "pessimistic manager" signal and mark down the stock price accordingly. You can also see why optimistic financial managers—and most managers *are* optimistic!—would view a common stock issue as a relatively expensive source of financing.

All these problems are avoided if the company can finance with internal funds, that is, with earnings retained and reinvested. But if external financing is required, the path of least resistance is debt, not equity. Issuing debt seems to have a trifling effect on stock prices. There is less scope for debt to be misvalued and therefore a debt issue is a less worrisome signal to investors.

pecking order theory Firms prefer to issue debt rather than equity if internal finance is insufficient.

These observations suggest a **pecking order theory** of capital structure. It goes like this:

1. Firms prefer internal finance because these funds are raised without sending any adverse signals that may lower the stock price.
2. If external finance is required, firms issue debt first and issue equity only as a last resort. This pecking order arises because an issue of debt is less likely than an equity issue to be interpreted by investors as a bad omen.

In this story, there is no clear target debt-equity mix, because there are two kinds of equity, internal and external. The first is at the top of the pecking order and the second is at the bottom. The pecking order explains why the most profitable firms generally borrow less; it is not because they have low target debt-ratios but because they don't need outside money. Less profitable firms issue debt because they do not have sufficient internal funds for their capital investment program and because debt is first in the pecking order for *external* finance.

The pecking order theory does not deny that taxes and financial distress *can* be important factors in the choice of capital structure. However, the theory says that these factors are less important than managers' preference for internal over external funds and for debt financing over new issues of common stock.

We saw in Chapter 13 that for most Canadian corporations, internal funds finance the majority of new investment, and most external financing comes from debt. These aggregate financing patterns are consistent with the pecking order theory. Yet the pecking order seems to work best for mature firms. Fast-growing high-tech firms often resort to a series of common stock issues to finance their investments. For this type of firm, common stock often comes at the *top* of the pecking order. The reasons why the pecking order theory works for some firms and not others are not well understood.

THE TWO FACES OF FINANCIAL SLACK

Other things being equal, it's better to be at the top of the pecking order than at the bottom. Firms that have worked down the pecking order and need external equity may end up living with excessive debt or bypassing good investments because shares can't be sold at what managers consider a fair price.

[11] We described this "announcement effect" in Chapter 14.

FINANCE IN ACTION

How Sealed Air's Change in Capital Structure Acted as a Catalyst to Organizational Change

Sealed Air Corporation manufactures a wide variety of packaging materials such as plastic packing bubbles and Jiffy padded envelopes.

As it entered 1989, Sealed Air was very conservatively financed with $33 million in total debt and over $54 million in cash. Thus, rather than borrowing cash, the company was actually a net lender. However, in June of that year, Sealed Air dramatically changed its capital structure by paying a special one-time dividend of $40 a share. With about 8.25 million shares trading, the total cash payout amounted to almost $330 million, or close to 90 percent of the total market value of the firm's common stock. To help finance this special dividend, the company borrowed a total of $307 million. Thus, the company went overnight from being a net lender to being a very heavy borrower. Debt now amounted to 125 percent of the book value of the assets and 65 percent of their market value.

Until the change in capital structure Sealed Air's performance was no better than that of the industry as a whole. But the change was a prelude to a sharp improvement in the company's operating performance. In the following 5 years, operating profit increased by 70 percent while the asset base grew by only 9 percent. This improvement in profitability was more than matched by the company's stock market performance. The initial effect of Sealed Air's announced change in capital structure was a jump of 10 percent in the stock price. Over the next 5.5 years the stock outperformed the market by 400 percent.

What, then, motivated the change in capital structure and what role, if any, did this change play in the company's subsequent performance?

Some of the gains from the change in capital structure may have come from the fact that the company was able to offset the interest payments against tax. But this does not appear to have been a primary motive. Instead, the change appears to have been management's response to the realization that life at Sealed Air was in many respects too comfortable. For years patents had insulated the company from competition. Cash was plentiful. So the company never needed to think hard about requests to invest in new projects, and there was no sense of urgency in removing inefficiencies. In the management's view, it would take nothing less than a crisis to shake employees out of their complacency. The change in capital structure was just such a crisis.

The sharp increase in debt levels meant that cash was no longer abundant for it was now needed to pay the debtholders and was literally essential to the company's survival. Thus, managers now felt under pressure to make those efficiency gains that previously had not seemed worthwhile. As employees became aware of the need for more effective operations, it was possible to decentralize decision making within the company and to install a more effective system of performance measurement and compensation. The result was a sharp increase in profit margins and a reduction in the working capital and fixed assets employed to generate each dollar of sales. It seemed that the capital structure change had succeeded in kickstarting a remarkable improvement in Sealed Air's performance.

Source: Adapted from K. H. Wruck, "Financial Policy as a Catalyst for Organizational Change: Sealed Air Corporation's Leveraged Special Dividend," *Journal of Applied Corporate Finance* 7 (Winter 1995), pp. 20–37.

financial slack Ready access to cash or debt financing.

In other words, **financial slack** is valuable. Having financial slack means having cash, marketable securities, readily saleable real assets, and ready access to the debt markets or to bank financing. Ready access basically requires conservative financing so that potential lenders see the company's debt as a safe investment.

In the long run, a company's value rests more on its capital investment and operating decisions than on financing. Therefore, you want to make sure your firm has sufficient financial slack so that financing is quickly available for good investments. Financial slack is most valuable to firms with plenty of positive-NPV growth opportunities. That is another reason why growth companies usually aspire to conservative capital structures.

There is also a dark side to financial slack. Too much of it may encourage managers to take it easy, expand their perks, or empire-build with cash that should be paid back to shareholders. Michael Jensen has stressed the tendency of managers with ample free cash flow (or unnecessary financial slack) to plow too much cash into mature businesses or ill-advised acquisitions. "The problem," Jensen says, "is how to motivate managers to disgorge the cash rather than investing it below the cost of capital or wasting it in organizational inefficiencies."[12]

If that's the problem, then maybe debt is an answer. Scheduled interest and principal payments are contractual obligations of the firm. Debt forces the firm to pay out cash. Perhaps the best debt level would leave just enough cash in the bank after debt service to finance all positive-NPV projects, with not a penny left over.

We do not recommend this degree of fine-tuning, but the idea is valid and important. For some firms, the threat of financial distress may have a good effect on managers' incentives. After all, skating on thin ice can be useful if it makes the skater concentrate. Likewise, managers of highly levered firms are more likely to work harder, run a leaner operation, and think more carefully before they spend money.

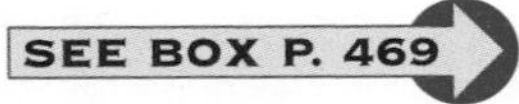

The nearby Finance in Action box tells the story of how Sealed Air Corporation borrowed more than $300 million (US), using the proceeds of the loan to pay a special cash dividend to shareholders. The net effect was to increase debt from a trivial level to a full 65 percent of the total value of the firm. The dramatic increase in debt committed the firm to pay out large sums of money as interest, leaving it with little opportunity to fritter its cash away in pursuit of a comfortable life. Sealed Air showed great improvements in efficiency after the change in capital structure.

15.5 Summary

1. What is the goal of the capital structure decision? What is the financial manager trying to do?

The goal is to maximize the overall market value of all the securities issued by the firm. Think of the financial manager as taking all the firm's real assets and selling them to investors as a package of securities. Some financial managers choose the simplest package possible: all-equity financing. Others end up issuing dozens of types of debt and equity securities. The financial manager must try to find the particular combination that maximizes the market value of the firm. If firm value increases, common shareholders will benefit.

2. Does firm value increase when more debt is used?

Not necessarily. Modigliani and Miller's (MM) famous **debt irrelevance proposition** states that firm value can't be increased by changing **capital structure.** Therefore, the proportions of debt and equity financing don't matter. **Financial leverage** does increase the expected rate of return to shareholders, but the risk of their shares increases proportionally. MM show that the extra return and extra risk balance out, leaving shareholders no better or worse off.

Of course MM's argument rests on simplifying assumptions. For example, the argument assumes efficient, well-functioning capital markets and ignores taxes and costs of financial distress. But even if these assumptions are incorrect in practice, MM's proposition is important. It exposes logical traps that financial managers sometimes fall into, particularly the idea that debt is "cheap financing" because the explicit cost of debt (the interest rate) is less than the cost of equity. Debt has an implicit cost too, because increased borrowing increases **financial risk** and cost of equity. When both costs are considered, debt is not cheaper than equity. MM show that if there are no corporate income taxes, the firm's weighted-average cost of capital does not depend on the amount of debt financing.

3. How do corporate income taxes modify MM's leverage irrelevance proposition?

Debt interest is a tax-deductible expense. Thus borrowing creates an **interest tax shield,** which equals the marginal corporate tax rate, T_c, times the interest payment $r_{\text{debt}} \times D$. Future interest tax shields are usually valued by discounting at the borrowing rate r_{debt}. In the special case of permanent debt,

$$\text{PV tax shield} = \frac{T_c\,(r_{\text{debt}} \times D)}{r_{\text{debt}}} = T_c D$$

[12] M. C. Jensen, "Agency Costs of Free Cash Flow, Corporate Finance and Takeovers," *American Economic Review* 26 (May 1986), p. 323.

Of course interest tax shields are valuable only for companies that are making profits and paying taxes.

4. If interest tax shields are valuable, why don't all tax-paying firms borrow as much as possible?

The more they borrow, the higher the odds of financial distress. The **costs of financial distress** can be broken down as follows:

- Direct bankruptcy costs, primarily legal and administrative costs.
- Indirect bankruptcy costs, reflecting the difficulty of managing a company when it is in bankruptcy proceedings.
- Costs of the threat of bankruptcy, such as poor investment decisions resulting from conflicts of interest between debtholders and shareholders.

5. Suppose I add interest tax shields and costs of financial distress to MM's leverage irrelevance proposition. What's the result?

The **trade-off theory** of optimal capital structure. The trade-off theory says that financial managers should increase debt to the point where the value of additional interest tax shields is just offset by additional costs of possible financial distress.

The trade-off theory says that firms with safe, tangible assets and plenty of taxable income should operate at high debt levels. Less profitable firms, or firms with risky, intangible assets, should borrow less.

6. What's the pecking order theory?

The **pecking order theory** says that firms prefer internal financing (that is, earnings retained and reinvested) over external financing. If external financing is needed, they prefer to issue debt rather than issue new shares. The pecking order theory starts with the observation that managers know more than outside investors about the firm's value and prospects. Therefore, investors find it difficult to value new security issues, particularly issues of common stock. Internal financing avoids this problem. If external financing is necessary, debt is the first choice.

The pecking order theory says that the amount of debt a firm issues will depend on its need for external financing. The theory also suggests that financial managers should try to maintain at least some **financial slack,** that is, a reserve of ready cash or unused borrowing capacity.

7. Is financial slack always valuable?

Not if it leads to slack managers. High debt levels (and the threat of financial distress) can create strong incentives for managers to work harder, conserve cash, and avoid negative-NPV investments.

8. Is there a rule for finding optimal capital structure?

Sorry, there are no simple answers for capital structure decisions. Debt may be better than equity in some cases, worse in others. But there are at least four dimensions for the financial manager to think about.

- *Taxes.* How valuable are interest tax shields? Is the firm likely to continue paying taxes over the full life of a debt issue? Safe, consistently profitable firms are most likely to stay in a tax-paying position.
- *Risk.* Financial distress is costly even if the firm survives it. Other things equal, financial distress is more likely for firms with high business risk. That is why risky firms typically issue less debt.
- *Asset type.* If distress does occur, the costs are generally greatest for firms whose value depends on intangible assets. Such firms generally borrow less than firms with safe, tangible assets.
- *Financial slack.* How much is enough? More slack makes it easy to finance future investments, but it may weaken incentives for managers. More debt, and therefore less slack, increases the odds that the firm may have to issue stock to finance future investments.

RELATED WEB LINKS

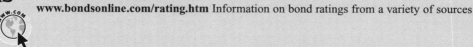

www.investinginbonds.com This Bond Market Association site has extensive information about bond markets and bond pricing

www.bondsonline.com/rating.htm Information on bond ratings from a variety of sources

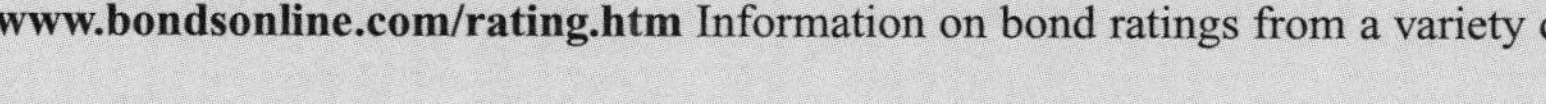

KEY TERMS

capital structure	446	financial leverage	451	costs of financial distress	459
restructuring	447	financial risk	451	trade-off theory	460
MM's proposition I (debt irrelevance proposition)	450	MM's proposition II	453	pecking order theory	468
operating risk, business risk	450	interest tax shield	455	financial slack	469

QUESTIONS AND PROBLEMS

*Answers in Appendix B

BASIC

1. **MM's Leverage Irrelevance Proposition.** True or false? MM's leverage irrelevance proposition says that
   a. the value of the firm does not depend on the fraction of debt versus equity financing.
   b. as financial leverage increases, the value of the firm increases by just enough to affect the additional financial risk absorbed by equity.
   c. the cost of equity increases with financial leverage only when the risk of financial distress is high.
   d. if the firm pays no taxes, the weighted-average cost of capital does not depend on the debt ratio.
2. **Effects of Leverage.** Increasing financial leverage can increase both the cost of debt, (r_{debt}), and the cost of equity, (r_{equity}). How can the overall cost of capital stay constant? (Assume the firm pays no taxes.)
3. **Tax Shields.** What is an interest tax shield? How does it increase the "pie" of after-tax income shareholders? Explain. *Hint:* Construct a simple numerical example showing how financial leverage affects the total cash flow available to debt and equity investors. Be sure to hold pretax operating income constant.

*4. **Value of Tax Shields.** Establishment Industries borrows $800 million at an interest rate of 7.6 percent. It expects to maintain this debt level into the far future. What is the present value of interest tax shields? Establishment will pay tax at an effective rate of 37 percent.

5. **Trade-Off Theory.** What is the trade-off theory of optimal capital structure? How does it define the optimal debt ratio?
6. **Financial Distress.** Give three examples of the types of costs incurred by firms in financial distress.
7. **Pecking Order Theory.** What is the pecking order theory of optimal capital structure? If the theory is correct, what types of firms would you expect to operate at high debt levels?
8. **Financial Slack.** Why is financial slack valuable? *Hint:* What does the pecking order theory say about financial slack? Are there circumstances where too much financial slack might actually *reduce* the market value of the firm?
9. **Earnings and Leverage.** Suppose that River Cruises, which currently is all-equity financed, issues $250,000 of debt and uses the proceeds to repurchase 25,000 shares. Assume the firm pays no taxes, and that debt finance has no impact on its market value. Rework Table 15.2 to show how earnings per share and share return now vary with operating income.
10. **Debt Irrelevance.** Suppose an investor is unhappy with River Cruises' decision to borrow $250,000 (see the previous problem). What modifications can she make to her own investment portfolio to offset the effects of the firm's additional borrowing?

*11. **Leverage and P/E Ratio.** Calculate the ratio of price to expected earnings for River Cruises both before and after it borrows the $250,000. Why does the P/E ratio fall after the increase in leverage?

12. **Tax Shields.** Now suppose that the corporate tax is $T_c = .35$. Demonstrate that when River Cruises borrows the $250,000, the combined after-tax income of its debtholders and equityholders increases (compared to all-equity financing) by 35 percent of the firm's interest expense regardless of the state of the economy.

PRACTICE

13. **Equity Return and Leverage.** The common stock and debt of Northern Sludge are valued at $70 million and $30 million, respectively. Investors currently require a 16 percent return on the common stock and an 8 percent return on the debt. If Northern Sludge issues an additional $10 million of common stock and uses this money to retire debt, what happens to the expected return on the stock? Assume that the change in capital structure does not affect the risk of the debt and that there are no taxes.

*14. **Earnings and Leverage.** Reliable Gearing currently is all-equity financed. It has 10,000 shares of equity outstanding, selling at $100 a share. The firm is considering a capital restructuring. The low-debt plan calls for a debt issue of $200,000 with the proceeds used to buy back stock. The high-debt plan would exchange $400,000 of debt for equity. The debt will pay an interest rate of 10 percent. The firm pays no taxes.

a. What will be the debt-to-equity ratio after each possible restructuring?
b. If earnings before interest and tax (EBIT) will be either $90,000 or $130,000, what will earnings per share be for each financing mix for both possible values of EBIT? If both scenarios are equally likely, what is expected (i.e., average) EPS under each financing mix? Is the high-debt mix preferable?
c. Suppose that EBIT is $100,000. What is EPS under each financing mix? Why are they the same in this particular case?

15. **Leverage and Risk Premiums.** Schuldenfrei A.G. is financed entirely by common stock and has a beta of 1.0. The firm pays no taxes. The stock has a price-earnings multiple of 10 and is priced to offer a 10 percent expected return. The company decides to repurchase half the common stock and substitute an equal value of debt. If the debt yields a *risk-free* 5 percent, calculate

a. the beta of the common stock after the refinancing.
b. the required return and risk premium on the common stock before the refinancing.
c. the required return and risk premium on the common stock after the refinancing.
d. the required return on the debt.
e. the required return on the company (i.e., stock and debt combined) after the refinancing.

Assume that the operating profit of the firm is expected to remain constant. Give

f. the percentage increase in earnings per share after the refinancing.
g. the new price-earnings multiple. *Hint:* Has anything happened to the stock price?

*16. **Leverage and Capital Costs.** Hubbard's Pet Foods is financed 80 percent by common stock and 20 percent by bonds. The expected return on the common stock is 12 percent and the rate of interest on the bonds is 6 percent. Assume that the bonds are default-free and that there are no taxes. Now assume that Hubbard's issues more debt and uses the proceeds to retire equity. The new financing mix is 40 percent equity and 60 percent debt. If the debt is still default-free, what happens to the expected rate of return on equity? What happens to the expected return on the package of common stock and bonds?

17. **Leverage and Capital Costs.** "MM totally ignore the fact that as you borrow more, you have to pay higher rates of interest." Explain carefully whether this is a valid objection.

18. **Debt Irrelevance.** What's wrong with the following arguments?

a. As the firm borrows more and debt becomes risky, both share- and bondholders demand higher rates of return. Thus by *reducing* the debt ratio we can reduce *both* the cost of debt and the cost of equity, making everybody better off.
b. Moderate borrowing doesn't significantly affect the probability of financial distress or bankruptcy. Consequently, moderate borrowing won't increase the expected rate of return demanded by shareholders.
c. A capital investment opportunity offering a 10 percent internal rate of return is an attractive project if it can be 100 percent debt-financed at an 8 percent interest rate.
d. The more debt the firm issues, the higher the interest rate it must pay. That is one important reason why firms should operate at conservative debt levels.

19. **Leverage and Capital Costs.** A firm currently has a debt-equity ratio of 1/2. The debt, which is virtually riskless, pays an interest rate of 6 percent. The expected rate of return on the equity is 12 percent. What would happen to the expected rate of return on equity if the firm reduced its debt-equity ratio to 1/3? Assume the firm pays no taxes.

20. **Leverage and Capital Costs.** If an increase in the debt-equity ratio makes both debt and equity more risky, how can the cost of capital remain unchanged?

21. **Tax Shields.** Look back to Table 2.2 where we provided a summary 2001 income statement for Molson. If the tax rate is 35 percent, what is Molson's annual interest tax shield? What is the present value of the annual tax shield if the company plans to maintain its current debt level indefinitely? Assume a discount rate of 8 percent.

*22. **WACC.** Here is Establishment Industries' market-value balance sheet (figures in millions):

Net working capital	$ 550	Debt	$ 800
Long-term assets	$2,150	Equity	$1,900
Value of firm	$2,700		$2,700

The debt is yielding 7.6 percent and the cost of equity is 14 percent. The tax rate is 37 percent. Investors expect this level of debt to be permanent.

a. What is Establishment's WACC?
b. Write out a market-value balance sheet assuming Establishment has no debt. Use your answer to problem 4.

*23. **Tax Shields and WACC.** Here are book- and market-value balance sheets of the United Frypan Company:

BOOK-VALUE BALANCE SHEET

Net working capital	$ 20	Debt	$40
Long-term assets	80	Equity	60
	$100		$100

MARKET-VALUE BALANCE SHEET

Net working capital	$ 20	Debt	$ 40
Long-term assets	140	Equity	120
	$160		$160

Assume that MM's theory holds except for taxes. There is no growth and the $40 of debt is expected to be permanent. Assume a 35 percent corporate tax rate.

a. How much of the firm's value is accounted for by the debt-generated tax shield?
b. What is United Frypan's after-tax weighted-average cost of capital (WACC)?
c. Now suppose that Parliament passes a law that eliminates the deductibility of interest for tax purposes after a grace period of 5 years. What will be the new value of the firm, other things being equal? Assume an 8 percent borrowing rate.

*24. **Bankruptcy.** What are the drawbacks of operating a firm that is close to bankruptcy? Give some examples.

25. **Costs of Financial Distress.** The Salad Oil Storage Company (SOS) has financed a large part of its facilities with long-term debt. There is a significant risk of default, but the company is not on the ropes yet. Explain why

a. SOS shareholders could lose by investing in a positive-NPV project financed by an equity issue.
b. SOS shareholders could gain by investing in a highly risky, negative-NPV project.

26. **Financial Distress.** Explain how financial distress can lead to conflicts of interest between debt and equity investors. Then explain how these conflicts can lead to costs of financial distress.

27. **Costs of Financial Distress.** For which of the following firms would you expect the costs of financial distress to be highest? Explain briefly.

a. a computer software company which depends on skilled programmers to produce new products.
b. a shipping company that operates a fleet of modern oil tankers.

28. **Trade-Off Theory.** Smoke and Mirrors currently has EBIT of $25,000 and is all-equity financed. EBIT is expected to stay at this level indefinitely. The firm pays corporate taxes equal to 35 percent of taxable income. The discount rate for the firm's projects is 10 percent.
    a. What is the market value of the firm?
    b. Now assume the firm issues $50,000 of debt paying interest of 6 percent per year and uses the proceeds to retire equity. The debt is expected to be permanent. What will happen to the total value of the firm (debt plus equity)?
    c. Recompute your answer to part (b) under the following assumptions. The debt issue raises the possibility of bankruptcy. The firm has a 30 percent chance of going bankrupt after 3 years. If it does go bankrupt, it will incur bankruptcy costs of $200,000. The discount rate is 10 percent. Should the firm issue the debt?
29. **Pecking Order Theory.** Alpha Corp. and Beta Corp. both produce turbo encabulators. Both companies' assets and operations are growing at the same rate and their annual capital expenditures are about the same. However, Alpha Corp. is the more efficient producer and is consistently more profitable. According to the pecking order theory, which company should have the higher debt ratio? Explain.
30. **Financial Slack.** Look back to the Sealed Air example in the Finance in Action box in Section 15.4, page 469. What was the value of financial slack to Sealed Air before its restructuring? What does the success of the restructuring say about optimal capital structure? Would you recommend that all firms restructure as Sealed Air did?

CHALLENGE

*31. **Costs of Financial Distress.** Let's go back to the Double-R Nutting Company. Suppose that Double-R's bonds have a face value of $50. Its current *market-value* balance sheet is

Assets		**Liabilities and Equity**	
Net working capital	$20	Bonds outstanding	$25
Fixed assets	10	Common stock	5
Total assets	$30	Total liabilities and shareholders' equity	$30

Who would gain or lose from the following manoeuvres?
    a. Double-R pays a $10 cash dividend.
    b. Double-R halts operations, sells its fixed assets for $6, and converts net working-capital into $20 cash. It invests its $26 in Treasury bills.
    c. Double-R encounters an investment opportunity requiring a $10 initial investment with NPV = $0. It borrows $10 to finance the project by issuing more bonds with the same security, seniority, and so on, as the existing bonds.
    d. Double-R finances the investment opportunity in part (c) by issuing more common stock.
32. **Trade-Off Theory.** Ronald Masulis[13] has analyzed the stock price impact of *exchange offers* of debt for equity, or vice versa. In an exchange offer, the firm offers to trade freshly issued securities for seasoned securities in the hands of investors. Thus a firm that wanted to move to a higher debt ratio could offer to trade new debt for outstanding shares. A firm that wanted to move to a more conservative capital structure could offer to trade new shares for outstanding debt securities. Masulis found that debt-for-equity exchanges were good news (stock price increased on announcement) and equity-for-debt exchanges were bad news.
    a. Are these results consistent with the trade-off theory of capital structure?
    b. Are the results consistent with the evidence that investors regard announcements of (1) stock

[13] R.W. Masulis, "The Effects of Capital Structure Change on Security Prices: A Study of Exchange Offers," *Journal of Financial Economics* 8 (June 1980), pp. 139–177, and "The Impact of Capital Structure Change on Firm Value," *Journal of Finance* 38 (March 1983), pp. 107–126.

issues as bad news, (2) stock repurchases as good news, and (3) debt issues as no news, or at most trifling disappointments?

33. **Pecking Order Theory.** Construct a simple example to show that a firm's existing shareholders gain if they can sell overpriced stock to new investors and invest the cash in a zero-NPV project. Who loses from these actions? If investors are aware that managers are likely to issue stock when it is overpriced, what will happen to the stock price when the issue is announced?
34. **Pecking Order Theory.** When companies announce an issue of common stock, the share price typically falls. When they announce an issue of debt, there is typically only a negligible change in the stock price. Can you explain why?
35. **Taxes.** MM's proposition I suggests that in the absence of taxes it makes no difference whether the firm borrows on behalf of its shareholders or whether they borrow directly. However, if there are corporate taxes, this is no longer the case. Construct a simple example to show that with taxes it is better for the firm to borrow than for the shareholders to do so.
36. **Taxes.** MM's proposition I, when modified to recognize corporate taxes, suggests that there is a tax advantage to firm borrowing. If there is a tax advantage to firm borrowing, there is also a tax *disadvantage* to firm lending. Explain why.

SOLUTIONS TO CHECK POINTS

15.1 Price per share will stay at $10, so with $350,000, River Cruises can repurchase 35,000 shares, leaving 65,000 outstanding. The remaining value of equity will be $650,000. Overall firm value stays at $1 million. Shareholders' wealth is unchanged: They start with shares worth $1 million, receive $350,000, and retain shares worth $650,000.

15.2 a. Data:

Number of shares	25,000
Price per share	$10
Market value of shares	$250,000
Market value of debt	$750,000

	State of the Economy		
	Slump	**Normal**	**Boom**
Operating income	$75,000	125,000	175,000
Interest	$75,000	75,000	75,000
Equity earnings	$ 0	50,000	100,000
Earnings per share	$ 0	2	4
Return on shares	0%	20%	40%

Every change of $50,000 in operating income leads to a change in the return to equityholders of 20 percent. This is double the swing in equity returns when debt was only $500,000.

b. The shareholder should lend out $3 for every $1 invested in River Cruises' stock. For example, he could buy one share for $10 and then lend $30. The payoffs are:

	State of the Economy		
	Slump	**Normal**	**Boom**
Earnings on one share	$0	2	4
Plus interest at 10%	$3	3	3
Net earnings	$3	5	7
Return on $40 investment	7.5%	12.5%	17.5%

15.3 Business risk is unaffected by capital structure. As the financing mix changes, whatever equity is outstanding must absorb the fixed business risk of the firm. The less equity, the more risk absorbed per share. Therefore, as capital structure changes, r_{assets} is held fixed while r_{equity} adjusts.

15.4 BCE, Inc.'s borrowing reduced taxable profits by $1,336 million. With a tax rate of 35 percent, tax was reduced by .35 x $1,336 = $467.6 million. If the borrowing is permanent, BCE, Inc., will save this amount of tax each year. The present value of the tax saving would be $467.6/.08 = $5,845 million.

15.5 In bankruptcy bondholders will receive $2 million less. This lowers the expected cash flow from the bond and reduces its present value. Therefore, the bonds will be priced lower and must offer a higher interest rate. This higher rate is paid by the firm today. It comes out of shareholders' income. Thus common stock value falls.

15.6 The conflicts are costly because they lead to poor investment decisions. The more debt the firm has today, the greater the chance of poor decisions in the future. Investors foresee this possibility and reduce today's market value of the firm.

15.7 The biotech company. Its assets are all intangible. If bankruptcy threatens and the best scientists accept job offers from other firms, there may not be much value remaining for the biotech company's debt and equity investors. On the other hand, bankruptcy would have little or no effect on the value of 50 producing oil wells and of the oil reserves still in the ground.

15.8 The electric utility has the most stable cash flow. It also has the highest reliance on tangible assets that would not be impaired by a bankruptcy. It should have the highest debt ratio. The software firm has the least dependence on tangible assets and the most on assets that have value only if the firm continues as an ongoing concern. It probably also has the most unpredictable cash flows. It should have the lowest debt ratio.

MINICASE

In March 2001, the management team of Londonderry Air (LA) met to discuss a proposal to purchase five shorthaul aircraft at a total cost of $25 million. There was general enthusiasm for the investment, and the new aircraft were expected to generate an annual cash flow of $4 million for 20 years.

The focus of the meeting was on how to finance the purchase. LA had $20 million in cash and marketable securities (see table on the following page), but Ed Johnson, the chief financial officer, pointed out that the company needed at least $10 million in cash to meet normal outflow and as a contingency reserve. This meant that there would be a cash deficiency of $15 million, which the firm would need to cover either by the sale of common stock or by additional borrowing. While admitting that the arguments were finely balanced, Johnson recommended an issue of stock. He pointed out that the airline industry was subject to wide swings in profits, and the firm should be careful to avoid the risk of excessive borrowing. He estimated that in market-value terms the long-term debt ratio was about 62 percent and that a further debt issue would raise the ratio to 64 percent.

Johnson's only doubt about making a stock issue was that investors might jump to the conclusion that management believed the stock was overpriced, in which case, the announcement might prompt an unjustified selloff by investors. He stressed therefore that the company needed to explain carefully the reasons for the issue. Also, he suggested that demand for the issue would be enhanced if at the same time LA increased its dividend payment. This would provide a tangible indication of management's confidence in the future.

These arguments cut little ice with LA's chief executive. "Ed," she said, "I know that you're the expert on all this, but everything you say flies in the face of common sense. Why should we want to sell more equity when our stock has fallen over the past year by nearly a fifth? Our stock is currently offering a dividend yield of 6.5 percent, which makes equity an expensive source of capital. Increasing the dividend would simply make it more expensive. What's more, I don't see the point of paying out more money to the shareholders at the same time that we are asking *them* for cash. If we hike the dividend, we will need to increase the amount of the stock issue; so we will just be paying the higher dividend out of the shareholders' own pockets. You're also ignoring the question of dilution. Our equity currently has a book value of $12 a share; it's not playing fair by our existing shareholders if we now issue stock for around $10 a share.

"Look at the alternative. We can borrow today at 5 percent. We get a tax break on the interest, so the after-tax cost of borrowing is .65 × 5 = 3.25 percent. That's about half the cost of equity. We expect to earn a return of 15 percent on these new aircraft. If we can raise money at 3.25 percent and invest it at 15 percent, that's a good deal in my book.

"You finance guys are always talking about risk, but as long as we don't go bankrupt, borrowing doesn't add any risk at all. In any case, my calculations show that the debt ratio is only 45 percent, which doesn't sound excessive to me.

"Ed, I don't want to push my views on this—after all, you're the expert. We don't need to make a firm recommendation to the board until next month. In the meantime, why don't you get one of your new business graduates to look at the whole issue of how we should finance the deal and what return we need to earn on these planes."

Summary financial statements for Londonderry Air, 2000 (figures are book values, in millions of dollars)

Balance Sheet			
Bank debt	$ 50	Cash	$ 20
Other current liabilities	20	Other current assets	20
10% bond, due 2020[1]	100	Fixed assets	250
Stockholders' equity[2,3]	120		
Total liabilities	$290	Total assets	$290
Income Statement			
Gross profit	57.5		
Depreciation	20.0		
Interest	7.5		
Pretax profit	30.0		
Tax	10.5		
Net profit	19.5		
Dividend	6.5		

Notes:

1. The yield to maturity on LA debt currently is 5 percent.
2. LA has 10 million shares outstanding, and a market price of $10 a share.
3. LA's equity beta is estimated at 1.25, the market risk premium is 8 percent, and the Treasury bill rate is 4 percent.

CHAPTER 16

Dividend Policy

16.1 How Dividends Are Paid

16.2 How Do Companies Decide on Dividend Payments?

16.3 Why Dividend Policy Should Not Matter

16.4 Why Dividends May Increase Firm Value

16.5 Why Pay Dividends? A Look at Tax Law Implications

16.6 Summary

In this chapter we explain how companies set their dividend payments, and we discuss the controversial question of how dividend policy affects value.

Why should you care about these issues? Of course, if you are responsible for deciding on your company's dividend payment, you will want to know how it affects the value of your stock. But there is a more general reason. When we discussed the company's investment decision, we assumed that it was not affected by financing policy. In that case, a good project is a good project, no matter how it is ultimately financed. If dividend policy does not affect value, this still holds true. But suppose that it *does* affect value. Then the attractiveness of a project would depend on where the money was coming from. For example, if investors prefer companies with high dividend payouts, then these firms might be reluctant to take on new projects that required them to cut back dividends.

We start the chapter with a discussion of how dividends are paid. We then show that in an ideal world, the value of a firm would be independent of its dividend policy. This demonstration is in the same spirit as the Modigliani and Miller debt-irrelevance proposition of the previous chapter.

That leads us to look at the real-world complications that might favour one dividend policy over another. These complications include transaction costs, taxes, and the signals that investors might read into the firm's dividend announcement.

After studying this chapter you should be able to

- Describe how dividends are paid and how companies decide on dividend payments.
- Explain why dividend policy would not affect firm value in an ideal world.
- Show how differences in the tax treatment of dividends and capital gains might affect dividend policy.
- Explain why dividends may be used by management to signal the prospects of the firm.

How Dividends Are Paid

CASH DIVIDENDS

cash dividend Payment of cash by the firm to its shareholders.

On July 30, 2001, Canadian Pacific (CP) announced a regular quarterly **cash dividend** of $.14 per share, making a total payment of $.56 for the year; soon after, its board of directors met and approved the decision. The term *regular* indicates that CP expected to maintain the payment in the future. If it did not want to give that kind of assurance, it could have declared both a regular and an *extra dividend.* In 1997, DuPont Canada did just that. As the nearby Finance in Action box points out, the cash-rich company declared a $278 million *special dividend* because it could not find any other way to spend its sizable cash flows. Investors realize that extra dividends are less likely to be repeated.[1]

Who receives the CP dividend? That may seem an obvious question, but because shares trade constantly, the firm's records of who owns its shares can never be fully up-to-date. So CP announced that it would send a dividend cheque to all shareholders recorded in its books on August 27. This is known as the *record date.*

ex-dividend date Date that determines whether a stockholder is entitled to a dividend payment; anyone holding stock before this date is entitled to a dividend.

The *payment date* for CP's dividend was September 28. On that date the dividend cheques were mailed to investors. If CP's records were not up-to-date, some of those cheques would be sent to the wrong investor. To handle this problem, stock exchanges fix a cut-off date, called the **ex-dividend date**, two business days prior to the record date. If you owned CP stock on the *with-dividend date*, which in this case was August 22, you were entitled to the dividend. If CP mistakenly sent that dividend to someone else, that person was obliged to pass it on to you. If you acquired the stock after August 22, you were not entitled to the dividend. If CP sent you that dividend by mistake, you had to send it on to the previous owner.

Through August 22, CP stock was said to be trading "with dividend" or "cum dividend." Beginning on August 23, the stock traded "ex dividend." The only difference between buying CP before and after the ex-dividend date is that in the second case you miss out on the dividend. Other things being equal, the stock is worth more when it is with dividend. Thus when the stock "goes ex," we would expect the stock price to drop by the amount of the dividend.

Figure 16.1 illustrates the sequence of the key dividend dates. This sequence is the same whenever companies pay a dividend (though of course the actual dates will differ).

Some of CP's shareholders may have desired the cash payment, but others preferred to reinvest the dividend in the company. To help these investors, CP had an automatic dividend reinvestment plan. If a shareholder belonged to this plan, his or her dividends were automatically used to buy additional shares.[2]

CHECK POINT 16.1

Mick Milekin buys 100 shares of Junk Bombs, Inc., on Tuesday, June 2. The company has declared a dividend of $1 per share payable on June 30 to shareholders on record as of Friday, June 5. If the ex-dividend date is June 1, is Mick entitled to the dividend? When will the cheques go out in the mail?

SOME LEGAL LIMITATIONS ON DIVIDENDS

Suppose that an unscrupulous board decided to sell all the firm's assets and distribute the money as dividends. That would not leave anything in the kitty to pay the company's

[1] Companies also use the term "special dividend" for payments that are unlikely to be repeated.

[2] Often the new shares in an automatic dividend investment plan are issued at a small discount from the market price; the firm offers this sweetener because it saves the underwriting costs of a regular share issue. Sometimes 10 percent or more of total dividends will be reinvested under such plans.

FINANCE IN ACTION

DuPont Canada Issues a Special Dividend

DuPont Canada, Inc. is paying shareholders, including its U.S. parent, $278 million in a special dividend because the cash-rich company can't find anywhere else to spend the money.

Retiring president Arthur Sawchuk announced an extraordinary dividend of $3 per common share at DuPont's annual shareholders meeting yesterday. The maker of high-tech speciality products had already spent $850 million on capital projects.

U.S.-based parent DuPont (E.I.) de Nemours & Co. will gain about $214 million from the dividend. Other shareholders including institutions and about 2,200 employees and retirees will collect the rest.

DuPont has generated about $1.4 billion in cash flow through the 1990s and used it to pay off all long-term debt, expand and overhaul operations and increase dividends.

But that still left the Mississauga-based company with about $400 million after exploring other options, including a share buy-back and acquisitions.

"Among other things, we've been looking at the possibility of buying something for the last five or six years but we couldn't find anything that fit," said Sawchuk.

After paying the dividend to shareholders, DuPont will be sitting on about $120 million in cash. DuPont, which makes everything from weed killers to nylon yarn for auto air bags, reported that profits climbed 9 percent to a record $200 million on revenue of $1.85 billion in 1996.

In the first quarter this year, profits improved 4 percent to $48 million on revenue of $471.2 million. The company also confirmed a dividend of $.13 for the second quarter.

The 62-year-old president told shareholders that the value of the company's stock has jumped from $13 to $33 a share since early 1992. Profits have jumped an average of 29 percent annually since the depths of the recession in 1991, he added.

Source: Excerpted from T. Van Alphen, "DuPont Issues $278 Million in Special Dividend," the *Toronto Star Syndicate*, Business section (April 26, 1997), p. E2.

debts. Therefore, bondholders often guard against this danger by placing limits on dividend payments.

Federal law under the Canadian Business Corporations Act as well as provincial acts may include provisions prohibiting firms from paying dividends under certain conditions. The intent of such provisions is to protect the firm's creditors against excessive dividend payments, which could push the firm toward insolvency. For example, payment of dividends could be prohibited if it results in the firm being unable to pay its liabilities when they become due, or if such liabilities exceed the firm's assets. Similarly, restrictions may be imposed when the dividend exceeds retained earnings, or when the dividend would be paid from the firm's invested capital.[3] Essentially, the spirit of such regulations is that dividends should be paid from retained earnings. Under certain conditions, firms are allowed to pay a "liquidating dividend." The laws give most corporations a large degree of flexibility in deciding what to pay out, but they help prevent unscrupulous managers from gutting the firm by paying out all its assets as dividends and then escaping creditors.

FIGURE 16.1
The key dates for Canadian Pacific's quarterly dividend

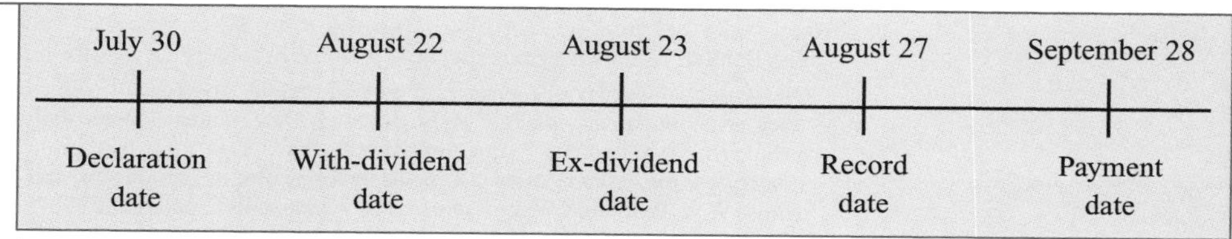

Note: Canadian Pacific's present dividend rate is $.56 per common share per annum paid in regular quarterly payments of $.14 per share. The above time line is for CP's fourth payout of 2001.

Source: Financial Post Online, "FP Dividends" at www.fpdata.finpost.com and Canadian Pacific's website at www.cp.ca.

[3] Invested capital consists of part or all the receipts from the issue of shares.

STOCK DIVIDENDS, STOCK SPLITS AND REVERSE SPLITS

stock dividend Distribution of additional shares to a firm's shareholders.

stock split Issue of additional shares to firm's shareholders.

CP's dividend was in the form of cash, but companies often declare **stock dividends**. For example, the Bank of Montreal declared a 100 percent stock dividend in January 2001, doubling the number of common shares. The American company Archer Daniels Midland has paid a yearly stock dividend of 5 percent for two decades. That means it sends each shareholder five additional shares for every 100 shares that are currently owned.

A stock dividend is very much like a **stock split.** In both cases the shareholder is given a fixed number of new shares for each share held. For example, in a two-for-one split, each investor would receive one additional share for each share already held. The investor ends up with two shares rather than one. A two-for-one stock split is therefore like a 100 percent stock dividend.[4] Both result in a doubling of the number of outstanding shares, but neither changes the total assets held by the firm. In both cases, therefore, we would expect the stock price to fall by half, leaving the total market value of the firm (price per share times shares outstanding) unchanged.[5]

More often than not, however, the announcement of a stock split does result in a rise in the market value of the firm, even though investors are aware that the company's assets and business are not affected. The reason: Investors take the decision to split as a signal of management's confidence in the company's propects.[6]

▸ EXAMPLE 16.1 *Stock Dividends and Splits*

Amoeba Products has issued two million shares currently selling at $15 each. Thus investors place a total market value on Amoeba of $30 million. The company now declares a 50 percent stock dividend. This means that each shareholder will receive one new share for every two shares that are currently held. So the total number of Amoeba shares will increase from two million to three million. The company's assets are not changed by this paper transaction and are still worth $30 million. The value of each share after the stock dividend is therefore $30/3 = $10.

If Amoeba split its stock three-for-two, the effect would be the same.[7] In this case two shares would split into three. (Amoeba's motto is "divide and conquer.") So each shareholder has 50 percent more shares with the same total value. Share price must decline by a third.

There are other types of noncash dividends. For example, companies sometimes send shareholders a sample of their product. The British company Dundee Crematorium once

[4] The Bank of Montreal's stock dividend effectively achieved a two-for-one stock split.

[5] One American survey of managers indicated that 93.7 percent of splits are motivated by the desire to bring the stock price into an acceptable "trading range." They seem to believe that if the price is too high, investors won't be able to afford to buy a "round lot" of 100 shares. Of course that might be a problem for you or us, but it isn't a worry for the Prudential or GM pension funds. See J. Lakonishok and B. Lev, "Stock Splits and Stock Dividends: Why, Who, and When," *Journal of Finance* 42 (September 1987), pp. 913–932.

[6] The insight that stock splits provide a signal to investors was proposed in E. F. Fama, L. Fisher, M. Jensen, and R. Roll, "The Adjustment of Stock Prices to New Information," *International Economic Review* 10 (February 1969), pp. 1–21. For evidence that companies which split their stock have above-average earnings prospects, see P. Asquith, P. Healy, and K. Palepu, "Earnings and Stock Splits," *Accounting Review* 64 (July 1989), pp. 387–403.

[7] The distinction between stock dividends and stock splits is a technical one. A stock dividend is shown on the balance sheet as a transfer from retained earnings to par value and additional paid-in capital, whereas a split is shown as a proportional reduction in the par value of each share. Neither affects the total book value of shareholders' equity.

offered its more substantial shareholders a discount cremation. Needless to say, you were not *required* to receive this dividend.

reverse split Issue of new shares in exchange for old shares, which results in the reduction of outstanding shares.

Sometimes a firm may decide to opt for a **reverse split**, which would effectively reduce its number of outstanding shares. For instance, in a one-for-two reverse split, shareholders would exchange two existing shares for one new share. Reverse splits occur much more infrequently than stock splits. An important consideration in a reverse-split decision appears to be an expectation of the resultant increase in share price. A company may wish to achieve such a share price increase in order to maintain minimum price per share requirements of the stock exchange (or exchanges) listing its stock. Also, for a low-priced stock, bringing the share price up to a higher, more acceptable trading range could increase its market participation and improve its liquidity. A more dubious reason could be to ease out minority shareholders who may end up with less than a required minimum number of shares following the reverse split.

SHARE REPURCHASE

stock repurchase Firm buys back stock from its shareholders.

When a firm wants to pay cash to its shareholders, it usually declares a cash dividend. But an alternative and increasingly popular method is for the firm to repurchase its own stock. In a **stock repurchase,** the company pays cash to repurchase shares from its shareholders. These shares are usually kept in the company's treasury and then resold if or when the company needs money.

To see why share repurchase is similar to a dividend, look at panel A of Table 16.1, which shows the market value of Hewlard Pocket's assets and liabilities. Shareholders hold 100,000 shares worth, in total, $1 million, so price per share equals $1 million/100,000 = $10.

Pocket is proposing to pay a dividend of $1 per share. With 100,000 shares outstanding, that amounts to a total payout of $100,000. Panel B shows the effect of this dividend payment. The cash account is reduced by $100,000, and the market value of the firm's assets falls to $900,000. Since there are still 100,000 shares outstanding, share price falls to $9. Suppose that before the dividend payment you owned 1,000 shares of Pocket worth $10,000. After the payment you would have $1,000 in cash and 1,000 shares worth $9,000.

Rather than paying out $100,000 as a dividend, Pocket could use the cash to buy back 10,000 shares at $10 each. Panel C shows what happens. The firm's assets fall to $900,000 just as in panel B, but only 90,000 shares remain outstanding, so price per share remains at $10. If you owned 1,000 shares before the repurchase, you would own 1 percent of the company. If you then sold 100 of your shares to Pocket, you would still own 1 percent of the company. Your sale would put $1,000 cash in your pocket and you would keep 900 shares worth $9,000. This is precisely the position that you would have been in if Pocket had paid a dividend of $1 per share.

It is not surprising that a cash dividend and a share repurchase are equivalent transactions. In both cases, the firm pays out some of its cash, which then goes into the shareholders' pockets. The assets that are left in the company are the same regardless of whether that cash was used to pay a dividend or to buy back shares. Later, however, we will see that how the company chooses to pay out cash may affect the tax that the investor is obliged to pay.

Share repurchases are generally used to make major adjustments to the firm's capital. For example, in August 2000, Canadian Pacific announced changes to its share repurchase program, increasing the number of shares it could repurchase in a 12-month period to 15.7 million, or approximately 5 percent of its outstanding common shares. Between 1998 and 2000, the company repurchased 28 million shares at a cost of over $985 million. Firms, occasionally, use share purchases when their cash resources have outrun good capital investment opportunities.

TABLE 16.1
Cash dividend versus share repurchase. Hewlard Pocket's market-value balance sheet

Assets		**Liabilities and Shareholders' Equity**	
A. Original balance sheet			
Cash	$ 150,000	Debt	$ 0
Other assets	850,000	Equity	1,000,000
Value of firm	$ 1,000,000	Value of firm	$ 1,000,000
Shares outstanding = 100,000			
Price per share = $1,000,000/100,000 = $10			
B. After-cash dividend			
Cash	$ 50,000	Debt	$ 0
Other assets	850,000	Equity	900,000
Value of firm	$ 900,000	Value of firm	$ 900,000
Shares outstanding =100,000			
Price per share = $900,000/100,000 = $9			
C. After-stock repurchase			
Cash	$ 50,000	Debt	$ 0
Other assets	850,000	Equity	900,000
Value of firm	$ 900,000	Value of firm	$ 900,000
Shares outstanding = 90,000			
Price per share = $900,000/90,000 = $10			

CHECK POINT 16.2

What would Table 16.1 look like if the dividend changes to $1.50 per share and the share repurchase to $150,000?

How Do Companies Decide on Dividend Payments?

What does the board of directors think about when it sets the dividend? To help answer this question, John Lintner conducted a classic series of interviews with corporate managers about their dividend policies.[8] His description of how dividends are determined can be summarized in four "stylized facts":

dividend payout ratio Percentage of earnings paid out as dividends.

1. Firms have long-run target **dividend payout ratios.** This ratio is the fraction of earnings paid out as dividends.
2. Managers focus more on dividend *changes* than on absolute levels. Thus paying a $2 dividend is an important financial decision if last year's dividend was $1, but it's no big deal if last year's dividend was $2.
3. Dividend changes follow shifts in long-run, sustainable levels of earnings rather than short-run changes in earnings. Managers are unlikely to change dividend payouts in response to temporary variations in earnings. Instead, they "smooth" dividends.
4. Managers are reluctant to make dividend changes that might have to be reversed. They are particularly worried about having to rescind a dividend increase.

[8] J. Lintner, "Distribution of Incomes of Corporations among Dividends, Retained Earnings, and Taxes," *American Economic Review* 46 (May 1956), pp. 97–113.

FIGURE 16.2

Canadian Pacific's earnings and dividends per common share

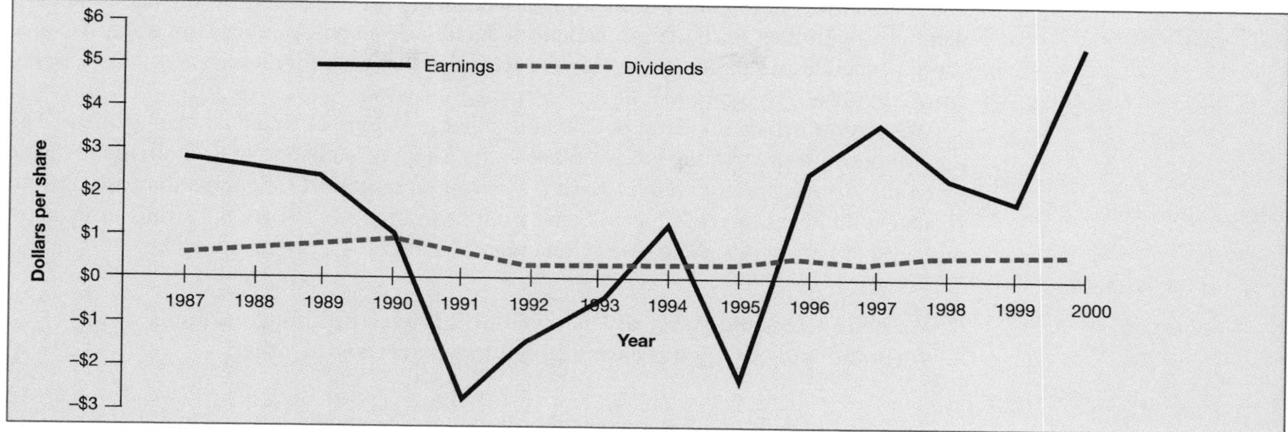

Source: 2000 Annual Report, Ten-year Summary, and 1996 Annual Report, Ten-year Summary at www.cp.ca.

A firm that always stuck to its target payout ratio would have to change its dividend whenever earnings changed. But the managers in Lintner's survey were loath to do this. They believed that shareholders prefer a steady progression in dividends. Therefore, even if circumstances appeared to warrant a large increase in their company's dividend, they would move only partway toward their target payment.

An extensive study by Fama and Babiak confirms Lintner's survey.[9] They found that if the company enjoys a good year, dividends may increase but to a lesser extent than earnings. Managers wait to see that the earnings increase is permanent before the dividend is fully adjusted.

If managers are reluctant to make dividend changes that might have to be reversed, we should also expect them to take *future* prospects into account when setting the payment. And that is what we find. When companies pay unexpectedly low dividends, earnings on the average subsequently decline. When they pay unexpectedly high dividends, earnings subsequently increase.[10] That is why investors pay close attention to the dividend decision.

To see Lintner's model at work, consider Figure 16.2, which plots the dividends and earnings per share of CP. While earnings per share fluctuate quite erratically, dividends per share do not. Dividends grow from $.54 per share in 1987 to $.92 in 1990, and are at $.56 per share in 2000. Dividends steadily increased between 1994 and 2000 as management seemed to wait cautiously for evidence that any dividend increase could be supported over the long-run. Following losses in 1991, CP slashed the dividend from $.63 per share in 1991 to $.32 the following year. It maintained the dividend at $.32 until 1994, although in 1992 and 1993, it continued to incur losses, albeit in smaller amounts. In 1995, CP actually increased the dividend to $.36 per share despite incurring a loss in that year.

16.3 Why Dividend Policy Should Not Matter

The first step toward understanding dividend policy is to recognize that the phrase means different things to different people. Therefore, we must start by defining what we mean by it.

[9] E. F. Fama and H. Babiak, "Dividend Policy: An Empirical Analysis," *Journal of the American Statistical Association* 63 (December 1968), pp. 1132–1161.

[10] See, for example, R. Watts, "The Information Content of Dividends," *Journal of Business* 46 (April 1973), pp. 191–211, for an analysis of the information effects in the United States.

A firm's decisions about dividends are often intertwined with other financing and investment decisions. Some firms pay low dividends because management is optimistic about the firm's future and wishes to retain earnings for expansion. In this case the dividend is a byproduct of the firm's capital budgeting decision. Another firm might finance capital expenditures largely by borrowing. This frees up cash for dividends. In this case the firm's dividend is a byproduct of the borrowing decision.

We wish to isolate dividend policy from other problems of financial management. The precise question we should ask is "What is the effect of a change in cash dividends paid, *given the firm's capital budgeting and borrowing decisions?*" Of course the cash used to finance a dividend increase has to come from somewhere. If we fix the firm's investment outlays and borrowing, there is only one possible source—an issue of stock.

We define *dividend policy* as the trade-off between retaining earnings on the one hand and paying out cash and issuing shares on the other.

One nice feature of economics is that it can accommodate not just two, but three opposing points of view—and so it is with dividend policy. On one side there is a group that believes high dividends increase firm value. On the other side there is a group that believes high dividends bring high taxes and therefore reduce firm value. And in the center there is a middle-of-the-road party that believes dividend policy makes no difference.

DIVIDEND POLICY IS IRRELEVANT IN COMPETITIVE MARKETS

The middle-of-the-road party was founded in 1961 by Modigliani and Miller (MM)[11]—the same two who showed that in idealized conditions capital structure is also irrelevant.

We can illustrate MM's views about dividend policy by considering the Pickwick Paper Company, which had set aside $100 million in cash to construct a new paper mill. But Pickwick's directors now propose to use the $100 million to increase the dividend payment. If Pickwick is to continue to build its new mill, that cash needs to be replaced. If the borrowing is fixed, there is only one place the money can come from, and that is the sale of new shares. The combination of the dividend payment and the new issue of shares leaves Pickwick and its shareholders in exactly the same position they started from. All that has happened is that Pickwick has put an extra $100 million in investors' pockets (the dividend payment) and then taken it out again (the share issue). In other words, Pickwick is simply recycling cash. To suggest that this makes investors better off is like advising the cook to cool the kitchen by leaving the refrigerator door open.

After Pickwick pays the additional dividend and replaces the cash by selling new shares, the company value is unchanged. The old shareholders now have an extra $100 million cash in their pockets, but they have given up a stake in the firm to those investors who buy the newly issued shares. The new shareholders are putting up $100 million and therefore will demand to receive shares *worth* $100 million. Since the total value of the company is the same, the value of the old shareholders' stake in the company falls by this $100 million. Thus the extra dividend that the old shareholders receive just offsets the loss in the value of the shares that they hold.

Does it make any difference to the old shareholders that they receive an extra dividend

[11] M. H. Miller and F. Modigliani, "Dividend Policy, Growth and the Valuation of Shares," *Journal of Business* 34 (October 1961), pp. 411–433.

payment plus an offsetting capital loss? It might if that were the only way they could get their hands on the cash. But as long as there are efficient capital markets, they can raise cash by selling shares. Thus Pickwick's old shareholders can "cash in" either by persuading the management to pay a higher dividend or by selling some of their shares. In either case there will be the same transfer of value from the old to the new shareholders.

Because investors do not need dividends to convert their shares to cash, they will not pay higher prices for firms with higher dividend payouts. In other words, dividend policy will have no impact on the value of the firm.

MM dividend-irrelevance proposition Under ideal conditions, the value of the firm is unaffected by dividend policy.

This conclusion is known as the **MM dividend-irrelevance proposition.**

The example of the Pickwick Paper Company showed that the firm cannot make shareholders better off by simply increasing the proportion of earnings paid out as dividends. But what about the reverse? Can a firm increase its value by *reducing* the dividend payout?

In the case of Pickwick, the extra cash paid out as a dividend needed to be replaced by a sale of stock. The same argument works in reverse: If investment and borrowing are held constant, any *reduction* in dividends must be balanced by a *purchase* of stock. For example, suppose that Old Curiosity Shops has $100 million surplus cash, which it had been proposing to pay out to shareholders as a dividend. If Old Curiosity now decides not to pay this dividend, then the surplus cash can be used only to buy back some of the company's shares. The shareholders miss out on $100 million of dividend payments, but they receive $100 million from the sale to the company of part of their shareholdings. Thus MM's dividend-irrelevance proposition holds true both for increases in dividends and for reductions.

As these examples illustrate, dividend policy is a trade-off between cash dividends and the issue or repurchase of common stock. In a perfect capital market, dividend choice would have no impact on firm value.

These examples may seem artificial at first because we do not observe firms scheduling a stock issue with every dividend payment. But there are many firms that pay dividends and also issue stock from time to time. They could avoid the stock issues by paying lower dividends and retaining more funds in the firm. Many other firms restrict dividends so that they *do not* have to issue shares. They could instead issue stock occasionally and increase the dividend.

Of course our demonstrations of dividend irrelevance have ignored taxes, issue costs, and a variety of other real-world complications. We will turn to these intricacies shortly, but before we do, we note that the crucial assumption in our proof is that the sale or purchase of shares occurs at a fair price. The shares that Pickwick sells to raise $100,000 must actually be worth $100,000; those that Old Curiosity buys for $100,000 must also be worth that figure. In other words, dividend irrelevance assumes efficient capital markets.

▶ EXAMPLE 16.2 *Dividend Irrelevance*

Table 16.2 shows that Consolidated Pasta is expected to pay annual dividends of $10 per share in perpetuity. Shareholders expect a 10 percent rate of return from Consolidated stock, and therefore the value of each share is

$$PV = \frac{10}{1.10} + \frac{10}{1.10^2} + \frac{10}{1.10^3} + \cdots = \frac{10}{.10} = \$100$$

TABLE 16.2
Consolidated Pasta is currently expected to pay a dividend of $10 million in perpetuity. However, the president is proposing to pay a one-time bumper dividend of $20 million in Year 1. To replace the lost cash, the firm will need to issue more shares, and the dividends that will need to be diverted to the new shareholders will exactly offset the effect of the higher dividend in Year 1.

	Old Dividend Plan		Revised Dividend Plan	
	Year 1	**Year 2 on**	**Year 1**	**Year 2 on**
Total dividend payments ($ million)	10	10	20	10
Total dividends paid to old shareholders ($ million)	10	10	20	9
Total dividends paid to new shareholders ($ million)	—	—	—	1

Note: New shareholders are putting up $10 million cash at the end of Year 1. Since they require a return of 10 percent, the total dividends paid to the new shares (starting in Year 2) must be 10 percent of $10 million, or $1 million.

Consolidated has issued one million shares. So the total forecast dividend payment in each year is 1 million × $10 = $10 million, and the total value of Consolidated Pasta equity is 1 million × $100 = $100 million. The president, Al Dente, has read that the value of a share depends on the dividends it pays. That suggests an easy way to keep shareholders happy—increase next year's dividend to $20 per share. That way, he reasons, share price should rise by the present value of the increase in the first-year dividend to a new value of

$$PV = \frac{20}{1.10} + \frac{10}{1.10^2} + \frac{10}{1.10^3} + \cdots = \frac{10}{1.10} + \frac{10}{.10} = \$109.91$$

The president's heart is obviously in the right place. Unfortunately, his head isn't. Let's see why.

Consolidated is proposing to pay out an extra $10 million in dividends. It can't do that *and* earn the same profits in the future, unless it also replaces the lost cash by an issue of shares. The new shareholders who provide this cash will require a return of 10 percent on their investment. So Consolidated will need to pay $1 million per year of dividends to the new shares ($1 million/$10 million = .10, or 10%). This is shown in the last line of Table 16.2.

As long as the company replaces the extra cash it pays out, it will continue to earn the same profits and to pay out $10 million of dividends each year from Year 2. However, $1 million of this total will be needed to satisfy the new shareholders, leaving only $9 million (or $9 per share) for the original shareholders. Now recalculate the value of the original shares under the revised dividend plan:

$$PV = \frac{20}{1.10} + \frac{9}{1.10^2} + \frac{9}{1.10^3} + \cdots = \frac{11}{1.10} + \frac{9}{.10} = \$100$$

The value of the shares is unchanged. The extra cash dividend in Year 1 is exactly offset by the reduction of dividends per share in later years. This reduction is necessary because some of the money paid out as dividends in later years is diverted to the new shareholders.[12]

CHECK POINT 16.3

Suppose that Consolidated Pasta had issued $10 million in preferred stock rather than common stock to pay the extra dividend. What would be the stock price?

[12] Notice that at the end of Year 1, when the new shareholders purchase their shares, the dividend per share they can look forward to receiving will be $9; since this dividend is expected to be a perpetuity, the share price at that time will be $9/.10 = $90. So the new shareholders will receive $10,000,000/$90 = 111,111 shares. Consistent with Table 16.2, the new shareholders therefore will receive total dividend payments of 111,111 × $9 = $1 million, and the old shareholders will receive total dividend payments of 1 million × $9 = $9 million. Notice also that after the extra $10 million dividend is paid in Year 1, the share price falls to $90, and the value of the shares held by the original shareholders falls by exactly $10 million to $90 million.

THE ASSUMPTIONS BEHIND DIVIDEND IRRELEVANCE

Many shareholders and businesspeople find it difficult to accept the suggestion that dividend policy is irrelevant. When faced with MM's argument, they often reply that dividends are cash-in-hand while capital gains are at best in the bush. It may be true, they say, that the recipient of an extra cash dividend forgoes an equal capital gain, but if the dividend is safe and the capital gain is risky, isn't the shareholder ahead?

It's correct that dividends are more predictable than capital gains. Managers can stabilize dividends but they cannot control stock price. From this it seems a small step to conclude that increased dividends make the firm less risky.[13] But the important point is, once again, that as long as investment policy and borrowing are held constant, a firm's *overall* cash flows are the same regardless of payout policy. The risks borne by *all* the firm's shareholders are likewise fixed by its investment and borrowing policies and unaffected by dividend policy.

If we really believed that existing shareholders are better off by trading a risky asset for cash, then we would also have to argue that the new shareholders—those who trade cash for the newly issued shares—are worse off. But this doesn't make sense: The new shareholders are bearing risk, but they are getting paid for it. They are willing to buy because the new shares are priced to offer an expected return adequate to compensate for the risk.

MM's argument for the irrelevance of dividend policy does not assume a world of certainty; it assumes an efficient capital market. Market efficiency means that the transfers of ownership created by shifts in dividend policy are carried out on fair terms. And since the *overall* value of (old and new) shareholders' equity is unaffected, nobody gains or loses.

16.4 Why Dividends May Increase Firm Value

MARKET IMPERFECTIONS

Most economists believe that MM's conclusions are correct, given their assumptions of perfect and efficient capital markets. However, nobody claims their model is an exact description of the so-called real world. Thus the impact of dividend policy finally boils down to arguments about imperfections and inefficiencies.

Those who believe that dividends are good argue that some investors have a natural preference for high-payout stocks. For example, some financial institutions are legally restricted from holding stocks lacking established dividend records. Trusts and endowment funds may prefer high-dividend stocks because dividends are regarded as spendable "income," whereas capital gains are "additions to principal," which may not be spent.[14]

In addition, many investors look to their stock portfolios for a steady source of cash to live on. In principle this cash can be generated from stocks paying no dividends at all; the investor can just sell off a small fraction of his or her holdings from time to time. For example, an investor who holds 1,000 shares of BCE stock can sell 10 shares (1 percent of the total holdings) this year. This "homemade dividend" is equivalent to an increase of one percentage point in BCE's annual dividend yield.

[13] In that case one might also argue that interest payments are even more predictable, so that a company's risk would be reduced by increasing the proportion of profits paid out as interest. How would you respond to that suggestion?

[14] Many colleges and universities are legally free to spend capital gains from their endowments, but this is rarely done.

However, instead of BCE's shareholders making regular sales, it is simpler and cheaper for the company to send them a dividend cheque. The costs of trading small numbers of shares can be extremely high. BCE's regular dividends relieve many of its shareholders of these transaction costs and considerable inconvenience.

All this is undoubtedly true, but it does not follow that you can increase the value of *your* firm by increasing the dividend payout. Smart managers already have recognized that there is a clientele of investors who would be prepared to pay a premium for high-payout stocks. High-payout fans already have a wide variety of stocks to choose from.

There are natural clienteles for high-payout stocks, but it does not follow that any particular firm can benefit by increasing its dividends. The high-dividend clienteles already have plenty of high-dividend stocks to choose from.

You don't hear businesspeople argue that because there is a clientele of car buyers, their company should manufacture cars. So why should you believe that because there is a clientele of investors who like high payouts, your company can increase value by manufacturing a high payout? That clientele was probably satisfied long ago.

CHECK POINT 16.4

Suppose an investor in BCE does not need a regular income. What could she do to offset BCE's "overly generous" payout policy? If there were no trading costs, would she have any reason to care about BCE's dividend payout policy? What if there is a brokerage fee on the purchase of new shares? What if BCE has a dividend reinvestment plan that allows the investor to buy shares at a 5 percent discount?

DIVIDENDS AS SIGNALS

Another line of argument for high payouts does not rely on market imperfections like trading costs. Think of a market in which investors receive very little reliable information about a firm's earnings. Such markets exist in some countries where a passion for secrecy and a tendency to construct many-layered corporate organizations produce earnings figures that are next to meaningless. Some people say that the situation is little better in the United States or Canada, thanks to creative accounting.

How might an investor in such a world separate marginally profitable firms from the real money makers? One clue is dividends. A firm that reports good earnings and pays a generous dividend is putting its money where its mouth is. Accounting numbers may lie, but dividends require the firm to come up with hard cash. We can understand why investors would favour firms with established dividend records. We can also see how investors would value the information content of dividends. Investors would refuse to believe a firm's reported earnings announcements unless they were backed up by an appropriate dividend policy.

Of course, firms can cheat in the short-run by overstating earnings and scraping up cash to pay a generous dividend. But it is hard to cheat in the long-run because a firm that is not making money will not have the cash flow to pay out. Only the firms with sufficient cash flow will find that it pays to signal their good fortune by choosing a high-dividend level. If a firm chooses a high-dividend payout without the cash flow to back it up, that firm ultimately will have to cut back on investment or turn to investors for additional debt or equity financing. All of these consequences are costly. Therefore, most managers don't increase dividends until they are confident that sufficient cash will flow in to pay them.

Investors can't read managers' minds, but they learn from managers' actions. When dividends increase, they infer managers' confidence in the firm's cash flow and earnings.

Because a high-dividend payout policy will be costly to firms that do not have the cash flow to support it, dividend increases signal a company's good fortune and its managers' confidence in future cash flow.

Healy and Palepu report that between 1970 and 1979 companies that made a dividend payment for the first time experienced relatively flat earnings growth until the year before the announcement.[15] In that year earnings grew by an average 43 percent. If managers thought that this was a temporary windfall, they might have been cautious about committing themselves to paying out cash. But it looks as if they had good reason to be confident about prospects, because over the next 4 years earnings grew by a further 164 percent.

Since dividends anticipate future earnings, it is no surprise to find that announcements of dividend cuts are usually taken as bad news (stock price typically falls) and that dividend increases are good news (stock price rises). This is called the **information content of dividends.**

information content of dividends Dividend increases send good news about cash flow and earnings. Dividend cuts send bad news.

It's important not to jump to the conclusion that investors like higher dividends for their own sake. A dividend initiation or increase may be welcomed *only* as a sign of higher future earnings. Even investors who prefer low-dividend policies might find that a drop in the dividend is unwelcome news about the firm's prospects.[16]

SEE PP. 492–493

The two nearby Finance in Action boxes discuss the signalling effects of dividend changes. The first Finance in Action box shows how dividend increases are viewed positively by investors, and are generally followed by stock price increases. The second Finance in Action box illustrates the signalling power of dividends and describes the effects of a dividend cut by the Florida Power & Light Company. When Florida Power & Light cut its dividend, the firm stressed that the cut was not a response to low or uncertain profits but part of a rethinking of its financial strategy for a deregulated world. Despite these reassurances, the stock price fell. The market apparently paid more attention to what the firm did than to what its management said. The stock price recovered only later as the market became convinced that the prospects of the firm were in fact OK.

Occasionally, when a company cuts dividends, investors react negatively and penalize it as well as others in the same industry. When TransCanada PipeLines shocked investors in December 1999 by cutting its dividend to $.80 from $1.12, its share price dropped to $11.65 from $23. The share price of TransAlta Corp., which didn't cut dividends, fell along with TransCanada despite assurances from top management that the company had no intention of cutting its dividend.

CHECK POINT 16.5

In 1974 Consolidated Edison announced that it would omit its regular $.45 per share cash quarterly dividend. It cited losses due to increased oil prices following the OPEC oil embargo. The stock price fell by about 30 percent in 1 day, from about $18 (US) per share to $12 per share. Why would omission of a $.45 per share dividend result in a stock price drop of $6 per share?

---

[15] P. Healy and K. Palepu, "Earnings Information Conveyed by Dividend Initiations and Omissions," *Journal of Financial Economics* 21 (1988), pp. 149–175.

[16] For example, in an article in *Fortune,* Carol Loomis tells the story of General Public Utilities, "A Case for Dropping Dividends," *Fortune* (June 15, 1968), p. 181ff. In 1968 its management decided to reduce its cash dividend to avoid a stock issue. Despite the company's assurances, it encountered considerable opposition. Individual shareholders advised the president to see a psychiatrist, institutional holders threatened to sell their stock, the share price fell nearly 10 percent, and eventually management capitulated.

FINANCE IN ACTION

Dividend Hikes Positive Signal for Investors

Twelve cents buys you peanuts (not many) these days, but it still can make a world of difference in the stock market.

Consider the case of Montreal-based cheese-maker Saputo, Inc. In the weeks after Saputo declared record profits and announced a hike in its share dividend to $.36 a year from $.24, the stock shot up more than 30 percent.

For investors, there are few signals more encouraging about a company's financial vigour than a dividend hike. And several publicly traded companies in Canada have been sending that signal lately.

The Bank of Nova Scotia, for one, raised its stock dividend last month to $.28 per quarter from $.24. As recently as 1997, Scotiabank shareholders received $.74 per year in dividends. This year, it'll be $1, and next year, $1.12.

Dividends tend to get overlooked in stock markets enamoured with high-flying high-tech titles, but they're something conservative investors still like to see. A pattern of dividend hikes is especially appealing.

In Canada, financial services companies, pipelines, and utilities have the best record of steadily growing dividends.

In the U.S., top recent performers include names like Paychex, Inc., Citigroup, Inc., Morgan Stanley, Dean Witter, Home Depot, Wal-Mart, Warner-Lambert, and Gillette Co.

Benoit Gauvin, senior manager of Canadian equities for Gestion de Placements Valorem in Montreal, said companies that raise their dividends usually are projecting at least three years ahead, and foresee no difficulty in finding the cash to make the extra payments.

A company wouldn't do it if it felt there was trouble ahead, because a dividend cut is just about the worst message a publicly traded company can send to investors, and the stock gets punished accordingly.

Witness TransCanada Pipe Lines, Ltd., whose shares went into free-fall on the Toronto Stock Exchange last year after it chopped its dividend by 29 percent. While there's been some recovery lately, it's still more than 30 percent below its 52-week high of $21.85.

While a dividend is not in itself sufficient reason to invest in a company, Mr. Gauvin said the ones that pay them generally are among the most stable, established, and non-cyclical.

On the high-tech side, however, dividends tend to be small to nonexistent. Growth companies would rather reinvest their earnings in research and development of new products than distribute them to shareholders, and that's probably for the best, Mr. Gauvin said.

Nortel Networks, for instance, has a stock price above $100 but pays a cash dividend of only about $.11 a year, and hasn't raised it since 1987.

"I'd rather it didn't have one at all," Mr. Gauvin said. "I'm buying it for growth."

Communications giant BCE, Inc., which earlier this year distributed its sizable Nortel stake to shareholders, pays $1.20 per year in dividends, a yield of roughly 3.7 percent at the current stock price.

Actual dividend yield of a stock depends on the purchase price. It ranges from less than one percent (the case for most) to between 3 and 5 percent for conservative companies like utilities and banks to 10 percent or more for titles whose share prices are more volatile or in the doghouse (and whose dividend payouts are consequently less assured).

Paget Warner, manager of the Scotia Canadian Dividend mutual fund, said he places greater importance on security of dividends than the yields, which are now at 20-year lows because they haven't kept pace with soaring stock prices.

In down markets, stocks with a good dividend "will have a much better time weathering the storm," Mr. Warner said.

Mr. Gauvin added that the yield and favourable tax treatment of dividend income make it an attractive alternative to interest-paying instruments like GICs.

Reinvestment plans, which automatically convert cash dividends into additional stock, are an effective way of adding to stockholdings without incurring further brokerage fees.

Source: P. Delean, "Dividend Hikes Positive Signal for Investors," the *Telegraph-Journal* (September 18, 2000), pp. D1–D2.

16.5 Why Pay Dividends? A Look at Tax Law Implications

DIVIDENDS VERSUS CAPITAL GAINS

Could paying dividends reduce firm value? If dividends are taxed more heavily than capital gains, any tax-paying investor would be attracted to companies that can convert dividends to capital gains by shifting their dividend policies. Firms should then pay the lowest

FINANCE IN ACTION

The Dividend Cut Heard 'Round the World

On May 9, 1994, FPL Group, the parent company of Florida Power & Light Company, announced a 32 percent reduction in its quarterly dividend payout, from $.62 per share to $.42. This was the first-ever dividend cut by a healthy utility. A number of utilities had reduced their dividends in the past, but only after cash flow problems—often associated with heavy investment in nuclear plants—had given them no other choice.

In its announcement, FPL stressed that it had studied the situation carefully and that, given the prospect of increased competition in the electric utility industry, the company's high-dividend payout ratio (which had averaged 90 percent in the past 4 years) was no longer in the shareholders' best interests. The new policy resulted in a dividend payout of about 60 percent of the prior year's earnings. Management also announced that, starting in 1995, the dividend payout would be reviewed in February instead of May to reinforce the linkage between dividends and annual earnings. In doing so, the company wanted to minimize unintended "signalling effects" from any future changes in the dividend.

At the same time it announced this change in dividend policy, FPL Group's board authorized the repurchase of up to 10 million shares of common stock over the next 3 years. FPL's management said that four million shares would be repurchased over the next 12 months, depending on market conditions. In adopting this strategy, the company noted that changes in the U.S. tax code since 1990 had made capital gains more attractive than dividends to shareholders.

Besides providing a more tax-efficient means of distributing excess capital to its shareholders, FPL's substitution of stock repurchases for dividends was also designed to increase the company's financial flexibility in preparation for a new era of deregulation and heightened competition among utilities. Although much of the cash savings from the dividend cut would be returned to investors in the form of stock repurchases, the rest would be used to retire debt at Florida Power & Light and so reduce the company's leverage ratio. This deleveraging and strengthening of FPL's financial condition were intended to prepare the company for an increase in business risk and to provide the financial resources to take advantage of future growth opportunities.

The stock market's initial reaction to FPL's announcement was negative. On the day of the announcement, the company's stock price fell from $31.88 to $27.50, a drop of nearly 14 percent. But, as analysts digested the news and considered the reasons for the reduction, they concluded that the action was not a signal of financial distress but rather a strategic decision that would improve the company's long-term financial flexibility and prospects for growth. This view spread throughout the financial community, and FPL's stock began to recover.

On May 31, less than a month after the announcement, FPL's stock closed at $32.17 (adjusted for the quarterly dividend of $.42), or about $.30 higher than the preannouncement price. By the middle of June, at least 15 major brokerage houses had placed FPL's common stock on their "buy" lists. On May 9, 1995—exactly one year after the announcement of the cut—FPL's stock price closed at $37.75, giving shareholders a one-year post-announcement return (including dividends) of 23.8 percent, more than double the 11.2 percent of the S&P Index and well above the 14.2 percent of the S&P utilities index over the same period.

Source: Modified from D. Soter, E. Brigham, and P. Evanson, "The Dividend Cut 'Heard 'Round the World': The Case of FPL," *Journal of Applied Corporate Finance* 9 (Spring 1996), pp. 4–15.

cash dividend they can get away with. Available cash should be retained and reinvested or used to repurchase shares.

In Chapter 2, we discussed the treatment of income from dividends and capital gains under Canadian tax laws. We saw that Canadian public corporations do not pay any tax on dividend income received from another Canadian corporation, whereas individual investors receive some tax relief through a *dividend tax credit* (DTC). The dividend tax credit reduces the burden of double taxation on shareholder income, which occurs because the cash flows that produce such income are taxed at both corporate and personal levels. On the other hand, corporations and individual investors pay tax on capital gains that are realized when the asset is sold. Presently, only 50 percent of such realized capital gains are taxable. Tax law is on the side of capital gains in another important respect. Taxes on dividends have to be paid immediately, but taxes on capital gains can be deferred until shares

TABLE 16.3
Effects of a shift in dividend policy when dividends are taxed more heavily than capital gains. The high-payout stock (firm B) must sell at a lower price in order to provide the same after-tax return.

	Firm A	Firm B
Next year's price	$112.50	$102.50
Dividend	$ 0	$ 10.00
Total *pretax* payoff	$112.50	$112.50
Today's stock price	$100	$ 98.90
Capital gain	$ 12.50	$ 3.60
Before-tax rate of return (%)	$\frac{12.5}{100} = .125 = 12.5\%$	$\frac{13.60}{98.90} = 0.138 = 13.8\%$
Tax on dividend at 30%	$0	.30 × $10 = $3.00
Tax on capital gain at 20%	.20 × $12.50 = $2.50	.20 × $3.60 = $.72
Total after-tax income (dividends plus capital gains less taxes)	(0 + 12.50) – 2.50 = $10.00	(10 + 3.60) – (3.00 + .72) = $9.88
After-tax rate of return (%)	$\frac{10}{100} = .10 = 10\%$	$\frac{9.88}{98.90} \cong .10 = 10\%$

are sold and capital gains are realized. Stockholders can choose when to sell their shares and thus when to pay the capital gains tax.[17]

Overall, for some investors, dividends are taxed more heavily than capital gains, whereas for others, capital gains suffer more tax than dividends. For instance, refer back to the solution to Check Point 2.6. Notice that an Ontario-based investor in the lowest tax bracket (combined tax rate of 22.2 percent) has a dividend tax rate of 4.68 percent, but a higher capital gains tax rate of 11.1 percent. On the other hand, the investor in the highest tax bracket with a combined tax rate of 42.39 percent has a dividend tax rate of 29.91 percent, but a lower capital gains tax rate of 21.19 percent.[18]

From the discussion above, some investors have a tax reason for preferring income from dividend instead of capital gains. These would include investors in low tax brackets and Canadian corporations. Suppose we call this group "Clientele D." There would also be a group of investors, particularly those in high tax brackets, who would prefer capital gains to dividends. We call this group "Clientele C."

Table 16.3 illustrates how taxes can affect firm value. It assumes that dividends and capital gains are taxed at rates applicable to the Ontario-based high-tax bracket investor, that is, a tax rate on dividends of 29.91 percent, but a lower capital gains tax rate of 21.19 percent. For convenience, we have rounded off these rates to 30 percent and 20 percent, respectively.

The table shows stocks of firms A and B, which are equally risky, and investors demand an expected after-tax rate of return of 10 percent on each. Investors expect A to be worth $112.50 per share next year. The share price of B is expected to be only $102.50, but a $10 dividend is also forecast, so the total pretax payoff is the same, $112.50.

Both stocks offer the same pretax dollar payoff. Yet, B's stock sells for less than A's and therefore offers a higher pretax rate of return. The reason is obvious: Investors are willing to buy stock A because its return comes in the form of low-taxed capital gains. After tax, each stock offers the same 10 percent return.[19]

[17] Suppose the discount rate is 8 percent, and an investor in a combined 40 percent federal and provincial tax bracket has a $100 capital gain. If the stock is sold today, the tax on capital gain will be $20 (that is, .5 x .4 × 100), but by virtue of delaying the sale for a year, the present value of the tax falls to $20/1.08 = $18.52. The effective tax rate falls to 18.52 percent. The longer the sale is deferred, the lower is the effective tax rate.

[18] See Chapter 2, Table 2.6, for a table of tax rates on ordinary income.

[19] Actually, stock B's after-tax return is being rounded off to 10 percent.

In this example, we have assumed tax rates on income from dividends, and capital gains from the point of view of the Clientele C group of investors. Notice that we would have arrived at the opposite conclusion if we had assumed tax rates from the standpoint of the Clientele D investor. Does any one of these clienteles play a dominant role in the market? If this is so, then the dominant clientele should have an influence on whether high-dividend yield stocks should sell for more or less than low-dividend yield stocks on the basis of taxes. Researchers have tried to find answers by examining whether high-yield stocks provide different expected rates of return than low-yield stocks. Unfortunately, it is difficult to measure such clientele effects, and the researchers have not been able to come up with definitive answers.[20]

Also, we must keep in mind that tax laws tend to change over time and the relationship between dividends and pretax rates of return should change as well. Capital gains were taxed for the first time in Canada in 1972. Before that year, many investors were taxed at higher rates on dividend income than on capital gains income. Consequently, we would expect high-dividend paying stocks to earn a higher pretax rate of return to compensate for the extra taxes. Since the 1980s, new reforms have increased the tax on capital gains. For example, a $100,000 lifetime capital gain exemption, introduced in the mid-1980s, was ended in 1994. In 2000, the federal budget lowered the taxable portion of capital gains from 75 percent to 50 percent. The net effect of these changes has been to reduce the difference in the taxes on dividends and capital gains. We would expect that the pretax rate of return on high-dividend paying stocks would get smaller.[21] While there may have been a predominance of Clientele D investors in Canada before the tax reforms, the tax savings from moving between the high- and low-dividend stocks are perhaps not as high as they used to be.

CHECK POINT 16.6

Look again at Table 16.3. What would happen to the price and pretax rate of return on stock B if the tax on capital gains were eliminated?

DIVIDEND CLIENTELE EFFECTS

dividend clientele effect Different investor groups prefer different dividend yields. Changing the firm's dividend policy may attract a new investor clientele but may not change firm value.

From our discussion above, we have seen that some groups of investors, such as rich individuals, prefer to receive capital gains and little or no dividends, while other groups, such as corporate investors, may prefer high-dividend payouts. Different investor groups, or clienteles, therefore prefer different payouts; this is the **dividend clientele effect**. The dividend-clientele-effect argument is that changing the dividend policy of the firm would attract a new investor clientele but may not change the value of the firm. Suppose a firm with a low-dividend payout switches to a high-dividend payout policy. It will now attract clienteles seeking high-dividend payout stocks. However, its share price may not go up as

[20] Some important early studies that provide insights on the issues involved in this research include F. Black and M. Scholes, "The Effects of Dividend Yield and Dividend Policy on Common Stock Prices and Returns," *Journal of Financial Economics* 1 (May 1974), pp. 1–22; R. H. Litzenberger and K. Ramaswamy, "The Effects of Dividends on Common Stock Prices: Tax Effects or Information Effect," *Journal of Finance* 37 (May 1982), pp. 429–443; and M. H. Miller, "Behavioural Rationality in Finance: The Case of Dividends," *Journal of Business* 59 (October 1986), pp. 451–468.

[21] Although a study by I. G. Morgan, "Dividends and Stock Price Behaviour in Canada," *Journal of Business Administration* 12 (Fall 1980), pp. 91–106, found no difference in the before-tax rates of return between high- and low-dividend paying stocks between 1972 and 1977. Another study which has examined the issue, B. Amoako-adu, M. Rashid, and M. Stebbens, "Capital Gains Tax and Equity Values: Empirical Test of Stock Price Reaction to the Introduction and Reduction of Capital Gains Tax Exemption," *Journal of Banking and Finance* 16 (1992), pp. 275–287.

long as enough firms satisfy the demand for high-dividend paying stocks. Essentially, this is a supply and demand argument. If the demand from investor clienteles is more for high-dividend paying stocks relative to the supply of such stocks, the prices of high-dividend paying stocks should rise. However, low-dividend paying firms will now find it advantageous to switch to high-dividend payout policies until prices stabilize and the "market for dividends" is in equilibrium. In such an environment, a dividend policy change by an individual firm will have no effect on its share value.

SHARE REPURCHASES INSTEAD OF CASH DIVIDENDS?

Many Canadian firms have active share repurchase programs in place. For example, Canadian Pacific's share repurchase program allows it to buy up to 5 percent of its outstanding common shares at prevailing market prices on the TSX and NYSE where its shares are listed. Other companies have similar programs in place.

Companies may repurchase their shares for a variety of reasons. A company may decide to repurchase some of its stock if it wishes to distribute temporary excess cash to its shareholders as an alternative form of dividend. Notice that a share repurchase can also reduce the firm's future-cash dividend requirement. Sometimes a company's management may decide to repurchase shares because they feel that the stock is undervalued, given their knowledge of the firm's future prospects. Share repurchases can be used to achieve other corporate goals such as "leveraging up" and altering the firm's capital structure, or as a take-over defence.

From the firm's point of view, a share repurchase is similar to paying a cash dividend. However, the tax treatment for shareholders may be quite different. When a company pays a cash dividend, the investor has no choice but to receive it and pay any applicable tax that may become due. However, if shares are repurchased on the open market, the shareholder pays taxes only if she has decided to sell the shares and incurs a taxable capital gain on the sale. As we have discussed earlier, by deferring a sale, the investor can lower the present value of the capital gains tax liability.

Sometimes, the investor could sell shares to another company making a tender offer to take over a target firm. In this case, any amount paid by the company for the repurchase of shares that exceeds their paid-up capital value is treated by the Income Tax Act as "deemed dividend" in the hands of investors. This removes any tax advantage of stock repurchases over dividends.

Shareholders who pay higher taxes on dividends than on capital gains (Clientele C) might be happy to sell some shares to the firm and receive income as capital gains. They will avoid paying the higher tax on the dividend income. We must caution firms to *not* stop paying dividends altogether and only make regular share repurchases. A firm that eliminates dividends and starts repurchasing stock on a regular basis may find that Canada Customs and Revenue Agency (CCRA) would recognize the repurchase program for what it really is and would tax the payments accordingly. That is why financial managers have never announced that they are repurchasing shares to save shareholders taxes; they give some other reason.[22]

Nevertheless, one could argue that firms which pay dividends, and as a result have to issue shares from time to time, are making a serious mistake. Any such firm is essentially

[22] They might say, "Our stock is a good investment," or "We want to have the shares available to finance acquisitions of other companies." What do you think of these rationales?

FINANCE IN ACTION

Whatever Happened to Dividends?

"The only thing that gives me pleasure," John D. Rockefeller once said, "is to see my dividends coming in." But Mr. Rockefeller would have less fun today, for many of America's corporate stars, such as Microsoft, Cisco, Sun Microsystems, Dell, and America Online, have *never* paid a dividend. In the 1950s, nine out of 10 American companies paid dividends. Today only one in five does. Dividends are disappearing so fast that professors Eugene Fama and Kenneth French have looked into the phenomenon.

Part of their explanation for it is straightforward: The sorts of companies that are traded on America's stock markets have changed radically. Until the early 1970s, an exchange listing was, by and large, the preserve of large, profitable firms—firms that one would expect to pay a dividend. All this changed after 1971, when the New York Stock Exchange was joined by a new rival, Nasdaq, which imposed less stringent listing conditions. The result was that many less profitable companies began to obtain a listing. Newly listed companies made returns on equity of about 18% in the 1970s, but only 3% in the mid-1990s, compared with 11% for corporate America as a whole. By 1997, only about half the new listings made any profits at all. Since then, as some cynics on Wall Street joke, making profits for any self-respecting "dot.com," has become uncool.

Companies that are making losses are ill-advised to pay a dividend. But even a company with profits should choose to retain them if it thinks that its own investment opportunities are better than those available to shareholders elsewhere. For both reasons, more "growth" companies will tend to mean fewer dividend-payers.

Even so, there is a puzzle about the disappearing dividend. It is not just growth companies that are opting out of dividends, but all companies, including those enjoying healthy flows of free cash. Among very profitable companies, only 32% pay dividends, half the proportion that did 20 years ago.

One possible explanation is that shareholders do not want dividends. These represent income, which is taxed at a top federal rate of 39.6%. By leaving profits in the firm, investors can defer this tax, and, if need be, cash in a capital gain, which is taxed at only 20%. But taxes do not in themselves explain the decline in dividend-paying. After all, income tax has long been higher than capital gains tax; it is unlikely that American investors have only just noticed.

Another theory says that dividends have not disappeared, but assumed a new guise: companies' purchases of their own shares. Such buybacks have risen from 3 to 5% of annual corporate profits during the 1970s to 26% in the 1980s and 1990s. But share buybacks are not replacing dividends as such, because most of the companies buying back shares also pay dividends. Mr. Fama and Mr. French find no evidence that companies stop paying dividends (or do not start) because they can buy back shares instead.

That does not mean dividends have become irrelevant. But it may mean that they have become less relevant. For most of the century the dividend yield was one of the most watched measures in the stock market. Whenever it dropped to 3% or less, traders assumed the market was overvalued and sold their holdings. Yet today the dividend yield on the S&P 500 shares is 1.2%. Optimists might argue that since dividends no longer play the role they once did, this does not, of itself, mean the market is wildly overvalued. But, given the uncertainty over what role dividends precisely play now, that is scarcely reassuring.

Source: Abridged from *The Economist*, November 20, 1999. www.economist.com.

financing its dividends by issuing stock; it should cut its dividends at least to the point where stock issues are unnecessary. This would not only save taxes for shareholders, it would also avoid the transaction costs of stock issues.

The above Finance in Action box notes that dividend payouts have, in fact, drastically declined in the last few decades, and it explores some explanations for this phenomenon.

16.6 Summary

1. How are dividends paid and how do companies decide on dividend payments?

Dividends come in many forms. The most common is the regular **cash dividend,** but sometimes companies pay an extra cash dividend, and sometimes they pay a **stock dividend.** A firm is not free to pay dividends at will. For example, it may have accepted restrictions on dividends as a condition for borrowing money.

Most managers seem to have a target **dividend payout ratio.** But if firms simply applied this target payout rate to each year's earnings, dividends could fluctuate wildly. Managers therefore try to smooth dividends by moving only partway toward the target payout in each year. Also, they don't look just at past earnings: They try to look into the future when they set the payment. Investors are aware of this and they know that a dividend increase is usually a sign of optimism on the part of management.

2. Why would dividend policy not affect firm value in an ideal world?

If we hold the company's investment policy and capital structure constant, then dividend policy is a trade-off between cash dividends and the issue or repurchase of common stock. In an ideally simple and perfect world, the choice would have no effect on market value. This is the **MM dividend-irrelevance proposition.** The dividend controversy centers on the effects of dividend policy in our flawed world. A common—though by no means universal—view is that high payout enhances share price. While there are natural clienteles for high-payout stocks, we find it difficult to explain a *general* preference for dividends except as an irrational prejudice.

3. How might differences in the tax treatment of dividends and capital gains affect dividend policy?

Instead of paying dividends, the company can repurchase its own stock. The Canada Customs and Revenue Agency (CCRA) taxes shareholders on the capital gains that they realize as a result of the repurchase.

Are capital gains taxed at lower rates than dividend income? For some investor groups, dividend income can offer some tax advantages over realized capital gains income. However, investors who do not realize capital gains can defer, and thereby, lower the present value of any capital gains tax liability. This suggests the existence of different investor clienteles preferring different dividend payouts. The **dividend-clientele-effect** argument is that changing the dividend policy of the firm would attract a new investor clientele but may not change the value of the firm.

If dividends are seriously tax-disadvantaged for some investors, we would expect such investors to demand a higher before-tax return on high-payout stocks. Instead of paying high dividends, companies should then use the cash to repurchase shares or to reduce the amount of share issues. In this way, the company would in effect convert dividend income into capital gains. This is one reason a low-dividend policy might be preferred.

4. Why may dividends be used by management to signal the prospects of the firm?

A firm that chooses a high-dividend policy without the cash flow to back it up will find that it ultimately has to either cut back on investments or turn to capital markets for additional debt or equity financing. Because this is costly, managers do not increase dividends unless they are confident that the firm is generating enough cash to pay them. This is the principal reason that we say that there is an **information content of dividends**—that is, dividend changes are liable to be interpreted as signals of a change in the firm's prospects.

If a sharp dividend change is necessary, then the company should provide as much forewarning and explanation as possible. Moreover, a firm should adopt a target payout that is sufficiently low to minimize its reliance on external equity. Why pay out cash to shareholders if that requires issuing new shares to get the cash back? It's better to hold on to the cash in the first place.

RELATED WEB LINKS

www.cfonews.com Current dividend news

www.e-analytics.com/splitd.htm Information about stock dividends during the last year and a discussion of cash versus stock dividends

www.dripcentral.com Information about dividend reinvestment plans

KEY TERMS

cash dividend	480	stock repurchase	483	information content of dividends	491
ex-dividend date	480	dividend payout ratio	484	dividend clientele effect	495
stock dividend	482	MM dividend-irrelevance proposition	487		
stock split	482				
reverse split	483				

QUESTIONS AND PROBLEMS

*Answers in Appendix B

BASIC

*1. **Dividend Sequence.** Cash Cow International paid a regular quarterly dividend of $.075 a share.

a. Connect each of the following dates to the correct term:

May 7	Record date
June 6	Payment date
June 7	Ex-dividend date
June 11	Last with-dividend date
July 2	Declaration date

b. On one of these dates the stock price is likely to fall by about the value of the dividend. Why?

c. The stock price in early January was $27. What was the prospective dividend yield?

d. The earnings per share were forecast at around $1.90. What was the percentage payout rate?

e. Suppose that the company paid a 10 percent stock dividend. What would be the expected fall in the stock price?

2. **Institutional Background.** True or false? If false, correct the statement.

a. A company may not generally pay a dividend out of legal capital.

b. A company may not generally pay a dividend if it is insolvent.

c. The *effective* tax rate on capital gains can be less than the stated tax rate on such gains.

d. Corporations are not taxed on dividends received from other corporations.

*3. **Splits and Dividends.** Shares in Raven Products are selling for $40 per share. There are one million shares outstanding. What will be the share price in each of the following situations? Ignore taxes.

a. The stock splits five-for-four.

b. The company pays a 25 percent stock dividend.

c. The company repurchases 100,000 shares.

4. **Dividend Irrelevance.** You own 1,000 shares of Patriot Corporation, which is about to raise its dividend from $.75 to $1 per share. The share price is currently $50. You would prefer that the dividend remain at its current level. What would you do to offset the effects of the increase in the dividend?

5. **DRIPs.** A firm considers initiating an aggressive dividend reinvestment plan (DRIP) in which it allows its investors to use dividends to buy shares at a discount of 40 percent from current market value. The firm's financial manager argues that the policy will benefit shareholders by giving them the opportunity to buy additional shares at a deep discount and will benefit the firm by providing a source of cash. Is the manager correct?

PRACTICE

6. **Dividends and Repurchases.** While dividend yields in the United States in the late 1990s were at historically low levels, share repurchases were at historical highs. Was this a coincidence?

7. **Dividend Irrelevance.** Respond to the following comment: "It's all very well saying that I can sell shares to cover cash needs, but that may mean selling at the bottom of the market. If the company pays a regular dividend, investors avoid the risk."

8. **Cash Dividends.** The stock of Payout Corp. will go ex-dividend tomorrow. The dividend will be $1 per share, and there are 20,000 shares of stock outstanding. The market-value balance sheet for Payout is shown below.

a. What price is Payout stock selling for today?
b. What price will it sell for tomorrow? Ignore taxes.

Assets		Liabilities and Equity	
Cash	$100,000	Equity	$1,000,000
Fixed assets	900,000		

*9. **Repurchases.** Now suppose that Payout from problem 8 announces its intention to repurchase $20,000 worth of stock instead of paying out the dividend.

a. What effect will the repurchase have on an investor who currently holds 100 shares and sells two of those shares back to the company in the repurchase?
b. Compare the effects of the repurchase to the effects of the cash dividend that you worked out in problem 8.

10. **Stock Dividend.** Now suppose that Payout again changes its mind and decides to issue a 2 percent stock dividend instead of either issuing the cash dividend or repurchasing 2 percent of the outstanding stock. How would this action affect a shareholder who owns 100 shares of stock? Compare with your answers to problems 8 and 9.

*11. **Dividend Irrelevance.** Suppose Mr. Dente from Example 16.2 changes his mind and cuts out Consolidated's Year 1 dividend entirely, instead spending $10 million to buy back stock. Are shareholders any better or worse off than if Consolidated had paid out $10 million as cash dividends? *Hints:* How many shares will be repurchased? The purchase price at Year 1 will be $110.

*12. **Dividends and Taxes.** Suppose that the tax rate on dividends is 28 percent, and the tax rate on capital gains is zero. Eagle Net Resources is about to pay a $2 per share dividend.

a. By how much will Eagle Net's share price fall when the stock goes ex-dividend?
b. Will anything happen to the share price on the payment date when the dividend cheques are sent out?

*13. **Stock Dividends and Splits.** Suppose that you own 1,000 shares of Nocash Corp., and the company is about to pay a 25 percent stock dividend. The stock currently sells at $50 per share.

a. What will be the number of shares that you hold and the total value of your equity position after the dividend is paid?
b. What will happen to the number of shares that you hold and the value of your equity position if the firm splits five-for-four instead of paying the stock dividend?

*14. **Dividends and Taxes.** Good Values, Inc., is all-equity financed. The total market value of the firm currently is $100,000, and there are 2,000 shares outstanding.

a. The firm has declared a $5 per share dividend. The stock will go ex-dividend tomorrow. At what price will the stock sell today? Ignore taxes.
b. Now assume that the federal marginal tax rate is 26 percent and the provincial marginal tax rate is 13.39 percent, the federal dividend tax credit is 13.33 percent of the grossed-up dividend and the provincial dividend tax credit is 5.13 percent of grossed-up dividend. The applicable gross-up for dividend tax credits is 25 percent. What is the dividend tax rate?
c. Using your result for the dividend tax rate from part (b) and assuming a capital gains tax rate of zero, at what price will the stock sell today?

15. **Repurchases and Taxes.** Now suppose that instead of paying a dividend, Good Values (from problem 14) plans to repurchase $10,000 worth of stock.

a. What will be the stock price before and after the repurchase?
b. Suppose an investor who holds 200 shares sells 20 of her shares back to the firm. If there are no taxes on dividends or capital gains, show that she should be indifferent toward the repurchase and the dividend.

c. For this part, use the dividend tax rate from your answer to part (b) in problem 14 and assume that capital gains are not taxed. Is the value of the firm higher or lower if it pursues the share repurchase instead of the dividend?

*16. **Dividends and Taxes.** Investors require an after-tax rate of return of 10 percent on their stock investments. Assume that the tax rate on dividends is 28 percent while capital gains escape taxation. A firm will pay a $2 per share dividend 1 year from now, after which, it is expected to sell at a price of $20.

a. Find the current price of the stock.
b. Find the expected before-tax rate of return for a 1-year holding period.
c. Now suppose that the dividend will be $3 per share. If the expected after-tax rate of return is still 10 percent, and investors still expect the stock to sell at $20 in 1 year, at what price must the stock now sell?
d. What is the before-tax rate of return? Why is it now higher than in part (b)?

*17. **Dividends and Taxes.** The expected pretax return on three stocks is divided between dividends and capital gains in the following way:

Stock	Expected Dividend	Expected Capital Gain
A	$ 0	$10
B	5	5
C	10	0

a. If each stock is priced at $100, what are the expected net returns on each stock to (1) a pension fund that does not pay taxes, (2) an Ontario corporation engaged in manufacturing activity, paying tax at a combined federal and provincial rate of 33 percent, and (3) an individual based in Ontario, paying a federal marginal tax rate of 29 percent and a provincial marginal tax rate of 13.39 percent. The gross-up for dividend tax credits is 25 percent. The federal dividend tax credit is 13.33 percent of the grossed-up dividend, and the provincial dividend tax credit is 5.13 percent of grossed-up dividend.
b. Suppose that stocks A, B, and C were priced to yield an 8 percent after-tax return to individual investors paying federal tax of 16 percent and provincial tax of 6.2 percent. The gross-up for dividend tax credits is 25 percent. The federal dividend tax credit is 13.33 percent of the grossed-up dividend and the provincial dividend tax credit is 5.13 percent of grossed-up dividend. What would A, B, and C each sell for?

18. **Dividends and Taxes.** Suppose all investments offered the same expected return *before* tax. Consider two equally risky shares, Hi and Lo. Hi shares pay a generous dividend and offer low expected capital gains. Lo shares pay low dividends and offer high-expected capital gains. Which of the following investors would prefer the Lo shares? Which would prefer the Hi shares? Which wouldn't care? Explain. Assume that any stock purchased will be sold after 1 year.

a. a pension fund
b. an individual
c. a corporation

19. **Signalling.** It is well documented that stock prices tend to rise when firms announce an increase in their dividend payouts. How then can it be said that dividend policy is irrelevant?

20. **Dividend Policy.** Here are several assertions about typical corporate dividend policies. Which of them are true? Write out a corrected version of any false statements.

a. Most companies set a target dividend payout ratio.
b. They set each year's dividend equal to the target payout ratio times that year's earnings.
c. Managers and investors seem more concerned with dividend changes than dividend levels.

d. Managers often increase dividends temporarily when earnings are unexpectedly high for a year or two.

21. **Dividend Policy.** For each of the following four groups of companies, state whether you would expect them to distribute a relatively high or low proportion of current earnings and whether you would expect them to have a relatively high or low price-earnings ratio.

    a. high-risk companies
    b. companies that have recently experienced a temporary decline in profits
    c. companies that expect to experience a decline in profits
    d. "growth" companies with valuable future investment opportunities

22. **Dividend Policy.** "Risky companies tend to have lower target payout ratios and more gradual adjustment rates." Explain what is meant by this statement. Why do you think it is so?

CHALLENGE

*23. **Dividends versus Repurchases.** Big Industries has the following market-value balance sheet. The stock currently sells for $20 a share, and there are 1,000 shares outstanding. The firm will either pay a $1 per share dividend or repurchase $1,000 worth of stock. Ignore taxes.

Assets		Liabilities and Equity	
Cash	$ 2,000	Debt	$10,000
Fixed assets	28,000	Equity	20,000

a. What will be the price per share under each alternative (dividend versus repurchase)?
b. If total earnings of the firm are $2,000 a year, find earnings per share under each alternative.
c. Find the price-earnings ratio under each alternative.
d. Adherents of the "dividends-are-good" school sometimes point to the fact that stocks with high dividend payout ratios tend to sell at above-average price-earnings multiples. Is this evidence convincing? Discuss this argument with regard to your answers to parts (a) through (c).

SOLUTIONS TO CHECK POINTS

16.1 The ex-dividend date is June 1. Therefore Mick buys the stock ex-dividend and will not receive the dividend. The cheques will be mailed on June 30.

16.2

Assets		Liabilities and Equity	
After-cash dividend			
Cash	$ 0	Debt	$ 0
Other assets	850,000	Equity	850,000
Value of firm	$850,000	Value of firm	$850,000

Shares outstanding = 100,000
Price per share = $850,000/100,000 = $8.50

After-stock repurchase			
Cash	$ 0	Debt	$ 0
Other assets	850,000	Equity	850,000
Value of firm	$850,000	Value of firm	$850,000

Shares outstanding = 85,000
Price per share = $850,000/85,000 = $10

If a dividend is paid, the stock price falls by the amount of the dividend. If the company instead uses the cash for a share repurchase, the stock price remains unchanged, but with fewer shares left outstanding, the market value of the firm falls by the same amount as if the dividend had been paid. If a shareholder wants to receive the same amount of cash as if the firm had paid a dividend, he or she must sell shares, and the market value of the remaining stock will be the same as if the firm had paid a dividend.

16.3 The total value of the firm remains at \$100 million. Since the firm issues \$10 million in new preferred stock and the total value of the firm is fixed, the total value of common equity must fall by \$10 million, which translates into the same \$1 per share price drop as when equity was issued. If the firm starts out all-equity financed, the market-value balance sheet of the firm will be as follows (in millions):

Assets		**Liabilities and Equity**	
Assets	\$100	Preferred stock	\$ 10
		Common equity	90
Value of firm	\$100	Value of firm	\$100

Shares outstanding = 1 million
Price per share = \$90 million/1 million = \$90

16.4 An investor who prefers a zero-dividend policy can reinvest any dividends received. This will cause the value of the shares held to be unaffected by payouts. The price drop on the ex-dividend date is offset by the reinvestment of the dividends. However, if the investor had to pay brokerage fees on the newly purchased shares, she would be harmed by a high-payout policy since part of the proceeds of the dividends would go toward paying the broker. On the other hand, if the firm offers a dividend reinvestment plan (DRIP) with a 5 percent discount, she is better off with a high-dividend policy. The DRIP is like a "negative trading cost." She can increase the value of her stock by 5 percent of the dividend just by participating in the DRIP.

16.5 The stock price dropped by more than the dividend because investors interpreted the news as a signal that in addition to omitting the current dividend Consolidated Edison would have to reduce future dividends. The omitted dividend conveyed bad news about the future prospects of the firm.

16.6 The price of the stock will equal the after-tax cash flows discounted by the required (after-tax) rate of return:

$$P = \frac{102.5 + 10 \times (1 - .3)}{1.10} = \$99.55$$

Notice that the after-tax proceeds from the stock would increase by the amount that previously went to pay capital gains taxes, .20 × \$3.60 = \$.72. The present value of this tax savings is \$.72/1.10 = \$.65. Therefore, the price increases to \$98.90 + \$.65 = \$99.55. The pretax rate of return falls to (102.50 – 99.55 + 10)/99.55 = .1301, or 13.01 percent, but the after-tax rate remains at 10 percent.

PART SIX

Financial Planning

17 FINANCIAL STATEMENT ANALYSIS

18 FINANCIAL PLANNING

19 WORKING CAPITAL MANAGEMENT AND SHORT-TERM PLANNING

CHAPTER 17

Financial Statement Analysis

17.1 Financial Ratios

17.2 The DuPont System

17.3 Analysis of the Statement of Cash Flows

17.4 Using Financial Ratios

17.5 Measuring Company Performance

17.6 The Role of Financial Ratios

17.7 Summary

Divide and conquer. That is the only practical strategy for presenting a complex topic like financial management. For that reason we have broken down the financial manager's job into separate areas: capital budgeting, dividend policy, equity financing, and debt policy. Ultimately the financial manager has to consider the combined effects of decisions in each of these areas on the firm as a whole. Therefore, we devote all of Part Six to financial planning. We begin in this chapter by looking at the analysis of financial statements.

Why do companies provide accounting information? Public companies have a variety of stakeholders: shareholders, bondholders, bankers, suppliers, employees, and management, for example. These stakeholders all need to monitor how well their interests are being served. They rely on the company's periodic financial statements to provide basic information on the profitability of the firm.

In this chapter we look at how you can use financial statements to analyze a firm's overall performance and assess its current financial standing. You may wish to understand the policies of a competitor or the financial health of a customer. Or you may need to check your own firm's financial performance in meeting standard criteria and determine where there is room for improvement.

We will look at how analysts summarize the large volume of accounting information by calculating some key financial ratios. We will then describe these ratios and look at some interesting relationships among them. Next we will show how the ratios are used and note the limitations of the accounting data on which most ratios are based. Finally, we will look at some measures of firm performance. Some of these are expressed in ratio form; some measure how much value the firm's decisions have added.

After studying this chapter you should be able to

- Calculate and interpret measures of a firm's leverage, liquidity, efficiency, and profitability.
- Use the DuPont formula to understand the determinants of the firm's return on its assets and equity.
- Examine the statement of cash flows.
- Evaluate the potential pitfalls of ratios based on accounting data.
- Understand some key measures of firm performance such as market value added and economic value added.

17.1 Financial Ratios

We have all heard stories of whizzes who can take a company's accounts apart in minutes, calculate a few financial ratios, and discover the company's innermost secrets. The truth, however, is that financial ratios are no substitute for a crystal ball. They are just a convenient way to summarize large quantities of financial data and to compare firms' performance. Ratios help you to ask the right questions: they seldom answer them.

We will describe and calculate four types of financial ratios:

- *Leverage ratios* show how heavily the company is in debt.
- *Liquidity ratios* measure how easily the firm can lay its hands on cash.
- *Efficiency* or *turnover ratios* measure how productively the firm is using its assets.
- *Profitability ratios* are used to measure the firm's return on its investments.

We will analyze the company Le Château (LC), a Canadian clothing manufacturer and retailer. Our objective is to assess the firm's recent financial performance.[1]

Before diving headlong into the numbers, it is important to examine the nature of the company's operations. Without an understanding of the business, reading their financial statements is like trying to put a puzzle together without knowing what it is a picture of—you may fit some pieces together but it's more difficult to finish the job. Start by reading the annual report. In addition to the financial statements, it contains a company profile, details about the firm's activities, and management's analysis of the company's operations and performance. Don't forget to read the notes to the financial statements—they have important information on how the accountants put the statements together and other details about the company not included in the financial statements.

The company's annual information form, required by the various Canadian securities commissions, is another useful source of information, which is also available online at www.sedar.com. Other information sources include the financial press and financial websites. For example, at www.globeinvestor.com you will find news reports relating to Le Château. Industry Canada's website, Strategis, www.strategis.ic.gc.ca, provides useful information on Canadian industries, including the apparel and retail industries.

According to its 2000 annual report, LC is a "leading retailer of moderately priced apparel, accessories, and footwear aimed at young, spirited, fashion-conscious men, women, and tweens." They operate 156 retail stores in Canada and five in the United States. They also research, design, and manufacture 65 percent of the goods they sell in their own Canadian production facilities.

You'll find LC's income statements and balance sheets for recent years in tables 17.1 and 17.3. Note that LC, like many retailers, selects the end of January for their fiscal year end. This allows a given year's Christmas sales to be in one set of financial statements. When we refer to 2000 revenues, we mean the revenues earned in the one-year period ending January 31, 2001.[2]

income statement Financial statement that shows the revenues, expenses, and net income of a firm over a period of time

The **income statement** summarizes the firm's revenues and expenses and the difference between the two, which is the firm's profit. You can see in Table 17.1 that LC sold $161.1 million of clothing in 2000. The costs of this clothing include the costs of producing or buying it and rent (i.e., the "cost of sales, buying, and occupancy"), and expenses for the retail sales staff, advertising and other marketing costs, and head-office expenses (i.e., the

[1] Le Château's 2000 annual report is available at www.sedar.com. SEDAR, the System for Electronic Document Analysis and Retrieval, is the website where Canadian public companies and mutual funds post their corporate documents and press releases as required by the Canadian securities commissions.

[2] LC follows this convention, too, reporting the financial statements for their January 2001 fiscal year end in the 2000 annual report.

TABLE 17.1
Income statement

INCOME STATEMENT FOR LE CHÂTEAU, INC., 2000 AND 1999
(figures in thousands of dollars)

	2000	1999
Sales	161,120	168,666
Cost of sales, buying, and occupancy	112,035	108,234
Selling, general, and administrative expenses	45,957	44,577
Earnings before interest, taxes, depreciation, and amortization (EBITDA)	3,128	15,855
Depreciation and amortization	6,687	6,370
Earnings before interest and taxes (EBIT)	–3,559	9,485
Interest	787	466
Earnings before taxes	–4,346	9,019
Provision for income taxes (recovered)	–1,739	3,750
Net earnings	–2,607	5,269
Cash dividends	1,974	1,974
Addition to retained earnings	–4,581	3,295
Net earnings per share (dollars)	($.53)	$1.07
Average number of shares outstanding	4,935,248	4,924,680

Source: Le Château, Inc., 2000 and 1999 annual reports.

"selling, general, and administrative expenses"). After deducting these expenses, LC had earnings before interest, taxes, depreciation, and amortization (EBITDA) of $3.1 million. In the process of making these sales, LC also used its fixed assets, including its retail stores, cash registers, and manufacturing facilities, and charged itself $6.687 million for depreciation and amortization of these assets. After deducting these charges, LC had earnings before interest and taxes (EBIT) of negative $3.559 million. This means that the expenses associated with operating the business were greater than the revenues earned. Businesses cannot survive if they make frequent operating losses. As management of LC put it, "Our 2000 loss was unacceptable to management, and clearly indicates that we did not deliver the goods our customers wanted."[3]

What happened to LC in 2000? The first two lines of the income statement reveal quite a lot. Even though LC added net two new stores, total sales fell 4.5 percent and the cost of the clothing sold increased 3.5 percent during 2000. The net impact of falling sales and rising costs was a staggering 80 percent drop in EBITDA. In effect, LC sold less stuff for lower prices. How did this happen? Many clothing retailers experienced sales declines during the same period, reflecting the poor weather and increased competition. In addition, LC's management acknowledged that they misread the fashion trends. Emilia Di Raddo, vice-president of finance, was quoted as saying, "We did go too avant-garde, and that was something customers just didn't go for. But when you are in the fashion industry that happens."[4]

While the entire retail sector was off, LC's finicky youth market segment was even more vulnerable. Richard Talbot, a retail consultant, commented, "That age group is very fickle. They'll drop one brand or store and move to another overnight. It's a very volatile market to be in, and to a certain extent, it's an oversaturated market. There are lots of players, there are big U.S. players coming in, and if you are not keeping at the leading edge, you're not

[3] Le Château, Inc., *Annual Report, 2000.*

[4] Hollie Shaw, "Investors Leave Le Château on the Rack: Shares Off 50% This Year. Clothing Retailer Misread Market, Posts Quarterly Loss," *National Post*, Sept. 27, 2000, p. D3.

TABLE 17.2
Common-size income statement

COMMON-SIZE INCOME STATEMENT FOR LE CHÂTEAU, INC., 2000 AND 1999
(all items expressed as a percentage of year's revenues)

	2000, %	1999, %
Sales	100	100
Cost of sales, buying, and occupancy	69.5	64.2
Selling, general, and administrative expenses	28.5	26.4
Earnings before interest, taxes, depreciation, and amortization (EBITDA)	1.9	9.4
Depreciation and amortization	4.2	3.8
Earnings before interest and taxes (EBIT)	–2.2	5.6
Interest	.5	.3
Earnings before taxes	–2.7	5.3
Provision for income taxes (recovered)	–1.1	2.2
Net earnings	–1.6	3.1
Cash dividends	1.2	1.2
Addition to retained earnings	–2.8	2

Source: Le Château, Inc., 2000 and 1999 annual reports.

going to make it, frankly." Furthermore, the fashions are inexpensive to begin with, and if they don't sell, the prices get slashed. Talbot added, "You get the fashion sense wrong for a couple of seasons and you're toast."[5]

In addition to the expenses of operating the business, LC paid $.787 million in interest. However, the operating loss meant the company did not have to pay taxes and was able to get a refund on past taxes paid. In spite of its poor financial performance, LC decided to pay dividends of $1.974 million to its common shareholders. The net result was that the addition to retained earnings was negative $4.581 million, representing a reduction in shareholders' equity. By contrast, in 1999 LC had positive earnings, and even after dividend payments, the addition to retained earnings was $3.295 million, representing the reinvestment of shareholders' earnings into the business.

common-size income statement Income statement that presents items as a percentage of revenues.

balance sheet Financial statement that shows the value of the firm's assets and liabilities at a particular time.

The income statement in Table 17.1 shows the number of dollars that LC earned in 1999 and 2000. When making comparisons between firms, analysts sometimes calculate a **common-size income statement.** In this case all items in the income statement are expressed as a percentage of revenues. Table 17.2 is LC's common-size income statement. You can see that the cost of sales consumed 69.5 percent of revenues in 2000, and selling and administrative expenses absorbed a further 28.5 percent. In contrast, costs as a percentage of sales were lower in 1999, reflecting LC's superior financial performance that year.

Whereas the income statement summarizes activity during a period, the **balance sheet** presents a "snapshot" of the firm at a given moment. For example, the balance sheet in Table 17.3 is a snapshot of LC's assets and liabilities at the end of 1998, 1999, and 2000.

As we pointed out in Chapter 2, the accountant lists first the assets that are most likely to be turned into cash in the near future. They include cash itself, short-term securities, receivables (that is, bills that have not yet been paid by the firm's customers), and inventories of raw materials, work-in-process, and finished goods. These assets are all known as *current assets.* The second main group of assets consists of *long-term assets* such as buildings, land, machinery, and equipment. Remember that the balance sheet does not show the market value of each asset. Instead, the accountant records the amount that the asset

[5] Hollie Shaw, "Investors Leave Le Château on the Rack: Shares Off 50% This Year. Clothing Retailer Misread Market, Posts Quarterly Loss," *National Post*, Sept. 27, 2000, p. D3.

TABLE 17.3
Balance sheet

BALANCE SHEET FOR LE CHÂTEAU, INC., 2000, 1999, AND 1998
(figures in thousands of dollars)

Assets	**2000**	**1999**	**1998**
Current assets			
Cash and cash equivalents	3,072	10,090	17,335
Accounts receivable and prepaid expenses	1,679	2,215	1,483
Inventories	22,123	20,362	17,017
Other current assets	2,427	761	0
Total current assets	29,301	33,428	35,835
Loans to director	686	686	686
Fixed assets			
Property, plant, and equipment, gross	58,382	55,787	48,469
Less accumulated depreciation	20,180	21,277	18,148
Net property, plant, and equipment	38,202	34,510	30,321
Total assets	68,189	68,624	66,842
Liabilities and Shareholders' Equity	**2000**	**1999**	**1998**
Current liabilities			
Accounts payable and accrued liabilities	12,027	10,719	11,155
Current portion of capital lease obligations	1,976	1,738	1,381
Current portion of long-term debt	1,000	892	833
Other current liabilities	494	494	716
Total current liabilities	15,497	13,843	14,085
Capital lease obligations	1,914	996	2,735
Long-term debt	1,112	226	1,118
Other long-term liabilities	3,866	3,179	2,107
Total liabilities	22,389	18,244	20,045
Shareholders' equity			
Capital stock	13,428	13,427	13,169
Retained earnings	32,372	36,953	33,658
Total shareholders' equity	45,800	50,380	46,827
Total liabilities and shareholders' equity	68,189	68,624	66,872

Source: Le Château, Inc., 2000, 1999, and 1998 annual reports.

originally cost and then, in the case of plant and equipment, deducts an annual charge for depreciation. LC also owns many valuable assets, such as its brand name, that are *not* shown on the balance sheet.

LC's liabilities show the claims on the firm's assets. These also are classified as current and long-term. *Current liabilities* are bills that the company expects to pay in the near future. They include debts that are due to be repaid within the next year and payables (that is, amounts the company owes to its suppliers). In addition to these short-term debts, LC has borrowed money that will not be repaid for several years. These are shown as *long-term liabilities*. Of the long-term debt, $1 million is to be repaid within one year and is included with the short-term liabilities. Total outstanding long-term debt is $2.112 million, the sum of the current ($1 million) and long-term ($1.112 million) portions of the long-term debt. As well, LC has entered into long-term rental agreements for fixed assets, such as cash registers and computer equipment. These leases are quite similar to debt because LC has committed to make fixed regular payments. Under GAAP, the present value of

TABLE 17.4
Common-size balance sheet

COMMON-SIZE BALANCE SHEET FOR LE CHÂTEAU, INC,. 2000 AND 1999
(all items expressed as a percentage of year's total assets)

Assets	**2000, %**	**1999, %**
Current assets		
Cash and cash equivalents	4.5	14.7
Accounts receivables and prepaid expenses	2.5	3.2
Inventories	32.4	29.7
Other current assets	3.6	1.1
Total current assets	43	48.7
Loans to director	1	1
Fixed assets		
Property, plant, and equipment, gross	85.6	81.3
Less accumulated depreciation	29.6	31
Net property, plant, and equipment	56	50.3
Total assets	100	100
Liabilities and Shareholders' Equity	**2000, %**	**1999, %**
Current liabilities		
Accounts payable and accrued liabilities	17.6	15.6
Current portion of capital lease obligations	2.9	2.5
Current portion of long-term debt	1.5	1.3
Other current liabilities	.7	.7
Total current liabilities	22.7	20.2
Capital lease obligations	2.8	1.5
Long-term debt	1.6	.3
Other long-term liabilities	5.7	4.6
Total liabilities	32.8	26.6
Shareholders' equity		
Capital stock	19.7	19.6
Retained earnings	47.5	53.8
Total shareholders' equity	67.2	73.4
Total liabilities and shareholders' equity	100	100

Source: Le Château, Inc., 2000 and 1999 annual reports.

these lease payments is reported as a long-term liability called *capital lease obligations*. LC has committed to repay an amount with a present value of $3.89 million to the leasing companies, the sum of the current portion and the long-term capital lease obligation. Likewise, LC's fixed assets include the value of the leased assets. Just as it depreciates the fixed assets it purchases, LC depreciates these leased assets.[6]

After taking account of all the firm's liabilities, the remaining assets belong to the common shareholders. The *shareholders' equity* is simply the total value of the assets less the current and long-term liabilities.[7] It is also equal to the amount that the firm has raised

[6] Not all leases are capitalized. As we shall soon see, LC does not capitalize leases for its retail space. You can find a more detailed look at leasing in Chapter 22.

[7] If LC had also issued preferred stock, we would also need to deduct this before calculating the equity that belonged to the common shareholders.

from shareholders ($13.428 million) plus the earnings that have been retained and reinvested on their behalf ($32.372 million).

common-size balance sheet Balance sheet that presents items as a percentage of total assets.

Just as it is sometimes useful to provide a common-size income statement, so we can also calculate a **common-size balance sheet.** In this case all items are re-expressed as a percentage of total assets. Table 17.4 is LC's common-size balance sheet. The table shows, for example, that inventories, a major asset for retailers, increased from 29.7 percent of total assets to 32.4 percent in 2000.

LEVERAGE RATIOS

When a firm borrows money, it promises to make a series of interest payments and then to repay the amount that it has borrowed. If profits rise, the debtholders continue to receive a fixed interest payment, so that all the gains go to the shareholders. Of course, the reverse happens if profits fall. In this case shareholders bear all the pain. If times are sufficiently hard, a firm that has borrowed heavily may not be able to pay its debts. The firm is then bankrupt and shareholders lose their entire investment. Because debt increases returns to shareholders in good times and reduces them in bad times, it is said to create *financial leverage.* Leverage ratios measure how much financial leverage the firm has taken on.

Debt Ratio. Financial leverage is usually measured by the ratio of long-term debt to total long-term capital. Here "long-term debt" should include not just bonds or other borrowing, but also the value of long-term leases. Total long-term capital, sometimes called *total capitalization,* is the sum of long-term debt and shareholders' equity. Thus for LC

$$\text{Long-term debt ratio} = \frac{\text{long-term debt} + \text{value of leases}}{\text{long-term debt} + \text{value of leases} + \text{equity}}$$

$$= \frac{2{,}112 + 3{,}890}{2{,}112 + 3{,}890 + 45{,}800} = .116$$

This means that 11.6 cents of every dollar of long-term capital is in the form of long-term debt. Another way to express leverage is in terms of the company's debt-equity ratio:

$$\text{Debt-equity ratio} = \frac{\text{long-term debt} + \text{value of leases}}{\text{equity}} = \frac{2{,}122 + 3{,}890}{45{,}800} = .13$$

These ratios would leave you with the impression that Le Château has low leverage. However, as is often the case when analyzing financial statements, first looks can be deceiving. If you read the notes to the financial statements, you will discover that LC rents all of its retail space and has entered into significant long-term leases that are not reported on its balance sheet. These leases are classified as operating leases and expensed, and are therefore a form of off-balance sheet financing.[8] For example, in 2001 its minimum operating lease payment is $20.564 million. If all of the reported future operating lease payments are capitalized, by calculating their present value, we get a value of $86.16 million.[9] That is, LC has an obligation with a present value of about $86 million that must be repaid over the next 6 years. If we include this with the other long-term liabilities, the long-term

[8] LC is following GAAP when it capitalizes some of its leases but not others. If a company bears substantively all of the economic risk and reward associated with owning the asset it leases, then it must capitalize the lease. Otherwise, it can expense the lease payments like other operating expenses.

[9] The reported minimum rental payments from 2001 to 2005, in millions of dollars, are $20,564, $18,787, $17,462, $14,256, and $12,045, respectively, and $29,316 for the years thereafter. The payments are discounted at the firm's cost of debt, which we assume is 8 percent.

debt ratio increases substantially to (2,112 + 3,980 + 86,160)/(2,112 + 3,890 + 86,160 + 45,800) = .668. Almost 67 cents of every dollar of long-term capital is in the form of long-term debt and leases, or equivalently, the debt-equity ratio is 2.

What do you think is a better measure of LC's financial leverage: including the value of the operating leases or not? If you were a loans officer at a bank considering a $5 million loan to LC, you would be very interested to know the extent of the operating leases. Just because the assets are leased does not mean that LC can ignore the payments. Be warned: financial statement analysis is a tricky business!

Notice that these measures make use of book (that is, accounting) values rather than market values.[10] The market value of the company determines whether the debtholders get their money back, so you would expect analysts to look at the face amount of the debt as a proportion of the total *market value* of debt and equity. One reason that they don't do this is that market values are often not readily available. Does it matter much? Perhaps not; after all, the market value of the firm includes the value of intangible assets generated by research and development, advertising, staff training, and so on. These assets are not readily saleable and, if the company falls on hard times, the value of these assets may disappear altogether. Thus when banks demand that a borrower keep within a maximum debt ratio, they are usually content to define this debt ratio in terms of book values and to ignore the intangible assets that are not shown in the balance sheet.

Notice also that these measures of leverage take account only of long-term debt. Managers sometimes also define debt to include all liabilities. Including the operating leases gives[11]

$$\text{Total debt ratio} = \frac{\text{total liabilities}}{\text{total assets}} = \frac{22{,}389 + 86{,}160}{68{,}189 + 86{,}160} = .70$$

Therefore, LC is financed 70 percent with debt, both long-term and short-term, and 30 percent with equity. We could also say that its ratio of total debt to equity is (22,389 + 86,160)/45,800 = 2.37.

Managers sometimes refer loosely to a company's debt ratio, but we have just seen that the debt ratio may be measured in several different ways. For example, LC could be said to have a debt ratio of .1 (the long-term debt ratio ignoring operating leases) or .70 (the total debt ratio including operating leases). The general point is there are a variety of ways to define most financial ratios and there is no law stating how they *should* be defined. Our advice: Don't accept a ratio at face value without understanding how it has been calculated.

Times Interest Earned Ratio. Another measure of financial leverage is the extent to which interest is covered by earnings. Banks prefer to lend to firms whose earnings are far in excess of interest payments. Therefore, analysts often calculate the ratio of earnings before interest and taxes (EBIT) to interest payments. For LC,

$$\text{Times interest earned (TIE)} = \frac{\text{EBIT}}{\text{interest payments}} = \frac{-3{,}559}{787} = -4.5$$

LC's profits were insufficient to cover the interest payment. In 1999, TIE was a more respectable 20.

[10] As we have seen, in the case of leased assets, accountants estimate the present value of the lease commitments. In the case of long-term debt they simply show the face value. This can sometimes be very different from present values. For example, the present value of low-coupon debt may be only a fraction of its face value.

[11] If operating leases are excluded, the total debt ratio becomes 22,389/68,189 or .328.

The regular interest payment is a hurdle that companies must keep jumping if they are to avoid default. The *times interest earned ratio* (also called the *interest cover ratio*) measures how much clear air there is between hurdle and hurdler.

Cash Coverage Ratio. We have pointed out that depreciation (and amortization) are deducted when calculating the firm's earnings, even though no cash goes out the door. Thus, rather than asking whether *earnings* are sufficient to cover interest payments, it might be more interesting to calculate the extent to which interest is covered by the cash flow from operations. This is measured by the cash coverage ratio. For LC,

$$\text{Cash coverage ratio} = \frac{\text{EBIT} + \text{depreciation and amortization}}{\text{interest payments}} = \frac{-3{,}559 + 6{,}687}{787} = 3.9$$

These two ratios tell only part of the story. For instance, they don't tell us whether LC is generating enough earnings or cash to repay debt as it comes due, or whether it can make its capital lease obligations. Other possible fixed charges include preferred share sinking-fund payments and preferred share dividends. A *fixed-charge coverage ratio* shows how many times greater EBIT plus depreciation and amortization is relative to the fixed charges the company is obliged to make.

When creating a fixed-charge coverage ratio, watch out for fixed payments that are made from after-tax earnings (or after-tax cash flows). Such nontax-deductible payments include debt principal repayment and payments to preferred shares. You must convert these payments to a before-tax basis by dividing by (1 – corporate tax rate). For example, if a company is obligated to pay $3 million in preferred share dividends and its tax rate is 35 percent, it must earn 3/(1 – .35) = 4.615 million in before-tax dollars.

In LC's case, we use a cash-flow coverage ratio that includes both its current portion of long-term debt and capital lease obligations. From the balance sheet, we see the current portion of long-term debt is $1,000 and current lease obligation is $1,976. With a 40 percent corporate tax rate,

$$\text{Fixed charge coverage ratio} = \frac{\text{EBIT} + \text{depreciation and amortization}}{\text{interest payments} + (\text{current debt repayment} + \text{current lease obligations})/(1 - \text{tax rate})}$$

$$= \frac{-3{,}559 + 6{,}687}{787 + (1{,}000 + 1{,}976)/(1 - .4)} = .544$$

The number is less than one, indicating insufficient cash flow from operations to cover the pending fixed charges.

☑ CHECK POINT 17.1

A firm repays $10 million par value of outstanding debt and issues $10 million of new debt with a lower rate of interest. What happens to its long-term debt ratio? What happens to its times interest earned and cash coverage ratios?

LIQUIDITY RATIOS

liquidity Ability of an asset to be converted to cash quickly at low cost.

If you are extending credit to a customer or making a short-term bank loan, you are interested in more than the company's leverage. You want to know whether it will be able to lay its hands on the cash to repay you. That is why credit analysts and bankers look at several measures of **liquidity.** Liquid assets can be converted into cash quickly and cheaply.

Think, for example, what you would do to meet a large, unexpected bill. You might have some money in the bank or some investments that are easily sold, but you would not find it so simple to convert your old sweaters into cash. Companies also own assets with different degrees of liquidity. For example, accounts receivable and inventories of finished goods are generally quite liquid. As inventories are sold and customers pay their bills, money flows into the firm. At the other extreme, real estate may be quite *illiquid.* It can be hard to find a buyer, negotiate a fair price, and close a deal at short notice.

Managers have another reason to focus on liquid assets: the accounting figures are more reliable. The book value of a catalytic cracker may be a poor guide to its true value, but at least you know what cash in the bank is worth.

Liquidity ratios also have some *less* desirable characteristics. Because short-term assets and liabilities are easily changed, measures of liquidity can rapidly become outdated. You might not know what the catalytic cracker is worth, but you can be fairly sure that it won't disappear overnight. Also, companies often choose a slack period for the end of their financial year. For example, like many other retailers, LC ends their financial year in January after the Christmas boom. At these times, the companies are likely to have more cash and less short-term debt than during busier seasons.

Net Working Capital to Total Assets Ratio. We have seen that current assets are those that the company expects to meet in the near future. The difference between the current assets and current liabilities is known as *net working capital.* It roughly measures the company's potential reservoir of cash. Net working capital is usually positive; however, it can be negative.

$$\text{Net working capital} = 29{,}301 - 15{,}497 = 13{,}804$$

Managers often express net working capital as a proportion of total assets. For LC,

$$\frac{\text{Net working capital}}{\text{Total assets}} = \frac{13{,}804}{68{,}189} = .20$$

Current Ratio. Another measure that serves a similar purpose is the current ratio:

$$\text{Current ratio} = \frac{\text{current assets}}{\text{current liabilities}} = \frac{29{,}301}{15{,}497} = 1.89$$

So LC has \$1.89 in current assets for every \$1 in current liabilities.

Rapid decreases in the current ratio sometimes signify trouble. For example, a firm that drags out its payables by delaying payment of its bills will suffer an increase in current liabilities and a decrease in the current ratio.

Changes in the current ratio can be misleading, however. For example, suppose that a company borrows a large sum from the bank and invests it in marketable securities. Current liabilities rise and so do current assets. Therefore, if nothing else changes, net working capital is unaffected but the current ratio changes. For this reason, it is sometimes preferable to net short-term investments against short-term debt when calculating the current ratio.

Quick (or Acid-Test) Ratio. Some assets are closer to cash than others. If trouble comes, inventory may not sell at anything above fire-sale prices. (Trouble typically comes *because* the firm can't sell its finished-product inventory for more than the production cost.) Thus managers often exclude inventories and other less liquid components of current assets when comparing current assets to current liabilities. They focus instead on cash, marketable securities, and bills that customers have not yet paid. This results in the quick ratio:

$$\text{Quick ratio} = \frac{\text{cash + marketable securities + receivables}}{\text{current liabilities}} = \frac{3{,}072 + 1{,}679}{15{,}497} = .31$$

CHECK POINT 17.2

a. A firm has $1.2 million in current assets and $1.0 million in current liabilities. If it uses $.5 million of cash to pay off some of its accounts payable, what will happen to the current ratio? What happens to net working capital?

b. A firm uses cash on hand to pay for additional inventories. What will happen to the current ratio? To the quick ratio?

Interval Measure. Instead of looking at a firm's liquid assets relative to its current liabilities, it may be useful to measure whether liquid assets are large relative to the firm's regular outgoings. We ask how long the firm could keep up with its bills using only its cash and other liquid assets. This is called the interval measure, which is computed by dividing liquid assets by daily expenditures:

$$\text{Interval measure} = \frac{\text{cash + marketable securities + receivables}}{\text{average daily expenditures from operations}}$$

For LC (in thousands of dollars), the cost of sales amounted to $112,035 in 2000, and selling and administrative costs were $45,957. Therefore,

$$\text{Interval measure} = \frac{3{,}072 + 1{,}679}{(112{,}035 + 45{,}957)/365} = 11.0$$

LC has only enough liquid assets to finance operations for 11 days if it does not sell another pair of pants or another shirt.

EFFICIENCY RATIOS

Financial analysts employ another set of ratios to judge how efficiently the firm is using its assets.

Asset Turnover Ratio. The asset turnover, or sales-to-assets, ratio shows how hard the firm's assets are being put to use. For LC, each dollar of assets produced $2.36 of sales:

$$\frac{\text{Sales}}{\text{Average total assets}} = \frac{161{,}120}{(68{,}189 + 68{,}624)/2} = 2.36$$

A high ratio compared with other firms in the same industry could indicate that the firm is working close to capacity. It may prove difficult to generate further business without additional investment.

Notice that since the assets are likely to change over the year, we use the *average* of the assets at the beginning and end of the year. Averages are often used when a flow figure (in this case *annual sales*) is compared with a snapshot figure (*total assets*).

Instead of looking at the ratio of sales to *total* assets, managers sometimes look at how hard particular types of capital are being put to use. For example, they might look at the value of sales per dollar invested in fixed assets. Or they might look at the ratio of sales to net working capital.

Thus for LC each dollar of fixed assets generated $4.43 of sales:

$$\frac{\text{Sales}}{\text{Average fixed assets}} = \frac{161{,}120}{(38{,}202 + 34{,}510)/2} = 4.43$$

Both the total-asset and fixed-asset turnover ratios are affected by the choice of lease accounting. For example, if Le Château's retail space leases were capitalized, an additional fixed asset, perhaps called "leased rental space", would show up on the balance sheet to reflect the present value of the lease payments. This increase in the fixed assets would produce lower asset turnover even though the firm's operations had not changed. This is important to remember if you are comparing two companies with very different leasing activities.

Average Collection Period. The average collection period measures the speed with which customers pay their bills. It expresses accounts receivable in terms of daily sales:

$$\text{Average collection period} = \frac{\text{average receivables}}{\text{average daily sales}} = \frac{(1{,}679 + 2{,}215)/2}{161{,}120/365} = 4.4 \text{ days}$$

LC's average collection period is only 4.4 days.

Often a comparatively low figure indicates a highly efficient collections department. Not this time; here is another example of the importance of knowing the nature of the company's business. LC is a retailer and most of its sales are by cash or credit card. Cash has a zero collection period, and with electronic credit-card billing, retailers are able to receive cash from the credit card companies quickly. The average collection period for credit card companies such as Visa and MasterCard will be much longer. If we knew LC's *credit* sales, we could measure its average collection period more sensibly. Note, too, that sometimes a low average collection period, especially when low compared to the firm's competitors, results from an unduly restrictive credit policy in which the firm offers credit only to customers who are certain to pay promptly. Again, this is not the case for Le Château.

Inventory Turnover Ratio. Managers may also monitor the rate at which the company is turning over its inventories. The balance sheet shows the *cost* of inventories rather than what the finished goods will eventually sell for. So, ideally, we compare the cost of inventories with the cost of goods sold, which is the value of the goods drawn out of inventory. Unfortunately, some firms lump various costs on the income statement, making it difficult to identify the cost of the goods sold. LC discloses the sum of its cost of sales, buying, and occupancy. These include LC's clothing manufacturing costs, the cost of finished clothing purchased from other manufacturers as well as the rent, heat, power, and so on, of its retail facilities. This seems like a reasonable measure of the cost of the goods sold.[12] LC's inventory turnover is

$$\text{Inventory turnover} = \frac{\text{cost of goods sold}}{\text{average inventory}} = \frac{112{,}035}{(22{,}123 + 20{,}362)/2} = 5.27$$

Efficient firms turn over their inventory rapidly and don't tie up more capital than they need in raw materials or finished goods. But firms that are living from hand to mouth may also cut their inventories to the bone.

Managers sometimes also look at how many days' sales are represented by inventories. This is equal to the average inventory divided by the daily cost of goods sold:

$$\text{Days' sales in inventories} = \frac{\text{average inventory}}{\text{cost of goods sold}/365} = \frac{(22{,}123 + 20{,}362)}{112{,}035/365} = 69.2 \text{ days}$$

You could say that on average LC has sufficient inventories to maintain sales for 69 days.[13]

[12] In situations where the cost of goods sold is not reported separately but included with other costs such as selling and administrative costs, analysts sometimes calculate inventory turnover as the ratio of operating costs to average inventory. An alternative is to use the ratio of sales to average inventory.

[13] This is a loose statement, because it ignores the fact that LC may have more than 69 days' supply of some materials and less of others.

CHECK POINT 17.3

The average collection period measures the number of days it takes LC to collect its bills. But LC also delays *paying* its own bills. Use the information in tables 17.1 and 17.3 to calculate the average number of days that it takes the company to pay its bills.

PROFITABILITY RATIOS

Profitability ratios focus on the firm's earnings, giving an overall indication of the firm's performance. One group of profitability measures, known as *profit margins*, looks at profit or earnings as a fraction of sales. The other group, called *return ratios*, measures profits earned as a fraction of the assets used.

The definition of profits (or earnings or income) used in a profitability ratio depends on what you want to measure. Let's look at a few profit margins and return ratios for Le Château.

Gross Profit Margin. Gross profits, or sales minus the cost of goods sold, reflects the mark-up over the cost of products sold as well as management's ability to control costs. For 2000, LC's gross profit margin was

$$\text{Gross profit margin} = \frac{\text{sales} - \text{cost of goods sold}}{\text{sales}} = \frac{161{,}120 - 112{,}035}{161{,}120} = .305, \text{ or } 30.5\%$$

In 1999, the gross profit margin was 35.8 percent. The decline in the gross profit margin is at the heart of LC's dismal 2000 performance.

Operating Profit Margin or Basic Earning Power. EBIT, also called operating profits, are the earnings after deducting all the costs associated with operating the business, including the cost of goods sold; selling, general, and administrative expenses; and depreciation and amortization. If you subtract taxes, you have after-tax operating profits, a sensible overall measure of the firm's operating performance.[14] The operating profit margin for LC in 2000 was

$$\text{Operating profit margin} = \frac{\text{EBIT} - \text{taxes}}{\text{sales}} = \frac{-3{,}559 + 1{,}739}{161{,}120} = -.011, \text{ or } -1.1\%$$

In 1999, the operating profit margin was 3.4 percent.

Net Profit Margin. If you want to know the proportion of revenue that finds its way to profits, you look at the net profit margin. This is commonly defined as

$$\text{Net profit margin} = \frac{\text{net income}}{\text{sales}} = \frac{-2{,}607}{161{,}120} = -.0162, \text{ or } -1.62\%$$

When companies are partly financed by debt, the profits are divided between the debtholders and the shareholders. We would not want to say that such a firm is less profitable simply because it employs debt finance and pays out part of its profits as interest. Therefore, when calculating the profit margin, it seems appropriate to add back the debt interest to net income. This would give

$$\text{Net profit margin} = \frac{\text{net income} + \text{interest}}{\text{sales}} = \frac{-2{,}607 + 787}{161{,}120} = -.0113, \text{ or } -1.13\%$$

[14] The operating margin is sometimes calculated as EBIT/sales. We prefer to subtract taxes as well because taxes are a cost of doing business.

In 1999, the net profit margin was 3.4 percent. When we refer to the profit margin, we mean this definition of the net profit margin.

Holding everything constant, a firm would naturally prefer a high profit margin. But all else cannot be held constant. A high-price and high-margin strategy typically will result in lower sales. So while Holt Renfrew might have a higher margin than Walmart, it will not necessarily enjoy higher profits. A low-margin but high-volume strategy can be quite successful. We return to this issue later.

Return on Assets (ROA). Managers often measure the performance of a firm by the ratio of net income to total assets. However, because net income measures profits net of interest expense, this practice makes the apparent profitability of the firm a function of its capital structure. It is better to use net income plus interest because we are measuring the return on *all* the firm's assets, not just the equity investment:

$$\text{Return on assets} = \frac{\text{net income + interest}}{\text{average total assets}} = \frac{-2{,}607 + 787}{(68{,}189 + 68{,}624)} = -.0266, \text{ or } -2.66\%$$

ROA for 1999 was 8.5 percent.

This definition of ROA is misleading if it is used to compare firms with different capital structures. The reason is that firms with more interest pay less in taxes. Thus the ROA ratio reflects differences in financial leverage as well as operating performance. If you want to measure operating performance alone, we suggest adjusting for leverage by subtracting that part of total income generated by interest tax shield (interest payments × marginal tax rate). This gives the income the firm would earn if it were all-equity finance.

$$\text{Adjusted return on assets} = \frac{\text{net income + interest − interest tax shields}}{\text{average total assets}}$$

For LC, with no interest tax shields, its adjusted ROA is the same as its ROA in 2000. For 1999, the adjusted ROA is 8.2 percent, assuming a 40 percent tax rate. Unless we say otherwise, we will use the first definition of ROA.

Return on Invested Capital. This ratio focuses on the return earned on total capital, debt, and capital leases, plus preferred and common equity invested in the company. Again the numerator should be the firm's earnings excluding the effects of the chosen financing strategies:

$$\text{Return on invested capital} = \frac{\text{net income + interest − interest tax shields}}{\text{average total debt + preferred and common equity}}$$

LC's average invested capital in 2000 was [(1,967 + 1,000 + 1,914 + 1,112 + 45,800) + (1,738 + 892 + 996 + 226 + 50,380)]/2 or $53.013 million. Thus its return on invested capital was (–2,607 + 787)/53.013 = –.0343, or – 3.43 percent. In 1999 the return on invested capital was 10.4 percent.

The assets in a company's books are valued on the basis of their original cost (less any depreciation). A high return on assets does not always mean that you could buy the same assets today and get a high return. Nor does a low return imply that the assets could be employed better elsewhere. But it does suggest that you should ask some searching questions.

In a competitive industry, firms can expect to earn only their cost of capital. Therefore, a high return on assets is sometimes cited as an indication that the firm is taking advantage of a monopoly position to charge excessive prices. For example, when a public utility commission tries to determine whether a utility is charging a fair price, much of the argument will center on a comparison between the cost of capital and the return that the utility is earning (its ROA).

Return on Equity (ROE). Another measure of profitability focuses on the return on the shareholders' equity:

$$\text{Return on equity} = \frac{\text{net income}}{\text{average equity}}$$

$$= \frac{-2{,}607}{(45{,}800 + 50{,}380)/2}$$

$$= -.0542, \text{ or } -5.42\%$$

ROE for 1999 was 10.8 percent.

Payout Ratio. The payout ratio measures the proportion of earnings that is paid out as dividends. Thus:

$$\text{Payout ratio} = \frac{\text{dividends}}{\text{earnings}} = \frac{1{,}974}{-2{,}607} = -.75$$

The 1999 payout ratio was 37.5%. We saw in Section 16.2 that managers don't like to cut dividends because of a shortfall in earnings. Therefore, if a company's earnings are particularly variable, management is likely to play it safe by setting a low average payout ratio.

When earnings fall unexpectedly, the payout ratio is likely to rise temporarily. Likewise, if earnings are expected to rise next year, management may feel that it can pay somewhat more generous dividends than it would otherwise have done.

In LC's case, dividends were unchanged despite negative net income. It is evident that LC's management was confident, or at least appeared to be confident, that the poor performance of 2000 would not be repeated. In a year with an operating loss, it is a brave act to pay out $1.974 million of cash to shareholders.

Earnings not paid out as dividends are retained, or plowed back into the business. The proportion of earnings reinvested in the firm is called the *plowback ratio*:

$$\text{Plowback ratio} = 1 - \text{payout ratio} = \frac{\text{earnings} - \text{dividends}}{\text{earnings}}$$

If you multiply this figure by the return on equity, you can see how rapidly shareholders' equity is growing as a result of plowing back part of its earnings each year. In 2000, with negative net income, shareholders' equity shrank, and therefore, it didn't make sense to talk about equity growth. However, in 1999, earnings plowed back into the firm increased the book value of equity by 7.1 percent:

$$\text{Growth in equity from plowback} = \frac{\text{earnings} - \text{dividends}}{\text{equity}}$$

$$= \frac{\text{earnings} - \text{dividends}}{\text{earnings}} \times \frac{\text{earnings}}{\text{equity}}$$

$$= \text{plowback ratio} \times \text{ROE}$$

$$= .625 \times .113 = .071, \text{ or } 7.1\%$$

If LC could continue to earn 11.3 percent on its book equity and plow back 62.5 percent of earnings, both earnings and equity would grow at 7.1 percent a year.[15]

[15] Analysts sometimes refer to this figure as the *sustainable rate of growth*. Notice that, when calculating the sustainable rate of growth, ROE is properly measured by earnings (in LC's case, $5,269 million) as a proportion of equity at the *start* of the year (in LC's case, $46,827 million), rather than the average of the equity at the start and end of the year. We discussed the sustainable rate of growth in Chapter 5 and we will return to it again in Chapter 18.

Is this a reasonable prospect? We know that LC had negative earnings and equity growth in 2000. In the long run, it is difficult for companies to grow faster than the economy. Add the increased competition from new competitors and changing demographics and tastes, and LC's growth in Canada is not likely to reach double-digit rates, even in the short run. How can LC grow? It recently expanded its U.S. operations with three new stores in New York City. We will watch to see if this pays off.

17.2 The DuPont System

DuPont system A breakdown of ROE and ROA into component ratios.

Some profitability or efficiency measures can be linked in useful ways. These relationships are often referred to as the **DuPont system,** in recognition of the chemical company that popularized them.

The first relationship links the return on assets (ROA) with the firm's turnover ratio and its net profit margin:[16]

$$\text{ROA} = \frac{\text{net income + interest}}{\text{assets}} = \underbrace{\frac{\text{sales}}{\text{assets}}}_{\text{asset turnover}} \times \underbrace{\frac{\text{net income + interest}}{\text{sales}}}_{\text{profit margin}} \qquad (17.1)$$

All firms would like to earn a higher return on their assets, but their ability to do so is limited by competition. If the expected return on assets is fixed by competition, firms face a trade-off between the turnover ratio and the profit margin. Thus we find that fast-food chains, which have high turnover, also tend to operate on low profit margins. Hotels have relatively low turnover ratios but tend to compensate for this with higher margins. Table 17.5 illustrates the trade-off. Both the fast-food chain and the hotel have the same return on assets. However, their profit margins and turnover ratios are entirely different.

Firms often seek to improve their profit margins by acquiring a supplier. The idea is to capture the supplier's profit as well as their own. Unfortunately, unless they have some special skill in running the new business, they are likely to find that any gain in profit margin is offset by a decline in the asset turnover.

A few numbers may help to illustrate this point. Table 17.6 shows the sales, profits, and assets of Admiral Motors and its components supplier Diana Corporation. Both earn a 10 percent return on assets, though Admiral has a lower profit margin (20 percent versus Diana's 25 percent). Since all of Diana's output goes to Admiral, Admiral's management reasons that it would be better to merge the two companies. That way the merged company would capture the profit margin on both the auto components and the assembled car.

The bottom line of Table 17.6 shows the effect of the merger. The merged firm does indeed earn the combined profits. Total sales remain at $20 million, however, because all the components produced by Diana are used within the company. With higher profits and

TABLE 17.5 *Fast-food chains and hotels may have similar returns on assets but different asset turnover ratios and profit margins.*

	Asset Turnover	×	Profit Margin	=	Return on Assets
Fast-food chains	2.0		5%		10%
Hotels	0.5		20		10

[16] Note that the profit margin we use is the *net* profit margin, the ratio of net income plus interest to sales. Also note that you can restate the DuPont relationship in terms of the adjusted ROA to remove the impact of the financing mix. To do this, use (net income + interest – interest tax shield)/sales as the profit margin in the formula.

TABLE 17.6
Merging with suppliers or customers will generally increase the profit margin, but this will be offset by a reduction in the turnover ratio.

	Millions of Dollars			Asset	Profit	
	Sales	Profits	Assets	Turnover	Margin	ROA
Admiral Motors	$20	$4	$40	.50	20%	10%
Diana Corp.	8	2	20	.40	25	10
Diana Motors (the merged firm)	20	6	60	.33	30	10

unchanged sales, the profit margin increases. Unfortunately, the asset turnover ratio is *reduced* by the merger since the merged firm operates with higher assets. This exactly offsets the benefit of the higher profit margin. The return on assets is unchanged.

We can also break down financial ratios to show how the return on equity (ROE) depends on the return on assets and leverage:

$$\text{ROE} = \frac{\text{earnings available for common stock}}{\text{equity}} = \frac{\text{net income}}{\text{equity}}$$

Therefore,

$$\mathbf{ROE} = \underbrace{\frac{\textbf{assets}}{\textbf{equity}}}_{\textbf{leverage ratio}} \times \underbrace{\frac{\textbf{sales}}{\textbf{assets}}}_{\textbf{asset turnover}} \times \underbrace{\frac{\textbf{net income + interest}}{\textbf{sales}}}_{\textbf{profit margin}} \times \underbrace{\frac{\textbf{net income}}{\textbf{net income + interest}}}_{\textbf{“debt burden”}} \qquad (17.2)$$

Notice that the product of the two middle terms is the return on assets. This depends on the firm's production and marketing skills and is unaffected by the firm's financing mix.[17] However, the first and fourth terms do depend on the debt-equity mix. The first term, assets/equity, which we call the leverage ratio, can be expressed as (equity + liabilities)/ equity, which equals 1 + total-debt-to-equity ratio. The last term, which we call the "debt burden," measures the proportion by which interest expense reduces profits.

Suppose that the firm is financed entirely by equity. In this case both the first and the fourth terms are equal to 1.0 and the return on equity is identical to the return on assets. If the firm is leveraged, the first term is greater than 1.0 (assets are greater than equity) and the fourth term is less than 1.0 (part of the profits are absorbed by interest). Thus leverage can either increase or reduce return on equity. In fact, we showed in Section 15.1 that leverage increases ROE when the firm's return on assets is higher than the interest rate on debt.

CHECK POINT 17.4

a. Sappy Syrup has a profit margin below the industry average, but its ROA equals the industry average. How is this possible?
b. Sappy Syrup's ROA equals the industry average, but its ROE exceeds the industry average. How is this possible?

OTHER IMPORTANT FINANCIAL RATIOS

Each of the financial ratios that we have described involves accounting data only. But managers also compare accounting numbers with the values that are established in the marketplace. For example, they may compare the total market value of the firm's shares with the

[17] This is not the whole picture because the amount of taxes paid depends on the financing mix. Use the adjusted profit margin in footnote 16 and change debt burden to (net income)/(net income + interest – interest tax shield).

book value (the amount that the company has raised from shareholders or reinvested on their behalf). If managers have been successful in adding value for shareholders, the *market-to-book ratio* should be greater than 1.0. In Chapter 5 we also discussed two other ratios that use accounting data, the *price-earnings ratio* and the *dividend yield.* These ratios provide additional measures of how highly the company is valued by investors.

You can probably think of a number of other ratios that could provide useful insights into a company's health. For example, a retail chain might compare its sales per square foot with those of its competitors, a steel producer might look at the cost per ton of steel produced, and an airline might look at revenues per passenger mile flown. A little thought and common sense should suggest which measures are likely to provide insights into your own company's efficiency.

17.3 Analysis of the Statement of Cash Flows

Like a corporate version of a bank statement, the cash-flow statement tracks the cash coming into and flowing out of a corporation over a specific time period. With this simple focus, the analysis of the cash-flow statement can tell you a lot about the financial health of the firm. By contrast, the income statement, with its emphasis on matching expenses to current period sales, gives a better sense of the long-run profitability of the firm. However, due to accrual accounting, a healthy-looking income statement can miss a current cash crunch.

To see how this can happen, consider a firm that spends $3 million in the year on a new production facility. The cash outflow is reported on that year's cash-flow statement as an investment activity reducing cash by $3 million. If you look at the income statement, you will not see the $3 million expenditure. Instead, once production starts, the cost of the building will be expensed as depreciation, gradually over the expected life of the building, perhaps 30 years. The company might look quite profitable while experiencing a severe shortage of cash.

The statement of cash flows has undergone significant changes and become more standardized in recent years. It replaced the statement of changes in financial position, which contained both cash and noncash transactions. The statement of cash flows for Le Château is in Table 17.7. As we saw in Chapter 2, cash flows are divided into three distinct categories: operating activities, investing activities, and financing activities. Each section reveals important information on where the cash came from and where it went.

An important cash flow number is the cash generated by the firm's operations after all of the necessary investments in net working capital and fixed assets. As we saw in Chapter 2, this is called either *cash flow from assets* or *free cash flow.*[18]

In Chapter 2, we showed you a fast way to measure free cash flow by rearranging the statement of cash flows. Using the information in Table 17.7, the following are LC's 1999 and 2000 free cash flows in millions:

	2000	1999
Cash flow from operating activities	$ 2,811	$ 6,537
– Cash flow for investing activities	– 10,379	– 10,628
= Cash flows from assets (free cash flow)	–$7,568	–$4,091

[18] No standard definition of cash flows from assets or free cash flows exists. A common variation of free cash flow treats interest expense as a cash flow to bondholders and not as an operating expense. To do this, add back interest expense to cash flows from assets. If you want to remove any impact of the choice of financing, add back interest expense but also subtract the interest tax shield. Then include after-tax interest expense as a cash flow to bondholders.

TABLE 17.7
Statement of cash flows

STATEMENT OF CASH FLOWS FOR LE CHÂTEAU, INC., 2000 AND 1999
(figures in thousands of dollars)

	2000	1999
Cash provided by operating activities		
Earnings (loss) from continuing operations	–2,607	5,259
Adjustments to determine net cash from operating activities		
Depreciation and amortization	6,687	6,370
Other adjustments	314	409
Cash provided by operations	4,394	12,038
Net change in noncash working capital items related to operations	–1,583	–5,501
Cash provided by operating activities	2,811	6,537
Investing activities		
Additions to fixed assets	–10,379	–10,628
Cash provided (used) by investing activities	–10,379	–10,628
Financing activities		
Proceeds of capital leases	3,778	
Retirement of capital lease obligations	–2,622	–1,382
Proceeds of long-term debt	2,248	
Retirement of long-term debt	–1,254	–833
Deferred lease inducements	373	732
Issue of capital stock	1	258
Dividends paid	–1,974	–1,969
Cash provided (used) by financing activities	550	–3,194
Increase (decrease) in cash and cash equivalents	–7,018	–7,285
Cash and cash equivalents, beginning of year	10,090	17,365
Cash and cash equivalents, end of year	3,072	10,080
Supplementary information		
Interest paid during the year	787	466
Income taxes paid during the year, net	–606	4,066

In 1999 and 2000, LC had negative cash flow from operations. In other words, it had insufficient cash flow from its operating activities to fund its investment requirements.

How did it finance this shortfall? The cash flow to bondholders and shareholders shows us. Using the information from the statement of cash flows, and remembering to reverse the signs of the entries, we see that in 2000 bondholders and shareholders invested $550 million of net new cash to the company. LC also reduced its cash balances by $7,018 million. The net financing flow in 2000 was –$550 – $7,018, or –$7,548 million. In 1999, LC's bondholders and shareholders received $3,194 million in cash flow. LC also reduced its cash balances by $7,285 million to give the net financing flow in 1999 of $3,194 – $7,285, or –$4,091 million. In each year, the financial shortfall was largely funded by using previously saved cash: LC used about $7 million of its spare cash to fund its activities. However, in 2000 it was also a net borrower.

It is not unusual for growing firms to have negative free cash flow during the growth period. Often, firms need to make significant investments in assets before they can produce goods to sell and generate cash. In 1999, LC added 13 new stores and renovated

FINANCE IN ACTION

Focus Shifts to Free Cash Flow in Return to Value Investing

When it comes to finance and investing "cash is king" they say. To determine how much excess cash a company generates from its operations after capital expenditures and other expenses, it pays to look at the metric free cash flow (FCF). The chemical industry, despite all the doom and gloom, tends to generate healthy amounts of FCF. As traditional investing becomes more fashionable in the wake of the ongoing massacre in the technology sector, the issue of FCF is getting pushed into the spotlight.

"Investors appear to be seeking safe havens where there is little risk of additional compression of P/E multiples, and where the general level of cash flow and free cash flow are both healthy and stable," says JP Morgan analyst Jeffrey Zekauskas. As one portfolio manager put it, "I am not interested in stories; I am interested in cash flow."

While Wall Street and investors tend to focus on net income and earnings per share, a truer metric for actual cash generation is FCF. Although just about every analyst has a slightly different definition for FCF, we will define it as net income plus depreciation and amortization minus capital expenditures minus change in working capital.

The benefit of using FCF is that it accounts for capital expenditures and working capital as uses of cash and adds back noncash expenses (D&A) to net income to get a clear picture of how much actual cash the business generated.

"For the chemical industry in general, earnings are often misleading as far as cash-flow generation capability of the companies because noncash charges are so large," Mr. Zekauskas points out. "Free cash flow provides a clearer picture of the quality of the cash flow that the company is throwing off."

"Looking at free cash flow instead of reported earnings per share is a better indicator of the kind of real value being created by the entity instead of clouding the underlying cash flow by accounting rules," says Lehman Brothers analyst Timothy Gerdeman. "It just gives you a better idea of the underlying cash the business is generating."

The difference between reported earnings and free cash flow can be substantial in many cases. For example, Lyondell Chemical Company posted 2000 adjusted net income of $70 million, or 59 cents per share.

However, to get a better sense of actual cash generation, take net income of $70 million, add $279 million in depreciation and amortization (noncash expenses), subtract $104 million in capital expenditures (cash expense) and add $254 million from the reduction in working capital (current assets minus current liabilities) from $865 million in 1999 to $611 million in 2000.

Lyondell's total free cash flow generation for 2000 comes out to $499 million, or $4.24 per share, of which $106 million paid shareholders' dividends. Much of the rest was used to pay off debt.

others. In 2000, LC continued to make significant investments in its facilities, largely to renovate existing stores; however, it was not followed by positive sales growth. If LC continues to lose money, it will have to seek new external debt or equity financing, reduce its dividends, and cut back on its capital expenditures to be able to meet its obligations to existing bondholders and shareholders. The Finance in Action box above presents a discussion of free cash flow in the chemical industry.

In addition to measuring free cash flow, analysts also calculate ratios using information from the statement of cash flows. Bond rating agencies often include cash-flow ratios in their assessment of the quality of firm's debt. For example, in Table 17.11 (page 532), one of the key financial ratios used by Standard and Poor's is the ratio of free operating cash flow to total debt. This ratio tells what fraction of the outstanding debt could be paid for with the current year's operating cash flow. However, unlike the ratios based on the income statement and balance sheet, cash-flow–based ratios have not become standard. We think this will change as more analysts get comfortable with the cash-flow statement.[19]

[19] See J. Mills and J. Yamamura, "The Power of Cash Flow Ratios," *Journal of Accountancy* (October 1998), p. 53, for some other cash-flow ratios.

In addition to dividends and paying down debt, FCF can be used to make acquisitions, buy back stock or invest in new projects or expansions. Measuring FCF gives investors an idea of what projects companies can fund just from the cash it generates.

Certain institutional investors look at free cash flow on a yield basis—that is, FCF per share divided by share price to get a percentage. "There are some institutions out there, primarily value investors, that really focus on FCF yield," notes Bank of America securities analyst Mark Gulley.

On a FCF yield basis, Octel Corporation, a producer of fuel additives and specialty chemicals, leads the list with a 2000 free cash flow yield of over 50 percent, according to research by JP Morgan's Mr. Zekauskas.

Octel reported 2000 net income of $18.3 million, or $1.41 per share, but free cash flow analysis tells another story. Adding back $80.2 million in depreciation and amortization (D&A) and subtracting $6.6 million in capital expenditures and $8.2 million to reflect an increase in working capital, leads to FCF of $83.7 million or a whopping $6.70 per share. With shares of Octel trading around $13, this represents an FCF yield of 52 percent.

Of course, this does not tell the whole story. One of the reasons Octel is so cheap is because sales of a fuel additive called tetraethyl lead (TEL), 71 percent of Octel's 2000 sales, is projected to decline 15 percent annually after falling 24 percent last year.

Despite its usefulness, there are some drawbacks to FCF as there are with all financial metrics. In any given year, a surge or sharp decline in capital expenditures or working capital could distort the picture.

"Let's say a new management comes in and slashes capital expenditures and works really hard on reducing working capital," says Bank of America's Mr. Gulley. "You could have one year of great FCF, but that would be a head fake." On the other hand, sharp increases in capital expenditures or working capital can reduce FCF to lower than normalized levels. For example, in 2000, Rohm and Haas' working capital increased by $570 million, leading to FCF of $33 million compared to net income of $381 million.

In the case of Lyondell, FCF of $499 million in 2000 benefited from a reduction in working capital of $254 million related to the sale of its polyols business in March 2000. Excluding the impact of the sale, working capital would have actually increased $98 million, according to the company, leading to an adjusted FCF figure of $147 million.

Because of the magnitude of the changes in capital expenditures and working capital from year to year, institutional investors tend to use normalized levels of capital expenditures and working capital in their FCF calculations, notes Bank of America's Mr. Gulley.

Source: Excerpted from Joseph Chang, "Chemical Cash Generation Capability Clouded by EPS," *Chemical Market Reporter*, March 19, 2001, p.1.

17.4 Using Financial Ratios

Many years ago a British bank chairperson observed that not only did the bank's accounts show its true position but the actual situation was a little better still.[20] Since that time accounting standards have been much more carefully defined, but companies still have considerable discretion in calculating profits and deciding what to show in the balance sheet. Thus when you calculate financial ratios, you need to look below the surface and understand some of the pitfalls of accounting data. The nearby Finance in Action box discusses some ways in which companies can manipulate reported earnings.

SEE BOX P. 526

For example, the assets shown in some companies' balance sheets include a figure for "intangibles." Molson, whose balance sheet is shown in Chapter 2, Table 2.1, had $1,519 billion in intangible assets. The major intangible consists of "goodwill," which is the difference between the amount that Molson paid when it acquired several companies and brand names and the book value of their assets. Molson writes off a proportion of this

[20] Speech by the chairman of the London and County Bank at the annual meeting, February 1901. Reported in *The Economist*, 1901, p. 204, and cited in C. A. E. Goodhart, *The Business of Banking 1891–1914* (London: Weidenfield and Nicholson, 1972), p. 15.

FINANCE IN ACTION

Think of a Number

The quality of mercy is not strain'd; the quality of American corporate profits is another matter. There may be a lot less to the published figures than meets the eye.

Warren Buffett, America's most admired investor, certainly thinks so. As he sagely put it recently, "A growing number of otherwise high-grade managers—CEOs you would be happy to have as spouses for your children or as trustees under your will—have come to the view that it is OK to manipulate earnings to satisfy what they believe are Wall Street's desires. Indeed, many CEOs think this kind of manipulation is not only OK, but actually their duty."

The question is: Do they under- or overstate profits? Unfortunately different ruses have different effects. Take first those designed to flatter profits. Thanks mainly to a furious lobbying effort by bosses, stock options are not counted as a cost. Smithers & Co., a London-based research firm, calculated the cost of these options and concluded that the American companies granting them had overstated their profits by as much as half in the 1998 financial year; overall, ignoring stock-option costs has exaggerated American profits as a whole by one to three percentage points every year since 1994.

Then there are corporate pension funds. The value of these has soared thanks to the stock market's vertiginous rise and, as a result, some pension plans have become overfunded (assets exceed liabilities). Firms can include this pension surplus as a credit in their income statements. Over $1 billion of General Electric's reported pretax profits of $13.8 billion in 1998 were "earned" in this way. The rising value of financial assets has allowed many firms to reduce, or even skip, their annual pension-fund contributions, boosting profits. As pension-fund contributions will almost certainly have to be resumed when the bull market ends, this probably paints a misleading impression of the long-term trend of profitability.

Mr. Buffett is especially critical of another way of dampening current profits to the benefit of future ones: restructuring charges (the cost, taken in one go, of a corporate reorganization). Firms may be booking much bigger restructuring charges than they should, creating a reserve of money to draw on to boost profits in a difficult future year.

Source: The Economist, September 11, 1999, pp. 107–108.

goodwill from each year's profits. We don't want to debate whether goodwill is really an asset, but we should warn you about the dangers of comparing ratios of firms whose balance sheets include a substantial goodwill element with those that do not.

Another pitfall arises because many of the company's liabilities are not shown in the balance sheet at all. We have already encountered leases. Whether a lease is capitalized and reported as a liability depends on certain tests—for example, leases lasting more than 75 percent of a leased asset's life are capitalized. But a lease lasting only 74 percent of asset life escapes the net and is shown only in the footnotes to the financial statements. Read the footnotes carefully; if you take the balance sheet uncritically, you may miss important obligations of the company. The nearby Finance in Action box discusses Enron and how sometimes even the notes don't fully reveal the extent of obligations.

SEE BOX P. 527

CHOOSING A BENCHMARK

We have shown you how to calculate the principal financial ratios for LC. In practice you may not need to calculate all of them, because many measure essentially the same thing. For example, often one debt ratio and one coverage ratio are sufficient to characterize the situation. However, for LC, debt ratios change dramatically with the treatment of the off-balance-sheet operating leases.

Once you have selected and calculated the important ratios, you still need some way of judging whether they are high or low. A good starting point is to compare them with the equivalent figures for the same company in earlier years. For example, you can see from the first two columns of Table 17.8 that, by every measure, LC's financial performance was worse in 2000 than in 1999. The most significant changes are to the liquidity and profitability ratios. This is not surprising given the loss that occurred. Efficiency ratios

Accounting for Enron

The story of the stunning financial collapse and bankruptcy of Enron, an energy trading company, is still unfolding. In the span of a few months, its stock price fell from $75 (US) to nothing, making it the largest bankruptcy in U.S. history. One aspect of their collapse was the way they managed to keep debt off their balance sheet and hid commitments to honour the debt. Without full disclosure, no one knew the true situation. The following is an excerpt from an article discussing financial disclosure by Enron and other companies.

When energy trader Enron Corp. admitted to hiding billions of dollars of liabilities in mysterious off-book entities, it trotted out the lame excuse of scoundrels: Everyone does it. And this time, it was the gospel truth.

Hundreds of respected U.S. companies are ferreting away trillions of dollars in debt in off-balance-sheet subsidiaries, partnerships, and assorted obligations, including leases, pension plans, and take-or-pay contracts with suppliers. Potentially bankrupting contracts are mentioned vaguely in footnotes to company accounts, at best. The goal is to skirt the rules of consolidation, the bedrock of the American financial reporting system and the source of much of its credibility. These rules, set clearly in 1959, aim to make public companies give a full and fair picture of their business—including all the assets and liabilities of any subsidiaries. But accountants, lawyers, and bankers have learned to drive a coach and horses through them.

Because of a gaping loophole in accounting practice, companies create arcane legal structures, often called special-purpose entities (SPE). Then, the parent can bankroll up to 97 percent of the initial investment in an SPE without having to consolidate it into its own accounts. Normally, once a company owns 50 percent or more of another, it must consolidate it under the 1959 rules. Outsiders need invest only 3 percent of an SPE's capital for it to be independent and off the balance sheet.

It's not just the energy industry that exploits the loophole and stashes major liabilities in the never-never land of SPEs. Increasingly, companies of all stripes routinely use them to offload potential balance-sheet bombshells such as loan guarantees or the financing of sales of their own products. For example, the accounts of data processor Electronic Data Systems Corp. don't show $500 million—half of last year's earnings—that it would owe if its customers were to cancel their contracts and leave it holding the bag for loans on their computer equipment. The arrangement is acknowledged only in a footnote. An EDS spokesman says the tactic is common in the industry and does not put the company at undue risk.

Airlines keep appearances aloft by shunting billions worth of airplane financing into off-balance-sheet vehicles, says credit analyst Philip Baggaley of Standard & Poor's. United Airlines, Inc.-parent UAL Corp.'s published balance sheet for 2000 shows $5 billion of long-term debt. But only a footnote describes the bulk of its lease payments, which Baggaley estimates have a present value of $12.7 billion due over 26 years on 233 airplanes. AMR Corp., parent of American Airlines, Inc., is on the hook for $7.9 billion in lease payments not on its balance sheet. "Everyone who's involved in the industry knows that the true leverage is higher" than what's shown on the balance sheet, says Baggaley. UAL and AMR declined to comment.

Companies argue that off-balance-sheet vehicles benefit investors because they enable management to tap extra sources of financing and hedge trading risks that could roil earnings. Maybe so, but they sure make the companies, and their executives, look good: return on capital looks better than it is because balance sheets understate the amount employed. And investors and regulators don't freak out as corporate debt balloons. But critics charge that the widespread use of off-balance-sheet schemes encourages contempt for accounting rules in the executive suite and spreads confusion among investors. "The nonprofessional has no idea of the extent of the real liabilities," says J. Edward Ketz, accounting professor at Pennsylvania State University. "Professionals can be easily fooled, too."

Worse yet, many SPEs have provisions that can throw their users into a full-blown financial crisis. To get assets off its books, a company typically sells them to an SPE, funding the purchase by borrowing cash from institutional investors. As a sweetener to protect investors, many SPEs incorporate triggers that require the parent to repay loans or give them new securities if its stock falls below a certain price or credit-rating agencies downgrade its debt. It was just such triggers in its notorious off-balance-sheet partnerships that sent Enron into a death spiral. And triggers fuelled the crises last year at Pacific Gas and Electric, Southern California Edison, and Xerox, according to Moody's Investors Service. "All of this hidden debt and these triggers could make the next economic downturn a lot worse than it would otherwise be," says Lynn Turner, who was chief accountant at the Securities and Exchange Commission until July.

From, "Who Else Is Hiding Debt—Moving Financial Obligations into Off-Book Vehicles Is a Common Ploy" by David Henry, with Heather Timmons and Steve Rosenbush, in New York, and Michael Arndt, in Chicago.

Source: *Business Week*, January 28, 2002, Issue 3767, p. 36.

TABLE 17.8
Financial ratios

FINANCIAL RATIOS FOR LE CHÂTEAU AND LES BOUTIQUES SAN FRANCISCO, 2000 AND 1999

	Le Château		Les Boutiques San Francisco	
	2000	**1999**	**2000**	**1999**
Leverage Ratios				
Long-term debt ratio, excluding operating leases	0.1	0.07	0.09	0.1
Long-term debt ratio, including operating leases	0.67	0.63	0.46	0.42
Total debt ratio, excluding operating leases	0.33	0.27	0.44	0.46
Total debt ratio, including operating leases	0.7	0.66	0.6	0.6
Times interest earned	–4.5	20.4	15.5	8.74
Liquidity Ratios				
Net working capital to assets	0.2	0.29	0.1	0.21
Current ratio	1.89	2.41	1.32	1.31
Quick ratio	0.31	0.89	0.26	0.43
Cash ratio	0.2	0.73	0.22	0.38
Interval measure (days)	11.0	29.4	17.0	31.2
Efficiency Ratios				
Asset turnover	2.36	2.49	1.98	1.98
Fixed asset turnover	4.43	5.2	4.3	3.73
Average collection period (days)	4.4	4.0	2.7	3.3
Inventory turnover[1]	5.27	5.79	6.21	6.65
Average payables period (days)	26.3	26.1	64.2	64.6
Profitability Ratios				
Net profit margin (%)	–1.13	3.29	2.86	2.74
Return on assets (%)	–2.66	8.19	5.59	5.22
Return on equity (%)	–5.42	10.8	9.57	8.72

[1] Les Boutique San Francisco does not report its cost of sales separately from its selling, general, and administrative expenses. Its inventory turnover is based on the cost of sales and selling, general, and administrative expenses. The comparable inventory turnover numbers for LC are 7.44 and 8.18, for 2000 and 1999 respectively.

were somewhat lower. We might have expected a sharp increase in the average payables period but LC has continued to pay its bills in 26 days on average.

It is also helpful to compare LC's financial position with that of other firms. However, you would not expect companies in different industries to have similar ratios. For example, a soft drink manufacturer is unlikely to have the same profit margin as a jeweler or the same leverage as a finance company. It makes sense, therefore, to limit comparison to other firms in the same industry. For example, the third and fourth columns of Table 17.8 show the financial ratios for Les Boutique San Francisco, a Canadian retailer of clothing for women, men, and children with a network of retail stores, including San Francisco and Bikini Village. San Francisco's performance was similar to LC's in 1999 but much better than LC's in 2000.

When making these comparisons remember our earlier warning about the need to dig behind the figures. For example, you might wonder why LC's average payment period is less than half that of San Francisco. Is LC not taking advantage of available trade credit? No, the difference reflects the fact that San Francisco buys a lot more of its products from manufacturers than LC does.

Financial ratios for industries are published by StatsCanada, Financial Post, Dun & Bradstreet, Robert Morris Associates, and others. Table 17.9 contains ratios for some major industry groups. This should give you a feel for some of the differences between industries.

TABLE 17.9
Financial ratios

FINANCIAL RATIOS FOR SELECTED INDUSTRY GROUPS, SECOND QUARTER, 2000								
	Wholesale and Retail	Biotechnology and Pharmaceuticals	Technology	Food and Beverage	Communi-cations and Media	Auto, Parts and Trans-portation	Oil and Gas	Steel
Long-term debt ratio[a]	0.26	0.14	0.15	0.51	0.69	0.19	0.34	0.47
Cash flow from operations/total debt	0.5	−0.46	−0.69	0.3	0.32	1.59	0.99	0.113
Current ratio	1.68	11.07	3.54	2.46	1.18	1.98	1.74	2.02
Quick ratio	0.66	7.21	2.96	0.83	0.86	1.17	1.5	0.79
Times interest earned	5.73	−10.26	−33.09	7.72	5.54	34.29	19.64	2.7
Total asset turnover	2.2	0.26	0.86	1.33	0.55	1.26	0.56	1.1
Operating profit margin	3.62	−33.56	−22.21	14.61	15.98	10.11	37.62	6.18
Return on total assets (%)	4.57	−14.55	−11.97	7.54	2.7	6.73	11.72	5.2
Return on equity (%)	7.89	−16.3	−18.8	16.36	−36.96	11.23	27.92	5.03

[a] Long-term debt/(Long-term debt + equity)
Source: Financial Post, Industry Reports.

CHECK POINT 17.5

Look at the financial ratios shown in Table 17.9. The wholesale and retail industry has a higher asset turnover and a lower operating profit margin than steel manufacturers. What do you think accounts for these differences?

17.5 Measuring Company Performance

The book value of the company's equity is equal to the total amount that the company has raised from its shareholders or retained and reinvested on their behalf. If the company has been successful in adding value, the market value of the equity will be higher than the book value. So investors are likely to look favourably on the managers of firms that have a high ratio of market to book value and to frown upon firms whose market value is less than book value. Of course, the market to book ratio does not tell you just how much richer the shareholders have become. Take Nortel, for example. At the end of 2001 the book value of Nortel's equity was $4,824 million (US), but investors valued its shares at $23,973 million (US). So every dollar that Nortel invested on behalf of its shareholders had increased 5 times in value (23,973/4,824 = 5). The difference between the market value of shares and their book value is often called the **market value added.** Nortel had added $23,973 − $4,824 = $19,149 million to the equity capital that it had invested.

market value added The difference between the market value of the firm's equity and its book value.

Table 17.10 ranks a number of large Canadian companies in terms of their MVA measured at the end of 2000. Stern Stewart, a management consulting company, generously provided these data.[21] You can see that Nortel heads the list in terms of market value added. At the end of 2000, Nortel had added $60,167 million to the equity capital it had

[21] Stern Stewart's annual ranking of 1,000 U.S. firms is published annually in *Fortune* magazine. On occasion, the *National Post* has published the Stern Stewart top 300 Canadian companies.

TABLE 17.10

MEASURES OF COMPANY PERFORMANCE (COMPANIES ARE RANKED BY MARKET VALUE ADDED) (all numbers in US dollars)				
Company Name	**Market-to Book Ratio**	**Market Value Added (millions)**	**Return on Assets, %**	**Economic Value Added (millions)**
Nortel Networks Corporation	2.3	60,167	−1.6%	−5,412
Bombardier Inc.	3.3	29,163	10.0%	109
Thomson Corporation	2.1	23,132	13.5%	978
BCE Inc.	1.4	13,457	11.2%	185
Rogers Communications Inc.	2.3	4,718	3.5%	−164
Alcan Aluminium Limited	1.3	3,557	7.3%	−301
Air Canada	1.2	1,537	5.0%	−166
Molson Inc.	1.6	1,508	7.3%	10
Le Château	0.7	−35	1.8%	−9
Quebecor Inc.	1.0	−675	9.7%	413
Canadian Pacific Limited	0.8	−2,831	12.0%	438

Source: Data provided by Stern Stewart & Co., www.sternstewart.com.

invested.[22] Canadian Pacific was at the bottom; the market value of CP's equity was $2,831 million *less* than the amount of shareholders' money that CP had invested.

Measures of company performance that are based on market values have two disadvantages. First, the market value of the company's shares reflects investors' expectations. Investors placed a high value on Nortel's shares partly because they believed that its management would *continue* to find profitable investments in the future. However, by the end of 2001, expectations of growth had diminished and Nortel's MVA had fallen from $60 billion to only $19 billion. Second, market values cannot be used to judge the performance of companies that are privately owned or the performance of divisions or plants that are part of larger companies. Therefore, financial managers also calculate accounting measures of performance.

Think again of how a firm creates value for its investors, both debtholders and shareholders. It can either invest in new plant and equipment or it can return the cash to investors, who can then invest the money for themselves by buying stocks and bonds in the capital market. The return that investors could expect to earn if they invested in the capital market is called the *cost of capital.* A firm that earns *more* than the cost of capital makes its investors better off: it is earning them a higher return than they could obtain for themselves. A firm that earns *less* than the cost of capital makes investors worse off: they could earn a higher return simply by investing their cash in the capital market. Therefore, naturally, financial managers are concerned whether the firm's return on its assets exceeds or falls short of the cost of capital. For example, look at the third column of Table 17.10,

[22] Stern Stewart measures market value added as the market value of debt *and* equity minus the book value of debt *and* equity. However, as we noted in Chapter 2, although book and market value of debt are not equal, typically, their difference is relatively small. The promised interest and principal payments on debt do not increase when a firm does well, which is unlike shareholders' dividends. The primary source of difference between book and market value of debt is variation in interest rates. Only in financial distress and bankruptcy does the market value of debt deviate substantially from its book value. We assume, for simplicity, that market and book values of debt are equal. In this case, Stern Stewart's market value added measure is the difference between market and book value of equity.

which shows the return on assets for our sample of companies. Thompson Corporation had the highest return on assets of 13.5 percent. Since the cost of capital for Thompson was around 8.73 percent, each dollar invested by Thompson was earning over 1.5 times the return that investors could have expected by investing in the capital market.

Let us work out how much this amounted to. Thompson's total capital in 2000 was $20,507 million. With a return of 13.5 percent, it earned profits on this figure of $.135 \times 20{,}507 = \$2{,}768$ million. The total cost of the capital employed by Thompson was about $.0873 \times 20{,}507 = \$1{,}790$ million. So after deducting the cost of capital, Thompson earned $2{,}768 - 1{,}790 = \$978$ million. This is called Thompson's **residual income.** It is also known as **economic value added,** or **EVA®,** a term coined by Stern Stewart, which has done much to develop and promote the concept.

residual income (also called economic value added or EVA) The net profit of a firm or division after deducting the cost of the capital employed.

economic value added (EVA®) See residual income

The final column of Table 17.10 shows the economic value added for our sample of large companies. Consider Alcan and Molson. Both had return on assets of 7.3 percent but only Molson had positive EVA. This occurred because Molson's cost of capital was only 6.9 percent, whereas riskier Alcan's cost of capital was 10.2 percent. Molson earned more than its investors' required return, creating economic value added of $10 million. By contrast, Alcan failed to earn enough to compensate investors, producing negative economic value added of $301 million. Nortel was the worst performer, with economic value added of –$5,412 million. Nortel's negative return on assets indicates that the company did not earn enough to cover its business costs, even before considering the cost of capital. A company cannot consistently have negative EVA and positive market value added. Unless its financial performance improves, investors will reassess their optimism about the future, and the share price will fall, lowering the market value added.

Residual income or EVA is a better measure of a company's performance than accounting profits. Profits are calculated after deducting all costs *except* the cost of capital. EVA recognizes that companies need to cover their cost of capital before they add value. If a plant or division is not earning a positive EVA, its management is likely to face some pointed questions about whether the assets could be better employed elsewhere—or by fresh management. Therefore, a growing number of firms now calculate EVA and tie managers' compensation to it.

17.6 The Role of Financial Ratios

In this chapter we have encountered a number of measures of a firm's financial position. Many of these were in the form of ratios; some, such as market value added and economic value added, were measured in dollars.

Before we leave the topic it might be helpful to emphasize the role of such accounting measures. Whenever two managers get together to discuss the state of the business, there is a good bet they will refer to financial ratios. Let's drop in on two conversations.

Conversation 1. The CEO was musing out loud: "How are we going to finance this expansion? Would the banks be happy to lend us the $30 million that we need?"

"I've been looking into that," the financial manager replies. "Our current debt ratio is .3. If we borrow the full cost of the project, the ratio would be about .45. When we took out our last loan from the bank, we agreed that we would not allow our debt ratio to get above .5. So if we borrow to finance this project, we wouldn't have much leeway to respond to possible emergencies. Also, the rating agencies currently give our bonds an investment-grade rating. They, too, look at a company's leverage when they rate its bonds. I have a table here (Table 17.11) which shows that, when firms are highly leveraged, their

TABLE 17.11

KEY INDUSTRIAL FINANCIAL RATIOS

U.S. industrial long-term debt Three-year (1997 to 1999) medians	AAA	AA	A	BBB	BB	B
EBIT interest coverage (×)	17.5	10.8	6.8	3.9	2.3	1.0
EBITDA interest coverage (×)	21.8	14.6	9.6	6.1	3.8	2.0
Funds from operations/total debt (%)	105.8	55.8	46.1	30.5	19.2	8.4
Free operating cash flow/total debt (%)	55.4	24.6	15.6	6.6	1.9	(4.5)
Return on capital (%)	28.2	22.9	19.9	14.0	11.7	7.2
Operating income/sales (%)	289.2	21.3	18.3	15.3	15.4	11.2
Long-term debt/capital (incl. STD) (%)	15.2	26.4	32.5	41.0	55.8	70.7
Total debt/capital (incl. STD) (%)	26.9	35.6	40.1	47.4	61.3	74.6

FORMULA FOR KEY RATIOS

1. EBIT interest coverage = $\dfrac{\text{Earnings from continuing operations* before interest and taxes}}{\text{Gross interest incurred before subtracting (1) capitalized interest and (2) interest income}}$

2. EBITDA interest coverage = $\dfrac{\text{Earnings from continuing operations* before interest, taxes, depreciation, and amortization}}{\text{Gross interest incurred before subtracting (1) capitalized interest and (2) interest income}}$

3. Funds from operatings/total debt = $\dfrac{\text{Net income from continuing operations plus depreciation, amortization, deferred income taxes, and other noncash items}}{\text{Long-term debt** + current maturities, commercial paper, and other short-term borrowings}}$

4. Free operating cash flow/total debt = $\dfrac{\text{Funds from operations – capital expenditures, – (+) the increase (decrease) in working capital (excluding changes in cash, marketable securities, and short-term debt)}}{\text{Long-term debt** + current maturities, commercial paper, and other short-term borrowings}}$

5. Return on capital = $\dfrac{\text{EBIT}}{\text{Average of beginning of year and end of year capital, including short-term debt, current maturities, long-term debt**, noncurrent deferred taxes, and equity}}$

6. Operating income/sales = $\dfrac{\text{Sales minus cost of goods manufactured (before depreciation and amortization), selling, general, and administrative, and research and development costs}}{\text{Sales}}$

7. Long-term debt/capital = $\dfrac{\text{Long-term debt**}}{\text{Long-term debt + shareholders' equity (including preferred stock) + minority interest}}$

8. Total debt/capital = $\dfrac{\text{Long-term debt** + current maturities, commercial paper, and other short-term borrowings}}{\text{Long-term debt + current maturities, commercial paper, and other short-term borrowings + shareholders' equity (including preferred stock) + minority interest}}$

*Including interest income and equity earnings; excluding nonrecurring items.
**Including amount for operating lease debt equivalent.

Source: Standard and Poor's, 2001 Corporate Ratings Criteria, www.standardandpoors.com.

bonds receive a lower rating. I don't know whether the rating agencies would downgrade our bonds if our debt ratio increased to .45, but they might. That wouldn't please our existing bondholders, and it could raise the cost of any new borrowing.

"We also need to think about our interest cover, which is beginning to look a bit thin. Debt interest is currently covered three times and, if we borrowed the entire $30 million, interest cover would fall to about two times. Sure, we expect to earn additional profits on the new investment but it could be several years before they come through. If we run into a recession in the meantime, we could find ourselves short of cash."

"Sounds to me as if we should be thinking about a possible equity issue," concluded the CEO.

Conversation 2. The CEO was not in the best of moods after her defeat at the company golf tournament by the manager of the packaging division: "I see our stock was down again yesterday," she growled. "It's now selling below book value and the stock price is only six times earnings. I work my socks off for this company; you would think that our shareholders would show a little more gratitude."

"I think I can understand a little of our shareholders' worries," the financial manager replies. "Just look at our return on assets. It's only 6 percent, well below the cost of capital. Sure we are making a profit, but that profit does not cover the cost of the funds that investors provide. Our economic value added is actually negative. Of course, this doesn't necessarily mean that the assets could be used better elsewhere, but we should certainly be looking carefully at whether any of our divisions should be sold off or the assets redeployed.

"In some ways we're in good shape. We have very little short-term debt and our current assets are three times our current liabilities. But that's not altogether good news because it also suggests that we may have more working capital than we need. I've been looking at our main competitors. They turn over their inventory 12 times a year compared with our figure of just 8 times. Also, their customers take an average of 45 days to pay their bills. Ours take 67. If we could just match their performance on these two measures, we would release $300 million that could be paid out to shareholders."

"Perhaps we could talk more about this tomorrow," said the CEO. "In the meantime, I intend to have a word with the production manager about our inventory levels and see the credit manager about our collections policy. You've also got me thinking about whether we should sell off our packaging division. I've always worried about the divisional manager there. Spends too much time practicing his backswing and not enough worrying about his return on assets."

17.7 Summary

1. **What are the standard measures of a firm's leverage, liquidity, profitability, asset management, and market valuation? What is the significance of these measures?**

If you are analyzing a company's financial statements, there is a danger of being overwhelmed by the sheer volume of data contained in the **income statement, balance sheet,** and **statement of cash flows.** Managers use a few salient ratios to summarize the firm's leverage, liquidity, efficiency, and profitability. They may also combine accounting data with other data to measure the esteem in which investors hold the company or the efficiency with which the firm uses its resources.

Table 17.12 summarizes the four categories of financial ratios that we have discussed in this chapter. Remember though that financial analysts define the same ratio in different ways or use different terms to describe the same ratio.

Leverage ratios measure the indebtedness of the firm. Liquidity ratios measure how easily the firm can obtain cash. Efficiency ratios measure how intensively the firm is using its assets. Profitability ratios measure the firm's return on its investments. Be selective in your choice of these ratios. Different ratios often tell you similar things.

Financial ratios crop up repeatedly in financial discussions and arrangements. For example, banks and bondholders commonly place limits on the borrower's leverage ratios. Ratings agencies also look at leverage ratios when they decide how highly to rate the firm's bonds.

2. **How does the DuPont formula help identify the determinants of the firm's return on its assets and equity?**

The **DuPont system** provides a useful way to link ratios to explain the firm's return on assets and equity. The formula states that the return on equity is the product of the firm's leverage ratio, asset turnover, profit margin, and debt burden. Return on assets is the product of the firm's asset turnover and profit margin.

3. **What are some potential pitfalls of ratio analysis based on accounting data?**

Financial ratio analysis will rarely be useful if practiced mechanically. It requires a large dose of good judgment. Financial ratios seldom provide answers but they do help you ask the right questions. Moreover, accounting data do not necessarily reflect market values properly, and so must be used with caution. You need a benchmark for assessing a company's financial position. Therefore, we typically compare financial ratios with the company's ratios in earlier years and with the ratios of other firms in the same business.

4. **How do measures such as market value added and economic value added help to assess the firm's performance?**

The ratio of the market value of the firm's equity to its book value indicates how far the value of the shareholders' investment exceeds the money that they have contributed. The *difference* between the market and book values is known as **market value added** and measures the number of dollars of value that the company has added.

Managers often compare the company's return on assets with the cost of capital, to see whether the firm is earning the return that investors require. It is also useful to deduct the cost of the capital employed from the company's profits to see how much profit the company has earned after all costs. This measure is known as **residual income,** also called **economic value added,** or **EVA.** Managers of divisions or plants are often judged and rewarded by their business's economic value added.

TABLE 17.12

Leverage ratios

$$\text{Long-term debt ratio} = \frac{\text{long-term debt}}{\text{long-term debt} + \text{equity}}$$

$$\text{Debt–equity ratio} = \frac{\text{long-term debt}}{\text{equity}}$$

$$\text{Total debt ratio} = \frac{\text{total liabilities}}{\text{total assets}}$$

$$\text{Times interest earned} = \frac{\text{EBIT}}{\text{interest payments}}$$

$$\text{Cash coverage ratio} = \frac{\text{EBIT} + \text{depreciation}}{\text{interest payments}}$$

$$\text{Fixed charge coverage ratio} = \frac{\text{EBIT} + \text{depreciation}}{\text{interest payments} + (\text{debt repayment})/(1 - \text{tax rate})}$$

Liquidity ratios

$$\text{NWC to assets} = \frac{\text{net working capital}}{\text{total assets}}$$

$$\text{Current ratio} = \frac{\text{current assets}}{\text{current liabilities}}$$

$$\text{Quick ratio} = \frac{\text{cash} + \text{marketable securities} + \text{receivables}}{\text{current liabilities}}$$

$$\text{Interval measure} = \frac{\text{cash} + \text{marketable securities} + \text{receivables}}{\text{average daily expenditures from operations}}$$

Efficiency ratios

$$\text{Total asset turnover} = \frac{\text{sales}}{\text{average total assets}}$$

$$\text{Average collection period} = \frac{\text{average receivables}}{\text{average daily sales}}$$

$$\text{Inventory turnover} = \frac{\text{cost of goods sold}}{\text{average inventory}}$$

$$\text{Days' sales in inventories} = \frac{\text{average inventory}}{\text{cost of goods sold}/365}$$

$$\text{Average payment period} = \frac{\text{average payables}}{\text{average daily expenses}}$$

Profitability ratios

$$\text{Gross profit margin} = \frac{\text{sales} - \text{cost of goods sold}}{\text{sales}}$$

$$\text{Operating profit margin} = \frac{\text{EBIT} - \text{taxes}}{\text{sales}}$$

$$\text{Net profit margin} = \frac{\text{net income} + \text{interest}}{\text{sales}}$$

$$\text{Return on assets} = \frac{\text{net income} + \text{interest}}{\text{average total assets}}$$

$$\text{Return on equity} = \frac{\text{net income}}{\text{average equity}}$$

$$\text{Payout ratio} = \frac{\text{dividends}}{\text{earnings}}$$

$$\text{Plowback ratio} = 1 - \text{payout ratio}$$

$$\text{Growth in equity from plowback} = \text{plowback ratio} \times \text{ROE}$$

Related Web Links

www.cfo.com/article/1,5309,1495,00.html A look at the DuPont model
www.globeinvestor.com/static/hubs/filters-company.html How investors use financial analysis to value or screen firms
www.onlinewbc.gov/docs/finance Basics of financial analysis, with tutorials and tools
www.corporateinformation.com Detailed information on 350,000 companies worldwide
www.hoovers.com Hoover's company directory reports on thousands of companies, IPOs, and industries
http://ca.finance.yahoo.com Useful financial profiles on thousands of firms
www.reportgallery.com Annual reports on thousands of companies
www.prars.com Public Register's Annual Report Service is the largest annual report service in the United States, providing annual reports, prospectuses, and 10-K reports
www.sternstewart.com Contains a good discussion of economic value added
www.sedar.com Annual reports, prospectuses, and other documents of Canadian companies
www.strategis.ic.gc.ca Canadian business information, tools, and links, operated by Industry Canada
www.globeinvestor.com Detailed information on publicly traded Canadian companies

Key Terms

income statement	506	common-size balance sheet	511	market value added	529
common-size income statement	508	liquidity	513	residual income	531
balance sheet	508	DuPont system	520	economic value added (EVA)	531

Questions and Problems

*Answers in Appendix B

Basic

*1. **Calculating Ratios.** Here are simplified financial statements of Phone Corporation from a recent year:

BALANCE SHEET
(figures in millions of dollars)

	End of Year	Start of Year
Assets		
Cash and marketable securities	89	158
Receivables	2,382	2,490
Inventories	187	238
Other current assets	867	932
Total current assets	3,525	3,818
Net property, plant, and equipment	19,973	19,915
Other long-term assets	4,216	3,770
Total assets	27,714	27,503
Liabilities and shareholders' equity		
Payables	2,564	3,040
Short-term debt	1,419	1,573
Other current liabilities	811	787
Total current liabilities	4,794	5,400
Long-term debt and leases	7,018	6,833
Other long-term liabilities	6,178	6,149
Shareholders' equity	9,724	9,121
Total liabilities and shareholders' equity	27,714	27,503

INCOME STATEMENT (figures in millions of dollars)	
Net sales	13,194
Cost of goods sold	4,060
Other expenses	4,049
Depreciation	2,518
Earnings before interest and taxes (EBIT)	2,566
Interest expenses	685
Income before tax	1,881
Taxes	570
Net income	1,311
Dividends	856

Calculate the following financial ratios:

a. Long-term debt ratio
b. Total debt ratio
c. Times interest earned
d. Cash coverage ratio
e. Current ratio
f. Quick ratio
g. Net profit margin
h. Inventory turnover
i. Days' sales in inventory
j. Average collection period
k. Return on equity
l. Return on assets
m. Payout ratio
n. Operating profit margin
o. Gross profit margin

2. **Interval Measure.** Suppose that Phone Corp. shut down operations. For how many days could it pay its bills?

*3. **Gross Investment.** What was Phone Corp.'s gross investment in plant and other equipment?

4. **Market Value Ratios.** If the market value of Phone Corp. stock was $17.2 billion at the end of the year, what was the market-to-book ratio? If there were 205 million shares outstanding, what were earnings per share? The price-earnings ratio?

*5. **Common-Size Balance Sheet.** Prepare a common-size balance sheet for Phone Corp. using its balance sheet from problem 1.

6. **DuPont Analysis.** Use the data for Phone Corp. to confirm that ROA = asset turnover × net profit margin.

*7. **DuPont Analysis.** Use the data for Phone Corp., to demonstrate that ROE = leverage ratio × asset turnover ratio × net profit margin × debt burden.

PRACTICE

8. **Asset Turnover.** In each case, choose the firm that you expect to have a higher asset turnover ratio.

a. Economics Consulting Group or Molson
b. Catalogue Shopping Network or Hudson's Bay
c. Electric Utility Co. or Standard Supermarkets

*9. **Defining Ratios.** There are no universally accepted definitions of financial ratios, but some of the following ratios make no sense at all. Substitute the correct definitions.

a. Debt-equity ratio = $\frac{\text{long-term debt}}{\text{long-term debt + equity}}$

b. Return on equity = $\frac{\text{EBIT} - \text{tax}}{\text{average equity}}$

c. Net profit margin = $\frac{\text{net income + interest}}{\text{sales}}$

d. Inventory turnover = $\frac{\text{total assets}}{\text{average inventory}}$

e. Current ratio = $\frac{\text{current liabilities}}{\text{current assets}}$

f. Interval measure = $\frac{\text{current assets} - \text{inventories}}{\text{average daily expenditure from operations}}$

g. Average collection period = $\frac{\text{sales}}{\text{average receivables/365}}$

h. Quick ratio = $\frac{\text{cash + marketable securities + receivables}}{\text{current liabilities}}$

*10. **Current Liabilities.** Suppose that at year-end LC had unused lines of credit which would have allowed it to borrow a further $10 million. Suppose also that it used this line of credit to borrow $10 million and invested the proceeds in marketable securities. Would the company have appeared to be (a) more or less liquid, (b) more or less highly leveraged? Calculate the appropriate ratios.

11. **Current Ratio.** How would each of the following actions affect a firm's current ratio?

a. Inventory is sold at cost.
b. The firm takes out a bank loan to pay its accounts due.
c. A customer pays its accounts receivable.
d. The firm uses cash to purchase additional inventories.

*12. **Liquidity Ratios.** A firm uses $1 million in cash to purchase inventories. What will happen to its current ratio? Its quick ratio?

13. **Receivables.** Chik's Chickens has average accounts receivable of $6,333. Sales for the year were $9,800. What is its average collection period?

*14. **Inventory.** Salad Daze maintains an inventory of produce worth $400. Its total bill for produce over the course of the year was $73,000. On average, how old is the lettuce it serves its customers?

15. **Inventory Turnover.** If a firm's inventory level of $10,000 represents 30 days' sales, what is the annual cost of goods sold? What is the inventory turnover ratio?

*16. **Leverage Ratios.** Lever Age pays an 8 percent coupon on outstanding debt with face value $10 million. The firm's EBIT was $1 million and its tax rate was 40 percent.

a. What is times interest earned?
b. If depreciation is $200,000, what is cash coverage?
c. If the firm must retire $300,000 of debt for the sinking fund each year, what is its fixed-charge coverage ratio?

17. **DuPont Analysis.** Keller Cosmetics maintains a net profit margin of 5 percent and asset turnover ratio of 3.

a. What is its ROA?
b. If its debt-equity ratio is 1.0, its interest payments are $8,000, its taxes are $3,600, and its EBIT is $20,000, what is its ROE?

*18. **DuPont Analysis.** Torrid Romance Publishers has total receivables of $3,000, which represent 20 days' sales. Average total assets are $75,000. The firm's net profit margin is 5 percent. Find the firm's ROA and asset turnover ratio.

19. **Leverage.** A firm has a long-term debt-equity ratio of .4. Shareholders' equity is $1 million. Current assets are $200,000 and the current ratio is 2.0. The only current liabilities are notes payable. What is the total debt ratio?

*20. **Leverage Ratios.** A firm has a debt-to-equity ratio of .5 and a market-to-book ratio of 2.0. What is the ratio of the book value of debt to the market value of equity?

21. **Times Interest Earned.** In the past year, TVG had revenue of $3 million, cost of goods sold of $2.5 million, and depreciation expense of $200,000. The firm has a single issue of debt outstanding with face value of $1 million, market value of $.92 million, and a coupon rate of 8 percent. What is the firm's times interest earned ratio?

*22. **DuPont Analysis.** CFA Corp. has a debt-equity ratio that is lower than the industry average, but its cash coverage ratio is also lower than the industry average. What might explain this seeming contradiction?

23. **Leverage.** Suppose that a firm has both floating rate and fixed rate debt outstanding. What effect will a decline in market interest rates have on the firm's times interest earned ratio? On the market value debt-to-equity ratio? Based on these answers, would you say that leverage has increased or decreased?

*24. **Interpreting Ratios.** In each of the following cases, explain briefly which of the two companies is likely to be characterized by the higher ratio:

a. Debt-equity ratio: a shipping company or a computer software company
b. Payout ratio: United Foods Inc. or Computer Graphics Inc.
c. Ratio of sales to assets: an integrated pulp and paper manufacturer or a grocery store
d. Average collection period: Regional Electric Power Company or Z-Mart Discount Outlets
e. Price-earnings multiple: Basic Sludge Company or Fledgling Electronics

25. **Using Financial Ratios.** For each category of financial ratios discussed in this chapter, give some examples of who would be likely to examine these ratios and why.

CHALLENGE

26. **Financial Statements.** As you can see, someone has spilled ink over some of the entries in the balance sheet and income statement of Transylvania Railroad. Can you use the following information to work out the missing entries?

Long-term debt ratio	0.5
Times interest earned	8.0
Current ratio	1.4
Quick ratio	1.0
Return on assets	28.0%
Return on equity	81.7%
Inventory turnover	5.0
Average collection period	71.175 days

INCOME STATEMENT (figures in millions of dollars)	
Net sales	•••
Cost of goods sold	•••
Selling, general, and administrative expenses	10
Depreciation	20
Earnings before interest and taxes (EBIT)	•••
Interest expense	•••
Income before tax	•••
Tax	•••
Net income	•••
Dividends	•••

BALANCE SHEET
(figures in millions of dollars)

	This Year	Last Year
Assets		
Cash and marketable securities	11	20
Receivables	•••	34
Inventories	•••	26
Total current assets	•••	80
Net property, plant, and equipment	•••	25
Total assets	•••	105
Liabilities and shareholders' equity		
Accounts payable	25	20
Notes payable	30	35
Total current liabilities	•••	55
Long-term debt	•••	20
Shareholders' equity	•••	30
Total liabilities and shareholders' equity	115	105

INTERNET PROBLEMS

1. Go to www.sedar.com and select "Search Database," then "Public Company." Select "Annual Report" as document type and pick an annual report to analyze. Read the report and its footnotes, and then, calculate the financial ratios in Table 17.12 and any other ratios you think would be useful. What did you learn about your company's financial performance?
2. Investors can use financial ratios to screen stocks. Go to www.globeinvestor.com and select "Filter." Choose a filter; for example, select the broadcasting industry. A list of stocks will appear. You will see three tabs: Price, Financial, and Estimate. If you pick "Financial" followed by "Ratios," the most recent ratios will be presented. What ratios are shown? Why do you think investors might be interested in these ratios? Check how each of the ratios has been calculated. Pick three companies and compare their ratios. What did you learn about the companies?
3. Financial ratios and performance measures are often used to provide incentives to employees to work in the shareholders' interests. Read the following two articles available at the website of *CFO Magazine*. The first deals with the DuPont model (www.cfo.com/article/1,5309,1495,00.html), and the second, with more recent value-based measures such as economic value added (www.cfo.com/article/1,5309,2182,00.html). Identify the issues associated with using financial ratios and value metrics for providing incentives to employees.

Solutions to Check Points

17.1 Nothing will happen to the long-term debt ratio computed using book values, since the face values of the old and new debt are equal. However, times interest earned and cash coverage will increase since the firm will reduce its interest expense.

17.2 a. The current ratio starts at 1.2/1.0 = 1.2. The transaction will reduce current assets to $.7 million and current liabilities to $.5 million. The current ratio increases to .7/.5 = 1.4. Net working capital is unaffected: current assets and current liabilities fall by equal amounts.

b. The current ratio is unaffected, since the firm merely exchanges one current asset (cash) for another (inventories). However, the quick ratio will fall since inventories are not included among the most liquid assets.

17.3 Average daily expenses are (112,035 + 45,957)/365 = $432.85 million. Average accounts payable are (12,027 + 10,719)/2 = $11,373 million. The average payment delay is therefore 11,373/432.85 = 26.3 days.

17.4 a. The firm must compensate for its below-average profit margin with an above-average turnover ratio. Remember that ROA is the *product* of margin × turnover.

b. If ROA equals the industry average but ROE exceeds the industry average, the firm must have above-average leverage. As long as ROA exceeds the borrowing rate, leverage will increase ROE.

17.5 Wholesalers' and retailers' profit margin on sales is relatively low, but they make up for that low margin by turning over goods rapidly. The high asset turnover allows retailers to earn an adequate return on assets even with a low profit margin, and competition prevents them from increasing prices and margins to a level that would provide a better ROA. In contrast, manufacturing firms have low turnover, and therefore, need higher profit margins to remain viable.

MINICASE

Burchetts Green had enjoyed the bank training course, but it was good to be starting his first real job in the corporate lending group. Earlier that morning the boss had handed him a set of financial statements for The Hobby Horse Company, Inc. (HH). "Hobby Horse," she said, "has got a $45 million loan from us due at the end of September, and it is likely to ask us to roll it over. The company seems to have run into some rough weather recently and I have asked Furze Platt to go down there this afternoon and see what is happening. It might do you good to go along with her. Before you go, take a look at these financial statements and see what you think the problems are. Here's a chance for you to use some of that stuff they taught you in the training course."

Burchetts was familiar with the HH story. Founded in 1990, it had rapidly built up a chain of discount stores selling materials for crafts and hobbies. However, last year a number of new store openings coinciding with a poor Christmas season had pushed the company into a loss. Management had halted all new construction and put 15 of its existing stores up for sale.

Burchetts decided to start with the 6-year summary of HH's balance sheet and income statement (Table 17.13). Then he turned to examine the latest position in more detail (Tables 17.14 and 17.15).

TABLE 17.13
Financial highlights for The Hobby Horse Company, Inc., year ending March 31

	2003	2002	2001	2000	1999	1998
Net sales	3,351	3,314	2,845	2,796	2,493	2,160
EBIT	–9	312	256	243	212	156
Interest	37	63	65	58	48	46
Taxes	3	60	46	43	39	34
Net income	–49	189	145	142	125	76
Earnings per share	–.15	.55	.44	.42	.37	.25
Current assets	669	469	491	435	392	423
Net fixed assets	923	780	753	680	610	536
Total assets	1,573	1,249	1,244	1,115	1,002	959
Current liabilities	680	365	348	302	276	320
Long-term debt	217	159	159	311	319	315
Shareholders' equity	676	725	599	502	407	324
Number of stores	240	221	211	184	170	157
Employees	13,057	11,835	9,810	9,790	9,075	7,825

TABLE 17.14

INCOME STATEMENT FOR THE HOBBY HORSE COMPANY, INC., YEAR ENDING MARCH 31, 2003 (all items in millions of dollars)	
Net sales	3,351
Cost of goods sold	1,990
Selling, general, and administrative expenses	1,211
Depreciation expense	159
Earnings before interest and taxes (EBIT)	–9
Net interest expense	37
Taxable income	–46
Income taxes	3
Net income	–49
Allocation of net income	
Addition to retained earnings	–49
Dividends	0

Note: Column sums subject to rounding error.

TABLE 17.15

CONSOLIDATED BALANCE SHEET FOR THE HOBBY HORSE COMPANY, INC.
(figures in millions of dollars)

Assets	**Mar. 31, 2003**	**Mar. 31, 2002**
Current assets		
Cash and marketable securities	14	72
Receivables	176	194
Inventories	479	203
Total current assets	669	469
Fixed assets		
Property, plant, and equipment, gross	1,077	910
Less accumulated depreciation	154	130
Net fixed assets	923	780
Total assets	1,592	1,249
Liabilities and Shareholders' Equity	**Mar. 31, 2003**	**Mar. 31, 2002**
Current Liabilities		
Debt due for repayment	484	222
Accounts payable	94	58
Other current liabilities	102	85
Total current liabilities	680	365
Long-term debt	236	159
Shareholders' equity		
Common stock	155	155
Addition to retained earnings	521	570
Total shareholders' equity	676	725
Total liabilities and shareholders' equity	1,592	1,249

Note: Column sums subject to rounding error.

CHAPTER 18

Financial Plannning

18.1 What Is Financial Planning?

18.2 Financial Planning Models

18.3 Planners Beware

18.4 External Financing and Growth

18.5 Summary

It's been said that a camel looks like a horse designed by committee. If a firm made all its financial decisions piecemeal, it would end up with a financial camel. Therefore, smart financial managers consider the overall effect of future investment and financing decisions. This process is called *financial planning,* and the end result is called a *financial plan.*

New investments need to be paid for. So investment and financing decisions cannot be made independently. Financial planning forces managers to think systematically about their goals for growth, investment, and financing. Planning should reveal any inconsistencies in these goals.

Planning also helps managers avoid some surprises and think about how they should react to those surprises that *cannot* be avoided. In Chapter 8 we stressed that good financial managers insist on understanding what makes projects work and what could go wrong with them. The same approach should be taken when investment and financing decisions are considered as a whole.

Finally, financial planning helps establish goals to motivate managers and provide standards for measuring performance.

We start the chapter by summarizing what financial planning involves and we describe the contents of a typical financial plan. We then discuss the use of financial models in the planning process. Finally, we examine the relationship between a firm's growth and its need for new financing.

After studying this chapter you should be able to

- Describe the contents and uses of a financial plan.
- Construct a simple financial planning model.
- Estimate the effect of growth on the need for external financing.

18.1 What Is Financial Planning?

Financial planning is a *process* consisting of

1. Analyzing the investment and financing choices open to the firm.
2. Projecting the future consequences of current decisions.
3. Deciding which alternatives to undertake.
4. Measuring subsequent performance against the goals set forth in the financial plan.

Notice that financial planning is not designed to minimize risk. Instead it is a process of deciding which risks to take and which risks are unnecessary or not worth taking.

Firms must plan for both the short-term and the long-term. Short-term planning rarely looks ahead further than the next 12 months. It is largely the process of making sure that the firm has enough cash to pay its bills and that short-term borrowing and lending are arranged to the best advantage. We discuss short-term planning in the next chapter.

planning horizon Time horizon for a financial plan.

Here we are more concerned with long-term planning, where a typical **planning horizon** is 5 years (although some firms look ahead 10 years or more). For example, it can take at least 10 years for an electric utility to obtain approval for, and then, design, build, and test a major generating plant.

FINANCIAL PLANNING FOCUSES ON THE BIG PICTURE

Many of the firm's capital expenditures are proposed by plant managers. But the final budget must also reflect strategic plans made by senior management. Positive-NPV opportunities occur in those businesses where the firm has a real competitive advantage. Strategic plans identify such businesses and look to expand them. These plans also seek to identify businesses to sell or liquidate as well as businesses that should be allowed to run down.

Strategic planning involves capital budgeting on a grand scale. In this process, financial planners try to look at the investment by each line of business and avoid getting bogged down in details. Of course, some individual projects are large enough to have significant individual impact. When Walt Disney announced its intention to build a new theme park in Hong Kong at a cost of $4 billion, you can bet that this project was explicitly analyzed as part of Disney's long-range financial plan. Normally, however, financial planners do not work on a project-by-project basis. Smaller projects are aggregated into a unit that is treated as a single project.

At the beginning of the planning process the corporate staff might ask each division to submit three alternative business plans covering the next 5 years:

1. A *best case* or *aggressive growth* plan calling for heavy capital investment and rapid growth of existing markets.
2. A *normal growth* plan in which the division grows with its markets but not significantly at the expense of its competitors.
3. A plan of *retrenchment* if the firm's markets contract. This is planning for lean economic times.

Of course, the planners might also want to look at the opportunities and costs of moving into a wholly new area where the company may be able to exploit some of its existing strengths. Often they may recommend entering a market for "strategic" reasons—that is, not because the *immediate* investment has a positive net present value, but because it establishes the firm in a new market and creates *options* for possibly valuable follow-up investments.

As an example, think of the decision by IBM to acquire Lotus Corporation for $3.3 billion. Lotus added less than $1 billion of revenues, but Lotus, with its Notes software, had considerable experience in helping computers talk to each other. This know-how gave IBM an option to produce and market new products in the future.

Because the firm's future is likely to depend on the options that it acquires today, we would expect planners to take a particular interest in these options.

In the simplest plans, capital expenditures might be forecast to grow in proportion to sales. In even moderately sophisticated models, however, the need for additional investments will recognize the firm's ability to use its fixed assets at varying levels of intensity by adjusting overtime or by adding additional shifts. Similarly, the plan will alert the firm to needs for additional investments in working capital. For example, if sales are forecast to increase, the firm should plan to increase inventory levels and should expect an increase in accounts receivable.

Most plans also contain a summary of planned financing. This part of the plan should logically include a discussion of dividend policy because the more the firm pays out, the more capital it will need to find from sources other than retained earnings.

Some firms need to worry much more than others about raising money. A firm with limited investment opportunities, ample operating cash flow, and a moderate dividend payout accumulates considerable "financial slack" in the form of liquid assets and unused borrowing power. Life is relatively easy for the managers of such firms, and their financing plans are routine. Whether that easy life is in the interests of their shareholders is another matter. For example, when we discussed capital structure in Chapter 15, we described how Sealed Air Corporation deliberately reduced its financial slack and increased its leverage in order to encourage its managers to run a tight ship.

Other firms have to raise capital by selling securities. Naturally, they give careful attention to planning the kinds of securities to be sold and the timing of the offerings. The plan might specify bank borrowing, debt issues, equity issues, or other means to raise capital.

Financial plans help managers ensure that their financing strategies are consistent with their capital budgets. They highlight the financing decisions necessary to support the firm's production and investment goals.

FINANCIAL PLANNING IS NOT JUST FORECASTING

Forecasting concentrates on the most likely future outcome. But financial planners are not concerned solely with forecasting. They need to worry about unlikely events as well as likely ones. If you think ahead about what could go wrong, then you are more likely to see the danger signals and can react faster to trouble.

Companies have developed a number of ways of asking what-if questions about both their projects and the overall firm. We examined some of these techniques in Chapter 8. Often planners work through the consequences of the plan under the most likely set of circumstances, and then, use *sensitivity analysis* to vary the assumptions one at a time. For example, they might look at what would happen if a policy of aggressive growth coincided with a recession. Companies using *scenario analysis* might look at the consequences of each business plan under different plausible scenarios in which several assumptions are varied at once. For example, one scenario might envisage high interest rates contributing to a slowdown in world economic growth and lower commodity prices. A second scenario might involve a buoyant domestic economy, high inflation, and a weak currency. The

SEE BOX P. 547

nearby Finance in Action box describes how Georgia Power Company used scenario analysis to help develop its business plans.

THREE REQUIREMENTS FOR EFFECTIVE PLANNING

Forecasting. The firm will never have perfectly accurate forecasts. If it did, there would be less need for planning. Still, managers must strive for the best forecasts possible.

Forecasting should not be reduced to a mechanical exercise. Naive extrapolation or fitting trends to past data is of limited value. Planning is needed because the future is *not* likely to resemble the past.

Do not forecast in a vacuum. By this we mean that your forecasts should recognize that your competitors are developing their own plans. For example, your ability to implement an aggressive growth plan and increase market share depends on what the competition is likely to do. So try putting yourself in the competition's shoes and think how they are likely to behave. Of course, if your competitors are also trying to guess *your* movements, you may need the skills of a good poker player to outguess them. For example, Boeing and Airbus both have schemes to develop new super-jumbo jets. But since there isn't room for two producers, the companies have been engaging in a game of bluff and counterbluff.

Planners draw on information from many sources. Therefore, inconsistency may be a problem. For example, forecast sales may be the sum of separate forecasts made by many product managers, each of whom may make different assumptions about inflation, growth of the national economy, availability of raw materials, and so on. In such cases, it makes sense to ask individuals for forecasts based on a common set of macroeconomic assumptions.

Choosing the Optimal Financial Plan. In the end, the financial manager has to choose which plan is best. We would like to tell you exactly how to make this choice—unfortunately, we can't. There is no model or procedure that encompasses all the complexity and intangibles encountered in financial planning.

You sometimes hear managers state corporate goals in terms of accounting numbers. They might say, "We want a 25 percent return on book equity and a profit margin of 10 percent." On the surface such objectives don't make sense. Shareholders want to be richer, not to have the satisfaction of a 10 percent profit margin. Also, a goal that is stated in terms of accounting ratios is not operational unless it is translated back into what that means for business decisions. For example, a higher profit margin can result from higher prices, lower costs, a move into new, high-margin products, or taking over the firm's suppliers.[1] Setting profit margin as a goal gives no guidance about which of these strategies is best.

So why do managers define objectives in this way? In part, such goals may be a mutual exhortation to work harder, like singing the company song before work. But we suspect that managers are often using a code to communicate real concerns. For example, a target profit margin may be a way of saying that in pursuing sales growth the firm has allowed costs to get out of control.

The danger is that everyone may forget the code and the accounting targets may be seen as goals in themselves.

[1] If you take over a supplier, total sales are not affected (to the extent that the supplier is selling to you), but you capture both the supplier's and your own profit margin. See Chapter 17, Table 17.6, for an example.

FINANCE IN ACTION

Contingency Planning at Georgia Power Company

The oil price hikes in 1973/1974 and 1979 caused consternation in the planning departments of electric utilities. Planners, who had assumed steady growth in energy usage and prices, found that their assumptions could no longer be relied on.

The planning department of the Georgia Power Company responded by developing a number of possible scenarios and exploring their implications for Georgia Power's business over the next 10 years. In planning for the future, the company was not simply interested in the most likely outcome; it also needed to develop contingency plans to cover any unexpected occurrences.

Georgia Power's planning process involved three steps: (1) identify the key factors affecting the company's prospects; (2) determine a range of plausible outcomes for each of these factors; and (3) consider whether a favourable outcome for one factor was likely to be matched by a favourable outcome for the other factors.

This exercise generated three principal scenarios. For example, in the most rosy scenario, the growth in gross national product was expected to exceed 3.2 percent a year. This higher economic growth was likely to be accompanied by high productivity growth and lower real interest rates as the baby boom generation matured. However, high growth was also likely to mean that economic prosperity would be more widely spread, so that the net migration to Georgia and the other sunbelt states was likely to decline. The average price of oil would probably remain below $18 a barrel as the power of OPEC weakened, and this would encourage industry to substitute oil for natural gas. The government was likely to pursue a free-market energy policy, which would tend to keep the growth in electricity prices below the rate of inflation.

Georgia Power's planners explored the implications of each scenario for energy demand and the amount of investment the company needed to make. That in turn allowed the financial managers to think about how the company could meet the possible demands for cash to finance the new investment.

Source: Georgia Power Company's use of scenario analysis is described in D. L. Goldfarb and W. R. Huss, "Building Scenarios for an Electric Utility," *Long Range Planning* 21 (1988), pp. 78–85.

Watching the Plan Unfold. Financial plans are out of date as soon as they are complete. Often they are out of date even earlier. For example, suppose that profits in the first year turn out to be 10 percent below forecast. What do you do with your plan? Scrap it and start again? Stick to your guns and hope profits will bounce back? Revise down your profit forecasts for later years by 10 percent? A good financial plan should be easy to adapt as events unfold and surprises occur.

Long-term plans can also be used as a benchmark to judge subsequent performance as events unfold. But performance appraisals have little value unless you also take into account the business background against which they were achieved. You are likely to be much less concerned if profits decline in a recession than if they decline when the economy is buoyant and your competitors' sales are booming. If you know how a downturn is likely to throw you off your plan, then you have a standard to judge your performance during such a downturn and a better idea of what to do about it.

18.2 Financial Planning Models

Financial planners often use a financial planning model to help them explore the consequences of alternative financial strategies. These models range from simple models, such as the one presented later in this chapter, to models that incorporate hundreds of equations.

Financial planning models support the financial planning process by making it easier and cheaper to construct forecast financial statements. The models automate an important part of planning that would otherwise be boring, time-consuming, and labour-intensive.

It used to consume large amounts of computer time and require high-priced talent to program these financial planning models. These days, standard spreadsheet programs such as Microsoft Excel are regularly used to solve complex financial planning problems.

COMPONENTS OF A FINANCIAL PLANNING MODEL

A completed financial plan for a large company is a substantial document. A smaller corporation's plan has the same elements but less detail. For the smallest, youngest businesses, financial plans may be entirely in the financial manager's head. However, the basic elements of the plans will be similar for firms of any size.

Financial plans include three components: inputs, the planning model, and outputs. The relationship among these components is represented in Figure 18.1. Let's look at these components in turn.

Inputs. The inputs to the financial plan consist of the firm's current financial statements and its forecasts about the future. Usually, the principal forecast is the likely growth in sales, since many of the other variables such as labour requirements and inventory levels are tied to sales. These forecasts are only in part the responsibility of the financial manager. Obviously, the marketing department will play a key role in forecasting sales. In addition, because sales will depend on the state of the overall economy, large firms will seek forecasting help from firms that specialize in preparing macroeconomic and industry forecasts.

The Planning Model. The financial planning model calculates the implications of the manager's forecasts for profits, new investment, and financing. The model consists of equations relating output variables to forecasts. For example, the equations can show how a change in sales is likely to affect costs, working capital, fixed assets, and financing requirements. The financial model could specify that the total cost of goods produced will increase by 80 cents for every $1 increase in total sales, that accounts receivable will be a fixed proportion of sales, and that the firm will need to increase fixed assets by 8 percent for every 10 percent increase in sales.

pro formas Projected or forecast financial statements.

Outputs. The output of the financial model consists of financial statements such as income statements, balance sheets, and cash-flow statements. These statements are called **pro formas,** which means that they are forecasts based on the inputs and the assumptions built into the plan. Usually the output of financial models also includes many of the financial ratios we discussed in the last chapter. These ratios indicate whether the firm will be financially fit and healthy at the end of the planning period.

AN EXAMPLE OF A PLANNING MODEL

We can illustrate the basic components of a planning model with a very simple example. In the next section we will start to add some complexity.

FIGURE 18.1
The components of a financial plan

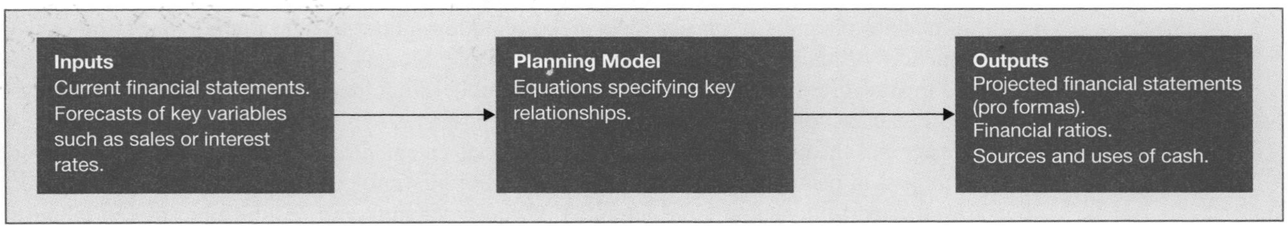

TABLE 18.1
Financial statements of Executive Cheese Company for the past year

INCOME STATEMENT			
Sales			$1,200
Costs			1,000
Net income			$ 200
BALANCE SHEET, YEAR-END			
Assets	$2,000	Debt	$ 800
		Equity	1,200
Total	$2,000	Total	$2,000

Suppose that Executive Cheese has prepared the simple balance sheet and income statement shown in Table 18.1. The firm's financial planners forecast that total sales next year will increase by 10 percent from this year's level. They expect that costs will be a fixed proportion of sales, so they too will increase by 10 percent. Almost all the forecasts for Executive Cheese are proportional to the forecast of sales. Such models are therefore called **percentage of sales models.** The result is the pro forma, or forecast, income statement in Table 18.2, which shows that next year's income will be $200 × 1.10 = $220.

percentage of sales models Planning model in which sales forecasts are the driving variables and most other variables are proportional to sales.

Executive Cheese has no spare capacity, and in order to sustain this higher level of output, it must increase plant and equipment by 10 percent, or $200. Therefore, the left-hand side of the balance sheet, which lists total assets, must increase to $2,200. What about the right-hand side? The firm must decide how it intends to finance its new assets. Suppose it decides to maintain its current debt-equity ratio. To do this, both debt and equity must be increased by the same percentage. We have already figured out that assets must grow by 10 percent, and since the balance sheet must balance, both debt and equity must also grow by 10 percent. This implies the firm must issue $80 in additional debt, 10 percent of the original debt of $800. Also, equity must increase by $120, 10 percent of the original $1,200 in equity. However, no new equity needs to be issued. The 10 percent increase in equity can be accomplished by retaining $120 of net income. The pro forma balance sheet for this financing plan is in Table 18.2.[2]

This raises a question, however. If income is forecast at $220, why does equity increase by only $120? The answer is that the firm must be planning to pay a dividend of $220 – $120 = $100. Notice that this dividend payment is not chosen independently but is a

TABLE 18.2
Pro forma financial statements of Executive Cheese for the next year, with fixed debt-equity ratio

PRO FORMA INCOME STATEMENT			
Sales			$1,320
Costs			1,100
Net income			$ 220
PRO FORMA BALANCE SHEET			
Assets	$2,200	Debt	$ 880
		Equity	1,320
Total	$2,200	Total	$2,200

[2] The new financing required can be figured out another way. If the debt-equity ratio is fixed, so too is the debt-asset ratio. The current debt-asset ratio is 800/2,000, or 40 percent. This tells us that the $200 increase in assets must be financed with 40 percent new debt, .4 × $200 = $80, and 60 percent new equity, .6 × $200 = $120, the same values we found above.

TABLE 18.3
Pro forma balance sheet of Executive Cheese, with dividends fixed at $180 and debt used as the balancing item

NEW PRO FORMA BALANCE SHEET			
Assets	$2,200	Debt	$ 960
		Equity	1,240
Total	$2,200	Total	$2,200

consequence of the other decisions. Given the company's need for funds and its decision to maintain the debt-equity ratio, dividend policy is completely determined. Any other dividend payment would be inconsistent with the two conditions that (1) the right-hand side of the balance sheet increase by $200, and (2) both debt and equity increase by 10 percent. For this reason we call dividends the **balancing item,** or *plug.* The balancing item is the variable that adjusts to make the sources of funds equal to the uses.

balancing item Variable that adjusts to maintain the consistency of a financial plan. Also called the *plug.*

Of course, most firms would be reluctant to vary dividends simply because they have a temporary need for cash; instead, they like to maintain a steady progression of dividends. In this case Executive Cheese could commit to some other dividend payment and allow the debt-equity ratio to vary. The amount of debt would therefore become the balancing item.

For example, suppose the firm commits to a dividend level of $180, and raises any extra money it needs by an issue of debt. In this case the amount of debt becomes the balancing item. With the dividend set at $180, the addition to retained earnings would be only $40, so the firm would have to issue $160 in new debt to help pay for the additional $200 of assets. Table 18.3 is the new balance sheet.

Is the second plan better than the first? It's hard to give a simple answer. The choice of dividend payment depends partly on how investors will interpret the decision. If last year's dividend was only $50, investors might regard a dividend payment of $100 as a sign of a confident management; if last year's dividend was $150, investors might not be so content with a payment of $100. The alternative of paying $180 in dividends and making up the shortfall by issuing more debt leaves the company with a debt-equity ratio of 77 percent. That is unlikely to make your bankers edgy but you may worry about how long you can continue to finance expansion predominantly by borrowing.

Our example shows how experiments with a financial model, including changes in the model's balancing item, can raise important financial questions. But the model does not answer these questions.

Financial models ensure consistency between growth assumptions and financing plans, but they do not identify the best financing plan.

CHECK POINT 18.1

Suppose that the firm is prevented by bond covenants from issuing more debt. It is committed to increasing assets by 10 percent to support the forecast increase in sales, and it strongly believes that a dividend payment of $180 is in the best interests of the firm. What must be the balancing item? What is the implication for the firm's financing activities in the next year?

AN IMPROVED MODEL

Now that you have grasped the idea behind financial planning models, we can move on to a more sophisticated example.

Table 18.4 shows current (year-end 2002) financial statements for Executive Fruit Company. Judging by these figures, the company is ordinary in almost all respects. Its

TABLE 18.4
Financial statements for Executive Fruit Co., 2002 (figures in thousands)

INCOME STATEMENT		Comment
Revenue	$2,000	
Cost of goods sold	1,800	90% of sales
EBIT	200	Difference = 10% of sales
Interest	40	10% of debt at start of year
Earnings before taxes	160	EBIT – interest
Corporate tax	64	40% of (EBIT – interest)
Net income	$ 96	EBIT – interest – taxes
Dividends	$ 64	Payout ratio = ⅔
Addition to retained earnings	$ 32	Net income – dividends
BALANCE SHEET		
Assets		
Net working capital	$ 200	10% of sales
Fixed assets	800	40% of sales
Total assets	$1,000	50% of sales
Liabilities and shareholders' equity		
Long-term debt	$ 400	
Shareholders' equity	600	
Total liabilities and shareholders' equity	$1,000	Equals total assets

earnings before interest and taxes were 10 percent of sales revenue. Net income was $96,000 after payment of taxes and 10 percent interest on $400,000 of long-term debt. The company paid out two-thirds of its net income as dividends.

Next to each item on the financial statements in Table 18.4 we have entered a comment about the relationship between that variable and sales. In most cases, the comment gives the value of each item as a percentage of sales. This may be useful for forecasting purposes. For example, it would be reasonable to assume that cost of goods sold will remain at 90 percent of sales even if sales grow by 10 percent next year. Similarly, it is reasonable to assume that net working capital will remain at 10 percent of sales.

On the other hand, the fact that long-term debt currently is 20 percent of sales does not mean that we should assume that this ratio will continue to hold next period. Many alternative financing plans with varying combinations of debt issues, equity issues, and dividend payouts may be considered without affecting the firm's operations.

Now suppose that you are asked to prepare pro forma financial statements for Executive Fruit for 2003. You are told to assume that (1) sales and operating costs are expected to be up 10 percent over 2002, (2) interest rates will remain at their current level, (3) the firm will stick to its traditional dividend policy of paying out two-thirds of earnings, and (4) fixed assets and net working capital will need to increase by 10 percent to support the larger sales volume.

In Table 18.5 we present the resulting first-stage pro forma calculations for Executive Fruit. These calculations show what would happen if the size of the firm increases along with sales, but at this preliminary stage, the plan does not specify a particular mix of new security issues.

Without any security issues, the balance sheet will not balance: assets will increase to $1,100,000 while debt plus shareholders' equity will amount to only $1,036,000. Somehow the firm will need to raise an extra $64,000 to help pay for the increase in assets. In this first

TABLE 18.5
First-stage pro forma statements for Executive Fruit Co., 2003 (figures in thousands)

FIRST-STAGE PRO FORMA INCOME STATEMENT		
		Comment
Revenue	$2,200	10% higher
Cost of goods sold	1,980	10% higher
EBIT	220	10% higher
Interest	40	Unchanged
Earnings before taxes	180	EBIT – interest
Corporate tax	72	40% of (EBIT – interest)
Net income	$ 108	EBIT – interest – taxes
Dividends	$ 72	⅔ of net income
Addition to retained earnings	$ 36	Net income – dividends

FIRST-STAGE PRO FORMA BALANCE SHEET		
Assets		
Net working capital	$ 220	10% higher
Fixed assets	880	10% higher
Total assets	$1,100	10% higher
Liabilities and shareholders' equity		
Long-term debt	$ 400	Temporarily held fixed
Shareholders' equity	636	Increased by addition to retained earnings
Total liabilities and shareholders' equity	$1,036	Sum of debt plus equity
Required external financing	$ 64	Balancing item or plug (= $1,100 – $1,036)

pass, external financing is the balancing item. Given the firm's growth forecasts and its dividend policy, the financial plan calculates how much money the firm needs to raise.

In the second-stage pro forma, the firm must decide on the financing mix that best meets its needs for additional funds. It must choose some combination of new debt and/or new equity that supports the contemplated acquisition of additional assets. For example, it could issue $64,000 of equity or debt, or it could choose to maintain its long-term debt-equity ratio at two-thirds by issuing both debt and equity.

Table 18.6 shows the second-stage pro forma balance sheet if the required funds are raised by issuing $64,000 of debt. Therefore, in Table 18.6, debt is treated as the balancing

TABLE 18.6
Second-stage pro forma balance sheet for Executive Fruit Co., 2003, with debt as the balancing item (figures in thousands)

SECOND-STAGE PRO FORMA BALANCE SHEET		
		Comment
Assets		
Net working capital	$ 220	10% higher
Fixed assets	880	10% higher
Total assets	$1,100	10% higher
Liabilities and shareholders' equity		
Long-term debt	$ 464	16% higher (new borrowing = $64; this is the balancing item)
Shareholders' equity	$ 636	Increased by addition to retained earnings
Total liabilities and shareholders' equity	$1,100	Again equals total assets

TABLE 18.7
Pro forma statement of sources and uses of funds for Executive Fruit, 2003 (figures in thousands)

Sources		Uses	
Retained earnings	$ 36	Investment in net working capital	$ 20
New borrowing	64	Investment in fixed assets	80
Total sources	$100	Total uses	$100

item. Notice that while the plan requires the firm to specify a financing plan *consistent* with its growth projections, it does not provide guidance as to the *best* financing mix.

Table 18.7 sets out the firm's sources and uses of funds. It shows that the firm requires an extra investment of $20,000 in working capital and $80,000 in fixed assets. Therefore, it needs $100,000 from retained earnings and new security issues. Retained earnings are $36,000, so $64,000 must be raised from the capital markets. Under the financing plan presented in Table 18.6, the firm borrows the entire $64,000. Tables 18.8 and 18.9 use the information in tables 18.4 and 18.6 to show cash flow from assets (free cash flow) and cash flow to bondholders and shareholders.[3] Table 18.8 clarifies that Executive Fruit will generate more than enough cash flow from its operating activities to cover the required investments in net working capital and fixed assets, leaving it with $8,000 in free cash flow. In Table 18.9, we see that the company needs to borrow $64,000 to produce sufficient cash to pay the promised dividend payment of $72,000.

We have spared you the trouble of actually calculating the figures necessary for tables 18.5, 18.7, 18.8, and 18.9. The calculations do not take more than a few minutes for this simple example, *provided* you set up the calculations correctly and make no arithmetic mistakes. If that time requirement seems trivial, remember that in reality you probably would be asked for four similar sets of statements covering each year from 2003 to 2006. Probably you would be asked for alternative projections under different assumptions (for example, 5 percent instead of 10 percent growth rate of revenue) or different financial strategies (for example, freezing dividends at their 2002 level of $64,000). This would be far more time-consuming. Moreover, actual plans will have many more line items than this simple one. Building a model and letting the computer toil in your place has obvious attractions.

Figure 18.2 is the spreadsheet we used for the Executive Fruit model. Column B contains the values that appear in Table 18.5, and column C presents the formulas that we used to obtain those values. Notice that we assumed the firm would maintain its dividend payout ratio at two-thirds (cell B13) and that we hold debt fixed at $400 (cell B23) and set shareholders' equity (cell B24) equal to its original value plus the addition to retained earnings from cell B14. These assumptions mean that the firm issues neither new debt nor new equity. As a result, the total of debt plus equity (cell B25) does not match the total assets (cell B20) necessary to support the assumed growth in sales. The difference between assets and total financing shows up as required external financing (cell B27).

Now that the spreadsheet is set up, it is easy to explore the consequences of various assumptions. For example, you can change the assumed growth rate (cell B3) or

TABLE 18.8
Pro forma cash flow from assets for Executive Fruit, 2003 (figures in thousands)

Pro Forma Cash Flow from Assets, 2003	
Net income	$108
Less: Investment in net working capital	− 20
Less: Investment in fixed assets	− 8
Total cash flow from assets	=$ 8

[3] Cash flow from assets (free cash flow) and cash flow to bondholders and shareholders are discussed in Chapter 2.

FIGURE 18.2
Executive Fruit spreadsheet

	A	B	C
1			
2			**Formula**
3	Assumed growth rate	0.1	0.1
4			
5	**INCOME STATEMENT**		
6	Revenue	2200	2000*(1+B3)
7	Cost of goods sold	1980	1800*(1+B3)
8	EBIT	220	B6-B7
9	Interest expense	40	0.1*B23
10	Earnings before taxes	180	B8-B9
11	Taxes	72	0.4*B10
12	Net income	108	B10-B11
13	Dividends	72	B12*(2/3)
14	Addition to retained earnings	36	B12-B13
15			
16	**BALANCE SHEET**		
17	Assets		
18	Net working capital	220	0.1*B6
19	Fixed assets	880	0.4*B6
20	Total assets	1100	B18 + B19
21			
22	Liabilities and equity		
23	Long-term debt	400	400
24	Shareholders' equity	636	600+B14
25	Total liabilities and shareholders' equity	1036	B23+B24
26			
27	Required external finance	64	B20-B25

TABLE 18.9
Pro forma cash flow to bondholders and shareholders for Executive Fruit, 2003 (figures in thousands)

Pro Forma Cash Flow to Bondholders and Shareholders, 2003	
New borrowing	–$64
Dividends	72
Total cash flow to bondholders and shareholders	$ 8

experiment with different policies, such as changing the dividend payout ratio or forcing debt or equity finance (or both) to absorb the required external financing.

CHECK POINT 18.2

a. Suppose that Executive Fruit is committed to its expansion plans and to its dividend policy. It also wishes to maintain its debt-equity ratio at two-thirds. What are the implications for external financing?

b. If the company is prepared to freeze dividends at the 2002 level, how much external financing would be needed?

18.3

Planners Beware

PITFALLS IN MODEL DESIGN

The Executive Fruit model is still too simple for practical application. You probably have already noticed several ways to improve it. For example, we ignored the capital cost allowance, CCA, associated with the fixed asset. CCA is important because it provides a tax shield. If Executive Fruit deducts CCA before calculating its tax bill, it could plow back more money into new investments and would need to borrow less. We also ignored the fact that there would probably be some interest to pay in 2003 on the new borrowing, which would cut into the cash for new investment.

You would certainly want to make these obvious improvements. But beware: there is always the temptation to make a model bigger and more detailed. You may end up with an exhaustive model that is too cumbersome for routine use.

Exhaustive detail gets in the way of the intended use of corporate planning models, which is to project the financial consequences of a variety of strategies and assumptions. The fascination of detail, if you give in to it, distracts attention from crucial decisions like stock issues and dividend policy and allocation of capital by business area.

THE ASSUMPTION IN PERCENTAGE OF SALES MODELS

When forecasting Executive Fruit's capital requirements, we assumed that both fixed assets and working capital increase proportionately with sales. For example, line (a) in Figure 18.3 shows that net working capital is a constant 10 percent of sales.

Percentage of sales models are useful first approximations for financial planning. However, in reality, assets may not be proportional to sales. For example, we will see in Chapter 20 that important components of working capital such as inventories and cash balances will generally rise *less* than proportionately with sales. Suppose that Executive Fruit looks back at past variations in sales and estimates that on average a \$1 rise in sales requires only a \$.075 increase in net working capital. Line (b) in Figure 18.3 shows the level of working capital

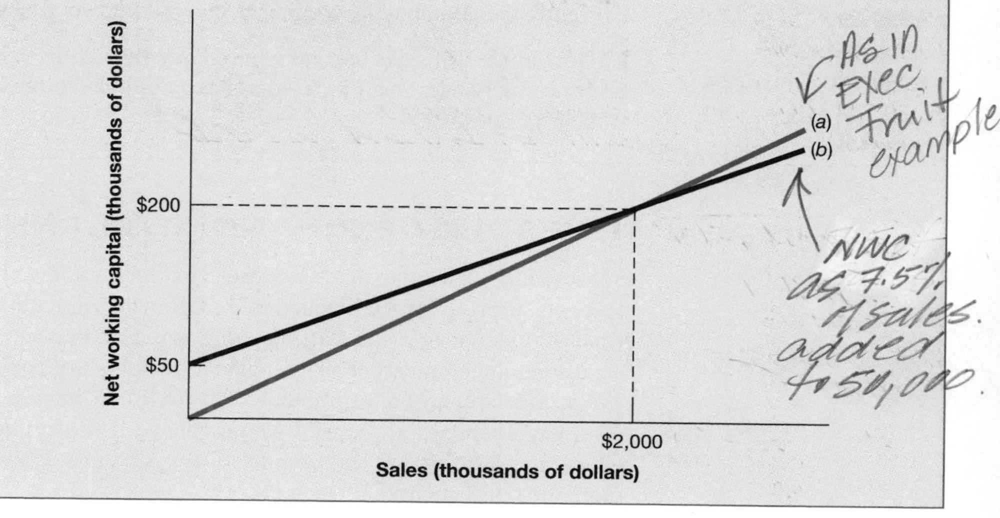

FIGURE 18.3
Net working capital (NWC) as a function of sales: line (a) shows net working capital equal to .10 × sales. Line (b) depicts net working capital as \$50,000 + (.075 × sales), so that NWC increases less than proportionately with sales.

FIGURE 18.4
If factories are operating below full capacity, sales can increase without investment in fixed assets (point A). Beyond some sales level (point B), new capacity must be added.

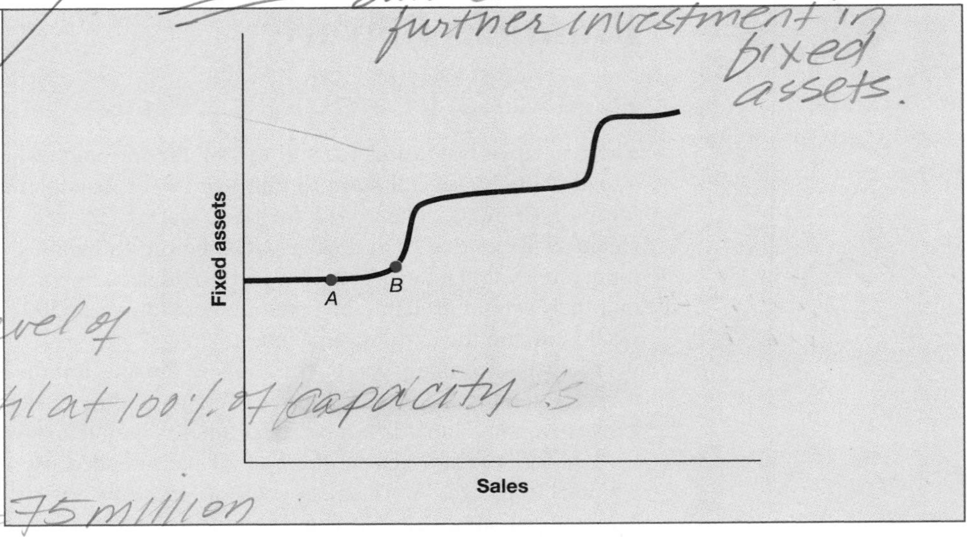

that would now be needed for different levels of sales. To allow for this in the Executive Fruit model, we would need to set net working capital equal to ($50,000 + .075 × sales).

A further complication is that typically fixed assets such as plant and equipment are not added in small increments as sales increase. Instead, the picture is more likely to resemble Figure 18.4. If Executive Fruit's factories are operating at less than full capacity (point *A*, for example), then the firm can expand sales without any additional investment in plant. Ultimately, however, if sales continue to increase, say beyond point *B*, Executive Fruit will need to add new capacity. This is shown by the occasional large changes to fixed assets in Figure 18.4. These "lumpy" changes to fixed assets need to be recognized when devising the financial plan. If there is considerable excess capacity, even rapid sales growth may not require big additions to fixed assets. On the other hand, if the firm is already operating at capacity, even small sales growth may call for large investment in plant and equipment.

CHECK POINT 18.3

Carter Tools has $50 million invested in fixed assets and generates sales of $60 million. Currently the company is working at only 80 percent of capacity.

a. How much can sales expand without any further investment in fixed assets?
b. How much investment in fixed assets would be required to support a 50 percent expansion in sales?

THE ROLE OF FINANCIAL PLANNING MODELS

Models such as the one that we constructed for Executive Fruit help the financial manager to avoid surprises. If the planned rate of growth will require the company to raise external finance, the manager can start planning how best to do so.

We commented earlier that financial planners are concerned about unlikely events as well as likely ones. For example, Executive Fruit's manager may wish to consider how the company's capital requirement would change if profit margins come under pressure and the company generated less cash from its operations. Planning models make it easy to explore the consequences of such events.

However, there are limits to what you can learn from planning models. Although they help to trace through the consequences of alternative plans, they do not tell the manager which plan is best. For example, we saw that Executive Fruit is proposing to grow its sales and earnings per share. Is that good news for shareholders? Well, not necessarily; it depends on the opportunity cost of the additional capital that the company needs to achieve that growth. In 2003 the company proposes to invest $100,000 in fixed assets and working capital. This extra investment is expected to generate $12,000 of additional income, equivalent to a return of 12 percent on the new investment. If the cost of that capital is less than 12 percent, the new investment will have a positive NPV and will add to shareholder wealth. But suppose that the cost of capital is higher at, say, 15 percent. In this case Executive Fruit's investment makes shareholders *worse off,* even though the company is recording steady growth in earnings per share and dividends. Executive Fruit's planning model tells us how much money the firm must raise to fund the planned growth, but it cannot tell us whether that growth contributes to shareholder value. Nor can it tell us whether the company should raise the cash by issuing new debt or equity.

CHECK POINT 18.4

Which of the following questions will a financial plan help to answer?

a. Is the firm's assumption for asset growth consistent with its plans for debt and equity issues and dividend policy?
b. Will accounts receivable increase in direct proportion to sales?
c. Will the contemplated debt-equity mix maximize the value of the firm?

18.4 External Financing and Growth

SEE BOX P. 558

Financial *plans* force managers to be consistent in their goals for growth, investments, and financing. The nearby Finance in Action box describes how one company was brought to its knees when it did not plan sufficiently for the cash that would be required to support its ambitions.

Financial *models,* such as the one that we have developed for Executive Fruit, can help managers trace through the financial consequences of their growth plans and avoid such disasters. But there is a danger that the complexities of a full-blown financial model can obscure the basic issues. Therefore, managers also use some simple rules of thumb to draw out the relationship between a firm's growth objectives and its requirement for external financing.

Recall that in 2002 Executive Fruit started the year with $1,000,000 of fixed assets and net working capital and it had $2,000,000 of sales. In other words, each dollar of sales required $.50 of net assets. The company forecasts that sales next year will increase by $200,000. Therefore, if the ratio of sales to net assets remains constant, assets will need to rise by .50 × 200,000 = $100,000.[4] Part of this increase can be financed by additional retained earnings, which are forecast to be $36,000. So the amount of external finance needed is

$$\begin{aligned}\text{Required external financing} &= \text{(net assets/sales)} \times \text{increase in sales} \\ &\quad - \text{addition to retained earnings} \\ &= .50 \times 200{,}000 - 36{,}000 = \$64{,}000\end{aligned}$$

[4] However, remember our earlier warning that the ratio of sales to net assets may change as the firm grows.

FINANCE IN ACTION

The Bankruptcy of W.T. Grant: A Failure in Planning

W.T. Grant was the largest and one of the most successful department store chains in the United States with 1,200 stores, 83,000 employees, and $1.8 billion of sales. Yet, in 1975, the company filed for bankruptcy, in what *Business Week* termed "the most significant bankruptcy in U.S. history."

The seeds of Grant's difficulties were sown in the mid-1960s when the company foresaw a shift in shopping habits from inner-city areas to out-of-town centres. The company decided to embark on a rapid expansion policy that involved opening up new stores in suburban areas. In addition to making a substantial investment in new buildings, the company needed to ensure that the new stores were stocked with merchandise and it encouraged customers by extending credit more freely. As a result, the company's investment in inventories and receivables more than doubled between 1967 and 1974.

W.T. Grant's expansion plan led to impressive growth. Sales grew from $900 million in 1967 to $1.8 billion in 1974. For a while, profits also boomed, growing from $63 million in 1967 to a peak of $90 million in 1970. Shareholders were delighted. By 1971 the share price had reached a high of $71, up from $20 in 1967.

To achieve the growth in sales, W.T. Grant needed to invest a total of $650 million in fixed assets, inventories, and receivables. However, it takes time for new stores to reach full profitability, so while profits initially increased, the return on capital fell. At the same time, the company decided to increase its dividends in line with earnings. This meant that the bulk of the money to finance the new investment had to be raised from the capital market. W.T. Grant was reluctant to sell more shares and chose instead to raise the money by issuing more than $400 million of new debt.

By 1974 Grant's debt-equity ratio had reached 1.8. This figure was high, but not alarmingly so. The problem was that rapid expansion combined with recession had begun to eat into profits. Almost all the operating cash flows in 1974 were used to service the company's debt. Yet the company insisted on maintaining the dividend on its common stock. Effectively, it was borrowing to pay the dividend. By the next year, W.T. Grant could no longer service its mountain of debt and had to seek postponement of payments on a $600 million bank loan.

W.T. Grant's failure was partly a failure of financial planning. It did not recognize and plan for the huge cash drain involved in its expansion strategy.

Sometimes it is useful to write this calculation in terms of growth rates. Executive Fruit's forecast increase in sales is equivalent to a rise of 10 percent. So, if net assets are a constant proportion of sales, the higher sales volume will also require a 10 percent addition to net assets. Thus

$$\begin{aligned}\text{New investment} &= \text{growth rate} \times \text{initial assets}\\ \$100{,}000 &= .10 \times \$1{,}000{,}000\end{aligned}$$

Part of the funds to pay for the new assets will be provided by the addition to retained earnings. The remainder must come from external financing. Therefore,

$$\begin{aligned}\textbf{Required external financing} &= \textbf{new investment} - \textbf{addition to retained earnings} \qquad (18.1)\\ &= (\textbf{growth rate} \times \textbf{assets}) - \textbf{addition to retained earnings}\end{aligned}$$

This simple equation highlights that the amount of external financing depends on the firm's projected growth. The faster the firm grows, the more it needs to invest and therefore the more it needs to raise new capital.

In the case of Executive Fruit,

$$\begin{aligned}\text{Required external financing} &= (.10 \times \$1{,}000{,}000) - \$36{,}000\\ &= \$100{,}000 - \$36{,}000\\ &= \$64{,}000\end{aligned}$$

FIGURE 18.5
External financing and growth

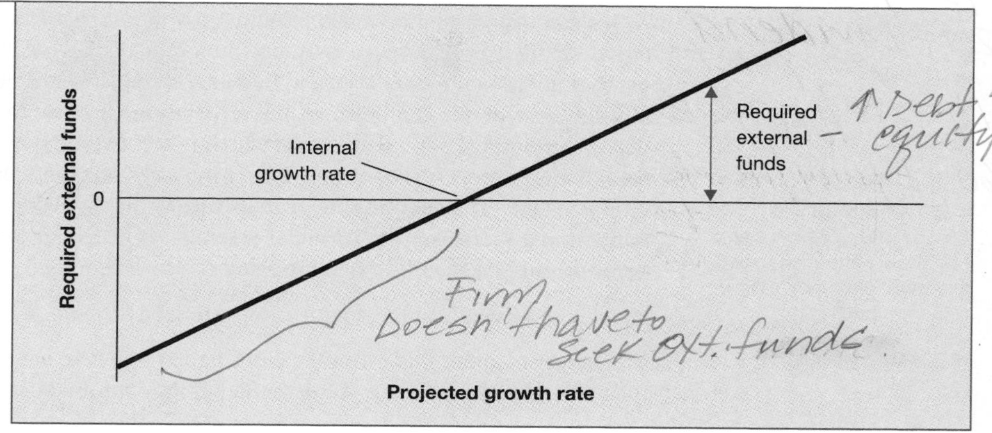

If Executive Fruit's assets remain a constant percentage of sales, then the company needs to raise \$64,000 to produce a 10 percent addition to sales.

The sloping line in Figure 18.5 illustrates how required external financing increases with the growth rate. At low growth rates, the firm generates more funds than necessary for expansion. In this sense, its requirement for further external funds is negative. It may choose to use its surplus to pay off some of its debt or buy back its stock. In fact, the vertical intercept in Figure 18.5, at zero growth, is the negative of the addition to retained earnings. When growth is zero, no funds are needed for expansion, so all the addition to retained earnings are surplus.

As the firm's projected growth rate increases, more funds are needed to pay for the necessary investments. Therefore, the plot in Figure 18.5 is upward-sloping. For high rates of growth the firm must issue new securities to pay for new investments.

Where the sloping line crosses the horizontal axis, external financing is zero: the firm is growing as fast as possible without resorting to new security issues. This is called the **internal growth rate.** The growth rate is "internal" because it can be maintained without resort to additional external sources of capital.

internal growth rate Maximum rate of growth without external financing.

Notice that if we set required external financing to zero, we can solve for the internal growth rate as

$$\textbf{Internal growth rate} = \frac{\textbf{addition to retained earnings}}{\textbf{assets}} \qquad (18.2)$$

Thus the firm's rate of growth without additional external sources of capital will equal the ratio of the addition to retained earnings to assets. This means that a firm with a high volume of retained earnings relative to its assets can generate a higher growth rate without needing to raise more capital.

We can gain more insight into what determines the internal growth rate by multiplying the top and bottom of the expression for internal growth by *net income* and *equity* as follows:

$$\begin{aligned}\textbf{Internal growth rate} &= \frac{\textbf{addition to retained earnings}}{\textbf{net income}} \times \frac{\textbf{net income}}{\textbf{equity}} \times \frac{\textbf{equity}}{\textbf{assets}} \\ &= \textbf{plowback ratio} \times \textbf{return on equity} \times \frac{\textbf{equity}}{\textbf{assets}}\end{aligned} \qquad (18.3)$$

A firm can achieve a higher growth rate without raising external capital if (1) it plows back a high proportion of its earnings, (2) it has a high return on equity (ROE), and (3) it has a low debt-to-asset ratio.

Instead of focusing on the maximum growth rate that can be supported without *any* external financing, firms also may be interested in the growth rate that can be sustained without additional *equity* issues. Of course, if the firm is able to issue enough debt, virtually any growth rate can be financed. It makes more sense to assume that the firm has settled on an optimal capital structure which it will maintain even as equity is augmented by the addition to retained earnings. The firm issues only enough debt to keep its debt-equity ratio constant. The **sustainable growth rate** is the highest growth rate the firm can maintain without increasing its financial leverage. It turns out that the sustainable growth rate depends only on the plowback ratio and return on equity:[5]

sustainable growth rate Steady rate at which a firm can grow without changing leverage; plowback ratio × return on equity.

$$\textbf{Sustainable growth rate} = \textbf{plowback ratio} \times \textbf{return on equity} \tag{18.4}$$

You may remember this formula from Chapter 5, where we first used it when we looked at the valuation of the firm and the dividend discount model.

EXAMPLE 18.1 *Internal and Sustainable Growth for Executive Fruit*

Executive Fruit has chosen a plowback ratio of one-third for 2003. As Table 18.4 shows, at the end of 2002, the outstanding assets were 1,000 and outstanding equity was 600. It also shows Executive Fruit's addition to retained earnings was 32. Hence, equity at the start of 2002 must have been 600 – 32 = 568. With net income of 96, Executive Fruit's return on equity[6] is ROE = 96/568 = .169. Its ratio of equity to assets is 600/1,000 = .60. If it is unwilling to raise new capital, its maximum growth rate is

$$\begin{aligned}\text{Internal growth rate} &= \text{plowback ratio} \times \text{ROE} \times \frac{\text{equity}}{\text{assets}}\\ &= \frac{1}{3} \times .169 \times .60\\ &= .0338, \text{ or } 3.38\%\end{aligned}$$

[5] Here is a proof:

$$\text{Required equity issues} = \text{growth rate} \times \text{assets} - \text{addition to retained earnings} - \text{new debt issues}$$

We find the sustainable growth rate by setting required new equity issues to zero and solving for growth:

$$\begin{aligned}\text{Sustainable growth rate} &= \frac{\text{addition to retained earnings} + \text{new debt issues}}{\text{assets}}\\ &= \frac{\text{addition to retained earnings} + \text{new debt issues}}{\text{debt} + \text{equity}}\end{aligned}$$

However, because both debt and equity are growing at the same rate, new debt issues must equal the additional retained earnings multiplied by the ratio of debt to equity, D/E. Therefore, we can write the sustainable growth rate as

$$\begin{aligned}\text{Sustainable growth rate} &= \frac{\text{addition to retained earnings} \times (1 + D/E)}{\text{debt} + \text{equity}}\\ &= \frac{\text{addition to retained earnings} \times (1 + D/E)}{\text{equity} \times (1 + D/E)} = \frac{\text{addition to retained earnings}}{\text{equity}}\\ &= \frac{\text{addition to retained earnings}}{\text{net income}} \times \frac{\text{net income}}{\text{equity}} = \text{plowback} \times \text{ROE}\end{aligned}$$

[6] Note that when we calculate internal or sustainable growth rates, ROE is properly measured by earnings as a proportion of equity at the *start* of the year rather than as a proportion of either end-of-year equity or the *average* of outstanding equity at the start and end of the year.

This is much less than the 10 percent growth it projects, which explains its need for external financing.

If Executive is prepared to maintain its current ratio of equity to total assets, it can issue an additional 40 cents of debt for every 60 cents of retained earnings. In this case, the maximum growth rate would be

$$\text{Substainable growth rate} = \text{plowback ratio} \times \text{ROE}$$
$$= \frac{1}{3} \times .169$$
$$= .0563, \text{ or } 5.63\%$$

Executive's planned growth rate of 10 percent requires not only new borrowing but an increase in the debt-equity ratio. In the long run the company will need to either issue new equity or cut back its rate of growth.[7]

CHECK POINT 18.5

Suppose Executive Fruit reduces the dividend payout ratio to 25 percent. Calculate its growth rate assuming that (1) no new debt or equity will be issued and (2) the firm maintains its equity-to-asset ratio at .60. For each case, check that the calculated growth rate is correct.

18.5 Summary

1. What are the contents and uses of a financial plan?

Most firms take financial planning seriously and devote considerable resources to it. The tangible product of the planning process is a financial plan describing the firm's financial strategy and projecting its future consequences by means of **pro forma** balance sheets, income statements, and statements of sources and uses of funds. The plan establishes financial goals and is a benchmark for evaluating subsequent performance. Usually it also describes why that strategy was chosen and how the plan's financial goals are to be achieved.

Planning, if it is done right, forces the financial manager to think about events that could upset the firm's progress and to devise strategies to be held in reserve for counterattack when unfortunate surprises occur. Planning is more than forecasting, because forecasting deals with the most likely outcome. Planners also have to think about events that may occur even though they are unlikely.

In long-range, or strategic, planning, the **planning horizon** is usually 5 years or more. This kind of planning deals with aggregate decisions; for example, the planner would worry about whether the broadax division should commit to heavy capital investment and rapid growth, but not whether the division should choose machine tool A versus tool B. In fact, planners must be constantly on guard against the fascination of detail, because giving in to it means slighting crucial issues like investment strategy, debt policy, and the choice of a target dividend payout ratio.

The plan is the end result. The process that produces the plan is valuable in its own right. Planning forces the financial manager to consider the combined effects of all the firm's investment and financing decisions. This is important because these decisions interact and should not be made independently.

2. How are financial planning models constructed?

There is no theory or model that leads straight to *the* optimal financial strategy. Consequently, financial planning proceeds by trial and error. Many different strategies may be projected under a range of assumptions about the future before one strategy is finally chosen. The dozens of separate projections that may be made during this trial-and-error process generate a heavy load of arithmetic and paperwork. Firms have responded by developing corporate planning models to forecast the financial consequences of specified strategies and assumptions about the future.

[7] As the firm issues more debt, its return on equity also changes. But Executive would need to have a very high debt-equity ratio before it could support a growth rate of 10 percent a year and maintain a constant debt ratio.

One very simple starting point may be a **percentage of sales model** in which many key variables are assumed to be directly proportional to sales. Planning models are efficient and widely used. But remember that there is not much finance in them. Their primary purpose is to produce accounting statements. The models do not search for the best financial strategy, they only trace out the consequences of a strategy specified by the model user.

2. **What is the effect of growth on the need for external financing?**

Higher growth rates will lead to greater need for investments in fixed assets and working capital. The **internal growth rate** is the maximum rate that the firm can grow if it relies entirely on reinvested profits to finance its growth, that is, the maximum rate of growth without requiring external financing. The **sustainable growth rate** is the rate at which the firm can grow without changing its leverage ratio.

RELATED WEB LINKS

www.bsa.cbsc.org Gateway to information on starting a business in Canada
www.cbsc.org/osbw/workshop.html Workshop on setting up a business
www.cbsc.org/osbw/finance.html Sources of financing for a start-up business
www.cbsc.org/osbw/whyplan.html Information on cash-flow planning

KEY TERMS

planning horizon	544	percentage of sales models	549	balancing item	550
pro formas	548			internal growth rate	559
				sustainable growth rate	560

QUESTIONS AND PROBLEMS

*Answers in Appendix B

BASIC

*1. **Financial Planning.** True or false? Explain.
   a. Financial planning should attempt to minimize risk.
   b. The primary aim of financial planning is to obtain better forecasts of future cash flows and earnings.
   c. Financial planning is necessary because financing and investment decisions interact and should not be made independently.
   d. Firms' planning horizons rarely exceed 3 years.
   e. Individual capital investment projects are not considered in a financial plan unless they are very large.
   f. Financial planning requires accurate and consistent forecasting.
   g. Financial planning models should include as much detail as possible.

2. **Financial Models.** What are the dangers and disadvantages of using a financial model? Discuss.

3. **Using Financial Plans.** Corporate financial plans are often used as a basis for judging subsequent performance. What can be learned from such comparisons? What problems might arise and how might you cope with such problems?

*4. **Growth Rates.** Find the sustainable and internal growth rates for a firm with the following ratios: asset turnover = 1.40; net profit margin = 6 percent; interest/sales = 1 percent; payout ratio = 25 percent; equity/assets = .60.

5. **Percentage of Sales Models.** Percentage of sales models usually assume that costs, fixed assets, and working capital all increase at the same rate as sales. When do you think that these assumptions do not make sense? Would you feel happier using a percentage of sales model for short-term or long-term planning?

6. **Relationships among Variables.** Comebaq Computers is aiming to increase its market share by slashing the price of its new range of personal computers. Are costs and assets likely to increase or decrease as a proportion of sales? Explain.

*7. **Balancing Items.** What are the possible choices of balancing items when using a financial planning model? Discuss whether some are generally preferable to others.

8. **Financial Targets.** Managers sometimes state a target growth rate for sales or earnings per share. Do you think that either one makes sense as a corporate goal? If not, why do you think that managers focus on them?

PRACTICE

*9. **Percentage of Sales Models.** Here are the abbreviated financial statements for Planners Peanuts:

INCOME STATEMENT, 2003	
Sales	$2,000
Costs	1,500
Net income	$ 500

BALANCE SHEET, YEAR-END					
	2002	2003		2002	2003
Assets	$2,500	$3,000	Debt	$ 833	$1,000
			Equity	1,667	2,000
Total	$2,500	$3,000	Total	$2,500	$3,000

If sales increase by 20 percent in 2004, and the company uses a strict percentage-of-sales planning model (meaning that all items on the income and balance sheet also increase by 20 percent), what must be the balancing item? What will be its value?

10. **Required External Financing.** If the dividend payout ratio in problem 9 is fixed at 50 percent, calculate the required total external financing for growth rates in 2004 of 15 percent, 20 percent, and 25 percent.

*11. **Feasible Growth Rates.** What is the maximum possible growth rate for Planners Peanuts (see problem 9) if the payout ratio remains at 50 percent and
   a. no external debt or equity is to be issued?
   b. the firm maintains a fixed debt ratio but issues no equity?

12. **Using Percentage of Sales.** Eagle Sports Supply has the following financial statements. Assume that Eagle's assets are proportional to its sales.

INCOME STATEMENT, 2003	
Sales	$950
Costs	250
EBIT	700
Taxes	200
Net income	$500

BALANCE SHEET, YEAR-END					
	2002	2003		2002	2003
Assets	$2,700	$3,000	Debt	$ 900	$1,000
			Equity	1,800	2,000
Total	$2,700	$3,000	Total	$2,700	$3,000

   a. Find Eagle's required external funds if it maintains a dividend payout ratio of 60 percent and plans a growth rate of 15 percent in 2004.
   b. If Eagle chooses not to issue new shares of stock, what variable must be the balancing item? What will its value be?
   c. Now suppose that the firm plans instead to increase long-term debt only to $1,100 and does not wish to issue any new shares of stock. Why must the dividend payment now be the balancing item? What will its value be? What is the dividend payout ratio?

*13. **Feasible Growth Rates.**

a. What is the internal growth rate of Eagle Sports (see problem 12) if the dividend payout ratio is fixed at 60 percent and the equity-to-asset ratio is fixed at two-thirds?

b. What is the sustainable growth rate?

14. **Building Financial Models.** How would Executive Fruit's financial model change if the dividend payout ratio were cut to one-third? Use the revised model to generate a new financial plan for 2003 assuming that debt is the balancing item. Show how the financial statements given in Table 18.6 would change. What would be required external financing?

*15. **Required External Financing.** Executive Fruit's financial manager believes that sales in 2003 could rise by as much as 20 percent or by as little as 5 percent.

a. Recalculate the first-stage pro forma financial statements (Table 18.5) under these two assumptions. How does the rate of growth in revenues affect the firm's need for external funds?

b. Assume any required external funds will be raised by issuing long-term debt and that any surplus funds will be used to retire such debt. Prepare the completed (second-stage) pro forma balance sheet.

16. **Building Financial Models.** The following tables contain financial statements for Dynastatics Corporation. Although the company has not been growing, it now plans to expand and will increase net fixed assets (that is, assets net of depreciation) by $200,000 per year for the next 5 years and forecasts that the ratio of revenues to total assets will remain at 1.5. Annual depreciation is 10 percent of net fixed assets at the start of the year. Fixed costs are expected to remain at $56,000 and variable costs at 80 percent of revenue. The company's policy is to pay out two-thirds of net income as dividends and to maintain a book debt ratio of 25 percent of total capital.

INCOME STATEMENT, 2003
(figures in thousands of dollars)

Revenue		$1,800
Fixed costs		56
Variable costs (80% of revenue)		1,440
Depreciation		80
Interest (8% of beginning-of-year debt)		24
Taxable income		200
Taxes (at 40%)		80
Net income		$ 120
Dividends	$80	
Addition to retained earnings	$40	

BALANCE SHEET, YEAR-END
(figures in thousands of dollars)

	2002	2003
Assets		
Net working capital	$ 400	$ 400
Fixed assets	800	800
Total assets	$1,200	$1,200
Liabilities and shareholders' equity		
Debt	$ 300	$ 300
Equity	900	900
Total liabilities and shareholders' equity	$1,200	$1,200

a. Produce a set of financial statements for 2004. Assume that net working capital will equal 50 percent of fixed assets.

b. Now assume that the balancing item is debt, and that no equity is to be issued. Prepare a completed pro forma balance sheet for 2004. What is the projected debt ratio for 2004?

*17. **Sustainable Growth.** Plank's Plants had net income of $2,000 on sales of $40,000 last year. The firm paid a dividend of $500. Total assets at the end of last year were $100,000, of which $40,000 was financed by debt.

a. What is the firm's sustainable growth rate?

b. If the firm grows at its sustainable growth rate, how much debt will be issued next year?

c. What would be the maximum possible growth rate if the firm did not issue any debt next year?

18. **Sustainable Growth.** A firm has decided that its optimal capital structure is 100 percent equity financed. It perceives its optimal dividend policy to be a 40 percent payout ratio. Asset turnover is sales/assets = .8, the net profit margin is 10 percent, and the firm has a target growth rate of 5 percent.

a. Is the firm's target growth rate consistent with its other goals?

b. If not, by how much does it need to increase asset turnover to achieve its goals?

c. How much would it need to increase the profit margin instead?

*19. **Internal Growth.** Go Go Industries is growing at 30 percent per year. It is all-equity financed and has total assets of $1 million. Its return on equity is 20 percent. Its plowback ratio is 40 percent.

a. What is the internal growth rate?

b. What is the firm's need for external financing this year?

c. By how much would the firm increase its internal growth rate if it reduced its payout ratio to zero?

d. By how much would such a move reduce the need for external financing? What do you conclude about the relationship between dividend policy and requirements for external financing?

20. **Sustainable Growth.** A firm's net profit margin is 10 percent and its asset turnover ratio is .5. It has no debt, has net income of $10 per share, and pays dividends of $4 per share. What is the sustainable growth rate?

*21. **Internal Growth.** An all-equity–financed firm plans to grow at an annual rate of at least 10 percent. Its return on equity is 15 percent. What is the maximum possible dividend payout rate the firm can maintain without resorting to additional equity issues?

22. **Internal Growth.** Suppose the firm in the previous question has a debt-equity ratio of one-third. What is the maximum dividend payout ratio it can maintain without resorting to any external financing?

*23. **Internal Growth.** A firm has an asset turnover ratio of 2.0. Its plowback ratio is 50 percent, and it is all-equity financed. What must its net profit margin be if it wishes to finance 8 percent growth using only internally generated funds?

24. **Internal Growth.** If the net profit margin of the firm in the previous problem is 6 percent, what is the maximum payout ratio that will allow it to grow at 8 percent without resorting to external financing?

*25. **Internal Growth.** If the net profit margin of the firm in problem 23 is 6 percent, what is the maximum possible growth rate that can be sustained without external financing?

26. **Using Percentage of Sales.** The 2003 financial statements for Growth Industries are presented here. Sales and costs in 2004 are projected to be 20 percent higher than in 2003. Both current assets and accounts payable are projected to rise in proportion to sales. The firm is currently operating at full capacity, so it plans to increase fixed assets in proportion to sales. What external financing will be required by the firm? Interest expense in 2004 will equal 10 percent of long-term debt outstanding at the start of the year. The firm will maintain a dividend payout ratio of .4.

INCOME STATEMENT, 2003	
Sales	$200,000
Costs	150,000
EBIT	50,000
Interest expense	10,000
Taxable income	40,000
Taxes (at 35%)	14,000
Net income	$ 26,000
Dividends	10,400
Addition to retained earnings	15,600

BALANCE SHEET, YEAR-END, 2003

Assets		Liabilities	
Current assets		Current liabilities	
Cash	$ 3,000	Accounts payable	$ 10,000
Accounts receivable	8,000	Total current liabilities	10,000
Inventories	29,000	Long-term debt	100,000
Total current assets	$ 40,000	Shareholders' equity	
Net plant and equipment	160,000	Common stock	15,000
		Retained earnings	75,000
Total assets	$200,000	Total liabilities and shareholders' equity	$200,000

CHALLENGE

*27. **Capacity Use and External Financing.** Now suppose that the fixed assets of Growth Industries (from the previous problem) are operating at only 75 percent of capacity. What is required external financing over the next year?

28. **Capacity Use and External Financing.** If Growth Industries from problem 26 is operating at only 75 percent of capacity, how much can sales grow before the firm will need to raise any external funds? Assume that once fixed assets are operating at capacity, they will need to grow thereafter in direct proportion to sales.

*29. **Internal Growth.** We will see in Chapter 20 that for many firms, cash and inventory needs may grow less than proportionally with sales. When we recognize this fact, will the firm's internal growth rate be higher or lower than the level predicted by the formula

$$\text{Internal growth rate} = \frac{\text{addition to retained earnings}}{\text{assets}}$$

30. **Spreadsheet Problem.** Use a spreadsheet like that in Figure 18.2 to answer the following questions about Executive Fruit:
    a. What would be required external financing if the growth rate is 15 percent and the dividend payout ratio is 60 percent?
    b. Given the assumptions in part (a), what would be the amount of debt and equity issued if the firm wants to maintain its debt-equity ratio at a level of two-thirds?
    c. What formulas would you put in cells C23 and C24 of the spreadsheet in Figure 18.2 to maintain the debt-equity ratio at two-thirds, while forcing the balance sheet to balance (that is, forcing debt + equity = total assets)?

INTERNET PROBLEMS

1. Go to strategis.ic.gc.ca/sc_mangb/stepstogrowth/engdoc/homepage.php, a website designed to help entrepreneurs get the funding they need. What are the nine steps suggested to securing the needed financing? What role does financial planning play in the process of raising funds for a business? What other important activities does the entrepreneur engage in? To see the steps in detail, read the case study for NewTech at strategis.ic.gc.ca/sc_mangb/stepstogrowth/engdoc/newtech/nt-0-1.php. Don't forget to look at the accompanying forecast (pro forma) financial statements, key assumptions, and sensitivity analysis.
2. Thinking about starting a business? Do you think you would enjoy running your own business? Go to www.cba.ca/eng/Tools/Brochures/tools_small.cfm, the Canadian Bankers Assocation website. Click on "Know Yourself" and answer the questions.

SOLUTIONS TO CHECK POINTS

18.1 The firm cannot issue debt, and its dividend payment is effectively fixed, which limits the addition to retained earnings to $40. Therefore, the balancing item must be new equity issues. The firm must raise $200 – $40 = $160 through equity sales in order to finance its plans for $200 in asset acquisitions.

18.2 a. The *total amount* of external financing is unchanged, since the dividend payout is unchanged. The $100,000 increase in total assets will now be financed by a mixture of debt and equity. If the debt-equity ratio is to remain at two-thirds, the firm will need to increase equity by $60,000 and debt by $40,000. Since addition to retained earnings already increases shareholders' equity by $36,000, the firm needs to issue an additional $24,000 of new equity and $40,000 of debt.

b. If dividends are frozen at $64,000 instead of increasing to $72,000 as envisioned in Table 18.5, then the required external funds fall by $8,000 to $56,000.

18.3 a. The company currently runs at 80 percent of capacity given the current level of fixed assets. Sales can increase until the company is at 100 percent of capacity; therefore, sales can increase to $60 million × (100/80) = $75 million.

b. If sales were to increase by 50 percent to $90 million, new fixed assets would need to be added. The ratio of assets to sales when the company is operating at 100 percent of capacity (from part a) is $50 million/$75 million = 2/3. Therefore, to support sales of $90 million, the company needs at least $90 million × 2/3 = $60 million of fixed assets. This calls for a $10 million investment in additional fixed assets.

18.4 a. This question is answered by the planning model. Given assumptions for asset growth, the model will show the need for external financing, and this value can be compared to the firm's plans for such financing.

b. Such a relationship may be assumed and built into the model. However, the model does not help to determine whether it is a reasonable assumption.

c. Financial models do not shed light on the best capital structure. They can tell us only whether contemplated financing decisions are consistent with asset growth.

18.5 a. If the payout ratio were reduced to 25 percent, the maximum growth rate assuming no external financing would be .75 × 16 percent × .6 = 7.2 percent. With a growth rate of 7.2 percent, the forecast increase in assets is .072 × 1,000 = 72. Since no new debt is raised, this increase in assets must be financed with equity. Equity must increase 72. Does the firm produce sufficient additional retained earnings?

Since forecast ROE is 16 percent and starting equity, 2,000, net income is forecast to be .16 × 2,000 = 96. Plowback is 75 percent, giving additional retained earnings of .75 × 96 = 72. So the company can grow at 7.2 percent if it uses only its internally generated funds (addition to retained earnings).

b. If the firm also can issue enough debt to maintain its equity-to-asset ratio unchanged, the sustainable growth rate will be .75 × 16 percent = 12 percent. At 12 percent growth, additional assets of .12 × 1,000 = 120 are needed. Of this increase in assets, 40 percent is financed with new debt. Equity must increase 120 – .4 × 120 = 72. Does the firm produce sufficient additional retained earnings?

In (a) we know that the forecast addition to retained earnings is 72. So the firm can grow at 12 percent if it borrows to maintain its capital structure and uses the additional retained earnings.

MINICASE

Jane Green, CEO and sole shareholder of Dog Delights, pored over the brochure showing the fully automated baking system capable of producing 1,000 dog biscuits an hour. "Wow!" she thought, "If we had that equipment, we could double our annual production. Just think of all the dog biscuits we could sell!" Then reality returned. The equipment cost $1.2 million and would be completely worn out in 10 years. How could the company finance such a huge expenditure? On the other hand, production was at capacity. Without new equipment, sales would only grow with inflation, expected to be 2 percent per year. The current resale value of the old equipment was $50,000.

Jane turned her attention to the recent financial statements of her company, shown in tables 18.10 to 18.12. What would be a reasonable sales forecast? Jane figured that if the company really worked hard, it could increase the nominal sales 20 percent in each of the next 2 years and maybe a further 10 percent in the third year. Sales would grow with inflation after that. They might have to hire a new salesperson and increase the advertising budget, which she expects would cost an incremental $100,000 a year. However, with new equipment, operating costs will be lower. Perhaps, Jane thought, we could shave 2 percentage points off our COGS/sales ratio. But what is our current COGS/sales? Have we been successful in controlling costs over the past few years? Our production manager has been off work a lot. Depreciation on the new machinery would run about $75,000 a year and she knew their tax rate was 35 percent.

Jane then turned her attention to the balance sheet. She noted that the company's stated credit terms were net 35 days. She remembered a conversation with the director of sales who had said that their competitors' average collection period was 40 days. The sales director recommended that Dog Delights be more relaxed in their collection efforts. Jane wondered how relaxed they had become. Inventories were another matter she needed to think about. She didn't think the new equipment would require any additional inventories, except to support the higher level of production.

Jane wondered how much of the $1.2 million the company could generate from its operations and how much she would need to raise from external sources. The manager of MoneyBank had said they could borrow at 8 percent if the debt-equity ratio was less than .6. Any borrowing beyond that would carry a 10 percent interest rate. And they had to continue to repay $10,000 a year on the existing 6 percent loan from Friendly Bank.

Jane knew she could ask her wealthy Uncle George for some equity financing. She knew he liked dividends and figured he would ask for dividends equal to 5 percent of his investment. On the other hand, he might want to meddle in the operation of the business. Did she really want to put up with him? The more of his money she used, the worse it would be.

Jane knew that she would have to review the recent financial performance of Dog Delight carefully. Perhaps they could implement some changes to improve their operating performance? Then she would estimate the NPV of the equipment purchase. Given the risks of the investment, she decided to use a WACC of 9 percent. If the resulting NPV was positive, she would then decide how to finance the purchase. She would consider the balance sheet, income statement and cash flows for the next 3 years. She figured her sales forecast was the most likely scenario but knew she had to consider the consequences of only 5 percent sales growth a year after the equipment purchase. "What to do?" she wondered as she settled down to work.

TABLE 18.10

INCOME STATEMENT FOR DOG DELIGHTS
for year-ends January 31, 2002 to 2004
(figures in thousands of dollars)

	2002	2003	2004
Sales	2,500	2,774	3,190
Cost of goods sold	1,850	2,081	2,488
Selling, general, and administrative expenses	250	305	383
Depreciation expense	16	18	19
Earnings before interest and taxes (EBIT)	384	370	300
Interest expense	27	26	26
Taxable income	357	344	274
Income taxes	125	120	96
Net income	232	224	178
Allocation of net income			
Addition to retained earnings	202	194	148
Dividends	30	30	30

TABLE 18.11

BALANCE SHEET FOR DOG DELIGHTS
for year-ends January 31, 2002 to 2004
(figures in thousands of dollars)

Assets	**2002**	**2003**	**2004**
Current assets			
Cash and marketable securities	50	176	240
Receivables	274	342	481
Inventories	313	370	456
Total current assets	636	888	1,176
Fixed assets			
Property, plant, and equipment	900	900	900
Less accumulated depreciation	187	205	224
Net fixed assets	713	695	676
Total assets	1,349	1,583	1,852
Liabilities and Shareholders' Equity	**2002**	**2003**	**2004**
Current liabilities			
Debt due for repayment	10	10	10
Accounts payable	152	200	327
Other current liabilities	26	28	32
Total current liabilities	188	238	369
Long-term debt	440	430	420
Shareholders' equity			
Common stock	70	70	70
Retained earnings	651	845	993
Total shareholders' equity	721	915	1,063
Total liabilities and shareholders' equity	1,349	1,582	1,852

TABLE 18.12

CASH FLOW FROM ASSETS AND CASH FLOW TO BONDHOLDERS AND SHAREHOLDERS (figures in thousands of dollars)

Cash flow from assets	**2003**	**2004**
Net income	224	178
Plus: Depreciation	18	19
Cash flow from operations	242	197
Less: Increase in noncash net working capital	76	93
Less: Capital expenditures	0	0
Cash flow from assets	166	104
Cash flow to bondholders and shareholders		
Repayment of debt	10	10
Dividends	30	30
Increase in cash	126	64
Total cash flow to bondholders and shareholders	166	104

CHAPTER 19

Working Capital Management and Short-Term Plannings

19.1 Working Capital

19.2 Links between Long-Term and Short-Term Financing

19.3 Tracing Changes in Cash and Working Capital

19.4 Cash Budgeting

19.5 A Short-Term Financing Plan

19.6 Sources of Short-Term Financing

19.7 The Cost of Bank Loans

19.8 Summary

Much of this book is devoted to long-term financial decisions such as capital budgeting and the choice of capital structure. These decisions are called *long-term* for two reasons. First, they usually involve long-lived assets or liabilities. Second, they are not easily reversed and thus may commit the firm to a particular course of action for several years.

Short-term financial decisions generally involve short-lived assets and liabilities, and usually they are easily reversed. Compare, for example, a 60-day bank loan for $50 million with a $50 million issue of 20-year bonds. The bank loan is clearly a short-term decision. The firm can repay it 2 months later and be right back where it started. A firm might conceivably issue a 20-year bond in January and retire it in March, but it would be extremely inconvenient and expensive to do so. In practice, such a bond issue is a long-term decision, not only because of the bond's 20-year maturity, but because the decision to issue it cannot be reversed on short notice.

A financial manager responsible for short-term financial decisions does not have to look far into the future. The decision to take the 60-day bank loan could properly be based on cash-flow forecasts for the next few months only. The bond-issue decision will normally reflect forecast cash requirements 5, 10, or more years into the future.

Short-term financial decisions do not involve many of the difficult conceptual issues encountered elsewhere in this book. In a sense, short-term decisions are easier than long-term decisions—but they are not less important. A firm can identify extremely valuable capital investment opportunities, find the precise optimal debt ratio, follow the perfect dividend policy, and yet founder because no one bothers to raise the cash to pay this year's bills. Hence the need for short-term planning.

In this chapter, we will review the major classes of short-term assets and liabilities, show how long-term financing decisions affect the firm's short-term financial planning, and describe how financial managers trace changes in cash and working capital. We will also describe how managers forecast month-by-month cash requirements or surpluses and how they develop short-term investment and financing strategies.

After studying this chapter you should be able to

- Understand *why* the firm needs to invest in net working capital.
- Show how long-term financing policy affects short-term financing requirements.
- Trace a firm's sources and uses of cash and evaluate its need for short-term borrowing.
- Develop a short-term financing plan that meets the firm's need for cash.

Working Capital

THE COMPONENTS OF WORKING CAPITAL

Short-term, or *current,* assets and liabilities are collectively known as *working capital.* Table 19.1 gives a breakdown of current assets and liabilities for all nonfinancial industries in Canada in the third quarter of 1998. Total current assets were over $391 billion and total current liabilities were $335 billion.

Current Assets. One important current asset is *accounts receivable.* Accounts receivable arise because companies do not usually expect customers to pay for their purchases immediately. These unpaid bills are a valuable asset that companies expect to be able to turn into cash in the near future. The bulk of accounts receivable consists of unpaid bills from sales to other companies and are known as *trade credit.* The remainder arises from the sale of goods to the final consumer. These are known as *consumer credit.*

Another important current asset is *inventory.* Inventories may consist of raw materials, work in process, or finished goods awaiting sale and shipment. Table 19.1 shows that firms in Canada had about 8 percent more invested in accounts receivable than in inventories in 1998.

The remaining current assets are cash and other current assets. The cash consists partly of dollar bills, but most of the cash is in the form of bank deposits. These may be *demand deposits* (money in chequing accounts that the firm can pay out immediately) and *time deposits* (money in savings accounts that can be paid out only with a delay). Other current assets include items such as marketable securities. The principal marketable security is *commercial paper* (short-term unsecured debt sold by other firms). Other securities

TABLE 19.1
Current assets and liabilities of the Canadian nonfinancial industry sector, third quarter 1998 (figures in millions)

Current Assets		Current Liabilities	
Cash	$ 60,485	Accounts payable and accrued liabilities	$196,580
Accounts receivable	169,706	Other current liabilities	138,657
Inventories	156,331		
Other current assets	5,122		
Total	$391,644	Total	$335,237

Note: Net working capital (current assets – current liabilities) equals $391,644 – $335,650 = $56,407 million.

Source: Table created using CANSIM series label numbers: D86228, D86229, D86230, D86237, D86252, D86254 (Statistics Canada, Financial Statistics for Enterprises, Total Non-Financial Industries).

include *Treasury bills,* which are short-term debts sold by the Canadian government, and provincial and local government securities.

In managing their cash, companies face much the same problem you do. There are always advantages to holding large amounts of ready cash—they reduce the risk of running out of cash and having to borrow more on short notice. On the other hand, there is a cost to holding idle cash balances rather than putting the money to work earning interest. In Chapter 20 we will tell you how the financial manager collects and pays out cash and decides on an optimal cash balance.

Current Liabilities. We have seen that a company's principal current asset consists of unpaid bills. One firm's credit must be another's debit. Therefore, it is not surprising that a company's principal current liability consists of *accounts payable*—that is, outstanding payments due to other companies.

The other major current liability consists of short-term borrowing. We will have more to say about this later in the chapter.

WORKING CAPITAL AND THE CASH CONVERSION CYCLE

net working capital
Current assets minus current liabilities. Often called *working capital.*

The difference between current assets and current liabilities is known as **net working capital,** but financial managers often refer to the difference simply (but imprecisely) as *working capital.* Usually current assets exceed current liabilities—that is, firms have positive net working capital. In 1998, for Canadian nonfinancial companies, current assets were on average about 17 percent higher than current liabilities.

To see why firms need net working capital, imagine a small company, Simple Souvenirs, that makes small novelty items for sale at gift shops. It buys raw materials such as leather, beads, and rhinestones for cash, processes them into finished goods like wallets or costume jewelry, and then sells these goods on credit. Figure 19.1 shows the whole cycle of operations.

If you prepare the firm's balance sheet at the beginning of the process, you see cash (a current asset). If you delay a little, you find the cash replaced first by inventories of raw materials and then by inventories of finished goods (also current assets). When the goods are sold, the inventories give way to accounts receivable (another current asset), and finally, when the customers pay their bills, the firm takes out its profit and replenishes the cash balance.

The components of working capital constantly change with the cycle of operations, but the amount of working capital is fixed. This is one reason why net working capital is a useful summary measure of current assets or liabilities.

FIGURE 19.1
Simple cycle of operations

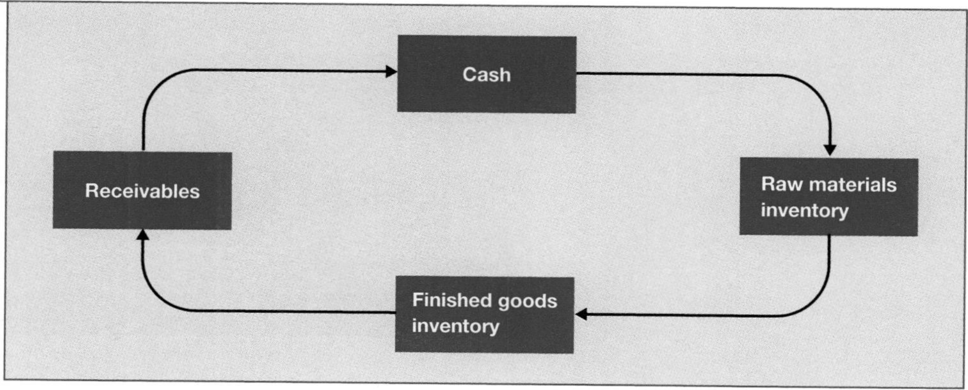

Figure 19.2 depicts four key dates in the production cycle that influence the firm's investment in working capital. The firm starts the cycle by purchasing raw materials, but it does not pay for them immediately. This delay is the *accounts payable period.* The firm processes the raw material and then sells the finished goods. The delay between the initial investment in inventories and the sale date is the *inventory period.* Some time after the firm has sold the goods its customers pay their bills. The delay between the date of sale and the date at which the firm is paid is the *accounts receivable period.*

The top part of Figure 19.2 shows that the *total* delay between initial purchase of raw materials and ultimate payments from customers is the sum of the inventory and accounts receivable periods: first the raw materials must be purchased, processed, and sold, and then the bills must be collected. However, the *net* time that the company is out of cash is reduced by the time it takes to pay its own bills. The length of time between the firm's payment for its raw materials and the collection of payment from the customer is known as the firm's **cash conversion cycle.** To summarize,

cash conversion cycle Period between firm's payment for materials and collection on its sales.

$$\textbf{Cash conversion cycle} = \textbf{(inventory period + receivables period)} - \textbf{accounts payable period} \quad (19.1)$$

The longer the production process, the more cash the firm must keep tied up in inventories. Similarly, the longer it takes customers to pay their bills, the higher the value of accounts receivable. On the other hand, if a firm can delay paying for its own materials, it may reduce the amount of cash it needs. In other words, accounts payable *reduce* net working capital.

In Chapter 17 we showed you how the firm's financial statements can be used to estimate the inventory period, also called days' sales in inventory:

$$\textbf{Inventory period} = \frac{\textbf{average inventory}}{\textbf{annual cost of goods sold/365}} \quad (19.2)$$

The denominator in this equation is the firm's daily output. The ratio of inventory to daily output measures the average number of days from the purchase of the inventories to the final sale.

FIGURE 19.2
Cash conversion cycle

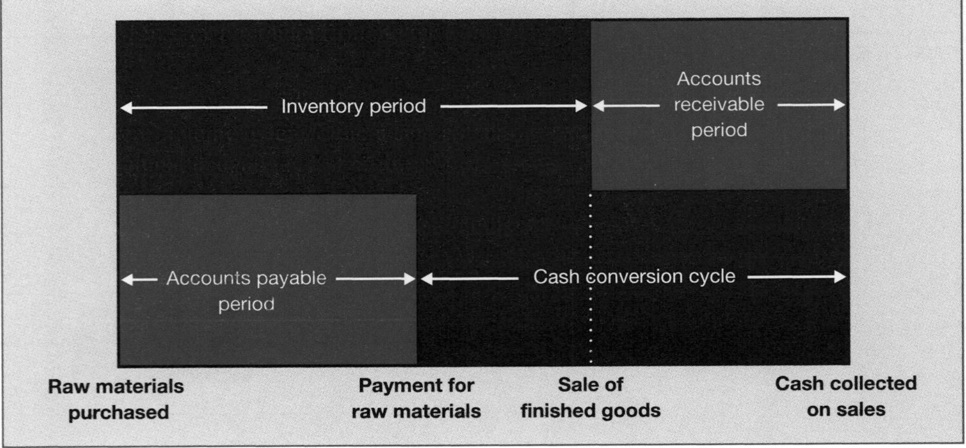

We can estimate the accounts receivable period and the accounts payable period in a similar way:[1]

$$\textbf{Accounts receivable period} = \frac{\textbf{average accounts receivable}}{\textbf{annual sales/365}} \qquad (19.3)$$

$$\textbf{Accounts payable period} = \frac{\textbf{average accounts payable}}{\textbf{annual cost of goods sold/365}} \qquad (19.4)$$

EXAMPLE 19.1 *Cash Conversion Cycle*

Table 19.2 provides the information necessary to compute the cash conversion cycle for nonfinancial firms in Canada in 2001. We can use the table to answer four questions. How long on average does it take Canadian non-finanial firms to produce and sell their product? How long does it take to collect bills? How long does it take to pay bills? And what is the cash conversion cycle?

The delays in collecting cash are given by the inventory and receivables period. The delay in paying bills is given by the payables period. The net delay in collecting payments is the cash conversion cycle. We calculate these periods as follows:

$$\textbf{Inventory period} = \frac{\textbf{average inventory}}{\textbf{annual cost of goods sold/365}} \qquad (19.5)$$

$$= \frac{(208{,}679 + 227{,}886)/2}{1{,}727{,}149/365} = 46.1 \text{ days}$$

$$\textbf{Receivables period} = \frac{\textbf{average accounts receivable}}{\textbf{annual sales/365}} \qquad (19.6)$$

$$= \frac{(182{,}062 + 187{,}450)/2}{1{,}785{,}371/365} = 37.8 \text{ days}$$

$$\textbf{Payables period} = \frac{\textbf{average accounts payable}}{\textbf{annual cost of goods sold/365}} \qquad (19.7)$$

$$= \frac{(256{,}313 + 274{,}992)/2}{1{,}727{,}149/365} = 56.1 \text{ days}$$

The cash conversion cycle is

$$\text{Inventory period} + \text{receivables period} - \text{accounts payable period}$$
$$= 46.1 + 37.8 - 56.1 = 27.8 \text{ days}$$

It is therefore taking Canadian nonfinancial enterprises an average of 28 days, or almost a month, from the time they lay out money on inventories to collect payment from their customers.

CHECK POINT 19.1

a. Suppose Canadian nonfinancial enterprises are able to reduce inventory levels to a year-average value of $150,000 million and average accounts receivable to $125,000 million. By how many days will this reduce the cash conversion cycle?

b. Suppose that with the same level of inventories, accounts receivable, and accounts payable, Canadian nonfinancial enterprises can increase production and sales by 10 percent. What will be the effect on the cash conversion cycle?

[1] Because inventories are valued at cost, we divide inventory levels by cost of goods sold rather than sales revenue to obtain the inventory period. This way, both numerator and denominator are measured by cost. The same reasoning applies to the accounts payable period. On the other hand, because accounts receivable are valued at product price, we divide average receivables by daily sales revenue to find the receivables period.

TABLE 19.2
These data can be used to calculate the cash conversion cycle for Canadian nonfinancial enterprises (figures in millions).

Income Statement Data		**Balance Sheet Data**		
Year Ending, First Quarter 2001			**End of First Quarter 2000**	**End of First Quarter 2001**
Sales	$1,785,371	Inventory	$208,679	$227,886
Cost of goods sold	1,727,149	Accounts receivable	182,062	187,450
		Accounts payable	256,313	274,992

Source: Table created using CANSIM series label numbers: D302059, D302060, D302067, D302085, D302090 (Statistics Canada, Financial Statistics for Enterprises, Total Non-Financial Industries).

THE WORKING CAPITAL TRADE-OFF

Of course the cash conversion cycle is not cast in stone. To a large extent it is within management's control. Working capital can be *managed.* For example, accounts receivable are affected by the terms of credit the firm offers to its customers. You can cut the amount of money tied up in receivables by getting tough with customers who are slow in paying their bills. (You may find, however, that in the future they take their business elsewhere.) Similarly, the firm can reduce its investment in inventories of raw materials. (Here the risk is that it may one day run out of inventories and production will grind to a halt.)

These considerations show that investment in working capital has both costs and benefits. For example, the cost of the firm's investment in receivables is the interest that could have been earned if customers had paid their bills earlier. The firm also forgoes interest income when it holds idle cash balances rather than putting the money to work in marketable securities. The cost of holding inventory includes not only the opportunity cost of capital but also storage and insurance costs and the risk of spoilage or obsolescence. All of these **carrying costs** encourage firms to hold current assets to a minimum.

carrying costs Costs of maintaining current assets, including opportunity cost of capital.

shortage costs Costs incurred from shortages in current assets.

While carrying costs discourage large investments in current assets, too low a level of current assets makes it more likely that the firm will face **shortage costs.** For example, if the firm runs out of inventory of raw materials, it may have to shut down production. Similarly, a producer holding a small finished goods inventory is more likely to be caught short, unable to fill orders promptly. There are also disadvantages to holding small "inventories" of cash. If the firm runs out of cash, it may have to sell securities and incur unnecessary trading costs. The firm may also maintain too low a level of accounts receivable. If the firm tries to minimize accounts receivable by restricting credit sales, it may lose customers.

An important job of the financial manager is to strike a balance between the costs and benefits of current assets, that is, to find the level of current assets that minimizes the sum of carrying costs and shortage costs.

The trade-off between carrying costs and shortage costs is depicted in Figure 19.3. The figure measures the amount of current assets on the horizontal axis and dollar costs on the vertical axis. With zero current assets, there are no carrying costs. However, as investment in current assets goes up, there is a corresponding increase in carrying costs. Shortage costs, on the other hand, are high at low levels of current assets but decline steadily as current assets increase. Total costs, shown as the sum of carrying costs and shortage costs, are lowest (at TC*) when the investment in current assets is at CA*. This is also the optimal level of investment in current assets.

In Chapter 17 we pointed out that in recent years many managers have tried to make their staff more aware of the cost of the capital that is used in the business. So, when they

FIGURE 19.3
The working capital trade-off and the optimal investment in current assets

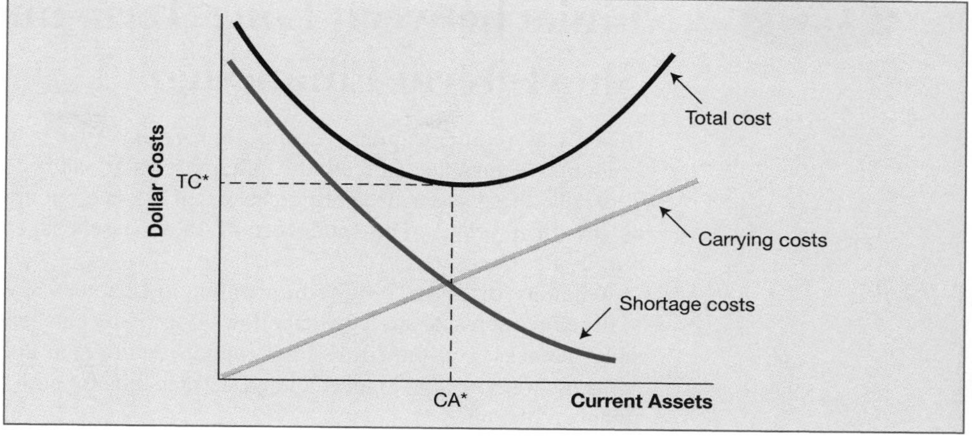

review the performance of each part of their business, they deduct the cost of the capital employed from its profits. This measure is known as *residual income* or *economic value added (EVA),* which is the term coined by the consulting firm Stern Stewart. Firms that employ EVA to measure performance have often discovered that they can make large savings on working capital. Herman Miller Corporation, the U.S. furniture manufacturer, found that after it introduced EVA, employees became much more conscious of the cash tied up in inventories. One sewing machine operator commented:

> *We used to have these stacks of fabric sitting here on the tables until we needed them . . . We were going to use the fabric anyway, so who cares that we're buying it and stacking it up there? Now no one has excess fabric. They only have stuff we're working on today. And it's changed the way we connect with suppliers, and we're having [them] deliver fabric more often.*[2]

The company also started to look at how rapidly customers paid their bills. It found that, any time an item was missing from an order, the customer would delay payment until all the pieces had been delivered. When the company cleared up the problem of missing items, it made its customers happier and it collected the cash faster.[3]

We will look more carefully at the costs and benefits of working capital in the next two chapters.

CHECK POINT 19.2

How will the following affect the size of the firm's optimal investment in current assets?

a. The interest rate rises from 6 percent to 8 percent.
b. A just-in-time inventory system is introduced that reduces the risk of inventory shortages.
c. Customers pressure the firm for a more lenient credit sales policy.

[2] A. Ehrbar, *EVA: The Real Key to Creating Wealth* (New York: John Wiley & Sons, 1998), pp. 130–131.

[3] A. Ehrbar and G. Bennett Stewart III, "The EVA Revolution," *Journal of Applied Corporate Finance* 12 (Summer 1999), pp. 18–31.

19.2 Links between Long-Term and Short-Term Financing

Businesses require capital—that is, money invested in plant, machinery, inventories, accounts receivable, and all the other assets it takes to run a company efficiently. Typically, these assets are not purchased all at once but are obtained gradually over time as the firm grows. The total cost of these assets is called the firm's *total capital requirement.*

When we discussed long-term planning in Chapter 18, we showed how the firm needs to develop a sensible strategy that allows it to finance its long-term goals and weather possible setbacks. But the firm's total capital requirement does not grow smoothly and the company must be able to meet temporary demands for cash. This is the focus of short-term financial planning.

Figure 19.4 illustrates the growth in the firm's total capital requirements. The upward-sloping line shows that as the business grows, it is likely to need additional fixed assets and current assets. You can think of this trendline as showing the base level of capital that is required. In addition to this base capital requirement, there may be seasonal fluctuations in the business that require an additional investment in current assets. Thus the wavy line in the illustration shows that the total capital requirement peaks late in each year. In practice, there would also be week-to-week and month-to-month fluctuations in the capital requirement, but these are not shown in Figure 19.4.

The total capital requirement can be met through either long- or short-term financing. When long-term financing does not cover the total capital requirement, the firm must raise short-term capital to make up the difference. When long-term financing *more* than covers the total capital requirement, the firm has surplus cash available for short-term investment. Thus the amount of long-term financing raised, given the total capital requirement, determines whether the firm is a short-term borrower or lender.

The three panels in Figure 19.5 illustrate this. Each depicts a different long-term financing strategy. The "relaxed strategy" in panel *a* always implies a short-term cash surplus. This surplus will be invested in marketable securities. The "restrictive" policy illustrated in panel *c* implies a permanent need for short-term borrowing. Finally, panel *b* illustrates an intermediate strategy: the firm has spare cash, which it can lend out during

FIGURE 19.4
The firm's total capital requirement grows over time. It also exhibits seasonal variation around the trend.

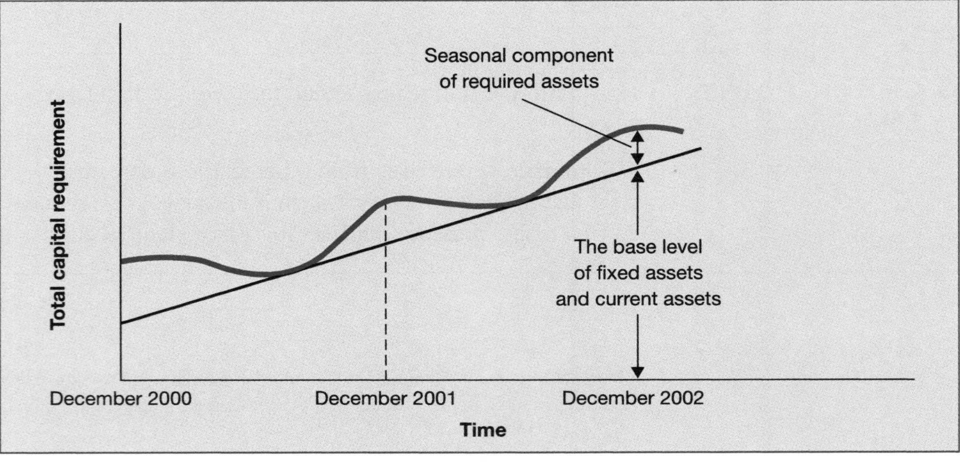

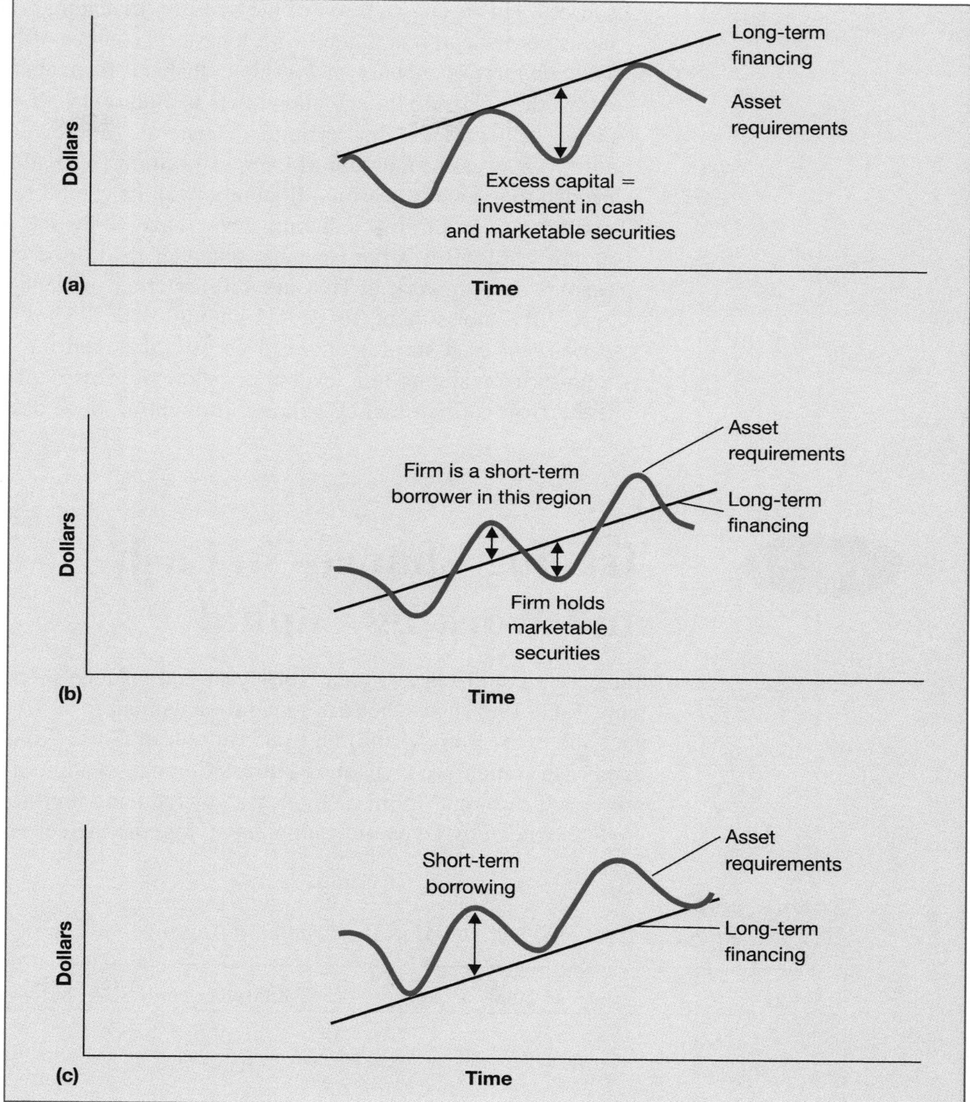

FIGURE 19.5
Alternative approaches to long- versus short-term financing.
(a) Relaxed strategy, where the firm is always a short-term lender.
(b) Middle-of-the-road policy.
(c) Restrictive policy, where the firm is always a short-term borrower.

the part of the year when total capital requirements are relatively low, but it is a borrower during the rest of the year when capital requirements are relatively high.

What is the *best* level of long-term financing relative to the total capital requirement? It is hard to say. We can make several practical observations, however.

1. *Matching maturities.* Most financial managers attempt to "match maturities" of assets and liabilities. That is, they finance long-lived assets like plant and machinery with long-term borrowing and equity. Short-term assets like inventory and accounts receivable are financed with short-term bank loans or by issuing short-term debt like commercial paper.
2. *Permanent working-capital requirements.* Most firms have a permanent investment in net working capital (current assets less current liabilities). By this we mean that they plan to have a positive amount of working capital at all times. This is financed from long-term

sources. This is an extension of the maturity-matching principle. Since the working capital is permanent, it is funded with long-term sources of financing.

3. *The comforts of surplus cash.* Many financial managers would feel more comfortable under the relaxed strategy illustrated in Figure 19.5*a* than the restrictive strategy in panel *c*. Consider, for example, General Motors. At the end of 1998 it was sitting on a cash mountain of over $10 billion (US), almost certainly far more than it needed to meet any seasonal fluctuations in its capital requirements. Firms with such a surplus of long-term financing never have to worry about borrowing to pay next month's bills. But is the financial manager paid to be comfortable? Firms usually put surplus cash to work in Treasury bills or other marketable securities. This is *at best* a zero-NPV investment for a tax-paying firm.[4] Thus we think that firms with a *permanent* cash surplus ought to go on a diet, retiring long-term securities to reduce long-term financing to a level at or below the firm's total capital requirement. That is, if the firm is described by panel *a*, it ought to move down to panel *b*, or perhaps even lower.

19.3 Tracing Changes in Cash and Working Capital

Table 19.3 compares 2000 and 2001 year-end balance sheets for Dynamic Mattress Company. Table 19.4 shows the firm's income statement for 2001. Note that Dynamic's cash balance increases from $4 million to $5 million in 2001. What caused this increase? Did the extra cash come from Dynamic Mattress Company's additional long-term borrowing? From reinvested earnings? From cash released by reducing inventory? Perhaps it came from extra credit extended by Dynamic's suppliers. (Note the increase in accounts payable.)

TABLE 19.3
Year-end balance sheets for Dynamic Mattress Company (figures in millions)

Assets	2000	2001	Liabilities and Shareholders' Equity	2000	2001
Current assets			Current liabilities		
Cash	$ 4	$ 5	Bank loans	$ 5	$ 0
Marketable securities	0	5	Accounts payable	20	27
Inventory	26	25	Total current liabilities	$25	$ 27
Accounts receivable	25	30	Long-term debt	5	12
Total current assets	$55	$ 65	Net worth (equity and retained earnings)	65	76
Fixed assets			Total liabilities and owners' equity	$95	$115
Gross investment	$56	$ 70			
Less depreciation	16	20			
Net fixed assets	$40	$ 50			
Total assets	$95	$115			

[4] Why do we say *at best* zero NPV? Not because we worry that the Treasury bills may be overpriced. Instead, we worry that when the firm holds Treasury bills, the interest income is subject to double taxation; first at the corporate level, and then again at the personal level when the income is passed through to investors as dividends. The extra layer of taxation can make corporate holdings of Treasury bills a negative-NPV investment, even if the bills would provide a fair rate of interest to an individual investor.

TABLE 19.4
Income statement for Dynamic Mattress Company, 2001 (figures in millions)

Sales	$350
Operating costs	321
Depreciation	4
EBIT	25
Interest	1
Pretax income	24
Tax at 50 percent	12
Net income	$ 12

Note: Dividend = $1 million; retained earnings = $11 million.

TABLE 19.5
Sources and uses of cash for Dynamic Mattress Company, 2001 (figures in millions)

Sources	
Issued long-term debt	$ 7
Reduced inventories	1
Increased accounts payable	7
Cash from operations	
Net income	12
Depreciation	4
Total sources	$31
Uses	
Repaid short-term bank loan	$ 5
Invested in fixed assets	14
Purchased marketable securities	5
Increased accounts receivable	5
Dividend	1
Total uses	$30
Increase in cash balance	$ 1

The correct answer? All of the above. There is rarely any point in linking a particular source of funds with a particular use. Instead, financial analysts list the various sources and uses of cash in a statement like the one shown in Table 19.5. The statement shows that Dynamic *generated* cash from the following sources:

1. It issued $7 million of long-term debt.
2. It reduced inventory, releasing $1 million.
3. It increased its accounts payable, in effect borrowing an additional $7 million from its suppliers.
4. By far the largest source of cash was Dynamic's operations, which generated $16 million. Note that the $12 million net income reported in Table 19.4 understates cash flow because depreciation is deducted in calculating income. Depreciation is *not* a cash outlay. Thus it must be added back in order to obtain operating cash flow.

Dynamic *used* cash for the following purposes:

1. It paid a $1 million dividend. (Note: The $11 million increase in Dynamic's equity is due to retained earnings: $12 million of equity income, less the $1 million dividend.)
2. It repaid a $5 million short-term bank loan.
3. It invested $14 million. This shows up as the increase in gross fixed assets in Table 19.3.
4. It purchased $5 million of marketable securities.
5. It allowed accounts receivable to expand by $5 million. In effect, it lent this additional amount to its customers.

CHECK POINT 19.3

How will the following affect *cash* and *net working capital?*

a. The firm takes out a short-term bank loan and uses the funds to pay off some of its accounts payable.
b. The firm uses cash on hand to buy raw materials.
c. The firm repurchases outstanding shares of stock.
d. The firm sells long-term bonds and puts the proceeds in its bank account.

Cash Budgeting

The financial manager's task is to forecast *future* sources and uses of cash. These forecasts serve two purposes. First, they alert the financial manager to future cash needs. Second, the cash-flow forecasts provide a standard, or budget, against which subsequent performance can be judged.

There are several ways to produce a quarterly cash budget. Many large firms have developed elaborate "corporate models"; others use a spreadsheet program to plan their cash needs. The procedures of smaller firms may be less formal. But no matter what method is chosen, there are three common steps to preparing a cash budget:

Step 1. Forecast the sources of cash. The largest inflow of cash comes from payments by the firm's customers.
Step 2. Forecast uses of cash.
Step 3. Calculate whether the firm is facing a cash shortage or surplus.

The financial *plan* sets out a strategy for investing a cash surplus or financing any deficit. We will illustrate these issues by continuing the example of Dynamic Mattress.

FORECAST SOURCES OF CASH

Most of Dynamic's cash inflow comes from the sale of mattresses. We therefore start with a sales forecast by quarter for 2002:[5]

Quarter:	First	Second	Third	Fourth
Sales, millions of dollars	87.5	78.5	116	131

However, unless customers pay cash on delivery, sales become accounts receivable before they become cash. Cash flow comes from *collections* on accounts receivable.

Most firms keep track of the average time it takes customers to pay their bills. From this they can forecast what proportion of a quarter's sales is likely to be converted into cash in that quarter and what proportion is likely to be carried over to the next quarter as accounts receivable. This proportion depends on the lags with which customers pay their bills. For example, if customers wait 1 month to pay their bills, then on average one-third of each quarter's bills will not be paid until the following quarter. If the payment delay is 2 months, then two-thirds of quarterly sales will be collected in the following quarter.

Suppose that 80 percent of sales are collected in the immediate quarter and the remaining 20 percent in the next. Table 19.6 shows forecast collections under this assumption.

[5] For simplicity, we present a quarterly forecast. However, most firms would forecast by month instead of by quarter. Sometimes weekly or even daily forecasts are made.

TABLE 19.6
Dynamic Mattress's collections on accounts receivable, 2002 (figures in millions)

	Quarter			
	First	Second	Third	Fourth
1. Receivables at start of period	$30	$ 32.5	$ 30.7	$ 38.2
2. Sales	87.5	78.5	116	131
3. Collections				
Sales in current period (80%)	70	62.8	92.8	104.8
Sales in last period (20%)	15[a]	17.5	15.7	23.2
Total collections	$85	$ 80.3	$108.5	$128
4. Receivables at end of period (4 = 1 + 2 – 3)	$32.5	$ 30.7	$ 38.2	$ 41.2

[a] Sales in the fourth quarter of the previous year were $75 million.

In the first quarter, for example, collections from current sales are 80 percent of $87.5 million, or $70 million. But the firm also collects 20 percent of the previous quarter's sales, or .20 × $75 million = $15 million. Therefore, total collections are $70 million + $15 million = $85 million.

Dynamic started the first quarter with $30 million of accounts receivable. The quarter's sales of $87.5 million were *added* to accounts receivable, but $85 million of collections was *subtracted*. Therefore, as Table 19.6 shows, Dynamic ended the quarter with accounts receivable of $30 million + $87.5 million – $85 million = $32.5 million. The general formula is

$$\textbf{Ending accounts receivable} = \begin{array}{c}\textbf{beginning accounts receivable}\\ \textbf{+ sales – collections}\end{array} \qquad (19.8)$$

The top section of Table 19.7 shows forecast sources of cash for Dynamic Mattress. Collection of receivables is the main source but it is not the only one. Perhaps the firm plans to dispose of some land or expects a tax refund or payment of an insurance claim. All such items are included as "other" sources. It is also possible that you may raise additional capital by borrowing or selling stock, but we don't want to prejudge that question. Therefore, for the moment we just assume that Dynamic will not raise further long-term finance.

TABLE 19.7
Dynamic Mattress's cash budget for 2002 (figures in millions)

	Quarter			
	First	Second	Third	Fourth
Sources of cash				
Collections on accounts receivable	$ 85	$ 80.3	$108.5	$128
Other	1.5	0	12.5	0
Total sources of cash	$ 86.5	$ 80.3	$121	$128
Uses of cash				
Payments of accounts payable	$ 65	$ 60	$ 55	$ 50
Labour and administrative expenses	30	30	30	30
Capital expenditures	32.5	1.3	5.5	8
Taxes, interest, and dividends	4	4	4.5	5
Total uses of cash	$131.5	$ 95.3	$ 95	$ 93
Net cash inflow equals sources minus uses	–$ 45	–$ 15	+$ 26	+$ 35

FORECAST USES OF CASH

There always seem to be many more uses for cash than there are sources. The second section of Table 19.7 shows how Dynamic expects to use cash. For simplicity, in Table 19.7 we condensed the uses into four categories:

1. *Payments of accounts payable.* Dynamic has to pay its bills for raw materials, parts, electricity, and so on. The cash-flow forecast assumes all these bills are paid on time, although Dynamic could probably delay payment to some extent. Delayed payment is sometimes called *stretching your payables.* Stretching is one source of short-term financing, but for most firms it is an expensive source, because by stretching they lose discounts given to firms that pay promptly. (This is discussed in more detail in Chapter 20.)
2. *Labour, administrative, and other expenses.* This category includes all other regular business expenses.
3. *Capital expenditures.* Note that Dynamic Mattress plans a major outlay of cash in the first quarter to pay for a long-lived asset.
4. *Taxes, interest, and dividend payments.* This includes interest on currently outstanding long-term debt and dividend payments to shareholders.

THE CASH BALANCE

The forecast net inflow of cash (sources minus uses) is shown on the bottom row of Table 19.7. Note the large negative figure for the first quarter: a $45 million forecast *outflow.* There is a smaller forecast outflow in the second quarter and then substantial cash inflows in the second half of the year.

Table 19.8 calculates how much financing Dynamic will have to raise if its cash-flow forecasts are right. It starts the year with $5 million in cash. There is a $45 million cash outflow in the first quarter, and so Dynamic will have to obtain at least $45 million – $5 million = $40 million of additional financing. This would leave the firm with a forecast cash balance of exactly zero at the start of the second quarter.

Most financial managers regard a planned cash balance of zero as driving too close to the edge of the cliff. They establish a *minimum operating cash balance* to absorb unexpected cash inflows and outflows. We will assume that Dynamic's minimum operating cash balance is $5 million. That means it will have to raise $45 million instead of $40 million in the first quarter, and $15 million more in the second quarter. Thus its *cumulative* financing requirement is $60 million in the second quarter. Fortunately, this is the peak; the cumulative requirement declines in the third quarter when its $26 million net cash inflow reduces its cumulative financing requirement to $34 million. (Notice that the

TABLE 19.8
Short-term financing requirements for Dynamic Mattress (figures in millions)

	Cash at start of period	$ 5	–$ 40	–$55	–$29
+	Net cash inflow (from Table 19.7)	– 45	– 15	+ 26	+ 35
=	Cash at end of period[a]	– 40	– 55	– 29	+ 6
	Minimum operating cash balance	5	5	5	5
	Cumulative short-term financing required (minimum cash balance minus cash at end of period)[b]	$45	$ 60	$34	–$ 1

[a] Of course firms cannot literally hold a negative amount of cash. This line shows the amount of cash the firm will have to raise to pay its bills.

[b] A negative sign indicates that no short-term financing is required. Instead the firm has a cash *surplus.*

change in cumulative short-term financing in Table 19.8 equals the net cash inflow in that quarter from Table 19.7.) In the final quarter Dynamic is out of the woods. Its $35 million net cash inflow is enough to eliminate short-term financing and actually increase cash balances above the $5 million minimum acceptable balance.

Before moving on, we offer two general observations about this example:

1. The large cash outflows in the first two quarters do not necessarily spell trouble for Dynamic Mattress. In part they reflect the capital investment made in the first quarter: Dynamic is spending $32.5 million, but it should be acquiring an asset worth that much or more. The cash outflows also reflect low sales in the first half of the year; sales recover in the second half.[6] If this is a predictable seasonal pattern, the firm should have no trouble borrowing to help it get through the slow months.
2. Table 19.7 is only a best guess about future cash flows. It is a good idea to think about the *uncertainty* in your estimates. For example, you could undertake a sensitivity analysis, in which you inspect how Dynamic's cash requirements would be affected by a shortfall in sales or by a delay in collections.

CHECK POINT 19.4

Calculate Dynamic Mattress's quarterly cash receipts, net cash inflow, and cumulative short-term financing required if customers pay for only 60 percent of purchases in the current quarter and pay the remaining 40 percent in the following quarter.

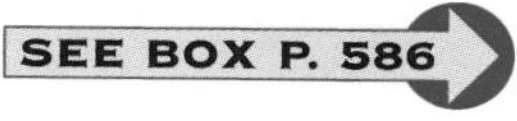
SEE BOX P. 586

Our next step will be to develop a short-term financing plan that covers the forecast requirements in the most economical way possible. Before presenting such a plan, however, we should pause briefly to point out that short-term financial planning, like long-term planning, is best done on a computer. The nearby Excel Spreadsheet box presents the spreadsheets underlying tables 19.6 to 19.8. The spreadsheet on the top presents the data appearing in the tables; the one on the bottom presents the underlying formulas. Examine those formulas and note which items are inputs (for example, rows 15–18) and which are calculated from equations. The formulas also indicate the links from one table to another. For example, in the spreadsheet, collections of receivables are calculated in Table 19.6 (row 6), and passed through as inputs in Table 19.7 (row 11). Similarly, net cash inflow in Table 19.7 (row 20) is passed along to Table 19.8 (row 24).

Once the spreadsheet is set up, it becomes easy to explore the consequences of many what-if questions. For example, Check Point 19.4 asks you to recalculate the quarterly cash receipts, net cash inflow, and cumulative short-term financing required if the firm's collections on accounts receivable slow down. You can obviously do this by hand, but it is quicker and easier to do it in a spreadsheet—especially when there might be dozens of scenarios that you are responsible to work through!

19.5 A Short-Term Financing Plan

OPTIONS FOR SHORT-TERM FINANCING

Suppose that Dynamic can borrow up to $40 million from the bank at an interest cost of 8 percent per year or 2 percent per quarter. Dynamic can also raise capital by putting off paying its bills and thus increasing its accounts payable. In effect, this is taking a loan from

[6] Maybe people buy more mattresses late in the year when the nights are longer.

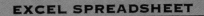

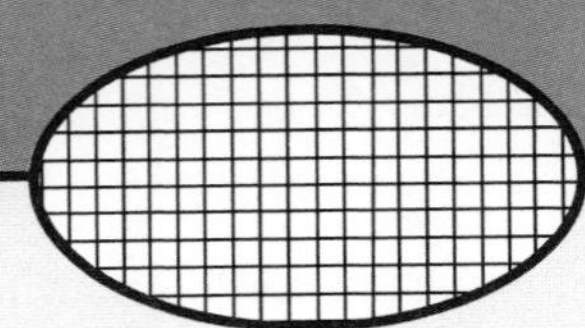

EXCEL SPREADSHEET

	A	B	C	D	E
1	**Quarter:**	**First**	**Second**	**Third**	**Fourth**
2					
3	**Accounts receivable (Table 19.6)**				
4	Receivables (beginning period)	30.0	32.5	3.7	38.2
5	Sales	87.5	78.5	116.0	131.0
6	Collections	85.0	80.3	108.5	128.0
7	Receivables (end period)	32.5	30.7	38.2	41.2
8					
9	**Cash budget (Table 19.7)**				
10	**Sources of cash**				
11	Collections of accounts receivable	85.0	80.3	108.5	128.0
12	Other	1.5	0.0	12.5	0.0
13	Total sources	86.5	80.3	121.0	128.0
14	**Uses**				
15	Payments of accounts payable	65.0	60.0	55.0	50.0
16	Labour & administrative expenses	30.0	30.0	30.0	30.0
17	Capital expenses	32.5	1.3	5.5	8.0
18	Taxes, interest & dividends	4.0	4.0	4.5	5.0
19	Total uses	131.5	95.3	95.0	93.0
20	**Net cash inflow**				
21					
22	**Short-term financing requirements (Table 19.8)**				
23	Cash at start of period	5.0	–40.0	–55.0	–29.0
24	+ Net cash inflow	–45.0	–15.0	26.0	35.0
25	= Cash at end of period	–40.0	–55.0	–29.0	6.0
26	Minimum operating balance	5.0	5.0	5.0	5.0
27	Cumulative short-term financing required	45.0	60.0	34.0	–1.0

	A	B	C	D	E
1	**Quarter:**	**First**	**Second**	**Third**	**Fourth**
2					
3	**Accounts receivable (Table 19.6)**				
4	Receivables (beginning period)	30	=B7	=C7	=D7
5	Sales	87.5	78.5	116.0	131.0
6	Collections	=75*0.2+B5*0.8	=B5*0.2+C5*0.8	=C5*0.2+D5*0.8	=D5*0.2+E5*0.8
7	Receivables (end period)	=B4+B5+B6	=C4+C5+C6	=D4+D5+D6	=E4+E5+E6
8					
9	**Cash budget (Table 19.7)**				
10	**Sources of cash**				
11	Collections of accounts receivable	=B6	=C6	=D6	=E6
12	Other	1.5	0.0	12.5	0.0
13	Total sources	=B11+B12	=C11+C12	=D11+D12	=E11+E12
14	**Uses**				
15	Payments of accounts payable	65.0	60.0	55.0	50.0
16	Labour & administrative expenses	30.0	30.0	30.0	30.0
17	Capital expenses	32.5	1.3	5.5	8.0
18	Taxes, interest & dividends	4.0	4.0	4.5	5.0
19	Total uses	=SUM(B15:B18)	=SUM(C15:C18)	=SUM(D15:D18)	=SUM(E15:E18)
20	**Net cash inflow**	=B13-B19	=C13-C19	=D13-D19	=E13-E19
21					
22	**Short-term financing requirements (Table 19.8)**				
23	Cash at start of period	5.0	=B25	=C25	=D25
24	+ Net cash inflow	=B20	=C20	=D20	=E20
25	= Cash at end of period	=B23+B24	=C23+C24	=D23+D24	=E23+E24
26	Minimum operating balance	5.0	=B26	=C26	=D26
27	Cumulative short-term financing required	=B26-B25	=C26-C25	=D26-D25	=E26-E25

its suppliers. The financial manager believes that Dynamic can defer the following amounts in each quarter:

Quarter:	First	Second	Third	Fourth
Amount deferrable, millions of dollars	52	48	44	40

That is, $52 million can be saved in the first quarter by *not* paying bills in that quarter. (Note that Table 19.7 was prepared assuming these bills *are* paid in the first quarter.) If deferred, these payments *must* be made in the second quarter. Similarly, $48 million of the second quarter's bills can be deferred to the third quarter and so on.

Stretching payables is often costly, however, even if no ill will is incurred.[7] This is because many suppliers offer discounts for prompt payment, so that Dynamic loses the discount if it pays late. In this example we assume the lost discount is 5 percent of the amount deferred. In other words, if a $52 million payment is delayed in the first quarter, the firm must pay 5 percent more, or $54.6 million in the next quarter. This is like borrowing at an annual interest rate of over 20 percent ($1.05^4 - 1 = .216$, or 21.6%).

With these two options, the short-term financing strategy is obvious: use the lower cost bank loan first. Stretch payables only if you can't borrow enough from the bank.

Table 19.9 shows the resulting plan. The first panel (cash requirements) sets out the cash that needs to be raised in each quarter. The second panel (cash raised) describes the

TABLE 19.9
Dynamic Mattress's financing plan (figures in millions)

	Quarter			
	First	**Second**	**Third**	**Fourth**
Cash requirements				
1. Cash required for operations[a]	$45	$15	–$26	–$35
2. Interest on bank loan[b]	0	0.8	0.8	0.6
3. Interest on stretched payables[c]	0	0	0.8	0
4. Total cash required	$45	$15.8	–$24.4	–$34.4
Cash raised				
5. Bank loan	$40	$ 0	$ 0	$ 0
6. Stretched payables	0	15.8	0	0
7. Securities sold	5	0	0	0
8. Total cash raised	$45	$15.8	$ 0	$ 0
Repayments				
9. Of stretched payables	0	0	$15.8	$ 0
10. Of bank loan	0	0	8.6	$31.4
Increase in cash balances				
11. Addition to cash balances	$ 0	$ 0	$ 0	$ 3
Line of credit				
12. Beginning of quarter	$ 0	$40	$40	$31.4
13. End of quarter	40	40	31.4	0

[a] From Table 19.7, bottom line. A negative cash requirement implies positive cash flow from operations.
[b] The interest rate on the bank loan is 2 percent per quarter applied to the bank loan outstanding at the start of the quarter. Thus the interest due in the second quarter is .02 × $40 million = $.8 million.
[c] The "interest" cost of the stretched payables is 5 percent of the amount of payment deferred. For example, in the third quarter, 5 percent of the $15.8 million stretched in the second quarter is about $.8 million.

[7] In fact, ill will is likely to be incurred. Firms that stretch payments risk being labelled as credit risks. Since stretching is so expensive, suppliers reason that only customers that cannot obtain credit at reasonable rates elsewhere will resort to it. Suppliers naturally are reluctant to act as the lender of last resort.

various sources of financing the firm plans to use. The third and fourth panels describe how the firm will use net cash inflows when they turn positive.

In the first quarter, the plan calls for borrowing the full amount available from the bank ($40 million). In addition, the firm sells the $5 million of marketable securities it held at the end of 2001. Thus, under this plan, it raises the necessary $45 million in the first quarter.

In the second quarter, an additional $15 million must be raised to cover the net cash outflow predicted in Table 19.7. In addition, $.8 million must be raised to pay interest on the bank loan. Therefore, the plan calls for Dynamic to maintain its bank borrowing and to stretch $15.8 million in payables. Notice that in the first two quarters, when net cash flow from operations is negative, the firm maintains its cash balance at the minimum acceptable level. Additions to cash balances are zero. Similarly, repayments of outstanding debt are zero. In fact, outstanding debt rises in each of these quarters.

In the third and fourth quarters, the firm generates a cash-flow surplus, so the plan calls for Dynamic to pay off its debt. First it pays off stretched payables, as it is required to do, and then it uses any remaining cash-flow surplus to pay down its bank loan. In the third quarter, all of the net cash inflow is used to reduce outstanding short-term borrowing. In the fourth quarter, the firm pays off its remaining short-term borrowing and uses the extra $3 million to increase its cash balances.

☑ CHECK POINT 19.5

Revise Dynamic Mattress's short-term financial plan assuming it can borrow up to $45 million through its line of credit. Assume that the firm will still sell its $5 million of short-term securities in the first quarter.

EVALUATING THE PLAN

Does the plan shown in Table 19.9 solve Dynamic's short-term financing problem? No—the plan is feasible but Dynamic can probably do better. The most glaring weakness of this plan is its reliance on stretching payables, an extremely expensive financing device. Remember that it costs Dynamic 5 percent *per quarter* to delay paying bills—20 percent per year at simple interest. This first plan should merely stimulate the financial manager to search for cheaper sources of short-term borrowing.

The financial manager would ask several other questions as well. For example:

1. Does Dynamic need a larger reserve of cash or marketable securities, say, to guard against its customers stretching *their* payables (thus slowing down collections on accounts receivable)?
2. Does the plan yield satisfactory current and quick ratios?[8] Its bankers may be worried if these ratios deteriorate.
3. Are there hidden costs to stretching payables? Will suppliers begin to doubt Dynamic's creditworthiness?
4. Does the plan for 2002 leave Dynamic in good financial shape for 2003? (Here the answer is yes, since Dynamic will have paid off all short-term borrowing by the end of the year.)
5. Should Dynamic try to arrange long-term financing for the major capital expenditure in the first quarter? This seems sensible, following the rule of thumb that long-term assets deserve long-term financing. It would also dramatically reduce the need for

[8] These ratios are discussed in Chapter 17.

short-term borrowing. A counterargument is that Dynamic is financing the capital investment *only temporarily* by short-term borrowing. By year-end, the investment is paid for by cash from operations. Thus Dynamic's initial decision not to seek immediate long-term financing may reflect a preference for ultimately financing the investment with retained earnings.

6. Perhaps the firm's operating and investment plans can be adjusted to make the short-term financing problem easier. Is there any easy way of deferring the first quarter's large cash outflow? For example, suppose that the large capital investment in the first quarter is for new mattress-stuffing machines to be delivered and installed in the first half of the year. The new machines are not scheduled to be ready for full-scale use until August. Perhaps the machine manufacturer could be persuaded to accept 60 percent of the purchase price on delivery and 40 percent when the machines are installed and operating satisfactorily.

Short-term financing plans must be developed by trial and error. You lay out one plan, think about it, then try again with different assumptions about financing and investment alternatives. You continue until you can think of no further improvements.

Sources of Short-Term Financing

We suggested that Dynamic's manager might want to investigate alternative sources of short-term borrowing. Here are some of the possibilities.

BANK LOANS

The simplest and most common source of short-term financing is an unsecured loan from a bank. For example, Dynamic might have a standing arrangement with its bank allowing it to borrow up to $40 million. The firm can borrow and repay whenever it wants so long as it does not exceed the credit limit. This kind of arrangement is called a **line of credit.**

line of credit Agreement by a bank that a company may borrow at any time up to an established limit.

Lines of credit are typically reviewed annually, and it is possible that the bank may seek to cancel it if the firm's creditworthiness deteriorates. If the firm wants to be sure that it will be able to borrow, it can enter into a *revolving credit agreement* with the bank. Revolving credit arrangements usually last for a few years and formally commit the bank to lending up to the agreed limit. In return the bank will require the firm to pay a **commitment fee**; for example, it could be .25 percent of the unused amount.

commitment fee Fee charged by the lender on the unused portion of a line of credit.

Most bank loans have durations of only a few months. For example, Dynamic may need a loan to cover a seasonal increase in inventories, and the loan is then repaid as the goods are sold. However, banks also make *term loans,* which last for several years. These term loans sometimes involve huge sums of money, and in this case they may be parcelled out among a syndicate of banks. For example, when Eurotunnel needed to arrange more than $10 billion (US) of borrowing to construct the tunnel between Britain and France, a syndicate of more than 200 international banks combined to provide the cash.

COMMERCIAL PAPER

When banks lend money, they provide two services. They match up would-be borrowers and lenders and they check that the borrower is likely to repay the loan. Banks recover the

commercial paper Short-term unsecured notes issued by firms

costs of providing these services by charging borrowers on average a higher interest rate than they pay to lenders. These services are less necessary for large, well-known companies that regularly need to raise large amounts of cash. These companies have increasingly found it profitable to bypass the bank and to sell short-term debt, known as **commercial paper,** directly to large investors. Banks have been forced to respond by reducing the interest rates on their loans to blue-chip customers.

In Canada, commercial paper can sometimes have a maturity of a year, although corporations mostly issue these instruments for periods of 1, 2 or 3 months. Commercial paper is not secured, but companies generally back up their issue of paper by arranging a special line of credit with a bank. This guarantees that they can find the money to repay the paper and the risk of default is therefore small.

Some companies regularly sell commercial paper in huge amounts. For example, the giant U.S. financial services company GE Capital Corporation has about $70 billion (US) of commercial paper in use. Canadian Pacific had about $898 million of outstanding commercial paper in 2000.

Rating organizations often provide information to investors regarding the quality and risk of different commercial paper issues. For instance, Dominion Bond Rating Service provides the following categories of ratings for commercial paper issues:[9]

R-1 (high, medium, or low): Prime credit quality securities
R-2 (high, medium, or low): Adequate credit quality securities
R-3 (high, medium, or low): Speculative securities

An R-1 (high) rating indicates the best possible credit rating whereas an R-3 (low) rating signifies a highly speculative issue. Firms with R-3–rated issues are likely to have unstable earnings and low profitability. The rate of return, or yield, on commercial paper tends to differ according to the issue's credit rating. Higher-rated issues carry lower yields than lower-rated ones. Commercial paper issues may carry yields of one or two percentage points below the prime rate, which tends to fluctuate with changing economic conditions and general levels of interest rates.

BANKER'S ACCEPTANCE

banker's acceptance A firm's time draft that has been accepted by a bank and may be sold to investors as a short-term unsecured note issued by the firm and guaranteed by the bank.

A firm may also seek short-term financing through a **banker's acceptance**. This instrument is created when a firm submits a time draft (which is much like a post-dated cheque) to the bank for acceptance. When the bank stamps "accepted" on the draft, it becomes a *banker's acceptance* and represents an unconditional promise of the bank to pay the amount stated on the draft when it matures. As such, a banker's acceptance becomes the bank's IOU and can be sold to portfolio investors in the acceptance market. Such investors may include money market funds, pension funds, and banks. We will revisit this topic in Chapter 21.

SECURED LOANS

Many short-term loans are unsecured, but sometimes the company may offer assets as security. Since the bank is lending on a short-term basis, the security generally consists of liquid assets such as receivables, inventories, or securities. For example, a firm may decide to borrow short-term money secured by its accounts receivable. When its customers pay

[9] For details, see Dominion Bond Rating Service's website at www.dbrs.com.

their bills, it can use the cash collected to repay the loan. Banks will not usually lend the full value of the assets that are used as security. For example, a firm that puts up $100,000 of receivables as security may find that the bank is prepared to lend only $75,000. The safety margin (or *haircut,* as it is called) is likely to be even larger in the case of loans that are secured by inventory.

Accounts Receivable Financing. When a loan is secured by receivables, the firm *assigns* the receivables to the bank. If the firm fails to repay the loan, the bank can collect the receivables from the firm's customers and use the cash to pay off the debt. However, the firm is still responsible for the loan even if ultimately the receivables cannot be collected. The risk of default on the receivables is therefore borne by the firm.

factoring A firm sells its accounts receivable at a discount for the purpose of obtaining short-term financing.

An alternative procedure is **factoring**, that is, to *sell* the receivables at a discount to a financial institution known as a *factor* and let it collect the money. In other words, some companies solve their financing problem by borrowing on the strength of their current assets; others solve it by selling their current assets. Once the firm has sold its receivables, the factor bears all the responsibility for collecting on the accounts. Therefore, the factor plays three roles: it administers collection of receivables, takes responsibility for bad debts, and provides finance.

EXAMPLE 19.2 *Factoring*

To illustrate factoring, suppose that the firm sells its accounts receivables to a factor at a 2 percent discount. This means that the factor pays 98 cents for each dollar of accounts receivable. If the average collection period is 1 month, then in a month the factor should be able to collect $1 for every 98 cents it paid today. Therefore, the implicit interest rate is 2/98 = 2.04 percent per month, which corresponds to an effective annual interest rate of $(1.0204)^{12} - 1 = .274$, or 27.4 percent.

While factoring would appear to be an expensive source of financing for the firm, from this example, part of the apparently steep interest rate represents payment for the assumption of default risk as well as for the cost of running the credit operation.

Inventory Financing. Banks also lend on the security of inventory, but they are choosy about the inventory they will accept. They want to make sure that they can identify and sell it if you default. Automobiles and other standardized, nonperishable commodities are good security for a loan; work in progress and ripe strawberries are poor collateral.

Banks need to monitor companies to be sure they don't sell their assets and run off with the money. Consider, for example, the story of the great salad oil swindle. Fifty-one banks and companies made loans for nearly $200 million (US) to the Allied Crude Vegetable Oil Refining Corporation in the belief that these loans were secured on valuable salad oil. Unfortunately, they did not notice that Allied's tanks contained false compartments which were mainly filled with seawater. When the fraud was discovered, the president of Allied went to jail and the 51 lenders were left out in the cold looking for their $200 million. The nearby Finance in Action box presents a similar story that illustrates the potential pitfalls of secured lending. Here, too, the loans were not as "secured" as they appeared: the supposed collateral did not exist.

To protect themselves against this sort of risk, lenders often insist on *field warehousing.* An independent warehouse company hired by the bank supervises the inventory pledged as collateral for the loan. As the firm sells its product and uses the revenue to pay back the

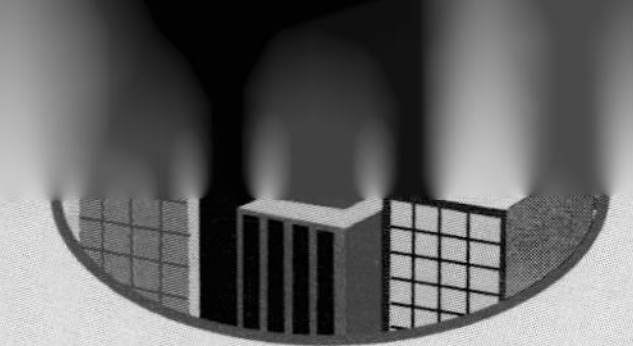

The Hazards of Secured Bank Lending

The National Safety Council of Australia's Victoria Division had been a sleepy outfit until John Friedrich took over. Under its new management, NSC members trained like commandos and were prepared to go anywhere and do anything. They saved people from drowning, they fought fires, found lost bushwalkers, and went down mines. Their lavish equipment included 22 helicopters, 8 aircraft, and a mini-submarine. Soon the NSC began selling its services internationally.

Unfortunately the NSC's paramilitary outfit cost millions of dollars to run—far more than it earned in revenue. Friedrich bridged the gap by borrowing $236 million (AUD) of debt. The banks were happy to lend because the NSC's debt appeared well secured. At one point the company showed $107 million (AUD) of receivables (that is, money owed by its customers), which it pledged as security for bank loans. Later checks revealed that many of these customers did not owe the NSC a cent. In other cases, banks took comfort in the fact that their loans were secured by containers of valuable rescue gear. There were more than 100 containers stacked around the NSC's main base. Only a handful contained any equipment, but these were the ones that the bankers saw when they came to check that their loans were safe. Sometimes a suspicious banker would ask to inspect a particular container. Friedrich would then explain that it was away on exercise, fly the banker across the country in a light plane and point to a container well out in the bush. The container would of course be empty, but the banker had no way to know that.

Six years after Friedrich was appointed CEO, his massive fraud was uncovered. But a few days before a warrant could be issued, Friedrich disappeared. Although he was eventually caught and arrested, he shot himself before he could come to trial. Investigations revealed that Friedrich was operating under an assumed name, having fled from his native Germany where he was wanted by the police. Many rumours continued to circulate about Friedrich. He was variously alleged to have been a plant of the CIA and the KGB, and the NSC was said to have been behind an attempted countercoup in Fiji. For the banks there was only one hard truth. Their loans to the NSC, which had appeared so well secured, would never be repaid.

Source: Adapted from Chapter 7 of T. Sykes, *The Bold Riders* (St. Leonards, NSW, Australia: Allen & Unwin, 1994).

loan, the bank directs the warehouse company to release the inventory back to the firm. If the firm defaults on the loan, the bank keeps the inventory and sells it to recover the debt.

19.7 The Cost of Bank Loans

Bank loans often extend for several years. Interest payments on these loans are sometimes fixed for the term of the loan but more commonly they are adjusted up or down as the general level of interest rates changes.

The interest rate on bank loans of less than a year is almost invariably fixed for the term of the loan. However, you need to be careful when comparing rates on these shorter term bank loans, for the rates may be calculated in different ways.

SIMPLE INTEREST

The interest rate on bank loans frequently is quoted as simple interest. For example, if the bank quotes an annual rate of 12 percent on a simple interest loan of $100,000 for 1 month, then at the end of the month you would need to repay $100,000 plus 1 month's interest. This interest is calculated as

$$\text{Amount of loan} \times \frac{\text{annual interest rate}}{\text{number of periods in the year}} = \$100{,}000 \times \frac{.12}{12} = \$1{,}000$$

Your total payment at the end of the month would be

$$\text{Repayment of face value } \textit{plus} \text{ interest} = \$100{,}000 + \$1{,}000 = \$101{,}000$$

In Chapter 3 you learned to distinguish between simple interest and compound interest. We have just seen that your 12 percent simple interest bank loan costs 1 percent per month. One percent per month compounded for 1 year cumulates to $1.01^{12} = 1.1268$. Thus the compound, or *effective,* annual interest rate on the bank loan is 12.68 percent, not the quoted rate of 12 percent.

The general formula for the equivalent compound interest rate on a simple interest loan is

$$\text{Effective annual rate} = \left(1 + \frac{\text{quoted annual interest rate}}{m}\right)^m - 1$$

where the annual interest rate is stated as a fraction (.12 in our example) and m is the number of periods in the year (12 in our example).

DISCOUNT INTEREST

The interest rate on a bank loan is often calculated on a discount basis. Similarly, when companies issue commercial paper, they also usually quote the interest rate as a discount. With a discount interest loan, the bank deducts the interest up front. For example, suppose that you borrow \$100,000 on a discount basis for 1 year at 12 percent. In this case the bank hands you \$100,000 less 12 percent, or \$88,000. Then at the end of the year you repay the bank the \$100,000 face value of the loan. This is equivalent to paying interest of \$12,000 on a loan of \$88,000. The effective interest rate on such a loan is therefore \$12,000/\$88,000 = .1364, or 13.64 percent.

Now suppose that you borrow \$100,000 on a discount basis for 1 *month* at 12 percent. In this case the bank deducts 1 percent up-front interest and hands you

$$\text{Face value of loan} \times \left(1 - \frac{\text{quoted annual interest rate}}{\text{number of periods in the year}}\right)$$
$$= \$100{,}000 \times \left(1 - \frac{.12}{12}\right) = \$99{,}000$$

At the end of the month you repay the bank the \$100,000 face value of the loan, so you are effectively paying interest of \$1,000 on a loan of \$99,000. The *monthly* interest rate on such a loan is \$1,000/\$99,000 = 1.01 percent and the compound, or effective, *annual* interest rate on this loan is $1.0101^{12} - 1 = .1282$, or 12.82 percent. The effective interest rate is higher than on the simple interest rate loan because the interest is paid at the beginning of the month rather than the end.

The general formula for the equivalent compound interest rate on a discount interest loan is

$$\text{Effective annual rate on a discount loan} = \left(\frac{1}{1 - \dfrac{\text{quoted annual interest rate}}{m}}\right)^m - 1$$

where the quoted annual interest rate is stated as a fraction (.12 in our example) and m is the number of periods in the year (12 in our example).

INTEREST WITH COMPENSATING BALANCES

Bank loans often require the firm to maintain some amount of money on balance at the bank. This is called a *compensating balance.* For example, a firm might have to maintain a balance of 20 percent of the amount of the loan. In other words, if the firm borrows \$100,000, it gets to use only \$80,000, because \$20,000 (20 percent of \$100,000) must be left on deposit in the bank.

If the compensating balance does not pay interest (or pays a below-market rate of interest), the actual interest rate on the loan is higher than the stated rate. The reason is that the borrower must pay interest on the full amount borrowed but has access to only part of the funds. For example, we calculated above that a firm borrowing $100,000 for 1 month at 12 percent simple interest must pay interest at the end of the month of $1,000. If the firm gets the use of only $80,000, the effective monthly interest rate is $1,000/$80,000 = .0125, or 1.25 percent. This is equivalent to a compound annual interest rate of $1.0125^{12} - 1 = .1608$, or 16.08 percent.

In general, the compound annual interest rate on a loan with compensating balances is

$$\begin{array}{c}\text{Effective annual rate on a} \\ \text{loan with compensating balances}\end{array} = \left(1 + \frac{\text{actual interest paid}}{\text{borrowed funds available}}\right)^m - 1$$

where m is the number of periods in the year (again, 12 in our example).

CHECK POINT 19.6

Suppose that Dynamic Mattress needs to raise $20 million for 6 months. Bank A quotes a simple interest rate of 7 percent but requires the firm to maintain an interest-free compensating balance of 20 percent. Bank B quotes a simple interest rate of 8 percent but does not require any compensating balances. Bank C quotes a discount interest rate of 7.5 percent and also does not require compensating balances. What is the effective (or compound) annual interest rate on each of these loans?

19.8 Summary

1. Why do firms need to invest in net working capital?

Short-term financial planning is concerned with the management of the firm's short-term, or *current,* assets and liabilities. The most important current assets are cash, marketable securities, inventory, and accounts receivable. The most important current liabilities are bank loans and accounts payable. The difference between current assets and current liabilities is called **net working capital.**

Net working capital arises from lags between the time the firm obtains the raw materials for its product and the time it finally collects its bills from customers. The **cash conversion cycle** is the length of time between the firm's payment for materials and the date that it gets paid by its customers. The cash conversion cycle is partly within management's control. For example, it can choose to have a higher or lower level of inventories. Management needs to trade off the benefits and costs of investing in current assets. Higher investments in current assets entail higher **carrying costs** but lower expected **shortage costs.**

2. How does long-term financing policy affect short-term financing requirements?

The nature of the firm's short-term financial planning problem is determined by the amount of long-term capital it raises. A firm that issues large amounts of long-term debt or common stock, or that retains a large part of its earnings, may find that it has permanent excess cash. Other firms raise relatively little long-term capital and end up as permanent short-term debtors. Most firms attempt to find a golden mean by financing all fixed assets and part of current assets with equity and long-term debt. Such firms may invest cash surpluses during part of the year and borrow during the rest of the year.

3. How do the firm's sources and uses of cash relate to its need for short-term borrowing?

The starting point for short-term financial planning is an understanding of sources and uses of cash. Firms forecast their net cash requirement by forecasting collections on accounts receivable, adding other cash inflows, and subtracting all forecast cash outlays. If the forecast cash balance is insufficient to cover day-to-day operations and to provide a buffer against contingencies, you will need to find additional finance. For example, you may borrow from a bank on an unsecured **line of credit,** you may borrow by offering receivables or inventory as security, or you may issue your own short-term notes known as **commercial paper.** You may also seek a short-term financing through a **banker's acceptance.**

4. **How do firms develop a short-term financing plan that meets their need for cash?**

The search for the best short-term financial plan inevitably proceeds by trial and error. The financial manager must explore the consequences of different assumptions about cash requirements, interest rates, limits on financing from particular sources, and so on. Firms are increasingly using computerized financial models to help in this process. Remember the key differences between the various sources of short-term financing—for example, the differences between bank lines of credit and commercial paper. Remember too that firms often raise money on the strength of their current assets, especially accounts receivable and inventories.

RELATED WEB LINKS

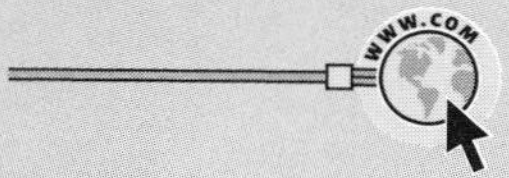

www.businessfinancemag.com *Business Finance* magazine has resources and software reviews for financial planning

www.toolkit.cch.com Financial planning resources of all kinds

http://edge.lowe.org Short-term financial management tools

www.ibcdata.com/index.html Short-term investment and money fund rates

www.dbrs.com Dominion Bond Rating Service

KEY TERMS

net working capital	573	shortage costs	576	commercial paper	590
cash conversion cycle	574	line of credit	589	banker's acceptance	590
carrying costs	576	commitment fee	589	factoring	591

QUESTIONS AND PROBLEMS

*Answers in Appendix B

BASIC

*1. **Working Capital Management.** Indicate how each of the following six different transactions that Dynamic Mattress might make would affect (1) cash and (2) net working capital:
   a. Paying out a $2 million cash dividend.
   b. A customer paying a $2,500 bill resulting from a previous sale.
   c. Paying $5,000 previously owed to one of its suppliers.
   d. Borrowing $1 million long-term and investing the proceeds in inventory.
   e. Borrowing $1 million short-term and investing the proceeds in inventory.
   f. Selling $5 million of marketable securities for cash.

*2. **Short-Term Financial Plans.** Fill in the blanks in the following statements:
   a. A firm has a cash surplus when its ________ exceeds its ________. The surplus is normally invested in ________.
   b. In developing the short-term financial plan, the financial manager starts with a(n) ________ budget for the next year. This budget shows the ________ generated or absorbed by the firm's operations and also the minimum ________ needed to support these operations. The financial manager may also wish to invest in ________ as a reserve for unexpected cash requirements.

3. **Sources and Uses of Cash.** State how each of the following events would affect the firm's balance sheet. State whether each change is a source or use of cash.
   a. An automobile manufacturer increases production in response to a forecast increase in demand. Unfortunately, the demand does not increase.
   b. Competition forces the firm to give customers more time to pay for their purchases.
   c. The firm sells a parcel of land for $100,000. The land was purchased 5 years earlier for $200,000.
   d. The firm repurchases its own common stock.
   e. The firm pays its quarterly dividend.
   f. The firm issues $1 million of long-term debt and uses the proceeds to repay a short-term bank loan.

4. **Cash Conversion Cycle.** What effect will the following events have on the cash conversion cycle?
   a. Higher financing rates induce the firm to reduce its level of inventory.
   b. The firm obtains a new line of credit that enables it to avoid stretching payables to its suppliers.
   c. The firm factors its accounts receivable.
   d. A recession occurs, and the firm's customers increasingly stretch their payables.

*5. **Managing Working Capital.** A new computer system allows your firm to more accurately monitor inventory and anticipate future inventory shortfalls. As a result, the firm feels more able to pare down its inventory levels. What effect will the new system have on working capital and on the cash conversion cycle?

6. **Cash Conversion Cycle.** Calculate the accounts receivable period, accounts payable period, inventory period, and cash conversion cycle for the following firm:

Income statement data:

Sales	5,000
Cost of goods sold	4,200

Balance sheet data:

	Beginning of Year	End of Year
Inventory	500	600
Accounts receivable	100	120
Accounts payable	250	290

*7. **Cash Conversion Cycle.** What effect will the following have on the cash conversion cycle?
   a. Customers are given a larger discount for cash transactions.
   b. The inventory turnover ratio falls from 8 to 6.
   c. New technology streamlines the production process.
   d. The firm adopts a policy of reducing outstanding accounts payable.
   e. The firm starts producing more goods in response to customers' advance orders instead of producing for inventory.
   f. A temporary glut in the commodity market induces the firm to stock up on raw materials while prices are low.

PRACTICE

8. **Compensating Balances.** Suppose that Dynamic Sofa (a subsidiary of Dynamic Mattress) has a line of credit with a stated interest rate of 10 percent and a compensating balance of 25 percent. The compensating balance earns no interest.
   a. If the firm needs $10,000, how much will it need to borrow?
   b. Suppose that Dynamic's bank offers to forget about the compensating balance requirement if the firm pays interest at a rate of 12 percent. Should the firm accept this offer? Why or why not?
   c. Redo part (b) if the compensating balance pays interest of 4 percent. *Warning:* You cannot use the formula in the chapter for the effective interest rate when the compensating balance pays interest. Think about how to measure the effective interest rate on this loan.

*9. **Compensating Balances.** The stated bank loan rate is 8 percent, but the loan requires a compensating balance of 10 percent on which no interest is earned. What is the effective interest rate on the loan? What happens to the effective rate if the compensating balance is doubled to 20 percent?

10. **Factoring.** A firm sells its accounts receivables to a factor at a 1.5 percent discount. The average collection period is 1 month. What is the implicit effective annual interest rate on the factoring arrangement? Suppose the average collection period is 1.5 months. How does this affect the implicit effective annual interest rate?

*11. **Discount Loan.** A discount bank loan has a quoted annual rate of 6 percent.

a. What is the effective rate of interest if the loan is for 1 year and is paid off in one payment at the end of the year?

b. What is the effective rate of interest if the loan is for 1 month?

12. **Compensating Balances.** A bank loan has a quoted annual rate of 6 percent. However, the borrower must maintain a balance of 25 percent of the amount of the loan, and the balance does not earn any interest.

a. What is the effective rate of interest if the loan is for 1 year and is paid off in one payment at the end of the year?

b. What is the effective rate of interest if the loan is for 1 month?

13. **Forecasting Collections.** Here is a forecast of sales by National Bromide for the first 4 months of 2003 (figures in thousands of dollars):

Month:	**1**	**2**	**3**	**4**
Cash sales	15	24	18	14
Sales on credit	100	120	90	70

On average, 50 percent of credit sales are paid for in the current month, 30 percent in the next month, and the remainder in the month after that. What are expected cash collections in months 3 and 4?

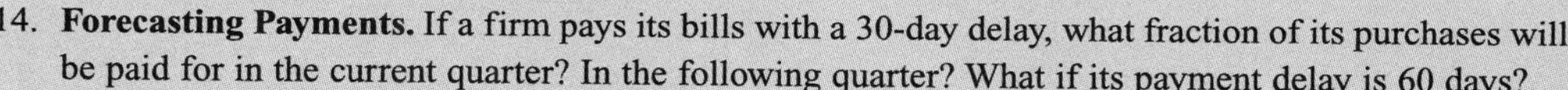

14. **Forecasting Payments.** If a firm pays its bills with a 30-day delay, what fraction of its purchases will be paid for in the current quarter? In the following quarter? What if its payment delay is 60 days?

*15. **Short-Term Planning.** Paymore Products places orders for goods equal to 75 percent of its sales forecast in the next quarter. What will be orders in each quarter of the year if the sales forecasts for the next five quarters are:

	Quarter in Coming Year				**Following Year**
	First	**Second**	**Third**	**Fourth**	**First quarter**
Sales forecast	$372	$360	$336	$384	$384

16. **Forecasting Payments.** Calculate Paymore's cash payments to its suppliers under the assumption that the firm pays for its goods with a 1-month delay. Therefore, on average, two-thirds of purchases are paid for in the quarter that they are purchased and one-third are paid in the following quarter.

*17. **Forecasting Collections.** Now suppose that Paymore's customers pay *their* bills with a 2-month delay. What is the forecast for Paymore's cash receipts in each quarter of the coming year? Assume that sales in the last quarter of the previous year were $336.

18. **Forecasting Net Cash Flow.** Assuming that Paymore's labour and administrative expenses are $65 per quarter and that interest on long-term debt is $40 per quarter, work out the net cash inflow for Paymore for the coming year using a table like Table 19.7.

*19. **Short-Term Financing Requirements.** Suppose that Paymore's cash balance at the start of the first quarter is $40 and its minimum acceptable cash balance is $30. Work out the short-term financing requirements for the firm in the coming year using a table like Table 19.8. The firm pays no dividends.

20. **Short-Term Financing Plan.** Now assume that Paymore can borrow up to $100 from a line of credit at an interest rate of 2 percent per quarter. Prepare a short-term financing plan. Use Table 19.9 to guide your answer.

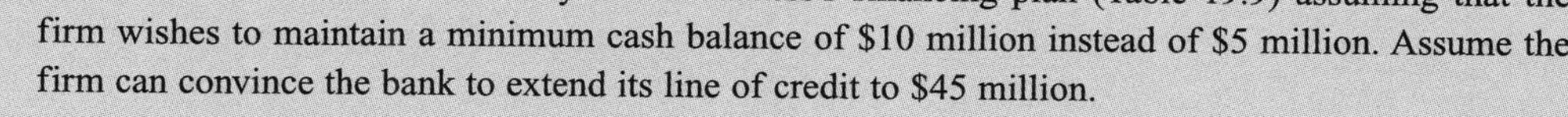

*21. **Short-Term Plan.** Recalculate Dynamic Mattress's financing plan (Table 19.9) assuming that the firm wishes to maintain a minimum cash balance of $10 million instead of $5 million. Assume the firm can convince the bank to extend its line of credit to $45 million.

*22. **Sources and Uses of Cash.** The accompanying tables show Dynamic Mattress's year-end 1999 balance sheet and its income statement for 2000. Use these tables (and Table 19.3) to work out a statement of sources and uses of cash for 2000.

YEAR-END BALANCE SHEET FOR 1999
(figures in millions of dollars)

Assets		**Liabilities**	
Current assets		Current liabilities	
Cash	4	Bank loans	4
Marketable securities	2	Accounts payable	15
Inventory	20	Total current liabilities	19
Accounts receivable	22	Long-term debt	5
Total current assets	48	Net worth (equity and retained earnings)	60
Fixed assets			
Gross investment	50		
Less depreciation	14	Total liabilities and net worth	84
Net fixed assets	36		
Total assets	84		

INCOME STATEMENT FOR 2000
(figures in millions of dollars)

Sales	300
Operating costs	–285
	15
Depreciation	–2
EBIT	13
Interest	–1
Pretax income	12
Tax at 50 percent	–6
Net income	6

Note: Dividend = $1 million and retained earnings = $5 million.

CHALLENGE

*23. **Cash Budget.** The following data are from the budget of Ritewell Publishers. Half the company's sales are transacted on a cash basis. The other half are paid for with a 1-month delay. The company pays all of its credit purchases with a 1-month delay. Credit purchases in January were $30 and total sales in January were $180.

	February	**March**	**April**
Total sales	200	220	180
Cash purchases	70	80	60
Credit purchases	40	30	40
Labour and administrative expenses	30	30	30
Taxes, interest, and dividends	10	10	10
Capital expenditures	100	0	0

Complete the following cash budget:

	February	March	April
Sources of cash			
Collections on current sales			
Collections on accounts receivable			
Total sources of cash			
Uses of cash			
Payments of accounts payable			
Cash purchases			
Labour and administrative expenses			
Capital expenditures			
Taxes, interest, and dividends			
Total uses of cash			
Net cash inflow			
Cash at start of period	100		
+ Net cash inflow			
= Cash at end of period			
+ Minimum operating cash balance	100	100	100
= Cumulative short-term financing required			

Solutions to Check Points

19.1 a. The new values for the accounts receivable period and inventory period are

$$\text{Days in inventory} = \frac{150{,}000}{1{,}727{,}149/365} = 31.7 \text{ days}$$

This is a reduction of 14.4 days from the original value of 46.1 days.

$$\text{Days in receivables} = \frac{125{,}000}{1{,}785{,}371/365} = 25.6 \text{ days}$$

This is a reduction of 12.2 days from the original value of 37.8 days
The cash conversion cycle falls by a total of 14.4 + 12.2 = 26.6 days.

b. The inventory period, accounts receivable period, and accounts payable period will all fall by a factor of 1.10. (The numerators are unchanged, but the denominators are higher by 10 percent.) Therefore, the conversion cycle will fall from 27.8 days to 27.8/1.10 = 25.3 days.

19.2 a. An increase in the interest rate will increase the cost of carrying current assets. The effect is to reduce the optimal level of such assets.

b. The just-in-time system lowers the expected level of shortage costs and reduces the amount of goods the firm ought to be willing to keep in inventory.

c. If the firm decides that more lenient credit terms are necessary to avoid lost sales, it must then expect customers to pay their bills more slowly. Accounts receivable will increase.

19.3 a. This transaction merely substitutes one current liability (short-term debt) for another (accounts payable). Neither cash nor net working capital is affected.

b. This transaction will increase inventory at the expense of cash. Cash falls but net working capital is unaffected.

c. The firm will use cash to buy back the stock. Both cash and net working capital will fall.

d. The proceeds from the sale will increase both cash and net working capital.

19.4

Quarter:	First	Second	Third	Fourth
Accounts receivable (Table 19.6)				
Receivables (beginning period)	30	35	31.4	46.4
Sales	87.5	78.5	116	131
Collections[a]	82.5	82.1	101	125
Receivables (end period)	35	31.4	46.4	52.4
Cash budget (Table 19.7)				
Sources of cash				
Collections of accounts receivable	82.5	82.1	101	125
Other	1.5	0	12.5	0
Total sources	84	82.1	113.5	125
Uses				
Payments of accounts payable	65	60	55	50
Labour and administrative expenses	30	30	30	30
Capital expenses	32.5	1.3	5.5	8
Taxes, interest, and dividends	4	4	4.5	5
Total uses	131.5	95.3	95	93
Net cash inflow	–47.5	–13.2	18.5	32
Short-term financing requirements (Table 19.8)				
Cash at start of period	5	–42.5	–55.7	–37.2
+ Net cash inflow	–47.5	–13.2	18.5	32
= Cash at end of period	–42.5	–55.7	–37.2	–5.2
Minimum operating balance	5	5	5	5
Cumulative short-term financing required	47.5	60.7	42.2	10.2

[a] Sales in fourth quarter of the previous year totalled $75 million.

19.5 The major change in the plan is the substitution of the extra $5 million of borrowing via the line of credit (bank loan) in the second quarter and the corresponding reduction in the stretched payables. This substitution is advantageous because the bank loan is a cheaper source of funds. Notice that the cash balance at the end of the year is higher under this plan than in the original plan.

Quarter:	First	Second	Third	Fourth
Cash requirements				
1. Cash required for operations	45	15	–26.0	–35
2. Interest on line of credit	0	0.8	0.9	0.6
3. Interest on stretched payables	0	0	0.5	0
4. Total cash required	45	15.8	–24.6	–34.4
Cash raised				
5. Bank loan	40	5	0	0
6. Stretched payables	0	10.8	0	0
7. Securities sold	5	0	0	0
8. Total cash raised	45	15.8	0	0
Repayments				
9. Of stretched payables	0	0	10.8	0
10. Of bank loan	0	0	13.8	31.2
Increase in cash balances				
11. Addition to cash balances	0	0	0	3.2
Bank loan				
12. Beginning of quarter	0	40	45	31.2
13. End of quarter	40	45	31.2	0

19.6 Bank A: The interest paid on the \$20 million loan over the 6-month period will be \$20 million × .07/2 = \$.7 million. With a 20 percent compensating balance, \$16 million is available to the firm. The effective annual interest rate is

$$\text{Effective annual rate on a loan with compensating balances} = \left(1 + \frac{\text{actual interest paid}}{\text{borrowed funds available}}\right)^m - 1$$

$$= \left(1 + \frac{\$.7\text{ million}}{\$16\text{ million}}\right)^2 - 1 = .0894, \text{ or } 8.94\%$$

Bank B: The compound annual interest rate on the simple loan is

$$\text{Effective annual rate} = \left(1 + \frac{\text{quoted interest rate}}{m}\right)^m - 1$$

$$= \left(1 + \frac{.08}{2}\right)^2 - 1 = 1.04^2 - 1 = .0816, \text{ or } 8.16\%$$

Bank C: The compound annual interest rate is

$$\text{Effective annual rate on a discount loan} = \left(\frac{1}{1 - \frac{\text{annual interest rate}}{m}}\right)^m - 1$$

$$= \left(\frac{1}{1 - \frac{.075}{2}}\right)^2 - 1 = \left(\frac{1}{.9625}\right)^2 - 1 = .0794, \text{ or } 7.94\%$$

MINICASE

Capstan Autos operated a dealership in the Maritime provinces for a major Japanese car manufacturer. Capstan's owner, Sidney Capstan, attributed much of the business's success to its no-frills policy of competitive pricing and immediate cash payment. The business was basically a simple one—the firm imported cars at the beginning of each quarter and paid the manufacturer at the end of the quarter. The revenues from the sale of these cars covered the payment to the manufacturer and the expenses of running the business, as well as providing Sidney Capstan with a good return on his equity investment.

By the fourth quarter of 2004, sales were running at 250 cars a quarter. Since the average sale price of each car was about \$20,000, this translated into quarterly revenues of 250 × \$20,000 = \$5 million. The average cost to Capstan of each imported car was \$18,000. After paying wages, rent, and other recurring costs of \$200,000 per quarter and deducting depreciation of \$80,000, the company was left with earnings before interest and taxes (EBIT) of \$220,000 a quarter and net profits of \$140,000.

The year 2005 was not a happy year for car importers in Canada. Recession led to a general decline in auto sales, while the fall in the value of the dollar shaved profit margins for many dealers in imported cars. Capstan, more than most firms, foresaw the difficulties ahead and reacted at once by offering 6 months' free credit while holding the sale price of its cars constant. Wages and other costs were pared by 25 percent to \$150,000 a quarter and the company effectively eliminated all capital expenditures. The policy appeared successful. Unit sales fell by 20 percent to 200 units a quarter, but the company continued to operate at a satisfactory profit (see table).

The slump in sales lasted for 6 months, but as consumer confidence began to return, auto sales began to recover. The company's new policy of 6 months' free credit was proving sufficiently popular that Sidney Capstan decided to maintain the policy. In the third quarter of 2005, sales had recovered to 225 units; by the fourth quarter they were 250 units; and by the first quarter of the next year they had reached 275 units. It looked as if the company could expect to sell 300 cars by the second quarter of 2006. Earnings before interest and tax were already in excess of their previous high and Sidney Capstan was able to congratulate himself on weathering what looked to be a tricky period. Over the 18-month period the firm had earned net profits of over half a million dollars, and the equity had grown from just under $1 million to about $2 million.

Sidney Capstan was first and foremost a superb salesman and always left the financial aspects of the business to his financial manager. However, there was one feature of the financial statements that disturbed Sidney Capstan—the mounting level of debt, which had reached $9.7 million by the end of the first quarter of 2006. This unease turned to alarm when the financial manager phoned to say that the bank was reluctant to extend further credit and was even questioning its current level of exposure to the company.

Capstan found it impossible to understand how such a successful year could have landed the company in financial difficulties. The company had always had good relationships with its bank, and the interest rate on its bank loans was a reasonable 8 percent per year (or about 2 percent per quarter). Surely, Capstan reasoned, when the bank saw the projected sales growth for the rest of 2006, it would realize that there were plenty of profits to enable the company to start repaying its loans.

Questions

1. Is Capstan Autos in trouble?
2. Is the bank correct to withhold further credit?
3. Why is Capstan's indebtedness increasing if its profits are higher than ever?

SUMMARY INCOME STATEMENT
(all figures except unit sales in thousands of dollars)

Year:	2004	2005				2006
Quarter:	4	1	2	3	4	1
1. Number of cars sold	250	200	200	225	250	275
2. Unit price	20	20	20	20	20	20
3. Unit cost	18	18	18	18	18	18
4. Revenues (1 × 2)	5,000	4,000	4,000	4,500	5,000	5,500
5. Cost of goods sold (1 × 3)	4,500	3,600	3,600	4,050	4,500	4,950
6. Wages and other costs	200	150	150	150	150	150
7. Depreciation	80	80	80	80	80	80
8. EBIT (4 – 5 – 6 – 7)	220	170	170	220	270	320
9. Net interest	4	0	76	153	161	178
10. Pretax profit (8 – 9)	216	170	94	67	109	142
11. Tax (.35 × 10)	76	60	33	23	38	50
12. Net profit (10 – 11)	140	110	61	44	71	92

SUMMARY BALANCE SHEETS
(figures in thousands of dollars)

	End of 3rd Quarter 2004	End of 1st Quarter 2005
Cash	10	10
Receivables	0	10,500
Inventory	4,500	5,400
Total current assets	4,510	15,910
Fixed assets, net	1,760	1,280
Total assets	6,270	17,190
Bank loan	230	9,731
Payables	4,500	5,400
Total current liabilities	4,730	15,131
Shareholders' equity	1,540	2,059
Total liabilities	6,270	17,190

PART SEVEN

Short-Term Financial Decisions

20 Cash and Inventory Management

21 Credit Management and Collection

CHAPTER 20

Cash and Inventory Management

20.1 Cash Collection, Disbursement, and Float

20.2 Canada's Payments System

20.3 Managing Float

20.4 Inventories and Cash Balances

20.5 Summary

In July 2001 citizens and corporations in Canada held nearly $115.5 billion in cash. This included about $35.5 billion held in demand deposits (chequing accounts) of commercial banks. Cash pays no interest. Why, then, do sensible people hold it? Why, for example, don't you take all your cash and invest it in interest-bearing securities? The answer is that cash gives more *liquidity* than securities. By this we mean it can be used it to buy things. It is hard enough getting Toronto cab drivers to give you change for a $50 bill, but try asking them to split a Treasury bill.

There could be myriad reasons for firms wanting to hold cash balances, but we can categorize the main ones as follows:

- **Meet Transactions Needs.** Firms have to carry certain minimum cash balances to meet day-to-day cash expenditures, which include routine items such as paying monthly bills or spending on regular supplies. Cash is also needed for major recurring expenses such as wage and salary disbursements as well as tax and dividend payments.
- **Hedge Against Uncertain Future.** Firms often hold some additional cash over and above their transaction requirement as a provision for the future. These funds are typically held as marketable securities. Alternatively, firms may choose to hedge against uncertainty by obtaining a line of credit. With a line of credit from a bank, the firm can borrow up to a specified maximum amount over a stipulated period of time. However, lines of credit generally require a commitment fee, whether they are used or not.
- **Speculation.** Firms may hold liquid assets in anticipation of taking advantage of unforeseen opportunities.
- **Compensate Balance Requirement.** A firm may be required to maintain a specified amount on deposit in its chequing account in lieu of loans and services provided by its bank. Usually, the amount of the compensating balance is determined by the size of the loan and the amount and range of services provided.

Of course, rational investors will not hold an asset like cash unless it provides the same benefit on the margin as other assets such as Treasury bills. The benefit from holding Treasury bills is the interest received; the benefit of holding cash is convenience of liquidity. When you have only a small proportion of your assets in cash, a little extra liquidity can be extremely useful; when you have a substantial holding, any additional liquidity is not worth much. Therefore, financial managers want to hold cash balances up to the point where the value of any additional liquidity is equal to the value of the interest forgone.

Cash is simply a raw material that companies need to carry out production. As we will explain later, the financial manager's decision to stock up on cash is in many ways similar to the production manager's decision to stock up on inventories of raw materials. We will therefore look at the problem of managing inventories and then show how this helps us to understand how much cash should be held.

But first you need to learn about the mechanics of cash collection and disbursement. This may seem a rather humdrum topic, but you will find that it involves some interesting and important decisions.

After studying this chapter you should be able to

- Measure float and explain why it arises and how it can be controlled.
- Calculate the value of changes in float.
- Understand the costs and benefits of holding inventories.
- Cite the costs and benefits of holding cash.
- Explain why an understanding of inventory management can be useful for cash management.

Cash Collection, Disbursement, and Float

Companies don't keep their cash in a little tin box; they keep it in a bank deposit. To understand how they can make best use of that deposit, you need to understand what happens when companies withdraw money from their accounts or pay money into them.

FLOAT

Suppose that the United Carbon Company has $1 million in a demand deposit (chequing account) with its bank. It now pays one of its suppliers by writing and mailing a cheque for $200,000. The company's records are immediately adjusted to show a cash balance of $800,000. Thus the company is said to have a *ledger balance* of $800,000.

But the company's bank won't learn anything about this cheque until it has been received by the supplier, deposited at the supplier's bank, and finally, presented to United Carbon's bank for payment. During this time United Carbon's bank continues to show in its ledger that the company has a balance of $1 million.

payment float Cheques written by a company that have not yet cleared.

While the cheque is clearing, the company obtains the benefit of an extra $200,000 in the bank. This sum is often called disbursement float, or **payment float.**

Company's ledger balance $800,000	+	Payment float $200,000

equals

Bank's ledger balance $1,000,000

Float sounds like a marvelous invention; every time you spend money, it takes the bank a few days to catch on. Unfortunately it can also work in reverse. Suppose that in addition to paying its supplier, United Carbon *receives* a cheque for $120,000 from a customer. It first processes the cheque and then deposits it in the bank. At this point both the company and the bank increase the ledger balance by $120,000:

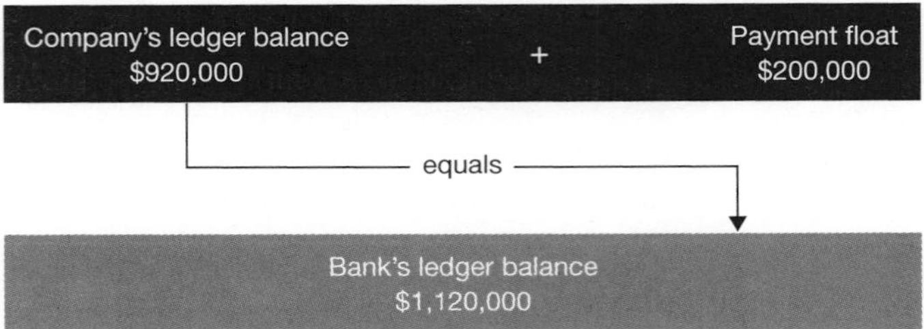

But this money isn't available to the company immediately. The bank doesn't actually have the money in hand until it has sent the cheque to the customer's bank and received payment. Since the bank has to wait, it makes United Carbon wait too—usually one or two business days. In the meantime, the bank will show that United Carbon still has an available balance of only $1 million. The extra $120,000 has been deposited but is not yet available. It is therefore known as **availability float.**

availability float Cheques already deposited that have not yet been cleared.

net float Difference between payment float and availability float.

Notice that the company gains as a result of the payment float and loses as a result of availability float. The **net float** available to the firm is the difference between payment and availability float:

Net float = payment float – availability float

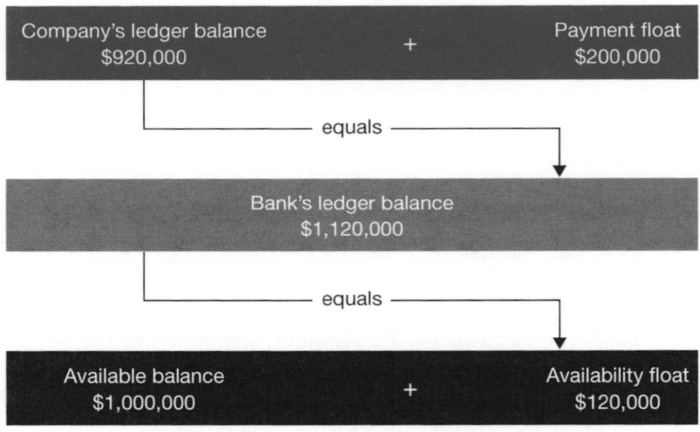

In our example, the net float is $80,000. The company's available balance is $80,000 greater than the balance shown in its ledger.

CHECK POINT 20.1

Your bank account currently shows a balance of $940. You deposit $100 into the account and write a cheque for $40.

a. What is the ledger balance in your account?
b. What is the availability float?
c. What is payment float?
d. What is the bank's ledger balance?
e. Show that your ledger balance plus payment float equals the bank's ledger balance, which in turn equals the available balance plus availability float.

VALUING FLOAT

Float results from the delay between writing a cheque and the reduction in the bank balance. The amount of float will therefore depend on the size of the cheque and the delay in collection.

EXAMPLE 20.1 *Float*

Suppose that your firm writes cheques worth $6,000 per day. It may take 3 days to mail these cheques to your suppliers, who then take a day to process the cheques and deposit them into their banks. Finally, it may be a further 3 days before the suppliers' banks send the cheques to your bank, which then debits your account. The total delay is 7 days and the payment float is 7 × $6,000 = $42,000. On average, the available balance at the bank will be $42,000 more than what is shown in your firm's ledger.

As a financial manager your concern is with the available balance not with the company's ledger balance. If you know that it is going to be a week before some of your cheques are presented for payment, you may be able to get by on a smaller cash balance. The smaller you can keep your cash balance, the more funds you can hold in interest-earning accounts or securities. This game is often called *playing the float.*

You can increase your available cash balance by increasing your net float. This means ensuring that cheques received from customers are cleared rapidly and those paid to suppliers are cleared slowly. Perhaps this may sound like small potatoes, but think what it could mean to a company like General Motors of Canada (GM). GM's daily sales average is over $115 million. If it could speed up collections by 1 day, and the interest rate is .02 percent per day (about 7.3 percent per year), it would increase earnings by .0002 × $115 million = $23,000 *per day.*

What would be the present value to GM if it could *permanently* reduce its collection period by 1 day? The extra interest income would then be a perpetuity, and the present value of the income would be $23,000/.0002 = $115 million, exactly equal to the reduction in float.

Why should this be? Think about the company's cash-flow stream. It receives $115 million per day. At any time, suppose that 4 days' worth of payments are deposited and "in the pipeline." When the company speeds up the collection period by a day, the pipeline will shrink to 3 days' worth of payments. At that point, GM receives an extra $115 million cash flow: it receives the "usual" payment of $115 million, and it also receives the $115 million for which it ordinarily would have had to wait an extra day. From that day forward, it continues to receive $115 million per day, exactly as before. So the net effect of reducing the payment pipeline from 4 days to 3 is that GM gets an extra up-front payment equal to 1 day of float, or $115 million. Therefore the present value of a permanent reduction in float is simply the amount by which float is reduced.

However, be careful not to become overenthusiastic about managing the float. Writing cheques on your account for the sole purpose of creating float and earning interest is called *cheque kiting* and is illegal. In 1985 the American brokerage firm E. F. Hutton pleaded guilty to 2,000 separate counts of mail and wire fraud. Hutton admitted that it had created nearly $1 billion of float by shuffling funds between its branches and through various accounts at different banks.

CHECK POINT 20.2

Suppose Ford's stock price is $50 (US) per share, and there are 1.14 billion shares of Ford outstanding. Assume that the daily sales average is $400 million (US). Now suppose that technological improvements in the cheque-clearing process reduce availability float from 4 days to 2 days. What would happen to the stock price? How much should Ford be willing to pay for a new computer system that would reduce availability float by 2 days?

Canada's Payments System

Every day, Canadians withdraw cash from banking machines, use cheques, debit cards, and preauthorized payments, or make other payments totalling, on average, more than $127 billion. Typically, these transactions result in financial institutions owing money to one another and settling payments over 15 million times daily. Canada's payments system includes the set of rules and procedures that guide the clearing, exchange, and mechanism for settling all of these different types of payments. The system is run by the Canadian Payments Association, a nonprofit organization, which was created by an act of Parliament in 1980. Its members are institutions such as banks, trust companies, credit unions, and caisses populaires that take deposits and offer chequing privileges. All members belong to deposit-insurance plans, which are statutory or regulated under special federal legislation.

The Bank of Canada and the Canadian Payments Association are responsible for clearing cheques and other types of payment. The CPA owns and operates two major payment systems in Canada, the *Automated Clearing Settlement System (ACSS)* and the *Large Value Transfer System (LVTS)*. The ACSS is the system by which cheques and certain types of automated payments (such as direct deposits) are cleared and settled. LVTS, introduced in 1999, is an electronic wire transfer system, which can be used by Canadian companies for their domestic and international payments.

There are essentially three steps in the process of clearing and settling payments:[1]

Step 1: Payment by cheque, debit card, direct deposit, or other means.
Step 2: Clearing, or the daily process by which CPA members exchange deposited payment items and then determine the net amounts owed to each other.
Step 3: Settlement, or the procedure by which CPA members use funds on deposit at the Bank of Canada to meet their net payment obligations to other member institutions.

For example, when you deposit a cheque at your bank, which is drawn on another financial institution, it is sent together with other cheques for sorting and clearance to a data centre operated by one of the Canadian Payments Association's (CPA) member financial institutions. These *direct clearers* clear their own cheques and have contracts to clear items on behalf of other financial institutions. After your cheque gets sorted, it will be forwarded to the data centre of the financial institution where the cheque is drawn. Most cheques, regardless of how far they have to travel, are received at the branch level no later than two days after they are deposited. Canadians usually receive credit immediately for the cheques they deposit, even if they do so at another branch on the other side of the country. The computerized network enables same-day settlement for cheques, keeping transit float to a minimum. In contrast, in the United States, a cheque may be placed on hold till it is verified that the person who wrote it has the funds in his or her account. In the United Kingdom, it could take an average of 4 days for a cheque to clear.[2]

[1] Much of our discussion here and elsewhere in this section is based on information provided in the Canadian Payment Association's website at www.cdnpay.ca.

[2] See "Introduction to the Canadian Payments Association," (March 2000), www.cdnpay.ca.

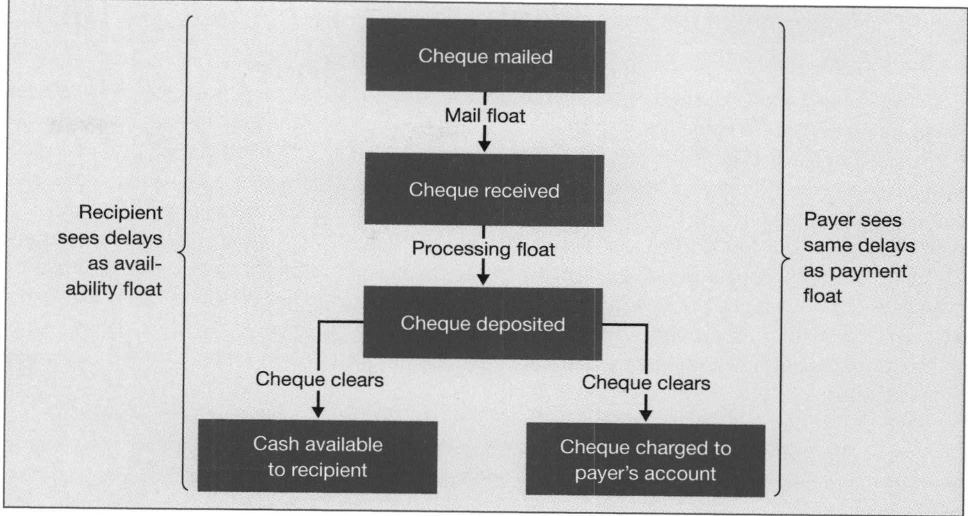

FIGURE 20.1
Delays create float. Each heavy arrow represents a source of delay. Recipients try to reduce delay to get available cash sooner. Payers prefer delay so they can use their cash longer.

20.3

Managing Float

Several kinds of delay create float, so people in the cash management business refer to several kinds of float. Figure 20.1 shows the three sources of float:

- the time it takes to mail a cheque
- the time it takes the company to process the cheque after it has been received
- the time it takes the bank to clear the cheque and adjust the firm's account[3]

The total collection time is the sum of these three sources of delay.

Delays that help the payer hurt the recipient. Recipients try to speed up collections. Payers try to slow down disbursements. Both attempt to minimize net float.

You probably have come across attempts by companies to reduce float in your own financial transactions. For example, many stores now encourage you to pay bills with your bank debit card instead of a credit card. The payment is automatically debited from your bank account on the day of the transaction, which eliminates the considerable float you otherwise would enjoy until you were billed by your credit card company and paid your bill. The stores save on any transaction costs that would have been payable to the credit card companies. Also, by receiving payment through debit cards, the stores have almost immediate use of cash and are able to eliminate accounts recievables. Similarly, many companies now arrange *preauthorized payments* or *preauthorized debits* (*PAD*s) with their customers. For example, if you have a mortgage payment on a house, the lender can arrange to have your bank account debited by the amount of the payment each month. The funds are automatically transferred to the lender. You save the work of paying the bill by hand. The lender saves the float time during which your cheque would

[3] In the earlier discussion of Canada's payments system, we saw that Canadians often receive immediate credit for the cheques they deposit, and so, this type of float is not significant here. However, this may be important if you are doing business in other countries such as the United States or the United Kingdom where the delay could be longer.

High-Tech Tactics Let Banks Keep the "Float"

If anybody knows time is money, it's banks.

And in the electronic age, banks are becoming more expert at the movement of money: racing it to themselves faster—but sometimes slamming on the brakes when you deposit a cheque. So don't expect your funds to be available to you any quicker.

To zip cheques along and reduce the "float"—or the downtime between when a cheque is written and when the funds are actually drawn from an account—banks are turning to everything from speedier cheque-reading machines to zooming jet planes loaded with bundles of cheques.

First Union Corp., for one, has begun installing scanning devices at HairCuttery salons, so when a patron hands over an ordinary cheque for a shampoo and cut, a machine reads it and swiftly deducts the amount from the chequing account—just as debit cards currently do.

But when it comes to moving funds into a customer's account, sometimes the pace is suddenly a lot slower.

There is big business in playing traffic cop to the flow of cheques. At any given moment, an estimated $140 billion in cheques are en route to a bank—a mountain of paper that could earn roughly $20 million in interest every day, estimates David Medeiros, an analyst at Tower Group, a bank consultancy in Needham, Mass.

Responding to the accelerated movement of money, the government may clamp down on banks. A pending Federal Reserve Board proposal, which banks oppose, would cut the maximum number of days a bank can put a hold on most cheques to four business days from the current five-day limit. The Fed started putting limits on how long banks can hold customers' funds about a decade ago, in response to numerous customer complaints that deposits were being tied up for no reason.

Clearly, paper cheques are moving faster now. About 83% of cheques currently arrive back at their bank of origin within five business days, up from 73% in 1990, according to the Fed. Major banks now use a fleet of 30 Lear jets owned by AirNet Systems Inc. of Columbus, Ohio to whiz cheques across the country.

But other bank-policy changes are reducing the breathing room people have long enjoyed with cheques. One new tactic is requiring that loan payments be received by their due date; in the past, banks usually considered a payment made if it was postmarked by the due date.

For the time being, the vast majority of cheques are covered by the Fed's five-day rule, but a cheque may be held longer by the bank under certain circumstances. A cheque, for instance, might be unusually large or it might be deposited by a customer who has repeatedly overdrawn his account. But even in those cases, the bank must notify the customer when a deposit will be held for a week or longer and explain exactly when the funds will be available for withdrawal.

Source: Rick Brooks, "High-Tech Tactics Let Banks Keep the 'Float,'" *The Wall Street Journal* (June 3, 1999), p. B1. Reprinted with permission of *The Wall Street Journal*.

have been processed through the banking system. In Section 20.2, we saw that in Canada the amount of float time saved would not be much as Canadians often receive immediate credit for deposited cheques, unlike other countries where it can take several days. The above Finance in Action box discusses tactics that American banks use to maximize their income from float.

Traditionally, insurance companies and mortgage providers, such as banks, have offered PADs as a convenient way for their customers to meet monthly premium and loan payments. In recent years, other businesses such as utility companies, and satellite and cable TV suppliers have realized the convenience and efficiency of this type of payment and are also offering PAD services. Many firms routinely deposit employees' paycheques directly into their bank accounts, which save the employees a few days of float.

SPEEDING UP COLLECTIONS

concentration banking System whereby customers make payments to a regional collection centre that transfers funds to a principal bank.

One way to speed up collections is by a method known as **concentration banking.** In this case customers in a particular area make payments to a local branch office rather than to company headquarters. The local branch office then deposits the cheques into a local bank account. Surplus funds are periodically transferred to a concentration account at one of the company's principal banks.

Concentration banking reduces float in two ways. First, because the branch office is nearer to the customer, mailing time is reduced. Second, because the customers are local, there is a good chance that they have local bank accounts, and therefore, the time taken to clear their cheques is also reduced. Another advantage is that concentration brings many small balances together in one large, central balance, which then can be invested in interest-paying assets through a single transaction. For example, when Amoco streamlined its U.S. bank accounts, it was able to reduce its daily bank balances in noninterest-bearing accounts by almost 80 percent.[4]

Unfortunately, concentration banking also involves additional costs. First, the company is likely to incur additional administrative costs. Second, the company's local bank needs to be paid for its services. Third, there is the cost of transferring the funds to the concentration bank. The fastest but most expensive arrangement is *wire transfer*; funds are transferred from one account to another via computer entries in the accounts. A slower but cheaper method is a *depository transfer cheque,* or *DTC.* This is a preprinted cheque used to transfer funds between specified accounts. The funds will become available within 2 days.

Wire transfer makes more sense when large funds are being transferred. For example, at a daily interest rate of .02 percent, the daily interest on a $10 million payment would be $2,000. Suppose a wire transfer costs $10. It clearly would pay to spend $10 to save 2 days' float. On the other hand, it would not be worth using wire transfer for just $5,000. The extra 2 days' interest that you pick up amounts to only $2, not nearly enough to justify the extra expense of the wire transfer.

▶ EXAMPLE 20.2 *Break-Even Wire Transfer Amount*

Suppose the daily interest rate is .02 percent and that a wire transfer saves 2 days of float but costs $10 more than a depository transfer cheque. How large a transfer is necessary to justify the additional cost of a wire transfer?

The interest savings are .02 percent per day × 2 days × funds to be transferred. So the break-even level of funds to be transferred is found by solving

$$.0004 \times \text{size of transfer} = \$10$$

$$\text{Size of transfer} = \frac{\$10}{.0004} = \$25{,}000$$

The cost of the wire transfer can be justified for any transfer above this amount.

---

lock-box system System whereby customers send payments to a post office box and a local bank collects and processes cheques.

Often concentration banking is combined with a **lock-box system.** In a lock-box system, you pay the local bank to take on the administrative chores. It works as follows: The company rents a locked post office box in each principal region. All customers within a region are instructed to send their payments to the post office box. The local bank empties the box at regular intervals (as often as several times per day) and deposits the cheques in your company's local account. Surplus funds are transferred periodically to one of the company's principal banks.

How many collection points do you need if you use a lock-box system or concentration banking? The answer depends on where your customers are and on the speed of Canada Post.

[4] "Amoco Streamlines Treasury Operations," The *Citibank Globe* (November/December 1998).

▸ EXAMPLE 20.3 *Lock-Box Systems*

Suppose that you are thinking of opening a lock box. The local bank shows you a map of mail delivery times. From that and knowledge of your customers' locations, you come up with the following data:

Average number of daily payments to lock box	= 150
Average size of payment	= $1,200
Rate of interest *per day*	= .02 percent
Saving in mailing time	= 1.2 days
Saving in processing time	= .8 of a day

On this basis, the lock box would reduce collection float by

$$150 \text{ items per day} \times \$1{,}200 \text{ per item} \times (1.2 + .8) \text{ days saved} = \$360{,}000$$

Invested at .02 percent per day, that gives a daily return of

$$.0002 \times \$360{,}000 = \$72$$

The bank's charge for operating the lock-box system depends on the number of cheques processed. Suppose that the bank charges $.26 per cheque. That works out to 150 × $.26 = $39 per day. You are ahead by $72 – $39 = $33 per day, plus whatever your firm saves from not having to process the cheques itself.

Our example assumes that the company has only two choices. It can do nothing or it can operate the lock box. But maybe there is some other lock-box location or some mixture of locations that would be still more effective. Of course, you can always find this out by working through all possible combinations, but many banks have computer programs that find the best locations for lock boxes.[5]

CHECK POINT 20.3

How will the following conditions affect the price that a firm should be willing to pay for a lock-box service?

a. The average size of its payments increases.
b. The number of payments per day increases (with no change in average size of payments).
c. The interest rate increases.
d. The average mail time saved by the lock-box system increases.
e. The processing time saved by the lock-box system increases.

CONTROLLING DISBURSEMENTS

Speeding up collections is not the only way to increase the net float. You can also do this by slowing down disbursements. One tempting strategy is to increase mail time. For example, United Carbon could pay its Halifax suppliers with cheques mailed from Prince George, B.C., and its Vancouver suppliers with cheques mailed from Charlottetown, P.E.I.

[5] These usually involve linear programming. Linear programming is an efficient method of hunting through the possible solutions to find the optimal one.

But on second thought you realize that these kinds of post office tricks are unlikely to help you. Suppose you have promised to pay a Halifax supplier on March 29. Does it matter whether you mail the cheque from Prince George on the 26th or from Halifax on the 28th? Such mailing games would buy you time only if your creditor cares more about the date you mailed the cheque than the day it arrives. This is unlikely: With the notable exception of tax returns sent to the Canada Customs and Revenue Agency, mailing dates are irrelevant. Of course you could use a remote mailing address as an *excuse* to pay late, but that's a trick easily seen through. If you have to pay late, you might as well mail late.

Remote Disbursement. You could try to pay the Toronto supplier with a cheque drawn on your account at the Prince George branch of your bank. This technique, known as *remote disbursement*, works in the United States where banks do not have widespread branches and the process for clearing cheques tends to be slow. Some American firms even maintain disbursement accounts in different parts of the country. The computer looks up each supplier's zip code and automatically produces a cheque on the most distant bank.[6] However, as we saw in Section 20.2 when we described Canada's payments system, this may not be of much use in Canada where most cheques are settled on the same day, and there is little scope for creating float through the clearing system.

Zero-Balance Accounts. A Toronto bank receives several cheque deliveries each day. Thus, if United Carbon uses a Toronto bank for paying its suppliers, it will not know at the beginning of the day how many cheques will be presented for payment. Either it must keep a large cash balance to cover contingencies or it must be prepared to borrow.

zero-balance account Regional bank account to which just enough funds are transferred daily to pay each day's bills.

However, instead of having a disbursement account with, say, TD Canada Trust in Toronto, United Carbon could open a **zero-balance account** with TD Canada Trust's affiliated bank in Sackville, New Brunswick. Because it is *not* in a major banking centre, this affiliated bank receives almost all cheque deliveries in the form of a single, early-morning delivery. Therefore, it can let the cash manager at United Carbon know early in the day exactly how much money will be paid out that day. The cash manager then arranges for this sum to be transferred from the company's concentration account to the disbursement account. Thus by the end of the day (and at the start of the next day), United Carbon has a zero balance in the disbursement account.

United Carbon does not need to keep extra cash in its Sackville branch account to cover contingencies because the bank can forecast early in the day how much money will be paid out.

ELECTRONIC FUNDS TRANSFER

electronic funds transfer Payments made electronically instead of using paper-based cheques.

electronic data interchange (EDI) Direct, electronic information exchange between enterprises, eliminating the mailing and handling of paper invoices.

Many cash payments involve pieces of paper, such as dollar bills or cheques. But, as shown in Table 20.1, the use of paper transactions is on the decline. In recent years, there has been a steady increase in the use of *electronic payment systems* or **electronic funds transfers**, which help businesses facilitate payments electronically. There is a growing practice of the exchange of financial information, or **Electronic Data Interchange (EDI)**, between enterprises. By making electronic payments, companies are eliminating the use of paper invoices and cheques, thereby avoiding the mail. Many firms deposit employees'

[6] This way, the company hopes to gain a few days of additional float. However, the suppliers won't object to these machinations because the U.S. Federal Reserve guarantees a maximum clearing time of 2 days on all cheques cleared through the Federal Reserve system. Therefore, the supplier never gives up more than 2 days of float; instead, the victim of remote disbursement is the Federal Reserve, which loses float if it takes more than 2 days to collect funds. The Fed has been trying to prevent remote disbursement.

TABLE 20.1
Percentage of paper versus electronic items flowing through the ACSS

Year		Paper	Electronic
2000	Volume	35.0	64.9
	Value	85.6	14.3
1999	Volume	38.6	61.4
	Value	91.0	9.0
1998	Volume	43.3	56.7
	Value	96.9	3.1
1997	Volume	47.5	52.5
	Value	97.3	2.7
1996	Volume	53.7	46.3
	Value	97.4	2.6
1995	Volume	61.8	38.2
	Value	98.3	1.7

Source: The Canadian Payments Association website at www.cdnpay.ca. Copyright © 2002 Canadian Payments Association.

debit card An automated-teller-machine card that allows retail customers to transfer funds directly from their bank accounts to a retailer's account.

paycheques directly into their bank accounts. Also, there is widespread use of **debit cards** among consumers allowing retail customers to transfer funds directly from their bank account to a retailer's account. Firms using this system eliminate accounts receivables and virtually have immediate use of cash. Electronic payment options, such as automated payments under the *ACSS* and electronic wire transfers through the *LVTS*, have enabled businesses to become more efficient in their cash management procedures. In the first half of 2001, total electronic remittances in Canada were valued at about $430 billion.[7]

For companies that are "wired" to their banks, electronic payment systems have several advantages:

- Record keeping and routine transactions are easy to automate when money moves electronically. For example, the Campbell Soup Company discovered it could handle cash management and short-term borrowing and lending with a total staff of seven.[8] The company's domestic cash flow was about $5 billion (US).
- The marginal cost of transactions on ACSS and LVTS is very low. For example, it can cost less than $10 to transfer huge sums of money through electronic wire transfers.
- Float is drastically reduced. This can generate substantial savings. For example, cash managers at Occidental Petroleum found that one plant was paying out about $8 million (US) per month, several days early, to avoid any risk of late fees if cheques were delayed in the mail. The solution was obvious: The plant's managers switched to paying large bills electronically, that way they could ensure cheques arrived exactly on time.[9]

20.4 Inventories and Cash Balances

So far we have focused on managing the *flow* of cash efficiently. We have seen how efficient float management can improve a firm's income and its net worth. Now we turn to the management of the *stock* of cash that a firm chooses to keep on hand and ask: How much cash does it make sense for a firm to hold?

[7] For details, visit the Canadian Payment Association's website at www.cdnpay.ca.

[8] J. D. Moss, "Campbell Soup's Cutting-Edge Cash Management," *Financial Executive* 8 (September/October 1992), pp. 39–42.

[9] R. J. Pisapia, "The Cash Manager's Expanding Role: Working Capital," *Journal of Cash Management* 10 (November/December 1990), pp. 11–14.

Recall that cash management involves a trade-off. If the cash were invested in securities, it would earn interest. On the other hand, you can't use securities to pay the firm's bills. If you had to sell those securities every time you needed to pay a bill, you would incur heavy transactions costs. The art of cash management is to balance these costs and benefits.

If that seems more easily said than done, you may be comforted to know that production managers must make a similar trade-off. Ask yourself why they carry inventories of raw materials, work in progress, and finished goods. They are not obliged to carry these inventories; for example, they could simply buy materials day by day, as needed. But then they would pay higher prices for ordering in small numbers, and they would risk production delays if the materials were not delivered on time. That is why they order more than the firm immediately needs. Similarly, the firm holds inventories of finished goods to avoid the risk of running out of product and losing a sale because it cannot fill an order.

But there are costs to holding inventories: Money tied up in inventories does not earn interest, storage and insurance must be paid for, and often there is spoilage and deterioration. Production managers must try to strike a sensible balance between the costs of holding too little inventory and holding too much.

In this sense, cash is just another raw material needed for production. There are costs to keeping an excessive inventory of cash (lost interest) and costs to keeping an inventory too small (the cost of repeated sales of securities).

MANAGING INVENTORIES

Let us take a look at what economists have had to say about managing inventories and then see whether some of these ideas can help us manage cash balances. Here is a simple inventory problem.

A builder's merchant faces a steady demand for engineering bricks. Every so often when the merchant runs out of inventory, it replenishes the supply by placing an order for more bricks from the manufacturer.

There are two costs associated with the merchant's inventory of bricks. First, there is the *order cost.* Each order placed with a supplier involves a fixed handling expense and delivery charge. The second type of cost is the *carrying cost.* This includes the cost of space, insurance, and losses due to spoilage or theft. The opportunity cost of the capital tied up in the inventory is also part of the carrying cost.

Here is the kernel of the inventory problem:

As the firm increases its order size, the number of orders fall and therefore the order costs decline. However, an increase in order size also increases the average amount in inventory, so that the carrying cost of inventory rises. The trick is to strike a balance between these two costs.

Let's insert some numbers to illustrate this point. Suppose that the merchant plans to buy one million bricks over the coming year. Each order that it places costs $90, and the annual carrying cost of the inventory is $.05 per brick. To minimize order costs, the merchant would need to place a single order for the entire one million bricks on January 1 and would then work off the inventory over the remainder of the year. The *average* inventory over the year would be 500,000 bricks and therefore carrying costs would be 500,000 × $.05 = $25,000. The first row of Table 20.2 shows that if the firm places just this one order, total costs are $25,090:

TABLE 20.2
How inventory costs vary with the number of orders

Order Size = Bricks per Order	Orders per Year = Annual Purchases / Bricks per Order	Average Inventory = Order Size / 2	Order Costs = $90 per Order	Carrying Costs = $.05 per Brick	Total Costs = Order Costs plus Carrying Costs
1,000,000	1	500,000	$ 90	$ 25,000	$ 25,090
500,000	2	250,000	180	12,500	12,680
200,000	5	100,000	450	5,000	5,450
100,000	10	50,000	900	2,500	3,400
60,000	16.7	30,000	1,500	1,500	3,000
50,000	20	25,000	1,800	1,250	3,050
20,000	50	10,000	4,500	500	5,000
10,000	100	5,000	9,000	250	9,250

$$\text{Total costs} = \text{order costs} + \text{carrying costs}$$
$$\$25{,}090 = \$90 + \$25{,}000$$

To minimize *carrying* costs, the merchant would need to minimize inventory by placing a large number of very small orders. For example, the bottom row of Table 20.2 shows the costs of placing 100 orders a year for 10,000 bricks each. The average inventory is now only 5,000 bricks, and therefore the carrying costs are only 5,000 × $.05 = $115. But the order costs have risen to 100 × $90 = $9,000.

Each row in Table 20.2 illustrates how changes in the order size affect the inventory costs. You can see that as the order size decreases and the number of orders rises, total inventory costs decline at first because carrying costs fall faster than order costs rise. Eventually, however, the curve turns up as order costs rise faster than carrying costs fall. Figure 20.2 illustrates this graphically. The downward-sloping curve charts annual order costs, and the upward-sloping straight line charts carrying costs. The U-shaped curve is the sum of these two costs. Total costs are minimized in this example when the order size is 60,000 bricks. About 17 times per year the merchant should place an order for 60,000 bricks, and it should work off this inventory over a period of about 3 weeks. Its inventory will therefore follow the sawtoothed pattern in Figure 20.3.

economic order quantity Order size that minimizes total inventory costs.

Note that it is worth increasing order size as long as the decrease in total order costs outweighs the increase in carrying costs. The optimal order size is the point at which these two effects offset each other. This order size is called the **economic order quantity.** There is a neat formula for calculating the economic order quantity. The formula is

$$\textbf{Economic order quantity} = \sqrt{\frac{\textbf{2} \times \textbf{annual sales} \times \textbf{cost per order}}{\textbf{carrying cost}}} \qquad (20.1)$$

In the present example,

$$\text{Economic order quantity} = \sqrt{\frac{2 \times 1{,}000{,}000 \times 90}{.05}} = 60{,}000 \text{ bricks}$$

You have probably already noticed several unrealistic features in our simple example. First, rather than allowing inventories of bricks to decline to zero, the firm would want to

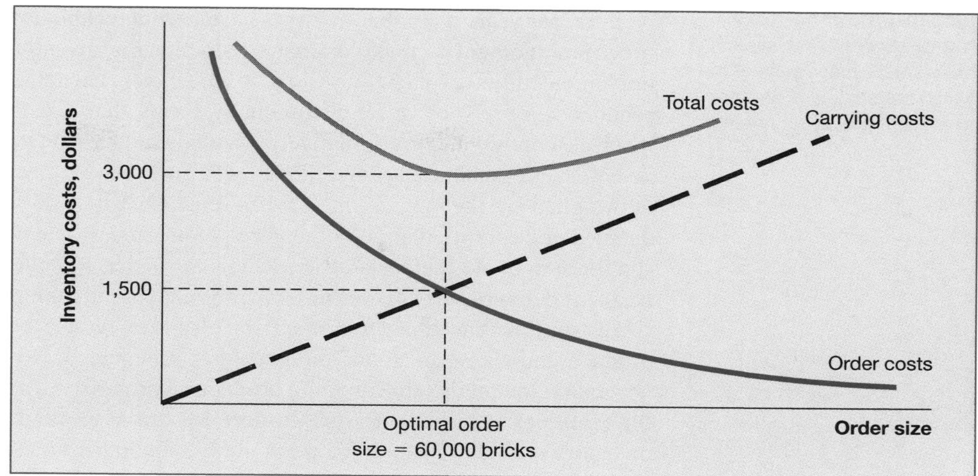

FIGURE 20.2
Determination of optimal order size

allow for the time it takes to fill an order. If it takes 5 days before the bricks can be delivered and the builder's merchant waits until it runs out of stock before placing an order, it will be out of stock for 5 days. In this case the firm should reorder when its stock of bricks falls to a 5-day supply.

The firm also might want to recognize that the rate at which it sells its goods is subject to uncertainty. Sometimes business may be slack; on other occasions, the firm may land a large order. In this case it should maintain a minimum *safety stock* below which it would not want inventories to drop.

The number of bricks the merchant plans to buy in the course of the year, in this case one million, is also a forecast that is subject to uncertainty. The optimal order size is proportional to the square root of the *forecast* of annual sales.

These are refinements: The important message of our simple example is that the firm needs to balance carrying costs and order costs. Carrying costs include both the cost of storing the goods and the cost of the capital tied up in inventory. So when storage costs or interest rates are high, inventory levels should be kept low. When the costs of restocking are high, inventories should also be high.

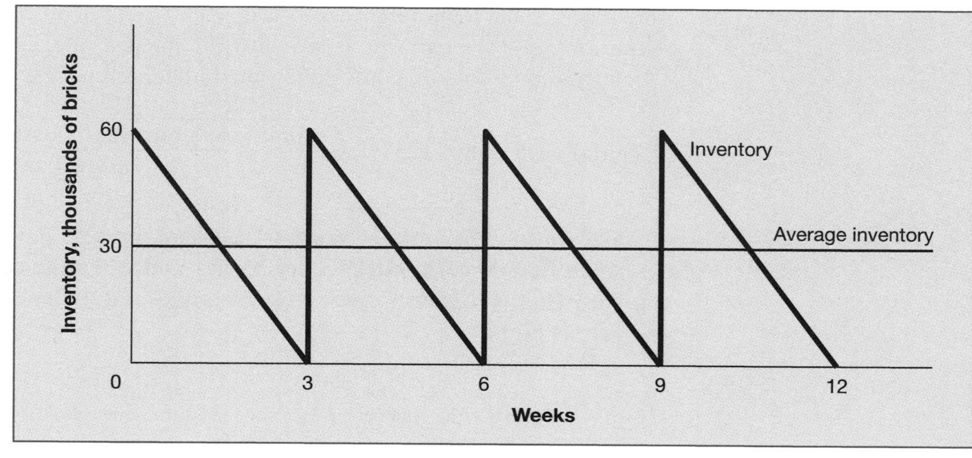

FIGURE 20.3
The builder's merchant minimizes inventory costs by placing about 17 orders per year for 60,000 bricks each. That is, it places orders at about 3-week intervals.

just-in-time inventory management A system of inventory management in which materials are delivered to the firm just when needed.

In recent years a number of firms have used a technique known as **just-in-time inventory management** to make dramatic reductions in inventory levels. This technique, first implemented by Toyota Motor Corp. in Japan, is particularly useful to manufacturers who produce a variety of different products. Firms that use the just-in-time system nearly receive a continuous flow of deliveries with no more than two or three hours' worth of parts inventory on hand at any time. For these firms the extra cost of restocking is completely outweighed by the savings in carrying cost. Just-in-time inventory management entails detailed and careful planning of material requirements and much greater coordination with suppliers to avoid the costs of stock-outs, however. Suppliers should be able to maintain frequent deliveries of smaller orders with meticulous timing.

Just-in-time inventory management also can reduce costs by allowing suppliers to produce and transport goods on a steadier schedule. However, just-in-time systems rely heavily on the predictability of the production process. A firm with shaky labour relations, for example, would adopt a just-in-time system at its peril, because it essentially has no inventory on hand, it would be particularly vulnerable to a strike.

CHECK POINT 20.4

The builder's merchant has experienced an increase in demand for engineering bricks. It now expects to sell 1.25 million bricks a year. Unfortunately, interest rates have risen and the annual carrying cost of the inventory has increased to $.09 per brick. Order costs have remained steady at $90 per order.

a. Rework Table 20.2 for each of the eight order sizes shown in the table.
b. Has the optimal inventory level risen or fallen? Explain why.

MANAGING INVENTORIES OF CASH

William Baumol was the first to notice that this simple inventory model can tell us something about the management of cash balances.[10] Suppose that you keep a reservoir of cash that is steadily drawn down to pay bills. When it runs out, you replenish the cash balance by selling short-term securities. In these circumstances your inventory of cash also follows a sawtoothed pattern like the pattern for inventories we saw in Figure 20.3.

In other words, your cash management problem is just like the problem of finding the optimal order size faced by the builder's merchant. You simply need to redefine the variables. Instead of bricks per order, the order size is defined as the value of short-term securities that are sold whenever the cash balance is replenished. Total cash outflow takes the place of the total number of bricks sold. Cost per order becomes the cost per sale of securities, and the carrying cost is just the interest rate. Our formula for the number of securities to be sold or, equivalently, the initial cash balance is therefore

$$\textbf{Initial cash balance} = \sqrt{\frac{\textbf{2} \times \textbf{annual cash outflows} \times \textbf{cost per sale of securities}}{\textbf{interest rate}}} \qquad (20.2)$$

The optimal number of short-term securities sold to raise cash will be higher when annual cash outflows are higher and when the cost per sale of securities is higher. Conversely, the initial cash balance falls when the interest rate is higher.

[10] See W. J. Baumol, "The Transactions Demand for Cash: An Inventory Theoretic Approach," *Quarterly Journal of Economics* 66 (November 1952), pp. 545–556.

▶ EXAMPLE 20.4 *The Optimal Cash Balance*

Suppose that you can invest spare cash in Canadian Treasury bills at an interest rate of 8 percent, but every sale of bills costs you $20. Your firm pays out cash at a rate of $105,000 per month, or $1,260,000 per year. Our formula for the initial cash balance tells us that the optimal number of Treasury bills that you should sell at one time is

$$\sqrt{\frac{2 \times 1{,}260{,}000 \times 20}{.08}} = \$25{,}100$$

Thus your firm would sell approximately $25,000 of Treasury bills four times a month—about once a week. Its average cash balance will be $25,000/2, or $12,500.

In Baumol's model a higher interest rate implies smaller sales of bills. In other words, when interest rates are high, you should hold more of your funds in interest-bearing securities and make small sales of these securities when you need the cash. On the other hand, if you use up cash at a high rate or there are high costs to selling securities, you want to hold large average cash balances. Think about that for a moment. *You can hold too little cash.* Many financial managers proudly point out the extra interest that they have earned; these benefits are highly visible. The costs are less visible but they can be very high. When you allow for the time that a manager spends in monitoring the cash balance, it may make some sense to forgo some of that extra interest.

CHECK POINT 20.5

Suppose now that the interest rate is only 4 percent. How will this affect the optimal initial cash balance derived in Example 20.4? What will be the average cash balance? What will be annual trading costs? Explain why the optimal cash position now involves fewer trades.

UNCERTAIN CASH FLOWS

Baumol's model stresses the essential similarity between the inventory problem and the cash management problem. It also demonstrates the relationship between the optimal cash balance on the one hand, and the level of interest rates and the cost of transactions on the other. However, it is clearly too simple for practical use. For example, firms do not pay out cash at a steady rate day after day and week after week. Sometimes the firm may collect a large unpaid bill and therefore receive a net *inflow* of cash. On other occasions it may pay its suppliers and so incur a net *outflow* of cash.

Economists and management scientists have developed a variety of more elaborate and realistic models that allow for the possibility of both cash inflows and outflows. For example, Figure 20.4 illustrates how the firm should manage its cash balance if it cannot predict day-to-day cash inflows and outflows. You can see that the cash balance meanders unpredictably until it reaches an upper limit. At this point the firm buys enough securities to return the cash balance to a more normal level. Once again the cash balance is allowed to meander until this time it hits a lower limit. This may be zero, a minimum safety margin above zero, or a balance necessary to keep the bank happy. When the cash balance hits the lower limit, the firm *sells* enough securities to restore the balance to a normal level. Thus the rule is to allow the cash holding to wander freely until it hits an upper or lower limit. When this happens, the firm should buy or sell securities to regain the desired balance.

FIGURE 20.4
If cash flows are unpredictable, the cash balance should be allowed to meander until it hits an upper or lower limit. At this point the firm buys or sells securities to restore the balance to the return point, which is the lower limit plus one-third of the spread between the upper and lower limits.

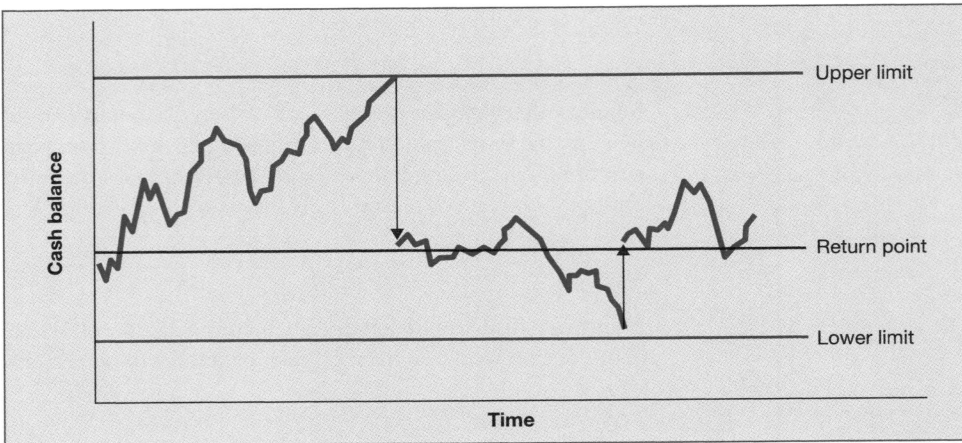

How far should the firm allow its cash balance to wander? The answer depends on three factors. If the day-to-day variability in cash flows is large or if the cost of buying and selling securities is high, then the firm should set the upper and lower limits far apart. The firm allows wider limits when cash-flow volatility is high to keep down the frequency of costly security sales and purchases. Similarly, the firm tolerates wider limits if the cost of security transactions is high. Conversely, if the rate of interest is high and the incentives to manage cash are correspondingly more important, the firm will set the limits close together.[11]

Have you noticed one odd feature about Figure 20.4? The cash balance does not return to a point halfway between the lower and upper limits. It always comes back to a point one-third of the distance from the lower to the upper limit. Always starting at this return point means the firm hits the lower limit more often than the upper limit. This does not minimize the number of transactions—that would require always starting exactly at the middle of the spread. However, always starting at the middle would mean a higher average cash balance and higher interest costs. The lower return point minimizes the sum of transaction costs and interest costs.

Recognizing uncertainty in cash flows is realistic, but few managers would concede that cash inflows and outflows are entirely unpredictable. The manager of Toys “R” Us knows that there will be substantial cash inflows around Christmas. Financial managers know when dividends will be paid and when taxes will be due. In Chapter 19 we described how firms forecast cash inflows and outflows and how they arrange short-term investment and financing decisions to supply cash when needed and put cash to work earning interest when it is not needed.

This kind of short-term financial plan is usually designed to produce a cash balance that is stable at some lower limit. But there are always fluctuations that financial managers cannot plan for, certainly not on a day-to-day basis. You can think of the decision rule depicted in Figure 20.4 as a way to cope with the cash inflows and outflows, which cannot be predicted or which are not *worth* predicting. Trying to predict *all* cash flows would chew up enormous amounts of management time.

You should therefore think of these cash management rules as helping us *understand* the problem of cash management. But they are not generally used for day-to-day management and would probably not yield substantial savings compared with policies based on a

[11] See M. H. Miller and D. Orr, “A Model of the Demand for Money by Firms,” *Quarterly Journal of Economics* 80 (August 1966), pp. 413–435.

manager's judgment, providing of course that the manager understands the trade-offs we have discussed.

CHECK POINT 20.6

How would you expect the firm's cash balance to respond to the following changes?

a. Interest rates increase.
b. The volatility of daily cash flow decreases.
c. The transaction cost of buying or selling marketable securities goes up.

CASH MANAGEMENT IN THE LARGEST CORPORATIONS

For very large firms, the transaction costs of buying and selling securities become trivial compared with the opportunity cost of holding idle cash balances. Suppose that the interest rate is 4 percent per year, or roughly 4/365 = .011 percent per day. Then the daily interest earned on \$1 million is .00011 × \$1,000,000 = \$110. Even at a cost of \$50 per transaction, which is generous, it pays to buy Treasury bills today and sell them tomorrow rather than leave \$1 million idle overnight.

A corporation with \$1 billion of annual sales has an average daily cash flow of \$1,000,000,000/365, about \$2.7 million. Firms of this size end up buying or selling securities once a day, every day, unless by chance they have only a small positive cash balance at the end of the day.

Why do such firms hold any significant amounts of cash? For two reasons. First, cash may be left in noninterest-bearing accounts to compensate banks for the services they provide. Second, large corporations may have, literally, hundreds of accounts with dozens of different banks. It is often less expensive to leave idle cash in some of these accounts than to monitor each account daily and make daily transfers between them.

One major reason for the proliferation of bank accounts is decentralized management. You cannot give a subsidiary operating freedom to manage its own affairs without giving it the right to spend and receive cash.

Good cash management nevertheless implies some degree of centralization. You cannot maintain your desired inventory of cash if all the subsidiaries in the group are responsible for their own private pools of cash. And you certainly want to avoid situations in which one subsidiary is investing its spare cash at 8 percent while another is borrowing at 10 percent. It is not surprising, therefore, that even in highly decentralized companies, generally, there is central control over cash balances and bank relations.

INVESTING IDLE CASH: THE MONEY MARKET

money market Market for short-term financial assets.

We have seen that when firms have excess funds, they can invest the surplus in interest-bearing securities. Treasury bills are only one of many securities that might be appropriate for such short-term investments. More generally, firms may invest in a variety of securities in the **money market,** the market for short-term financial assets.

Only fixed-income securities with maturities less than 1 year are considered to be part of the money market. In fact, however, most instruments in the money market have considerably shorter maturity. Limiting maturity has two advantages for the cash manager. First, short-term securities entail little interest rate risk. Recall from Chapter 4 that price risk due to interest rate fluctuations increases with maturity. Very short-term securities, therefore, have almost no interest rate risk. Second, it is far easier to gauge financial stability over very short horizons. It isn't necessary to worry as much about deterioration in financial strength over a 90-day horizon compared to the 30-year life of a bond. These considerations imply that high-quality money market securities are a safe "parking spot" to keep idle balances until they are converted back to cash.

Most money market securities are also highly marketable, or *liquid,* meaning that it is easy and cheap to sell the asset for cash. This property, too, is an attractive feature of securities used as temporary investments until cash is needed. Some important money market instruments are described below.[12] Also, Table 20.3 provides information on recent rates for some Canadian money market securities.

Treasury bills. These are the most liquid of assets and are traded actively over-the-counter by banks and security dealers. Treasury bills are issued by the Canadian government with original maturities ranging from 1 month to a year. These securities are sold at weekly auctions.

Commercial paper. This is the short-term, usually unsecured, debt of large and well-known companies. While maturities can range up to 365 days, commercial paper usually is issued with maturities ranging from 1 to 3 months. Because there is no active trading in commercial paper, it has low marketability. Therefore, it would not be an appropriate investment for a firm that could not hold it until maturity.[13] Dominion Bond Rating Service rates commercial paper in terms of the default risk of the issuer.

Certificates of deposit. CDs are time deposits at banks, usually in denominations greater than $100,000. Unlike demand deposits (chequing accounts), time deposits cannot be withdrawn from the bank on demand: The bank pays interest and principal only at the maturity of the deposit. However, short-term CDs (maturities less than 3 months) are actively traded, so a firm can easily sell the security if it needs cash.

Repurchase agreements. Also known as *repos*, or *buybacks,* repurchase agreements are in effect collateralized loans. A government bond dealer sells Treasury bills to an investor,

TABLE 20.3
Money rates

Administered Rates	
Bank of Canada	4.25%
Target overnight rate	4.00%
Central bank call range	3.75–4.25%
Canadian prime	5.75%
Money Market Rates	
(for transactions of $1 million or more)	
3-month Treasury bills	3.72%
6-month Treasury bills	3.67%
1-year Treasury bills	3.65%
10-year Canadian bonds	5.29%
30-year Canadian bonds	5.82%
1-month banker's acceptance	4.03%
2-month banker's acceptance	3.97%
3-month banker's acceptance	3.85%
Commercial Paper (R-1 Low)	
1-month	4.03%
3-month	3.90%
Call money	4.00%

Source: The *Globe and Mail* (September 8, 2001), p. B20.

[12] We have not included a discussion of the *banker's acceptance* here. This instrument is discussed in detail in chapters 19 and 21.

[13] Firms which issue commercial paper often repurchase it directly before maturity.

with an agreement to repurchase them at a later date at a higher price. The increase in price serves as implicit interest, so the investor, in effect, is lending money to the dealer, first giving money to the dealer and later getting it back with interest. The bills serve as collateral for the loan: If the dealer fails and cannot buy back the bill, the investor can keep it. Repurchase agreements are usually very short term, with maturities of only a few days and sometimes overnight. These are usually transacted in minimum denominations of $100,000.

20.5 Summary

1. **What is float and why can it be valuable?**

   The cash shown in the company ledger is not the same as the available balance in its bank account. When you write a cheque, it takes time before your bank balance is adjusted downward. This is **payment float.** During this time the available balance will be larger than the ledger balance. When you deposit a cheque, there is a delay before it gets credited to your bank account. In this case the available balance will be smaller than the ledger balance. This is **availability float.** The difference between payment float and availability float is the **net float.** If you can predict how long it will take cheques to clear, you may be able to "play the float" and get by on a smaller cash balance. The interest you can thereby earn on the net float is a source of value.

2. **What are some tactics to increase net float?**

   You can manage the float by speeding up collections and slowing down payments. One way to speed collections is by **concentration banking.** Customers make payments to a regional office, which then pays the cheques into a local bank account. Surplus funds are transferred from the local account to a concentration bank. A related technique is **lock-box banking.** In this case customers send their payments to a local post office box. A local bank empties the box at regular intervals and clears the cheques. Concentration banking and lock-box banking reduce mailing time and the time required to clear cheques. Finally, a **zero-balance account** is a regional bank account to which just enough funds are transferred each day to pay that day's bills.

3. **What are the costs and benefits of holding inventories?**

   The benefit of higher inventory levels is the reduction in order costs associated with restocking and the reduced chances of running out of material. The costs are the carrying costs, which include the cost of space, insurance, spoilage, and the opportunity cost of the capital tied up in inventory. The **economic order quantity** is the order size that minimizes the sum of order costs plus carrying costs.

4. **What are the costs and benefits of holding cash?**

   Cash provides liquidity, but it doesn't pay interest. Securities pay interest, but you can't use them to buy things. As financial manager, you want to hold cash up to the point where the incremental or marginal benefit of liquidity is equal to the cost of holding cash, that is, the interest that you could earn on securities.

5. **Why is an understanding of inventory management useful for cash management?**

   Cash is simply a raw material—like inventories of other goods—that you need to do business. Capital that is tied up in large inventories of *any* raw material rather than earning interest is expensive. So why do you hold inventories at all? Why not order materials when you need them? The answer is that placing many small orders is also expensive. The principles of optimal inventory management and optimal cash management are similar.

   Try to strike a balance between holding an inventory of cash that's too large (and losing interest on the money) and making too many small adjustments to your inventory (and incurring additional transaction or administrative costs). If interest rates are high, you want to hold relatively small inventories of cash. If your cash needs are variable and your transaction or administrative costs are high, you will want to hold relatively large inventories.

6. **Where do firms invest excess funds until they are needed to pay bills?**

   Firms can invest idle cash in the **money market,** the market for short-term financial assets. These assets tend to be short-term, low risk, and highly liquid, making them ideal instruments in which to invest funds for short periods of time before cash is needed.

Related Web Links

www.smallbusinessbc.ca Guide to preparing a cash-flow forecast
www.fpsc.com/firstunion First Union's quarterly magazine with a focus on cash management
www.ioma.com An online management library with some articles on cash management
www.nacha.org Automated collection systems for cash management
www.cdnpay.ca Canadian Payments Association
www.gmcanada.com General Motors of Canada

Key Terms

payment float	605	zero-balance account	613	economic order quantity	616
availability float	606	electronic funds transfer	613	just-in-time inventory	618
net float	606	electronic data interchange (EDI)	613	money market	621
concentration banking	610	debit card	614		
lock-box system	611				

Questions and Problems

*Answers in Appendix B

Basic

*1. **Float.** On January 25, Coot Company has $250,000 deposited with a local bank. On January 27, the company writes and mails cheques of $20,000 and $60,000 to suppliers. At the end of the month, Coot's financial manager deposits a $45,000 cheque received from a customer in the morning mail and picks up the end-of-month account summary from the bank. The manager notes that only the $20,000 payment of the 27th has cleared the bank. What are the company's ledger balance and payment float? What is the company's net float?

2. **Float.** A company has the following cash balances:

   Company's ledger balance = $600,000
   Bank's ledger balance = $625,000
   Available balance = $550,000

   a. Calculate the payment float and availability float.
   b. Why does the company gain from the payment float?
   c. Suppose the company adopts a policy of writing cheques on a remote bank. How is this likely to affect the three measures of cash balance?

*3. **Float.** General Products writes cheques that average $20,000 daily. These cheques take an average of 6 days to clear. It receives payments that average $22,000 daily. It takes 3 days before these cheques are available to the firm.

   a. Calculate payment float, availability float, and net float.
   b. What would be General Products' annual savings if it could reduce availability float to 2 days? The interest rate is 6 percent per year. What would be the present value of these savings?

4. **Lock Boxes.** Anne Teak, the financial manager of a furniture manufacturer, is considering operating a lock-box system. She forecasts that 300 payments per day will be made to lock boxes with an average payment size of $1,500. The bank's charge for operating the lock boxes is $.40 per cheque. The interest rate is .015 percent per day.

   a. If the lock box saves 2 days in collection float, is it worthwhile to adopt the system?
   b. What minimum reduction in the time to collect and process each cheque is needed to justify use of the lock-box system?

5. **Cash Management.** Complete the following passage by choosing the appropriate term from the following list: lock-box banking, wire transfer, payment float, concentration banking, availability float, net float, depository transfer cheque.

   The firm's available balance is equal to its ledger balance plus the ________ and minus the ________. The difference between the available balance and the ledger balance is often called the ________.

Firms can increase their cash resources by speeding up collections. One way to do this is to arrange for payments to be made to regional offices which pay the cheques into local banks. This is known as ________. Surplus funds are then transferred from the local bank to one of the company's main banks. Transfer may be by the quick but expensive ________ or by the slightly slower but cheaper ________. Another technique is to arrange for a local bank to collect the cheques directly from a post office box. This is known as ________.

PRACTICE

*6. **Lock Boxes.** Sherman's Sherbet currently takes about 6 days to collect and deposit cheques from customers. A lock-box system could reduce this time to 4 days. Collections average $10,000 daily. The interest rate is .02 percent per day.

a. By how much will the lock-box system reduce collection float?
b. What is the daily interest savings of the system?
c. Suppose the lock-box service is offered for a fixed monthly fee instead of payment per cheque. What is the maximum monthly fee that Sherman's should be willing to pay for this service? (Assume a 30-day month.)

7. **Lock Boxes.** The financial manager of JAC Cosmetics is considering opening a lock box in Calgary. Cheques cleared through the lock box will amount to $300,000 per month. The lock box will make cash available to the company 3 days earlier.

a. Suppose that the bank offers to run the lock box for a $20,000 compensating balance. Is the lock box worthwhile?
b. Suppose that the bank offers to run the lock box for a fee of $.10 per cheque cleared instead of a compensating balance. What must the average cheque size be for the fee alternative to be less costly? Assume an interest rate of 6 percent per year.
c. Why did you need to know the interest rate to answer (b) but not to answer (a)?

*8. **Collection Policy.** Major Manufacturing has a big market for its' products in the United States. It currently has one bank account located in New York to handle all of its collections. The firm keeps a compensating balance of $300,000 (US) to pay for these services (see Section 19.7). It is considering opening a bank account with West Coast National Bank to speed up collections from its many California-based customers. Major estimates that the West Coast account would reduce collection time by 1 day on the $1 million a day of business that it does with its California-based customers. If it opens the account, it can reduce the compensating balance with its New York bank to $200,000 since it will do less business in New York. However, West Coast also will require a compensating balance of $200,000. Should Major open the new account?

9. **Economic Order Quantity.** Assume that Everyman's Bookstore uses up cash at a steady rate of $200,000 per year. The interest rate is 2 percent and each sale of securities costs $20.

a. How many times a year should the store sell securities?
b. What is its average cash balance?

*10. **Economic Order Quantity.** Genuine Gems orders a full month's worth of precious stones at the beginning of every month. Over the course of the month, it sells off its stock, at which point it restocks inventory for the following month. It sells 200 gems per month, and the monthly carrying cost is $1 per gem. The fixed order cost is $20 per order. Should the firm adjust its inventory policy? If so, should it order smaller stocks more frequently or larger stocks less frequently?

11. **Economic Order Quantity.** Patty's Pancakes orders pancake mix once a week. The mix is used up by the end of the week, at which point more is reordered. Each time Patty orders pancake mix, she spends about a half hour of her time, which she estimates is worth $20. Patty sells 200 pounds of pancakes each week. The carrying cost of each pound of the mix is $.05 per week. Should Patty

restock more or less frequently? What is the cost-minimizing order size? How many times per month should Patty restock?

12. **Economic Order Quantity.** A large consulting firm orders photocopying paper by the carton. The firm pays a $30 delivery charge on each order. The total cost of storing the paper, including forgone interest, storage space, and deterioration comes to about $1.50 per carton per month. The firm uses about 1,000 cartons of paper per month.

    a. Fill in the following table:

	Order Size			
	100	**200**	**250**	**500**
Orders per month	_______	_______	_______	_______
Total order cost	_______	_______	_______	_______
Average inventory	_______	_______	_______	_______
Total carrying costs	_______	_______	_______	_______
Total inventory costs	_______	_______	_______	_______

    b. Calculate the economic order quantity. Is your answer consistent with your findings in part (a)?

*13. **Economic Order Quantity.** Micro-Encapsulator Corp. (MEC) expects to sell 7,200 miniature home encapsulators this year. The cost of placing an order from its supplier is $250. Each unit costs $50 and carrying costs are 20 percent of the purchase price.

    a. What is the economic order quantity?

    b. What are total costs—order costs plus carrying costs—of inventory over the course of the year?

14. **Inventory Management.** Suppose now that the supplier in the previous problem offers a 1 percent discount on orders of 1,800 units or more. Should MEC accept the supplier's offer?

*15. **Inventory Management.** A just-in-time inventory system reduces the cost of ordering additional inventory by a factor of 100. What is the change in the optimal order size predicted by the economic order quantity model?

*16. **Cash Management.** A firm maintains a separate account for cash disbursements. Total disbursements are $100,000 per month, spread evenly over the month. Administrative and transaction costs of transferring cash to the disbursement account are $10 per transfer. Marketable securities yield 1 percent per month. Determine the size and number of transfers that will minimize the cost of maintaining the special account.

17. **Float Management in the United States and Canada.** The Automated Clearinghouse (ACH) system in the United States uses electronic communication to provide next-day delivery of payments. The processing cost of making a payment through the ACH system is roughly half the cost of making the same payment by cheque.

    a. Why then do American firms often rationally choose to make payments by cheque?

    b. Two major payment systems in Canada are the Automated Clearing Settlement System (ACSS) and the Large Value Transfer System (LVTS). Would your answer in the context of Canada's payment system be different from part (a) above.

18. **Float Management.** A parent company settles the collection account balances of its subsidiaries once a week. (That is, each week it transfers any balances in the accounts to a central account.) The cost of a wire transfer is $10. A depository transfer cheque costs $.80. Cash transferred by wire is available the same day, but the parent must wait 3 days for depository transfer cheques to clear. Cash can be invested at 12 percent per year. How much money must be in a collection account before it pays to use a wire transfer?

*19. **Float Management.** Knob, Inc., is a nationwide distributor of furniture hardware. The company now uses a central billing system for credit sales of $182.5 million annually. The Bank of Montreal, Knob's principal bank, offers to establish a new concentration banking system for a flat fee of $100,000 per year. The bank estimates that mailing and collection time can be reduced by 3 days.

a. By how much will Knob's availability float be reduced under the new system?
b. How much extra interest income will the new system generate if the extra funds are used to reduce borrowing under Knob's line of credit with the Bank of Montreal? Assume the interest rate is 12 percent.
c. Finally, should Knob accept the Bank of Montreal's offer if collection costs under the old system are $40,000 per year?

*20. **Cash Management.** If cash flows change unpredictably, the firm should allow the cash balance to move within limits.

a. What three factors determine how far apart these limits are?
b. How far should the firm adjust its cash balance when it reaches the upper or lower limit?
c. Why does it not restore the cash balance to the halfway point?

*21. **Optimal Cash Balances.** Suppose that your weekly cash expenses are $80. Every time you withdraw money from the automated teller at your bank, you are charged $.15. Your bank account pays interest of 3 percent annually.

a. How often should you withdraw funds from the bank?
b. What is the optimal-sized withdrawal?
c. What is your average amount of cash on hand?

*22. **Cash Management.** Suppose that the rate of interest increases from 4 to 8 percent per year. Would firms' cash balances go up or down relative to sales? Explain.

23. **Cash and Inventory Management.** According to the economic-order-quantity-inventory model and the Baumol model of cash management, what will happen to cash balances and inventory levels if the firm's production and sales both double? What is the implication of your answer for percentage of sales financial planning models (see Section 18.2)?

CHALLENGE

24. **Float Management.** Some years ago, Merrill Lynch, the American investment bank, increased its float by mailing cheques drawn on West Coast banks to customers in the east and cheques drawn on East Coast banks to customers in the west. A subsequent class action suit against Merrill Lynch revealed that in 28 months from September 1976, Merrill Lynch disbursed $1.25 billion (US) in 365,000 cheques to New York State customers alone. The plaintiff's lawyer calculated that by using a remote bank Merrill Lynch had increased its average float by 1.5 days.[14]

a. How much did Merrill Lynch disburse per day to New York State customers?
b. What was the total gain to Merrill Lynch over the 28 months, assuming an interest rate of 8 percent?
c. What was the present value of the increase in float, if the benefits were expected to be permanent?
d. Suppose that the use of remote banks had involved Merrill Lynch in extra expenses. What was the maximum extra cost per cheque that Merrill Lynch would have been prepared to pay?

SOLUTIONS TO CHECK POINTS

20.1 a. The ledger balance is $940 + $100 – $40 = $1,000.
b. Availability float is $100, since you do not yet have access to the funds you have deposited.
c. Payment float is $40, since the cheque that you wrote has not yet cleared.

[14] See I. Ross, "The Race Is to the Slow Player," *Fortune* (April 1983), pp. 75–80.

d. The bank's ledger balance is $940 + $100 = $1,040. The bank is aware of the cheque you deposited but is not aware of the cheque you wrote.

e. Ledger balance plus payment float = $1,000 + $40 = $1,040, which equals the bank's ledger balance. Available balance + availability float = $940 + $100 = $1,040, also equal to the bank's ledger balance.

20.2 The current market value of Ford is $57 billion. The 2-day reduction in float is worth $800 million. This increases the value of Ford to $57.8 billion. The new stock price will be 57.8/1.14 = $50.70 per share. Ford should be willing to pay up to $800 million for the system, since the present value of the savings is $800 million. (All amounts are in U.S. dollars.)

20.3 The benefit of the lock-box system, and the price the firm should be willing to pay for the system, is higher when

a. payment size is higher (since interest is earned on more funds).
b. payments per day are higher (since interest is earned on more funds).
c. the interest rate is higher (since the cost of float is higher).
d. mail time saved is higher (since more float is saved).
e. processing time saved is higher (since more float is saved).

20.4 a.

Order Size	**Orders per Year**	**Average Inventory**	**Order Costs**	**Carrying Costs**	**Total Costs**
Bricks per Order	**1,250,000 / Bricks per Order**	**Order Size / 2**	**$90 per Order**	**$.09 per Brick**	**Order Costs plus Carrying Costs**
1,000,000	1.25	500,000	$ 113	$45,000	$45,113
500,000	2.50	250,000	225	22,500	22,725
200,000	6.25	100,000	563	9,000	9,563
100,000	12.50	50,000	1,125	4,500	5,625
60,000	20.83	30,000	1,875	2,700	4,575
50,000	25.00	25,000	2,250	2,250	4,500
20,000	62.50	10,000	5,625	900	6,525
10,000	125.00	5,000	11,250	450	11,700

b. The optimal order size decreases to 50,000 bricks:

$$\text{Economic order quantity} = \sqrt{\frac{2 \times \text{annual sales} \times \text{costs per order}}{\text{carrying cost}}}$$

$$= \sqrt{\frac{2 \times 1{,}250{,}000 \times 90}{.09}} = 50{,}000$$

Therefore, the average inventory level will fall to 25,000 bricks. The effect of the higher carrying costs more than offsets the effect of the higher sales.

20.5 At an interest rate of 4 percent, the optimal initial cash balance is

$$\sqrt{\frac{2 \times 1{,}260{,}000 \times 20}{.04}} = \$35{,}496$$

The average cash balance will be one-half this amount, or $17,748. The firm will need to sell securities 1,260,000/35,496 = 35.5 times per year. Therefore, annual trading costs will be 35.5 × $20 = $710 per year. Because the interest rate is lower, the firm is willing to hold larger cash balances.

20.6 a. Higher interest rates will lead to lower cash balances.
b. Higher volatility will lead to higher cash balances.
c. Higher transaction costs will lead to higher cash balances.

CHAPTER 21

Credit Management and Collection

21.1 Terms of Sale

21.2 Credit Agreements

21.3 Credit Analysis

21.4 The Credit Decision

21.5 Collection Policy

21.6 Bankruptcy

21.7 Summary

When companies sell their products, they sometimes demand cash on delivery, but in most cases they allow a delay in payment. The customers' promises to pay for their purchases constitute a valuable asset; therefore, the accountant enters these promises in the balance sheet as accounts receivable. If you turn back to the balance sheet in Table 19.1, you can see that accounts receivable constitute, on the average, more than one-third of a firm's current assets. These receivables include both trade credit to other firms and consumer credit to retail customers. The former is by far the larger and will therefore be the main focus of this chapter.

Customers may be attracted by the opportunity to buy goods on credit, but there is a cost to the seller who provides the credit. Take Molson, Inc., for example. In Chapter 2 we saw that in 2001, Molson had sales of $1,857 million, or about $5 million a day. Receivables during the year averaged $128 million.[1] Thus Molson's customers were taking an average of 128/5 = 25.6 days to pay their bills. Suppose that Molson could collect this cash 1 day earlier without affecting sales. In that case receivables would decline by $5 million, and Molson would have an extra $5 million in the bank, which it could either hand back to shareholders or invest to earn interest.

Credit management involves the following steps, which we will discuss in turn.

First, you must establish the *terms of sale* on which you propose to sell your goods. How long are you going to give customers to pay their bills? Are you prepared to offer a cash discount for prompt payment?

Second, you must decide what evidence you need to have that shows the customer owes you money. Do you just ask the buyer to sign a receipt, or do you insist on a more formal IOU?

Third, you must consider which customers are likely to pay their bills. This is called *credit analysis.* Do you judge this from the customer's past payment record or past financial statements? Do you also rely on bank references?

Fourth, you must decide on *credit policy.* How much credit are you prepared to extend to each customer? Do you play it safe by turning down any doubtful prospects? Or do you accept the risk of a few bad debts as part of the cost of building up a large, regular clientele?

[1] This is an average of receivables at the start of the year and at the end of the year.

Fifth, after you have granted credit, you have the problem of collecting the money when it becomes due. This is called *collection policy.* How do you keep track of payments and pursue slow payers? If all goes well, this is the end of the matter. But sometimes you will find that the customers go bankrupt and cannot pay. In this case you need to understand how bankruptcy works.

After studying this chapter you should be able to

- Measure the implicit interest rate on credit.
- Understand when it makes sense to ask the customer for a formal IOU.
- Explain how firms can assess the probability that a customer will pay, and decide whether it makes sense to grant credit to that customer.
- Summarize the bankruptcy procedures when firms cannot pay their creditors.

Terms of Sale

terms of sale Credit, discount, and payment terms offered on a sale.

Whenever you sell goods, you need to set the **terms of sale.** For example, if you are supplying goods to a wide variety of irregular customers, you may require cash on delivery (COD). And if you are producing goods to the customer's specification or incurring heavy delivery costs, then it may be sensible to ask for cash before delivery (CBD).

Some contracts provide for *progress payments* as work is carried out. For example, a large consulting contract might call for 30 percent payment after completion of field research, 30 percent more on submission of a draft report, and the remaining 40 percent when the project is finally completed.

In many other cases, payment is not made until after delivery, so the buyer receives *credit.* Each industry seems to have its own typical credit arrangements. These arrangements have a rough logic. For example, the seller will naturally demand earlier payment if its customers are financially less secure, if their accounts are small, or if the goods are perishable or quickly resold.

When you buy goods on credit, the supplier will state a final payment date. To encourage you to pay *before* the final date, it is common to offer a cash discount for prompt settlement. For example, a manufacturer may require payment within 30 days but offer a 5 percent discount to customers who pay within 10 days. These terms would be referred to as 5/10, net 30:

5	/	10,	net 30
↑		↑	↑
percent discount for early payment		number of days that discount is available	number of days before payment is due

Similarly, if a firm sells goods on terms of 2/30, net 60, customers receive a 2 percent discount for payment within 30 days or else must pay in full within 60 days. If the terms are simply net 30, then customers must pay within 30 days of the invoice date, and no discounts are offered for early payment.

CHECK POINT 21.1

Suppose that a firm sells goods on terms of 2/10, net 20. On May 1 you buy goods from the company with an invoice value of $20,000. How much would you need to pay if you took the cash discount? What is the latest date on which the cash discount is available? By what date should you pay for your purchase if you decide not to take the cash discount?

For many items that are bought regularly, it is inconvenient to require separate payment for each delivery. A common solution is to pretend that all sales during the month in fact occur at the end of the month (EOM). Thus goods may be sold on terms of 8/10, *EOM*, net 60. This allows the customer a cash discount of 8 percent if the bill is paid within 10 days of the end of the month; otherwise, the full payment is due within 60 days of the invoice date.

When purchases are subject to seasonal fluctuations, manufacturers often encourage customers to take early delivery, allowing them to delay payment until the usual order season. This practice is known as *season dating*. For example, summer products might have terms of 2/10, net 30, but the invoice might be dated May 1, even if the sale takes place in February. The discount is then available until May 10, and the bill is not due until May 30.

A firm that buys on credit is in effect borrowing from its supplier. It saves cash today but will have to pay later. This, of course, is an implicit loan from the supplier.

Of course, a free loan is always worth having. But if you pass up a cash discount, then the loan may prove to be very expensive. For example, a customer who buys on terms of 3/10, net 30, may decide to forgo the cash discount and pay on the 30th day. The customer obtains an extra 20 days' credit by deferring payment from 10 to 30 days after the sale but pays about 3 percent more for the goods. This is equivalent to borrowing money at a rate of 74.3 percent a year. To see why, consider an order of \$100. If the firm pays within 10 days, it gets a 3 percent discount and pays only \$97. If it waits the full 30 days, it pays \$100. The extra 20 days of credit increase the payment by the fraction 3/97 = .0309, or 3.09 percent. Therefore, the implicit interest charged to extend the trade credit is 3.09 percent *per 20 days*. There are 365/20 = 18.25 20-day periods in a year, so the effective annual rate of interest on the loan is $(1.0309)^{18.25} - 1 = .743$, or 74.3 percent.

The general formula for calculating the implicit annual interest rate for customers who do not take the cash discount is

$$\textbf{Effective annual rate} = \left(1 + \frac{\textbf{discount}}{\textbf{discounted price}}\right)^{\textbf{365/extra days credit}} - 1 \qquad (21.1)$$

The discount divided by the discounted price is the percentage increase in price paid by a customer who forgoes the discount. In our example, with terms of 3/10, net 30, the percentage increase in price is 3/97 = .0309, or 3.09 percent. This is the per-period implicit rate of interest. The period of the loan is the number of extra days of credit that you can obtain by forgoing the discount. In our example, this is 20 days. To annualize this rate, we compound the per-period rate by the number of periods in a year.

Of course any firm that delays payment beyond day 30 gains a cheaper loan but damages its reputation for creditworthiness.

EXAMPLE 21.1 *Trade Credit Rates*

What is the implied interest rate on the trade credit if the discount for early payment is 5/10, net 60?

The cash discount in this case is 5 percent and customers who choose not to take the discount receive an extra 60 – 10 = 50 days credit. So the effective annual interest is

$$\text{Effective annual rate} = \left(1 + \frac{\text{discount}}{\text{discounted price}}\right)^{365/\text{extra days credit}} - 1$$

$$= \left(1 + \frac{5}{95}\right)^{365/50} - 1 = .454, \text{ or } 45.4\%$$

In this case the customer who does not take the discount is effectively borrowing money at an annual interest rate of 45.4 percent.

You might wonder why the effective interest rate on trade credit is typically so high. Part of the rate should be viewed as compensation for the costs the firm anticipates in collecting from slow payers. After all, at such steep effective rates, most purchasers will choose to pay early and receive the discount. Therefore, you might interpret the choice to stretch payables as a sign of financial difficulties. It makes sense that the charged interest rate should be high.

CHECK POINT 21.2

What would be the effective annual interest rate in Example 21.1, if the terms of sale were 5/10, net 50? Why is the rate higher?

Credit Agreements

open account Agreement whereby sales are made with no formal debt contract.

The terms of sale define the amount of credit but not the nature of the contract. Repetitive sales are almost always made on **open account** and involve only an implicit contract. There is simply a record in the seller's books and a receipt signed by the buyer.

Sometimes you might want a more formal agreement stating that the customer owes you money. When the order is very large and there is no complicated cash discount, the customer may be asked to sign a *promissory note.* This is just a straightforward IOU, worded along the following lines:

> Vancouver
> April 1, 2001
>
> Sixty days after date, ABC, Inc., promises to pay to the order of the XYZ Company ten thousand dollars ($10,000) for value received.
>
> Signature

Such an arrangement is not common but it does eliminate the possibility of any subsequent disputes about the amount and existence of the debt; the customer knows that he or she may be sued immediately for failure to pay on the due date.

If you want a clear commitment from the buyer, it is more useful to have it *before* you deliver the goods. In this case the common procedure is to arrange a *commercial draft.* This is simply jargon for an order to pay.[2] It works as follows. The seller prepares a draft ordering payment by the customer and sends this draft to the customer's bank. If immediate payment is required, the draft is termed a *sight draft;* otherwise it is known as a *time draft.* Depending on whether it is a sight or a time draft, the customer either tells

[2] For example, a cheque is an example of a draft. Whenever you write a cheque, you are ordering the bank to make a payment.

the bank to pay up or acknowledges the debt by adding the word *accepted* and a signature. Once accepted, a time draft is like a postdated cheque and is called a *trade acceptance.* This trade acceptance is then forwarded to the seller, who holds it until the payment becomes due.

If the customer's credit is for any reason suspect, the seller may ask the customer to arrange for his or her bank to accept the time draft. In this case, the bank guarantees the customer's debt and the draft is called a *banker's acceptance.* Banker's acceptances are often used in overseas trade. They are actively bought and sold in the money market, the market for short-term high-quality debt.

If you sell goods to a customer who proves unable to pay, you cannot get your goods back. You simply become a general creditor similar to other unfortunate companies. You can avoid this situation by making a *conditional sale,* so that ownership of the goods remains with the seller until full payment is made. The conditional sale is common in Europe. In Canada it is used only for goods that are bought on installment. In this case, if the customer fails to make the agreed number of payments, then the equipment can be immediately repossessed by the seller.

Credit Analysis

credit analysis
Procedure to determine the likelihood a customer will pay its bills.

There are a number of ways to find out whether customers are likely to pay their debts, that is, to carry out **credit analysis.** The most obvious indication is whether they have paid promptly in the past. Prompt payment is usually a good omen, but beware of the customer who establishes a high credit limit based on small payments, and then disappears, leaving you with a large unpaid bill.

If you are dealing with a new customer, you will probably check with a credit agency. Dun & Bradstreet, which is by far the largest of these agencies, provides credit ratings on several million American and international firms, including more than one million Canadian businesses. In addition to its rating service, Dun & Bradstreet provides, on request, a full credit report on a potential customer. Similarly Trans Union Canada offers consumer credit-related products and services throughout Canada to its subscribers.

Credit agencies usually report the experience that other firms have had with your customer, but you can also get this information by contacting those firms directly or through a credit bureau.

Your bank can also make a credit check. It will contact the customer's bank and ask for information on the customer's average bank balance, access to bank credit, and general reputation.

In addition to checking with your customer's bank, it might make sense to check what everybody else in the financial community thinks about your customer's credit standing. Does that sound expensive? Not if your customer is a public company. You just look at Dominion Bond Rating Service's or Standard & Poor's rating for the customer's bonds.[3] You can also compare prices of these bonds to the prices of other firms' bonds. (Of course the comparisons should be between bonds of similar maturity, coupon, and so on.) Finally, you can look at how the customer's stock price has been behaving recently. A sharp fall in price doesn't mean that the company is in trouble, but it does suggest that prospects are less bright than they were formerly.

[3] Standard & Poor's has recently acquired Canadian Bond Rating Service, which used to be a major Canadian rating organization. Of course, many Canadian companies borrow regularly in the United States and other countries, and their bonds are rated by other prominent rating firms such as Moody's. We described bond ratings in Chapter 4, Section 4.2.

FINANCIAL RATIO ANALYSIS

We have suggested a number of ways to check whether your customer is a good risk. You can ask your collection manager, a specialized credit agency, credit bureau, banker, or the financial community at large. But if you don't like relying on the judgment of others, you can do your own homework. Ideally this would involve a detailed analysis of the company's business prospects and financing, but this is usually too expensive. Therefore, credit analysts concentrate on the company's financial statements, using rough rules of thumb to judge whether the firm is a good credit risk. The rules of thumb are based on *financial ratios.* Chapter 17 described how these ratios are calculated and interpreted.

NUMERICAL CREDIT SCORING

Analyzing credit risk is like detective work. You have a lot of clues—some important, some fitting into a neat pattern, others contradictory. You must weigh these clues to come up with an overall judgment.

When the firm has a small, regular clientele, the credit manager can easily handle the process informally and make a judgment about what are often termed the *five Cs of credit:*

1. customer's *character*
2. customer's *capacity* to pay
3. customer's *capital*
4. *collateral* provided by the customer[4]
5. *condition* of the customer's business

When the company is dealing directly with consumers or with a large number of small trade accounts, some streamlining is essential. In these cases it may make sense to use a scoring system to prescreen credit applications.

For example, if you apply for a credit card or a bank loan, you will be asked about your job, home, and financial position. The information that you provide is used to calculate an overall credit score. Applicants who do not make the grade on the score are likely to be refused credit or subjected to more detailed analysis.

Banks and the credit departments of industrial firms also use mechanical credit scoring systems to cut the costs of assessing commercial credit applications. One bank claimed that by introducing a credit scoring system, it cut the cost of reviewing loan applications by two-thirds. It cited the case of an application for a $5,000 credit line from a small business. A clerk entered information from the loan application into a computer and checked the firm's deposit balances with the bank, as well as the owner's personal and business credit files. Immediately the loan officer could see the applicant's score: 240 on a scale of 100 to 300, well above the bank's cut-off figure. All that remained for the bank was to check that there was nothing obviously suspicious about the application. "We don't want to lend to set up an alligator farm in the desert," said one bank official.[5]

Firms use several statistical techniques to separate the creditworthy customers from the impecunious ones. One common method employs *multiple discriminant analysis* to produce a measure of solvency called a *Z score.* For example, a study by Edward Altman suggested the following relationship between a firm's financial ratios and its creditworthiness (Z):[6]

[4] For example, the customer can offer bonds as collateral. These bonds can then be seized by the seller if the customer fails to pay.

[5] Quoted in S. Hansell, "Need a Loan? Ask the Computer; 'Credit Scoring' Changes Small-Business Lending," the *New York Times* (April 18, 1995), p. D1.

[6] EBIT is earnings before interest and taxes. E. I. Altman, "Financial Ratios, Discriminant Analysis and the Prediction of Corporate Bankruptcy," *Journal of Finance* 23 (September 1968), pp. 589–609.

$$Z = 3.3 \frac{\text{EBIT}}{\text{total assets}} + 1.0 \frac{\text{sales}}{\text{total assets}} + .6 \frac{\text{market value of equity}}{\text{total book debt}} + 1.4 \frac{\text{retained earnings}}{\text{total assets}} + 1.2 \frac{\text{working capital}}{\text{total assets}}$$

This equation did a good job at distinguishing between the bankrupt and nonbankrupt firms. Of the former, 94 percent had Z scores *less* than 2.7 before they went bankrupt. In contrast, 97 percent of the nonbankrupt firms had Z scores *above* this level.[7]

▶ EXAMPLE 21.2 *Credit Scoring*

Consider a firm with the following financial ratios:

$$\frac{\text{EBIT}}{\text{total assets}} = .12 \qquad \frac{\text{sales}}{\text{total assets}} = 1.4 \qquad \frac{\text{market equity}}{\text{book debt}} = .9$$

$$\frac{\text{retained earnings}}{\text{total assets}} = .4 \qquad \frac{\text{working capital}}{\text{total assets}} = .12$$

The firm's Z score is thus

$$(3.3 \times .12) + (1.0 \times 1.4) + (.6 \times .9) + (1.4 \times .4) + (1.2 \times .12) = 3.04$$

This score is above the cut-off level for predicting bankruptcy, and thus, would be considered favourable in terms of evaluating the firm's creditworthiness.

The nearby Finance in Action box describes how statistical scoring systems similar to the Z score can provide timely first-cut estimates of creditworthiness. These assessments can streamline the credit decision and free up labour for other, less mechanical tasks. These scoring systems can be used in conjunction with large databases, such as Dun & Bradstreet's, to provide quick credit scores for thousands of firms.

WHEN TO STOP LOOKING FOR CLUES

We told you earlier where to start looking for clues about a customer's creditworthiness, but we never said anything about when to *stop*. A detailed credit analysis costs money, so you need to keep the following basic principle in mind:

Credit analysis is worthwhile only if the expected savings exceed the cost.

This simple rule has two immediate implications:

1. *Don't undertake a full credit analysis unless the order is big enough to justify it.* If the maximum profit on an order is $100, it is foolish to spend $200 to check whether the customer is a good prospect. Rely on a less detailed credit check for the smaller orders and save your energy and your money for the big orders.
2. *Undertake a full credit analysis for the doubtful orders.* If a preliminary check suggests that a customer is almost certainly a good prospect, then searching further is unlikely

[7] This equation was fitted with hindsight. The equation did slightly less well when used to *predict* bankruptcies after 1965.

FINANCE IN ACTION

System Cuts the Risks

Case Study/Hunter Timber

When Hunter Timber, an offshoot of the Wickes Group, appointed a credit director who describes himself as primarily a business analyst, it got more than it bargained for. Risk assessment is now undertaken by a powerful credit monitoring system developed in conjunction with Dun & Bradstreet, the business information group. Not only does the program eliminate many of the mundane duties which were executed by credit analysts, it also assists the operations of the marketing department.

The system, called Decision Index, was created for the company after the arrival of John Griffiths as credit director. Mr. Griffiths, who is now merchanting director at the company, found the methods of traditional credit management too labour-intensive. Particularly unsatisfactory, he thought, were the response times, averaging four to five days, to credit requests from Hunter's branches. To speed up such response times and generally streamline the credit analysis operation, Mr. Griffiths wanted a system that would cut the paperwork involved in many credit applications and free credit analysts to meet customers.

Hunter Timber's approach to Dun & Bradstreet to work on the production of a credit monitoring system was a natural one as the company had used D&B's financial information services for a number of years. D&B's business information service had been contemplating the development of such a program. The system took 12 months to complete, and Hunter's credit management implemented it last August. Mr. Griffiths believes it has transformed the role of credit analysis. "The response time to branches has been reduced from days to just minutes. Also, we are able to pre-credit customers and give answers to their credit requests far more quickly."

Decision Index functions by tapping into a large database supplied by Dun & Bradstreet and cross-referring to Hunter's own customer information and credit demands. In the databases comprehensive information is filed on several thousand companies, which supply their details to D&B. In addition to the detailed information, basic business dossiers are potentially available on 38,000 companies worldwide and nearly 2,000 in the U.K.

The detailed files in the databases used by Decision Index enable sales data updates and payment records to be accessed. Another important feature of the system, according to Mr. Philip Mellor, senior analyst at D&B, is that the information is dynamically updated. "It is updated overnight with any information that we may receive on a company from a variety of sources such as payment data." However, Mr. Mellor is quick to stress that such a monitoring device is no substitute for human credit management. Rather it is a sophisticated filter after which significant decisions are still the responsibility of the credit analyst. "It doesn't work without people being involved. If a score goes to a certain level then that is fine and it is accepted by the system, but if it doesn't reach the required level then we don't necessarily say we won't deal with the customer. A credit analyst will then look more closely at the proposal," says Mr. Griffiths.

Source: Christine Buckley, "System Cuts the Risks: Case Study/ Hunter Timber," *Financial Times Survey of Credit Management* (March 6, 1995).

to justify the costs. That is why many firms use a numerical credit scoring system to identify borderline applicants, who are then the subject of a full-blown detailed credit check. Other applicants are either accepted or rejected without further question.

21.4 The Credit Decision

credit policy Standards set to determine the amount and nature of credit to extend to customers.

You have taken the first three steps toward an effective credit operation. In other words, you have fixed your terms of sale; you have decided whether to sell on open account or to ask your customers to sign an IOU; and you have established a procedure for estimating the probability of customers paying up. Your next step is to decide on **credit policy.**

If there is no possibility of repeat orders, the credit decision is relatively simple. Figure 21.1 summarizes your choice. On the one hand, you can refuse credit and pass up the sale. In this case you make neither profit nor loss. The alternative is to offer credit. If you offer credit and the customer pays, you benefit by the profit margin on the sale. If the customer defaults, you lose the cost of the goods delivered.

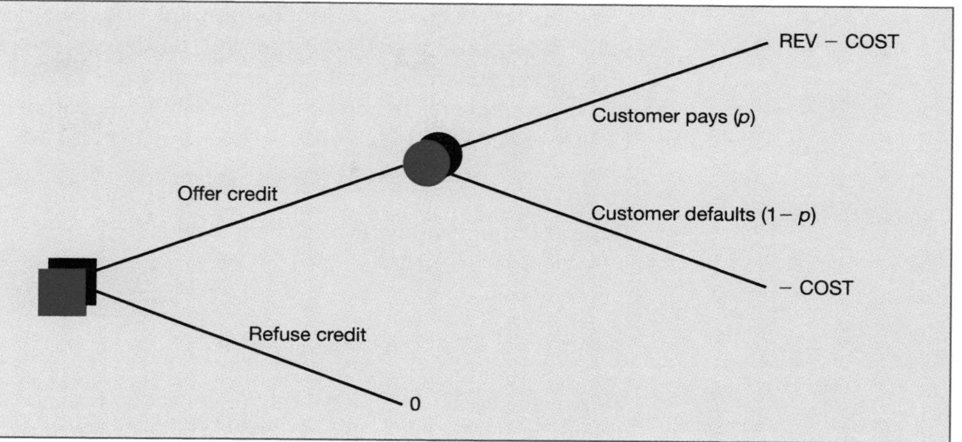

FIGURE 21.1
If you refuse credit, you make neither profit nor loss. If you offer credit, there is a probability (p) *that the customer will pay and you will make REV – COST; there is a probability (1 –* p*) that the customer will default and you will lose COST.*

The decision to offer credit depends on the probability of payment. You should grant credit if the expected profit from doing so is greater than the profit from refusing.

Suppose that the probability that the customer will pay up is p. If the customer does pay, you receive additional revenues (REV), and you deliver goods that you incurred costs to produce; your net gain is the present value of REV – COST. Unfortunately, you can't be certain that the customer will pay; there is a probability $(1 - p)$ of default. Default means you receive nothing but still incur the additional costs of the delivered goods. The *expected profit*[8] from the two sources of action is therefore as follows:

$$\begin{aligned} &\textbf{Refuse credit:} \quad \mathbf{0} \\ &\textbf{Grant credit:} \quad p \times \mathbf{PV(REV - COST)} - (\mathbf{1} - p) \times \mathbf{PV(COST)} \end{aligned} \qquad (21.2)$$

You should grant credit if the expected profit from doing so is positive.

▸ EXAMPLE 21.3 *The Credit Decision*

Consider the case of the Cast Iron Company. On each nondelinquent sale, Cast Iron receives revenues with a present value of \$1,200 and incurs costs with a present value of \$1,000. Therefore, the company's expected profit if it offers credit is

$$p \times \text{PV(REV} - \text{COST)} - (1 - p) \times \text{PV(COST)} = p \times 200 - (1 - p) \times 1{,}000$$

If the probability of collection is 5/6, Cast Iron can expect to break even:

$$\text{Expected profit} = 5/6 \times 200 - (1 - 5/6) \times 1{,}000 = 0$$

Thus Cast Iron's policy should be to grant credit whenever the chances of collection are better than 5 out of 6.

[8] Notice that we use the present values of costs and revenues. This is because there sometimes are significant lags between costs incurred and revenues generated. Also, while we follow convention in referring to the "expected profit" of the decision, it should be clear that our equation for expected profit is, in fact, the net present value of the decision to grant credit. As we emphasized in Chapter 1, the manager's task is to add value not to maximize accounting profits.

In this last example, the net present value of granting credit is positive if the probability of collection exceeds 5/6. In general, this break-even probability can be found by setting the net present value of granting credit equal to zero, and solving for p. It turns out that the formula for the break-even probability is simply the ratio of the present value of costs to revenues:

$$p \times \text{PV(REV} - \text{COST)} - (1 - p) \times \text{PV(COST)} = 0$$

Break-even probability of collection, then, is

$$p = \frac{\text{PV(COST)}}{\text{PV(REV)}}$$

CHECK POINT 21.3

What is the break-even probability of collection if the present value of the revenues from the sale is \$1,100 rather than \$1,200? Why does the break-even probability increase? Use your answer to decide whether firms that sell high-profit-margin or low-margin goods should be more willing to issue credit.

CREDIT DECISIONS WITH REPEAT ORDERS

What effect does the possibility of repeat orders have on your credit decision? One of the reasons for offering credit today is that you may get yourself a good, regular customer.

Cast Iron has been asked to extend credit to a new customer. You can find little information on the firm, and you believe that the probability of payment is no better than .8. If you grant credit, the expected profit on this order is

$$\begin{aligned}\text{Expected profit on initial order} &= p \times \text{PV(REV} - \text{COST)} - (1 - p) \times \text{PV(COST)} \\ &= (.8 \times 200) - (.2 \times 1{,}000) = -\$40\end{aligned}$$

You decide to refuse credit.

This is the correct decision *if* there is no chance of a repeat order. But now consider the future. If the customer does pay up, there will be a reorder next year. Having paid once, the customer will seem less of a risk. For this reason, any repeat orders are very profitable.

Think back to Chapter 8, and you will recognize that the credit decision bears many similarities to our earlier discussion of real options. By granting credit now, the firm retains the option to grant credit on an entire sequence of potentially profitable repeat sales. This option can be very valuable and can tilt the decision toward granting credit. Even a dubious prospect may warrant some initial credit if there is a chance that it will develop into a profitable steady customer.

EXAMPLE 21.4 *Credit Decisions with Repeat Orders*

To illustrate, let's look at an extreme case. Suppose that if a customer pays up on the first sale, you can be *sure* you will have a regular and completely reliable customer. In this case, the value of such a customer is not the profit of one order but an entire stream of profits from repeat purchases. For example, suppose that the customer will make one purchase each year from Cast Iron. If the discount rate is 10 percent and the profit on each order is \$200 per year, then the present value of an indefinite stream of business from a good customer is not \$200 but \$200/.10 = \$2,000. There is a probability (p) that Cast Iron will secure a good customer with a value of \$2,000. There is a probability of $(1 - p)$ that the customer will default, resulting in a loss of \$1,000. So, once we recognize the benefits of securing a good and permanent customer, the expected profit from granting credit is

$$\text{Expected profit} = (p \times 2{,}000) - (1 - p) \times 1{,}000$$

This is positive for any probability of collection above .33. Thus the break-even probability falls from 5/6 to 1/3.

If one sale may lead to profitable repeat sales, the firm should be inclined to grant credit on the initial purchase.

CHECK POINT 21.4

How will the break-even probability vary with the discount rate? Try a rate of 20 percent in Example 21.4. What is the thinking behind your answer?

SOME GENERAL PRINCIPLES

Real-life situations are generally far more complex than our simple examples. Customers are not all good or all bad. Many pay late consistently; you get your money, but it costs more to collect, and you lose a few months' interest. And estimating the probability that a customer will pay up is far from an exact science.

Like almost all financial decisions, credit allocation involves a strong dose of judgment. Our examples are intended as reminders of the issues involved rather than as "cookbook" formulas. Here are the basic things to remember:

1. *Maximize profit.* As credit manager, your job is not to minimize the number of bad accounts; it is to maximize profits. You are faced with a trade-off. The best that can happen is that the customer pays promptly; the worst is default. In the one case the firm receives the full additional revenues from the sale less the additional costs; in the other it receives nothing and loses the costs. You must weigh the chances of these alternative outcomes. If the margin of profit is high, you are justified in a liberal credit policy; if it is low, you cannot afford many bad debts.
2. *Concentrate on the dangerous accounts.* You should not expend the same effort on analyzing all credit decisions. If an application is small or clear-cut, your decision should be largely routine; if it is large or dubious, you might do better to move forward to a detailed credit appraisal. Most credit managers don't make credit decisions on an order-by-order basis. Instead they set a credit limit for each customer. The sales representative is required to refer the order for approval only if the customer exceeds this limit.
3. *Look beyond the immediate order.* Sometimes it may be worth accepting a relatively poor risk as long as there is a likelihood that the customer will grow into a regular and reliable buyer. (This is why credit card companies are eager to sign up college students even though few students can point to an established credit history.) New businesses must be prepared to incur more bad debts than established businesses because they have not yet formed relationships with low-risk customers. This is part of the cost of building up a good customer list.

Collection Policy

It would be nice if all customers paid their bills by the due date. But they don't, and since you may also "stretch" your payables, you can't really blame them.

Slow payers impose two costs on the firm. First, they require the firm to spend more resources in collecting payments. They also force the firm to invest more in working capital. Recall from Chapter 17 that accounts receivable are proportional to the average collection period (also known as days' sales in receivables):

$$\text{Accounts receivable} = \text{daily sales} \times \text{average collection period}$$

When your customers stretch payables, you end up with a longer collection period and a greater investment in accounts receivable. Thus you must establish a **collection policy.**

collection policy Procedures to collect and monitor receivables.

aging schedule Classification of accounts receivable by time outstanding.

The credit manager keeps a record of payment experiences with each customer. In addition, the manager monitors overdue payments by drawing up a schedule of the aging of receivables. The **aging schedule** classifies accounts receivable by the length of time they are outstanding. This may look similar to Table 21.1. The table shows that customer A, for example, is fully current: There are no bills outstanding for more than a month. Customer Z, however, might present problems, as there are $15,000 in bills that have been outstanding for more than 3 months.

When a customer is in arrears, the usual procedure is to send a *statement of account* and to follow this at intervals with increasingly insistent letters, telephone calls, or fax messages. If none of these has any effect, most companies turn the debt over to a collection agency or an attorney.

CHECK POINT 21.5

Suppose a customer who buys goods on terms 1/10, net 45, always forgoes the cash discount and pays on the 45th day after sale. If the firm typically buys $10,000 of goods per month, spread evenly over the month, what will the aging schedule look like?

There is always a potential conflict of interest between the collection department and the sales department. Sales representatives commonly complain that they no sooner win new customers than the collection department frightens them off with threatening letters. The collection manager, on the other hand, bemoans the fact that the sales force is concerned only with winning orders and does not care whether the goods are subsequently paid for. This conflict is another example of the agency problem introduced in Chapter 1.

TABLE 21.1
An aging schedule of receivables

Customer's Name	Less than 1 Month	1–2 Months	2–3 Months	More than 3 Months	Total Owed
A	$ 10,000	$ 0	$ 0	$ 0	$ 10,000
B	8,000	3,000	0	0	11,000
•	•	•	•	•	•
•	•	•	•	•	•
•	•	•	•	•	•
Z	5,000	4,000	6,000	15,000	30,000
Total	$200,000	$40,000	$15,000	$43,000	$298,000

Good collection policy balances conflicting goals. The company wants cordial relations with its customers. It also wants them to pay their bills on time.

There are instances of cooperation between sales managers and the financial managers who worry about collections. For example, the specialty chemicals division of a major pharmaceutical company actually made a business loan to an important customer that had been suddenly cut off by its bank. The pharmaceutical company bet that it knew its customer better than the customer's bank did—and the pharmaceutical company was right. The customer arranged alternative bank financing, paid back the pharmaceutical company, and became more of a loyal customer. It is a nice example of financial management supporting sales.

21.6 Bankruptcy

We have reviewed some of the techniques that firms use to evaluate the creditworthiness of their customers and to decide whether to issue credit. It would be helpful if these techniques were refined enough to distinguish between customers that will pay their bills and those that will go belly up, but this is not realistic. In any event, we have seen that granting credit to a financially shaky customer may pay off if there is a chance that the offer will lead to a profitable future relationship. Therefore, it is not uncommon for firms to have to deal with an insolvent customer.

According to the Office of the Superintendent of Bankruptcy (OSB), about 75,000 individuals and 10,000 businesses filed for bankruptcy in 2000. Individual liabilities totalled $4.09 billion while business liabilities were roughly $4.49 billion.[8] Our focus here is on business **bankruptcy**. Business bankruptcies account for only about 12 percent of the total number of bankruptcies, but because they are larger than individual bankruptcies, they involve about half of all claims by value. There are also more complications when a business declares bankruptcy compared to when an individual does. Table 21.2 provides details regarding business bankruptcies by type of industry in 2000.

bankruptcy The reorganization or liquidation of a firm that cannot pay its debts.

BANKRUPTCY PROCEDURES

A corporation that cannot pay its debts will often try to come to an informal agreement with its creditors. This is known as a **workout.** A workout may take several forms. For example, the firm may negotiate an *extension,* that is, an agreement with its creditors to delay payments. Or the firm may negotiate a *composition,* in which the firm makes partial payments to its creditors in exchange for relief of its debts.

workout Agreement between a company and its creditors establishing the steps the company must take to avoid bankruptcy.

The advantage of a negotiated agreement is that the costs and delays of formal bankruptcy are avoided. However, the larger the firm, and the more complicated its capital structure, the less likely it is that a negotiated settlement can be reached. (For example, the American firm, Wickes Corp. tried—and failed—to reach a negotiated settlement with its 250,000 creditors.)

Regulations pertaining to bankruptcies are provided in the Bankruptcy and Insolvency Act, 1992. Some companies are also governed by the Companies' Creditors Arrangement Act and the Winding-up and Restructuring Act. These laws provide mechanisms by which the firm's assets can be **liquidated**—that is, sold—and the proceeds used to pay creditors.

liquidation Sale of bankrupt firm's assets.

[8] These and other statistics are available at OSB's website, www.osb-bsf.gc.ca.

TABLE 21.2
Business bankruptcies reported in the calendar year 2000, by type of industry

Type of Industry	Number of Cases	Total Assets $	Total Liabilities $	Total Deficiency $
Agriculture & related services industries	263	54,860,506	90,590,256	35,729,751
Fishing & trapping industries	18	2,556,998	6,594,624	4,037,626
Logging & forestry industries	143	11,976,857	30,613,541	18,636,684
Mining, quarrying & oil well industries	66	297,555,345	590,348,431	292,793,086
Manufacturing industries	776	190,830,132	438,844,648	248,014,516
Construction industries	1,490	314,388,323	428,000,886	113,612,563
Transportation & storage industries	861	70,068,356	138,006,412	67,938,056
Communication & other utility industries	118	11,991,052	27,370,851	15,379,799
Wholesale trade industries	552	92,705,702	343,471,739	250,766,037
Retail trade industries	1,821	138,154,023	355,072,379	216,918,356
Finance & insurance industries	87	12,769,304	103,760,888	90,991,584
Real estate operations & insurance agencies industries	190	74,818,914	246,197,840	171,378,926
Business service industries	753	84,625,129	276,190,450	191,565,321
Government service industries	27	7,341,473	9,064,726	1,723,253
Educational service industries	36	1,999,034	9,033,925	7,034,891
Health & social service industries	133	11,407,002	28,264,544	16,857,543
Accommodation, food & beverage service industries	1,310	93,000,900	261,531,007	168,530,106
Other service industries	1,411	471,966,477	1,104,731,434	632,764,957
Total	**10,055**	**1,943,015,526**	**4,487,688,581**	**2,544,673,055**

Source: Office of the Superintendent of Bankruptcy Canada, "Annual Statistical Report for the 2000 Calendar Year," at www.osb-bsf.gc.ca. Reprinted with permission of the Minister of Public Works and Government Services Canada, 2002.

Liquidation usually involves a process wherein a petition is first filed in a federal court, either voluntarily by the debtor company, or involuntarily, if it is filed on behalf of the company by its creditors. A trustee in bankruptcy is then elected by the creditors to take over and liquidate the assets of the company. Proceeds from liquidating the assets are distributed among the creditors after paying bankruptcy administration costs. If any assets remain after meeting expenses and payments to creditors, they are distributed to preferred and common shareholders. This priority for distribution of claims may not always be followed at the discretion of the courts. Secured creditors are paid from the proceeds of sales of assets to which they have title, while unsecured creditors share in what is left over. If, however, the sale of the secured property does not generate sufficient cash to cover the amount owed, the secured creditors join with the unsecured creditors in dividing the liquidated value of remaining assets. In contrast, if secured assets are liquidated for proceeds greater than the secured claim, the net proceeds are used to pay unsecured creditors and others. In large bankruptcies involving numerous secured and unsecured claimants, creditors sometimes take controversial actions in their attempt at securing a piece of a shrinking asset pool. The nearby Finance in Action box describes the controversy surrounding Enron, the energy giant, and its recent bankruptcy filing and one of its large lenders, Citigroup.

SEE BOX P. 643

There is also a pecking order of unsecured creditors. First come claims for expenses that arise after bankruptcy is filed, such as attorneys' fees or employees' compensation earned

FINANCE IN ACTION

Citigroup's Enron Financing Challenged by Other Lenders

When Enron Corp. turned to its bankers for money in late October, the energy company needed a quick, big loan to restore investor confidence in its finances.

Citigroup, Inc., came up with the cash—but with a catch.

Enron owed Citigroup $250 million (US) in unsecured debt that was coming due in early December; just one portion of the overall debt Enron owes the bank. So Citigroup told Enron it would provide $600 million of a new $1 billion loan—as long as $250 million was used to pay back existing Citigroup debt, according to people familiar with the transaction.

Now, a number of bankers in the lending syndicate are crying foul. Citigroup, they say, used its influence as a new secured lender to improve the standing of unsecured loans it had already extended at the expense of other lenders. The bankers say they discovered, only later, that part of the loan facility was used to prop a Citigroup debt position. Thus, the bankers are likely to challenge Citigroup's arrangement as part of Enron's bankruptcy filing in a New York bankruptcy court.

Few can blame Citigroup for trying to reduce its exposure to Enron. But some analysts say the manoeuvre raises questions about whether Citigroup moved unfairly to grab assets. And the deal effectively reduced the pool of collateral, available to all of Enron's other creditors in the bankruptcy proceedings.

At a minimum, the controversy over the Citigroup financing underscores how contentious Enron's bankruptcy process could become, as numerous creditors fight to secure a piece of a shrinking asset pie. In addition, it continues to raise more questions about the multiple hats worn by large lenders such as Citigroup, and the conflicts that may be created with Enron's other creditors.

In most bankruptcy cases, unsecured creditors examine all loans extended before the filing to see whether the collateral was granted properly.

If an unsecured debt was to be paid off, or turned into a secured debt within 90 days of a bankruptcy, that lender is sometimes accused of receiving a "preference" over other lenders.

Because such "preferences" clash with a basic aim of bankruptcy law—to stop a race to the courthouse by treating all similarly situated creditors the same—they can be challenged in court.

If the Citigroup financing is successfully challenged, the $250 million claim would once again become unsecured, freeing up the collateral for the potential pool of assets to be divided up by unsecured creditors.

Source: Excerpt from Sapsford, Jathon and Pacelle, Mitchell, "Citigroup's Enron Financing Challenged by Other Lenders," the *Globe and Mail* (January 16, 2002) p. B2. (Reprinted from *The Wall Street Journal*.)

after the filing. If such postfiling claims did not receive priority, no firm in bankruptcy proceedings could continue to operate. Next come claims for wages and employee benefits earned in the period immediately prior to the filing. Taxes are next in line, together with debts to some government agencies such as the Workers' Compensation Board. Finally come general unsecured claims such as bonds or unsecured trade debt.

reorganization Restructuring of financial claims on failing firm to allow it to keep operating.

The alternative to a liquidation is to seek a **reorganization,** which keeps the firm as a going concern and usually compensates creditors with new securities, often including equity, in the reorganized firm. Such reorganizations are generally in the shareholders' interests—they have little to lose if things deteriorate further and everything to gain if the firm recovers.

Firms attempting reorganization may seek refuge under specific provisions of the Bankruptcy and Insolvency Act, 1992, the Companies' Creditors Arrangement Act, or the Winding-up and Restructuring Act. Such provisions are designed to keep the firm alive and operating and to protect the value of its assets while a plan of reorganization is being worked out. During this period, other proceedings against the firm are halted, and the company is operated by existing management or by a court-appointed trustee.[10] Recently, Consumers Packaging, Inc., a large glass manufacturer, which supplies 85 percent of all

[10] In the United States, firms attempting to reorganize would seek protection under Chapter 11 of the Bankruptcy Reform Act.

FINANCE IN ACTION

Laidlaw to Seek Bankruptcy Protection

Struggling Laidlaw, Inc., will seek bankruptcy court protection here and in the U.S. during the next few days in its reorganization and survival efforts. The Burlington-based transportation giant will apply to courts in Toronto and Buffalo for protection from creditors, so the company can proceed with a vote on a reorganization and repayment plan, sources said yesterday.

"There's an 80 to 90 percent chance it may come down (today)," said one insider familiar with the negotiations.

The source said creditors would get between $.70 and $.80 on the dollar under the proposal.

It would come in the form of $.17 in cash, $.25 in new notes and the remainder in shares in a newly restructured Laidlaw company.

Most of the senior creditors, including Canadian banks, support the plan, according to the source.

The company, which is trying to overcome the weight of a huge debt load, has been working on restructuring debts of more than $3.4 billion (US) and a reorganization plan since last year.

Laidlaw indicated late last year the company would likely complete a plan by spring and then apply for a brief period under bankruptcy court protection, in both countries, for further negotiations and a creditors' vote on the plan.

Laidlaw, North America's biggest public and school bus operator, ran into serious debt problems after an expansion drive during the last decade.

The acquisitions included interests in U.S. health-care operations, primarily in ambulance and hospital emergency services.

The company lost $90 million on revenues of $1.56 billion in the six months ended Feb. 28.

In fiscal 2000, Laidlaw reported an operating loss of $961 million on revenues of $2.92 billion.

Laidlaw reports its results in U.S. dollars.

However, Laidlaw's net loss climbed to a whopping $2.23 billion as the company wrote down investments in its health-care holdings and Safety-Kleen Corp.

Safety-Kleen, which is trying to overcome lawsuits and an accounting scandal, filed for bankruptcy protection last year.

Laidlaw suspended interest payments on its bank and bond debt more than a year ago. The company closed a $150 million (Cdn) financing deal to help provide working capital for all its operating companies, except the Greyhound Lines division early this year.

Laidlaw completed the deal with a group of banks, led by the Canadian Imperial Bank of Commerce, for a $100 million line of credit. It also secured another $50 million in short-term financing.

Greyhound, the biggest intercity bus line on the continent, got its own $125 million credit line last fall.

Laidlaw won't have to hold its annual meeting until Jan. 15, 2002, because of the restructuring efforts after receiving permission from the Ontario Court of Justice. Laidlaw's stock has traded as high as $.93 in the last year but is currently languishing at less than $.20 a share.

The stock closed at $.18 on the Toronto Stock Exchange yesterday.

Source: T. Van Alphen and S. Josey, "Laidlaw to Seek Bankruptcy Protection, Sources Say," the *Toronto Star Syndicate* (June 27, 2001) p. E01.

the wine, beer, and jam bottles used in Canada, filed for and obtained protection under the Companies' Creditors Arrangement Act, effectively putting its creditors on hold. The Ontario Superior Court has allowed the company time to restructure its $245 million (US) debt, mostly held by bondholders in the United States. The above Finance in Action box describes the restructuring and survival efforts of Laidlaw, Inc., as it prepared to seek protection from its creditors in Canadian and U.S. courts.

The responsibility for developing a plan of reorganization may fall on the debtor firm. Otherwise, a plan may also be submitted by others—for example, a trustee, if appointed, or a committee of creditors.

The reorganization plan is basically a statement of who gets what; each class of creditors gives up its claim in exchange for new securities. (Sometimes creditors receive cash as well.) The problem is to design a new capital structure for the firm that will (1) satisfy the creditors, and (2) allow the firm to solve the *business* problems that got the firm into trouble in the first place. Sometimes only a plan of baroque complexity can satisfy these two requirements. When the Penn Central Corporation was finally reorganized in the United States in 1978 (7 years after it became the largest railroad bankruptcy ever), more than a dozen new securities were created and parcelled out among 15 classes of creditors.

The reorganization plan goes into effect if it is accepted by creditors and confirmed by the court. Acceptance requires approval by a majority of each class of creditor. Once a plan is accepted, the court normally approves it, provided that *each* class of creditors has approved it and that the creditors will be better off under the plan than if the firm's assets were liquidated and distributed. The court may, under certain conditions, confirm a plan even if one or more classes of creditors vote against it. This is known as a *cram-down.*

The terms of a cram-down are open to negotiation among all parties. For example, unsecured creditors may threaten to slow the process as a way of extracting concessions from secured creditors. The secured creditors may take less than 100 cents on the dollar and give something to unsecured creditors in order to expedite the process and reach an agreement.

Restructuring efforts under court protection are often successful, and the patient emerges fit and healthy. But in other cases, cures prove impossible and the assets are sold or liquidated. Sometimes the firm may emerge from bankruptcy protection for a brief period before it is once again submerged by disaster and back in bankruptcy. For example, the American airline company, TWA, came out of Chapter 11 bankruptcy at the end of 1993 and was back again less than 2 years later, prompting jokes about "Chapter 22." The once successful Canadian clothing retailer, Dylex, emerged from bankruptcy protection in 1995. Five years later, the company was once again on the brink of bankruptcy and had sold most of its well-known retail outlets, such as BiWay, Tip Top Tailors, Thriftys, and Braemar.

THE CHOICE BETWEEN LIQUIDATION AND REORGANIZATION

Here is an idealized view of the bankruptcy decision. Whenever a payment is due to creditors, management checks the value of the firm. If the firm is worth more than the promised payment, the firm pays up (if necessary, raising the cash by an issue of shares). If not, the equity is worthless, and the firm defaults on its debt and petitions for bankruptcy. If in the court's judgment the assets of the bankrupt firm can be put to better use elsewhere, the firm is liquidated and the proceeds are used to pay off the creditors. Otherwise, the creditors simply become the new owners and the firm continues to operate.

In practice, matters are rarely so simple. For example, we observe that firms often petition for bankruptcy even when the equity has a positive value. And firms are often reorganized even when the assets could be used more efficiently elsewhere. The nearby Finance in Action box provides a striking example. There are several reasons.

SEE BOX P. 646

First, although the reorganized firm is legally a new entity, it is entitled to any tax-loss carry-forwards belonging to the old firm. If the firm is liquidated rather than reorganized, any tax-loss carry-forwards disappear. Thus there is an incentive to continue in operation even if assets are better used by another firm.

Second, if the firm's assets are sold off, it is easy to determine what is available to pay the creditors. However, when the company is reorganized, it needs to conserve cash as far as possible. Therefore, claimants are generally paid in a mixture of cash and securities. This makes it less easy to judge whether they have received their entitlement. For example, each bondholder may be offered $300 in cash and $700 in a new bond, which pays no interest for the first 2 years and a low rate of interest thereafter. A bond of this kind in a company that is struggling to survive may not be worth much, but the bankruptcy court usually looks at the face value of the new bonds and may decide that the bondholders have received as much as they would have if the firm was liquidated and, therefore, regard them as paid in full.

FINANCE IN ACTION

The Grounding of Eastern Airlines

Chapter 11 bankruptcy proceedings often involve a conflict between the objective of keeping the company afloat and that of protecting the interests of the lenders. Seldom has that conflict been more apparent than in the case of Eastern Airlines.

Eastern Airlines operated in the very competitive East Coast corridor and had services to South America and the Caribbean. For some years before it filed for bankruptcy, the company had had a record of high operating costs and poor labour relations. Its boss, Frank Lorenzo, had a reputation for union busting and one trade unionist had termed him "the Typhoid Mary of organized labour." Lorenzo's attempts to force Eastern's employees to take a wage cut led to a strike by machinists in March 1989 and almost immediately Eastern filed for bankruptcy under Chapter 11.

When Eastern filed for bankruptcy, it had saleable assets, such as planes and gates, worth over $4 billion. This would have been more than sufficient to pay off the company's creditors and preferred stockholders. But the bankruptcy judge decided that it was important to keep Eastern flying at all costs for the sake of its customers and employees.

Eastern did keep flying, but the more it flew, the more it lost. Management presented the bankruptcy court with three different plans to reorganize the company, but each time it immediately became clear that the plan was not viable. Eventually, the creditors' patience with management ran out, and they demanded the appointment of an independent trustee to run the company. However, the deficits continued to accumulate. In less than two years the airline had piled up additional losses of nearly $1.3 billion. Eventually, Eastern could no longer raise the cash to continue flying, and in January 1991 its planes were finally grounded.

Nearly four more years were to elapse before the court was able to settle on a plan to pay off Eastern's creditors and a further year passed before the last of the company's assets were sold. A large part of the proceeds from asset sales had been eaten up by the operating losses and just over $100 million had been seeped away in legal costs. Less than $900 million was left to pay off the creditors. The secured creditors received about 80 percent of what they were owed and unsecured creditors received just over 10 percent.

Source: The description of the bankruptcy of Eastern Airlines is based on L. A. Weiss and K. H. Wruck, "Information Problems, Conflicts of Interest, and Asset Stripping: Chapter 11's Failure in the Case of Eastern Airlines," *Journal of Financial Economics* 48 (1998), pp. 55–97.

Senior creditors who know they are likely to get a raw deal in a reorganization are likely to press for a liquidation. Shareholders and junior creditors prefer a reorganization. They hope that the court will not interpret the pecking order too strictly and that they will receive some crumbs.

Third, although shareholders and junior creditors are at the bottom of the pecking order, they have a secret weapon: They can play for time. Bankruptcies of large companies often take several years before a plan is presented to the court and agreed to by each class of creditor. The bankruptcy proceedings of the Missouri Pacific Railroad, in the United States, took a total of 22 years. When they use delaying tactics, the junior claimants are betting on a turn of fortune that will rescue their investment. On the other hand, the senior creditors know that time is working against them, so they may be prepared to accept a smaller payoff as part of the price for getting a plan accepted. Also, prolonged bankruptcy cases are costly (the liquidators handling the Eaton's bankruptcy reportedly received $80 million). Senior claimants may see their money seeping into lawyers' pockets and therefore decide to settle quickly.

Fourth, while a reorganization plan is being drawn up, the company is allowed to buy goods on credit and borrow money. Postpetition creditors (those who extend credit to a firm already in bankruptcy proceedings) have priority over the old creditors and their debt may even be secured by assets that are already mortgaged to existing debtholders. This also gives the prepetition creditors an incentive to settle quickly, before their claim on assets is diluted by the new debt.

Finally, profitable companies may file for bankruptcy to protect themselves against "burdensome" suits. For example, in 1982, Manville Corporation was threatened by 16,000 damage suits alleging injury from asbestos. Manville filed for bankruptcy under Chapter 11 of the Bankruptcy Reform Act in the United States, and the bankruptcy judge agreed to put the damage suits on hold until the company was reorganized. This took 6 years. Of course legislators worry that these actions are contrary to the original intent of the bankruptcy acts.

21.7 Summary

1. What are the usual steps in credit management?

The first step in credit management is to set normal **terms of sale.** This means that you must decide the length of the payment period and the size of any cash discounts. In most industries these conditions are standardized.

Your second step is to decide the form of the contract with your customer. Most domestic sales are made on **open account.** In this case the only evidence that the customer owes you money is the entry in your ledger and a receipt signed by the customer. Sometimes, you may require a more formal commitment before you deliver the goods. For example, the supplier may arrange for the customer to provide a trade acceptance.

The third task is to assess each customer's creditworthiness. When you have made an assessment of the customer's credit standing, the fourth step is to establish sensible credit policy. Finally, once the credit policy is set, you need to establish a collection policy to identify and pursue slow payers.

2. How do we measure the implicit interest rate on credit?

The effective interest rate for customers who buy goods on credit rather than taking the discount for quicker payment is

$$\left(\frac{1 + \text{discount}}{\text{discounted price}}\right)^{365/\text{extra days credit}} - 1$$

3. When does it make sense to ask the customer for a formal IOU?

When a customer places a large order, and you want to eliminate the possibility of any subsequent disputes about the existence, amount, and scheduled payment date of the debt, a formal IOU or promissory note may be appropriate.

4. How do firms assess the probability that a customer will pay?

Credit analysis is the process of deciding which customers are likely to pay their bills. There are various sources of information: your own experience with the customer, the experience of other creditors, the assessment of a credit agency, a check with the customer's bank, the market value of the customer's securities, and an analysis of the customer's financial statements. Firms that handle a large volume of credit information often use a formal system for combining the various sources into an overall credit score.

5. How do firms decide whether it makes sense to grant credit to a customer?

Credit policy refers to the decision to extend credit to a customer. The job of the credit manager is not to minimize the number of bad debts; it is to maximize profits. This means that you need to weigh the odds that the customer will pay, providing you with a profit, against the odds that the customer will default, resulting in a loss. Remember not to be too shortsighted when reckoning the expected profit. It is often worth accepting the marginal applicant if there is a chance that the applicant may become a regular and reliable customer.

If credit is granted, the next problem is to set a **collection policy.** This requires tact and judgment. You want to be firm with the truly delinquent customer, but you don't want to offend the good one by writing demanding letters just because a cheque has been delayed in the mail. You will find it easier to spot troublesome accounts if you keep a careful **aging schedule** of outstanding accounts.

6. What happens when firms cannot pay their creditors?

A firm that cannot meet obligations may try to arrange a **workout** with its creditors to enable it to settle its debts. If this is unsuccessful, the firm may file for **bankruptcy,** in which case the business may be liquidated or reorganized. **Liquidation** means that the firm's assets are sold and the proceeds used to pay creditors. **Reorganization** means that the firm is maintained as an ongoing concern, and creditors are compensated with securities in the reorganized firm. Ideally, reorganization should be chosen over liquidation when the firm as a going concern is worth more than its liquidation value. However, the conflicting interests of the different parties can result in violations of this principle.

RELATED WEB LINKS

www.nacm.org National Association of Credit Management

www.dnb.com Dun & Bradstreet's site; the premier guide to corporate credit decisions

www.osb–bsf.gc.ca Website of the Office of the Superintendent of Bankruptcy. This site provides a variety of information, including statistics on personal and business bankruptcies, relevant acts and laws, etc.

www.ny.frb.org/pihome/addpub/credit.html The Federal Reserve Bank of New York's guide to credit management

www.creditworthy.com Useful tips and online resources for credit management

www.ftc.gov/bcp/conline/pubs/credit/scoring.htm A discussion of the credit scoring process

http://bankrupt.com Resources for firms that have made some bad decisions

www.tuc.ca TransUnion Canada

www.strategis.gc.ca Website maintained by Industry Canada, providing a variety of trade, business, and consumer information

www.insolvency.ca The Insolvency Institute of Canada

KEY TERMS

terms of sale	630	collection policy	640	workout	641
open account	632	aging schedule	640	liquidation	641
credit analysis	633	bankruptcy	641	reorganization	643
credit policy	636				

QUESTIONS AND PROBLEMS

*Answers in Appendix B

BASIC

*1. **Trade Credit Rates.** Company X sells on a 1/20, net 60, basis. Customer Y buys goods with an invoice of $1,000.

a. How much can Company Y deduct from the bill if it pays on day 20?

b. How many extra days of credit can Company Y receive if it passes up the cash discount?

c. What is the effective annual rate of interest if Y pays on the due date rather than day 20?

2. **Terms of Sale.** Complete the following passage by selecting the appropriate terms from the following list (some terms may be used more than once): acceptance, open, commercial, trade, Canada, his or her own, note, draft, account, promissory, bank, banker's, the customer's.

Most goods are sold on ________ ________. In this case the only evidence of the debt is a record in the seller's books and a signed receipt. When the order is very large, the customer may be asked to sign a(n) ________ ________, which is just a simple IOU. An alternative is for the seller to arrange a(n) ________ ________ ordering payment by the customer. In order to obtain the goods, the customer must acknowledge this order and sign the document. This signed acknowledgment is known as a(n) ________ ________. Sometimes the seller may also ask ________ ________ bank to sign the document. In this case it is known as a(n) ________ ________.

3. **Terms of Sale.** Indicate which firm, of each pair, you would expect to grant shorter or longer credit periods:

a. One firm sells hardware; the other sells bread.

b. One firm's customers have an inventory turnover ratio of 10; the other firm's customers have a turnover of 15.

c. One firm sells mainly to electric utilities; the other to fashion boutiques.

*4. **Payment Lag.** The lag between purchase date and the date at which payment is due is known as the *terms lag.* The lag between the due date and the date on which the buyer actually pays is termed the *due lag,* and the lag between the purchase and actual payment dates is the *pay lag.* Thus

$$\text{Pay lag} = \text{terms lag} + \text{due lag}$$

State how you would expect the following events to affect each type of lag:

a. The company imposes a service charge on late payers.
b. A recession causes customers to be short of cash.
c. The company changes its terms from net 10 to net 20.

*5. **Bankruptcy.** True or false?

a. It makes sense to evaluate the credit manager's performance by looking at the proportion of bad debts.
b. When a company becomes bankrupt, it is usually in the interests of the equityholders to seek a liquidation rather than a reorganization.
c. A reorganization plan must be presented for approval by each class of creditor.
d. The Canada Customs and Revenue Agency has first claim on the company's assets in the event of bankruptcy.
e. In a reorganization, creditors may be paid off with a mixture of cash and securities.
f. When a company is liquidated, one of the most valuable assets to be sold is often the tax-loss carry-forward.

6. **Trade Credit Rates.** A firm currently offers terms of sale of 3/20, net 40. What effect will the following actions have on the implicit interest rate charged to customers that pass up the cash discount? State whether the implicit interest rate will increase or decrease.

a. The terms are changed to 4/20, net 40.
b. The terms are changed to 3/30, net 40.
c. The terms are changed to 3/20, net 30.

PRACTICE

*7. **Trade Credit and Receivables.** A firm offers terms of 2/15, net 30. Currently, two-thirds of all customers take advantage of the trade discount; the remainder pay bills at the due date.

a. What will be the firm's typical value for its accounts receivable period? (See Chapter 19, Section 19.1 for a review of the accounts receivable period.)
b. What is the average investment in accounts receivable if annual sales are $20 million?
c. What would likely happen to the firm's accounts receivable period if it changed its terms to 3/15, net 30?

8. **Terms of Sale.** Microbiotics currently sells all of its frozen dinners cash on delivery, but believes it can increase sales by offering supermarkets 1 month of free credit. The price per carton is $50 and the cost per carton is $40.

a. If unit sales will increase from 1,000 cartons to 1,060 per month, should the firm offer the credit? The interest rate is 1 percent per month, and all customers will pay their bills.
b. What if the interest rate is 1.5 percent per month?
c. What if the interest rate is 1.5 percent per month, but the firm can offer the credit only as a special deal to new customers, while old customers will continue to pay cash on delivery.

*9. **Credit Decision/Repeat Sales.** Locust Software sells computer training packages to its business customers at a price of $101. The cost of production (in present value terms) is $95. Locust sells its packages on terms of net 30 and estimates that about 7 percent of all orders will be not collectable. An order comes in for 20 units. The interest rate is 1 percent per month.

a. Should the firm extend credit if this is a one-time order? The sale will not be made unless credit is extended.
b. What is the break-even probability of collection?
c. Now suppose that if a customer pays this month's bill, it will place an identical order in each month indefinitely and can be safely assumed to pose no risk of default. Should credit be extended?
d. What is the break-even probability of collection in the repeat-sales case?

10. **Bankruptcy.** Explain why equity can sometimes have a positive value even when companies petition for bankruptcy.

*11. **Credit Decision.** Look back at Example 21.3. Cast Iron's costs have increased from $1,000 to $1,050. Assuming there is no possibility of repeat orders, and that the probability of successful collection from the customer is $p = .9$, answer the following:

   a. Should Cast Iron grant or refuse credit?
   b. What is the break-even probability of collection?

12. **Credit Analysis.** Financial ratios were described in Chapter 17. If you were the credit manager, to which financial ratios would you pay most attention?

13. **Credit Decision.** The Branding Iron Company sells its irons for $50 apiece wholesale. Production cost is $40 per iron. There is a 25 percent chance that a prospective customer will go bankrupt within the next half year. The customer orders 1,000 irons and asks for 6 months' credit. Should you accept the order? Assume a 10 percent per year discount rate, no chance of a repeat order, and that the customer will pay either in full or not at all.

14. **Credit Policy.** As treasurer of the Universal Bed Corporation, Aristotle Procrustes is worried about his bad debt ratio, which is currently running at 6 percent. He believes that imposing a more stringent credit policy might reduce sales by 5 percent and reduce the bad debt ratio to 4 percent. If the cost of goods sold is 80 percent of the selling price, should Mr. Procrustes adopt the more stringent policy?

15. **Credit Decision/Repeat Sales.** Surf City sells its network browsing software for $15 per copy to computer software distributors and allows its customers 1 month to pay their bills. The cost of the software is $10 per copy. The industry is very new and unsettled, however, and the probability that a new customer granted credit will go bankrupt within the next month is 25 percent. The firm is considering switching to a cash-on-delivery credit policy to reduce its exposure to defaults on trade credit. The discount rate is 1 percent per month.

   a. Should the firm switch to a cash-on-delivery policy? If it does so, its sales will fall by 40 percent.
   b. How would your answer change if a customer which is granted credit, pays its bills, and is expected to generate repeat orders with negligible likelihood of default for each of the next 6 months? Similarly, customers which pay cash also will generate on average 6 months of repeat sales.

*16. **Credit Policy.** A firm currently makes only cash sales. It estimates that allowing trade credit on terms of net 30 would increase monthly sales from 200 to 220 units per month. The price per unit is $101 and the cost (in present value terms) is $80. The interest rate is 1 percent per month.

   a. Should the firm change its credit policy?
   b. Would your answer to part (a) change if 5 percent of all customers fail to pay their bills under the new credit policy?
   c. What if 5 percent of only the *new* customers fail to pay their bills? The current customers take advantage of the 30 days of free credit but remain safe credit risks.

CHALLENGE

*17. **Credit Analysis.** Use the data in Example 21.3. Now suppose, however, that 10 percent of Cast Iron's customers are slow payers, and that slow payers have a probability of 30 percent of defaulting on their bills. If it costs $5 to determine whether a customer has been a prompt or slow payer in the past, should Cast Iron undertake such a check? *Hint:* What is the expected savings from the credit check? It will depend on both the probability of uncovering a slow payer and the savings from denying these payers credit.

18. **Credit Analysis.** Look back at the previous problem, but now suppose that if a customer defaults on a payment, you can eventually collect about half the amount owed to you. Will you be more or less tempted to pay for a credit check once you account for the possibility of partial recovery of debts?

*19. **Credit Policy.** Jim Khana, the credit manager of Velcro Saddles, is reappraising the company's credit policy. Velcro sells on terms of net 30. Cost of goods sold is 85 percent of sales. Velcro classifies customers on a scale of 1 to 4. During the past 5 years, the collection experience was as follows:

Classification	Defaults as Percentage of Sales	Average Collection Period in Days for Nondefaulting Accounts
1	0	45
2	2	42
3	10	50
4	20	80

The average interest rate was 15 percent. What conclusions (if any) can you draw about Velcro's credit policy? Should the firm deny credit to any of its customers? What other factors should be taken into account before changing this policy?

20. **Credit Analysis.** Galenic, Inc., is a wholesaler for a range of pharmaceutical products. Before deducting any losses from bad debts, Galenic operates on a profit margin of 5 percent. For a long time the firm has employed a numerical credit scoring system based on a small number of key ratios. This has resulted in a bad debt ratio of 1 percent.

Galenic has recently commissioned a detailed statistical study of the payment record of its customers over the past 8 years and, after considerable experimentation, has identified five variables that could form the basis of a new credit-scoring system. On the evidence of the past 8 years, Galenic calculates that for every 10,000 accounts it would have experienced the following default rates:

	Number of Accounts		
Credit Score under Proposed System	**Defaulting**	**Paying**	**Total**
Better than 80	60	9,100	9,160
Worse than 80	40	800	840
Total	100	9,900	10,000

By refusing credit to firms with a poor credit score (less than 80), Galenic calculates that it would reduce its bad debt ratio to 60/9,160 net, or just under .7 percent. While this may not seem like a big deal, Galenic's credit manager reasons that this is equivalent to a decrease of one-third in the bad debt ratio and would result in a significant improvement in the profit margin.

a. What is Galenic's current profit margin allowing for bad debts?
b. Assuming that the firm's estimates of default rates are right, how would the new credit-scoring system affect profits?
c. Why might you suspect that Galenic's estimates of default rates will not be realized in practice?
d. Suppose that one of the variables in the proposed new scoring system is whether the customer has an existing account with Galenic (new customers are more likely to default). How would this affect your assessment of the proposal? *Hint:* Think about repeat sales.

SOLUTIONS TO CHECK POINTS

21.1 To get the cash discount, you have to pay the bill within 10 days, that is, by May 11. With the 2 percent discount, the amount that needs to be paid by May 11 is $20,000 × .98 = $19,600. If you forgo the cash discount, you do not have to pay your bill until May 21, but on that date, the amount due is $20,000.

21.2 The cash discount in this case is 5 percent and customers who choose not to take the discount receive an extra 50 – 10 = 40 days credit. So the effective annual interest is

$$\text{Effective annual rate} = \left(1 + \frac{\text{discount}}{\text{discounted price}}\right)^{365/\text{extra days credit}} - 1$$

$$= \left(1 + \frac{5}{95}\right)^{365/40} - 1 = .597, \text{ or } 59.7\%$$

In this case the customer who does not take the discount is effectively borrowing money at an annual interest rate of 59.7 percent. This is higher than the rate in Example 21.1 because fewer days of credit are obtained by forfeiting the discount.

21.3 The present value of costs is still $1,000. Present value of revenues is now $1,100. The break-even probability is defined by

$$p \times 100 - (1 - p) \times 1{,}000 = 0$$

which implies that $p = .909$. The break-even probability is higher because the profit margin is now lower. The firm cannot afford as high a bad debt ratio as before since it is not making as much on its successful sales. We conclude that high-margin goods will be offered with more liberal credit terms.

21.4 The higher the discount rate the less important future sales are. Because the value of repeat sales is lower, the break-even probability on the initial sale is higher. For instance, we saw that the break-even probability was 1/3 when the discount rate was 10 percent. When the discount rate is 20 percent, the value of a perpetual flow of repeat sales falls to $200/.20 = $1,000, and the break-even probability increases to 1/2:

$$1/2 \times \$1{,}000 - 1/2 \times \$1{,}000 = 0$$

21.5 The customer pays bills 45 days after the invoice date. Because goods are purchased daily, at any time there will be bills outstanding with "ages" ranging from 1 to 45 days. At any time, the customer will have 30 days' worth of purchases, or $10,000, outstanding for a period of up to 1 month, and 15 days' worth of purchases, or $5,000, outstanding for between 1 month and 45 days. The aging schedule will appear as follows:

Age of Account	Amount
< 1 month	$10,000
1–2 months	$ 5,000

MINICASE

George Stamper, a credit analyst with Micro-Encapsulators Corp. (MEC), needed to respond to an urgent e-mail request from the western Canada sales office. The local sales manager reported that she had an opportunity to clinch an order from Surrey Spice (SS) for 50 encapsulators at $10,000 each. She added that she was particularly keen to secure this order since SS was likely to have a continuing need for 50 encapsulators a year and could therefore prove to be a very valuable customer. However, orders of this size for a new customer generally required head office agreement. It was therefore George's responsibility to make a rapid assessment of SS's creditworthiness and to approve or disapprove the sale.

George knew that SS was a medium-sized company with a patchy earnings record. After growing rapidly in the 1980s, SS had encountered strong competition in its principal markets and earnings had fallen sharply. George Stamper was not exactly sure to what extent this was a bad omen. New management had been brought in to cut costs and there were some indications that the worst was over for the company. Investors appeared to agree with this assessment, because the stock price had risen to $5.80 from its low of $4.25 the previous year. George had in front of him SS's latest financial statements, which are summarized in Table 21.2. He rapidly calculated a few key financial ratios and the company's *Z* score.

George also made a number of other checks on SS. The company had a small issue of bonds outstanding, which were rated BB by Dominion Bond Rating Service. Inquiries through MEC's bank indicated that SS had unused lines of credit totalling $5 million but had entered into discussions with its bank for a renewal of a $15 million bank loan that was due to be repaid at the end of the year. Telephone calls to SS's other suppliers suggested that the company had recently been 30 days late in paying its bills.

George also needed to take into account the profit that the company could make on SS's order. Encapsulators were sold on standard terms of 2/30, net 60. So if SS paid promptly, MEC would receive additional revenues of 50 × $9,800 = $490,000. However, given SS's cash position, it was more than likely that it would forgo the cash discount and would not pay until sometime after the 60 days. Since interest rates were about 8 percent, any such delays in payment would reduce the present value to MEC of the revenues. George also recognized that there were production and transportation costs in filling SS's order. These worked out at $475,000, or $9,500, a unit. Corporate profits were taxed at 35 percent.

Questions

1. What can you say about Surrey Spice's creditworthiness?
2. What is the break-even probability of default? How is it affected by the delay before SS pays its bills?
3. How should George Stamper's decision be affected by the possibility of repeat orders?

TABLE 21.3
Surrey Spice: summary financial statements (figures in millions of dollars)

	2001	2000
Assets		
Current assets		
Cash and marketable securities	5.0	12.2
Accounts receivable	16.2	15.7
Inventories	27.5	32.5
Total current assets	48.7	60.4
Fixed assets		
Property, plant, and equipment	228.5	228.1
Less accumulated depreciation	129.5	127.6
Net fixed assets	99.0	100.5
Total assets	147.7	160.9
Liabilities and shareholders' equity		
Current liabilities		
Debt due for repayment	22.8	28.0
Accounts payable	19.0	16.2
Total current liabilities	41.8	44.2
Long-term debt	40.8	42.3
Shareholders' equity		
Common stock[a]	10.0	10.0
Retained earnings	55.1	64.4
Total shareholders' equity	65.1	74.4
Total liabilities and shareholders' equity	147.7	160.9
Income Statement		
Revenue	149.8	134.4
Cost of goods sold	131.0	124.2
Other expenses	1.7	8.7
Depreciation	8.1	8.6
Earnings before interest and taxes	9.0	– 7.1
Interest expense	5.1	5.6
Income taxes	1.4	– 4.4
Net income	2.5	– 8.3
Allocation of net income		
Addition to retained earnings	1.5	– 9.3
Dividends	1.0	1.0

[a] 10 million shares.

PART EIGHT

Special Topics

22 Leasing

23 Mergers, Acquisitions, and Corporate Control

24 International Financial Management

25 Options

26 Risk Management

CHAPTER 22

Leasing

22.1 What is a Lease?

22.2 Why Lease?

22.3 Valuing Leases

22.4 When Do Financial Leases Pay?

22.5 Summary

Most of us occasionally rent a car, bicycle, or boat, and usually, these kinds of rentals are short-term—we rent them for a day or a week or so. But in corporate finance longer term rentals are common. A rental agreement that extends for a year or more and involves a series of fixed payments is called a **lease**.[1]

Firms often lease as an alternative to buying capital equipment. Computers are often leased; so are trucks, railroad cars, aircraft, and ships. Just about every kind of asset has been leased some time by somebody including electric and nuclear power plants, handball courts, and even horses.

Every lease involves two parties. The *user* of the asset is called the **lessee**. The lessee makes periodic payments to the *owner* of the asset, who is called the **lessor**. For example, if you sign an agreement to rent an apartment for a year, you are the lessee and the owner is the lessor.

Firms lease assets for a variety of reasons. One reason firms lease is for convenience, if the asset is only needed for a short period of time. Another reason is for the flexibility of cancelling the lease if the asset is no longer needed. However, tax reduction is the main reason for long-term leasing. Companies pay fewer taxes if they acquire the asset by leasing rather than borrowing. The tax savings occur because in a lease arrangement, it is the asset owner not the asset user who can deduct the asset's capital cost allowance (CCA) from its taxable income. By transferring the CCA from a lower taxed user to a higher taxed owner, total taxes are lowered and both parties are better off.

After reading this chapter you should be able to

- Understand the different kinds of leases and some of the reasons for their use.
- Assess the net present value of a long-term lease and understand how it is an alternative to debt financing.

[1] Our discussion of leasing is drawn, in part, from Chapter 25 of R. Brealey and S. Myers, *Principals of Corporate Finance*, 6th ed., (Boston, MA: McGraw-Hill, 2000).

22.1 What is a Lease?

lease Rental agreement for the use of an asset extending for more than 1 year and involving a series of fixed payments.

lessee User of the asset in a lease. Responsible for making regular payments to lessor.

lessor Owner of the asset in a lease. Receives regular payments from lessee.

operating lease Short-term, cancellable lease.

financial lease Long-term, noncancellable lease. It is also known as *capital* or *full-payout lease*.

Leases come in many forms, but in all cases the lessee (user) promises to make a series of payments to the lessor (owner). The lease contract specifies the monthly or semiannual payments; the first payment is usually due as soon as the contract is signed. The payments are usually level, but their time pattern can be tailored to the user's needs. For example, suppose that a manufacturer leases a machine to produce a complex new product. There will be a year's "shakedown" period before volume production starts. In this case, it might be possible to arrange for lower payments during the first year of the lease.

When a lease is terminated, the leased equipment reverts to the lessor. However, the lease agreement often gives the user the option to purchase the equipment or take out a new lease.

Some leases provide for the *temporary* use of an asset. Generally known as **operating leases**, these leases are either short-term or cancellable during the contract period at the option of the lessee. On the other hand, a **financial lease** provides for *long-term* use of an asset. With a financial lease, the lessee has the asset for most of its estimated economic life, and the lease cannot be cancelled, or can be cancelled only if the lessor is reimbursed for any losses. This type of lease is also called a *capital* or *full-payout* lease.[2]

Financial leases are a *source of financing*. Signing a financial lease contract is like borrowing money. There is an immediate cash inflow because the lessee is relieved of having to pay for the asset. But the lessee also assumes a binding obligation to make the payments specified in the lease contract. The user could have borrowed the full purchase price of the asset by accepting a binding obligation to make interest and principal payments to the lender. Thus the cash-flow consequences of leasing and borrowing are similar. In either case, the firm raises cash now and pays it back later. A large part of this chapter will be devoted to comparing leases and borrowing as financing alternatives.

Leases also differ in the services provided by the lessor. Under a *full-service,* or *rental* lease, the lessor promises to maintain and insure the equipment and to pay any property taxes due on it. In a *net* lease, the lessee agrees to maintain the asset, insure it, and pay any property taxes. Financial leases are usually net leases.

Most financial leases are arranged for brand new assets. The lessee identifies the equipment, arranges for the leasing company to buy it from the manufacturer, and signs a contract with the leasing company. This is called a *direct* lease. In other cases, the firm sells an asset it already owns and leases it back from the buyer. These *sale and lease-back* arrangements are common in real estate. For example, a company may wish to raise cash by selling a factory, but still retain use of it. It could do this by selling the factory for cash to a leasing company and simultaneously signing a long-term lease for the factory. Legal ownership of the factory passes to the leasing company, but the right to use it stays with the company.

You may also encounter *leveraged* leases. These are financial leases in which the lessor borrows part of the purchase price of the leased asset, using the lease contract as security for the loan. This does not change the lessee's obligations, but it can complicate the lessor's analysis considerably.

The *leasing industry* is made up of various types of companies that are in the business of providing leases. Some of the largest lessors are equipment manufacturers. For example, IBM is a large lessor of computers, and Xerox is a large lessor of copiers. By offering leasing, they are able to sell more products.

The other two major groups of lessors are banks and independent leasing companies. In

[2] In the shipping industry, a financial lease is called a *bareboat charter* or a *demise hire*.

Canada, banks are currently not permitted to engage in consumer car leasing but are active in other types of leasing. Independent leasing companies have grown significantly in number and exist in many different sizes. For example, GE Capital, a large company, operates in many different countries and leases a wide range of assets. Its subsidiary, GE Capital Aviation Services, owned and leased out about 1,100 commercial aircraft in 2001. A large fraction of the world's airlines rely entirely on leasing to finance their fleet. Some of the independent lessors are small- and medium-sized businesses who specialize in the financing of particular kinds of equipment and vehicles.

Leasing has grown substantially since the 1950s when the first independent leasing companies, completely separate from the manufacturers, were established. Now, leasing provides significant amounts of financing to businesses worldwide. In Canada, it is estimated that 20 to 25 percent of total business investment in machinery and equipment is financed by asset-based financing and leasing.[3]

EXAMPLE 22.1 *Operating and Financial Lessors*

GE Capital, with assets of more than $345 billion (US), is a major global, diversified financial services company. Its businesses include providing operating and financial leases for many different types of assets including cars, trucks and trailers, jets, and commercial equipment. As an operating lessor, GE Capital has a significant number of "off-lease assets"—assets available to be leased but are currently not leased. Sometimes off-lease assets are sold, rather than leased again. On its website at www.gecapital.com, GE Capital has a long list of off-lease assets for sale. Items for sale include logging equipment, helicopters, and injection molding production lines.

By contrast, lessors specializing in providing financial leases do not end up with off-lease assets. Typically, at the end of the financial lease, the lessee purchases the asset from the lessor. For example, TD Asset Finance primarily offers financial leases and supplies relatively few operating leases; they do not want to be in the used-equipment business.

Why Lease?

You hear many suggestions about why companies should lease equipment rather than buy it. Let us look at some sensible reasons and then at four more dubious ones.

SENSIBLE REASONS FOR LEASING

Short-Term Leases Are Convenient. Suppose you want the use of a car for a week. You could buy one and sell it 7 days later, but that would be silly. Apart from the fact that registering ownership is a nuisance, you would spend some time selecting a car, negotiating its purchase, and arranging insurance. Then at the end of the week you would negotiate resale and cancel the registration and insurance. When you need a car for only a short time, it clearly makes sense to rent it. You save the trouble of registering ownership, and you know the effective cost. In the same way, it pays a company to lease equipment that it needs for only a year or two. Of course, this kind of lease is always an operating lease.

[3] Canadian Finance and Leasing Association backgrounder on the asset-based financing, equipment and vehicle leasing industry in Canada, December 2000, found at the CFLA website, www.cfla-acfl.ca.

Sometimes the cost of short-term rentals may seem prohibitively high, or you may find it difficult to rent at any price. This can happen for equipment that is easily damaged by careless use. The owner knows that short-term users are unlikely to take the same care they would with their own equipment. When the danger of abuse becomes too high, short-term rental markets do not survive. Thus, it is easy enough to buy a Lamborgini Diablo, provided your pockets are deep enough, but nearly impossible to rent one.

Cancellation Options Are Valuable. Some leases that *appear* expensive really are fairly priced once the option to cancel is recognized.

Maintenance Is Provided. Under a full-service lease, the user receives maintenance and other services. Many lessors are well-equipped to provide efficient maintenance. However, bear in mind that these benefits will be reflected in higher lease payments.

EXAMPLE 22.2 *Leasing a Horse*

Did you know that you can lease a horse? Horse leasing is a good way to find out if you are ready to own a horse without the long-term commitment of purchasing one. It can also make sense for meeting the changing needs of growing teenagers whose horse-riding skills are improving. Rather than buying and selling a succession of horses, it may be cheaper to lease. Leases can include the cost of board, vet, and farrier (someone who puts shoes on the horse) on top of the lease fee. The terms of the lease may include how often the horse can be ridden, what feed it gets, and who pays in the event the horse gets hurt. Like other short-term leases, a horse lease is more expensive than buying the horse itself. If you think you want the horse for many years, you would be better off buying it.

Standardization Leads to Low Administrative and Transaction Costs. Suppose that you operate a leasing company that specializes in financial leases for trucks. You are effectively lending money to a large number of firms (lessees), which may differ considerably in size and risk. But because the underlying asset is, in each case, the same saleable item (a truck), you can safely "lend" the money (lease the truck) without conducting a detailed analysis of each firm's business. You can also use a simple, standard lease contract. This standardization makes it possible to "lend" small sums of money without incurring large investigative, administrative, or legal costs.

For these reasons leasing is often a relatively cheap source of cash for the small company. It offers financing on a flexible, piecemeal basis and has lower transaction costs than in a private placement or a public bond, or stock issue.

Tax Shields Can Be Used. The lessor owns the leased asset and deducts the asset's capital cost allowance (CCA) from taxable income. If the lessor can make better use of CCA tax shields than an asset's user can, it may make sense for the leasing company to own the equipment and pass on some of the tax benefits to the lessee in the form of lower lease payments.

SOME DUBIOUS REASONS FOR LEASING

Leasing Avoids Capital Expenditure Controls. In many companies lease proposals are scrutinized as carefully as capital expenditure proposals, but in others, leasing may enable an operating manager to avoid the elaborate approval procedures needed to buy an asset.

Although this is a dubious reason for leasing, it may be influential, particularly in the public sector. For example, hospitals have sometimes found it politically more convenient to lease their medical equipment than to ask the government to provide funds for purchase.

Leasing Preserves Capital. Leasing companies provide "100 percent financing"; they advance the full cost of the leased asset. Consequently, they often claim that leasing preserves capital, allowing the firm to save its cash for other things.

But the firm can also "preserve capital" by borrowing money. If Greenfield Construction leases a $100,000 backhoe rather than buying it, it does conserve $100,000 cash. It could also (1) buy the backhoe for cash, and (2) borrow $100,000, using the backhoe as security. Its bank balance ends up the same whether it leases or buys and borrows. It has the backhoe in either case, and it incurs a $100,000 liability in either case. What's so special about leasing?

Leases May Be Off-Balance-Sheet Financing. The rules for reporting leases in a firm's financial statements vary internationally. In some countries, such as Germany, financial leases are **off-balance-sheet financing**; that is, a firm can acquire an asset, finance it through a financial lease, and show neither the asset nor the lease contract on its balance sheet. All lease payments are recognized as an expense of the lessee and reported as lease income by the lessor. No distinction is made between operating leases, which give temporary use of an asset, and financial leases, which are commitments of the lessee to use and pay for the asset over the bulk of the asset's economic life.

off-balance-sheet financing Financing that is not shown as a liability in a company's balance sheet.

Both the Canadian Accounting Standards Board (AcSB) and the U.S. Financial Accounting Standards Board (FASB) require that leases be accounted for according to who bears the risks and rewards of ownership of the assets. In an operating lease, the lessor bears the risks and rewards of ownership because the lease is short term. At the end of the lease period, the lessor gets the asset back and bears the risk of finding another lessee. The asset stays on the lessor's balance sheet and the lessor reports lease payments as income. Likewise, the lessee is just a temporary user of the asset and the lease payments are another business expense.

With a financial lease, although the lessor is the legal owner of the leased assets, the lessee bears essentially all of the risk and rewards of ownership. As we noted, a financial lease is primarily a means of providing financing so that the lessee can acquire the asset without actually buying it upfront. Canadian and U.S. accounting rules require that the financial statements reflect the true economic consequences of a financial lease. In other words, the leased assets are reported along with the other assets on the balance sheet of the lessee. Likewise, the lease financing shows up as liability on the lessee's balance sheet. To do this, the lease is *capitalized*.

To capitalize a lease, the present value of the lease payments is calculated and listed along with debt on the right-hand side of the balance sheet. The same amount is shown as an asset on the left-hand side. This leased asset would typically be included with other fixed assets and is amortized over the life of the lease. The amortization is deducted from book income, just as depreciation is deducted for a purchased asset.

According to the *CICA Handbook*, a lease is normally considered to be a financial lease when at least one of the following conditions is present at the start of the lease:[4]

1. There is reasonable assurance that the lessee will obtain ownership of the leased property at the end of the lease term. This would occur if the lease provides for automatic transfer of title to the lessee at the end of the lease, or if the lessee is entitled to purchase the asset at a bargain price (below its expected value) at the end of the lease.

[4] These criteria are from *CICA Handbook*, para. 3065.06, as summarized in Beechy and Conrod, *Intermediate Accounting, Volume 2*, McGraw-Hill Ryerson (2000), pp. 1004–1005. CICA, the Canadian Institute of Chartered Accountants, is the professional association and regulator of Canadian chartered accountants.

2. The lessee will receive all of the economic benefits expected to be derived through the use of the leased asset. Since assets are most productive in the earlier years of their lives, this condition is presumed to be satisfied if the lease term is at least 75 percent of the asset's economic life.

3. The lessor is assured of recovering the investment in the leased asset plus a return on its investment over the lease term. This condition is presumed to be satisfied if the present value of the lease payments is equal to at least 90 percent of the fair value of the asset at the inception of the lease.

The Canadian criteria are similar to those used in the United States. In Canada and the U.S., all other leases are operating leases as far as accountants are concerned.

Many financial managers have tried to take advantage of this arbitrary boundary between operating and financial leases. Suppose that you want to finance a computer-controlled machine tool costing $1 million. The machine tool's life is expected to be 12 years. You could sign a lease contract for 8 years, 11 months (just missing requirement 2) with lease payments having a present value of $899,000 (just missing requirement 3). You could also make sure the lease contract avoids requirement 1. Result? You have off-balance-sheet financing. This lease would not have to be capitalized, although it is clearly a long-term fixed obligation.

Now we come to the big question: Why should anyone *care* whether financing is off balance sheet or on balance sheet? Shouldn't the financial manager worry about substance rather than appearance? Indeed, the International Accounting Standards Committee thinks the distinction made between operating and financial leases is arbitrary. In a recent discussion paper, a proposal was made that all leases, both operating and financial, be accounted for in terms of the rights and obligations of lease obligation. This would result in capitalization of operating leases, so that the present value of the minimum lease payments would be reported as a liability of the lessee and no longer treated as off-balance-sheet financing.

When a firm obtains off-balance-sheet financing, the conventional measures of financial leverage, such as the debt-equity ratio, understate the true degree of financial leverage. Some believe that financial analysts do not always notice off-balance-sheet lease obligations (which are still referred to in footnotes) or the greater volatility of earnings that result from the fixed lease payments. They may be right, but we would not expect such an imperfection to be widespread.

When a company borrows money, it must usually consent to certain restrictions on future borrowing. Early bond indentures did not include any restrictions on financial leases.Therefore leasing was seen as a way to circumvent restrictive covenants. Loopholes such as these are easily stopped, and most bond indentures now include limits on leasing.

Long-term lease obligations ought to be regarded as debt whether or not they appear on the balance sheet. Financial analysts may overlook moderate leasing activity, just as they overlook minor debts. But major lease obligations are generally recognized and taken into account.

SEE BOX P. 662

Debt-rating agencies, such as Moody's and Standard and Poor's, do not ignore operating leases when assessing a company's financial leverage. In the nearby Finance in Action box, you can read about Moody's treatment of operating leases.

Leasing Affects Book Income. Leasing can make the firm's balance sheet and income statement *look* better by increasing book income or decreasing book asset value, or both.

A lease which qualifies as off-balance-sheet financing affects book income in only one way: The lease payments are an expense. If the firm buys the asset instead and borrows to finance it, both depreciation and interest expense are deducted. Leases are usually set up

FINANCE IN ACTION

Off-Balance-Sheet Leases: Capitalization and Ratings Implications

Out of Sight But Not Out of Mind

Should creditors to a company engaged in off-balance-sheet leases be concerned about the existence of these transactions? The argument is that leases are secured by their own assets and could effectively be ignored for the purpose of analyzing on-balance-sheet debt. However, we beg to differ, and firmly believe that leases represent use of a company's debt capacity and could meaningfully impact the recovery prospects of a balance sheet creditor in a stress scenario.

Debt capacity may be loosely defined as a company's ability to *incur additional* debt. Simply put, a use of debt capacity and a corresponding increase in leverage, arises from any transaction that stakes a claim to a company's cash flow.

It is not difficult to see why leases do utilize a company's debt capacity. Lease agreements are contractual obligations, resulting in a claim on cash flow through fixed lease payments over the life of the lease. Failure to comply with the terms of the lease agreement would constitute default. Besides, in the absence of a lease financing option, the company would likely borrow the money and buy the asset.

Our discussion will focus on operating lease transactions. Our objectives are two-fold: to accurately depict a firm's effective leverage and to achieve comparability in analyzing firms employing different financing tools (e.g., lease vs. buy).... The choice of capitalization method is ultimately a judgement call, though we believe the present value approach (or variations thereof) may be the lesser of the evils.... We calculate the net present value of the future minimum lease payments using an appropriate discount rate.

Once an "appropriate" capitalization amount [for the operating leases] is determined we may incorporate it into the analysis and rating of the various debt issues. It is more meaningful to incorporate capitalized lease if the amount is significant and the leased assets are essential to the business.

Source: Moody's Investors Services, Global Credit Research, "Off-Balance Sheet Leases: Capitalization and Rating Implications," (October 1999).

so that payments in the early years are less than depreciation plus interest under the buy-and-borrow alternative. Consequently, leasing increases book income in the early years of an asset's life. The book rate of return can increase even more dramatically because the book value of assets (the denominator in the book-rate-of-return calculation) is understated if the leased asset never appears on the firm's balance sheet.

Leasing's impact on book income should in itself have no effect on firm value. In efficient capital markets, investors will look through the firm's accounting results to the true value of the asset and the liability incurred to finance it.

22.3 Valuing Leases

OPERATING LEASES

Leases can be attractive for a variety of reasons. However, the decision to lease requires careful calculation of the cash inflows and outflows from the lease. If you are considering an *operating* lease, decide whether it is cheaper to lease the asset for the time that you need it or to buy it. Figure out the *equivalent annual cost*[5] of buying the asset and compare it to the annual lease payment charged by the lessor. In other words, can you "lease" the asset to yourself more cheaply than you can lease it from a lessor? Generally, the longer you need the asset, the more sense it makes to buy it rather than arranging an operating lease.

[5] Look back to Chapter 6 for a review of equivalent annual cost and an example of the analysis of an operating lease.

An attractive feature of an operating lease is the option to cancel the lease, avoiding the risks of obsolescence. The options embedded in an operating lease can be very valuable but are rather tricky to assess and are beyond this book. In general, operating leases make sense when the user needs the equipment for a short time, when the lessor is better able to bear the risks of obsolescence, or when the lessor can offer a good deal on maintenance.

FINANCIAL LEASES

When you are considering a *financial* lease, the decision amounts to "lease versus borrow." Financial leases extend over most of the economic life of the lease equipment. They are *not* cancellable. The lease payments are fixed obligations equivalent to *debt service*, the sum of interest and principal repayment on the debt.

Financial leases make sense when the company is prepared to take on the business risks of owning and operating the leased asset. Suppose a company is thinking about getting a stretch limousine. If they aren't sure whether they will use it enough, they will want to consider an operating lease to give them the option of cancelling the lease: They will avoid the risk of owning the limo. If the company signs a financial lease, it is stuck with the limo for a long time. The financial lease is just another way of borrowing to pay for the asset.

Financial leases do offer special advantages to some firms in some circumstances. However, there is no point in discussing this further until you know how to value financial lease contracts.

CASH FLOWS OF A FINANCIAL LEASE

Imagine yourself in the position of Jane Jones, president of Greenfield Construction. Your firm was established by your grandfather, who was quick to capitalize on the growing demand of residential housing in Busy Town. The company has always owned all of its construction equipment since the time the company was formed; you are now reconsidering this policy. Your operating manager wants to buy a new backhoe-loader costing \$100,000. The backhoe will last 7 years before going to the scrap yard. You are convinced that the investment in the additional equipment is worthwhile. A representative of the equipment manufacturer has pointed out that her firm is willing to lease the backhoe to you if you make seven annual payments of \$18,500, payable at the start of each year. Greenfield would remain responsible for all maintenance, insurance, and operating expenses.

Table 22.1 shows the direct cash-flow consequences of signing the lease contract rather than purchasing the backhoe. (An important indirect effect is considered later.) The consequences are:

1. Greenfield does not have to pay for the backhoe. This is equivalent to a cash inflow of \$100,000.
2. Greenfield would not own the backhoe, and so it cannot claim any CCA. Therefore it gives up a valuable CCA tax shield. Calculation of the tax shield is shown in Table 22.1. We assume that the backhoe is a Class 38 asset with a 30 percent CCA rate. To simplify the calculations, we assume that Greenfield is able to hold this asset alone in its own asset pool. After 7 years of operation, the backhoe is scrapped and a terminal loss equal to the remaining undepreciated capital cost is taken.
3. Greenfield must pay \$18,500 per year for 7 years to the lessor. The first payment is due immediately.
4. However, these lease payments are fully tax-deductible. At a 35 percent marginal tax rate, each lease payment generates an annual tax shield of .35 × \$18,500, or \$6,475. The after-tax lease payment is \$18,500 – \$6,475, or \$12,025.

In Table 22.1, the first CCA deduction occurs at Year 0 because we assume that the backhoe is purchased at the end of Year 0.[6] Table 22.1 also assumes that the backhoe will be worthless when it goes to the scrap yard at the end of Year 7. Otherwise there would be an entry for salvage value lost, and the undepreciated capital cost would have been reduced by the salvage value before we took the terminal loss.

CHECK POINT 22.1

Suppose the backhoe-loader cost $85,000, has zero-expected salvage value, and the annual lease payments are $15,000, payable in advance. If the lease is for 7 years, what are Greenfield's after-tax cash flows from leasing, rather than buying the backhoe, assuming everything else is unchanged?

WHO REALLY OWNS THE LEASED ASSET?

To a lawyer or a tax accountant, that would be a silly question: The lessor is clearly the *legal* owner of the leased asset. That is why the lessor is allowed to deduct depreciation from taxable income.

From an *economic* point of view, you might say that the *user* is the real owner, because in a *financial* lease, the user faces the risks and receives the rewards of ownership. Greenfield cannot cancel a financial lease. If the new backhoe turns out be hopelessly expensive and unsuited for Greenfield, that is Greenfield's problem not the lessor's. If it turns out to be a great success, the profit goes to Greenfield not the lessor. The success or failure of the firm's business operations does not depend on whether the backhoes are financed by leasing or some other financial instrument.

In many respects, a financial lease is equivalent to a secured loan. The lessee must make a series of fixed payments; if the lessee fails to do so, the lessor can repossess the asset.

TABLE 22.1

Cash flow consequences to Greenfield Construction by accepting the lease contract rather than purchasing the backhoe-loader (figures in dollars; some columns may not add up due to rounding)

	Year							
Lease Cash Flows	0	1	2	3	4	5	6	7
Saved cost of a new backhoe-loader	+100,000							
Lost CCA tax shield (calculated below)	–5,250	–8,925	–6,248	–4,373	–3,061	–2,143	–1,500	–3,500
Lease payment	–18,500	–18,500	–18,500	–18,500	–18,500	–18,500	–18,500	
Lease payment tax shield	+6,475	+6,475	+6,475	+6,475	+6,475	+6,475	+6,475	
Cash flow of lease	82,725	–20,950	–18,273	–16,398	–15,086	–14,168	–13,525	–3,500
Tax Shield Calculation								
UCC	100,000	85,000	59,500	41,650	29,155	20,409	14,286	10,000
CCA (CCA rate = 30%)	15,000	25,500	17,850	12,495	8,747	6,123	4,286	
CCA tax shield (tax rate = 35%)*	5,250	8,925	6,248	4,373	3,061	2,143	1,500	3,500

Notes:

* At the very end of Year 7 the backhoe is scrapped, generating a terminal loss of $10,000, equal to the undepreciated capital cost. The terminal loss creates a tax savings of .35 x $10,000, or $3,500.

[6] In Chapter 6, the first CCA deduction always occurred in Year 1 because we implicitly assumed that the asset was purchased in Year 1. However, it is only an assumption—the asset could have been purchased at the end of Year 0 and the first CCA deduction taken in Year 0. In practice, a company will think about the tax consequences of the timing of significant asset purchases.

Thus we can think of a balance sheet like this

Greenfield Construction (figures in thousands of dollars)

Backhoe-loader	100	100	Loan secured by backhoe-loader
All other assets	1,000	450	Other loans
		550	Equity
Total assets	1,100	1,100	Total liabilities

as being economically equivalent to a balance sheet like this:

Greenfield Construction (figures in thousands of dollars)

Backhoe-loader	100	100	Financial lease
All other assets	1,000	450	Other loans
		550	Equity
Total assets	1,100	1,100	Total liabilities

Having said this, we must immediately add two qualifications. First, legal ownership can make a big difference when a financial lease expires because the lessor gets the salvage value of the asset. Once a secured loan is paid off, the user owns the asset free and clear.

Second, whether you are lessor or a secured creditor makes a difference in bankruptcy or reorganization. When a lessee fails to make a lease payment, the lessor is entitled to take back its asset. However, what if the value of that asset is much less than the present value of the future lease payments the lessee had promised to pay? The lessor loses. The lessor can try to recover its loss from the firm but the lessor is only an unsecured creditor.

By contrast, if the firm defaults on a secured lender, the secured lender is entitled to receive the full amount of the principal and unpaid interest, secured by the asset. In default, the lender can sell the asset to recover the full amount owed. If this asset is worth less than the amount the lender is owed, the lender is entitled to make a claim for the full amount of the difference. This claim has priority over the other unsecured lenders of the firm.

Of course, neither the lessor nor the secured lender can be sure it will be paid the full amount they are owed. Our point is that lessors and secured creditors have different rights when the asset user gets into financial trouble.

LEASING AND THE CANADA CUSTOMS AND REVENUE AGENCY (CCRA)

We have already noted that the lessee loses the CCA of the leased asset but can deduct the lease payment in full. The *lessor,* as legal owner, uses the CCA tax shield but must report the lease payments as taxable rental income.

However, the CCRA is suspicious by nature and will not allow the lessee to deduct the entire lease payment unless it is satisfied that the arrangement is a genuine lease and not a disguised installment purchase or secured loan agreement. Here are examples of lease provisions that will arouse its suspicion:[7]

1. Giving the lessee the option to acquire the asset, say for $1, when the lease expires. Such a provision would effectively give the asset's salvage value to the lessee.
2. The lessee automatically acquires title to the property after payment of a specified amount in lease payments.
3. The lessee is required to buy the asset at the end of lease contract.

[7] This list is based on information contained in *CCRA Interpretation Bulletin*, IT 233-R. However, this bulletin was cancelled in June 2001 because it was being misused. The CCRA stated that whether a contract is a lease or sale it is based on the legal relationship created by the terms of the agreement. Further clarification of this in the near future is expected.

FIRST PASS AT VALUING A FINANCIAL LEASE CONTRACT

When we left Jane Jones, president of Greenfield Construction, she was thinking about whether to buy or to lease the required new backhoe-loader. She had set down in Table 22.1 the incremental cash flows from leasing the backhoe rather than purchasing it. To recap, by leasing and not purchasing the equipment, Greenfield does not pay upfront for the backhoe. However, in each of the subsequent years, the lease payments must be made and the CCA tax shields are foregone. If leasing is preferred to purchasing, the net present value of these lease cash flows must be positive. In other words, the cash saved upfront must be greater than the present value of the future cash outflows required to service the lease obligation. If the NPV is negative, Greenfield pays out more in future cash flows than the cash saved initially. In this case, shareholders of Greenfield are worse off by leasing than purchasing the backhoe.

What is the appropriate discount rate to use in calculating the NPV of the lease? That depends on the nature of the risks of the cash flows. The lease cash flows are typically assumed to be about as safe as the interest and principal payments on a secured loan issued by the lessee. This assumption is reasonable for the lease payments because the lessor is effectively lending money to the lessee. But the various tax shields might carry enough risk to deserve a higher discount rate. For example, Greenfield might be confident that it could make the lease payments but not confident that it could earn enough taxable income to use these tax shields. In that case the cash flows generated by the tax shields would probably deserve a higher discount rate than the borrowing rate used for the lease payments.

A lessee might, in principle, end up using a separate discount rate for each line of Table 22.1, each rate chosen to fit the risk of that line's cash flow. But established, profitable firms usually find it reasonable to simplify by discounting the types of flows shown in Table 22.1 at a single rate based on the rate of interest the firm would pay if it borrowed rather than leased. We will assume Greenfield's borrowing rate is 10 percent.

We have determined that the risk of the lease cash flows is equal to the risk of its secured debt. However, we must make one further adjustment: The discount rate must be the firm's *after-tax* cost of its secured debt. When a company lends money, it pays tax on the interest it receives. Its net return is the after-tax interest rate. When a company borrows money, it can *deduct* interest payments from its taxable income. The net cost of borrowing is the after-tax interest rate. Therefore, to value the incremental cash flows stemming from the lease, we need to discount them at the after-tax interest rate.

Since Greenfield can borrow at 10 percent, we should discount the lease cash flows at $r_D(1 - T) = .10(1 - .35) = .065$, or 6.5 percent. This gives

$$\text{NPV lease} = 82{,}725 - \frac{20{,}950}{1.065} - \frac{18{,}273}{(1.065)^2} - \frac{16{,}398}{(1.065)^3} - \frac{15{,}086}{(1.065)^4} - \frac{14{,}168}{(1.065)^5} - \frac{13{,}525}{(1.065)^6} - \frac{3{,}500}{(1.065)^7}$$

$$= -221, \text{ or } -\$221$$

Since the lease has a negative NPV, Greenfield is better off buying the backhoe.

CHECK POINT 22.2

What is the NPV of the lease in Check Point 22.1? Assume that Greenfield can borrow at 10 percent, before tax.

A positive or negative NPV is not an abstract concept; in this case, Greenfield's shareholders are really $221 poorer if the company leases. Let's now check how this situation comes about.

The lease cash outflows are contractual obligations like the principal and interest payments, or debt service, on secured debt. The cash inflow in Year 0 of the lease is like the amount of money borrowed through the loan. This is gives us another way to examine the attractiveness of the lease. Let's compare it to an **equivalent loan**, a loan with identical annual cash outflows as the lease.

equivalent loan Present value of the lease cash outflows, discounted at the after-tax cost of borrowing.

Suppose Jane went to the bank and asked, "How much would you lend me today if I promised to make the following after-tax loan payments?" (principal and interest):

Year	1	2	3	4	5	6	7
Payments	–20,950	–18,273	–16,398	–15,086	–14,168	–13,525	–3,500

Note that Greenfield's loan payments are identical to the lease cash flows shown in years 1 to 7 of Table 22.1. This equivalent loan would carry a 10 percent interest rate, Greenfield's borrowing rate. The bank would be willing to lend Jane an amount equal to the present value of the lease cash outflows, discounted at Greenfield's after-tax borrowing rate:

$$\text{Equivalent loan} = \text{Present value of lease cash outflows in years 1 to 7}$$

$$= \frac{20{,}950}{1.065} + \frac{18{,}273}{(1.065)^2} + \frac{16{,}398}{(1.065)^3} + \frac{15{,}086}{(1.065)^4} + \frac{14{,}168}{(1.065)^5} + \frac{13{,}525}{(1.065)^6} + \frac{3{,}500}{(1.065)^7}$$

$$= 82{,}946, \text{ or } \$82{,}946$$

Table 22.2 shows the details of a loan for \$82,946 at 10 percent interest rate with *exactly* the same annual cash outflows as the lease. At the end of each year, interest on the outstanding loan amount is paid. Also, Greenfield repays part of the loan principal to make that year's total loan payment equal to the lease cash flow they would have paid had they leased the equipment. For example, at the end of the first year, Greenfield would need to pay interest of .10 × \$82,946, or \$8,295. Greenfield would *receive* a tax shield on this interest of .35 × 8,295, or \$2,903. In other words, their after-tax interest expense is \$8,295 – \$2,903, or \$5,391. Greenfield could then repay \$15,559 of the loan principal, giving a net cash outflow of \$5,391 + \$15,559 = \$20,950, exactly the same as the cash outflow in the first year of the lease. The loan amount outstanding at the start of Year 2 is now the original amount borrowed less the principal repaid in Year 1, \$82,946 – \$15,559, or \$67,387. We repeat the calculation of interest owed and pay down the principal of the loan such that the total cash outflow in Year 2 is \$18,273, exactly equal to Year 2's lease cash flow.

CHECK POINT 22.3

Look again at Table 22.2. Explain the calculations for the equivalent loan payments made in Year 2.

CHECK POINT 22.4

The bank receives interest before Greenfield pays tax. Show that the present value of the cash flows received by the bank, discounted at the required 10 percent, equals the equivalent loan of \$82,946.

As you walk through the calculations in Table 22.2, you see that it costs exactly the same to service a loan that brings an immediate cash flow of \$82,946 as it does to service the lease, which brings in only \$82,725. The lease is not as attractive as the loan. The difference between the cash inflow of the lease and cash inflow of an equivalent loan equals the net present value of the lease: \$82,725 – \$82,946 = – \$221. If Greenfield leases

TABLE 22.2

Details of equivalent loan offered to Greenfield Construction (figures in dollars; some columns may not add up due to rounding)

	Year							
	0	1	2	3	4	5	6	7
Amount borrowed at year-end	82,946	67,388	53,495	40,574	28,125	15,785	3,286	0
Interest paid at 10%		–8,295	–6,739	–5,350	–4,057	–2,813	–1,579	–329
Interest tax shield (35% tax rate)		2,903	2,359	1,872	1,420	984	552	115
Interest paid after tax*		–5,391	–4,380	–3,477	–2,637	–1,828	–1,026	–214
Principal repaid		–15,559	–13,892	–12,921	–12,449	–12,340	–12,499	–3,286
Net cash flow of equivalent loan**	82,946	–20,950	–18,273	–16,398	–15,086	–14,168	–13,525	–3,500

Notes:

* Interest paid after tax = interest paid + interest tax shield

** Net cash flow of equivalent loan = interest paid after tax + principal repaid

the backhoe rather than raising an equivalent loan,[8] there will be $221 less in Greenfield's bank account.

Our example illustrates two general points about leases and equivalent loans. First, if you can devise a borrowing plan that gives the same cash flow as the lease in every future period but a higher immediate cash flow, then you should not lease. If, however, the equivalent loan provides the same future cash outflows as the lease but a lower immediate inflow, then leasing is the better choice.

Second, our example suggests two ways to value a lease:

1. *Hard way*. Construct a table like Table 22.2 showing the equivalent loan.
2. *Easy way*. Discount the lease cash flows at the after-tax interest rate that the firm would pay on an equivalent loan. Both methods give the same answer—in our case an NPV of –$221.

FINANCIAL LEASE EVALUATION

We concluded that the lease contract offered to Greenfield Construction was *not* attractive because the lease provided $221 less financing than the equivalent loan. The underlying principle is as follows: A financial lease is superior to buying and borrowing if the financing provided by the lease exceeds the financing generated by the equivalent loan.

The principle implies this formula:

Net value of lease = initial financing provided – value of equivalent loan

Initial financing provided equals the cost of the leased asset minus any immediate lease payment or other cash outflow attributable to the lease.

Notice that the value of the lease is its incremental value relative to borrowing via an equivalent loan. A positive lease value means that *if* you acquire the asset, lease financing is advantageous. It does not prove you should acquire the asset.

However, sometimes favourable lease terms rescue a capital investment project. Suppose that Greenfield had decided *against* buying a new backhoe because the NPV of the

[8] When we compare the lease to its equivalent loan, we do not mean to imply that the backhoe alone could support all of the loan. Some part of the loan would be supported by Greenfield's other assets. Some part of the lease would likewise be supported by the other assets.

\$100,000 investment was –\$5,000 assuming normal financing. The equipment manufacturer could rescue the deal by offering a lease with a value of, say, +\$8,000. By offering such a lease, the manufacturer would in effect cut the price of the backhoe to \$92,000, giving the backhoe-lease package a positive value to Greenfield. The total NPV of acquiring the backhoe is the sum of the NPV of the investment in a new backhoe, assuming normal financing, plus the NPV of the lease:

$$\begin{aligned}\text{NPV of backhoe investment} + \text{lease financing} &= \text{NPV of project} + \text{NPV of lease}\\ &= -5{,}000 + 8{,}000 = +\$3{,}000\end{aligned}$$

Notice also that this approach applies to *net* financial leases. Any insurance, maintenance, and other operating costs picked up by the lessor have to be evaluated separately and added to the value of the lease. If the asset has salvage value at the end of the lease, that value should be taken into account also.

▸ EXAMPLE 22.3 *Lease Variations: A Net Financial Lease and Asset Salvage Value*

The backhoe manufacturer offers to provide routine maintenance that would otherwise cost Greenfield \$2,000 per year after tax. However, Ms. Jones reconsiders and decides that the backhoe will probably be worth \$10,000 after 7 years, rather than nothing. The value of the lease increases by the present value of the maintenance savings and decreases by the present value of the lost salvage value. In addition, the lost tax savings from giving up the terminal loss (or CCA) will also be lower if the machine has a positive salvage value.

Maintenance and salvage value are harder to predict than the cash flows shown in Table 22.1, and so they normally deserve a higher discount rate. Suppose that Ms. Jones uses 12 percent, the project's (after-tax) discount rate. We assume the maintenance expenses are paid at the start of each year and the salvage value is measured at the end of Year 7. Then the maintenance savings are worth[9]

$$\$2{,}000 \times \text{Annuity due present value factor for 7 year annuity with 12\% interest rate}$$

$$= \$2{,}000\left[1 + \frac{1}{.12} - \frac{1}{.12(1.12)^6}\right] = \$10{,}223$$

The lost salvage is worth $\$10{,}000/(1.12)^7$, or \$4,524. The salvage value would also be subtracted from the asset pool and any balance remaining would be taken as a terminal loss (assuming that the asset pool is closed). From Table 22.1, you see that at the end of Year 7, the backhoe's undepreciated capital cost was \$10,000. Once the asset is sold, the asset pool is empty and there is no terminal loss. Originally, when salvage value was assumed to be 0, there was a tax shield from the terminal loss worth \$3,500 (.35 × \$10,000) and it had a present value of $\$3{,}500/(1.065)^7$, or \$2,252. By leasing, Greenfield gave up the tax savings from this terminal loss. Now, with the \$10,000 salvage value, there is no terminal loss and no lost tax savings.

The original lease was worth –\$221. We add the value of the maintenance to be provided by the lessor, \$10,223, but subtract the salvage value we give up by not owning the backhoe, \$4,524. We also add back the tax savings from the terminal loss originally expected when the salvage value was zero, \$2,252. The revised value is therefore –\$221 + \$10,223 – \$4,524 + \$2,252 = \$7,730. Now the lease looks like a good deal.

[9] Look in Chapter 3 for the formula for the present value of an annuity due.

▶ EXAMPLE 22.4 *Another Variation: Asset Pool Does Not Close*

Food Express, a grocery chain, needs new electronic cash registers. The cost to purchase them is \$150,000. They will last 4 years and be scrapped with zero value. The allowable CCA is 30 percent and the company has many assets of this type. Thus, if they buy the equipment, the CCA tax savings will continue after 4 years. The equipment manufacturer is offering to lease the cash registers for \$45,000 a year, payable in advance. The tax rate is 35 percent and the company's cost of borrowing is 8 percent. Should they lease or buy the cash registers?

The cash flows of the lease are found in Table 22.3. With the asset pool not closing, CCA would continue to be taken in the 5th year, 6th year, and so on, if the cash registers are purchased. By leasing, Food Express gives up the tax savings from these additional CCA deductions. At the end of the 4th year, the remaining undepreciated capital cost (UCC) is \$43,732 (\$62,475 – \$18,743). The present value of the tax savings from CCA on the UCC, at the end of Year 4, is[10]

$$\text{PV(tax savings from UCC, at end of Year 4)} = \frac{\text{UCC} \times \text{CCA rate} \times \text{tax rate}}{\text{CCA rate} + \text{interest rate}}$$

$$= \frac{43{,}732 \times .3 \times .35}{.3 + .08} = \$12{,}084$$

Table 22.3 shows that if Fast Food leases rather than buys the cash registers, it will be ahead \$4,699.

22.4 When Do Financial Leases Pay?

We have examined the value of a lease from the viewpoint of the lessee. However, the lessor's criterion is simply the reverse. As long as lessor and lessee are in the same tax bracket, every cash outflow to the lessee is an inflow to the lessor, and vice versa. In our numerical example, the backhoe manufacturer would project cash flows in a table like

TABLE 22.3 *Cash flow consequences and lease NPV for Food Express if they lease rather than buy the new cash registers (figures in dollars)*

		Year				
		0	1	2	3	4
Saved cost of new cash registers		+150,000				
Lost CCA tax shield (calculated below)			–13,388	–9,371	–6,560	–12,084
Lease payment		–45,000	–45,000	–45,000	–45,000	
Tax shield of lease payment		+15,750	+15,750	+15,750	+15,750	
Cash flow of lease		120,750	–42,638	–38,621	–35,810	–12,084
NPV of lease cash flows	4,699					
Tax Shield Calculation						
UCC		150,000	127,500	89,250	62,475	43,732
CCA (CCA rate = 30%)		22,500	38,250	26,775	18,743	
CCA tax shield (tax rate = 35%)		13,388	13,388	9,371	6,560	12,084

[10] If the cash registers have a salvage value, subtract it from the UCC, reducing the asset value in the pool before calculating the tax savings.

Table 22.1, but with the signs reversed. The value of the lease to the backhoe manufacturer would be

$$\text{Value of lease to lessor} = -82{,}725 + \frac{20{,}950}{1.065} + \frac{18{,}273}{(1.065)^2} + \frac{16{,}398}{(1.065)^3} + \frac{15{,}086}{(1.065)^4} + \frac{14{,}168}{(1.065)^5} + \frac{13{,}525}{(1.065)^6} + \frac{3{,}500}{(1.065)^7}$$

$$= +221, \text{ or } \$221$$

In this case, the values to lessee and lessor offset exactly. The lessor can win only at the lessee's expense.

But both lessee and lessor can win if their tax rates differ. Suppose that Greenfield paid no tax ($T_c = 0$). Then the only cash flows of the equipment lease would be

Year	0	1	2	3	4	5	6
Cost of new backhoe	+100,000						
Lease payment	–18,500	–18,500	–18,500	–18,500	–18,500	–18,500	–18,500

These flows would be discounted at 10 percent, because $r_D(1 - T_C) = r_D$ when $T_C = 0$. The value of the lease is

$$\text{Value of lease} = +100{,}000 - 18{,}5000 \times \begin{array}{c}\text{annuity due factor for 7-year annuity}\\ \text{with 10\% interest rate}\end{array}$$

$$= +100{,}000 - 18{,}500\left[1 + \frac{1}{.1} - \frac{1}{.1(1.1)^6}\right] = 928, \text{ or } \$928$$

In this case there is a net gain of \$221 to the lessor (who has the 35 percent tax rate) *and* a net gain of \$928 to the lessee (who pays zero tax). This mutual gain is at the expense of the government. On one hand, the government gains from the lease contract because it can tax the lease payments. On the other hand, the contract allows the lessor to take advantage of CCA and interest tax shields which are of no use to the lessee. However, because the CCA is accelerated and the interest rate is positive, the government suffers a net loss in the present value of its tax receipts as a result of the lease.

Now you should begin to understand the curcumstances in which the government incurs a loss on the lease and the other two parties gain. Other things being equal, the potential gains to lessor and lessee are highest when

- the lessor's tax rate is substantially higher than the lessee's.
- the CCA tax shield is received early in the lease period.
- the lease period is long and the lease payments are concentrated toward the end of the period.
- the interest rate, r_D, is high—if it were zero, there would be no advantage in present value terms to postponing tax.

22.5 Summary

1. **What is a lease?**

A lease is just an extended rental agreement. The owner of the equipment (the lessor) allows the user (the lessee) to operate the equipment in exchange for regular lease payments.

There is a wide variety of possible arrangements. Short-term, cancellable leases are known as **operating leases**. In these leases the lessor bears the risks of ownership. Long-term, noncancellable leases are called **full-payout**, **financial**, or **capital** leases. In these leases the lessee bears the risks. Financial leases are **sources of financing** for assets the firm wishes to acquire and use for an extended period.

Many vehicle or office equipment leases include insurance and maintenance. They are **full-service** leases. If the lessee is responsible for insurance and maintenance, the lease is a **net** lease.

Frequently the lessor acquires the asset directly from the manufacturer. This is a **direct** lease. Sometimes the lessor acquires the asset from the user and then leases it back to the user. This is a **sale and lease-back.**

2. **How do you value an operating lease?**

Operating leases are attractive to equipment users if the lease payment is less than the **user's** equivalent annual cost of buying the equipment. Operating leases make sense when the user needs the equipment only for a short time, when the lessor is better able to bear the risks of obsolescence, or when the lessor can offer a good deal on maintenance. Remember too that operating leases often have valuable options attached.

3. **How do you value a financial lease?**

A financial lease extends over most of the economic life of the leased asset and cannot be cancelled by the lessee. Signing a financial lease is like signing a secured loan to finance purchase of the leased asset. With financial leases, the choice is not "lease versus buy" but "lease versus borrow."

Many companies have sound reasons for financing via leases. For example, companies that are not paying taxes can usually strike a favourable deal with a tax-paying lessor. Also, it may be less costly and time-consuming to sign a standardized lease contract than to negotiate a long-term secured loan.

When a firm borrows money, it pays the after-tax rate of interest on its debt. Therefore, the opportunity cost of lease financing is the after-tax rate of interest on the firm's bonds. To value a financial lease, we need to discount the incremental cash flows from leasing by the after-tax interest rate.

An equivalent loan is one that commits the firm to exactly the same future cash flow as a financial lease. When we calculate the net present vale of the lease, we are measuring the difference between the amount of financing provided by the lease and the financing provided by the equivalent loan:

Net present value of lease = financing provided by lease – value of equivalent loan

We can also analyze leases from the lessor's side of the transaction using the same approaches we developed for the lessee. If lessee and lessor are in the same tax bracket, they will receive exactly the same cash flows but with signs reversed. Thus, the lessee can gain only at the lessor's expense, and vice versa. However, if the lessee's tax rate is lower than the lessor's, then both can gain at the government's expense.

Related Web Links

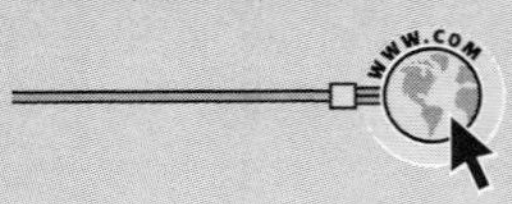

www.cfla-acfl.ca The website of the Canadian Finance and Leasing Association
www.executivecaliber.ws/sys-tmpl/door Lots of information, excellent glossary on leasing
www.gecapital.com Large Canadian lessor
www.leasingcanada.com Information on leasing in Canada

Key Terms

lease	657	operating lease	657	off-balance-sheet financing	660
lessee	657	financial lease	657	equivalent loan	667
lessor	657				

QUESTIONS AND PROBLEMS

*Answers in Appendix B

BASIC

*1. **Lease Terms.** The following terms are often used to describe leases:

i. Direct
ii. Full-service
iii. Operating
iv. Financial
v. Rental
vi. Net
vii. Leveraged
viii. Sale and lease-back
ix. Full-payout

Match one or more of these terms with each of the following statements:

a. The initial lease period is shorter than the economic life of the asset.
b. The initial lease period is long enough for the lessor to recover the cost of the asset.
c. The lessor provides maintenance and insurance.
d. The lessee provides maintenance and insurance.
e. The lessor buys the equipment from the manufacturer.
f. The lessor buys the equipment from the prospective lessee.
g. The lessor finances the lease contract by issuing debt and equity claims against it.

*2. **Why lease?** Some of the following reasons for leasing are rational. Others are irrational or assume imperfect or inefficient capital markets. Which of the following reasons are the rational ones?

a. The lessee's need for the leased asset is only temporary.
b. Specialized lessors are better able to bear the risk of obsolescence.
c. Leasing provides 100 percent financing and thus preserves capital.
d. Leasing allows firms with low tax rates to "sell" CCA tax shields.
e. Leasing increases earnings per share.
f. Leasing reduces the transaction cost of obtaining external financing.
g. Leasing avoids restrictions on capital expenditures.

*3. **Reasons to Lease.** True or False? Explain your answers.

a. It makes sense to enter into an operating lease if you are sure that you want to keep the asset for a long time.
b. Leasing is advantageous because it provides a company with off-balance-sheet financing, allowing it to hide its financial obligations.

4. **Understanding Leases.** True or false?

a. Lease payments are usually made at the start of each period. Thus the first payment is usually made as soon as the lease contract is signed.
b. Financial leases can still provide off-balance-sheet financing.
c. The cost of capital for a financial lease is the interest rate the company would pay on a bank loan.
d. An equivalent loan's principal plus after-tax interest payments exactly match the after-tax cash flows of the lease.
e. A financial lease should not be undertaken unless it provides more financing than the equivalent loan.
f. It makes sense for firms that pay no taxes to lease from firms that do.
g. Other things being equal, the net tax advantage of leasing increases as nominal interest rates increase.

*5. **Lease Valuation.** Suppose that National Waferonics has before it a proposal for a 4-year financial lease. The firm constructs a table like Table 22.1. The bottom line of its table shows the lease cash flows:

Year	0	1	2	3
Lease cash flow	+62,000	–26,800	–22,200	–17,600

These flows reflect the cost of the machine, CCA tax shields, and the after-tax lease payments. Ignore salvage value. Assume the firm could borrow at 10 percent and faces a 35 percent marginal tax rate.

a. What is the value of the equivalent loan?
b. What is the value of the lease.
c. Suppose the machine's NPV under normal financing is –$5,000. Should National Waferonics invest? Should it sign the lease?

PRACTICE

*6. **Lease as Financing.** A lessee does not have to pay to buy the leased asset. Thus it's said that "leases provide 100 percent financing." Explain why this is not a true advantage to the lessee.

*7. **Lease Valuation.** ABC Brickworks proposes to lease a $75,000 forklift. Five annual lease payments of $15,000 are due in advance. ABC's tax rate is 35 percent. If it purchases the forklift, it will be in its own 25 percent CCA class. The half-year rule applies and after 6 years, the forklift will be worthless. The interest rate is 9 percent.

a. Using Table 22.1 as a guide, determine the cash flows of leasing rather than purchasing the forklift.
b. What are the equivalent loan and NPV of the lease?
c. If the forklift is expected to have a $10,000 salvage value after 6 years and the project's discount rate is 12 percent, what is the NPV of the lease?

8. **Lease Valuation.** Printing World thinks they may need a new colour printing press. The press will cost $500,000 but will substantially reduce annual operating costs by $215,000 a year, before tax. The press has a 30 percent CCA rate and will be in its own asset pool. It will operate for 4 years and then be worthless. The cost of equity for Printing World is 12 percent, the cost of debt is 8 percent, and the company's target debt-equity ratio is .5. The company's tax rate is 30 percent.

a. What is the NPV of buying the press?
b. The equipment manufacturer is offering to lease the press for $112,000 a year, for 4 years, payable in advance. Should Printing World accept their offer?

9. **Why Lease?** Why do you think that leasing of trucks, airplanes, and computers is such big business? What efficiencies offset the costs of running these leasing operations?

10. **Operating Lease.** Financial leases make sense when the lessee faces a lower marginal tax rate than the lessor. Does this tax advantage carry over to *operating* leases?

The following questions all apply to financial leases.

*11. **Lease Valuation.** Look again at the backhoe-loader lease described in Table 22.1 Consider each question separately.

a. What is the value of the lease if Greenfield's tax rate is 20 percent?
b. What would the lease value be if Greenfield's first CCA payment was at the end of Year 1?
c. What would the lease value be if Greenfield had many other assets in the equipment asset pool? In this case, the equipment asset pool would not be closed.

*12. **Setting Lease Payments.** In Section 22.4 we showed that the lease offered to Greenfield Construction had a positive NPV of $928 if Greenfield paid no tax *and* a +$221 NPV to a lessor paying 35 percent tax.

a. What is the minimum lease payment the lessor could accept under these circumstances?
b. What is the maximum amount that Greenfield could pay?

*13. **Gains From Leasing.** In Section 22.4 we listed four circumstances in which there are potential gains from leasing. Check them out by conducting a sensitivity analysis on the Greenfield Construction lease, assuming that Greenfield does not pay tax. Try, in turn, (a) a lessor tax rate of 50 percent (rather than 35 percent), (b) a CCA rate of 35 percent rather than 30 percent, (c) a 4-year lease with four annual payments (rather than a 7-year lease), and (d) an interest rate of 20 percent (rather than 10 percent). In each case, find the minimum rental that would satisfy the lessor and calculate the NPV to the lessee.

14. **Taxes and Leasing.** In Section 22.4 we stated that if the interest rate was zero, there would be no advantage in postponing tax and therefore no advantage in leasing. Value the Greenfield Construction lease with an interest rate of zero. Assume that Greenfield does not pay tax. Can you devise any lease terms that would make both a lessee and a lessor happy? (If you can, we would like to hear from you.)

15. **Structured Lease.** A lease with varying rental schedule is known as a *structured lease.* Try structuring the Greenfield Construction lease to increase value to the lessee while preserving the value to the lessor. Assume that Greenfield does not pay tax. (*Note:* In practice the tax authorities will allow some structuring of rental payments but might be unhappy with some of the schemes you devise.)

*16. **Lease NPV.** Nodhead College needs a new computer. It can either buy it for $250,000 or lease it from Compulease. The lease terms require Nodhead to make six annual payments (prepaid) of $55,000. Nodhead pays no tax. Compulease pays tax at 35 percent. Compulease can depreciate the computer for tax purposes at a CCA rate of 30 percent, and will close the asset pool at the end of the 6th year. The computer will have no residual value at the end of Year 5. The interest rate is 8 percent.

   a. What is the NPV of the lease for Nodhead College?
   b. What is the NPV for Compulease?
   c. What is the overall gain from leasing?

17. **Lease NPV.** The Safety Razor Company has a large tax-loss carryforward and does not expect to pay taxes for another 10 years. The company is therefore proposing to lease $100,000 of new machinery. The lease terms consist of eight equal lease payments prepaid annually. The lessor will take CCA on the machinery at a 30 percent rate and the pool will never close. There is no salvage value at the end of the machinery's economic life. The tax rate is 35 percent, and the rate of interest is 10 percent. Wilbur Occam, the president of Safety Razor, wants to know the maximum lease payment that the lessor is likely to accept. Can you help him? *Hint:* Use the perpetual CCA tax savings formula, Equation 7.1 from Chapter 7.

*18. **Lease Rate of Return.** Many companies calculate the internal rate of return of the incremental after-tax cash flows from financial leases. What problems to you think this may give rise to? To what rate should the IRR be compared?

19. **Why Lease?** Discuss the following two opposite statements. Which do you think makes more sense?

   a. "Leasing is tax avoidance and should be legislated against."
   b. "Leasing ensures that the government's investment incentives work. It does so by allowing companies in nontaxpaying positions to take advantage of CCA deductions."

CHALLENGE

20. **Lease NPV.** Magna Charter has been asked to operate a Beaver bush plane for a mining company exploring in the Yukon. Magna will have a 1-year contract with the mining company and expects that the contract will be renewed after 1 year, for the remaining 4 years of the exploration program. If the mining company renews after I year, it will commit to use the plane for 4 more years.

    Magna Charter has the following choices:

    - Buy the plane for $500,000.
    - Arrange a 5-year, noncancellable, net financial lease at a rate of $75,000 per year, paid in advance.

    How would you advise Agnes Magna, the charter company's CEO? Assume that the CCA rate is 25 percent and Magna has many other airplanes in its asset pool. The company's tax rate is 35 percent. The weighted-average cost of capital for the bush plane business is 14 percent, but Magna can borrow at 9 percent.

Ms. Magna thinks the plane will be worth $300,000 after 5 years. She also thinks that there is a 20 percent chance that the contract will not be renewed at Year 1. If the contract is not renewed, the plane will have to be sold on short notice for $400,000.

If Magna Charters takes the 5-year financial lease and the mining company cancels at Year 1, Magna can sublet the plane, that is, rent it out to another user.

Make additional assumptions as necessary.

21. **Lease NPV.** Recalculate the value of the lease to Greenfield Construction if the company pays no taxes until Year 3. Calculate the lease cash flows by modifying Table 22.1. Remember that the after-tax borrowing rate for years 1 and 2 differs from the rate for years 3 through 7.

INTERNET PROBLEMS

1. Canadian Capital Leasing's website at www.leasingcanada.com/leaseguide.htm has information about leasing in Canada. Go to the glossary "Your Guide to Leasing Terms" and identify the terms that deal with the possibility of terminating (or not terminating) a lease. Likewise, identify the various ways the asset can be disposed of at the end of lease.
2. In the same website as above, click on "Leasing for Business," and read their arguments about why businesses should consider leasing. What do you think about their arguments?
3. The "Lease or Buy Calculator" at strategis.ic.gc.ca/SSG/so02019e.html, the website of Industry Canada, shows the cash flows of a lease versus a loan. This calculator assumes that the asset pool is not closed at the end of the lease. A neat feature of this calculator is that it allows you to look up the CCA rate for the asset you are purchasing. Suppose the lease is for a $100,000 Class 38 asset, that will have zero salvage value and last for 3 years. The company's tax rate is 40 percent and the cost of debt is 10 percent. If the loan is also 3 years, can you figure out what the monthly lease payment must be to be indifferent between borrowing and leasing? See if you can figure out the numbers the calculator produces.

SOLUTIONS TO CHECK POINTS

22.1 The lease cash flows are in Table 22.4.

22.2 $$\text{NPV lease} = 72{,}013 - \frac{16{,}111}{1.065} - \frac{13{,}835}{(1.065)^2} - \frac{12{,}242}{(1.065)^3} - \frac{11{,}127}{(1.065)^4} - \frac{10{,}346}{(1.065)^5} - \frac{9{,}800}{(1.065)^6} - \frac{2{,}975}{(1.065)^7}$$
$$= \$9{,}720$$

22.3 Interest paid in Year 2 is 10 percent of the amount borrowed during the year .1 × 67,388 = $6,739. However, Greenfield gets an interest tax shield of 35 percent of the interest paid, .35 × $6,739 = $2,359, so the interest paid after tax is $6,739 – $2,359 = $4,380. To match the Year 2 lease cash outflow of $18,273, Greenfield can repay principal equal to $18,273 – $4,380, or $13,892.

TABLE 22.4

Lease cash flows for Check Point 22.1 (amounts in dollars)

	Year							
Lease Cash Flows	0	1	2	3	4	5	6	7
Saved cost of a new backhoe-loader	+85,000							
Lost CCA tax shield (calculated below)	–4,463	–7,586	–5,310	–3,717	–2,602	–1,821	–1,275	–2,975
Lease payment	–15,000	–15,000	–15,000	–15,000	–15,000	–15,000	–15,000	
Lease payment tax shield	+6,475	+6,475	+6,475	+6,475	+6,475	+6,475	+6,475	
Cash flow of lease	72,013	–16,111	–13,835	–12,242	–11,127	–10,346	–9,800	–2,975
Tax Shield Calculation								
UCC	85,000	72,250	50,575	35,403	24,782	17,347	12,143	8,500
CCA (CCA rate = 30%)	12,750	21,675	15,173	10,621	7,435	5,204	3,643	
CCA tax shield (tax rate = 35%)	4,463	7,586	5,310	3,717	2,602	1,821	1,275	2,975

22.4 The cash flows received by the bank are the interest paid and the principal repayments. For example, in Year 1 the bank is paid \$8,295 + \$15,559 = \$23,854. The present value of the cash flows received by the bank is:

$$= \frac{23{,}853}{1.1} + \frac{20{,}631}{(1.1)^2} + \frac{18{,}271}{(1.1)^3} + \frac{16{,}506}{(1.1)^4} + \frac{15{,}152}{(1.1)^5} + \frac{14{,}078}{(1.1)^6} + \frac{3{,}615}{(1.1)^7} = \$82{,}946$$

The bank is willing to lend \$82,946 to Greenfield because it receives interest and principal repayment with an equal present value.

MINICASE

Helen James, a newly recruited financial analyst at Halverton Corporation, had just been asked to analyze a proposal to acquire a new dredger.

She reviewed the capital appropriation request. The dredger would cost \$3.5 million and was expected to generate cash flows of \$470,000 a year for 9 years. After that point, the dredger would almost surely be obsolete and have no significant salvage value. The company's weighted-average cost of capital was 16 percent.

Helen proposed a standard DCF analysis, but this suggestion was brushed off by Halverton's top management. They seemed to be convinced of the merits of the investment but were unsure of the best ways to finance it. Halverton could raise the money by issuing a secured 8-year note at an interest rate of 12 percent. However, Halverton had large tax-loss carryforwards from a disastrous foray into foreign exchange options. As a result, the company was unlikely to be in a tax-paying position for many years. Halverton's CEO thought it might be better to lease the dredger rather than to buy it.

Helen's first step was to invite two leasing companies, Mount Zircon Finance and First Cookham Bank, to submit proposals. Both companies were in a tax-paying position and could claim CCA on the dredger. The dredger is a Class 38 asset with a 30 percent CCA rate.

Helen received the following letters, the first from Mount Zircon Finance:

February 29, 2004

Dear Helen,

We appreciated the opportunity to meet you the other day and to discuss the possibility of providing lease finance for your proposed new JLT4 dredger. As you know, Mount Zircon has extensive experience in this field, and because of our large volumes and low borrowing costs, we are able to offer very attractive terms.

We would envisage offering a 9-year lease with 10 annual payments of \$550,000, with the initial lease payment due on entering into the lease contract. This is equivalent to a borrowing cost of 11.8 percent per annum (i.e., 10 payments of \$550,000 paid at the beginning of each year discounted at 11.5 percent amounts to \$3,500,000).

We hope that you agree with us that this is an attractive rate. It is well below your company's overall cost of capital. Our leasing proposal will cover the entire \$3.5 million cost of the dredger, thereby preserving Halverton's capital for other uses. Leasing will also allow a very attractive return on equity from your company's acquisition of this new equipment.

This proposal is subject to a routine credit check and review of Halverton's financial statements. We expect no difficulties on that score, but you will understand the need for due diligence.

Thank you for contacting Mount Zircon Finance. We look forward to hearing your response.

Sincerely yours,

Henry Attinger
For and on behalf of Mount Zircon Finance

The next letter was from First Cookham.

February 29, 2004

Dear Helen,

It was an honour to meet you the other day and to discuss how First Cookham Bank can help your company to finance its new dredger. First Cookham has a small specialized leasing operation. This enables us to tailor our proposals to our clients' needs.

We recommend that Halverton consider leasing the dredger on a 7-year term. Subject to documentation and routine review of Halverton's financial statements, we could offer a 7-year lease on the basis of eight payments of \$619,400 due at the beginning of each year. This is equivalent to a loan at an interest rate of 11.41 percent.

We expect that this lease payment will be higher than quoted by the large, mass-market leasing companies, but our financial analysts have determined that by offering a shorter lease, we can quote a lower interest rate.

We are confident that this is a highly competitive offer, and we look forward to your response.

Yours sincerely,

George Bucknall
First Cookham Bank

Both proposals appeared to be attractive. However, Helen realized the need to undertake careful calculations before deciding whether leasing made sense and which firm was offering the better deal. She also wondered whether the terms offered were really as attractive as the two lessors claimed. Perhaps she could persuade them to cut their prices.

CHAPTER 23

Mergers, Acquisitions, and Corporate Control

23.1 The Market for Corporate Control

23.2 Sensible Motives for Mergers

23.3 Dubious Reasons for Mergers

23.4 Evaluating Mergers

23.5 Merger Tactics

23.6 Leverage Buyouts

23.7 Mergers and the Economy

23.8 Summary

In recent years the scale and pace of merger activity have been remarkable. For example, Table 23.1 lists just a few of the important Canadian mergers of 2000 and 2001. In recent years many of the largest mergers have involved European as well as American firms. A few Canadian deals are big by world standards.

The mergers listed in Table 23.1 all involved *big* money. During periods of intense merger activity, financial managers spend considerable time either searching for firms to acquire or worrying whether some other firm is about to take over their company.

When one company buys another, it is making an investment, and the basic principles of capital investment decisions apply. You should go ahead with the purchase if it makes a net contribution to shareholders' wealth. But mergers are often awkward transactions to evaluate, and you have to be careful to define benefits and costs properly.

Many mergers are arranged amicably, but in other cases one firm will make a hostile takeover bid for the other. We describe the principal techniques of modern merger warfare, and since the threat of hostile takeovers has stimulated corporate restructurings and leveraged buyouts (LBOs), we describe them, too, and attempt to explain why these deals have generated rewards for investors. We close with a look at who gains and who loses from mergers and we discuss whether mergers are beneficial on balance.

After studying this chapter you should be able to

- Describe ways that companies change their ownership or management.
- Explain why it may make sense for companies to merge.
- Estimate the gains and costs of mergers to the acquiring firm.
- Describe takeover defences.
- Summarize the evidence on whether mergers increase efficiency and how the gains from mergers are distributed between shareholders of the acquired and acquiring firms.
- Explain some of the motivations for leveraged and management buyouts of the firm.

TABLE 23.1
Some important recent mergers involving Canadian companies

Year	Buying Company	Selling Company	Value (in millions)
2000	Vivendi (France)	Seagram	$41,650
2000	Nortel Networks Corp.	Alteon WebSystems Inc.	11,523
2000	Alcatel SA	Newbridge Networks Corp.	10,800
2001	Sun Life Financial Services	Clarica Life Insurance	6,800
2001	Conoco Inc.	Gulf Canada Resources	6,700
2000	BCE Inc.	Teleglobe Inc.	6,400
2000	Shire Pharmaceuticals Group	BioChem Pharma	5,900
2000	Abitibi-Consolidated	Donohue	5,600
2001	Duke Energy Corp.	Westcoast Energy Inc.	5,500
2001	Newmont Mining Corp.	Franco-Nevada Mining Corp. and Normandy Mining	5,281
2000	Nortel Networks Corp.	Xros	4,750
2001	Investors Group Inc.	Mackenzie Financial Corp.	4,149
2000	Telus	Clearnet Communications	4,091
2000	CanWest Global Communications	Hollingers (newspapers)	3,200
2000	PMC-Sierra	Quantum Effect Devices	3,170

23.1 The Market for Corporate Control

The shareholders are the owners of the firm. But many shareholders do not feel like the boss, and with good reason. Try buying a share of Royal Bank stock and marching into the boardroom for a chat with your employee, the chief executive officer.

The *ownership* and *management* of large corporations are substantially separated. Shareholders do not directly appoint or supervise the firm's managers. They elect the board of directors, who act as their agents in choosing and monitoring the managers of the firm. Shareholders have a direct say in very few matters. Control of the firm is in the hands of the managers, subject to the general oversight of the board of directors.

The separation of the ownership and management or control of the firm creates potential *agency costs.* Agency costs occur when managers or directors take actions adverse to shareholders' interests.

The temptation to take such actions may be ever-present, but there are many forces and constraints working to keep managers' and shareholders' interests in line. As we pointed out in Chapter 1, managers' paycheques in large corporations are almost always tied to the profitability of the firm and the performance of its shares. Boards of directors take their responsibilities seriously—they may face lawsuits if they don't—and therefore are reluctant to rubber-stamp obviously bad financial decisions.

But what ensures that the board has engaged the most talented managers? What happens if managers are inadequate? What if the board of directors is derelict in monitoring the performance of managers? Or what if the firm's managers are fine, but resources of the firm could be used more efficiently by merging with another firm? Can we count on managers to pursue arrangements that would put them out of jobs?

These are all questions about *the market for corporate control,* the mechanisms by which firms are matched up with management teams and owners who can make the most of the firm's resources. You should not take a firm's current ownership and management for granted. If it is possible for the value of the firm to be enhanced by changing management or by reorganizing under new owners, there will be incentives for someone to make a change.

There are four ways to change the management of a firm. These are (1) a successful proxy contest in which a group of shareholders votes in a new group of directors, who then pick a new management team; (2) the purchase of one firm by another in a merger or acquisition; (3) a leveraged buyout of the firm by a private group of investors; and (4) a divestiture, in which a firm either sells part of its operations to another company or spins it off as an independent firm.

We will briefly review each of these methods.

METHOD 1: PROXY CONTESTS

Shareholders elect the board of directors to keep watch on management and replace unsatisfactory managers. If the board is lax, shareholders are free to elect a different board. In theory this ensures that the corporation is run in the best interests of shareholders.

In practice things are not so clear-cut. Ownership in large corporations is sometimes widely dispersed and even the largest single shareholder may hold only a small fraction of the shares. Most shareholders have little notion who is on the board or what the members stand for. Management, on the other hand, deals directly with the board and has a personal relationship with its members. In many corporations, management sits on the committee that nominates candidates for the board. It is not surprising that some boards seem less than aggressive in forcing managers to run a lean, efficient operation and act primarily in the interests of shareholders.

proxy contest Takeover attempt in which outsiders compete with management for shareholders' votes. Also called proxy fight.

When a group of investors believes that the board and its management team should be replaced, they can launch a **proxy contest.** A proxy is the right to vote another shareholder's shares. In a proxy contest, the dissident shareholders attempt to obtain enough proxies to elect their own slate to the board of directors. Once the new board is in control, management can be replaced. A proxy fight is therefore a direct contest for control of the corporation.

But most proxy contests fail. Dissidents who engage in such fights must use their own money, while management can use the corporation's funds and lines of communication with shareholders to defend itself. Such fights can cost millions of dollars.[1]

Institutional shareholders such as large pension funds have become more aggressive in pressing for managerial accountability. These funds have been able to gain concessions from firms without initiating proxy contests. For example, firms have agreed to split the jobs of chief executive officer and chairperson of the board of directors. This ensures that an outsider is responsible for keeping watch over the company. Also, more firms now bar corporate insiders from serving on the committee that nominates candidates to the board. Perhaps as a result of shareholder pressure, boards also seem to be getting more aggressive. For example, outside directors were widely credited for hastening the replacement of top management at Coca-Cola and British Airways.

▶ EXAMPLE 23.1 *Fishery Products International Proxy Fight*

In the spring of 2001, a group of dissident shareholders of Fishery Products International (FPI) initiated a proxy fight to change the board and management of the company. Led by John Risley, president and sole shareholder of Clearwater Fine Foods, the dissidents argued

[1] J. H. Mulherin and A. B. Poulsen provide an analysis of proxy fights in "Proxy Contests and Corporate Change: Implications for Shareholder Wealth," *Journal of Financial Economics* 47 (1998), pp. 279–313.

that FPI's stock price would benefit from new leadership and modernized plants. Through Clearwater, which owned 13.4 percent of FPI's shares, Risley was FPI's largest shareholder. A special law established by the Newfoundland government permits a single shareholder to own a maximum of 15 percent of shares.

Unlike many proxy fights, this fight was successful, with 82 percent of shareholders voting in favour of the slate of new board members nominated by the dissident shareholders. In an interesting turn of events in September 2001, FPI announced plans to purchase Clearwater's shares from Risley, its sole shareholder. Risley was to become CEO of the combined companies. However, the deal was cancelled in February 2002 after the Newfoundland government announced legislation that limits the ownership of FPI.

METHOD 2: MERGERS AND ACQUISITIONS

Proxy contests are rare, and successful ones are rarer still. Poorly performing managers face a greater risk from acquisition. If the management of one firm observes another firm underperforming, it can try to acquire the business and replace the poor managers with its own team. In practice, corporate takeovers are the arenas where contests for corporate control are usually fought.

There are three ways for one firm to acquire another firm: (1) merge with it, (2) purchase a majority of its shares, or (3) purchase some or all of its assets. Laws and regulations (the details of which are well beyond this book) govern each method.

merger or statutory amalgamation
Combination of the assets and liabilities of two firms into one.

In Canada, when people talk about a **merger**, a situation in which the assets and liabilities of two companies are combined into one, they are really referring to a **statutory amalgamation**. The laws governing statutory amalgamations are found in the federal and provincial business corporations acts. For a statutory amalgamation—or merger—to succeed, a large majority of shareholders (typically, two-thirds) must approve it by voting in favour of the merger at a special shareholders meeting.

In many mergers there is a clear acquiring company whose management then runs the enlarged firm. In these cases the acquiring company assumes all of the assets and all of the liabilities of the target and the target company ceases to exist. The former shareholders of the target firm receive cash and/or securities in the acquiring firm. However, sometimes an entirely new company is created through the statutory amalgamation and both original companies disappear. Such is the case when the companies involved are considered equals, with management from both firms having a major say in the running of the new company.[2] For example, the $350 billion (US) merger between Time Warner and AOL is a merger of equals.

▸ EXAMPLE 23.2 *The Creation of Aliant*

In 1999, the four principal telecommunications companies operating in Atlantic Canada—Bruncor Inc., Island Telecom Inc., Maritime Telegraph and Telephone Company, and New Tel Enterprises—determined that by combining their businesses they would create a stronger company. Through a statutory amalgamation they created a new company, Aliant Inc. Shareholders of each of the four selling companies exchanged their old shares for

[2] In the United States, the term *merger* refers to the situation in which one company is subsumed into another company and ceases to exist. The terms *amalgamation* and *consolidation* refer to the situation in which both companies end their legal existence and become an entirely new company.

shares in the new company. The number of new shares received was based on the prices of the companies' shares before merging.

A second alternative is for the acquiring firm to buy the target firm's stock in exchange for cash, shares, or other securities. The acquired firm may continue to exist as a separate entity, but it is now owned by the acquirer. The approval and cooperation of the target firm's managers are generally sought, but even if they resist, the acquirer can attempt to purchase a majority of the outstanding shares. By offering to buy shares directly from shareholders, the acquiring firm can bypass the target firm's management altogether. The offer to purchase stock is called a **tender offer.** If the tender offer is successful, the buyer obtains control and can, if it chooses, toss out incumbent management.

tender offer Takeover attempt in which outsiders directly offer to buy the stock of the firm's shareholders.

Frequently, a tender offer is the first step toward the final goal of complete acquisition of the publicly traded target company. Consequently, many tender offers are conditional on acquiring two-thirds of the outstanding shares. Why two-thirds, you ask? With two-thirds of the shares, the acquiring firm ensures it will win the subsequent vote to approve statutory amalgamation of the target company with the acquirer.

EXAMPLE 23.3 *Tender Offer for Royal Airlines*

In February 2001, Canada 3000 made a tender offer to purchase all of the common shares of Royal Aviation (Royal Airlines). Each Royal share tendered was to receive .4 of a Canada 3000 share. The deal was worth about $3.40 per Royal share, a premium of 33 percent of the preannouncement Royal price of $2.56. The offer was conditional on the requirement that least two-thirds of Royal share be tendered. Over 94 percent of the shares were tendered. Canada 3000 then merged the assets of Royal Airlines with its own. Subsequently, unable to cope with its debt when revenues plummeted after the terrorist attacks of September 11, 2001, Canada 3000 went bankrupt later that fall.

The third approach for one firm to acquire another is to buy the target firm's assets. In this case ownership of the assets needs to be transferred, and payment is made to the selling firm rather than directly to its shareholders. Usually, the target firm sells only some of its assets, but occasionally it sells *all* of them. In this case, the selling firm continues to exist as an independent entity, but it becomes an empty shell—a corporation engaged in no business activity.

The terminology of mergers and acquisitions (M&A) can be confusing. These phrases are used loosely to refer to any kind of corporate combination or takeover. But strictly speaking, *merger* or *statutory amalgamation* means the combination of all the assets and liabilities of two firms. The purchase of the stock or assets of another firm is an **acquisition.**

acquisition Takeover of a firm by purchase of that firm's common stock or assets.

METHOD 3: LEVERAGED BUYOUTS

Sometimes a group of investors takes over a firm by means of a **leveraged buyout,** or **LBO.** The LBO group takes the firm private, so its shares no longer trade in the securities markets. Usually a considerable proportion of LBO financing is borrowed, hence the term *leveraged* buyout.

leveraged buyout (LBO) Acquisition of the firm by a private group using substantial borrowed funds.

If the investor group is led by the management of the firm, the takeover is called a **management buyout,** or **MBO.** In this case, the firm's managers actually buy the firm from the shareholders and continue to run it. They become owner-managers. We will discuss LBOs and MBOs later in the chapter.

management buyout (MBO) Acquisition of the firm by its own management in a leveraged buyout.

▶ EXAMPLE 23.4 *Management Buyout of Cotton Ginny*

In July 2001, senior management of Cotton Ginny Limited completed a successful buyout of Cotton Ginny from its previous owner, a Florida holding company. Cotton Ginny Limited owns Tabi International, Tabi Woman and Cotton Ginny brand names. The management group, which included both the president/chief executive officer and the chief financial officer of Cotton Ginny, teamed with Catterton Partners, a U.S. private equity firm, to purchase the company for an undisclosed amount. Catterton provided the majority of the financing.

METHOD 4: DIVESTITURES AND SPIN-OFFS

Firms not only acquire businesses; they also sell them. *Divestitures* are part of the market for corporate control. In recent years the number of divestitures has been about half the number of mergers.

Instead of selling a business to another firm, companies may *spin off* the business by separating it from the parent firm and distributing stock in the newly independent company to the shareholders of the parent company. For example, BCE decided to spin off almost all of its holdings of Nortel Networks to BCE shareholders. Although at one time BCE owned all of Nortel, by January 2000, it was a minority shareholder, owning 39 percent of Nortel's stock. These shares accounted for about 78 percent of BCE's value. BCE management and some analysts felt that the non-Nortel assets of BCE were not being fully valued, overshadowed by the Nortel holdings. BCE shareholders received .78 Nortel share for each BCE share. On the announcement of the widely anticipated spin-off, BCE's share price rose about 5 percent. Given the colossal crash of Nortel's stock value in 2001, BCE's management looks pretty smart (or lucky) to have disconnected from Nortel.

▶ EXAMPLE 23.5 *Canadian Pacific Starburst Split*

Another major Canadian spin-off was announced in February 2001 when Canadian Pacific revealed its plans to divide the company into five separate companies, all of which were to be publicly traded. In July 2001, the details of division were finalized. Each common share of Canadian Pacific was to be exchanged for the following: .5 Canadian Pacific Railway common shares, .25 Canadian Pacific Ships common shares, .25 Fairmont Hotel and Resorts common shares, .684 PanCanadian Energy common shares, and .166 Fording common shares. CP stated that the reorganization was designed to maximize value for CP shareholders by unlocking the current value of the businesses and strengthening their ability to pursue further success as independent companies. The stated hope of CP management was that the sum of the value of shares of the new companies would exceed the current market value of the pre-split Canadian Pacific common shares. CP's investors clearly welcomed the split: the stock price jumped nearly 11 percent on the day the plan was announced.

Probably the most frequent motive for spin-offs is improved efficiency. Companies sometimes refer to a business as being a "poor fit." By spinning off a poor fit, the management of the parent company can concentrate on its main activity. If each business must stand on its own feet, there is no risk that funds will be siphoned off from one in order to support unprofitable investments in the other. Moreover, if the two parts of the business are independent, it is easy to see the value of each and to reward managers accordingly.

OWNERSHIP STRUCTURE AND THE MARKET FOR CORPORATE CONTROL

The ownership structure, or how shares are distributed among shareholders, affects both the extent of the separation of ownership and control and also the effectiveness of the various corporate control mechanisms. At one extreme are privately owned companies with no publicly traded common shares and only one or a few shareholders. In Canada the largest private companies are owned by other corporations. General Motors of Canada, ranked the largest private Canadian company with 2000 revenues of $42 billion, is owned 100 percent by General Motors Corporation, its American parent. Some private corporations are owned by individuals or families. For example, McCain Foods, the seventh largest private company in Canada, with 2000 revenues of $5.3 billion, is wholly owned by the McCain family.[3]

In a private company, typically shareholders are actively involved in the management of the company, often holding senior management positions, as well as sitting on the board of directors. Thus problems of the separation of ownership from control are much less important than in a publicly owned company. Of course, if the sole shareholder of the company is another company, the shareholders of the parent company are still separated from the control of the various companies they own. A privately held company will never be sold unless the shareholders want it to happen. Proxy contests and hostile tender offers cannot occur.

Some publicly traded companies have a controlling shareholder or shareholder group that owns a significant percentage of the votes. Typically, the controlling shareholders hold at least 40 percent of the votes. These closely held but publicly traded companies use a variety of methods to maintain control while still allowing outsiders to invest in the company's equity. Multiple classes of equity is a commonly used structure. For example, Molson's, a company we studied in Chapter 2, has two classes of equity: one with one vote per share and the other with no votes. The Molson family controls about 60 percent of the voting shares. Many Canadian public companies have a controlling shareholder.

A closely held public company has less separation between management and the *controlling* shareholders. However, minority, noncontrolling shareholders have less influence and are unlikely to be able to change management through the market for corporate control mechanisms. If the large shareholder owns more than 50 percent of the votes, any proxy fight or hostile bid is doomed to fail. If the controlling shareholder does not want to sell their shares, control cannot be changed.[4]

Finally, some companies are widely held, where no one shareholder or shareholder group owns a significant number of votes. In these companies, the separation of ownership from control is the most evident. Likewise, the corporate control mechanisms have the greatest chance to succeed.

23.2 Sensible Motives for Mergers

We now look more closely at mergers and acquisitions and consider when they do and do not make sense. Mergers are often categorized as *horizontal, vertical,* or *conglomerate.* A horizontal merger is one that takes place between two firms in the same line of business; the merged firms are former competitors. Most of the mergers around the turn of the 20th

[3] The corporations' rankings are from the *Report on Business* magazine, July 2001.

[4] To protect non-controlling public shareholders, securities commissions have implemented special rules governing non–arms' length transactions by controlling shareholders. For example, if the majority shareholder wants to take the company private by purchasing all the shares held by other shareholders, the company must get an independent valuation of the company and a majority of the minority shareholders must approve the transaction.

century were of this type and are still common today. Recent examples of Canadian horizontal mergers have occurred in transportation, the acquisition of Canadian Airlines by Air Canada; communications, the acquisition of Clearnet by Telus; and oil and gas, Husky Oil's acquisition of Renaissance Energy and Devon Energy's acquisition of Anderson Exploration.

During the 1920s, vertical mergers were predominant. A vertical merger is one in which the buyer expands backward toward the source of raw material or forward in the direction of the ultimate consumer. Thus a soft drink manufacturer might buy a sugar producer (expanding backward) or a fast-food chain as an outlet for its product (expanding forward). Pepsi owns Burger King, for example.

A conglomerate merger involves companies in unrelated lines of business. For example, before it went belly-up in 1999, the Korean conglomerate, Daewoo, had nearly 400 different subsidiaries and 150,000 employees. It built ships in Korea, manufactured microwaves in France, TVs in Mexico, cars in Poland, fertilizers in Vietnam, and managed hotels in China and a bank in Hungary. No Canadian or U.S. company is as diversified as Daewoo, but in the 1960s and 1970s it was common in both Canada and the United States for unrelated businesses to merge. However, the number of conglomerate mergers declined in the 1980s. In fact much of the action in the 1980s came from breaking up the conglomerates that had been formed 10 to 20 years earlier.

CHECK POINT 23.1

Are the following hypothetical mergers horizontal, vertical, or conglomerate?

a. IBM acquires Apple Computer.
b. BCE acquires Stop & Shop (a supermarket chain).
c. Loblaws acquires Fishery Products International (a frozen fish processor).
d. Alcan acquires Canada Bread.

We have already seen that one motive for a merger is to replace the existing management team. If this motive is important, one would expect that poorly performing firms would tend to be targets for acquisition; this seems to be the case.[5] However, firms also acquire other firms for reasons that have nothing to do with inadequate management. Many mergers and acquisitions are motivated by possible gains in efficiency from combining operations. These mergers create *synergies.* By this we mean that the two firms are worth more together than apart.

A merger adds value only if synergies, better management, or other changes make the two firms worth more together than apart.

It would be convenient if we could say that certain types of mergers are usually successful and other types fail. Unfortunately, there are no such simple generalizations. Many mergers that appear to make sense nevertheless fail because managers cannot handle the complex task of integrating two firms with different production processes, accounting methods, and corporate cultures. Moreover, the value of most businesses depends on *human* assets—managers, skilled workers, scientists, and engineers. If these people are not happy in their new roles in the acquiring firm, many of them will leave. Beware of paying

[5] For example, Palepu found that investors in firms that were subsequently acquired earned relatively low rates of return for several years before the merger. See K. Palepu, "Predicting Takeover Targets: A Methodological and Empirical Analysis," *Journal of Accounting and Economics* 8 (March 1986), pp. 3–36.

too much for assets that go down in the elevator and out to the parking lot at the close of each business day.

With this caveat in mind, we will now consider possible sources of synergy.

INCREASED REVENUES

Mergers are frequently justified on the belief that revenues of the combined companies will exceed the sum of the revenues of the two companies if they were to remain separate. However, revenue synergies are difficult to estimate accurately because they are out of the direct control of management. For revenues to increase, customers must buy more than they used to or be willing to pay a higher price, and also, competitors must not lower their prices in response to the acquisition.

Potentially, the most effective way to increase revenues is a horizontal merger. By combining with a competitor in the same business, market share and market power of the companies may be increased, allowing the merged company to raise its prices and increase revenues. Although this may sound like a great idea to an enterprising capitalist, from society's perspective, mergers that lessen competition to the detriment of customers are not acceptable. In Canada, the Federal Competition Act, administered by the Competition Bureau and the Competition Tribunal, prohibits mergers that severely limit competition. However, merger proposals are rarely turned down for anti-competitive reasons in Canada. Instead, the Competition Bureau requests that the companies sell some of their assets to a third company, thereby limiting the reduction in competition. For example, the Competition Bureau requested that Canada Trust and TD Bank sell branches to competitors in particular geographic areas to reduce the anti-competitive impact of the proposed merger of those two companies.

As we write this, a landmark merger case is under consideration. The Competition Bureau opposed the proposed merger of Superior Propane with ICG Propane, which would give the merged companies 70 percent of the Canadian propane market and a complete monopoly in some parts of Canada, on the grounds that consumers would face higher prices. However, in 2000, the Competition Tribunal, the court that hears applications under the Competition Act, ruled that the merger should be allowed for efficiency reasons as permitted by the Act. With the approval of the Tribunal, Superior and ICG merged their operations.

Subsequently, the decision was overturned by a federal appeals court and was sent back to the Competition Tribunal with instructions to think about protecting consumers' interests. In April 2002, once again the Competition Tribunal approved the merger. The Competition Bureau launched another appeal to the federal court. They still believe the merger is contrary to the law and will request that the merged company be broken up.

In contrast to the Canadian experience, mergers are frequently disallowed in the United States on anti-competitive grounds.

ECONOMIES OF SCALE

Just as most of us believe that we would be happier if only we were a little richer, so managers always seem to believe their firm would be more competitive if only it were just a little bigger. They hope for *economies of scale,* that is, the opportunity to spread fixed costs across a larger volume of output. The banking industry provides many examples. By the 1970s, it was clear that the United States had too many small, local banks. Some (now very large) banks grew by systematically buying up smaller banks and streamlining their operations. Most of the cost savings came from consolidating "back-office" operations, such as computer systems for processing cheques and credit-card transactions and payments.

Similarly, TD Bank management argued they should be permitted to merge with their competitor Canada Trust to increase the scale and scope of their operations, and thereby, better compete with their larger domestic and foreign competitors. In addition to increasing the scale of back-office operations, the merger permitted the companies to reduce the number of branches. The effect is to create increased economies of scale, with higher volume at the remaining branches and lower costs per transaction.

These economies of scale are the natural goal of horizontal mergers. But they have been claimed in conglomerate mergers, too. The architects of these mergers have pointed to the economies that come from sharing central services such as accounting, financial control, and top-level management.

ECONOMIES OF VERTICAL INTEGRATION

Large industrial companies commonly like to gain as much control and coordination as possible over the production process by expanding back toward the output of the raw material and forward to the ultimate consumer. One way to achieve this is to merge with a supplier or a customer. Consider DuPont's purchase of an oil company, Conoco. This was vertical integration because petroleum is the ultimate raw material for much of DuPont's chemical production.

Do not assume that more vertical integration is necessarily better than less. Carried to extremes, it is absurdly inefficient. For example, before the Polish economy was restructured, LOT, the Polish state airline, found itself raising pigs to make sure that its employees had fresh meat on their tables. (Of course, in a centrally managed economy it may prove necessary to grow your own meat, since you can't be sure you'll be able to buy it.)

Some people mistakenly think that vertical integration is a good idea because if you own your supplier, you will pay less for materials. However, if you pay less, the supplier's profits will fall. No synergy is created if the merger simply moves profits but does not increase total profit. The gains from vertical integration are achieved through improved coordination and control of production.

Vertical integration is now less popular. The advent of just-in-time inventory systems and computerized ordering systems makes it much easier for a company to manage its supply chain without having to own its suppliers. Many companies are finding it more efficient to *outsource* many activities. For example, automobile manufacturers used to manufacture most of the parts used to make cars. Now companies like General Motors and Ford are primarily car assemblers, building vehicles with components purchased from parts manufacturers, like Magna International. Even DuPont seems to have become less convinced of the benefits of vertical integration: in 1999, it sold off Conoco.

COMBINING COMPLEMENTARY RESOURCES

Many small firms are acquired by large firms that can provide the missing ingredients necessary for the firm's success. The small firm may have a unique product but lack the engineering and sales organization necessary to produce and market it on a large scale. The firm could develop engineering and sales talent from scratch, but it may be quicker and cheaper to merge with a firm that already has ample talent. The two firms have *complementary resources*—each has what the other needs—so it may make sense for them to merge. Also the merger may open up opportunities that neither firm would pursue otherwise. Federal Express's purchase of Caliber System, a trucking company, is an example. Federal Express specializes in shipping packages by air, mostly for overnight delivery. Caliber's subsidiary RMS moves nonexpress packages by truck. RMS greatly increases

Federal Express's capability to move packages on the ground. At the same time, RMS-originated business can move easily on the Federal Express system when rapid or distant delivery is essential. Combining complementary resources may increase total revenues, decrease total costs, or both.

EXAMPLE 23.6 *Complementary Resources*

Of course two large firms may also merge because they have complementary resources. Consider the 1989 merger between two electric utilities, Utah Power & Light and PacifiCorp, which serves customers in California. Utah Power's peak demand comes in the summer, for air conditioning. PacifiCorp's peak comes in the winter, for heating. The savings from combining the two firms' generating systems were estimated at $45 million annually.

MERGING TO REDUCE TAXES

The tax implications of a merger or acquisition are often very complicated. However, it may be possible to reduce the total taxes of the combined companies if one of the companies has tax shields it is unable to use. For example, if a company has operating losses, by joining with another company in the same business that has taxable income, the losses may be a valuable tax deduction. However, merging for the sole purpose of using operating losses is not permitted and the CCRA may disallow the tax deductions.

Unused interest tax shield is another merger motive. As we saw in Chapter 15, the interest on debt generates an interest tax shield. A company with unused debt capacity, perhaps due to poor management, may be an attractive target. The acquirer will increase the target's debt/equity ratio, taking advantage of the interest deduction to reduce taxes and increase target firm value. This is one explanation offered for leveraged buyouts.

MERGERS AS A USE FOR SURPLUS FUNDS

Suppose that your firm is in a mature industry. It is generating a substantial amount of cash but has few profitable investment opportunities. Ideally such a firm should distribute the surplus cash to shareholders by increasing its dividend payment or by repurchasing its shares. Unfortunately, energetic managers are often reluctant to shrink their firm in this way. Furthermore, some shareholders may pay taxes on the dividends and repurchased shares.

If the firm is not willing to purchase its own shares, it can instead purchase someone else's. Thus firms with a surplus of cash and a shortage of good investment opportunities often turn to mergers *financed by cash* as a way of deploying their capital. This also avoids the tax consequences of dividends and share repurchases.

Firms that have excess cash and do not pay it out or redeploy it by acquisition often find themselves targets for takeover by other firms that propose to redeploy the cash for them. During the oil price slump of the early 1980s, many cash-rich oil companies found themselves threatened by takeover. This was not because their cash was a unique asset. The acquirers wanted to capture the companies' cash flow to make sure it was not frittered away on negative-NPV oil exploration projects. We return to this *free-cash-flow* motive for takeovers later in this chapter.

We have discussed how mergers may make economic sense, but things can still go wrong when managers don't do their homework. That was the case for Converse Inc., which produces athletic shoes. In May 1995 Converse announced that it was acquiring Apex One, a leading maker of sportswear. Apex brought with it a number of valuable licences for professional and college teams. As one enthusiast observed, "By letting them outfit athletes from head to toe, the Apex deal potentially puts them on an even keel with Nike and Reebok." However, 85 days later, Converse closed down Apex One after incurring a $46 million loss on its investment.

What went wrong? The problem appears to have begun when Apex was several months late in introducing its fall product lines. Converse's management complained that, in light of these delays, Apex's $100 million revenue projection at the time of the purchase had been unrealistic, and over the next 3 months projections were progressively scaled back to $40 million. Inevitably, the closure of Apex was followed by a volley of legal suits.[6]

23.3 Dubious Reasons for Mergers

The benefits that we have described so far all make economic sense. Other arguments sometimes given for mergers are more dubious. Here are two.

DIVERSIFICATION

We have suggested that the managers of a cash-rich company may prefer to see that cash used for acquisitions. That is why we often see cash-rich firms in stagnant industries merging their way into fresh woods and new pastures. What about diversification as an end in itself? It is obvious that diversification reduces risk. Isn't that a gain from merging?

The trouble with this argument is that diversification is easier and cheaper for the shareholder than for the corporation. Why should firm A buy firm B to diversify when the shareholders of firm A can buy shares in firm B to diversify their own portfolios? It is far easier and cheaper for individual investors to diversify than it is for firms to combine operations.

THE BOOTSTRAP GAME

During the 1960s some conglomerate companies made acquisitions which offered no evident economic gains. Nevertheless, the conglomerates' aggressive strategy produced several years of rising earnings per share. To see how this can happen, let us look at the acquisition of Muck and Slurry by the well-known conglomerate World Enterprises.

EXAMPLE 23.7 *The Bootstrap Game*

The position before the merger is set out in the first two columns of Table 23.2. Notice that because Muck and Slurry has relatively poor growth prospects, its stock sells at a lower price-earnings ratio than World Enterprises (line 3). The merger, we assume, produces no economic benefits, so the firms should be worth exactly the same together as apart. The value of World Enterprises after the merger is therefore equal to the sum of the separate values of the two firms (line 6).

[6] This description of the Apex One purchase draws on M. Maremount, "How Converse Got Its Laces All Tangled," *Business Week,* September 4, 1995, p. 37, and A. Bernstein, "Converse, Apex Sellers Point Fingers in Court Battle," *Sporting Goods Business,* May 1996, p. 8.

TABLE 23.2
Impact of merger on market value and earnings per share of World Enterprises

	World Enterprises (before merger)	Muck and Slurry	World Enterprises (after acquiring Muck and Slurry)
1. Earnings per share	$2	$2	$2.67
2. Price per share	$40	$20	$40
3. Price-earnings ratio	20	10	15
4. Number of shares	100,000	100,000	150,000
5. Total earnings	$200,000	$200,000	$400,000
6. Total market value	$4,000,000	$2,000,000	$6,000,000
7. Current earnings per dollar invested in stock (line 1 divided by line 2)	$.05	$.10	$.067

Note: When World Enterprises purchases Muck and Slurry, there are no gains. Therefore, total earnings and total market value should be unaffected by the merger. But earnings per share increase. World Enterprises issues only 50,000 of its shares (priced at $40) to acquire the 100,000 Muck and Slurry shares (priced at $20).

Since World Enterprises stock is selling for double the price of Muck and Slurry stock (line 2), World Enterprises can acquire the 100,000 Muck and Slurry shares for 50,000 of its own shares. Thus World will have 150,000 shares outstanding after the merger.

World's total earnings double as a result of the acquisition (line 5), but the number of shares increases by only 50 percent. Its earnings *per share* rise from $2 to $2.67. We call this a *bootstrap effect* because there is no real gain created by the merger and no increase in the two firms' combined value. Since World's stock price is unchanged by the acquisition of Muck and Slurry, the price-earnings ratio falls (line 3).

Before the merger, $1 invested in World Enterprises bought 5 cents of current earnings and rapid growth prospects. On the other hand, $1 invested in Muck and Slurry bought 10 cents of current earnings but slower growth prospects. If the *total* market value is not altered by the merger, then $1 invested in the merged firm gives World shareholders 6.7 cents of immediate earnings but slower growth than before the merger. Muck and Slurry shareholders get lower immediate earnings but faster growth. Neither side gains or loses *provided* that everybody understands the deal.

Financial manipulators sometimes try to ensure that the market does *not* understand the deal. Suppose that investors are fooled by the exuberance of the president of World Enterprises and mistake the 33 percent postmerger increase in earnings per share for *sustainable* growth. If they do, the price of World Enterprises stock rises and the shareholders of both companies receive something for nothing.

You should now see how to play the bootstrap game. Suppose that you manage a company enjoying a high price-earnings ratio. The reason it is high is that investors anticipate rapid growth in future earnings. You achieve this growth not by capital investment, product improvement, or increased operating efficiency, but by purchasing slow-growing firms with low price-earnings ratios. The long-run result will be slower growth and a depressed price-earnings ratio, but in the short run earnings per share can increase dramatically. If this fools investors, you may be able to achieve the higher earnings per share without suffering a decline in your price-earnings ratio. But in order to *keep* fooling investors, you must continue to expand by merger *at the same compound rate.* Obviously you cannot do this forever; one day expansion must slow down or stop. Then earnings growth will cease, and your house of cards will fall.

Buying a firm with a lower P/E ratio can increase earnings per share. But the increase should not result in a higher share price. The short-term increase in earnings should be offset by lower future earnings growth.

CHECK POINT 23.2

Suppose that Muck and Slurry has even worse growth prospects than in our example and its share price is only $10. Recalculate the effects of the merger in this case. You should find that earnings per share increase by a greater amount, since World Enterprises can now buy the same current earnings for fewer shares.

23.4 Evaluating Mergers

If you are given the responsibility for evaluating a proposed merger, you must think hard about the following two questions:

1. Is there an overall economic gain to the merger? In other words, is the merger value-enhancing? Are the two firms worth more together than apart?
2. Do the terms of the merger make my company and its shareholders better off? There is no point in merging if the cost is too high and all the economic gain goes to the other company.

Answering these deceptively simple questions is rarely easy. Some economic gains can be nearly impossible to quantify, and complex merger financing can obscure the true terms of the deal. But the basic principles for evaluating mergers are not too difficult.

MERGERS FINANCED BY CASH

We will concentrate on a simple numerical example. Your company, Cislunar Foods, is considering acquisition of a smaller food company, Targetco. Cislunar is proposing to finance the deal by purchasing all of Targetco's outstanding stock for $19 per share. Some financial information on the two companies is given in the left and center columns of Table 23.3.

Question 1. Why would Cislunar and Targetco be worth more together than apart? Suppose that operating costs can be reduced by combining the companies' marketing,

TABLE 23.3
Cislunar Foods is considering an acquisition of Targetco. The merger would increase the companies' combined earnings by $4 million.

	Cislunar Foods	Targetco	Combined Companies	
Revenues	$150	$20	$172	(+2)
Operating costs	118	16	132	(–2)
Earnings	$ 32	$ 4	$ 40	(+4)
Cash	$ 55	$ 2.5		
Other assets' book value	185	17		
Total assets	$240	$19.5		
Price per share	$ 48	$16		
Number of shares	10	2.5		
Market value	$480	$40		

Note: Figures in millions except price per share.

distribution, and administration. Revenues can also be increased in Targetco's region. The rightmost column of Table 23.3 contains projected revenues, costs, and earnings for the two firms operating together: annual operating costs postmerger will be \$2 million less than the sum of the separate companies' costs, and revenues will be \$2 million more. Therefore, projected earnings increase by \$4 million.[7] We will assume that the increased earnings are the only synergy to be generated by the merger.

The economic gain to the merger is the present value of the extra earnings. If the earnings increase is permanent (a level perpetuity), and the cost of capital is 20 percent,

$$\text{Economic gain} = \text{PV (increased earnings)} = \frac{4}{.20} = \$20 \text{ million}$$

This additional value is the basic motivation for the merger.

Question 2. What are the terms of the merger? What is the cost to Cislunar and its shareholders?

Targetco's management and shareholders will not consent to the merger unless they receive at least the stand-alone value of their shares. They can be paid in cash or by new shares issued by Cislunar. In this case we are considering a cash offer of \$19 per Targetco share, \$3 per share over the prior share price. Targetco has 2.5 million shares outstanding, so Cislunar will have to pay out \$47.5 million, a premium of \$7.5 million over Targetco's prior market value. On these terms, Targetco shareholders will capture \$7.5 million out of the \$20 million gain from the merger. That ought to leave \$12.5 million for Cislunar.

This is confirmed in the Cash Purchase column of Table 23.4. Start at the *bottom* of the column, where the total market value of the merged firms is \$492.5 million. This is derived as follows:

Cislunar market value prior to merger	\$480 million
Targetco market value	40
Present value of gain to merger	20
Less cash paid out to Targetco shareholders	–47.5
Postmerger market value	\$492.5 million

The postmerger share price for Cislunar will be \$49.25, an increase of \$1.25 per share. There are 10 million shares now outstanding, so the total increase in the value of Cislunar shares is \$12.5 million.

Now let's summarize. The merger makes sense for Cislunar for two reasons. First, the

TABLE 23.4
Financial forecasts after the Cislunar–Targetco merger: The left column assumes a cash purchase at \$19 per Targetco share. The right column assumes Targetco shareholders receive one new Cislunar share for every three Targetco shares.

	Cash Purchase	Exchange of Shares
Earnings	\$ 40	\$ 40
Cash	\$ 10	\$ 57.5
Other assets' book value	202	202
Total assets	\$212	\$259.5
Price per share	\$ 49.25	\$ 49.85
Number of shares	10	10.833
Market value	\$492.5	\$540

Note: Figures in millions except price per share.

[7] To keep things simple, the example ignores taxes and assumes that both companies are all-equity financed. We also ignore the interest income that could have been earned by investing the cash used to finance the merger.

merger adds $20 million of overall value. Second, the terms of the merger give only $7.5 million of the $20 million overall gain to Targetco's shareholders, leaving $12.5 million for Cislunar. You could say that the *cost* of acquiring Targetco is $7.5 million, the difference between the cash payment and the value of Targetco as a separate company.

$$\text{Cost} = \text{cash paid out} - \text{Targetco value} = \$47.5 - 40 = \$7.5 \text{ million}$$

Of course the Targetco shareholders are ahead by $7.5 million. *Their gain is your cost.* As we've already seen, Cislunar shareholders come out $12.5 million ahead. This is the merger's NPV for Cislunar:

$$\text{NPV} = \text{economic gain} - \text{cost} = \$20 - 7.5 = \$12.5 \text{ million}$$

Writing down the economic gain and cost of a merger in this way separates the motive for the merger (the economic gain, or value added) from the terms of the merger (the *division* of the gain between the two merging companies).

CHECK POINT 23.3

Killer Shark Inc. makes a surprise cash offer of $22 a share for Goldfish Industries. Before the offer, Goldfish was selling for $18 a share. Goldfish has 1 million shares outstanding. What must Killer Shark believe about the present value of the improvement it can bring to Goldfish's operations?

MERGERS FINANCED BY STOCK

What if Cislunar wants to conserve its cash for other investments, and therefore decides to pay for the Targetco acquisition with new Cislunar shares? The deal calls for Targetco shareholders to receive one Cislunar share in exchange for every three Targetco shares.

It's the same merger, but the financing is different. The right column of Table 23.4 works out the consequences. Again, start at the *bottom* of the column. Note that the market value of Cislunar's shares after the merger is $540 million, $47.5 million higher than in the cash deal, because that cash is kept rather than paid out to Targetco shareholders. On the other hand, there are more shares outstanding, since 833,333 new shares have to be issued in exchange for the 2.5 million Targetco shares (a 1 to 3 ratio). Therefore, the price per share is 540/10.833 = $49.85, which is 60 cents higher than in the cash offer.

Why do Cislunar shareholders do better from the share exchange? The economic gain from the merger is the same, but the Targetco shareholders capture less of it. They get 833,333 shares at $49.85, or $41.5 million, a premium of only $1.5 million over Targetco's prior market value.

$$\begin{aligned}\text{Cost} &= \text{value of shares issued} - \text{Targetco value}\\ &= \$41.5 - 40 = \$1.5 \text{ million}\end{aligned}$$

The merger's NPV to Cislunar's original shareholders is

$$\text{NPV} = \text{economic gain} - \text{cost} = 20 - 1.5 = \$18.5 \text{ million}$$

Note that Cislunar stock rises by $1.85 from its prior value. The total increase in value for Cislunar's original shareholders, who retain 10 million shares, is $18.5 million.

Evaluating the terms of a merger can be tricky when there is an exchange of shares. The target company's shareholders will retain a stake in the merged firms, so you have to figure out what the firm's shares will be worth *after* the merger is announced and its benefits appreciated by investors. Notice that we started with the total market value of Cislunar and

Targetco postmerger, took account of the merger terms (833,333 new shares issued), and worked back to the postmerger share price. Only then could we work out the division of the merger gains between the two companies.

SEE BOX P. 696

There is a key distinction between cash and stock for financing mergers. If cash is offered, the cost of the merger is not affected by the size of the merger gains. If stock is offered, the cost depends on the gains because the gains show up in the postmerger share price, and these shares are used to pay for the acquired firm. The nearby Finance in Action box illustrates how complex a stock offer can be. When Gillette offered to buy Duracell, giving Duracell shareholders about a 20 percent stake in the merged firm, the attractiveness of the deal depended on the stock market's valuation of *both* firms.

Stock financing also mitigates the effects of over- or undervaluation of either firm. Suppose, for example, that A overestimates B's value as a separate entity, perhaps because it has overlooked some hidden liability. Thus A makes too generous an offer. Other things equal, A's shareholders are better off if it is a stock rather than a cash offer. With a stock offer, the inevitable bad news about B's value will fall partly on B's former shareholders.

CHECK POINT 23.4

Suppose Targetco shareholders demand one Cislunar share for every 2.5 Targetco shares. Otherwise they will not accept the merger. Under these revised terms, is the merger still a good deal for Cislunar?

A WARNING

The cost of a merger is the premium the acquirer pays for the target firm over its value as a separate company. If the target is a public company, you can measure its separate value by multiplying its stock price by the number of outstanding shares. Watch out, though: if investors expect the target to be acquired, its stock price may overstate the company's separate value. The target company's stock price may already have risen in anticipation of a premium to be paid by an acquiring firm.

ANOTHER WARNING

Some companies begin their merger analyses with a forecast of the target firm's future cash flows. Any revenue increases or cost reductions attributable to the merger are included in the forecasts, which are then discounted back to the present and compared with the purchase price:

$$\text{Estimated net gain} = \begin{array}{l}\text{DCF valuation of target including merger benefits} \\ \qquad - \text{cash required for acquisition}\end{array}$$

This is a dangerous procedure. Even the brightest and best-trained analyst can make large errors in valuing a business. The estimated net gain may come up positive not because the merger makes sense but simply because the analyst's cash-flow forecasts are too optimistic. On the other hand, a good merger may not be pursued if the analyst fails to recognize the target's potential as a stand-alone business.

A better procedure *starts* with the target's current and stand-alone market value and concentrates instead on the *changes* in cash flow that would result from the merger. Always ask why the two firms should be worth more together than apart. Remember, you add value only if you can generate *additional economic benefits*—some competitive edge that other firms can't match and that the target firm's managers can't achieve on their own.

FINANCE IN ACTION

Blades, Batteries, and a Fifth of Gillette

Back in 1988, when Kraft Inc. decided to unload its battery subsidiary, Gillette Co. was tempted. But the bidding went up and up and out of Gillette's reach. Kohlberg Kravis Roberts & Co. eventually bought the battery maker—it was Duracell, of course—for a seemingly extravagant $1.8 billion.

After 8 years of due diligence, Gillette has finally agreed to fork over stock valued at more than $7 billion for the very same Duracell International Inc. Just as KKR now looks shrewd, rear-view analysts may snicker at Gillette for buying dear what it could have had then for, let us assume, only $2 billion in stock.

In fact, Gillette shareholders should thank their lucky stars the earlier deal didn't happen. In share-for-share acquisitions, what you are getting is only half the picture; what you are giving up is just as important. The standard analysis values such deals according to the dollar value of the target, but that approach is flawed. The key question isn't whether Duracell is worth $7 billion, because Gillette isn't giving up $7 billion. It is giving up a part—in this case 20%—of itself.

Schematically, Gillette is trading razor blades for batteries (not bucks for batteries), and the results can be very different. Since 1988, for instance, the blade business, at least under Gillette's management, has performed much better than batteries. While Duracell's stock has quadrupled, Gillette's has multiplied eight times. Thus if Gillette had in fact made that "cheap" $2 billion acquisition, it would have acquired a jack rabbit but given up a prize thoroughbred. The passed-over purchase back then would have cost Gillette *more than one-third* of its stock; today, it is buying the same business for only a fifth of its stock.

Clearly, taking a pass was the right move. Duracell was cheap in 1988, but Gillette was cheaper. And shopping with inexpensive currency, meaning issuing undervalued stock, amounts to selling the company (or a piece of it) on the cheap.

Going forward, the same analysis holds. The imputed dollar value of the deal will forever drift with Gillette's share price; the one constant is that each shareholder is trading away one-fifth of his interest in the old Gillette. Whether Duracell will be worth it, a subject no analyst has addressed, is what matters.

Such deals are manna for investment bankers (and bound to wind up in B-school texts) because you need to size up two businesses instead of one.

On balance, the blade business is more distinct, and better, than batteries. But how much better? Duracell for one-fifth of Gillette works out to this: For each dollar of Gillette earnings that shareholders are giving up, they are getting roughly $1.30 in cash earnings from batteries.

Blades should trade at a premium, but this one is steep. That premium, of course, reflects the current very high price of Gillette's stock, which in turn reflects a view that Gillette will forever keep profit growing twice as fast as its sales. Gillette's managers wouldn't come out and say that 34 times earnings reflects unwarranted optimism, or even a bull-market joie de vivre, but if that is what they thought, trading part of their company at that price for a cheaper one would be a smart move. And that is what they are doing.

Source: Republished with permission of Dow Jones, from "Blades, Batteries, and a Fifth of Gillette," from R. Lowenstein, "Intrinsic Value," *The Wall Street Journal*, September 19, 1996, p. C1; permission conveyed through Copyright Clearance Center.

It makes sense to keep an eye on the value that investors place on the gains from merging. If A's stock price falls when the deal is announced, investors are sending a message that the merger benefits are doubtful *or* that A is paying too much for these benefits.

A NOTE ON TAX COMPLICATIONS

When shareholders sell their shares, normally they must pay capital gains tax on the increase in their shares' value. This is the case in a *taxable* acquisition, where the selling shareholders receive cash for their shares. However, it is possible for the acquisition to be *tax-free*. In a tax-free acquisition, the selling shareholders cannot receive cash but get shares of the acquirer or of the merged company. The rules determining the tax-free status of amalgamations, stocks, and assets are complex but the basic message is the same: the selling shareholders must continue to be shareholders or capital gains will be assessed from the share sale.

The tax status of the acquisition also affects the taxation of the company afterwards. In a taxable acquisition, the assets of the target are revalued, allowing the acquirer to take more CCA deductions and reduce taxable income. This is called *stepping up the asset pool*. In a tax-free acquisition, the assets are not revalued and no incremental tax savings are generated.

As you can see, the selling shareholders would prefer a tax-free acquisition, while the buyer pays less tax in the future if the acquisition is taxable. If possible, the merger deal will be struck to reduce the total tax consequences of the transaction.

23.5 Merger Tactics

In recent years, most mergers have been agreed upon by both parties, but occasionally, an acquirer goes over the heads of the target firm's management and makes a *tender offer* directly to its shareholders. The management of the target firm may advise shareholders to accept the tender, or it may attempt to fight the bid in the hope that the acquirer will either raise its offer or throw in the towel.

The rules of merger warfare are largely set by the Ontario Securities Act and are administered by the Ontario Securities Commission (OSC). Ontario dominates in this area because the Toronto Stock Exchange is located in Ontario. However, the various provincial securities acts tend to be similar, and the provincial securities commissions try to work together.

EXAMPLE 23.8 *A Hostile Takeover Bid: Trilogy/Indigo Goes after Chapters*

In late November 2000, Trilogy Retail Enterprises, a private company owned by Gerald Schwartz, CEO of Onex Corp., and his wife, Heather Reisman, CEO of Indigo Books, offered \$63.5 million (\$13 cash per share) for 50.1 percent of Chapters, Canada's largest Canadian book retailer at the time. Schwartz and Reisman, majority shareholders of Indigo, the second largest Canadian book retailer, suggested that they would combine Chapters and Indigo and reduce the number of stores. Chapters and Indigo had been engaged in a tough battle for supremacy in the bookselling business and both had expanded aggressively and were losing a lot of money.

Gerald Schwartz and Heather Reisman were well known in the business community. Schwartz had created Onex Corp., the Toronto-based merchant-banking firm that had grown into a multibillion-dollar enterprise with interests in many dull but lucrative businesses—everything from airline catering (SC International Services Inc.) to auto parts (DuraAutomotive Systems Inc.), and from computer equipment (Celestica Inc.) to sugar refining (B.C. Sugar Refinery Ltd.). The key to Onex's success was acquiring undervalued businesses, often with extensive use of debt financing, and then, successfully turning them around and ultimately reselling the transformed businesses. Schwartz was known as the LBO (leveraged buyout) king of Canada.

The market reacted favourably, increasing Chapters' price to \$11.10 from the previous day's price of \$9.10. However, the offer was far below Chapters' peak of \$35 in mid-1999.

Quickly, Chapters' board of directors advised shareholders to reject the bid. Chapters CEO Larry Stevenson called the offer "completely inadequate."

"Shareholders are much better served by us continuing to run this company the way it should be and doing the things we can to maximize shareholder value," he said in an interview. "Shareholders should hold on to their shares."[8]

In a move viewed by many as defensive, Chapters also announced a $25.5-million plan to buy back the 31 percent of Chapters Online shares it did not own for $3.40 per share. Funds for the buyback would be raised through additional borrowing by Chapters, which would make the company less attractive to a buyer. Those Chapters Online shares had been sold in an initial public offering in September 1999 at $13.50 per share.

Trilogy continued to purchase Chapters shares on the open market, increasing its stake from 9 percent to 14 percent. In early January, Trilogy raised its bid to $15 per share, for a 50.1 percent stake in Chapters.

Chapters' management felt the bid was too low and disliked the fact that it was a partial bid—offering to purchase only 50.1 percent of the shares. They were concerned that accepting Trilogy's partial bid left shareholders in the dark about the potential value of the shares not taken up in the tender offer.

Chapters' management worked hard to thwart the takeover. On several occasions they asked the OSC to order Reisman to allow Chapters to look at Indigo's financial statements. They wanted to estimate the postmerger price of the remaining Chapters shares. The OSC determined that it was not necessary for Indigo to reveal its financial situation to Chapters.

shareholders' rights plan or poison pill Measures taken by the target firm to avoid acquisition; for example, the right of existing shareholders to buy additional shares at an attractive price if a bidder acquires a significant holding.

Trilogy, on the other hand, appealed to the OSC to kill Chapters' **shareholders' rights plan**. The rights plan, or **poison pill**, had been put in place in April 2001 stipulating that anyone who acquired 20 percent or more of the company without meeting the requirements of the Chapters board would find their shareholding diluted through a rights issue. All shareholders other than the raider would be given rights to purchase Chapters shares at a low price. This would severely dilute the raider's shareholding.

The daily reporting of the very hostile, very public battle for Chapters filled the business press for several months as both sides argued why they were right and the other side was wrong.

white knight Friendly potential acquirer sought by a target company that is threatened by an unwelcome bidder.

On January 18, 2001, Future Shop unexpectedly entered as a **white knight**. Supported by Chapters' board and management, Future Shop bid $200 million for all of Chapters' common shares. The bid was $16 cash or two Future Shop shares for each Chapters share, with a maximum $100 million in cash. Had Trilogy been trumped? Would they come back with a higher bid? The business press speculated that Schwartz and Reisman had been beaten and would likely not proceed.

However, on January 20, 2001, Trilogy raised its bid to $121.5 million, $17 a share for all Chapters shares except the 30 percent locked up in the Future Shop deal. It was revealed that Schwartz and Reisman would be providing half of the money to pay for the purchase, with the other half from bank financing. However, a condition of the revised bid was the removal of Chapters' poison pill. At an unusual Sunday hearing of the OSC on January 21, it was ruled that Chapters' shareholders' rights plan had served its purpose and it was in the public interest to kill it. Schwartz and Reisman had won this round.

Now with two bids on the table for Chapters, its board of directors formed a special committee of independent (nonmanagement) directors to carefully examine the bids and

[8] G. Livingston, "Indigo CEO Reisman and Husband Gerry Schwartz Bid for Bookseller Chapters," *Canadian Press Newswire*, November 28, 2000.

inform shareholders which bid was better. The board also defended the poison pill plan, arguing that it had forced Trilogy to increase its original bid by giving Chapters enough time to find another buyer.

A separate, but crucial, series of hearings and meetings between Schwartz and Reisman with the federal Competition Bureau also occurred during this time. The Competition Bureau, concerned about lessening of competition if the top two book retailers were allowed to merge, indicated they needed time to fully review the merits of a possible merger. Schwartz and Reisman agreed to temporarily place the control of Indigo into a third-party trust if they succeeded in acquiring Chapters.

In the end, Chapters' board recommended the Trilogy bid. Schwartz and Reisman got the shares they wanted. The Competition Bureau gave its approval, conditional on the sale of 13 superstores and 10 mall stores of Chapters and Indigo.

The Chapters–Indigo battle illustrates many of the features of Canadian merger warfare. Firms frequently attempt to deter potential bidders by adopting poison pills, which make the company unappealing. In a typical poison pill, or shareholders' rights plan, existing shareholders are given the right to buy the company's shares at a low price as soon as the bidder acquires more than 20 percent of the shares. The bidder is not entitled to the discount and finds itself unable to acquire the needed shares.

In Canada, shareholders' rights plans are rarely triggered, and are often killed by the OSC at the request of the bidder. Their main accomplishment is to extend the time the bid is open, giving other bidders time to make an offer.

Bidders and targets often approach the Ontario Securities Commission and the courts to make rulings to prevent or require their opponent to take some action. In the Chapters–Indigo battle, both parties made requests of the OSC.

The search for a *white knight* is also typical of many hostile bids in Canada and the United States. White knights play an important role in raising the bid. Sometimes they successfully acquire the target, sometimes they lose the battle.

shark repellent Amendments to a company charter made to forestall takeover attempts

Another merger tactic, less common in Canada but used frequently in the United States, is known as **shark repellent**. Managers who are worried about the possibility of a hostile bid will ask shareholders to agree to changes in the corporate charter that make it more difficult for a successful bidder to get control of the board of directors. For example, the charter may be amended to stagger the election of board members, making only one-third of the board up for re-election each year. This means that the bidder cannot obtain majority control of the board immediately after acquiring a majority of the shares. Another example is to require a supermajority of 80 percent of the shares to approve the merger rather than the normal 50 percent. In Canada, most mergers require a two-thirds majority by law.

WHO GETS THE GAINS?

Is it better to own shares in the acquiring firm or the target? In general, shareholders of the target firm do best. Franks, Harris, and Titman studied 399 acquisitions by large U.S. firms between 1975 and 1984. They found that shareholders who sold following the announcement of the bid received a healthy gain averaging 28 percent.[9] On the other hand, it appears that investors expected acquiring companies to just about break even. The prices of their

[9] J. R. Franks, R. S. Harris, and S. Titman, "The Postmerger Share-Price Performance of Acquiring Firms," *Journal of Financial Economics* 29 (March 1991), pp. 81–96.

shares fell by 1 percent.[10] The value of the *total* package—buyer plus seller—increased by 4 percent. Of course, these are averages; selling shareholders sometimes obtain much higher returns. When IBM took over Lotus, it paid a premium of 100 percent, or about $1.7 billion, for Lotus stock.

Why do sellers earn higher returns? The most important reason is the competition among potential bidders. Once the first bidder puts the target company "in play," one or more additional suitors often jump in, sometimes as white knights at the invitation of the target firm's management. Every time one suitor tops another's bid, more of the merger gain slides toward the target. At the same time the target firm's management may mount various legal and financial counterattacks, ensuring that capitulation, if and when it comes, is at the highest attainable price.

Of course, bidders and targets are not the only possible winners. Unsuccessful bidders often win, too, by selling off their holdings in target companies at substantial profits. Such shares may be sold on the open market or, in the U.S., sold back to the target company.[11] Sometimes they are sold to the successful suitor.

Other winners include investment bankers, lawyers, accountants, and in some cases, arbitrageurs, or "arbs," who speculate on the likely success of takeover bids.

"Speculate" has a negative ring, but it can be a useful social service. A tender offer may present shareholders with a difficult decision. Should they accept, should they wait to see if someone else produces a better offer, or should they sell their stock in the market? This quandary presents an opportunity for the arbitrageurs. In other words, they buy from the target's shareholders and take on the risk that the deal will not go through.[12]

23.6 Leveraged Buyouts

Leveraged buyouts, or *LBOs,* differ from ordinary acquisitions in two ways. First, a large fraction of the purchase price is debt-financed. Some, perhaps all, of this debt is junk, that is, below investment grade. Second, the shares of the LBO no longer trade on the open market. The remaining equity in the LBO is privately held by a small group of (usually institutional) investors. When this group is led by the company's management, the acquisition is called a *management buyout (MBO).* Many LBOs are in fact MBOs.

In the 1970s and 1980s many management buyouts were arranged for unwanted divisions of large, diversified companies. Smaller divisions outside the companies' main lines of business often lacked top management's interest and commitment, and divisional management chafed under corporate bureaucracy. Many such divisions flowered when spun off as MBOs. Their managers, pushed by the need to generate cash for debt service and encouraged by a substantial personal stake in the business, found ways to cut costs and compete more effectively.

During the 1980s MBO/LBO activity expanded to include buyouts of entire businesses, including large, mature public corporations. The largest, most dramatic, and best-documented LBO of them all was the $25 billion takeover of RJR Nabisco[13] in 1988 by

[10] The small loss to the shareholders of acquiring firms is not statistically significant. Other studies using different samples have observed a small positive return.

[11] When a potential acquirer sells the shares back to the target, the transaction is known as *greenmail.* Greenmail is illegal in Canada. All sharesholders of a particular class must be treated equally.

[12] Strictly speaking, an arbitrageur is an investor who makes a riskless profit. Arbitrageurs in merger battles often take very large risks indeed. Their activities are sometimes known as "risk arbitrage."

[13] The story of the RJR Nabisco buyout is reconstructed by B. Burrough and J. Helyar in *Barbarians at the Gate: The Fall of RJR Nabisco* (New York: Harper & Row, 1990) and is the subject of a movie with the same title.

Kohlberg Kravis Roberts (KKR). The players, tactics, and controversies of LBOs are writ large in this case.

Since the 1990s the use of leveraged buyouts to acquire entire companies has become infrequent, although LBOs continue to be used to facilitate the sale of unwanted divisions. For example, in 2000, CIBC World Markets, the investment banking division of the Canadian Imperial Bank of Commerce, along with Deutsche Bank arranged $425 million (US) in loans to help fund a leveraged buyout of Monsanto Co.'s artificial sweetener business by an investment group. The loans were provided by institutional investors and provided almost 75 percent of the $570 million (US) of cash needed to purchase the sweetener business.

EXAMPLE 23.9 *RJR Nabisco*

On October 28, 1988, the board of directors of RJR Nabisco revealed that Ross Johnson, the company's chief executive officer, had formed a group of investors prepared to buy all the firm's stock for $75 per share in cash and take the company private. Johnson's group was backed up and advised by Shearson Lehman Hutton, the investment bank subsidiary of American Express.

RJR's share price immediately moved to about $75, handing shareholders a 36 percent gain over the previous day's price of $56. At the same time RJR's bonds fell, since it was clear that existing bondholders would soon have a lot more company.

Johnson's offer lifted RJR onto the auction block. Once the company was in play, its board of directors was obliged to consider other offers, which were not long in coming. Four days later, a group of investors led by LBO specialists Kohlberg Kravis Roberts bid $90 per share, $79 in cash plus preferred stock valued at $11.

The bidding finally closed on November 30, some 32 days after the initial offer was revealed. In the end it was Johnson's group against KKR. KKR offered $109 per share, after adding $1 per share (roughly $230 million) at the last hour. The KKR bid was $81 in cash, convertible subordinated debentures valued at about $10, and preferred shares valued at about $18. Johnson's group bid $112 in cash and securities.

But the RJR board chose KKR. True, Johnson's group had offered $3 per share more, but its security valuations were viewed as "softer" and perhaps overstated. Also, KKR's planned asset sales were less drastic; perhaps their plans for managing the business inspired more confidence. Finally, the Johnson group's proposal contained a management compensation package that seemed extremely generous and had generated an avalanche of bad press.

But where did the merger benefits come from? What could justify offering $109 per share, about $25 billion in all, for a company that only 33 days previously had been selling for $56 per share?

KKR and other bidders were betting on two things. First, they expected to generate billions of additional dollars from interest tax shields, reduced capital expenditures, and sales of assets not strictly necessary to RJR's core businesses. Asset sales alone were projected to generate $5 billion. Second, they expected to make those core businesses significantly more profitable, mainly by cutting back on expenses and bureaucracy. Apparently there was plenty to cut, including the RJR "Air Force," which at one point operated 10 corporate jets.

In the year after KKR took over, new management was installed. This group sold assets and cut back operating expenses and capital spending. There were also layoffs. As expected, high interest charges meant a net loss of $976 million for 1989, but pretax operating income actually increased, despite extensive asset sales, including the sale of RJR's European food operations.

While management was cutting costs and selling assets, prices in the junk bond market were rapidly declining, implying much higher future interest charges for RJR and stricter terms on any refinancing. In mid-1990 KKR made an additional equity investment, and later that year the company announced an offer of cash and new shares in exchange for $753 million of junk bonds. By 1993 the burden of debt had been reduced from $26 billion to $14 billion. For RJR, the world's largest LBO, it seemed that high debt was a temporary, not permanent, virtue.

BARBARIANS AT THE GATE?

The buyout of RJR crystallized views on LBOs, the junk bond market, and the takeover business. For many it exemplified all that was wrong with finance in the 1980s, especially the willingness of "raiders" to carve up established companies, leaving them with enormous debt burdens, basically in order to get rich quick.

There was plenty of confusion, stupidity, and greed in the LBO business. Not all the people involved were nice. On the other hand, LBOs generated enormous increases in market value, and most of the gains went to selling shareholders not raiders. For example, the biggest winners in the RJR Nabisco LBO were the company's shareholders.

We should therefore consider briefly where these gains may have come from before we try to pass judgment on LBOs. There are several possibilities.

The Junk Bond Markets. LBOs and debt-financed takeovers may have been driven by artificially cheap funding from the junk bond markets. With hindsight it seems that investors in junk bonds underestimated the risks of default. Default rates climbed painfully between 1989 and 1991. At the same time, the junk bond market became much less liquid after the demise of Drexel Burnham Lambert, the chief market-maker. Yields rose dramatically, and new issues dried up. Suddenly junk-financed LBOs seemed to disappear from the scene.[14]

Leverage and Taxes. As we explained in Chapter 15, borrowing money saves taxes. But taxes were not the main driving force behind LBOs. The value of interest tax shields was just not big enough to explain the observed gains in market value.

Of course, if interest tax shields were the main motive for LBOs' high debt, then LBO managers would not be so concerned to pay off debt. We saw that this was one of the first tasks facing RJR Nabisco's new management.

Other Stakeholders. It is possible that the gain to the selling shareholders is just someone else's loss and that no value is generated overall. Therefore, we should look at the total gain to *all* investors in an LBO, not just the selling shareholders.

Bondholders are the obvious losers. The debt they thought was well-secured may turn into junk when the borrower goes through an LBO. We noted how market prices of RJR Nabisco debt fell sharply when Ross Johnson's first LBO offer was announced. But again, the value losses suffered by bondholders in LBOs are not nearly large enough to explain shareholder gains.

Leverage and Incentives. Managers and employees of LBOs work harder and often smarter. They have to generate cash to service the extra debt. Moreover, managers'

[14] There was a sharp revival of junk bond sales in 1992 and 1993 and 1996 was a banner year. But many of these issues simply replaced existing bonds. It remains to be seen whether junk bonds will make a lasting recovery.

personal fortunes are riding on the LBO's success. They become owners rather than organization men or women.

It is hard to measure the payoff from better incentives, but there is some evidence of improved operating efficiency in LBOs. Kaplan, who studied 48 management buyouts between 1980 and 1986, found average increases in operating income of 24 percent over the following 3 years. Ratios of operating income and net cash flow to assets and sales increased dramatically. He observed cutbacks in capital expenditures but not in employment. Kaplan suggests that these operating changes "are due to improved incentives rather than layoffs or managerial exploitation of shareholders through inside information."[15]

Free Cash Flow. The free-cash-flow theory of takeovers is basically that mature firms with a surplus of cash will tend to waste it. This contrasts with standard finance theory, which says that firms with more cash than positive-NPV investment opportunities should give the cash back to investors through higher dividends or share repurchases. But we see firms like RJR Nabisco spending on corporate luxuries and questionable capital investments. One benefit of LBOs is to put such companies on a diet and force them to pay out cash to service debt.

The free-cash-flow theory predicts that mature, "cash cow" companies will be the most likely targets of LBOs. We can find many examples that fit the theory, including RJR Nabisco. The theory says that the gains in market value generated by LBOs are just the present values of the future cash flows that would otherwise have been frittered away.[16]

We do not endorse the free-cash-flow theory as the sole explanation for LBOs. We have mentioned several other plausible rationales, and we suspect that most LBOs are driven by a mixture of motives. Nor do we say that all LBOs are beneficial. On the contrary, there are many mistakes, and even soundly motivated LBOs can be dangerous, as the bankruptcies of Campeau, Revco, National Gypsum, and many other highly leveraged companies prove. However, we do take issue with those who portray LBOs *simply* as Bay Street or Wall Street barbarians breaking up the traditional strengths of corporate North America. In many cases LBOs have generated true gains.

In the next section we sum up the long-run impact of mergers and acquisitions, including LBOs, using the United States economy as an example. We warn you, however, that there are no neat answers. Our assessment has to be mixed and tentative.

23.7 Mergers and the Economy

MERGER WAVES

Mergers come in waves. The first episode of intense merger activity occurred at the turn of the 20th century and the second in the 1920s. There was a further boom from 1967 to 1969 and then again in the 1980s and 1990s. Each episode coincided with a period of buoyant stock prices, though in each case there were substantial differences in the types of companies that merged and how they went about it.

We don't really understand why merger activity is so volatile. If mergers are prompted

[15] S. Kaplan, "The Effects of Management Buyouts on Operating Performance and Value," *Journal of Financial Economics* 24 (October 1989), pp. 217–254.

[16] The free-cash-flow theory's chief proponent is Michael Jensen. See M. C. Jensen, "The Eclipse of the Public Corporation," *Harvard Business Review* 67 (September–October 1989), pp. 61–74, and "The Agency Costs of Free Cash Flow, Corporate Finance and Takeovers," *American Economic Review* 76 (May 1986), pp. 323–329.

by economic motives, at least one of these motives must be "here today, gone tomorrow," and it must somehow be associated with high stock prices. But none of the economic motives that we review in this chapter has anything to do with the general level of the stock market. None of the motives burst on the scene in 1967, departed in 1970, reappeared for most of the 1980s, and reappeared again in the mid-1990s.

Some mergers may result from mistakes in valuation on the part of the stock market. In other words, the buyer may believe that investors have underestimated the value of the seller or may hope that they *will* overestimate the value of the combined firm. Why don't we see just as many firms hunting for bargain acquisitions when the stock market is low? It is possible that "suckers are born every minute," but it's difficult to believe that they can be harvested only in bull markets.

During the 1980s merger boom in the U.S., only the very largest companies were immune from attack by a rival management team. For example, in 1985, Pantry Pride, a small supermarket chain recently emerged from bankruptcy, made a bid for the cosmetics company Revlon. Revlon's assets were more than five times those of Pantry Pride. What made the bid possible (and eventually successful) was the ability of Pantry Pride to finance the takeover by borrowing $2.1 billion. The growth of leveraged buyouts during the 1980s depended on the development of a junk bond market that allowed bidders to place low-grade bonds rapidly and in high volume.

By the end of the decade the merger environment had changed. Many of the obvious targets had disappeared, and the battle for RJR Nabisco highlighted the increasing cost of victory. Institutions were reluctant to increase their holdings of junk bonds. Moreover, the market for these bonds had depended to a remarkable extent on one individual, Michael Milken, of the investment bank Drexel Burnham Lambert. By the late 1980s Milken and his employer were in trouble. Milken was indicted by a U.S. grand jury on 98 counts and was subsequently sentenced to jail and ordered to pay $600 million. Drexel filed for bankruptcy, but by that time the junk bond market was moribund and the finance for highly leveraged buyouts had largely dried up.[17] Finally, in reaction to the perceived excess of the merger boom, U.S. state legislatures and courts began to lean against takeovers.

The decline in merger activity proved temporary; by the mid-1990s stock markets and mergers were booming again. However, LBOs remained out of fashion, and relatively few mergers were intended simply to replace management. Instead, companies began to look once more at the possible benefits from combining two businesses.

DO MERGERS GENERATE NET BENEFITS?

There are undoubtedly good acquisitions and bad acquisitions, but economists find it hard to agree on whether acquisitions are beneficial *on balance.* We do know that mergers generate substantial gains to shareholders of acquired firms.

Since buyers seem roughly to break even and sellers make substantial gains, it seems that there are positive gains to mergers. But not everybody is convinced. Some believe that investors analyzing mergers pay too much attention to short-term earnings gains and don't notice that these gains are at the expense of long-term prospects.

Since we can't observe how companies would have fared in the absence of a merger, it is difficult to measure the effects on profitability. Studies of recent merger activity suggest that mergers *do* seem to improve real productivity. For example, Healy, Palepu, and Ruback examined 50 large mergers between 1979 and 1983 and found an average increase

[17] For a history of the role of Milken in the development of the junk bond market, see C. Bruck, *The Predator's Ball: The Junk Bond Raiders and the Man Who Staked Them* (New York: Simon and Schuster, 1988).

in the companies' pretax returns of 2.4 percentage points.[18] They argue that this gain came from generating a higher level of sales from the same assets. There was no evidence that the companies were mortgaging their long-term futures by cutting back on long-term investments; expenditures on capital equipment and research and development tracked the industry average.

If you are concerned with public policy toward mergers, you do not want to look only at their impact on the shareholders of the companies concerned. For instance, we have already seen that in the case of RJR Nabisco some part of the shareholders' gain was at the expense of the bondholders and the Internal Revenue Service (through the enlarged interest tax shield). The acquirer's shareholders may also gain at the expense of the target firm's employees, who in some cases are laid off or are forced to take pay cuts after takeovers.

Many people believe that the merger wave of the 1980s led to excessive debt levels and left many companies ill-equipped to survive a recession. Also, many savings and loan companies and some large insurance firms invested heavily in junk bonds. Defaults on these bonds threatened, and in some cases, extinguished, their solvency.

Perhaps the most important effect of acquisition is felt by the managers of companies that are *not* taken over. For example, one effect of LBOs was that the managers of even the largest corporations could not feel safe from challenge. Perhaps the threat of takeover spurs the whole corporate community to try harder. Unfortunately, we don't know whether on balance the threat of merger makes for more active days or sleepless nights.

We do know that merger activity is very costly. For example, in the RJR Nabisco buyout, the total fees paid to the investment banks, lawyers, and accountants amounted to over $1 billion.

Even if the gains to the community exceed these costs, one wonders whether the same benefits could not be achieved more cheaply another way. For example, are leveraged buyouts necessary to make managers work harder? Perhaps the problem lies in the way that many corporations reward and penalize their managers. Perhaps many of the gains from takeover could be captured by linking management compensation more closely to performance.

23.8 Summary

1. In what ways do companies change the composition of their ownership or management?

If the board of directors fails to replace an inefficient management, there are four ways to effect a change: (1) shareholders may engage in a **proxy contest** to replace the board; (2) the firm may be acquired by another; (3) the firm may be purchased by a private group of investors in a leveraged buyout, or (4) it may sell off part of its operations to another company.

There are three ways for one firm to acquire another: (1) it can **merge** all the assets and liabilities of the target firm into those of its own company; (2) it can buy the stock of the target; or (3) it can buy the individual assets of the target. The offer to buy the stock of the target firm is called a **tender offer.** The purchase of the stock or assets of another firm is called an **acquisition.**

2. Why may it make sense for companies to merge?

A merger may be undertaken in order to replace an inefficient management. But sometimes two business may be more valuable together than apart. Gains may stem from increased revenues, economies of scale, economies of vertical integration, the combination of complementary resources, reduced taxes, or redeployment of surplus funds. We don't know how frequently these benefits occur, but they do make economic sense. Sometimes mergers are undertaken to diversify risks or artificially increase growth of earnings per share. These motives are dubious.

[18] See P. Healy, K. Palepu, and R. Ruback, "Does Corporate Performance Improve after Mergers?" *Journal of Financial Economics* 31 (April 1992), pp. 135–175. The study examined the pretax returns of the merged companies relative to industry averages.

3. **How should the gains and costs of mergers to the acquiring firm be measured?**

A merger generates an economic gain if the two firms are worth more together than apart. The *gain* is the difference between the value of the merged firm and the value of the two firms run independently. The *cost* is the premium that the buyer pays for the selling firm over its value as a separate entity. When payment is in the form of shares, the value of this payment naturally depends on what those shares are worth after the merger is complete. You should go ahead with the merger if the gain exceeds the cost.

4. **What are some takeover defences?**

Mergers are often amicably negotiated between the management and directors of the two companies; but if the seller is reluctant, the would-be buyer can decide to make a tender offer for the stock. We sketched some of the offensive and defensive tactics used in takeover battles. These defenses include **shark repellents** (changes in the company charter meant to make a takeover more difficult to achieve), **shareholders' rights plans** or **poison pills** (measures that make takeover of the firm more costly), and the search for **white knights** (the attempt to find a friendly acquirer before the unfriendly one takes over the firm).

5. **Do mergers increase efficiency and how are the gains from mergers distributed between shareholders of the acquired and acquiring firms?**

We observed that when the target firm is acquired, its shareholders typically win: target firms' shareholders earn abnormally large returns. The bidding firm's shareholders roughly break even. This suggests that the typical merger appears to generate positive net benefits, but competition among bidders and active defense by management of the target firm pushes most of the gains toward selling shareholders.

Mergers seem to generate economic gains, but they are also costly. Investment bankers, lawyers, and arbitrageurs thrived during the 1980s merger and LBO boom. Many companies were left with heavy debt burdens and had to sell assets or improve performance to stay solvent. By the end of 1990, the new-issue junk bond market had dried up, and the corporate jousting field was strangely quiet. But by the end of the 1990s, once again, stock markets and mergers were booming. However, with the crash of the tech stocks, a general slowdown of the economy, and the terrorist attacks of September 11, 2001, markets and merger activity once again dropped off.

6. **What are some of the motivations for leveraged and management buyouts of the firm?**

In a **leveraged buyout** (LBO) or **management buyout** (MBO), all public shares are repurchased and the company "goes private." LBOs tend to involve mature businesses with ample cash flow and modest growth opportunities. LBOs and other debt-financed takeovers are driven by a mixture of motives, including (1) the value of interest tax shields; (2) transfers of value from bondholders, who may see the value of their bonds fall as the firm piles up more debt; and (3) the opportunity to create better incentives for managers and employees, who have a personal stake in the company. In addition, many LBOs have been designed to force firms with surplus cash to distribute it to shareholders rather than plowing it back. Investors feared such companies would otherwise channel free cash flow into negative-NPV investments.

RELATED WEB LINKS

www.crosbieco.com/M&A.html Canadian merger data
www.mergernetwork.com Information about mergers and acquisitions
http://viking.som.yale.edu/will/finman540/acquira3.htm A sample case looking at an acquisition
www.lens-inc.com Active corporate governance strategies
www.corpgov.net The Corporate Governance Network

KEY TERMS

Term	Page
proxy contest	681
merger or statutory amalgamation	682
tender offer	683
acquisition	683
leveraged buyout (LBO)	683
management buyout (MBO)	683
shareholders' rights plan or poison pill	698
white knight	698
shark repellent	699

QUESTIONS AND PROBLEMS

*Answers in Appendix B

BASIC

*1. **Merger Motives.** Which of the following motives for mergers make economic sense?

a. Merging to achieve economies of scale.
b. Merging to reduce risk by diversification.
c. Merging to redeploy cash generated by a firm with ample profits but limited growth opportunities.
d. Merging to increase earnings per share.

*2. **Merger Motives.** Explain why it might make good sense for Northeast Heating and Northeast Air Conditioning to merge into one company.

3. **Empirical Facts.** True or false?

a. Sellers almost always gain in mergers.
b. Buyers almost always gain in mergers.
c. Firms that do unusually well tend to be acquisition targets.
d. Merger activity in Canada varies dramatically from year to year.
e. On the average, mergers produce substantial economic gains.
f. Tender offers require the approval of the selling firm's management.
g. The cost of a merger is always independent of the economic gain produced by the merger.

*4. **Merger Tactics.** Connect each term to its correct definition or description:

A. LBO	1. Attempt to gain control of a firm by winning the votes of its shareholders.
B. Poison pill	2. Changes in corporate charter designed to deter an unwelcome takeover.
C. Tender offer	3. Friendly potential acquirer sought by a threatened target firm.
D. Shark repellent	4. Shareholders are issued rights to buy shares if a bidder acquires a large stake in the firm.
E. Proxy contest	5. Offer to buy shares directly from shareholders.
F. White knight	6. Company or business bought out by private investors, largely debt-financed.

5. **Empirical Facts.** True or false?

a. One of the first tasks of an LBO's financial manager is to pay down debt.
b. Shareholders of bidding companies earn higher abnormal returns when the merger is financed with stock than in cash-financed deals.
c. Targets for LBOs in the 1980s tended to be profitable companies in mature industries with limited investment opportunities.

PRACTICE

*6. **Merger Gains.** Acquiring Corp. is considering a takeover of Takeover Target Inc. Acquiring has 10 million shares outstanding, which sell for $40 each. Takeover Target has 5 million shares outstanding, which sell for $20 each. If the merger gains are estimated at $20 million, what is the highest price per share that Acquiring should be willing to pay to Takeover Target shareholders? What is Acquiring's NPV if it pays the maximum price?

7. **Mergers and P/E Ratios.** If Acquiring Corp. from problem 6 has a price-earnings ratio of 12, and Takeover Target has a P/E ratio of 8, what should be the P/E ratio of the merged firm? Assume in this case that the merger is financed by an issue of new Acquiring Corp. shares. Takeover Target will get one Acquiring share for every two Takeover Target shares held.

*8. **Merger Gains and Costs.** Velcro Saddles is contemplating the acquisition of Pogo Ski Sticks, Inc. The values of the two companies as separate entities are $20 million and $10 million, respectively. Velcro Saddles estimates that by combining the two companies, it will reduce marketing and administrative costs by $500,000 per year in perpetuity. Velcro Saddles is willing to pay $14 million cash for Pogo. The opportunity cost of capital is 10 percent.

a. What is the gain from merger?
b. What is the cost of the cash offer?
c. What is the NPV of the acquisition under the cash offer?

9. **Stock versus Cash Offers.** Suppose that instead of making a cash offer as in problem 8, Velcro Saddles considers offering Pogo shareholders a 50 percent holding in Velcro Saddles.

a. What is the value of the stock in the merged company held by the original Pogo shareholders?
b. What is the cost of the stock alternative?
c. What is its NPV under the stock offer?

10. **Merger Gains.** Immense Appetite, Inc., believes that it can acquire Sleepy Industries and improve efficiency to the extent that the market value of Sleepy will increase by $5 million. Sleepy currently sells for $20 a share, and there are 1 million shares outstanding.

a. Sleepy's management is willing to accept a cash offer of $25 a share. Can the merger be accomplished on a friendly basis?
b. What will happen if Sleepy's management holds out for an offer of $28 a share?

11. **Mergers and P/E Ratios.** Castles in the Sand currently sells at a price-earnings multiple of 10. The firm has 2 million shares outstanding and sells at a price per share of $40. Firm Foundation has a P/E multiple of 8, 1 million shares outstanding, and sells at a price per share of $20.

a. If Castles acquires the other firm by exchanging one of its shares for every two of Firm Foundation's, what will be the earnings per share of the merged firm?
b. What should be the P/E of the new firm if the merger has no economic gains? What will happen to Castles's price per share? Show that shareholders of neither Castles nor Firm Foundation realize any change in wealth.
c. What will happen to Castles's price per share if the market does not realize that the P/E ratio of the merged firm ought to differ from Castles's pre-merger ratio?
d. How are the gains from the merger split between shareholders of the two firms if the market is fooled as in part (c)?

*12. **Stock versus Cash Offers.** Sweet Cola Corp. (SCC) is bidding to take over Salty Dog Pretzels (SDP). SCC has 3,000 shares outstanding, selling at $50 per share. SDP has 2,000 shares outstanding, selling at $17.50 a share. SCC estimates the economic gain from the merger to be $10,000.

a. If SDP can be acquired for $20 a share, what is the NPV of the merger to SCC?
b. What will SCC sell for when the market learns that it plans to acquire SDP for $20 a share? What will SDP sell for? What are the percentage gains to the shareholders of each firm? What fraction of the economic gain do SCC's shareholders receive? What fraction goes to SDP's shareholders?
c. Now suppose that the merger takes place through an exchange of stock. Based on the pre-merger prices of the firms, SCC sells for $50, so instead of paying $20 cash, SCC issues .40 of its shares for every SDP share acquired. What will be the price of the merged firm?
d. What is the NPV of the merger to SCC when it uses an exchange of stock? What fraction of the economic gain do SCC's shareholders receive? Why does your answer differ from part (a)?

CHALLENGE

*13. **Bootstrap Game.** The Muck and Slurry merger has fallen through (see Section 23.3). But World Enterprises is determined to report earnings per share of $2.67. It therefore acquires the Wheelrim and Axle Company.

Once again there are no gains from merging. In exchange for Wheelrim and Axle shares, World Enterprises issues just enough of its own shares to ensure its $2.67 earnings per share objective. Here are the facts you are given:

	World Enterprises	Wheelrim and Axle	Merged Firm
Earnings per share	$2	$2.50	$2.67
Price per share	$40	$25	_____
Price-earnings ratio	20	10	_____
Number of shares	100,000	200,000	_____
Total earnings	$200,000	$500,000	_____
Total market value	$4,000,000	$5,000,000	_____

a. Complete the above table for the merged firm.
b. How many shares of World Enterprises are exchanged for each share of Wheelrim and Axle?
c. What is the cost of the merger to World Enterprises?
d. What is the change in the total market value of those World Enterprises shares that were outstanding before the merger?

14. **Merger Gains and Costs.** As treasurer of Leisure Products, Inc., you are investigating the possible acquisition of Plastitoys. You have the following basic data:

	Leisure Products	Plastitoys
Forecast earnings per share	$5	$1.50
Forecast dividend per share	$3	$.80
Number of shares	1,000,000	600,000
Stock price	$90.00	$20.00

You estimate that investors currently expect a steady growth of about 6 percent in Plastitoys's earnings and dividends. You believe that Leisure Products could increase Plastitoys's growth rate to 8 percent per year, after 1 year, without any additional capital investment required.

a. What is the economic gain from the acquisition?
b. What is the cost of the acquisition if Leisure Products pays $25 in cash for each share of Plastitoys? What is the NPV to Leisure of acquiring Plastitoys?
c. What is the cost of the acquisition if Leisure Products offers 1 share of Leisure Products for every 3.96 shares of Plastitoys? What is the NPV to Leisure of acquiring Plastitoy?
d. Suppose immediately after the completion of the merger, everyone realizes that the expected growth rate will not be improved. Reassess the cost and NPV of the cash and share offers. Explain what you find.

INTERNET PROBLEMS

1. *Mergers and Acquisitions in Canada* reports on current merger activity in Canada. It is available in libraries and parts of it can be found at www.crosbieco.com/M&A.html. Select "Press Releases" for recent summaries of merger activity in Canada. Read the most current and the oldest press releases and compare them. Is the same industry experiencing the greatest M&A activity? How have the cross-border transactions changed?
2. The Ontario Teachers Pension Plan Board (Teachers), www.otpp.com, and the Ontario Municipal Employees Retirement System (OMERS), www.omers.com, manage very large investment portfolios.
   a. What are the current sizes of their portfolios?
   b. As active shareholders, they closely monitor the activities of the companies they own. Review their corporate governance policies. What issues are they concerned with?
   c. Click on the "Proxy-Voting Records" at the Teachers website and then "Upcoming Meetings" and pick a company. You will see a list of issues to be voted at an upcoming shareholders meeting and how Teachers intends to vote. Click on the little "i" and read the reasons for Teachers' position. Do you agree with them?

3. You might be interested in becoming a Chartered Business Valuator, CBV, an expert in business valuation. You can read about this program of study at the website of the Canadian Institute of Chartered Business Valulators, www.cicbv.ca. They also provide a list of valuation terms.

Solutions to Check Points

23.1 a. Horizontal merger. IBM is in the same industry as Apple Computer.
b. Conglomerate merger. BCE and Stop & Shop are in different industries.
c. Vertical merger. Loblaws is expanding backward to acquire one of its suppliers, Fishery Products International.
d. Conglomerate merger. Alcan and Canada Bread are in different industries.

23.2 Given current earnings of $2 a share, and a share price of $10, Muck and Slurry would have a market value of $1,000,000 and a price-earnings ratio of only 5. It can be acquired for only half as many shares of World Enterprises, 25,000 shares. Therefore, the merged firm will have 125,000 shares outstanding and earnings of $400,000, resulting in earnings per share of $3.20, higher than the $2.67 value in the third column of Table 23.2.

23.3 The cost of the merger is $4 million: the $4 per share premium offered to Goldfish shareholders times 1 million shares. If the merger has positive NPV to Killer Shark, the gain must be greater than $4 million.

23.4 Yes. Look again at Table 23.4. Total market value is still $540, but Cislunar will have to issue 1 million shares to complete the merger. Total shares in the merged firm will be 11 million. The post-merger share price is $49.09, so Cislunar and its shareholders still come out ahead.

MINICASE

McPhee Food Halls operated a chain of supermarkets in the west of Scotland. The company had had a lacklustre record and, since the death of its founder in late 2002, it had been regarded as a prime target for a takeover bid. In anticipation of a bid, McPhee's share price moved up from £4.90 in March 2003 to a 12-month high of £5.80 on June 10, despite the fact that the London stock market index as a whole was largely unchanged.

Almost nobody anticipated a bid coming from Fenton, a diversified retail business with a chain of clothing and department stores. Though Fenton operated food halls in several of its department stores, it had relatively little experience in food retailing. Fenton's management, however, had been contemplating a merger with McPhee for some time. They not only felt that they could make use of McPhee's food retailing skills within their department stores, but they believed that better management and inventory control in McPhee's business could result in cost savings worth £10 million.

Fenton's offer of 8 Fenton shares for every 10 McPhee shares was announced after the market close on June 10. Since McPhee had 5 million shares outstanding, the acquisition would add an additional $5 \times (8/10) = 4$ million shares to the 10 million Fenton shares that were already outstanding. While Fenton's management believed that it would be difficult for McPhee to mount a successful takeover defence, the company and its investment bankers privately agreed that the company could afford to raise the offer if it proved necessary.

Investors were not persuaded of the benefits of combining a supermarket with a department store company, and on June 11, Fenton's shares opened lower and drifted down £.10 to close the day at £7.90. McPhee's shares, however, jumped to £6.32 a share.

Fenton's financial manager was due to attend a meeting with the company's investment bankers that evening, but before doing so, he decided to run the numbers once again. First he reestimated the gain and the cost of the merger. Then he analyzed that day's fall in Fenton's stock price to see whether investors believed there were any gains to be had from merging. Finally, he decided to revisit the issue of whether Fenton could afford to raise its bid at a later stage. If the effect was simply a further fall in the price of Fenton stock, the move could be self-defeating.

CHAPTER 24

International Financial Management

24.1 Foreign Exchange Markets

24.2 Some Basic Relationships

24.3 Hedging Exchange Rate Risk

24.4 International Capital Budgeting

24.5 Summary

Thus far we have talked principally about doing business at home. But many companies have substantial overseas interests. Of course the objectives of international financial management are still the same. You want to buy assets that are worth *more* than they cost, and you want to pay for them by issuing liabilities that are worth *less* than the money raised. But when you try to apply these criteria to an international business, you come up against some new wrinkles.

You must, for example, know how to deal with more than one currency. Therefore we open this chapter with a look at foreign exchange markets.

The financial manager must also remember that interest rates differ from country to country. For example, in early September 2001 the short-term rate of interest was about .01 percent in Japan, 3.55 percent in Canada, 3.24 percent in the United States, and 4.2 percent in the euro countries. We will discuss the reasons for these differences in interest rates, along with some of the implications for financing overseas operations.

Exchange rate fluctuations can knock companies off course and transform black ink into red. We will therefore discuss how firms can protect themselves against exchange risks.

We will also discuss how international companies decide on capital investments. How do they choose the discount rate? You'll find that the basic principles of capital budgeting are the same as for domestic projects, but there are a few pitfalls to watch for.

After studying this chapter you should be able to

- Understand the difference between spot and forward exchange rates.
- Understand the basic relationships between spot exchange rates, forward exchange rates, interest rates, and inflation rates.
- Formulate simple strategies to protect the firm against exchange rate risk.
- Perform an NPV analysis for projects with cash flows in foreign currencies.

Foreign Exchange Markets

A Canadian company that imports goods from Switzerland may need to exchange its dollars for Swiss francs in order to pay for its purchases. A Canadian company exporting to Switzerland may *receive* Swiss francs, which it sells in exchange for dollars. Both firms must make use of the foreign exchange market, where currencies are traded.

The foreign exchange market has no central marketplace. All business is conducted by computer and telephone. The principal dealers are the large commercial banks, and any corporation that wants to buy or sell currency usually does so through a commercial bank.

Turnover in the foreign exchange markets is huge. In London alone about $640 billion (US) of currency changes hands each day. That is equivalent to an annual turnover of $159 trillion (US) ($159,000,000,000,000). New York and Tokyo together account for a further $500 billion of turnover per day. Compare this to trading volume of the New York Stock Exchange, where no more than $30 billion (US) of stock might change hands on a typical day.

exchange rate Amount of one currency needed to purchase one unit of another.

Suppose you ask someone the price of bread. He may tell you that you can buy two loaves for a dollar, or he may say that one loaf costs 50 cents. Similarly, if you ask a foreign exchange dealer to quote you a price for Ruritanian francs, she may tell you that you can buy two francs for a dollar *or* that one franc costs $.50. The first quote (the number of francs that you can buy for a dollar) is known as an *indirect quote* of the **exchange rate.** The second quote (the number of dollars that it costs to buy one franc) is known as a *direct quote.* Of course, both quotes provide the same information. If you can buy two francs for a dollar, then you can easily calculate that the cost of one franc is 1/2 = $.50.

Now look at Table 24.1, which has been adapted from the daily table of exchange rates in the *Globe and Mail*. The table provides exchange rate information for 65 currencies on September 20, 2001. The price of the U.S. dollar is expressed as indirect and direct quotes, while all other currency prices are expressed as direct quotes. Thus you could buy .1657 Canadian dollars with one Mexican peso, or converting to an indirect quote, 6.0350 pesos for one Canadian dollar.[1]

EXAMPLE 24.1 *A Yen for Trade*

How many yen will it cost a Japanese importer to purchase $1,000 worth of potatoes from a P.E.I. farmer? How many dollars will it take for that farmer to buy a Japanese VCR priced in Japan at 30,000 yen (¥)?

The exchange rate is $.013550 per yen. The $1,000 of potatoes will require the Japanese importer to come up with 1,000 ÷ .013550 = ¥73,800. The VCR will require the Canadian importer to come up with 30,000 × .013550 = $406.50.

CHECK POINT 24.1

Use the exchange rates in Table 24.1. How many euros can you buy for one dollar (an indirect quote)? How many dollars can you buy for one yen (a direct quote)?

---

spot rate of exchange Exchange rate for an immediate transaction.

Table 24.1 provides information on spot and forward rates. The **spot rate of exchange** is the price of currency for immediate delivery. For example, the spot rate of exchange for

[1] In the United States, prices of most currencies are customarily expressed as indirect quotes in terms of the U.S. dollar. However, the price of the euro and the British pound are generally expressed as direct quotes.

TABLE 24.1

Currency exchange rates on September 20, 2001

Mid-market rates in Toronto at noon, Sept. 20, 2001.
Prepared by BMO Nesbitt Burns, Capital Markets

		$1 U.S. in Cdn. $ =	$1 Cdn. in U.S. =
U.S./Canada spot		1.5703	.6368
1 month forward		1.5715	.6363
2 months forward		1.5723	.6360
3 months forward		1.5729	.6358
6 months forward		1.5739	.6354
12 months forward		1.5752	.6348
3 years forward		1.5796	.6331
5 years forward		1.5908	.6286
7 years forward		1.5943	.6273
10 years forward		1.6203	.6172
Canadian dollar	High	1.4901	.6711
in 2001:	Low	1.5825	.6319
	Average	1.5368	.6507

Country	Currency	Cdn. $ per unit	U.S. $ per unit
Britain	Pound	2.3017	1.4658
1 month forward		2.2997	1.4634
2 months forward		2.2971	1.4610
3 months forward		2.2948	1.4590
6 months forward		2.2859	1.4524
12 months forward		2.2687	1.4403
Europe	Euro	1.4546	.9263
1 month forward		1.4543	.9254
3 months forward		1.4529	.9237
6 months forward		1.4501	.9213
12 months forward		1.4473	.9188
Japan	Yen	.013550	.008629
1 month forward		.013591	.008648
3 months forward		.013662	.008686
6 months forward		.013754	.008739
12 months forward		.013963	.008865
Algeria	Dinar	.02157	.0137
Antigua, Granada, and St. Lucia	E.C. Dollar	.5881	.3745
Argentina	Peso	1.57077	1.00030
Australia	Dollar	.7749	.4935
Austria	Schill	.10571	.06732
Bahamas	Dollar	1.5703	1.0000
Barbados	Dollar	.7891	.5025
Belgium	Franc	.03606	.02296
Bermuda	Dollar	1.5703	1.0000
Brazil	Real	.5748	.3660
Bulgaria	Lev	.746128	.4751
Chile	Peso	.002262	.001441
China	Renminbi	.1897	.1208
Cyprus	Pound	2.5319	1.6124
Czech Republic	Koruna	.0423	.0270

Country	Currency	Cdn. $ per unit	U.S. $ per unit
Denmark	Krone	.1955	.1245
Egypt	Pound	.3701	.2357
Fiji	Dollar	.6878	.4380
Finland	Markka	.2446	.1558
France	Franc	.2218	.1412
Germany	Mark	.7437	.4736
Greece	Drachma	.004269	.002718
Hong Kong	Dollar	.2013	.1282
Hungary	Forint	.00563	.00358
Iceland	Krona	.01570	.01000
India	Rupee	.03276	.02086
Indonesia	Rupiah	.000167	.000106
Ireland	Punt	1.8470	1.1762
Israel	N Shekel	.3626	.2309
Italy	Lira	.000751	.000478
Jamaica	Dollar	.03447	.02196
Jordan	Dinar	2.2179	1.4124
Lebanon	Pound	.001037	.000661
Luxembourg	Franc	.03606	.02296
Malaysia	Ringgit	.4133	.2632
Mexico	N Peso	.1657	.1055
Netherlands	Guildr	.6601	.4204
New Zealand	Dollar	.6477	.4125
Norway	Krone	.1831	.1166
Pakistan	Rupee	.02454	.01563
Panama	Balboa	1.5703	1.0000
Philippines	Peso	.03067	.01953
Poland	Zloty	.3780	.2407
Portugal	Escudo	.00726	.00462
Romania	Leu	.000052	.000033
Russia	Ruble	.053361	.033981
Saudi Arabia	Royal	.4188	.2667
Singapore	Dollar	.9045	.5760
Slovakia	Koruna	.0332	.0211
South Africa	Rand	.1808	.1151
South Korea	Won	.001219	.000776
Spain	Peseta	.00874	.00557
Sudan	Dinar	.00607	.0039
Sweden	Krona	.1485	.0946
Switzerland	Franc	.9867	.6284
Taiwan	Dollar	.04550	.0290
Thailand	Baht	.03558	.0227
Trinidad, Tobago	Dollar	.2591	.1650
Turkey	Lira	.0000010	.0000007
Venezuala	Bolivar	.002113	.00135
Zambia	Kwacha	.000436	.000278
Spec. Draw Right S.D.R		2.0328	1.2945

Source: "Foreign Exchange," *Globe and Mail,* September 21, 2001, B19.

Canadian dollars in terms of Mexican pesos is \$.1657/pesos. In other words, it costs .1657 dollars to buy one Mexican peso. We could also express the spot rate of exchange for Mexican pesos as 1/.1657 = 6.0350 pesos/\$. That is, it will cost 6.0350 pesos to buy one dollar. Notice that the table provides spot and forward rates for a few selected currencies: the U.S. dollar, British pound, euro, and Japanese yen. Only spot rates are available for currencies of 61 other countries.

Many countries allow their currencies to float, so that the exchange rate fluctuates from day to day, and from minute to minute. When the currency increases in value, meaning that you need less of the foreign currency to buy one dollar, the currency is said to *appreciate.* When you need more of the currency to buy one dollar, the currency is said to *depreciate.*

CHECK POINT 24.2

Table 24.1 shows the exchange rate for the Swiss franc on September 20, 2001. The next day the spot rate of exchange for the Swiss franc was \$.9909/SFr, or SFr1.0092/\$. Thus you could buy fewer Swiss francs for your dollar than one day earlier. Had the Swiss franc appreciated or depreciated?

Some countries try to avoid fluctuations in the value of their currency and seek instead to maintain a fixed exchange rate. But fixed rates seldom last forever. If everybody tries to sell the currency, eventually the country will be forced to allow the currency to depreciate. When this happens, exchange rates can change dramatically. For example, when Indonesia gave up trying to fix its exchange rate in fall 1997, the value of the Indonesian rupiah fell by 80 percent in a few months.

These fluctuations in exchange rates can get companies into hot water. For example, suppose you have agreed to buy a shipment of Japanese VCRs for ¥100 million and to make the payment when you take delivery of the VCRs at the end of 12 months. You could wait until the 12 months have passed and then buy 100 million yen at the spot exchange rate. If the spot rate is unchanged at \$.013550/¥, then the VCRs will cost you 100 million × .013550 = \$1.355 million. But you are taking a risk by waiting, for the yen may become more expensive. For example, if the yen appreciates from the existing rate of 1/.013550 = ¥73.80/\$ to ¥70/\$, then you will have to pay out 100 million/70 = \$1.429 million.

You can avoid exchange rate risk and fix the dollar cost of VCRs by "buying the yen forward," that is, by arranging *now* to buy yen in the future. A foreign exchange *forward contract* is an agreement to exchange at a future date a given amount of currency at an exchange rate agreed to *today.* The **forward exchange rate** is the price of currency for delivery at some time in the future. Table 24.1 shows forward exchange rates for four currencies, namely, the U.S. dollar, British pound, euro, and Japanese yen.[2] For example, the 12-month forward rate for the yen is quoted at .013963 dollars per yen, or 71.62 yen per dollar. If you buy 100 million yen forward, you don't pay anything today; you simply fix today the price which you will pay for your yen in the future. At the end of the year you receive your 100 million yen and hand over 100 million/71.62 = \$1.3963 million in payment.

forward exchange rate Exchange rate for a forward transaction.

Notice that if you buy Japanese yen forward, you get fewer yen for your dollar than if you buy spot. In this case, the yen is said to trade at a forward *premium* relative to the dollar. Expressed as a percentage, the 12-month forward premium is

[2] Although forward rates are not quoted for the remaining currencies in Canadian dollars, such rates are available for several currencies in terms of the U.S. dollar, which is recognized as the major international trading currency. For instance, daily spot and forward rate quotes in U.S. dollars are available for Greek drachma, Swedish krona, Mexican pesos, and Australian, Hong Kong, and Singapore dollars.

$$\frac{73.80 - 71.62}{71.62} \times 100 = 3.04\%$$

You could also say that the dollar was selling at a *forward discount* of about 3.04 percent.[3]

A forward purchase or sale is a made-to-order transaction between you and the bank. It can be for any currency, any amount, and any delivery day. You could buy, say, 99,999 Vietnamese dong or Haitian gourdes for a year and a day forward as long as you can find a bank ready to deal. From Table 24.1, we see that forward rates are quoted for most currencies for periods ranging from 1 month to a year. However, banks are prepared to buy or sell the U.S. dollar, Canada's major trading currency, for up to 10 years forward.

There is also an organized market for currency for future delivery known as the currency *futures* market. Futures contracts are highly standardized versions of forward contracts—they exist only for the main currencies, they are for specified amounts, and choice of delivery dates is limited. The advantage of this standardization is that there is a very low-cost market in currency futures. Huge numbers of contracts are bought and sold daily on the futures exchanges. In North America, the most important market for foreign currency futures is the International Monetary Market (IMM), a division of the Chicago Mercantile Exchange.

CHECK POINT 24.3

A skiing vacation in Switzerland costs SFr1,500.

a. How many dollars does that represent? Use the exchange rates in Table 24.1.
b. Suppose the dollar depreciates by 10 percent relative to the Swiss franc, so that each dollar buys 10 percent fewer Swiss francs than before. What will be the new value of the (1) direct exchange rate and (2) indirect exchange rate?
c. If the Swiss vacation continues to cost the same number of Swiss francs, what will happen to the cost in dollars?
d. If the tour company that is offering the vacation keeps the price fixed in dollars, what will happen to the number of Swiss francs that it will receive?

24.2 Some Basic Relationships

The financial manager of an international business must cope with fluctuations in exchange rates and must be aware of the distinction between spot and forward exchange rates. She must also recognize that two countries may have different interest rates. To develop a consistent international financial policy, the financial manager needs to understand how exchange rates are determined and why one country may have a lower interest rate than another. These are complex issues, but as a first cut we suggest that you think of spot

[3] Here is a minor point that sometimes causes confusion. To calculate the forward premium, we divide by the *forward* rate as long as the exchange quotes are *indirect*. If you use *direct* quotes, the correct formula is

$$\text{Forward premium} = \frac{\text{forward rate} - \text{spot rate}}{\text{spot rate}}$$

In our example, the corresponding direct quote for spot yen is 1/73.80 = .013550, while the direct forward quote is 1/71.62 = .013963. Substituting these rates in our revised formula gives

$$\text{Forward premium} = \frac{.013963 - .013550}{.013550} = .0304, \text{ or } 3.04\%.$$

The two methods give the same answer.

and forward exchange rates, interest rates, and inflation rates as being linked as shown in Figure 24.1. Let's explain.

EXCHANGE RATES AND INFLATION

Consider first the relationship between changes in the exchange rate and inflation rates (the two boxes on the right of Figure 24.1). The idea here is simple: if country X suffers a higher rate of inflation than country Y, then the value of X's currency will decline relative to Y's. The decline in value shows up in the spot exchange rate for X's currency.

But let's slow down and consider why changes in inflation and spot interest rates are linked. Think first about the prices of the *same* good or service in two different countries and currencies.

Suppose you notice that gold can be bought in Toronto for \$450 an ounce and sold in Mexico City for 4,000 pesos an ounce. If there are no restrictions on the import of gold, you could be on to a good thing. You buy gold for \$450 and put it on the first plane to Mexico City, where you sell it for 4,000 pesos. Then (using the exchange rates from Table 24.1) you can exchange your 4,000 pesos for 4,000/6.0350 = \$662.8. You have made a gross profit of \$212.8 an ounce. Of course, you have to pay transportation and insurance costs out of this, but there should still be something left over for you.

You returned from your trip with a sure-fire profit. But sure-fire profits don't exist—not for long. As others notice the disparity between the price of gold in Mexico and the price in Toronto, the price will be forced down in Mexico and up in Toronto until the profit opportunity disappears. This ensures that the dollar price of gold is about the same in the two countries.[4]

Gold is a standard and easily transportable commodity, but to some degree you might expect that the same forces would be acting to equalize the domestic and foreign prices of other goods. Those goods that can be bought more cheaply abroad will be imported, and that will force down the price of the domestic product. Similarly, those goods that can be bought more cheaply in Canada will be exported, and that will force down the price of the foreign product.

FIGURE 24.1
Some simple theories linking spot and forward exchange rates, interest rates, and inflation rates

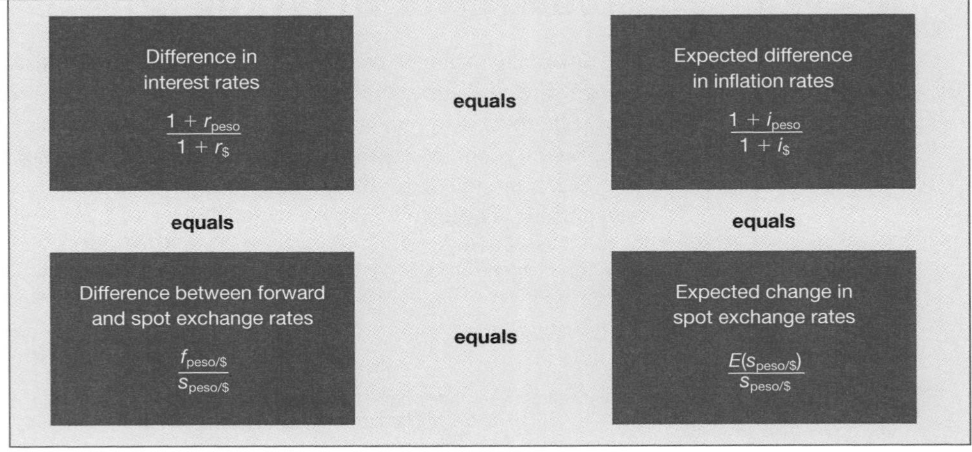

[4] Activity of this kind is known as *arbitrage.* The arbitrageur makes a riskless profit by noticing discrepancies in prices.

TABLE 24.2
Price of a Big Mac in different countries

	Price in Local Currency	Exchange Rate, 17/04/01 (currency/U.S. dollar)	Local Price Converted to U.S. Dollars
Australia	A$3.00	1.98	1.52
Canada	C$3.33	1.56	2.14
China	Yuan9.90	8.28	1.20
Euro area	€2.57	1.136	2.27
France	FFr18.50	7.44	2.49
Germany	DM5.10	2.22	2.30
Hong Kong	HK$10.70	7.80	1.37
Italy	Lire4,300	2,195	1.96
Japan	¥294	124	2.38
Malaysia	M$4.52	3.80	1.19
Mexico	Peso21.90	9.29	2.36
Poland	Zloty5.90	4.03	1.46
Russia	Ruble35.00	28.90	1.21
Switzerland	SFr6.30	1.73	3.65
United Kingdom	£1.99	.699	2.85
United States			2.54

Source: Adapted from "Big Mac Currencies," *The Economist*, April 21, 2001, p. 74.

law of one price Theory that prices of goods in all countries should be equal when translated to a common currency.

This conclusion is often called the **law of one price.** Just as the price of goods in Provigo must be roughly the same as the price of goods in Sobey's, so the price of goods in Mexico, when converted into dollars must be roughly the same as the price in Canada:

$$\text{Dollar price of goods in Canada} = \frac{\text{peso price of goods in Mexico}}{\text{number of pesos per dollar}}$$

$$\$450 = \frac{\text{peso price of gold in Mexico}}{6.0350}$$

$$\text{Price of gold in Mexico} = 450 \times 6.0350 = 2{,}716 \text{ pesos}$$

No one who has compared prices in foreign stores with prices at home really believes that the law of one price holds exactly. Look at the first column of Table 24.2, which shows the price of a Big Mac in different countries in 2001. Using the exchange rates at that time (second column), we can convert the local price to U.S. dollars (third column). You can see that the price varies considerably across countries. For example, Big Macs were 43 percent more expensive in Switzerland than in the United States, but they were a little less than half the price in Malaysia.[5]

This suggests a possible way to make a quick buck. Why don't you buy a hamburger-to-go in Malaysia for $1.19 and take it for resale to Switzerland where the price in dollars is $3.65? The answer, of course, is that the gain would not cover the costs. The law of one price works very well for commodities like gold, where transportation costs are relatively small; it works far less well for Big Macs, and very badly indeed for haircuts and appendectomies, which cannot be transported at all.

[5] Of course, it could also be that Big Macs come with a bigger smile in Switzerland. If the quality of the hamburgers or the service differs, we are not comparing like with like.

▸ EXAMPLE 24.2 *The Beer Standard*

There are very few McDonald's branches in Africa, so we can't use Big Macs to test the law of one price there. But barley beer is a common and relatively homogeneous product throughout Africa. So we can test the law of one price using the beer standard.

Table 24.3 shows the price of a bottle of beer in several African countries expressed in local currencies and converted into South African rand using the spot exchange rate. For example, beer in Kenya cost 41.25 shillings; at an exchange rate of 10.27 Kenyan shillings per rand, this is equivalent to a price of 41.25/10.27 = 4.02 rand. This is 1.75 times the cost of beer in South Africa; for the costs to be equal, the shilling would need to depreciate by 75 percent to a new exchange rate of 10.27 × 1.75 = 17.9 shillings per rand. Therefore, we might say that this comparison suggests the shilling is 75 percent overvalued against the rand.

TABLE 24.3
The price of a beer in different countries

Country	Beer Prices: In Local Currency	Beer Prices: In Rand	Actual Rand Exchange Rate, March 1999	Rand, % Valuation against the Under (–)/Over (+)
South Africa	Rand2.30	2.30		
Botswana	Pula2.20	2.94	.75	+28
Ghana	Cedi 1,200	3.17	379.10	+38
Kenya	Shilling41.25	4.02	10.27	+75
Malawi	Kwacha 18.50	2.66	6.96	+16
Mauritius	Rupee 15.00	3.72	4.03	+62
Namibia	N$2.50	2.50	1.00	+9
Zambia	Kwacha 1,200	3.52	340.68	+53
Zimbabwe	Z$9.00	1.46	6.15	–36

Source: The Economist, May 8, 1999.

purchasing power parity (PPP) Theory that the cost of living in different countries is equal and exchange rates adjust to offset inflation differentials across countries.

A weaker version of the law of one price is known as **purchasing power parity,** or **PPP.** PPP states that although some goods may cost different amounts in different countries, the *general* cost of living should be the same in any two countries.

Purchasing power parity implies that the relative costs of living in two countries will not be affected by differences in their inflation rates. Instead, the different inflation rates in local currencies will be offset by changes in the exchange rate between the two currencies.

For example, between 1993 and 2001 Russia experienced high inflation. Each year between 1993 and 1999, the purchasing power of the ruble declined by nearly 35 percent compared with other countries' currencies. As prices in Russia increased, Russian exporters would have found it impossible to sell their goods if the exchange rate had not also changed. But, of course, the exchange rate did adjust. In fact, each year the ruble bought over 33 percent less foreign currency than before. Thus a 35 percent annual decline in purchasing power was offset by a 33 percent decline in the value of the Russian currency.

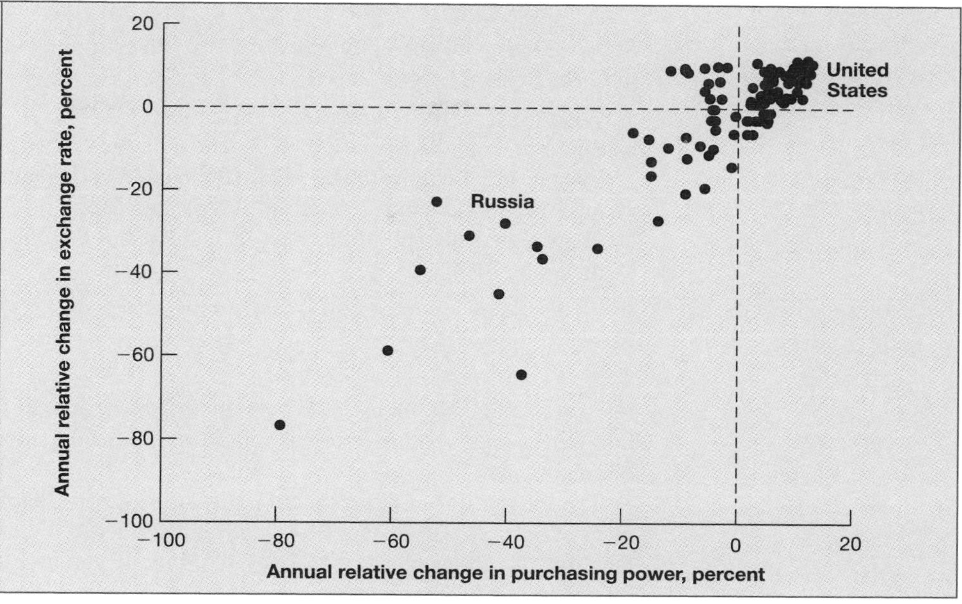

FIGURE 24.2
Countries with high inflation rates tend to see their currencies depreciate.

In Figure 24.2 we have plotted the relative change in purchasing power for a sample of countries against the change in the exchange rate. Russia is toward the bottom left; United States is closer to the top right. You can see that although the relationship is far from exact, large differences in inflation rates are generally accompanied by an offsetting change in the exchange rate. In fact, if you have to make a long-term forecast of the exchange rate, it is very difficult to do much better than to assume that it will offset the effect of any differences in the inflation rates.

If purchasing power parity holds, then your forecast of the difference in inflation rates is also your best forecast of the change in the spot rate of exchange. Thus the expected difference between inflation rates in Mexico and the United States is given by the right-hand boxes in Figure 24.1:

Expected difference in inflation rates		Expected change in spot exchange rate
$\frac{1 + i_{peso}}{1 + i_{\$}}$	equals	$\frac{E(s_{peso/\$})}{s_{peso/\$}}$

For example, from Table 24.1, the present spot exchange rate between the U.S. dollar and Mexican peso is U.S.$.1055/peso, or pesos 9.4787/U.S.$. If inflation is 2 percent in the United States and 6 percent in Mexico, then purchasing power parity implies that the expected spot rate for the peso at the end of the year is peso9.851/U.S.$:

$$\text{Current spot rate} \times \text{expected difference in inflation rates} = \text{expected spot rate}$$

$$9.479 \times \frac{1.06}{1.02} = 9.851$$

CHECK POINT 24.4

Suppose that gold currently costs \$330 an ounce in the United States and £220 an ounce in Great Britain.

a. What must be the pound/dollar exchange rate?
b. Suppose that gold prices rise by 2 percent in the United States and by 5 percent in Great Britain. What will be the price of gold in the two currencies at the end of the year? What must be the exchange rate at the end of the year?
c. Show that at the end of the year each dollar buys about 3 percent more pounds, as predicted by PPP.

INFLATION AND INTEREST RATES

Interest rates in Russia in 2001 were about 25 percent. So why didn't you (and a few million other investors) put your cash in a Russian bank deposit where the return seemed to be so attractive?

The answer lies in the distinction that we made in Chapter 3 between nominal and real rates of interest. Bank deposits usually promise you a fixed nominal rate of interest but they don't promise what that money will buy. If you invested 100 rubles for a year at an interest rate of 25 percent, you would have 25 percent more rubles at the end of the year than you did at the start. But you wouldn't be 25 percent better off. A good part of the gain would be needed to compensate for inflation.

The nominal rate of interest in 2001 was much lower in Canada, but then so was the inflation rate. The real rates of interest were much closer than the nominal rates.

There is a general law at work here. Just as water always flows downhill, so capital always flows where returns are greatest. But it is the *real* returns that concern investors, not the *nominal* returns. Two countries may have different nominal interest rates but the same expected real interest rate.

international Fisher effect Theory that real interest rates in all countries should be equal, with differences in nominal rates reflecting differences in expected inflation.

Do you remember Irving Fisher's theory from Chapter 3 that changes in the expected inflation rate are reflected in the nominal interest rate? We have just described here the **international Fisher effect**—international variations in the expected inflation rate are reflected in the nominal interest rates:

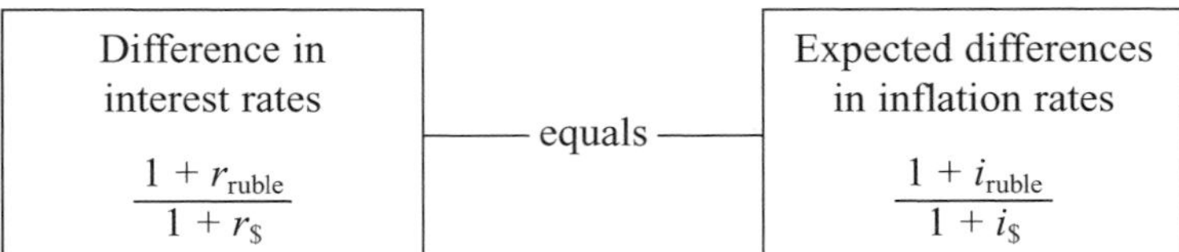

In other words, capital market equilibrium requires that real interest rates be the same in any two countries.

▸ EXAMPLE 24.3 *International Fisher Effect*

If the nominal interest rate in Russia is 25 percent and the expected inflation is 20 percent, then

$$r_{\text{ruble}}(\text{real}) = \frac{1 + r_{\text{ruble}}}{E(1 + i_{\text{ruble}})} - 1 = \frac{1.25}{1.20} - 1 = .042, \text{ or } 4.2\%$$

In Canada, where the nominal interest rate is about 3.5 percent and the expected inflation rate is about 2 percent,

$$r_{\$}(\text{real}) = \frac{1 + r_{\$}}{E(1 + i_{\$})} - 1 = \frac{1.035}{1.02} - 1 = .015, \text{ or } 1.5\%$$

The real interest rate is higher in Russia than in Canada, but the difference in the real rates is much smaller than the difference in nominal rates.

How similar are real interest rates around the world? It is hard to say, because we cannot directly observe *expected* inflation. In Figure 24.3 we have plotted the average interest rate in each of 40 countries against the inflation that in fact occurred. You can see that the countries with the highest interest rates generally had the highest inflation rates.

CHECK POINT 24.5

Canadian investors can invest $1,000 at an interest rate of 4 percent. Alternatively, they can convert those funds to 234,247 drachma at the current exchange rate and invest at 8 percent in Greece. If the expected inflation rate in Canada is 2 percent, what must be investors' forecast of the inflation rate in Greece?

INTEREST RATES AND EXCHANGE RATES

You are an investor with $1 million to invest for 1 year. Suppose the interest rate in Canada is 3.55 percent and in Japan it is .5 percent. Is it better to make a yen loan or a dollar loan?

FIGURE 24.3

Countries with the highest interest rates generally have the highest subsequent inflation rates. In this diagram, each point represents a different country.

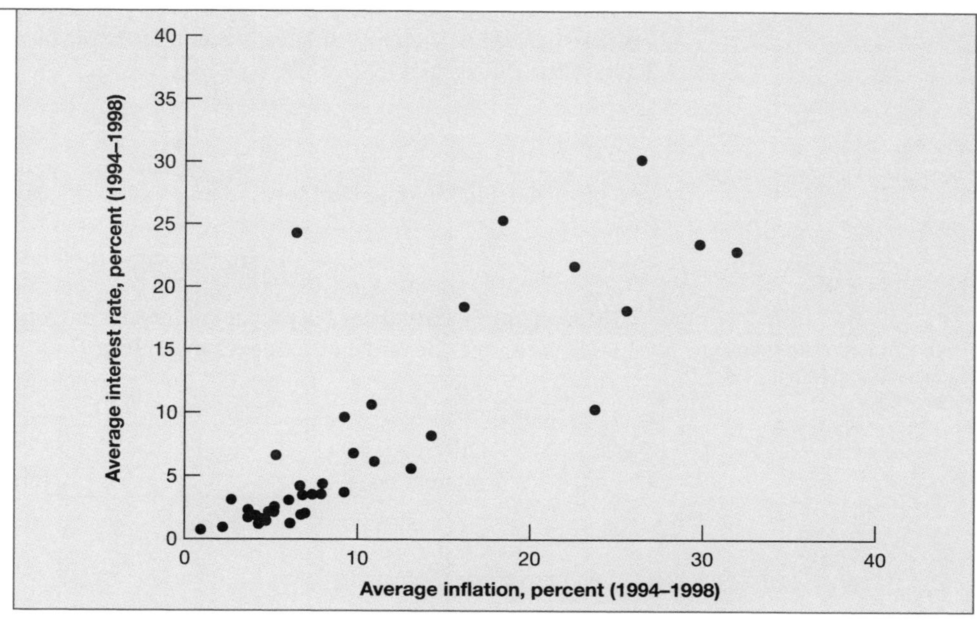

The answer seems obvious: Isn't it better to earn an interest rate of 3.55 percent in Canada than .5 percent in Japan? But appearances may be deceptive. If you lend in Japan, you first need to convert your $1 million into yen. When the loan is repaid at the end of the year, you need to convert your yen back into dollars. Of course you don't know what the exchange rate will be at the end of the year but you can fix the future value of your yen by selling them forward. If the forward rate of exchange is sufficiently high, you may do just as well investing your money in Japan.

Let's use the data from Table 24.1 to check which loan is the better deal:

- *Dollar loan:* The rate of interest on a dollar loan is 3.55 percent. Therefore, at the end of the year you get 1,000,000 × 1.0355 = $1,035,500.
- *Yen loan:* The current rate of exchange (from Table 24.1) is $.013550/¥. Therefore, for $1 million, you can buy 1,000,000 ÷ .013550 = 73,800,738 yen. The rate of interest on a 1-year yen loan is .5 percent. So at the end of the year, you get ¥73,800,738 × 1.005 = ¥74,169,742. Of course, you don't know what the exchange rate will be at the end of the year. But that doesn't matter. You can nail down the price at which you sell your yen. The 12-month forward rate is $.013963/¥. Therefore, by selling the ¥74,169,742 forward, you make sure that you will get 74,169,742 × .013963 = $1,035,632.

Thus the two investments offer almost exactly the same rate of return. They have to—they are both risk-free. If the domestic interest rate were different from the "covered" foreign rate, you would have a money machine: you could borrow in the market with the lower rate and lend in the market with the higher rate.

A difference in interest rates must be offset by a difference between spot and forward exchange rates. If the risk-free interest rate in country X is higher than in country Y, then country X's currency will buy less of Y's in a forward transaction than in a spot transaction.

When you make a yen loan, you lose because you get a lower interest rate. But you gain because you sell the yen forward at a higher price than you have to pay for them today. The interest rate differential is

$$\frac{1 + r_{¥}}{1 + r_{\$}} = \frac{1.005}{1.0355} = .9706$$

and the differential between the forward and spot exchange rates is virtually identical:[6]

$$\frac{f_{¥/\$}}{s_{¥/\$}} = \frac{71.62}{73.80} = .9704$$

interest rate parity Theory that forward premium equals interest rate differential.

Interest rate parity theory says that the interest rate differential must equal the differential between the forward and spot exchange rates. Thus

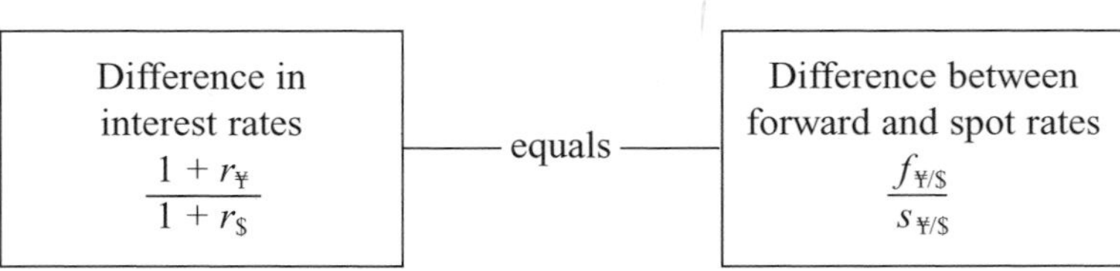

[6] In our discussion so far, are have used direct quotes from Table 24.1 The indirect quote for the forward rate, *f*yen/$, is 1/.013963 = ¥71.62/$. The indirect spot quote, *s*yen/$ = 1/.01355 = ¥73.80.

▸ EXAMPLE 24.4 *What Happens If Interest Rate Parity Theory Does Not Hold?*

Suppose that the forward rate on the yen is not ¥71.62/$ (or $.013963/¥) but ¥73.00/$ (or $.013699/¥). Here is what you do. Borrow 1 million yen at an interest rate of .5 percent and change these yen into dollars at the spot exchange rate of ¥73.80/$ (or $.013550/¥). This gives you $13,550, which you invest for a year at 3.55 percent. At the end of the year you will have 13,550 × 1.0355 = $14,031. Of course, this is not money to spend because you must repay your yen loan. The amount that you need to repay is 1,000,000 × 1.005 = ¥1,005,000. If you buy these yen forward, you can fix in advance the number of dollars that you will need to lay out. With a forward rate of ¥73.00/$, you need to set aside 1,005,000/73.00 = $13,767. Thus, after paying off your yen loan, you walk away with a risk-free profit of $14,031 – $13,767 = $264. While this amount is small, notice that you would have made a profit of $2,640 had you invested 10 million yen. It is a pity that in practice interest rate parity almost always holds and the opportunities for such easy profits are rare.

CHECK POINT 24.6

Look at the exchange rates in Table 24.1. Does the British pound sell at a forward premium or discount on the dollar? Does this suggest that the interest rate in Britain is higher or lower than in Canada? Use the interest rate parity relationship to estimate the 1-year interest rate in Britain. Assume the Canadian interest rate is 3.55 percent.

THE FORWARD RATE AND THE EXPECTED SPOT RATE

If you buy yen forward, you get fewer yen for your dollar than if you buy them spot. So the yen is selling at a forward premium. Now let us think how this premium is related to expected changes in spot rates of exchange.

The 12-month forward rate for the yen is ¥71.62/$. Would you sell yen at this rate if you expected the yen to rise in value? Probably not. You would be tempted to wait until the end of the year and get a better price for your yen in the spot market. If other traders felt the same way, nobody would sell yen forward and everybody would want to buy. The result would be that the number of yen that you could get for your dollar in the forward market would fall. Similarly, if traders expected the yen to fall sharply in value, they might be reluctant to *buy* forward and, in order to attract buyers, the number of yen that you could buy for a dollar in the forward market would need to rise.[7]

expectations theory of exchange rates Theory that expected spot exchange rate equals the forward rate.

This is the reasoning behind the **expectations theory of exchange rates,** which predicts that the forward rate equals the expected future spot exchange rate: $f_{¥/\$} = E(s_{¥/\$})$. Equivalently, we can say that the *percentage* difference between the forward rate and today's spot rate is equal to the expected *percentage* change in the spot rate:

Difference between forward and spot rates $\frac{f_{¥/\$}}{s_{¥/\$}}$	equals	Expected change in spot exchange rate $\frac{E(s_{¥/\$})}{s_{¥/\$}}$

This is the final leg of our quadrilateral in Figure 24.1.

[7] This reasoning ignores risk. If a forward purchase reduces your risk sufficiently, you *might* be prepared to buy forward even if you expected to pay more as a result. Similarly, if a forward sale reduces risk, you *might* be prepared to sell forward even if you expected to receive less as a result.

The expectations theory of forward rates does not imply that managers are perfect forecasters. Sometimes the *actual* future spot rate will turn out to be above the previous forward rate. Sometimes it will fall below. But if the theory is correct, we should find that *on the average* the forward rate is equal to the future spot rate.

The theory passes this simple test reasonably well. This is important news for the financial manager; it means that a company which always covers its foreign exchange commitments by buying or selling currency in the forward market does not have to pay a premium to avoid exchange rate risk. *On average,* the forward price at which it agrees to exchange currency will equal the eventual spot exchange rate, no better but no worse.

We should, however, warn you that the forward rate does not tell you very much about the future spot rate. For example, when the forward rate appears to suggest that the spot rate is likely to appreciate, you will find that the spot rate is about equally likely to head off in the opposite direction.

SOME IMPLICATIONS

Our four simple relationships ignore many of the complexities of interest rates and exchange rates. But they capture the more important features and emphasize that international capital markets and currency markets function well and offer no free lunches. When managers forget this, it can be costly. For example, in the late 1980s, several Australian banks observed that interest rates in Switzerland were about 8 percentage points lower than those in Australia and advised their clients to borrow Swiss francs. Was this advice correct? According to the international Fisher effect, the lower Swiss interest rate indicated that investors were expecting a lower inflation rate in Switzerland than in Australia and this in turn would result in an appreciation of the Swiss franc relative to the Australian dollar. Thus it was likely that the advantage of the low Swiss interest rate would be offset by the fact that it would cost the borrowers more Australian dollars to repay the loan. As it turned out, the Swiss franc appreciated very rapidly, and the Australian banks found that they had a number of very irate clients and agreed to compensate them for the losses they had incurred. The moral: Don't assume automatically that it is cheaper to borrow in a currency with a low nominal rate of interest.

☑ CHECK POINT 24.7

In October 1998, Stellar Corporation borrowed 100 million Japanese yen at an attractive interest rate of 2 percent, when the exchange rate between the yen and U.S. dollar was ¥123.97/U.S.$. One year later, when Stellar came to repay its loan, the exchange rate was ¥107.52/U.S.$. Calculate in U.S. dollars the amount that Stellar borrowed and the amounts that it paid in interest and principal (assume annual interest payments). What was the effective U.S. dollar interest rate on the loan?

Here is another case where our simple relationships can stop you from falling into a trap. Managers sometimes talk as if you make money simply by buying currencies that go up in value and selling those that go down. But if investors anticipate the change in the exchange rate, then it will be reflected in the interest rate differential; therefore, what you gain on the currency you will lose in terms of interest income. You make money from currency speculation only if you can predict whether the exchange rate will change by more or less than the interest rate differential. In other words, you must be able to predict whether the exchange rate will change by more or less than the forward premium.

▸ EXAMPLE 24.5 *Measuring Currency Gains*

The financial manager of Universal Waffle is proud of his acumen. Instead of keeping his cash in U.S. dollars, he for many years invested it in German deutschemark deposits. He calculates that between the end of 1980 and 1998, the deutschemark increased in value by nearly 47 percent, or about 2.1 percent a year. But did the manager really gain from investing in foreign currency? Let's check.

The compound rate of interest on U.S. dollar deposits during the period was 9.0 percent, while the compound rate of interest on deutschemark deposits was only 6.9 percent. So the 2.1 percent a year appreciation in the value of the deutschemark was almost exactly offset by the lower rate of interest on deutschemark deposits.

The interest rate differential (which by interest rate parity is equal to the forward premium) is a measure of the market's expectation of the change in the value of the currency. The difference between the German and United States interest rates during this period suggests that the market was expecting the deutschemark to appreciate by just over 2 percent a year,[8] and that is almost exactly what happened.

Hedging Exchange Rate Risk

Firms with international operations are subject to exchange rate risk. As exchange rates fluctuate, the dollar value of the firm's revenues or expenses also fluctuates. It helps to distinguish two types of exchange rate risk: contractual and noncontractual. By *contractual risk,* we mean that the firm is committed either to pay or to receive a known amount of foreign currency. For example, our VCR importer was committed to pay ¥100 million at the end of 12 months. If the value of the yen appreciates rapidly over this period, those VCRs will cost more dollars than the firm expected.

Noncontractual risk arises because exchange rate fluctuations can affect the competitive position of the firm. For example, during 1991 and 1992 the value of the deutschemark appreciated relative to that of other major currencies. As a result, Porsche and other German luxury car manufacturers found it increasingly difficult to compete in the United States and Canada. North American dealers that had a franchise to sell German luxury cars also took a bath. Thus the German car producers and their dealers in the United States and Canada were exposed to exchange rate changes even if they had no fixed obligations to pay or receive dollars.

Exchange rate changes can get companies into *big* trouble and therefore most companies aim to limit at least their contractual exposure to currency fluctuations. Let us look at an example of how this can be done.

In 1989 a British company, Enterprise Oil, bought some oil properties from Texas Eastern for $440 million (US).[9] Since the payment was delayed a couple of months, Enterprise's plans for financing the purchase could have been thrown out of kilter if the dollar had strengthened during this period.

Enterprise therefore decided to avoid, or *hedge,* this risk. It did so by borrowing pounds, which it converted into U.S. dollars at the current spot rate and invested for 2 months. In

[8] If the interest rate is 9 percent on U.S. dollar deposits and 6.9 percent on deutschemark deposits, our simple relationship implies that the expected change in the value of the deutschemark was $(1 + r_{\text{U.S.\$}})/(1 + r_{\text{DM}}) - 1 = 1.090/1.069 - 1 = .020$, or 2 percent per year.

[9] See "Enterprise Oil's Mega Forex Option," *Corporate Finance* 53 (April 1989), p. 13.

that way Enterprise guaranteed it would have just enough U.S. dollars available to pay for the purchase. Of course it was possible that the U.S. dollar would *depreciate* over the 2 months, in which case Enterprise would have regretted that it did not wait and buy the dollars spot. Unfortunately, you cannot have your cake and eat it too. By fixing its dollar cost, Enterprise forfeited the chance of pleasant as well as unpleasant surprises.

Was there any other way that Enterprise could hedge against exchange loss? Of course. It could buy $440 million (US) 2 months forward. No cash would change hands immediately but Enterprise would fix the price at which it buys its U.S. dollars at the end of 2 months. It would therefore eliminate all exchange risk on the deal. Interest rate parity theory tells us that the difference between buying spot and buying forward is equal to the difference between the rate of interest that you pay at home and the interest that you earn overseas. In other words, the two methods of eliminating risk should be equivalent.

Let us check this. In March 1989 the 2-month interest rate in the United States was about 9.7 percent and the interest rate in the United Kingdom was 13 percent. The spot exchange rate was U.S.$1.743 to the pound and the 2-month forward rate was U.S.$1.730/£. Table 24.4 shows that the cash flows from the two methods of hedging the dollar payment for Texas Eastern were almost identical.[10]

What is the cost of such a hedge? You sometimes hear managers say that it is equal to the difference between the forward rate and *today's* spot rate. This is wrong. If Enterprise did not hedge, it would pay the spot rate for U.S. dollars at the time that the payment for Texas Eastern was due. Therefore, the cost of hedging is the difference between the forward rate and the *expected* spot rate when payment is received.

Hedge or speculate? We generally vote for hedging. First, it makes life simpler for the

TABLE 24.4
Enterprise Oil could hedge its future U.S. dollar payment either by borrowing sterling and lending U.S. dollars or by buying U.S. dollars forward.

	Cash Flow, Millions	
	£	**U.S.$**
Method 1: Borrow sterling, convert proceeds to U.S. dollars, and invest dollars until needed		
Now:		
Borrow £248.6m at 13%	+248.6	
Convert to U.S.$ at $1.743/£	–248.6	+433.3
Invest U.S.$433.3m for 2 months at 9.7%		–433.3
Net cash flow, Now	0	0
Month 2:		
Repay £ loan with interest	–253.7	
Receive payment on U.S.$ loan		+440
Pay for oil properties		–440
Net cash flow, Month 2	–253.7	0
Method 2: Buy dollars forward		
Now:		
Buy U.S.$440m forward at U.S.$1.73/£	0	0
Month 2:		
Pay for U.S.$	–254.3	+440
Pay for oil properties		–440
Net cash flow, Month 2	–254.3	0

[10] We are not sure of Enterprise's borrowing rate but the company is rumoured to have hedged at an effective forward rate of U.S.$1.73/£.

firm and allows it to concentrate on its own business. Second, it does not cost much. (In fact, the cost is zero if the forward rate equals the expected spot rate, as our simple relations imply.) Third, the foreign exchange market seems reasonably efficient, at least for the major currencies. Speculation should be a zero-sum game unless financial managers have superior information to the pros who make the market.

CHECK POINT 24.8

Suppose that the current spot rate for the euro is \$1.4546/€ and that the 6-month forward rate is \$1.4501/€. What is the cost to a Canadian company of hedging its future need for euros by buying them in the forward market? Assume the expectations theory of exchange rates.

International Capital Budgeting

NET PRESENT VALUE ANALYSIS

KW Corporation is a Canadian firm manufacturing flat-packed kit wardrobes. Its export business has risen to the point that it is considering establishing a small manufacturing operation overseas in Narnia. KW's decision to invest overseas should be based on the same criteria as a decision to invest in Canada—that is, the company needs to forecast the incremental cash flows from the project, discount the cash flows at the opportunity cost of capital, and accept those projects with a positive NPV.

Suppose KW's Narnian facility is expected to generate the following cash flows *in Narnian leos:*

Year	0	1	2	3	4	5
Cash flow (millions of leos)	–7.6	2.0	2.5	3.0	3.5	4.0

The interest rate in Canada is 5 percent. KW's financial manager estimates that the company requires an additional expected return of 10 percent to compensate for the risk of the project, so the opportunity cost of capital for the project is 5 + 10 = 15 percent.

Notice that KW's opportunity cost of capital is stated in terms of the return on a dollar-denominated investment, but the cash flows are given in leos. A project that offers a 15 percent expected return in leos could fall far short of offering the required return in dollars if the value of the leo is expected to decline. Conversely, a project that offers an expected return of less than 15 percent in leos may be worthwhile if the leo is likely to appreciate.

You cannot compare the project's return measured in one currency with the return that you require from investing in another currency. If the opportunity cost of capital is measured as a dollar-denominated return, consistency demands that the forecast cash flows should also be stated in dollars.

To translate the leo cash flows into dollars, KW needs a forecast of the leo/dollar exchange rate. Where does this come from? We suggest using the simple parity relationships in Figure 24.1. These tell us that the expected annual change in the spot rate (the southeast box in Figure 24.1) is equal to the difference between the interest rates in the two countries (the northwest box). For example, suppose that the financial manager looks in the newspaper and finds that the current exchange rate is 2 leos to the dollar ($s_{L/\$} = 2.0$), while the interest rate is 5 percent in Canada ($r_\$ = .05$) and 10 percent in Narnia ($r_L = .10$). Thus the manager sees right away that the leo is likely to depreciate by about 5 percent a year.[11] For example, at the end of 1 year

$$\text{Expected spot rate in Year 1} = \text{spot rate in Year 0} \times \text{expected change in spot rate}$$

$$= 2.0 \times \frac{1.10}{1.05} = \text{L}2.095/\$$$

The forecast exchange rates for each year of the project are calculated in a similar way, as follows:

Year	Forecast Exchange Rate		
0	Spot exchange rate	=	L2.0/$
1	$2.0 \times (1.10/1.05)$	=	L2.095/$
2	$2.0 \times (1.10/1.05)^2$	=	L2.195/$
3	$2.0 \times (1.10/1.05)^3$	=	L2.300/$
4	$2.0 \times (1.10/1.05)^4$	=	L2.409/$
5	$2.0 \times (1.10/1.05)^5$	=	L2.524/$

The financial manager can use these projected exchange rates to convert the leo cash flows into dollars:[12]

Year	0	1	2	3	4	5
Cash flow ($ millions)	$-\frac{7.6}{2.00}$	$\frac{2.0}{2.095}$	$\frac{2.5}{2.195}$	$\frac{3.0}{2.300}$	$\frac{3.5}{2.409}$	$\frac{4.0}{2.524}$
	= –$3.8	= $.95	= $1.14	= $1.30	= $1.45	= $1.58

Now the manager discounts these *dollar* cash flows at the 15 percent *dollar* cost of capital:

$$\text{NPV} = -3.8 + \frac{.95}{1.15} + \frac{1.14}{1.15^2} + \frac{1.30}{1.15^3} + \frac{1.45}{1.15^4} + \frac{1.58}{1.15^5}$$

$$= \$.36 \text{ million, or } \$360{,}000$$

Notice that the manager discounted cash flows at 15 percent, not the Canadian risk-free interest rate of 5 percent. The cash flows are risky, so a risk-adjusted interest rate is appropriate. The positive NPV tells the manager that the project is worth undertaking; it increases shareholder wealth by $360,000.

CHECK POINT 24.9

Suppose that the nominal interest rate in Narnia is 3 percent rather than 10 percent. The spot exchange rate is still L2.0/$ and the forecast leo cash flows on KW's project are also the same as before.

a. What do you deduce about the likely difference in the inflation rates in Narnia and Canada?
b. Would you now forecast that the leo will appreciate or depreciate against the dollar?
c. Do you think that the NPV of KW's project will now be higher or lower than the figure we calculated above? Check your answer by calculating NPV under this new assumption.

[11] The financial manager could use the forward exchange rate ($f_{L/\$}$) equally well to estimate the expected spot rate. In practice, it is usually easier to find interest rates in the financial press than yearly forward rates.

[12] Suppose KW's managers do not go along with what market prices are telling them. For example, perhaps they believe that the leo is likely to appreciate relative to the dollar. Should they plug their own currency forecasts into their present value calculations? We think not. It would be unwise to undertake what might be an unprofitable investment just because management is optimistic about the currency. Given its exchange rate forecast, KW would do better to pass up the investment in wardrobe manufacturing and buy leos instead.

THE COST OF CAPITAL FOR FOREIGN INVESTMENT

We did not say how KW arrived at a 15 percent dollar discount rate for its Narnian project. That depends on the risk of overseas investment and the reward that investors require for taking this risk. These are issues on which few economists can agree, but we will tell you where we stand.[13]

Remember that the risk of an investment cannot be considered in isolation; it depends on the securities that the investor holds in his or her portfolio. For example, suppose KW's shareholders invest mainly in companies that do business in Canada. They would find that the value of KW's Narnian venture was relatively unaffected by fluctuations in the value of Canadian shares. So an investment in the Narnian furniture business would appear to be a relatively low-risk project to KW's shareholders. That would not be true of a Narnian company, whose shareholders are already exposed to the fortunes of the Narnian market. To them an investment in the Narnian furniture business might seem a relatively high-risk project. They would therefore demand a higher return *(measured in dollars)* than KW's shareholders.

POLITICAL RISK

When multinational companies invest abroad, their financial mangers need to consider the political risks that are involved. By this we mean the threat that governments will change the rules of the game *after* an investment is made. At worst, the government may expropriate the company's assets without compensation. Or it may simply insist that the company keep any profits it makes in the country.

political risk A change in firm value arising from political events.

Political risk refers to any change in the value of a firm arising from political events, which are often unanticipated. Firms operating in domestic as well as international environments can face such risks; businesses in every country are exposed to the risk of unanticipated actions by governments or the courts. But in some parts of the world, foreign companies are particularly vulnerable. Several organizations publish regular rankings of countries in terms of their political risk. For example, the PRS Group places countries on a scale of 1 to 100 based on factors such as regime stability, financial transfer, and turmoil. Table 24.5 presents the 10 least risky and 10 riskiest countries based on these factors. The nearby Finance in Action box describes the recent experiences of the biggest Canadian oil company operating in Russia.

SEE BOX P. 730

AVOIDING FUDGE FACTORS

We certainly don't pretend that we can put a precise figure on the cost of capital for foreign investment. But you can see that we disagree with the frequent practice of *automatically* increasing the domestic cost of capital when foreign investment is considered. We suspect that managers mark up the required return for foreign investment because it is more costly to manage an operation in a foreign country and to cover the risk of expropriation, foreign exchange restrictions, or unfavourable tax changes. A fudge factor is added to the discount factor to cover costs associated with political risk.

We think managers should leave the discount rate alone and reduce expected cash flows instead. For example, suppose that KW is expected to earn L2.5 million in the first year *if*

[13] Why don't economists agree? One fundamental reason is that economists have never been able to agree on what makes one country different from another. Is it just that they have different currencies? Or is it that their citizens have different tastes? Or is it that they are subject to different regulations and taxes? The answer affects the relationship between security prices in different countries.

FINANCE IN ACTION

Russian Raider Gains Control of Canadian Oil Firm's Accounts

A Russian corporate raider, backed by dozens of armed security guards, has won control of a Canadian oil company's bank accounts, triggering fears that as much as $30 million (US) in assets could be removed from the Canadian firm.

The move is another serious blow for Yugraneft, the biggest Canadian-owned oil firm in Russia, which has been reeling from repeated attacks by its Russian minority shareholder, Tyumen Oil Co.

A local administrator in Siberia yesterday decided to give Yugraneft's corporate seal to Tyumen, allowing it to take control of the company's bank accounts and other assets. "It allows them to go to the bank, take the money, and do anything they want," said Alex Rotzang, president of Calgary-based Norex Petroleum Ltd., which says it owns 98 percent of Yugraneft.

Tyumen, part of the powerful Alfa Group empire of Moscow, deployed about 20 heavily armed men in a military-style operation to seize Yugraneft's headquarters in the Siberian city of Nizhnevartovsk on June 29, citing a court order that the Canadians have disputed. The Russians then dispatched other gunmen to seize Yugraneft's oil field, about 90 kilometres away.

The Canadian embassy in Moscow has sharply protested the takeover, calling it "an illegal confiscation of assets" and "a major negative signal to Canadian and foreign investors."

Norex Petroleum says it rehabilitated the Yugraneft oil field at considerable expense in the early 1990s, and it now produces about 10,000 barrels of oil a day. It has been taking legal action to seek about $50 million from Tyumen to compensate for oil deliveries that it says it was never paid for.

But Tyumen organized a shareholders' meeting last month, without any Norex representatives, and appointed its own managers to take control of Yugraneft. The Canadian embassy says the shareholders' meeting was "fraudulent."

After the takeover, Norex obtained a court order to remove the armed men. It also received a letter from a prosecutor who said the shareholders' meeting was illegal.

Tyumen, however, simply removed one set of security guards and installed a new team. "They have over 1,000 armed men around the city," Mr. Rotzang said. "That's more than the police have."

Yesterday Tyumen won its biggest victory when the local administrator gave it control of the Yugraneft corporate seal, allowing the Russians to gain access to about $30 million in the company's bank accounts.

Mr. Rotzang calls it robbery. "I feel awful about it," he said. "We showed him all the documents, he knows the local prosecutor's opinion, he promised he wouldn't allow it, and then he turned around and did this."

Other asset-stripping moves could follow. The newly installed manager has already tried to sell Yugraneft oil to Tyumen at about one-third of the normal price. The pipeline company refused to send the oil at the below-market price, but after yesterday's move it might have no choice.

The chairman of Tyumen, Sergei Sobyanin, is the powerful governor of the oil-rich Tyumen Region. He enjoys considerable influence over the courts and police forces in his region, including those who acted in the Yugraneft case, Mr. Rotzang noted. "Wouldn't you see a conflict of interest in this situation?"

For its part, Tyumen says it owns 40 percent of Yugraneft, not the 2 percent that Norex says it owns. "We discovered that Yugraneft was being run as if it was completely owned by Norex," Tyumen spokesman Dmitry Ivanov told the English-language *Moscow Times* last week. "We approached Norex. They didn't want to work with us. We took action."

Tyumen has a long history of battles with foreign investors, including Canadians. In 1996, it won control of the oil field licences of Vancouver-based Ivanhoe Energy Inc., which denounced it as an illegal takeover. Ivanhoe eventually accepted about $29 million in compensation but analysts said it had invested about $60 million in the project.

Source: Excerpted from Geoffrey York, "Russian Raider Gains Control of Canadian Oil Firm's Accounts," *Globe and Mail*, July 11, 2001, B1.

no penalties are placed on the operations of foreign firms. Suppose also that there is a 20 percent chance that KW's cash flow may be expropriated without compensation. The *expected* cash flow is not L2.5 million but .8 × 2.5 million = L2 million.

The end result may be the same if you pretend that the expected cash flow is L2.5 million but add a fudge factor to the discount rate. Nevertheless, adjusting cash flows brings management's assumptions about "political risk" out in the open for scrutiny and sensitivity analysis.

TABLE 24.5
The top 10 least risky and top 10 most risky countries for investment

10 Least Risky Countries	10 Riskiest Countries
1. Switzerland	1. Ecuador
2. Bulgaria	2. Iraq
3. Singapore	3. Cuba
4. Belgium	4. Russia
5. Ireland	5. Myanmar
6. Finland	6. Sudan
7. Austria	7. Vietnam
8. Canada	8. Cameroon
9. Netherlands	9. Pakistan
10. United Kingdom	10. Nigeria

Source: PRS Group website, www.prsgroup.com, as at September 26, 2001. The ratings are based on the Political Risk Services' Coplin-O'Leary risk rating system. Courtesy of Political Risk Services © The PRS Group, Inc.

24.5 Summary

1. **What is the difference between spot and forward exchange rates?**

The **exchange rate** is the amount of one currency needed to purchase one unit of another currency. The **spot rate of exchange** is the exchange rate for an immediate transaction. The **forward rate** is the exchange rate for a forward transaction, that is, a transaction at a specified future date.

2. **What are the basic relationships between spot exchange rates, forward exchange rates, interest rates, and inflation rates?**

To produce order out of chaos, the international financial manager needs some model of the relationships between exchange rates, interest rates, and inflation rates. Four very simple theories prove useful:

- In its strictest form, **purchasing power parity** states that $1 must have the same purchasing power in every country. You only need to take a vacation abroad to know that this doesn't square well with the facts. Nevertheless, *on average,* changes in exchange rates match differences in inflation rates, and if you need a long-term forecast of the exchange rate, it is difficult to do much better than to assume that the exchange rate will offset the effect of any differences in the inflation rates.
- In an open world-capital market, *real* rates of interest would have to be the same. Thus differences in *nominal* interest rates result from differences in expected inflation rates. The **international Fisher effect** suggests that firms should not simply borrow where interest rates are lowest. Those countries are also likely to have the lowest inflation rates and the strongest currencies.
- **Interest rate parity theory** states that the interest differential between two countries must be equal to the difference between the forward and spot exchange rates. In the international markets, arbitrage ensures that parity almost always holds.
- The **expectations theory of exchange rates** tells us that the forward rate equals the expected spot rate (though it is very far from being a perfect forecaster of the spot rate).

3. **What are some simple strategies to protect the firm against exchange rate risk?**

Our simple theories about forward rates have two practical implications for the problem of hedging overseas operations. First, the expectations theory suggests that hedging exchange risk is on average cost-free. Second, there are two ways to hedge against exchange risk—one is to buy or sell currency forward, the other is to lend or borrow abroad. Interest rate parity tells us that the cost of the two methods should be the same.

4. **How do we perform an NPV analysis for projects with cash flows in foreign currencies?**

Overseas investment decisions are no different in principle from domestic decisions. You need to forecast the project's cash flows and then discount them at the opportunity cost of capital. But it is important to remember that if the opportunity cost of capital is stated in dollars, the cash flows must also be converted to dollars. This requires a forecast of foreign exchange rates. We suggest that you rely on the simple parity relationships and use the interest rate differential to produce these forecasts. In international capital budgeting, the return that shareholders require from foreign investments must be estimated. Adding a premium for the "extra risks," such as political risk, of overseas investment is not a good solution.

Related Web Links

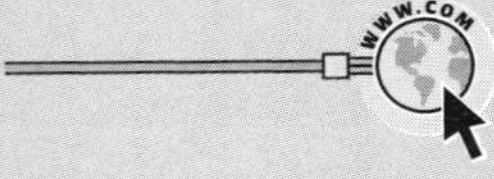

www.cme.com/products/currency/products_currency_eurofx.cfm The Chicago Mercantile Exchange's information centre on managing European foreign exchange risk with euro contracts
www.bloomberg.com/markets Data on current exchange rates as well as securities
www.global-investor.com Global Investor directory with information about major international markets
www.emgmkts.com/index.htm Analysis of economic, political, and financial events in emerging markets
www.jpmorgan.com/research Information about emerging markets
www.florin.com/v4/valore4.html Issues in currency risk management
www.globeandmail.ca *Globe and Mail* website
http://news.ft.com *Financial Times* website
www.cibs.commerce.ubc.ca Foreign exchange data, teaching- and research-related information from the Centre for International Business Studies, University of British Columbia

Key Terms

exchange rate	712	purchasing power parity (PPP)	718	expectations theory of exchange rates	723
spot rate of exchange	712	international Fisher effect	720	political risk	729
forward exchange rate	714	interest rate parity	722		
law of one price	717				

Questions and Problems

*Answers in Appendix B

Basic

*1. **Exchange Rates.** Use Table 24.1 to answer these questions:
   a. How many euros can you buy for $100? How many dollars can you buy for 100 euros?
   b. How many Swiss francs can you buy for $100? How many dollars can you buy for 100 Swiss francs?
   c. If the euro depreciates with respect to the dollar, will the direct exchange rate quoted in Table 24.1 increase or decrease? What about the indirect exchange rate?
   d. Is a United States or an Australian dollar worth more?

2. **Exchange Rate Relationships.** Look at Table 24.1.
   a. How many Japanese yen do you get for your dollar?
   b. What is the 12-month forward rate for the yen?
   c. Is the yen at a forward discount or premium on the dollar?
   d. Calculate the annual percentage discount or premium on the yen.
   e. If the interest rate on dollars is 3.5 percent, what do you think is the interest rate on yen?
   f. According to the expectations theory, what is the expected spot rate for the yen in 1 year's time?
   g. According to purchasing power parity, what is the expected difference in the rate of price inflation in Canada and Japan?

*3. **Exchange Rate Relationships.** Define each of the following theories in a sentence or simple equation:
   a. Interest rate parity theory
   b. Expectations theory of forward rates
   c. Law of one price
   d. International Fisher effect (relationship between interest rates in different countries)

*4. **International Capital Budgeting.** Which of the following items do you need if you do all your capital budgeting calculations in your own currency?
   a. Forecasts of future exchange rates
   b. Forecasts of the foreign inflation rate
   c. Forecasts of the domestic inflation rate
   d. Foreign interest rates
   e. Domestic interest rates

5. **Foreign Currency Management.** Rosetta Stone, the treasurer of International Reprints, Inc., has noticed that the interest rate in Switzerland is below the rates in most other countries. She is therefore suggesting that the company should make an issue of Swiss franc bonds. What considerations should she first take into account?

*6. **Hedging Exchange Rate Risk.** An importer in Canada is due to take delivery of silk scarves from Europe in 6 months. The price is fixed in euros. Which of the following transactions could eliminate the importer's exchange risk?

a. Buy euros forward.
b. Sell euros forward.
c. Borrow euros, buy dollars at the spot exchange rate.
d. Sell euros at the spot exchange rate, lend dollars.

PRACTICE

7. **Currency Risk.** Sanyo produces audio and video consumer goods and exports a large fraction of its output to the United States under its own name and the Fisher brand name. It prices its products in yen, meaning that it seeks to maintain a fixed price in terms of yen. Suppose the yen moves from ¥115.02/U.S.$ to ¥110/U.S.$. What currency risk does Sanyo face? How can it reduce its exposure?

*8. **Managing Exchange Rate Risk.** A firm in the United States is due to receive payment of 1 million Australian dollars in 8 years' time. It would like to protect itself against a decline in the value of the Australian dollar but finds it difficult to arrange a forward sale for such a long period. Is there any other way that it can protect itself?

9. **Interest Rate Parity.** The following table shows interest rates and exchange rates for the U.S. dollar and Mexican peso. The spot exchange rate is 9.5 pesos per U.S. dollar. Complete the missing entries:

	1 Month	1 Year
U.S. dollar interest rate (annually compounded)	5.5%	7%
Peso interest rate (annually compounded)	20%	___
Forward pesos per U.S. dollar	___	11.2

Hint: When calculating the 1-month forward rate, remember to translate the annual interest rate into a monthly interest rate.

*10. **Exchange Rate Risk.** An American investor buys 100 shares of London Enterprises at a price of £50 when the exchange rate is U.S.$1.60/£. A year later the shares are selling at £52. No dividends have been paid.

a. What is the rate of return to an American investor if the exchange rate is still U.S.$1.60/£?
b. What if the exchange rate is U.S.$1.70/£?
c. What if the exchange rate is U.S.$1.50/£?

*11. **Interest Rate Parity.** Look at Table 24.1. If the 3-month interest rate on dollars is 6 percent (annualized), what do you think is the 3-month sterling (U.K.) interest rate? Explain what would happen if the rate were substantially above your figure. *Hint:* In your calculations remember to convert the annually compounded interest rate into a rate for 3 months.

12. **Expectations Theory.** Table 24.1 shows the 12-month forward rate on the U.S. dollar.

a. Is the U.S. dollar at a forward discount or a premium on the Canadian dollar?
b. What is the annualized *percentage* discount or premium?
c. If you have no other information about the two currencies, what is your best guess about the spot rate in 1 year?
d. Suppose that you expect to receive 100,000 U.S. dollars in 1 year. How many Canadian dollars is this likely to be worth?

13. **Interest Rate Parity.** Suppose the interest rate on 1-year loans in the United States is 5 percent while in the United Kingdom the interest rate is 6 percent. The spot exchange rate is U.S.$1.55/£ and the forward rate is U.S.$1.54/£. In what country would you choose to borrow? To lend? Can you profit from this situation?

*14. **Purchasing Power Parity.** Suppose that the inflation rate in the United States is 4 percent and in Canada it is 5 percent. What would you expect is happening to the exchange rate between the United States and Canadian dollars?

15. **Cross Rates.** Look at Table 24.1. How many Swiss francs can you buy for $1? How many yen can you buy? What rate do you think a Japanese bank would quote for buying or selling Swiss francs? Explain what would happen if it quoted a rate that was substantially less than your figure.

*16. **International Capital Budgeting.** Suppose that you apply your own views about exchange rates when valuing an overseas investment proposal. Specifically, suppose that you believe that the leo will depreciate by 2 percent per year. Recalculate the NPV of KW's project.

17. **Currency Risk.** You have bid for a possible export order that would provide a cash inflow of €1 million in 6 months. The spot exchange rate is €.687/$ and the 12-month forward rate is €.691/$. There are two sources of uncertainty: (1) the euro could appreciate or depreciate, and (2) you may or may not receive the export order. Illustrate in each case the profits or losses that you would make if you sell €1 million forward by filling in the following table. Assume that the exchange rate in 1 year will be either €.65/$ or €.74/$.

	Profit/Loss	
Spot Rate	**Receive Order**	**Lose Order**
€.65/$	________	________
€.74/$	________	________

*18. **Managing Currency Risk.** General Gadget Corp. (GGC) is a Canada-based multinational firm that makes electrical coconut scrapers. These gadgets are made only in Canada using local inputs. The scrapers are sold mainly to Asian and West Indian countries where coconuts are grown.

a. If GGC sells scrapers in Trinidad, what is the currency risk faced by the firm?
b. In what currency should GGC borrow funds to pay for its investment in order to mitigate its foreign exchange exposure?
c. Suppose that GGC begins manufacturing its products in Trinidad using local (Trinidadian) inputs and labour. How does this affect its exchange rate risk?

19. **Currency Risk.** If investors recognize the impacts of inflation and exchange rate changes on a firm's cash flows, changes in exchange rates should be reflected in stock prices. How would the stock price of each of the following Swiss companies be affected by an unanticipated appreciation in the Swiss franc of 10 percent, only 2 percent of which could be justified by comparing Swiss inflation to that in the rest of the world?

a. *Swiss Air:* More than two-thirds of its employees are Swiss. Most revenues come from international fares set in U.S. dollars.
b. *Nestlé:* Fewer than 5 percent of its employees are Swiss. Most revenues are derived from sales of consumer goods in a wide range of countries with competition from local producers.
c. *Union Bank of Switzerland:* Most employees are Swiss. All non–Swiss franc monetary positions are fully hedged.

CHALLENGE

20. **International Capital Budgeting.** A Canadian firm is evaluating an investment in Indonesia. The project costs 500 billion Indonesian rupiah and it is expected to produce an income of 250 billion Indonesian rupiah a year in *real* terms for each of the next 3 years. The expected inflation rate in Indonesia is 12 percent per year and the firm estimates that an appropriate discount rate for the project would be about 8 percent above the risk-free rate of interest. Calculate the net present value of the project in dollars. Exchange rates are given in Table 24.1. The interest rate is about 15 percent in Indonesia and 5 percent in Canada.

21. **Hedging Exchange Rate Risk.** You have decided to purchase a deluxe condominium apartment in a newly built residential complex in South Florida. Your agreement with the real estate developer specifies that construction of the apartment will be completed and its keys will be handed to you 3 months from today. The purchase price is U.S.$200,000 to be paid at the time of possession. The current spot exchange rate is $1.5700/U.S.$ and the current 3-month forward rate is $1.6200/U.S.$.

    You intend to pay for the apartment using your dollar savings from a bank account in Canada. These dollars are earning interest at 6 percent per annum in Canada. Interest rates in the United States are 3 percent per annum.

    What options are available to you to pay for the condominium apartment if you want to avoid all foreign exchange risk associated with the transaction? Show which of the choices will work out best for you.

INTERNET PROBLEMS

1. The *Financial Times* maintains a "special reports" website on the euro: http://specials.ft.com/euro/index.html. Go to the site and trace the chronology of events which led to the European Monetary Union and the creation of this single currency.
2. The euro has replaced 12 national currencies. Return to the website from problem 1 and list these 12 countries. What is the permanent conversion rate of the euro against these eurozone currencies?
3. Go to http://cibs.commerce.ubc.ca, the website of the Centre for International Business Studies, Faculty of Commerce and Business Administration, University of British Columbia. Can you retrieve information on the most recent purchasing-power parity rates for all of the OECD countries?

SOLUTIONS TO CHECK POINTS

24.1 Direct quote: $1.4546/€
Indirect quote: 1/1.4546 = €.6875/$
Direct quote: $.013550/¥
Indirect quote: 1/0.013550 = ¥73.80/$

24.2 The dollar buys fewer Swiss francs, so the franc has appreciated with respect to the dollar.

24.3 a. $1,500 × .9867 = $1,480 using the direct (i.e., $/SFr) quote. Using the indirect quote, we get $1,500/1.01348 = $1,480.
b. (1) Direct exchange rate: SFr1 = .9867/.9 = $1.0963
(2) Indirect exchange rate: $1 = .9 × 1.01348 = .91213 francs
c. 1,500 × 1.0963 = $1,644
d. 1,480/1.0963 = 1,350 francs

24.4 a. £220 = $330. Therefore £1 = 330/220 = $1.50.
b. In the United States, price = $330 × 1.02 = $336.60. In the United Kingdom, price = £220 × 1.05 = £231. The new exchange rate = $336.60/£231 = $1.457/£.
c. Initially $1 buys 1/1.50 = £.667. At the end of the year, $1 buys 1/1.457 = £.686, which is about 3 percent higher than the original value of £.667.

24.5 The real interest rate in Canada is 1.04/1.02 – 1 = .02, or 2%. If the real rate is the same in Greece, then expected inflation must be

$$(1 + \text{nominal rate})/(1 + \text{real rate}) - 1 = 1.08/1.02 - 1 = .059, \text{ or } 5.9\%.$$

24.6 The pound is at a forward discount (that is, you get more pounds for $1, or conversely, fewer dollars for £1 in the forward market). This implies that the interest rates in Great Britain are higher than those in Canada.

The interest rate in Canada is 3.55 percent. Interest rate parity states

$$(1 + r_{£})/(1 + r_{\$}) = f_{£/\$}/s_{£/\$}$$

Therefore, $r_{£} = 1.0355 \times (.4408/.4345) - 1 = .051$, or 5.1%.

24.7 Stellar borrows ¥100 million in 1998. It pays ¥2 million in interest at the end of 1999, when it also repays the loan. Cash flows in U.S. dollars are

$$1998: \quad \frac{100 \text{ million}}{123.97} = \text{U.S.\$806,647}$$

$$1999: \quad \text{Interest} = \frac{2 \text{ million}}{107.52} = \$18,601$$

$$\text{Principal} = \frac{100 \text{ million}}{107.52} = \$930,059$$

$$\text{Total} = \text{U.S.\$948,661}$$

To find the U.S.dollar interest rate, solve

$$806,647 \times (1 + r_{U.S.\$}) = 948,661$$

$$r_{U.S.\$} = \frac{948,661}{806,647} - 1 = .176 = 17.6\%$$

24.8 According to the expectations theory of exchange rates, the forward rate equals the expected future spot exchange rate. Therefore, the expected cost of the hedge—the difference between the forward rate and expected spot rate—is zero!

24.9 a. The lower interest rate in Narnia than in Canada suggests that forecast inflation is lower in Narnia. If real interest rates are the same in the two countries, then the difference in inflation rates is about 5 – 3 = 2 percent.

b. The lower interest rate (and lower expected inflation rate) in Narnia suggests that investors are expecting the leo to appreciate against the dollar.

c. Since KW can now expect to change its leo cash flows into more dollars than before, the project's NPV is increased. Forecast exchange rates will be as follows:

Year	Forecast Exchange Rate		
0	Spot exchange rate	=	L2.0/$
1	$2.0 \times (1.03/1.05)$	=	L1.962/$
2	$2.0 \times (1.03/1.05)^2$	=	L1.925/$
3	$2.0 \times (1.03/1.05)^3$	=	L1.888/$
4	$2.0 \times (1.03/1.05)^4$	=	L1.852/$
5	$2.0 \times (1.03/1.05)^5$	=	L1.817/$

The expected dollar cash flows from the project are

Year	**0**	**1**	**2**	**3**	**4**	**5**
Cash flow (millions of dollars)	$\frac{-7.6}{2.00}$ = –\$3.8	$\frac{2.0}{1.962}$ = \$1.02	$\frac{2.5}{1.925}$ = \$1.30	$\frac{3.0}{1.888}$ = \$1.59	$\frac{3.5}{1.852}$ = \$1.89	$\frac{4.0}{1.817}$ = \$2.20

Discounting these dollar cash flows at the 15 percent *dollar* cost of capital gives

$$\text{NPV} = -3.8 + \frac{1.02}{1.15} + \frac{1.30}{1.15^2} + \frac{1.59}{1.15^3} + \frac{1.89}{1.15^4} + \frac{2.20}{1.15^5}$$

$$= \$1.29 \text{ million, or } \$1{,}290{,}000$$

The project is worth more because the reduced interest rate in Narnia suggests that investors expect the leo to appreciate in value. Thus the dollar cash flows from the project are higher than in Section 24.4.

MINICASE

"Jumping jackasses! Not another one!" groaned George Luger. This was the third memo he had received that morning from the CEO of VCR Importers. It read as follows:

From: CEO's Office
To: Company Treasurer

George,

I have been looking at some of our foreign exchange deals and they don't seem to make sense.

First, we have been buying yen forward to cover the cost of our imports. You have explained that this insures us against the risk that the dollar may depreciate over the next year, but it is incredibly expensive insurance. Each dollar buys only 71.3 yen when we buy forward, compared with the current spot rate of 76.8 yen to the dollar. We could save a fortune by buying yen as and when we need them rather than buying them forward.

Another possibility has occurred to me. If we are worried that the dollar may depreciate (or do I mean "appreciate"?), why don't we buy yen at the low spot rate of ¥76.8 to the dollar and then put them on deposit until we have to pay for the VCRs? That way we can make sure we get a good rate for our yen.

I am also worried that we are missing out on some cheap financing. We are paying about 8 percent to borrow dollars for one year, but Ben Hur was telling me at lunch that we could get a 1-year yen loan for about 1.75 percent. I find that a bit surprising, but if that's the case, why don't we repay our dollar loans and borrow yen instead?

Perhaps we could discuss these ideas at next Wednesday's meeting. I would be interested in your views on the matter.

Jill Edison

CHAPTER 25

Options

25.1 Calls and Puts

25.2 What Determines Option Values?

25.3 Spotting the Option

25.4 Summary

25.5 Appendix 25A: The Black-Scholes Option Valuation Model

When the Chicago Board Options Exchange (CBOE) was established in 1973, few observers guessed what a success it would be. By creating standardized, listed stock options, the CBOE revolutionized options trading. Today the CBOE is the world's largest options exchange, each year trading options to buy or sell more than 15 billion shares of stock in 1,200 companies. Other exchanges around the world have copied the CBOE model, and in addition to options on individual stocks, options can be traded on stock indexes, bonds, commodities, and foreign exchanges. For example, options on Canadian stocks and bonds are traded on the Bourse de Montréal, home of the Canadian Derivatives Exchange, www.m-x.ca.

You will see that options can be valuable tools for managing the risk characteristics of an investment portfolio. But why should the financial manager of an industrial company read further? There are several reasons. First, most capital budgeting projects have options embedded in them that allow the company to expand at a future date or to bail out. These options allow the company to profit if things go well but give downside protection when they don't.

Second, many of the securities that firms issue include an option. For example, companies often issue convertible bonds. The holder has the option to exchange the bond for common stock. Some corporate bonds also contain a call provision, meaning that the issuer has the option to buy back the bond from the investor.

Finally, managers routinely use currency, commodity, and interest rate options to protect the firm against a variety of risks. (We will have more to say about this in Chapter 26.)

In one chapter we can provide you with only a brief introduction to options. Our first goal in this chapter is to explain how options work and how option value is determined. Then we will tell you how to recognize some of the options that crop up in capital investment proposals and in company financing.

After studying this chapter you should be able to

- Calculate the payoff to buyers and sellers of call and put options.
- Understand the determinants of option values.
- Recognize options in capital investment proposals.
- Identify options that are provided in financial securities.

25.1 Calls and Puts

call option Right to buy an asset at a specified exercise price on or before the exercise date.

A **call option** gives its holder the right to buy stock for a fixed *exercise price* (also called the *strike price*) on or before a specified exercise date.[1] For example, if you buy a call option on IBM that has an expiration date in October and an exercise price of $100, you have the right to buy shares of IBM at a price of $100 at any time until October.

You need not exercise a call option; it will be profitable to do so only if the share price exceeds the exercise price. If it does not, the option will be left unexercised and will prove to be valueless. But suppose IBM shares are selling above the $100 exercise price, say at $120, just before the call option expires. You will choose to exercise your option to pay $100 to buy shares worth $120. Your net proceeds upon exercise equal the difference between the $100 paid and the $120 you can realize for the shares. More generally, the proceeds would equal the difference between the stock price and the exercise price.

In summary, the value of the call option at expiration is as follows:

Stock Price at Expiration	Value of Call at Expiration
Greater than exercise price	Stock price – exercise price
Less than exercise price	Zero

Of course, the ultimate value of the option is not all profit: You have to pay for the option. The price of the call is called the option *premium.* Option buyers pay the premium for the right to exercise later. Your profit equals the ultimate payoff to the call option (which may be zero) minus the initial premium.

EXAMPLE 25.1 *Call Options on Bombardier*

On September 20, 2001, a call option on Bombardier Class B shares with a January 2002 expiration and an exercise price of $14.50 per share sold for $.65. If you had purchased the call on this date, you would have had the right to purchase shares of Bombardier for $14.50 anytime until the option expired in January. On September 20, Bombardier shares sold for $12.94. Immediate exercise of the call would have resulted in net proceeds of $12.94 – $14.50 = –$1.56. Obviously, anyone who paid $.65 for the call on September 20 had no intention of exercising it immediately. A buyer of the call was betting on an increase in the stock price, which would make the option turn out to be a profitable investment. For example, if Bombardier sold in January for $16, the proceeds from exercising the call would have been

$$\text{Proceeds} = \text{stock price} - \text{exercise price} = \$16 - \$14.50 = \$1.50$$

and the net profit on the call would have been

$$\text{Profits} = \text{proceeds} - \text{original investment} = \$1.50 - \$.65 = \$.85$$

In 6 months, you would have earned a return of $.85/$.65 = 1.31, or 131 percent.

put option Right to sell an asset at a specified exercise price on or before the exercise date.

A call option gives you the right to buy a share of stock whereas a **put option** gives you the right to *sell* it for the exercise price. If you hold a put on a share of stock and the stock price turns out to be greater than the exercise price, you will not want to exercise your option

[1] In some cases, the option can be exercised only on one particular day, which is conventionally known as a *European call;* in other cases, it can be exercised on or before that day, which is called an *American call.*

TABLE 25.1
Option values on expiration date as a function of stock price on that date (exercise price = $14.50)

Stock and Option Values						
Bombardier value	$11	$13	$14.50	$16	$18	$20
Call value	0	0	0	$ 1.50	$ 3.50	$ 5.50
Put value	$ 3.50	$ 1.50	0	0	0	0

to sell the shares for the exercise price. The put will be left unexercised and will expire valueless. But if the stock price turns out to be less than the exercise price, it will pay to buy the share at the low price and then exercise your option to sell it for the exercise price. The put would then be worth the difference between the exercise price and the stock price.

EXAMPLE 25.2 *Put Options on Bombardier*

On September 20, 2001, it cost $2.10 to buy a put option on Bombardier Class B shares with a January 2002 expiration and an exercise price of $14.50. Suppose Bombardier is selling for $11 just before the put option expires. Then if you hold a put, you can buy a share of stock for $11 and exercise your right to sell it for $14.50. The put will be worth $14.50 – $11 = $3.50. Because you paid $2.10 for the put originally, your net profit is $1.40. If, however, the stock price is above $14.50 on the maturity date, you will let the put option expire worthless. Your loss equals the $2.10 you originally spent to purchase the put.

In general, the value of the put option at expiration is as follows:

Stock Price at Expiration	Value of Put Option at Expiration
Greater than exercise price	Zero
Less than exercise price	Exercise price – stock price

Table 25.1 shows the value on their expiration date of call and put options on Bombardier stock with exercise price $14.50 as a function of Bombardier's share price on that date. You can see that once the stock price is above $14.50, the call value rises dollar for dollar with the stock price, and that once the stock price is below $14.50, the put value rises $1 for each dollar *decrease* in the stock price. Figure 25.1 plots the values of each option on the expiration date.

Figure 25.2 is an excerpt of listed stock quotations from the *Globe and Mail* showing options for shares of Bombardier. The value $12.94, next to the stock name BmbrB, is the current price of the stock. In the column below the stock name is the expiration month for

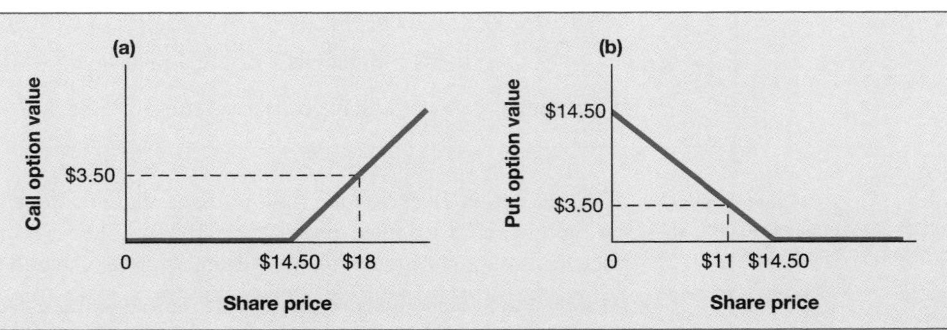

FIGURE 25.1
Values of call options and put options on Bombardier stock on option expiration date (exercise price = $14.50)

FIGURE 25.2
Prices of options on shares of Bombardier, September 20, 2001

Stock Series		Bid	Close Ask	Last	Total Vol	Op. Int.
BmbrB		$12.94			1315	49501
Oct 01	$12.50	1.00	1.25	1.20	107	154
	$12.50p	0.55	0.80	0.60	185	185
	$15.00	0.35	0.50	0.40	60	487
	$15.00p	2.30	2.55	2.45	10	35
	$22.50P	9.55	9.95	9.70	25	438
	$25.00		0.05	0.04	5	4547
Jan 02	$10.50	2.60	2.85	3.60	10	148
	$10.50p	0.25	0.50	0.45	20	54
	$11.50	1.85	2.10	2.05	15	501
	$11.50P	0.40	0.65	0.65	5	66
	$12.50	1.35	1.50	1.50	112	626
	$12.50P	1.05	1.10	1.05	28	160
	$13.50	0.90	1.05	1.05	144`	4034
	$13.50p	1.35	1.60	1.45	30	220
	$14.50	0.70	0.85	0.65	108	394
	$14.50p	2.05	2.30	2.10	5	86
	$15.50	0.50	0.65	0.65	52	902
	$17.50	0.20	0.35	0.35	40	728
	$20.00p	7.00	7.25	6.00	10	521
	$22.50	0.05	0.25	0.25	14	1495
	$22.50p	9.65	10.05	9.40	10	722
	$25.00		0.25	0.20	25	3349
	$27.50p	14.70	15.20	15.15	9	88
Apr 02	$12.50	1.70	2.75	1.95	92	319
	$12.50p	1.20	1.45	1.15	15	45
	$15.00	1.00	1.15	1.20	83	177
	$15.00p	2.85	3.10	2.80	5	40
	$17.50	0.50	0.70	0.75	10	251
	$22.50	0.05	0.30	0.25	3	278
Jan 03	$15.00	1.80	2.20	2.25	13	20
	$17.50	1.85	1.90	2.20	25	979
	$20.00	1.30	1.35	1.20	4	1526
Jan 04	$12.50	5.00	5.30	5.50	22	30
	$22.50p	9.55	10.05	9.20	2	49
	$25.00	0.90	1.20	1.70	5	110
	$25.00p	12.00	12.50	12.05	7	54

Source: The *Globe and Mail* (September 21, 2001), p. B22.

each option.[2] Next to the expiration month is the exercise price of the option. If the exercise price has the letter "p" next to it, the option is a put; otherwise, the option is a call. The next two numbers in the row are the bid and ask prices for the option at the market close.[3] The next number is the price of the last trade of the day. The final two numbers on the line are the volume of option contracts traded during the day and open interest.[4] Looking back at the first line of the listing, you will see the total trading volume and open interest for all of the Bombardier equity options for the day.

You can see from the listings that for any particular maturity, or expiration month, calls are worth more when the exercise price is lower, while puts are worth more when the exercise price is higher. This makes sense: You would rather have the right to buy at a low price and the right to sell at high price.

☑ CHECK POINT 25.1

a. What will be the proceeds and net profits (i.e., net of the option premium) to an investor who purchases the January-maturity Bombardier call options with exercise price of \$17.50 if the stock price at maturity is \$10? What if the stock price at maturity is \$20? Use the price of the last trade of the day in Figure 25.2.
b. Now answer part (a) for an investor who purchases a January-maturity Bombardier put option with exercise price \$13.50.

SELLING CALLS AND PUTS

The traded options that you see quoted in the financial pages are not sold by the companies themselves but by other investors. If one investor buys an option on Bombardier stock,

[2] For the Bourse de Montréal, the expiry date is the Saturday following the last trading day of the expiration month. The last trading day is the third Friday of the expiration month, providing it is a business day; if not, the first preceding business day. These details vary among the options exchanges.

[3] The bid price is the price at which an options dealer is willing to buy the option; the ask price is the price at which the dealer is willing to sell. The dealer gets the difference between bid and ask prices, the bid-ask spread, as compensation for his or her willingness to engage in trading of the options. On the other hand, an ordinary investor, thinking of buying an option, pays the ask price when buying and receives the bid price when selling.

[4] Volume is reported as the number of option contracts traded. Each contract is for 100 shares of stock. For example, if a call price is reported as \$2, you would pay \$200 to buy one contract, which would give you the right to buy 100 shares of stock. You would pay the exercise price for each share. Open interest is the number of option contracts outstanding at the end of the day.

some other investor must be on the other side of the bargain. We will look now at the position of the investor who sells an option.[5]

We have already seen that the January-maturity Bombardier calls with exercise price $14.50 are trading at $.65. Thus if you *sell* the January call option on Bombardier stock, the buyer pays you $.65. However, in return you promise to sell Bombardier shares at a price of $14.50 if the call buyer decides to exercise his option. The option seller's obligation to *sell* Bombardier is just the other side of the coin to the option holder's right to *buy* the stock. The buyer *pays* the option premium for the right to exercise advantageously; the seller *receives* the premium but may be required at a later date to deliver the stock for an exercise price that is less than the market price of the stock. If the share price is below the exercise price of $14.50 when the option expires in January, holders of the call will not exercise their option, and you, the seller, will have no further liability. However, if the price of Bombardier is greater than $14.50, the option will be exercised and you must give up your shares for $14.50 each. You therefore lose the difference between the share price and the $14.50 that you receive from the buyer.

Suppose that Bombardier's stock price turns out to be $20. In this case the buyer will exercise the call option and will pay $14.50 for stock that can be resold for $20. The buyer therefore has a payoff of $5.50—not bad on an investment of only $.65. Of course, that positive payoff for the *buyer* means a negative payoff for you, the *seller,* for you are obliged to sell Bombardier stock worth $20 for only $14.50.

In general, the seller's loss is the buyer's gain, and vice versa. Figure 25.3*a* shows the payoffs to the call option seller. Note that Figure 25.3*a* is just Figure 25.1*a* drawn upside down.

The position of an investor who sells the Bombardier put option can be shown in just the same way by standing Figure 25.1*b* on its head. The put *buyer* has the right to sell a share for $14.50; so the *seller* of the put has agreed to pay $14.50 for the share if the put buyer should demand it. Clearly the seller will be safe as long as the share price remains above $14.50, but will lose money if the share price falls below this figure. The worst thing that can happen to the put seller is for the stock to be worthless. The seller would then be obliged to pay $14.50 for a worthless stock. The payoff to the seller would be –$14.50. Note that the advantage always lies with the option buyer, the obligation with the seller. Therefore, the buyer must pay the seller to acquire the option.

The purchaser of an option has the right to buy or sell an asset at a fixed and possibly advantageous price. The option seller is obliged to sell or buy at this price if the buyer wants to exercise. The option buyer pays the seller to take on this obligation.

FIGURE 25.3
Payoffs to sellers of call and put options on Bombardier stock (exercise price = $14.50)

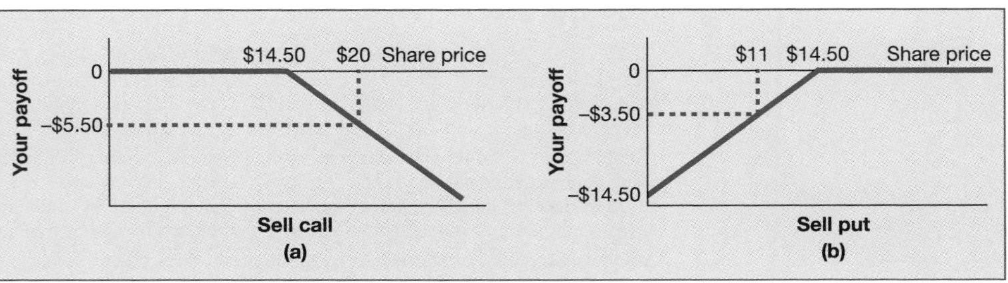

[5] The option seller is known as the *writer.*

TABLE 25.2
Rights and obligations of various options positions

	Buyer	Seller
Call option	Right to buy asset	Obligation to sell asset
Put option	Right to sell asset	Obligation to buy asset

Table 25.2 summarizes the rights and obligation of buyers and sellers of calls and puts.

CHECK POINT 25.2

a. What will be the proceeds and net profits to an investor who sells the January-maturity Bombardier call options with exercise price $17.50 if the stock price at maturity is $10? What if the stock price at maturity is $20? Use the data price of the last trade of the day in Figure 25.2.
b. Now answer part (a) for an investor who sells a January-maturity Bombardier put option with exercise price $13.50.

FINANCIAL ALCHEMY WITH OPTIONS

Now we can see how options can be used to modify the risk characteristics of a portfolio. Suppose, for example, that you are generally optimistic about Bombardier's prospects, but you understand that a large investment in the stock is a risk and would cause you to have sleepless nights. Here is a strategy that might appeal to you: Buy the stock, but also buy a put option on the stock with exercise price $14.50. If the stock price rises, your put turns out to be worthless, but you win on the stock investment. If the stock price falls, your losses are limited, since the put gives you the right to sell the stock for the $14.50 exercise price. Thus the value of your stock-plus-put position cannot be less than $14.50.

Here is another way to view your overall position. You hold the stock and the put option. The value of each component of the portfolio will be as follows:

	Stock Price < $14.50	Stock Price ≥ $14.50
Value of stock	Stock price	Stock price
Value of put option	$14.50 – stock price	0
Total value	$14.50	Stock price

No matter how far the stock price falls, the total value of your portfolio cannot fall below the $14.50 exercise price.

The value of your position when the options expire is graphed in Figure 25.4. You have downside protection at $14.50 but still share in potential gains on the stock. This strategy is called a *protective put,* because the put option gives protection against losses. Of course, such protection is not free. Look again at Figure 25.2 and you will find the cost of such protection. "Stock price insurance" at a level of $14.50 between September 2001 and January 2002 cost $2.10 per share; this was the price of the put option with exercise price $14.50 and January expiration.

EXAMPLE 25.3 *Profiting from Volatility*

Suppose you believe that Bombardier is going to be subject to considerable volatility over the next few months. Perhaps a new product due to come to the market soon will be either a fabulous success or, if technological bugs cannot be overcome, a dismal failure. How can you bet on the expected volatility of the stock?

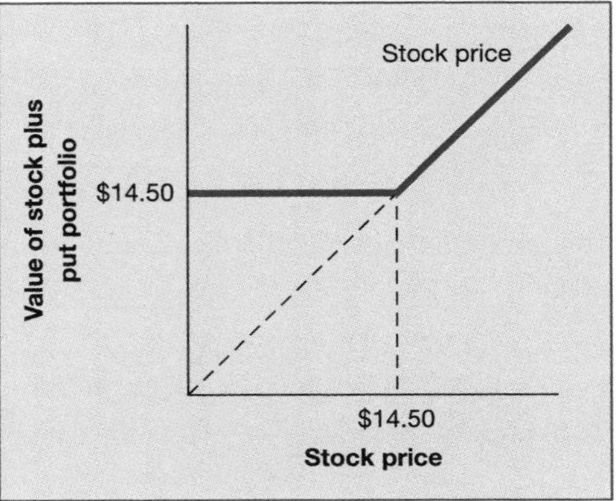

FIGURE 25.4
Payoff to protective put strategy. If the ultimate stock price exceeds $14.50, the put is valueless but you own the stock. If it is less than $14.50, you can sell the stock for the exercise price.

Try buying one call and one put option, both with exercise price $14.50. This position—holding a call and a put—is called a *straddle.* If the stock price falls, the put will be profitable; if the stock price rises, the call will be profitable. Figure 25.5 illustrates your position. The green line is the value of the call. The blue line is the value of the put. You hold the call *and* the put, so the total value of your holdings is a V-shaped profile.

Of course, there is no free lunch here. Although the value of the position cannot be negative, remember that you have to pay to establish this position: You pay for both the call and the put. Unless the ultimate payoff exceeds the cost of the two options, you will lose money. Thus the *profit* on this strategy is given by the dashed V-shaped line in Figure 25.5. Unless the stock moves far enough that the profit on either the call or the put covers the initial cost of the two options, your profits will be negative.

Of course there are many other interesting option strategies that one might envision. These instruments give you considerable leeway to tailor the risk features of a portfolio. Try your skill at financial alchemy with Check Point 25.3.

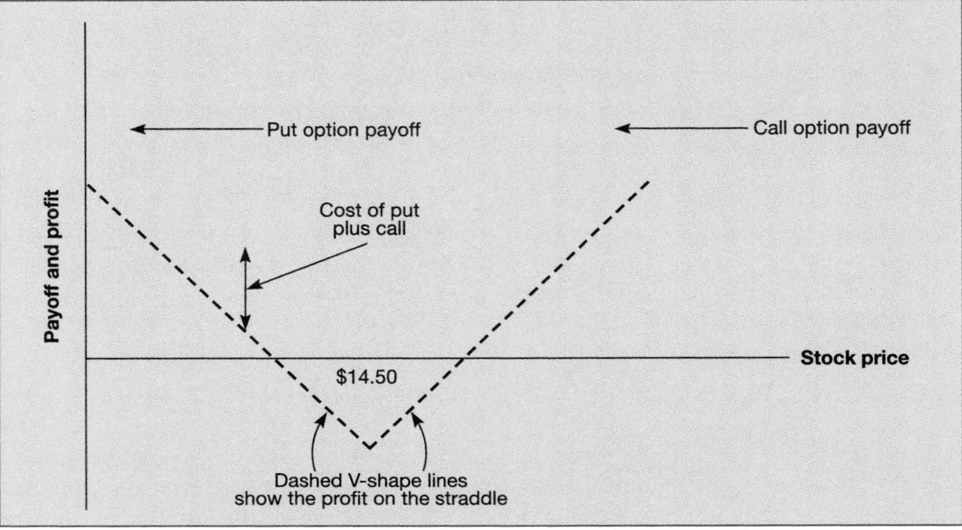

FIGURE 25.5
Payoff and profit on a straddle. Call option is drawn in green, put option in blue.

CHECK POINT 25.3

What strategy using a call, a put, and a share of stock can create a payoff that depends on the price of Bombardier stock in the manner depicted in Figure 25.6? Why might someone establish this position?

FIGURE 25.6

This strategy provides a total payoff of $11.50 if the stock price is below $11.50, a payoff of $15.50 if the stock price is above $15.50, and a payoff equal to the stock price for values between $11.50 and $15.50. Can you create this payoff?

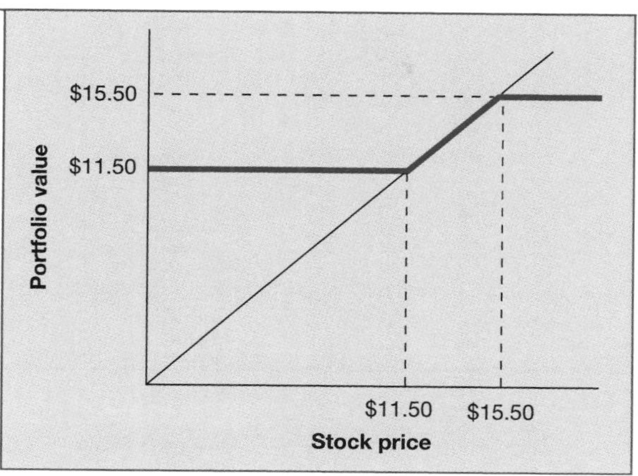

25.2 What Determines Option Values?

We have seen that $14.50 January-maturity calls on Bombardier are trading at $.65. But we have said nothing about how the market values of options are determined.

UPPER AND LOWER LIMITS ON OPTION VALUES

We know what an option is worth when it expires. Consider, for example, the option to buy stock at $30. If the stock price is below $30 at the expiration date, the call will be worthless; if the stock price is above $30, the call will be worth the value of the stock minus the $30 exercise price. The relationship is depicted by the heavy green line in Figure 25.7.

Even before expiration, the price of the option can never remain *below* the heavy green line in Figure 25.7. For example, if our option were priced at $5 and the stock at $40, it would pay any investor to buy the option, exercise it for an additional $30, and then sell the stock for $40. That would give a "money machine" with a profit of $40 – $35 = $5. The demand for options from investors using this strategy would quickly force the option price up at least to the heavy green line in the figure. The heavy green line is therefore a *lower* limit on the market price of the option. Thus

Lower limit on value of call option = the greater of *zero* or (*stock price* – *exercise price*)

The diagonal light blue line in Figure 25.7, which is the plot of the stock price, is the *upper* limit to the option price. Why? Because the stock itself gives a higher final payoff whatever happens. If when the option expires the stock price ends up above the exercise price, the option is worth the stock price *less* the exercise price. If the stock price ends up below the exercise price, the option is worthless, but the stock's owner still has a valuable security. Thus the extra payoff to holding the stock rather than the option is as follows:

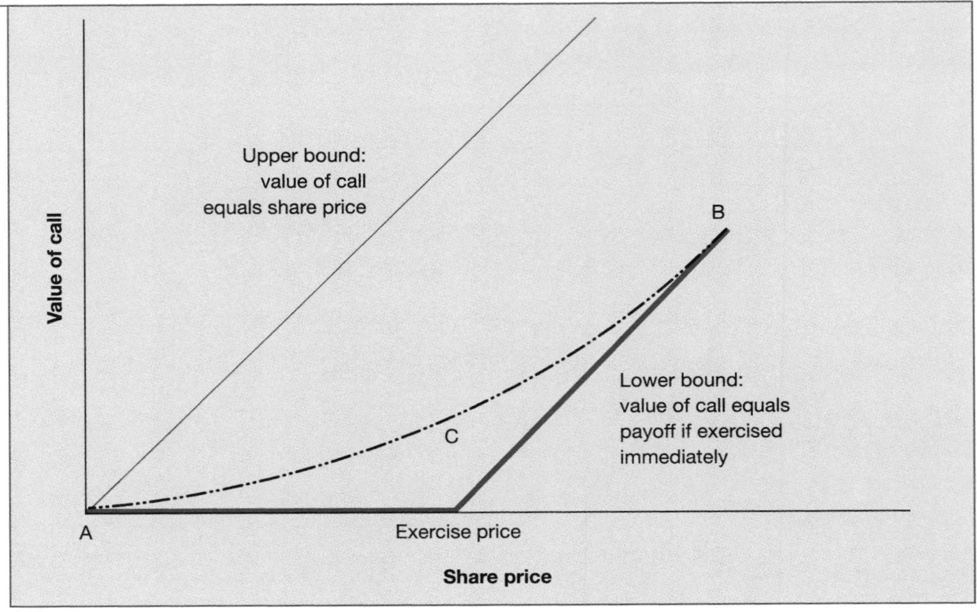

FIGURE 25.7
Value of a call before its expiration date (dashed line). The value depends on the stock price. The call is always worth more than its value if exercised now (heavy green line). It is never worth more than the stock price itself.

Stock Price at Expiration	Stock Payoff	Option Payoff	Extra Payoff from Holding Stock Rather than Option
Greater than $30	Stock price	Stock price – $30	$30
Less than or equal to $30	Stock price	$0	Stock price

THE DETERMINANTS OF OPTION VALUE

The option price must lie between the upper and lower limits in Figure 25.7. In fact, the price will lie on a curved, upward-sloping line like the dashed curve shown in the figure. This line begins its travels where the upper and lower bounds meet (at zero). Then it rises, gradually becoming parallel to the lower bound. This line tells us an important fact about option values: Given the exercise price, *the value of a call option increases as the stock price increases.*

That should be no surprise. Owners of call options clearly hope for the stock price to rise and are happy when it does. But let us look more carefully at the shape and location of the dashed line. Three points, *A, B,* and *C,* are marked on the dashed line. As we explain each point, you will see why the option price has to behave as the dashed line predicts.

Point *A*. *When the stock is worthless, the option is worthless.* A stock price of zero means that there is no possibility the stock will ever have any future value.[6] If so, the option is sure to expire unexercised and worthless, and it is worthless today.

Point *B*. *When the stock price becomes very high, the option price approaches the stock price less the present value of the exercise price.* Notice that the dashed line representing the option price in Figure 25.7 eventually becomes parallel to the ascending heavy green

[6] If a stock *can* be worth something in the future then investors will pay *something* for it today, although possibly a very small amount.

line representing the lower bound on the option price. The reason is as follows. The higher the stock price, the greater the odds that the option will eventually be exercised. If the stock price is high enough, exercise becomes a virtual certainty; the probability that the stock price will fall below the exercise price before the option expires becomes trivial.

If you own an option that you *know* will be exchanged for a share of stock, you effectively own the stock now. The only difference is that you don't have to pay for the stock (by handing over the exercise price) until later, when formal exercise occurs. In these circumstances, buying the call is equivalent to buying the stock now with deferred payment and delivery. The value of the call is therefore equal to the stock price less the present value of the exercise price.[7]

This brings us to another important point about options. Investors who acquire stock by way of a call option are buying on "installment credit." They pay the purchase price of the option today, but they do not pay the exercise price until they actually exercise the option. The delay in payment is particularly valuable if interest rates are high and the option has a long maturity. Thus *the value of a call option increases with both the rate of interest and the time to expiration.*

CHECK POINT 25.4

How would the value of a put option be affected by an increase in the exercise price? Explain.

Point *C*. *The option price always exceeds its minimum value* (except at maturity or when stock price is zero). We have seen that the dashed and heavy lines in Figure 25.7 coincide when stock price is zero (point *A*), but elsewhere the lines diverge; that is, the option price must exceed the minimum value given by the heavy line. You can see why by examining point *C*.

At point *C*, the stock price exactly equals the exercise price. The option therefore would be worthless if it expired today. However, suppose that the option will not expire until 3 months hence. Of course we do not know what the stock price will be at the expiration date. There is roughly a 50 percent chance that it will be higher than the exercise price, and a 50 percent chance that it will be lower. The possible payoffs to the option are therefore:

Outcome	Payoff
Stock price rises (50 percent probability)	Stock price – exercise price (option is exercised)
Stock price falls (50 percent probability)	Zero (option expires worthless)

If there is some chance of a positive payoff, and if the worst payoff is zero, then the option must be valuable. That means the option price at point *C* exceeds its lower bound, which at point *C* is zero. In general, the option price will exceed the lower bound as long as there is time left before expiration.

One of the most important determinants of the *height* of the dashed curve (that is, of the difference between actual and lower-bound value) is the likelihood of substantial movements in the stock price. An option on a stock whose price is unlikely to change by more than 1 or 2 percent is not worth much; an option on a stock whose price may halve or double is very valuable.

[7] We assume here that the stock pays no dividends until after the option matures. If dividends were paid, you *would* care about when you get to own the stock because the option holder misses out on any dividends.

For example, suppose that a call option has an exercise price of $30, and the stock price will be either $25 or $35 when the option expires. The possible payoffs to the option are as follows:

Stock price at expiration	$25	$35
Call value at expiration	$ 0	$ 5

Now suppose that the value of the stock when the option expires can be $20 or $40. The *average* of the possible stock prices is the same as before, but the volatility is greater. In this case the payoffs to the call are

Stock price at expiration	$20	$40
Call value at expiration	$ 0	$10

A comparison of the two cases highlights the valuable asymmetry that options offer. If the stock price turns out to be below the exercise price when the option expires, the option is valueless regardless of whether the shortfall is a cent or a dollar. However, the option holder reaps all the benefits of stock price advances. Thus in our example the option is worth only $5 if the stock price reaches $35, but it is worth $10 if the stock price rises to $40. Therefore, volatility helps the option holder.

The probability of large stock price changes during the remaining life of an option depend on two things: (1) the variability of the stock price *per unit of time,* and (2) the length of time until the option expires. Other things being equal, you would like to hold an option on a volatile stock. Given volatility, you would like to hold an option with a long life ahead of it, since that longer life means that there is more opportunity for the stock price to change.

The value of an option increases with both the variability of the share price and the time to expiration.

It's hard to keep all these properties straight at first reading. Therefore, we have summed them up in Table 25.3.

CHECK POINT 25.5

Rework our numerical example for a put option with an exercise price of $30. Show that put options also are more valuable when the stock price is more volatile.

OPTION-VALUATION MODELS

If you want to value an option, you need to go beyond the qualitative statements of Table 25.3; you need an exact option-valuation model—a formula that you can plug numbers into and come up with a figure for option value.

TABLE 25.3
What the price of a call option depends on

If the following variables *increase,* . . .	. . . the value of a call option will
stock price	increase
exercise price	decrease
interest rate	increase
time to expiration	increase
volatility of stock price	increase

Valuing complex options is a high-tech business and well beyond the scope of this book. Our aim here is not to instantly make you into option whizzes but to illustrate the basics of option valuation by walking you through an example. The trick to option valuation is to find a combination of borrowing and an investment in the stock that exactly replicates the option. The nearby Financial Calculator box illustrates a simple version of one of these option-valuation models.

This model achieves simplicity by assuming that the share price can take on only two values at the expiration date of the option. This assumption is clearly unrealistic, but it turns out that this approach can be generalized to allow for a large number of possible future share prices rather than just the two values in our example.

In 1973, Fischer Black, Myron Scholes, and Robert Merton came up with a formula that showed that even when share prices are changing continuously, you can still replicate an option by a series of levered investments in the stock. The Black-Scholes formula is regularly used by option traders, investment bankers, and financial managers to value a wide variety of options. Scholes and Merton shared the 1997 Nobel Prize in economics for their work on the development of this formula.[8] In Appendix 25A we present the basics of their remarkable option pricing formula.

Today, there are many more sophisticated variants of the Black-Scholes formula that can better capture some aspect of real-life markets. As computer power continues to increase, these models can be made more complex and increasingly accurate.

CHECK POINT 25.6

Use the Financial Calculator box on page 750 as a model to help you answer this question. Suppose that the price of Alcan stock is \$47 and could either double to \$94 or halve to \$23.5 over the next 3 months. Show that the following two strategies have exactly the same payoffs regardless of whether the stock price rises or falls: Strategy A—Buy three call options with an exercise price of \$47; Strategy B—Buy two shares and borrow the present value of \$47. What is your cash outflow today if you follow Strategy B? What does this tell you about the value of three call options? Assume that the interest rate is 1 percent per 3 months.

25.3 Spotting the Option

In our discussion so far we may have given you the impression that financial managers are concerned only with traded options to buy or sell shares. But once you have learned to recognize the different kinds of options, you will find that they are everywhere. Unfortunately, they rarely come with a large label attached. Often the trickiest part of the problem is to identify the option.

We will start by looking briefly at options on real assets and then turn to options on financial assets. You should find that you have already encountered many of these options in earlier chapters.

OPTIONS ON REAL ASSETS

In Chapter 8 we pointed out that the capital investment projects that you accept today may affect the opportunities you have tomorrow.[9] Today's capital budgeting decisions need to

[8] Fischer Black passed away in 1995.

[9] See Section 8.4.

FINANCIAL CALCULATOR

A Simple Option-Valuation Model

It is September 2001 and you are contemplating the purchase of a call option on Ballard Power System (Ballard) stock. The call has a January 2002 exercise date and an exercise price of \$32.50. Ballard's stock price is currently \$25, so the option will be valueless unless the stock price appreciates over the next 4 months. The outlook for Ballard stock is uncertain, and all you know is that at the end of the 6 months it will be either \$16 or \$38. Finally we assume that the rate of interest on a bank loan is 13 percent a year, or about 1 percent for four months.

The following table depicts the outlook for three alternative investments:

Ballard Stock		Call Option		Bank Loan	
Sept.	**January**	**Sept.**	**January**	**Sept.**	**January**
	\$38		\$5.50		\$101
\$25		?		\$100	
	\$16		\$0		\$101

The first investment is Ballard stock. Its current price is \$25 but the price could rise to \$38 or fall to \$16. The second investment is the call option. When the call expires in January, the option will be valueless if the stock price falls to \$16, and it will be worth \$38 – \$32.50 = \$5.50 if the stock price rises to \$38. We don't know (yet) how much the call is worth today, so for the time being we put a question mark against the July value. Our third investment is a bank loan at an interest rate of 1 percent per 4 months. The payoff on a \$100 bank loan is \$101 no matter what happens to the price of Ballard stock.

Consider now two investment strategies. The first (Strategy A) is to buy four call options. The second (Strategy B) is to buy one Ballard share and to borrow the present value of \$16 from the bank. Table 25.4 shows the possible payoffs from the two strategies. Notice that when you borrow from the bank, you receive a *positive* cash flow now but have a *negative flow* when the loan is repaid in January.

You can see that *regardless of whether the stock price falls to \$16 or rises to \$38,* the payoffs from the two strategies are identical. To put it another way, you can exactly *replicate* an investment in call options by a combination of a bank loan and an investment in the stock.[1] If two investments give the same payoffs in all circumstances, then their value must be the same today. In other words, the cost of buying four call options must be exactly the same as borrowing PV(\$16) (i.e., \$16/1.01 = \$15.84) from the bank and buying one Ballard share:

$$\text{Price of 4 calls} = \$25 - \$15.84 = \$9.16$$

$$\text{Price of 1 call} = \frac{\$9.16}{4} = \$2.29$$

Presto! You have just valued a call option.

TABLE 25.4
It is possible to replicate the payoffs from Ballard call options by borrowing to invest in Ballard stock.

	Cash Flow in September 2001	Payoff in January 2002 if Stock Price Equals: \$16	\$38
Strategy A			
Buy four calls	?	\$0	+\$22 (= 4 × \$5.5)
Strategy B			
Buy one share	–\$ 25	+\$16	+\$38
Borrow PV(\$16)	+\$15.84	–16	–16
	–\$ 9.16	\$ 0	+\$22

Note: PV(\$16) at an interest rate of 1 percent for 4 months is 16/1.01 = \$15.84.

[1] The only tricky part in valuing the Ballard option is to work out the number of shares that are needed to replicate one option. Fortunately, there is a simple formula that says that the number of shares needed is equal to

$$\frac{\text{Spread of possible option prices}}{\text{Spread of possible stock prices}} = \frac{\$5.50 - \$0}{\$38 - \$16} = .25$$

To replicate a call option, you need to buy .25 of a share of stock. To replicate four calls, you need to buy one share of stock. This ratio is called the hedge ratio or the option delta.

recognize these future opportunities. We looked in Chapter 8 at several ways that companies may build future flexibility into a project.

Other things being equal, a capital investment project that generates new opportunities is more valuable than one that doesn't. A flexible project—one that doesn't commit management to a fixed operating strategy—is more valuable than an inflexible one. When a project is flexible or generates new opportunities for the firm, it is said to contain **real options.** Here are a few specific examples.

real options Options embedded in real assets.

The Option to Expand. Many capital investment proposals include an option to buy additional equipment in the future. For instance, a drug company may invest in a patent that allows it to exploit a new technology, an airline may acquire an option to buy a new aircraft, or a retailer may purchase adjoining land that has no immediate value but offers an opportunity to expand at a later date.

EXAMPLE 25.4 *Options to Expand*

Here is another disguised option that might arise in a capital budgeting analysis. You are considering the purchase of a tract of desert land that is known to contain gold deposits. Unfortunately, the cost of extraction is higher than the current price of gold. Does that mean the land is almost worthless? Not at all. You are not obliged to mine the gold, but ownership of the land gives you the *option* to do so. Of course, if you know that the gold price will remain below the extraction cost, then the option is worthless. But if there is uncertainty about future gold prices, you could be lucky and make a killing.

Buying the mine gives you an option to extract the gold. The exercise price of that option is the cost of extraction. In effect, you have a call option to acquire gold for the extraction cost. If there is a chance that gold prices will increase enough to make extraction profitable, the option will have value and might justify its cost, which is the purchase price of the land.

The Option to Abandon. Suppose that you need a new plant ready to produce turboencabulators in 3 years. You have a choice of designs. If design A is chosen, construction must begin immediately. Design B is more expensive but you can wait a year before breaking ground.

If you know with certainty that the plant will be needed, you should opt for design A. But suppose that there is some possibility that demand for turboencabulators will fall off and that in a year's time, you will decide the plant is not required. Then design B may be preferable because it gives you the option to bail out at low cost any time during the next 12 months.

You can think of the option to abandon as a put option. The exercise price of the put is the amount that you could recover if you abandon the project. The abandonment option makes design B more attractive by limiting the downside exposure; the worst outcome is that you receive the project's salvage value. The more uncertain is the need for the new plant, the more valuable is the downside protection offered by the abandonment option. As always, options are more valuable when the value of the underlying asset is more volatile.

It is also possible that, once built, design B can be readily converted to producing retrochrysalids, while design A has no alternative uses. Again, the extra flexibility provided by design B may tip the balance in its favour.

These are only two examples of options encountered in capital investment decisions. The others could fill (and have filled) entire books. If you look out for real options, you'll

FINANCE IN ACTION

Enron Builds a Real Option

In 1999 Enron Corporation planned to open gas-fired power plants in Mississippi and Tennessee. These plants were expected to sit idle most of the year, and, when operating, to produce electricity at a cost at least 50 percent higher than the most efficient state-of-the-art facilities. Is it time for the firm's board of directors to look for new management? Hardly. Enron's decision to build these power plants resulted from a sophisticated application of real options analysis.

The firm observed that electricity prices in an increasingly free energy market can be wildly volatile. For example, during some power shortages in the Midwest during the hot summer months of 1999, the cost of one megawatt-hour of electricity increased briefly from a typical level of $40 to several thousand dollars. The option to obtain additional energy in these situations obviously would be quite valuable.

Enron concluded that it would pay to build some cheap power plants, even if they were relatively high-cost electricity producers. Most of the time, the plants will sit idle, with market prices for electricity below the marginal cost of production. But every so often, when electricity prices spike, the plants can be fired up to produce electricity—at a great profit. Even if they operate only a few weeks a year, they can be positive-NPV investments.

These plants are in effect call options on electrical power. The options are currently out of the money, but the possibility that prices will increase makes these calls worth more than their price—the cost of building the plant. The decision to build them therefore makes Enron more valuable.

Note: This discussion is based on information found in the following article: "Exploiting Uncertainty: The 'Real Options' Revolution in Decision-Making," *Business Week*, June 7, 1999.

find them almost everywhere. The above Finance in Action box describes how a real options perspective was central to Enron's analysis of an investment in new power plants.

Whenever management can decide in the future how best to operate a project—for example, to expand, contract, delay, or abandon it—the project contains a real option.

CHECK POINT 25.7

A real estate developer buys 70 acres of land in a rural area, planning to build a subdivision on the land if and when the population from the city begins to expand into the area. If population growth is less than anticipated, the developer believes that the land can be sold to a country club that would build a golf course on the property.

a. In what way does the possibility of sale to the country club provide a put option to the developer?
b. What is the exercise price of the option? The asset value?
c. How does the golf course option increase the NPV of the land project to the developer?

OPTIONS ON FINANCIAL ASSETS

When companies issue securities, they often include an option in the package. Here are a few examples of the options that are associated with new financing.

warrant Right to buy shares from a company at a stipulated price before a set date.

Warrants. A **warrant** is a long-term call option on the company's stock. Unlike the Bombardier option that we considered earlier, a warrant is issued by the company. The company sells the warrant; the investor buys it.

A company that issues a bond will sometimes add some warrants as a "sweetener." Since these warrants are valuable to investors, they are prepared to pay a higher price for a package of bonds and warrants than for the bond on its own. Managers sometimes look with delight at this higher price, forgetting that in return the company has incurred a liability to sell its shares to the warrant holders at what, with hindsight, may turn out to be a low price.

Warrants may also be issued when a firm becomes bankrupt; the bankruptcy court offers the firm's bondholders warrants in the reorganized company as part of the settlement. For example, when Federated Department Stores was reorganized, it issued warrants, each of which entitled the owner to buy one share of Federated stock on or before December 19, 2001, at $29.92. Investors who held these warrants bet that the stock price would rise above $29.92, if not, their warrants would be worthless. The stock closed on December 19, 2001, at $36.25, a testimony to Federated's successful recovery from bankruptcy and generating a payoff of $6.33 (= $36.25 – $29.92) per share.

convertible bond Bond that the holder may exchange for a specified number of shares.

Convertible Bonds. The **convertible bond** is a close relative of the bond-warrant package. It allows the bondholder to exchange the bond for a given number of shares of common stock. Therefore, it is a package of a straight bond (that is, a bond that is not convertible) with a call option. The exercise price of the call option is the value of the straight bond. If the value of the stock exceeds the value of the straight bond, it will be profitable to convert.

EXAMPLE 25.5 *Convertible Bonds*

In November 2000 TELUS Corporation issued 10-year convertible bonds with a coupon rate of 6.75 percent. Each bond could be converted at any time before maturity into 25.2 shares of TELUS non-voting stock. In other words, the owner had a 10-year option to return the bond to TELUS and receive 25.2 shares in exchange. The number of shares that are received for each bond is called the bond's *conversion ratio.* The conversion ratio of the TELUS bond was 25.2.

In order to receive 25.2 shares of TELUS stock you had to surrender bonds with a face value of $1,000. Therefore, to receive *one* share, you had to surrender a face amount of 1,000/ 25.2 = $39.68. This figure is called the *conversion price.* Anybody who bought the bond at $1,000 in order to convert into 25.2 shares paid the equivalent of $39.68 per share.

The owner of a convertible bond owns a bond and a call option on the firm's stock. So does the owner of a package of a bond and a warrant. However, there are differences, the most important being that a convertible bond's owner must give up the bond to exercise the option. The owner of a package of bonds and warrants exercises the warrants for cash and keeps the bond.

The value of a convertible bond depends on its *bond value* and its *conversion value.* The bond value is what the bond would sell for if it could *not* be converted into stock. The conversion value is what the bond would be worth if it were converted immediately.

Since the owner of the convertible always has the option *not* to convert, bond value establishes a lower bound, or *floor,* to the price of a convertible. Of course, this floor is not completely flat. If the firm falls on hard times, the bond may not be worth much. In the extreme case where the firm becomes worthless, the bond is also worthless.

Conversion value is the value of the convertible bond if it were converted immediately. For example, the TELUS convertible in Example 25.5 could be exchanged for 25.2 shares. When the bonds were issued, the price of TELUS stock was $37.35. Thus the conversion value on this date was 25.2 × $37.35 = $941.32. A convertible can never sell for *less* than its conversion value. If it did, smart investors would buy the convertible, exchange it for stock, and sell the stock. Their profit would be the difference between the conversion value and the price of the convertible.

This means that there are two lower bounds to the price of any convertible: its bond value and its conversion value. When the firm does well, conversion value exceeds bond value; the investor would choose to convert if forced to make an immediate choice. Bond value exceeds conversion value when the firm does poorly. In these circumstances the investor would hold on to the bonds if forced to choose.

Convertible holders do not have to make a now-or-never choice for or against conversion. They can wait and then, with the benefit of hindsight, take whatever course turns out to give them the highest payoff. Thus a convertible is always worth *more* than both its bond value and its conversion value (except when time runs out at the bond's maturity).

Convertible bonds provide their holders with some protection if the price of the stock falls. But if the stock price zooms up, convertible bondholders share in the rise. In February 2001, the price of TELUS nonvoting shares hit $40, and the price of the convertible was $1150. By October 2001, the TELUS nonvoting shares had fallen to $18.70, but the convertible bond fell to $945. The stock price had fallen 53 percent but the bond price had fallen only 17.8 percent.

We stated earlier that it is useful to think of a convertible bond as a package of a straight bond and an option to buy the common stock in exchange for the straight bond. The value of this call option is equal to the difference between the convertible's selling price and its bond value.

CHECK POINT 25.8

a. What is the conversion value of the TELUS convertible bond if the stock price is $60? What is its conversion price?
b. Suppose that a straight (nonconvertible) bond issued by TELUS had been priced to yield 10 percent. What would the bond value of the TELUS 6.75 percent convertibles be at the time of issue? (Assume annual coupon payments.)

---

callable bond Bond that may be repurchased by the issuer before maturity at specified call price.

Callable Bonds. Unlike warrants and convertibles, which give the *investor* an option, a **callable bond** gives an option to the *issuer.* A company that issues a callable bond has an option to buy the bond back at the stated exercise or "call" price. Therefore, you can think of a callable bond as a *package* of a straight bond (a bond that is not callable) and a call option held by the issuer.

The option to call the bond is obviously attractive to the issuer. If interest rates decline and bond prices rise, the company has the opportunity to repurchase the bond at a fixed call price. Therefore, the option to call the bond puts a ceiling on the bond price.

Of course, when the company issues a callable bond, investors are aware of this ceiling on the bond price and will pay less for a callable bond than for a straight bond. The difference between the value of a straight bond and a callable bond with the same coupon rate and maturity is the value of the call option that investors have given to the company:

$$\text{Value of callable bond} = \text{value of straight bond} - \text{value of the issuer's call option}$$

CHECK POINT 25.9

"Extendable bonds" allow the investor to redeem the bond at par or let the bond remain outstanding until maturity. Suppose a 20-year extendable bond is issued with the investor allowed after 5 years to redeem the bond at par.

a. These bonds are sometimes called put bonds. Why? Who holds an implicit put option?
b. On what asset is the option written? (What asset do the option holders have the right to sell?)
c. What is the exercise price of the option?
d. In what circumstances will the option be exercised?

25.4 Summary

1. What is the payoff to buyers and sellers of call and put options?

There are two basic types of options. A **call option** is the right to buy an asset at a specific exercise price on or before the exercise date. A **put** is the right to sell an asset at a specific exercise price on or before the exercise date. The payoff to a call is the value of the asset minus the exercise price, if the difference is positive, and zero otherwise. The payoff to a put is the exercise price minus the value of the asset if the difference is positive, and zero otherwise. The payoff to the seller of an option is the negative of the payoff to the option buyer.

2. What are the determinants of option values?

The value of a call option depends on the following considerations:

- To exercise the call option you must pay the exercise price. Other things being equal, the less you are obliged to pay, the better. Therefore, the value of the option is higher when the exercise price is low relative to the stock price.
- Investors who buy the stock by way of a call option are buying on installment credit. They pay the purchase price of the option today, but they do not pay the exercise price until they exercise the option. The higher the rate of interest and the longer the time to expiration, the more this "free credit" is worth.
- No matter how far the stock price falls, the owner of the call cannot lose more than the price of the call. On the other hand, the more the stock price rises above the exercise price, the greater the profit on the call. Therefore, the option holder does not lose from increased variability if things go wrong, but gains if they go right. The value of the option increases with the variability of stock returns. Of course the longer the time to the final exercise date, the more opportunity there is for the stock price to vary.

3. What options may be present in capital investment proposals?

The importance of building flexibility into investment projects (discussed in Chapter 8) can be reformulated in the language of options. For example, many capital investments provide the flexibility to expand capacity in the future if demand turns out to be unusually buoyant. They are in effect providing the firm with a call option on the extra capacity. Firms also think about alternative uses for their assets if things go wrong. The option to abandon a project is a put option; the put's exercise price is the value of the project's assets if shifted to an alternative use. The ability to expand or to abandon are both examples of **real options.**

4. What options may be provided in financial securities?

Many of the securities that firms issue contain an option. For example, a **warrant** is nothing but a long-term call option issued by the firm. **Convertible bonds** give the investor the option to buy the firm's stock in exchange for the value of the underlying bond. Unlike warrants and convertibles, which give an option to the investor, **callable bonds** give the option to the issuing firm. If interest rates decline and the value of the underlying bond rises, the firm can buy the bonds back at a specified exercise price.

Related Web Links

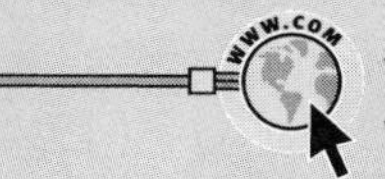

www.cbot.com The Chicago Board of Trade offers information, simulations, and product descriptions on options and futures

www.cme.com The Chicago Mercantile Exchange is a major centre for options and futures trading

www.cboe.com Chicago Board Options Exchange

www.m-x.ca Bourse de Montréal, Canadian Derivatives Exchange

www.pmpublishing.com/volatility Analyses of options data from the major commodity exchanges, including historical implied volatilities and volatility graphs, along with comprehensive online pricing function

www.numa.com/index.htm Information about financial derivatives of all kinds

www.ace.uiuc.edu/ofor The Office for Futures and Options Research at the University of Illinois at Urbana-Champaign

www.real-options.com The real-options approach to valuing projects

www.adtrading.com/beginners/index.cfm Information on trading options and futures
www.canola.ab.ca Options and futures quotes for grains, and information about canola
www.futuresindustry.org Current information on trading options

KEY TERMS

call option	739	real options	751	convertible bond	753
put option	739	warrant	752	callable bond	754

QUESTIONS AND PROBLEMS

*Answers in Appendix B

BASIC

*1. **Option Payoffs.** Turn back to Figure 25.2, which lists prices of various Bombardier options. Use the data in the figure to calculate the payoff and the profits for investments in each of the following April 2002 maturity options, assuming that the stock price on the expiration date is $15.

a. call option with exercise price of $12.50
b. put option with exercise price of $12.50
c. call option with exercise price of $15
d. put option with exercise price of $15
e. call option with exercise price of $17.50
f. call option with exercise price of $22.50

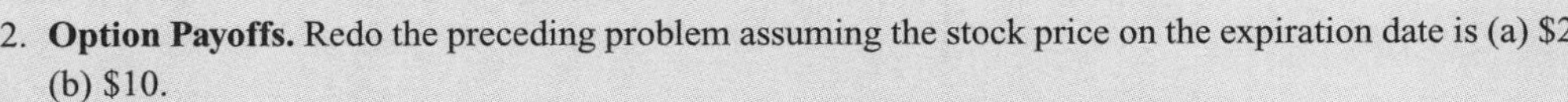

2. **Option Payoffs.** Redo the preceding problem assuming the stock price on the expiration date is (a) $21 (b) $10.

*3. **Determinants of Option Value.** Look at the data in Figure 25.2

a. What is the price of a call option with an exercise price of $15 and expiration in October? What if expiration is in April?
b. Why do you think the April calls cost more than the October calls?
c. Is the same true of put options? Why?

4. **Option Contracts.** Fill in the blanks by choosing the appropriate terms from the following list: call, exercise, put.

A(n) ________ option gives its owner the opportunity to buy a stock at a specific price which is generally called the ________ price. A(n) ________ option gives its owner the opportunity to sell stock at a specified ________ price.

*5. **Option Payoffs.** Note Figure 25.8*a* and 25.8*b*. Match each figure with one of the following positions and draw the figures for the positions not shown:

a. call buyer
b. call seller
c. put buyer
d. put seller

6. **Puts versus Calls.** The buyer of a call and the seller of a put both hope that the stock price will rise. Therefore the two positions are identical. Is this true? Illustrate with a simple example and show graphically.

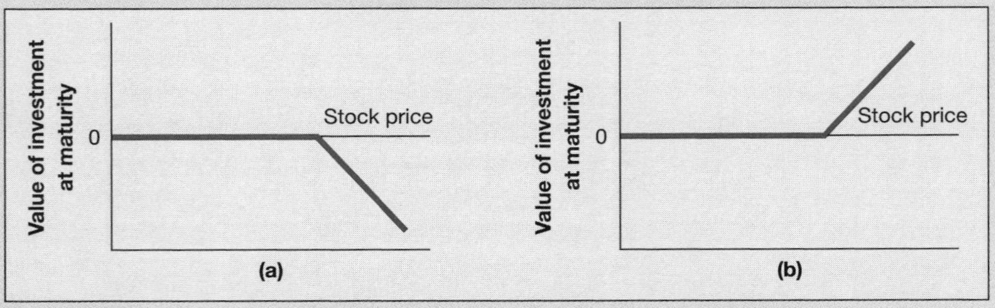

FIGURE 25.8
See problem 5

*7. **Hedging with Options.** Suppose that you hold a share of stock and a put option on that share with an exercise price of $100. Show algebraically and graphically the value of your portfolio when the option expires if

a. the stock price is below $100.
b. the stock price is above $100.

PRACTICE

8. **Option Portfolios.** Mixing options and securities can often create interesting payoffs. For each of the following combinations show what the payoff would be when the option expires if (1) the stock price is below the exercise price, and (2) the stock price is above the exercise price. Illustrate the payoffs with graphs. Assume that each option has the same exercise price and expiration date.

a. Buy a call and invest the present value of the exercise price in a bank deposit.
b. Buy a share and a put option on the share.
c. Buy a share, buy a put option on the share, and sell a call option on the share.
d. Buy a call option and a put option on the share.

*9. **Option Values.** What is the lower bound to the price of a call option? What is the upper bound?

10. **Option Values.** What is a call option worth if

a. the stock price is zero?
b. the stock price is extremely high relative to the exercise price?

*11. **Option Valuation.** Figure 25.2 shows call options on Bombardier stock with the same exercise date in January and with exercise prices $11.50, $12.50, and $13.50. Notice that the price of the middle call option (with exercise price $12.50) is less than halfway between the prices of the other two calls (with exercise prices $11.50 and $13.50). Suppose that this were not the case. For example, suppose that the price of the middle call were the average of the prices of the other two calls. Show that if you sell two of the middle calls and use the proceeds to buy one each of the other calls, your proceeds in January may be positive but cannot be negative despite the fact that your net outlay today is zero. What can you deduce from this example about option pricing?

12. **Put Prices.** How does the price of a *put* option respond to the following changes, other things being equal? Does the put price go up or down?

a. Stock price increases.
b. Exercise price is increased.
c. Risk-free interest rate increases.
d. Expiration date of the option is extended.
e. Volatility of the stock price falls.
f. Time passes, so the option's expiration date comes closer.

*13. **Option Values.** As manager of United Bedstead you own substantial executive stock options. These options entitle you to buy the firm's shares during the next 5 years at a price of $100 a share. The plant manager has just outlined two alternative proposals to re-equip the plant. Both proposals have the same net present value but one is substantially riskier than the other. At first you are undecided about which to choose, but then you remember your stock options. How might these influence your choice?

14. **Real and Financial Options.** Are these put or call options? Fill in the blanks:

a. An oil company acquires mining rights to a silver deposit. It is not obliged to mine the silver, however. The company has effectively acquired a ________ option, where the exercise price is the cost of opening the mine and extracting the silver.
b. Some preferred shareholders have the right to redeem their shares at par value after a specified date. (If they hand over their shares, the firm sends them a cheque equal to the shares' par value.) These shareholders have a ________ option.

c. A firm buys a standard machine with a ready secondhand market. The secondhand market gives the firm a ________ option.

*15. **Real Options.** What is the option in each of the following cases. Is it a call or a put?

a. Western Telecom commits to production of digital switching equipment specifically designed for the European market. As a stand-alone venture, the project has a negative NPV, but it is justified by the need for a strong market position in the rapidly growing, and potentially very profitable, market.

b. Western Telecom vetoes a fully integrated automated production line for the new digital switches. It will rely on standard, less expensive equipment even though the automated production line would be more efficient overall using the specialized equipment, according to a discounted-cash-flow calculation.

16. **Real Options**. Describe each of the following situations in the language of options.

a. Drilling rights to undeveloped heavy crude oil in Alberta. Development and production of the oil now is a negative-NPV endeavour. The break-even price is $32 per barrel, versus a spot price of $20. However, the decision to develop can be put off for up to 5 years.

b. A restaurant producing net cash flows, after all out-of-pocket expenses of $700,000 per year. There is no upward or downward trend in the cash flows, but they fluctuate. The real estate occupied by the restaurant is owned, and it could be sold for $5 million.

*17. **Real Options.** Price support systems for various agricultural products have allowed farmers to sell their crops to the government for a specified "support price." What kind of option has the government given to the farmers? What is the exercise price?

18. **Implicit Options.** Some investment management contracts give the portfolio manager a bonus proportional to the amount by which a portfolio return exceeds a specified threshold.

a. In what way is this an implicit call option on the portfolio?

b. Can you think of a way in which such contracts can lead to incentive problems? For example, what happens to the value of the prospective bonus if the manager invests in high-volatility stocks?

*19. **Implicit Options.** The Rank and File Company is considering a stock issue to raise $50 million. An underwriter offers to guarantee the success of the issue by buying any unwanted stock at the $25 issue price. The underwriter's fee is $2 million.

a. What kind of option does Rank and File acquire if it accepts the underwriter's offer?

b. What determines the value of the option?

20. **Implicit Options.**

a. Some banks have offered their customers an unusual type of time deposit. The deposit does not pay any interest if the market falls, but instead the depositor receives a proportion of any rise in the Standard & Poor's Index. What implicit option do the investors hold? How should the bank invest the money in order to protect itself against the risk of offering this deposit?

b. You can also make a deposit with a bank that does not pay interest if the market index rises but which makes an increasingly large payment as the market index falls. How should the bank protect itself against the risk of offering this deposit?

*21. **Loan Guarantees.** The CDIC (Canadian Deposit Insurance Corporation), insures bank deposits. If a bank's assets are insufficient to pay off all depositors, the CDIC will contribute enough money to ensure that all depositors can be paid off in full. (We ignore the $60,000 maximum coverage on each account.) In what way is this guarantee of deposits the provision of a put option by the CDIC? *Hint*: Write out the funds the CDIC will have to contribute when bank assets are less than deposits owed to depositors. What is the exercise price of the put option?

22. **Real Options.** After dramatic increases in oil prices in the 1970s, the United States government funded several projects to create synthetic oil or natural gas from abundant U.S. supplies of coal and

oil shale. Although the cost of producing such synthetic fuels at the time was greater than the price of oil, it was argued that the projects still could be justified for their insurance value, since the cost of synthetic fuel would be essentially fixed while the price of oil was risky. Evaluate the synthetic fuel program as an option on fuel sources. Is it a call or a put option? What is the exercise price? How would uncertainty in the future price of oil affect the amount the United States should have been willing to spend on such projects?

*23. **Arbitrage Opportunities.**

a. Circular File stock is selling for $25 a share. You see that call options on the stock with exercise price of $20 are selling at $3. What should you do? What will happen to the option price as investors identify this opportunity?

b. Now you observe that put options on Circular File with exercise price $30 are selling for $4. What should you do?

24. **Implicit Options.** A 10-year maturity convertible bond with a 6 percent coupon on a company with a bond rating of AAA is selling for $1,050. Each bond can be exchanged for 20 shares, and the stock price currently is $50 per share. Other AAA-rated bonds with the same maturity would sell at a yield to maturity of 8 percent. What is the value of the implicit call option on the bond? Why is the bond selling for more than the value of the shares it can be converted into?

CHALLENGE

25. **Option Pricing.** Look again at the Ballard Power System call option that we valued in Section 25.3. Suppose that by the end of January the price of Ballard stock could rise to $40.50 or fall to $14.50. Everything else is unchanged from our example.

a. What would be the value of the Ballard call at the end of January if the stock price is $40.50? If it is $14.50?

b. Show that a strategy of buying 13 calls provides exactly the same payoffs as borrowing the present value of $58 from the bank and buying four shares.

c. What is the net cash flow in September from the policy of borrowing PV($58) and buying four shares?

d. What does this tell you about the value of the call option?

e. Why is the value of the call option different from the value that we calculated in Section 25.2? What does this tell you about the relationship between the value of a call and the volatility of the share price?

*26. **Option Pricing.** Look once more at the Ballard call option that we valued in Section 25.3. Suppose that the interest rate on bank loans is zero. Recalculate the value of the Ballard call option. What does this tell you about the relationship between interest rates and the value of a call?

INTERNET PROBLEMS

1. Visit the Canadian Derivatives Exchange at the Bourse de Montréal, www.m-x.ca, and look up current prices of call and put options on Canadian equity by clicking on "Options List." Find examples to illustrate the effect on the prices of call and put options from an increase in the exercise price. Repeat for an increase in the time to expiration.

2. What other options are traded on the Canadian Derivatives Exchange? Try to explain what these options are.

3. The application of option pricing models to real options is a rapidly expanding field of finance. Although much of the details are beyond this textbook in scope, check out the visual discussion of real options at www.puc-rio.br/marco.ind/faqs.html. A good list of readings is found at www.realoptions-software.com/articles.htm.

Solutions to Check Points

25.1 a. The call with exercise price $17.50 costs $.35. If the stock price at maturity is $10, the call expires valueless and the investor loses the entire $.35. If the stock price is $20, the value of the call is $20 – $17.50 = $2.50, and the investor's profit is $2.50 – $.35 = $2.15.

b. The put costs $1.45. If the stock price at maturity is $10, the put value at expiration is $13.50 – $10 = $3.50 and the investor's profit is $3.50 – $1.45 = $2.05. If the stock price is $20, the value of the put is zero, and the investor's loss is the price paid for the put, $1.45.

25.2 a. The call seller receives $.35 for writing the call. If the stock price at maturity is $10, the call expires valueless, and the investor keeps the entire $.35 as a profit. If the stock price is $20, the value of the call is $20 – $17.50 = $2.50. In other words, the option seller must deliver a stock worth $20 for an exercise price of only $17.50. The investor's net profit is $.35 – $2.50 = –$2.15. The call seller will clear a positive net profit as long as the stock price remains below $17.85 (the exercise price plus option selling price).

b. The put seller receives $1.45 for writing the put. If the stock price at maturity is $10, the put value at expiration is $13.50 – $10 = $3.50. In other words, the put option seller must pay an exercise price of $13.50 to buy a stock worth only $10. The seller's loss is $3.50 – $1.45 = $2.05. If the stock price is $20, the final value of the put is zero, and the investor's profit is the price originally received for the put, $1.45.

25.3 This payoff can be achieved by buying a share of stock, *buying* a put option on the stock with exercise price $11.50, and *selling* a call option on the stock with exercise price $15.50. If the stock price falls below $11.50, the call will expire valueless, and the put will allow you to sell the share for $11.50. Therefore, the strategy offers protection against the stock price falling below $11.50. If the stock price rises above $15.50, the put will be valueless and the call will be exercised against you; you will have to deliver the stock for an exercise price of $15.50. Thus the maximum value of the position will be $15.50.

Such a strategy might be appropriate for an investor who wishes to take a position in the stock, wants downside protection, and is willing to pay for that protection by selling a call option and thereby forfeiting upside potential beyond a price of $15.50. The call sold offsets the cost of the put purchased. Extremely poor investment performance is eliminated at the cost of also eliminating the potential for extremely good returns.

25.4 The value of a put option is higher when the exercise price is higher. You would be willing to pay more for the right to sell a stock at a high price than the right to sell it at a low price.

25.5 First consider the payoff to the put holder in the lower volatility scenario:

Stock price	$25	$35
Put value	$ 5	$ 0

In the higher volatility scenario, the value of the stock can be $20 or $40. Now the payoff to the put is

Stock price	$20	$40
Put value	$10	$ 0

The expected value of the payoff of the put doubles.

25.6 The payoffs are as follows:

		Payoff in 3 Months if Stock Price Equals	
	Cash Flow Today	**$23.50**	**$94**
Strategy A	?	$ 0	+$141 (= 3 × [94 – 47])
Buy three calls			
Strategy B			
Buy two shares	–$94	+$47	+$188
Borrow PV($47)	– 46.53	– 47	– 47
	–$47.47	$ 0	+$141

Note: PV($47) at an interest rate of 1 percent for 3 months is 47/1.01 = $46.53.

The initial net cash outflow from strategy B is $47.47. Since the three calls offer the same payoffs in the future, they also cost $47.47. One call is worth 47.47/3 = $15.82.

25.7 a. The developer has the option to sell the potential housing development to the country club. This abandonment option is like a put that guarantees a minimum payoff from the investment.

b. The exercise price of the option is the price at which it can be sold to the country club at. The asset value is the present value of the project if maintained as a housing development. If this value is less than the value as a golf course, the project will be sold.

c. The abandonment option increases NPV by placing a lower bound on the possible payoffs from the project.

25.8 a. Conversion value = 25.2 × $60 = $1,512
Conversion price = $1,000/25.2 = $39.68 (unchanged)

b. Bond value = $67.50 × 10-year annuity factor at 10% + $1,000 × 10-year PV factor at 10%
= $414.76 + 385.54 = $800.3

25.9 a., b. In 5 years, the bond will be a 15-year maturity bond. The bondholder can sell the bond back to the firm at par value. The bondholder therefore has a put option to sell a 15-year bond for par value even if interest rates have risen and the bond would otherwise sell below par.

c. The exercise price is the par value of the bond.

d. The bondholder will extend the loan if interest rates decrease.

Appendix 25A: The Black-Scholes Option Valuation Model[1]

In this appendix you will learn how to price call options with the famous Black-Scholes option pricing formula.

We showed you a simple option-valuation model on page 750. Known as the *binomial model*, it illustrates the general principal of option valuation: Find a combination of borrowing and an investment in the stock that exactly replicates the payoffs from the option. If we can price the stock and the loan, we can also price the option. In general,

Value of call option = [delta × current stock price] – [bank loan]

The delta, or hedge ratio, is the number of shares to purchase. The bank loan is the present value of the amount needed to make the combination of the stock and loan cash flows equal to the option's cash flows at the option's expiry.

In the binomial model, the delta is equal to the ratio of the spread of possible option prices to the spread of possible stock prices at the time of the option's expiry. The bank loan is the present value of the difference between the payoffs from the option and the payoffs from the shares at the option's expiry.

In our Ballard example, we determined the price of a 4-month call option with an exercise price of $32.50. Let's use the formula to price the option.

EXAMPLE 25A.1

The current Ballard stock price is $25. We assume that the stock price will be either $16 or $38 in 4 months. Thus the call option will be worth either $0, or $38 – $32.50 = $5.50 at expiry.

The delta of the leveraged investment in the stock is ($5.50 – 0)/($38 – $16), or .25. Thus you should buy one-quarter of a share. The cost of the stock purchase is one-quarter of $25, or $6.25.

The bank loan is the present value of difference between the possible option payoffs and payoffs from one-quarter of a share at maturity. If the stock price turns out to be $16, the payoff from owning one-quarter of a share is .25 × $16 = $4, and the payoff from the option is zero. The difference in the payoffs is $4 – 0, or $4. Likewise, if the stock price turns out to be $38, the payoff from one-quarter of a share is .25 × $38, or $9.50, and from the option is $5.50, also giving a difference of $4. With a 1 percent 4-month interest rate, the bank loan needed is $4/(1.01) = $3.96.

Putting all the pieces together gives the value of Ballard's $32.50 4-month call option:

Value of call option = [delta × current stock price] – [bank loan] = $6.25 – $3.96 = $2.29

The concept of valuing an option by valuing a levered investment that replicates the option's cash flows is completely general. However, the binomial method allows the stock price only two possible changes, giving only two possible future stock prices. This might be reasonable over a very short time but not sensible over a longer time period.

We could make the problem slightly more realistic by assuming that there were two possible changes in the stock price in each two-month period. That would give a wider range of 4-month prices. But why stop at two-month periods? Take shorter and shorter intervals,

[1] This appendix draws on Chapter 20 of R. Brealey and S. Myers, *Principals of Corporate Finance*, 6th ed. (Boston, MA: McGraw-Hill, 2000).

allowing two price changes per each period. Eventually, we would reach a situation in which the stock price was changing continuously and generating a continuum of possible prices at the end of 4 months.

Calculating the value of this levered investment may sound like a hopelessly tedious business, but Black and Scholes derived a formula that does the trick. Although it looks unpleasant, it is very powerful:

$$\text{Value of call option} = [\text{delta} \times \text{current stock price}, P] - [\text{bank loan}]$$
$$= [N(d_1) \times P] - [N(d_2) \times \text{PV(EX)}]$$

where

$d_1 = \dfrac{\ln [\text{P/PV(EX)}]}{\sigma\sqrt{t}} + \dfrac{\sigma\sqrt{t}}{2}$

$d_2 = d_1 - \sigma\sqrt{t}$

$N(d)$ = cumulative standard normal probability density function[2]

EX = exercise price of option; PV(EX) is calculated by discounting at the risk-free interest rate, r_f

t = number of periods to expiration date

P = price of stock now

σ = standard deviation per period of (continuously compounded) rate of return on stock, also called volatility

To derive their formula, Black and Scholes assumed that there is a continuum of stock prices, and therefore to replicate an option, investors must continuously adjust their holdings of stocks. Of course, this can't be done in the real world. Despite this, the formula works remarkably well in practice, where stocks trade intermittently and prices jump from one level to another. The Black-Scholes model has also proven very flexible; it can be adapted to value options on a variety of assets with special features, such as foreign currency, bonds, and futures. It is not surprising therefore that is has been extremely influential and become the standard model for valuing options. Every day, dealers on options exchanges use this formula to make huge trades. These dealers are not for the most part trained in the formula's mathematical derivation; they just use a computer or a special programmed calculator to find the value of the option.

EXAMPLE 25A.2

Let's apply the Black-Scholes formula to the pricing of a 6-month call option with an exercise price of $90 on a stock with a current price of $85. The standard deviation of the annual stock return is 32 percent. The 6-month interest rate is 2.5 percent.

Price of stock now = P = $85

Exercise price = $85

Standard deviation of continuously compounded annual returns = σ = .32, or 32 percent

Years to maturity = $t = 6/12 = .5$

Interest rate per 6 month = r = 2.5 percent

[2] That is, $N(d)$ is the probability that a standardized, normally distributed random variable, z, will be less than or equal to d. $N(d_1)$ in the Black-Scholes formula is the option delta, the number of shares to purchase. Thus the formula tells us that the value of a call is equal to an investment of $N(d_1)$ in the common stock, less borrowing of $N(d_2) \times$ PV(EX).

Step 1: Calculate d_1 and d_2. Just plug the numbers into the formula, noting that "ln" means *natural log*:

$$d_1 = \ln[P/PV(EX)]/\sigma\sqrt{t} + \sigma\sqrt{t}/2$$
$$= \ln[85/(85/1.025)] / (.32 \times \sqrt{.5}) + (.32 \times \sqrt{.5})/2 = .2223$$
$$d_2 = d_1 - \sigma\sqrt{t} = .2223 - (.32 \times \sqrt{.5}) = -.004$$

Step 2: Find N(d_1) and N(d_2). N(d_1) is the probability of observing a standard normal variable of less than d_1. A simple way to find N(d_1) is to use the Excel function "Normsdist." For example, if you enter Normsdist(.2223) into an Excel spreadsheet, you will find that there is a .5879 probability that a standard normal variable will be less than .2223. Likewise, N(d_2) can be found as Normsdist(-.004) = .4984.

You can also use a cumulative normal probability table, such as Table 25A.1. The table shows the probability (N(d)) of observing a value less than or equal to d. To get the probability for negative value of d, find the probability for the positive value and subtract it from 1. With d_1 = .2223, round it to .22, and then from the table you'll find the probability is .5871. For a more accurate number, interpolate between the probabilities for d_1 = .22 and d_1 = .23. To find the cumulative probability for d_2 = –.004, round it first to zero, which has a probability of .5. To interpolate, also look up the value for +.01 which is .5040. Since .004 is 40 percent of the distance between 0 and 1, the interpolated probability of .004 is .5 + .4 (.504 – .5) = .5016. Now subtract it from 1 to get N(d_2) = 1 – .5016 = .4984.

Step 3: Plug these numbers into the Black-Scholes formula. You can now calculate the value of the call:

$$= [\text{delta} \times \text{current stock price}, P] - [\text{bank loan}]$$
$$= [N(d_1) \times P] - [N(d_2) \times PV(EX)]$$
$$= [.5879 \times 85] - [0.4984 \times 90/1.025] = 6.46$$

The Black-Scholes call option price is $6.46.

CHECK POINT 25A.1

Using the data from Example 25A.1, price the Ballard call option using the Black-Scholes formula. Assume the stock's return standard deviation is 80 percent per year. Recalculate it with a volatility of 30 percent per year. Explain what you find.

In all of the examples so far, the risk-free interest rate has equalled the length of the option. To get the interest rate to use in the formula, calculate the 6-month interest rate equivalent to the annual rate: $r = (1.08)^{.5} - 1$, or 3.923 percent.[3]

[3] To be completely accurate, the interest rate should be continuously compounded. To learn more, consult an options pricing book, such as John Hull's, *Fundamentals of Futures and Options Markets*, 4th ed. (Englewood Cliffs, NJ: Prentice-Hall, 2002).

TABLE 25A.1
Cumulative probabilty [N(d)] that a normally distributed variable will be less than d *standard deviations above the mean*

d	0	0.01	0.02	0.03	0.04	0.05	0.06	0.07	0.08	0.09
0	.5000	.5040	.5080	.5120	.5160	.5199	.5239	.5279	.5319	.5359
0.1	.5398	.5438	.5478	.5517	.5557	.5996	.5636	.5675	.5714	.5753
0.2	.5793	.5832	.5871	.5910	.5948	.5987	.6026	.6064	.6103	.6141
0.3	.6179	.6217	.6255	.6293	.6331	.6368	.6406	.6443	.6480	.6517
0.4	.6554	.6591	.6628	.6664	.6700	.6736	.6772	.6808	.6844	.6879
0.5	.6915	.6950	.6985	.7019	.7054.	7088	.7123	.7157	.7190	.7224
0.6	.7257	.7291	.7324	.7357	.7389	.7422	.7454	.7486	.7517	.7549
0.7	.7580	.7611	.7642	.7673	.7704	.7734	.7764	.7794	.7823	.7852
0.8	.7881	.7910	.7939	.7967	.7995	.8023	.8051	.8078	.8106	.8133
0.9	.8159	.8126	.8212	.8238	.8264	.8289	.8315	.8340	.8365	.8389
1	.8413	.8438	.8461	.8485	.8508	.8531	.8554	.8577	.8599	.8621
1.1	.8643	.8665	.8686	.8708	.8729	.8749	.8770	.8790	.8810	.8830
1.2	.8849	.8869	.8888	.8907	.8925	.8944	.8962	.8980	.8997	.9015
1.3	.9032	.9049	.9066	.9082	.9099	.9115	.9131	.9147	.9162	.9177
1.4	.9192	.9207	.9222	.9236	.9251	.9265	.9279	.9292	.9306	.9319
1.5	.9332	.9345	.9357	.9370	.9382	.9394	.9406	.9418	.9429	.9441
1.6	.9452	.9483	.9474	.9484	.9495	.9506	.9515	.9525	.9835	.9545
1.7	.9554	.9564	.9573	.9582	.9591	.9599	.9608	.9616	,9625	.9633
1.8	.9641	.9649	.9656	.9664	.9671	.9678	.9685	.9693	.9699	.9706
1.9	.9713	.9719	.9726	.9732	.9738	.9744	.9750	.9756	.9761	.9767
2	.9772	.9778	.9783	.9788	.9793	.9798	.9803	.9808	.9812	.9817
2.1	.9821	.9826	.9830	.9834	.9838	.9842	.9846	.9850	.9854	.9857
2.2	.9861	.9864	.9868	.9871	.9875	.9878	.9881	.9884	.9887	.9890
2.3	.9803	.9896	.9898	.9901	.9904	.9906	.9909	.9911	.9913	.9916
2.4	.9918	.9920	.9922	.9925	.9927	.9929	.9931	.9932	.9934	.9936
2.5	.9918	.9940	.9941	.9943	.9945	.9946	.9948	.9949	.9951	.9952

E.g.: If $d = .22$, N(d) = .5871 (i.e., there is a .5871 probability that a normally distributed variable will be less than .22 standard deviations above the mean). If $d = -.51$, N(d) = 1 – N (+ .51) = 1 – .6950 = .305.

QUESTIONS AND PROBLEMS

*Answers in Appendix B

BASIC

1. **Binomial Model.** Over the coming year Chance Manufacturing's stock price will halve to $50 from its current level of $100, or it will rise to $200. The 1-year interest rate is 10 percent.
   a. What is the delta of a 1-year call option on Chance stock with an exercise price of $100?
   b. Create a table showing the cash flows from an investment in the stock and borrowing to replicate the option's cash flows. Explain what you have done.
   c. What is the price of the call option?
2. **Black-Scholes Formula**. A call option written on a stock selling for $10 has an exercise price of $12. The call expires in 9 months. The stock's standard deviation of return is 30 percent per year and the risk-free interest rate is 1 percent per month.
   a. What is the Black-Scholes price of the call?
   b. What is the price if the call expires in 3 months? Why is it lower than the price you found in part (a)?

PRACTICE

3. **Using Black-Scholes Formula.** Instead of using the Black-Scholes formula to estimate option values in reference to volatility, it is sometimes useful to turn the question around and back out the volatility

implied in option prices. A 3-month call option with a \$10 exercise price is trading for \$.558, and the current stock price is \$9.75. If the risk-free interest rate is 2 percent per 3 months (or $(1.02)^4 - 1 = .0824$ per year), what is the implied volatility of the stock?

Solutions to Check Point

25A.1 With P = \$25, EX = \$32.50, t = 4/12, or 1/3, r = 0.01 and $\sigma = .8$, the values of d_1 and d_2 are

$d_1 = \ln[25/(32.5/1.01)]/(.8 \times \sqrt{.333}) + (.8 \times \sqrt{.333})/2 = -.3159$

$d_2 = -.3159 - (.80 \times \sqrt{.333}) = -.7776$

Next, find $N(d_1)$ and $N(d_2)$:

The value of d_1 is 59 percent way between –.31 and –.32. Look up the probabilities of +.31 and +.32 in Table 25A.1. We see that N(+.31) =.6217 and N(+.32) = .6255. Thus N(+.3159) = .6217 + .59(.6255 – .6217) = .6239. Thus, $N(d_1) = 1 - .6239 = .3761$. Note that d_2 is 76 percent of the distance between –.77 and –.78. Thus N(+.7776) = .7794 + .76(.7823 –.7794) = .7816 and $N(d_2) = 1 - .7816 = .2184$

Substitute into the Black-Scholes formula:

Price of call = [.3761 × 25] – [.2184 × 32.5/1.01] = 9.403 – 7.028 = 2.38.

With 80 percent volatility, the call price is \$2.38.

With only 30 percent volatility, the value of d_1 is –1.3715 and d_2 is –1.5446. $N(d_1)$ is .0851 and $N(d_2)$ is 1 – [.9382 + .46(.9394 – .9382)] = .0612. The price of the call option is = [.0851 × 25] – [.0612 × 32.5/1.01] = .158, or about \$.16.

With a standard deviation of the stock return of 80 percent, compared to 30 percent, there is a much higher probability that the stock price will be at least \$32.50 when the option expires. Therefore, with 80 percent volatility, call option is worth much more than with only 30 percent volatility.

Note: Your answer may vary slightly depending on the number of decimal places you use in your calculations.

CHAPTER 26

Risk Management

26.1 Why Hedge?
26.2 Reducing Risk with Options
26.3 Futures Contracts
26.4 Forward Contracts
26.5 Swaps
26.6 Is "Derivative" a Four-Letter Word
26.7 Summary

We often assume that risk is beyond our control. A business is exposed to unpredictable changes in raw material costs, tax rates, technology, and a long list of other variables. There's nothing the manager can do about it.

This is not wholly true. To some extent a manager can *select* the risks of an asset or business. For example, in the last chapter we saw that companies can consciously affect the risk of an investment by building in flexibility. A company that reduces the cost of bailing out of a project by using standardized equipment is taking less risk than a similar firm that uses specialized equipment with no alternative uses. In this case the option to resell the equipment serves as an insurance policy.

Sometimes, rather than building flexibility into the project, companies accept the risk but then use financial instruments to offset it. This practice of taking offsetting risks is known as *hedging.* In this chapter we will explain how hedging works and we will describe some of the specialized financial instruments that have been devised to help manage risk. These instruments include options, futures, forwards, and swaps. Each of these instruments provides a payoff that depends on the price of some underlying commodity or financial asset. Because their payoffs derive from the prices of other assets, they are often known collectively as *derivative instruments* (or *derivatives* for short).[1]

After reading this chapter you should be able to

- Understand why companies hedge to reduce risk.
- Use options, futures, and forward contracts to devise simple hedging strategies.
- Explain how companies can use swaps to change the risk of securities that they have issued.

[1] Derivatives often conjure up an image of wicked speculators. Derivative instruments attract their share of speculators, some of whom may be wicked, but they are also used by sober and prudent businesspeople who simply want to reduce risk.

26.1

Why Hedge?

In this chapter we will explain *how* companies use derivatives to hedge the risks of their business. But first we should give some of the reasons *why* they do it.

Hedging is seldom free. Most businesses hedge to reduce risk, not to make money. Why then bother to hedge? For one thing, reducing the risk makes financial planning easier and reduces the odds of an embarrassing shortfall. A shortfall might mean only an unexpected trip to the bank, but in extreme cases it could trigger bankruptcy. Why not reduce the odds of these awkward outcomes with a hedge?

We saw in our discussion of debt policy in Chapter 15 that financial distress can result in indirect as well as direct costs to a firm. Costs of financial distress arise from disruption to normal business operations as well as from the effect financial distress has on the firm's investment decisions. The better the risk management policies, the less the risk and expected costs of financial distress. As a side benefit, better risk management increases the firm's debt capacity.

In some cases hedging also makes it easier to decide whether an operating manager deserves a stern lecture or a pat on the back. Suppose that your export division shows a 50 percent decline in profits when the dollar unexpectedly strengthens against other currencies. How much of that decrease is due to the exchange rate shift and how much to poor management? If the company had protected itself against the effect of exchange rate changes, it's probably bad management. If it wasn't protected, you have to make a judgment with hindsight, probably by asking, "What would profits have been *if* the firm had hedged against exchange rate movements?"

Finally, hedging extraneous events can help focus the operating manager's attention. We know we shouldn't worry about events outside our control, but most of us do anyway. It's naive to expect the manager of the export division not to worry about exchange rate movements if his bottom line and bonus depend on them. The time spent worrying could be better spent if the company hedged itself against such movements.

A sensible risk strategy must answer the following questions:

- *What are the major risks that the company faces and what are the possible consequences?* Some risks are scarcely worth a thought, but there are others that might bankrupt the company.
- *Is the company being paid for taking these risks?* Managers are not paid to avoid all risks, but if they can reduce their exposure to risks for which there are no compensating rewards, they can afford to place larger bets when the odds are stacked in their favour.
- *Can the company take any measures to reduce the probability of a bad outcome or to limit its impact?* For example, most businesses install alarm and sprinkler systems to prevent damage from fire and invest in backup facilities in case damage does occur.
- *Can the company purchase fairly priced insurance to offset any losses?* Insurance companies have some advantages in bearing risk. In particular, they may be able to spread the risk across a portfolio of different insurers.
- *Can the company use derivatives, such as options or futures, to hedge the risk?* In the remainder of this chapter we explain when and how derivatives may be used.

26.2

Reducing Risk with Options

In the last chapter we introduced you to put and call options. Managers regularly buy options on currencies, interest rates, and commodities to limit their downside risk. Many of these options are traded on options exchanges, but often they are simply private deals between the corporation and a bank.

Petrochemical Parfum, Inc., is concerned about potential increases in the price of heavy crude oil, which is one of its major inputs. To protect itself against such increases, Petrochemical buys 6-month options to purchase 1,000 barrels of crude oil at an exercise price of $20. These options might cost $.50 per barrel.

If the price of crude is above the $20 exercise price when the options expire, Petrochemical will exercise the options and will receive the difference between the oil price and the exercise price. If the oil price falls below the exercise price, the options will expire worthless. The net cost of oil will therefore be

	Oil Price, Dollars per Barrel		
	$18	**$20**	**$22**
Cost of 1,000 barrels	$18,000	$20,000	$22,000
− Payoff on call option	0	0	2,000
Net cost	$18,000	$20,000	$20,000

You can see that by buying options Petrochemical protects itself against increases in the oil price while continuing to benefit from oil price decreases. If prices fall, it can discard its call option and buy its oil at the market price. If oil prices rise, however, it can exercise its call option to purchase oil for $20 a barrel. Therefore, options create an attractive asymmetry. Of course, this asymmetry comes at a price—the $500 cost of the options.

EXAMPLE 26.1 *Hedging with Options*

Consider now the problem of Onnex, Inc., which supplies Petrochemical with crude oil. Its problem is the mirror image of Petrochemical's; it loses when oil prices fall and gains when oil prices rise.

Onnex wants to lock in a minimum price of oil but still benefit from rising oil prices. It can do so by purchasing *put* options that give it the right to *sell* oil at an exercise price of $20 per barrel. If oil prices fall, it will exercise the put. If they rise, it will discard the put and sell oil at the market price:

	Oil Price, Dollars per Barrel		
	$18	**$20**	**$22**
Revenue from 1,000 barrels	$18,000	$20,000	$22,000
+ Payoff on put option	2,000	0	0
Net revenues	$20,000	$20,000	$22,000

If oil prices rise, Onnex reaps the benefit. But if oil prices fall below $20 a barrel the payoff of the put option exactly offsets the revenue shortfall. As a result, Onnex realizes net revenues of at least $20 a barrel, which is the exercise price of the put option.

Once again you don't get something for nothing. The price that Onnex pays for insurance against a fall in the price of oil is the cost of the put option. Similarly, the price that Petrochemical paid for insurance against a rise in the price of oil was the cost of the call option. Options provide protection against adverse price changes for a fee—the option premium.

FIGURE 26.1
Onnex can buy put options to place a floor on its overall revenues.

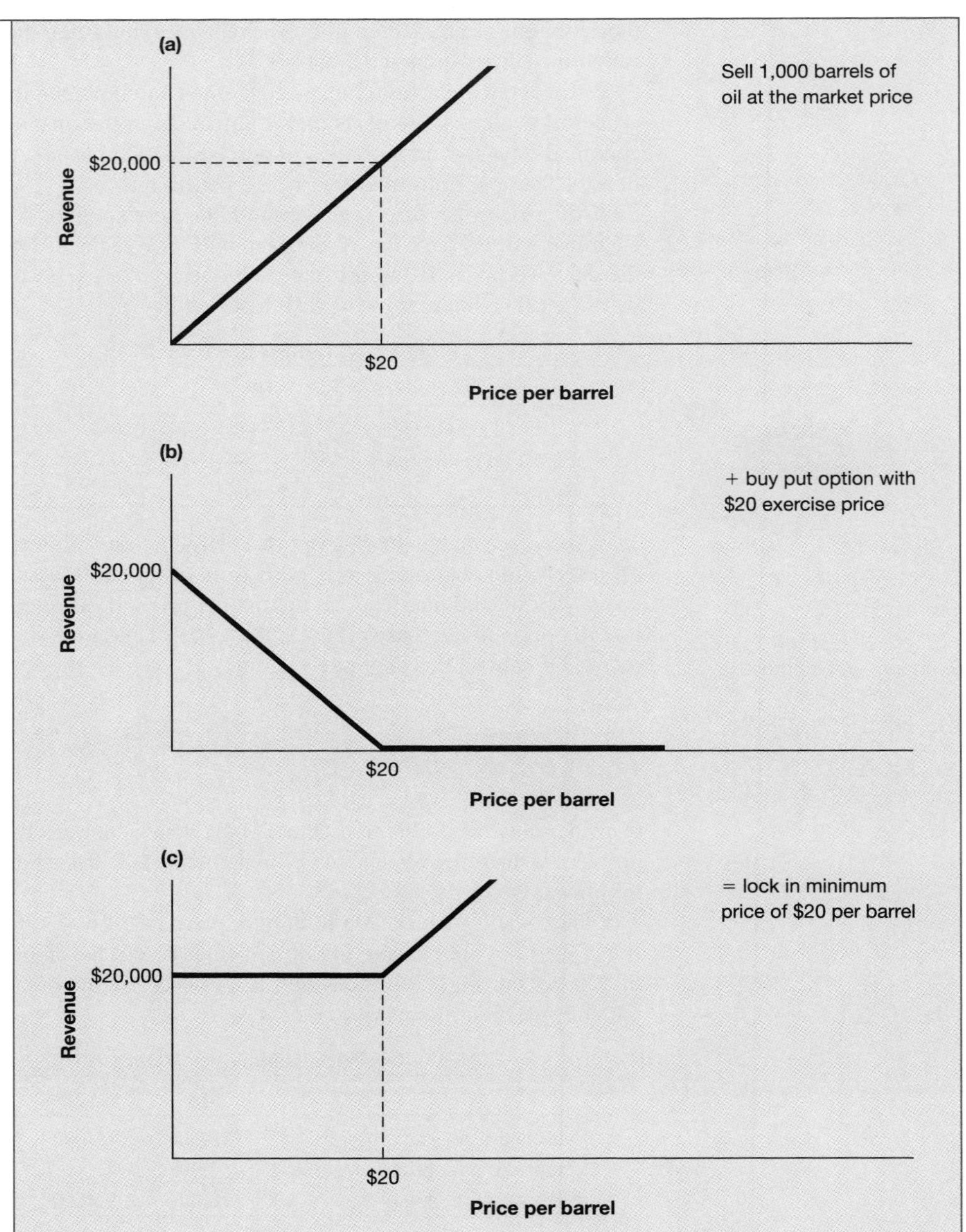

Notice that both Petrochemical and Onnex use options to insure against an adverse move in oil prices. But the options do not remove all uncertainty. For example, Onnex may be able to sell oil for much more than the exercise price of the option.

Figure 26.1 illustrates the nature of Onnex's hedge. Panel *a* shows the total revenue derived from selling the 1,000 barrels of oil. The firm is currently exposed to oil price risk: as prices fall, so will the firm's revenue. But, as panel *b* illustrates, the payoff on a put option to sell 1,000 barrels rises as oil prices fall below $20 a barrel, and therefore, can offset the firm's exposure. Panel c shows the firm's net revenues after it buys the put option. For prices below $20 per barrel, revenues are $20,000. But revenues rise $1,000 for every dollar that oil prices rise above $20. The profile in panel *c* should be familiar to you: think back to the protective put strategy we first saw in Example 26.1. In both cases, the put provides a floor on the value of the overall position.

CHECK POINT 26.1

Draw three graphs like those in Figure 26.1 to illustrate how Petrochemical hedges its costs by purchasing call options on oil.

Futures Contracts

Suppose you are a canola farmer.[2] You are optimistic about next year's canola crop, but still you can't sleep. You are worried that when the time comes to sell the canola, prices may have fallen through the floor. The cure for insomnia is to sell canola *futures*. In this case, you agree to deliver so many tonnes of canola in (say) November at a price that is set today. Do not confuse this **futures contract** with an option, where the holder has a *choice* whether or not to make delivery; your futures contract is a firm promise to deliver canola at a fixed selling price.

futures contract Exchange-traded promise to buy or sell an asset in the future at a prespecified price.

A canola oil processor is in the opposite position. She needs to *buy* canola after the harvest. If she would like to fix the price of this canola ahead of time, she can do so by *buying* canola futures. In other words, she agrees to take delivery of canola in the future at a price that is fixed today. The oil processor also does not have an option; if she still holds the futures contract when it matures, she is obliged to take delivery.

Let's suppose the farmer and the oil processor strike a deal. They enter a futures contract. What happens? First, no money changes hands when the contract is initiated.[3] The oil processor agrees to buy canola at the futures price on a stated *future* date (the contract maturity date). The farmer agrees to sell at the same price and date. Second, the futures contract is a binding obligation, not an option. Options give the right to buy or sell *if* buying or selling turns out to be profitable. The futures contract *requires* the farmer to sell and the oil processor to buy regardless of who profits and who loses.

No money changes hands when a futures contract is entered into. The contract is a binding obligation to buy or sell at a fixed price at contract maturity.

The profit on the futures contract is the difference between the initial futures price and the ultimate price of the asset when the contract matures. For example, if the futures price is originally $300 per tonne and the market price of canola turns out to be $340, the farmer delivers and the oil processor receives the canola for a price $40 below market value. The

[2] Canola is a grain used to make canola oil, which has very low saturated fat and is believed to be healthier than many other oils. Canada produces about 15 percent of the world's output of canola.

[3] Actually, each party will be required to set up a margin account to guarantee performance on the contract. Despite this, the futures contract may still be considered as essentially requiring no money down. First, the amount of margin is small. Second, it may be posted in interest-bearing securities, so that the parties to the trade need not suffer opportunity cost from placing assets in the margin account.

farmer loses $40 per tonne and the canola oil processor gains $40 per tonne as a result of the futures transaction. In general, the seller of the contract benefits if the price initially locked in turns out to exceed the price that could have been obtained at contract maturity. Conversely, the buyer of the contract benefits if the ultimate market price of the asset turns out to exceed the initial futures price. Therefore, the profits on the futures contract to each party are

Profit to seller = initial futures price – ultimate market price (26.1)

Profit to buyer = ultimate market price – initial futures price (26.2)

Now it is easy to see how the farmer and the oil processor can both use the contract to hedge. Consider the farmer's overall cash flows:

	Cash Flow
Sale of canola	Ultimate price of canola
Futures profits	Futures price – ultimate price of canola
Total	Futures price

The profits on the futures contract offset the risk surrounding the sales price of canola and lock in total revenue equal to the futures price. Similarly, the oil processor's all-in cost for the canola is also fixed at the futures price. Any increase in the cost of canola will be offset by a commensurate increase in the profit realized on the futures contract.

Both the farmer and the oil processor have less risk than before. The farmer has hedged (that is, offset) risk by selling canola futures; the oil processor has hedged risk by buying canola futures.[4]

▸ EXAMPLE 26.2 *Hedging with Futures*

Suppose that the farmer originally sold 50 tonnes of November canola futures at a price of $300 per tonne. In November, when the futures contract matures, the price of canola is only $250 per tonne. The farmer buys back the canola futures at $250 just before maturity, giving him a profit of $50 a tonne on the sale and subsequent repurchase. At the same time he sells his canola at the spot price of $250 a tonne. His total receipts are therefore $300 a tonne:

Profit on sale and repurchase of futures	$50
Sale of canola at the November spot price	$250
Total receipts	$300

You can see that the futures contract has allowed the farmer to lock in total proceeds of $300 a tonne.

Figure 26.2 illustrates how the futures contract enabled the farmer in Example 26.2 to hedge his position. Panel *a* is the value of 50 tonnes of canola as a function of the spot price of canola. The value rises by $50 for every dollar increase in canola prices. Panel *b* is the profit on a futures contract to deliver 50 bushels of canola at a futures price of $300

[4] Neither has eliminated all risk. For example, the farmer still has quantity risk. He does not know for sure how many bushels of canola he will produce.

FIGURE 26.2
The farmer can use canola futures to hedge the value of the crop. See Example 26.2.

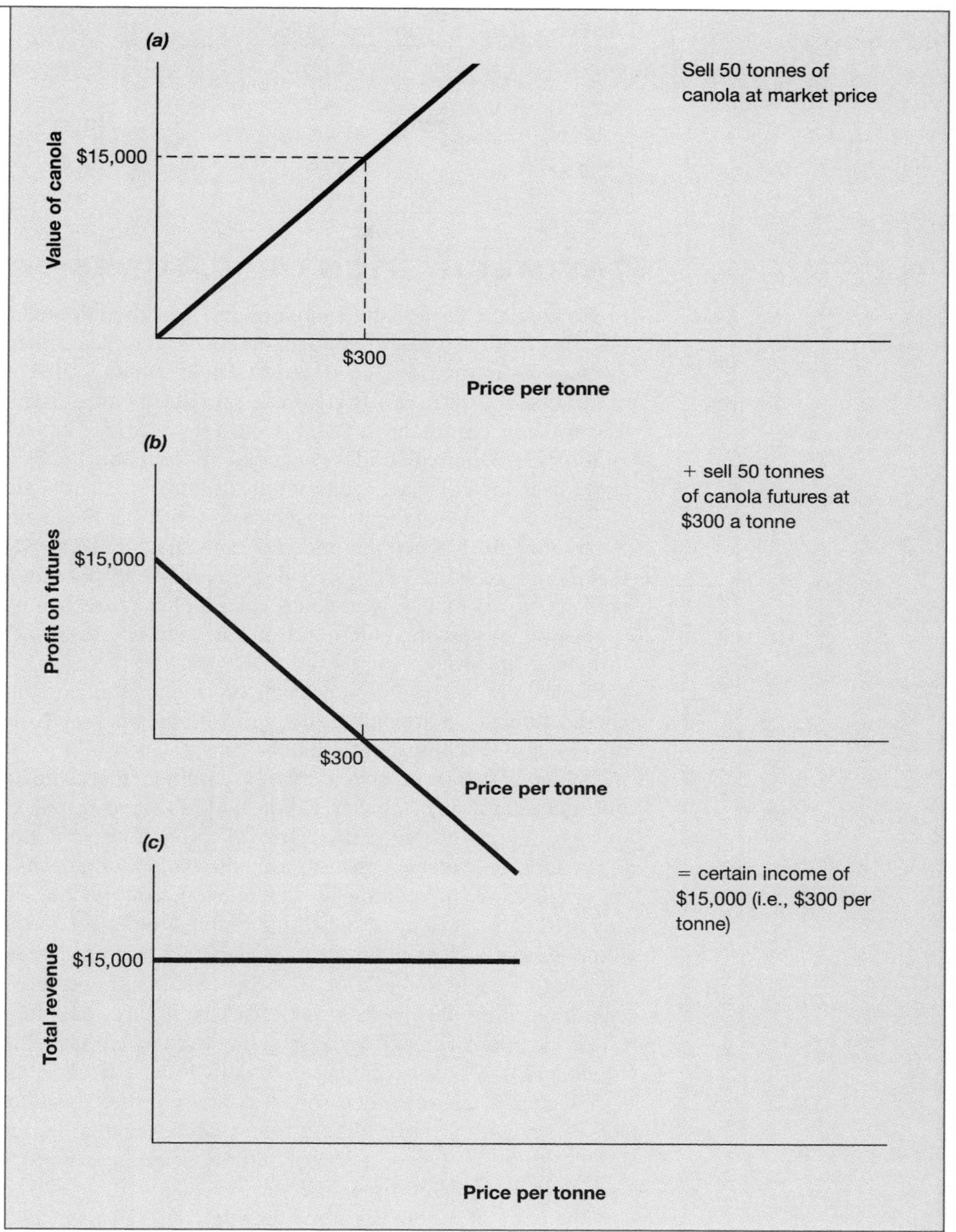

per tonne. The profit will be zero if the ultimate price of canola equals the original futures price, \$300. The profit on the contract to deliver at \$300 rises by \$50 for every dollar the price of canola *falls* below \$300. The exposures to the price of canola depicted in panels *a* and *b* obviously cancel out. Panel *c* shows that the total value of the 50 tonnes plus the futures position is unaffected by the ultimate price of canola, and equals $\$300 \times 50 = \$15{,}000$. In other words, the farmer has locked in proceeds per tonne equal to the original futures price.

TABLE 26.1
The price of canola futures at the Winnipeg Commodity Exchange, reported in the Globe and Mail, *September 21, 2001*

Delivery Date	Price per Tonne
November 2001	\$342.0
January 2002	341.8
March 2002	341.9
May 2002	341.1
July 2002	340.0

THE MECHANICS OF FUTURES TRADING

In practice, the farmer and canola oil processor would not sign the futures contract face to face. Instead, each would go to an organized futures exchange. The largest of these futures exchanges are the Chicago Board of Trade, which traded 253 million futures and options contracts in 2000, and the Eurex, the European derivatives exchange, which traded 454 million contracts in 2000. Futures are traded on two exchanges in Canada. The Bourse |de Montréal trades financial futures and the Winnipeg Commodity Exchange (www.wce.mb.ca) trades commodities futures on canola and other grains.

Table 26.1 shows the price of canola futures at the Winnipeg Commodity Exchange in September 2001, when the price for immediate delivery was about \$332.4 a tonne. Notice that there is a choice of possible delivery dates. If, for example, you were to sell canola for delivery in November, you would get a higher price than by selling January futures.

The oil processor would not be prepared to buy futures contracts if the farmer were free to deliver half-rotten canola to a leaky barn at the end of a cart track. Futures trading is possible only because the contracts are highly standardized. For example, in the case of canola futures, each contract calls for the delivery of 20 tonnes of canola of a specified quality at a warehouse in Saskatchewan.

When you buy or sell a futures contract, the price is fixed today, but payment is not made until later. However, you will be asked to put up some cash or securities as a *margin* to demonstrate that you are able to honour your side of the bargain.

In addition, futures contracts are *marked to market.* This means that each day any profits or losses on the contract are calculated; you pay the exchange any losses and receive any profits. For example, our farmer agreed to deliver 50 tonnes of canola at \$300 a tonne. Suppose that the next day the price of canola futures increases to \$305 a tonne. The farmer now has a loss on his sale of $50 \times \$5 = \$250$ and must pay this sum to the exchange. You can think of the farmer as buying back his futures position each day and then opening up a new position. Thus after the first day the farmer has realized a loss on his trade of \$5 a tonne and now has an obligation to deliver canola for \$305 per tonne.

Of course our oil processor is in the opposite position. The rise in the futures price leaves her with a *profit* of \$5 a tonne. The exchange will therefore pay her this profit. In effect the oil processor sells her futures position at a profit and opens a new contract to take delivery at \$305 per tonne.

The price of canola for immediate delivery is known as the *spot price.* When the farmer sells canola futures, the price that he agrees to take for his canola may be very different from the spot price. But the future eventually becomes the present. As the date for delivery approaches, the futures contract becomes more and more like a spot contract and the price of the futures contract approaches the spot price.

The farmer may decide to wait until the futures contract matures and then deliver canola to the buyer. But in practice such delivery is rare, for it is more convenient for the farmer to buy back the canola futures just before maturity.[5]

[5] In the case of some of the financial futures described later, you *cannot* deliver the asset. At maturity the buyer simply receives (or pays) the difference between the spot price and the price at which he or she has agreed to purchase the asset.

TABLE 26.2
Some financial futures contracts

Future	Principal Exchange
Government of Canada Bonds	ME
Standard & Poor's Canada 60 Index	ME
U.S. Treasury notes	CBT
U.S. Treasury bonds	CBT
Eurodollar deposits	IMM
Standard & Poor's Index	IMM
Euro	IMM
Yen	IMM
German government bonds (Bunds)	Eurex

Key to abbreviations:

CBT	Chicago Board of Trade (www.cbot.com)
IMM	International Monetary Market (at the Chicago Mercantile Exchange) (www.cme.com)
ME	Bourse de Montréal (formerly the Montreal Exchange) (www.m-x.ca)
Eurex	European Derivatives Exchange (www.eurexchange.com)

☑ CHECK POINT 26.2

Suppose that 2 days after taking out the futures contracts the price of November canola increases to $320 a tonne. What additional payments will be made by or to the farmer and the oil processor? What will be their remaining obligations at the end of this second day?

COMMODITY AND FINANCIAL FUTURES

We have shown how the farmer and the oil processor can both use canola futures to hedge their risk. It is also possible to trade futures in a wide variety of other commodities, such as sugar, soybean oil, pork bellies, orange juice, crude oil, and copper.

Commodity prices can bounce up and down like a bungee jumper. For example, in early 1999, raw sugar prices fell from 8.8 cents a pound to 4.5 cents before rising to 6.3 cents in August. For a large buyer of sugar, such as Hershey, these price fluctuations could knock the company badly off course. Hershey therefore reduces its exposure to movements in sugar and cocoa prices by hedging with commodity futures.

For many firms, the wide fluctuations in interest rates and exchange rates have become at least as important a source of risk as changes in commodity prices. You can use *financial futures* to hedge against these risks.

Financial futures are similar to commodity futures but, instead of placing an order to buy or sell a commodity at a future date, you place an order to buy or sell a financial asset at a future date. You can use financial futures to protect yourself against fluctuations in short- and long-term interest rates, exchange rates, and the level of share prices.

Financial futures have been a remarkable success. They were invented in 1972; within a few years, trading in financial futures significantly exceeded trading in commodity futures. Figure 26.3 shows the explosive growth of trading on the Chicago Board of Trade. While financial futures barely registered in 1976, they now dominate the market. Table 26.2 above lists some of the more popular financial futures contracts.

FIGURE 26.3

Trading on the Chicago Board of Trade has come to be dominated by financial futures and options.

Financial Futures and Options
Agriculture Futures and Options
Metals

Contracts (in millions)

Year	1986	1987	1988	1989	1990	1991	1992	1993	1994	1995	1996	1997	1998	1999	2000
Total	99.0	124.5	141.8	137.2	153.3	138.7	149.7	178.6	219.5	210.7	222.4	241.8	277.4	250.4	229.7
Agriculture	22.1	26.8	43.1	35.4	38.8	37.0	36.9	42.2	42.3	50.3	65.4	62.0	58.7	59.4	60.3
Metals	.8	.7	.7	.4	.2	.1	.1	.1	.1	.1	.1	.05	.05	.03	.02

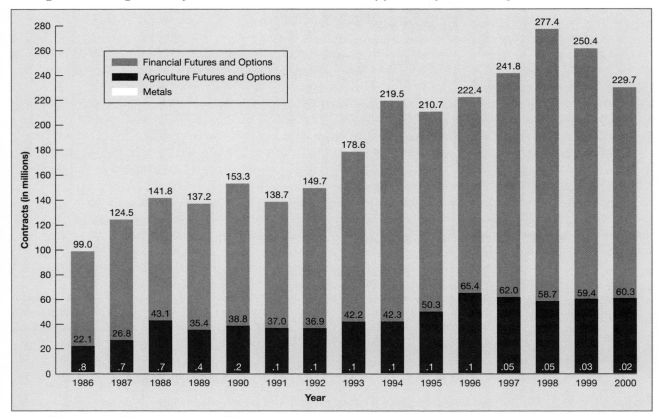

Source: Chicago Board of Trade Historical Annual Volume.

CHECK POINT 26.3

You plan to issue long-term bonds in 9 months but are worried that interest rates may have increased in the meantime. How could you use financial futures to protect yourself against a general rise in interest rates?

Forward Contracts

Each day billions of dollars of futures contracts are bought and sold. We have seen that this liquidity is possible only because futures contracts are standardized. Futures contracts mature on a limited number of dates each year (take another look at the canola contracts in Table 26.1), and the contract size is standardized. For example, a contract may call for delivery of 5,000 bushels of wheat, 100 ounces of gold, or 62,500 British pounds. If the terms of a futures contract do not suit your particular needs, you may be able to buy or sell a **forward contract**.

forward contract Agreement to buy or sell an asset in the future at an agreed price.

Forward contracts are custom-tailored futures contracts.[6] You can write a forward con-

[6] One difference between forward and futures contracts is that forward contracts are not marked to market. Thus with a forward contract you settle up any profits or losses when the contract matures.

tract with any maturity date for delivery of any quantity of goods. For example, suppose that you know that you will need to pay out yen in 3 months time. You can fix the price today that you will pay for the yen by arranging with your bank to buy yen forward. At the end of the 3 months, you pay the agreed upon sum and take delivery of the yen.

EXAMPLE 26.3 *A Pizza Forward Contract*

Have you ever ordered a pizza by phone? If so, you have entered into a forward contract! Your order specifies the pizza type (cheese, pepperoni, and green olives), size (large), the delivery time and location (to be delivered in 30 minutes to your front door) and the price ($15). You don't pay until the product is delivered but you agree on the price at the time the contract is established. You might even be able to trade your forward contract—that is, if your roommate suddenly arrives home very hungry and is willing to buy your pizza contract from you.

EXAMPLE 26.4 *Foreign Currency Forward Contracts*

Computer Parts Inc. has ordered memory chips from its supplier in Japan. The bill for ¥53 million must be paid on July 27. The company can arrange with its bank today to buy this number of yen forward for delivery on July 27 at a forward price of ¥110 per dollar. Therefore, on July 27, Computer Parts pays the bank 53 million/110 = $481,818 and receives ¥53 million, which it can use to pay its Japanese supplier. By committing forward to exchange $481,818 for ¥53 million, its dollar costs are locked in. Notice that if the firm had not used the forward contract to hedge and the dollar had depreciated over this period, the firm would have had to pay a greater amount of dollars. For example, if the exchange rate had fallen to ¥100/dollar, the firm would have had to exchange $530,000 for the ¥53 million necessary to pay its bill. The firm could have used a futures contract to hedge its foreign exchange exposure, but standardization of futures would not allow for delivery of precisely ¥53 million on precisely July 27.

The most active trading in forwards is in foreign currencies, but in recent years, companies have increasingly entered into forward rate agreements that allow them to fix the interest rate at which they borrow or lend in advance.

26.5 Swaps

Suppose Computer Parts from Example 26.4 decides to produce memory chips instead of purchasing them from outside suppliers. It has issued $100 million in floating-rate bonds to help finance the construction of a new plant. (Recall from Chapter 13 that floating-rate bonds make interest payments that go up and down with the general level of interest rates. The coupon payments on the bonds are tied to a specific short-term interest rate.) But the financial manager is concerned that interest rates are becoming more volatile, and she would like to lock in the firm's interest expenses. One approach would be to buy back the floating-rate bonds and replace them with a new issue of fixed-rate debt. But it is costly to issue new debt to the public; in addition, buying back the outstanding bonds in the market will result in considerable trading costs.

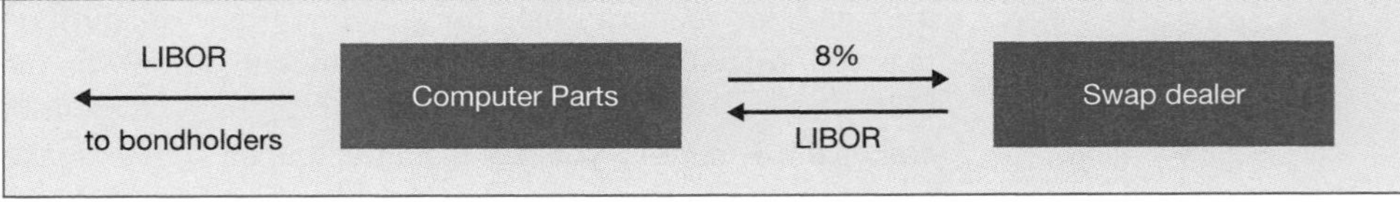

FIGURE 26.4
Interest rate swap: Computer Parts currently pays the LIBOR rate on its outstanding bonds (the arrow on the left). If the firm enters a swap to pay a fixed rate of 8 percent and receive a floating rate of LIBOR, its exposure to LIBOR will cancel out, and its net cash outflow will be a fixed rate of 8 percent.

swap Arrangement by two counterparties to exchange one stream of cash flows for another.

A better approach to hedge out its interest rate exposure is for the firm to enter an interest rate **swap.** The firm will pay or "swap" a fixed payment for another payment that is tied to the level of interest rates. Thus, if rates do rise, increasing the firm's interest expense on its floating-rate debt, its cash flow from the swap agreement will rise as well, offsetting its exposure.

Suppose the firm pays the LIBOR rate on its floating-rate bonds. (Recall that LIBOR, or London Interbank Offer Rate, is the interest rate at which banks borrow from each other in the Eurodollar market. It is the most frequently used short-term interest rate in the swap market.) The firm's interest expense each year therefore equals the LIBOR rate times $100 million. It would like to transform this obligation into one that will not fluctuate with interest rates.

Suppose that current rates in the swaps market are LIBOR for 8 percent fixed. This means that Computer Parts can enter into a swap agreement to *pay* 8 percent on "notional principal" of $100 million to a swap dealer and *receive* payment of the LIBOR rate on the same amount of notional principal. The firm pays the dealer .08 × $100 million and receives LIBOR × $100 million. The dealer and the firm are called *counterparties* in the swap. The firm's *net* cash payment to the dealer is therefore (LIBOR – .08) × $100 million. (If LIBOR exceeds 8 percent, the firm receives money from the dealer; if it is less than 8 percent, the firm pays money to the dealer.) Figure 26.4 illustrates the cash flows paid by Computer Parts and the swap dealer.

Table 26.3 shows Computer Parts' net payments for three possible interest rates. The total payment on the bond-with-swap agreement equals $8,000,000 regardless of the interest rate. The swap has transformed the floating-rate bond into synthetic fixed-rate debt with an effective coupon rate of 8 percent. The firm has thus hedged away its interest rate exposure without actually having to replace its floating-rate bonds with fixed-rate bonds. Swaps offer a much cheaper way to "rearrange the balance sheet."[7]

There are many other applications of interest rate swaps. A portfolio manager who is holding a portfolio of long-term bonds but is worried that interest rates might increase, causing a capital loss on the portfolio, can enter a swap to pay a fixed rate and receive a

TABLE 26.3
An interest rate swap can transform floating-rate bonds into synthetic fixed-rate bonds.

	LIBOR Rate		
	7.5%	**8.0%**	**8.5%**
Interest paid on floating-rate bonds (= LIBOR × $100 million)	$7,500,000	$8,000,000	$8,500,000
+ Cash payment on swap [= (.08 – LIBOR) × notional principal of $100 million]	500,000	0	–500,000
Total payment	$8,000,000	$8,000,000	$8,000,000

[7] You might wonder what's in this arrangement for the swap dealer. The dealer will profit by charging a bid-ask spread. Since the dealer pays LIBOR in return for 8 percent in this swap, it might search for another trader who wishes to receive a fixed rate and pay LIBOR. The dealer will pay a 7.9 percent rate to that trader in return for the LIBOR rate. So the dealer pays a fixed rate and receives floating with one trader but pays floating and receives fixed with the other. Its net cash flow is thus riskless and equal to .1 percent of notional principal.

floating rate, thereby converting the holdings into a synthetic floating-rate portfolio (see Check Point 26.4). Or a pension fund manager might identify some money market securities that are paying excellent yields compared to other comparable-risk short-term securities. However, the manager might believe that such short-term assets are inappropriate for the portfolio. The fund can hold these high-yielding securities and enter a swap in which it receives a fixed rate and pays a floating rate. It thus captures the benefit of the advantageous *relative* yields on these securities, but still establishes a portfolio with the fixed-interest-rate risk characteristic of long-term bonds.

CHECK POINT 26.4

Consider the portfolio manager who is holding a $100 million portfolio of long-term bonds and wishes to reduce price risk by transforming the holdings into a synthetic floating-rate portfolio. Assume the portfolio currently pays an 8 percent fixed rate and that swap dealers currently offer terms of 8 percent fixed for LIBOR. What swap would the manager establish? Show the total income on the fund in a table like Table 26.3, and illustrate the cash flows in a diagram like Figure 26.4.

There are many variations on the interest rate swap. For example, currency swaps allow firms to exchange a series of payments in dollars (which may be tied to a fixed or floating rate) for a series of payments in another currency (which also may be tied to a fixed or floating rate). These swaps can therefore be used to manage exposure to exchange rate fluctuations.

EXAMPLE 26.4 *Currency Swaps*

Suppose that the Moose Company wishes to borrow Swiss francs (SFr) to help finance its European operations. Since Moose is better known in Canada, the financial manager believes that the company can obtain more attractive terms on a dollar loan than on a Swiss franc loan. Therefore, the company borrows $10 million for 5 years at 5 percent in Canada. At the same time Moose arranges with a bank to trade its future dollar liability for Swiss francs. Under this arrangement the bank agrees to pay Moose sufficient dollars to service its dollar loan, and in exchange, Moose agrees to make a series of annual payments in Swiss francs to the bank.

Moose's cash flows are set out in Table 26.4. Line 1 shows that when Moose takes out its dollar loan, it promises to pay annual interest of $.5 million and repay the $10 million that it has borrowed. Lines 2a and 2b show the cash flows from the swap, assuming that the spot exchange rate for Swiss francs is $1 = SFr2. Moose hands over to the bank the $10 million that it borrowed and receives in exchange 2 × $10 million = SFr20 million. In each

TABLE 26.4
Cash flows from Moose's dollar loan and currency swap (figures in millions)

	Year 0		Years 1–4		Year 5	
	$	SFr	$	SFr	$	SFr
1. Issue dollar loan	+10		–.5		–10.5	
2. Arrange currency swap						
a. Moose receives $	–10		+.5		+10.5	
b. Moose pays SFr		+20		–1.2		–21.2
3. Net cash flow	0	+20	0	–1.2	0	–21.2

of the next 4 years the bank pays Moose \$.5 million, which it uses to pay the annual interest on its loan. In Year 5 the bank pays Moose \$10.5 million, which covers both the final year's interest and the repayment of the loan. In return for these future dollar receipts, Moose agrees to pay the bank SFr1.2 million in each of the next 4 years and SFr21.2 million in Year 5.

The combined effect of Moose's two steps (line 3) is to convert its 5 percent dollar loan into a 6 percent Swiss franc loan. The device that makes this possible is the currency swap.

CHECK POINT 26.5

Suppose that the spot exchange rate had been \$1 = SFr3 and that Swiss interest rates were 8 percent. Recalculate the Swiss franc cash flows that the bank would agree to (line 2b of Table 26.4) and Moose's net cash flows (line 3).

26.6 Is "Derivative" a Four-Letter Word?

Our earlier examples of the farmer and the oil processor showed how derivatives—futures, options, or swaps, for example—can be used to reduce business risk. However, if you were to copy the farmer and sell canola futures without an offsetting holding of canola, you would not be *reducing* risk; you would be *speculating.*

A successful futures market needs speculators who are prepared to take on risk and provide the farmer and the canola oil processor with the protection they need. For example, if an excess of farmers wished to sell canola futures, the price of futures would be forced down until enough speculators were tempted to buy in the hope of a profit. If there is a surplus of oil processors wishing to buy canola futures, the reverse will happen. The price will be forced up until speculators are drawn in to sell.

Speculation may be necessary to a thriving derivatives market, but it can get companies into serious trouble. For example, for 10 years a Japanese trading company, Sumitomo Corporation, used the futures market to place huge bets on the price of copper. Its chief trader, known in the business simply as "Mr. Copper," was lauded for his contributions to the firm's profits. However, in June 1996 the copper market was battered by the revelation that the man with the Midas touch had managed to hide losses amounting to about \$1 billion.

Sumitomo has plenty of company. In 1995, Baring Brothers, a blue-chip British merchant bank, became insolvent. The reason: Nick Leeson, a trader in its Singapore office, had lost \$1.4 billion speculating in futures contracts on the Japanese stock market index. The same year Daiwa Bank reported that a bond trader in its New York office had managed to hide losses over 11 years of \$1.1 billion. Procter & Gamble, the blue-chip consumer products company, was painfully embarrassed in 1994 when a bet against rising interest rates lost over \$100 million. At least it didn't join the billion-dollar-loss club.

The nearby Finance in Action box discusses another billion-dollar debacle. In this case, Metallgesellschaft claimed to be using futures markets to hedge but it still managed to lose well over \$1 billion. Whether the firm really was hedging, however, is a matter that is still subject to debate.

Do these horror stories mean that firms should ban the use of derivatives? Of course not. But they do illustrate that derivatives need to be used with care. Our view is this:

FINANCE IN ACTION

Meltdown at Metallgesellschaft

Metallgesellschaft AG was one of Germany's most respected companies with more than 20,000 employees and revenues of some $10 billion. Its 251 subsidiaries were engaged in engineering, mining, financial services, and commodities trading, and its major shareholders included such blue-chip German companies as Deutsche Bank, Daimler-Benz, and Allianz.

However, in 1993, Metallgesellschaft was nearly brought to its knees by losses of $1.4 billion from trading in oil futures. The problem arose in one of its U.S. subsidiaries, MGRM. MGRM offered its customers firm price guarantees for up to 10 years on any oil that they agreed to buy. These guarantees proved very popular, so that by the end of 1993 the company had entered into long-term contracts to supply 160 million barrels of oil worth more than $3 billion.

There was only one problem. MGRM did not own the oil that it had promised to deliver and would therefore have to buy it from the major oil companies. If the price of oil rose above the price that customers had agreed to pay, MGRM would make a loss on every barrel of oil that it had sold. The apparent solution was for MGRM to hedge its exposure by buying oil futures. This would fix the price at which the company could buy oil when it needed to deliver it. The company would have liked to buy oil futures that matured on the same dates as it was obliged to deliver the oil, but, unfortunately, most futures trading takes place in contracts that mature within a year. MGRM's solution was to buy short-term oil futures and to replace them when they matured.

During the second half of 1993 oil prices fell by 25 percent and MGRM's contracts to deliver oil at a predetermined price looked increasingly attractive. However, at the same time, the company started to pile up large losses on its purchases of oil futures. This was not in itself a cause for concern. If MGRM was truly hedged, the profits on the oil contracts should have exactly offset the losses on the futures.

So what went wrong? One view is that management focused on the accumulating losses on the futures positions and failed to recognize the gains on the oil contracts. When the losses became sufficiently large, management's nerve cracked and it sold out of its futures positions at the wrong time. Moreover, because MGRM's futures positions were marked to market, the company had to find the cash each day to cover the losses on these positions. This problem of financing the hedge may have contributed to management's decision to abandon its strategy.

Other commentators are less convinced that all would have come out right if only management had not panicked. They argue that the company's strategy of hedging long-term liabilities with short-term futures was fundamentally flawed. The problem was that MGRM could not predict the price at which it would be able to replace each futures contract when it matured. If the price of the new future was *below* that of the maturing one, MGRM would make a profit from the trade. But unfortunately for MGRM, the reverse proved to be the case, so that the company incurred a loss each time it replaced the maturing futures contract with a new one.

While financial experts continued to debate the cause of MGRM's losses, the company's bankers struggled to put together a rescue package. A massive $1.9 billion loan from 150 international banks was needed to keep the company from foundering.

Speculation is foolish unless you have reason to believe that the odds are stacked in your favour. If you are not better informed than the highly paid professionals in banks and other institutions, you should use derivatives for hedging, not for speculation.

26.7 Summary

1. Why do companies hedge to reduce risk?

Fluctuations in commodity prices, interest rates, or exchange rates can make planning difficult and can throw companies badly off course. Financial managers therefore look for opportunities to manage these risks, and a number of specialized instruments have been invented to help them. These are collectively known as *derivative instruments.*

2. How can options, futures, and forward contracts be used to devise simple hedging strategies?

In the last chapter we introduced you to put and call options. **Options** are often used by firms to limit their downside risk. For example, if you own an asset and have the option to sell it at the current price, then you have effectively insured yourself against loss.

Futures contracts are agreements made today to buy or sell an asset in the future. The price is fixed today, but the final payment does not occur until the delivery date. Futures contracts are highly standardized and are traded on organized exchanges. Commodity futures allow firms to fix the future price that they pay for a wide range of agricultural commodities, metals, and oil. Financial futures help firms to protect themselves against unforeseen movements in interest rates, exchange rates, and stock prices.

Forward contracts are equivalent to tailor-made futures contracts. For example, firms often enter into forward agreements with a bank to buy or sell foreign exchange or to fix the interest rate on a loan to be made in the future.

3. **How can companies use swaps to change the risk of securities they have issued?**

Swaps allow firms to exchange one series of future payments for another. For example, the firm might agree to make a series of regular payments in one currency in return for receiving a series of payments in another currency.

Related Web Links

www.finance.wat.ch Information about derivative contracts and their use in risk management
www.cisco-futures.com Data on a variety of contracts, including simulations and other information
www.intltreasurer.com Information for the treasury manager with emphasis on risk management
http://home.earthlink.net/~green/whatisan.htm Information about swaps
www.stuart.iit.edu/fmtreview/fmtrev2.htm One company's approach to encouraging managers to manage financial risk
www.wce.mb.ca Winnipeg Commodity Exchange
www.cbot.com Chicago Board of Trade
www.cme.com International Monetary Market (at the Chicago Mercantile Exchange)
www.m-x.ca Bourse de Montréal
www.eurexchange.com European Derivatives Exchange

Key Terms

futures contract	771	forward contract	776	swap	778

Questions and Problems

*Answers in Appendix B

Basic

*1. **Risk Management.** Large businesses spend millions of dollars annually on insurance. Why? Should they insure against all risks or does insurance make more sense for some risks than others?

2. **Hedging.**
   a. An investor currently holding $1 million in long-term government bonds becomes concerned about increasing volatility in interest rates. She decides to hedge her risk using government bond futures contracts. Should she buy or sell such contracts?
   b. The treasurer of a corporation that will be issuing bonds in 3 months is also concerned about interest rate volatility and wants to lock in the price at which he could sell 8 percent coupon bonds. How would he use government bond futures contracts to hedge his firm's position?

3. **Commodity Futures.** What commodity futures are traded on futures exchanges? Who do you think could usefully reduce risk by buying each of these contracts? Who do you think might wish to sell each contract?

*4. **Hedging.** "The farmer does not avoid risk by selling canola futures. If canola prices stay above $340 per tonne, then he will actually have lost by selling canola futures at $340." Is this a fair comment?

5. **Marking to Market.** Suppose that in the 5 days following a farmer's sale of September wheat futures at a futures price of $3.83 the futures price is

Day	1	2	3	4	5
Price	$3.83	$3.98	$3.70	$3.50	$3.70

At the end of day 5 the farmer decides to quit wheat farming and buys back his futures contract. What payments are made between the farmer and the exchange on each day? What is the total payment over the 5 days? Would the total payment be any different if the contract was not marked to market? The contract size is 5,000 bushels.

*6. **Futures versus Spot Positions.** What do you think are the advantages of holding futures rather than the underlying commodity? What do you think are the disadvantages?

PRACTICE

*7. **Hedging with Futures versus Puts.** A gold mining firm is concerned about short-term volatility in its revenues. Gold currently sells for $300 an ounce, but the price is extremely volatile and could fall as low as $280 or rise as high as $320 in the next month. The company will bring 1,000 ounces to the market next month.
   a. What will be total revenues if the firm remains unhedged for gold prices of $280, $300, and $320 an ounce?
   b. The futures price of gold for 1-month-ahead delivery is $301. What will be the firm's total revenues at each gold price if the firm enters a 1-month futures contract to deliver 1,000 ounces of gold?
   c. What will total revenues be if the firm buys a 1-month put option to sell gold for $300 an ounce? The puts cost $2 per ounce.

8. **Hedging with Calls.** A large dental lab plans to purchase 1,000 ounces of gold in 1 month. Assume again that gold prices can be $280, $300, or $320 an ounce.
   a. What will total expenses be if the firm purchases call options on 1,000 ounces of gold with an exercise price of $300 an ounce? The options cost $3 per ounce.
   b. What will total expenses be if the firm purchases call options on 1,000 ounces of gold with an exercise price of $295 an ounce? These options cost $7 per ounce.

*9. **Forward Contract.** Assume that the 1-year interest rate is 10 percent and the 2-year interest rate is 12 percent per year. You approach a bank and ask at what rate the bank will promise to make a 1-year loan in 12 months' time. The bank offers to make a forward commitment to lend to you at 15 percent. Would you accept the offer? Can you think of a simple, cheaper alternative?

10. **Hedging Project Risk.** Your firm has just tendered for a contract in Japan. You won't know for 3 months whether you get the contract but if you do, you will receive a payment of ¥10 million 1 year from now. You are worried that if the yen declines in value, the dollar value of this payment will be less than you expect and the project could even show a loss. Discuss the possible ways that you could protect the firm against a decline in the value of the yen. Illustrate the possible outcomes if you do get the contract and if you don't.

*11. **Hedging with Futures.** Show how Petrochemical Parfum (see Section 26.2) can also use futures contracts to protect itself against a rise in the price of crude oil. Show how the payoffs would vary if the oil price is $18, $20, or $22 a barrel. What are the advantages and disadvantages for Petrochemical of using futures rather than options to reduce risk? Repeat the exercise for Onnex.

*12. **Futures Contracts.** Look in the *Globe and Mail* or *National Post* at the prices of gold futures quoted on the COMEX futures exchange. What is the date of the most distant contract? Suppose that you buy 100 ounces of gold futures for this date. When do you receive the gold? When do you pay for it? Is the futures price higher or lower than the current spot price? Can you suggest why?

13. **Hedging Currency Risk.** We saw in Chapter 24 that when the deutschemark strengthened in 1991 and 1992, German luxury car manufacturers found it increasingly difficult to compete in the United States market. How could they have hedged themselves against this risk? Would a company that was hedged have been in a better position to compete? Explain why or why not.

*14. **Swaps.** What is a currency swap? An interest rate swap? Give one example of how each might be used.

CHALLENGE

15. **Swaps.** Firms A and B face the following borrowing rates for a 5-year fixed-rate debt issue in U.S. dollars or euros:

	U.S. Dollars	Euros
Firm A	10%	7%
Firm B	8%	6%

Suppose that A wishes to borrow U.S. dollars and B wishes to borrow euros. Show how a swap could be used to reduce the borrowing costs of each company. Assume a spot exchange rate of 1 euro to the dollar.

INTERNET PROBLEMS

1. The International Finance Risk Institute provides three case studies on the sources, types, and control of financial risk at http://newrisk.ifci.ch/introduction.htm. Read the Sumitomo story for insights into the financial trading scandal.
2. Risk management extends beyond using financial instruments to hedge. This website offers some ideas on how to manage a business crisis: http://entrepreneurs.about.com/cs/riskmanagement/.
3. In Canada, futures are traded on the Bourse de Montréal, www.m-x.ca. What futures contracts are offered for trading? Why would an investor be interested in purchasing a bond futures?
4. Algorithmics is a world leader in risk management systems and a Canadian company. Read a few job descriptions on their careers page, www.algorithmics.com/careers/index.shtml, and summarize what skills it takes to be a financial risk management professional.

SOLUTIONS TO CHECK POINTS

26.1 See Figure 26.5 on page 786.

26.2 The farmer has a further loss of $15 a tonne ($320 – $305) and will be required to pay this amount to the exchange. The oil processor has a further profit of $15 a tonne ($320 – $305) and will receive this from the exchange. The farmer is now committed to delivering canola in November for $320 a tonne and the oil processor is committed to paying $320 a tonne.

26.3 You sell long-term bond futures with a delivery date of 9 months. Suppose, for example, that you agree to deliver long-term bonds in 9 months at a price of 100. If interest rates fall, the price of the bond futures will rise to (say) 105. (Remember that when interest rates fall, bond prices rise.) In this case the profit that you make on your bond futures offsets the lower price that the firm is likely to receive on the sale of its own bonds. Conversely, if interest rates fall, the company will make a loss on its futures position but will receive a higher price for its own bonds.

26.4 The manager should enter a swap to pay an 8 percent fixed rate and receive LIBOR on notional principal of $100 million. The cash flows will then rise in tandem with the LIBOR rate:

	LIBOR Rate		
	7.5%	8.0%	8.5%
Interest received on fixed-rate bonds (= .08 × $100 million)	$8,000,000	$8,000,000	$8,000,000
+ Cash flow on swap [= (LIBOR – .08) × notional principal of $100 million]	–500,000	0	+500,000
Total payment	$7,500,000	$8,000,000	$8,500,000

The diagram describing the cash flows of each party to the swap is as follows:

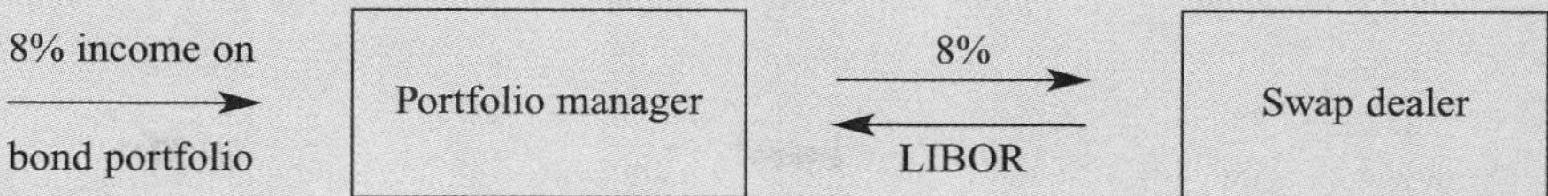

The manager nets a cash flow proportional to the LIBOR rate.

26.5 The following table shows revised cash flows from Moose's dollar loan and currency swap (figures in millions):

	Year 0		Years 1–4		Year 5	
	$	**SFr**	**$**	**SFr**	**$**	**SFr**
1. Issue dollar loan	+10		−.5		−10.5	
2. Arrange currency swap						
a. Moose receives $	−10		+.5		+10.5	
b. Moose pays SFr		+30		−2.4		−32.4
3. Net cash flow	0	+30	0	−2.4	0	−32.4

Notice that in exchange for $10 million today the bank is now prepared to pay SFr30 million. Since the Swiss interest rate is now 8 percent, the bank will expect to earn $.08 \times 30 =$ SFr2.4 million interest on its Swiss franc outlay.

FIGURE 26.5
Diagrams for Check Point 26.1.

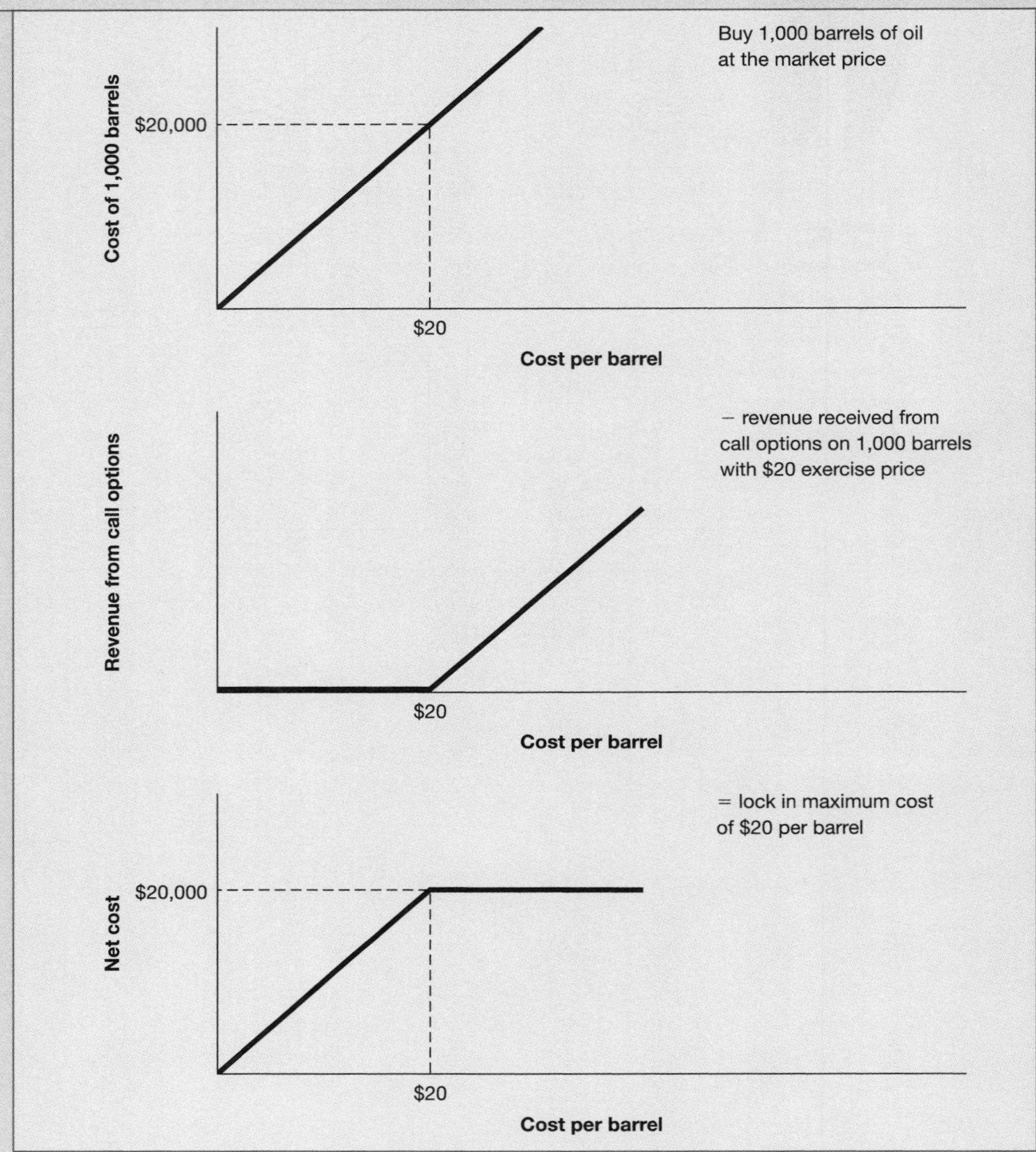

Appendix A

PRESENT VALUE TABLES

APPENDIX A TABLE A.1

FUTURE VALUE OF $1 AFTER t YEARS = $(1 + r)^t$

Number of Years	Interest Rate per Year 1%	2%	3%	4%	5%	6%	7%	8%	9%	10%	11%	12%	13%	14%	15%
1	1.010	1.020	1.030	1.040	1.050	1.060	1.070	1.080	1.090	1.100	1.110	1.120	1.130	1.140	1.150
2	1.020	1.040	1.061	1.082	1.102	1.124	1.145	1.166	1.188	1.210	1.232	1.254	1.277	1.300	1.323
3	1.030	1.061	1.093	1.125	1.158	1.191	1.225	1.260	1.295	1.331	1.368	1.405	1.443	1.482	1.521
4	1.041	1.082	1.126	1.170	1.216	1.262	1.311	1.360	1.412	1.464	1.518	1.574	1.630	1.689	1.749
5	1.051	1.104	1.159	1.217	1.276	1.338	1.403	1.469	1.539	1.611	1.685	1.762	1.842	1.925	2.011
6	1.062	1.126	1.194	1.265	1.340	1.419	1.501	1.587	1.677	1.772	1.870	1.974	2.082	2.195	2.313
7	1.072	1.149	1.230	1.316	1.407	1.504	1.606	1.714	1.828	1.949	2.076	2.211	2.353	2.502	2.660
8	1.083	1.172	1.267	1.369	1.477	1.594	1.718	1.851	1.993	2.144	2.305	2.476	2.658	2.853	3.059
9	1.094	1.195	1.305	1.423	1.551	1.689	1.838	1.999	2.172	2.358	2.558	2.773	3.004	3.252	3.518
10	1.105	1.219	1.344	1.480	1.629	1.791	1.967	2.159	2.367	2.594	2.839	3.106	3.395	3.707	4.046
11	1.116	1.243	1.384	1.539	1.710	1.898	2.105	2.332	2.580	2.853	3.152	3.479	3.836	4.226	4.652
12	1.127	1.268	1.426	1.601	1.796	2.012	2.252	2.518	2.813	3.138	3.498	3.896	4.335	4.818	5.350
13	1.138	1.294	1.469	1.665	1.886	2.133	2.410	2.720	3.066	3.452	3.883	4.363	4.898	5.492	6.153
14	1.149	1.319	1.513	1.732	1.980	2.261	2.579	2.937	3.342	3.797	4.310	4.887	5.535	6.261	7.076
15	1.161	1.346	1.558	1.801	2.079	2.397	2.759	3.172	3.642	4.177	4.785	5.474	6.254	7.138	8.137
16	1.173	1.373	1.605	1.873	2.183	2.540	2.952	3.426	3.970	4.595	5.311	6.130	7.067	8.137	9.358
17	1.184	1.400	1.653	1.948	2.292	2.693	3.159	3.700	4.328	5.054	5.895	6.866	7.986	9.276	10.76
18	1.196	1.428	1.702	2.026	2.407	2.854	3.380	3.996	4.717	5.560	6.544	7.690	9.024	10.58	12.38
19	1.208	1.457	1.754	2.107	2.527	3.026	3.617	4.316	5.142	6.116	7.263	8.613	10.20	12.06	14.23
20	1.220	1.486	1.806	2.191	2.653	3.207	3.870	4.661	5.604	6.727	8.062	9.646	11.52	13.74	16.37
25	1.282	1.641	2.094	2.666	3.386	4.292	5.427	6.848	8.623	10.83	13.59	17.00	21.23	26.46	32.92
30	1.348	1.811	2.427	3.243	4.322	5.743	7.612	10.06	13.27	17.45	22.89	29.96	39.12	50.95	66.21

Number of Years	Interest Rate per Year														
	16%	17%	18%	19%	20%	21%	22%	23%	24%	25%	26%	27%	28%	29%	30%
1	1.160	1.170	1.180	1.190	1.200	1.210	1.220	1.230	1.240	1.250	1.260	1.270	1.280	1.290	1.300
2	1.346	1.369	1.392	1.416	1.440	1.464	1.488	1.513	1.538	1.563	1.588	1.613	1.638	1.664	1.690
3	1.561	1.602	1.643	1.685	1.728	1.772	1.816	1.861	1.907	1.953	2.000	2.048	2.097	2.147	2.197
4	1.811	1.874	1.939	2.005	2.074	2.144	2.215	2.289	2.364	2.441	2.520	2.601	2.684	2.769	2.856
5	2.100	2.192	2.288	2.386	2.488	2.594	2.703	2.815	2.932	3.052	3.176	3.304	3.436	3.572	3.713
6	2.436	2.565	2.700	2.840	2.986	3.138	3.297	3.463	3.635	3.815	4.002	4.196	4.398	4.608	4.827
7	2.826	3.001	3.185	3.379	3.583	3.797	4.023	4.259	4.508	4.768	5.042	5.329	5.629	5.945	6.275
8	3.278	3.511	3.759	4.021	4.300	4.595	4.908	5.239	5.590	5.960	6.353	6.768	7.206	7.669	8.157
9	3.803	4.108	4.435	4.785	5.160	5.560	5.987	6.444	6.931	7.451	8.005	8.595	9.223	9.893	10.60
10	4.411	4.807	5.234	5.695	6.192	6.728	7.305	7.926	8.594	9.313	10.09	10.92	11.81	12.76	13.79
11	5.117	5.624	6.176	6.777	7.430	8.140	8.912	9.749	10.66	11.64	12.71	13.86	15.11	16.46	17.92
12	5.936	6.580	7.288	8.064	8.916	9.850	10.87	11.99	13.21	14.55	16.01	17.61	19.34	21.24	23.30
13	6.886	7.699	8.599	9.596	10.70	11.92	13.26	14.75	16.39	18.19	20.18	22.36	24.76	27.39	30.29
14	7.988	9.007	10.15	11.42	12.84	14.42	16.18	18.14	20.32	22.74	25.42	28.40	31.69	35.34	39.37
15	9.266	10.54	11.97	13.59	15.41	17.45	19.74	22.31	25.20	28.42	32.03	36.06	40.56	45.59	51.19
16	10.75	12.33	14.13	16.17	18.49	21.11	24.09	27.45	31.24	35.53	40.36	45.80	51.92	58.81	66.54
17	12.47	14.43	16.67	19.24	22.19	25.55	29.38	33.76	38.74	44.41	50.85	58.17	66.46	75.86	86.50
18	14.46	16.88	19.67	22.90	26.62	30.91	35.85	41.52	48.04	55.51	64.07	73.87	85.07	97.86	112.5
19	16.78	19.75	23.21	27.25	31.95	37.40	43.74	51.07	59.57	69.39	80.73	93.81	108.9	126.2	146.2
20	19.46	23.11	27.39	32.43	38.34	45.26	53.36	62.82	73.86	86.74	101.7	119.1	139.4	162.9	190.0
25	40.87	50.66	62.67	77.39	95.40	117.4	144.2	176.9	216.5	264.7	323.0	393.6	478.9	581.8	705.6
30	85.85	111.1	143.4	184.7	237.4	304.5	389.8	497.9	634.8	807.8	1026	1301	1646	2078	2620

(e.g., if the interest rate is 10 percent per year, the investment of $1 today will be worth $1.611 at Year 5.)

APPENDIX A TABLE A.2

DISCOUNT FACTORS: PRESENT VALUE OF $1 TO BE RECEIVED AFTER t YEARS = $1/(1 + r)^t$

Number of Years	Interest Rate per Year 1%	2%	3%	4%	5%	6%	7%	8%	9%	10%	11%	12%	13%	14%	15%
1	.990	.980	.971	.962	.952	.943	.935	.926	.917	.909	.901	.893	.885	.877	.870
2	.980	.961	.943	.925	.907	.890	.873	.857	.842	.826	.812	.797	.783	.769	.756
3	.971	.942	.915	.889	.864	.840	.816	.794	.772	.751	.731	.712	.693	.675	.658
4	.961	.924	.888	.855	.823	.792	.763	.735	.708	.683	.659	.636	.613	.592	.572
5	.951	.906	.863	.822	.784	.747	.713	.681	.650	.621	.593	.567	.543	.519	.497
6	.942	.888	.837	.790	.746	.705	.666	.630	.596	.564	.535	.507	.480	.456	.432
7	.933	.871	.813	.760	.711	.665	.623	.583	.547	.513	.482	.452	.425	.400	.376
8	.923	.853	.789	.731	.677	.627	.582	.540	.502	.467	.434	.404	.376	.351	.327
9	.914	.837	.766	.703	.645	.592	.544	.500	.460	.424	.391	.361	.333	.308	.284
10	.905	.820	.744	.676	.614	.558	.508	.463	.422	.386	.352	.322	.295	.270	.247
11	.896	.804	.722	.650	.585	.527	.475	.429	.388	.350	.317	.287	.261	.237	.215
12	.887	.788	.701	.625	.557	.497	.444	.397	.356	.319	.286	.257	.231	.208	.187
13	.879	.773	.681	.601	.530	.469	.415	.368	.326	.290	.258	.229	.204	.182	.163
14	.870	.758	.661	.577	.505	.442	.388	.340	.299	.263	.232	.205	.181	.160	.141
15	.861	.743	.642	.555	.481	.417	.362	.315	.275	.239	.209	.183	.160	.140	.123
16	.853	.728	.623	.534	.458	.394	.339	.292	.252	.218	.188	.163	.141	.123	.107
17	.844	.714	.605	.513	.436	.371	.317	.270	.231	.198	.170	.146	.125	.108	.093
18	.836	.700	.587	.494	.416	.350	.296	.250	.212	.180	.153	.130	.111	.095	.081
19	.828	.686	.570	.475	.396	.331	.277	.232	.194	.164	.138	.116	.098	.083	.070
20	.820	.673	.554	.456	.377	.312	.258	.215	.178	.149	.124	.104	.087	.073	.061
25	.780	.610	.478	.375	.295	.233	.184	.146	.116	.092	.074	.059	.047	.038	.030
30	.742	.552	.412	.308	.231	.174	.131	.099	.075	.057	.044	.033	.026	.020	.015

Number of Years	Interest Rate per Year 16%	17%	18%	19%	20%	21%	22%	23%	24%	25%	26%	27%	28%	29%	30%
1	.862	.855	.847	.840	.833	.826	.820	.813	.806	.800	.794	.787	.781	.775	.769
2	.743	.731	.718	.706	.694	.683	.672	.661	.650	.640	.630	.620	.610	.601	.592
3	.641	.624	.609	.593	.579	.564	.551	.537	.524	.512	.500	.488	.477	.466	.455
4	.552	.534	.516	.499	.482	.467	.451	.437	.423	.410	.397	.384	.373	.361	.350
5	.476	.456	.437	.419	.402	.386	.370	.355	.341	.328	.315	.303	.291	.280	.269
6	.410	.390	.370	.352	.335	.319	.303	.289	.275	.262	.250	.238	.227	.217	.207
7	.354	.333	.314	.296	.279	.263	.249	.235	.222	.210	.198	.188	.178	.168	.159
8	.305	.285	.266	.249	.233	.218	.204	.191	.179	.168	.157	.148	.139	.130	.123
9	.263	.243	.225	.209	.194	.180	.167	.155	.144	.134	.125	.116	.108	.101	.094
10	.227	.208	.191	.176	.162	.149	.137	.126	.116	.107	.099	.092	.085	.078	.073
11	.195	.178	.162	.148	.135	.123	.112	.103	.094	.086	.079	.072	.066	.061	.056
12	.168	.152	.137	.124	.112	.102	.092	.083	.076	.069	.062	.057	.052	.047	.043
13	.145	.130	.116	.104	.093	.084	.075	.068	.061	.055	.050	.045	.040	.037	.033
14	.125	.111	.099	.088	.078	.069	.062	.055	.049	.044	.039	.035	.032	.028	.025
15	.108	.095	.084	.074	.065	.057	.051	.045	.040	.035	.031	.028	.025	.022	.020
16	.093	.081	.071	.062	.054	.047	.042	.036	.032	.028	.025	.022	.019	.017	.015
17	.080	.069	.060	.052	.045	.039	.034	.030	.026	.023	.020	.017	.015	.013	.012
18	.069	.059	.051	.044	.038	.032	.028	.024	.021	.018	.016	.014	.012	.010	.009
19	.060	.051	.043	.037	.031	.027	.023	.020	.017	.014	.012	.011	.009	.008	.007
20	.051	.043	.037	.031	.026	.022	.019	.016	.014	.012	.010	.008	.007	.006	.005
25	.024	.020	.016	.013	.010	.009	.007	.006	.005	.004	.003	.003	.002	.002	.001
30	.012	.009	.007	.005	.004	.003	.003	.002	.002	.001	.001	.001	.001	.000	.000

(e.g., if the interest rate is 10 percent per year, the present value of $1 received at Year 5 is $.621.)

APPENDIX A TABLE A.3

ANNUITY TABLE: PRESENT VALUE OF \$1 *PER YEAR* FOR EACH OF t YEARS = $1/r - 1/[r(1 + r)^t]$

Number of Years	Interest Rate per Year														
	1%	2%	3%	4%	5%	6%	7%	8%	9%	10%	11%	12%	13%	14%	15%
1	.990	.980	.971	.962	.952	.943	.935	.926	.917	.909	.901	.893	.885	.877	.870
2	1.970	1.942	1.913	1.886	1.859	1.833	1.808	1.783	1.759	1.736	1.713	1.690	1.668	1.647	1.626
3	2.941	2.884	2.829	2.775	2.723	2.673	2.624	2.577	2.531	2.487	2.444	2.402	2.361	2.322	2.283
4	3.902	3.808	3.717	3.630	3.546	3.465	3.387	3.312	3.240	3.170	3.102	3.037	2.974	2.914	2.855
5	4.853	4.713	4.580	4.452	4.329	4.212	4.100	3.993	3.890	3.791	3.696	3.605	3.517	3.433	3.352
6	5.795	5.601	5.417	5.242	5.076	4.917	4.767	4.623	4.486	4.355	4.231	4.111	3.998	3.889	3.784
7	6.728	6.472	6.230	6.002	5.786	5.582	5.389	5.206	5.033	4.868	4.712	4.564	4.423	4.288	4.160
8	7.652	7.325	7.020	6.733	6.463	6.210	5.971	5.747	5.535	5.335	5.146	4.968	4.799	4.639	4.487
9	8.566	8.162	7.786	7.435	7.108	6.802	6.515	6.247	5.995	5.759	5.537	5.328	5.132	4.946	4.772
10	9.471	8.983	8.530	8.111	7.722	7.360	7.024	6.710	6.418	6.145	5.889	5.650	5.426	5.216	5.019
11	10.37	9.787	9.253	8.760	8.306	7.887	7.499	7.139	6.805	6.495	6.207	5.938	5.687	5.453	5.234
12	11.26	10.58	9.954	9.385	8.863	8.384	7.943	7.536	7.161	6.814	6.492	6.194	5.918	5.660	5.421
13	12.13	11.35	10.63	9.986	9.394	8.853	8.358	7.904	7.487	7.103	6.750	6.424	6.122	5.842	5.583
14	13.00	12.11	11.30	10.56	9.899	9.295	8.745	8.244	7.786	7.367	6.982	6.628	6.302	6.002	5.724
15	13.87	12.85	11.94	11.12	10.38	9.712	9.108	8.559	8.061	7.606	7.191	6.811	6.462	6.142	5.847
16	14.72	13.58	12.56	11.65	10.84	10.11	9.447	8.851	8.313	7.824	7.379	6.974	6.604	6.265	5.954
17	15.56	14.29	13.17	12.17	11.27	10.48	9.763	9.122	8.544	8.022	7.549	7.120	6.729	6.373	6.047
18	16.40	14.99	13.75	12.66	11.69	10.83	10.06	9.372	8.756	8.201	7.702	7.250	6.840	6.467	6.128
19	17.23	15.68	14.32	13.13	12.09	11.16	10.34	9.604	8.950	8.365	7.839	7.366	6.938	6.550	6.198
20	18.05	16.35	14.88	13.59	12.46	11.47	10.59	9.818	9.129	8.514	7.963	7.469	7.025	6.623	6.259
25	22.02	19.52	17.41	15.62	14.09	12.78	11.65	10.67	9.823	9.077	8.422	7.843	7.330	6.873	6.464
30	25.81	22.40	19.60	17.29	15.37	13.76	12.41	11.26	10.27	9.427	8.694	8.055	7.496	7.003	6.566

Number of Years	Interest Rate per Year														
	16%	17%	18%	19%	20%	21%	22%	23%	24%	25%	26%	27%	28%	29%	30%
1	.862	.855	.847	.840	.833	.826	.820	.813	.806	.800	.794	.787	.781	.775	.769
2	1.605	1.585	1.566	1.547	1.528	1.509	1.492	1.474	1.457	1.440	1.424	1.407	1.392	1.376	1.361
3	2.246	2.210	2.174	2.140	2.106	2.074	2.042	2.011	1.981	1.952	1.923	1.896	1.868	1.842	1.816
4	2.798	2.743	2.690	2.639	2.589	2.540	2.494	2.448	2.404	2.362	2.320	2.280	2.241	2.203	2.166
5	3.274	3.199	3.127	3.058	2.991	2.926	2.864	2.803	2.745	2.689	2.635	2.583	2.532	2.483	2.436
6	3.685	3.589	3.498	3.410	3.326	3.245	3.167	3.092	3.020	2.951	2.885	2.821	2.759	2.700	2.643
7	4.039	3.922	3.812	3.706	3.605	3.508	3.416	3.327	3.242	3.161	3.083	3.009	2.937	2.868	2.802
8	4.344	4.207	4.078	3.954	3.837	3.726	3.619	3.518	3.421	3.329	3.241	3.156	3.076	2.999	2.925
9	4.607	4.451	4.303	4.163	4.031	3.905	3.786	3.673	3.566	3.463	3.366	3.273	3.184	3.100	3.019
10	4.833	4.659	4.494	4.339	4.192	4.054	3.923	3.799	3.682	3.571	3.465	3.364	3.269	3.178	3.092
11	5.029	4.836	4.656	4.486	4.327	4.177	4.035	3.902	3.776	3.656	3.543	3.437	3.335	3.239	3.147
12	5.197	4.988	4.793	4.611	4.439	4.278	4.127	3.985	3.851	3.725	3.606	3.493	3.387	3.286	3.190
13	5.342	5.118	4.910	4.715	4.533	4.362	4.203	4.053	3.912	3.780	3.656	3.538	3.427	3.322	3.223
14	5.468	5.229	5.008	4.802	4.611	4.432	4.265	4.108	3.962	3.824	3.695	3.573	3.459	3.351	3.249
15	5.575	5.324	5.092	4.876	4.675	4.489	4.315	4.153	4.001	3.859	3.726	3.601	3.483	3.373	3.268
16	5.668	5.405	5.162	4.938	4.730	4.536	4.357	4.189	4.033	3.887	3.751	3.623	3.503	3.390	3.283
17	5.749	5.475	5.222	4.990	4.775	4.576	4.391	4.219	4.059	3.910	3.771	3.640	3.518	3.403	3.295
18	5.818	5.534	5.273	5.033	4.812	4.608	4.419	4.243	4.080	3.928	3.786	3.654	3.529	3.413	3.304
19	5.877	5.584	5.316	5.070	4.843	4.635	4.442	4.263	4.097	3.942	3.799	3.664	3.539	3.421	3.311
20	5.929	5.628	5.353	5.101	4.870	4.657	4.460	4.279	4.110	3.954	3.808	3.673	3.546	3.427	3.316
25	6.097	5.766	5.467	5.195	4.948	4.721	4.514	4.323	4.147	3.985	3.834	3.694	3.564	3.442	3.329
30	6.177	5.829	5.517	5.235	4.979	4.746	4.534	4.339	4.160	3.995	3.842	3.701	3.569	3.447	3.332

(e.g., if the interest rate is 10 percent per year, the present value of $1 received in each of the next 5 years is $3.791.)

APPENDIX A TABLE A.4

ANNUITY TABLE: FUTURE VALUE OF $1 *PER YEAR* FOR EACH OF t YEARS = $[(1 + r)^t - 1]/r$

Number of Years	Interest Rate per Year														
	1%	2%	3%	4%	5%	6%	7%	8%	9%	10%	11%	12%	13%	14%	15%
1	1.000	1.000	1.000	1.000	1.000	1.000	1.000	1.000	1.000	1.000	1.000	1.000	1.000	1.000	1.000
2	2.010	2.020	2.030	2.040	2.050	2.060	2.070	2.080	2.090	2.100	2.110	2.120	2.130	2.140	2.150
3	3.030	3.060	3.091	3.122	3.153	3.184	3.215	3.246	3.278	3.310	3.342	3.374	3.407	3.440	3.473
4	4.060	4.122	4.184	4.246	4.310	4.375	4.440	4.506	4.573	4.641	4.710	4.779	4.850	4.921	4.993
5	5.101	5.204	5.309	5.416	5.526	5.637	5.751	5.867	5.985	6.105	6.228	6.353	6.480	6.610	6.742
6	6.152	6.308	6.468	6.633	6.802	6.975	7.153	7.336	7.523	7.716	7.913	8.115	8.323	8.536	8.754
7	7.214	7.434	7.662	7.898	8.142	8.394	8.654	8.923	9.200	9.487	9.783	10.089	10.405	10.730	11.067
8	8.286	8.583	8.892	9.214	9.549	9.897	10.260	10.637	11.028	11.436	11.859	12.300	12.757	13.233	13.727
9	9.369	9.755	10.159	10.583	11.027	11.491	11.978	12.488	13.021	13.579	14.164	14.776	15.416	16.085	16.786
10	10.462	10.950	11.464	12.006	12.578	13.181	13.816	14.487	15.193	15.937	16.722	17.549	18.420	19.337	20.304
11	11.567	12.169	12.808	13.486	14.207	14.972	15.784	16.645	17.560	18.531	19.561	20.655	21.814	23.045	24.349
12	12.683	13.412	14.192	15.026	15.917	16.870	17.888	18.977	20.141	21.384	22.713	24.133	25.650	27.271	29.002
13	13.809	14.680	15.618	16.627	17.713	18.882	20.141	21.495	22.953	24.523	26.212	28.029	29.985	32.089	34.352
14	14.947	15.974	17.086	18.292	19.599	21.015	22.550	24.215	26.019	27.975	30.095	32.393	34.883	37.581	40.505
15	16.097	17.293	18.599	20.024	21.579	23.276	25.129	27.152	29.361	31.772	34.405	37.280	40.417	43.842	47.580
16	17.258	18.639	20.157	21.825	23.657	25.673	27.888	30.324	33.003	35.950	39.190	42.753	46.672	50.980	55.717
17	18.430	20.012	21.762	23.698	25.840	28.213	30.840	33.750	36.974	40.545	44.501	48.884	53.739	59.118	65.075
18	19.615	21.412	23.414	25.645	28.132	30.906	33.999	37.450	41.301	45.599	50.396	55.750	61.725	68.394	75.836
19	20.811	22.841	25.117	27.671	30.539	33.760	37.379	41.446	46.018	51.159	56.939	63.440	70.749	78.969	88.212
20	22.019	24.297	26.870	29.778	33.066	36.786	40.995	45.762	51.160	57.275	64.203	72.052	80.947	91.025	102.444
25	28.243	32.030	36.459	41.646	47.727	54.865	63.249	73.106	84.701	98.347	114.413	133.334	155.620	181.871	212.793
30	34.785	40.568	47.575	56.085	66.439	79.058	94.461	113.283	136.308	164.494	199.021	241.333	293.199	356.787	434.745

Number of Years	Interest Rate per Year 16%	17%	18%	19%	20%	21%	22%	23%	24%	25%	26%	27%	28%	29%	30%
1	1.000	1.000	1.000	1.000	1.000	1.000	1.000	1.000	1.000	1.000	1.000	1.000	1.000	1.000	1.000
2	2.160	2.170	2.180	2.190	2.200	2.210	2.220	2.230	2.240	2.250	2.260	2.270	2.280	2.290	2.300
3	3.506	3.539	3.572	3.606	3.640	3.674	3.708	3.743	3.778	3.813	3.848	3.883	3.918	3.954	3.990
4	5.066	5.141	5.215	5.291	5.368	5.446	5.524	5.604	5.684	5.766	5.848	5.931	6.016	6.101	6.187
5	6.877	7.014	7.154	7.297	7.442	7.589	7.740	7.893	8.048	8.207	8.368	8.533	8.700	8.870	9.043
6	8.977	9.207	9.442	9.683	9.930	10.183	10.442	10.708	10.980	11.259	11.544	11.837	12.136	12.442	12.756
7	11.414	11.772	12.142	12.523	12.916	13.321	13.740	14.171	14.615	15.073	15.546	16.032	16.534	17.051	17.583
8	14.240	14.773	15.327	15.902	16.499	17.119	17.762	18.430	19.123	19.842	20.588	21.361	22.163	22.995	23.858
9	17.519	18.285	19.086	19.923	20.799	21.714	22.670	23.669	24.712	25.802	26.940	28.129	29.369	30.664	32.015
10	21.321	22.393	23.521	24.709	25.959	27.274	28.657	30.113	31.643	33.253	34.945	36.723	38.593	40.556	42.619
11	25.733	27.200	28.755	30.404	32.150	34.001	35.962	38.039	40.238	42.566	45.031	47.639	50.398	53.318	56.405
12	30.850	32.824	34.931	37.180	39.581	42.142	44.874	47.788	50.895	54.208	57.739	61.501	65.510	69.780	74.327
13	36.786	39.404	42.219	45.244	48.497	51.991	55.746	59.779	64.110	68.760	73.751	79.107	84.853	91.016	97.625
14	43.672	47.103	50.818	54.841	59.196	63.909	69.010	74.528	80.496	86.949	93.926	101.465	109.612	118.411	127.913
15	51.660	56.110	60.965	66.261	72.035	78.330	85.192	92.669	100.815	109.687	119.347	129.861	141.303	153.750	167.286
16	60.925	66.649	72.939	79.850	87.442	95.780	104.935	114.983	126.011	138.109	151.377	165.924	181.868	199.337	218.472
17	71.673	78.979	87.068	96.022	105.931	116.894	129.020	142.430	157.253	173.636	191.735	211.723	233.791	258.145	285.014
18	84.141	93.406	103.740	115.266	128.117	142.441	158.405	176.188	195.994	218.045	242.585	269.888	300.252	334.007	371.518
19	98.603	110.285	123.414	138.166	154.740	173.354	194.254	217.712	244.033	273.556	306.658	343.758	385.323	431.870	483.973
20	115.380	130.033	146.628	165.418	186.688	210.758	237.989	268.785	303.601	342.945	387.389	437.573	494.213	558.112	630.165
25	249.214	292.105	342.603	402.042	471.98	554.24	650.96	764.61	898.09	1054.79	1238.64	1454.20	1706.80	2002.62	2348.80
30	530.312	647.439	790.948	966.712	1181.88	1445.15	1767.08	2160.49	2640.92	3227.17	3942.03	4812.98	5873.23	7162.82	8729.99

(e.g., if the interest rate is 10 percent per year, the future value of $1 received in each of the next 5 years is $6.105.)

Appendix B

SOLUTIONS TO SELECTED END-OF-CHAPTER PROBLEMS

CHAPTER 1

1. real, executive airplanes, brand names, financial, stock, investment, capital budgeting, financing
7. a. financial
   b. financial
   c. real
   d. real
   e. real
   f. financial
   g. real
   h. financial
10. Mutual funds; Pension funds; Venture capital firms
15. The contingency arrangement aligns the interests of the lawyer and the client.
17. Such a plan would burden them with a considerable personal risk tied to the fortunes of the firm.
18. Managers who are more securely entrenched in their positions are more able to pursue their own interests.
22. If you know that you will engage in business with another party on a repeated basis, you will be less likely to take advantage of your business partner should the opportunity to do so arise.

CHAPTER 2

1.

Assets		Liabilities and Shareholders' Equity	
Cash	$ 10,000	Accounts payable	$ 17,000
Receivables	22,000	Long-term debt	170,000
Inventory	200,000		
Store and property	100,000	Shareholders' equity	145,000
Total assets	$332,000	Liabilities and shareholders' equity	$332,000

5. a. Federal + Alta. taxes = $3,200 + $2,000 = $5,200
   Marginal and average tax rates are 26%
   Federal + Nfld. taxes = $3,200 + $2,114 = $5,314
   Marginal and average tax rates are 26.57%.
   b. Federal + Alta. taxes = $11,355 + $6,000 = $17,355
   Average tax rate = 28.92%
   Marginal tax rate = 32%
   Federal + Nfld. taxes = $11,355 + $8,057 = $19,412
   Average tax rate = 32.35%
   Marginal tax rate = 40.02%.
   c. Federal + Alta. taxes = $21,692 + $10,000 = $31,692
   Average tax rate = 31.69%
   Marginal tax rate = 36%
   Federal + Nfld. taxes = $21,692 + $15,265 = $36,957
   Average tax rate = 36.96%
   Marginal tax rate = 44.02%
   d. Federal + Alta. taxes = $775,692 + $300,000 = $1,075,692
   Average tax rate = 35.86%
   Marginal tax rate = 36%
   Federal + Nfld. taxes = $775,692 + $537,845 = $1,313,537
   Average tax rate = 43.78%
   Marginal tax rate = 44.02%
9. Dividends = $600,000
10. Total taxes are reduced by $4,533.50 (from $28,130.5 to $23,597).
11. a. Book value = $200,000
    Market value = $50,200,000
    b. Price per share = $25.10
    Book value per share = $.10
12.

Sales	$ 10,000
Cost of goods sold	6,500
G & A expenses	1,000
Depreciation expense	1,000
EBIT	1,500
Interest expense	500
Taxable income	1,000
Taxes (35%)	350
Net income	$ 650

Cash flow = net income + depreciation = $1,650

15. Cash flow will be $3,000 less than profits.
17. a. Net income = $1.95 million
    Cash flow from operations = $3.95 million
    Cash flow from assets = $2.95 million
    b. Both cash flows increase by $.35 million
    Net income decreases by $.65 million
    Depreciation reduces net income, but since it is not a cash outflow, it does not reduce cash flow. However, assuming this depreciation is deductible for tax purposes (it really is CCA), it reduces taxes which increases cash flow.
    c. Positive impact. Investors should care more about cash flow than book income.
    d. Net income and both cash flows decrease by $.65 million. Unlike depreciation, interest expense is an actual cash outflow.
20. a. 2002: Equity = 890 – 650 = 240
    2003: Equity = 1,040 – 810 = 230
    b. 2002: NWC = 90 – 50 = 40
    2003: NWC = 140 – 60 = 80
    c. Taxable income = 1,950 – 1,030 – 350 – 240 = 330
    Taxes paid = .35 x 330 = 115.50
    d. Cash flow from operations = 524.5
    e. Gross investment = 450
    f. Other current liabilities increased by 45.

g. Cash flow from assets = 524.5 – 450 = 74.5
Cash flow to bondholders and shareholders = (750 – 600) + (230 – 240) + 214.5 = 74.5

22. Noncash net working capital increased by 50.

24. Earnings per share in 2002 = $1.70
Earnings per share in 2003 = $1.52

28. Price per share = $6,650,000/500,000 = $13.30

CHAPTER 3

1. a. 38.55
b. 14.86
c. 61.39
d. 37.69

3. $100 × (1.05)^{113} = $24,797
$100 × (1.10)^{113} = $4,757,441

5. PV = $523

6. 5%
8%
0%

7.

	Discount Rate	PV of 10-Year $1,000 Annuity	PV of 15-Year $800 Annuity
a.	5%	$7,722	$8,304
b.	20%	4,192	3,740

9. PV = $812.44

10. a. $t = 23.36$
b. $t = 11.91$
c. $t = 6.17$

11. Effective annual rate:
12.68%
8.24%
10.25%

12. APR = 9.57%
APR = 6%
APR = 8%

13. $n = 9.01$ years

15. APR = 52%; EAR = 67.77%

20. The PV for the quarterback is $10.81 million. The PV for the receiver is $7.21 million plus $4 million immediate payment, or $11.21 million.

23. a. EAR = 6.78%
b. PMT = 573.14

25. a. $r = 11.11\%$
b. $r = 1/(1 - d) - 1 = d/(1 - d)$

27. APR = 15.58%, EAR = 16.74%

30. The value of the lease payments is $40,801. It is cheaper to buy the truck.

31. Installment plan: PV = 91.83% of stated price
Pay in full: Payment net of discount is only 90% of stated price

33. a. PMT = 277.41
b. PMT = 247.69

34. PV = $61,796.71

35. Monthly mortgage payment = $1,119.66.
Balance remaining after 5 years is $157,208.

36. Paying $1,225.73 every two weeks (26 payments a year) pays off the mortgage in 534 bi-weekly periods, or about 20.5 years, reducing the life of the mortgage by 4.5 years.

40. Real rate of interest is zero. Annual consumption = $450,000/30 = $15,000.

45. $100 × $e^{.10 \times 6}$ = $182.21
$100 × $e^{.06 \times 10}$ = $182.21

46. $n = 44.74$ months

47. The present value of your payments is $671. The present value of your receipts is $579. This is a bad deal.

49. $r = 8\%$

52. a. The present value of the payoff is $1,228. This is a good deal.
b. PV is $771. This is a bad deal.

54. APR = 35.08%; EAR = 41.3%

61. $4,126.57

62. a. $408,334.38
b. $3,457.40

65. a. Nominal rate = 4%
b. Nominal rate = 8.16%
c. Nominal rate = 10.24%

67. a. $79.38
b. $91.51
c. Real interest rate = 4.854%
d. $91.51/(1.04854)^3 = $79.38

69. a. $264,439
b. $16,172

70. 18 years

71. Inflation = 1,099% per year

76. $1.188, $0.8418

77. $3,947.90

CHAPTER 4

1. a. Coupon rate remains unchanged.
b. Price will fall.
c. Yield to maturity increases.
d. Current yield increases.

3. Bond price = \$1,066.67

4. Coupon rate = 8.0%
   Current yield = 8.42%
   Yield to maturity = 9.12%

9. 15%

10. 12%

11. Rate of return on both bonds = 10%

12. a. Price will be \$1,000.
    b. Rate of return = 2.86%
    c. Real return = –.14%

13. a. Bondholder receives \$80 per year.
    b. Price = \$940.05
    c. The bond will sell for \$1,065.15.

14. a. 8.97%
    b. 8%
    c. 7.18%

15. 20 years

20. a. Price = \$721.67
    b. r = 11.97%

21. a. Yield to maturity = 7.23%
    b. Rate of return = 15.31%

24. a. 9.89%
    b. 8%
    c. 6.18%

26. a. 7.5% per year
    b. 7.63% per year
    c. 8.64% per year

27. 8.64 % per year

28. Initial price = \$978.16
    New price = \$959.39

29. a. 3.92%
    b. 1.92%
    c. 0
    d. –1.85%

33. a. 5.19%
    b. 5.25%
    c. 5.70

CHAPTER 5

3. a. \$58.33
   b \$58.33
   c. Dividend yield = 12%; capital gains yield = 0%; expected return = 12%

6. a. 14%
   b. P_0 = \$20

8. a. DIV_1 = \$1.04
      DIV_2 = \$1.0816
      DIV_3 = \$1.1249
   b. P_0 = \$13
   c. P_3 = \$14.62
   d. Your payments are:

	Year 1	Year 2	Year 3
DIV	1.04	1.0816	1.1249
Sales price			14.6232
Total cash flow	1.04	1.0816	15.7481
PV of cash flow	0.9286	0.8622	11.2092

   Sum of PV = \$13.00

10. a. P_0 = \$21
    b. P_0 = \$30

12. a. 9.26%
    b. 3.74%
    c. 12.5%

15. a. (1) Reinvest 0% of earnings
           P_0 = \$33.33
       (2) Reinvest at 40%
           P_0 = \$33.33
       (3) Reinvest at 60%
           P_0 = \$33.33
    b. (1) Reinvest at 0%
           P_0 = \$33.33
       (2) Reinvest at 40%
           P_0 = 42.86
           PVGO = \$9.53
       (3) Reinvest at 60%
           P_0 = \$66.67
           PVGO = \$33.34
    c. In part (a), the return on reinvested earnings was equal to the discount rate.
       In part (b), the return on reinvested earnings was greater than the discount rate.

16. a. P_0 = \$18.10
    b. DIV_1/P_0 = 5.52%

18. a. 6%
    b. 23.33
    c. 6.66
    d. 11.67
    e. 8.33
    f. High P/E ratios reflect expectations of high PVGO.

20. a. P/E = 33.33/4 = 8.33
    b. P/E increases to 10

22. a. P_0 = \$125
    b. Assets in place = \$80
       PVGO = \$45

25. a. Market-to-book ratio = $400/$100 = 4
    b. Market-to-book ratio = ½

27. a. $2.4
    b. $28.02

29. Before-tax return is 7.8%, after-tax return is 5.96%.

33. a. Expected return = 8%
    b. PVGO = $16.67
    c. P_0 = $106.22

CHAPTER 6

1. Both projects are worth pursuing.

3. NPV_A = $11.93 and NPV_B = $12.29. Choose B.

5. No.

7. Project A has a payback period of 2.5 years. Project B has a payback period of 2 years.

10.

	Year	Book Return
Project A	1	.15
	2	.20
	3	.30
	4	.60
Project B	1	.167
	2	.25
	3	.50

13 .2378

16. IRR_A = 25.7%
    IRR_B = 20.7%
    Project B is best.

17. NPV = –$197.7. Reject.

18. a. r = 0 implies NPV = $15,750.
    r = 50% implies NPV = $4,250.
    r = 100% implies NPV = 0.
    b. IRR = 100%

20. $NPV_{9\%}$ = $2,139.28 and $NPV_{14\%}$ = –$1,444.54. The IRR is 11.81%.

23. NPV must be negative.

25. a.

Project	Payback	Discounted Payback
A	3	4+
B	2	2.12
C	3	3.30

    b. Project B
    c. Project B
    d.

Project	NPV
A	–1,011
B	3,378
C	2,405

    e. False

28. a.

Year	Book Rate of Return
1	10%
2	12.5%
3	16.7%
4	25%
5	50%

    b. NPV = $1,978
    c.

Year	Book Rate of Return
1	–60%
2	50%
3	66.7%
4	100%
5	200%

    d. NPV unaffected

32. a. If r = 2%, choose A.
    b. If r = 12%, choose B.
    c. Larger cash flows for project A come later and are more sensitive to discount rate increases.

34. $22,774

36. b. At 5%, NPV = –$.443
    c. At 20%, NPV = $.840
    At 40%, NPV = –$.634

37. a. The equivalent annual cost of owning and operating Econo-cool is $252.53. The equivalent annual cost of Luxury Air is $234.21.
    b. Luxury Air.
    c. Econo-cool equivalent annual cost is $229.14. Luxury Air equivalent annual cost is $193.72.

40. a. The equivalent cost of owning and operating the new machine is $4,590. The old machine costs $5,000 a year to operate. You should replace.
    b. If r = 10%, do not replace.

CHAPTER 7

3. $2.2 million

5. Increase in net cash flow = $106 million

6.

Revenue	$ 160,000
Rental costs	35,000
Variable costs	45,000
Depreciation	10,000
Pretax profit	$ 70,000
Taxes (35%)	24,500
Net income	$ 45,500

8. Cash flow = $3,300

10. Total operating cash flow in thousands (Years 1-6) = $339.45
    Net cash flow at time 0 = –$1,000

11. a.

Year	CCA Rate
1	6,000
2	10,200
3	7,140

b. and c. See Solutions Manual.

16. After-tax cash flow = $17.3 million

18. a. Total incremental operating CF = $7,457 in years 1–6
    Net cash flow at time 0 = –$4,000
    b. NPV = $901.25
    c. NPV = –4,000 + 1,300 × annuity factor (15%, 6 years) = $919.83; IRR = 23.21%

21. a. Initial investment = $58,000
    b.

Year	Cash Flow ($000)
1	18.9
2	17.2
3	12.5
4	8.1

c. NPV = (in $ thousands) = –8.14

23. NPV = –10,894. Don't buy.

25. Equivalent annual (net-of-tax) capital costs:
    Quick and Dirty: $2.12 million
    Do-It-Right: $1.84 million
    Choose Do-It-Right.

27. NPV = –$372,964

29. NPV = –$1.82

31. NPV = $24.92 million
    IRR = 31.33%
    NPV (with CCA) = $5.25 million

CHAPTER 8

1. Variable costs = $.50 per burger
   Fixed costs = $1.25 million

4. a. $1.836 million
   $3.673 million
   b. $544,588
   c. $3 million

5. a. NPV = $5.1 million
   b. NPV = $2.5 million
   c. NPV = $6.2 million
   d. Price = $1.61 per jar

9. a. 4,286 diamonds annually
   b. 5,978 diamonds per year

11. Accounting break-even is unaffected. NPV break-even increases.

12. CF break-even is less than zero-profit break-even sales level.

14. a. Accounting break-even sales level is $6,400 per year. NPV break-even sales level is $7,166.
    b. Accounting break-even is unchanged. NPV break-even is $7,676.

15. a. Accounting break-even increases.
    b. NPV break-even falls.
    c. The switch to CCA makes the project more attractive.

17. NPV will be negative.

20. DOL = 1

23. a. Average CF = 0
    b. Average CF = $15,000

27. a. Expected NPV = –$681,728. The firm will reject the project.
    b. Expected NPV = $69,855. The project is now worth pursuing.

CHAPTER 9

1. Return = 15%
   Dividend yield = 5%
   Capital gains yield = 10%

3. a. Rate of return = 0
   Real rate = –4.76%
   b. Rate of return = 5%
   Real rate = 0
   c. Rate of return = 10%
   Real rate = 4.76%

5.

Asset Class	Real Rate
Treasury bills	2.01%
Government bonds	2.59
Common stock	8.05

7.

Week	Average Price of Stock in Market	Equal-Weight Index	Value-Weighted Index
1	85.90	100.00	100.00
2	85.00	98.95	96.77
3	84.80	98.72	94.56
4	85.70	99.77	93.96
5	88.60	103.14	96.61
6	86.00	100.12	96.65
7	85.20	99.19	96.94
8	83.60	97.32	96.04
9	78.60	91.50	89.44

9\. a.

Year	TSX Risk Premium	Long Bond Risk Premium
1996	23.86	9.80
1997	11.68	14.15
1998	–6.39	9.32
1999	26.88	–11.98
2000	1.92	8.15
Average	11.59	5.89

b. Average TSX risk premium = 11.59%; Average long bond risk premium = 5.89%

c. TSX risk premium standard deviation = 14.16%; Long bond risk premium standard deviation = 10.24%. The riskier TSX will have a more variable historic risk premium, with a higher standard deviation than less risk long bonds.

14\. Expected return = 23.3%
Standard deviation = 77.63%

15\. The bankruptcy lawyer, whose business does well in a recession and poorly in a boom, will see the Tower of Pita stock as risk-reducing, lowering variability of her total income. The casino owner's business likely does well in a boom, just like Tower of Pita's stock.The stock will not lower variability of his total income.

17\. b. r_{stock} = 13%
r_{bonds} = 8.4%
Standard deviation (stocks) = 9.8%
Standard deviation (bonds) = 3.2%

19\. Our estimate of "normal" risk premiums will fall. It is sensbile to assume that each additional year of data reveals new information about the "normal" behaviour of the market portfolio. Update our beliefs as additional observations about the market become available.

21\. a. General Steel
b. Club Med

23\. Sassafras is *not* a risky investment to a diversified investor. Its return is better when the economy enters a recession. In contrast, the Leaning Tower of Pita has returns that are positively correlated with the rest of the economy.

25\. a., b.

	Average return	Standard deviation
TSX	16.17%	14.00%
Long Bond	10.47	9.97
Treasury Bill	4.58	0.81
Portfolio	10.41	3.69
Average	11.59	5.89

b. The average standard deviation of the three securities is 8.25%, much higher than the portfolio standard deviation of 3.69%, showing the benefit of diversification.

CHAPTER 10

1\. a. False
b. False
c. False
d. True
e. True

3\. It is not well diversified. The actual returns vary above and below the regression line, indicating that the fund is subject to diversifiable risk. The variation in return is affected by more than just market-wide events.

7\. Required return = $r_f + \beta(r_m - r_f)$ = 16%
Expected return = 14%
The security is overpriced.

9\. a. Nike, which has a beta of 1.20.
b. Nike, with standard deviation of 31%.
c. $\beta = .78$
d. The portfolio beta = .61
Portfolio standard deviation = 12.2%
e. Exxon: r = 8.88%
Polaroid: r = 8.24%
Nike: r = 13.60%

11\. a. $\beta_A = 1.2$
$\beta_D = .75$
D is more defensive because its return is less sensitive to the return of the overall market.
b. r_m = 12%
r_A = 14%
r_D = 9%
c. $r = r_f + \beta(r_m - r_f)$
r_A = 13.6%
r_D = 10%
d. Stock A

13\. NPV = –$34.92

15\. P_1 = $53

19\. $400,000

21\.

Company	Expected Return;
Alliance Atlantis	8.83%
Big Rock Brewery	7.36
Intrawest	10.65
Nortel	19.75

23\. $\beta = .5$

25\. a. False
b. True
c. False
d. True
e. False

26. $r = r_f + \beta(r_m - r_f) = 9.6\%$
    The 9% expected return is too low relative to its risk.

31. a. 10.3%
    b. 13.8% because it reflects the risk of ChemCo.
    c. $91.84 million
    d. .94

CHAPTER 11

1. 5.50%
3. 9.9%
4. 13.75%
6. No, the riskof the project determines the appropriate discount rate. Use Geothermal's WACC.
8. The cost of equity capital is 10.4%.
   WACC = 8.78%
10. WACC = 12.4%
14. a. 10.55%
    b. 6.86%
15.

	Dollars	Percent
Bonds	$ 9.36 million	30.3%
Preferred stock	1.50 million	4.9
Common stock	20.00 million	64.8
Total	$30.86 million	100.0%

17. The IRR is less than the WACC of firms in the computer industry. Reject the project.
18. a. $r = 19\%$
    b. Weighted-average beta = 1.0
    c. WACC = 14.67%
    d. Discount rate = 14.67%
    e. $r = 16\%$

CHAPTER 12

1. weak, semistrong, strong, fundamental, strong, technical, weak
4. diversification, tax planning and management, risk management
8. Investments in financial markets such as stocks or bonds are available to all participants in the marketplace. Prices of these investments are bid up to "fair" levels. In contrast, investments in product markets are made by firms with various forms of protection from full competition.
11. If the price of the firm already reflects this fact, the stock may not be a bargain.
13. The market has no memory. Just because long-term interest rates are high relative to past levels doesn't mean they won't go higher still.
14. a. No.
    b. No.
    c. Earnings per share will fall by half.
    d. The firm's stock price will fall by half.
    e. Shareholders' wealth is unaffected.
16. A downward-sloping yield curve might indicate that investors anticipate future short-term rates lower than today's.

CHAPTER 13

1. a. 80,000 shares
   b.

After new issue:	
Common shares	$110,000
Retained earnings	$ 30,000
Common equity	$140,000
Note:	
Authorized shares	$100,000
Issued shares	$ 30,000

3. a. funded
   b. eurobond
   c. subordinated
   d. sinking fund
   e. call
   f. prime rate
   g. floating rate
   h. private placement, public issue
   i. lease
   j. convertible
   k. warrant
6. a. 90 votes
   b. 900 votes
7. a. 200,001 shares
   b. 80,000 shares
11. Similarity: The firm promises to make specified payments. Advantage of income bonds: interest payments are tax-deductible expenses.

CHAPTER 14

1. a. Subsequent issue
   b. Bond issue
   c. Bond issue
3. a. A large issue
   b. A bond issue
   c. Private placements
4. Less underwriter risk; less signalling effect from debt; easier to value

7. a. 10%
   b. Average return = 3.94%
   c. I have suffered the winner's curse.

10. No.

12. 12% of the value of funds raised.

14. a. Net proceeds of public issue = \$9,770,000
    Net proceeds of private placement = \$9,970,000
    b. The public issue
    c. The private placement can be custom-tailored and its terms can be more easily renegotiated.

15. a. \$12.5 million
    b. \$5.80 per share

17. a. \$10
    b. \$18.333
    c. \$8.333
    d. 200 rights

CHAPTER 15

4. \$296 million

11. P/E = 10/1.25 = 8 (no leverage)
    P/E = 10/1.33 = 7.5 (leveraged)

14. a. Low-debt plan: D/E = .25
    High-debt plan: D/E = .67

b.

	Low-Debt Plan		High-Debt Plan	
EPS	8.75	13.75	8.33	15.00
Expected EPS	\$11.25		\$11.67	

c.

	Low-Debt	High-Debt
EPS	10	10

16. r_{equity} = 18%

22. a. 11.27%
    b. Without the tax shield, the value of equity would fall by \$296 million. E falls to 1,900 – 296 = 1,604. Market-value balance sheet:

Assets	Liabilities and Equity	
2,404	Debt	800
	Equity	1,604

23. a. PV tax shield = \$14
    b. PV tax shield = \$4.47. Value of firm falls by \$14 – \$4.47 = \$9.53, from \$160 to \$150.47.
    c. \$150.47

24. Distorted investment decisions, impeded relations with other firms and creditors

31. a. Stockholders gain; bondholders lose.
    b. Bondholders gain; stockholders lose.
    c. Bondholders lose; stockholders gain.
    d. Original stockholders lose; bondholders gain.

CHAPTER 16

1. a. May 7: Declaration date
   June 6: Last with-dividend date
   June 7: Ex-dividend date
   June 11: Record date
   July 2: Payment date
   b. The ex-dividend date, June 7
   c. Dividend yield = 1.1%
   d. Payout ratio = 15.8%
   e. New stock price = \$24.55

3. a. Price = \$32
   b. Price = \$32
   c. Price = \$40, unchanged

9. a. No effect on total wealth
   b. Identical to position after the stock repurchase

11. No impact on wealth

12. a. The after-tax dividend, \$1.44
    b. No

13. a. 1,250 shares. Value of equity remains at \$50,000.
    b. Same effect as the stock dividend

14. a. \$50
    b. 26.16%
    c. \$48.692

16. a. Price = \$19.49
    b. Before-tax return = 12.9%
    c. Price = \$20.15
    d. Before-tax return = 14.1%

17. a.

Stock	Pension	Corporation	Individual
A	10.00%	8.35%	7.88%
B	10.00	9.175	7.44
C	10.00	10	7.01

b.

Stock	Price
A	\$111.13
B	\$115.19
C	\$119.19

23. a. \$20 per share
    b. If the firm pays a dividend, EPS = \$2. If the firm does the repurchase, EPS = \$2.105.
    c. If the dividend is paid, the P/E ratio = 9.5. If the stock is repurchased, the P/E ratio = 9.5.

CHAPTER 17

1. a. Long-term debt ratio = .42
   b. Total debt ratio = .65
   c. Times interest earned = 3.75
   d. Cash coverage ratio = 7.42
   e. Current ratio = .74
   f. Quick ratio = .52
   g. Net profit margin = .151
   h. Inventory turnover = 19.11
   i. Days sales in inventory = 19.10 days
   j. Average collection period = 67.39 days
   k. ROE = .139
   l. ROA = .072
   m. Payout ratio = .65
   n. Operating profit margin = .151
   o. Gross profit margin = .692
3. Gross investment = $2,576 million
5. Common-size balance sheet for Phone Corp.:

	Common-Size Balance Sheet (% amounts)	
	End of Year	**Start of Year**
Assets		
Cash and marketable securities	0.32%	0.57%
Receivables	8.59	9.05
Inventories	0.67	0.87
Other current assets	3.13	3.39
Total current assets	12.72%	13.88%
Net property, plant, and equipment	72.07	72.41
Other long-term assets	15.21	13.71
Total assets	100.00%	100.00%
Liabilities and Shareholders' Equity		
Payables	9.25%	11.05%
Short-term debt	5.12	5.72
Other current liabilities	2.93	2.86
Total current liabilities	17.30%	19.63%
Long-term debt and leases	25.32	24.84
Other long-term liabilities	22.29	22.36
Shareholders' equity	35.09	33.16
Total liabilities and shareholders' equity	100.00%	100.00%

7. $$\frac{\text{assets}}{\text{equity}} \times \frac{\text{sales}}{\text{assets}} \times \frac{\text{NI + interest}}{\text{sales}} \times \frac{\text{NI}}{\text{NI + interest}}$$

$$\frac{27{,}608.5}{9{,}422.5} \times \frac{13{,}194}{27{,}608.5} \times \frac{2{,}566 - 570}{13{,}194}$$

$$\times \frac{2{,}566 - 570 - 685}{2{,}566 - 570} = .139$$

9. a. Debt-equity ratio $= \dfrac{\text{long-term debt}}{\text{equity}}$
   b. Return on equity $= \dfrac{\text{earnings available for common stock}}{\text{average equity}}$
   c. Net profit margin $= \dfrac{\text{net income + interest}}{\text{sales}}$
   d. Inventory turnover $= \dfrac{\text{cost of goods sold}}{\text{average inventory}}$
   e. Current ratio $= \dfrac{\text{current assets}}{\text{current liabilities}}$
   f. Interval measure $= \dfrac{\text{cash + marketable securities + receivables}}{\text{average daily expenditures from operations}}$
   g. Average collection period $= \dfrac{\text{average receivables}}{\text{average daily sales}}$
   h. Quick ratio $= \dfrac{\text{cash + marketable securities + accounts receivable}}{\text{current liabilities}}$
10. a. Liquidity ratios:
    NWC/TA = .177 (decreases)
    Current ratio = 1.54 (decreases)
    Quick ratio = .579 (increases)
    b. Leverage ratios:
    Long-term debt = no change
    Total debt/Total assets = .414 (increases)
    (excluding operating leases)
12. The current ratio is unaffected. The quick ratio falls.
14. Days sales in inventory = 2
16. a. Times interest earned = 1.25
    b. Cash coverage ratio = 1.5
    c. Fixed-charge coverage ratio = 0.923
18. Total sales = $54,750
    Asset turnover = .73
    ROA = 3.65%
20. $\dfrac{\text{Book debt}}{\text{Book equity}} = .5$

    $\dfrac{\text{Market equity}}{\text{Book equity}} = 2$

    $\dfrac{\text{Book debt}}{\text{Market equity}} = \dfrac{.5}{2} = .25$
22. Perhaps the firm has a lower ROA than its competitors; perhaps it pays a higher interest rate on its debt.
24. a. The shipping company
    b. United Foods
    c. The grocery store
    d. The power company
    e. Fledgling Electronics

CHAPTER 18

1. a. False
   b. False
   c. True
   d. False
   e. True
   f. True
   g. False
4. Sustainable growth rate = 8.75%
   Internal growth rate = 5.25%
7. Possible balancing items: dividends, borrowing or equity issues. With the tendency to keep dividends steady and raise equity in large amounts, borrowing is the most frequently used balancing item.
9. The balancing item is dividends. Dividends must be $200.
11. a. Internal growth rate = 10%
    b. Sustainable growth rate = 15%
13. a. Internal growth rate = 7.4%
    b. Sustainable growth rate = 11.1%
15. a.

Income Statement	**20% growth**
Revenue	2,400
Cost of goods sold	2,160
EBIT	240
Interest expense	40
Earnings before taxes	200
State and federal taxes	80
Net income	120
Dividends	80
Retained earnings	40

Balance Sheet	
Assets	
Net working capital	240
Fixed assets	960
Net assets	1,200
Liabilities and Shareholders' Equity	
Long-term debt	400
Shareholders' equity	640
Total liabilities and shareholders' equity	1,040
Required external financing	160

b. **Second-Stage Pro Forma**

Balance Sheet	
Assets	
Net working capital	240
Fixed assets	960
Net assets	1,200
Liabilities and Shareholders' Equity	
Long-term debt	560
Shareholders' equity	640
Total liabilities and shareholders' equity	1,200

17. a. g = .02564
    b. Issue $1,025.6 in new debt.
    c. g = .0154
19. a. Internal growth rate = 8%
    b. External financing = $220,000
    c. Internal growth rate = 20%
    d. External financing = $100,000. Reduction in dividend payout reduce requirements for external financing.
21. Payout ratio can be at most 1/3.
23. Net profit margin = 8%
25. g = 12%
27. Required external financing is zero.
29. Higher

CHAPTER 19

1.

	Cash	**Net Working Capital**
a.	$2 million decline	$2 million decline
b.	$2,500 increase	Unchanged
c.	$5,000 decline	Unchanged
d.	Unchanged	$1 million increase
e.	Unchanged	Unchanged
f.	$5 million increase	Unchanged

2. a. long-term financing, total capital requirement, marketable securities
   b. cash, cash, cash balance, marketable securities
5. Lower inventory period and cash conversion cycle; reduce net working capital.
7. a. Cash conversion cycle falls.
   b. Cash conversion cycle increases.
   c. Cash conversion cycle falls.
   d. Cash conversion cycle increases.
   e. Cash conversion cycle falls.
   f. Cash conversion cycle increases.
9. Effective rate = 8.89%. If the compensating balance is 20%, the effective rate is 10%.

11. a. 6.38%
    b. 6.20%

15. The order is .75 times the following quarter's sales forecast:

Quarter	Order
1	270
2	252
3	288
4	288

17.

Quarter	Collections
1	348
2	368
3	352
4	352

19.

	Quarter			
	First	Second	Third	Fourth
Cash at start of period	$40	$10	$15	–$14
+ Net cash inflow (from problem 18)	–30	+5	–29	–41
= Cash at end of period	10	15	–14	–55
Minimum operating cash balance	30	30	30	30
Cumulative short-term financing required (minimum cash balance minus cash at end of period)	$20	$15	$44	$85

21.

	Quarter			
	First	Second	Third	Fourth
Cash requirements				
1. Cash required for operations	$45	$15	–$26	–$35
2. Interest on line of credit	0	0.9	0.9	0.6
3. Interest on stretched payables	0	0	0.8	0
4. Total cash required	$45	$15.9	–$24.3	–$34.4
Cash raised				
5. Line of credit (bank loan)	$45	$ 0	$0	$0
6. Stretched payables	0	15.9	0	0
7. Securities sold	5	0	0	0
8. Total cash raised	$50	$15.9	$0	$0
Repayments				
9. Of stretched payables	0	0	$15.9	0
10. Of line of credit (bank loan)	0	0	8.4	34.4
Increase in cash balances				
11. Addition to cash balances	$ 5	$0	$0	$0
Line of credit (bank loan)				
12. Beginning of quarter	$ 0	$45	$45	$36.6
13. End of quarter	45	45	36.6	2.2

22.

Sources of Cash	
Sale of marketable securities	2
Increase in bank loans	1
Increase in accounts payable	5
Cash from operations:	
Net income	6
Depreciation	2
Total	16
Uses of Cash	
Increase in inventories	6
Increase in accounts receivable	3
Investment in fixed assets	6
Dividend paid	1
Total	16
Change in cash balance	0

23.

	February	March	April
Sources of cash			
Collections on current sales	$100	$110	$ 90
Collections on accounts receivable	90	100	110
Total sources of cash	$190	$210	$200
Uses of cash			
Payments of accounts payable	$ 30	$ 40	$ 30
Cash purchases	70	80	60
Labour and administrative expenses	30	30	30
Capital expenditures	100	0	0
Taxes, interest, and dividends	10	10	10
Total uses of cash	$240	$160	$130
Net cash inflow (sources – uses)	–$ 50	+$ 50	+$ 70
Cash at start of period	$100	$ 50	$100
+ Net cash inflow	–50	+50	+70
= Cash at end of period	$ 50	$100	$170
Minimum operating cash balance	$100	$100	$100
Cumulative short-term financing required (minimum cash balance minus cash at end of period)	$ 50	$ 0	–$ 70

CHAPTER 20

1. Ledger balance = $215,000
   Net float = $15,000

3. a. Payment float = $120,000
      Availability float = 66,000
      Net float = 54,000
   b. Annual interest earnings = $1,320
      Present value of earnings = $22,000

6. a. $20,000
   b. $4
   c. $120

8. Yes

10. The economic order quantity = 90 gems. The firm should place smaller but more frequent orders.

13. a. Economic order quantity = 600
    b. Total costs = $6,000

15. Economic order quantity falls by a factor of 10.

16. Cash balance = $14,142
    Transfers per month = 7.07

19. a. $1.5 million
    b. $180,000
    c. Yes

20. a. The interest rate, the cost of each transaction, and the variability of each cash flow.
    b. It should restore it to one-third of the distance from the lower to the upper limit.

21. a. Once every 2½ weeks
    b. $204
    c. $102

22. Cash balances fall relative to sales.

CHAPTER 21

1. a. $10
   b. 40 days
   c. 9.6%

4. a. Due lag and pay lag fall.
   b. Due lag and pay lag increase.
   c. Terms lag and pay lag increase.

5. a. False
   b. False
   c. True
   d. False
   e. True
   f. False

7. a. 20 days
   b. $1.096 million
   c. Average days in receivables will fall.

9. a. The expected profit from a sale is –2. Do not extend credit.
   b. $p = .95$
   c. The present value of a sale, net of default, is positive, $458.35
   d. $p = 16\%$

11. a. The expected profit of a sale is positive, $30.
    b. $p = .875$

16. a. Yes
    b. Credit should not be advanced.
    c. Net benefit from advancing credit = $100

17. PV (REV) = $1,200
    PV (COST) = $1,000
    Slow payers have a 70% probability of paying their bills. The expected profit of a sale to a slow payer is therefore .70 ($1,200 – $1,000) – .30 ($1,000) = –$160.
    Expected savings = $16. The credit check costs $5, so it is cost effective.

19. Sell only to groups 1, 2, and 3.

CHAPTER 22

1. a. 1, 3; b. 4, 9; c. 2, 5; d. 6; e. 1; f. 8; g. 7.
2. a, b, d, f
3. a. False. Operating leases are costly because of the lessee's option to cancel the lease. Don't buy an option you don't need.
   b. False. Lease obligations are disclosed in footnotes or capitalized. Lease financing is not hidden.
5. a. $59,307i.3
   b. $2,692.7
   c. NPV = –$2,307.3; do not lease.
6. Same cash flows can be arranged by borrowing.
7. a. Lease cash flows:

	0	1	2	3	4	5	6
Saved cost	75,000						
CCA tax shield	–3,281	–5,742	–4,307	–3,230	–2,422	–1,817	–5,451
Lease payment	–15,000	–15,000	–15,000	–15,000	–15,000	–15,000	
Lease tax shield	5,250	5,250	5,250	5,250	5,250	5,250	0
Lease cash flows	61,969	–15,492	–14,057	–12,980	–12,172	–11,567	–5,451

   b. Equivalent loan = $60,403; NPV = $1,566
   c. NPV = $1,566 – $5,066 = –$3,500
11. a. $188
    b. $1,471
    c. $60
12. a. Minimum lease payment acceptable to lessor = $18,441.5
    b. Maximum lease payment acceptable to lessee - $18,673
16. a. NPV to Nodhead = –$13,493
    b. NPV to Compulease = $9,639
    c. Overall gain = –$13,493 + $9,639 = –$3,855
18. Same problems encountered for IRR in Chapter 6. These include multiple IRRs, inability to handle cash flows of different risks, and inability to use IRR method to choose between alternative lease bids with different lives or payment patterns.

CHAPTER 23

1. a. Economies of scale is a valid reason.
   b. Diversification is not a valid reason.
   c. Possibly a valid reason.
   d. The bootstrap strategy is not a valid reason.
2. By merging, the firms can even out the workload over the year, increasing capacity utilization and lowering operating costs.
4. LBO: 6
   Poison pill: 4
   Tender offer: 5
   Shark repellent: 2
   Proxy contest: 1
   White knight: 3
6. $24 per share, NPV = 0.
8. a. $5 million
   b. $4 million
   c. NPV = $1 million
12. a. NPV = $5,000
    b. SCC will sell for $51.67; SDP will sell for $20; Wealth increase: SCC = 3.3%, SDP = 14.29%; Fraction of economic gain: SCC = 50%, SDP = 50%.
    c. Price = $51.32
    d. NPV = $3,947; SCCs fraction of economic gain = 39.5%. SDP shareholders capture most of the merger gains because the deal is based on the pre-merger price of SCC shares. When the impact of the deal is reflected in SCC shares, SDP shareholders end up with more than $20 per share.
13. a. Total market value = $4,000,000 + 5,000,000 = $9,000,000
       Total earnings = $200,000 + 500,000 = $700,000
       Number of shares = 262,172
       Price per share = $9,000,000/262,172 = $34.33
       Price-earnings ratio = 34.33/2.67 = 12.9
    b. .81 share
    c. $567,365
    d. $567,365

CHAPTER 24

1. a. 68.75 euros; $145.46
   b. 101.35 Swiss francs; $98.67
   c. Direct exchange rate will decrease and indirect exchange rate will increase.
   d. U.S. dollar is worth more.
3. a. $\frac{1 + r_x}{1 + r_\$} = \frac{f_{x/\$}}{s_{x/\$}}$
   b. $\frac{f_{x/\$}}{s_{x/\$}} = \frac{E(s_{x/\$})}{s_{x/\$}}$
   c. $\frac{E(1 + i_x)}{E(1 + i_\$)} = \frac{E(s_{x/\$})}{s_{x/\$}}$
   d. $\frac{1 + r_x}{1 + r_\$} = \frac{E(1 + i_x)}{E(1 + i_\$)}$
4. Foreign inflation rate forecasts
   Future exchange rates forecasts
   Domestic interest rates
6. a
8. Borrow the present value of 1 million Australian dollars, sell

them for U.S. dollars in the spot market, and invest the proceeds in an 8-year U.S. dollar loan. In 8 years, it can repay the Australian loan with the anticipated Australian dollar payment.

10. a. 4.0%
    b. 10.5%
    c. –2.5%

11. 7.27%

14. Canadian dollar should be depreciating relative to the U.S. dollar.

16. Net present value = \$.72 million

18. a. Depreciation of Trinidadian dollars
    b. Borrow in Trinidad.
    c. Its exposure is mitigated.

CHAPTER 25

1.

	Payoff	Profit
a. Call option, $X = 12.5$	2.5	0.55
b. Put option, $X = 12.5$	0	–1.15
c. Call option, $X = 15$	0	–1.20
d. Put option, $X = 15$	0	–2.80
e. Call option, $X = 17.50$	0	–0.75
f. Put option, $X = 22.50$	0	–0.25

3. a. The October call costs 0.40. The April call costs 1.20.
   b. Longer time to expiry increases the probability that the stock price will go up, making the call more valuable.
   c. This is true of puts as well.

5. Figure 25.8*a* represents a call seller; Figure 25.8*b* represents a call buyer.

7.

	a. $S<100$	b. $S>100$
Value of put	$100 - S$	0
Value of stock	S	S
Total	100	S

9. Lower bound is either zero or the stock price minus the exercise price, whichever is greater. The upper bound is the stock price.

11.

	Payoff of Option Position at Expiration			
	$S<11.50$	$11.50<S<12.50$	$12.50<S<13.50$	$S>13.50$
Buy call ($X = 11.50$)	0	$S - 11.50$	$S - 11.50$	$S - 11.50$
Sell 2 calls ($X = 12.50$)	0	0	$-2(S - 12.50)$	$-2(S - 12.50)$
Buy call ($X = 13.50$)	0	0	0	$S - 13.50$
Total	0	$S - 25$	$30 - S$	0

13. You will be more tempted to choose the high-risk proposal.

15. a. Call option to pursue a project.
    b. Put option to sell the equipment.

17. Put option with exercise price equal to support price.

19. a. Option to put (sell) the stock to the underwriter.
    b. Volatility of the stock value; the length of the period for which the underwriter guarantees the issue; the interest rate; the price at which the underwriter is obligated to buy the stock; and the market value of the stock.

21. Put option on the bank assets with exercise price equal to the deposits owed to bank customers.

23. a. Buy a call option for \$3. Exercise the call to purchase stock. Pay the \$20 exercise price. Sell the share for \$25. Riskless profit equals \$2.
    b. Buy a share and put option. Exercise the put. Riskless profit equals \$1.

26. Call price = \$2.25

CHAPTER 26

1. Both activities eliminate the firm's exposure to a particular source of risk, reducing uncertainty about firm's cash flows. Insure risk with big impact on the firm's performance. However, there is no need to protect against events that cannot materially affect the firm.

4. No

6. Advantages: liquidity, no storage costs, no spoilage. Disadvantages: no income or benefits that could accrue from holding asset in portfolio.

7.

	Gold Price		
	\$280	\$300	\$320
a. Revenues	\$280,000	\$300,000	\$320,000
Futures contract	21,000	1,000	–19,000
b. Total	\$301,000	\$301,000	\$301,000
c. Revenues	\$280,000	\$300,000	\$320,000
+ Put option payoff	20,000	0	0
– Put option cost	2,000	2,000	2,000
Net revenue	\$298,000	\$298,000	\$318,000

9. Create a synthetic loan: Lend \$100 today, for one year, at 10 percent and borrow \$100 today, for two years, at 12 percent. Your net cash flow today is zero. In one year you receive \$110 and will owe $\$100 \times (1.12)^2 = \$125.44$ for payment one more year hence. This is effectively a one-year borrowing agreement at rate 125.44/110 = .14, which is the forward rate for Year 2. Borrowing at 14% through the synthetic loan is less expensive than the bank's offer to lend at 15%. Reject the bank's offer.

11. Assume that the futures price for oil is $20 per barrel. Petrochemical will take a long position to hedge its cost of buying oil. Onnex will take a short position to hedge its revenue from selling oil.

	Oil Price ($ per barrel)		
	$18	**$20**	**$22**
Cost for Petrochemical:			
Cash flow on purchase of oil	–18,000	–20,000	–22,000
+ Cash flow on long futures position	– 2,000	0	+ 2,000
Total cash flow	–20,000	–20,000	–20,000
Revenue for Onnex:			
Revenue from 1,000 barrels	$18,000	$20,000	$22,000
+ Payoff on short futures position	2,000	0	(2,000)
Net revenue	$20,000	$20,000	$20,000

The benefit of futures is the ability to lock in a riskless position without paying any money. The benefit of the option hedge is that you benefit if prices move in one direction without losing if they move in the other direction. However, this asymmetry comes at a price: the cost of the option.

12. The futures price is greater than the spot price for gold. This reflects the fact that the futures contract ensures your receipt of the gold without tying up your money now. The difference between the spot price and the futures price reflects compensation for the time value of money. Another way to put it is that the spot price must be lower than the futures price to compensate investors who buy and store gold for the opportunity cost of their funds until the futures maturity date.

14. A currency swap is an agreement to exchange a series of payments in one currency for a given series of payments in another currency. An interest rate swap is an exchange of a series of fixed payments for a series of payments that are linked to market interest rates.

GLOSSARY

acquisition: Takeover of a firm by purchase of that firm's common stock or assets.

additional paid-in capital: Difference between issue price and par value of stock, also called capital surplus.

agency problems: Conflicts of interest between the firm's owners and managers.

aging schedule: Classification of accounts receivable by time outstanding.

angel: A wealthy individual investor in early-stage ventures.

annual percentage rate (APR): Interest rate that is annualized using simple interest.

annuity: Equally spaced and level stream of cash flows.

annuity due: Level stream of cash flows starting immediately.

annuity factor: Present value of a $1 annuity.

asset class: Eligible depreciable assets are grouped into specified asset classes by CCRA. Each asset class has a prescribed CCA rate.

authorized share capital: Maximum number of shares that the company is permitted to issue as specified in the firm's articles of incorporation.

availability float: Cheques already deposited that have not yet been cleared.

average tax rate: Total taxes owed divided by total income.

balance sheet: Financial statement that shows the value of the firm's assets and liabilities at a particular time.

balancing item: Variable that adjusts to maintain the consistency of a financial plan. Also called the plug.

banker's acceptance: A firm's time draft that has been accepted by a bank and may be sold to investors as a short-term unsecured note issued by the firm and guaranteed by the bank.

bankruptcy: The reorganization or liquidation of a firm that cannot pay its debts.

bear market: A market in which stock or bond prices are generally falling.

beta: Sensitivity of a stock's return to the return on the market portfolio.

bond: Security that obligates the issuer to make specified payments to the bondholder.

book rate of return: Accounting income divided by book value. Also called accounting rate of return.

book value: Net worth of the firm according to the balance sheet.

bought deal: The underwriter buys securities from the issuing company and sells them to investors.

break-even analysis: Analysis of the level of sales at which the company breaks even.

bull market: A market in which stock or bond prices are generally rising.

call option: Right to buy an asset at a specified exercise price on or before the exercise date.

callable bond: Bond that may be repurchased by the firm before maturity at a specified call price.

capital asset pricing model (CAPM): Theory of the relationship between risk and return which states that the expected risk premium on any security equals its beta times the market risk premium.

capital budget: List of planned investment projects.

capital budgeting decision: Decision as to which real assets the firm should acquire.

capital cost allowance: The amount of write-off on depreciable assets allowed by Canada Customs and Revenue Agency (CCRA) against taxable income.

capital markets: Markets for long-term financing.

capital rationing: Limit set on the amount of funds available for investment.

capital structure: A firm's mix of long-term financing.

CAPM: See *capital asset pricing model.*

carrying costs: Costs of maintaining current assets, including opportunity cost of capital.

cash conversion cycle: Period between firm's payment for materials and collection on its sales.

cash cow: Business that produces a lot of cash but few growth prospects.

cash dividend: Payment of cash by the firm to its shareholders.

cash flow from assets, or free cash flow: Cash flow generated by the firm after investment in net working capital and fixed assets; also equal to *cash flow to bondholders and shareholders.*

CCA tax shield: Tax savings arising from the capital cost allowance charge.

CEO: Acronym for chief executive officer.

CFO: Acronym for chief financial officer.

chief financial officer (CFO): Officer who oversees the treasurer and controller and sets overall financial strategy.

collection policy: Procedures to collect and monitor receivables.

commercial paper: Short-term unsecured notes issued by firms.

commitment fee: Fee charged by the lender on the unused portion of a line of credit.

common stock: Ownership shares in a publicly held corporation.

common-size balance sheet: Balance sheet that presents items as a percentage of total assets.

common-size income statement: Income statement that presents items as a percentage of revenues.

company cost of capital: Expected rate of return demanded by investors in a company, determined by the average risk of the company's assets and operations.

compound interest: Interest earned on interest.
concentration banking: System whereby customers make payments to a regional collection centre that transfers funds to a principal bank.
constant-growth dividend discount model: Version of the dividend discount model in which dividends grow at a constant rate.
controller: Officer responsible for budgeting, accounting, and auditing.
convertible bond: Bond that the holder may exchange for a specified amount of another security.
corporation: Business owned by shareholders who are not personally liable for the business's liabilities.
correlation coefficient: Measure of how closely two variables move together.
costs of financial distress: Costs arising from bankruptcy or distorted business decisions before bankruptcy.
coupon: The interest payments paid to the bondholder.
coupon rate: Annual interest payment as a percentage of face value.
credit analysis: Procedure to determine the likelihood a customer will pay its bills.
credit policy: Standards set to determine the amount and nature of credit to extend to customers.
cumulative voting: Voting system in which all the votes one shareholder is allowed to cast can be cast for one candidate for the board of directors.
current yield: Annual coupon payments divided by bond price.
debit card: An automated-teller machine card that allows retail customers to transfer funds directly from their bank accounts to a retailer's account.
decision tree: Diagram of sequential decisions and possible outcomes.
declining balance depreciation: This is computed by applying the depreciation rate to the asset balance for each year.
default premium or credit spread: The additional yield on a bond investors require for bearing credit risk.
default risk or credit risk: The risk that a bond issuer may default on its bonds.
degree of operating leverage (DOL): Percentage change in profits given a 1 percent change in sales.
depreciation tax shield: Reduction in taxes attributable to the depreciation allowance.
discount factor: Present value of a $1 future payment.
discount rate: Interest rate used to compute present values of future cash flows.
discounted payback period: The time until discounted cash flows recover the initial investment in the project.
diversification: Strategy designed to reduce risk by spreading the portfolio across many investments.
dividend: Periodic cash distribution from the firm to its shareholders.
dividend clientele effect: Different investor groups prefer different dividend yields. Changing the firm's divided policy may attract a new investor clientele but might not change firm value.
dividend discount model: Discounted cash-flow model of today's stock price which states that share value equals the present value of all expected future dividends.
dividend payout ratio: Percentage of earnings paid out as dividends.
Dow Jones Industrial Average: U.S. index of the investment performance of a portfolio of 30 "blue-chip" stocks.
DuPont system: A breakdown of ROE and ROA into component ratios.
economic order quantity: Order size that minimizes total inventory costs.
economic value added (EVA®): See *residual income*. Term coined by the consulting firm Stern Stewart.
effective annual interest rate (EAR): Interest rate that is annualized using compound interest.
efficient capital markets: Financial markets in which security prices rapidly reflect all relevant information about asset values.
electronic data interchange (EDI): Direct, electronic information exchange between enterprises, eliminating the mailing and handling of paper invoices.
electronic funds transfer: Payments made electronically instead of using paper-based cheques.
equivalent annual cost: The cost per period with the same present value as the cost of buying and operating a machine.
equivalent loan: Present value of lease cash outflows, discounted at the after-tax cost of borrowing.
eurobond: Bond that is denominated in the currency of one country but issued to investors in other countries.
eurodollars: Dollars held on deposit in a bank outside the United States.
EVA®: See *economic value added*.
exchange rate: Amount of one currency needed to purchase one unit of another.
ex-dividend date: Date that determines whether a shareholder is entitled to a dividend payment; anyone holding stock before this date is entitled to a dividend.
expectations theory of exchange rates: Theory that expected spot exchange rate equals the forward rate.
ex-rights date: This date is usually four business days before the holder-of-record date.
face value: Payment at the maturity of the bond. Also called *par value,* or *maturity value*, or *principal*.
factoring: A firm sells its accounts receivable at a discount for the purpose of obtaining short-term financing.
financial assets: Claims to the income generated by real assets. Also called securities.
financial intermediary: Firm that raises money from many small investors and provides financing to businesses or other organizations by investing in their securities.
financial lease: Long-term, noncancellable lease. It is also known as *capital* or *full-payout lease*.
financial leverage: Debt financing to amplify the effects of changes in operating income on the returns to shareholders.
financial markets: Markets in which financial assets are traded.
financial risk: Risk to shareholders resulting from the use of debt.
financial slack: Ready access to cash or debt financing.
financing decision: Decision as to how to raise the money to pay for investments in real assets.
fixed costs: Costs that do not depend on the level of output.
floating-rate preferred: Preferred stock paying dividends that vary with short-term interest rates.
floating-rate security: Security paying dividends or interest that vary with short-term interest rates.
flotation costs: The costs incurred when a firm issues new securities to the public.

foreign bond: ***Bond*** issued in the currency of its country but the borrower is from another country.

forward contract: Agreement to buy or sell an asset in the future at an agreed price.

forward exchange rate: Exchange rate for a forward transaction.

free cash flow: See *cash flow from assets.*

fundamental analysts: Analysts who attempt to find under- or overvalued securities by analyzing fundamental information, such as earnings, asset values, and business prospects.

future value: Amount to which an investment will grow after earning interest.

future value factor: Future value of a current cash flow of $1.

futures contract: Exchange-traded promise to buy or sell an asset in the future at a prespecified price.

GAAP: See *generally accepted accounting principles.*

general cash offer: Sale of securities open to all investors by an already public company.

generally accepted accounting principles (GAAP): Procedures for preparing financial statements.

growing annuity: A finite stream of cash flows growing at a constant rate.

growing perpetuity: An infinite stream of cash flows growing at a constant rate.

half-year rule: Only one-half of the purchase cost of the asset is added to the asset class and used to compute CCA in the year of purchase.

holder-of-record date: The date on which shareholders appearing on company records are entitled to receive the stock rights.

income statement: Financial statement that shows the revenues, expenses, and net income of a firm over a period of time.

inflation: Rate at which prices as a whole are increasing.

information content of dividends: Dividend increases send good news about cash flow and earnings. Dividend cuts send bad news.

initial public offering (IPO): First offering of stock to the general public.

interest rate parity: Theory that forward premium equals interest rate differential.

interest rate risk: The risk in bond prices due to fluctuations in interest rates.

interest tax shield: Tax savings resulting from deductibility of interest payments.

internal growth rate: Maximum rate of growth without external financing.

internal rate of return (IRR): Discount rate at which project NPV = 0.

internally generated funds: Cash reinvested in the firm: depreciation plus earnings not paid out as dividends.

international Fisher effect: Theory that real interest rates in all countries should be equal, with differences in nominal rates reflecting differences in expected inflation.

investment grade: Bonds rated Baa or above by Moody's, or BBB or above by Standard & Poor's or DBRS.

IPO: See *initial public offering.*

IRR: See *internal rate of return.*

issued shares: Shares that have been issued by the company.

junk bond: Bond with a rating below Baa or BBB.

just-in-time inventory management: A system of inventory management in which materials are delivered to the firm just when needed.

law of one price: Theory that prices of goods in all countries should be equal when translated to a common currency.

lease: Rental agreement for the use on an asset extending for more than 1 year and involving a series of fixed payments.

lessee: User of the asset in a lease; responsible for making regular payments to lessor.

lessor: Owner of the asset in a lease; receives regular payments from lessee.

leveraged buyout (LBO): Acquisition of the firm by a private group using substantial borrowed funds.

limited liability: The owners of the corporation are not personally responsible for its obligations.

line of credit: Agreement by a bank that a company may borrow at any time up to an established limit.

liquidation: Sale of bankrupt firm's assets.

liquidation value: Net proceeds that would be realized by selling the firm's assets and paying off its creditors.

liquidity: Ability of an asset to be converted to cash quickly at low cost.

lock-box system: System whereby customers send payments to a post office box and a local bank collects and processes cheques.

long position: Purchase of an investment.

long-term debt: Debt with more than 1 year remaining to maturity.

majority voting: Voting system in which each director is voted on separately.

management buyout (MBO): Acquisition of the firm by its own management in a leveraged buyout.

M&A: Abbreviation for mergers and acquisitions.

marginal tax rate: Additional taxes owed per dollar of additional income.

market index: Measure of the investment performance of the overall market.

market portfolio: Portfolio of all assets in the economy. In practice, a broad stock market index, such as the S&P/TSX or S&P 500 Composite Index, is used to represent the market.

market risk: Economywide (macroeconomic) sources of risk that affect the overall stock market. Also called systematic risk.

market risk premium: Risk premium of market portfolio. The difference between market return and return on risk-free Treasury bills.

market value added: The difference between the market value of the firm's equity and its book value.

market-value balance sheet: Financial statement that uses the market value of all assets and liabilities.

maturity premium: Extra average return from investing in long-term bonds versus short-term Treasury securities.

merger or statutory amalgamation: Combination of the assets and liabilities of two firms into one.

MM dividend-irrelevance proposition: Under ideal conditions, the value of the firm is unaffected by dividend policy.

MM's proposition I (debt irrelevance proposition): The value of a firm is unaffected by its capital structure.

MM's proposition II: The required rate of return on equity increases as the firm's debt-equity ratio increases.

money market: Market for short-term financial assets.

mutually exclusive projects: Two or more projects that cannot be pursued simultaneously.

net float: Difference between payment float and availability float.

net present value (NPV): Present value of cash flows minus initial investment.

net working capital: Current assets minus current liabilities. Often called *working capital.*

net worth: Book value of common shareholders' equity plus preferred stock.

nominal interest rate: Rate at which money invested grows.

NPV: See *net present value.*

off-balance-sheet financing: Financing that is not shown as a liability in a company's balance sheet.

open account: Agreement whereby sales are made with no formal debt contract.

operating lease: Short-term, cancellable lease.

operating leverage: Degree to which costs are fixed.

operating risk, or business risk: Risk in a firm's operating income.

opportunity cost: Benefit or cash flow forgone as a result of an action.

opportunity cost of capital: Expected rate of return given up by investing in a project.

OTC: See *over-the-counter.*

outstanding shares: Shares that have been issued by the company and are held by investors.

oversubscription privilege: Given to shareholders in a rights issue, enabling them to purchase any unsold shares at the subscription price.

over-the-counter (OTC): Shares traded off an organized exchange. Also used to refer to the Nasdaq market.

par value: Value of security shown on certificate.

partnership: Business owned by two or more people who are personally responsible for all its liabilities.

payback period: Time until cash flows recover the initial investment of the project.

payment float: Cheques written by a company that have not yet cleared.

payout ratio: Fraction of earnings paid out as dividends.

P/E: See *price-earnings multiple.*

pecking order theory: Firms prefer to issue debt rather than equity if internal finance is insufficient.

percentage of sales models: Planning models in which sales forecasts are the driving variables and most other variables are proportional to sales.

perpetuity: Stream of level cash payments that never end.

planning horizon: Time horizon for a financial plan.

plowback ratio: Fraction of earnings retained by the firm.

political risk: A change in firm value arising from political events.

preferred stock: Stock that takes priority over common stock in regard to dividends.

present value (PV): Value today of a future cash flow.

present value of growth opportunities (PVGO): Net present value of a firm's future investments.

price-earnings (P/E) multiple: Ratio of stock price to earnings per share.

primary market: Market for the sale of newly issued securities, sold by corporations to raise cash.

prime rate: Benchmark interest rate charged by banks.

private placement: Sale of securities to a limited number of investors without a public offering.

pro formas: Projected or forecast financial statements.

profitability index: Ratio of net present value to initial investment.

project cost of capital: Minimum acceptable expected rate of return on a project given its risk.

prompt offering prospectus (POP) system: Allows qualified firms quicker access to capital markets by enabling them to use a short-form filing process rather than a full prospectus.

prospectus: Formal summary that provides information on an issue of securities.

protective covenant: Restriction on a firm to protect bondholders.

proxy contest: Takeover attempt in which outsiders compete with management for shareholders' votes. Also called proxy fight.

purchasing power parity (PPP): Theory that the cost of living in different countries is equal and exchange rates adjust to offset inflation differentials across countries.

pure play approach: Estimating project cost of capital using the cost of capital of another company involved exclusively in the same type of project.

put option: Right to sell an asset at a specified exercise price on or before the exercise date.

PV: See *present value.*

random walk: Security prices change randomly without predictable trends or patterns.

rate of return: Total income per period per dollar invested.

real assets: Assets used to produce goods and services.

real interest rate: Rate at which the purchasing power of an investment increases.

real options: Options embedded in real assets.

real return bonds: Bonds with a nominal coupon payment, determined by a fixed real coupon payment and the inflation rate.

real value of $1: Purchasing power–adjusted value of a dollar.

recaptured depreciation: If the sale of an asset causes a negative balance in an asset class, the amount of the negative balance is known as recaptured depreciation and is added to taxable income.

refunding: When an old bond issue is replaced with a new one by the firm. Often, this is done when interest rates decline, and the firm can save on the interest cost of the new issue.

reorganization: Restructuring of financial claims on failing firm to allow it to keep operating.

residual income (also called economic value added, or EVA®): The net profit of a firm or division after deducting the cost of the capital employed.

restructuring: Process of changing the firm's capital structure without changing its assets.

retained earnings: Earnings not paid out as dividends.

reverse split: Issue of new shares in exchange for old shares, which results in the reduction of outstanding shares.

rights issue: Issue of securities offered only to current shareholders.

risk premium: Expected return in excess of risk-free return as compensation for risk.

S&P: Abbreviation for Standard & Poor's stock market indexes.

S&P/TSX Capped Composite Index: Index based on the prices of the TSX stocks, with no stock weighted more than 10 percent. Formerly the TSE 300 Capped Index.

S&P/TSX Composite Index: Index of the investment performance of a portfolio of the major stocks listed on the Toronto Stock Exchange. Also called the TSX. Formerly called the TSE 300.

scenario analysis: Project analysis given a particular combination of assumptions.

seasoned offering: Sale of securities by a firm that is already publicly traded.

secondary market: Market in which already-issued securities are traded among investors.
secured debt: Debt that has first claim on specified collateral in the event of default.
security market line: Relationship between expected return and beta.
semi-strong-form efficiency: Market prices reflect all publicly available information.
sensitivity analysis: Analysis of the effects of changes in sales, costs, and so on, on project profitability.
shareholders' rights plan or poison pill: Measures taken by the target firm to avoid acquisition; for example, the right of existing shareholders to buy additional shares at an attractive price if a bidder acquires a significant holding.
shark repellent: Amendments to a company charter made to forestall takeover attempts.
shelf registration: A procedure followed in the U.S. that allows firms to file one registration statement for several issues of the same security.
shortage costs: Costs incurred from shortages in current assets.
simple interest: Interest earned only on the original investment; no interest is earned on interest.
simulation analysis: Estimation of the probabilities of different possible outcomes, e.g., from an investment project.
sinking fund: Fund established to retire debt before maturity.
sole proprietor: Sole owner of a business which has no partners and no shareholders. The proprietor is personally liable for all the firm's obligations.
spot rate of exchange: Exchange rate for an immediate transaction.
spread: Difference between public offer price and price paid by underwriter.
stakeholder: Anyone with a financial interest in the firm.
Standard & Poor's Composite Index: U.S. index of the investment performance of a portfolio of 500 large stocks. Also called the S&P 500.
standard deviation: Square root of variance. Another measure of volatility.
standby underwriting agreement: The underwriter stands ready to purchase any unsold shares.
statement of cash flows: Financial statement that shows the firm's cash receipts and cash payments over a period of time.
statutory amalgamation or merger: Combination of the assets and liabilities of two firms into one.
stock dividend: Distribution of additional shares to a firm's shareholders.
stock repurchase: Firm buys back stock from its shareholders.
stock split: Issue of additional shares to firm's shareholders.
straight-line depreciation: Constant depreciation for each year of the asset's accounting life.
strong-form efficiency: Market prices rapidly reflect all information that is potentially available to determine true value.
subordinated debt: Debt that may be repaid in bankruptcy only after senior debt is paid.
sunk costs: Costs that have been incurred and cannot be recovered.
sustainable growth rate: Steady rate at which a firm can grow without changing leverage; plowback ratio X return on equity.
swap: Arrangement by two counterparties to exchange one stream of cash flows for another.
technical analysts: Investors who attempt to identify over- or undervalued stocks by searching for patterns in past prices.
tender offer: Takeover attempt in which outsiders directly offer to buy the stock of the firm's shareholders.
terminal loss: When an asset class has a positive balance following the disposal of all assets in the class, this balance is called terminal loss. The UCC of the asset class is set to zero after a terminal loss is recognized.
terms of sale: Credit, discount, and payment terms offered on a sale.
trade-off theory: Debt levels are chosen to balance interest tax shields against the costs of financial distress.
treasurer: Manager responsible for financing, cash management, and relationships with financial markets and institutions.
TRIV: See *TSX Total Return Index Value.*
TSX: See *S&P/TSX Composite Index.*
TSX Total Return Index Value (TRIV): Measure of the composite index based on the prices plus dividends paid by the stocks in the S&P/TSX Composite Index. Formerly the TSE Total Return Index.
undepreciated capital cost (UCC): The balance remaining in an asset class that has not yet been depreciated in that year.
underpricing: Issuing securities at an offering price set below the true value of the security.
underwriter: Firm that buys an issue of securities from a company and resells it to the public.
unique risk: Risk factors affecting only the particular firm. Also called diversifiable risk.
variable costs: Costs that change as the level of output changes.
variance: Average value of squared deviations from mean. A measure of volatility.
venture capital: Money invested to finance a new firm.
WACC: See *weighted-average cost of capital.*
warrant: Right to buy shares from a company at a stipulated price before a set date.
weak-form efficiency: Market prices rapidly reflect all information contained in the history of past prices.
weighted-average cost of capital (WACC): Expected rate of return on a portfolio of all the firm's securities, adjusted for tax savings due to interest payments.
white knight: Friendly potential acquirer sought by a target company that is threatened by an unwelcome bidder.
working capital: See *net working capital.*
workout: Agreement between a company and its creditors establishing the steps the company must take to avoid bankruptcy.
yield curve: Graph of the relationship between time to maturity and yield to maturity.
yield to maturity: Interest rate for which the present value of the bond's payments equals the price.
zero-balance account: Regional bank account to which just enough funds are transferred daily to pay each day's bills.

INDEX

724 Solutions, 139, 414

Abandonment options, 259–260, 751–752
Accounting
  accounting for differences, 47–48
  accrual accounting, 42
  aging schedule, 640
  balance sheet, 35–39
    book values, 37–39
    market value, 37–39
  break-even analysis, 249–251
  dangerous accounts, 639
  history of, 28–29
  income statement, 40–42
    profits versus cash flow, 41–42
  statement of cash flow, 42–46
Accounting income versus cash flows, 183
Accounting rate of return, 182
Accounting standards, 47
Accounts payable, 36
  payments of, 584
Accounts payable period, 574, 575
Accounts receivable, 35
Accounts receivable financing, 591
Accounts receivable period, 574, 575
Acid-test ratio
  see quick ratio
Acquisition, 683
Additional economic benefits, 695
Additional paid-in capital, 378
Adjusted cost of disposal, 217
Advantages of leasing, 658–659
Agency costs, 680
Agency problems, 21
Aggressive growth plan, 544
Aging schedule, 640
Air Canada, 297, 389, 426, 462, 686
Airlines, 296
AirNet Systems Inc., 610
Alcan Aluminum, 11, 291–292, 391, 531
Aliant Inc., 682–683
Alliance Atlantis Communications, Inc., 385
Allied Crude Vegetable Oil Refining Corporation, 591
Allocated overhead costs, 209
Alta Group, 730
American Airlines, 527
American Express, 701
America Online, 415
Amortization, 84
Amortization loan, 84
Anderson Exploration, 686
Angel investing, 410, 436–437
Annually compound rate
  see effective annual interest rate
Annual percentage rate (APR), 96
Annuity, 78
  due, 82–83
  factor, 80
  future value of, 86–88
  problem solving on calculators, 89
  valuation of, 79–80
Annuity dye, present value, 82–83
AOL, 682
Apex One, 690
Apple Computer, 3, 23
A Random Walk Down Wall Street, 366
Aristotle, 28
Articles of incorporation, 4
Asked price, 114
Asset-backed bonds, 392–393
Asset class, 215
  system, 215–217
Asset pool
  and leasing, 670
  termination of, 215–217
Asset risk, 286–289
Assets, 215–217
  on balance sheet, 35–37
  cash flow from, 44, 45
  and costs of distress, 465–466
  current, 35, 507
  financial, 6, 7, 11
  fixed, 35, 36
  historical return, 275–278
  intangible, 36, 62
  leased, 664–665
  liquid, 35
  long-term, 507
  long- versus short-lived, 186–187
  negative-risk, 288
  real, 6, 11
  real versus financial, 6, 11
  sale of, 217
  tangible, 36, 62
  termination of pool, 217–218
Asset turnover ratio, 515–516
AT&T, 158
Atlantic Canada Opportunities Agency (ACOA), 438
Auction markets, 140
AudioNet, 415
Authorized share capital, 378
Automated Clearing Settlement System (ACSS), 608
Availability float, 606
Average collection period, 516
Average tax rate, 51

Baggaley, Philip, 527
Balance sheet, 35, 508
  common-sized, 511
  market value versus book value, 39
Balancing item, 550
Ballard Power Systems, 434, 750
Bank accounts interest on, 97
Bank debt, 36
Banker's acceptance, 590
Bank loans, 589
  case, 601–602
  cost of, 592–594
  types of, 589–591
Bank of Canada, 608
Bank of Montreal, 17
Bank of Nova Scotia, 492
Bank of Tokyo-Mitsubishi, 389
Bankruptcy
  and asset types, 465–466
  case, 653–654
  costs of, 461
  direct versus indirect costs, 462
  evidence on, 461–462
  financial distress without, 462–465
  liquidation, 641–642, 645–646
  procedures, 641–645
  reorganization, 643, 645–646
  workout, 641
Bankruptcy and Insolvency Act, 641, 643
Banks, 9–10, 13, 15
Banque Nationale de Paris, 389
Barclays Bank, 389
Barings Bank, 29, 780
Basic earning power, 517
BCE, Inc., 492, 684
B.C. Sugar Refinery Ltd., 697–698
Bear Stearns, 158
Beer standard, 718
Benchmark for ratio analysis, 526–528
Berra, Yogi, 446
Best-case growth plan, 544
Beta
  in capital asset pricing model, 316–317
  measuring, 305–308
  of portfolio, 309–311
Bid price, 113–114
Big Mac index, 717
Binomial valuation model, 762
Biomira, 144
Black, Fischer, 749

Black-Scholes formula, 749
Black-Scholes option valuation model, 762–764
BMO Nesbitt Burns, 3, 393
Board of directors, 4, 23, 24
Boeing, 7
Bombardier Inc., 7, 381, 382, 385, 739, 740
Bond
  valuation, 116
Bondholders
  cash flow to, 45–46
Bond prices, 115–118
  current yield versus yield to maturity, 118–121
  inflation-indexed, 128
  interest rate risk, 125
  and interest rates, 117
  and nominal/real interest rates, 126–128
  and rate of return, 121–123
  semiannual coupon payments, 116–117
  varying with interest rates, 117–118
  and yield curve, 126
Bond ratings, 129–130
Bonds
  asset-backed, 392–393
  calculating the rate of return, 121–123
  callable, 754
  characteristics, 113–114
  convertible, 131, 394, 753–754
  corporate, 129–131
  default premium, 129
  default risk, 129
  expected return, 343
  floating-rate, 131
  foreign, 389
  high-yield, 129
  indexed, 392
  international, 389
  investment grade, 129
  junk, 129
  junk bonds, 129
  long-term fluctuations, 126
  reading financial pages, 114
  retail traders, 115
  reverse floaters, 393–394
  Treasury Inflation-Protected Securities (TIPS), 128
  valuation, 120
  zero-coupon, 131
Bond value, 753
Book income
  and leasing, 661–662
Book rate of return, 182–183
Book value, 142, 145
  on balance sheet, 37, 38
  versus market value, 39, 379–380
Bootstrap effect, 691
Bootstrap game, 690–692
Borrowing, 13
  based on asymmetric information, 467
  effect on earnings per share, 448–450
  effect on risk and return, 450–452
  effect on value, 446–455
  financing choice theories, 466–470
  by government, 113
  resulting in financial distress, 462–466
Bottom-up investment choice, 243
Bought deal, 423
Break-even analysis, 249–256
  accounting, 249–251
  net present value, 251–254
Break-even wire transfer, 611
British Airways, 681
British Gas, 412
British Petroleum, 418–419
Broadcast.com, 415
Brookfield Properties, 393
Bruncor Inc., 682
Buffett, Warren, 157, 526
Burger King, 686
Burgundy Asset Management Ltd., 24
Business Development Bank of Canada (BDC), 437–438
Business organizations
  characteristics, 5
  corporations, 3–5
  hybrid forms, 5–6
  partnerships, 3
  sole proprietorship, 3
Business Week, 463
Buybacks
  see repurchase agreements

Caisse de dépôt et placement du Québéc, 10, 381
Caisses populaires, 10
Caliber System, 688
Callable bonds, 754
Callable fund, 387
Call options, 739–745
  selling, 741–742
Campbell Soup Company, 614
Campeau, 703
Canada 3000, 683
Canada Business Corporation Act, 3
Canada Customs and Revenue Agency (CCRA), 3, 49, 51, 496
  and leasing, 665
Canada Economic Development for Québec Regions: Financing, 438
Canadair, 7
Canadian Accounting Standards Board (AcSB), 48, 660
Canadian Airlines, 25, 686
Canadian Bank of Commerce, 644
Canadian Business Corporations Act, 378, 481
Canadian Federation of Labour, 434
Canadian Imperial Bank of Commerce, 701
Canadian Institute of Actuaries, 275
Canadian National Railway, 413
Canadian Pacific, Ltd., 378–379, 382, 384, 396, 397, 480, 530, 684
Canadian Pacific Railway, 684
Canadian Pacific Ships, 684
Canadian Payments Association (CPA), 608
Canadian Tax Foundation, 49
Canadian Tire, 382, 393
Canadian Venture Exchange, 12, 420
CanWest Global, 321
Capital
  external sources, 396–398
  internal sources, 395–396
Capital asset pricing model (CAPM), 312–319, 313, 316–318, 344
Capital budget, 243
Capital budgeting decision, 7–8
Capital budgeting/project analysis, 169, 243–262
  break-even analysis, 249–256
    accounting, 249–251
    degree of operating leverage, 255–256
    example, 252–254
    net present value, 251–254
    operating leverage, 254–256
  case, 269
  flexibility in
    abandonment options, 259–260
    decision trees, 256–258
    expansion options, 258–259
    investment timing, 260–261
    production facilities, 260
  international
    avoiding fudge factors, 729–730
    cost of capital, 729
    net present value analysis, 727–728
  investment process organization, 243–245
    capital budget, 243
    eliminating conflicts of interest, 244
    ensuring consistent forecasts, 244
    problems and solutions, 244
    project authorization, 243–244
    reducing forecast bias, 244–245
    valid projects, 245
  practices in Canadian firms, 261
  and project risk, 319–323
  value of information, 247
  what-if questions, 245–249
    scenario analysis, 248–249
    sensitivity analysis, 245–248
    simulation analysis, 248–249
Capital cost allowance, 49, 215
  and depreciation, 215
Capital expenditures, 584
Capital gains, 53, 145, 146, 272
Capital gains tax, 53
Capital investment, 183, 212
Capital investment project, 169
Capitalized lease, 660
Capital lease, 657
Capital loss, 145
Capital markets, 8
  efficient, 360
  history, 282–280
  international, 389
Capital rationing
  hard, 192–193
  soft, 192
Capital structure, 333
  case, 477–478
  corporate taxes, 455–459
  costs of distress, 459–466
  effects of borrowing, 446–455
  and expected returns, 348–349
  financial slack, 468–470
  MM propositions, 487
  pecking order theory, 467–468
  trade-off theory, 466–467
Capital structure decision, 8
Capital surplus, 378

CAPM
 see Capital asset pricing model
Carrying costs, 576
Cash
 forecasting sources of, 582–583
 forecasting uses of cash, 584–585
 generation of, 581
 inventories and balances of, 614–623
 managing inventories of, 618
 optimal balance, 619
 tracing changes in cash, 580–582
Cash balance
 584-585
Cash budgeting
 cash balance, 584–585
 forecasting cash sources, 582–583
 forecasting uses of cash, 584–585
 steps in preparing, 582
Cash conversion cycle, 573–576
Cash coverage ratio, 513
Cash dividends, 480
Cash flow, 7
 from assets, 44, 45
 to bondholders and shareholders, 45–46
 calculating, 211–214
 and capital rationing, 192
 current dollar, 92
 of financial lease, 663–664
 free, 44
 incremental, 206–209
 and inflation, 210–211
 levels, 78–90
 multiple, 75–78
 versus profits, 41–42, 204–206
 real versus nominal, 91–92
 statement of, 42–46
 stream of, 75
Cash flow from assets, 522
Cash flow from investments, 212
Cash flow from operating, 213–214
Cash management
 of cash balances, 618–619
 concentration banking, 611–612
 controlling disbursements, 612–613
 electronic funds transfer, 613–614
 float, 605–607
 inventory costs, 615–618
 investing idle cash, 621–623
 in large corporations, 621
 lockbox system, 611–612
 managing float, 609–614
 speeding up collections, 610–611
 uncertain cash flows, 619–621
 zero-balance accounts, 613
Cash payments, valuating, 92, 94
Cash up front versus installment plan, 77–78
CCA tax shield, 215
Celestica Inc., 697–698
Certificates of paper, 622
Chaebols, 383
Channel Tunnel, 169, 174
Chapter 11 bankruptcy, 645, 646
Chapters, 25, 697–699
Chicago Mercantile Exchange, 29
Chief executive officer (CEO)
 compensation, 24
 removing, 25
Chief financial officer (CFO), 14–15
Chrysalix Energy, 434
Chum, Ltd., 385
CIBC World Markets, 3, 11, 16, 393, 426, 701
CICA Handbook, 660, 661
Citicorp, 389
Citigroup, Inc., 492, 642, 643
Citron, Robert, 394
Clearnet, 686
Clearwater Fine Foods, 681–682
Closely held corporations, 4
Coattail provision, 382
Coca-Cola, 69, 72, 681
Coin-toss game, 280–283
Collection policy, 629, 640–641
Commercial draft, 632
Commercial paper, 572, 589–590, 622
Commitment fee, 589
Commodity future, 775
Common-size balance sheet, 511
Common-size income statement, 508
Common stock, 139, 378–383
 authorized share capital, 378
 case, 167
 cash payoff, 145
 classes of, 381–382
 and convertible bonds, 131
 and corporate governance, 382–383
 in crash of 1987, 368–369
 dividend discount model, 147–149
  constant growth, 151–152
  estimating rate of return, 152–153
  nonconstant growth, 154
  with no growth, 150–151
 dividends, 380
 entire business valuing, 157–158
 expected return, 344–345
 growth stock, 155–158
 income stock, 155–158
 issuance, 139–140
 market portfolio, 278
 market risk, 305–311
 market risk premium, 279
 in mergers and acquisitions, 139–140
 price-earnings ratio, 157
 risks of, 275–276
 shareholders' rights, 380
 terminal value, 155
 today's/tomorrow's price, 145–147
 valuation of, 145–150
 voting procedures, 381
Companies' Creditors Agreement Act, 643
Company cost of capital, 319–320
Company risk, 319–320
Compaq, 25
Compensating balance, 593–594
Compensation plans, 23, 24
Competition Bureau, 687, 699
Competition Tribunal, 687
Complementary resources, 688, 689
Compound growth, 28, 66
Compound interest, 63–66
Concentration banking
 lockbox system, 611–612
Confederation Bridge, 169
Conglomerate mergers, 686
Conoco, 688
Constant dollars, 92
Constant-growth dividend discount model, 151–152
Consumer credit, 572
Consumer Price Index (CPI), 90, 91
Consumers Packaging, Inc., 643–644
Continental Airlines, 462
Continuous compounding, 97
Controller, 14
Converse Inc., 689–690
Conversion price, 753
Conversion ration, 753
Convertible bonds, 131, 394, 753–754
Convertible securities, 394–395
Coolidge, Calvin, 277
Corel Corporation, 4
Corporate bonds, 129–131
 variations in, 131
Corporate control
 divestitures and spin-offs, 684
 leveraged buyout, 683
 management buyout, 683–684
 market for, 680–685
 mergers and acquisitions, 682–683
 ownership structure, 685
 proxy contests, 681–682
 tender offer, 683
Corporate debt, 386–394
 country/currency, 389
 default risk, 389
 forms of, 387–391
 innovations
  asset-backed bonds, 392–393
  indexed bonds, 392
  reversed floaters, 393–394
 interest rate, 387
 leases, 390
 maturity, 387
 protective covenants, 390
 public versus private placements, 390
 repayment provisions, 387–388
 security, 388
 seniority, 388
 sinking fund, 387
Corporate financing
 borrowing, 446–455
 efficient market theory, 361–370
  and financial illusions, 370–371
  and market memory, 370
  crash of 1987, 368–369
  imperfections in, 365–367
  no free lunch, 371
  random walk, 361
  technical analysts, 362–363
  three forms of, 363–365
 financial slack, 468–470
 initial public offering (IPO), 412–418
 long- versus short-term, 578–580
 pecking order theory, 467–468
 primary versus secondary offering, 412
 trade-off theory, 466–467
 venture capital, 410–412
Corporate financing patterns
 capital surplus, 378
 common stock, 378–383
 convertible securities, 394–395

with debt, 387–394
external sources of capital, 396–398
internally generated funds, 395–396
preferred stock, 383–386
retained earnings, 378
Corporate governance, 382–383
Corporate taxes, 4, 48–51
and weighted-average cost of capital, 349
Corporate tax rate, 48–51
Corporate venture capital funds, 434
Corporations, 21
book value, 142, 145
countercyclical, 286
cyclical, 286
goals of
ethics, 19–21
manager role, 17–25
market value, 17, 19, 21–25
going-concern value, 143–144
growth companies, 144
initial public offering (IPO), 11
limited liability, 6
liquidation value, 143, 145
market-value balance sheet, 145
nature of, 3–5
present value of growth opportunities, 156
professional, 6
sustainable growth rates, 156
taxes, 48–51
valuation of entire business, 157–158
Correlation coefficient, 289
Cost of capital, 530
see also Weighted-average cost of capital
calculating weighted average, 334–341
and capital structure, 333
company, 336–337
dividend discount model, 344–345
estimating, 278–280
flotation costs, 350
for foreign investment, 729
market versus book weights, 337–338
meaning of, 271
nominal, 209–210
required rate of return, 343–3
on bonds, 343
on common stock, 344–345
on preferred stock, 345
Costs
agency, 680
carrying, 576
fixed, 248
shortage, 576
variable, 248
Costs of financial distress, 459–466, 461
bankruptcy costs, 461–465
types of assets, 465–466
without bankruptcy, 462–465
Cotton Ginny Limited, 684
Country/currency debt issues, 389
Coupon, 113
Coupon payments, 116
Coupon rate, 113
Cram-down, 645
Credit, 70
five Cs of, 634
Credit agencies, 633
Credit agreements, 632–633
Credit analysis, 629, 633–636
costs and results, 635–636
financial ratio analysis, 634
multiple discriminant analysis, 634–635
numerical credit scoring, 634–635
Credit decisions, 636–639
general principles, 639
with repeat orders, 638–639
Credit management
and bankruptcy, 641–647
collection policy, 640–641
credit agreement, 632–633
credit analysis, 633–636
credit decisions, 636–639
numerical credit scoring, 634–635
steps, 629
terms of sale, 630–632
Credit policy, 629, 636
Credit rating, 633
Credit risk, 129
Credit spread, 129
Credit unions, 10
Cuban, Mark, 415
Cumulative voting, 381
Currency appreciation/depreciation, 714
Currency futures market, 715, 716–720
Currency swaps, 779–780
Current assets, 35, 507
Current dollar cash flows, 94
Current dollars, 92
Current liabilities, 36, 509–510
Current ratio, 514
Current yield, 118
versus yield to maturity, 118–121
Current yield, Treasury bonds, 118–120

Daewoo, 686
Daimler-Benz AG, 47
Daiwa Bank, 780
Dangerous accounts, 639
David Bowie, 392
Dealer market, 140
Dean Witter, 492
Debit card, 614
Debt-equity trade-off, 466–467
Debt financing
and corporate taxes, 455–459
and cost of equity, 452–455
and earnings per share, 448–450
effects on risk and return, 450–452
and financial distress, 462–466
financial leverage, 451, 511
and financial slack, 468–470
impact on value, 446–455
interest tax shield, 455–457
MM proposition, 450
pecking order theory, 467–468
trade-off theory, 466–467
weighted average cost of capital, 457–458
Debt ratio, 511–512
Debt service, 663
Decision Index, 636
Decision trees, 257
Declining balance depreciation, 215
Default premium, 129
Default risk, 129, 389
Degree of operating leverage, 255
Demand deposits, 572
Depository transfer cheque (DTC), 611
Depreciation, 215, 271
and capital cost allowance, 215
declining balance, 215
recaptured, 218
straight-line, 215
Depreciation tax shield, 215, 218–220, 239
Derivatives, 780–781
Desjardins-Laurentian Financial Corporation, 17
Deutsche Bank, 389, 701
Devon Energy, 686
Di Raddo, Emilia, 507
Direct exchange rate quotes, 712
Disadvantages of leasing, 659–660
Discounted cash flow analysis, 204–228
allocated overhead costs, 209
calculating cash flow, 211–214
capital investment, 212
cash flow from operations, 213–214
and depreciation, 215–217
depreciation tax shield, 218–221
versus financing decision, 211
incremental cash flows, 206–209
and indirect effects, 206–207
and inflation, 210–211
investment in working capital, 212
net working capital in, 208–209
nominal cost of capital, 209–211
opportunity costs, 207–208
profits versus cash flows, 204–206
salvage value, 228
straight-line depreciation, 215
sunk costs in, 207
working capital investment in, 208–209
Discounted cash flow rate of return, 177
Discounted payback period, 181–182
Discounted payback rule, 181
Discounted value
see present value
Discount factor, 69
Discount interest, 593
Discount rate, 210
Discount rates, 67, 322–323
Diversification
and risk, 285–294
Dividend discount model, 147–149, 344–345
constant growth, 151–152
cost of equity estimates, 344–345
estimating expected rates of return, 152–153
no growth, 150–151
nonconstant growth, 154
Dividend payout ratio, 484
Dividend policy
assumption behind irrelevance, 489
definition, 486
irrelevant in competitive markets, 486–488
as trade-off, 486
Dividends, 141
calculating tax on, 53
versus capital gains, 492–495
clientele effects, 495–496

common stock, 380
ex-dividend date, 480
extra, 480
and firm value
dividends as signals, 490–492
market imperfections, 489–490
grossed-up, 52
information content, 491
payment date, 480
payment of
cash dividend, 480
decisions on, 484–485
limitations on, 480–481
stock dividends, 482–483
stock repurchase, 483
payout ratio, 155
preferred stock, 383–386
record date, 480
versus stock repurchase, 496–497
stock splits, 482–483
tax credit, 52
taxes on, 492–497
types of, 482–483
Dividend tax credit (DTC), 493
Dividend yield, 272, 522
Dominion Bond Rating Service, 393, 633
Dow Chemical Venture Capital, 434
Dow Jones Industrial Average, 274
Drexel Burnham Lambert, 704
Dun & Bradstreet, 528, 633, 635, 636
DuPont Canada, 480, 481, 688
DuPont system, 520–522
DuraAutomotive Systems Inc., 697–698
Duracell International Inc., 696
Dylex, 645

Earning power, 143
Earnings, 157
meaning of, 157
Earnings before interest and taxes (EBIT), 40, 50
Eastern Airlines, 646
East India Company, 28
Eastman Kodak, 23
Economic order quantity, 616–617
Economic value added (EVA), 531
Economies of scale, 687
Economy
new paradigm, 157
Effective annual interest rate (EAR), 95–98
on bank accounts, 97
Efficiency ratios, 515–517
Efficient capital markets, 361–372
Efficient market theory
imperfections, 365–368
lessons in, 370–371
three forms of, 363–365
Eisner, Michael, 23
Electric utilities, 297
Electronic communication networks (ECN), 140
Electronic Data Interchange (EDI), 613
Electronic Data Systems, 527
Electronic funds transfer, 613
Electronic payment systems
see electronic funds transfer
Enron Corp., 527, 642, 643, 752
Enterprise Oil, 725–726
Equivalent annual cost, 157, 186–187, 662
Equivalent loan, 667
Ethics of management objectives, 19–21
Eurobond, 389
Euro Disney, 8
Eurodollar market, 29
Eurodollars, 389
European Monetary Union (EMU), 29
Eurotunnel, 71, 589
Eurotunnel Corporation, 174
EValhalla.com, 437
Exchange rate, 712
beer standard, 718
Big Mac index, 717
expectations theory, 723–724
expected spot rate, 723–724
fixed, 714
floating, 714
fluctuations, 712, 714
hedging risk, 725–727
and inflation, 716–720
and interest rates, 721–723
and law of one price, 717
and purchasing power parity (PPP), 718
Exchange rate risk
hedging, 725–727
Ex-dividend date, 480
Executive compensation, 23–24
Exercise price, 739
Expansion option, 258–259, 751
Expectations theory of exchange rates, 723–724
Expected rate of return, 171
in dividend discount model, 152–154
opportunity cost of capital, 171
Expected rate of return formula, 152
Expected return
on bonds, 343
and capital structure, 348–349
on common stock, 344–345
on preferred stock, 345
using capital asset pricing model, 317–319
Expected spot rate, 723–724
Expenses, 584
Ex-rights date, 422
Extensions, 641
External financing and growth, 557–561
Extra dividend, 480
Extra earning power, 143

Face value, 113
Factoring, 591
Fair behaviour, 22
Fairmont Hotel and Resorts, 684
Fairvest Proxy Monitor, 385
Federal Competition Act, 687
Federal dividend tax credit, 53
Federal Economic Development Initiative in Northern Ontario (FedNor), 438
Federal Express, 688
Federated Department Stores, 753
Field warehousing, 591
Finance
careers, 15–17, 18
merger waves, 703–704
representative salaries, 17–18
Financial assets, 6, 7, 11
Financial calculators, 72–73
and annuity, 89
and bond valuation, 120
for future value, 72
and internal rate of return, 179
and net present value, 179
for present value, 73
Financial decision, 7, 8–9
Financial decisions, 578–580
Financial distress
and asset types, 465–466
bankruptcy costs, 461–462
costs of, 459–466
stockholder reaction, 463–465
without bankruptcy, 462–465
Financial futures, 29, 775
Financial illusions, 370–371
Financial institutions
functions, 13
kinds of, 9–11
Financial intermediary, 9
Financial lease, 657, 658, 663, 665–669
cash flows of, 663–664
cost of, 670–671
evaluation of, 668–669
Financial leverage, 451, 511
Financial managers
capital budgeting decisions, 7–8
careers, 15–17, 18
decision makers, 5
financing decisions, 7, 8–9
increasing market value, 17–19
maximizing firm value, 21–25
role of, 6–7
types of, 14–15
Financial markets, 6–7, 11–13, 360–372
competitive, 361
functions, 13
fundamental analysts, 363
lessons of efficiency, 370–372
technical analysts, 362
Financial pages, 113–114
Financial planning
alternative business plan, 544
big-picture focus, 544–545
characteristics, 544–547
definition, 544, 546
external financing and growth, 557–561
models, 547–554
balancing item, 550
design pitfalls, 555–557
financial statement analysis, 549–554
improved, 550–554
inputs, 548
outputs, 548
percentage of sales, 549, 555–556
planning models, 548–550
role of, 556–557
process steps, 544
requirements
choosing optimal plan, 546
forecasting, 545, 546
unfolding plan, 547
Financial ratio analysis, 634
Financial ratios

benchmark for, 526, 528
case, 540–542
for credit management, 634
dividend yield, 522
efficiency ratios, 515–517
for financial statement analysis, 506–511
leverage ratios, 511–513
liquidity ratios, 513–515
major industry groups, 529
market-to-book, 522
as performance measures, 531–533
price-earnings ratio, 522
profitability ratios, 517–520
role of, 531–533
summary of, 533–534
types of, 506
using, 525–528
Financial risk, 451
from debt, 450
Financial slack, 468–470
Financial statement analysis
comparing financial position, 529–530
dividend yield, 522
DuPont system, 520–22
efficiency ratios, 515–517
asset turnover, 515–516
average collection period, 516
inventory turnover, 516
for financial planning, 547–554
measures of performance, 531
financial ratios
role of, 531–533
leverage ratios, 511–513
cash coverage, 513
debt ratio, 511–512
times interest earned, 511–512
liquidity ratios, 513–515
cash ratio, 513
current ratio, 514
interval measure, 515
net working capital to total assets, 514
quick ratio, 514–515
market-to-book ratio, 522
measuring company performance, 529–531
market value added, 529
residual income, 531
price-earnings ratio, 522
profitability ratios, 517–520
net profit margin, 517–518
payout ratio, 519–520
return on assets, 518
return on assets, 520
return on equity, 519, 521
Financial Times Stock Exchange Index, 275
Financing decision, 7
versus investment decision, 211
Financing planning
case, 568–570
Fire insurance, 296
First Union Corp., 610
Fisher, Irving, 29, 720
Fishery Products International, 681–682
Five Cs of credit, 634
Fixed assets, 35, 36
Fixed-charge coverage ratio, 513
Fixed costs, 246, 248
Fixed exchange rates, 714
Flexible production facilities, 260
Float
kept by banks, 605–606
managing, 609–614
concentration banking, 610–611
controlling disbursements, 612–613
electronic funds transfer, 613
speeding up collections, 610–611
zero-balance accounts, 613
types of, 605–606
valuing, 607
Floating exchange rates, 714
Floating interest rate, 387
Floating-rate bonds, 131
Floating-rate preferred stock, 386
Floor price, 753
Florida Power and Light, 493
Flotation costs, 350, 416
Fonds de Solidarité des Travailleurs du Québec, 434
Food companies, 296
Fording, 684
Ford Mondeo, 169
Forecasting
in capital budgeting process, 244–245
and financial planning, 545–546
sources of cash, 582–583
uses of cash, 584
Foreign bond, 389
Foreign exchange market, 712–715
Foreign investment, 727–729
forward contracts, 714
forward discounts, 715
Forrester Research, 415
Forward contracts, 714
for risk management, 776–777
Forward discount, 715
Forward exchange rate, 714, 716–720, 717
FPL Group, 493
Franks, Harris, and Titman, 699
Free cash flow, 44, 522, 689, 703
Free credit
value of, 70–73
Fudge factors, avoiding, 729–730
Full-payout lease, 657
Full-service lease, 657
Fundamental analysts, 363
Futures contracts
commodity, 775
financial, 775
hedging with, 772–774
market to market, 774
Future Shop, 698
Futures trading, 774–775
Future value, 63–65
of annuity, 86–88
compared to present value, 67–69
and compound interest, 63–66
factor, 65
of multiple cash flows, 75

Gauvin, Benoit, 492
GE Capital, 658
General cash offer, 423–424
costs of, 424
rights issue, 421–423
seasoned offering, 421
and shelf registration, 424
stock market reaction to, 424–426
General Electric, 274, 526
Generally accepted accounting principles (GAAP), 37, 47
General Motors of Canada, 23, 607
Georgia Power Company, 547
Gerdeman, Timothy, 524
Gestion de Placements Valorem, 492
Gillette Co., 212, 492, 696
Going-concern value, 143–144
Goldman Sachs, 3, 417, 418
Gordon growth model, 152
Gordon, Myron, 152
Government funds, 434
Grass, Martin, 25
Great-West Life Assurance, 17
Griffiths, John, 636
Grossed-up dividends, 52
Gross profit margin, 517
Groupe Videotron Ltée, 381
Growing perpetuity, 88
Growth
best-case plan, 544
and external financing, 557–561
normal plan, 544
Growth company, 144
Growth in equity from plowback, 519
Growth stocks, 155–158

Half-year rule, 215
Hammurabi, Code of, 28
Hard capital rationing, 192
Hardie, Mark, 415
Healy, Palepu, and Ruback, 704
Hedging
exchange rate risk, 725–727
with financial futures, 775
with forward contracts, 776–777
with futures, 771–775
with options, 769–771
as risk management, 768–771
with swaps, 777–780
Herman Miller Corporation, 577
Hewlett-Packard, 89, 120, 179
High dividend payout policy, 490–491
High-yield bonds, 129
Historical cost, 37
Holder-of-record date, 422
Home Depot, 492
Horizontal mergers, 686
Hudson's Bay Company, 28
Hunter Timber, 636
Hybrid business forms, 5–6
Hydro-Quebec Capitech, Inc., 434
Hyperinflation, 73

Ibbotson, Sindelar, and Ritter, 414
IBM, 23, 145, 297, 545, 657, 739
ICG Propane, 687
Imperial Oil, 297
Implicit annual interest rate, 631
Inco, 308
Income statement, 40–42, 506–507
common-sized, 508
limitations, 42

profits versus cash flows, 41–42
Income stocks, 155–158
Income taxes, 48–54
Incremental cash flows, 206–209
Index funds, 310
Indigo Books, 697–698
Indirect effects, in DCF analysis, 206–207
Indirect exchange rate quotes, 712
Industry Canada, 438, 506
Inflation, 29, 90–95
and book value, 145
and cash flows, 210–211
and exchange rates, 716–720
and interest rates, 720–721
international Fisher effect, 424–426
real versus nominal cash flows, 90–92
and Treasury bonds, 127–128
valuing real cash payments, 94–95
Inflation-indexed debt, 29
Information content of dividends, 491
Initial public offering (IPO), 11, 139, 412–418
arranging, 412–414
case, 432
costs of, 417–418
flotation costs, 416
primary versus secondary, 412
spread, 413
underpricing, 414–416
underwriters, 413, 418–420
Inputs, 548
Installment plan, 77–78
Insurance companies, 10
Insurance industry, 17
Intangible assets, 36, 62, 143
Intel Corporation, 37, 206, 412, 432
Interest
compound, 63–66
simple, 63
Interest cover ratio
see cash coverage ratio
Interest/Interest rates
and inflation, 720
international Fisher effect, 720–721
Interest rate differential, 721–722, 724
Interest rate parity, 722, 722–723
Interest rate risk, 125
Interest rates
annual percentage rate, 96
and bond prices, 117
effective annual rate, 96
and exchange rates, 720–721
finding, 72–73
and inflation, 92–93, 720
installment plan, 77–78
nominal, 92
origin of, 28
real, 92
Rule of 72, 74
varying with bond prices, 117–118
Interest rate swaps, 777–780
Internal growth rate, 559
Internal rate of return, 176, 177, 178
calculating, 177
long-lived projects, 177–178
and mutually exclusive projects, 188–190
pitfalls, 188–182
Internal rate of return rule, 188–192
Internal Revenue Service, 705
International Accounting Standards Committee (IAS), 661–662
International Accounting Standards (IASC), 48
International Angel Investors Group, 437
International banking, 28
International capital budgeting, 727–731
International financial management
basic relationships
forward rate and expected spot rate, 723–724
inflation and exchange rates, 716–720
inflation and interest rates, 720–721
capital budgeting
avoiding fudge factors, 729–730
cost of capital for foreign investment, 729
net present value analysis, 727–728
political risk, 729
hedging exchange rate risk, 725–727
implications, 724
interest rate and exchange rates, 721–723
International Fisher Effect, 720–721
International Monetary Market (IMM), 715
Interval measure, 515
Inventories
carrying costs, 616
and cash balances, 614–623
economic order quantity, 616–617
just-in-time systems, 618
managing, 615–618
managing cash, 618–619
safety stock, 617
Inventory financing, 591
Inventory period, 574, 575
Inventory turnover ratio, 516
InvestAngel Network, 437
Investment dealers, 16
Investment decision, 7
book rate of return, 182–183
and capital rationing, 192–193
discounted cash flow rate of return, 177
and equivalent annual cost, 186–187
versus financing decision, 211, 360
internal rate of return, 176–179, 188–190
long- versus short-lived equipment, 186–187
mutually exclusive projects, 183–184, 188–190
net present value analysis, 170–175
net present value profile, 176–177
payback period, 180–182
pitfalls of IRR rule, 190–192
profitability index, 193–194
and project interactions, 183–192
and rate of return, 272–273
on replacement, 187–188
timing of, 184–185
unsafe, 174–175
Investment grade bonds, 129
Investment horizon, 154
Investment Returns 2000, 275
Investments
future value, 144
Investors Group, 17
Island Telecom Inc., 682
Issued shares, 378
Ivanhoe Energy Inc., 730

Jarislowsky, Stephen, 157
Jean Coutu Group, 3
Johnson, Ross, 701
Joint stock companies, 28
JP Morgan, 524
Junk bonds, 129
Just-in-time inventory systems, 618

Keiretsu, 383
KenDavis Industries, 464
Ketz, Edward J., 527
Khurana, Rakesh, 25
Kohlberg Kravis Roberts & Co., 696, 701
Kraft, 297
Kraft Inc., 696

Labour-sponsored funds, 433
Laidlaw, Inc., 644
Large Value Transfer System (LVTS), 608
Latin Monetary Union, 29
Law of one price, 717
Learjet, 7
Lease, 390
Leasing
assets, 664–665
and Canada Customs and Revenue Agency, 665
case, 677–678
definition, 657
effect on book income, 661–662
financial, 665–669, 670–671
industry, 657–658
reasons for leasing, 658–662
types of, 657–658
valuation of, 662–670
Le Château (LC), 506–511
Leeson, Nick, 29, 780
Lehman Brothers, 158, 524
Lending, 13
Lessee, 657
Lessor, 657
Level cash flows
future value of an annuity, 86–88
valuing annuities, 79–82
valuing annuity due, 82–83
valuing perpetuities, 78–79
Leveraged buyout (LBO), 683
case, 701–702
free-cash-flow theory, 703
and incentives, 702–703
junk bond markets, 702
and stakeholders, 702
and taxes, 702
Leveraged lease, 657
Leverage ratios, 511–513
Liabilities
on balance sheet, 36
current, 509–510
Limited liability, 4
Limited liability corporations (LLC), 6
Limited liability partnerships (LLP), 5
LIN Broadcasting, 158
Line of credit, 589

Liquid assets, 35
Liquidation
versus reorganization, 645–647
Liquidation value, 143, 145
value of stocks, 145–147
Liquidity, 513
Liquidity ratios, 513–515
Lockbox system, 611–612
Lockheed Corporation, 207
London Interbank Offered Rate (LIBOR), 387, 778
London Stock Exchange, 275
Long-lived equipment, 186–187
Long-lived projects
internal rate of return, 177–179
net present value, 172–175
Long-term assets, 507
Long-term debt, 387
Long-term financing, 11
alternative approaches, 578–579
versus short-term financing, 578–580
Lorenzo, Frank, 646
LOT airlines, 688
Lotus Development Corporation, 412, 545
Lower limits, option value, 745

Machine tool manufacturers, 296
Mackenzie, Bill, 385
Macro risk, 296-297; *see also* Market risk
Magna International, 382, 688
Majority voting, 381
Malkiel, Burton, 366
Management
corporate, 4–5
and ethics, 19–21
Management buyout (MBO), 683–684, 700
Managers
agency problem, 25
and company goals, 17–25
maximizing company value, 21–25
maximizing market value, 17–19
specialist monitoring, 25
Manhattan Island, 66
Marginal tax rate, 51
Maritime Telegraph and Telephone Company, 682
Marked to market, 774
Market indexes, 273–275
Market-out clause, 423
Market portfolio, 305
Market price, 171
Market risk, 293–294, 312–319
betas, 305
causes, 305
measuring betas, 305–308
measuring portfolio betas, 309–311
Market risk premium, 312
Market-to-book ratio, 522
Market to market, 774
Market value, 145, 171, 512
on balance sheet, 37–39
versus book value, 39
Market value added, 529
Market-value balance sheet, 145
Matching maturities, 579

Maturities
and yield curve, 126
Maturity premium, 276
McCaw Cellular, 158
McGraw-Hill Ryerson, 37
Medeiros, David, 610
Mellor, Philip, 636
Merck, 467
Merger, 682
Mergers and acquisitions, 29
dubious reasons for
bootstrap game, 690–692
diversification, 690
and economy, 703–704
evaluation of
financed by cash, 692–694
financed by stock, 694–695
warnings about, 695–696
gains from, 699–700
merger waves, 703–704
sensible reasons for, 685–690
combining complementary resources, 688–689
economies of scale, 687–688
economies of vertical integration, 688
increased revenues, 687
reduction of taxes, 689
use for surplus funds, 689–690
shark repellent, 699
synergies from, 686
and tactics, 697–700
white knight, 698
Mergers waves, 703–704
Merrill Lynch, 3
Merton, Robert, 749
Metallgesellschaft AG, 780, 781
Microsoft, 3, 145, 432
Milken, Michael, 704
Miller, Merton, 446, 486
Minimum operating cash balance, 584
Missouri Pacific Railroad, 646
MM debt-irrelevance proposition, 450
MM dividend-irrelevance proposition, 487
Modigliani, Franco, 446, 486
Molson Inc., 35–37, 40–41, 43–45, 142, 525, 531
Money
purchasing power, 90–91
real value of $1, 91
Rule of 72, 74
Money market, 621–623
Monsanto Co., 701
Moody's Investors Service, 527, 661
Morgan Stanley, 3, 158, 492
Morgan Stanley Capital International (MSCI), 275, 312
Mortgages, 84–85
figuring out, 97–98
Mouvement des caisses Desjardins, 10
Multi-class mortgage pass-through certificates, 393
Multi-jurisdictional disclosure system (MJDS), 47
Multiple cash flows, 75–78
future value of, 75
present value of, 76

Multiple discriminant analysis, 634–635
Multiple rates or return, 191
Multiple voting shares, 382
Mutual fund, 17
Mutual funds
risk, 310
Mutually exclusive projects, 183–184
and internal rate of return rule, 188–192

Nasdaq, 12, 275, 414
Nasdaq Canada, 420
National Bank of Canada, 17
National Gypsum, 703
NatWest, 25
Negative-risk asset, 288
Net float, 606
Net lease, 657
Net present value formula, 171
Net present value (NPV), 169, 171, 171–175, 176–177, 192–193
break-even analysis, 251–254
and capital rationing, 192–193
definition, 171
discounted payback period, 181–182
focus on cash flows, 204–205
and international capital budgeting, 727–728
investment timing, 184–185
long-lived projects, 172–175, 177–179
mutually exclusive projects, 183–184
and present value, 171–172
of replacement decisions, 187–188
and risk, 171–172
rule of, 171
Net present value profit, 176–177
Net present value rule, 171
Net profit margin, 517–518
Net working capital, 208, 573
in DCF analysis, 208–209
to total assets ratio, 514
Net worth, 383
New Tel Enterprises, 682
New York Stock Exchange (NYSE), 28, 275
Nikkei 225 Index, 275
Nintendo, 8
Nippon Telegraph and Telephone, 412
No-free-lunch assertion, 371
No-growth dividend discount model, 150–151
Nominal cost of capital, 209–211
Nominal interest rate, 92
and real, 126–128
Nominal rate of return, 273
Nonconstant growth dividend discount model, 154
Noncontractual risk, 725
Nonexecutive directors, 380
Nonvoting shares, 382
Norex Petroleum Ltd., 730
Normal growth plan, 544
Nortel Networks, 8, 23, 144, 492, 529, 530, 684
Numerical credit scoring, 634–635

Occidental Petroleum, 614
Odd lots, 142
Off-balance-sheet financing, 660–662

Office of the Superintendent of Bankruptcy (OSB), 641
Onex Corporation, 697–699
Ontario Securities Act, 697
Ontario Securities Commission (OSC), 20, 381, 413, 697
Open account, 632
Operating cash flow, 213–214
Operating expenses, 183
Operating lease, 657, 658, 662–663
Operating leverage
  break-even analysis, 254–256
  degree of, 255
Operating profit margin, 517
Opportunity cost, in DCF analysis, 207–208
Opportunity cost of capital, 171, 278
  and project rate of return, 176–177
  and project returns, 318–319
Optimal cash balance, 619
Option premium, 739
Options
  calls and puts, 739–745
  financial alchemy with, 743–744
  on financial assets
    callable bonds, 754
    convertible bonds, 753–754
    warrants, 752–753
  on real assets, 749, 751–752
  for risk management, 768–771
  selling calls and puts, 741–742
  straddle position, 744
Option valuation
  determinants, 746–748
  models, 748–749, 750
  models Black-Scholes valuation, 762–764
  upper and lower limits, 745–746
Orange County, California, 393
Ottawa Capital Network, 437
Outsourcing, 688
Outstanding shares, 378
Overhead costs, 209
Over-the-counter market, 12, 114
Ownership, 685

Pacific Gas and Electric, 527
Pacific Northern Gas, 144
PacifiCorp, 689
Paid-in surplus, 378
PanCanadian Energy, 684
Pantry Pride, 704
Partnership, 3
  agreement, 3
  limited, 5
  limited liability, 5
Par value, 378
Pasternak, Stan, 393
Payback period, 180–182
Payback rule, 180
Paychex, Inc., 492
Payment date, 480
Payment float, 605
Payment mechanism, 13
Payments of accounts payable, 584
Payment system, 608
Payout ratio, 155, 519–520
Pecking order theory, 467–468
Penn Central Corporation, 493, 640, 644
Penn Central Railroad, 462, 463
Pentagon Law of Large Projects, 175
Pepsi, 686
Percentage capital gain, 272
Percentage of sales model, 549, 555–556
Performance measures
  cost of capital, 530
  financial ratios, 529–530, 531
  market value, 529
  residual income, 531
Perpetuity, 78
  growing, 88
  valuation of, 78–79
Personal tax, 51–53
Pet.com, 432
Pfeiffer, Eckhard, 25
Planning horizon, 544
Plowback ratio, 155, 519, 560
Plug, 550
Poison pill, 698
Political risk, 729
Pooling risk, 13
Porsche, 725
Portfolio betas, 309–311
Portfolio diversifications, 309–311
Portfolio risk, 286–289
Power Corporation, 382
Preauthorized debits, 609–610
Preauthorized payment, 609
Preferred stock, 383–386
  expected return, 345
  floating-rate, 386
Premium
  maturity, 276
  risk, 276
Present value of growth opportunities (PVGO), 156
Present values, 67–75
  of annuity, 79–82
  of annuity due, 82–83
  of CCA tax shields, 218–221
  Channel Tunnel, 174
  finding interest rate, 72–73
  and free credit, 70–71
  of growth opportunities, 150
  home mortgage, 84
  of multiple cash flows, 76
  of perpetuity, 78–79
  stock price formula, 150
  using compound interest, 63
Price-earnings (P/E) multiple, 142
Price-earnings ratio, 157, 522
PricewaterhouseCooper, 49, 142
Primary issue, 12
Primary market, 12, 139
Primary offering, 412
Prime rate, 387
Private independent firms, 433
Private placement, 390, 426–427
Procter and Gamble, 780
Professional corporations, 6
Profitability index, 170, 192–193
  pitfalls of, 193
Profitability ratios, 517–520
Profit maximization, 19
Profits
  versus cash flow, 41–42, 204–206
Pro formas statements, 548
Progress payments, 630
Project authorizations, 243–244
Project cost of capital, 320, 349–350
Project interactions, 183–192
Project rate of return, 176–179
Project risk, 319–320, 319–322
  determinants of, 320–322
Promissory note, 632
Prompt Offering Prospectus (POP), 424
Prospectus, 413
Protective covenants, 390
Protective put, 743
Provincial and regional lending programs, 438
Proxy contest, 381, 681–682
PRS Group, 729
Public companies, 5
Purchasing power parity (PPP), 718
Pure play approach, 321–322
Put options, 739–745
  protective, 743
  selling, 741–742

Quebecor, Inc., 381, 382
Quick ratio, 514–515

Random walk, 361
Rate of return, 121
  calculating
    expected rate on bonds, 343
    expected return on common stock, 344–345
    expected return on preferred stock, 345
    on two-year bond, 125
  capital market history, 273–280
    estimating cost of capital, 278–280
    historical record, 275–278
    market indexes, 273–275
  estimation for dividend discount model, 152–153
  market portfolio, 305
  market risk premium, 276
  maturity premium, 276
  nominal, 273
  overview, 272–273
  and portfolio diversification, 285–294
  real, 273
  required, 343–345
    on bonds, 343
    on common stock, 344–345
    on preferred stock, 345
  and taxes, 123–125
  variation in stock returns, 283–284
  weighted average cost of capital, 347–348
  versus yield to maturity, 122–123
Rate of return rule, 176–177
RBC Dominion Securities, 11, 16, 419
Real assets, 6, 11
  options on, 749, 751–752
Real dollars, 92
Real interest rate, 92
  and forward exchange rate, 714
  and spot rate of exchange, 712, 714

Real options, 751
 option to abandon, 751–752
 option to expand, 751
Real rate of return, 273
Real rates of interest
 and nominal, 126–128
Real return bonds, 127
Real value of $1, 91
Recaptured depreciation, 218
Recession, 287
Record date, 480
Red herring, 413
Refunding, 387
Regression line, 308
Reisman, Heather, 697–699
Remote disbursement, 613
Renaissance Energy, 686
Rental lease, 657
Reorganization
 under bankruptcy, 643
 versus liquidation, 645–647
Repayment provisions, 387–388
Repeat orders, 638–639
Replacement decision, 187–188
Report on Canadian Economic Statistics 1924-2000, 275
Repurchase agreements, 622–623
Research in Motion, 412, 432, 466
Residual income, 530, 531
Restricted shares, 382
Retail bond traders, 115
Retained earnings, 378
 plowback ratio, 155, 519
Retention ratio, 155
Retrenchment, 544
Return on assets (ROA), 518, 520
Return on equity (ROE), 126, 519, 521
 and plowback ratio, 155, 519
Return on invested capital, 518
Revco, 703
Reverse floaters, 393–394
Reverse split, 483
Revlon, 704
Revolving credit agreement, 589
Rights issues, 421–426
 equation of, 423
 market reaction to stock issues, 424–426
Risk
 capital asset pricing model, 322–323
 capital budgeting and project risk
  company versus project risk, 319–320
  determinants of risk, 320–322
  fudge factors, 322–323
 and diversification, 285–294
 diversification
  asset versus portfolio risk, 286–289
  view of dangerous risks, 294–296
 effect on borrowing, 450–452
 macro risks, 296
 market risk, 296–297
  beta, 305
  causes, 305
  measuring, 205–311
  measuring betas, 305–308
 market risk versus unique risk, 293–294
 measuring, 297
  calculating variance, 280–283
  market risk, 305–311
  variance and standard deviation, 280–283
  variation in stock returns, 283–285
 of mutual funds, 310
 and net present value, 171–177
 political, 729
 pooling, 13
 portfolio, 286–289
 of portfolios of securities, 286–288
 in stocks, 139
 systematic, 293
Risk and return, 312–319
 capital asset pricing model, 312–313, 316–318
 market risk premium, 312
 opportunity cost of capital, 318–319
 project returns, 318–319
 security market line, 314–315
 using capital asset pricing model, 317–318
Risk-free interest rate, 279
Risk management
 with derivatives, 780
 with forward contracts, 776–777
 with futures contracts, 771–775
 by hedging, 768, 769
 with options, 768–771
 with swaps, 777–780
Risk premium, 276
Rite Aid, 25
RJR Nabisco, 29, 700–702, 704, 705
Robert Morris Associates, 528
Rogers Communications, Inc., 381
Rogers Sugar Ltd., 426
Rooney, Richard, 24
Roth, John, 23
Rotzang, Alex, 730
Round lots, 142
Royal Airlines, 683
Royal Bank Financial Group, 16, 434
Royal Bank of Canada, 28
Royal Bank Ventures, Inc., 434
Royal Dutch/Shell Group, 434
Rule of 72, 74

Sable Island Offshore Energy Project, 169
Safety-Kleen Corp., 644
Safety stock, 617
Sales department, 640
Salomon, 3, 20
Saputo Inc., 3, 492
Sawchuck, Arthur, 481
Scenario analysis, 248, 545
Scholes, Myron, 749
Schwartz, Gerald, 697–699
SC International Services Inc., 697–698
Scotia Canadian Dividend, 492
Scotia Capital, 3, 16
Sealed Air Corporation, 469
Season dating, 631
Seasoned offerings, 139, 142
Secondary market, 12, 139
Secondary offering, 412
Secondary transactions, 12
Secured debt, 388
Secured loans, 590–591
Securities
 initial public offering (IPO), 11–12
 issuance of
  general cash offering, 423–424
  initial public offerings, 412–418
  market reaction to, 424–426
  private placement, 426–427
  underwriters, 413, 418–420
  venture capital, 410–412
 in primary market, 12
 in secondary market, 12
Securities
 portfolio diversification, 289–291
Securities and Exchange Commission, 527
Securities and Exchange Committee (SEC), 49
Security market line, 314–315
Semiannual coupon payments, 116–117
Semi-strong-form efficiency, 364
Sensitivity analysis, 245–248, 545
Shareholders, 4
 cash flow to, 45–46
 dissident, 24
 maximizing market value, 17–19
Shareholders' equity, 36, 37, 510–511
Shareholders' rights, 380
Shareholders' rights plan, 698
Shark repellent, 699
Sharp calculator, 89, 120, 179
Shaw Communications, 385
Shearson Lehman Hutton, 701
Shelf registration, 424
Shell Canada, 258
Shortage costs, 576
Short-lived equipment, 186–187
Short-term financing
 case, 601–602
 cost of bank loans, 592–594
  discount interest, 593
  interest with compensating balances, 593–594
  simple interest, 592–593
 versus long-term financing, 578–580
 options, 585–588
 sources, 589–592
  accounts receivable financing, 591
  banker's acceptance, 590
  bank loans, 589
  commercial paper, 589–590
  factoring, 591
  inventory financing, 591
  secured loans, 590–591
Sight draft, 632
Simple interest, 63, 592–593
Simulation analysis, 248–249
Sinking fund, 387
Sloan School of Management, 25
Small business financing, 437–438
Smith, Adam, 19
Smith Barney, 3
Smith, Clifford W. Jr., 20
Smithers & Co., 526
Sobyanin, Sergei, 730
Soft capital rationing, 192
Sole proprietorship, 3
Southern California Edison, 527
South Sea Bubble, 28

Special dividend, 480
Specialist monitoring, 25
Special-purpose entities (SPE), 527
Speculation, 28, 780
Speculative-grade bonds, 129
Spot price, 774
Spot rate of exchange, 712, 714
Spreadsheets, 226–227
Stakeholder, 21, 22
Standard & Poor's Composite Index, 243, 274, 305, 368
Standard & Poor's Corp., 129, 527, 633, 661
Standard & Poor's Corp/TSX Canadian Small Cap Index, 275
Standard deviation, 280
Star Wars, 169
Statement of cash flows, 42–46
- analysis of, 522–525

StatsCanada, 528
Statutory amalgamation, 682
Stepping up the asset pool, 697
Stevenson, Larry, 698
Stewart, Stern, 529
Stock, 139–142
- auction markets, 140
- book value, 142–145
- common, 139
- common, valuation of, 145–150
- dividend discount model, 147–149
- dividends, 141
- initial public offering (IPO), 139
- liquidation value, 143
- market risk, 305–311
- market value, 142–145
- market-value balance sheet, 145
- odd lots, 142
- portfolio diversification, 289–291
- price appreciation, 157
- price-earnings (P/E) multiple, 142
- primary market, 12, 139
- reading stock market listings, 140–142
- return variations, 283–284
- risks of, 139
- round lots, 142
- seasoned offerings, 139
- secondary market, 12, 139
- terminal value, 155

Stockbrokerage firms, 17
Stock dividend, 482
Stockholders, 4
- and financial distress, 463–465

Stock market, 139–142
- auction market, 140
- crashes, 28–29
- crash of 1929, 277
- crash of 1987, 277, 368–369
- dealer market, 140
- electronic communications network, 140
- indexes, 273–275
- listing, 420–421
- primary market, 139
- reaction to stock issues, 424–426
- secondary market, 139
- types of, 140

Stock price formula, 150
Stock repurchase, 483
Stock split, 482
Straight-line depreciation, 215
Stream of cash flows, 75
Strike price, 739
Strong-form efficiency, 364
Subordinated debt, 388
Sumitomo Corporation, 780
Suncor Energy, 258
Sunk costs, 207
Superior Propane, 687
Sustainable growth rate, 156, 560–561
Swaps, 777–780
- currency swaps, 779–780
- interest rate, 778

"Sweetner", 752
Synergies, 686
Systematic risk, 293
System for Electronic Documents and Retrieval (SEDAR), 414

Takeovers, 24, 25
Talbot, Richard, 507
Tangible assets, 36, 62
Taxable dividends, 52
Taxes
- average rates, 51
- capital gains, 53
- corporate, 48–51
- dividend tax credit, 493
- federal dividend credit, 53
- and leasing, 659
- marginal rates, 51
- merging to reduce taxes, 689
- personal, 51–54
- present value of CCA shields, 218–221
- and rate of return, 123–125
- and weighted-average cost of capital, 338–339

TD Canada Trust, 613, 687
TD Securities, 393
TD Waterhouse, 140
Technical analysts, 362
Telus, 686
Telus Corporation, 753–754
Tenaga Nasional, 71
Tender offer, 683, 697
Terminal loss, 218
Terminal value, 155
Term loans, 589
Terms of sale, 630–632
Texas Eastern, 725–726
Texas Instruments, 89, 120, 179
Thomson Corporation, 3, 531
Thomson, Roy, 3
Time deposits, 572
Times interest earned ratio, 512–513
Time value of money, 62
- and inflation, 90–95
  - interest rates, 92–95
  - real versus nominal cash flows, 90–92
  - valuing real cash payments, 94–95

Time Warner, 682
Tokyo Stock Exchange, 275
Top-down investment choice, 243
Toronto Stock Exchange, 12, 28, 139, 275, 368, 382, 413, 416, 420
Total assets, 514
Total assets ratio, 514
Total capitalization, 511
Total capital requirements, 578
Tower Group, 610
Toys "R" Us, 620
Trade acceptance, 633
Trade credit, 572
- rates, 631–632

Trade-off of working capital, 576–577
Trade-off theory, 460, 466–467
TransAlta Corp., 491
TransCanada Pipe Lines, 491, 492
Trans Union Canada, 633
Treasurer, 14
Treasury bills, 275, 276, 278, 573, 622
- rates of return, 276

Treasury bonds, 275–276
- calculating rate of return, 118–119
- current yield, 118–121
- nominal versus real interest rates, 126–128
- price and coupon payments, 116–117
- prices and interest rates, 117–118
- rate of return, 121–123
- and yield curve, 126
- yield to maturity, 119–121

Treasury Inflation-Protected Securities (TIPS), 128
Triax Growth Fund, 434
Trilogy Retail Enterprises, 697–699
Turner, Lynn, 527
TWA, 645
Tyumen Oil Co., 730

Undepreciated capital cost (UCC), 215
Underpricing, 414–416
Underpricing of initial public offering (IPO), 414–416
- and investor returns, 416

Underwriter, 413, 418–420
Union Bank of Switzerland, 389
Unique risk, 293–294
United Airlines, Inc., 143, 527
Unlimited liability, 3, 531
Upper limits, option value, 745
U.S. Financial Accounting Standards Board, 48
U.S. Financial Accounting Standards Board (FASB), 660
Utah Power and Light, 689

Valuation
- bond prices and yields
  - calculating, 119
  - current yield, 118–119
  - default risk, 129–130
  - face value, 113
  - interest rate risk, 125
  - nominal versus real interest rates, 126–128
  - on financial pages, 113–114
  - rate of return, 121–123
  - semiannual coupon payment, 116–117
  - varying with interest rates, 117
  - yield curve, 126
  - yield to maturity, 118–120, 122–123
- common stock
  - case, 167–168

dividend discount model, 147–155
entire business valuing, 157–158
growth stock, 155–158
income stock, 155–158
meaning of earnings, 157
price-earnings ratio, 157
today's/tomorrow's price, 145–147
investments, 144
Value of future investments, 144
Valuing entire business, 157–158
Valuing leases
financial, 663
operating, 662–663
Variable costs, 246, 248
Variance
calculating, 280
and standard deviation, 280
Venture capital, 410–412
Venture capital in Canada, 410–418, 432–438
angel investing, 436–437
recent activity, 436
small business financing, 437–438
stages of development, 434–435
types of, 433–434
VentureDrive.com, 437
Vertical integration, 688
Vertical mergers, 686

Wagner, Todd, 415
Wal-Mart, 492
Walt Disney Company, 7, 23, 544
Wanless, Derek, 25
Warner-Lambert, 492
Warrant, 394, 752–753
Wasserstein Perella, 158
Weak-form efficiency, 363
Weighted-average cost of capital
calculating, 334–341
changing capital structure, 348–349
common mistakes, 347–348
corporate tax rates, 349
and debit policy, 458
interpreting, 347–350
market versus book weights, 337–338
and taxes, 338–339
three or more financing sources, 339–340
when not to use, 347
Westcoast Energy, 308, 434
Western Economic Diversification Canada: Financing, 438
Westons, 297
What-if questions, 245–249
White knight, 699
Wickes Group, 636, 641
Wildcat oil wells, 295–296
Winding-up and Restructuring Act, 643
Winnipeg Commodity Exchange, 28
Winterthur, 392
With-dividend date, 480
Wolfond, Greg, 414
Working capital
case, 601–602
cash budgeting, 582–585
cash conversion cycle, 573–576
components
current assets, 572–573
current liabilities, 573
cost of bank loans, 592–594
in DCF analysis, 206–209
investment in, 208–209, 212
long- versus short-term, 578–580
permanent requirements, 579–580
short-term financing, 585–589
evaluating plan, 588–589
options, 585–588
sources, 589–592
surplus cash, 580
tracing changes in cash, 580–582
trade-off, 576–577
Working ventures, 434
World Enterprises, 690–691
W.T. Grant, 558

Xerox, 527, 657

Yahoo!, 415
Yield curve, 126
Yield to maturity, 114, 119
calculating for Canada Bond, 119
versus current yield, 118–119, 118–121
promised versus expected, 130
versus rate of return, 122–123
treasury bonds, 119–121
Yugraneft, 730

Zekauskas, Jeffrey, 524
Zenon environmental, 146
Zero-coupon bonds, 131, 387
Z score, 634